THE NON-LEAGUE
FOOTBALL YEARBOOK
1996

EDITED BY KERRY MILLER
& JAMES WRIGHT

Published by Paper Plane Publishing Ltd
© Copyright Non-League Football Yearbook Ltd 1996
Printed by Unwin Brothers
ISBN 1-871-872-15-4

CONTENTS

Intro	3
FA Cup	8
FA Vase	14
FA Trophy	19
Vauxhall Conference	22
Altrincham	23
Bath City	26
Bromsgrove Rovers	29
Dover Athletic	32
Farnborough Town	35
Gateshead	38
Halifax Town	41
Hayes	44
Hednesford Town	47
Kettering Town	49
Kidderminster Harriers	52
Macclesfield Town	55
Morecambe	58
Northwich Victoria	61
Rushden & Diamonds	64
Slough Town	67
Southport	70
Stalybridge Celtic	73
Stevenage Borough	76
Telford United	79
Welling United	82
Woking	85

Dr Martens League	89
Eastern Counties League	226
Midland Alliance	268
Wessex League	290
Kent League	311
Sussex County League	333
Hellenic League	363
United Counties League	382
Western League	420
Unibond NPL	454
North West Counties League	550
Northern Counties East League	590
Northern League	626
ICIS League	665
Essex Senior League	808
Spartan League	819
South Midlands League	834
Combined Counties League	849
Midland Combination	865
West Midlands League	876
Central Midlands League	891
League of Wales	907
South Western League	925
County Senior Cups	936
Miscellaneous Tables	953
Minor Club Directory	962
Index	1018

THE NON-LEAGUE FOOTBALL YEARBOOK 1996-97

Non-League football has rarely been given the publicity it needs and deserves, and it is hoped that through this book, the tens of thousands of people up and down the land who for whatever reason either have turned to our game through frustration with League football, or have been raised on the game at grass roots level, can get a better insight.

With Murdoch's millions being pumped into the top end of the market, prices are spiralling out of all proportion, alienating the working man and creating an elitist, sanitised footballing supporter who will happily pay £25 to watch a Premiership game, and shell out £2 for a programme and 90p for a cup of tea.

It has also brought such an influx of foreign imports that so many home grown footballers have been forced to seek a living in places like Norway or Austria, or bite the bullet and go part time in non-League football. This has led through natural progression to a better standard and with ground gradings becoming stricter each year, the football is played in better conditions.

The only thing which does not appear to have gained momentum is the coverage our game gets in the national media. However, with Non-League Monthly having come onto the market at the back end of last season, the public who take an interest in the general scene are well catered for, and James Wright's superb weekly results service in Non-League Newsdesk has become essential fare for supporters, programme editors and statisticians alike. Bill Berry has for a number of years provided the impetus for many to visit non-League football grounds through his essential weekly Non-League Traveller magazine, and the final part of the jigsaw is hopefully this yearbook.

It would be pointless and somewhat churlish to simply produce another version of what has been on the market for some time, and that is not the object of the exercise, moreover it has been the intention to compile a companion which gives that that has not been available before.

When first deciding on the format for the book, it was thought that rather than cram it full of information that may well be out of date within weeks, it would be wiser to go for a more humble approach, and then possibly expand with subsequent seasons, as neither Rome nor Rushden and Diamonds were built in a day. With that in mind the decision was made to even up the ration of pages per club slightly, so that those in the top flights did not dominate the book to the detriment of those lower down.

With James' database able to provide results and scorers for the Conference sides, those clubs were allocated three pages. The Southern League's three divisions were given two pages each, as their results were also available in full, and the top two divisions of the Isthmian League were likewise given two pages. The Northern Premier League is similarly treated, which leaves the various feeders, which in truth were allocated space relative to the amount of information which became available either from clubs or the leagues themselves.

All of the feeders to the three main leagues, ie NPL, Isthmian and Southern were catered for, with those lower down in the main either given a page each or in some cases less, depending again on the amount of information available. In most cases, the results and scorers for the main leagues are in full, but where League records did not show them and clubs did not publish, then the known scorers only have been included.

In the case of the three NPL feeders, they were able to be well catered for as the questionnaire returns were good and the leagues themselves provided the all important handbooks. In the Midlands with the West Midland Regional League and the Combination now being feeders to a feeder, and with many clubs groundsharing and either folding or moving around, the coverage is less, with the lower divisions being incorporated into the rear section in alphabetical order.

With the help of people such as Steve Penney, editor of the Norwich Pink 'Un, Colin and Jane

Sinden from Hoddesdon Town FC, Mike Simpkins at Bolehall Swifts, Sid Pittman from the excellent Sussex County League and Stan Wilton from the Central Midlands League, amongst others, a number of leagues were covered more fully. Sadly, with little co-operation from one or two other leagues and in some cases a virtual blank on the return of the forms, a couple of prominent clubs who are in the lower part of their league at the moment find themselves at the back of the book.

Indeed, the inability to spot the potential of free advertising, simply by replying to a freepost address, is one which has perplexed James Wright and myself in the many occasions we have had to correspond with clubs over the years. Happily there are many around the country who can be relied on to provide excellent material for their clubs, such as Neil Harvey at Cambridge City, John Weaver at Braintree Town, Andy Dakin at Northwich Vics, Mike Odgers at Falmouth Town, Neil Marsdin at Morecambe, John Tebbitt at Slough Town, Wallace Brown at Newport AFC and Tony Booth at Harrow Borough amongst many others. Conversely it has become apparent that a number of clubs will not be adequately covered in this or any further publication unless a willing correspondent is found. It was suggested that a list be made of those who deem themselves too important to waste time on replying to non-League publications, but it would be counter productive. These people know who they are and all they do is deprive the very clubs which they purport to serve. If your club fits this category then PLEASE CONTACT EITHER JAMES WRIGHT OR MYSELF, and you will be welcomed with open arms. Without giving too much away, three Gloucestershire based Southern League clubs, one Cheshire side recently relegated to the NPL and a North London Isthmian League side spring readily to mind as urgently needing somebody to act as a liaison, as well as many others further down the scale whose section looks a bit on the skinny side. Also we could do with somebody from the Eastern based Southern League feeder who would be prepared to make our life a bit easier.

As the reader makes his way through the book, it will soon become obvious where the problems lie. The original questionnaire was structured so as to gain the most important information, with a few other embellishments to make life easier for such as programme editors. A quick scan of a club's page will soon indicate whether a reply was received, for each was asked to name their Manager, Assistant Manager, Chairman and Vice Chairman as well as more static information such as capacities, biggest wins, record goalscorers and honours won.

Where clubs did not have the courtesy to reply, then favours had to be called in from a number of friends and regular correspondents around the country, and many hundreds of phone calls were made to clubmen, a number of whom were openly annoyed at being contacted at home. It again begs the question as to why they are bothering in the first place. To complete the entry, a club history was included, many of which were culled and re-written from the many hundreds of programmes available to us. My involvement in the writing of the History of Non-League Football Grounds as well as the club histories for Taunton Town, Tiverton Town and Walton and Hersham meant that that was easily the most pleasurable of the tasks which were undertaken. The vast majority were informed and accurate, and those which fell short were tidied up using excellent research material. Leigh Edwards' History of the Southern League, James Wright's FA Cup Club-by-Club Records, Doug and Sandie Webb's Western League Centenary, Brian Hunt's superb Northern Goalfields, Barry Hugman's Football League Players Records and works by Simon Inglis, Norman Gannaway and many others proved invaluable. There were the odd one or two which proved elusive, but during this season they will be added and others amended as history multiplies, or indeed more research reveals previously forgotten facts.

It is fascinating to discover how some far less prominent clubs have somehow always kept their act together and maintained facts and figures and are able to list even the most obscure Hospital Cup wins from the Great War days, seemingly without ever having had the full history researched. It is equally interesting to see how some of the top clubs appear to have no idea of even basic historic information such as their all time top scorer, biggest attendance or previous leagues any further back than the 50's. That is where hopefully as the year goes on, this Yearbook can act as a database which will be added to as more clubs are researched.

The years of 1896, 1897, 1946 and 1947 are particularly relevant to football historians, as so many

clubs were being founded around 100 years ago, and even more either sprung up or were re-formed 50 years ago after the Second War. Happily a number of new club histories are believed to be in the process of being researched or have already been completed, including those of Sudbury Town, Marine, Dudley Town, Leatherhead, Southport, Diss Town, Bideford and Taunton Town. A number of others were completed recently and the list is growing.

With regard to league and cup names, throughout the book it will become apparent that sponsors have only been named in exceptional circumstances, as well as at the front of each section. Throughout the years since sponsorship became an integral part of our game, virtually every competition has gone through several name changes, some mid-season, and now we have the spectre of individual divisions having different sponsors.

Of course this would lead to chaos within the honours sections of each club, and so to make things easier, instead of the faintly ridiculous Interlink Express Midland Alliance Industrial Rewinds League Cup, which was won last year by Blakenall, it simply becomes the Midland Alliance League Cup. Similarly the Southern League Cup remains just that, as do many other competitions which have been afflicted with quite staggering monickers in the quest for a few bob in sponsorship. Where a cup has been named after a former player or administrator years after the same competition began under its common name, then it has normally remained unchanged, although some obscure references may or may not have been League Cups in distant past. It will also be noticed that other than FA Amateur Cup, FA Cup, Vase and Trophy appearances in finals or semi-finals, only the winners have been included, and runners up spots have been omitted. Sadly this has led to a couple of long established club's honours boards reading blank, until such time as they come up with a Hospital Cup win somewhere!

Should anyone be in the position to assist with either adding to the records listed or indeed correcting any that need correcting, however obscure, then it will be very welcome, and indeed if the club's mini history itself, which is maybe sent to opponents for their programme, has since been updated, then that too will be warmly received.

Another area where the book is hopefully going to prove useful is in the road maps, which were included where possible in the major leagues entries. It has often been said that directions to many grounds are obscure and that one minor error can lead to a wild goose chase. With landmark buildings going, garages closing and the old Red Lion becoming the Giraffe and Virgin, navigation is not always straight forward and so road maps seemed the logical alternative.

Elsewhere on the pages, information such as previous grounds, previous names and former leagues played in were incorporated into the histories where known, and where clubs had either not replied or the information was simply not known, then it was not included.

As to the highest attendance at the various grounds, many of those given were obviously only in the individuals recent memory or vague recollections which have been altered like Chinese whispers over the years. One club insisted that their highest ever attendance was 500, despite being one of the top amateur clubs of the post War years and having reached Amateur Cup finals, and another insisted that they played Crystal Palace in the FA Cup in the 20's despite not having entered the competition until 1946. Many others listed their highest attendance as being for Showbiz X1's, Dennis Waterman's teams, All Star XI or Eastenders charity games. In the main, any function which has the likes of Eric Hall running around with a cigar and a mobile phone and is refereed by Mr Blobby does not get a mention. That being the case, what is perceived at the time as being a straight forward match, albeit a testimonial, was usually accepted as were multiple answers where several different grounds have been used.

Many clubs have no idea as to their highest fee ever paid, record appearance holder or record goalscorer, as in many cases they were not kept and will never be known. Even where clubs have had in depth histories researched, the information is not, and will not ever be available.

As to what was not included, it was agreed that with the more mercenary attitude of many players and the constant merry go round of managers, players listings were erroneous, especially as here in

the West Country and in many other parts, many players sign for clubs in three or four different leagues to make sure of a regular pay day whatever the fixture list brings. Team photos were requested but not chased with any great gusto because again a significant percentage of those captured on film will not be around by the time the book is published.

As for programmes, as any supporter will know, particularly in the lower echelons, they are never guaranteed and indeed many clubs are solely reliant upon one individual and are often at the mercy of the flu bug. On iffy weather days it is regularly prudent for a club's copier to conveniently pack up rather than risk printing a programme that will not be used, and for those reasons it was decided not to include information on them. For those whose main aim is to collect a programme when visiting a new ground, then it is pot luck and this book would hate to be responsible for a wasted journey!

A look at other yearly publications will show that other information such as local papers, radio stations, club sponsors and club shops were included. Again all these are liable to change at a moment's notice. It is far easier to confirm with the club on the day as to whether the shop is open, and as to news and radio, our game is ever fitted in around the national stuff, and non-League items are always the first to go if Gazza pulls a muscle or Jamie Moralee pulls another Page 3 girl.

With all that in mind, it is hoped that the style and content will entice the reader to want more next year and will be a valuable and essential item for the season. Whilst this is the first edition and will therefore hit the shops well into the season, next year's will write itself as the campaign progresses and will grow and grow.

NON-LEAGUE NEWSDESK

One tie up which is unique to the Yearbook and will undoubtedly prove to be a boon, is the service provided by James Wright's Non-League Newsdesk. Each week throughout the season any relevant changes to Secretaries, grounds, floodlights, telephone numbers etc will be relayed through Newsdesk to enable the reader to keep up to date rather than have to wait until next August when the new edition becomes available. Newsdesk is published every Monday through the season and is available from James at 25 Stephen St, Taunton, Somerset TA1 1LD. Telephone him for details on 01823 327720 during office hours.

Without the invaluable help of many people around the country, the Non-League Football Yearbook could not possibly have been born this season and in late July when everything was going decidedly pear-shaped, it was only the intervention of some of those very people that kept it all going.

Inevitably there will be some whose name is not mentioned, and if so then please accept my grateful thanks now, and if and when we meet then it is my round!

Special thanks must go to those who supplied batches of club histories for their respective leagues. Colin and Jane Sinden, whose astonishing Hoddesdon Town programme has been voted the best in the country in recent times provided the bulk of the South Midlands League clubs information, and Jeremy Biggs came up trumps with his United Counties League handbook, plus other managerial information, all of which was most welcome and readily made available. Mike Simpkins is a regular non-League man from the South who is currently exiled at Bolehall Swifts, and his data base provided the bulk of last year's Midland Alliance club histories. John Stancombe is another who was most helpful in upgrading the Spartan League entries after just one phone call and Stan Wilton of Heanor Town and the Central Midlands League provided valuable help with histories of some of his member clubs. Elsewhere, John Mills of AFC Lymington provided a batch of Wessex League material within 18 hours despite a heavy personal workload and Rob Smith at Slade Green also came up trumps at short notice. Steve Penney from Downham Town FC and the Norwich Pink 'Un provided a batch of mini-histories for Eastern Counties Division One sides and Alan Evans from Northwood FC, whose programme stood proud over the rest last season, provided a number of Isthmian histories.

Other thanks must go to friends such as Richard Rundle at Bideford, Stan Strickland at Burscough, John Tebbitt at Slough Town, John Whatford in Bitterne, and many others.

There have also been many league men who always back any project that James or myself have been involved in and again our heartfelt thanks go out to them.

Amongst those who helped are...

Trevor Brock - Wessex League

Duncan Bayley - Northern Premier League

Nick Robinson - Isthmian League

Frank Clayton - North-West Counties League

Barry Wood - Northern Counties East League

Ernie Davies - Mid-Cheshire League

Kevin Parkinson - West Yorkshire League

Bill Gardner - Northern Alliance

J.C.Harpley - Anglian Combination

Jeremy Biggs - United Counties League

Dennis Cordell - Spartan League

Rob Errington - Essex Senior League

John Mugridge - Kent County League

Paul Rivers - Kent League

Kevin Folds - Herts Senior County League

Phil Hiscox - Devon County League

Phil Mitchell - South Midlands League

Sid Pittman - Sussex County League

Norman Harvey - Midland Combination

Steve Carr and Mick Moseley - West Midlands Regional League

Stan Wilton and Frank Harwood - Central Midlands League

Trevor Scorah - Dorset Combination

John Deakin - League of Wales

David Jamieson - Leicestershire Senior League

Gordon Stafford - Notts Alliance

Neil Morrell and Tony Ford - Chiltonian League

John Moody - Hampshire League

Dave Robinson - Midland Regional Alliance

There are of course a few glaring omissions in this list, and if anybody at all can either persuade those in charge to change their way of thinking, or indeed usurp them and assist us throughout the year, then they will have our eternal gratitude.

Please contact myself on 01823 698961 at any time, or on 0402 502039 if I'm not available at home. In that case you will almost certainly catch me at a game somewhere!

Finally it remains for me to thank my friend and colleague James Wright for coming in with me on this book, which we have every intention of repeating next year, and to each of you out there who trusted us sufficiently to buy it.

Best wishes to you all and good luck for the season. May you never see another 0-0 draw in the rain!

KERRY MILLER

Stantons Cottage

East Lyng

Somerset

TA3 5AU

September 1996

F.A. Cup

Preliminary Round

Epsom & Ewell	Tooting & Mitch	4-0	
Abingdon Town	Andover	3-2	136
Aldershot Town	Selsey	5-0	1644
Alnwick Town	Glasshoughton W	1-3	45
Armthorpe Welfare	Bradford PA	1-1	85
Arnold Town	Maine Road	2-0	
Aveley	Stowmarket Town	0-0	
A.F.C. Lymington	Calne Town	0-2	50
A.F.C. Totton	Fleet Town	3-1	
Backwell United	Elmore	0-1	
Banstead Athletic	Burgess Hill Town	3-1	52
Barking	Royston Town	1-0	101
Barnstaple Town	Minehead	2-0	123
Basildon United	Saffron Walden T	1-2	
Bedfont	Langford	0-0	22
Bedford Town	Edgware Town	1-4	413
Belper Town	Worksop Town	2-3	261
Bemerton Heath H	Ryde Sports	2-3	52
Bicester Town	Ringmer	0-1	97
Biggleswade Town	Berkhamsted Town	0-4	42
Bilston Town	Blakenall	0-0	131
Blidworth Welfare	Rossendale United	0-0	
Bognor Regis Town	Whitehawk	4-3	200
Bournemouth	Wimborne Town	0-4	
Bracknell Town	Kingsbury Town	0-0	
Brandon United	Chester-le-St T	1-4	30
Brierley Hill Town	Sandwell Borough	0-0	19
Brigg Town	Clitheroe	1-1	68
Brimsdown Rovers	Barton Rovers	0-2	
Brockenhurst	Swanage T & H	0-0	
Brook House	Welwyn GC	0-0	
Burnham Ramblers	Holbeach United	1-3	74
Burscough	Northallerton	2-2	134
Bury Town	Collier Row	1-2	214
Chadderton	Eastwood Town	0-1	96
Chasetown	Halesowen Harriers	2-1	82
Chatham Town	Whyteleafe	3-1	116
Cheshunt	Wealdstone	0-1	155
Chippenham Town	Paulton Rovers	0-0	118
Chipstead	Horsham	0-4	75
Clapton	Leighton Town	2-1	46
Clevedon Town	Mangotsfield United	1-5	407
Concord Rangers	Wootton Blue Cross	2-1	8
Corinthian-Casuals	Stamco	3-0	104
Crook Town	Kimberley Town	3-2	99
Crowborough Athletic	Godalming & G	1-3	70
Croydon	Dorking	5-2	82
Darlington C S	Billingham Syn	0-3	9
Dartford	Egham Town	3-1	123
Denaby United	Hucknall Town	4-0	80
Desborough Town	Rocester	0-0	62
Devizes Town	Bristol Manor Farm	1-1	58
East Ham United	Sudbury Wanderers	0-7	100
East Thurrock United	Tiptree United	1-1	54
Eccleshill United	Atherton L.R.	3-2	37
Esh Winning	Stockton	3-1	7
Eynesbury Rovers	Witham Town	4-1	70
Falmouth Town	Frome Town	3-0	
Fareham Town	Weymouth	1-1	152
Farsley Celtic	Oldham Town	2-2	103
Felixstowe Town	Burnham	1-1	
Fisher	Merstham	0-0	124
Flackwell Heath	Potters Bar Town	1-0	
Folkestone Invicta	Peacehaven & Tel	1-1	182
Forest Green Rovers	Exmouth Town	4-0	114
Glastonbury	Tuffley Rovers	1-5	
Glossop North End	Nantwich Town	1-2	200
Goole Town	Great Harwood T	2-2	99
Gorleston	Diss Town	1-5	301
Gosport Borough	Eastleigh	2-0	111
Great Yarmouth Town	Bourne Town	2-1	86
Guisborough Town	Gretna	1-0	101
Hadleigh United	Southall	1-0	63
Halstead Town	Stamford	1-1	
Hanwell Town	Wingate & Finchley	2-4	40
Harefield United	Hoddesdon Town	0-1	18
Harlow Town	Thamesmead Town	2-3	114
Haverhill Rovers	Hampton	0-1	
Herne Bay	Horsham Y.M.C.A.	1-1	144
Hertford Town	Ware	2-1	154
Hillingdon Borough	Cornard United	2-0	58
Hinckley Athletic	Ashton United	1-1	218
Hornchurch	Bowers United	3-0	45
Hungerford Town	Poole Town	5-0	66
King's Lynn	Wivenhoe Town	3-0	621
Knypersley Victoria	Stratford Town	0-3	47
Leicester United	Barwell	0-0	59
Leigh R.M.I.	Flixton	2-0	60
Lewes	Lancing	2-1	64
Leyton Pennant	Clacton Town	2-2	
Lincoln United	Stocksbridge P S	3-2	164
Littlehampton Town	Southwick	1-1	96
Liversedge	Blackpool Rovers	1-4	51
Louth United	Harworth C I	4-0	26
Lowestoft Town	Chalfont St Peter	2-2	170
Maltby M W	Mossley	3-3	60
March Town United	Fakenham Town	1-0	
Melksham Town	Bridport	1-2	80
Metropolitan Police	Viking Sports	7-0	70
Milton Keynes	Leatherhead	0-4	50
Netherfield	Evenwood Town	10-1	116
Newbury Town	Buckingham Town	walkover	
Newmarket Town	Boston Town	0-1	116
Newport Pag T	Boldmere St M	0-2	25
North Ferriby United	Heanor Town	2-4	84
Northampton Spencer	Cogenhoe United	2-2	44
Northwood	Ford United	3-2	102
Oldbury United	Darlaston	4-0	69
Ossett Albion	Hatfield Main	1-3	42

Ossett Town	Castleton Gabriels	3-2	47
Pelsall Villa	Dudley Town	1-1	142
Pershore Town	Evesham United	1-1	259
Pontefract Collieries	Oakham United	4-1	50
Prescot	Atherton Collieries	3-0	28
Prudhoe Town	Consett	1-3	30
Radcliffe Borough	Alfreton Town	3-2	118
Raynes Park Vale	Canterbury City	3-0	40
Redditch United	Bridgnorth Town	2-2	153
Redhill	Tunbridge Wells	3-1	121
Rothwell Town	Rushall Olympic	2-0	95
Ryhope C A	Morpeth Town	2-2	43
R.T.M. Newcastle	Harrogate R A	1-2	48
Salford City	Newcastle Town	1-2	
Saltash United	Torrington	3-2	
Seaham Red Star	Billingham Town	1-2	32
Sheffield	Caernarfon Town	9-1	
Sheppey United	Arundel	2-0	72
Shepshed Dynamo	Grantham Town	0-1	211
Shifnal Town	Willenhall Town	0-0	86
Shoreham	Corinthian	4-2	87
Shotton Comrades	Shildon	1-1	
Slade Green	Langney Sports	0-2	61
Soham Town Rangers	Stotfold	1-1	115
South Shields	Pickering Town	3-4	
Spalding United	Harwich & P	2-3	128
St Helens Town	Bootle	1-2	112
Stapenhill	Lye Town	1-2	32
Steyning Town	Cove	3-0	42
Stourport Swifts	Armitage	0-1	
Tadcaster Albion	Bedlington Terriers	1-1	80
Tamworth	Hinckley Town	3-1	514
Thackley	Cheadle Town	5-2	100
Thame United	Maidenhead United	4-0	161
Thatcham Town	Oakwood	2-1	79
Three Bridges	Camberley Town	0-5	141
Tilbury	Woodbridge Town	1-2	53
Tonbridge Angels	Croydon Athletic	3-1	487
Trafford	Fleetwood	2-1	101
Tufnell Park	Potton United	1-0	21
Uxbridge	Kempston Rovers	4-0	98
Washington	Garforth Town	1-9	56
Wednesfield	Banbury United	2-2	78
Wellingborough Town	Bolehall Swifts	0-4	40
Welton Rovers	Odd Down Athletic	2-0	71
West Midlands Police	Raunds Town	1-1	82
Westbury United	Basingstoke Town	2-2	
Westfields	Corby Town	1-1	122
Weston-super-Mare	St Blazey	7-0	180
Whitley Bay	Easington Colliery	3-0	142
Whitstable Town	Hailsham Town	3-2	142
Wick	Portfield	3-2	148
Willington	Dunston Fed	0-0	
Winterton Rangers	Darwen	2-0	32
Wisbech Town	Tring Town	4-0	338
Witney Town	B.A.T. Sports	5-0	127
Worcester City	Yate Town	1-2	595
Workington	Hebburn	8-1	253

Wroxham	Canvey Island	0-0	187
Yorkshire Amateur	Borrowash Victoria	2-4	63
Immingham Town	Rossington Main	1-1	20
Long Buckby	S & L Corby	2-1	35

Preliminary Round First Replay

Clitheroe	Brigg Town	1-0	140
Dudley Town	Pelsall Villa	1-0	161
Mossley	Maine Road	4-0	163
Willenhall Town	Shifnal Town	0-1	101
Banbury United	Wednesfield	0-3	110
Barwell	Leicester United	1-1	76
Basingstoke Town	Westbury United	5-1	196
Blakenall	Bilston Town	2-1	103
Bridgnorth Town	Redditch United	1-4	101
Bristol Manor Farm	Devizes Town	3-1	55
Burnham	Felixstowe Town	2-3	
Canvey Island	Wroxham	3-1	251
Chalfont St Peter	Lowestoft Town	4-1	106
Clacton Town	Leyton Pennant	0-4	92
Cogenhoe United	Northampton Sp	1-0	108
Dunston Fed	Willington	5-2	115
East Thurrock United	Tiptree United	6-2	91
Evesham United	Pershore Town	3-2	206
Horsham Y.M.C.A.	Herne Bay	1-4	142
Kingsbury Town	Bracknell Town	0-0	63
Langford	Bedfont	1-1	
Merstham	Fisher	0-2	175
Morpeth Town	Ryhope C A	3-1	79
Oldham Town	Farsley Celtic	0-2	75
Paulton Rovers	Chippenham Town	1-1	
Peacehaven & Tel	Folkestone Invicta	4-1	221
Rocester	Desborough Town	2-4	48
Sandwell Borough	Brierley Hill Town	5-3	20
Southwick	Littlehampton Town	1-0	160
Stamford	Halstead Town	3-3	170
Stotfold	Soham Town R	4-1	88
Swanage T & H	Brockenhurst	1-1	
Welwyn Garden City	Brook House	0-2	
Weymouth	Fareham Town	3-2	807
Ashton United	Hinckley Athletic	2-4	170
Bedlington Terriers	Tadcaster Albion	3-0	127
Bradford P A	Armthorpe Welfare	1-0	148
Corby Town	Westfields	7-5	217
Northallerton	Burscough	1-2	115
Raunds Town	West Mids Police	3-2	109
Rossendale United	Blidworth Welfare	3-0	92
Shildon	Shotton Comrades	2-1	84
Stowmarket Town	Aveley	3-4	119
Great Harwood Town	Goole Town	3-2	112
Rossington Main	Immingham Town	1-4	```

Preliminary Round Second Replays

Barwell	Leicester United	3-4	79
Bedfont	Langford	0-4	
Brockenhurst	Swanage T & H	1-0	
Chippenham Town	Paulton Rovers	0-2	
Kingsbury Town	Bracknell Town	1-1	
Stamford	Halstead	1-2	

Preliminary Round Third Replay

Bracknell Town	Kingsbury Town	3-2	80

First Qualifying Round

Abingdon Town	Newport I.O.W.	2-3	168
Accrington Stanley	Ossett Town	2-1	429
Aldershot Town	Pagham	4-0	1614
Arlesey Town	Leyton Pennant	3-0	156
Ashford Town	Tonbridge Angels	2-0	732
Atherstone United	Armitage	2-2	258
Baldock Town	Metropolitan Police	2-1	176
Bamber Bridge	Heanor Town	4-1	453
Barking	Clapton	1-3	154
Barrow	Consett	3-0	1029
Basingstoke Town	Havant Town	2-1	212
Berkhamsted Town	Hillingdon Borough	3-2	75
Bideford	Elmore	2-2	120
Billericay Town	Aveley	2-0	
Billingham Synthonia	Shildon	3-1	95
Bishop Auckland	Harrogate R A	2-1	156
Bishop's Stortford	Boston Town	2-2	352
Blyth Spartans	Garforth Town	6-0	498
Boldmere St M	Bedworth United	1-2	108
Bolehall Swifts	Tamworth	0-1	803
Boreham Wood	Chalfont St Peter	1-0	151
Boston United	Wisbech Town	1-2	983
Bracknell Town	Thamesmead Town	1-1	43
Bridport	Merthyr Tydfil	0-3	311
Bromley	Herne Bay	3-1	338
Burton Albion	Stratford Town	4-0	746
Cambridge City	Canvey Island	2-3	268
Carshalton Athletic	Sheppey United	3-1	289
Chasetown	Solihull Borough	1-3	122
Chatham Town	Ramsgate	1-1	131
Chelmsford City	Collier Row	1-0	991
Cheltenham Town	Yate Town	5-0	659
Chertsey Town	Shoreham	2-2	272
Chorley	Farsley Celtic	2-2	251
Concord Rangers	Hayes	0-3	150
Congleton Town	Pontefract Collieries	3-1	139
Corinthian-Casuals	Margate	2-5	120
Crook Town	Curzon Ashton	1-1	118
Croydon	Hastings Town	2-3	166
Dagenham & Red	Hornchurch	4-0	539
Denaby United	Bootle	3-0	114
Diss Town	Heybridge Swifts	0-2	406
Dorchester Town	Wimborne Town	2-2	764
Dover Athletic	Bognor Regis Town	1-2	578
Dulwich Hamlet	Southwick	7-1	298
Durham City	Blackpool Rovers	1-1	237
Eastwood Town	Buxton	2-1	229
Eccleshill United	Lincoln United	2-3	73
Edgware Town	Chesham United	0-1	226
Emley	Thackley	6-0	186
Erith & Belvedere	Redhill	4-1	87
Esh Winning	West Auckland T	1-2	98
Eynesbury Rovers	Halstead Town	7-1	150
Falmouth Town	Weston-super-Mare	1-1	225
Farnborough Town	Dartford	1-0	602
Fisher	Lewes	7-0	181
Forest Green Rovers	Mangotsfield United	2-1	179
Frickley Athletic	Prescot	0-0	160
Gainsborough Trinity	Arnold Town	2-0	385
Gateshead	Dunston Feds	3-2	492
Gloucester City	Bristol Manor Farm	8-0	514
Gravesend & N	Godalming & G	7-0	443
Grays Athletic	Wealdstone	2-2	291
Great Yarmouth Town	Mirrlees Blackstone	2-1	102
Gresley Rovers	Dudley Town	1-2	541
Guisborough Town	Murton	1-0	120
Guiseley	Leigh R.M.I.	3-0	484
Halesowen Town	Blakenall	3-2	618
Hampton	Staines Town	1-2	218
Harrogate Town	Bedlington Terriers	1-2	183
Harrow Borough	Leatherhead	2-1	198
Harwich & Parkeston	Braintree Town	0-1	269
Hatfield Main	Ilkeston Town	0-2	185
Hednesford Town	Corby Town	3-1	732
Hendon	Flackwell Heath	8-0	156
Hinckley Athletic	Kidsgrove Athletic	3-1	271
Hoddesdon Town	Woodbridge Town	0-2	50
Horsham	Sittingbourne	0-5	376
Hyde United	Winterton Rangers	6-0	240
Knowsley United	Bradford P A	0-0	74
Lancaster City	Pickering Town	2-1	208
Langney Sports	Windsor & Eton	1-3	236
Leek Town	Clitheroe	1-1	202
Long Buckby	Sutt Coldfield Town	2-1	82
Lye Town	Eastwood Hanley	1-2	68
March Town United	Holbeach United	0-3	98
Marine	Louth United	4-0	259
Matlock Town	Great Harwood T	5-2	290
Molesey	Whitstable Town	4-1	130
Morecambe	Sheffield	7-0	469
Morpeth Town	Whickham	1-2	70
Mossley	Hallam	1-0	176
Nantwich Town	Droylsden	3-0	84
Netherfield	Peterlee Newtown	2-4	128
Newcastle Town	Immingham Town	5-0	59
Newport A.F.C.	Brockenhurst	5-0	1011
Northwich Victoria	Burscough	5-0	655
Northwood	Uxbridge	0-5	143
Oxford City	Witney Town	1-1	376
Paget Rangers	Wednesfield	1-0	85
Paulton Rovers	Welton Rovers	1-1	117
Purfleet	Felixstowe Town	4-0	105
R C Warwick	Oldbury United	1-0	108
Raunds Town	Desborough Town	3-0	112
Raynes Park Vale	Banstead Athletic	1-2	58
Redditch United	Moor Green	1-3	210
Romford	Hadleigh United	1-0	196
Rossendale United	Colwyn Bay	1-4	102
Rushden & Diamonds	Grantham Town	4-1	1681
Ryde Sports	Weymouth	1-1	250
Saffron Walden Town	King's Lynn	0-2	230
Salisbury City	Hungerford Town	5-2	373

Saltash United	Taunton Town	1-2	
Sandwell Borough	Cogenhoe United	2-1	28
Spennymoor United	Glasshoughton W	1-0	247
St Albans City	Barton Rovers	4-1	407
Stafford Rangers	Rothwell Town	6-1	306
Stevenage Borough	Brook House	0-0	814
Stotfold	Hemel Hempstead	2-1	60
Stourbridge	Evesham United	2-2	141
Sudbury Town	Tiptree United	3-0	334
Sudbury Wanderers	Watton United	3-1	42
Telford United	Shifnal Town	4-0	837
Thame United	A.F.C. Totton	1-1	
Thatcham Town	Steyning Town	5-1	91
Tiverton Town	Barnstaple Town	9-0	448
Tooting & Mitch	Peacehaven & Tsl	0-0	197
Tow Law Town	Chester-le-St Town	3-3	
Trowbridge Town	Gosport Borough	8-1	282
Tuffley Rovers	Cinderford Town	0-4	124
Tufnell Park	Hertford Town	2-2	
V.S. Rugby	Leicester United	1-2	307
Walton & Hersham	Camberley Town	4-0	164
Warrington Town	Trafford	2-2	87
Waterlooville	Calne Town	5-0	223
Welling United	Wick	2-0	547
Wembley	Langford	3-0	39
Whitby Town	Billingham Town	0-1	157
Whitley Bay	Workington	1-2	277
Wingate & Finchley	Ruislip Manor	2-3	170
Winsford United	Borrowash Victoria	1-0	357
Wokingham Town	Ringmer	3-1	226
Worksop Town	Radcliffe Borough	4-0	357
Worthing	Buckingham Town	1-1	464

First Qualifying Round Replays

Clitheroe	Leek Town	2-2	237
Welton Rovers	Paulton Rovers	2-1	173
Armitage	Atherstone United	3-3	229
Blackpool Rovers	Durham City	1-5	41
Boston Town	Bishop's Stortford	5-2	183
Brook House	Stevenage Borough	1-5	167
Buckingham Town	Worthing	0-0	84
Chester-le-St Town	Tow Law Town	1-3	129
Curzon Ashton	Crook Town	3-1	108
Elmore	Bideford	2-6	75
Evesham United	Stourbridge	3-0	154
Hertford Town	Tufnell Park	5-1	62
Peacehaven & Tel	Tooting & Mitch	0-1	291
Prescot	Frickley Athletic	2-2	32
Ramsgate	Chatham Town	0-2	105
Shoreham	Chertsey Town	1-3	236
Thamesmead Town	Bracknell Town	2-3	43
Trafford	Warrington Town	4-3	118
Wealdstone	Grays Athletic	4-3	209
Weston-super-Mare	Falmouth Town	5-0	250
Weymouth	Ryde Sports	2-1	609
Wimborne Town	Dorchester Town	0-2	604
Witney Town	Oxford City	3-1	341
Bradford P A	Knowsley United	3-2	158

Farsley Celtic	Chorley	1-2	221
A.F.C. Totton	Thame United	0-4	203

First Qualifying Round Second Replays

Armitage	Atherstone United	5-4	275
Clitheroe	Leek Town	0-0	258
Prescot	Frickley Athletic	0-1	50
Worthing	Buckingham Town	2-2	277

First Qualifying Round Third Replays

Buckingham Town	Worthing	6-1	100
Leek Town	Clitheroe	1-0	181

Second Qualifying Round

Accrington Stanley	Bradford P A	1-2	553
Arlesey Town	Sudbury Wanderers	1-2	157
Armitage	Solihull Borough	2-3	118
Ashford Town	Hastings Town	3-1	966
Baldock Town	Hayes	0-1	319
Bamber Bridge	Mossley	0-2	583
Banstead Athletic	Bognor Regis Town	0-3	
Bedlington Terriers	Whickham	1-0	132
Berkhamsted Town	Dagenham & Red	1-2	292
Bideford	Taunton Town	4-3	170
Billericay Town	Great Yarmouth T	2-0	298
Billingham Synthonia	Blyth Spartans	0-2	246
Billingham Town	West Auckland T	1-0	32
Bishop Auckland	Tow Law Town	2-1	311
Boreham Wood	Staines Town	0-1	314
Bracknell Town	Harrow Borough	2-1	
Burton Albion	Stafford Rangers	1-1	1014
Canvey Island	Braintree Town	2-0	301
Carshalton Athletic	Windsor & Eton	4-3	360
Chorley	Colwyn Bay	1-2	234
Clapton	Hendon	2-3	158
Congleton Town	Hinckley Athletic	1-1	203
Denaby United	Hyde United	1-2	185
Dorchester Town	Basingstoke Town	2-0	609
Dulwich Hamlet	Chatham Town	2-1	293
Durham City	Guisborough Town	2-1	308
Emley	Winsford United	1-1	253
Erith & Belvedere	Sittingbourne	2-2	247
Evesham United	Bedworth United	2-0	223
Eynesbury Rovers	Wisbech Town	3-3	320
Fisher	Farnborough Town	1-4	335
Forest Green Rovers	Cheltenham Town	3-0	544
Frickley Athletic	Eastwood Town	2-4	201
Gainsborough Trinity	Nantwich Town	5-0	375
Gateshead	Barrow	2-2	721
Gloucester City	Cinderford Town	0-1	921
Guiseley	Leek Town	4-0	507
Halesowen Town	Moor Green	1-0	620
Hertford Town	Wealdstone	1-0	262
Holbeach United	Chelmsford City	0-0	350
King's Lynn	Boston Town	5-1	1157
Lancaster City	Peterlee Newtown	3-0	217
Leicester United	Paget Rangers	3-2	53
Lincoln United	Northwich Victoria	1-4	354

Matlock Town	Ilkeston Town	1-2	759
Molesey	Gravesend & North	0-6	295
Newcastle Town	Marine	0-1	313
Purfleet	Chesham United	3-1	220
R C Warwick	Long Buckby	2-0	159
Raunds Town	Telford United	1-2	225
Romford	Stotfold	4-1	188
Rushden & D	Eastwood Hanley	1-0	1652
Salisbury City	Newport I.O.W.	1-3	412
Sandwell Borough	Dudley Town	2-1	90
Sudbury Town	Heybridge Swifts	2-1	502
Tamworth	Hednesford Town	1-2	1138
Thame United	Witney Town	1-1	334
Thatcham Town	Buckingham Town	0-1	130
Tooting & Mitch	Chertsey Town	2-2	253
Trafford	Curzon Ashton	1-2	108
Uxbridge	Stevenage Borough	0-1	460
Walton & Hersham	Margate	2-2	225
Welling United	Bromley	2-2	722
Welton Rovers	Trowbridge Town	1-2	374
Wembley	Ruislip Manor	3-0	108
Weston-super-Mare	Tiverton Town	1-1	701
Weymouth	Waterlooville	1-0	754
Wokingham Town	Aldershot Town	1-2	1469
Woodbridge Town	St Albans City	1-1	292
Workington	Spennymoor United	2-4	487
Worksop Town	Morecambe	2-3	529
Newport A.F.C.	Merthyr Tydfil	3-3	1816

Second Qualifying Round Replays

Chelmsford City	Holbeach United	3-1	858
Winsford United	Emley	2-1	248
Barrow	Gateshead	1-0	1908
Bromley	Welling United	3-3	451
Chertsey Town	Tooting & Mitch	1-2	327
Hinckley Athletic	Congleton Town	1-0	213
Margate	Walton & Hersham	0-1	189
Merthyr Tydfil	Newport A.F.C.	1-2	887
St Albans City	Woodbridge Town	2-0	358
Stafford Rangers	Burton Albion	2-3	610
Wisbech Town	Eynesbury Rovers	6-1	422
Witney Town	Thame United	2-3	273
Sittingbourne	Erith & Belvedere	6-1	556
Tiverton Town	Weston-super-Mare	1-0	801

Second Qualifying Round Second Replay

Welling United	Bromley	1-2	701

Third Qualifying Round

Barrow	Durham City	1-1	1413
Bishop Auckland	Lancaster City	0-1	298
Blyth Spartans	Bedlington Terriers	3-1	648
Bognor Regis Town	Dulwich Hamlet	4-2	780
Bracknell Town	Wembley	4-1	169
Bradford P A	Curzon Ashton	2-1	202
Bromley	Sittingbourne	1-1	692
Buckingham Town	Aldershot Town	0-1	916
Burton Albion	R C Warwick	2-0	867
Chelmsford City	Billericay Town	1-1	2074
Dagenham & Red	Purfleet	1-1	718
Farnborough Town	Walton & Hersham	3-2	761
Forest Green Rovers	Cinderford Town	1-1	335
Gravesend & North	Carshalton Athletic	2-1	685
Guiseley	Mossley	6-1	608
Hednesford Town	Solihull Borough	2-2	1013
Hendon	Hayes	0-3	376
Hertford Town	Sudbury Wanderers	0-2	205
Hyde United	Colwyn Bay	1-2	414
King's Lynn	Canvey Island	1-0	1737
Leicester United	Evesham United	0-1	169
Marine	Ilkeston Town	0-0	499
Morecambe	Gainsborough T	6-2	805
Northwich Victoria	Eastwood Town	0-0	742
Sandwell Borough	Rushden & D	1-6	250
Spennymoor United	Billingham Town	6-1	337
St Albans City	Romford	3-1	648
Stevenage Borough	Staines Town	2-0	1176
Telford United	Halesowen Town	4-1	904
Thame United	Newport I.O.W.	1-1	308
Tiverton Town	Bideford	4-1	653
Tooting & Mitch	Ashford Town	0-1	540
Trowbridge Town	Newport A.F.C.	2-0	623
Weymouth	Dorchester Town	2-3	2527
Winsford United	Hinckley Athletic	3-2	236
Wisbech Town	Sudbury Town	1-0	705

Third Qualifying Round First Replays

Purfleet	Dagenham & Red	2-1	683
Billericay Town	Chelmsford City	2-1	1704
Cinderford Town	Forest Green Rovers	1-1	684
Eastwood Town	Northwich Victoria	1-2	640
Ilkeston Town	Marine	1-2	801
Newport I.O.W.	Thame United	3-1	863
Durham City	Barrow	0-1	764
Sittingbourne	Bromley	3-2	1030
Solihull Borough	Hednesford Town	1-2	421

Third Qualifying Round Second Replay

Forest Green Rovers	Cinderford Town	1-3	671

Fourth Qualifying Round

Ashford Town	Aldershot Town	2-0	2016
Aylesbury United	Stevenage Borough	1-3	1480
Billericay Town	Wisbech Town	1-1	1106
Blyth Spartans	Guiseley	2-0	775
Burton Albion	Bracknell Town	3-1	1008
Canvey Island	Hednesford Town	2-0	710
Cinderford Town	Bath City	3-2	730
Farnborough Town	Yeovil Town	2-1	1409
Gravesend & North	Marlow	1-1	814
Hayes	Sudbury Wanderers	4-0	420
Hitchin Town	St Albans City	2-1	1147
Kettering Town	Bromsgrove Rovers	0-0	2427
Kingstonian	Trowbridge Town	3-1	781
Macclesfield Town	Northwich Victoria	0-1	1707
Marine	Bradford P A	2-0	626

Newport I.O.W.	Bashley	1-1	1061
Nuneaton Borough	Evesham United	6-1	1415
Purfleet	Rushden & D	1-1	650
Runcorn	Halifax Town	2-1	901
Sittingbourne	Dorchester Town	1-2	1232
Spennymoor United	Lancaster City	1-0	621
Stalybridge Celtic	Colwyn Bay	2-2	617
Sutton United	Crawley Town	4-1	1637
Telford United	Southport	3-0	898
Tiverton Town	Bognor Regis Town	1-4	1101
Winsford United	Barrow	0-3	714
Witton Albion	Morecambe	3-2	931
Yeading	Slough Town	0-2	473

Fourth Qualifying Round First Replays

Bashley	Newport I.O.W.	2-3	558
Bromsgrove Rovers	Kettering Town	2-2	1246
Colwyn Bay	Stalybridge Celtic	3-0	617
Marlow	Gravesend & North	3-3	814
Rushden & D	Purfleet	3-1	2850
Wisbech Town	Billericay Town	2-0	

Fourth Qualifying Round Second Replays

Gravesend & North	Marlow	4-0	1346
Kettering Town	Bromsgrove Rovers	1-2	2283

First Round Proper

Altrincham	Crewe Alexandra	0-2	
Barnet	Woking	2-2	3034
Barrow	Nuneaton Borough	2-1	2869
Bognor Regis Town	Ashford Town	1-1	2200
Bradford City	Burton Albion	4-3	4920
Brentford	Farnborough Town	1-1	4711
Bury	Blyth Spartans	0-2	3076
Cinderford Town	Bromsgrove Rovers	2-1	1850
Gravesend & North	Colchester United	2-0	3128
Hereford United	Stevenage Borough	2-1	3321
Hitchin Town	Bristol Rovers	2-1	3101
Kidderminster H	Sutton United	2-2	2513
Kingstonian	Wisbech Town	5-1	1396
Newport I.O.W.	Enfield	1-1	1818
Northampton Town	Hayes	1-0	5389
Northwich Victoria	Scunthorpe United	1-3	2685
Oxford United	Dorchester Town	9-1	3819
Runcorn	Wigan Athletic	1-1	2844
Rushden & D	Cardiff City	1-3	4212
Shrewsbury Town	Marine	11-2	2845
Slough Town	Plymouth Argyle	0-2	3013
Spennymoor United	Colwyn Bay	0-1	824
Telford United	Witton Albion	2-1	1277
Canvey Island	Brighton & H A	2-2	3403

First Round Proper Replays

Ashford Town	Bognor Regis Town	0-1	2542
Brighton & H A	Canvey Island	4-1	7008
Enfield	Newport I.O.W.	2-1	2034
Sutton United	Kidderminster H	1-1	1804
	Pens(3-2)		

Wigan Athletic	Runcorn	4-2	3224
Woking	Barnet	2-1	3535
Farnborough Town	Brentford	0-4	3581

Second Round Proper

Barrow	Wigan Athletic	0-4	3500
Blackpool	Colwyn Bay	2-0	4581
Cinderford Town	Gravesend & North	1-1	2067
Enfield	Woking	1-1	3477
Gillingham	Hitchin Town	3-0	7142
Hereford United	Sutton United	2-0	2908
Peterborough United	Bognor Regis Town	4-0	5004
Stockport County	Blyth Spartans	2-0	5693
Telford United	Notts County	0-2	2831
Kingstonian	Plymouth Argyle	1-2	2961

Second Round Proper Replays

Woking	Enfield	2-1	2253
Gravesend & North	Cinderford Town	3-0	2851

Third Round Proper

Gravesend & North	Aston Villa	0-3	26021
Swindon Town	Woking	2-0	10322

F A CARLSBERG VASE

First Qualifying Round

Abingdon United	B.A.T. Sports	3-0	32
Alnwick Town	Ryhope C A	1-1	46
Ashford T (Middx)	Southwick	6-0	86
Bedfont	Ramsgate	2-3	
Bemerton Heath	Kintbury Rangers	5-2	44
Blackpool Rovers	Newcastle Town	0-2	37
Boldmere St Michaels	Knypersley Victoria	6-0	48
Bracknell Town	Redhill	2-0	75
Brantham Athletic	Stowmarket Town	walkover	
Bridgwater Town	Larkhall Athletic	2-0	174
Brockenhurst	Ryde Sports	0-4	47
Burgess Hill Town	Oakwood	3-0	64
Carterton Town	Swanage Town & H	2-0	
Castleton Gabriels	Wythenshawe A	2-3	57
Chasetown	Bloxwich Town	1-2	86
Chippenham Town	Clyst Rovers	2-0	105
Chipstead	Beckenham Town	3-1	64
Clapton	Leverstock Green	4-2	45
Cornard United	Witham Town	1-4	63
Cowes Sports	Gosport Borough	1-2	103
Cradley Town	Holwell Sports	1-0	90
Crediton United	Glastonbury	1-3	
Crowborough Ath	Lancing	1-2	
Dartford	Steyning Town	2-2	275
Didcot Town	A.F.C. Totton	2-3	47
Downham Town	Southend Manor	2-3	50
East Grinstead	Folkestone Invicta	1-4	58
Eastbourne Town	Littlehampton Town	0-1	104
Eccleshill United	Worsborough Bridge	3-0	30
Eppleton Colliery	Seaton Delaval Am	2-2	
Exmouth Town	Warminster Town	1-2	54
Fairford Town	Backwell United	2-3	45
Fakenham Town	Sudbury Wanderers	2-0	30
Ford United	Tilbury	1-3	102
Furness	Sheppey United	1-1	80
Garforth Town	Nuthall	1-1	83
Glasshoughton W	Atherton Collieries	0-0	38
Grove United	Pontefract Collieries	3-3	19
Hall Road Rangers	Nettleham	0-3	
Hallam	Selby Town	0-1	
Hanwell Town	Bedford Town	1-2	69
Harlow Town	Beaconsfield	2-0	48
Harpenden Town	Ware	1-4	41
Harrogate Railway	Shotton Comrades	0-0	65
Haverhill Rovers	Harwich & Park	1-3	
Hemel Hempstead	Stansted	1-3	45
Heswall	Sandiacre Town	2-1	37
Horsham Y.M.C.A.	Epsom & Ewell	2-1	120
Jarrow Roofing	Evenwood Town	2-3	
Kempston Rovers	Amersham Town	0-1	32
Kidsgrove Athletic	Formby	4-1	83
Kingsbury Town	Rayners Lane	2-1	41
Langney Sports	Mile Oak	3-2	174
Liversedge	Daisy Hill	3-0	48
Long Eaton United	Merseyside Police	1-2	70
Maghull	Denaby United	2-3	58
Maltby Miners W	Kimberley Town	4-2	53
March Town United	Hullbridge Sports	4-0	87
Merstham	Chichester City	1-4	60
Milton Keynes	Edgware Town	1-2	50
Newhaven	Canterbury City	1-3	70
Norwich United	Stamford	2-5	42
Odd Down Athletic	Hallen	1-0	52
Ponteland United	Billingham Town	4-3	39
Portfield	Broadbridge Heath	2-0	53
Priory (Eastwood)	Harworth C I	Walkover	
Rocester	Northampton Sp	1-3	
Rossington Main	Louth United	2-3	
Rushall Olympic	Highgate United	3-1	38
Salford City	Sheffield	2-1	45
Saltdean United	Sidley United	2-0	72
Sherborne Town	Portsmouth RN	5-3	
Shifnal Town	Northfield Town	5-1	79
Shirebrook Town	Cheadle Town	1-3	45
Shortwood United	Ilfracombe Town	4-0	60
St Blazey	D.R.G.	3-0	36
Stourport Swifts	Brierley Hill Town	4-0	
Swindon Super	Downton	2-1	70
Tadcaster Albion	Ossett Town	1-2	
Tetley Walker	South Normanton A	1-4	41
Tiptree United	Sawbridgeworth T	2-3	39
Tividale	Stafford Town	0-3	70
Totternhoe	Feltham	2-3	24
Wealdstone	East Ham United	10-0	305
Wellingborough T	Pegasus Juniors	6-0	30
West Allotment C	North Shields A	1-0	66
Romford	Tufnell Park	2-1	

Replayed match in Second Round

Darlaston	Gedling Town	3-2	100

First Qualifying Round Replays

Ashton Collieries	Glasshoughton W	3-3	
Pontefract Collieries	Grove United	0-1	
Sheppey United	Furness	0-3	75
Steyning Town	Dartford	0-4	124
Ryhope C A	Alnwick Town	2-3	22
Shotton Comrades	Harrogate R A	2-1	43
Seaton Delaval Am	Eppleton C W	2-2	
Nuthall	Garforth Town	3-2	100

First Qualifying Round Second Replays

Glasshoughton W	Atherton Collieries	0-2	54
Eppleton C W	Seaton Delaval Am	0-2	30

Second Qualifying Round

Almondsbury Town	Devizes Town	1-2	61
Alnwick Town	Esh Winning	1-2	44
Amersham Town	Hoddesdon Town	0-0	30

Andover	Abingdon United	3-1	171
Annfield Plain	Norton & Stockton A	2-1	
Anstey Nomads	Radford	4-1	111
Ash United	Shoreham	0-6	37
Ashfield United	Heswall	5-1	66
Ashford T (Middx)	Raynes Park Vale	2-1	48
Ashington	Darlington C B	3-0	
A.F.C. Lymington	Carterton Town	1-0	112
A.F.C. Totton	Milton United	2-1	88
Backwell United	Bristol Manor Farm	3-0	72
Banbury United	Birstall United	2-2	133
Barkingside	Harefield United	2-1	40
Barwell	Stratford Town	1-0	31
Bedford Town	Brook House	1-0	248
Bedlington Terriers	Horden CW	5-1	89
Bicester Town	Ryde Sports	1-1	55
Bishop Sutton	Welton Rovers	2-2	78
Blakenall	Desborough Town	1-0	61
Bloxwich Town	Wednesfield	3-1	57
Bootle	Grove United	2-1	65
Borrowash Victoria	Cheadle Town	1-4	43
Bourne Town	Great Yarmouth T	2-1	120
Brentwood	Welwyn Garden City	1-1	55
Brigg Town	Rossendale United	9-0	78
Brimsdown Rovers	Romford	0-4	
Brislington	Torrington	0-2	72
Burgess Hill Town	Selsey	3-1	96
Chard Town	Dawlish Town	2-0	56
Chatham Town	Camberley Town	5-2	86
Cheshunt	Stansted	1-0	44
Chichester City	Canterbury City	1-0	50
Cirencester Town	Old Georgians	1-5	47
Clitheroe	Immingham Town	4-0	154
Cockfosters	Edgware Town	1-2	120
Cogenhoe United	Barrow Town	2-0	96
Concord Rangers	Potters Bar Town	2-0	49
Cove	Wick	0-2	110
Cradley Town	Halesowen Harriers	2-3	145
Cranleigh	Egham Town	3-1	99
Croydon Athletic	Bracknell Town	0-0	33
Darlaston	Northampton Spencer	4-1	82
Dartford	Furness	1-3	408
Darwen	Ossett Albion	0-3	104
Deal Town	Langney Sports	2-1	156
Denaby United	Ossett Town	0-1	80
Easington Colliery	West Allotment Celtic	4-2	18
Endsleigh	Bridgwater Town	0-1	
Eton Wick	Stotfold	2-6	35
Evenwood Town	Crook Town	1-3	92
Eynesbury Rovers	Mirrlees Blackstone	2-2	80
Felixstowe Town	Harwich & Parkeston	1-2	135
Feltham	Biggleswade Town	2-3	28
Ferryhill Athletic	Yorkshire Amateur	0-1	28
First Tower United	Bournemouth	1-2	50
Flackwell Heath	Hornchurch	1-0	102
Flixton	Poulton Victoria	2-1	92
Friar Lane Old Boys	Oldbury United	0-1	98
Frome Town	Torpoint Athletic	1-2	92
Godalming & G	Three Bridges	1-0	134
Gosport Borough	Calne Town	3-1	56
Great Wakering R	Clacton Town	1-2	101
Greenwich Borough	Chalfont St Peter	0-1	74
Hailsham Town	Portfield	4-0	130
Hampton	Viking Sports	3-0	88
Harlow Town	East Thurrock Utd	5-4	52
Harrow Hill	Bideford	3-4	47
Hatfield Main	Parkgate	7-1	84
Heanor Town	Maine Road	2-2	
Herne Bay	Cray Wanderers	1-0	112
Hertford Town	Eton Manor	3-1	70
Histon	Fakenham Town	1-3	40
Holbeach United	Sawbridgeworth T	1-4	148
Horsham	Crockenhill	3-0	141
Horsham Y.M.C.A.	Faversham Town	0-0	61
Hungerford Town	Wantage Town	3-1	108
Ipswich Wanderers	Gorleston	0-3	91
Kidsgrove Athletic	Chadderton	3-0	96
Kingsbury Town	Northwood	0-1	60
Knowle	Pershore Town	2-3	36
Lancing	Corinthian	2-3	81
Langford	London Colney	3-2	52
Letchworth GC	Leighton Town	Walkover	
Liversedge	Newcastle Town	0-1	56
Long Buckby	Stourport Swifts	4-1	47
Long Sutton Athletic	Brightlingsea United	Walkover	
Lowestoft Town	Mildenhall Town	5-2	114
Maldon Town	Burnham Ramblers	3-1	77
Maltby Miners W	Nuthall	0-2	40
Meir K.A.	Walsall Wood	0-5	61
Melksham Town	Saltash United	0-1	65
Merseyside Police	North Ferriby Utd	2-3	
Minehead	Warminster Town	0-1	39
Nantwich Town	Harworth C I	3-0	81
Netherne	Lewes	3-1	41
Nettleham	Louth United	1-1	30
Newcastle Ben Pk	Whickham	2-3	
Newport Pag T	Wellingborough T	3-3	40
Newquay	Bridport	0-3	133
Oakham United	Blidworth MW	2-1	40
Odd Down Athletic	Glastonbury	2-0	25
Oldham Town	Prescot	3-2	45
Pagham	Arundel	4-3	81
Penrith	Willington	0-1	79
Petersfield Town	North Leigh	0-1	50
Pickering Town	Washington	3-4	76
Porthleven	Keynsham Town	0-0	64
Potton United	Aveley	1-2	110
Ramsgate	Hassocks	1-2	90
Ringmer	Whitstable Town	2-3	144
Rushall Olympic	Upton Town	3-1	70
Saffron Walden Town	Swaffham Town	1-2	101
Salford City	Atherton Collieries	3-0	52
Saltdean United	Corinthian-Casuals	3-2	245
Sandhurst Town	Peppard	2-3	53
Sandwell Borough	Lye Town	0-3	39
Seaton Delaval Am	Marske United	1-5	
Selby Town	Armthorpe Welfare	2-0	52
Shepshed Dynamo	Kings Heath	4-0	169

Sherborne Town	Christchurch	3-1	39
Shifnal Town	Bolehall Swifts	1-1	107
Shillington	Clapton	2-4	60
Shortwood United	Tuffley Rovers	3-1	77
Shotton Comrades	Morpeth Town	1-0	19
Slade Green	Leatherhead	5-1	68
Soham Town Rangers	Ely City	1-4	240
South Normanton Ath	Hucknall Town	0-5	180
Southall	Royston Town	1-3	
Southend Manor	Newmarket Town	0-2	50
St Blazey	Chippenham Town	0-3	65
St Helens Town	Eccleshill United	4-0	99
Stafford Town	Willenhall Town	2-4	91
Stamford	St Neots Town	0-1	105
Stapenhill	West Mids Police	1-2	68
Stewarts & Lloyds	Boldmere St Michaels	1-3	32
Stockton	Ponteland United	0-1	32
Swindon Super	Thatcham Town	2-1	62
Thamesmead Town	Chipstead	1-0	36
Tilbury	Waltham Abbey	2-1	45
Trafford	Staveley MW	4-2	89
Tring Town	Wingate & Finchley	2-4	
Truro City	Cadbury Heath	6-2	151
Warboys Town	March Town United	2-0	129
Ware	Bowers United	3-0	70
Watton United	Stowmarket Town	0-1	68
Wealdstone	St Margaretsbury	1-1	241
Wellington	Liskeard Athletic	2-4	65
West Wickham	Eastbourne United	2-0	69
Westbury United	Bemerton Heath H	0-1	105
Westfields	Brackley Town	0-2	61
Windsor & Eton	Folkestone Invicta	2-2	149
Winterton Rangers	Rainworth MW	3-1	50
Witham Town	Spalding United	1-1	59
Woodbridge Town	Chatteris Town	5-0	85
Wootton Blue Cross	Hillingdon Borough	4-3	50
Worthing United	Littlehampton Town	1-4	68
Wroxham	Somersham Town	7-3	73
Wythenshawe Amateur	Arnold Town	3-2	94

Second Qualifying Round Replays

Welton Rovers	Bishop Sutton	0-1	71
Bolehall Swifts	Shifnal Town	1-3	59
Bracknell Town	Croydon Athletic	4-3	51
Faversham Town	Horsham Y.M.C.A.	3-4	66
Folkestone Invicta	Windsor & Eton	4-5	141
Hoddesdon Town	Amersham Town	4-0	40
Louth United	Nettleham	0-1	38
Maine Road	Heanor Town	5-2	48
Mirrlees Blackstone	Eynesbury Rovers	2-1	67
Ryde Sports	Bicester Town	3-1	70
Spalding United	Witham Town	2-1	112
Wellingborough T	Newport Pagnell T	3-0	30
Welwyn Garden City	Brentwood	1-0	
Keynsham Town	Porthleven	4-2	85
Birstall United	Banbury United	1-3	110
St Margaretsbury	Wealdstone	0-2	194

FIRST ROUND

Andover	Furness	1-4	203
Anstey Nomads	Oldbury United	2-1	115
Ashington	North Ferriby Utd	0-3	152
Aveley	Hertford Town	2-1	97
A.F.C. Lymington	Croydon	3-0	147
Backwell United	Bridport	1-2	85
Banstead Athletic	Chatham Town	1-0	63
Barwell	Dunkirk	1-1	48
Bedlington Terriers	Kidsgrove Athletic	4-0	110
Bideford	Tiverton Town	2-1	465
Blakenall	Lye Town	1-4	84
Bloxwich Town	St Andrews	1-0	64
Boston Town	Shepshed Dynamo	2-6	109
Bourne Town	Bedford Town	0-1	221
Brackley Town	Banbury United	3-0	220
Brandon United	Ossett Albion	0-2	46
Bridgwater Town	Bishop Sutton	1-2	197
Brigg Town	Stocksbridge Park St	2-1	79
Brightlingsea United	Newmarket Town	0-1	84
Burgess Hill Town	Bournemouth	2-1	157
Chalfont St Peter	Maldon Town	3-1	88
Chard Town	Saltash United	2-1	
Chichester City	Deal Town	2-0	80
Clapton	Leighton Town	1-2	58
Clitheroe	Bootle	5-1	
Collier Row	Clacton Town	8-1	114
Corinthian	A.F.C. Totton	2-1	89
Cranleigh	Peppard	3-2	102
Crook Town	Ashfield United	2-0	133
Darlaston	Walsall Wood	1-1	102
Devizes Town	Bemerton Heath H	0-3	66
Easington Colliery	Wythenshawe Amateur	2-1	58
Eastleigh	Hailsham Town	2-1	131
Eastwood Hanley	Shotton Comrades	2-0	82
Edgware Town	Wingate & Finchley	4-1	206
Elmore	Chippenham Town	1-4	52
Esh Winning	Winterton Rangers	2-5	86
Falmouth Town	Liskeard Athletic	3-0	
Flixton	Glossop North End	3-0	130
Gorleston	Biggleswade Town	4-0	173
Hadleigh United	Mirrlees Blackstone	4-2	77
Halstead Town	Wisbech Town	1-2	401
Harlow Town	Barkingside	2-1	52
Harwich & Parkeston	Warboys Town	2-0	231
Hatfield Main	Selby Town	0-2	82
Hinckley Athletic	Wellingborough T	3-2	
Horsham	Hassocks	6-3	217
Horsham Y.M.C.A.	Wick	1-3	94
Hucknall Town	Shifnal Town	2-1	
Langford	Hoddesdon Town	3-1	90
Mangotsfield United	Truro City	3-0	185
Netherne	Bracknell Town	3-4	50
Nettleham	Nantwich Town	2-0	59
Newcastle Town	Burscough	3-1	119
Northwood	Stotfold	3-0	114
Oadby Town	Boldmere St Michaels	2-5	88
Oakham United	Washington	3-2	45
Oldham Town	Annfield Plain	6-1	

Ossett Town	Willington	7-3	64
Pagham	Windsor & Eton	1-2	135
Paulton Rovers	Shortwood United	2-0	167
Peacehaven & Tels	North Leigh	4-0	187
Pelsall Villa	Halesowen Harriers	3-1	104
Ponteland United	Thackley	2-5	76
Romford	Fakenham Town	2-4	241
Royston Town	Cheshunt	1-2	79
Rushall Olympic	Cogenhoe United	2-1	
Salford City	Nuthall	0-1	34
Sawbridgeworth T	Concord Rangers	1-0	55
Shoreham	Gosport Borough	1-0	131
Slade Green	Saltdean United	5-1	128
South Shields	Maine Road	1-6	192
Spalding United	Ely City	1-3	131
St Neots Town	Tilbury	1-4	150
Stamco	Godalming & G	1-2	485
Stowmarket Town	Woodbridge Town	2-2	209
Swaffham Town	Brentwood	2-3	158
Swindon Super	Keynsham Town	1-2	67
Thamesmead Town	Ashford T (Middx)	1-0	71
Torpoint Athletic	Odd Down	3-1	80
Torrington	Sherborne Town	3-0	81
Trafford	St Helens Town	2-0	74
Tunbridge Wells	Hungerford Town	1-6	155
Ware	Basildon United	4-2	100
Warminster Town	Barnstaple Town	3-2	130
West Mids Police	Pershore Town	3-4	36
West Wickham	Herne Bay	0-3	96
Whickham	Marske United	3-2	50
Whitehawk	Littlehampton Town	5-1	95
Whitstable Town	Ryde Sports	4-0	210
Willenhall Town	Long Buckby	1-0	87
Wimborne Town	Old Georgians	2-1	185
Wootton Blue Cross	Flackwell Heath	2-2	64
Wroxham	Lowestoft Town	2-0	131
Yorkshire Amateur	Cheadle Town	2-0	40
Wealdstone	Hampton	0-3	333

FIRST ROUND REPLAYS

Flackwell Heath	Wootton Blue Cross	1-2	
Walsall Wood	Darlaston	0-1	
Woodbridge Town	Stowmarket	2-1	
Dunkirk	Barwell	0-2	50

SECOND ROUND

Anstey Nomads	Shepshed Dynamo	4-1	300
Arlesey Town	Thamesmead Town	1-2	477
Armitage	Rushall Olympic	0-2	77
A.F.C. Lymington	Warminster Town	2-0	170
Belper Town	Bloxwich Town	3-1	250
Brackley Town	Aveley	2-3	100
Bridport	Bemerton Heath Harl	2-0	190
Brigg Town	Tow Law Town	3-0	128
Burgess Hill Town	Wootton Blue Cross	3-2	110
Burnham	Windsor & Eton	0-4	176
Cheshunt	Bedford Town	2-3	
Clitheroe	R.T.M. Newcastle	2-1	170
Collier Row	Woodbridge Town	5-4	164

Cranleigh	Banstead Athletic	0-2	
Diss Town	Herne Bay	2-0	429
Dorking	Bishop Sutton	2-2	56
Flixton	Hucknall Town	5-1	118
Furness	Sawbridgeworth T	0-0	95
Godalming & Guild	MangotsfieldUtd	2-5	215
Gorleston	Fakenham Town	3-2	216
Hadleigh United	Edgware Town	0-2	104
Hampton	Ware	5-2	128
Harwich & Parkeston	Tilbury	2-3	192
Horsham	Falmouth Town	0-2	302
Keynsham Town	Chard Town	0-1	129
Langford	Whitstable Town	0-1	155
Leighton Town	Chalfont St Peter	1-1	149
Maine Road	Eastwood Hanley	1-4	66
Metropolitan Police	Canvey Island	1-3	165
Nettleham	Pershore Town	1-4	81
North Ferriby United	Oldham Town	7-0	107
Northwood	Ely City	2-1	146
Nuthall	Boldmere St Michaels	1-3	50
Oakham United	Lye Town	1-4	45
Paulton Rovers	Bideford	2-0	182
Peacehaven & Tels	Harlow Town	2-0	214
Pelsall Villa	Barwell	2-4	155
Raunds Town	Hinckley Athletic	2-2	210
Selby Town	Billingham Synthonia	3-2	158
Shildon	Mossley	1-2	116
Shoreham	Chichester City	1-2	83
Slade Green	Newmarket Town	2-0	86
Taunton Town	Bracknell Town	3-3	377
Thackley	Bedlington Terriers	0-1	80
Torpoint Athletic	Eastleigh	1-0	127
Trafford	Darlaston	3-0	112
Whitehawk	Corinthian	3-1	89
Wick	Chippenham Town	0-1	180
Willenhall Town	Newcastle Town	3-1	107
Wimborne Town	Torrington	1-2	152
Winterton Rangers	Northallerton	1-0	70
Wisbech Town	Wivenhoe Town	2-3	538
Wroxham	Brentwood	1-2	115
Yorkshire Amateur	West Auckland T	1-1	57
Chester-le-St Town	Whickham	5-1	
Dunston Fed Brewery	Cammell Laird	2-0	96
Easington Colliery	Ossett Town	2-1	31
Hebburn	Ossett Albion	2-1	53
Durham City	Whitby Town	4-1	254
Guisborough Town	Crook Town	1-1	107
Murton	Consett	2-1	46
Prudhoe Town	Goole Town	2-0	48
Seaham Red Star	Peterlee Newtown	2-1	40

SECOND ROUND REPLAYS

Bracknell Town	Taunton Town	1-2	103
Chalfont St Peter	Leighton Town	2-0	85
Hinckley Athletic	Raunds Town	0-2	355
Sawbridgeworth T	Furness	1-1	60
West Auckland Town	Yorkshire Amateur	2-1	
Bishop Sutton	Dorking	2-0	81
Crook Town	Guisborough Town	1-2	

SECOND ROUND SECOND REPLAY

Sawbridgeworth T	Furness	1-2	118

THIRD ROUND

A.F.C. Lymington	Bishop Sutton	4-0	177
Barwell	Mossley	3-1	130
Boldmere St Michaels	Trafford	0-2	83
Bridport	Windsor & Eton	2-4	205
Brigg Town	Guisborough Town	2-0	82
Burgess Hill Town	Pershore Town	2-1	225
Canvey Island	Bedford Town	2-0	511
Chester-le-St Town	Lye Town	1-3	145
Clitheroe	West Auckland T	6-0	210
Easington Colliery	Anstey Nomads	2-3	65
Hampton	Collier Row	0-1	242
Hebburn	Durham City	0-4	65
Hungerford Town	Mangotsfield United	0-0	175
Murton	Selby Town	3-5	
North Ferriby United	Eastwood Hanley	4-2	109
Northwood	Gorleston	0-1	158
Paulton Rovers	Falmouth Town	2-0	275
Prudhoe Town	Dunston Fed Brewery	1-2	
Raunds Town	Furness	1-1	196
Rushall Olympic	Bedlington Terriers	0-4	100
Seaham Red Star	Belper Town	1-2	130
Taunton Town	Chippenham Town	4-0	408
Torpoint Athletic	Chard Town	4-2	111
Torrington	Chichester City	1-2	157
Whitehawk	Banstead Athletic	0-2	108
Whitstable Town	Peacehaven & Tels	0-1	295
Willenhall Town	Chalfont St Peter	2-1	122
Winterton Rangers	Flixton	0-4	104
Wivenhoe Town	Edgware Town	3-1	113

THIRD ROUND REPLAYS

Mangotsfield United	Hungerford Town	5-1	186
Slade Green	Diss Town	0-2	322
Thamesmead Town	Brentwood	3-1	71
Tilbury	Aveley	2-4	158
Furness	Raunds Town	1-1	150

THIRD ROUND SECOND REPLAYS

Raunds Town	Furness	5-2	210

SEMI FINALS 1ST LEGS

Brigg Town	Flixton	0-0	1128
Mangotsfield United	Clitheroe	1-0	998

FOURTH ROUND

A.F.C. Lymington	Torpoint Athletic	1-3	331
Brigg Town	Bedlington Terriers	2-1	180
Burgess Hill Town	Collier Row	0-1	365
Canvey Island	Gorleston	1-0	604
Chichester City	Thamesmead Town	1-3	310
Clitheroe	Willenhall Town	3-0	451
Diss Town	Banstead Athletic	1-2	682
Durham City	Belper Town	2-3	570
Flixton	Dunston Fed Brewery	2-0	180
Lye Town	Barwell	0-2	310
North Ferriby United	Anstey Nomads	2-3	204
Raunds Town	Taunton Town	4-1	290
Trafford	Selby Town	0-0	151
Windsor & Eton	Peacehaven & Tels	0-1	278
Wivenhoe Town	Aveley	4-0	301

FOURTH ROUND REPLAYS

Selby Town	Trafford	1-1	320
Paulton Rovers	Mangotsfield Utd	0-3	447

FOURTH ROUND SECOND REPLAY

Selby Town	Trafford	0-3	550

FIFTH ROUND

Banstead Athletic	Peacehaven & Tels	2-3	250
Brigg Town	Trafford	1-0	320
Collier Row	Anstey Nomads	6-0	430
Flixton	Barwell	3-1	328
Wivenhoe Town	Mangotsfield Utd	2-2	543
Thamesmead Town	Canvey Island	1-2	811
Belper Town	Clitheroe	0-3	754
Raunds Town	Torpoint Athletic	2-0	296

FIFTH ROUND REPLAY

Mangotsfield United	Wivenhoe Town	3-0	446

QUARTER FINALS

Brigg Town	Collier Row	2-0	560
Clitheroe	Peacehaven & Tels	1-0	850
Flixton	Canvey Island	3-0	860
Mangotsfield United	Raunds Town	2-2	725

QUARTER FINAL REPLAY

Raunds Town	Mangotsfield Utd	0-1	638

SEMI FINALS 2ND LEGS

Clitheroe	Mangotsfield Utd	2-0	2000
Flixton	Brigg Town	0-1	1540

FINAL (AT WEMBLEY STADIUM)
May 12th 1996

BRIGG TOWN   **3**   **CLITHEROE**   **0**

Stead (2), Lampkin og

Attendance: 7350

First Qualifying Round

Abingdon Town	Bishop's Stortford	1-1	182
Accrington Stanley	Bradford PA	2-2	415
Alfreton Town	Congleton Town	5-0	202
Ashford Town	Sudbury Town	0-2	569
Atherstone United	Lincoln United	2-1	278
Atherton L.R.	Chorley	1-2	298
Barking	Baldock Town	0-0	136
Barrow	Hinckley Town	3-0	1119
Barton Rovers	Crawley Town	1-3	331
Bashley	Margate	1-1	220
Berkhamsted Town	Purfleet	1-2	98
Billericay Town	Wembley	0-4	261
Bridgnorth Town	Leigh R.M.I.	1-1	90
Buckingham Town	Braintree Town	1-1	65
Bury Town	Trowbridge Town	1-2	170
Carshalton Athletic	Dulwich Hamlet	1-1	
Chertsey Town	Poole Town	9-0	326
Curzon Ashton	Worksop Town	4-3	170
Droylsden	Matlock Town	0-3	173
Erith & Belvedere	Basingstoke Town	0-6	112
Fareham Town	Maidenhead United	2-4	90
Farsley Celtic	Bedworth United	3-1	159
Fleetwood Town	Whitley Bay	2-1	119
Forest Green Rovers	Sittingbourne	1-2	101
Harrogate Town	Grantham Town	1-4	191
Harrow Borough	Marlow	1-1	244
Hastings Town	Havant Town	2-2	392
Hendon	Waterlooville	2-2	179
King's Lynn	Uxbridge	1-2	833
Knowsley United	Moor Green	3-2	80
Lancaster City	Solihull Borough	3-0	173
Leyton Pennant	Fleet Town	0-1	66
Newport I.O.W.	Chesham United	1-3	463
Racing Club Warwick	Warrington Town	1-0	130
Radcliffe Borough	Redditch United	3-1	107
Ruislip Manor	Cinderford Town	3-1	142
Salisbury City	Fisher	2-0	319
Staines Town	Wokingham Town	2-1	244
Stourbridge	Frickley Athletic	1-2	126
Sutt Coldfield Town	Bilston Town	1-1	116
Tamworth	Caernarfon Town	walkover	
Weston-super-Mare	Bognor Regis Town	2-6	226
Weymouth	Tonbridge Angels	4-0	714
Whyteleafe	Tooting & Mitch	1-2	161
Winsford United	Paget Rangers	1-1	183
Workington	Leicester United	1-1	286
Worthing	Thame United	1-1	372
Yate Town	Witney Town	3-2	156

First Qualifying Round Replays

Baldock Town	Barking	3-2	136
Bilston Town	Sutt Coldfield Town	4-4	85
Bishop's Stortford	Abingdon Town	5-1	208
Braintree Town	Buckingham Town	1-0	103
Dulwich Hamlet	Carshalton Athletic	1-1	292
Leicester United	Workington	5-0	125
Leigh R.M.I.	Bridgnorth Town	7-0	51
Margate	Bashley	1-2	157
Marlow	Harrow Borough	1-4	261
Thame United	Worthing	2-0	152
Waterlooville	Hendon	0-1	110
Bradford PA	Accrington Stanley	2-3	258
Havant Town	Hastings Town	1-0	141
Paget Rangers	Winsford United	0-2	124

First Qualifying Round Second Replays

Bilston Town	Sutt Coldfield Town	2-1	154
Dulwich Hamlet	Carshalton Athletic	1-2	301

Second Qualifying Round

Alfreton Town	Dudley Town	2-2	260
Atherstone United	Accrington Stanley	1-3	422
Barrow	Winsford United	0-1	1222
Basingstoke Town	Uxbridge	0-2	165
Bilston Town	Leicester United	5-2	100
Bognor Regis Town	Sittingbourne	2-2	400
Braintree Town	Harrow Borough	4-0	203
Carshalton Athletic	Weymouth	5-1	379
Chertsey Town	Chesham United	2-2	518
Clevedon Town	Worcester City	0-4	420
Crawley Town	Bashley	0-1	609
Curzon Ashton	Lancaster City	1-1	278
Eastwood Town	Chorley	0-1	86
Emley	R C Warwick	2-1	225
Evesham United	Aldershot Town	0-2	465
Grantham Town	Farsley Celtic	1-3	303
Great Harwood Town	Frickley Athletic	3-2	105
Hendon	Gravesend & North	3-0	391
Leigh R.M.I.	Matlock Town	0-2	90
Maidenhead United	Thame United	0-5	93
Newport A.F.C.	Fleet Town	2-1	679
Nuneaton Borough	Knowsley United	3-2	1017
Purfleet	Corby Town	6-1	108
Radcliffe Borough	Fleetwood	2-0	136
Salisbury City	Sudbury Town	2-2	332
Staines Town	Havant Town	3-1	207
Tamworth	Netherfield	3-1	409
Tooting & Mitch	Baldock Town	2-1	174
Trowbridge Town	Bishop's Stortford	1-0	361
Walton & Hersham	Oxford City	0-0	201
Wembley	Ruislip Manor	1-1	85
Yate Town	Heybridge Swifts	1-2	163

Second Qualifying Round Replays

Ruislip Manor	Wembley	1-2	
Chesham United	Chertsey Town	2-3	397
Lancaster City	Curzon Ashton	3-0	206
Oxford City	Walton & Hersham	5-2	96
Sudbury Town	Salisbury City	2-2	251

Dudley Town	Alfreton Town	2-0	183
Sittingbourne	Bognor Regis Town	1-2	674

Second Replays

Sudbury Town	Salisbury City	3-2	249
Accrington Stanley	Gresley Rovers	2-3	542
Ashton United	Lancaster City	1-1	229
Bishop Auckland	Witton Albion	0-0	239

Third Qualifying Round

Blyth Spartans	Gretna	3-2	453
Boreham Wood	Heybridge Swifts	3-0	204
Bromley	Oxford City	1-1	250
Burton Albion	Bamber Bridge	3-3	964
Cambridge City	Hendon	2-0	234
Carshalton Athletic	Braintree Town	1-1	309
Chelmsford City	Yeading	2-1	828
Chertsey Town	Purfleet	0-1	266
Chorley	Winsford United	3-1	297
Dorchester Town	Hayes	2-3	515
Dudley Town	V.S. Rugby	4-3	283
Emley	Great Harwood Town	3-1	224
Gloucester City	Aldershot Town	5-1	1041
Halesowen Town	Bilston Town	0-0	601
Hitchin Town	Bognor Regis Town	1-2	394
Ilkeston Town	Gainsborough T	0-5	626
Leek Town	Boston United	0-0	370
Matlock Town	Buxton	1-0	516
Molesey	Staines Town	2-2	150
Radcliffe Borough	Farsley Celtic	3-1	155
Rothwell Town	Uxbridge	3-2	126
Spennymoor United	Nuneaton Borough	0-2	486
St Albans City	Thame United	4-2	456
Stafford Rangers	Tamworth	1-1	647
Sudbury Town	Tooting & Mitch	2-0	418
Sutton United	Trowbridge Town	0-1	612
Wembley	Bashley	2-0	116
Worcester City	Aylesbury United	3-0	863
Newport A.F.C.	Grays Athletic	1-0	679

Third Qualifying Round Replays

Bamber Bridge	Burton Albion	2-3	502
Bilston Town	Halesowen Town	1-4	307
Braintree Town	Carshalton Athletic	0-5	260
Lancaster City	Ashton United	0-2	228
Oxford City	Bromley	3-2	248
Staines Town	Molesey	5-0	208
Tamworth	Stafford Rangers	0-3	741
Witton Albion	Bishop Auckland	0-0	461
Boston United	Leek Town	2-0	819

Third Qualifying Round Second Replays

Bishop Auckland	Witton Albion	3-1	222

First Round

Ashton United	Blyth Spartans	1-3	535
Bognor Regis Town	Worcester City	1-0	524
Boston United	Chorley	1-1	808
Bromsgrove Rovers	Bishop Auckland	1-0	999
Burton Albion	Telford United	3-1	950
Cambridge City	Boreham Wood	1-2	287
Carshalton Athletic	Woking	3-1	1485
Chelmsford City	Newport A.F.C.	0-1	1130
Colwyn Bay	Altrincham	3-3	596
Dover Athletic	Cheltenham Town	2-2	904
Dudley Town	Halesowen Town	4-2	769
Farnborough Town	Slough Town	1-1	856
Gainsborough Trinity	Nuneaton Borough	4-1	867
Gloucester City	Staines Town	5-0	748
Halifax Town	Southport	2-1	966
Hayes	Enfield	0-0	502
Hednesford Town	Northwich Victoria	1-1	935
Kettering Town	St Albans City	1-1	1577
Kidderminster H	Gateshead	0-0	1312
Macclesfield Town	Runcorn	1-0	1401
Marine	Hyde United	0-0	467
Morecambe	Emley	2-2	656
Oxford City	Merthyr Tydfil	1-2	352
Radcliffe Borough	Matlock Town	3-2	241
Rothwell Town	Welling United	2-2	238
Rushden & D	Purfleet	0-1	1906
Stafford Rangers	Guiseley	1-1	689
Stalybridge Celtic	Gresley Rovers	1-1	638
Stevenage Borough	Dagenham & Red	3-2	1348
Trowbridge Town	Sudbury Town	2-2	319
Wembley	Kingstonian	2-1	214
Bath City	Yeovil Town	1-1	2225

First Round Replays

Guiseley	Stafford Rangers	2-1	365
Hyde United	Marine	0-0	416
Altrincham	Colwyn Bay	2-0	527
Cheltenham Town	Dover Athletic	1-1	640
Chorley	Boston United	2-1	294
Emley	Morecambe	3-1	412
Enfield	Hayes	2-2	436
Gresley Rovers	Stalybridge Celtic	1-0	603
Northwich Victoria	Hednesford Town	2-0	636
Slough Town	Farnborough Town	4-3	742
St Albans City	Kettering Town	2-3	705
Sudbury Town	Trowbridge Town	1-1	224
Yeovil Town	Bath City	2-3	2731
Gateshead	Kidderminster H	2-0	383
Welling United	Rothwell Town	3-0	312

First Round Second Replays

Enfield	Hayes	2-2	398
Dover Athletic	Cheltenham Town	1-0	598
Hyde United	Marine	3-0	374
Trowbridge Town	Sudbury Town	1-1	327

First Round Third Replays

Hayes	Enfield	2-0	369
Sudbury Town	Trowbridge Town	4-3	368

Second Round

Bath City	Hayes	2-0	699
Blyth Spartans	Gresley Rovers	1-2	626
Bognor Regis Town	Radcliffe Borough	1-3	539
Boreham Wood	Dover Athletic	2-1	506
Carshalton Athletic	Newport A.F.C.	2-1	682
Emley	Gateshead	1-2	668
Guiseley	Altrincham	4-0	690
Halifax Town	Bromsgrove Rovers	0-1	887
Hyde United	Welling United	4-1	680
Macclesfield Town	Purfleet	2-1	1003
Slough Town	Kettering Town	1-2	1058
Stevenage Borough	Burton Albion	2-1	1362
Wembley	Northwich Victoria	0-2	268
Chorley	Gainsborough T	2-0	425
Dudley Town	Merthyr Tydfil	1-2	268
Sudbury Town	Gloucester City	3-1	262

Third Round

Boreham Wood	Chorley	1-1	525
Guiseley	Gresley Rovers	1-2	790
Hyde United	Carshalton Athletic	3-2	854
Macclesfield Town	Sudbury Town	1-0	1140
Merthyr Tydfil	Northwich Victoria	1-1	528
Radcliffe Borough	Gateshead	1-2	716
Stevenage Borough	Kettering Town	3-0	2219
Bath City	Bromsgrove Rovers	1-1	1276

Third Round Replays

Bromsgrove Rovers	Bath City	2-1	1113
Chorley	Boreham Wood	4-3	833
Northwich Victoria	Merthyr Tydfil	2-2	800

Third Round Second Replays

Northwich Victoria	Merthyr Tydfil	3-0	765

Quarter-Finals

Bromsgrove Rovers	Northwich Victoria	0-1	1807
Chorley	Gateshead	3-1	1136
Gresley Rovers	Macclesfield Town	0-2	1727
Hyde United	Stevenage Borough	3-2	2012

Semi Finals 1st Leg

Hyde United	Northwich Victoria	1-2	2253
Macclesfield Town	Chorley	3-1	2260

Semi Finals 2nd Leg

Chorley	Macclesfield Town	1-1	3048
Northwich Victoria	Hyde United	1-0	2809

FINAL

(At Wembley Stadium)

19th May 1996

NORTHWICH VICTORIA	**1**	**MACCLESFIELD TOWN**	**3**
Williams		Payne, Burgess og, Hemmings	

Attendance: 8672

VAUXHALL CONFERENCE

FINAL TABLE 1995-96

Stevenage Boro	42	27	10	5	101	44	91
Woking	42	25	8	9	83	54	83
Hednesford Town	42	23	7	12	71	46	76
Macclesfield T	42	22	9	11	66	49	75
Gateshead	42	18	13	11	58	46	67
Southport	42	18	12	12	77	64	66
Kidderminster H	42	18	10	14	78	66	64
Northwich Vics	42	16	12	14	72	64	60
Morecambe	42	17	8	17	78	72	59
Farnborough T	42	15	14	13	63	58	59
Bromsgrove Rov	42	15	12	13	59	57	59
Altrincham	42	15	13	14	59	64	58
Telford United	42	15	10	17	51	56	55
Stalybridge Celt	42	16	7	19	59	68	55
Halifax Town	42	13	13	16	49	63	52
Kettering Town	42	13	9	20	68	84	48
Slough Town	42	13	8	21	63	76	47
Bath City	42	13	7	22	45	66	46
Welling United	42	10	15	17	42	53	45
Dover Athletic	42	11	7	24	51	74	40
Runcorn	42	9	8	25	48	87	35
Dagenham & Red	42	7	12	23	43	73	33

ALTRINCHAM
MOSS LANE, ALTRINCHAM, CHESHIRE WA15 8AP
TEL: 0161 928 1045. FAX 0161 926 9934.

Secretary: Graham Heathcote, c/o Altrincham FC

Press officer: Mark Harris, 11 Hatchmere Close, Timperley, Cheshire WA15 7LN Tel 0161 904 8821

Nickname: The Robins

Colours: Red and White stripes

Capacity: 6,000 by end 1996

Seating: 1,000 (will rise to 1,500)

Covered standing: Yes

Clubhouse on ground: Yes

Record attendance: 10,275 for Altrincham Boys v Sunderland Boys, English Schools Shield Feb 28th 1925

Biggest win: 9-2 v Merthyr Tydfil Conference 1991

Record appearances: John Davison, 677, 1971-86

Record goalscorer in total: Jack Swindells 252 1965-71

Record fee paid: £10,000 to Telford Utd for Ken McKenna June 1990

Record fee received: Undisclosed for Paul Edwards to Crewe Alex 1988

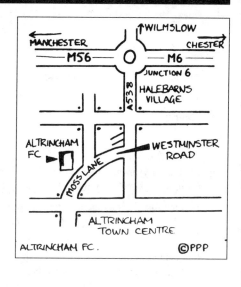

HONOURS

FA Trophy Winners 1978 and 1986, Alliance Premier League 1980 and 1981, Cheshire County League 1966 and 1967, Manchester League 1905 and 1907, Cheshire Senior Cup 1905, 1934, 1967, 1982, Cheshire Amateur Cup 1904, Bob Lord Trophy 1981, Northern Premier League Cup 1970, NPL Shield 1980, Cheshire County League Cup 1933, 1951, 1953, 1964.

Manager 1996-97: John King

Assistant manager: Graham Heathcote

Chairman: Gerry Berman

Vice Chairman: Len Rosenfield

Altrincham FC was formed in 1903 and within a year won its first honours by winning the Cheshire Amateur Cup, a year later taking the Manchester League and the Senior Cup. 1907 saw the league won again, from where they moved to the Lancs Combination where they were runners up in 1912.

They became founder members of the Cheshire County League in 1919, tasting success in the 30's when the Robins won the League Cup in 1933 and the Senior Cup before finishing second to Wigan in 1935 and 1936.

The Robins missed the first season after the War but soon reached three League Cup finals in four years, losing two. The club's fortunes then declined dramatically to the point of near extinction until local businessmen Noel White and the late Peter Swales bought the club.

With the appointment of Freddie Pye as manager they won the Cheshire League Cup in 1964 and 1966, when they did the double and also reached the FA Cup 3rd Round.

After retaining the title in 1967 and finishing second a year later, they became founder members of the Northern Premier League. During the 11 year membership the club established a reputation as Cup fighters, holding Everton at Goodison Park in 1975 and winning the Trophy at Wembley in 1978. Two League Cup finals were reached and they ended their career as runners up.

The Alliance Premier League heralded their most successful period ever. Under Tony Sanders and skipper John King the championship was won for the first two years before automatic promotion, and they missed the Football League by one vote. 1978-79 was the fourth year running that Alty had reached the 3rd Round of the Cup and in 1981 they went to Anfield and were a credit in their 4-1 defeat at the hands of Liverpool.

The 80's bought two FA Trophy finals. The 82 final defeat in extra time was forgotten when Runcorn were beaten in 1986. In the same year Alty became the second non-League club to beat a First Division club on its own ground, when beating Birmingham City. 1991 saw Barnet pip the club to promotion and it took three seasons for them to recover and by February 1994 they were in dire trouble. The appointment of John King led to a tremendous late run and in 1995 they mounted a strong challenge scoring over 100 goals in again reaching the 3rd Round of the Cup, where they lost to Spurs.

ALTRINCHAM 1995/96 SEASON

Date	Comp	Opponent	Att	Score	Scorers
19/08/95	L	KETTERING TOWN	969	1-3	Bolland 42
22/08/95	L	Telford United	840	0-2	
26/08/95	L	Dagenham & Redbridge	662	0-1	
28/08/95	L	GATESHEAD	640	1-1	Oliver 35
02/09/95	L	KIDDERMINSTER H.	881	1-1	Green 10
05/09/95	L	Southport	1127	2-1	Ward 88(og), Carmody 90
09/09/95	L	BROMSGROVE ROVERS	773	3-0	Whalley 24, Terry 42 80
12/09/95	L	MORECAMBE	755	3-0	Allan 22, Hardy 61 84
16/09/95	L	Slough Town	991	2-1	Hardy 13, Sharratt 55
23/09/95	L	HALIFAX TOWN	1085	3-2	Sharratt 17, Green 34, Hardy 53
30/09/95	L	Stevenage Borough	1615	1-1	Green 36
07/10/95	L	BATH CITY	1057	1-2	Terry 6
14/10/95	L	Woking	2081	0-2	
21/10/95	L	Kidderminster Harriers	2429	1-1	Terry 56
28/10/95	L	DOVER ATHLETIC	929	2-2	Sharratt 61 75
04/11/95	L	Welling United	623	1-1	Royle 55
18/11/95	L	MACCLESFIELD TOWN	1648	0-4	
22/11/95	C1	CREWE ALEXANDRA		0-2	
25/11/95	L	Kettering Town	1369	2-4	Terry 8(p), Heesom 77
28/11/95	C2	WARRINGTON TOWN	273	4-0	Green(2), Sharratt, Terry
02/12/95	L	RUNCORN	707	2-2	Terry 71(p) 88(p)
05/12/95	C3	Morecambe	546	4-6	
09/12/95	L	Stalybridge Celtic	654	0-1	
16/12/95	L	TELFORD UNITED	633	1-0	Hardy 23
26/12/95	L	Northwich Victoria	1278	1-2	France 71
01/01/96	L	NORTHWICH VICTORIA	1076	3-4	Sharratt 20 60, Butler 54
06/01/96	L	Bromsgrove Rovers	852	0-0	
13/01/96	L	SLOUGH TOWN	648	0-1	
20/01/96	C4	Colwyn Bay	596	3-3	Hughes, Terry, France
23/01/96	FAT1R	COLWYN BAY	527	2-0	Reid, France
30/01/96	L	Macclesfield Town	1301	3-2	Terry 16(p) 26(p), Pritchard 54
03/02/96	L	WELLING UNITED	762	1-0	Doherty 1
10/02/96	FAT2	Guiseley	690	0-4	
17/02/96	L	Morecambe	983	0-7	
20/02/96	Ches. SCSF(1)	Witton Albion	460	1-1	Royce
24/02/96	L	FARNBOROUGH TOWN	580	2-2	Pritchard 6 31
02/03/96	L	SOUTHPORT	851	1-1	Kelly 38
05/03/96	L	Runcorn	607	1-0	Terry 74
09/03/96	L	WOKING	971	2-0	Butler 37, France 41
12/03/96	Ches. SCSF(2)	WITTON ALBION	481	1-2	France
16/03/96	L	Halifax Town	755	1-1	Terry 77
27/03/96	L	Gateshead	357	3-2	Terry 22(p), Hardy 62, France 88
30/03/96	L	STEVENAGE BOROUGH	838	0-2	
06/04/96	L	Hednesford Town	1010	1-2	Doherty 90
08/04/96	L	Farnborough Town	706	1-1	Terry 90(p)
13/04/96	L	Dover Athletic	1070	4-1	Dougherty 4 25, Harris 52 65
20/04/96	L	HEDNESFORD TOWN	731	2-1	Hardy 21, Doherty 53
23/04/96	L	STALYBRIDGE CELTIC	608	1-0	France 63
27/04/96	L	Bath City	489	2-2	Hardy 73 76
04/05/96	L	DAGENHAM & REDBRIDGE	748	3-1	Hardy 14, Terry 47, Perry 72

C1=FAC1, C2=Ches. SCQF, C3=SC2, C4=FAT1

Secretary: Bob Twyford, c/o Bath City FC

Nickname: The Romans

Capacity: 8,995

Seating: 1,053

Covered standing: 3,165.

Clubhouse on ground: Yes

Record Attendance: 18,020 v Brighton
in FA Cup

Record goalscorer in one season: Paul Randall

Record fee paid: £15,000 Mickey Tanner

Record fee received: Undisclosed for Jason Dodd
from Southampton

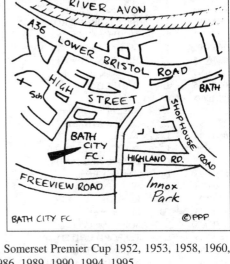

Honours

Southern League 1960, 1978 and League Cup 1979, Somerset Premier Cup 1952, 1953, 1958, 1960, 1966, 1968, 1970, 1978, 1981, 1982, 1984, 1985, 1986, 1989, 1990, 1994, 1995

Manager for 1996-97:Steve Millard

Assistant Manager: Richard Crowley

Chairman: Ray Stock

Vice Chairman: Dave Turner

Bristol Rovers shared Twerton Park from 1986, and after 10 years they have moved to Bristol Rugby Club. It is believed that this was the longest ground share in the country.

Bath City began life in local football, not joining the Western League until 1908. They played on a pitch in East Twerton called the Belvoir ground, tight against the railway line on a site now covered by Stothert and Pitts just a goal kick away from Twerton. After the Great War, with the club having moved from the basic Belvoir to the more advanced Lambridge, they joined the powerful Southern League, winning the Western Section in 1930. Their new ground was owned by the Bath Horse Show Committee who leased it to the club for the staggering sum of £100 per year, irrespective of the fact that if there was a show, then it was not available. On the days when it was the club had to contend with the River Avon and a problem where the horse show had to improvise on a water jump by digging a huge whole in the pitch. Despite all that, Lambridge boasted a huge wooden stand which helped when the FA Cup came along, as it was only the big matches that kept City from going under more than once.

A couple of transfer fees and another Cup run later, City found themselves in a position to buy their own ground, and a £2,000 bid secured a site just off Twerton High Street on the steeply sloping Innox Park. Whilst continuing in the Southern League at Lambridge, the new ground was being hewed out, and some 15,000 tonnes of soil in three years later, Bristol Rovers Reserves were the visitors for the first ever Southern League fixture at Twerton Park. City have remained there ever since, whereas Lambridge is now used as a rugby training ground, sadly minus any trace of the old stand.

Since those exciting days Bath have steadily remained as one of the top non-League sides in the country, winning the Southern League twice and reaching the FA Cup 3rd Round three times, the second time under Malcolm Allison. The Romans were founder members of the Alliance, but were relegated in 1988, bouncing back in 1990 as runners-up. During the last ten years, Twerton Park has staged League football, as Bristol Rovers have been tenants following their enforced move from Eastville. However, 1996-97 will see them move back to Bristol leaving a large void in the finances of this proud club.

FORMER GROUNDS

Lambridge, situated along A4 opposite junction with A46, is still there and used as a rugby ground. Also played at Belvoir Ground which was further along A4 from Twerton close to pub of same name.

BATH CITY 1995/96 SEASON

Date		Opponent	Att	Score	Scorers
19/08/95	L	Stevenage Borough	1355	0-2	
22/08/95	L	Woking	1708	0-2	
26/08/95	L	BROMSGROVE ROVERS	510	0-1	
28/08/95	L	DOVER ATHLETIC	439	2-1	Mings 7, Smart 83
02/09/95	L	Macclesfield Town	1225	1-0	Spencer 87
05/09/95	L	Slough Town	980	1-1	Mings 48
09/09/95	L	SOUTHPORT	584	4-0	Smart 38(p) 52(p), Mings 54, Birkby 65
12/09/95	L	WELLING UNITED	458	1-1	Cousins 77
16/09/95	L	Kettering Town	1767	0-3	
19/09/95	C[1]	FARNBOROUGH TOWN	257	0-3	
23/09/95	L	Runcorn	519	0-1	
30/09/95	L	STALYBRIDGE CELTIC	580	0-4	
03/10/95	C[2]	Farnborough Town	374	2-3	Mings, Chiverton 70
07/10/95	L	Altrincham	1057	2-1	Chiverton 4, Vernon 82
10/10/95	L	WOKING	720	0-3	
14/10/95	L	HEDNESFORD TOWN	661	1-0	Birkby 45
21/10/95	C[3]	Cinderford Town	730	2-3	Birkby, Mings
28/10/95	L	GATESHEAD	481	0-1	
31/10/95	L	Welling United	403	1-2	Birkby 22
04/11/95	L	Halifax Town	811	1-3	Chiverton 52
11/11/95	L	Morecambe	1007	0-1	
14/11/95	C[4]	KEYNSHAM TOWN	197	3-0	Birkby, Chenoweth(2)
18/11/95	L	NORTHWICH VICTORIA	417	0-3	
25/11/95	L	Bromsgrove Rovers	796	1-4	Crisp 21(og)
02/12/95	L	Kidderminster Harriers	1833	2-1	Sugar 47, Chiverton 50
09/12/95	L	KETTERING TOWN	612	3-1	Withey 5 43 90
16/12/95	L	Dover Athletic	826	0-1	
01/01/96	L	Farnborough Town	779	0-0	
06/01/96	L	Northwich Victoria	708	2-2	Withey 25, Vernon 74
13/01/96	L	TELFORD UNITED	517	0-3	
21/01/96	C[5]	YEOVIL TOWN	2225	1-1	Sugar
23/01/96	C[6]	Yeovil Town	2731	3-2	Burton(og), Cousins, Vernon
05/02/96	C[7]	Bristol City		2-3	Withey, Adcock
10/02/96	C[8]	HAYES	699	2-0	Withey(2)
17/02/96	L	Hednesford Town	1004	1-2	Adcock 57
20/02/96	L	FARNBOROUGH TOWN	290	2-1	Vernon 48, Mings 52
24/02/96	L	HALIFAX TOWN	547	2-1	Withey 18, Mings 56
03/03/96	C[9]	BROMSGROVE ROVERS	1276	1-1	Clarke(og)
05/03/96	C[10]	Bromsgrove Rovers	1113	1-2	Chiverton
09/03/96	L	MORECAMBE	511	3-2	Withey 12, Adcock 24 90
16/03/96	L	Gateshead	583	1-3	Adcock 24
25/03/96	L	Dagenham & Redbridge	695	1-0	Withey 11
30/03/96	L	RUNCORN	503	3-0	Finley 22(og), Chiverton 29, Smart 37
03/04/96	L	SLOUGH TOWN	397	3-1	Smart 62(p), Mings 81 88
06/04/96	L	Stalybridge Celtic	506	0-1	
08/04/96	L	DAGENHAM & REDBR	541	0-2	
13/04/96	L	Southport	643	1-2	Withey 16
16/04/96	L	KIDDERMINSTER HARRIERS	412	1-1	James 49
20/04/96	L	STEVENAGE BOROUGH	806	1-2	Withey 62
27/04/96	L	ALTRINCHAM	489	2-2	Scott 39, Withey 43
30/04/96	L	MACCLESFIELD TOWN	361	1-1	Cousins 74
04/05/96	L	Telford United	831	1-3	Scott 33

C[1]=SC1(1), C[2]=SC1(2), C[3]=FACupQ4, C[4]=Som.PC2, C[5]=FA Trophy1, C[6]=FA Trophy1 rep, C[7]=Som.PC3, C[8]=FA Trophy2, C[9]=FA Trophy3, C[10]=FA Trophy 3 rep

BROMSGROVE ROVERS
VICTORIA GROUND, BIRMINGHAM ROAD, BROMSGROVE, WORCS, B61 0DR TEL 01527 876949

Commercial Dept: 01527 876949

Victoria Club: 01527 878260

Hotline: 0891 884496

Secretary: Mr B.A.Henings 21 Carol Avenue, Bromsgrove, Worcs B61 8RN Tel 01527 831182

Nickname: Greens or Rovers

Capacity: 4,423

Seating: 394

Covered standing: 1,344

Clubhouse on ground: Yes

Record attendance: 7,389 v Worcester City in 1957

Biggest win: 11-0 v Hinckley Athletic

Biggest defeat: 0-12 v Aston Villa 1939

Record appearances: Shaun O'Meara

Record goalscorer in total: Chris Hanks 238

Record fee: £30,000 Martin O'Connor in 1992

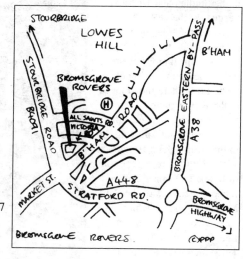

HONOURS

Worcester Junior Cup 1896,

Studley and District Cup 1894,

Chatrian Cup 1897,

Birmingham Comb League 1947,

West Midlands League 1961,

Southern League1992, Midland Division 1986, Champions Cup 1987 and 1993, Bill Dellow Cup 1986,

Worcester Senior Cup 1947, 1948, 1960, 1986, 1987, 1992, 1994, 1995, 1996,

Birmingham Senior Cup 1947,

Towns Cup 1960,

Tillotson Cup 1940,

Border Counties Cup 1975,

Border Counties Floodlit Cup 1976,

Bob Lord Trophy 1995 and 1996

Manager for 1996-97: Brian Kenning,
Chairman: Mr K McMaster, Vice Chairman: Mr J.Sharkey

BRIEF HISTORY

Bromsgrove Rovers were founded in 1885 and competed in their early days in the Studley and District League. In the 1897-98 season they won the title and were promoted into the Birmingham Junior League where they remained until 1908. From there they moved to the Birmingham Combination and stayed there for 43 years, until moving up to the Birmingham League in 1953. With the re-organisation of football, Bromsgrove were founder members of the West Midlands League, which succeeded the Birmingham League and from there, in 1972, they were accepted into the Southern League.

Rovers celebrated their centenary year by winning the Midland Division championship, as well as the Bill Dellow League Cup, the Worcestershire Senior Cup and the League Merit Cup. After 6 good years in the top flight they were promoted to the Conference as champions of the Southern League.

The first season ended with Rovers runners-up but the next three were a struggle, although last May saw them finish in mid table, after retaining the Bob Lord Trophy and the Worcester Senior Cup.

Rovers first played on Old Station Road for two years before moving to the Recreation Ground in Market Street. From there they went to Churchfields for two more years which is now the grounds of the Parkside School, and then Well Lane, which is where North Bromsgrove High School is now. The Victoria Ground was opened in 1910 and has been home to Rovers ever since.

BROMSGROVE ROVERS 1995/96 SEASON

Date	Comp	Opponent	Att	Score	Scorers
19/08/95	L	GATESHEAD	789	3-1	Crisp 6 45, Gaunt 29
22/08/95	L	Kettering Town	2006	2-2	Gaunt 50, Carter 76
26/08/95	L	Bath City	510	1-0	Dale 52
28/08/95	L	WOKING	1290	2-1	Crisp 16, Carter 90
02/09/95	L	DOVER ATHLETIC	1082	3-0	Crisp 7, Smith 41, Carter 87
05/09/95	L	Welling United	602	2-5	Skelding 28(p), Gaunt 63
09/09/95	L	Altrincham	773	0-3	
12/09/95	L	DAGENHAM & REDBRIDGE	728	2-0	Dale 10, Skelding 61(p)
16/09/95	L	STEVENAGE BOROUGH	1067	1-1	Crisp 26
23/09/95	L	Slough Town	931	3-2	Crisp 8, Radburn 13, Grocutt 45
26/09/95	L	Telford United	743	0-0	
30/09/95	L	RUNCORN	973	2-0	Smith 3, Grocutt 82
07/10/95	L	Macclesfield Town	1137	1-2	Crisp 30
14/10/95	L	FARNBOROUGH TOWN	1145	1-2	Smith 65
21/10/95	C[1]	Kettering Town	2427	0-0	
24/10/95	C[2]	KETTERING TOWN	1246	2-2	
28/10/95	L	Morecambe	955	1-4	Hunt 37
30/10/95	C[3]	Kettering Town	2283	2-1	Power, Grocutt
04/11/95	L	STALYBRIDGE CELTIC	1033	1-1	Brighton 74(p)
11/11/95	C[4]	Cinderford Town	1850	1-2	Skelding
18/11/95	L	Farnborough Town	930	0-1	
21/11/95	L	HEDNESFORD TOWN	952	1-4	Crisp 32
25/11/95	L	BATH CITY	796	4-1	Carter 1, Amos 67, Hunt 76 90
02/12/95	L	Halifax Town	843	1-1	Skelding 56(p)
05/12/95	C[5]	TELFORD UNITED	548	3-1	Amos, Grocutt, Smith
09/12/95	L	Stevenage Borough	1565	3-3	Amos 27, Carter 78 80(p)
16/12/95	L	WELLING UNITED	721	1-1	Gaunt 30
19/12/95	C[6]	MOOR GREEN	315	5-0	Grocutt(2), Carter(2), Hunt
26/12/95	L	K.MINSTER HARRIERS	4398	2-1	Smith 38, Carter 44
30/12/95	L	Dagenham & Redbridge	1020	2-2	Carter 38, Clarke 73
01/01/96	L	Kidderminster Harriers	4481	0-1	
06/01/96	L	ALTRINCHAM	852	0-0	
13/01/96	L	Runcorn	547	0-0	
20/01/96	C[7]	BISHOP AUCKLAND	999	1-0	Carter
30/01/96	L	Northwich Victoria	609	2-2	Carter 42, Skelding 78(p)
03/02/96	L	Woking	2481	1-1	Batty 62(og)
10/02/96	C[8]	Halifax Town	887	1-0	Smith
17/02/96	L	MACCLESFIELD TOWN	1481	1-0	Carter 70
24/02/96	L	Dover Athletic	1011	2-0	Brighton 12(p), Marlowe 83
27/02/96	C[9]	Dover Athletic	464	1-0	Skelding 11(p)
03/03/96	C[10]	Bath City	1276	1-1	Brighton
05/03/96	C[11]	BATH CITY	1113	2-1	Amos, Carter
09/03/96	L	Southport	894	2-1	Hunt 79, Skelding 85(p)
12/03/96	L	TELFORD UNITED	746	0-2	
16/03/96	L	Hednesford Town	1119	2-4	Carter 19, Hunt 49
19/03/96	C[12]	KETTERING TOWN	650	2-0	Power 6, Dale 45
23/03/96	C[13]	NORTHWICH VICTORIA	1807	0-1	
25/03/96	C[14]	Solihull Borough	183	2-2	Brighton, Grocutt
30/03/96	L	SLOUGH TOWN	687	0-0	
03/04/96	C[15]	Kettering Town	773	1-2	Burgher 19
06/04/96	L	SOUTHPORT	729	4-1	Crisp 21 39 75 77
08/04/96	L	Stalybridge Celtic	463	1-2	Clarke 21
16/04/96	C[16]	SOLIHULL BOROUGH	524	3-1	Carter(2), Richardson
20/04/96	L	KETTERING TOWN	824	3-2	Carter 41 74, Amos 87
22/04/96	C[17]	Stourbridge	527	1-2	Amos
24/04/96	C[18]	Macclesfield Town	547	1-1	Howarth 81(og)
27/04/96	L	Gateshead	762	0-1	
28/04/96	L	NORTHWICH VICTORIA		1-1	Grocutt
30/04/96	L	MORECAMBE	626	1-0	Hunt 46
04/05/96	L	HALIFAX TOWN	887	0-1	
06/05/96	C[19]	MACCLESFIELD TOWN	1341	3-1	Grocutt 41, Hunt 59, Carter
09/05/96	C[20]	STOURBRIDGE		3-1	

C[1]=FA CupQ4, C[2]=FA Cup Q4 rep, C[3]=FA CupQ4 rep(2), C[4]=FA Cup1, C[5]=SC2, C[6]=Worcs SCQF, C[7]=FA Trophy1, C[8]=FA Trophy2, C[9]=SCQF, C[10]=FA Trophy3, C[11]=FA Trophy 3 rep, C[12]=SCSF(1), C[13]=FA TrophyQF, C[14]=Worcs SCSF, C[15]=SCSF(2), C[16]=Worcs SCSF rep, C[17]=Worcs SCF(1), C[18]=SCF(1), C[19]=SCF(2), C[20]=Worcs SCF(2)

DOVER ATHLETIC
CRABBLE ATHLETIC GROUND, LEWISHAM ROAD, RIVER, DOVER
TEL: 01304 240041

Secretary: John Durrant, 7 Alison Close, Whitfield, Dover CT16 3LW. Tel: 01304 823429

Prog Editor: Chris Collings 16 Pardoners Way, Dover, Kent CT16 2DE. Tel: 01304 822074

Colours: White and Black

Nickname: Lilywhites

Capacity: 6,500

Seating: 1,200

Covered standing: 4,900

Clubhouse on ground: Yes

Record attendance: 4,035 v Bromsgrove Rovers, League April 1992

Biggest Win: 7-0 v Weymouth, April 3rd 1990

Biggest: 1-7 v Poole Town April 4th 1984

Record Appearances: Jason Bartlett 539

Record Goalscorer In One Season: Lennie Lee 38 in 1987-88

Record Goalscorer In Aggregate: Lennie Lee 160

Record Fee Paid Or Received: £50,000 to Farnborough Town for David Leworthy

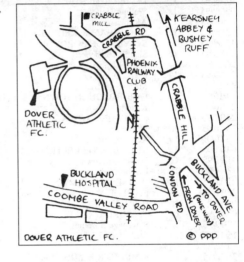

HONOURS

Southern League champions 1989-90 and 92-93,

Southern Div Champs 1987-88,

Southern League Cup 1990-91,

Kent Senior Cup 1990-91,

Dover Supporters fanzine is available, called "Tales from the River End"

Manager for: 1996-97 Joe O'Sullivan

Chairman: John Husk

Vice Chairman: Alan Husk

Dover Athletic was formed in the summer of 1983 following the demise of Dover FC. The new club took the old one's place in the Southern League and finished 13th. In 1985 the new club struggled but a year later under Chris Kinnear, they finished fourth, reaching the Kent Senior Cup final before losing to Welling United at Gillingham. It was 1988 that saw Athletic take the Southern League Southern Division with 94 points and only two defeats, the season neatly finished off with the Knight Floodlight Cup.

The first season in the Premier Division saw a good start slowly ebb away but it was a taster, for in 1990 the fledgling club took the Southern League title with a record 102 points, the first ten games and the last eleven all being won in a row, to beat off the challenge of Bath City. Sadly they were denied promotion due to the work on the Crabble being incomplete at the specified time, and Bath were promoted, but after wins in the Championship match and the Inter-League Cup, they won the Kent Senior Cup in May 1991. Again in 1992 the club went so close, finishing runners up to Bromsgrove Rovers whilst winning the League Cup, but finally and deservedly they clinched the title again in 1993 and were given the green light for Conference status.

The original Dover FC came into being in 1891, playing in the old Kent League before disbanding in 1910 and, after the Great War in 1920, Dover United won the Kent League (Eastern Section) from 1921 to 1924. Their success did not last as they were wound up in 1933, but less than a year later Dover FC were formed to join the Kent Amateur League. It was not long after the Second War that they turned professional and joined the Kent League in 1947. They were champions in 1952 and League Cup winners in 1957, coming second three times before entering the Southern League in 1959, the First Division title coming in 1967.

They won the Kent Senior Cup four times in six seasons and the new Southern Division title in 1979, but were wound up with heavy debts to make way for Dover Athletic.

DOVER ATHLETIC 1995/96 SEASON

Date	Competition	Opponent	Att	Score	Scorers
19/08/95	L	Northwich Victoria	824	2-1	Chambers 17, Leworthy 81
22/08/95	L	STEVENAGE BOROUGH	1157	1-2	Leworthy 45
26/08/95	L	HEDNESFORD TOWN	866	1-3	Strouts 42
28/08/95	L	Bath City	439	1-2	Darlington 13
02/09/95	L	Bromsgrove Rovers	1082	0-3	
05/09/95	L	FARNBOROUGH TOWN	779	1-3	Theodosiou 84
09/09/95	FA Cup Q1	BOGNOR REGIS TOWN	578	1-2	Leworthy
12/09/95	L	Slough Town	846	2-3	Leworthy 37, Carruthers 87
16/09/95	L	MACCLESFIELD TOWN	822	2-3	Leworthy 82(p) 85
19/09/95	SCC1(1)	Welling United	409	2-1	
26/09/95	L	SLOUGH TOWN	619	0-1	
30/09/95	L	Halifax Town	905	0-1	
07/10/95	L	Kidderminster Harriers	2259	1-1	Leworthy 85
10/10/95	SC1(2)	WELLING UNITED	664	3-0	
14/10/95	L	RUNCORN	1277	4-2	Restarick 41, Strouts 55, Leworthy 68 Milton 90
21/10/95	L	Gateshead	512	1-1	Hayes 26
28/10/95	L	Altrincham	929	2-2	Lindsey 71, Leworthy 77
31/10/95	L	DAGENHAM & REDBRIDGE	1164	0-1	
04/11/95	L	KIDDERMINSTER HARRIERS	1124	2-1	Sowerby 6 85
07/11/95	Kent SC 1	ASHFORD TOWN	505	1-2	Lewis
11/11/95	L	Hednesford Town	1147	2-2	Milton 52, Essex 59(og)
18/11/95	L	Morecambe	1047	1-3	Lewis 19
21/11/95	E. F'lit Cup	Folkestone Invicta		0-2	
25/11/95	L	STALYBRIDGE CELTIC	1069	1-3	Hayes 32(p)
28/11/95	SC2	Farnborough Town		3-1	
02/12/95	L	KETTERING TOWN	1045	2-1	Sowerby 69 79
09/12/95	L	Dagenham & Redbridge	862	0-3	
16/12/95	L	BATH CITY	826	1-0	Restarick 25
01/01/96	L	Welling United	1006	0-1	
06/01/96	L	TELFORD UNITED	1030	1-0	Daniels 82
13/01/96	L	Kettering Town	1332	2-2	Daniels 83, Pilkington 88
20/01/96	FA Trophy 1	CHELTENHAM TOWN	904	2-2	Rogers, Darlington
23/01/96	FA Trophy 1 rep	Cheltenham Town	640	1-1	Leworthy
31/01/96	FA Trophy 1 rep (2)	CHELTENHAM TOWN	598	1-0	Rogers
10/02/96	FA Trophy 2	Boreham Wood	506	1-2	Restarick
13/02/96	L	WOKING	976	4-3	Leworthy 39 51 88 90(p)
17/02/96	L	Telford United	733	0-1	
24/02/96	L	BROMSGROVE ROVERS	1011	0-2	
27/02/96	SCC QF	BROMSGROVE ROVERS	464	0-1	
28/02/96	E. F'lit Cup	ASHFORD TOWN		0-4	
02/03/96	L	HALIFAX TOWN	895	3-2	Harris 17 50, Leworthy 67
04/03/96	L	Stevenage Borough	1062	2-3	Leworthy 38(p), Harris 50
09/03/96	L	Runcorn	433	3-1	Darlington 37, Leworthy 57, Harris 85
16/03/96	L	SOUTHPORT	1142	0-1	
19/03/96	L	Farnborough Town	416	2-3	Pilkington 78, Leworthy 90
23/03/96	L	Woking	2438	0-1	
26/03/96	L	WELLING UNITED	1001	2-1	Milton 16, Leworthy 90
30/03/96	L	MORECAMBE	1090	2-3	Leworthy 2, Lavelle 35(og)
06/04/96	L	NORTHWICH VICTORIA	976	0-1	
08/04/96	L	Macclesfield Town	1482	1-0	Harris 63
13/04/96	L	Altrincham	1070	1-4	Leworthy 85
20/04/96	L	Stalybridge Celtic	533	0-2	
27/04/96	L	Southport	849	0-0	
04/05/96	L	Gateshead	1103	1-1	Leworthy 39

FARNBOROUGH TOWN
JOHN ROBERTS GROUND, CHERRYWOOD ROAD, FARNBOROUGH, HANTS GU14 8UD TEL: 01252 541469

Secretary: Terry Parr, 3 Cambrian Rd, Farnborough, Hants GU14 9JF

Tel: 01252 546387

Colours: Yellow and Blue

Nickname: The Boro

Capacity: 4,900

Seating: 561

Covered Standing: 350

Clubhouse on ground: Yes

Record Attendance: 3,581 v Brentford FA Cup 1st Rd Replay 1995

Biggest win: 11-0 v Chertsey Town in Spartan League 1972-3

Biggest Defeat: 2-10 v Worplesdon in Surrey Senior League 1968

Record appearances Brian Broome 500 1980-1994

Record Goalscorer In One Season: Simon Read 53 1988-89

Record Goalscorer in Aggregate: Simon Read

HONOURS

Spartan League 72-73, 73-74, 74-75,

London Spartan 75-76,

Athenian League 77-78,

Isthmian League Div 2 78-79, Div 1 84-85,

Southern League 90-91

Spartan League Cup 74-75,75-76,

Hants Senior Cup 74-75, 81-82, 83-84, 85-86, 90-91.

FA Vase semi-finals 1976 and 1977

MANAGER FOR 1996-97: Alan Taylor

ASSISTANT MANAGER: Ken Ballard

CHAIRMAN: Tony Alper

PRESS OFFICER: Vince Williams c/o FTFC

DIRECTIONS
M3 exit 4, A325 towards Farnborough, right into Prospect Avenue (club signposted), 2nd right into Cherrywood Rd, ground on right. 20-30 min walk from Farnborough Main, Farnborough North and Frimley BR stations. Whippet mini-bus route 19 passes ground.

Farnborough Town's record has been one of remarkable progress since their formation in 1967. After a couple of quiet years in the late 60's, they moved forward when Ted Pearce was appointed manager, a position he was to hold for 23 years. They gained promotion to the Surrey Senior League Premier Division and won the title for the next four seasons, the last two being part of the League and Cup double. Lack of facilities at Queens Road was holding the club up and so a new ground in Cherrywood Road was begun.

The club moved to the Athenian League where they immediately won the Division Two championship and were accepted by an expanding Isthmian League. They narrowly missed promotion from Division Two in the first season but a year later they took the title by 10 points. The following six years were spent in Division One before in 1985 they were champions, this time by 7 points. Town were soon established in the top division and in the fourth season up they led the league for months before losing out to Leytonstone and Iford. Due to ground grading problems for the champions, the door was open for Farnborough and they moved into the Conference. The first season came as a shock and despite a good start they faded and were forced to suffer relegation for the first time, only to bounce back as champions, this time of the Southern League Premier Division at the first attempt. The second Conference year was vastly more successful, ending with a fifth place, but 1992-93 again proved a struggle and problems on and off the pitch once again saw them relegated to the Southern League. Ted Pearce stood down to be replaced by ex-West Ham man Alan Taylor, and his side successfully took the Southern league for the second time to make another quick return to the Conference, where they remain. The last two seasons have seen the club stabilise with lower mid-table positions, which has not diverted attention away from their cup exploits. Before last season the club had already caught the public's imagination by reaching the FA Cup 1st round on eight occasions, before in 1991 they overcame Torquay United 4-3 in a dramatic televised replay after drawing at Plainmoor. It gave the club a tie with West Ham United which was switched on police advice and in front of 23,000 at Upton Park, the club battled for a draw, and in the replay, also at Upton Park, only a last minute goal beat them.

Last season saw the ground attendance record broken when after drawing at Griffin Park against Brentford, the replayed First Round tie drew 3,581 to Cherrywood Rd.

FARNBOROUGH TOWN 1995/96 SEASON

19/08/95	L	KIDDERMINSTER HARRIERS	840	3-1	Horton 9, Boothe 65, Senior 71
21/08/95	L	Dagenham & Redbridge	758	2-2	Harlow 48, Boothe 88
26/08/95	L	Telford United	809	2-3	Boothe 22, Horton 89
28/08/95	L	KETTERING TOWN	1037	1-1	Boothe 67
02/09/95	L	NORTHWICH VICTORIA	808	0-1	
05/09/95	L	Dover Athletic	779	3-1	Senior 70, Robson 75 90
09/09/95	C1	DARTFORD	602	1-0	Harlow
16/09/95	L	STALYBRIDGE CELTIC	707	1-1	Senior 71
19/09/95	C2	Bath City	257	3-0	Boothe 9 16, Day 47
23/09/95	C3	Fisher	335	4-1	Robson, Boothe(2), Baker
26/09/95	L	DAGENHAM & REDBRIDGE	494	2-0	Coney 3, Boothe 73(p)
30/09/95	L	MACCLESFIELD TOWN	740	6-1	Senior 2 77, Boothe 34 61 85, Denny 74
03/10/95	C4	BATH CITY	374	3-2	Boothe 8(p) 60, Denny 66
07/10/95	C5	WALTON & HERSHAM	761	3-2	Boothe(2), Senior
14/10/95	L	Bromsgrove Rovers	1145	2-1	Harlow 40, Boothe 50
21/10/95	C6	YEOVIL TOWN	1409	2-1	Stemp, Boothe
28/10/95	L	HALIFAX TOWN	908	0-0	
31/10/95	L	Slough Town	891	1-1	Boothe 41
02/11/95	C7	NEW STREET		6-1	
04/11/95	L	Southport	819	1-7	Day 18
11/11/95	C8	Brentford	4711	1-1	Senior
18/11/95	L	BROMSGROVE ROVERS	930	1-0	Boothe 50
22/11/95	C9	BRENTFORD	3581	0-4	
25/11/95	L	Macclesfield Town	1721	0-1	
28/11/95	C10	DOVER ATHLETIC		1-3	
02/12/95	L	Northwich Victoria	687	3-1	Denny 37, Boothe 39, Underwood 60
09/12/95	L	HEDNESFORD TOWN	716	1-3	Gavin 4
12/12/95	L	Welling United	403	1-0	Robson 79
16/12/95	L	Kettering Town	1260	2-0	Boothe 7, Baker 53
19/12/95	C11	D.C.A. BASINGSTOKE		1-4	
01/01/96	L	BATH CITY	779	0-0	
06/01/96	L	MORECAMBE	729	3-1	Gavin 38, Harlow 41, Boothe 57
08/01/96	L	Stevenage Borough	1745	0-0	
13/01/96	L	Gateshead	881	1-1	Robson 65
20/01/96	C12	SLOUGH TOWN	856	1-1	Gavin
23/01/96	C13	Slough Town	742	3-4	
03/02/96	L	SOUTHPORT	738	1-0	Robson 82
10/02/96	L	Stalybridge Celtic	521	2-2	Gavin 58, Boothe 68
17/02/96	L	Runcorn	429	3-0	Gavin 12, Boothe 72, Baker 84
20/02/96	L	Bath City	290	1-2	Wingfield 9-
24/02/96	L	Altrincham	580	2-2	Boothe 27, Gavin 60
02/03/96	L	SLOUGH TOWN	1069	0-1	
05/03/96	L	WELLING UNITE	470	0-1	
09/03/96	L	Hednesford Town	1010	1-4	Wingfield 69
12/03/96	L	WOKING	1497	0-2	
16/03/96	L	RUNCORN	619	0-1	
19/03/96	L	DOVER ATHLETIC	416	3-2	Baker 33, Boothe 36, Gavin 71
23/03/96	L	Morecambe	726	3-2	Boothe 28, Underwood 45, Gavin 58
30/03/96	L	Halifax Town	697	0-0	
06/04/96	L	GATESHEAD	625	2-3	Gavin 11, Wingfield 57
08/04/96	L	ALTRINCHAM	706	1-1	McAvoy 13
16/04/96	L	Woking	3166	1-2	Robson 74
20/04/96	L	TELFORD UNITED	784	2-1	Boothe 72, Wingfield 75
27/04/96	L	Kidderminster Harriers	1559	3-3	Harlow 4, Gavin 42, Wingfield 77
04/05/96	L	STEVENAGE BOROUGH	1413	2-2	Boothe 27, Baker 42

C1=FA CupQ1, C2=SC1(1), C3=FA CupQ2, C4=SC1(2), C5=FA CupQ3, C6=FA CupQ4, C7=HantsSC2, C8=FA Cup1,
C9=FA Cup1 rep, C10=SC2, C11=Hants SC3, C12-FA Trophy1, C13=FA Trophy1

General Manager: Mark Donnelly, Gateshead FC

Press Sec : Andy Wilson

Colours: Black and white halves

Nickname: The Tynesiders

Capacity: 11,750

Seating: 3,300

Covered Standing: None, it is all seater

Clubhouse On Ground: No

Record Attendance: 11,750 v Newcastle Utd Friendly 1995

Biggest Win: 8-0 v Netherfield

Biggest Defeat: 0-9 v Sutton Utd Sept 22nd 1990

Record Appearances: Simon Smith 405

Record Goalscorer In One Season: Bob Topping

HONOURS

Northern Premier League 1982-83, 1985-86

Manager For 1996-97: Colin Richardson

Assistant Manager: George Cook

Chairman: John Gibson

Vice Chairman: Peter Robinson

DIRECTIONS

From the South follow A1 (M) to Granada services (Birtley), take right hand fork off motorway marked A194 (Tyne Tunnel, South Shields) follow A194 to first roundabout. Turn right at traffic lights into Neilson Road. By Rail to Newcastle Central Station transfer to Metro System to Gateshead Stadium.

The current club are the latest of several who have taken the title over the years. Formed from the ashes of South Shields FC and Gateshead Town FC, they are not related to the Football League club which perished in the 60's despite media insistence that they are whenever their name is mentioned. They have been fortunate to have had the use of the International Stadium, known previously as the Brendon Foster Stadium at first, which has been passed by the powers that be as a potential Football League ground, hardly surprising when it is an 11,000 all seater home.

Former Grounds

The former Gateshead and South Shields sides used a number of important and much mourned grounds. Early South Shields FC in the League played at Horsley Hill, later a greyhound stadium until it was covered by a housing estate. The club became Gateshead and moved to Redheugh Park, close to the bridge of that name, which remained home until the end, later being demolished, although at the time of writing the site is still undeveloped.

South Shields FC played at the huge Simonside Hall in the NPL before losing their ground and identity to Gateshead, the 20,000 capacity ground is now under a council housing estate just a stone's throw from the new Filtrona Park home of the latest South Shields club.

GATESHEAD 1995/96 SEASON

Date	Comp	Opponent	Att	Score	Scorers
19/08/95	L	Bromsgrove Rovers	789	1-3	Thompson 90
23/08/95	L	STALYBRIDGE CELTIC	524	1-0	Thompson 52
26/08/95	L	MACCLESFIELD TOWN	650	0-1	
28/08/95	L	Altrincham	640	1-1	Trott 32
02/09/95	L	STEVENAGE BOROUGH	610	2-2	Proudlock 54 73
05/09/95	L	Halifax Town	743	0-2	
09/09/95	C1	DUNSTON FED	492	3-2	
13/09/95	L	RUNCORN	375	1-0	Proudlock 63
16/09/95	L	Telford United	750	0-0	
20/09/95	L	HALIFAX TOWN	559	3-2	Thompson 22, Marquis 28, Cramman 44
23/09/95	C2	BARROW	721	2-2	Thompson(2)
26/09/95	C3	Barrow	1908	0-1	
30/09/95	L	Woking	1939	0-2	
07/10/95	L	Welling United	588	2-1	Thompson 40, Dobson 74(p)
10/10/95	L	Stalybridge Celtic	480	2-0	Cramman 8, Harkus 52
14/10/95	L	DAGENHAM & REDBRIDGE	587	2-0	Trott 29 89
21/10/95	L	DOVER ATHLETIC	512	1-1	Cramman 63
28/10/95	L	Bath City	481	1-0	Ord 76
04/11/95	L	SLOUGH TOWN	642	2-1	Harkus 11 19(p)
11/11/95	L	Dagenham & Redbridge	712	4-0	Harkus 1, Proudlock 8, Trott 55 80
18/11/95	L	KETTERING TOWN	712	1-1	Ord 11
25/11/95	L	Southport	1008	0-1	
02/12/95	L	HEDNESFORD TOWN	841	0-3	
09/12/95	L	NORTHWICH VICTORIA	612	1-1	Cramman 72
16/12/95	L	Macclesfield Town	1161	0-1	
01/01/96	L	Morecambe	1400	3-2	Harkus 2, Trott 8, Proudlock 54
06/01/96	L	Slough Town	768	2-1	Trott 10, Harkus 45(p)
10/01/96	C4	HALIFAX TOWN	327	4-0	
13/01/96	L	FARNBOROUGH TOWN	881	1-1	Trott 46
20/01/96	C5	Kidderminster Harriers	1312	0-0	
24/01/96	C6	KIDDERMINSTER HARRIERS	383	2-0	Robson, Cramman
31/01/96	L	MORECAMBE	478	3-0	Harkus 25 70 88
10/02/96	C7	Emley	668	2-1	Cramman(2)
17/02/96	L	Stevenage Borough	1364	1-1	Harkus 41
24/02/96	L	TELFORD UNITED	813	1-2	Ord 68
27/02/96	L	Runcorn	333	1-1	Watson 33
02/03/96	C8	Radcliffe Borough	716	2-1	Thompson, Kitchen
05/03/96	C9	Southport	315	1-2	Thompson 82
09/03/96	L	Kettering Town	1179	0-1	
16/03/96	L	BATH CITY	583	3-1	Thompson 58 73(p)
18/03/96	L	Hednesford Town	1017	1-0	Cramman 82
23/03/96	C10	Chorley	1136	1-3	Proudlock
27/03/96	L	ALTRINCHAM	357	2-3	Cramman 13, Harkus 17
30/03/96	L	WELLING UNITED	510	1-1	Ord 11
02/04/96	L	Northwich Victoria	602	2-1	Harkus 18(p), Proudlock 54
06/04/96	L	Farnborough Town	625	3-2	Harkus 13, Lowe 58, Thompson 86
08/04/96	L	KIDDERMINSTER HARRIERS	687	4-1	Thompson 17, Harkus 31 36, Ord 48
13/04/96	L	WOKING	919	0-1	
20/04/96	L	Kidderminster Harriers	1509	1-1	Harkus 85
24/04/96	L	SOUTHPORT	469	2-2	Harkus 38 45
27/04/96	L	BROMSGROVE ROVERS	762	1-0	Hine 73
04/05/96	L	Dover Athletic	1103	1-1	Harkus 75

C1=FA CupQ1, C2=FA CupQ2, C3=FA CupQ2 rep, C4=SC2, C5=FA Trophy1, C6=FA Trophy1 rep, C7=FA Trophy2, C8=SCQF, C9=FA TrophyQF, C10=FA Trophy3

HALIFAX TOWN
THE SHAY, HALIFAX, WEST YORKSHIRE, HX1 2YS
TEL: 01422 345543 FAX: 01422 349487

Secretary: Derek A Newiss, 216 Highfield Rd, Keighley, BD21 2RL

Tel:01535 661690

Club Admin Address: Halifax Town AFC 18 Prescott St, Halifax HX1 2LG

Colours: Blue and White

Nickname: The Shaymen

Capacity: 5,194

Seating: Yes

Covered standing: Yes

Clubhouse on ground: No

Record attendance: 36,885 v Tottenham Hotspur FA Cup 5th Round, 14th Feb 1953

Biggest win: 2-0 v West Vale Ramblers FA Cup 1st Qual Rd 1913

Biggest defeat: 0-13 v Stockport County Div 3 North 1933-34

Record appearances: John Pickering 367

Record goalscorer in one season: Albert Valentine 34 Div 3 North 1934-35

Record goalscorer in aggregate: Ernest Dixon 129

Record fee received: £250.000 for Wayne Allison to Watford

Record transfer paid: £50,000 for Ian Juryeff from Herford Utd in 1990

HONOURS

Yorkshire Electricity Cup 1991 and 1993

Bradford Hospitals Cup 1914

Promoted to Division Three in 1969

Manager for 1996-97: John Carroll

Assistant Manager: Billy Rodaway

Chairman: John Stockwell

Vice Chairman: Chris Holland

Halifax Town were founded on May 24th 1911, after a meeting at the Saddle Hotel. They turned professional straight away and began playing in the Yorkshire Combination on a pitch at Sandhall which was to remain home until the Great War when the site was taken over for a munitions factory. They played just one season in the Comb before moving into the stronger Midland League in 1912, where they remained until 1921. The club played briefly at Exley until the Shay was ready for football, having like many others been a rubbish tip. A stand had been brought from Manchester City's Hyde Road ground and a hut was provided for changing. Despite the spartan surroundings the club were voted into the Football League in 1921, to play in Division Three North. The Shaymen remained with a conspicuous lack of success in Division Three North until 1958 when the league was re-organised into a 3rd and 4th division, and Town had five years in the 3rd before being relegated in 1963.

The following season the club enjoyed a run to the 4th Round of the League Cup and in 1969 they were promoted back to Division 3, where they stayed until relegation came again in 1976.

In 1980 the club enjoyed another Cup run, where TV cameras witnessed their famous victory over Manchester City, which was to be their last moment of glory as a League club for they dropped into the Conference in 1993.

The Shay once held a crowd of 36,885 for a match with Tottenham Hotspur in 1953 and, after the tragedies which befell Bradford and Hillsbrough, it was reduced to around 16,000, but today, having been altered to account for life in non-League football it has gone from 8,000 to 5,194.

HALIFAX TOWN 1995/96 SEASON

Date	Comp	Opponent	Att	Score	Scorers
19/08/95	L	Hednesford Town	1650	0-3	
22/08/95	L	MACCLESFIELD TOWN	1169	1-0	Stoneman 85
26/08/95	L	SLOUGH TOWN	917	1-2	Johnson 33
28/08/95	L	Stalybridge Celti	905	0-1	
02/09/95	L	WELLING UNITED	766	2-1	O'Regan 17, Johnson 21
05/09/95	L	GATESHEAD	743	2-0	Beddard 25, Midwood 83
09/09/95	L	Woking	2065	0-2	
12/09/95	L	NORTHWICH VICTORIA	829	2-0	Stoneman 31, Simpson 66(og)
16/09/95	L	KIDDERMINSTER HARRIERS	1008	0-2	
20/09/95	L	Gateshead	559	2-3	Worthington 62, Midwood 72
23/09/95	L	Altrincham	1085	2-3	Trotter 46, Worthington 68
26/09/95	L	MORECAMBE	910	1-1	Midwood 40
30/09/95	L	DOVER ATHLETIC	905	1-0	Hendrick 48
07/10/95	L	Runcorn	637	1-0	Midwood 45
14/10/95	L	STEVENAGE BOROUGH	858	2-3	Brown 27, Johnson 31
21/10/95	C1	Runcorn	901	1-2	Worthington
28/10/95	L	Farnborough Town	908	0-0	
04/11/95	L	BATH CITY	811	3-1	Midwood 13 45, Cochrane 20
11/11/95	L	KETTERING TOWN	929	2-0	Worthington 15 33
18/11/95	L	Dagenham & Redbridge	701	1-1	Midwood 34
25/11/95	L	Welling United	666	0-0	
02/12/95	L	BROMSGROVE ROVERS	843	1-1	Worthington 13
05/12/95	C2	OSSETT TOWN		5-1	O'Regan, Midwood(3), Johnson
09/12/95	L	Slough Town	862	3-2	Beddard 71 74, Midwood 75
16/12/95	L	RUNCORN	834	1-3	Johnson 45
01/01/96	L	Southport	1318	0-0	
06/01/96	L	DAGENHAM & REDBRIDGE	729	3-0	Cochrane 6, Johnson 29, O'Regan 67
10/01/96	SC	2Gateshead	327	0-4	
13/01/96	L	Stevenage Borough	1841	0-2	
20/01/96	C3	SOUTHPORT	966	2-1	Johnson, Cochrane
03/02/96	L	HEDNESFORD TOWN	859	1-3	Brook 75
10/02/96	C4	BROMSGROVE ROVERS	887	0-1	
14/02/96	C5	Farsley Celtic	211	0-1	
17/02/96	L	Northwich Victoria	879	1-1	Brook 22
24/02/96	L	Bath City	547	1-2	Sansan 1
02/03/96	L	Dover Athletic	895	2-3	Lee 48, Midwood 90
05/03/96	L	STALYBRIDGE CELTIC	509	2-3	Trotter 76, O'Regan 78
09/03/96	L	Macclesfield Town	1348	0-7	
12/03/96	L	Morecambe	648	1-0	Cochrane 66
16/03/96	L	ALTRINCHAM	755	1-1	Stoneman 68
18/03/96	L	Kidderminster Harriers	1168	1-6	Johnson 37
26/03/96	L	SOUTHPORT	694	2-2	Horner 25, O'Regan 78
30/03/96	L	FARNBOROUGH TOWN	697	0-0	
06/04/96	L	TELFORD UNITED	771	0-0	
08/04/96	L	Kettering Town	1317	2-1	Daws 14, Hendrick 64
13/04/96	L	Telford United	708	1-1	Trotter 26
20/04/96	L	WOKING	1064	2-2	Brook 16 66
04/05/96	L	Bromsgrove Rovers	887	1-0	Midwood 59

C1=FA CupQ4, C2=W. Riding2, C3=W. Riding2, C4=FA Trophy2, C5=W. RidingQF

HAYES
TOWNFIELD HOUSE, CHURCH ROAD, HAYES, MIDDX. UB3 2LE
TEL: 0181 573 4598 CLUB 2075

Secretary: John Price, 18 Ickenham Close, West Ruislip, Middx HA4 7DJ

Tel: 01895 631933

General Manager: Terry Brown c/o Hayes FC

Press officer: Trevor Griffith: 01895 638013

Colours: Red and White stripes

Nickname: The Missioners

Capacity: 6,500

Seating: 450

Covered standing: 2,000

Clubhouse on ground: Yes

Record attendance: 15,370 v Bromley in FA Amateur Cup February 10th 1951

Record appearances: Reg Leather and Johnny Reay

Record fee received: £30,000 for Les Ferdinand with subsequent moving on fee clause which brought in £600,000 when he moved to Newcastle Utd

Record fee paid: £6,000 for A Cox

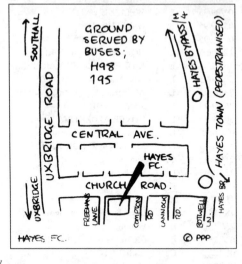

HONOURS

Great Western Suburban League from 1920 to 1924 (4 wins),Spartan League 1927-28,

Athenian League 1956-57,Premier Midweek Floodlit League 1975-76, Suburban League North 1988-89 and 1991-92. ICIS League 1995-96.

London Senior Cup 1932 and 1981, Middx Senior Cup 1920, 21, 26, 31, 36, 40, 50, 82.

Middx Charity Cup 16 times, London Charity Cup 1961, Middx Minor Cup 1911, Middx Premier Cup 1987, 88, 89

Former Grounds

Botwell Common, roughly at the junction of Pump Lane and Station Road at the end of Coldharbour Lane until 1920. Moved to Cox's Meadow which is the current ground in Church Road

Hayes Football Club was formed in 1909 by Eileen Shackle, a well known social worker. It was originally a boys team, playing under the name of Botwell Mission and her intention was to introduce the boys to religion, rather than just football.

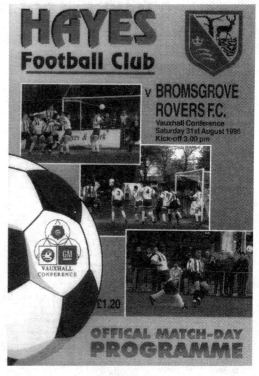

Within three years they had won their first trophy, the Middlesex Minor Cup. After the Great War they stepped into senior football and entered the Great Western Combination, finishing runners up behind Maidenhead in the first season. Four more years were spent in that league before a move to the Spartan League, with all four seasons ending with the title. With the Middlesex Senior Cup also won twice, the move to the current ground, then called Cox's Meadow, was in a very successful period. In 1928 the Spartan title was won with 106 goals in 28 games and this prompted a name change in 1929 to Hayes FC. They joined the Athenian League a year later from where they reached the Amateur Cup Final, after playing through nine rounds, all away. In the final, they sadly lost to Wycombe Wanderers at Highbury. The Athenian League closed down for six years during the War and on resumption Hayes were runners up before eventually winning the title in 1957 on goal average over Finchley. That year was also notable for another Amateur Cup run to the semi-final, where they lost to Bishop Auckland at Newcastle.

At the turn of the 70's, when Maidstone and Wealdstone left to turn professional, Hayes joined the Isthmian. It heralded a quiet time, with the odd cup run locally, but until, last May, their main fame has come in the FA Cup, where they reached the First Round proper for six seasons on the trot, losing to Swansea, Aldershot, Peterborough and AFC Bournemouth, before their greatest ever result, winning 2-0 at Craven Cottage in 1991 against Fulham.

1995 saw a fine league season end in third spot, but last May, after an epic battle, the title was won on the last day with a win over Carshalton Athletic, which meant promotion to the Conference.

Hayes immediate future was secured during the last year, when former player Les Ferdinand moved from QPR to Newcastle Utd, thus activating a sell on clause which netted them a cool £600,000 and brought national attention.

HAYES 1995/96 SEASON

Date	Comp		Opponent	Att	Score	Scorers
12/08/95	IFL	P	Bromley	419	1-0	Cox
19/08/95	IFL	P	DULWICH HAMLET	327	2-2	Goodliffe, Randall
22/08/95	IFL	P	Hendon	262	2-0	Kelly, Driscoll
26/08/95	IFL	P	Sutton United	611	2-2	Pearce, Stevens
02/09/95	IFL	P	MOLESEY	318	2-0	Goodliffe, Baker
05/09/95	C1	1	GRAYS ATHLETIC	109	0-1	
09/09/95	C2		Concord Rangers	150	3-0	Baker, T Kelly, W Kelly
16/09/95	IFL	P	WALTON & HERSHAM	293	2-0	Baker, Pearce
23/09/95	C3		Baldock Town	319	1-0	Kellman
30/09/95	IFL	P	Purfleet	181	0-0	
03/10/95	IFL	P	WORTHING	240	2-0	T Kelly(2)
07/10/95	C4		Hendon	376	3-0	Kellman, Randall(2)
14/10/95	IFL	P	Enfield	1023	1-1	Kellman
21/10/95	C5		SUDBURY WANDERERS	420	4-0	Kellman(3), Pearce
24/10/95	IFL	P	Chertsey Town	603	3-1	Kellman, T Kelly, Pearce
28/10/95	IFL	P	YEADING	437	0-0	
31/10/95	IFL	P	Kingstonian	432	0-1	
07/11/95	C6		Cockfosters	94	3-2	Brady(2), Flitter
11/11/95	C7	1	Northampton Town	5389	0-1	
13/11/95	C8	1	Purfleet	58	0-2	
18/11/95	IFL	P	HITCHIN TOWN	303	1-1	Pearce
21/11/95	IFL	P	Boreham Wood	308	0-0	
25/11/95	C9		Dorchester Town	515	3-2	Pearson, Kelly, Brady
02/12/95	IFL	P	AYLESBURY UNITED	393	0-1	
09/12/95	IFL	P	Yeovil Town	2025	0-3	
16/12/95	IFL	P	CARSHALTON ATHLETIC	283	1-2	Baker
19/12/95	IFL	P	ST ALBANS CITY	238	0-0	
23/12/95	IFL	P	Molesey	200	2-0	Cox, Kelly
02/01/96	IFL	P	Grays Athletic	226	3-3	Haynes, T Kelly, Hyatt
06/01/96	IFL	P	BROMLEY	267	5-1	Brady(2), Haynes, Cox, Pearce
09/01/96	C10		Kingsbury Town		4-0	Williams(2), Cox, Mee
13/01/96	IFL	P	HENDON	347	3-1	Haynes(2), Pearce
20/01/96	C11		ENFIELD	502	0-0	
23/01/96	C12		Enfield	436	2-2	Cox, Randall
29/01/96	C13		Enfield	398	2-2	Cox, Stevens
01/02/96	C14		ENFIELD	369	2-0	Goodliffe, Randall
03/02/96	IFL	P	Worthing	305	3-0	Williams, Haynes, Brady
10/02/96	C15		Bath City	699	0-2	
13/02/96	C16		FELTHAM		6-2	
17/02/96	IFL	P	Walton & Hersham	302	1-0	Haynes
21/02/96	IFL	P	Hitchin Town	164	3-1	Williams, Cox, Randall
24/02/96	IFL	P	Yeading	403	1-0	W Kelly
02/03/96	IFL	P	KINGSTONIAN	431	2-1	Cox, Pearce
05/03/96	IFL	P	BISHOP'S STORTFORD	243	3-1	Pearce, Haynes, Hyatt
09/03/96	IFL	P	ENFIELD	625	3-1	Baker, W Kelly, Pearce
12/03/96	C17		HARROW BOROUGH		2-1	
16/03/96	IFL	P	St Albans City	765	3-0	Stevens, Flynn, Brady
19/03/96	IFL	P	Dulwich Hamlet	448	1-1	W Kelly
23/03/96	IFL	P	Bishop's Stortford	427	2-1	Williams, Stevens
26/03/96	IFL	P	PURFLEET	371	2-1	Wilkinson, Williams
30/03/96	IFL	P	CHERTSEY TOWN	507	4-0	Hyatt, Randall, Brady, Sugrue
06/04/96	IFL	P	GRAYS ATHLETIC	583	5-1	Cox(3), E Williams, Marsh(og)
08/04/96	C18		Hampton	813	3-2	(played at Yeading F.C.)
13/04/96	IFL	P	BOREHAM WOOD	707	1-1	Haynes
16/04/96	IFL	P	SUTTON UNITED	516	0-0	
20/04/96	IFL	P	Aylesbury United	809	3-1	Stevens, G Williams, Randall
23/04/96	IFL	P	HARROW BOROUGH	716	2-1	Marshall(og), G Williams
27/04/96	IFL	P	YEOVIL TOWN	1537	1-1	G Williams
01/05/96	IFL	P	Harrow Borough	1212	1-1	Cox
04/05/96	IFL	P	Carshalton Athletic	1025	3-0	Williams(2), Haynes

C1=GIC1, C2=FA CupQ1, C3=FA CupQ2, C4=FA CupQ3, C5=FA CupQ4, C6=MiddxSC1, C7=FA Cup, C8=CC1,
C9=FA TrophyQ3, C10=MiddxSC12, C11=FA Trophy1, C12=FA Trophy1, C13=FA Trophy1 rep2,
C14=FA Trophy1rep3, C15=FA Trophy2, C16=Middx SCQF, C17=Middx SCSF, C18=Middx SCF

HEDNESFORD TOWN
KEYS PARK, HEDNESFORD, CANNOCK, STAFFS WS12 5DW
TEL: 01543 422870

Secretary: Ritchie Murning, 26 Linden View, Chase Heights, Hednesford, Staffs WS12 5AU

Comercial Manager: Terry Brumpton or Joanne Smith full time at club during midweek 9am - 5pm

Colours: White and Black

Nickname: The Pitmen

Capacity: 3,500   Seating: 770

Covered Standing:1000   Clubhouse on ground: Yes

Record attendance: 3,500 v Wolverhampton Wanderers Nov 1995. At Cross Keys 10,000 v Walsall Birmingham League Easter 1922

Biggest win: 12-1 v Birmingham City 1940-41 and Redditch Utd 1952-53

Biggest defeat: 0-15 v Burton 1924-25 Birmingham League

Record appearances: Kevin Foster

Record goalscorer in one season: Tosh Griffiths

Record goalscorer in total: Tosh Griffiths

Record fee paid: £12,000 for Steve Burr

Record fee received: £50,000 for Dave Hanson to Leyton Orient 1995

DIRECTIONS

From South: Leave M6 at Junction 11 and follow A460 for Cannock to Longford Island. Proceed on A5 through lights and under bridge to Churchbridge Island. Turn left and follow A460 for Rugeley over 5 islands till Sawyers pub (6th Island) turn right (3rd exit) and follow road to next island. Entrance to ground is straight ahead.

From North: Leave M6 at Junction 12 and follow A5 to Longford Island (McDonalds on right). Proceed through lights and under bridge to Churchbridge Island. Turn left and follow A460 for Rugeley over 5 islands till Sawyers pub (6th Island) turn right (3rd exit) and follow road to next island. Entrance to ground is straight ahead.

HONOURS

Welsh Cup runners up 1992. West Midlands League 1978 and League Cup 1984.
Birmingham Combination 1910 and 1951. Staffs Senior Cup 1970 and 1974.
Birmingham Senior Cup 1936.
Southern League Premier Division 1995

**Manager for 96-97:
John Baldwin.**

Assistant manager: John Allen

Chairman: Mick Smith.

Vice Chairman: John Baldwin.

**Press officer:
Terry Brumpton as above**

HEDNESFORD TOWN 1995/96 SEASON

Date		Opponent	Att	Score	Scorers
12/08/95	C1	Hastings Town	356	4-0	Hanson, O'Connor, Devine, Wright
19/08/95	L	HALIFAX TOWN	1650	3-0	Essex 57, Lambert 70, Wright 83
21/08/95	L	Kidderminster Harriers	1681	1-3	O'Connor 84
26/08/95	L	Dover Athletic	866	3-1	O'Connor 4, Essex 24, Devine 72
28/08/95	L	WELLING UNITED	1732	1-1	Berry 13(og)
02/09/95	L	WOKING	1711	2-1	O'Connor 31, Lambert 68
04/09/95	L	Dagenham & Redbridge	837	2-1	Hanson 57, Fitzpatrick 72
09/09/95	C2	CORBY TOWN	732	3-1	Essex, Street, Wright
11/09/95	L	TELFORD UNITED	2480	4-0	O'Connor 45, Carty 53, Hanson 73 75
16/09/95	L	Northwich Victoria	1100	2-0	O'Connor 4 17
18/09/95	C3	Kidderminster Harriers	1326	1-4	
23/09/95	C4	Tamworth	1138	2-1	Hackett, O'Connor
25/09/95	C5	WILLENHALL TOWN		6-1	
30/09/95	L	Slough Town	971	2-0	Carty 3, O'Connor 69
02/10/95	C6	KIDDERMINSTER HARRIERS	1626	2-0	
07/10/95	C7	SOLIHULL BOROUGH	1013	2-2	Devine, Wright
11/10/95	C8	Solihull Borough	421	2-1	Essex, McNally
14/10/95	L	Bath City	661	0-1	
21/10/95	C9	Canvey Island	710	0-2	
28/10/95	L	SOUTHPORT	1355	2-1	Burr 26, Devine 45
31/10/95	C10	Armitage		3-1	
04/11/95	L	MACCLESFIELD TOWN	2019	0-1	
11/11/95	L	DOVER ATHLETIC	1147	2-2	Street 18, O'Connor 75
13/11/95	C11	WEST BROMWICH ALBION	1200	2-3	Carty, Jennings
18/11/95	L	Stalybridge Celtic	687	1-0	Foreman 3
21/11/95	L	Bromsgrove Rovers	952	4-1	Street 42, O'Connor 50 55, Fitzpatrick 83
25/11/95	L	MORECAMBE	1271	1-2	Devine 77
27/11/95	L	STALYBRIDGE CELTIC	895	0-1	
02/12/95	L	Gateshead	841	3-0	O'Connor 15 27, Foreman 45
09/12/95	L	Farnborough Town	716	3-1	O'Connor 12, Yates 34, Foreman 70
16/12/95	L	KIDDERMINSTER HARRIERS	1392	1-3	Foreman 2
01/01/96	L	Kettering Town	1712	0-2	
06/01/96	L	RUNCORN	1008	2-0	Collins 69, Lambert 75
13/01/96	L	NORTHWICH VICTORIA	1017	2-1	Lambert 15, Yates 47
20/01/96	C12	NORTHWICH VICTORIA	935	1-1	McNally
23/01/96	C13	Northwich Victoria	636	0-2	
31/01/96	C14	Paget Rangers	102	1-2	Carty
03/02/96	L	Halifax Town	859	3-1	Devine 18, O'Connor 54 88
10/02/96	L	Southport	811	2-2	Carty 12(p), Lake 41
17/02/96	L	BATH CITY	1004	2-1	Lake 38, Essex 42
24/02/96	L	Stevenage Borough	1626	0-1	
02/03/96	L	Morecambe	961	1-0	O'Connor 32
04/03/96	L	KETTERING TOWN	1049	1-0	Street 75
09/03/96	L	FARNBOROUGH TOWN	1010	4-1	Devine 20, Russell 64, McNally 66, O'Connor 82
12/03/96	L	Welling United	400	1-1	Russell 63(p)
16/03/96	L	BROMSGROVE ROVERS	1119	4-2	Russell 35, O'Connor 45 51, Lake 84
18/03/96	L	GATESHEAD	1017	0-1	
23/03/96	L	Runcorn	507	2-2	Lambert 32, O'Connor 64
25/03/96	L	STEVENAGE BOROUGH	1651	2-1	Russell 59, Lambert 76
30/03/96	L	Woking	3194	0-3	
02/04/96	L	Telford United	967	1-2	Ridings 87
06/04/96	L	ALTRINCHAM	1010	2-1	Essex 63, Ridings 75
13/04/96	L	DAGENHAM & REDBRIDGE	946	0-0	
20/04/96	L	Altrincham	731	1-2	O'Connor 87
27/04/96	L	SLOUGH TOWN	1031	3-1	Simpson 33, O'Connor 62, Lake 88
04/05/96	L	Macclesfield Town	1236	1-1	O'Connor 26

C1=BHL Shield, C2=FA CupQ1, C3=SC1(1), C4=FA CupQ2, C5=Staffs SC1, C6=SC1(2), C7=SC1(2), C8=SC1(2), C9=FA CupQ4, C10=Staffs SC2, C11=Staffs SC2, C12=Staffs SC2, C13=FA Trophy1 rep, C14=Staffs SCQF

KETTERING TOWN
ROCKINGHAM RD, KETTERING, NORTHANTS, NN16 9AW
TEL: 01536 83028/410815 OFFICE: 01536 410962 CLUB FAX: 01536 412273

Secretary: Mr Gerry Knowles c/o Club

Nickname: Poppies

Capacity: 6,035

Seating: 1,800

Covered standing

Clubhouse on ground: Yes

Record Attendance: 11,536 v Peterborough Utd

Biggest win: 20-3 v Higham East Midlands League Circa 1934

Biggest defeat: 0-13 v Mardy Southern League 1912

Record appearances: Roger Ashby

Record goalscorer in total: Roy Clayton 171

Record fee received: £150,000 from Newcastle Utd for Andy Hunt

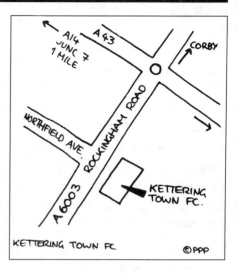

HONOURS

Midland League 1896 and 1900

Southern League 1928, 1957, 1973

East Midlands League 1934

Birmingham League 1948

Alliance League (GMAC) Cup 1987

Northants Senior Cup 1884, 1896, 1898, 1901, 1907, 1921, 1932, 1933, 1936, 1939, 1947, 1949, 1953, 1956, 1957, 1969, 1973, 1979, 1980, 1984, 1985, 1986, 1987, 1990, 1992, 1993, 1996

Maunsell Cup 1914, 1920, 1924 jt, 1925, 1929, 1948, 1952, 1955, 1960, 1984,

Manager for 1996-97: Gary Johnson

Assistant Manager: Bob Mullan

Chairman: Peter Mallinger

Vice Chairman: Peter Oliver

Kettering Town were formed in 1872, when the Northampton Mercury announced the beginning of a football club by Messrs GW Roughton and W Shrives to satisfy the want of outdoor amusement on Saturday afternoons. The first game was on December 19th against a team from Uppingham School on George Eldred's Field, in Green Lane. The first of over two dozen Northampton Senior Cup triumphs came in 1884 and by the end of the 1890's they had gathered a large scale support, many of whom travelled to Leicester to see them beat the Fosse in the FA Cup. In 1899, after again beating Leicester, over 5,500 people packed into the newly acquired and heavily sloping Rockingham Road enclosure to see the Poppies take on Notts County, and draw 1-1.

The new century saw the club in the Southern League after eight years in the Midland League where they were twice champions. They played league games against the likes of Tottenham Hotspur, West Ham United, Portsmouth and Queens Park Rangers for a while before finances dictated they resign to join the Northants League (UCL). They returned in 1909 for another brief spell of three years to return to Northants football but in 1923 had a third spell which saw them take the title in 1928 and lose the championship play off a year later. Again they endured money problems and were forced to go amateur until the Second War.

In peacetime they joined the Birmingham League and in 1950 re-joined the Southern League for a fourth spell, winning it in 1957. It began a spell which lasted until 1979, and in that time the club took the FA Cup scalps of Swindon Town and Millwall, and after suffering relegation, they bounced back to take the championship under Ron Atkinson in 1973, also beating Swansea in the FA Cup. Again the club developed serious financial troubles and in 1981, despite a runners up spot in the new Alliance Premier League and a visit to Wembley for the FA Trophy within the last two years, the club were on the brink of bankruptcy.

They were saved in 1982 but nearly went under again three years later when the ground was sold and then leased back, but since then the superb Rockingham Road ground has blossomed as the club have established themselves in the Conference

Former Grounds

George Eldred's Field, Green Lane, situated close to the Police Station until moving to North Park, which still exists. Moved to Rockingham Road in 1897

KETTERING TOWN 1995/96 SEASON

Date	Comp	Opponent	Att	Score	Scorers
29/07/95	F	RUSHDEN & DIAMONDS		2-2	(1995-96 Northants Senior Cup Final Won 3-1 on penalties)
19/08/95	L	Altrincham	969	3-1	Alford 2 49, Stringfellow 53
22/08/95	L	BROMSGROVE ROVERS	2006	2-2	Oxbrow 12, Alford 35
26/08/95	L	RUNCORN	1583	4-0	Stott 27, Alford 59, Stringfellow 72 80
28/08/95	L	Farnborough Town	1037	1-1	Scott 9
02/09/95	L	SOUTHPORT	1944	1-1	Pope 24
04/09/95	L	Kidderminster Harriers	1949	0-1	
09/09/95	L	Macclesfield Town	1320	1-1	Stringfellow 20
12/09/95	L	WOKING	1671	3-0	Alford 44 87, Oxbrow 63
16/09/95	L	BATH CITY	1767	3-0	Alford 44, Pope 49, Stringfellow 50
18/09/95	L	Stevenage Borough	2033	1-5	Oxbrow 36
23/09/95	L	Stalybridge Celtic	627	2-3	Scott 16, Stott 18
30/09/95	L	Telford United	952	4-3	Pope 20, Oxbrow 26, Scott 30, Alford 72
07/10/95	L	SLOUGH TOWN	1902	2-0	Scott 28, Alford 36
14/10/95	L	Morecambe	1098	3-5	Stott 7, Alford 53, Scott 65
21/10/95	C1	BROMSGROVE ROVERS	2427	0-0	
24/10/95	C2	Bromsgrove Rovers	1246	2-2	
28/10/95	L	Runcorn	569	2-4	Hunter 36 63
30/10/95	C3	BROMSGROVE ROVERS	2283	1-2	Alford
04/11/95	L	DAGENHAM & REDBRIDGE	1616	2-0	Alford 22, Stringfellow 82
11/11/95	L	Halifax Town	929	0-2	
14/11/95	L	WELLING UNITED	1232	1-3	Scott 48
18/11/95	L	Gateshead	712	1-1	Alford 1
25/11/95	L	ALTRINCHAM	1369	4-2	Alford 1 47 71, Scott 90
02/12/95	L	Dover Athletic	1045	1-2	Alford 57
05/12/95	C4	Stewarts & Lloyds Corby		0-2	
09/12/95	L	Bath City	612	1-3	Parsons
16/12/95	L	FARNBOROUGH TOWN	1260	0-2	
01/01/96	L	HEDNESFORD TOWN	1712	2-0	Hayworth 14, Alford 60
06/01/96	L	Southport	916	1-6	Norman 10
09/01/96	L	NORTHWICH VICTORIA	912	2-2	Alford 49 60
13/01/96	L	DOVER ATHLETIC	1332	2-2	Pope 43, Haworth 85
20/01/96	C5	ST ALBANS CITY	1577	1-1	Pope
23/01/96	C6	St Albans City	705	3-2	Ibrahim, Alford, Pope
10/02/96	C7	Slough Town	1058	2-1	Scott, Gynn
13/02/96	C8	SLOUGH TOWN	646	2-0	
17/02/96	L	Slough Town	766	2-1	Nyamah 77, Alford 90
24/02/96	L	Woking	2637	1-1	Alford 68
27/02/96	C9	Rothwell Town	402	0-5	
02/03/96	C10	Stevenage Borough	2219	0-3	
04/03/96	L	Hednesford Town	1049	0-1	
09/03/96	L	GATESHEAD	1179	1-0	Alford 34
16/03/96	L	MACCLESFIELD TOWN	1433	2-2	Nyanah 41 42
19/03/96	C11	Bromsgrove Rovers	650	0-2	
23/03/96	L	KIDDERMINSTER HARRIERS	1376	2-0	Harmon 23, Mustafa 47
03/04/96	C12	BROMSGROVE ROVERS	773	2-1	Gynn 6, Mustafa 43
06/04/96	L	Dagenham & Redbridge	730	2-1	Crooks 57(og), Thomas 83
08/04/96	L	HALIFAX TOWN	1317	1-2	Benjamin 88
13/04/96	L	MORECAMBE	1124	2-3	Oxbrow 7, Benjamin 71
16/04/96	L	STEVENAGE BOROUGH	1414	1-2	Mustafa 11
20/04/96	L	Bromsgrove Rovers	824	2-3	Benjamin 45, Dowling 68
23/04/96	L	Welling United	603	0-1	
30/04/96	L	TELFORD UNITED	851	0-3	
02/05/96	L	Northwich Victoria	632	2-6	Pope 7 65
04/05/96	L	STALYBRIDGE CELTIC	962	1-6	Dowling 79

C1=FA CupQ4, C2, C3=FA CupQ4 rep(2), C4=N'hants SCQF=FA CupQ4 rep, C5=FA Trophy1, C6=FA Trophy1, C7=FA Trophy2, C8=SCQF, C9=N'hants SCSF, C10=FA Trophy3, C11=SCSF(1), C12=SCSF(2)

Secretary: Roger Barlow c/o Aggborough Stadium

Commercial Manager: Mark Searl

Colours: Red and White

Nickname: Harriers

Capacity: 6,290

Seating: 1,100

Covered standing: 4,690

Clubhouse on ground: Yes

Record attendance 9, 155 v Hereford United FA Cup 1st Round Replay 1948

Biggest Win: 25-0 v Hereford in Birmingham Senior Cup 1889

Biggest Defeat: 0-13 v Darwen (A) FA Cup 1st Round 24th January 1891

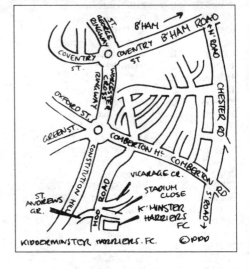

Record appearances: Brendan Wassall 686 1962-74

Record goalscorer in total: Peter Wassall 432 1963-74

Record fee received: £100,000 for Paul Jones from Wolverhampton Wanderers

in 1991 and for Richard Forsyth from Birmingham City in 1996.

HONOURS

F.A Trophy Winners 1987

Runners Up: 1991 and 1995

Welsh F A Cup Runners up 1986 and 1989

GMV Conference 1994

Southern League Cup 1980

Worcester Senior Cup 19 times

Birmingham Senior Cup 7 times

Staffs Senior Cup 4 times

West Midland League 6 times

League Cup 7 times

Keys Cup 7 times

Border Counties Floodlit League 3 times

Bass County Vase

Manager for 1996-97: Graham Allner

Assistant manager: Jim Conway

Chairman: David L Reynolds

Vice Chairman: Lionel Newton

Kidderminster Harriers were, as the name suggests, originally an athletics club, as well as a rugby club, and for the first nine years they played under the rugby code. For the next three years they played friendlies, but the Football League's formation spawned many new leagues and when the Birmingham and District League (now the West Midlands League) was formed, Harriers took their place.

In the first season they finished runners-up but when professional reserve sides came in things went downhill, and despite regularly finishing in the top four a title did not arrive until 1938. They joined the Southern League in 1939 but War broke out after just two games, and on the resumption they went back into that league and remained until 1960 when rejoining the Birmingham League. Through the 60's Harriers developed into a major non-League club, reaching the FA Cup 1st Round on four occasions and in 1970, with Aggborough having been steadily developed, they returned to the Southern League, progressing to the Alliance in 1983. Wembley beckoned during the last decade with Burton beaten in the Trophy final in 1987 before the all conquering Wycombe Wanderers won in 1991. Four years later Harriers were again beaten, this time by Woking, but by then they had reached the peak and in 1994 they won the Conference, only to be cruelly denied a place in the Football League by ground grading problems.

That same season saw them eclipse Birmingham and Preston in the FA Cup before losing to West Ham United at Aggborough, a situation which allowed a club such as West Ham United to play an FA Cup tie, but not the likes of Scarborough, Rochdale and Hartlepool in the League.

With much rebuilding having been accomplished, the ground has now been passed as worthy of the league, so all Harriers now have to do is win the Conference again!

Former Grounds

The original clubs, Olympic and Harriers, played at Chester Road and Old Aggborough, but the amalgamated club have always played at the current site

KIDDERMINSTER HARRIERS 1995/96 SEASON

Date		Opponent	Att	Score	Scorers
19/08/95	L	Farnborough Town	840	1-3	May 25
21/08/95	L	HEDNESFORD TOWN	1681	3-1	May 17, Casey 69, Davies 88
26/08/95	L	MORECAMBE	1702	4-2	Davies 7 62(p), Casey 26, Deakin 80
28/08/95	L	Slough Town	1092	4-5	Yates 21 90, Casey 63, May 79(p)
02/09/95	L	Altrincham	881	1-1	Deakin 73
04/09/95	L	KETTERING TOWN	1949	1-0	Davies 30
09/09/95	L	STALYBRIDGE CELTIC	1962	3-0	Davies 49, Casey 86, May 90
12/09/95	L	Macclesfield Town	1202	2-0	Hughes 11, Cartwright 69
16/09/95	L	Halifax Town	1008	2-0	Casey 64, May 90
18/09/95	C1	HEDNESFORD TOWN	1326	4-1	Casey(2), Brindley, May
23/09/95	L	WOKING	2716	2-0	Davies 3, Casey 75
30/09/95	L	Southport	1164	2-0	Davies 57 87
02/10/95	C2	Hednesford Town	1626	0-2	
07/10/95	L	DOVER ATHLETIC	2259	1-1	Yates 38
09/10/95	L	TELFORD UNITED	2433	2-0	May 6, Davies 44
14/10/95	L	Northwich Victoria	1106	2-5	Deakin 58, Hughes 84
21/10/95	L	ALTRINCHAM	2429	1-1	Davies 90
28/10/95	L	Dagenham & Redbridge	756	2-4	Yates 3 45
04/11/95	L	Dover Athletic	1124	1-2	Yates 89
11/11/95	C3	SUTTON UNITED	2513	2-2	Hughes, Webb
18/11/95	L	RUNCORN	1879	4-1	Hughes 8, Davies 23, May 53 66
21/11/95	C4	Sutton United	1804	1-1	Casey
25/11/95	L	Woking	2264	0-0	
28/11/95	C5	Macclesfield Town	566	1-4	Hughes
02/12/95	L	BATH CITY	1833	1-2	Casey 45
09/12/95	L	SOUTHPORT	1664	2-3	Casey 79, Webb 86
16/12/95	L	Hednesford Town	1392	3-1	May 24, Davies 43, Dearlove 69
18/12/95	C6	DUDLEY TOWN	370	2-1	Dearlove, Shepherd
26/12/95	L	Bromsgrove Rovers	4398	1-2	May 1
01/01/96	L	BROMSGROVE ROVERS	4481	1-0	Yates 83
06/01/96	L	Stalybridge Celtic	605	2-2	Shepherd 15 86
13/01/96	L	MACCLESFIELD TOWN	2703	0-4	
20/01/96	C7	GATESHEAD	1312	0-0	
24/01/96	C8	Gateshead	383	0-2	
03/02/96	L	DAGENHAM & REDBRIDGE	1439	5-1	Hughes 2 15 43(p), Casey 5, Willetts 21
10/02/96	L	Runcorn	475	1-0	Brindley 66
17/02/96	L	Welling United	556	0-0	
20/02/96	L	Telford United	918	1-1	Hughes 72
24/02/96	L	SLOUGH TOWN	1715	4-3	Davies 13, Casey 29 43, Hughes 65
02/03/96	C9	STOURBRIDGE	750	1-2	Davies
09/03/96	L	WELLING UNITED	1685	3-0	Hughes 19, May 74, Yates 89
16/03/96	L	Stevenage Borough	2012	1-4	Casey 41
18/03/96	L	HALIFAX TOWN	1168	6-1	Brindley 12, Hughes 15, Casey 20, 54, May 31, Davies 73
23/03/96	L	Kettering Town	1376	0-2	
30/03/96	L	NORTHWICH VICTORIA	1604	2-1	Cartwright 50, Dearlove 62
08/04/96	L	Gateshead	687	1-4	Shepherd 79
16/04/96	L	Bath City	412	1-1	Shepherd 28
20/04/96	L	GATESHEAD	1509	1-1	Hughes 62
22/04/96	L	STEVENAG BOROUGH	2060	0-1	
27/04/96	L	FARNBOROUGH TOWN	1559	3-3	Deakin 31, Willetts 36, Hughes 52
04/05/96	L	Morecambe	1213	1-3	May 27

C1=SC1(1), C2=SC1(2),C3=SC1(2), C4=FA Cu1 rep, C5=SC2, C6=Worcs SCQF, C7=FA Trophy1,
C8=FA Trophy1 rep, C9=Worcs SCSF

MACCLESFIELD TOWN
MOSS ROSE, LONDON ROAD, MACCLESFIELD, CHESHIRE SK11 7SP
TEL: 01625 264686 COMMERCIAL OFFICE: 01625 424324

Secretary and Press Officer: Colin Garlick, 26 Kenilworth Rd, Macclesfield, Cheshire SK11 8PE

Tel: 01625 614181

(H) 0161 428 0976/4258

(B) 0370 420141 (mobile)

Club news and information on: 0891 884482

Colours: Blue and White

Nickname: The Silkmen

Capacity: 6,212

Seating: 1,072

Covered standing: 3,000

Clubhouse on ground: Yes

Record attendance: 9,003 v Winsford Utd Cheshire Senior Cup Rd 2, Feb 4th 1948

Biggest win: 15-0 v Chester St Mary's Cheshire Senior Cup Feb 16th 1886

Biggest defeat: 1-13 v Tranmere Rovers Res. April 3rd 1929

DIRECTIONS
Exit M6 Junction 18 eastwards on A541, then A535 to Chelford, turn right A537 to Macclesfield. The ground is at the south end of town on the main road to Leek (A523) on the right hand side.
Nearest Railway: Macclesfield one mile
Bus Service: Opposite Railway stn. Leek service.
Car Parking: Ample parking all around the ground.

ZENECA Pharmaceuticals
OFFICIAL CLUB SPONSORS

The Silkmen were formed in 1874 as an association side, having played for many years under the rugby code. Bowfield Lane, and later Victoria Road, on the home of the cricket club, were the early venues, but the original club went bankrupt near the turn of the century after they had moved to Moss Rose in 1891. A rival side, Hallfield FC moved in, changing their name to Macclesfield FC in 1904.

The club were champions of the Manchester and District league twice and won the Cheshire Senior Cup 5 times as they grew steadily in time with the ground, and with wins in the Cheshire County League and the Senior Cup, the 30's were a boom time. During the 1933-34 season the goalscoring record was set by Albert Valentine with 83 goals. After the War, with crowds at their peak, over 10,000 saw the Cheshire Senior Cup Final between Northwich Vics and Winsford Utd and a year later Macc's biggest crowd of just over 9,000 saw another match involving Winsford.

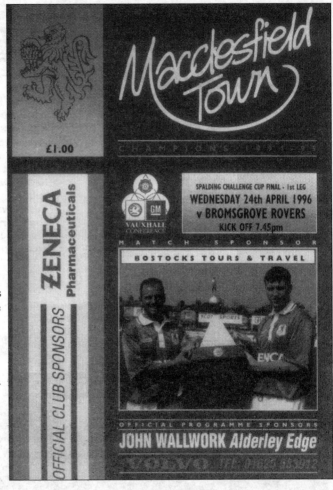

The club were founder members of the Northern Premier League, walking away with the title and in 1970 went to Wembley for the first FA Trophy Final, beating Telford Utd 2-0. The mid-eighties again saw the club dominate, winning the treble of League, League Cup and President's Cup, reaching the FA Cup 3rd Round a year later. Since then, Macc have been to Wembley thrice more, losing twice before beating Northwich Vics back in May of this year. The appointment of former Manchester United and Northern Ireland star Sammy McIlroy heralded a golden period for the club which continues today. 1994-95 was arguably the best ever, as not only did they enjoy cup runs in three competitions but the Conference title was taken by a street, at one stage leading by 22 points. A run of ten consecutive wins was a record and three players were named in the Conference team of the year. Their most disappointing times came when denied a place in the Football League due to ground grading, but they hope that this latest triumph in winning the FA Trophy last May can be the springboard once more.

FORMER GROUNDS..Bowfield Lane, Macclesfield Cricket Club in Victoria Road, Bowfield Lane again and Moss Rose in 1891

MACCLESFIELD TOWN 1995/96 SEASON

Date	Comp	Opponent	Att	Score	Scorers
19/08/95	L	WOKING	1370	3-2	Coates 14, Lyons 35, Marginson 75
22/08/95	L	Halifax Town	1169	0-1	
26/08/95	L	Gateshead	650	1-0	Power 21
28/08/95	L	DAGENHAM & REDBRIDGE	1172	3-1	Bradshaw 22 65, McDonald 71(p)
02/09/95	L	BATH CITY	1225	0-1	
05/09/95	L	Morecambe	1414	4-2	Cavell 2 14, Power 53, Lyons 63
09/09/95	L	KETTERING TOWN	1320	1-1	Cavell 8
12/09/95	L	KIDDERMINSTER HARRIERS	1202	0-2	
16/09/95	L	Dover Athletic	822	3-2	Power 4, Cavell 6 19
19/09/95	CS	WOKING	636	3-2	Coates(2), Lyons
23/09/95	L	SOUTHPORT	1282	3-1	Cavell 11, Sorvel 68, Power 80
26/09/95	C1	PELSALL VILLA	228	1-1	Coates
30/09/95	L	Farnborough Town	740	1-6	Coates 62
03/10/95	C2	Pelsall Villa	152	1-0	Coates
07/10/95	L	BROMSGROVE ROVERS	1137	2-1	Cavell 57, Lyons 90
10/10/95	L	MORECAMBE	1034	2-0	Coates 44, Sorvel 56
14/10/95	L	Slough Town	1007	2-2	Cavell 27, Howarth 87
21/10/95	C3	NORTHWICH VICTORIA	1707	0-1	
24/10/95	L	Runcorn	600	0-0	
28/10/95	L	WELLING UNITED	988	2-1	Bradshaw 63, Coates 71
31/10/95	L	Stalybridge Celtic	884	2-1	Sorvel 27, Cavell 44
04/11/95	L	Hednesford Town	2019	1-0	Coates 4
11/11/95	L	STALYBRIDGE CELTIC	1457	1-0	Lyons 15(p)
18/11/95	L	Altrincham	1648	4-0	Coates 17 52, Lyons 62 74
21/11/95	C4	Vauxhall G.M.	161	4-0	Lyons(2), Sorvel, Coates
25/11/95	L	FARNBOROUGH TOWN	1721	1-0	Sorvel 90
28/11/95	C5	KIDDERMINSTER HARRIERS	566	4-1	Coates(2), Lyons, Cavell
02/12/95	L	Stevenage Borough	2021	0-4	
05/12/95	C6	BOLDMERE ST MICHAELS	124	5-2	Hutchinson(2), Gardiner, Lyons, Payne
16/12/95	L	GATESHEAD	1161	1-0	Howarth 87
06/01/96	L	STEVENAGE BOROUGH	2126	0-0	
09/01/96	C7	BILSTON TOWN	298	1-2	Power
13/01/96	L	Kidderminster Harriers	2703	4-0	Power 38 57 84, Gardener 75
20/01/96	C8	RUNCORN	1401	1-0	Power
30/01/96	L	ALTRINCHAM	1301	2-3	Power 12, Hemmings 49
10/02/96	C9	PURFLEET	1003	2-1	Bradshaw, Payne
13/02/96	L	TELFORD UNITED	866	1-0	Lyons 35
17/02/96	L	Bromsgrove Rovers	1481	0-1	
24/02/96	L	RUNCORN	1410	1-0	Hutchinson 17
26/02/96	C10	Hyde United	716	1-2	Lyons
02/03/96	C11	SUDBURY TOWN	1140	1-0	Coates
05/03/96	C12	QFMorecambe	625	4-1	Coates 2, Hulme 21 47, Hemmings 31
09/03/96	L	HALIFAX TOWN	1348	7-0	Hulme 17 28, Payne 23, Power 61 76, Lyons 75(p), Hemmings 79
12/03/96	C13	HYDE UNITED	707	1-1	Hemmings
16/03/96	L	Kettering Town	1433	2-2	Wood 84, Towers 87
19/03/96	C14	SF(1)Southport	561	4-4	Own-Goal, Sorvel, Power, Hemmings
23/03/96	C15	Gresley Rovers	1727	2-0	Bradshaw, Power
26/03/96	L	NORTHWICH VICTORIA	1117	0-0	
30/03/96	L	Telford United	1015	2-1	Coates 11 89
03/04/96	C16	SF(2)SOUTHPORT	510	2-1	Coates 56, Power 80
06/04/96	L	Woking	4583	2-3	Power 19 28
08/04/96	L	DOVER ATHLETIC	1482	0-1	
13/04/96	C17	CHORLEY	2260	3-1	Thorpe 51(og), Coates 84, Power 87
16/04/96	L	Northwich Victoria	936	2-1	Tinson 62, Wood 72
20/04/96	C18	Chorley	3048	1-1	Sorvel
22/04/96	L	Southport	736	1-2	Lyons 19(p)
24/04/96	C19	BROMSGROVE ROVERS	547	1-1	Coates 12
27/04/96	L	Dagenham & Redbridge	660	0-3	
28/04/96	L	Welling United	558	2-1	Hulme 54, Woods 65
30/04/96	L	Bath City	361	1-1	Hulme 72
02/05/96	L	SLOUGH TOWN	591	1-1	Coates 76
04/05/96	L	HEDNESFORD TOWN	1236	1-1	Coates 59
06/05/96	C20	Bromsgrove Rovers	1341	1-3	Sorvel 21(p)
19/05/96	C21	Northwich Victoria	8672	3-1	Payne, Buress og, Hemmmings

C1=Staffs SC1, C2=Staffs SC1 rep, C3=FA CupQ4, C4=Ches.SCQF, C5=SC2, C6=Staffs SC2, C7=Staffs SCQF, C8=FA Trophy1, C9=FA Trophy2, C10=Ches. SCSF(1), C11=FA Trophy3, C12=SCQF, C13=Ches. SCSF(2), C14=SCSF(1), C15=FA TrophyQF, C16=SCSF(2), C17=FA TrophySF(1), C18=FA TrophySF(2), C19=SCF(1), C20=SCF(2), C21=FA TrophyF

MORECAMBE
CHRISTIE PARK, LANCASTER RD, MORECAMBE, LANCS. LA4 5TJ
TEL 01524 411797 FAX 01524 411797

Secretary Neil Marsdin, c/o MFC

Colours: Red and White stripes

Nickname: The Shrimps

Capacity: 4,300

Seating: 1,100

Covered: standing 1,000

Clubhouse on ground: Yes

Record attendance: 9,324 v Weymouth FA Cup 3rd Rd Jan 4th 1962

Biggest win: 16-0 Rossendale Utd Lancs Combination Sept 1967

Biggest defeat: 0-7 v Darwen Nov 7th 1953

Record appearances: Steve Done 530 1968-1978

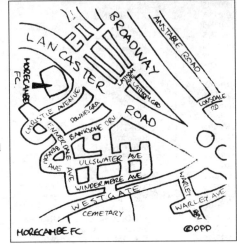

Record goalscorer in one season: Keith Borrowdale 51 in 1961-62

Record goalscorer in one game: Arnold Timmins 8 v Rossendale Lancs Comb 1967

Record goalscorer in total Keith Borrowdale: 289 1956-68 and 1978-9 in Lancs Combination and John Coleman 130 from 1990-95 in NPL

Record fee paid: £7,500 Ian Cain from Fleetwood in 1989

Record fee received: £5,000 for Barrie Stimpson to Colne Dynamoes 1990

and Paul Lodge to Southport in 1993

HONOURS

FA TROPHY WINNERS 1974

Northern Premier League President's Cup 1992

Lancs Combination 1925, 1962, 1963, 1967, 1968

League Cup 1927, 1946, 1965, 1967, 1968

Lancs Junior Cup (ATS Trophy) 1926, 1927, 1962, 1963, 1969, 1986, 1987, 1993, 1996

Lancs Senior Cup 1968

Manager 1996-97: Jim Harvey

Assistant Manager: Tony Hesketh

Chairman: Ken Parker

Vice Chairman: Graham Hodgson

After a number of abortive attempts to form a football team, the local cricket club called a meeting on May 7th 1920 at the West View Hotel and agreed to enter a team in the Lancs Combination.

The first season saw them share the cricket ground and over 3,000 saw the first game against Fleetwood. At the end of the season a new ground had to be found as the two games were becoming incompatible, and land was found. The present site was developed and initially called Roseby Park. The early seasons had been difficult but 1925 saw the Reds claim the league title for the first time. The following year the club were runners up and won the prestigious Lancashire Junior Cup with over 36,000 watching the twice replayed final against Chorley.

Mr J.B. Christie, the club's President, bought and bequeathed the ground to the club in 1927, at which point the committee renamed it Christie Park in gratitude. It was then that the club became a Limited Company with a share issue of £1,000. Despite this, the club struggled to stay afloat until after the War, when after another period of struggle, Ken Horton was appointed manager in 1956. It was the beginning of the club's golden era. They reached the first round of the FA Cup in 1957 and over the next 20 years got to the same stage no less than 11 times. They won four championships, three League Cups and a Lancs Senior Cup, at that point the only non-League club to do so. With a number of minor honours as well, the Golden Era seemed to end with a visit to Wembley for the FA Trophy final of 1974.

The next ten years were as barren as any that had gone before, with relegation and extinction both real possibilities. Again the tide turned in 1986 when the club finished third in the Northern Premier League.

Although never winning it, the runners up spot in 1995 was enough to send the club to the Conference. Christie Park had undergone a massive facelift to enable the club to take their place and a final place of ninth was nicely topped off with the ATS (Lancs Junior) Trophy.

MORECAMBE 1995/96 SEASON

Date	Comp	Opponent	Att	Score	Scorers
19/08/95	L	TELFORD UNITED	1532	2-0	Burns 82(p), Cain 90
22/08/95	L	RUNCORN	1425	3-1	Burns 13(p) 58(p), McCluskie 66
26/08/95	L	Kidderminster Harriers	1702	2-4	Cain 2, Coleman 44
28/08/95	L	Northwich Victoria	941	1-2	Coleman 64
02/09/95	L	SLOUGH TOWN	1120	1-2	Cain 81
05/09/95	L	MACCLESFIELD TOWN	1414	2-4	Grimshaw 35, Ceraole 82
09/09/95	C1	SHEFFIELD	469	7-0	Ceraolo(3), Coleman(2), Burns, Own-Goal
12/09/95	L	Altrincham	755	0-3	
16/09/95	L	Dagenham & Redbridge	834	2-2	Grimshaw 10, Burns 64(p)
19/09/95	C2	STALYBRIDGE CELTIC	604	4-1	Knowles, Coleman, Ceraolo, Norman
23/09/95	C3	Worksop Town	529	3-2	Ceraolo, Coleman, McCluskie
26/09/95	L	Halifax Town	910	1-1	Norman 32
30/09/95	L	WELLING UNITED	845	1-0	Coleman 4
07/10/95	C4	GAINSBOROUGH TRINITY	805	6-2	Coleman(4), Norman, Grimshaw
10/10/95	L	Macclesfield Town	1034	0-2	
14/10/95	L	KETTERING TOWN	1098	5-3	Coleman 54 69 90, Cain 59, Norman 63
21/10/95	C5	Witton Albion	931	2-3	Burns, Knowles
28/10/95	L	BROMSGROVE ROVERS	955	4-1	Cain 14, McCluskie 46, Norman 51, Ceraolo 81
04/11/95	L	Woking	2679	0-3	
07/11/95	C6	Stalybridge Celtic	467	2-5	Cain, Ceraolo
11/11/95	L	BATH CITY	1007	1-0	Burns 22
18/11/95	L	DOVER ATHLETIC	1047	3-1	Tomlinson 45, Coleman 67, McCluskie 84
25/11/95	L	Hednesford Town	1271	2-1	Knowles 45, Burns 53(p)
02/12/95	L	SOUTHPORT	1745	4-3	Monk 3 8, McCluskie 15, Coleman 73
05/12/95	C7	ALTRINCHAM	546	6-4	McCluskie(3), Comstive, Coleman, Cain
09/12/95	L	Telford United	728	2-2	Comstive 7, Coleman 78
16/12/95	L	STALYBRIDGE CELTIC	1143	2-0	Grimshaw 45, Ceraolo 90
01/01/96	L	GATESHEAD	1400	2-3	McCluskie 47 74
06/01/96	L	Farnborough Town	729	1-3	McCluskie 44
13/01/96	L	WOKING	1312	4-5	Monk 39, Knowles 41, Dullaghan 80, Coleman 89
16/01/96	C8	LEIGH R.M.I.	266	2-0	Monk, Ceraolo
20/01/96	C9	EMLEY	656	2-2	Coleman, Cain
23/01/96	C10	Emley	412	1-3	McCluskie
31/01/96	L	Gateshead	478	0-3	
10/02/96	L	DAGENHAM & REDBRIDGE	787	2-2	Monk 2 67
13/02/96	C11	RADCLIFFE BOROUGH	318	3-0	Norman, Monk, Byrne
17/02/96	L	ALTRINCHAM	983	7-0	Ceraolo 39 44, Norman 54 77 84, Burns 56(p), Monk 62
20/02/96	L	NORTHWICH VICTORIA	830	2-2	Armstrong 14, Cain 47
24/02/96	L	Stalybridge Celtic	585	2-0	Cain 7, Coleman 47
27/02/96	C12	SOUTHPORT	910	2-1	Burns, Coleman
02/03/96	L	HEDNESFORD TOWN	961	0-1	
05/03/96	C13	MACCLESFIELD TOWN	625	1-4	McCluskie 10
09/03/96	L	Bath City	511	2-3	Norman 72, Cain 86
12/03/96	L	HALIFAX TOWN	648	0-1	
16/03/96	L	Welling United	508	0-1	
23/03/96	L	FARNBOROUGH TOWN	726	2-3	West 20, Ceraolo 78
30/03/96	L	Dover Athletic	1090	3-2	Ceraolo 50 82, Cain 66
06/04/96	L	STEVENAGE BOROUGH	1227	1-0	Ceraolo 13
08/04/96	L	Runcorn	681	3-1	Monk 7 86, McCluskie 77
13/04/96	L	Kettering Town	1124	3-2	Jackson 10, McCluskie 38, Norman 89
16/04/96	L	Southport	729	1-1	Jackson 72
20/04/96	L	Slough Town	882	1-1	McCluskie 31
24/04/96	C14	Bamber Bridge	1708	1-0	Jackson (at Preston North End)
27/04/96	L	Stevenage Borough	2556	1-1	Ceraolo 32
30/04/96	L	Bromsgrove Rovers	626	0-1	
04/05/96	L	KIDDERMINSTER HARRIERS	1213	3-1	Monk 1, Ceraolo 47, McCluskie 87

C1=FA Cup Q1, C2=SC1(1), C3=FA Cup Q2, C4=FA Cup Q3, C5=FA Cup Q4, C6=SC1(2), C7=SC2, C8=Lancs ATS2, C9=FA Trophy 1, C10=FA Trophy 1 rep, C11=Lancs ATSQF, C12=Lancs ATSSF, C13=SCQF, C14=Lancs ATSF

NORTHWICH VICTORIA
THE DRILL FIELD, DRILL FIELD ROAD, NORTHWICH, CHESHIRE
TEL: 01606 41450 FAX: 01606 330577

Secretary: Mr Derek Nuttall, c/o Northwich Vics FC

Colours: Green and White

Nickname: The Vics

Capacity: 14,000, currently restricted to 3,500.

Seating: 660

Covered standing: 2,000

Clubhouse on ground: Yes

Record attendance: 11,290 v Witton Albion Cheshire League Good Friday 1949

Record appearances: 970 Ken Jones 1969-85

Record goalscorer in total: Peter Burns 160 1955-65

Record fee received: £50,000 from Chester for Neil Morton 1990

Record fee paid: £10,000 to Hyde United for Mal O'Connor 1988

and also £10,000 for Delwyn Humphries from Kidderminster Harriers 1995

Club shop Contact: Andy Dakin on 01606 45509

Programme Editor: William Hughes 01606 853925

DIRECTIONS

M6 motorway to Knutsford Service Station (Junction 19) take Chester Road (A556) to Davenham roundabout, and head for town centre (6 miles from M6). Ground 50 yards short of first main traffic lights. Nearest Railway Station: Hartford Northwich (2 miles from ground).

HONOURS

FA Trophy Winners 1984

Runners Up 1996

Manchester League 1902-03

Cheshire League 1956-57

North-West Floodlit League 1966-67 and 75-76,

Bob Lord Trophy 1980 and 1993

Northern Premier League Cup 1973

Cheshire Senior Cup 1881, 1882,1883,1884,1885,1886, 1929, 1937, 1950,1955,1972,1977, 1979,1984,1985.

Staffordshire Senior Cup 1979, 1980, 1990.

Northwich Senior Cup 1949, 1959, 1960, 1964, 1965, 1966, 1968, 1969, 1970, 1972, 1975.

Mid-Cheshire Senior Cup 1985, 1986, 1988, 1990.

Manager for 1996-97: Mark Hancock

Assistant Manager: John Williams

Chairman: R J Stitch

Vice Chairman: D Stone

G.M. Vauxhall Conference
NORTHWICH VICTORIA v
WELLING UNITED
Saturday, 4th May, 1996
Kick-off 3-00 p.m.

Club Sponsor HARVEY'S TYRE & EXHAUST

The club's history is one of the most fascinating of all, not harmed by the fact that their home, the Drill Field, is believed to be the oldest continually used football ground in the world. Certainly the club are known to have been formed in 1874, playing friendlies at a ground called Stumpers Field before joining the Combination and then entering the Football League for two years, in 1892. After their brief sojourn in the 2nd Division it was back to the Combination before the Cheshire League and then the Manchester League through the First War. From then on it was the strong Cheshire County League until becoming founder members of the Northern Premier League in 1968, and again founder members of the Alliance Premier League, now the Conference, in 1979. The club have consistently maintained a good standard of football, the evidence of which is shown in the impressive list of honours, including 15 Senior Cup wins, Cheshire County League and Manchester League titles, Welsh Cup runners up spots and a little matter of three appearances at Wembley for FA Trophy finals, winning one in 1983 against Bangor City in a replay. Last season's run to Wembley ended in sadness as Vics went down to local rivals Macclesfield Town, but having suffered the real prospect of losing the Drill Field in recent times, a determined fund-raising effort successfully secured its future as Vics aim to progress and perhaps rejoin the Football League that they left over 100 years ago.

NORTHWICH VICTORIA 1995/96 SEASON

Date	Comp	Opponent	Att	Score	Scorers
19/08/95	L	DOVER ATHLETIC	824	1-2	Vicary 50
22/08/95	L	Southport	1542	2-2	Clayton 54, McAuley 86
26/08/95	L	Welling United	538	1-1	Butler 90
28/08/95	L	MORECAMBE	941	2-1	Clayton 4, McAuley 69
02/09/95	L	Farnborough Town	808	1-0	Duffy 45
05/09/95	L	STALYBRIDGE CELTIC	816	1-0	Walters 73
09/09/95	C1	BURSCOUGH	655	5-0	Williams(2), Walters, Butler, Clayton, Vicary
12/09/95	L	Halifax Town	829	0-2	
16/09/95	L	HEDNESFORD TOWN	1100	0-2	
19/09/95	C2	Telford United	512	2-1	Walters, Cooke
23/09/95	C3	Lincoln United	354	4-1	Butler, Cooke, Vicary, Williams
26/09/95	C4	RUNCORN	502	3-1	Cooke, Williams, Walters
30/09/95	L	Dagenham & Redbridge	646	3-0	Butler 2(p), Williams 17, Vicary 19
03/10/95	C5	TELFORD UNITED	514	0-3	
07/10/95	C6	EASTWOOD TOWN	742	0-0	
10/10/95	C7	Eastwood Town	640	2-1	Bush(og), Vicary
14/10/95	L	KIDDERMINSTER HARRIERS	1106	5-2	Clayton 26, Williams 37 47 77 86
21/10/95	C8	Macclesfield Town	1707	1-0	Duffy
28/10/95	L	Stevenage Borough	1645	1-5	Simpson 32
31/10/95	L	SOUTHPORT	724	1-2	Williams 86
04/11/95	L	RUNCORN	1007	4-3	Cooke 6, Walter 39 78, Williams 70
11/11/95	C9	SCUNTHORPE UNITED	2685	1-3	Cooke
18/11/95	L	Bath City	417	3-0	Butler 28(p), Burgess 55, Williams 78
21/11/95	C10	Witton Albion	1006	0-2	
25/11/95	L	Slough Town	703	1-1	Vicary 21
02/12/95	L	FARNBOROUGH TOWN	687	1-3	Clayton 81
09/12/95	L	Gateshead	612	1-1	Vicary 75
16/12/95	L	STEVENAGE BOROUGH	673	1-3	Oghani 73(p)
19/12/95	L	TELFORD UNITED	503	2-0	Butler 16(p) 78(p)
26/12/95	L	ALTRINCHAM	1278	2-1	Butler 42 64
01/01/96	L	Altrincham	1076	4-3	Ward 25 45, Butler 48(p) Cooke 69
06/01/96	L	BATH CITY	708	2-2	Cooke 11, Butler 28(p)
09/01/96	L	Kettering Town	912	2-2	Vicary 1, Williams 24
13/01/96	L	Hednesford Town	1017	1-2	Cooke 77
20/01/96	C11	Hednesford Town	935	1-1	Vicary
23/01/96	C12	HEDNESFORD TOWN	636	2-0	
30/01/96	L	BROMSGROVE ROVERS	609	2-2	Williams 51, Butler 53
10/02/96	C13	Wembley	268	2-0	Butler, Cooke
17/02/96	L	HALIFAX TOWN	879	1-1	Jones 65
20/02/96	L	Morecambe	830	2-2	Vicary 23, Cooke 56
24/02/96	L	DAGENHAM & REDBRIDGE	727	1-0	Butler 31
27/02/96	C14	Witton Albion	667	2-3	Cooke, Walters
02/03/96	C15	Merthyr Tydfil	528	1-1	Abel
05/03/96	C16	MERTHYR TYDFIL	800	2-2	Vicary, Butler
09/03/96	L	Telford United	712	0-1	
11/03/96	C17	MERTHYR TYDFIL	765	3-0	Butler(2), Humphreys
16/03/96	L	SLOUGH TOWN	634	0-3	
23/03/96	C18	Bromsgrove Rovers	1807	1-0	Cooke
26/03/96	L	Macclesfield Town	1117	0-0	
30/03/96	L	Kidderminster Harriers	1604	1-2	Williams 8
02/04/96	L	GATESHEAD	602	1-2	Butler 66
06/04/96	L	Dover Athletic	976	1-0	Williams 90
13/04/96	C19	Hyde United	2253	2-1	Cooke 45, Humphreys 71
16/04/96	L	MACCLESFIELD TOWN	936	1-2	Vicary 49
20/04/96	C20	HYDE UNITED	2809	1-0	Abel
23/04/96	L	Runcorn	653	4-3	Butler 56, Steele 66, Williams 73 90
25/04/96	L	Stalybridge Celtic	514	5-1	Williams 22, Steele 64 80 90, Butler 71
27/04/96	L	WOKING	842	3-0	Steele 17, Butler 56, Humphreys 71
28/04/96	L	Bromsgrove Rovers		1-1	Tait
30/04/96	L	Woking	1771	0-0	
02/05/96	L	KETTERING TOWN	632	6-2	Vicary 5 47, Williams 43 54, Walters 45 80
04/05/96	L	WELLING UNITED	875	1-2	Cooke 21
19/05/96	C21	MACCLESFIELD TOWN	8672	1-3	Williams 53.

C1=FA Cup Q1, C2=SC1(1), C3=FA Cup Q2, C4=Ches. SC1, C5=SC1(2), C6=FA Cup Q3, C7=FA Cup Q3 rep, C8=FA Cup Q4, C9=FA Cup 1,C10=Ches. SCQF, C11=FA Trophy 1,C12=FA Trophy 1 rep,C13=FA Trophy 2, C14=Mid-Ches .SF, C15=FA Trophy 3, C16=FA Trophy 3 rep, C17=FA Trophy 3 rep(2), C18=FA Trophy QF, C19=FA Trophy SF(1), C20=FA Trophy SF(2), C21=FA Trophy F

RUSHDEN AND DIAMONDS
NENE PARK, STATION RD, IRTHLINGBOROUGH, NORTHANTS
TEL: 01933 652000 FAX: 01933 650418

Secretary: David Joyce, 54 Ferrestone Rd, Wellingborough, Northants NN9 5QF

Colours: Red and White

Nickname: Diamonds

Capacity: 4,200 until December 1996 then 6,500

Seating: 2,300

Covered standing: Whole ground under cover by December 1st

Clubhouse on ground: Yes

Record attendance: 4,664

Biggest win: 8-0

Biggest defeat: 1-4

Record appearances: Andy Peaks and Dale Watkins 129 each

Record goalscorer in one season: Darren Collins 39

Record goalscorer in total: Dale Watkins 88

Record fee paid: £85,000 for Carl Alford

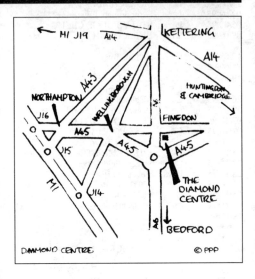

HONOURS

RUSHDEN TOWN

United Counties League 1903, 1927, 1930, 1932, 1935, 1936, 1937, 1938, 1964, 1973

League Cup 1934, 1935, 1937, 1938, 1947

Northants Senior Cup 1926, 1927, 1928, 1930, 1931, 1935, 1937, 1958, 1978

IRTHLINGBOROUGH DIAMONDS

United Counties League 1971, 1977, 1979, 1983

League Cup 1979 and 1981

Northants Senior Cup 1981

RUSHDEN AND DIAMONDS

Southern League Midland Division 1994

Southern League Premier 1996

Northants Senior Cup 1994

Northants Premier Cup 1994

Manager 1996-97 Roger Ashby

Assistant Manager: Billy Jeffrey

Chairman: W M Griggs CBE

Vice Chairman: A C Jones

Rushden and Diamonds Football Club was formed at the end of the 1991-92 season following a merger of Rushden Town and Irthlingborough Diamonds. Rushden were formed in 1889 and competed in the Midland and Northants Leagues before joining the United Counties League. They had a brief spell in the Central Alliance before returning to the UCL in the late 50's. In 1983 came election to the Southern League Midland Division with further progress in 1991 following promotion. After a year the club were told that their ground no longer qualified as up to standard and they were relegated again.

Irthlingborough Diamonds were founded in 1946 as a youth team and played for ten years in Under 18 football until moving into Rushden and District and Kettering Amateur football. They achieved senior status in 1964 and moved to the UCL which they won for the first time in 1971. In addition they reached two FA Vase semi-finals, but their good fortune faded at the same time as Rushden's, and when Mr Max Griggs was approached concerning possible sponsorship, a merger was agreed, and casting decades of rivalry aside, the new club was formed, playing at Diamond's Nene Park ground.

The history from then until now is one of the most astonishing anywhere in football, as the modest ground has been transformed into one which is possibly only a year away from staging League football. It will hold 6,500 by Christmas and is geared to go higher should the club progress. The Midland Division title was followed by the Southern League championship last year and they are expected to go close this season to fulfilling the dream of entering the Football League to compete with Northampton Town on level terms.

RUSHDEN AND DIAMONDS 1995/96 SEASON

Date	Comp		Opponent	Att	Score	Scorers
19/08/95	BHL	P	SALISBURY CITY	1532	3-0	Wilkin, Kirkup, Collins
21/08/95	BHL	P	Chelmsford City	1003	2-1	Spooner, Watkins
26/08/95	BHL	P	CRAWLEY TOWN	1661	3-1	Butterworth, Watkins(2)
28/08/95	BHL	P	Burton Albion	901	2-4	Watkins, Collins
02/09/95	BHL	P	Hastings Town	552	1-0	Watkins
05/09/95	BHL	P	V.S. RUGBY	1624	6-1	Ashby, Wilkin, Watkins(3), Bailey
09/09/95	C1		GRANTHAM TOWN	1681	4-1	Collins(3), Wilkin
16/09/95	BHL	P	Worcester City	960	0-0	
19/09/95	BHL	P	CHELMSFORD CITY	1747	2-1	Bird(og), Collins
23/09/95	C2		EASTWOOD HANLEY	1652	1-0	Collins
30/09/95	BHL	P	Cheltenham Town	1122	2-0	Kirkup, Collins
07/10/95	C3		Sandwell Borough	250	6-1	Wilkin(3), Collins(3)
14/10/95	BHL	P	Gresley Rovers	808	3-0	Hannigan, Collins, Butterworth
21/10/95	C4		Purfleet	650	1-1	Hannigan
24/10/95	C5		PURFLEET	2850	3-1	Watkin, Collins, Wilkins
28/10/95	BHL	P	Merthyr Tydfil	464	3-0	Collins, Kirkup, Watkin
31/10/95	DMC	1(1)	KING'S LYNN	1098	1-0	
04/11/95	BHL	P	STAFFORD RANGERS	2078	5-1	Wooding, Watkins, Wilkin(2), Hackett
07/11/95	C6		LONG BUCKBY	574	4-0	Nuttell(2), Kirkup, Watkins
11/11/95	FA Cup	1	CARDIFF CITY	4212	1-3	Hannigan
15/11/95	BHL	P	V.S. Rugby	741	3-1	Wilkin(3)
18/11/95	BHL	P	Gravesend & Northfleet	658	3-1	Wilkin, Collins, Smith
21/11/95	BHL	P	BURTON ALBION	1651	2-0	Wilkin, Collins
25/11/95	BHL	P	ATHERSTONE UNITED	2231	7-3	Hackett, Hannigan, Collins(4), Ashby
28/11/95	BHL	P	BALDOCK TOWN	1922	3-0	Collins, Kirkup, Wilkin
02/12/95	BHL	P	Crawley Town	1118	2-2	Wooding, Collins
05/12/95	DMC	1(2)	King's Lynn	432	0-2	
09/12/95	BHL	P	Dorchester Town	684	1-1	Wilkin
12/12/95	BHL	P	GLOUCESTER CITY	1666	3-2	Kirkup, Collins(2)
16/12/95	BHL	P	HASTINGS TOWN	1924	1-1	Watkins
23/12/95	BHL	P	ILKESTON TOWN	2312	3-0	Wilkin, Hackett, Watkins
13/01/96	BHL	P	Atherstone United	605	3-1	Wilkin, Collins(2)
20/01/96	C7		PURFLEET	1906	0-1	
30/01/96	C8		RAUNDS TOWN	904	1-0	Collins
03/02/96	BHL	P	WORCESTER CITY	2197	1-0	Collins
10/02/96	BHL	P	GRAVESEND & NORTHFLEET	1841	2-3	Watkins, Collins
13/02/96	BHL	P	Baldock Town	854	3-0	Stott, Collins(2)
17/02/96	BHL	P	CHELTENHAM TOWN	2472	4-1	Watkins, Kirkup(2), Wilkin
24/02/96	BHL	P	Newport A.F.C.	1170	1-1	Ashby
05/03/96	BHL	P	SUDBURY TOWN	1409	3-1	Collins, Hackett, Kirkup
16/03/96	BHL	P	Cambridge City	750	2-0	Collins, Taylor
19/03/96	BHL	P	Halesowen Town	1725	0-0	
23/03/96	BHL	P	Ilkeston Town	1009	1-1	Hackett
26/03/96	C9		Rothwell Town	511	0-1	
30/03/96	BHL	P	HALESOWEN TOWN	3481	1-2	Alford
04/04/96	BHL	P	DORCHESTER TOWN	1823	0-1	
06/04/96	BHL	P	CAMBRIDGE CITY	2135	2-1	Collins, Alford
08/04/96	BHL	P	Sudbury Town	918	1-4	Alford
13/04/96	BHL	P	NEWPORT A.F.C.	2914	3-0	Collins, Alford, Ashby
16/04/96	BHL	P	GRESLEY ROVERS	2250	2-1	Collins, Alford
20/04/96	BHL	P	Gloucester City	1226	1-2	Collins
24/04/96	BHL	P	Salisbury City	569	2-0	Collins, Kirkup
27/04/96	BHL	P	Stafford Rangers	1160	4-0	Alford, Kirkup(2), Hackett
04/05/96	BHL	P	MERTHYR TYDFIL	4664	3-2	Alford, Butterworth, Collins

C1=FA CupQ1, C2=FA CupQ2 C3=FA CupQ3, C4=FA CupQ4, C5=FA CupQ4 rep, C6=N'hants SCQF,C7=FA Trophy1, C8=N'hants SCSF,C9=N'hants SCF

SLOUGH TOWN
WEXHAM PARK STADIUM, WEXHAM RD, SLOUGH, BERKSHIRE SL2 5QL
TEL: 01753 523358 FAX: 01753 516956

Secretary: David Stanley, c/o Slough Town FC

Programme Editor: David Stanley

Contributors: Mal Keenan and John Tebbitt

Commercial Manager: Bob Breen

Club Shop: Yes, possibly to be run by Supporters Association this season

Colours: Amber and Blue   Nickname: The Rebels

Capacity: 5,000   Seating: 450

Covered standing: 1,890

Clubhouse on ground: Yes, with large screen viewing after matches, golf room and bar, garden, Mayfair Banqueting Suite and Conference Centre.

Record attendance: 8,000 Slough v Liverpool National Schools U-15 final 1976

Biggest win: 17-0 v Railway Clearing House 1921-22

Biggest defeat: 1-11 v Chesham Town 1922

Record appearances: Terry Reardon 487 1964-81

Record goalscorer in one season: Terry Norris 85 in 1925-26

Record fee paid: £18,000 for Colin Fielder from Farnborough Town 1991

Record fee received: £22,000 from Wycombe Wanderers for Steve Thompson

DIRECTIONS

From North: M25 junction 16 East London M40 junction 1 - South A412 through Iver Heath to George Green. 2nd set lights turn right by George PH, George Green. Church Lane 1 mile to end, then small roundabout, turn left, ground 1/4 mile on right. **From East:** M25 J15/M4 J5 to A4 West to Co-op Superstore on right, A412 North (Uxbridge), dual carriageway to 4th set lights. Church Lane, then as from North. **From South:** If M25 then as from East. **From Windsor** A355 under M4 J6 to A4, turn right, pass Brunel Bus station on left, Tesco Superstore, also on left, then first left, Wexham Road, signposted Wexham Park Hospital, ground just over 1 mile on left. **From West:** If M4 junction 6 then as from South.

HONOURS

FA AMATEUR CUP Runners up 1973

Corinthian League 1951

Athenian League 1968, 1972, 1973

Division One 1965, League Cup 1965, 1972, 1973

Isthmian League 1981, 1990

League Cup 1981 and 1990

Berks and Bucks Senior Cup 1903, 1920, 1924, 1936, 1955, 1971, 1972, 1977, 1981

Manager 1996-97: Brian McDermott,   **Assistant Manager: David Brown,**

Chairman: Mr A Thorn,   **Vice Chairman: Mr B A Thorn**

Press Officer: David Stanley

Slough Town FC fanzine 'Banging with Manning' available from club shop

Football began as early as 1860 with the Swifts who lost the FA Cup semi-final to the Royal Engineers in 1874 and who amalgamated with Slough Albion and the Young Men's Friendly Society to form Slough FC. They joined the Southern Alliance in 1892, playing on what was to become the Dolphin Stadium. They quickly moved to the Berks and Bucks League and then the Great Western Suburban, but there was little progress and after the Great War the club lost out on a vote for membership of the Isthmian League and so moved to the Spartans, where they remained until the Second War. The club played through Wartime, although the Dolphin Stadium became unavailable due to a clash with greyhound racing and the problem of blackout restrictions. They briefly used the Slough Cricket Ground in Chalvey Road and then shared with Maidenhead United for two years, before another amalgamation took place when they moved in with Slough Centre FC and began playing on the Centre Stadium in 1943 as Slough United FC.

When peace returned the club were active in creating a new league of a higher standard, and thus the Corinthian League was born and the nickname 'The Rebels' came about. In 1946 they returned to the Dolphin and when Slough Centre re-formed elsewhere, United became Town. In 1951, after 60 years of football, they won their first title, taking the Corinthian League, but with promotion not available it was another dozen years before Slough won the Athenian League Division One after it was expanded with the Corinthians and took the Premier championship three times in five years.

In Cups, Slough had much more success early after the War, reaching the last eight of the Amateur Cup in 1953 and winning the County Cup, but later they got to the Semi-finals in 1971, quarter-finals a year later and the final itself at Wembley in 1973, losing to a last minute Walton and Hersham goal.

Later they reached a Trophy semi-final, but to date 1973 is their only Wembley visit.

In 1973 the club finally moved into the Isthmian League as founder members of Division One and were promoted in the first year, but they were difficult times, and with the Dolphin Stadium being closed and subsequently demolished, it needed much co-operation from the authorities for them to create Wexham Park to be ready for the next season.

They soon settled and established themselves in the top half of the league and were champions in 1981, but turned down the chance to join the Alliance Premier League. Later in the club's Centenary year, they were champions again and this time they moved up, but the first two seasons were difficult and financial problems saw them go into receivership. They were bought in 1992 by a consortium previously connected with Millwall FC and a revival saw them finish third in 1993. It was temporary, as relegation followed a year later, but they bounced back and in 1995 returned to the Conference once more.

SLOUGH TOWN 1995/96 SEASON

Date	Comp	Opponent	Att	Score	Scorers
19/08/95	L	SOUTHPORT	942	2-5	West 25, Blackman 41
22/08/95	L	Welling United	747	3-0	Baron 13, Bushay 38 40
26/08/95	L	Halifax Town	917	2-1	Baron 56 90
28/08/95	L	KIDDERMINSTER HARRIERS	1092	5-4	West 17, Blackman 27 49, Lay 60 68(p)
02/09/95	L	Morecambe	1120	2-1	Blackman 33, Pickett 55
05/09/95	L	BATH CITY	980	1-1	West 16
09/09/95	L	Runcorn	480	3-4	Fiore 35, West 49 75
12/09/95	L	DOVER ATHLETIC	846	3-2	Bushay 46, West 49 65
16/09/95	L	ALTRINCHAM	991	1-2	Blackman 37
18/09/95	C1	Dagenham & Redbridge	403	3-0	Pickett, Blackman, Bushay
23/09/95	L	BROMSGROVE ROVERS	931	2-3	West 15(p), Bushay 58
26/09/95	L	Dover Athletic	619	1-0	Walker 73(og)
30/09/95	L	HEDNESFORD TOWN	971	0-2	
03/10/95	C2	DAGENHAM & REDBRIDGE	456	3-0	West(2), Bushay
07/10/95	L	Kettering Town	1902	0-2	
14/10/95	L	MACCLESFIELD TOWN	1007	2-2	West 38(p) 80
21/10/95	C3	Yeading	473	2-0	Bushay(2)
28/10/95	L	Telford United	808	0-2	
31/10/95	L	FARNBOROUGH TOWN	891	1-1	West 83
04/11/95	L	Gateshead	642	1-2	West 30
11/11/95	C4	PLYMOUTH ARGYLE	3013	0-2	
18/11/95	L	WOKING	1659	2-3	Bushay 17, Baron 63
20/11/95	L	Dagenham & Redbridge	712	3-1	Catlin 24 45 55
25/11/95	L	NORTHWICH VICTORIA	703	1-1	West 15
02/12/95	L	Stalybridge Celtic	558	1-0	Hercules 52
09/12/95	L	HALIFAX TOWN	862	2-3	Hercules 45, Catlin 55
16/12/95	SC2	WOKING	774	3-0	West 6 86, Hercules 54
01/01/96	L	Stevenage Borough	2123	1-3	West 77
06/01/96	L	GATESHEAD	768	1-2	Hercules 41
13/01/96	L	Altrincham	648	1-0	West 65(p)
20/01/96	C5	Farnborough Town	856	1-1	West
23/01/96	C6	FARNBOROUGH TOWN	742	4-3	
30/01/96	C8	Reading	525	2-3	West(2)
03/02/96	L	TELFORD UNITED	682	1-2	Hercules 9
10/02/96	C7	KETTERING TOWN	1058	1-2	Pickett
13/02/96	C9	Kettering Town	646	0-2	
17/02/96	L	KETTERING TOWN	766	1-2	Pickett 18
24/02/96	L	Kidderminster Harriers	1715	3-4	West 26, Harvey 37, Bushay 40
02/03/96	L	Farnborough Town	1069	1-0	Hercules 30
09/03/96	L	DAGENHAM & REDBRIDGE	912	5-0	Bushay 1, West 33(p) 50, Bateman 62, Catlin 64
12/03/96	L	STEVENAGE BOROUGH	1126	2-6	Hercules 34, West 45
16/03/96	L	Northwich Victoria	634	3-0	Fiore 6, Clement 78 85
19/03/96	L	Woking	1911	0-3	
23/03/96	L	STALYBRIDGE CELTIC	748	2-1	West 46, Blackman 85
30/03/96	L	Bromsgrove Rovers	687	0-0	
03/04/96	L	Bath City	397	1-3	Bushay 3
08/04/96	L	Southport	677	0-2	
13/04/96	L	WELLING UNITED	785	0-0	
20/04/96	L	MORECAMBE	882	1-1	Hercules 46
27/04/96	L	Hednesford Town	1031	1-3	West 43
02/05/96	L	Macclesfield Town	591	1-1	Smart 60
04/05/96	L	RUNCORN	835	0-1	

C1=SC1(1), C2=SC1(2), C3=FA Cup Q4,C4=FA Cup 1, C5=FA Trophy 1, C6=FA Trophy 1 rep, C8=B&B SC1, C7=FA Trophy 2, C9=SCQF,

69

Secretary: Roy Morris, Manikata, 3 Stretton Dr, Southport, PR9 7DR

Tel: 01704 211428

Colours: Old Gold and Black

Nickname: The Sandgrounders

Capacity: 6,012

Covered seating: 1,880

Covered standing: 1,100

Clubhouse on ground: Yes

Record attendance: 20,000 v Newcastle Utd FA Cup 1932

Biggest win: 8-1 v Nelson in 1931

Biggest defeat: 0-11 v Oldham Athletic 1962

Record appearances: Arthur Peat 401 1962-72

Record goalscorer in total: Alan Spence

Record fee received: £25,000 for Steve Whitehall to Rochdale

DIRECTIONS
From M6 join M58 (Junction 26) to Ounskirk then Southport. Haig Avenue is on the right a mile before town centre, ground signposted from all entrances to town.

HONOURS

Football League Division Four 1973

Third Division North Section Cup 1938

Liverpool Senior Cup 1931, 1932, 1944, 1958 jt, 1964 jt, 1975, 1991, 1993

Lancs Senior Cup 1905

Lancs Junior (ATS) Cup 1920, 1993

Northern Premier League 1993

League Cup 1991

League Shield 1994

Southport FC was originally a rugby club which, after some heavy defeats changed codes in 1881. In 1888 following a merger with Southport Wanderers and a move to a new ground on Scarisbrick New Road, Southport Central were born and soon joined the Lancashire League. In 1894 they reached the First Round of the FA Cup losing to Everton in front of 5,000. In 1903 they joined the Lancashire Combination, winning the B Division a year later and after taking the Senior Cup in 1905 they moved to their present ground, in Ash Lane, later re-named Haig Avenue.

They became founder members of the Central League in 1911 and immediately after the Great War they were taken over as a company by the Vulcan Motor Company, playing a single season as Southport Vulcan. Following re-formation they became Southport FC and as such were founder members of the Football League Division Three North in 1921.

In 1931 Southport reached the Sixth Round of the FA Cup, and a year later in Round Four, Newcastle Utd drew 20,010 to Haig Avenue, winning after two replays. Financial problems all but brought the club down, but transfers saved the day and when War broke out they had been challenging for promotion only months earlier. After the War the club struggled, though 1955-56 saw them challenging again, but the re-organisation into four divisions saw Southport in the basement and it was not until 1967 that they were promoted under Billy Bingham. Relegation sadly came in 1970 but under Jimmy Meadows the club won Division Four with 62 points. Then the club seemed to fall apart, financial problems led to managerial changes and relegation and after three successive re-election applications, the members pulled the plug and Southport were voted out by one vote in 1978.

Despite hardships they battled on in the Northern Premier League, but with little reward until 1989 when they won the League Cup and Liverpool Senior Cup. As the club began to climb off the floor, their improvement dramatically increased and they stormed to the title in 1993 with only four defeats and over 100 goals. Off the field the crumbling Haig Avenue was completely rebuilt on three sides after the covered terracing was condemned and Southport today enjoy life in the Conference with a ground which is good enough to make the re-entry into the Football League.

SOUTHPORT 1995/96 SEASON

Date	Comp	Opponent	Att	Score	Scorers
19/08/95	L	Slough Town	942	5-2	Gamble 16(p) 20(p), Haw 19 71 78
22/08/95	L	NORTHWICH VICTORIA	1542	2-2	Whittaker 49, Blackstone 63
26/08/95	L	STEVENAGE BOROUGH	1179	0-1	
28/08/95	L	Runcorn	708	1-1	Gamble 28
02/09/95	L	Kettering Town	1944	1-1	Whittaker 7
05/09/95	L	ALTRINCHAM	1127	1-2	Ward 21
09/09/95	L	Bath City	584	0-4	
12/09/95	L	Stalybridge Celtic	496	4-1	Davenport 4, Griffiths 31 39, Gamble 70
16/09/95	L	WELLING UNITED	915	2-0	Davenport 7, Griffiths 79
19/09/95	L	RUNCORN	1004	1-1	Griffiths 32
23/09/95	L	Macclesfield Town	1282	1-3	Gamble 15
30/09/95	L	KIDDERMINSTER HARRIERS	1164	0-2	
14/10/95	L	TELFORD UNITED	812	3-2	Clark 8, Davenport 41, Haw 90
21/10/95	C1	Telford United	898	0-3	
28/10/95	L	Hednesford Town	1355	1-2	Farley 43
31/10/95	L	Northwich Victoria	724	2-1	Davenport 21 45
04/11/95	L	FARNBOROUGH TOWN	819	7-1	Baker(og), Davenport, Horner, Griffiths, Whittaker(2), Gambl
18/11/95	L	Stevenage Borough	1785	3-1	Whittaker 9, Dove 63, Berry 90(og)
25/11/95	L	GATESHEAD	1008	1-0	Haw 35
28/11/95	C2	Runcorn		5-1	
02/12/95	L	Morecambe	1745	3-4	Fuller 5, Davenport 62, Gamble 69(p)
09/12/95	L	Kidderminster Harriers	1664	3-2	Davenport 32, Haw 45, Farley 48
16/12/95	L	DAGENHAM & REDBRIDGE	904	2-1	Farley 79, Whittaker 84
01/01/96	L	HALIFAX TOWN	1318	0-0	
06/01/96	L	KETTERING TOWN	916	6-1	Whittaker 40 50 68, Davenport 48, Blackstone 55 74
13/01/96	L	Dagenham & Redbridge	964	2-1	Whittaker 31, Davenport 85
16/01/96	C3	MARINE	543	1-0	Whittaker
20/01/96	C4	Halifax Town	966	1-2	Whittaker
03/02/96	L	Farnborough Town	738	0-1	
10/02/96	L	HEDNESFORD TOWN	811	2-2	Whittaker 18, Griffiths 79
14/02/96	C5	BARROW	321	3-1	Whittaker, Gamble, Harold(og)
17/02/96	L	WOKING	1074	2-2	McDonald 21, Whittaker 26
24/02/96	L	Welling United	600	1-0	Davenport 80
27/02/96	C6	Morecambe	910	1-2	
02/03/96	L	Altrincham	851	1-1	Haw 19, Whittaker 90
09/03/96	L	BROMSGROVE ROVERS	894	1-2	Haw 66
16/03/96	L	Dover Athletic	1142	1-0	Whittaker 37
19/03/96	C7	MACCLESFIELD TOWN	561	4-4	Davenport 33 83, Cunningham 41, Whittaker 84
23/03/96	L	Telford United	758	1-2	McDonald 88(p)
26/03/96	L	Halifax Town	694	2-2	Davenport 29, Whittaker 76
30/03/96	L	STALYBRIDGE CELTIC	704	5-3	McDonald 14(p), Whittaker 27, Mitchell 42, Haw 44 66
03/04/96	C8	Macclesfield Town	510	1-2	Whittaker 10
06/04/96	L	Bromsgrove Rovers	729	1-4	Davenport 4
08/04/96	L	SLOUGH TOWN	677	2-0	Mitchell 6 90
13/04/96	L	BATH CITY	643	2-1	Goulding 22, Dove 58
16/04/96	L	MORECAMBE	729	1-1	Fuller 62
22/04/96	L	MACCLESFIELD TOWN	736	2-1	Lodge 40, Mitchell 90
24/04/96	L	Gateshead	469	2-2	Whittaker 46, Clark 60
27/04/96	L	DOVER ATHLETIC	849	0-0	
04/05/96	L	Woking	2543	0-4	

C1=FA Cup Q4, C2=SC2, C3=Lancs ATS2, C4=FA Trophy 1, C5=Lancs ATSQF, C6=Lancs ATSSF, C7=SCSF(1), C8=SCSF (2)

Secretary: Martyn Torr c/o Stalybridge Celtic FC

Colours: All Blue

Nickname: Celtic

Capacity: 6,000

Seating: 600

Covered standing: 1,300

Clubhouse on ground: Yes

DIRECTIONS

Directions: M6 to A556 to M63 to M67; end of Motorway through roundabout to traffic lights, left; left at end into Molttram Road, up hill, down hill into Stalybridge, ground on left next to Hare & Hounds pub.

Record attendance: 9,753 v West Bromwich Albion FA Cup replay 1922-23

Biggest win: 16-2 v Manchester North End May 1st 1925 and v Nantwich Oct 22nd 1932

Record appearances: Kevin Booth 354

Record goalscorer in one season: Chris Camden 45 in 1991-92

HONOURS

Northern Premier League and Challenge Shield 1992

North-West Counties League and Champions Trophy 1984 and 1987

Lancs Floodlight Cup 1989

Cheshire County League 1980

Challenge Shield 1978

League Cup 1922

Lancs Combination Div 2 1912

Cheshire Senior Cup 1953

Manchester Intermediate Cup 1958 and 1969

Manchester Junior Cup 1963

Edward Case Cup 1978

Manager for 1996/97: Brian Kettle

Stalybridge Celtic have a long and proud history having been founded in 1909 by local businessman Herbert Rhodes, beginning life as amateurs. They turned professional in 1911 when they joined the Lancashire Combination. They found immediate success winning the Second Division in their only season before moving to the Central League where they played until the Great War. In 1921 they became founder members of the Football League Division Three and spent two seasons there, finishing seventh and eleventh. In 1922 they played West Bromwich Albion in the 1st Round of the FA Cup and after a draw, some 9,753 packed into Bower Fold for the replay, a record which will not be beaten. After leaving the Football League Celtic joined the Cheshire County League, but had to wait until 1980 before taking the title.

The league was absorbed into the new North-West Counties League and in 1984 Celtic were champions, and again in 1987, which led to them joining the Northern Premier League, where they were runners up and promoted in the first term.

A runners up spot in the Premier League was followed by the title in 1992, which saw the club and the wonderful old Bower Fold ground, elevated to within one division of a return to the Football League after 70 years.

STALYBRIDGE CELTIC 1995/96 SEASON

Date	Comp	Opponent	Att	Score	Scorers
19/08/95	L	DAGENHAM & REDBRIDGE	547	2-1	Shaw 44, Burke 60
23/08/95	L	Gateshead	524	0-1	
26/08/95	L	Woking	1613	1-2	Jones 73
28/08/95	L	HALIFAX TOWN	905	1-0	Wheeler 90
02/09/95	L	TELFORD UNITED	619	2-2	Jones 54, Burke 79
05/09/95	L	Northwich Victoria	816	0-1	
09/09/95	L	Kidderminster Harriers	1962	0-3	
12/09/95	L	SOUTHPORT	496	1-4	Ryan 23
16/09/95	L	Farnborough Town	707	1-1	Higginbotham 90
19/09/95	C1	Morecambe	604	1-4	
23/09/95	L	KETTERING TOWN	627	3-2	Higginbotham 5, Wheeler 68, Burke 85
30/09/95	L	Bath City	580	4-0	Wheeler 6, Higginbotham 45 47, Ryan 75
03/10/95	C2	Congleton Town	146	6-2	Allis, Burke(2), Wheeler, Higginbotham, Jones
10/10/95	L	GATESHEAD	480	0-2	
14/10/95	L	WELLING UNITED	605	2-1	Frain 52, Wheeler 81
21/10/95	C3	COLWYN BAY	617	2-2	Burke, Wheeler
24/10/95	C4	Colwyn Bay	617	0-3	
28/10/95	L	WOKING	754	2-4	Arnold 22, Goodacre 36
31/10/95	L	MACCLESFIELD TOWN	884	1-2	Burke 46
04/11/95	L	Bromsgrove Rovers	1033	1-1	Arnold 71
07/11/95	C5	MORECAMBE	467	5-2	
11/11/95	L	Macclesfield Town	1457	0-1	
18/11/95	L	HEDNESFORD TOWN	687	0-1	
21/11/95	C6	HYDE UNITED	614	0-3	
25/11/95	L	Dover Athletic	1069	3-1	Ryan 12, Goodacre 80, O'Shaughnessy 90
27/11/95	L	Hednesford Town	895	1-0	Burke
02/12/95	L	SLOUGH TOWN	558	0-1	
09/12/95	L	ALTRINCHAM	654	1-0	Goodacre 13
16/12/95	L	Morecambe	1143	0-2	
06/01/96	L	KIDDERMINSTER HARRIERS	605	2-2	Arnold 40 72
13/01/96	L	Welling United	626	1-1	Frain
20/01/96	C7	GRESLEY ROVERS	638	1-1	Goodacre
23/01/96	C8	Gresley Rovers	603	0-1	
10/02/96	L	FARNBOROUGH TOWN	521	2-2	Ellison 25, Burke 27(p)
17/02/96	L	Dagenham & Redbridge	706	1-4	Ellis 24
24/02/96	L	MORECAMBE	585	0-2	
02/03/96	L	Telford United	783	1-0	Goodacre 17
05/03/96	L	Halifax Town	509	3-2	Goodacre 15 29, S Jones 31
09/03/96	L	STEVENAGE BOROUGH	843	2-5	Goodacre 44, Burke 48(p)
19/03/96	L	RUNCORN	478	2-0	Burke 46, Jones 53
23/03/96	L	Slough Town	748	1-2	Jones 78
30/03/96	L	Southport	704	3-5	Powell 62, Coathup 75, Goodacre 87
06/04/96	L	BATH CITY	506	1-0	Powell 25
08/04/96	L	BROMSGROVE ROVERS	463	2-1	Goodacre 47, Burke 77
13/04/96	L	Stevenage Borough	1767	2-2	Powell 48, Burke 82
16/04/96	L	Runcorn	352	1-0	Burke 87
20/04/96	L	DOVER ATHLETIC	533	2-0	Goodacre 28, Coathup 45
23/04/96	L	Altrincham	608	0-1	
25/04/96	L	NORTHWICH VICTORIA	514	1-5	Jones 26
04/05/96	L	Kettering Town	962	6-1	Arnold 12 82(p), Goodacre 18 20, Megson 34, Burke 54

C1=SC1 (1), C2=Ches. SC1, C3=FA Cup Q4, C4=FA Cup Q4 rep, C5=SC1 (2), C6=Ches. SCQF, C7=FA Trophy 1, C8=FA Trophy 1 rep

STEVENAGE BOROUGH
STEVENAGE STADIUM, BROADHALL WAY, STEVENAGE, HERTS SG2 8TH
TEL: 01438 743322 FAX: 743666

Secretary: Janice Hutchings, c/o Football Club

Nickname: The Stripes

Colours: Red and White

Capacity: 3,700

Seating: 488

Covered Standing: 2,000

Clubhouse On Ground: Yes

Record Attendance: 3,976 v Woking April 8th 1996

Biggest Win: 11-1 v British Timken Ath. UCL 1980-81

Biggest Defeat: 0-7 v Southwick Isthmian League 1987-88

Record appearances: Martin Gittings

Record Goalscorer In One Season: Barry Hayles

Record Goalscorer In Total: Barry Hayles

Record Goalscorer In Total: Undisclosed

DIRECTIONS
Stevenage South exit off A1 (M) - ground on right at second roundabout. One mile from Stevenage BR station. Buses SB4 and SB5.

HONOURS

Conference 1996

Isthmian League 1994

Division One 1992 and Divs 2 North 1986 and 1991

United Counties League Div 1 and Div 1 Cup 1981

Eastern Professional Floodlit Cup 1982, 1986, 1987, 1989, 1991, 1992

Southern Counties Combination Cup 1992

Manager For 1996-97: Paul Fairclough

Assistant Manager: Paul Peterson

Chairman: Victor Green

Press Officer: Simon Mortimer, 40 Prestatyn Close, Stevenage, Herts 0585 188600 Mobile

Borough were formed as recently as 1976 and have had a meteoric rise through the ranks of Non-League football. There have been three different clubs in the town that have used Broadhall Way, all of whom have played a high standard, with Borough being the natural successor within touching distance of the Football League. Stevenage Town played on a substantial ground on London Road until moving to Broadhall Way, along with their old stand, around 1961. The new site was farmland until it began to be developed, but the initial enthusiasm waned and the club folded in 1968 to be replaced by Stevenage Athletic, who played in the Metropolitan League before also joining the Southern League. This club lasted until 1976 until sadly going the way of Town, which left Broadhall Way to be sold and it lay dormant and soon derelict.

Stevenage FC meanwhile had been formed in 1976 and were playing youth football on a Playing Field but the ground was rescued and the club moved in.

They played in the Chiltern Youth League before becoming Intermediate and moving to the Southern Combination where they added 'Borough' to the club name. The next step was the United Counties League on gaining senior status and they completed the double of Division One championship and League Cup on their debut season. Three years later after a spell in the top division they moved across the pyramid and joined the Isthmian League Division Two North, where they finished fourth. 1986 saw them crowned champions as well as reaching the last eight of the FA Vase. To cap it they lost the Herts Senior Cup final.

They suffered a poor season in 1986-87 which saw them relegated back to Division Two North, but the appointment of Paul Fairclough and Vic Clarke was the start of their rise to the top. They took the title with 122 goals and a 100% home record and in 1992 took Division One remaining unbeaten at home and cruising it by 14 points. The 45th match against Dulwich was the first home loss in a season which ended with Borough in 7th, but it was a taster for 1993, when the Isthmian League championship was won with 31 wins and 97 points. With vast amounts being spent on rebuilding the ground slowly, the real prospect of another Hertfordshire club in the League came nearer and last season Stevenage swept all before them to take the Conference title from Woking in second place. However, the dream of the club and the chairman was shattered earlier in the season when the deadline for the work came and went and the Football League rejected them to add them to an increasing list of Conference champions.

STEVENAGE BOROUGH 1995/96 SEASON

Date		Opponent	Att	Score	Scorers
15/08/95	C1	HITCHIN TOWN	818	3-0	
19/08/95	L	BATH CITY	1355	2-0	Nugent 29, Lynch 36
22/08/95	L	Dover Athletic	1157	2-1	Lynch 59, Hayles 89
26/08/95	L	Southport	1179	1-0	Marshall
28/08/95	L	TELFORD UNITED	2023	0-1	
02/09/95	L	Gateshead	610	2-2	Nugent 57, Hayles 76
05/09/95	L	Woking	1864	1-4	Venables 89
09/09/95	C2	BROOK HOUSE	814	0-0	
12/09/95	C3	Brook House	167	5-1	
16/09/95	L	Bromsgrove Rovers	1067	1-1	Barrowcliff 22
18/09/95	L	KETTERING TOWN	2033	5-1	Smith 13,Barrowcliff 19,Crawshaw 45(p),Browne 53, Marshall90
23/09/95	C4	Uxbridge	460	1-0	Marshall
30/09/95	L	ALTRINCHAM	1615	1-1	Smith 54
07/10/95	C5	STAINES TOWN	1176	2-0	Lynch, Crawshaw
14/10/95	L	Halifax Town	858	3-2	Lynch 16, Smith 23, Sodje 41
21/10/95	C6	Aylesbury United	1480	3-1	Crawshaw(2), Browne
23/10/95	L	WELLING UNITED	1713	4-1	Hayles 13, Webster 31, Browne 46, Barrowcliff 70
28/10/95	L	NORTHWICH VICTORIA	1645	5-1	Crawshaw 3(p) 40, Smith 34, Browne 44, Hayles 51
04/11/95	L	Telford United	883	3-1	Browne 31, Crawshaw 61, Sodje 80
11/11/95	C7	Hereford United	3321	1-2	Crawshaw
18/11/95	L	SOUTHPORT	1785	1-3	Venables 23
25/11/95	L	Runcorn	442	8-0	Hayles 2 20 49, Venables 34 60, Berry 57, Browne 62, Smith 7
02/12/95	L	MACCLESFIELD TOWN	2021	4-0	Berry 9, Lynch 65, Sodje 76, Hayles 78
05/12/95	C8	WATFORD		0-0	
09/12/95	L	BROMSGROVE ROVERS	1565	3-3	Barrowcliff 2, Lynch 7, Hayles 40
11/12/95	L	Dagenham & Redbridge	762	2-1	Webster 72, Hayles 80
16/12/95	L	Northwich Victoria	673	3-1	Browne 26, Hayles 48 65
01/01/96	L	SLOUGH TOWN	2123	3-1	Lynch 43, Marshall 65, Browne 90
03/01/96	C9	Watford		0-0	
06/01/96	L	Macclesfield Town	2126	0-0	
08/01/96	L	FARNBOROUGH TOWN	1745	0-0	
13/01/96	L	HALIFAX TOWN	1841	2-0	Venables(2)
20/01/96	C10	DAGENHAM & REDBRIDGE	1348	3-2	Hayles, Venables, Marshall
03/02/96	L	RUNCORN	1432	4-1	Hayles 4 71 79, Lynch 8
05/02/96	C11	HEMEL HEMPSTEAD		0-0	
10/02/96	C12	BURTON ALBION	1362	2-1	Venables, Hayles
13/02/96	L	Welling United	572	3-0	Lynch 46 76, Hayles 55
17/02/96	L	GATESHEAD	1364	1-1	Browne 62
24/02/96	L	HEDNESFORD TOWN	1626	1-0	Hayles 14
26/02/96	C13	HEMEL HEMPSTEAD		2-1	
02/03/96	C14	KETTERING TOWN	2219	3-0	Smith, Hayles(2)
04/03/96	L	DOVER ATHLETIC	1062	3-2	Hayles 1 23, Marshall 58
09/03/96	L	Stalybridge Celtic	843	5-2	Hayles 2 29 30, Venables 40, Browne 86
12/03/96	L	Slough Town	1126	6-2	Browne 4 7,Webster 10(p),Hayles 47,Barrowcliffe 62, Venables
16/03/96	L	KIDDERMINSTER HARRIERS	2012	4-1	Smith 38, Browne 53 82, Hayles 58
23/03/96	C15	Hyde United	2012	2-3	Venables, Hayles
25/03/96	L	Hednesford Town	1651	1-2	Venables 53
30/03/96	L	Altrincham	838	2-0	Browne 21, Webster 44(p)
06/04/96	L	Morecambe	1227	0-1	
08/04/96	L	WOKING	3967	4-0	Venables 3, Hayles 28, Sodje 67, Trebble 75
13/04/96	L	STALYBRIDGE CELTIC	1767	2-2	Hayles 87, Beavor 90
16/04/96	L	Kettering Town	1414	2-1	Hayles 69 80
20/04/96	L	Bath City	806	2-1	Hayles 21, Beevor 49
22/04/96	L	Kidderminster Harriers	2060	1-0	Trebble 37
27/04/96	L	MORECAMBE	2556	1-1	Browne 76
29/04/96	L	DAGENHAM & REDBRIDGE	2379	1-0	Barrowcliff 4
04/05/96	L	Farnborough Town	1413	2-2	Mitchell 26(p), Day 30(og)
10/08/96	C16	St Albans City		4-2	

C1=Herts CCQF, C2=FA Cup Q1, C3=FA Cup Q1 rep, C4=FA Cup Q2, C5=FA Cup Q3, C6=FA Cup Q4,
C7=FA Cup 1, C8=Herts SC2, C9=Herts SC2 rep, C10=FA Trophy 1, C11=Herts CCSF, C12=FA Trophy 2,
C13=Herts CCSF rep, C14=FA Trophy 3, C15=FA Trophy QF, C16=Herts CCF

TELFORD UTD
BUCKS HEAD GROUND, WATLING STREET, WELLINGTON, SHROPSHIRE TF1 2NJ TEL:01952 270767 FAX 246431

Secretary: Mike Ferriday, 199 Trench Rd, Telford, TF2 7DX

Tel: 01952 605193

Press Sec: Rob Cave

Tel: 01952 299444

Nickname: The Bucks or Lilywhites

Capacity: 4,600

Seating: 200

Covered standing: 1,000

Clubhouse On Ground: Yes

Record Attendance: 13,000 v Shrewsbury Town in 1936

Record Fee Received :£50,000 from Scarborough for Stephen Norris

DIRECTIONS
Leave M54 at Junction 6, take A518. Straight on at first island and then left at second island onto B5061. At traffic lights go straight on, ground is immediately on right.

HONOURS
FA TROPHY 1971, 1983, 1989.

WELSH CUP 1901-02, 1905-06, 1938-40.

Birmingham League 1920-21, 1934-35, 1935-36.

Cheshire League 1945-46, 1946-47, 1951-52.

Birmingham Senior Cup 1946-47.

Walsall Senior Cup 1946-47.

Birmingham League Challenge Cup 1946-47.

Southern League Cup 1970-71.

Midland Floodlit Cup 1970-71, 1982-83, 1988-89.

Shropshire Senior Cup 30 times

Manager:Wayne Clarke   Assistant Manager: Brian Caswell   Chairman: Tony Esp

The Bucks Head ground has seen football since the mid-1880's, when the old club, Wellington FC began playing there after using various sites, including Barnfield Farm, Haygate Admaston, the Red Lion Ground and Spraggs Rec in Street Lane. They entered the Shropshire League and then the Birmingham League before the turn of the century, staying until just before the Second World War.

The Bucks Head had by then grown and the delightful West Stand had been built, which gained dressing rooms and offices a decade later. On leaving the Birmingham League, Wellington entered the Cheshire League which they won in 1946, 47 and 52 and, with further success in various cups, they stepped up into the Southern League in 1958, enjoying a continued stay in the top division for twenty years until becoming founder members of the Alliance. Ten years earlier, after a financial upheaval, the ground was sold to the Development Corporation and the club name changed to Telford United. A new stand was built on the east side and eventually United bought the ground back from the Corporation. 1970 saw the start of a tremendous run of success with FA Trophy Final appearances and the now famous FA Cup runs began in earnest in 1983-4 when the club knocked out Stockport County, Northampton Town and Rochdale before taking Derby County all the way. Twelve months on, Utd beat Lincoln City, Preston North End, Bradford City, and Darlington before losing to Everton in the Fifth Round and since then Stockport again, Burnley and Stoke City have all found the Bucks too hot to handle.

Although the last few years have been relatively peaceful, Telford United remain in the Conference averaging around 1,000 for home games last season.

TELFORD UTD 1995/96 SEASON

Date	Cup	Opponent	Att	Score	Scorers
31/07/95	C1	Bridgnorth Town		2-1	
19/08/95	L	Morecambe	1532	0-2	
22/08/95	L	ALTRINCHAM	840	2-0	Clarke 29, Myers 35
26/08/95	L	FARNBOROUGH TOWN	809	3-2	Bignot 12, Clarke 53, Myers 78
28/08/95	L	Stevenage Borough	2023	1-0	Langford 75
02/09/95	L	Stalybridge Celtic	619	2-2	Clarke 21, Myers 43
05/09/95	L	RUNCORN	1008	1-2	Gray 33
09/09/95	C2	SHIFNAL TOWN	837	4-0	
11/09/95	L	Hednesford Town	2480	0-4	
16/09/95	L	GATESHEAD	750	0-0	
19/09/95	C3	NORTHWICH VICTORIA	512	1-2	
23/09/95	C4	Raunds Town	225	2-1	Clarke, Langford
26/09/95	L	BROMSGROVE ROVERS	743	0-0	
30/09/95	L	KETTERING TOWN	952	3-4	Myers 3 49, Clarke 34(p)
03/10/95	C5	Northwich Victoria	514	3-0	
07/10/95	C6	HALESOWEN TOWN	904	4-1	Clarke, Myers, Fowler, Langford
09/10/95	L	Kidderminster Harriers	2433	0-2	
14/10/95	L	Southport	812	2-3	Gray 18 88
21/10/95	C7	SOUTHPORT	898	3-0	Langford(2), Myers
28/10/95	L	SLOUGH TOWN	808	2-0	Myers 9, Fereday 61
04/11/95	L	STEVENAGE BOROUGH	883	1-3	Bignot 81
11/11/95	C8	WITTON ALBION	1277	2-1	Foster, Langford
18/11/95	L	Welling United	613	1-3	Langford 66
25/11/95	L	DAGENHAM & REDBRIDGE	711	0-0	
02/12/95	C9	NOTTS COUNTY	2831	0-2	
05/12/95	C10	Bromsgrove Rovers	548	1-3	Clarke
09/12/95	L	MORECAMBE	728	2-2	Simpkin 39, Robinson 59
16/12/95	L	Altrincham	633	0-1	
19/12/95	L	Northwich Victoria	503	0-2	
06/01/96	L	Dover Athletic	1030	0-1	
13/01/96	L	Bath City	517	3-0	Myers 14 43 44
20/01/96	C11	Burton Albion	950	1-3	Gray
03/02/96	L	Slough Town	682	2-1	Clarke 62, Turner 90
10/02/96	L	Woking	2384	1-5	Langford 54
13/02/96	L	Macclesfield Town	866	0-1	
17/02/96	L	DOVER ATHLETIC	733	1-0	Gray 47
20/02/96	L	KIDDERMINSTER HARRIERS	918	1-1	Langford 84
24/02/96	L	Gateshead	813	2-1	Langford 31, Hine 49(og)
02/03/96	L	STALYBRIDGE CELTIC	783	0-1	
09/03/96	L	NORTHWICH VICTORIA	712	1-0	Langford 68
12/03/96	L	Bromsgrove Rovers	746	2-0	Niblett 4, Gray 81
16/03/96	L	Dagenham & Redbridge	668	1-1	Niblett 89
23/03/96	L	SOUTHPORT	758	2-1	Gray 1 8
26/03/96	L	WOKING	736	1-2	Adams 70(p)
30/03/96	L	MACCLESFIELD TOWN	1015	1-2	Purdie 53
02/04/96	L	HEDNESFORD TOWN	967	2-1	Wilcox 12, Turner 63
06/04/96	L	Halifax Town	771	0-0	
08/04/96	L	WELLING UNITED	782	0-0	
13/04/96	L	HALIFAX TOWN	708	1-1	Eccleston 50
20/04/96	L	Farnborough Town	784	1-2	Adams 65
27/04/96	L	Runcorn	401	3-2	Gray 18, Turner 31, Purdie 72
30/04/96	L	Kettering Town	851	3-0	Gray 25 75, Adams 41
04/05/96	L	BATH CITY	831	3-1	Niblett 39, Bignot 66, Adams 75

C1=Shrops SCSF, C2=FA Cup Q1, C3=SC1 (1), C4=FA Cup Q2, C5=SC1 (2), C6=FA Cup Q3, C7=FA Cup Q4, C8=FA Cup 1, C9=FA Cup 2, C10=SC2, C11=FA Trophy 1

WELLING UNITED
PARK VIEW ROAD GROUND, WELLING, KENT DA16 1SY
TEL; 0181 301 1196 FAX 0811 301 5676

Secretary: Barrie Hobbins, Welling United FC

Nickname: The Wings

Colours: Red and White

Capacity: 5,500

Seating: 500

Covered standing: 1,500

Clubhouse on ground: Yes

Record attendance: 4,100 v Gillingham FA Cup 1991

Biggest win: 7-1

Biggest defeat: 0-7

Record appearances: Nigel Ransom 1066 and Ray Burgess 1045

Record goalscorer in one season: John Bartley 55

Record goalscorer in total: John Bartley 533

Record fee paid: £30,000 for Gary Abbott

Record fee received: £70,000 + for Steve Finnan to Birmingham City

DIRECTIONS

M25 then A2 towards London. Take Welling turn-off, ground 1 mile. By rail to Welling station (BR) - ground 3/4 mile.

HONOURS

London Spartan League 1978,
Southern League Premier Div1986
Kent Senior Cup 1986
London Senior Cup 1990
London Challenge Cup 1992
Manager for 1996-97: Kevin Hales
Assistant Manager: Ray Burgess
Chairman: Paul Websdale
Vice Chairman: Steve Pain

Welling United are now 33 years old, having begun in Youth football back in 1963. From there the club played Sunday football for four years before the club turned to Saturday football and the Intermediate section of the Metropolitan London League. Senior status followed in 1977 and with it came promotion to the Premier Division of what is now the Spartan League.

A year later came the move from a sports ground at Eltham to the present stadium at Park View Road, in Welling. The ground was the former home of Bexley United, and Bexleyheath and Welling who used it before the War. It has been a football ground for over 70 years and lay derelict twice in its lifetime, once after the war as the club did not re-emerge until 1952. Again when Bexley United went under in 1976 the ground was left to rot, but Welling gained the lease and began playing there in August 1977 as an Athenian League club. They were in that league for three years until successfully applying for the Southern League, having been turned down a year earlier. The league re-formed its Premier League and Welling United were founder members and within four years were champions, taking their place in the Conference.

The first year found the club wanting and only the internal problems at Nuneaton Borough kept them up, but determined not to be caught again improved and had five comfortable years before again surviving due to a feeder league club not making the grade.

Over the 33 years, the Wings have won many honours including the London Challenge Cup, London Senior Cup, Kent Senior Cup and Spartan League Cup, but the highlight was in 1990 when they reached the 3rd Round of the FA Cup, hosting Blackburn Rovers in front of a capacity 4,000 crowd.

WELLING UNITED 1995/96 SEASON

Date	Comp	Opponent	Att	Score	Scorers
19/08/95	L	Runcorn	410	3-1	Farley 18, Gamble 22 82
22/08/95	L	SLOUGH TOWN	747	0-3	
26/08/95	L	NORTHWICH VICTORIA	538	1-1	Berry 72
28/08/95	L	Hednesford Town	1732	1-1	Simpson 75(og)
02/09/95	L	Halifax Town	766	1-2	Copley 42
05/09/95	L	BROMSGROVE ROVERS	602	5-2	Wordsworth 25, Barnes 44 82 86, Henry 47
09/09/95	C1	WICK	547	2-0	Farley, Sykes
12/09/95	L	Bath City	458	1-1	Farley 10
16/09/95	L	Southport	915	0-2	
19/09/95	C2	DOVER ATHLETIC	409	1-2	O'Keefe
23/09/95	C3	BROMLEY	722	2-2	Gorman, Brown
26/09/95	C4	Bromley	451	3-3	
30/09/95	L	Morecambe	845	0-1	
02/10/95	C5	BROMLEY	701	1-2	
07/10/95	L	GATESHEAD	588	1-2	Morah 23
10/10/95	C6	Dover Athletic	664	0-3	
14/10/95	L	Stalybridge Celtic	605	1-2	Morah 38(p)
17/10/95	C7	DEAL TOWN	157	1-0	Appiah
21/10/95	L	WOKING	1066	1-2	Morah 73(p)
23/10/95	L	Stevenage Borough	1713	1-4	Morah 57
28/10/95	L	Macclesfield Town	988	1-2	Morah 10
31/10/95	L	BATH CITY	403	2-1	Henry 34, Morah 50(p)
04/11/95	L	ALTRINCHAM	623	1-1	Henry 10
14/11/95	L	Kettering Town	1232	3-1	Brown 12, Wordsworth 40, Rutherford 53
18/11/95	L	TELFORD UNITED	613	3-1	Henry 30, Fowler 57(og), Brown 64
21/11/95	C8	SOUTHALL	101	12-0	Morah(5), Henry(4), Wordsworth(2), Gorman
25/11/95	L	HALIFAX TOWN	666	0-0	
02/12/95	L	Dagenham & Redbridge	805	1-1	Morah 70
12/12/95	L	FARNBOROUGH TOWN	403	0-1	
16/12/95	L	Bromsgrove Rovers	721	1-1	Copley 86
01/01/96	L	DOVER ATHLETIC	1006	1-0	Wordsworth 66
09/01/96	C9	ASHFORD TOWN	202	2-3	Morah, Watts
13/01/96	L	STALYBRIDGE CELTIC	626	1-1	Gorman
20/01/96	C10	Rothwell Town	238	2-2	Morah, Tierling
01/02/96	C11	ROTHWELL TOWN	312	3-0	Tierling, Morah, Wordsworth
03/02/96	L	Altrincham	762	0-1	
10/02/96	C12	Hyde United	680	1-4	Henry
13/02/96	L	STEVENAGE BOROUGH	572	0-3	
15/02/96	C13	Tooting & Mitcham United		1-2	Sykes
17/02/96	L	KIDDERMINSTER HARRIERS	556	0-0	
24/02/96	L	SOUTHPORT	600	0-1	
02/03/96	L	Woking	2286	2-3	Hansen 28 35
05/03/96	L	Farnborough Town	470	1-0	
09/03/96	L	Kidderminster Harriers	1685	0-3	
12/03/96	L	HEDNESFORD TOWN	400	1-1	Farley 26
16/03/96	L	MORECAMBE	508	1-0	Dimmock 55
23/03/96	L	DAGENHAM & REDBRIDGE	623	0-0	
26/03/96	L	Dover Athletic	1001	1-2	Hansen 62
30/03/96	L	Gateshead	510	1-1	Rutherford 18
06/04/96	L	RUNCORN	616	1-1	Morah 7
08/04/96	L	Telford United	782	0-0	
13/04/96	L	Slough Town	785	0-0	
23/04/96	L	KETTERING TOWN	603	1-0	Morah 17
28/04/96	L	MACCLESFIELD TOWN	558	1-2	Gardner 82(og)
04/05/96	L	Northwich Victoria	875	2-1	Abel 39(og), Morah 45

C1=FA Cup Q1, C2=SC1 (1) D, C3=FA Cup Q2, C4=FA Cup Q2 rep, C5=FA Cup Q2 rep (2), C6=SC1 (2), C7=Kent SC1, C8=London CC1, C9=Kent SCQF, C10-FA Trophy 1, C11=FA Trophy 1 rep, C12=FA Trophy 2, C13=London CCQF

Secretary: P J Ledger J P, 16 Bowsey Lane, Westfield, Woking, Surrey GU22 9AA

Tel: 01483 725295 (h) 0831 271369 (mob)

Best contact when confirming fixture:

D N Powell, 30 Warwick Rd, Ash Vale, Aldershot, Hants GU12 5PL

Tel: 01252 545803 (h) 01483 740740 (b) 0378 269 105 (mob)

Press Officer: P Beard 01483 760355 (h)

Colours: Red and White halves

Nickname: The Cardinals

Capacity: 6,049

Seating: 2,536

Covered standing: 1,389

Clubhouse on ground: Yes

Record attendance: 6,000 v Swansea City FA Cup 1978-79

Biggest win: 17-4 v Farnham in 1912-13

Biggest defeat: 0-16 v New Crusaders in 1905-06

Record appearances: B Finn 564 from 1962-74

Record Goalscorer in total: C Mortimore 331 1953-65

Record fee received: £35,000 for Mark Tucker from Rushden & Diamonds 1996

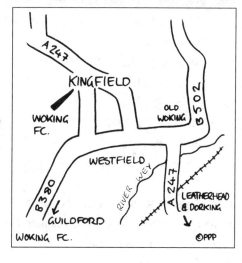

HONOURS

FA TROPHY WINNERS 1994 AND 1995

FA AMATEUR CUP WINNERS 1958

Isthmian League 1992 and Charity Shield 1992 and 1993

Isthmian League Cup 1991 and Division Two South 1987

West Surrey League 4 times

Surrey Senior Cup 1913, 1927, 1956, 1957, 1972, 1991, 1994, 1996

Surrey Senior Shield 9 times

Surrey Premier Cup twice

Surrey Invitation Cup 1967

Surrey Intermediate Cup twice

Channel Islands Victory Cup twice

MANAGER FOR 1996-97: Geoff Chapple

ASSISTANT MANAGER: Colin Lippiatt

CHAIRMAN: PJ Ledger J P

VICE CHAIRMAN: J Davies

Woking were founded in 1889, competing in the West Surrey League before moving to the Isthmian League in 1911. They had a series of homes, playing their first game on a field in Brewery Road. In the early 1900's, they moved to Pembroke Road until the First War. On resumption the Cards played at Hobbs Meadow, which was part of the original Kingfield, where spectators walked through Woking Rec and a rubbish tip and over the River Bourne to reach the ground which had a temporary stand with dressing rooms.

In 1922 the club joined a sports ground association and acquired 10 acres at Kingfield where tennis, cricket, hockey and football was played and they have remained there ever since, albeit on the site which is now enclosed with the original acreage built on.

Success in the league was not a regular occurrence, but with wins in the Surrey Senior Shield, and the Surrey Senior Cup the club continued until its finest hour in 1958, when they took the FA Amateur Cup with a 3-0 win over Ilford. It was not until 1980, when they Cards had long since turned professional, that they again came close to gracing Wembley, losing in the Trophy semi-final to Dagenham, but in 1994 and 1995 they eclipsed all by beating Runcorn and Kidderminster Harriers.

It was the culmination of a wonderful career for manager Geoff Chapple, who had seen the club plummet down the league only to rise again with a strong base of support and a ground designated as good enough by the Football League. The promotions on the back of a flood of goals were topped off nicely by the memorable FA Cup day when the Surrey side demolished West Bromwich Albion at the Hawthorns, chiefly through a Tim Buzaglo hat-trick. It has seen Woking rise to the Conference where they pushed Stevenage all the way last year and will be looking to go even better in 1997.

WOKING 1995/96 SEASON

Date	Comp	Opponent	Att	Score	Scorers
19/08/95	L	Macclesfield Town	1370	2-3	Steele 62 83
22/08/95	L	BATH CITY	1708	2-0	Steele 36, Hay 65
26/08/95	L	STALYBRIDGE CELTIC	1613	2-1	Brown 21, Wye 74
28/08/95	L	Bromsgrove Rovers	1290	1-2	Ellis 45
02/09/95	L	Hednesford Town	1711	1-2	Walker 12
05/09/95	L	STEVENAGE BOROUGH	1864	4-1	Hay 43, Reid 50, Peters 57, Walker 75
09/09/95	L	HALIFAX TOWN	2065	2-0	Walker 29(p), Steele 68
12/09/95	L	Kettering Town	1671	0-3	
16/09/95	L	RUNCORN	1620	2-1	Fielder 12, Hay 46
19/09/95	CS	Macclesfield Town	636	2-3	
23/09/95	L	Kidderminster Harriers	2716	0-2	
30/09/95	L	GATESHEAD	1939	2-0	Steele 65, Hay 90
10/10/95	L	Bath City	720	3-0	Walker 24 66, Ellis 44
14/10/95	L	ALTRINCHAM	2081	2-0	Hay 35, Walker 54
21/10/95	L	Welling United	1066	2-1	Steele 49, Brown 82
28/10/95	L	Stalybridge Celtic	754	4-2	Walker 29 49(p) 76, Ellis 35
04/11/95	L	MORECAMBE	2679	3-0	Steele 4 54, Hay 52
11/11/95	C1	Barnet	3034	2-2	Hay, Steele
18/11/95	L	Slough Town	1659	3-2	Walker 28(p) 62(p), Steele 45
21/11/95	C2	BARNET	3535	2-1	Hay, Steele
25/11/95	L	KIDDERMINSTER HARRIERS	2264	0-0	
02/12/95	C3	Enfield	3477	1-1	Walker
09/12/95	L	Runcorn	707	3-2	Hay 18, Ellis 32, Fielder 43(p)
12/12/95	C4	ENFIELD	2253	2-1	Hay(2)
16/12/95	SC	2Slough Town	774	0-3	
26/12/95	L	DAGENHAM & REDBRIDGE	2874	2-2	Crooks 13(og), Hay 78
01/01/96	L	Dagenham & Redbridge	1358	0-0	
06/01/96	C5	Swindon Town	10322	0-2	
13/01/96	L	Morecambe	1312	5-4	Hunter 18 58 77 81, Thompson 52
16/01/96	C6	EPSOM & EWELL		6-0	
20/01/96	C7	Carshalton Athletic	1485	1-3	Steele
23/01/96	C8	MOLESEY		8-1	
03/02/96	L	BROMSGROVE ROVERS	2481	1-1	Ellis 80
10/02/96	L	TELFORD UNITED	2384	5-1	Hunter 1 24 90, Wanless 52, Steele 57
13/02/96	L	Dover Athletic	976	3-4	Hunter 45 70, Hay 89
15/02/96	C9	CRYSTAL PALACE		0-0	
17/02/96	L	Southport	1074	2-2	Hunter 55, Walker 83
24/02/96	L	KETTERING TON	2637	1-1	Hunter 20
02/03/96	L	WELLING UNITED	2286	3-2	Steele 18, Crumplin 57, Hay 89
09/03/96	L	Altrincham	971	0-2	
12/03/96	L	Farnborough Town	1497	2-0	Walker 24 84
16/03/96	C10	CRYSTAL PALACE		4-1	
19/03/96	L	SLOUGH TOWN	1911	3-0	Harvey 2(og), Hay 69, Ellis 75
23/03/96	L	DOVER ATHLETIC	2438	1-0	Fielder 17
26/03/96	L	Telford United	736	2-1	Hay 39, Girdler 40
30/03/96	L	HEDNESFORD TOWN	3194	3-0	Ellis 36, Walker 52 74
06/04/96	L	MACCLESFIELD TOWN	4583	3-2	Hunter 10, Adams 55 64
08/04/96	L	Stevenage Borough	3967	0-4	
13/04/96	L	Gateshead	919	1-0	Hay 59
16/04/96	L	FARNBOROUGH TOWN	3166	2-1	Harlow 82(og), Adams 84
20/04/96	L	Halifax Town	1064	2-2	Walker 80, Baron 86
23/04/96	C11	TOOTING & MITCHAM UNITED		2-0	
27/04/96	L	Northwich Victoria	842	0-3	
30/04/96	L	NORTHWICH VICTORIA	1771	0-0	
04/05/96	L	SOUTHPORT	2543	4-0	Hay 27, Crumplin 70, Steele 76, Walker 78

C1=FA Cup 1, C2=FA Cup 1 rep, C3=FA Cup 2, C5=FA Cup 2 rep, C5=FA Cup 3, C6=Surrey SC1, C7=FA Trophy 1, C8=Surrey SCQF, C9=Surrey SCSF, C10=Surrey SCSF rep, C12=Surrey SCF

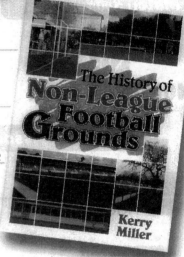

PREMIER DIVISION

Rushden & D	42	29	7	6	99	41	94
Halesowen Town	42	27	11	4	70	36	92
Cheltenham Town	42	21	11	10	76	57	74
Gloucester City	42	21	8	13	65	47	71
Gresley Rovers	42	20	10	12	70	58	70
Worcester City	42	19	12	11	61	43	69
Merthyr Tydfil	42	19	6	17	67	59	63
Hastings Town	42	16	13	13	68	55	61
Crawley Town	42	15	13	14	57	56	58
Sudbury Town	42	15	10	17	69	71	55
Gravesend & N	42	15	10	17	60	62	55
Chelmsford City	42	13	16	13	46	53	55
Dorchester Town	42	15	8	19	62	57	53
Newport A.F.C.	42	13	13	16	53	59	52
Salisbury City	42	14	10	18	57	69	52
Burton Albion	42	13	12	17	55	56	51
Atherstone United	42	12	12	18	57	75	48
Baldock Town	42	11	14	17	51	56	47
Cambridge City	42	12	10	20	56	68	46
Ilkestone Town	42	11	10	21	53	87	43
Stafford Rangers	42	11	4	27	58	90	37
V.S. Rugby	42	5	10	27	37	92	25

MIDLAND DIVISION

Nuneaton Borough	42	30	5	7	82	35	95
King's Lynn (-2)	42	27	5	10	85	43	84
Bedworth Utd (-1)	42	24	10	8	76	42	81
Moor Green	42	22	8	12	81	47	74
Paget Rangers	42	21	9	12	70	45	72
Tamworth	42	22	3	17	97	64	69
Solihull Borough	42	19	9	14	77	64	66
Rothwell Town	42	17	14	11	79	62	65
Buckingham Town	42	18	9	15	74	62	63
Dudley Town	42	15	16	11	83	66	61
Stourbridge	42	17	8	17	60	63	59
Bilston Town	42	16	9	17	61	62	57
Sutt Coldfield T	42	16	9	17	62	67	57
Grantham Town	42	17	5	20	71	83	56
Redditch United	42	14	11	17	57	77	53
Leicester United	42	13	13	16	58	72	52
Hinckley Town	42	14	7	21	62	83	49
R C Warwick	42	10	13	19	67	90	43
Evesham United	42	11	6	25	59	94	39
Corby Town	42	9	7	26	52	95	34
Bury Town	42	8	8	26	57	95	32
Bridgnorth Town	42	7	6	29	53	112	27

SOUTHERN DIVISION

Sittingbourne	42	28	4	10	102	44	88
Ashford Town	42	25	9	8	75	44	84
Waterlooville	42	24	8	10	87	44	80
Newport I.O.W.	42	24	6	12	75	58	78
Braintree Town (-3)	42	24	8	10	93	70	77
Weymouth	42	24	4	14	75	55	76
Havant Town (-6)	42	23	11	8	73	42	74
Forest Gr Rovers	42	22	8	12	85	55	74
Trowbridge Town	42	18	8	16	86	51	62
Yate Town	42	17	8	17	85	71	59
Margate	42	18	5	19	68	62	59
Witney Town	42	16	11	15	60	54	59
Weston-Super-Mare	42	16	9	17	78	68	57
Cinderford Town	42	16	8	18	74	77	56
Fisher	42	14	13	15	58	59	55
Bashley	42	14	11	17	63	61	53
Clevedon Town	42	15	6	21	70	80	51
Tonbridge Angels	42	13	10	19	58	79	49
Fleet Town	42	14	5	23	58	79	47
Fareham Town	42	12	5	25	71	97	41
Erith & Belvedere	42	4	4	34	38	111	16
Poole Town	42	0	1	41	17	188	1

ASHFORD TOWN

The Homelands, Ashford Road, Kingsnorth, Ashford, Kent TN26 1NJ.Tel: 01233 611838

Secretary: Alan Lancaster, 128 Kingsnorth Rd, Ashford, Kent TN23 6HY. Tel: 01233 621325

Chairman: Ernie Warren, 8 Hawks Way, Ashford, Kent TN23 2UN. Tel: 01233 634125

Nickname: Nuts and Bolts

Colours: Green and White stripes

Capacity: 3,565   Seating: 498

Covered seating: 1,100   Clubhouse on ground: Yes

Record attendance: 6,525 v Crystal Palace FA Cup Rd 1 1958

Biggest win: 10-1 v Barry Town Southern League Feb 1964

Biggest defeat: 0-8 v Crawley Town November 1964

Record appearances: Peter McRobert 758

Record goalscorer in one season: Alan Morton

Record goalscorer in total: David Arter

Record fee received: £20,000 for Lee McRobert to Sittingbourne

DIRECTIONS

M20 jct 10, follow A2070 signs towards Brenzett & Lydd airport, dual carriageway to junction of old A2070, ground one mile left through village of Kingsworth. 4 miles south of Ashford — special bus service leaves railway station at 13.35 (Saturday) and 18.35 (midweek matches)

HONOURS

FA Trophy semi-final 1973; Kent League 1949; League Cup 1939; Kent Senior Cup 1959, 1963, 1993, 1996

Manager for 1996/97: Neil Cugley   **Assistant Manager: Dave Williams**

Vice Chairman and Press Officer: Roger West, 16 Spring Lane, Seabrook, Hythe, Kent CT21 5TJ. Tel: 01303 239476

The club was formed in 1930 and is a full member of the Football Association and was incorporated as a company without share capital limited by guarantee in 1959, shortly after joining the Southern League.

Following the disbanding of the old Railway Works team, the Town club was born and for the first two years used the old Railway Ground "Underneath the Arches", and it was from there that the familiar chant of 'Come Along the Nuts and Bolts' originated and the nickname has stuck ever since.

In 1932 the club moved to Essella Park, owned by the President Mr Fred Norman. Prior to joining the Southern League, the club was able to purchase the freehold of Essella Park for £1,500, which turned out to be a shrewd investment as it enabled The Homelands to be built many years later.

Originally members of the old Kent League, they were champions in 1949, but it was Cup football which brought their success. FA Cup 2nd Round once and 1st Round five times, winners of the Kent Senior Cup three times and semi-finalists in the FA Trophy in 1973. Despite all that the club had but three seasons in the Premier Division before going down in 1991.

The old but homely Essella Park was home for 56 years until on reaching the Premier Division, the club were forced to play at Folkestone while the new ground was completed, and moved in a year later.

Last season Ashford Town, under Neil Cugley in his 7th season as manager, finished runners up and were promoted once again to the Premier Division. To crown a memorable season the Nuts and Bolts took the Kent Senior Cup for only the 4th time, beating Charlton Athletic in the final.

ASHFORD TOWN 1995/96 SEASON

Date	Comp	Rnd	Opponent	Att	Score	Scorers
19/08/95	BHL	S	POOLE TOWN	433	1-0	Arter
22/08/95	BHL	S	SITTINGBOURNE	891	0-0	
26/08/95	BHL	S	Bashley	242	0-2	
28/08/95	BHL	S	Braintree Town	251	1-1	Griffiths
02/09/95	BHL	S	HAVANT TOWN	405	1-1	Griffiths
05/09/95	BHL	S	Margate	373	1-0	Stanton
09/09/95	FA Cup	Q1	TONBRIDGE ANGELS	732	2-0	"Griffiths, Stanton"
16/09/95	BHL	S	NEWPORT I.O.W.	412	4-2	Stanton(2), Allon, Arter
20/09/95	BHL	S	Sittingbourne	947	0-4	
23/09/95	FA Cup	Q2	HASTINGS TOWN	966	3-1	Stanton, Allon, Ross
30/09/95	BHL	S	TROWBRIDGE TOWN	490	1-0	Stanton
03/10/95	DMC	1(1)	Tonbridge Angels	408	3-5	Arter(2), Stanton
07/10/95	FA Cup	Q3	Tooting & Mitcham United	540	1-0	Woods(og)
14/10/95	FA Trophy	Q1	SUDBURY TOWN	569	0-2	
21/10/95	FA Cup	Q4	ALDERSHOT TOWN	2016	2-0	Warrilow, Arter
24/10/95	BHL	S	BRAINTREE TOWN	436	7-1	Carruthers(2), Arter(3), Lemoine, Wheeler
28/10/95	BHL	S	CINDERFORD TOWN	564	4-0	Wynter, Arter, Warrilow, Stanton
31/10/95	DMC	1(2)	TONBRIDGE ANGELS	440	1-1	Wynter
04/11/95	BHL	S	WESTON-SUPER-MARE	515	2-2	Arter(2)
07/11/95	Kent	SC1	Dover Athletic	505	2-1	Stanton, Carruthers
11/11/95	FA Cup	1	Bognor Regis Town	2200	1-1	Allon
14/11/95	BHL	S	MARGATE	499	2-0	Arter(2)
18/11/95	BHL	S	YATE TOWN	554	4-2	(og), Carruthers, Arter(2)
21/11/95	FA Cup	1 rep	BOGNOR REGIS TOWN	2542	0-1	
25/11/95	BHL	S	Fisher	290	0-0	
02/12/95	BHL	S	Newport I.O.W.	341	1-2	Stanton
09/12/95	BHL	S	BASHLEY	405	1-4	Stanton
16/12/95	BHL	S	Fleet Town	117	2-3	Allon, Arter
01/01/96	BHL	S	Erith & Belvedere	162	3-2	Carruthers(2), Ross
06/01/96	BHL	S	Havant Town	168	1-2	Stanton
09/01/96	Kent SC	QF	Welling United	202	3-2	
13/01/96	BHL	S	Weston-super-Mare	249	1-1	Arter
16/01/96	E. F'lit	Gp 1	FOLKESTONE INVICTA		2-1	
20/01/96	BHL	S	Fareham Town	126	3-0	Carruthers, Arter(2)
03/02/96	BHL	S	Yate Town	114	1-0	Morris
10/02/96	BHL	S	WATERLOOVILLE	395	3-2	Wynter, Milkins(og), Stanton
17/02/96	BHL	S	FISHER	489	1-0	Allon
28/02/96	E. F'lit	Gp 1	Dover Athletic		4-0	
02/03/96	BHL	S	Poole Town	122	4-0	Arter, Wheeler, White, Ross
09/03/96	BHL	S	Trowbridge Town	346	1-1	White
12/03/96	Kent SC	SF	GILLINGHAM	439	3-1	Arter, Ross(2)
16/03/96	BHL	S	WITNEY TOWN	423	2-0	Wynter, Morris
20/03/96	BHL	S	Forest Green Rovers	131	3-2	Wynter, Ross, Morris
23/03/96	BHL	S	CLEVEDON TOWN	457	2-1	Arter, Carruthers
30/03/96	BHL	S	Weymouth	766	2-0	Wynter, Warrilow
02/04/96	BHL	S	FOREST GREEN ROVERS	441	3-0	Carruthers, Arter, Allon
06/04/96	BHL	S	ERITH & BELVEDERE	558	2-0	Ross, Arter
08/04/96	BHL	S	Tonbridge Angels	761	1-2	Arter
10/04/96	E. F'lit	QF	BISHOP'S STORTFORD	253	0-2	
13/04/96	BHL	S	Cinderford Town	245	1-0	Arter
16/04/96	BHL	S	WEYMOUTH	587	1-0	Warrilow
18/04/96	BHL	S	Witney Town	112	2-1	Warrilow(2)
20/04/96	BHL	S	FLEET TOWN	711	1-0	Pearson
23/04/96	BHL	S	Clevedon Town	157	2-4	Chambers, Arter
27/04/96	BHL	S	FAREHAM TOWN	688	2-1	Arter, Allon
30/04/96	BHL	S	TONBRIDGE ANGELS	1036	0-0	
04/05/96	BHL	S	Waterlooville	266	1-1	Chambers
06/05/96	Kent SC	F	CHARLTON ATHLETIC	1200	3-0	Arter, Allon, Carruthers

ATHERSTONE UNITED

Sheepy Rd, Atherstone, Warwicks. Tel: 01827 717829

Secretary: Neil Dykes, 18 Greendale Close, Atherstone, CV9 1PR. Tel: 01827 714326

Colours: Red and White

Nickname: The Adders

Capacity: 4,500

Seating: 353

Covered standing: 1,000

Clubhouse on ground: Yes

Record attendance: 2,873 v VS Rugby FA Cup 1st Rd 1987

Biggest win: 12-2 v Tipton Town, West Midlands Lge 1986-87

Biggest defeat: 1-7 v Rushden & Diamonds Southern League 1994-95

Record appearances: Lee Spencer

Record goalscorer in one season: Alan Bourton 41

Record goalscorer in total: Alan Bourton

Record fee received: £40,000 for Andy Rammell from Manchester United

DIRECTIONS
Half mile north of town centre on B4116 Twycross/Ashby Road.

HONOURS

Southern League Midland Div 1989; West Midlands League: Div 1 1982; Premier Division 1987; League Cup 1984 and 1987; Walsall Senior Cup 1986.

Manager 1996-97: Ron Bradbury   **Assistant Manager: Bob Stockley**

Chairman: Stan Holland

Vice Chairman: Lee Spencer

Football began in the town in 1887 with friendlies until leagues began in 1894. From local football the original club moved to the Birmingham Combination in 1911, with success coming mainly in cups, the Birmingham Junior Cup with three finals and one win. During that pre-Great War spell the club twice reached the semi-finals of the Amateur Cup.

After the Second War they did the league and Cup double and in 1954 they moved to the West Midlands League although with little good fortune until 1972 when they were runners up and moved up to the Southern League a year later. Under Gil Merrick they finished third behind Wimbledon and Yeovil and won the Birmingham Senior Cup.

Sadly they went into liquidation in 1979 but, after a handful of people got into talks with the FA and the local council, Atherstone United were born, taking over the old club's reserve fixtures in the West Midlands League. Two seasons later the double was achieved and promotion came again, and in 1989, when finishing second to Gloucester City, United were in the Premier Division.

In 1985 United reached the semi-final of the FA Vase in only their second season in the competition and with success in the FA Cup, the new club were soon established.

ATHERSTONE UNITED 1995/96 SEASON

Date	Competition	Round	Opponent	Att	Score	Scorers
08/08/95	Mids F'lit	94-95 QF	HINCKLEY ATHLETIC	224	0-3	
19/08/95	BHL	P	Dorchester Town	604	1-0	Wright
22/08/95	BHL	P	ILKESTON TOWN	359	3-3	Judd, Wright, Knight
26/08/95	BHL	P	GRAVESEND & NORTHFLEET	286	2-0	Russell, Wright
28/08/95	BHL	P	Stafford Rangers	522	4-1	Ellison, Campbell, Read, Tomlinson
02/09/95	BHL	P	CHELMSFORD CITY	303	1-2	Judge
05/09/95	BHL	P	Gresley Rovers	702	0-1	
09/09/95	FA Cup	Q1	ARMITAGE	258	2-2	Read(2)
12/09/95	FA Cup	Q1 rep	Armitage	229	3-3	Russell, Donovan(2)
16/09/95	BHL	P	CHELTENHAM TOWN	402	1-2	Randall
18/09/95	FA Cup	Q1 rep(2)	Armitage	275	4-5	Randall, Knight, Judd, Donovan
30/09/95	BHL	P	BALDOCK TOWN	235	2-2	Russell, Albrighton
03/10/95	DMC	1(1)	TAMWORTH	423	4-3	Tomlinson, Albrighton, Russell, Ellison
07/10/95	BHL	P	Cambridge City	191	1-3	Wade
14/10/95	FA Trophy	Q1	LINCOLN UNITED	278	2-1	Ellison(2)
17/10/95	Birm SC	1	Gornal Athletic	101	0-0	
21/10/95	BHL	P	SUDBURY TOWN	234	0-0	
24/10/95	BHL	P	STAFFORD RANGERS	263	2-2	Russell(2)
28/10/95	BHL	P	Halesowen Town	694	4-5	Albrighton, Russell(2), Randall
31/10/95	DMC	1(2)	Tamworth	617	3-2	Ellison, Judd
02/11/95	Birm SC	1 rep	GORNAL ATHLETIC	120	4-2	D Albrighton(2), S Campbell, Parker
04/11/95	FA Trophy	Q2	ACCRINGTON STANLEY	422	1-3	Knight
11/11/95	BHL	P	Chelmsford City	789	1-1	Judd
14/11/95	BHL	P	GRESLEY ROVERS	454	1-2	Parker
18/11/95	BHL	P	DORCHESTER TOWN	222	3-4	Russell, Ellison, Albrighton
20/11/95	Birm SC	2	COVENTRY CITY	266	0-3	
25/11/95	BHL	P	Rushden & Diamonds	2231	3-7	Russell, Judd, D Albrighton
02/12/95	BHL	P	Salisbury City	333	0-2	
09/12/95	BHL	P	CRAWLEY TOWN	244	2-1	M Albrighton, Hart
12/12/95	DMC	2	NUNEATON BOROUGH	467	1-3	Russell
23/12/95	BHL	P	Gloucester City	615	2-1	Ellison, Russell
06/01/96	BHL	P	Baldock Town	251	1-1	Judd
13/01/96	BHL	P	RUSHDEN & DIAMONDS	605	1-3	Russell
20/01/96	BHL	P	Hastings Town	407	0-5	
23/01/96	Mids F'lit	1(1)	GORNAL ATHLETIC	78	5-0	Judd, Nduku, D Albrighton(3)
03/02/96	BHL	P	Cheltenham Town	516	1-1	Russell
10/02/96	BHL	P	Worcester City	588	0-1	
17/02/96	BHL	P	Gravesend & Northfleet	511	1-2	Russell
24/02/96	BHL	P	SALISBURY CITY	244	3-1	Russell(2), Albrighton
27/02/96	BHL	P	MERTHYR TYDFIL	229	0-2	
02/03/96	BHL	P	NEWPORT A.F.C.	328	0-0	
05/03/96	Mids F'lit	1(2)	Gornal Athletic	40	1-3	Higgs
09/03/96	BHL	P	V.S. Rugby	620	0-3	
12/03/96	BHL	P	BURTON ALBION	278	0-3	
16/03/96	BHL	P	HALESOWEN TOWN	339	0-1	
19/03/96	BHL	P	Ilkeston Town	377	1-1	Ellison
23/03/96	BHL	P	GLOUCESTER CITY	284	2-1	Bennett, Speedie
26/03/96	BHL	P	V.S. Rugby	344	4-1	Ellison, Speedie, Blair, Higgs
30/03/96	BHL	P	Merthyr Tydfil	402	0-4	
03/04/96	BHL	P	Newport A.F.C.	504	2-1	Speedie, Ellison
06/04/96	BHL	P	WORCESTER CITY	326	1-1	Greenman(og)
08/04/96	BHL	P	Burton Albion	538	2-2	Judd, Bennett
13/04/96	BHL	P	HASTINGS TOWN	301	1-0	Speedie
20/04/96	BHL	P	Sudbury Town	390	1-0	Osman(og)
27/04/96	BHL	P	Crawley Town	732	1-0	Speedie
04/05/96	BHL	P	CAMBRIDGE CITY	865	2-2	Albrighton, Ellison

BALDOCK TOWN

Norton Road, Baldock, Herts SG7 5AU. Tel: 01462 895449

Secretary: C.T.Hammond, 2 Elmwood Ct, 65 High Street, Baldock, Herts SG7 6AY Tell: 01462 894253

Nickname: The Reds

Capacity: 3,000   Seating: 250

Covered standing: 1,250   Clubhouse on ground: Yes

Record attendance: 1,588 v Stevenage Borough, FA Cup October 1996

Record appearances: Keith (Paddy) Stanton 440

Record fee received: £30,000 for Kevin Phillips to Watford

HONOURS

South Midlands League 1928, 1966, 1968, 1970, Div 1 1950; League Cup 1984 and 1987; Herts Charity Cup 1992 and 1995; Herts Charity Shield 1958 and 1970; Wallspan Floodlit Cup 1986; Hinchingbrooke Cup 1987; TSI Floodlit Cup 1989; Woolwich Equitable Cup 1984; Herts Intermediate Cup 1987.

> ## DIRECTIONS
> Off A1 (M) at Letchworth/Baldock sign, left to 3rd island, A505 to Baldock, Norton Road is left off A505, left pass Orange Tree pub, ground on right after railway bridge. From North or East turn left into town, Hitchin Street, right into Norton then proceed as above. From Baldock station (Kings Cross to Royston line) — left down Ickneild Way and right into Norton Road (800 yards).

Manager for 1996/97: Brian Stein

Joint Chairmen: Mike Watson-Challis and Ray Childerstone

Press Officer: David Hammond, 51 London Road, Baldock, Herts Tel: 01462 892797

Baldock Town FC were founded in 1889, making it one of the oldest clubs in Hertfordshire. During the early years, the team played in the North Herts, Herts County and even Northampton Leagues, before joining the Beds and District, in 1925. In 1929 Baldock reached the final of the Herts Senior Cup, losing to Watford OB's in extra time. The club were playing at Bakers Close and just prior to the war they built a new pavilion. After the war, The Reds finished runners up in the Premier Division of the league which had become the South Midlands League, but seven years later they moved to pastures new with entry into the London based Parthenon League. It was not a success and in 1963 they returned to the South Midlands League, where two years later they won the League and the Championship Shield double. The following years proved to be the best ever for the club, for in 1970 they again did the double, winning the Herts Charity Shield as well.

The 70's were quiet times for the club, although they were always respected as one of the better sides, but plans were in hand at the end of the decade and in 1980 the club accepted an offer from the Council and moved from Bakers Close into their current ground in Norton Road, which was officially opened by Sir Stanley Rous in 1982.

He returned two years later to switch on the new floodlights in front of a record crowd of 1,250 to watch a match with Arsenal.

Baldock moved to the United Counties League Premier Division for the 1983-84 season, finishing runners up and reaching the last 16 of the FA Vase. In 1987 they were again runners up, but that was sufficient to gain promotion to the Southern League.

Baldock continued to grow in stature and the next few years, under Paul Bowgett and Ian Allinson, they enjoyed a number of Cup runs, including taking the Herts Charity Cup for the first time in 1992.

1994-95 saw some upheaval when Kevin Phillips, the club's top scorer was sold to Watford for £30,000 with the manager walking out two days later. Despite that the team went 29 games unbeaten to clinch a place as runners up, and promotion to the Premier Division, from where last May, they reached the League Cup final, only to lose to Nuneaton Borough.

BALDOCK TOWN 1995/96 SEASON

Date	Competition		Opponent	Att	Score	Scorers
12/08/95	Herts CC	1	BERKHAMSTED TOWN		2-0	
19/08/95	BHL	P	Merthyr Tydfil	453	0-1	
22/08/95	BHL	P	V.S. RUGBY	352	2-0	Cook, Kamara
26/08/95	BHL	P	DORCHESTER TOWN	281	2-1	Howell, Cook
28/08/95	BHL	P	Hastings Town	527	2-2	Russell, Debnam
02/09/95	BHL	P	GRESLEY ROVERS	277	0-1	
04/09/95	BHL	P	Chelmsford City	902	2-0	Cook, Russell
09/09/95	FA Cup	Q1	METROPOLITAN POLICE	176	2-1	Fenton, Debnam
16/09/95	BHL	P	CRAWLEY TOWN	401	0-0	
20/09/95	BHL	P	V.S. Rugby	333	6-0	Russell(3), Guile(3)
23/09/95	FA Cup	Q2	HAYES	319	0-1	
30/09/95	BHL	P	Atherstone United	235	2-2	Cook(2)
03/10/95	DMC	1(1)	Bury Town	107	2-0	Woolgar, Bates
07/10/95	BHL	P	STAFFORD RANGERS	281	5-0	Guile(2), Fenton, Russell, Debnam
14/10/95	FA Trophy	Q1	Barking	136	0-0	
17/10/95	FA Trophy	Q1 rep	BARKING	136	3-2	Howell, Stanton, Bruce
21/10/95	BHL	P	Ilkeston Town	475	2-3	Howell(2)
24/10/95	BHL	P	HASTINGS TOWN	183	1-3	Chattoe
28/10/95	BHL	P	Sudbury Town	406	1-2	Chattoe
31/10/95	DMC	1(2)	BURY TOWN	110	1-1	Howell
04/11/95	FA Trophy	Q2	Tooting & Mitcham United	174	1-2	Bruce
14/11/95	BHL	P	CHELMSFORD CITY	282	2-1	Wallace(2)
18/11/95	BHL	P	Gloucester City	584	1-3	Russell
20/11/95	Herts SC	2	HATFIELD TOWN	107	3-1	Wallace(2), Fenton
25/11/95	BHL	P	MERTHYR TYDFIL	237	1-1	Wallace
28/11/95	BHL	P	Rushden & Diamonds	1922	0-3	
02/12/95	BHL	P	Dorchester Town	560	2-1	Debnam, Cook
09/12/95	BHL	P	Cheltenham Town	751	1-3	Wallace
12/12/95	DMC	2	MARGATE	81	1-0	Wallace
16/12/95	BHL	P	ILKESTON TOWN	238	1-1	Hagg
23/12/95	BHL	P	Salisbury City	351	2-1	Wallace(2)
01/01/96	BHL	P	Cambridge City	332	0-0	
06/01/96	BHL	P	ATHERSTONE UNITED	251	1-1	Fenton
09/01/96	DMC	3	KING'S LYNN	275	2-0	Fenton, Russell
13/01/96	BHL	P	Burton Albion	611	0-1	
20/01/96	BHL	P	GRAVESEND & NORTHFLEET	360	2-2	Russell, Wallace
23/01/96	Herts SC	QF	LONDON COLNEY	110	4-3	Wallace(2), Chattoe, Howell
30/01/96	DMC	QF	Crawley Town	237	2-2	Cook, Russell
03/02/96	BHL	P	Stafford Rangers	511	1-0	Fenton
06/02/96	Herts CC	QF	Boreham Wood	99	1-0	
13/02/96	BHL	P	RUSHDEN & DIAMONDS	854	0-3	
17/02/96	BHL	P	Crawley Town	546	2-1	Wallace(2)
24/02/96	BHL	P	CHELTENHAM TOWN	283	1-1	Wallace
27/02/96	DMC	QF rep	CRAWLEY TOWN	107	1-1	Wallace
05/03/96	BHL	P	WORCESTER CITY	220	0-1	
09/03/96	BHL	P	Gresley Rovers	657	0-3	
12/03/96	BHL	P	HALESOWEN TOWN	163	0-2	
16/03/96	BHL	P	NEWPORT A.F.C.	307	1-2	Haag
19/03/96	Herts SC	SF	Watford	182	1-2	Wallace
23/03/96	BHL	P	SALISBURY CITY	280	4-2	Chattoe, Cullum, Wallace, Russell
27/03/96	BHL	P	CAMBRIDGE CITY	222	0-0	
30/03/96	BHL	P	Worcester City	555	0-0	
03/04/96	DMC	SF(1)	SALISBURY CITY	104	0-0	
06/04/96	BHL	P	SUDBURY TOWN	382	1-3	Bruce
08/04/96	BHL	P	Gravesend & Northfleet	506	1-1	Debnam
10/04/96	DMC	SF(2)	Salisbury City	355	1-1	Russell
13/04/96	BHL	P	GLOUCESTER CITY	261	0-1	
16/04/96	DMC	F(1)	NUNEATON BOROUGH	469	1-3	Wallace
20/04/96	BHL	P	Newport A.F.C.	724	1-1	Bruce
27/04/96	BHL	P	Halesowen Town	1053	0-1	
30/04/96	DMC	F(2)	Nuneaton Borough	1248	1-2	Fenton
04/05/96	BHL	P	BURTON ALBION	442	1-1	Howell

BURTON ALBION

Eton Park, Princess Way, Burton-On-Trent, Staffs DE14 2RU. Tel: 01283 565938

Secretary: Tony Kirkland, 40 Hurst Drive, Stretton, Burton-on-Trent, Staffs DE13 0ED

Tel: 01283 536510 (h) 0374 102485 (mobile)

Press: Mr D J Twigg, 12 Gatcombe Close, Stretton, Burton-on-Trent DE13 0EP Tel 01283 562013

Colours: Yellow and Black stripes   Nickname: The Brewers

Capacity: 4,500   Seating: 300

Covered standing: 2,500

Clubhouse on ground: Yes

Record attendance: 5,860 v Weymouth Southern League Cup Final 2nd Leg 1964

Biggest win: 12-1 Coalville Town Sept 6th 1954

Record appearances: Phil Annable 567

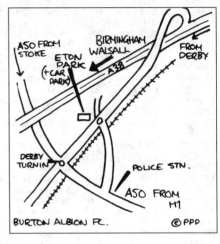

Record goalscorer in one season: Stan Round 59 in 1965-66

Record goalscorer in aggregate: Richie Barker 157

Record fee received: £60,000 for Darren Carr from Crystal Palace in 1989

Record fee paid: £21,000 to Kidderminster Harriers for R Jones and J Pearson

HONOURS

FA TROPHY Runners-up 1987; Staffs Senior Cup 1956; Birmingham Senior Cup 1954 and 1971; Southern League Cup 1964; Northern Premier League Cup 1983; Bass Charity Vase 1982 and 1986; Bass Challenge Cup 1985.

Manager for 1996/97: John Barton

Assistant Manager: John Newman

Chairman: Mr C B Robinson

Senior football was restored to the town of Burton in 1950 after a ten year absence, when the Brewers were formed, playing in the Birmingham League. It was not long before success arrived, the club reaching the 3rd Round of the FA Cup in 1956, eventually losing to Charlton Athletic. Two years later they joined the Southern League, moving from their Wellington Street home to a new ground, built on part of Eatough's sports ground in Derby Road, and purchased for £2,000. Work began on a new £6,000 stand as the club progressed, and the League Cup was won, as a first division side, when beating Weymouth in the final in front of a record crowd.

The Brewers joined the Northern Premier League in 1979, finishing third in 1983 when they also won the Challenge Cup and were runners-up in the President's Cup. Success continued in 1987 when they reached the FA Trophy Final at Wembley, drawing 0-0 before losing the replay to Kidderminster Harriers at West Bromwich Albion. The FA Cup also brought the club fame during this period when reaching the 3rd Round after beating Wootton Blue Cross, Stevenage Borough, Willenhall Town, Wycombe Wanderers, Staines Town and Aldershot before losing to Derby County after the first game was ordered to be replayed following a missile throwing incident where keeper Paul Evans was struck.

In recent times Burton have remained in the top division of the Southern League which they rejoined in 1987.

FORMER GROUNDS: From founding until 1958, Burton used the Lloyds Foundry ground in Wellington Street, where 5,000 people crammed in for the first ever league match against Gloucester City. That ground is now covered by industry.

BURTON ALBION 1995/96 SEASON

Date	Comp	Round	Opponent	Att	Score	Scorers
19/08/95	BHL	P	HASTINGS TOWN	672	1-1	Devaney
22/08/95	BHL	P	Cambridge City	331	2-3	Redfern, Rhodes
26/08/95	BHL	P	Sudbury Town	380	0-3	
28/08/95	BHL	P	RUSHDEN & DIAMONDS	901	4-2	Devaney(2), Rhodes(2)
02/09/95	BHL	P	CRAWLEY TOWN	950	2-1	Rhodes, Redfern
05/09/95	BHL	P	Stafford Rangers	730	3-2	Rhodes(2), Devaney
09/09/95	FA Cup	Q1	STRATFORD TOWN	746	4-0	Redfern, Devaney(2), Rhodes
16/09/95	BHL	P	Gloucester City	867	1-2	Stride
19/09/95	BHL	P	CAMBRIDGE CITY	764	0-0	
23/09/95	FA Cup	Q2	STAFFORD RANGERS	1014	1-1	Rookyard
26/09/95	FA Cup	Q2 rep	Stafford Rangers	610	3-2	Redfern, Hadley, Rhodes
30/09/95	BHL	P	Worcester City	978	1-1	Rhodes
03/10/95	DMC	1(1)	GRESLEY ROVERS	1143	0-2	
07/10/95	FA Cup	Q3	RACING CLUB WARWICK	867	2-0	Rookyard(2)
14/10/95	BHL	P	Merthyr Tydfil	451	3-4	Gretton, Stride, Rookyard
17/10/95	BHL	P	V.S. RUGBY	518	0-0	
21/10/95	FA Cup	Q4	BRACKNELL TOWN	1008	3-1	Keast, Davies, Hadley
28/10/95	BHL	P	Gravesend & Northfleet	609	2-1	Redfern, Devaney
31/10/95	DMC	1(2)	Gresley Rovers	990	2-1	Devaney, Gretton
04/11/95	BHL	P	Hastings Town	421	3-0	Stride(2), Devaney
11/11/95	FA Cup	1	Bradford City	4920	3-4	Rhodes, Stride(2)
14/11/95	BHL	P	STAFFORD RANGERS	803	5-1	Devaney, Redfern, Keast, Davis, Stride
18/11/95	BHL	P	WORCESTER CITY	942	2-0	Stride, Rhodes
21/11/95	BHL	P	Rushden & Diamonds	1651	0-2	
25/11/95	FA Trophy	Q3	BAMBER BRIDGE	964	3-3	Stride(2), Redfern
28/11/95	FA Trophy	Q3 rep	Bamber Bridge	502	3-2	Rhodes(2), Devaney
02/12/95	BHL	P	Newport A.F.C.	817	1-0	Rhodes
05/12/95	Birm SC	2	NUNEATON BOROUGH	343	2-1	Rhodes(2)
09/12/95	BHL	P	V.S. Rugby	524	1-3	Devaney
16/12/95	BHL	P	MERTHYR TYDFIL	658	1-3	Keast
19/12/95	BHL	P	SALISBURY CITY	466	0-1	
23/12/95	BHL	P	CHELMSFORD CITY	652	1-1	Devaney
01/01/96	BHL	P	GRESLEY ROVERS	1609	1-1	Redfern
06/01/96	BHL	P	Crawley Town	657	1-1	Rhodes
09/01/96	Birm SC	3	WALSALL	433	0-0	
13/01/96	BHL	P	BALDOCK TOWN	611	1-0	Payne
20/01/96	FA Trophy	1	TELFORD UNITED	950	3-1	Rhodes, Devaney, Payne
22/01/96	Birm SC	3 rep	Walsall	202	0-3	
03/02/96	BHL	P	SUDBURY TOWN	769	2-3	Keast, Donnelly
10/02/96	FA Trophy	2	Stevenage Borough	1362	1-2	Rhodes
17/02/96	BHL	P	Salisbury City	376	0-2	
24/02/96	BHL	P	GLOUCESTER CITY	672	1-0	Davis
27/02/96	BHL	P	DORCHESTER TOWN	458	1-0	Stride
02/03/96	BHL	P	HALESOWEN TOWN	816	1-1	Rhodes
09/03/96	BHL	P	Cheltenham Town	608	0-1	
12/03/96	BHL	P	Atherstone United	278	3-0	Nuttell, Stride, Devaney
16/03/96	BHL	P	Gresley Rovers	1172	1-2	Redfern
23/03/96	BHL	P	Chelmsford City	755	0-0	
30/03/96	BHL	P	ILKESTON TOWN	830	1-2	Stride
06/04/96	BHL	P	Halesowen Town	902	1-1	Payne
08/04/96	BHL	P	ATHERSTONE UNITED	538	2-2	Nuttell, Devaney
13/04/96	BHL	P	Dorchester Town	647	1-2	Gretton
16/04/96	BHL	P	Ilkeston Town	692	0-1	
20/04/96	BHL	P	CHELTENHAM TOWN	532	3-2	Redfern, Keast, Rhodes
23/04/96	BHL	P	GRAVESEND & NORTHFLEET	444	1-2	Nuttell
27/04/96	BHL	P	NEWPORT A.F.C.	599	0-1	
04/05/96	BHL	P	Baldock Town	442	1-1	Stride

CAMBRIDGE CITY

City Ground, Milton Rd, Cambridge, CB4 1UY. Tel: 01223 357973

Secretary: Stuart Hamilton, 55 Crowhill, Godmanchester, Huntingdon, Cambs
Tel 01480 412266

Club shop: Neil Harvey, 19 Water Lane, Impington, Cambridge CB4 4XW
Tel 01223 235991

DIRECTIONS

50 yards on left from beginning of A1309, Cambridge to Ely Road. Half hour walk from Cambridge BR station.

Colours: White and Black   Nickname: Lilywhites

Capacity: 3,000   Seating: 400

Covered standing: 800   Clubhouse on ground: Yes

Record attendance: 12,058 v Leytonstone Amateur Cup 1949 (on old ground)

Biggest win: 15-1 v RAF in East Anglian League 1942-43

Biggest defeat: 1-11 v Hendon Athenian League 1957-58

Record appearances: Mal Keenan   Record goalscorer in total: Gary Grogan

Record fee paid : £7,000 for Andy Beattie from Barnet in 1991   Received: £15,500 Kevin Wilkin

HONOURS

FA Amateur Cup semi-final 1928; Southern League and Championship Cup 1963; Southern Division 1986; East Anglian Cup 1931, 36, 43, 44, 46, 48, 60, 65, 76; Eastern Professional Floodlit League 1966, 73; Cambs Professional Cup 1961, 62, 63, 71, 73, 75; Cambs Invitation Cup 1951, 77, 79, 86, 89, 90, 93; Spartan League 1948 and 1949, and Eastern Division 1946; Southern Amateur League 1921, 28, 29, 31, 32; Bury and District League 1910, 11, 13, 20; East Anglian League 1910, 40, 41, 42, 43, 45; AFA Senior Cup 1931, 47, 48 jt, 1949, 50; AFA Invitation Cup 1951; Hunts Premier Cup 1963 and 1965; Suffolk Senior Cup 1910; Du Nord International Trophy 1912.

Manager 1996-97: Steve Fallon   **Assistant Manager: Michael Cook**

Cambridge City were formed in August 1908 as Cambridge Town FC, adopting the present title in April 1951. In its formative years, the club played in the Bury and District, East Anglian and Southern Olympian Leagues, before their first honour came in 1910, when they won the Suffolk Senior Cup.

They began their successful association with the Southern Amateur League after the Great War, winning the title in 1921, a year before the move to Milton Road. The club had used a number of sports grounds in the town up to that point including Purbeck Road, Perse School, Hills Road, now the site of a cattle market, Trinity New Field, Jesus College, Grange Road, Corpus Christi, Magdelene College, St Johns College, the Amalgamation ground and the Old County Ground. Most of them still exist, and when the club finally began developing Milton Road, known later as the Town Ground, it was to become their final move, although events would see the ground change dramatically in the 80's.

They again won the league in 1928, 1929, 1931 and 1932 at a time when one of the main rivals were Ipswich Town and a crucial league match at Milton Road between them attracted 11,900 spectators. The previous season saw the best ever FA Amateur Cup run, to the semi-finals where they lost to Leyton at Craven Cottage.

Town joined the Spartan League in 1935 but it was after the War before they had success, winning it three times in the late forties. The Spartan League was suspended during the war, and Town played through it in the East Anglian League, which they won every season accept one, no doubt helped by the likes of Dixie Dean, who scored 8 against RAF (B) in a record 15-1 win in 1942. The 40's were a boom time for the club as they also reached the FA Cup 1st round twice and won the East Anglian Cup four times and the AFA Senior Cup four times. They built on the success by joining the Athenian League in 1950 and they lost the first game 7-0 to Bromley in front of 7,000 people, and things got no better reaching a lowest point when losing 11-1 to Hendon with the crowd below 1,000.

In a bid to halt the decline, the club turned professional and moved to the Southern League in 1958. Gates soared to over 4,000 with 11,000 seeing the floodlight match with West Ham United in 1959. Sadly within five years City were relegated, but returned in 1970 where they were runners up to Yeovil Town. Relegation came again in 1976 and lean years followed by neighbours Cambridge United having forged ahead into the Football League. Gates at one point fell to 120 as the club hit bottom of the league, but following a decision to knock down the stadium and rebuild at right angles just a few yards away, meant that the club played away all year. The return was triumphant as they won the Southern Division on goal difference from Salisbury. Since then there have been a couple of third places but last year was a disaster and only a last minute reprieve saw them escape relegation.

CAMBRIDGE CITY 1995/96 SEASON

Date	Competition	Round	Opponent	Att	Score	Scorers
19/08/95	BHL	P	Stafford Rangers	550	4-2	Harrington, Flack, Coe(2)
22/08/95	BHL	P	BURTON ALBION	331	3-2	Flack, Pincher, I Cambridge
26/08/95	BHL	P	GLOUCESTER CITY	342	0-4	
28/08/95	BHL	P	V.S. Rugby	338	1-0	Coe
02/09/95	BHL	P	NEWPORT A.F.C.	495	0-1	
05/09/95	BHL	P	Gravesend & Northfleet	471	0-2	
09/09/95	FA Cup	Q1	CANVEY ISLAND	268	2-3	Coe, Ryan
16/09/95	BHL	P	MERTHYR TYDFIL	257	1-2	Harrington
19/09/95	BHL	P	Burton Albion	764	0-0	
30/09/95	BHL	P	Hastings Town	441	1-3	Coe
03/10/95	DMC	1(1)	SUDBURY TOWN	180	1-1	Cambridge
07/10/95	BHL	P	ATHERSTONE UNITED	191	3-1	Pincher(2), Flack
10/10/95	E. Anglian	1	HISTON	107	6-1	Saddington, Ryan(2), Cambridge, Pincher, Confrey(og)
14/10/95	BHL	P	CHELTENHAM TOWN	289	1-2	Ryan
21/10/95	BHL	P	Worcester City	825	1-2	McLean
24/10/95	BHL	P	V.S. RUGBY	233	4-1	McLean(2), Coe(2)
28/10/95	BHL	P	ILKESTON TOWN	276	2-3	Robinson(og), Coe
31/10/95	DMC	1(2)	Sudbury Town	226	3-1	Povey, Coe, Cambridge
04/11/95	BHL	P	Cheltenham Town	764	3-2	Lockhart, Tovey(2)
14/11/95	BHL	P	GRAVESEND & NORTHFLEET	267	2-1	Fowler, McLean
18/11/95	BHL	P	STAFFORD RANGERS	257	2-0	McLean, Hurcock
25/11/95	FA Trophy	Q3	HENDON	234	2-0	Tovey, Pincher
02/12/95	BHL	P	Chelmsford City	853	0-0	
05/12/95	DMC	2	Buckingham Town	56	0-1	
09/12/95	BHL	P	Gloucester City	666	1-3	Lockhart
12/12/95	BHL	P	SUDBURY TOWN	141	1-0	McIntosh(og)
19/12/95	E. Anglian	2	Warboys Town	94	4-2	Harrington(2), McLean, Lockhart
01/01/96	BHL	P	BALDOCK TOWN	332	0-0	
06/01/96	BHL	P	Ilkeston Town	435	2-2	Tovey(2)
09/01/96	Cambs IC	QF	Mildenhall Town	114	1-2	Harrington
13/01/96	BHL	P	HALESOWEN TOWN	409	0-1	
20/01/96	FA Trophy	1	BOREHAM WOOD	287	1-2	Lockhart
23/01/96	BHL	P	Crawley Town	343	3-3	Cambridge, Gawthrop, Retallick
03/02/96	BHL	P	Merthyr Tydfil	239	1-2	Harrington
10/02/96	BHL	P	SALISBURY CITY	257	1-3	McLean
27/02/96	BHL	P	Sudbury Town	279	1-1	Harrington
02/03/96	BHL	P	Salisbury City	272	0-1	
05/03/96	BHL	P	HASTINGS TOWN	139	0-3	
09/03/96	BHL	P	Newport A.F.C.	828	2-1	Pincher, Donovan(og)
12/03/96	BHL	P	Dorchester Town	300	2-1	Pincher, Coe
16/03/96	BHL	P	RUSHDEN & DIAMONDS	750	0-2	
19/03/96	E. Anglian	3	Potton United	70	2-0	Cambridge, Coe
27/03/96	BHL	P	Baldock Town	222	0-0	
30/03/96	BHL	P	CRAWLEY TOWN	218	1-2	Cambridge
04/04/96	E. Anglian	QF	Concord Rangers	50	0-1	
06/04/96	BHL	P	Rushden & Diamonds	2135	1-2	Cambridge
08/04/96	BHL	P	CHELMSFORD CITY	341	0-0	
13/04/96	BHL	P	Halesowen Town	952	1-2	Williams
20/04/96	BHL	P	WORCESTER CITY	243	4-2	Williams(2), Lockhart, Dolby
25/04/96	BHL	P	Gresley Rovers	483	2-2	Coe, Fallon
27/04/96	BHL	P	DORCHESTER TOWN	256	1-2	Coe
30/04/96	BHL	P	GRESLEY ROVERS	303	2-3	Lockhart, Cambridge
04/05/96	BHL	P	Atherstone United	865	2-2	Beattie, Williams

CHELMSFORD CITY

The Stadium, New Writtle Street, Chelmsford, CM2 0RP. Tel: 01245 353052

Secretary: David Gore c/o Club address

Press office: Steve Dorrington Tel: 01245 251667

Colours: All Claret   Nickname: Clarets

Capacity: 2,850 police limit   Seating: 500

Covered standing: 250   Clubhouse on ground: Yes

Record attendance: 16,807 v Colchester Utd Southern League 1949

Biggest win: 10-3 v Billericay Town Essex Senior Cup 1993

Biggest defeat: 2-10 v Barking FA Trophy 1978

Record appearances: Derek Tiffin 550 1950-1963

Record goalscorer in total: Tony Butcher 287 1957-71

Record goalscorer in one season: Syd Plunkett 40 league goals in 1949-50

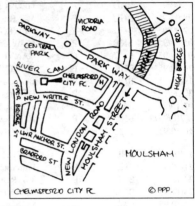

Record fee paid: £10,000 for Tony Rogers from Dover Ath in 1992

Record fee received: £20,000 for Ian Brown to Bristol City

HONOURS

Southern League 1946, 68, 72 and Southern Div 1989; War-time East 1940 and League Cup 1946, 60; Essex Pro Cup 1958, 70, 71, 74, 75; Essex Senior Cup 1986, 89, 92; East Anglian Cup 1949; Eastern Counties League 1947, 48, 49 and League Cup 1960; Eastern Floodlit League 1967, 75, 78, 82, 83, 87; League Cup 1973 and 1975; Metropolitan League and Pro Cup 1968.

Manager 1996-97: Roy McDonough   **Assistant Manager: Paul Roberts**

Chairman: Trevor Wright   **Vice Chairman: Don Walker**

City were formed on Nov 26th 1937, as a professional team and they immediately were accepted into the Southern League. There had been an amateur club in existence for 50 years before City, but they folded after playing at New Writtle Street since 1922. In the first season the club reached the 4th Round beating Darlington and Southampton before losing to Birmingham in front of 45,000 people. After the War the club was one of the top clubs in the country as many players preferred the financial rewards of the Southern League to the Football League's maximum wage, and they won the title in 1946, and were highly placed in the next five seasons. The success was at a heavy price, for the early fifties saw the club struggle to survive, although they rose again and in 1968 and 1972 were champions again.

However, more financial problems after saw the club merge with Brentwood Town, but it could not save the club from relegation.

The original Limited Company was wound up in 1980 and a new club Chelmsford City 1980 was formed and steady progress was made with promotion in 1986 but they were relegated again a year later only to bounce back again winning the league ahead of Gravesend. In 1992 a new board was appointed but finances got no better and in 1994 the company was wound up.

Strenuous efforts were made by supporters, players and new directors to save the club and with crowds of 1,000 or more, there is hope once again.

The club has won the Southern League Cup three times and has reached the FA Cup 1st and 2nd Rounds many times, once playing Ipswich Town in front of 15,000, the record being 16,807 for a League game with Colchester.

New Writtle Street once had a capacity of 18,000, which included a huge barn along the opposite side to the main stand, but a scheme to turn the pitch around saw it demolished and yet more financial problems has seen uncertainty in recent years. The ground was bought by the neighbouring County Cricket Club and City are hopeful of a move to a new ground to Conference standards.

CHELMSFORD CITY 1995/96 SEASON

Date	Comp	Round	Opponent	Att	Score	Scorers
19/08/95	BHL	P	Gloucester City	764	0-5	
21/08/95	BHL	P	RUSHDEN & DIAMONDS	1003	1-2	Garvey
26/08/95	BHL	P	ILKESTON TOWN	827	1-0	Garvey
28/08/95	BHL	P	Crawley Town	1146	2-3	Mayes, Garvey
02/09/95	BHL	P	Atherstone United	303	2-1	Keen, Bellingham
04/09/95	BHL	P	BALDOCK TOWN	902	0-2	
09/09/95	FA Cup	Q1	COLLIER ROW	991	1-0	Docking
16/09/95	BHL	P	Gresley Rovers	545	2-0	Docking, Garvey
19/09/95	BHL	P	Rushden & Diamonds	1747	1-2	Bellingham
23/09/95	FA Cup	Q2	Holbeach United	350	0-0	
25/09/95	FA Cup	Q2 rep	HOLBEACH UNITED	858	3-1	Keen, Bellingham(2)
30/09/95	BHL	P	HALESOWEN TOWN	1185	1-0	Bellingham
03/10/95	DMC	1(1)	Gravesend & Northfleet	386	1-3	Bird
07/10/95	FA Cup	Q3	BILLERICAY TOWN	2074	1-1	Davidson
10/10/95	FA Cup	Q3 rep	Billericay Town	1704	1-2	Hudson
14/10/95	BHL	P	V.S. Rugby	454	2-2	Bellingham, Hunter
21/10/95	BHL	P	GLOUCESTER CITY	804	1-1	Garvey
23/10/95	BHL	P	CRAWLEY TOWN	1149	0-0	
28/10/95	BHL	P	Dorchester Town	714	1-1	Greene
04/11/95	BHL	P	GRESLEY ROVERS	947	1-2	Heasman
11/11/95	BHL	P	ATHERSTONE UNITED	789	1-1	Keen
14/11/95	BHL	P	Baldock Town	282	1-2	Bellingham
18/11/95	BHL	P	Newport A.F.C.	896	2-1	Bellingham, Garvey
20/11/95	DMC	1(2)	GRAVESEND & NORTHFLEET	534	1-0	Garvey
25/11/95	FA Trophy	Q3	YEADING	828	2-1	Garvey, Kane
02/12/95	BHL	P	CAMBRIDGE CITY	853	0-0	
04/12/95	Essex SC	2	TILBURY	309	3-0	Garvey(2), Kane
09/12/95	BHL	P	Merthyr Tydfil	409	1-0	Keen
12/12/95	E. F'lit	Gp 2	Sawbridgeworth Town		6-1	
16/12/95	BHL	P	SUDBURY TOWN	771	2-1	Mansfield, Hunter
23/12/95	BHL	P	Burton Albion	652	1-1	Kane
01/01/96	BHL	P	Hastings Town	616	3-2	Moseley, Mayes(2)
06/01/96	BHL	P	Cheltenham Town	788	1-2	Mayes
09/01/96	Essex SC	3	Braintree Town	305	2-3	Keen, Davidson
13/01/96	BHL	P	STAFFORD RANGERS	990	1-0	Roberts
15/01/96	E. F'lit	Gp 2	SAWBRIDGEWORTH TOWN		0-0	
20/01/96	FA Trophy	1	NEWPORT A.F.C.	1130	0-1	
12/02/96	BHL	P	GRAVESEND & NORTHFLEET	618	6-1	Garvey(2), Mansfield, Davidson, Blewden(og), Mayes
14/02/96	E. F'lit	Gp 2	St Albans City		2-0	
17/02/96	BHL	P	Worcester City	743	0-0	
24/02/96	BHL	P	Sudbury Town	604	0-2	
27/02/96	Essex TST	2	Witham Town		1-2	
02/03/96	BHL	P	WORCESTER CITY	710	1-0	Garvey
04/03/96	BHL	P	DORCHESTER TOWN	552	2-2	Garvey, Keen
06/03/96	E. F'lit	Gp 2	ST ALBANS CITY		3-3	
09/03/96	BHL	P	Halesowen Town	693	0-3	
11/03/96	BHL	P	SALISBURY CITY	556	0-0	
16/03/96	BHL	P	CHELTENHAM TOWN	713	3-3	Keen(2), Lock
23/03/96	BHL	P	BURTON ALBION	755	0-0	
30/03/96	BHL	P	Salisbury City	355	0-0	
31/03/96	BHL	P	NEWPORT A.F.C.	804	0-0	
06/04/96	BHL	P	HASTINGS TOWN	648	0-3	
08/04/96	BHL	P	Cambridge City	341	0-0	
10/04/96	E. F'lit	QF	Clacton Town		1-3	
13/04/96	BHL	P	MERTHYR TYDFIL	715	1-4	Garvey
20/04/96	BHL	P	Stafford Rangers	460	0-3	
23/04/96	BHL	P	Ilkeston Town	592	1-1	Docking
27/04/96	BHL	P	Gravesend & Northfleet	670	1-0	Docking
04/05/96	BHL	P	V.S. RUGBY	722	3-0	Docking(3)

CHELTENHAM TOWN

Whaddon Road, Cheltenham, Glos. GL52 5NA. Tel: 01242 513397

Secretary: Reg Woodward 3 Harveys Lane, Winchcombe, Glos GL54 5QS Tel: 01242 602261

Colours: Red and White stripes

Nickname: Robins

Capacity: 5,000

Seating: 1,000

Covered standing: 3,000

Clubhouse on ground: Yes

Record attendance: 8,326 v Reading FA Cup 1st Rd 1956

Record appearances: Roger Thorndale 701 1958-76

Record goalscorer in total: Dave Lewis 290 1970-83

Record fee paid: £20,000 for Kim Casey from Kidderminster Harriers

Record fee received: £60,000 for Christer Warren to Southampton

HONOURS

Southern League 1985 and Midland Division 1983; League Cup 1958 and Championship Shield 1959; North Gloucestershire Pro Cup 30 times; Midland Floodlit Cup 1986, 1987, 1988.

Cheltenham Town FC were formed in 1892 and thus celebrated their centenary four years ago. Traditionally known as the Robins, they play at Whaddon Road, where they moved to from their previous home in Whaddon Lane. It was opened and owned by Cheltenham Original Brewers in 1927, and Town moved in having played Northern Senior League football at the old site, 200 yards away and now covered by a road. Previous to that and from the start, they used Carters Field.

They played in local Gloucestershire football from the early days until joining the Comb, and during the 30's they reached the First Round of the FA Cup for the first time.

Their growth as a club saw them accepted into the Southern League in 1935, but it was many years before they enjoyed any success, being runner up to Guildford City in 1956. Sadly 1962 saw the club relegated back to the First Division, but it was a fleeting visit as they returned to the Premier Division in 1965. They were fourth in 1968, just four points behind, but a year on they were again relegated by .002 of a goal, enduring the added heartache of losing the League Cup final to Cambridge United.

After two poor seasons the league was regionalised and in Division One North they were third three years in a row and eventually went up in 1977 as runners up to Worcester City. Further re-structuring took place in 1980 which saw Town in the Midland Division, which they won by a point over Sutton Coldfield in 1983.

In 1985 their long association with the league finished for a while when they won the title and moved into the Alliance Premier, clinching it on the last day in front of 1,200 people at Whaddon Road.

They had seven years at the top before losing their place in 1992, and since then they have gone close with three runners up spots, Dover Athletic, Farnborough Town and Hednesford Town denying the Robins a return.

CHELTENHAM TOWN 1995/96 SEASON

Date	Comp	Round	Opponent	Att	Score	Scorers
19/08/95	BHL	P	Crawley Town	917	1-4	Tucker
22/08/95	BHL	P	DORCHESTER TOWN	624	3-0	Howells, Smith(2)
26/08/95	BHL	P	V.S. RUGBY	730	4-0	Howells, Eaton, Smith, Tucker
28/08/95	BHL	P	Halesowen Town	843	1-0	Eaton
02/09/95	BHL	P	Worcester City	1212	2-1	Licata(2)
05/09/95	BHL	P	ILKESTON TOWN	788	4-0	Tucker, Eaton, Wring, Howell
09/09/95	FA Cup	Q1	YATE TOWN	659	5-0	Tucker, Smith(2), Howell, Boyle
16/09/95	BHL	P	Atherstone United	402	2-1	Smith(2)
19/09/95	BHL	P	Dorchester Town	689	0-4	
23/09/95	FA Cup	Q2	Forest Green Rovers	544	0-3	
30/09/95	BHL	P	RUSHDEN & DIAMONDS	1122	0-2	
03/10/95	DMC	1(1)	Weston-super-Mare	195	2-1	Barton(og), Eaton
07/10/95	BHL	P	GRESLEY ROVERS	607	2-0	Smith(2)
14/10/95	BHL	P	Cambridge City	289	2-1	Smith(2)
17/10/95	DMC	1(2)	WESTON-SUPER-MARE	211	4-2	Smith(2), Jones, Licata
24/10/95	BHL	P	HALESOWEN TOWN	534	2-2	Wring, Eaton
28/10/95	BHL	P	Salisbury City	547	3-3	Smith, Eaton, Wright
31/10/95	Glos NSC	SF	YATE TOWN	131	2-0	Smith, Howell
04/11/95	BHL	P	CAMBRIDGE CITY	764	2-3	Wright, Smith
11/11/95	BHL	P	NEWPORT A.F.C.	1092	2-0	Wring, Smith
14/11/95	BHL	P	Ilkeston Town	610	4-1	Eaton(2), Smith, Howells
18/11/95	BHL	P	Sudbury Town	349	4-3	Banks, Wright, Eaton(2)
25/11/95	BHL	P	CRAWLEY TOWN	715	1-1	Eaton
02/12/95	BHL	P	Gresley Rovers	662	2-0	Eaton, Smith
05/12/95	DMC	2	GLOUCESTER CITY	551	4-0	Chenoweth, Wright, Smith(2)
09/12/95	BHL	P	BALDOCK TOWN	751	3-1	Wring, Smith, Eaton
16/12/95	BHL	P	WORCESTER CITY	1010	1-3	Chenoweth
23/12/95	BHL	P	Hastings Town	523	1-4	Wring
06/01/96	BHL	P	CHELMSFORD CITY	788	2-1	Wright, Eaton
09/01/96	DMC	3	GRESLEY ROVERS	308	3-3	Banks, Smith, Wring
13/01/96	BHL	P	Gravesend & Northfleet	884	0-1	
20/01/96	FA Trophy	1	Dover Athletic	904	2-2	Wring(2)
23/01/96	FA Trophy	1 rep	DOVER ATHLETIC	640	1-1	Banks
31/01/96	FA Trophy	1 rep(2)	Dover Athletic	598	0-1	
03/02/96	BHL	P	ATHERSTONE UNITED	516	1-1	Eaton
17/02/96	BHL	P	Rushden & Diamonds	2472	1-4	Elsey
24/02/96	BHL	P	Baldock Town	283	1-1	Wring
27/02/96	BHL	P	GLOUCESTER CITY	1010	0-0	
02/03/96	BHL	P	GRAVESEND & NORTHFLEET	549	0-0	
05/03/96	DMC	3 rep	Gresley Rovers	407	2-2	Smith, Dunphy
09/03/96	BHL	P	BURTON ALBION	608	1-0	Freeman
16/03/96	BHL	P	Chelmsford City	713	3-3	Eaton, Wright, Smith
18/03/96	BHL	P	Newport A.F.C.	646	3-2	Wring, Smith(2)
23/03/96	BHL	P	HASTINGS TOWN	608	1-2	Eaton
26/03/96	BHL	P	Merthyr Tydfil	277	1-0	Eaton
30/03/96	BHL	P	Stafford Rangers	654	1-0	Eaton
02/04/96	Glos NSC	F	GLOUCESTER CITY	437	0-0	(Won 3-1 on penalties)
06/04/96	BHL	P	MERTHYR TYDFIL	603	1-0	Wring
08/04/96	BHL	P	Gloucester City	1523	3-0	Eaton(2), Elsey
13/04/96	BHL	P	SUDBURY TOWN	602	1-1	Chenoweth
16/04/96	BHL	P	STAFFORD RANGERS	425	4-0	Smith(2), Banks, Chenoweth
20/04/96	BHL	P	Burton Albion	532	2-3	Banks, Eaton
27/04/96	BHL	P	V.S. Rugby	291	1-1	Wright
04/05/96	BHL	P	SALISBURY CITY	548	3-3	Smith, Eaton(2)

CRAWLEY TOWN

Town Mead, Ifield Avenue, West Green, Crawley, Sussex. Tel: 01293 410000

Secretary: Stan Markham, 105 Winchester Rd, Tilgate, Crawley, Sussex RH10 5HW. Tel: 01293 522371

Nickname: Red Devils   Colours: Red and White

Capacity: 4,750   Seating: 400

Covered standing: 1,400   Clubhouse on ground: Yes

Record attendance: 4,104 v Barnet FA Cup Round 2 December 4th 1993

Biggest win: 10-0 v Chichester United Sussex County League Div 2 December 17th 1955

Biggest defeat: 0-10 v Dartford (H) Mid-Surrey Professional Floodlit League April 8th 1985

Record appearance holder: John Maggs 652 from 1963-73 and 1975-1979

Record goalscorer in one season: Terry Robbins 51 in 1985-86

Record goalscorer in aggregate: Phil Basey 108 1968-72

Record fee received: £50,000 for Craig Whittington from Scarborough 1993

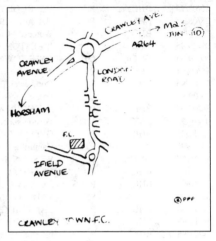

HONOURS

Sussex Senior Cup 1990 and 1991; Sussex Intermediate Cup 1928; Sussex Professional Cup 1970; Sussex Floodlit Cup 1991, 1992, 1993; Gilbert Rice Floodlit Cup 1980 and 1984; Southern Counties Comb Floodlit Cup 1986; Metropolitan League Cup 1959; Mid-Sussex Senior Cup 1903; Montgomery Cup 1926.

Manager for 1996/97: Dave Haining   **Assistant Manager: Gary Brown**

Chairman: John Maggs

Crawley Town were formed 100 years ago and played for the first half century in local football. They have had at least three home grounds, playing at Malthouse Farm until the Great War, before moving to Victoria Hall and the Rectory Fields between the Wars. Yetmans Field was home for the first seven years following the resumption until moving to Town Mead in 1952. Malthouse Farm stood roughly a mile south-east of the current ground on the other side of the railway, but Victoria Hall was much nearer, around 200 yards away. Yetmans Field was behind the old bus garage in Northgate.

Town joined the Sussex County League in 1951, relegation coming four years later, but having returned to Div 1 as runners-up the committee took the club into the Metropolitan League, which catered for amateur and professional sides. Still staying amateur they won the League Cup in 1959 and lost in the County Cup Final to Worthing. They went professional in 1962 and moved to the Southern League in the following year, only tasting Premier Division football briefly in 1969-70 before dropping back, but in 1984 they finished runners-up to the short-lived RS Southampton and thus returned to the Premier Division.

The 93 and 94 seasons saw Crawley challenging for the title, finishing fifth and then sixth, which have been the nearest they have come. There has been other cup successes, with the Professional Cup won in 1970, when they beat Brighton and Hove Albion, the Gilbert Rice Floodlit Cup twice, the Southern Counties Floodlight Cup in 1986 and the Sussex Senior Cup twice, and twice runners up.

The 70's saw success in the FA Cup, reaching the First Round twice but all that had gone before paled when in 1991-92 the Reds reached the Third Round, attracting a gate of over 18,000 to the Goldstone Ground. There had already been considerable income from earlier rounds, as 2,208 and 3,427 saw the two matches with Horsham, whereas 3,370 and over 4,000 saw the matches with Northampton and Hayes. Finances gained from that season enabled the club to press ahead with many ground improvements to gear themselves for the Conference, despite persistent talk of a move to a purpose built out of town ground.

CRAWLEY TOWN 1995/96 SEASON

Date	Comp	Round	Opponent	Att	Score	Scorers
19/08/95	BHL	P	CHELTENHAM TOWN	917	4-1	Sakala(2), Dineen, Hudson
22/08/95	BHL	P	Sudbury Town	370	2-1	Sakala, Dineen
26/08/95	BHL	P	Rushden & Diamonds	1661	1-3	Sakala
28/08/95	BHL	P	CHELMSFORD CITY	1146	3-2	Meade, Jeffery, Geddes
02/09/95	BHL	P	Burton Albion	950	1-2	Speedie
05/09/95	BHL	P	SALISBURY CITY	722	2-0	Meade(2)
16/09/95	BHL	P	Baldock Town	401	0-0	
19/09/95	BHL	P	SUDBURY TOWN	822	2-2	Meade, Mockler
23/09/95	BHL	P	WORCESTER CITY	1004	1-3	Speedie
30/09/95	BHL	P	Dorchester Town	709	1-3	Speedie
03/10/95	DMC	1(1)	HASTINGS TOWN	425	1-1	Speedie
07/10/95	BHL	P	GLOUCESTER CITY	855	0-0	
14/10/95	FA Trophy	Q1	Barton Rovers	331	3-1	Speedie, Meade, McNally(og)
21/10/95	FA Cup	Q4	Sutton United	1637	1-4	Pates
23/10/95	BHL	P	Chelmsford City	1149	0-0	
28/10/95	BHL	P	NEWPORT A.F.C.	853	0-0	
31/10/95	DMC	1(2)	Hastings Town	328	3-1	Meade, Geddes
04/11/95	FA Trophy	Q2	BASHLEY	609	0-1	
11/11/95	BHL	P	Worcester City	887	0-2	
18/11/95	BHL	P	ILKESTON TOWN	618	1-0	Clark
21/11/95	Sussex SC	2	Lancing	179	4-0	Speedie(2), Cheal(og), Sakala
25/11/95	BHL	P	Cheltenham Town	715	1-1	Speedie
02/12/95	BHL	P	RUSHDEN & DIAMONDS	1118	2-2	Hudson, Speedie
09/12/95	BHL	P	Atherstone United	244	1-2	M Albrighton(og)
19/12/95	DMC	2	Gravesend & Northfleet	189	2-1	Meade(2)
26/12/95	BHL	P	HASTINGS TOWN	757	3-2	Sakala, Meade, Ford
01/01/96	BHL	P	Gravesend & Northfleet	633	1-3	Lester
06/01/96	BHL	P	BURTON ALBION	657	1-1	Meade
10/01/96	Sussex SC	3	Selsey	250	3-1	Meade(2), Sakala
13/01/96	BHL	P	Newport A.F.C.	827	1-1	Meade
16/01/96	DMC	3	TONBRIDGE ANGELS	289	3-0	Shepstone, Speedie, Sakala
20/01/96	BHL	P	Salisbury City	272	1-2	Smith
23/01/96	BHL	P	CAMBRIDGE CITY	343	3-3	Meade(2), Sakala
30/01/96	DMC	QF	BALDOCK TOWN	237	2-2	Meade, Speedie
03/02/96	BHL	P	Gloucester City	606	1-1	Speedie
05/02/96	Sussex SC	QF	Worthing	314	4-1	Meade, Jeffery, Hudson, Gamble(og)
10/02/96	BHL	P	Halesowen Town	681	0-2	
17/02/96	BHL	P	BALDOCK TOWN	546	1-2	Hudson
24/02/96	BHL	P	Stafford Rangers	679	0-3	
27/02/96	DMC	QF rep	Baldock Town	107	1-1	Ford
09/03/96	BHL	P	Ilkeston Town	547	4-1	Restarick, Theodosiou(2), Meade
12/03/96	Sussex SC	SF	WICK	236	4-1	Meade(2), Restarick, Ford
23/03/96	BHL	P	V.S. RUGBY	671	3-1	Restarick(2), Kruszynski
26/03/96	BHL	P	GRESLEY ROVERS	437	2-0	Rogers, Restarick
30/03/96	BHL	P	Cambridge City	218	2-1	Geddes, Restarick
01/04/96	BHL	P	DORCHESTER TOWN	601	1-1	Restarick
06/04/96	BHL	P	GRAVESEND & NORTHFLEET	843	1-0	Geddes
08/04/96	BHL	P	Hastings Town	713	1-0	Geddes
13/04/96	BHL	P	STAFFORD RANGERS	740	2-1	Rogers, Restarick
16/04/96	BHL	P	MERTHYR TYDFIL	534	1-0	Geddes
20/04/96	BHL	P	Merthyr Tydfil	404	1-1	Geddes
24/04/96	BHL	P	V.S. Rugby	220	4-1	Restarick(2), Geddes, Sakala
27/04/96	BHL	P	ATHERSTONE UNITED	732	0-1	
30/04/96	BHL	P	HALESOWEN TOWN	802	1-3	Theodosiou
04/05/96	BHL	P	Gresley Rovers	611	0-1	
06/05/96	Sussex SC	F	HASTINGS TOWN	1153	0-1	(played at Worthing FC)

DORCHESTER TOWN

Avenue Stadium, Weymouth Ave, Dorchester, DT1 2RYTel: 01305 262451

Secretary: Albert Miller, 29 Shaston Crescent, Dorchester DT1 2EB Tel 01305 264843

Nickname: The Magpies

Capacity: 7,210

Seating: 710

Covered standing: 4,000

Clubhouse on ground: Yes

DIRECTIONS

At junction of southern bypass (A35) and Weymouth Road (A354).

Record attendance:4,000 v Chelsea Ground Opening. At old ground 5,500 v York City FA Cup 2nd Rd 1954 and competitive at new ground 3,027 v Weymouth Southern League Boxing Day 1992

Biggest win: 7-0 Canterbury (A) Southern League 1986-87

Biggest defeat: 0-6 several occasions

Record appearances: Trevor Townsend 377

Record goalscorer in one season: Dennis Cheney 61

Record fee paid: £12,000 for Chris Townsend from Gloucester City in 1990

Record fee received: £35,000 for Trevor Senior from Portsmouth in 1981

HONOURS

Southern League Cup 1987

Western League 1955

Dorset Senior Cup 1951, 1961, 1968, 1969, 1972, 1994

Dorset League 1938

Founded in 1880, Dorchester Town Football Club participated in the Dorset League from 1896 to 1947, before joining the Western League Division Two in 1947, winning promotion in 1950 and the championship in 1955. The Magpies won the Dorset League in 1938 to claim their first major trophy and it was not until 1950, when the promotion team also won the Senior Cup, that more honours came their way.

After joining the Southern League the early years were a struggle. They first tasted success when finishing runners-up to Margate in Division 1 South, but following the formation of the Alliance Premier League they ended up back in the re-formed Southern Division.

Their centenary was celebrated by winning Division One South in 1980 by a point from Aylesbury, but again went down in 1984 amidst a severe financial crisis, only to bounce back as Champions in 1987. For most of the time back in the Premier they have been mid-table, and a final position of 13th last May was little different.

Dorchester originally played on the Recreation Ground just a few hundred yards back up the road, until moving next door in 1929. A railway coach was pressed into action for changing until a pavilion was built, followed by a wooden stand in 1930. The whole site was owned by the Duchy of Cornwall who resisted temptation to sell the freehold, and insisted that any deals went through them. Thus when Tesco supermarkets took over the site of the football ground, Dorchester Town moved next door to the site of the rugby ground, and that club relocated to Coburg Park. What transpired was one of the very best new non-League football Grounds anywhere in the country.

DORCHESTER TOWN 1995/96 SEASON

Date	Comp	Round	Opponent	Att	Score	Scorers
19/08/95	BHL	P	ATHERSTONE UNITED	604	0-1	
22/08/95	BHL	P	Cheltenham Town	624	0-3	
26/08/95	BHL	P	Baldock Town	281	1-2	Pickard
28/08/95	BHL	P	NEWPORT A.F.C.	944	0-3	
02/09/95	BHL	P	Ilkeston Town	654	0-1	
05/09/95	BHL	P	MERTHYR TYDFIL	502	7-1	Richardson, Gater, Pickard(3), Wilkinson, Killick
09/09/95	FA Cup	Q1	WIMBORNE TOWN	764	2-2	Killick, Reeve
12/09/95	FA Cup	Q1 rep	Wimborne Town	604	2-0	Pickard(2)
16/09/95	BHL	P	Hastings Town	466	1-1	Pickard
19/09/95	BHL	P	CHELTENHAM TOWN	689	4-0	Richardson, Killick(2), Kilgour
23/09/95	FA Cup	Q2	BASINGSTOKE TOWN	609	2-0	Pickard(2)
30/09/95	BHL	P	CRAWLEY TOWN	709	3-1	Pickard, Killick, Richardson
03/10/95	DMC	1(1)	HAVANT TOWN	302	1-0	Killick
07/10/95	FA Cup	Q3	Weymouth	2527	3-2	Pickard(3)
14/10/95	BHL	P	Stafford Rangers	382	3-0	Pickard, Wilkinson, Kilgour
21/10/95	FA Cup	Q4	Sittingbourne	1232	2-1	Evans, Pickard
25/10/95	BHL	P	Newport A.F.C.	1077	2-3	Killick, Wilkinson
28/10/95	BHL	P	CHELMSFORD CITY	714	1-1	Pickard
31/10/95	DMC	1(2)	Havant Town	65	1-0	Pickard
04/11/95	Dorset	2	STURMINSTER NEWTON UTD	308	10-0	Pickard(5), Tallon, Wilkinson, Taylor, Reeves
11/11/95	FA Cup	1	Oxford United	3819	1-9	Killick
14/11/95	BHL	P	Merthyr Tydfil	222	1-3	Evans
18/11/95	BHL	P	Atherstone United	222	4-3	Taylor, Richardson, Pickard(2)
25/11/95	FA Trophy	Q3	HAYES	515	2-3	Pickard, Kilgour
28/11/95	Dorset	QF	Weymouth	987	2-0	Pickard(2)
02/12/95	BHL	P	BALDOCK TOWN	560	1-2	Kilgour
06/12/95	DMC	2	Salisbury City	145	1-2	Taylor
09/12/95	BHL	P	RUSHDEN & DIAMONDS	684	1-1	Pickard
16/12/95	BHL	P	Halesowen Town	534	0-1	
26/12/95	BHL	P	SALISBURY CITY	1032	0-2	
30/12/95	BHL	P	GRAVESEND & NORTHFLEET	607	2-2	Reeve, Lamb(og)
06/01/96	BHL	P	HASTINGS TOWN	510	1-4	Killick
13/01/96	BHL	P	Sudbury Town	344	1-2	Reeve
10/02/96	BHL	P	V.S. RUGBY	660	4-0	Richardson, Wilkinson, Pickard, Killick
17/02/96	BHL	P	Gresley Rovers	640	2-0	Pickard, Cooper
24/02/96	BHL	P	ILKESTON TOWN	755	3-0	Tallon(2), Evans
27/02/96	BHL	P	Burton Albion	458	0-1	
02/03/96	Dorset	SF	BOURNEMOUTH SPORTS	272	0-0	
04/03/96	BHL	P	Chelmsford City	552	2-2	Reeves, Tallon
09/03/96	Dorset	SF rep	Bournemouth Sports	283	2-2	Reeves, Sullivan
12/03/96	BHL	P	CAMBRIDGE CITY	300	1-2	Morgan
16/03/96	Dorset	SF rep(2)	Bournemouth Sports	200	1-0	Pickard
19/03/96	BHL	P	SUDBURY TOWN	408	2-0	Richardson, Killick
23/03/96	BHL	P	WORCESTER CITY	705	1-2	Pickard
26/03/96	BHL	P	HALESOWEN TOWN	454	0-0	
30/03/96	BHL	P	Gravesend & Northfleet	427	1-4	Wilkinson
01/04/96	BHL	P	Crawley Town	601	1-1	Killick
04/04/96	BHL	P	Rushden & Diamonds	1823	1-0	Killick
06/04/96	BHL	P	GLOUCESTER CITY	770	0-1	
08/04/96	BHL	P	Salisbury City	422	0-1	
13/04/96	BHL	P	BURTON ALBION	647	2-1	Richardson, Pickard
15/04/96	BHL	P	Worcester City	537	1-0	Wilkinson
16/04/96	Dorset	F	St Pauls (Jersey)	362	3-1	Pickard(2), Evans (at Wimbourne Town)
20/04/96	BHL	P	V.S. Rugby	277	0-0	
23/04/96	BHL	P	GRESLEY ROVERS	536	2-1	Pickard, Tallon
27/04/96	BHL	P	Cambridge City	256	2-1	Pickard, Killick
30/04/96	BHL	P	Gloucester City	523	0-1	
04/05/96	BHL	P	STAFFORD RANGERS	688	4-2	Killick, Sullivan(2), Richardson

GLOUCESTER CITY

Meadow Park, Sudmeadow Park, Hempsted, Gloucester GL2 6HS. Tel: 01452 523883

Secretary: Ken Turner, 24 Ladysmith Rd, Cheltenham, Glos GL52 5LQ
Tel 01242 522514

Nickname: The Tigers   Colours: Yellow and black

Capacity: 5,000   Seating: 560

Covered standing: 2,000   Clubhouse on ground: Yes

Record attendance: At Longlevens: 10,500 v Tottenham Hotspur 1952 and at
Meadow Park, 3,952 v Arsenal July 1987

Record appearances: Stan Myers and Frank Tredgett in the 50's

Record goalscorer in aggregate: Reg Weaver 250

HONOURS

Southern League Cup 1956; Southern League Midland Division 1989; Glos Northern Sen Lge 1934;
Gloucester Professional Cup 1938, 50, 51, 52, 53, 54, 55, 56, 57, 58, 66, 69, 71, 75, 79, 80, 82, 83, 84, 91, 93

Manager for 1996-97: Leroy Rosenior   **Chairman: Keith Gardner**

The Gloucester Journal reported in March 1883 that an Association Football Club had been formed in the city.
However, the club's first recorded match was against Eastville Rovers on Jan 2nd 1886, when Gloucester lost
1-0 in Bristol. On October 5th 1889 Gloucester were beaten by Clifton 6-0 with that match refereed by none
other than WG Grace. In 1893 the club entered the Bristol and District League (subsequently the Western
League), but withdrew with financial problems before moving to the Gloucester and District League where
they were champions. They remained there, changing their name to Gloucester City in 1902, until 1906, when
they were reconstituted and moved to the North Gloucestershire League. After the Great War many players
attached themselves to the YMCA club which had been founded in 1910. In fact to many they were City under
another name, and indeed after being founder members of the Gloucestershire Northern Senior League in 1920,
five years later they were called Gloucester City. They were runners up in the first season and became
champions eight years later, having previously won the Northern Senior Cup.

1935 saw City turn professional and enter the strong Birmingham Combination, taking over the Longlevens
Ground, and they stayed for four years, until the War saw them enter the restricted Southern League. They
rejoined after the War and have been members ever since. Success was sporadic with a League Cup win in
1956 following a spell of three seasons in the First Round of the FA Cup, and after moving to Horton Road in
1964, lean years came, until 1982 when promotion to the Premier Division came, with relegation soon to
follow. The move to their current Meadow Park home coincided with an upturn in fortunes as they were
promoted once again and two years later they came within a whisker of making it to the Conference only to be
denied late on the last day

FORMER GROUNDS: Gloucester have had a number of well established grounds in their history, although the
early homes are vague. It is known that the Budding Field was home until 1895, with the Avenue Ground off
Tuffley Road also used for a while, the two being used on and off for another 20 years, as was the Co-Op
ground in India Road. From 1925 City were at the Avenue again for two years until moving to a field in
Sutgrove, which had two entrances and could accommodate large crowds. There was a stand and dressing
rooms with work beginning on a second stand when problems arose and soon they were away again, this time
to the Bon Marche ground in Estcourt Road, with the old stand and a much larger pavilion going up with
changing rooms. After turning pro a new field was bought in Longlevens, which developed into a ground
ample enough to hold 10,000, with two stands and banked wooden terracing, floodlights being installed in
1952. Its out of town site caused problems however, as did the lack of parking and it was sold for housing in
1960, with a 14 acre site in Horton Road being purchased.

A lack of support for City at the time meant that the original plans for Horton Road were never fulfilled and
the ground remained virtually unchanged for its existence, until once again, housing needs overtook it and,
with it already looking run down and with severe drainage problems, it was sold and work began at
Sudmeadow Road in 1979.

GLOUCESTER CITY 1995/96 SEASON

Date	Comp	Rnd	Opponent	Att	Score	Scorers
19/08/95	BHL	P	CHELMSFORD CITY	764	5-0	Rouse, Adebowale, Knight, Holmes, Hallam
23/08/95	BHL	P	Newport A.F.C.	1524	0-1	
26/08/95	BHL	P	Cambridge City	342	4-0	Adebowale, Knight, Portway, Hallam
28/08/95	BHL	P	SALISBURY CITY	1576	2-0	Portway, Kemp
02/09/95	BHL	P	GRAVESEND & NORTHFLEET	851	3-1	Holmes(2), Knight
05/09/95	BHL	P	Halesowen Town	678	1-2	Knight
09/09/95	FA Cup	Q1	BRISTOL MANOR FARM	514	8-0	Portway(2), Adebowale, Webb, Rouse, Warner, Adams, Knight
16/09/95	BHL	P	BURTON ALBION	867	2-1	Adebowale, Holmes
19/09/95	BHL	P	NEWPORT A.F.C.	1412	1-1	Knight
23/09/95	FA Cup	Q2	CINDERFORD TOWN	921	0-1	
30/09/95	BHL	P	Sudbury Town	421	2-0	Holmes, Knight
03/10/95	Glos NSC	1	Forest Green Rovers	215	2-1	Holmes, Adebowale
07/10/95	BHL	P	Crawley Town	855	0-0	
10/10/95	DMC	1(1)	Witney Town	177	0-1	
14/10/95	BHL	P	WORCESTER CITY	1285	2-1	Adebowale, Hallam
17/10/95	DMC	1(2)	WITNEY TOWN	276	3-0	Holmes, Hallam(2)
21/10/95	BHL	P	Chelmsford City	804	1-1	Milsom
25/10/95	BHL	P	Salisbury City	483	3-3	Milsom(2), Phillips
28/10/95	BHL	P	HASTINGS TOWN	712	0-2	
31/10/95	Glos NSC	SF	CINDERFORD TOWN	296	2-0	Hallam, Milsom
04/11/95	BHL	P	Ilkeston Town	751	2-1	Kemp, Phillips
11/11/95	BHL	P	Stafford Rangers	324	4-3	Webb, Holmes, Phillips, Milsom
14/11/95	BHL	P	HALESOWEN TOWN	578	0-2	
18/11/95	BHL	P	BALDOCK TOWN	584	3-1	Holmes, Milsom(2)
25/11/95	FA Trophy	Q3	ALDERSHOT TOWN	1041	5-1	Milsom, Holmes(2), Adebowale, Webb
02/12/95	BHL	P	Worcester City	1109	3-1	Benton(og), Hallam, Webb
05/12/95	DMC	2	Cheltenham Town	551	0-4	
09/12/95	BHL	P	CAMBRIDGE CITY	666	3-1	Phillips(2), Knight
12/12/95	BHL	P	Rushden & Diamonds	1666	2-3	Milsom, Adebowale
23/12/95	BHL	P	ATHERSTONE UNITED	615	1-2	
06/01/96	BHL	P	V.S. Rugby	446	2-1	Rouse, Hallam
13/01/96	BHL	P	MERTHYR TYDFIL	781	3-1	Webb, Hallam(2)
20/01/96	FA Trophy	1	STAINES TOWN	748	5-0	Hallam(2), Phillips, Knight, Portway
03/02/96	BHL	P	CRAWLEY TOWN	606	1-1	Hallam
15/02/96	FA Trophy	2	Sudbury Town	262	1-3	Hallam
20/02/96	Glos NSC	SF rematch	CINDERFORD TOWN	246	3-2	Adebowale, C Smith(og), Hallam
24/02/96	BHL	P	Burton Albion	672	0-1	
27/02/96	BHL	P	Cheltenham Town	1010	0-0	
02/03/96	BHL	P	V.S. RUGBY	509	1-1	Holmes
09/03/96	BHL	P	Merthyr Tydfil	456	0-1	
12/03/96	BHL	P	STAFFORD RANGERS	435	3-2	Webb, Milsom, Adebowale
16/03/96	BHL	P	SUDBURY TOWN	509	1-0	Webb
19/03/96	BHL	P	Gresley Rovers	511	0-1	
23/03/96	BHL	P	Atherstone United	284	1-2	Milsom
26/03/96	BHL	P	Gravesend & Northfleet	383	0-0	
30/03/96	BHL	P	GRESLEY ROVERS	613	1-2	Holloway
02/04/96	Glos NSC	F	Cheltenham Town	437	0-0	(Lost 1-3 on penalties)
06/04/96	BHL	P	Dorchester Town	770	1-0	Vernon
08/04/96	BHL	P	CHELTENHAM TOWN	1523	0-3	
13/04/96	BHL	P	Baldock Town	261	1-0	Black
20/04/96	BHL	P	RUSHDEN & DIAMONDS	1226	2-1	Mardenborough, Milsom
27/04/96	BHL	P	ILKESTON TOWN	607	3-1	Kemp, Howell, Holloway
30/04/96	BHL	P	DORCHESTER TOWN	523	1-0	Black
04/05/96	BHL	P	Hastings Town	504	0-2	

GRAVESEND AND NORTHFLEET

Stonebridge Road, Northfleet, Kent DA11 9BA. Tel: 01474 363424

Secretary Bill Hornby c/o Football Club

PR Director/Press Secretary/Programme Editor Lionel RH Ball
Tel: 01474 569985

Nickname: Fleet   Capacity: 3,000   Seating: 400

Covered Standing: 2,200   Clubhouse on ground: Yes

Record attendance: 12,036 v Sunderland FA Cup 4th Rd 1963

Biggest win: 8-1 v Clacton Southern League 1962-63

Biggest defeat: 0-9 v Trowbridge Town Southern League 1991-92

Record appearances: Ken Burrett 537

Record goalscorer in one season: Steve Portway 62 in 1992-93

Record goalscorer in aggregate: Bert Hawkins

Record fee paid: £8,000 for Richard Newbery from Wokingham in 1996

Record fee received: £!7,500 from Gloucester City for Steve Portway in 1994

DIRECTIONS

From A2 take Northfleet/Southfleet exit (B262), follow to Northfleet then B2175 (Springhead Road) to junction with A226, turn left (The Hill, Northfleet), road becomes Stonebridge Road, ground is on right at bottom of steep hill after 1 mile - car parking behind for 400-500 cars. 2 mins walk from Northfleet BR station.

HONOURS

Southern League 1958; Southern Division 1975 and 1995; League Cup 1978; Championship Cup 1978; Kent Senior Cup 1949, 1953, 1981.

Manager for 1996/97: Steve Lovell

Chairman: Lionel GF Ball   **Vice Chairman: David Stevens**

Gravesend and Northfleet have commemorated their 50 years with an Official Golden Jubilee Book, priced at £9.99 + £1.50pp. 128 pages with over 100 photos from 1946 to the present day. Also available is `Fleet's Great FA Cup Adventure' video covering the 1996 FA Cup exploits including interviews and coverage of Cinderford Town match Price £9.99 +£1.50p

The club was formed in 1946, but for nearly 60 years previous the two towns had been amongst the leaders of Kent football. Northfleet United was formed in 1890 and Gravesend United three years later and there was always great rivalry between the two in the early days when they were both in the Southern League. If the two clubs had combined then, they must surely have reached the Football League, but they remained separate and diluted their strength. When World War Two ended, Northfleet were a spent force, as their benefactor and guiding light, Mr Lingham, had died and all they had left was the excellent Stonebridge Road ground. Gravesend United were still playing and it was agreed that the two clubs should merge and play in the Southern League in the old red and white of Northfleet.

The new club was ambitious and named a succession of ex-Internationals to manage the team, including Lionel Smith of Arsenal, Waford and England. It was he who steered Fleet to the Southern League title in 1958, only just missing out on the league and Cup double. Before this, Fleet had become the first Kent club to install floodlights in 1954, which enabled them to play a number of prestige friendlies against Foreign and Football League sides. Smith's five year reign came to an end in 1960 and this brought a downturn in the club's fortunes. Eventually relegation came in 1964, although the club had consolation in a record-breaking FA Cup run. It began with a first qualifying round win over Chatham Town on September 8th and continued until February 18th with a defeat by Sunderland in a fourth round replay. The Fleet's five month ten day Cup run, extended by the big freeze, still stands as a record. It took eight seasons before they returned to the Premier Division, but relegation followed after one season due to the promotion side breaking up. Things looked up again when Tony Sitford became manager in 1974. They won the Championship that season and the League Cup in 1978, becoming a founder member of the Alliance Premier League in 1979, finishing fifth. Two years on the Kent Senior Cup was won for only the third time. It was not long before fortunes turned sour again. Sitford left after a dispute with Chairman Roger Easterby and relegation and near bankruptcy followed. Lionel Ball took over the club and the massive debts were slowly cleared, although relegation to the Southern Division came in 1986 and it took three years before they returned. 1990-91 started poorly but the club ended by reaching the final of the Senior Cup and gaining promotion, although once again in 1992 they were back down. 1992-93 saw a better season as the club regrouped and the following year saw the Southern Division title won and the FA Cup 1st Round reached.

The current season is the club's Golden Jubilee and the famous FA Cup run which ended at Aston Villa has made it one to remember, with over 7,000 Fleet fans travelling for a carnival day.

Significant steps have been made to secure the future of the ground thanks to the support of the council and the granting of a ten year lease is hoped for. When Northfleet first played on Stonebridge Road, it was described as "a nice little plot of level ground". It had a 7ft fence, changing rooms, a tea bar and a small shelter and was opened in time for the first game against East Ham on September 2nd 1905. From those humble beginnings, the ground has survived two Wars and is widely thought to be one of the classic unspoiled football grounds of the non-League world.

GRAVESEND AND NORTHFLEET 1995/96 SEASON

Date	Comp	Rd	Opponent	Att	Score	Scorers
19/08/95	BHL	P	GRESLEY ROVERS	527	1-1	Cotter
22/08/95	BHL	P	Hastings Town	584	3-1	Cotter, Best, Munday
26/08/95	BHL	P	Atherstone United	286	0-2	
28/08/95	BHL	P	SUDBURY TOWN	536	3-3	Munday, Blewden, Lamb
02/09/95	BHL	P	Gloucester City	851	1-3	Powell
05/09/95	BHL	P	CAMBRIDGE CITY	471	2-0	Cotter(2)
09/09/95	FA Cup	Q1	GODALMING & GUILDFORD	443	7-0	Munday(2), Powell(2), Mortley, Cotter, Thomas
16/09/95	BHL	P	V.S. Rugby	384	1-0	Munday
19/09/95	BHL	P	HASTINGS TOWN	500	4-0	Munday, Mortley, Powell
23/09/95	FA Cup	Q2	Molesey	295	6-0	Powell(2), Jackson, Munday(3)
30/09/95	BHL	P	Salisbury City	425	0-2	
03/10/95	DMC	1(1)	CHELMSFORD CITY	386	3-1	Gooding, Munday, Cotter
07/10/95	FA Cup	Q3	CARSHALTON ATHLETIC	685	2-1	Lamb, Mortley
14/10/95	BHL	P	ILKESTON TOWN	595	3-1	Munday, Powell, Clark(og)
17/10/95	BHL	P	Sudbury Town	411	3-5	Munday(2), Cotter
21/10/95	FA Cup	Q4	MARLOW	814	1-1	Munday
24/10/95	FA Cup	Q4 rep	Marlow	814	3-3	Powell, Lamb, Blewden
28/10/95	BHL	P	BURTON ALBION	609	1-2	Cotter
30/10/95	FA Cup	Q4 rep(2)	MARLOW	1346	4-0	Powell(3), Jackson
04/11/95	FA Trophy	Q2	Hendon	291	0-3	
07/11/95	Kent SC	1	MARGATE	241	2-1	Powell, Gibbs
11/11/95	FA Cup	1	COLCHESTER UNITED	3128	2-0	Jackson, Mortley
14/11/95	BHL	P	Cambridge City	267	1-2	Munday
18/11/95	BHL	P	RUSHDEN & DIAMONDS	658	1-3	Gooding
20/11/95	DMC	1(2)	Chelmsford City	534	0-1	
02/12/95	FA Cup	2	Cinderford Town	2067	1-1	Blewden
09/12/95	BHL	P	Gresley Rovers	537	1-3	Jackson
14/12/95	FA Cup	2 rep	CINDERFORD TOWN	2851	3-0	Best, Munday, Powell
16/12/95	BHL	P	STAFFORD RANGERS	462	0-3	
19/12/95	DMC	2	CRAWLEY TOWN	189	1-2	Best
30/12/95	BHL	P	Dorchester Town	607	2-2	Munday(2)
01/01/96	BHL	P	CRAWLEY TOWN	633	3-1	Gibbs, Cotter, Munday
06/01/96	FA Cup	3	ASTON VILLA	26021	0-3	(Played at Aston Villa)
13/01/96	BHL	P	CHELTENHAM TOWN	884	1-0	Mortley
20/01/96	BHL	P	Baldock Town	360	2-2	Jackson(2)
23/01/96	Kent SC	QF	Fisher	140	0-2	
03/02/96	BHL	P	Halesowen Town	675	1-2	Powell
10/02/96	BHL	P	Rushden & Diamonds	1841	3-2	Munday, Cotter, Mortley
12/02/96	BHL	P	Chelmsford City	618	1-6	Gubbins
17/02/96	BHL	P	ATHERSTONE UNITED	511	2-1	Jackson, Mortley
24/02/96	BHL	P	Merthyr Tydfil	411	2-2	Mortley, Cotter
27/02/96	BHL	P	V.S. RUGBY	426	2-0	Cotter, Munday
02/03/96	BHL	P	Cheltenham Town	549	0-0	
05/03/96	BHL	P	SALISBURY CITY	429	1-1	Powell
09/03/96	BHL	P	Stafford Rangers	635	0-1	
16/03/96	BHL	P	WORCESTER CITY	472	0-1	
23/03/96	BHL	P	Newport A.F.C.	777	1-0	Cotter
26/03/96	BHL	P	GLOUCESTER CITY	383	0-0	
30/03/96	BHL	P	DORCHESTER TOWN	427	4-1	Cotter(2), Jackson, Newbery
02/04/96	BHL	P	MERTHYR TYDFIL	395	1-0	Jackson
06/04/96	BHL	P	Crawley Town	843	0-1	
08/04/96	BHL	P	BALDOCK TOWN	506	1-1	Powell
13/04/96	BHL	P	Ilkeston Town	598	1-1	Munday
16/04/96	BHL	P	NEWPORT A.F.C.	449	4-0	Jackson, Munday(3)
20/04/96	BHL	P	HALESOWEN TOWN	679	0-1	
23/04/96	BHL	P	Burton Albion	444	2-1	Powell, Munday
27/04/96	BHL	P	CHELMSFORD CITY	670	0-1	
04/05/96	BHL	P	Worcester City	702	1-3	Munday

GRESLEY ROVERS

The Moat Ground, Moat Street, Church Gresley, Swadlincote, Derbys DE11 9RE. Tel: 01283 216315

Secretary: Neil Betteridge, 88 Midway Rd, Midway, Swadlincote, Derbyshire, DE11 7PG Tel & Fax: 01283 221881

Nickname: The Moatmen   Capacity: 2,000   Seating: 400

Covered standing: 800   Clubhouse on ground: Yes

Record attendance: 3,950 v Burton Albion Birmingham League 1957-58

Biggest win: 23-0 v Holy Cross Priory, Leicestershire Junior Cup 1889-90.

Biggest defeat: 1-15 v Burton Crusaders 1886-87

Record appearances: Dennis King 579

Record goalscorer in one season: Gordon Duggins 75

Record goalscorer in total: Gordon Duggins 306

Record fee received: £30,000 for Justin O'Reilly to Port Vale in 1995-96

DIRECTIONS

Travel to A444 via either the A5, A38, A5121 or M42 North to Aplleby Magna. On reaching A444 head for Castle Gresley. Turn onto A514 to Derby; at island take second exit (Church Street), then second left (School Street) then first left into Moat Street. Five miles from Burton-on-Trent (BR). Buses from Swadlincote and Burton.

HONOURS

FA VASE RUNNERS UP 1991; FA VASE semi-finals 1993; West Mids League 1991 and 1992; League Cup 1989; Leicestershire Senior League 1901, 1947, 1948; Leicestershire Senior Cup 1899, 1947; Derbyshire Senior Cup 1988, 1989, 1990, 1991, 1994, 1996, and (South) 1902 and 1903; Coalville Charity Cup 1947; Derby's Divisional Cup 1949; Bass Vase 1911, 1929, 1931, 1949, 1950, 1967; Central Alliance 1965 and 1967; League Cup 1953; East Mids Regional League 1968 and 1970.

Manager for 1996-97: Paul Futcher   **Assistant manager: Garry Birtles**

Chairman: Peter Hall   **Vice Chairman: Dennis Everitt**

Gresley Rovers are currently working on a new ground which hopefully will be ready for the 1997-98 season.

Formed in 1882, Gresley Rovers spent their formative years in the Burton, Leicestershire and Derbyshire Leagues, until the turn of the century when they moved up into the Midland League, a competition which contained a number of clubs destined for the Football League. It was a struggle on the field and in 1905 they reverted back to local football, eventually playing in the Central Alliance where they remained until the First War. In 1925 Rovers moved across to join the Birmingham Combination, from where they reached the first round proper of the FA Cup in 1933, losing to York City with only five minutes left. Despite this success they struggled financially, and after moving to the Central Combination they moved to the Leicestershire Senior League, until the Second War.

The immediate post War years were spectacularly successful for Gresley, winning the league in 1947 and 48 and finishing runners-up in the next two terms, which prompted a move to the Central Alliance and then Birmingham and District League before re-joining the Alliance in 1960, where they stayed until 1974, by which time the league was called the East Midlands Regional. Again, success was forthcoming during that period with four championships and a lowest finish of fifth in 14 years. However, the standard of opposition meant that often away matches were played on park pitches, and so a move to the West Midlands League came in 1975. It was the beginning of a barren spell until a vast improvement a decade later when a run of six seasons saw two championships, a runners-up spot and four Derbyshire Senior Cup wins. The 1990-91 season almost saw them pull off a marvellous treble, of League, Senior Cup and the big prize, the FA Vase, fighting back from 3-0 down at Wembley before losing the replay at Sheffield United. Despite the success, they were denied entry into the Southern League, but within 12 months they had again won the league, and were promoted. Since then the Derbyshire Senior Cup has been won again and their wonderful Moat Ground has been given the last rites as plans for a new ground are advanced.

The Moat is without doubt one of the few truly classic grounds left in the country, having been home to Rovers since 1909. It was originally a works cricket ground with a derelict waste site a one end, but gradually it was fashioned into a football ground, with the old cricket pavilion put to good use, as indeed it still is. The early days were spent in Albert Village, half a mile away across the border in Leicestershire, shared with cricket, until after 13 seasons they moved to Church Street, close to the Moat, until the site was sold. The site in Albert Village was eventually quarried and obliterated, and part of the Church Street was used for housing.

GRESLEY ROVERS 1995/96 SEASON

Date	Competition	Round	Opponent	Att	Score	Scorers
19/08/95	BHL	P	Gravesend & Northfleet	527	1-1	Taylor
22/08/95	BHL	P	HALESOWEN TOWN	704	1-1	Mann
26/08/95	BHL	P	MERTHYR TYDFIL	580	3-1	Mann(2), Taylor
28/08/95	BHL	P	Ilkeston Town	979	0-0	
02/09/95	BHL	P	Baldock Town	277	1-0	Fowkes
05/09/95	BHL	P	ATHERSTONE UNITED	702	1-0	Taylor
09/09/95	FA Cup	Q1	DUDLEY TOWN	541	1-2	Taylor
16/09/95	BHL	P	CHELMSFORD CITY	545	0-2	
19/09/95	BHL	P	Halesowen Town	584	1-1	Mann
30/09/95	BHL	P	NEWPORT A.F.C.	788	1-3	Taylor
03/10/95	DMC	1(1)	Burton Albion	1143	2-0	Taylor, Marsden
07/10/95	BHL	P	Cheltenham Town	607	0-2	
14/10/95	BHL	P	RUSHDEN & DIAMONDS	808	0-3	
24/10/95	BHL	P	ILKESTON TOWN	637	2-3	Horseman, Taylor
28/10/95	BHL	P	Stafford Rangers	582	5-3	O'Reilly(3), Taylor(2)
31/10/95	DMC	1(2)	BURTON ALBION	990	1-2	Marsden
04/11/95	BHL	P	Chelmsford City	947	2-1	Denby, Wardle
11/11/95	BHL	P	V.S. RUGBY	689	4-0	Taylor(2), Marsden, Garner
14/11/95	BHL	P	Atherstone United	454	2-1	Garner, Fowkes
18/11/95	BHL	P	Merthyr Tydfil	336	1-2	Foster
25/11/95	FA Trophy	Q3	Accrington Stanley	542	3-2	Garner(2), Marsden
02/12/95	BHL	P	CHELTENHAM TOWN	662	0-2	
06/12/95	DMC	2	Paget Rangers	127	3-2	O'Reilly(3)
09/12/95	BHL	P	GRAVESEND & NORTHFLEET	537	3-1	Fowkes, O'Reilly(2)
13/12/95	Derbys SC	3	Staveley Miners Welfare	180	4-1	Taylor(4)
16/12/95	BHL	P	Newport A.F.C.	655	1-0	Garner
01/01/96	BHL	P	Burton Albion	1609	1-1	O'Reilly
06/01/96	BHL	P	WORCESTER CITY	677	1-0	O'Reilly
09/01/96	DMC	3	Cheltenham Town	308	3-3	Castledine, Taylor(2)
13/01/96	BHL	P	Salisbury City	337	4-1	Marsden, Stanborough, O'Reilly, Castledine
20/01/96	FA Trophy	1	Stalybridge Celtic	638	1-1	O'Reilly
23/01/96	FA Trophy	1 rep	STALYBRIDGE CELTIC	603	1-0	Marsden
10/02/96	FA Trophy	2	Blyth Spartans	626	2-1	O'Reilly, Garner
13/02/96	Derbys SC	QF	BUXTON	401	2-0	O'Reilly(2)
17/02/96	BHL	P	DORCHESTER TOWN	640	0-2	
24/02/96	BHL	P	Worcester City	630	3-3	Fowkes(2), Marsden
02/03/96	FA Trophy	3	Guiseley	790	2-1	Evans, O'Reilly
05/03/96	DMC	3 rep	CHELTENHAM TOWN	407	2-2	Marsden, Garner
09/03/96	BHL	P	BALDOCK TOWN	657	3-0	Garner, Marsden, O'Reilly
12/03/96	BHL	P	SUDBURY TOWN	402	5-2	Alsop(3), Marsden, Garner
14/03/96	DMC	QF	Nuneaton Borough	606	1-4	Taylor
16/03/96	BHL	P	BURTON ALBION	1172	2-1	Garner, P Wardle
19/03/96	BHL	P	GLOUCESTER CITY	511	1-0	O'Reilly
23/03/96	FA Trophy	QF	MACCLESFIELD TOWN	1727	0-2	
26/03/96	BHL	P	Crawley Town	437	0-2	
30/03/96	BHL	P	Gloucester City	613	2-1	Fowkes, Allsop
02/04/96	BHL	P	HASTINGS TOWN	538	1-1	Allsop
06/04/96	BHL	P	STAFFORD RANGERS	656	1-1	Allsop
08/04/96	BHL	P	V.S. Rugby	364	2-1	Evans, Fowkes
10/04/96	Derbys SC	SF	GLOSSOP NORTH END	383	3-0	Ringland(og), Master, Allsop
13/04/96	BHL	P	SALISBURY CITY	582	2-2	Allsop(2)
16/04/96	BHL	P	Rushden & Diamonds	2250	1-2	Fowkes
20/04/96	BHL	P	Hastings Town	380	4-2	Garner, Cox, Castledine, Marsden
23/04/96	BHL	P	Dorchester Town	536	1-2	Allsop
25/04/96	BHL	P	CAMBRIDGE CITY	483	2-2	Garner, Allsop
27/04/96	BHL	P	Sudbury Town	320	1-3	Marsden
30/04/96	BHL	P	Cambridge City	303	3-2	Marsden, Fowkes, Wardle
04/05/96	BHL	P	CRAWLEY TOWN	611	1-0	Marsden
09/05/96	Derbys SC	F(1)	BELPER TOWN	505	0-0	
13/05/96	Derbys SC	F(2)	Belper Town	662	2-1	Evans, Garner

HALESOWEN TOWN

The Grove, Old Hawne Lane, Halesowen, West Mids. Tel: 0121 550 2179 & Social club: 0121 602 5305

Secretary: Stewart Tildesley, 83 Bloomfield St, Halesowen, West Mids B63 3RF Tel: 0121 550 8443

Press office: Paul Floud, 112 Blackberry Lane, Halesowen, West Mids Tel: 0121 550 8999

Colours: Blue and white stripes   Nickname: Yeltz

Capacity: 5,000   Seating: 380   Covered standing: 1,000

Clubhouse on ground: Around 150 yds away

Record attendance: 5,000 v Hendon FA Cup 1st Rd 1954

Biggest win: 13-1 v Coventry Amateurs 1956

Biggest defeat: 0-8 v Bilston West Mids Lge 1962

Record appearances: Paul Joinson 608

Record goalscorer in one season: Paul Joinson 49 1989-90

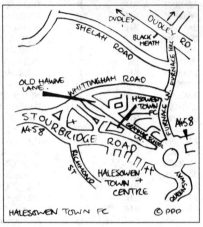

HALESOWEN TOWN FC   © PPP

Record goalscorer in total: Paul Joinson 369

Record fee received: £30,000 for Dean Spink to Aston Villa 1989

Record fee paid: £ 5,000 for Richard Massey from Stourbridge 1992

HONOURS

FA VASE 1985 AND 1986; FA VASE Runners up in 1983; Southern League Midland Div 1990; Birmingham League 1947; West Mids League 1984, 85, 86; League Cup 1983 and 1985; Birmingham Senior Cup 1984; Staffs Senior Cup 1989; Worcester Senior Cup 1952 and 1962.

Manager 1996-97: Stewart Hall   **Assistant Manager: Colin Brookes**

Chairman: Ron Moseley   **Vice Chairman: Nigel Pitt**

Formed in 1873, Halesowen Town FC is one of the oldest clubs in the country, and as far as records show, have always played at their current home, The Grove. The first competition of any standing the club appeared in was the Birmingham Combination and they remained members of that league until 1939 without winning any major honours. In 1946 they joined the re-formed Birmingham and District League, later named the West Midlands League, and with only ten clubs competing won the league at the first attempt. Honours were few, though they did win the Worcestershire Senior Cup in 1952 beating Hednesford Town, and again in 1962 when defeating Kidderminster Harriers. In 1955 they reached the 1st Round of the FA Cup for the first time when a crowd of 5,000 saw them lose 4-2 at home to Hendon, then one of the leading amateur clubs in the country. Halesowen, nicknamed the Yeltz, saw an upswing in fortune in the 1980's and between 1982-83 and 1985-86 they won four successive West Midlands League titles and two League Cups. It was the FA Vase that really put Halesowen on the map, and the first of three Wembley appearances came in 1983 when losing 1-0 to VS Rugby. Two years later they returned to beat Fleetwood Town 3-1 and a year later they were back again comfortably defeating Southall 3-0.

Success also came in the FA Cup and in 1985 they again reached the First Round before losing to Frickley Athletic. It was the first of seven consecutive seasons in that round. Locally there have been wins in the Birmingham Senior Cup in 1984 and 1989 in the Staffs Senior Cup, but more good times came with the move up to the Southern League in 1986. The title was won in 1990 and the club have been in the Premier Division ever since. Several Yeltz players have gone on to Football League clubs in recent years. Dean Spink was transferred to Aston Villa for a record fee, and Stuart Cash went to Nottingham Forest. Andy Pearce joined Coventry City, as did Tim Clarke and Sean Flynn. Town continue to progress and are confident of Conference football very soon after last season's near miss.

HALESOWEN TOWN 1995/96 SEASON

Date	Comp	Round	Opponent	Att	Score	Scorers
19/08/95	BHL	P	SUDBURY TOWN	660	3-3	Wright, Crisp, Bradley
22/08/95	BHL	P	Gresley Rovers	704	1-1	Harrison
28/08/95	BHL	P	CHELTENHAM TOWN	843	0-1	
02/09/95	BHL	P	V.S. Rugby	443	1-0	Crisp
05/09/95	BHL	P	GLOUCESTER CITY	678	2-1	Crisp(2)
09/09/95	FA Cup	Q1	BLAKENALL	618	3-2	Snape, Wright, Bradley
16/09/95	BHL	P	Ilkeston Town	597	3-1	Crisp, Harrison, Owen
19/09/95	BHL	P	GRESLEY ROVERS	584	1-1	Crisp
23/09/95	FA Cup	Q2	MOOR GREEN	620	1-0	Crisp
30/09/95	BHL	P	Chelmsford City	1185	0-1	
03/10/95	DMC	1(1)	WORCESTER CITY	441	0-2	
07/10/95	FA Cup	Q3	Telford United	904	1-4	Rodwell
14/10/95	BHL	P	NEWPORT A.F.C.	855	3-1	Crisp, Harrison, Hackett
21/10/95	BHL	P	STAFFORD RANGERS	678	2-2	Harrison, Wright
24/10/95	BHL	P	Cheltenham Town	534	2-2	Crisp, Wright
28/10/95	BHL	P	ATHERSTONE UNITED	694	5-4	Harrison(2), Wright(2), Rodwell
30/10/95	DMC	1(2)	Worcester City	627	1-4	Owen
07/11/95	Worcs SC	1	Bridgnorth Town	180	3-0	Harrison, Wright(2)
11/11/95	BHL	P	ILKESTON TOWN	636	3-2	Shearer, Harrison, Owen
14/11/95	BHL	P	Gloucester City	578	2-0	Crisp, Wright
18/11/95	BHL	P	Salisbury City	391	3-2	Wright(3)
25/11/95	FA Trophy	Q3	BILSTON TOWN	601	0-0	
28/11/95	FA Trophy	Q3 rep	Bilston Town	307	4-1	Crisp, Snape, Wright(2)
02/12/95	BHL	P	HASTINGS TOWN	627	0-1	
05/12/95	Birm SC	2	Tamworth	264	1-1	Massey
09/12/95	BHL	P	Sudbury Town	345	2-1	Wright(2)
12/12/95	Birm SC	2 rep	TAMWORTH	275	1-2	Bradley
16/12/95	BHL	P	DORCHESTER TOWN	534	1-0	Harrison
23/12/95	BHL	P	Merthyr Tydfil	703	2-0	Williams, Crisp
26/12/95	BHL	P	WORCESTER CITY	1119	3-3	Williams(2), Harrison
06/01/96	BHL	P	SALISBURY CITY	652	2-0	Coates, Williams
09/01/96	Worcs SC	QF	Stourbridge	421	0-1	
13/01/96	BHL	P	Cambridge City	409	1-0	Wright
20/01/96	FA Trophy	1	Dudley Town	769	2-4	Snape, Wright
03/02/96	BHL	P	GRAVESEND & NORTHFLEET	675	2-1	Wright, Shearer
10/02/96	BHL	P	CRAWLEY TOWN	681	2-0	Wright(2)
13/02/96	BHL	P	Stafford Rangers	602	0-1	
17/02/96	BHL	P	Hastings Town	512	2-0	Bradley, Wright
24/02/96	BHL	P	V.S. RUGBY	737	0-0	
02/03/96	BHL	P	Burton Albion	816	1-1	Wright
09/03/96	BHL	P	CHELMSFORD CITY	693	3-0	Harrison(3)
12/03/96	BHL	P	Baldock Town	163	2-0	Wright, Crisp
16/03/96	BHL	P	Atherstone United	339	1-0	Wright
19/03/96	BHL	P	RUSHDEN & DIAMONDS	1725	0-0	
23/03/96	BHL	P	MERTHYR TYDFIL	680	2-1	Wright, Hopcroft
26/03/96	BHL	P	Dorchester Town	454	0-0	
30/03/96	BHL	P	Rushden & Diamonds	3481	2-1	Harrison, Bradley
06/04/96	BHL	P	BURTON ALBION	902	1-1	Crisp
08/04/96	BHL	P	Worcester City	1221	1-0	Wright
13/04/96	BHL	P	CAMBRIDGE CITY	952	2-1	Crisp, Owen
20/04/96	BHL	P	Gravesend & Northfleet	679	1-0	Bellingham
27/04/96	BHL	P	BALDOCK TOWN	1053	1-0	Crisp
30/04/96	BHL	P	Crawley Town	802	3-1	Hackett, Crisp, Wright
04/05/96	BHL	P	Newport A.F.C.	1180	2-1	Wright, Wood

HASTINGS TOWN

Pilot Field, Elphinstone Road, Hastings, TN34 2AX Tel: 01424 444635

Secretary and Press officer R.A.Cosens, 22 Baldslow Road, Hastings, TN24 2EZ Tel: 01424 427867

Nickname: The Town   Capacity: 5,000

Seating: 800   Covered standing: 600

Clubhouse on ground: Yes

Record attendance: 1,774 v Dover Athetic Southern League April 12th 1993

Record goalscorer in one season: Dean White 28

Record fee paid: £10,000 for Steve Cuggy

HONOURS

Southern League Southern Division 1992

Division Two B: 1910

Southern League Cup: 1995

Sussex County League Cup 1981 and Div 2 Cup 1980

Sussex Senior Cup 1926, 1938, 1996, AFA Senior Cup 1938

Gilbert Rice Floodlit Cup 1990, Roy Hayden Trophy 1996

Manager for 1996-97: Garry Wilson   **Assistant manager: Peter Carman**

Chairman: David Nessling   **Vice Chairman: Charles Pilbeam**

DIRECTIONS

From A21 turn left at 1st mini roundabout into St Helens Road, left after 1 mile into St Helens Park Road, this leads into Downs Road, at end of Downs Road (T-junction) turn left, ground 200yds on right. From town centre take Queens Road (A2101). Right at roundabout into Elphinstone Road - ground 1 mile on right. One and a half miles from Hastings BR station - infrequent bus service from town centre to ground.

Hastings Town were formed in 1894 and until 11 years ago were playing in the Sussex County League. They were known until recent years as Hastings and St Leonards. They soon found success in their early days, winning the Sussex RUR Cup in 1901 and 1902 whilst still playing in local football. In 1921 they joined the Sussex County League which had been formed a year earlier and in their first season finished runners up to Worthing. They again finished second in 1927, but then reverted back to Hastings League football for a while. They won the Sussex Senior Cup in 1936 and 1938 as well as the RUR Cup again twice, before rejoining the County League in 1952. Hastings finished in second place in Division Two in 1960. After changing their name to Hastings Town, they went through a lean spell but in 1980 they won Division Two and also took the Division's League Cup. The following season they took the full League Cup. 1984-85 was to be the last for Town in the County League, for following Hastings United's demise, Town applied for and were elected into the Southern League, gaining a new lease for the Pilot Field. After several seasons under Peter Sillett, the club finally won promotion to the Premier Division, taking the title by 13 points from Weymouth. The history of football in Hastings continues to get more complex. St Leonards were formed in 1904 and played at the Central Ground, amalgamating with St Leonards Utd before folding. Rock-A-Nore FC were next, and they played on the top pitch at Pilot Field from it opening in 1920, and merged with All Saints FC to become Hastings and St Leonards FC. When the Council brought forward a scheme to create the Pilot Field's lower pitch, St Leonards moved on and remained until the war. In 1948, a newly formed professional club, Hastings United, took over the main pitch with its huge stand, with St Leonards going back to the top pitch, where apart from a spell whilst it was rebuilt, they stayed, having changed their name to Hastings Town in 1976. Now called the Firs, the ground was home until Pilot Field became available and they were allowed to move to their home after nearly 40 years. Since then the Firs has become home to STAMCO FC, who have reached the Southern League, and through the ultimate irony, have renamed themselves St Leonards FC Stamcroft.

HASTINGS TOWN 1995/96 SEASON

Date	Comp	Round	Opponent	Att	Score	Scorers
12/08/95	S		HEDNESFORD TOWN	356	0-4	
19/08/95	BHL	P	Burton Albion	672	1-1	Cussey
22/08/95	BHL	P	GRAVESEND & NORTH F	584	1-3	White
26/08/95	BHL	P	Salisbury City	334	4-3	White(2), Ullathorne, Cuggy
28/08/95	BHL	P	BALDOCK TOWN	527	2-2	White, Ullathorne
02/09/95	BHL	P	RUSHDEN & DIAMONDS	552	0-1	
05/09/95	BHL	P	Sudbury Town	320	0-0	
09/09/95	FA Cup	Q1	Croydon	166	3-2	O'Shaughnessey, Simmonds, White
16/09/95	BHL	P	DORCHESTER TOWN	466	1-1	O'Shaughnessy
19/09/95	BHL	P	Gravesend & Northfleet	500	0-4	
23/09/95	FA Cup	Q2	Ashford Town	966	1-3	Simmonds
30/09/95	BHL	P	CAMBRIDGE CITY	441	3-1	Tuppenny, O'Shaughnessy, Playford
03/10/95	DMC	1(1)	Crawley Town	425	1-1	Cuggy
07/10/95	BHL	P	Worcester City	723	0-1	
14/10/95	FA Trophy	Q1	HAVANT TOWN	392	2-2	Ullathorne, Beard
18/10/95	FA Trophy	Q1 rep	Havant Town	141	0-1	
21/10/95	BHL	P	MERTHYR TYDFIL	381	2-1	Parris, Cuggy
24/10/95	BHL	P	Baldock Town	183	3-1	Ullathorne(2), Simmonds
28/10/95	BHL	P	Gloucester City	712	2-0	White, Cuggy
31/10/95	DMC	1(2)	CRAWLEY TOWN	328	1-3	Cuggy
04/11/95	BHL	P	BURTON ALBION	421	0-3	
11/11/95	BHL	P	SALISBURY CITY	444	6-2	Cuggy(4), Ullathorne, White
18/11/95	BHL	P	V.S. Rugby	389	1-1	Parris
25/11/95	Sussex SC	2	Peacehaven & Telscombe	269	2-1	White, Beard
29/11/95	Hastings S	SF	Stamco	240	3-5	Simmonds(3)
02/12/95	BHL	P	Halesowen Town	627	1-0	White
16/12/95	BHL	P	Rushden & Diamonds	1924	1-1	Playford
23/12/95	BHL	P	CHELTENHAM TOWN	523	4-1	Callaway(2), Cuggy(2)
26/12/95	BHL	P	Crawley Town	757	2-3	Playford, Smith
01/01/96	BHL	P	CHELMSFORD CITY	616	2-3	Beard, Ullathorne
06/01/96	BHL	P	Dorchester Town	510	4-1	Cuggy, Ullathorne(2), O'Shaughnessy
09/01/96	Sussex SC	3	STAMCO	1418	2-1	Cuggy, Playford
13/01/96	BHL	P	V.S. RUGBY	530	2-2	Cuggy, Parris
20/01/96	BHL	P	ATHERSTONE UNITED	407	5-0	Smith, Cuggy, Burt, Ullathorne(2)
03/02/96	BHL	P	ILKESTON TOWN	402	2-1	Ullathorne, Smith
10/02/96	Sussex SC	QF	BURGESS HILL TOWN	361	4-0	Willard, Beard, Playford, Parris
17/02/96	BHL	P	HALESOWEN TOWN	512	0-2	
02/03/96	BHL	P	Ilkeston Town	413	0-1	
05/03/96	BHL	P	Cambridge City	139	3-0	Cuggy(2), Simmonds
09/03/96	BHL	P	WORCESTER CITY	440	0-0	
13/03/96	Sussex SC	SF	LANGNEY SPORTS	430	6-0	Playford, Cuggy(2), White, Ullathorne, Simmonds
16/03/96	BHL	P	STAFFORD RANGERS	451	0-2	
23/03/96	BHL	P	Cheltenham Town	608	2-1	Cuggy, Playford
26/03/96	BHL	P	Stafford Rangers	500	1-1	Playford
30/03/96	BHL	P	NEWPORT A.F.C.	463	1-1	O'Shaughnessy
02/04/96	BHL	P	Gresley Rovers	538	1-1	Willard
06/04/96	BHL	P	Chelmsford City	648	3-0	Tuppenney, Calloway, Cuggy
08/04/96	BHL	P	CRAWLEY TOWN	713	0-1	
13/04/96	BHL	P	Atherstone United	301	0-1	
20/04/96	BHL	P	GRESLEY ROVERS	380	2-4	Cuggy, White
23/04/96	BHL	P	SUDBURY TOWN	363	2-1	Cuggy, Hume
27/04/96	BHL	P	Merthyr Tydfil	387	1-1	White
28/04/96	BHL	P	Newport A.F.C.	611	1-1	Calloway
04/05/96	BHL	P	GLOUCESTER CITY	504	2-0	Playford(2)
06/05/96	Sussex SC	F	Crawley Town	1153	1-0	Simmonds (at Worthing FC)

KING'S LYNN

The Walks Stadium, Tennyson Rd, King's Lynn PE30 5PB. Tel: 0116 276 0060

Secretary: John Franks, The Lyntons, Stamford Rd Marholm, Peterborough PE6 7HX. Tel: 01733 267272

Nickname: The Linnets

Colours: Royal Blue and Gold

Capacity: 8,000

Seating: 1,200

Covered standing: 5,000

Clubhouse on ground: Yes

Record attendance: 12,937 Exeter City FA Cup 1951

Record appearance holder: Mick Wright 1,152

Record goalscorer in aggregate: Malcolm Lindsay 321

DIRECTIONS

At mini roundabout arriving from A10/A447 take Vancouse Avenue. Ground on left after a half mile. Quarter mile from King's Lynn (BR), half mile from bus station.

HONOURS

FA AMATEUR CUP Runner up 1901

Northern Premier League President's Cup 1983

Eastern Counties League and League Cup 1954

Norfolk and Suffolk League 8 times

Norfolk Senior Cup 1883, 1884, 1887, 1890, 1899, 1908, 1924, 1925, 1932, 1934, 1937, 1939, 1952, 1954, 1955, 1956, 1957, 1958

Norfolk Invitation Cup 1995

Norfolk Premier Cup 1969 jt, 1974

East Anglian Cup 1966, 1967, 1968, 1985

Eastern Pro Floodlit League 1969

King's Lynn FC was formed in 1879 and until 1935 it was a member of the Norfolk and Suffolk League, winning the championship on eight occasions. From there they entered the Eastern Counties League and stayed until the war. In 1946 the club joined the United Counties League, but on turning professional in 1948 returned to the ECL. After twice finishing runners up they completed the League and Cup double in 1954, joining the Midland League until 1958 when it progressed to the Southern League. Due to its geographical position, the club were compelled to move to the Northern Premier League in 1980 but three seasons later they were back in Southern territory. During the Northern period they won the President's Cup and they followed that by finishing second in 1985. It was the end of the era for in 1987 they were relegated back to the Midland Division and for some while the years were disappointing.

Last May saw Lynn finally make it back, after finishing second to Nuneaton Borough, a season which saw the biggest crowd for a league match for decades. The record attendance at the Walks ground is 13,000 for an FA Cup tie in 1951, where as the best performance in that competition came in 1962 when they lost a 3rd Round tie at Everton in front of 45,000 people. In the Amateur Cup Lynn reached the final in 1901, losing a replay to Crook Town, but locally they have taken the Norfolk Senior Cup 19 times with 20 other appearances as runners up.

The Walks has been home to Lynn since the start, but was only fenced off as an enclosure in 1907 after an FA Cup tie at Aston Villa brought in some money. It now has a capacity for 8,000 and is hosting Premier Division football again.

KINGS LYNN 1995/96 SEASON

Date	Comp	Rd	Opponent	Att	Score	Scorers
19/08/95	BHL	M	Moor Green	215	2-0	McNamara, Setchell
22/08/95	BHL	M	ROTHWELL TOWN	641	2-0	McNamara, Hudson
26/08/95	FA Cup	P	WIVENHOE TOWN	621	3-0	Setchell, Pascoe, McNamara
28/08/95	BHL	M	Grantham Town	272	1-0	McNamara
02/09/95	BHL	M	Racing Club Warwick	150	1-2	McNamara
05/09/95	BHL	M	HINCKLEY TOWN	761	3-1	McNamara, Setchell, Munton
09/09/95	FA Cup	Q1	Saffron Walden Town	230	2-0	McNamara(2)
16/09/95	BHL	M	Bridgnorth Town	117	3-2	McNamara, Skelly, Setchell
19/09/95	BHL	M	Rothwell Town	242	2-1	Pascoe, McNamara
23/09/95	FA Cup	Q2	BOSTON TOWN	1157	5-1	Stanhope, Setchell, McNamara, Pascoe, Dolby
30/09/95	BHL	M	Solihull Borough	187	2-2	McNamara, Dolby
07/10/95	FA Cup	Q3	CANVEY ISLAND	1737	1-0	McNamara
14/10/95	FA Trophy	Q1	UXBRIDGE	833	1-2	Setchell
24/10/95	BHL	M	GRANTHAM TOWN	728	6-2	Campbell(og), Gethfield(2 ogs), McNamara(2), Dolby
28/10/95	BHL	M	Nuneaton Borough	1202	1-1	Hudson
31/10/95	DMC	1(1)	Rushden & Diamonds	1098	0-1	
04/11/95	BHL	M	BUCKINGHAM TOWN	787	1-4	Munton
11/11/95	BHL	M	RACING CLUB WARWICK	619	2-0	Pascoe, Munton
14/11/95	BHL	M	Hinckley Town	114	3-4	Bloodworth, McNamara,Matthews
18/11/95	BHL	M	Stourbridge	133	2-1	Setchell, Skelly
21/11/95	BHL	M	TAMWORTH	596	0-3	
28/11/95	BHL	M	Leicester United	156	3-0	McNamara(2), Hudson
02/12/95	BHL	M	SUTTON COLDFIELD TOWN	590	2-1	McNamara(2)
05/12/95	DMC	1(2)	RUSHDEN & DIAMONDS	432	2-0	Munton, Cooper
16/12/95	BHL	M	DUDLEY TOWN	527	2-1	McNamara(2)
19/12/95	DMC	2	Rothwell Town	189	1-0	Coe(og)
23/12/95	BHL	M	PAGET RANGERS	1051	2-0	McNamara, Cooper
26/12/95	BHL	M	Bury Town	378	5-1	Munton, Hudson, Stanhope(2), McNamara
01/01/96	BHL	M	CORBY TOWN	1148	1-0	Stanhope
06/01/96	BHL	M	Buckingham Town	170	4-0	Munton, Stanhope(2), Satchell
09/01/96	DMC	3	Baldock Town	275	0-2	
13/01/96	BHL	M	SOLIHULL BOROUGH	1028	3-0	Hudson, Fearon(og), Munton
20/01/96	BHL	M	Tamworth	845	0-1	
10/02/96	BHL	M	LEICESTER UNITED	913	0-0	
17/02/96	BHL	M	Dudley Town	164	2-2	Setchell, Hopkins
02/03/96	BHL	M	MOOR GREEN	840	2-0	McNamara, McLaughlin
05/03/96	BHL	M	Redditch United	128	1-2	Hudson
09/03/96	BHL	M	Sutton Coldfield Town	203	4-1	McLaughlin, Hudson(2), Skelly
12/03/96	BHL	M	BILSTON TOWN	700	1-3	Pascoe
16/03/96	BHL	M	BEDWORTH UNITED	770	2-0	Skelly, Hudson
23/03/96	BHL	M	Paget Rangers	225	2-0	Hudson, Setchell
26/03/96	BHL	M	Evesham United	137	3-2	Hudson(2), McNamara
30/03/96	BHL	M	EVESHAM UNITED	922	2-0	McLaughlin(2)
02/04/96	BHL	M	REDDITCH UNITED	1030	3-0	McLaughlin, McNamara, Stanhope
06/04/96	BHL	M	BURY TOWN	1221	3-0	McNamara(2), Hudson
08/04/96	BHL	M	Corby Town	402	1-1	Hudson
13/04/96	BHL	M	NUNEATON BOROUGH	3635	0-1	
20/04/96	BHL	M	Bedworth United	701	0-1	
27/04/96	BHL	M	Bilston Town	211	0-2	
30/04/96	BHL	M	BRIDGNORTH TOWN	1492	4-0	Harrison, Pascoe, Hudson, Cooper
04/05/96	BHL	M	STOURBRIDGE	1688	2-1	Hudson, McNamara

MERTHYR TYDFIL

Penydarren Park, Merthyr Tydfil, Mid Glamorgan. Tel: 01685 371395

Secretary: Phil Dauncey, c/o MTFC

Colours: White and black   Nickname: Martyrs

Capacity: 10,000   Seating: 1,500

Covered standing: 5,000

Clubhouse on ground: Yes

Record attendance: 21,000 v Reading FA Cup 2 Rd 1946

Biggest win: 11-0   Biggest defeat: 2-9

Record fee paid: £10,000 to Cardiff City for Robbie James in 1992

Record fee received: £12,000 from Exeter City for Ray Pratt in 1981

HONOURS

WELSH FA CUP Winners 1949, 1951, 1987

Southern League 1948, 1950, 1951, 1952, 1954, 1989

Midland Division 1988

League Cup 1948 and 1951

DIRECTIONS

From the South: M4 to Jct 32, take the A470 dual carriageway to Merthyr Tydfil; at end of dual carriageway head for town centre; straight on at next roundabout, passing Vauxhall garage on your right. At the next roundabout, take second exit onto the Avenue De Clichy, follow the road through traffic lights, passing fire station on your left. At next mini roundabout, turn right, passing the Wellington pub on your left. Turn left at the second pedestrian crossing and first right at the Catholic church, right again and follow the road round; the ground is situated just after the Tregenna Hotel.

From the North: Take M50 through Ross on Wye, heading for Abergavenny, A465 Heads of the Valley road sign posted Merthyr Tydfil, follow this road for approx. 16/18 miles until you come to a roundabout with a McDonalds on the left (after the roundabout). Take the town centre road, passing through the villages of Dowlais and Penydarren and passing three roundabouts. At the first set of lights, turn right; approx. 100 yards up turn right again, then first right at the Catholic church, right again and follow the road round; the ground is situated just after the Tregenna Hotel.

Merthyr Tydfil Football Club were re-formed after the Second War, winning promotion to the Southern League in 1946. In seven seasons up to 1954 they took the title on five occasions and were runners up and third in the other two. They also won the Welsh Cup twice during that period and and were beaten finalists in 1947. Unfortunately due to the closed shop attitude of the Football League at the time, they were unable to break through and gain sufficient votes, the previous club having been members before the War.

After that great spell, the Martyrs settled to a more moderate history, where promotion was often followed by relegation, but in 1986 a new Board took over and the club went from strength to strength, winning the Welsh Cup, but a home defeat on the last day deprived them of promotion.

It was a temporary loss, for in 1988 the club won the Midland Division championship and the Merit Cup, with the highlight being the two legged European Cup Winners Cup tie with Atalanta.

Martyrs won the first leg 2-1 at Penydarren but went down 2-0 in Italy, losing on aggregate.

Success came again a year later when the club won the Premier Division and gained Conference status, and around this time, the ground was completely refurbished enough for the Under 21 and Youth International teams to play there.

The advent of the League of Wales caused a major problem at the club, when they insisted that they join them instead of the Conference but that has been dealt with for the time being and Merthyr remain in English football. The last two seasons in the Conference were traumatic and after surviving one year they were eventually relegated and are now back in the Southern League.

MERTHYR TYDFIL 1995/96 SEASON

Date	Comp	Round	Opponent	Att	Score	Scorers
19/08/95	BHL	P	BALDOCK TOWN	453	1-0	Pearson
23/08/95	BHL	P	Salisbury City	402	0-0	
26/08/95	BHL	P	Gresley Rovers	580	1-3	Evans
28/08/95	BHL	P	WORCESTER CITY	424	0-1	
02/09/95	BHL	P	STAFFORD RANGERS	323	3-1	Evans(2), Pearson
05/09/95	BHL	P	Dorchester Town	502	1-7	Loss
09/09/95	FA Cup	Q1	Bridport	311	3-0	Loss, Jones, Evans
16/09/95	BHL	P	Cambridge City	257	2-1	Saddington(og), Evans
19/09/95	BHL	P	SALISBURY CITY	321	1-0	Mitchell
24/09/95	FA Cup	Q2	Newport A.F.C.	1816	3-3	Abraham(2), William
26/09/95	FA Cup	Q2 rep	NEWPORT A.F.C.	887	1-2	Mitchell
30/09/95	BHL	P	ILKESTON TOWN	321	10-1	Evans, Loss(2), Jenkins(3), Mitchell(3), Williams
03/10/95	DMC	P(1)	Cinderford Town	177	4-1	Loss, Evans, Jenkins(2)
14/10/95	BHL	P	BURTON ALBION	451	4-3	Abraham, Williams, Jenkins, Mitchell
21/10/95	BHL	P	Hastings Town	381	1-2	Mitchell
23/10/95	BHL	P	Worcester City	1094	2-4	Jenkins, Evans
28/10/95	BHL	P	RUSHDEN & DIAMONDS	464	0-3	
04/11/95	BHL	P	V.S. RUGBY	312	2-3	Mitchell, Loss
07/11/95	DMC	P(2)	CINDERFORD TOWN	144	4-3	Evans(4)
11/11/95	BHL	P	Sudbury Town	324	2-1	Jones, Nichols
14/11/95	BHL	P	DORCHESTER TOWN	222	3-1	Beattie(3)
18/11/95	BHL	P	GRESLEY ROVERS	336	2-1	Evans, Williams
22/11/95	DMC	1(1)	Newport A.F.C.	572	1-2	Walker
25/11/95	BHL	P	Baldock Town	237	1-1	Jenkins
28/11/95	DMC	1(2)	NEWPORT A.F.C.	347	1-1	Evans
02/12/95	BHL	P	Stafford Rangers	487	2-1	Evans, Summers
09/12/95	BHL	P	CHELMSFORD CITY	409	0-1	
16/12/95	BHL	P	Burton Albion	658	3-1	Summers(2), Evans
23/12/95	BHL	P	HALESOWEN TOWN	703	0-2	
06/01/96	BHL	P	SUDBURY TOWN	417	2-1	M Williams(2)
13/01/96	BHL	P	Gloucester City	781	1-3	Evans
20/01/96	FA Trophy	1	Oxford City	352	2-1	Evans, Williams
03/02/96	BHL	P	CAMBRIDGE CITY	239	2-1	Jones, Jenkins
13/02/96	FA Trophy	2	Dudley Town	268	2-1	Jenkins, Evans
17/02/96	BHL	P	Ilkeston Town	434	1-0	Perrett
24/02/96	BHL	P	GRAVESEND & NORTHFLEET	411	2-2	Evans(2)
27/02/96	BHL	P	Atherstone United	229	2-0	Summers, Jenkins
02/03/96	FA Trophy	3	NORTHWICH VICTORIA	528	1-1	Summers
05/03/96	FA Trophy	3 rep	Northwich Victoria	800	2-2	Evans(2)
09/03/96	BHL	P	GLOUCESTER CITY	456	1-0	Beattie
11/03/96	FA Trophy	3 rep(2)	Northwich Victoria	765	0-3	
16/03/96	BHL	P	V.S. Rugby	317	2-1	A Evans, P Evans
23/03/96	BHL	P	Halesowen Town	680	1-2	Evans
26/03/96	BHL	P	CHELTENHAM TOWN	277	0-1	
30/03/96	BHL	P	ATHERSTONE UNITED	402	4-0	O'Brien, Summers(2), Evans
02/04/96	BHL	P	Gravesend & Northfleet	395	0-1	
06/04/96	BHL	P	Cheltenham Town	603	0-1	
08/04/96	BHL	P	NEWPORT A.F.C.	735	0-1	
13/04/96	BHL	P	Chelmsford City	715	4-1	Summers(3), S Williams
16/04/96	BHL	P	Crawley Town	534	0-1	
20/04/96	BHL	P	CRAWLEY TOWN	404	1-1	Evans
24/04/96	BHL	P	Newport A.F.C.	839	0-0	
27/04/96	BHL	P	HASTINGS TOWN	387	1-1	Evans
04/05/96	BHL	P	Rushden & Diamonds	4664	2-3	Evans, Knight

NEWPORT AFC

Newport Stadium, Spytty Park, Langland Way, Newport, Gwent NP9 0PT. Tel: 01633 271771

Secretary: Mike Everett, 66 Gibbs Rd, Newport, NP9 8AU Tel: 01633 280932

Press Officer: Wallace Brown 10 Fairoak Avenue, Newport, Gwent NP9 8FX Tel: 01633 265500

Colours: All Amber

Nickname: The Exiles

Capacity: 3,300

Seating: 1,200

Covered standing: None

Clubhouse on ground: No, but club headquarters are at The King, 76 Somerton Rd, Newport, Gwent NP9 0JX

Record attendance: 2,475 v Redditch Utd Aug 24th 1994

Biggest win: 9-0 v Pontlottyn Blast Furnace Welsh Cup 1990

Biggest defeat: 1-6 v Stafford Rangers Southern League 1995-96

Record appearances: Mark Price

Record goalscorer in one season: Ceri Williams 36 in 1994-95

Record goalscorer in total: Chris Lilygreen 93

DIRECTIONS

From M4 junction 24, follow sign for Industrial Area, turn left at first roundabout, continue over next two roundabouts. Pass stadium on left, take next left turning (adjacent to Empress Car Sales), then turn left and road leads to the stadium car park.

HONOURS

Hellenic League and League Cup 1990

Glos Senior Cup 1994

Southern League Midland Division 1995

Manager 1996-97: Nigel Vaughan(temp)

Chairman: David Hando

Vice Chairman: Wallace Brown

"A Champion Campaign 1994-95", a review of the promotion season, still has copies available.

Also fanzine "Run Lads, Shout Lads" issued during season.

Newport AFC was formed in June 1989 by supporters of Newport County, whose long history in the game had been ended by bankruptcy just four months earlier. The aim of the new club is to restore Football League status to the town and substantial progress has already been made, in the shape of two promotions.

Unfortunately the club has had to resort to expensive, and extensive legal action to protect itself from being forced into Welsh domestic football. That litigation proved successful, both in maintaining their ambition and enabling them to have a permanent home in Wales after spending three of the first five years in exile in Gloucestershire.

The inaugural season at Moreton-in-Marsh saw "The Exiles" win the Hellenic League double and in 1995 they won the Southern League Midland Division by 14 points. After Moreton, the club played at Gloucester City before returning home to the brand new Council built Spytty Park.

NEWPORT AFC 1995/96 SEASON

Date	Comp	Round	Opposition	Att	Score	Scorers
19/08/95	BHL	P	V.S. Rugby	648	3-1	Foley(2), Webley
23/08/95	BHL	P	GLOUCESTER CITY	1524	1-0	Vaughan
26/08/95	BHL	P	STAFFORD RANGERS	1279	2-1	Webley, Lowndes
28/08/95	BHL	P	Dorchester Town	944	3-0	Tucker, Spencer, Webley
02/09/95	BHL	P	Cambridge City	495	1-0	Webley
06/09/95	BHL	P	WORCESTER CITY	1407	1-1	Tucker
09/09/95	FA Cup	Q1	BROCKENHURST	1011	5-0	Tucker(2), John, Vaughan, Lowndes
16/09/95	BHL	P	Sudbury Town	454	1-3	Tucker
19/09/95	BHL	P	Gloucester City	1412	1-1	Donovan
24/09/95	FA Cup	Q2	MERTHYR TYDFIL	1816	3-3	C Williams, Tucker, Jones
26/09/95	FA Cup	Q2 rep	Merthyr Tydfil	887	2-1	Tucker, Jones
30/09/95	BHL	P	Gresley Rovers	788	3-1	Tucker(3)
07/10/95	FA Cup	Q3	Trowbridge Town	623	0-2	
14/10/95	BHL	P	Halesowen Town	855	1-3	Jones
21/10/95	BHL	P	V.S. RUGBY	921	5-2	C Williams(2), Webley, Spencer, K Rogers
25/10/95	BHL	P	DORCHESTER TOWN	1077	3-2	Webley, C Williams, Lowndes
28/10/95	BHL	P	Crawley Town	853	0-0	
04/11/95	FA Trophy	Q2	FLEET TOWN	679	2-1	Evans(2)
11/11/95	BHL	P	Cheltenham Town	1092	0-2	
13/11/95	BHL	P	Worcester City	1447	0-2	
18/11/95	BHL	P	CHELMSFORD CITY	896	1-2	S Williams
22/11/95	DMC	1(1)	MERTHYR TYDFIL	572	2-1	Dowd, Hall
26/11/95	FA Trophy	Q3	GRAYS ATHLETIC	679	1-0	Jones
28/11/95	DMC	1(2)	Merthyr Tydfil	347	1-1	Jones
02/12/95	BHL	P	BURTON ALBION	817	0-1	
06/12/95	DMC	2	Forest Green Rovers	185	4-2	M Price, Williams, Book(og), Jones
09/12/95	BHL	P	Ilkeston Town	564	1-1	Jones
16/12/95	BHL	P	GRESLEY ROVERS	655	0-1	
06/01/96	BHL	P	Stafford Rangers	634	1-6	Webley
10/01/96	DMC	3	WATERLOOVILLE	418	1-0	Lowndes
13/01/96	BHL	P	CRAWLEY TOWN	827	1-1	Webley
20/01/96	FA Trophy	1	Chelmsford City	1130	1-0	Evans
10/02/96	FA Trophy	2	Carshalton Athletic	682	1-2	Tucker
17/02/96	BHL	P	SUDBURY TOWN	576	5-1	Webley, Tucker(3), Nichols
24/02/96	BHL	P	RUSHDEN & DIAMONDS	1170	1-1	Webley
26/02/96	DMC	QF	SALISBURY CITY	541	1-2	Webley
28/02/96	BHL	P	Salisbury City	340	3-1	Webley(2), Porretta
02/03/96	BHL	P	Atherstone United	328	0-0	
09/03/96	BHL	P	CAMBRIDGE CITY	828	1-2	Tucker
16/03/96	BHL	P	Baldock Town	307	2-1	Lowndes, Webley
18/03/96	BHL	P	CHELTENHAM TOWN	646	2-3	Webley, Donovan
23/03/96	BHL	P	GRAVESEND & NORTHFLEET	777	0-1	
27/03/96	BHL	P	ILKESTON TOWN	542	2-3	Brown, Nichols
30/03/96	BHL	P	Hastings Town	463	1-1	Webley
31/03/96	BHL	P	Chelmsford City	804	0-0	
03/04/96	BHL	P	ATHERSTONE UNITED	504	1-2	Porretta
06/04/96	BHL	P	SALISBURY CITY	648	1-1	Nichols
08/04/96	BHL	P	Merthyr Tydfil	735	1-0	Tucker
13/04/96	BHL	P	Rushden & Diamonds	2914	0-3	
16/04/96	BHL	P	Gravesend & Northfleet	449	0-4	
20/04/96	BHL	P	BALDOCK TOWN	724	1-1	Webley
24/04/96	BHL	P	MERTHYR TYDFIL	839	0-0	
27/04/96	BHL	P	Burton Albion	599	1-0	Webley
28/04/96	BHL	P	HASTINGS TOWN	611	1-1	Brown
04/05/96	BHL	P	HALESOWEN TOWN	1180	1-2	Brown

NUNEATON BOROUGH

Manor Park, Beaumont Rd, Nuneaton, Warks CV10 0SY. Tel: 01203 385738

Secretary: Peter Humphreys, 29 Amington Rd, Shirley, Solihull, B90 2RF Tel: 0121 745 2031

Commercial Manager: Philip J Wright: C/O NBFC 01203 342690

Boro Newsline 0891 122909 updated every day

Club shop newly revamped open matchdays, 1st team, reserves and youths

Coventry City Res are playing at Manor Park in 1996-97

Nickname: The Boro   Colours: Blue and White

Capacity: 6,500   Seating: 550

Covered standing: 3,000   Clubhouse on ground: Yes

Record attendance: 22,114 v Rotherham Utd FA Cup 3rd Rd 1967

DIRECTIONS

A444 to Nuneaton from M6 jct 3, second exit at 1st roundabout, left at second roundabout then 2nd right into Greenmoor Road, turn right at the end ground is on the left. From town centre ring-road, ground is at the end of Queens Road. Parking for 100 cars at Manor Park School, Beaumont Road, 50p each. Ground 1 mile from Nuneaton Trent Valley (BR) station.

Biggest win: 11-1 in 1945-46 and 1955-56   Biggest defeat: 1-8 in 1955-56 1968-69

Record appearances: Alan Jones 545   Record goalscorer in total: Paul Culpin

Record goalscorer in one season: Paul Culpin 55 in 1992-93

HONOURS

Southern League Midland Div 1982, 93, 96; League Cup 1996; Birmingham League 1956 and North Div 1955; Birmingham Senior Cup 1949, 56, 60, 78, 80, 93; Midland Floodlit Cup 1969, 1974, 1980, 1984 jt.

Manager for 1996-97: Brendan Phillips   **Assistant Manager: Colin Welsh**

Chairman: Howard Kerry   **Press Secretary: Gordon Chislett c/o NBFC**

Nuneaton Borough AFC was formed in 1937 following the demise of the Nuneaton Town club. The original club was formed in 1889 as Nuneaton St Nicholas by members of the local parish church and following a name change they became founder members of the North Warwickshire League. Five years later they entered the FA Cup as members of the Leicestershire Senior League. The club recorded its first success when champions of the Coventry and North Warwickshire League in 1905. Prompted by this they turned semi-professional and joined the Birmingham Junior League, winning it at the first attempt. The second title came in 1915 by which time the league was called the Birmingham Combination.

Town moved to Manor Park in 1919 and won more titles in 1929 and 1931, winning the Birmingham Senior Cup also in the latter year. However, the club came to an end in 1937 after an extra-ordinary meeting of the share holders. Within two days and aided by several Town players, Borough was formed and they joined the Central Amateur League in 1937. A year later the new club turned pro and joined the Combination, taking over the fixtures of Evesham Town. After the war came a decade of success. They were runners up in the Combination in 1946, 1949 and 1951 before moving to the Birmingham League where they took the title in 1955 and 1956. During this time they reached the 3rd Round of the FA Cup and won the Birmingham Senior Cup three times.

In 1958 Borough took the step up to the Southern League becoming founder members of the Premier Division in 1959. After relegation they were promoted again in 1963 and in 1967 finished runners up in the League to Romford, again reaching the 3rd Round of the Cup. The visit of Rotherham United to Manor Park set the attendance record of 22,114. The highlight of the 70's was in 1975 when they were again runners up, this time to Wimbledon. At the end of the decade Borough became founder members of the Alliance Premier League. They stayed just two years but bounced straight back as Southern League champions. By the mid-Eighties the club were well established having finished Alliance runners up twice. However the era came to a sad end in 1987 when they were relegated due to ground problems at Manor Park, and a year later they were in the Midland Division. Problems continued and with huge debts the club faced a winding up order, but in the summer of 1991 a consortium of businessmen took over the club. Success returned in 1993 when they reached the 1st Round of the FA Cup, won the Birmingham Senior Cup and took the Midland Division title. Sadly relegation came yet again, despite a marvellous season in the Cup where Swansea were beaten after a replay and

AFC Bournemouth were also taken to two games.

Once again last season Borough returned to the Premier Division after walking away with the Midland title by 11 points from King's Lynn and neighbours Bedworth Utd. The Doc Martens League Cup win over Baldock gave the club a wonderful double.

NUNEATON BOROUGH 1995/96 SEASON

Date	Comp	Round	Opponent	Att	Score	Scorers
19/08/95	BHL	M	SUTTON COLDFIELD TOWN	1002	1-2	Statham
23/08/95	BHL	M	Dudley Town	357	1-0	Drewitt
26/08/95	BHL	M	Solihull Borough	381	1-0	Drewitt
28/08/95	BHL	M	RACING CLUB WARWICK	1010	1-0	Drewitt
02/09/95	BHL	M	Moor Green	571	2-0	Drewitt(2)
05/09/95	BHL	M	REDDITCH UNITED	1056	4-1	Williams, Clark, Drewitt(2)
09/09/95	BHL	M	Hinckley Town	895	3-0	Drewitt, Straw(2)
16/09/95	BHL	M	EVESHAM UNITED	1049	6-3	Straw(3), Crowley, Drewitt, Clark
19/09/95	BHL	M	DUDLEY TOWN	1186	3-4	Drewitt, Straw, Smith
23/09/95	BHL	M	Grantham Town	543	2-1	Drewitt, Donald
30/09/95	BHL	M	Bridgnorth Town	475	0-1	
04/10/95	DMC	1(1)	V.S. Rugby	651	4-2	R Smith, Simpson, Drewitt, Carr
07/10/95	BHL	M	CORBY TOWN	1075	1-0	Drewitt
21/10/95	FA Cup	Q4	EVESHAM UNITED	1415	6-1	Drewitt, Statham(2), Simpson, Andersen, Straw
24/10/95	BHL	M	Racing Club Warwick	450	2-2	Drewitt, Straw
28/10/95	BHL	M	KING'S LYNN	1202	1-1	Simpson
31/10/95	DMC	1(2)	V.S. Rugby	629	2-1	Donnelly, Williams
04/11/95	FA Trophy	Q2	KNOWSLEY UNITED	1017	3-2	Donnelly, Straw, Simpson
11/11/95	FA Cup	1	Barrow	2869	1-2	Simpson
14/11/95	BHL	M	Redditch United	385	5-1	Straw, Carr, Drewitt, Culpin(2)
18/11/95	BHL	M	BUCKINGHAM TOWN	1103	1-1	Drewitt
25/11/95	FA Trophy	Q3	Spennymoor United	486	2-0	Straw, Donnelly
02/12/95	BHL	M	BILSTON TOWN	943	2-1	Straw, Statham
05/12/95	Birm SC	2	Burton Albion	343	1-2	Carr
09/12/95	BHL	M	Sutton Coldfield Town	498	3-0	Straw(2), Drewitt
12/12/95	DMC	2	Atherstone United	467	3-1	Straw, Simpson, Drewitt
16/12/95	BHL	M	SOLIHULL BOROUGH	869	2-1	Andersen, Straw
23/12/95	BHL	M	STOURBRIDGE	975	1-0	Drewitt
01/01/96	BHL	M	BEDWORTH UNITED	1936	1-2	Carr
06/01/96	BHL	M	BURY TOWN	935	5-1	Carr, Statham, Straw, Simpson(2)
10/01/96	DMC	3	Buckingham Town	127	3-1	Straw(2), Statham
13/01/96	BHL	M	Paget Rangers	760	2-2	Simpson, Drewitt
20/01/96	FA Trophy	1	Gainsborough Trinity	867	1-4	Straw
03/02/96	BHL	M	HINCKLEY TOWN	1061	1-0	Straw
10/02/96	BHL	M	Evesham United	460	3-0	Simpson, Straw(2)
17/02/96	BHL	M	GRANTHAM TOWN	1031	2-1	Simpson, Andersen
20/02/96	BHL	M	Leicester United	223	2-1	Simpson, Straw
24/02/96	BHL	M	Bilston Town	489	2-0	Straw(2)
27/02/96	BHL	M	Bury Town	218	3-1	Statham, Straw(2)
02/03/96	BHL	M	Corby Town	602	3-1	Straw, Simpson, Hardwick
09/03/96	BHL	M	PAGET RANGERS	1179	0-2	
14/03/96	DMC	QF	GRESLEY ROVERS	606	4-1	Straw, Simpson, Burton(2)
16/03/96	BHL	M	MOOR GREEN	937	3-1	Drewitt(2), Straw
19/03/96	DMC	SF(1)	MOOR GREEN	528	2-0	Simpson, Straw
23/03/96	BHL	M	Stourbridge	507	1-0	Straw
26/03/96	BHL	M	Tamworth	1635	3-0	Straw(2), Drewitt
30/03/96	BHL	M	ROTHWELL TOWN	901	0-0	
02/04/96	DMC	SF(2)	Moor Green	340	1-1	Straw
06/04/96	BHL	M	Bedworth United	1540	0-1	
08/04/96	BHL	M	TAMWORTH	1388	1-0	Simpson
13/04/96	BHL	M	King's Lynn	3635	1-0	Drewitt
16/04/96	DMC	F(1)	Baldock Town	469	3-1	Andersen, Straw(2)
20/04/96	BHL	M	BRIDGNORTH TOWN	1245	2-0	Drewitt(2)
23/04/96	BHL	M	Rothwell Town	412	0-2	
27/04/96	BHL	M	LEICESTER UNITED	1055	2-0	Williams, Massey
30/04/96	DMC	F(2)	BALDOCK TOWN	1248	2-1	Drewitt, Simpson
04/05/96	BHL	M	Buckingham Town	472	3-2	Massey, Statham, Simpson

SALISBURY CITY

Victoria Park, Castle Road, Salisbury, Wilts SP1 3ER.Tel: 01722 336689

Secretary: Sean Gallagher, 49 Sunnyhill Rd, Salisbury, Wilts SP1 3JQ. Tel: 01722 324932

Colours: White and Black

Nickname: The Whites

Capacity: 3,400

Seating: 320

Covered standing: 1,100

Clubhouse on ground: Yes

DIRECTIONS

A345 (Amesbury) road north from city centre/ring-road, Victoria Park is on the left 800 yds after the ring road. One mile from Salisbury (BR). Buses 208 & 209 run every 15 minutes from city centre.

Record attendance: 8,902 v Weymouth Western League 1948

Biggest win: 9-1 v Westbury Utd FA Cup 1st Qual Rd 1978

Biggest defeat: 0-7 v Minehead Southern League 1975

Record appearances: Barry Fitch 713

Record goalscorer in total: Allan Green 113 (Southern League)

Record fee received: £16,000 for Ian Thompson to AFC Bournemouth 1983

Record fee paid: £ 5,750 for Peter Loveridge to Dorchester Town 1990

HONOURS

Southern League Southern Division 1995

Western League 1958 and 1961, and Division Two 1948, and League Cup 1956

Hants Senior Cup 1962 and 1964

Alan Young Cup 1960, 1961, 1963

Wilts Premier Shield 1957, 1960, 1961, 1962, 1967, 1968, 1971, 1978, 1979, 1996

The club was formed in 1947 as the natural successor to the old Salisbury City and Salisbury Corinthians. The new club played at Hudson's Field and entered the Western League Division Two. They won promotion at the first attempt and shortly after a Supporters Club was formed to help the parent club.

Salisbury enjoyed success, winning the title in 1958 and 1961, having moved to Victoria Park in 1951, and the ground saw another five runners up spots as the club were consistent through to the late 60's when floodlights were installed. This did not hinder the club's application for the Southern League which was accepted in 1968.

They stayed in the lower division until 1986 when they were promoted, but it lasted only one season before they were back. Since then, although hampered by ground problems, the club have been runners up in 1993 and champions in 1995, which along with expensive additions to the ground, enabled them to be promoted.

In the FA Cup Salisbury reached the 2nd Round in 1959, losing to Newport with a trip to Spurs on offer and in 1962 were beaten by Peterborough United in the 1st Round. The Whites reached the competition proper in 1967 and 1979 when they switched a home tie with Millwall to the Dell, which attracted 9,000 people.

For some time the club have been close to finalising a move to a new ground up at Old Sarum, but for the time being they remain at Victoria Park.

SALISBURY CITY 1995/96 SEASON

19/08/95	BHL	P	Rushden & Diamonds	1532	0-3	
23/08/95	BHL	P	MERTHYR TYDFIL	402	0-0	
26/08/95	BHL	P	HASTINGS TOWN	334	3-4	Emms, Chalk, Manson
28/08/95	BHL	P	Gloucester City	1576	0-2	
02/09/95	BHL	P	SUDBURY TOWN	345	3-0	Paskins(2), Harbutt
05/09/95	BHL	P	Crawley Town	722	0-2	
09/09/95	FA Cup	Q1	HUNGERFORD TOWN	373	5-2	Chalk(2), Manson, Browne, Guy
16/09/95	BHL	P	STAFFORD RANGERS	379	2-1	Manson, Chalk
19/09/95	BHL	P	Merthyr Tydfil	321	0-1	
23/09/95	FA Cup	Q2	NEWPORT I.O.W.	412	1-3	Browne
30/09/95	BHL	P	GRAVESEND & NORTHFLEET	425	2-0	Manson(2)
04/10/95	DMC	1(1)	POOLE TOWN	239	5-0	Emms, Blackler, Paskins, Hewitt, Clemments
14/10/95	FA Trophy	Q1	FISHER	319	2-0	Chalk, Emms
18/10/95	DMC	1(2)	Poole Town	117	6-0	Chalk(3), Emms, Clemmence, Brown
25/10/95	BHL	P	GLOUCESTER CITY	483	3-3	Manson(2), Emms
28/10/95	BHL	P	CHELTENHAM TOWN	547	3-3	Brown, Noble, Clemments
04/11/95	FA Trophy	Q2	SUDBURY TOWN	332	2-2	Carroll, Paskins
07/11/95	FA Trophy	Q2 rep	Sudbury Town	251	2-2	Chalk, Noble
11/11/95	BHL	P	Hastings Town	444	2-6	Blackler, Manson
13/11/95	FA Trophy	Q2 rep(2)	Sudbury Town	249	2-3	Noble, Tracey
18/11/95	BHL	P	HALESOWEN TOWN	391	2-3	Manson, Hobson
02/12/95	BHL	P	ATHERSTONE UNITED	333	2-0	Manson, Clements
06/12/95	DMC	2	DORCHESTER TOWN	145	2-1	Chalk, Sandry
09/12/95	BHL	P	Stafford Rangers	433	1-2	Browne
16/12/95	BHL	P	V.S. RUGBY	302	1-0	Masters
19/12/95	BHL	P	Burton Albion	466	1-0	Manson
23/12/95	BHL	P	BALDOCK TOWN	351	1-2	Hobson
26/12/95	BHL	P	Dorchester Town	1032	2-0	Masters, Sandry
06/01/96	BHL	P	Halesowen Town	652	0-2	
13/01/96	BHL	P	GRESLEY ROVERS	337	1-4	Carroll
20/01/96	BHL	P	CRAWLEY TOWN	272	2-1	Browne, Lovell
10/02/96	BHL	P	Cambridge City	257	3-1	Browne, Lovell, Manson
13/02/96	DMC	3	Trowbridge Town	303	1-1	Emms
17/02/96	BHL	P	BURTON ALBION	376	2-0	Emms, Chalk
21/02/96	DMC	3 rep	TROWBRIDGE TOWN	238	2-1	Carroll(2)
24/02/96	BHL	P	Atherstone United	244	1-3	Chalk
26/02/96	DMC	QF	Newport A.F.C.	541	2-1	Sandry, Manson
28/02/96	BHL	P	NEWPORT A.F.C.	340	1-3	Chalk
02/03/96	BHL	P	CAMBRIDGE CITY	272	1-0	Carroll
05/03/96	BHL	P	Gravesend & Northfleet	429	1-1	Lovell
09/03/96	BHL	P	Sudbury Town	325	3-3	Sanders, Chalk, Carroll
11/03/96	BHL	P	Chelmsford City	556	0-0	
16/03/96	BHL	P	Ilkeston Town	340	1-2	Carroll
18/03/96	BHL	P	Worcester City	435	0-2	
20/03/96	BHL	P	V.S. Rugby	250	1-0	Sandrey
23/03/96	BHL	P	Baldock Town	280	2-4	Manson, Guy
27/03/96	Wilts PS	SF	TROWBRIDGE TOWN	168	2-1	De-Gordon(2)
30/03/96	BHL	P	CHELMSFORD CITY	355	0-0	
03/04/96	DMC	SF(1)	Baldock Town	104	0-0	
06/04/96	BHL	P	Newport A.F.C.	648	1-1	Chalk
08/04/96	BHL	P	DORCHESTER TOWN	422	1-0	Carroll
10/04/96	DMC	SF(2)	BALDOCK TOWN	355	1-1	Jones(og)
13/04/96	BHL	P	Gresley Rovers	582	2-2	Webb, Chalk
20/04/96	BHL	P	ILKESTON TOWN	381	0-2	
24/04/96	BHL	P	RUSHDEN & DIAMONDS	569	0-2	
27/04/96	BHL	P	WORCESTER CITY	316	3-1	Browne, Webb, Spencer
01/05/96	Wilts PS	F	CHIPPENHAM TOWN	170	2-0	Harbut(2) (played at Westbury United)
04/05/96	BHL	P	Cheltenham Town	548	3-3	Emms, Carroll, Spencer

SITTINGBOURNE

Central Park, Eurolink, Sittingbourne, Kent ME10 3SB. Tel: 01795 475577

Secretary: Christina Hadaway, C/O Sittingbourne FC

Colours: Red and Black stripes

Nickname: The Brickies

Capacity: 8,000

Seating: 2,000

Covered standing: 1,300

Clubhouse on ground: Yes

DIRECTIONS

Through Sittingbourne on main A2, club signposted clearly and regularly from both east and west. 1 mile from Sittingbourne BR station.

Record attendance: 5,951 v Tottenham Hotspur Friendly Jan 26th 1993 At the Bull Ground 5,583 v Gravesend and Northfleet FA Cup

Record fee paid or received: £210,000 for Neil Emblen and Micheal Harle from Millwall in 1993

HONOURS

Southern League South 1993; Kent League 1898, 1903, 1958, 1959, 1976, 1984, 1991; Kent League Cup 1926, 1959, 1974, 1981; Div 2 Cup 1955, 1958, 1984, 1987, 1988; Kent Senior Cup 1902, 1929, 1930, 1958; Kent Senior Shield 1926, 1928, 1954; Kent Senior Trophy 1990; Thames and Medway Cup 1956 and 1959; Thames and Medway Combination 1903, 1908, 1912, 1925, 1926; Chatham Charity Cup 1904, 1920.

The forerunners of the club commenced playing on the newly opened Recreation Ground in 1881, being known as Sittingbourne United. In 1886 it was decided to fold the old club and form a new team, Sittingbourne FC. There was another local club, named Nil Desperadums, who grew quickly, often sharing players with Bourne and in 1888 they merged, moving to the Gore Cricket Ground in 1890. By 1892, the club were having ground problems and so a field at the rear of the Bull Hotel, called Vallnces Meadow was obtained, which was leased, fenced and became home for the next 107 years. 1894 saw the club gain senior status, entering the Kent Senior, FA and Amateur Cups, around the time that the first wooden stand was built at the ground. Bourne were founder members of the Kent League, winning it in 1898, turning professional the same year. The league was won again in 1906, and joined the South-Eastern League for one season before going back until the Great War. Between Wars the club were prominent in the Kent, and Thames and Medway Leagues, winning the Kent Senior Shield in 1927 and 1928 and the Senior Cup the following two years, coinciding with their entry into the Southern League which lasted three years.

After surviving a financial crisis the club was re-formed in 1946 and eight years later the Bull Ground was purchased with the help of a £3,000 loan from the FA, which heralded the start of another boom time in the Kent League with wins in league and cup until again joining the Southern League in 1959 along with a number of fellow Kent clubs. Promotion did not come and after a lean spell they reverted back to the reformed Kent League in 1967, immediately winning the title, and repeating it nine years later, finishing runners-up on three other occasions. During the 80's the Brickies were consistently amongst the top sides in cup and league which saw them in good fettle to make the most important decision in the 100 plus years when they sold the Bull Ground for development. The finances enabled them to move to a 23 acre site nearby which despite another major cash crisis has been built with Football League in mind. A fabulous final season in the Kent League saw them promoted as undefeated champions, but after gaining promotion severe cut-backs saw the club relegated to the Southern Division. Last season saw the awaited renaissance and the Brickies are back in the Premier Division for 1996-97.

SITTINGBOURNE 1995/96 SEASON

Date	Comp	Round	Opponent	Att	Score	Scorers
19/08/95	BHL	S	BASHLEY	549	2-2	Donohue, Seager
22/08/95	BHL	S	Ashford Town	891	0-0	
26/08/95	BHL	S	Cinderford Town	229	2-3	Miller(2)
28/08/95	BHL	S	TONBRIDGE ANGELS	749	3-1	Walker, Miller, Hearn
02/09/95	BHL	S	Weymouth	711	3-0	Kimble(2), Planck
06/09/95	BHL	S	ERITH & BELVEDERE	526	1-0	Planck
09/09/95	FA Cup	Q1	Horsham	376	5-0	Kimble(2), Lovell, Thompson, Seager
16/09/95	BHL	S	Yate Town	155	2-2	Lovell, Walker
20/09/95	BHL	S	ASHFORD TOWN	947	4-0	Walker(2), Planck, Hearn
23/09/95	FA Cup	Q2	Erith & Belvedere	247	2-2	Lovell, Planck
27/09/95	FA Cup	Q2 rep	ERITH & BELVEDERE	556	6-1	Searle, Planck, Lovell, Walker(2), Kimble
30/09/95	BHL	S	FLEET TOWN	646	3-2	Planck(2), Kimble
04/10/95	DMC	1(1)	MARGATE	467	1-3	Donoghue
07/10/95	FA Cup	Q3	Bromley	692	1-1	Planck
11/10/95	FA Cup	Q3 rep	BROMLEY	1030	3-2	Lovell, Walker, Kimble
14/10/95	FA Trophy	Q1	Forest Green Rovers	101	2-1	Hearn, Lovell
18/10/95	Kent SC	1	ERITH & BELVEDERE	249	3-3	Miller(2), Seager
21/10/95	FA Cup	Q4	DORCHESTER TOWN	1232	1-2	Walker
24/10/95	BHL	S	Tonbridge Angels	588	4-1	Walker(2), Miller, Searle
28/10/95	BHL	S	WATERLOOVILLE	701	1-2	Pearson
31/10/95	DMC	1(2)	Margate	154	0-1	
02/11/95	Kent SC	1 rep	Erith & Belvedere	76	5-2	Donoghue(3), Thompson, Smith
04/11/95	FA Trophy	Q2	Bognor Regis Town	400	2-2	Planck, Miller
08/11/95	FA Trophy	Q2 rep	BOGNOR REGIS TOWN	674	1-2	Planck
11/11/95	BHL	S	Poole Town	102	5-0	Planck, Lovell(3), Hough
18/11/95	BHL	S	CLEVEDON TOWN	598	5-1	Walker, Eeles, Lovell, Seager, Kimble
25/11/95	BHL	S	Forest Green Rovers	169	0-2	
02/12/95	BHL	S	YATE TOWN	547	0-1	
09/12/95	BHL	S	Fareham Town	104	2-0	Seager, Lovell
16/12/95	BHL	S	HAVANT TOWN	546	0-1	
23/12/95	BHL	S	NEWPORT I.O.W.	675	1-2	Lovell
26/12/95	BHL	S	Margate	506	2-1	Walker, Kimble
01/01/96	BHL	S	BRAINTREE TOWN	674	2-1	Hearn, Lovell
06/01/96	BHL	S	CINDERFORD TOWN	597	4-0	Lovell, Seager(2), Kimble
16/01/96	BHL	S	Trowbridge Town	243	0-3	
20/01/96	BHL	S	POOLE TOWN	611	8-1	Walker(2), Lovell(4), Pearson, Kimble
29/01/96	Kent SC	QF	CHARLTON ATHLETIC	476	1-3	Planck
03/02/96	BHL	S	TROWBRIDGE TOWN	629	2-1	Pearson, Planck
06/02/96	BHL	S	Erith & Belvedere	213	3-0	Lovell, Planck, Seagar
13/02/96	BHL	S	Weston-super-Mare	220	2-1	Donoghue(2)
17/02/96	BHL	S	Waterlooville	276	0-1	
24/02/96	BHL	S	FOREST GREEN ROVERS	750	5-1	Lovell, Donohue, Searle, Seagar, Planck
02/03/96	BHL	S	Bashley	171	1-0	Planck
09/03/96	BHL	S	WEYMOUTH	805	2-1	Miller, Kimble
16/03/96	BHL	S	Clevedon Town	218	3-2	Lovell, Kimble, Walker
20/03/96	BHL	S	WESTON-SUPER-MARE	554	2-0	Planck, Lovell
23/03/96	BHL	S	Newport I.O.W.	385	1-3	Walker
30/03/96	BHL	S	FISHER	647	3-0	Lovell, Eeles, Kimble
06/04/96	BHL	S	Braintree Town	303	7-0	Planck(3), Eeles, Seagar, Kimble, Walker
08/04/96	BHL	S	MARGATE	1085	3-1	Walker, Searle, Planck
13/04/96	BHL	S	Fleet Town	388	1-3	Planck
16/04/96	BHL	S	Witney Town	124	2-0	Bourne, Lovell
20/04/96	BHL	S	FAREHAM TOWN	795	3-0	Walker, Lovell, Planck
23/04/96	BHL	S	Fisher	411	2-0	Kimble, Pearson
27/04/96	BHL	S	WITNEY TOWN	1072	4-2	Pearson, Planck(3)
04/05/96	BHL	S	Havant Town	465	2-2	Planck, Seager

SUDBURY TOWN

Priory Stadium, Priory Walk, Sudbury, Suffolk. Tel: 01787 379095

Secretary: David Webb, 6 Melford Rd, Sudbury, Suffolk CO10 6LS. Tel: 01787 372352

Press officer: Richie Powling at club

Club shop and programme: Darren Witt, 4 Highfield Rd, Sudbury, Suffolk CO10 6QY Tel: 01787 212234 Mobile: 0402 159375

Nickname: Borough   Colours: All Yellow

Capacity: 5,000   Seating: 300

Covered standing: 1,000   Clubhouse on ground: Yes

DIRECTIONS

From Sudbury town centre follow Halstead/Chelmsford signs for about 1 mile. Take 1st right after railway bridge at foot of steep hill, and 1st right after sharp lefthand bend.

Record attendance: 4,700 v Ipswich Town Testimonial 1978

Biggest win: 14-1 v Leiston (h) FA Cup 1st Qual Rd Sept 24th 1955

Biggest defeat: 0-9 v Tottenham Hotspur Eastern Co Lge Feb 25th 1961

Record goalscorer in one season: Steve McGavin 58

Record fee achieved: £10,000 for Steve McGavin   Record fee paid: Undisclosed for Jamie Reilly

HONOURS

FA VASE Runners-up 1989 and semi-finalists 1988 and 1992; Southern League Cup 1994; Eastern Counties League 1974, 1975, 1976, 1986, 1987, 1989, 1990,; League Cup 1970, 1977, 1983, 1987, 1989, 1990; Suffolk Premier Cup 1973, 1974, 1976, 1981, 1982, 1983, 1985, 1987, 1988, 1989, 1990, 1992, 1993; Suffolk Senior Cup 1957 and 1987; East Anglian Cup 1986, 1987 retained but final not played, 1992; Essex and Suffolk Border League 1949, 1950, 1952, 1953, 1954.

Manager for 1996/97: Richie Powling   **Assistant Manager: David Crown**

Chairman: Graeme Garden

A clubshop catalogue will be available 50p + sae from start of season.

The club produce an occasional Fanzine and regular programmes for reserve and youth matches. Work has started on an official history by John Chaplin and Darren Witt

Formed in 1885, Sudbury Town were founder members of the Suffolk County FA and made their first home in Friars Street, sharing with the Cricket Club. They played in the Suffolk and Ipswich, and later Essex and Suffolk Border Leagues, winning the latter six times in eight seasons under manager Pat Kearney in the late 40's and early 50's. In 1951 a Limited Company was formed and a former water meadow close to the cricket ground was purchased. Much work then went into raising the ground level to counter flooding from the adjacent river, but eventually the club's glorious ornate grandstand was moved from Friar Street and they moved in. They were elected to the Eastern Counties League and won the first major trophy in 1957, the Suffolk Senior Cup. After going close in 1966, it took until 1974 for the club to finally win the league, and from then success snowballed with seven championships and six runners up spots as well as six wins in the League Cup and over 20 appearances in the Suffolk Premier Cup final.

As the 90's approached, so did the possibility of a Wembley Final, and although Borough lost in the FA Vase semi-final to Colne Dynamoes, the following season saw them reach Wembley after a season which saw 74 matches. Although the club drew at Wembley against Tamworth, they lost the replay at Peterborough, but they had the consolation of winning the League and Cup double as well the Premier Cup. The following year saw another three titles and more importantly, election to the Southern League. In 1992 Sudbury again failed at the Vase semi-final stage, losing to Guiseley, but in 1994 the club were promoted to the Premier Division as runners-up.

The last two seasons have seen Sudbury struggle in 1995, with relegation a distinct possibility, but a win and a draw were enough to guarantee safety. In reserve, the club were promoted to the Premier Division of the Eastern Counties League, and last May, the club finished a more comfortable tenth, with a Trophy run which lasted 11 matches as a highlight. They reached the final of the East Anglian Cup before losing to local rivals Braintree Town, but after 65 matches there was no silverware.

SUDBURY TOWN 1995/96 SEASON

Date	Comp	Round	Opponent	Att	Score	Scorers
19/08/95	BHL	P	Halesowen Town	660	3-3	Wallis, Brown, Girling
22/08/95	BHL	P	CRAWLEY TOWN	370	1-2	Brown
26/08/95	BHL	P	BURTON ALBION	380	3-0	Stafford, Greaves, Wallis
28/08/95	BHL	P	Gravesend & Northfleet	536	3-3	Hammond(2), Smith
02/09/95	BHL	P	Salisbury City	345	0-3	
05/09/95	BHL	P	HASTINGS TOWN	320	0-0	
09/09/95	FA Cup	Q1	TIPTREE UNITED	334	3-0	Brown(3)
16/09/95	BHL	P	NEWPORT A.F.C.	454	3-1	McLean, Stafford, Brown
19/09/95	BHL	P	Crawley Town	822	2-2	Smith, Ashdjian
23/09/95	FA Cup	Q2	HEYBRIDGE SWIFTS	502	2-1	Smith, French
30/09/95	BHL	P	GLOUCESTER CITY	421	0-2	
03/10/95	DMC	1(1)	Cambridge City	180	1-1	Reilly
07/10/95	FA Cup	Q3	Wisbech Town	705	0-1	
11/10/95	Suffolk PC	QF	BURY TOWN	154	1-2	Smith
14/10/95	FA Trophy	Q1	Ashford Town	569	2-0	Brown, McClean
17/10/95	BHL	P	GRAVESEND & NORTHFLEET	411	5-3	Tracey, Reilly, Thompson(2), Brown
21/10/95	BHL	P	Atherstone United	234	0-0	
24/10/95	E. Anglian	1	Woodbridge Town	220	1-0	McLean
28/10/95	BHL	P	BALDOCK TOWN	406	2-1	Wallis, Brown
31/10/95	DMC	1(2)	CAMBRIDGE CITY	226	1-3	Cutmore
04/11/95	FA Trophy	Q2	Salisbury City	332	2-2	Smith(2)
07/11/95	FA Trophy	Q2 rep	SALISBURY CITY	251	2-2	Osman, McIntosh
11/11/95	BHL	P	MERTHYR TYDFIL	324	1-2	Smith
13/11/95	FA Trophy	Q2 rep(2)	SALISBURY CITY	249	3-2	Brown(3)
18/11/95	BHL	P	CHELTENHAM TOWN	349	3-4	McIntosh, Thompson, Osman
25/11/95	FA Trophy	Q3	TOOTING & MITCHAM UTD	418	2-0	Stafford, Thompson
02/12/95	BHL	P	ILKESTON TOWN	349	1-0	McIntosh
09/12/95	BHL	P	HALESOWEN TOWN	345	1-2	Brown
12/12/95	BHL	P	Cambridge City	141	0-1	
16/12/95	BHL	P	Chelmsford City	771	1-2	Reilly
06/01/96	BHL	P	Merthyr Tydfil	417	1-2	Ashdjian
10/01/96	E. Anglian	2	Stowmarket Town	100	2-1	Brown, Girling
13/01/96	BHL	P	DORCHESTER TOWN	344	2-1	Tracey, Brown
20/01/96	FA Trophy	1	Trowbridge Town	319	2-2	McClean, Smith
23/01/96	FA Trophy	1 rep	TROWBRIDGE TOWN	224	1-1	Brown
03/02/96	BHL	P	Burton Albion	769	3-2	Brown, Tracey, Callinan
05/02/96	FA Trophy	1 rep(2)	Trowbridge Town	327	1-1	Smith
10/02/96	FA Trophy	1 rep(3)	TROWBRIDGE TOWN	368	4-3	McLean(2), French, Greaves
15/02/96	FA Trophy	2	GLOUCESTER CITY	262	3-1	McLean, Smith(2)
17/02/96	BHL	P	Newport A.F.C.	576	1-5	Brown
24/02/96	BHL	P	CHELMSFORD CITY	604	2-0	Brown, Grice
27/02/96	BHL	P	CAMBRIDGE CITY	279	1-1	Smith
02/03/96	FA Trophy	3	Macclesfield Town	1140	0-1	
05/03/96	BHL	P	Rushden & Diamonds	1409	1-3	Ashdjian
09/03/96	BHL	P	SALISBURY CITY	325	3-3	McLean, Brown(2)
12/03/96	BHL	P	Gresley Rovers	402	2-5	Callinan, Brown
16/03/96	BHL	P	Gloucester City	509	0-1	
19/03/96	BHL	P	Dorchester Town	408	0-2	
23/03/96	BHL	P	STAFFORD RANGERS	347	3-1	McLean, Smith, Brown
25/03/96	BHL	P	Worcester City	448	1-1	Tracey
28/03/96	E. Anglian	3	IPSWICH WANDERERS		2-0	
30/03/96	BHL	P	V.S. Rugby	302	2-0	Ball, Crown
02/04/96	BHL	P	Stafford Rangers	440	1-0	Brown
06/04/96	BHL	P	Baldock Town	382	3-1	Crown, Reilly, Brown
08/04/96	BHL	P	RUSHDEN & DIAMONDS	918	4-1	Brown(4)
11/04/96	E. Anglian	QF	Fakenham Town	277	2-1	Brown, Tracey
13/04/96	BHL	P	Cheltenham Town	602	1-1	McLean
16/04/96	BHL	P	V.S. RUGBY	301	3-2	Ball, Crown(2)
20/04/96	BHL	P	ATHERSTONE UNITED	390	0-1	
23/04/96	BHL	P	Hastings Town	363	1-2	Crown
25/04/96	E. Anglian	SF	Concord Rangers	120	2-0	Grice(2)
27/04/96	BHL	P	GRESLEY ROVERS	320	3-1	Smith, Brown, Adams
30/04/96	BHL	P	WORCESTER CITY	263	0-0	
04/05/96	BHL	P	Ilkeston Town	534	2-4	Brown(2)
07/05/96	E. Anglian	F	Braintree Town	643	0-3	

WORCESTER CITY

St George's Lane, Barbourne, Worcester WR1 1QT. Tel: 01905 23003

Secretary: Steve Bond, 4 Ferry Close, St Johns, Worcester
Tel: 01905 423120 or 01905 25427

Nickname: The City

Capacity: 4,749

Seating: 1,223

Covered standing: 2,000

Clubhouse on ground: Yes

Record attendance: 17,042 v Sheffield United
FA Cup 4th Rd Jan 24th 1959

Biggest win: 18-1 v Bilston Birmingham League
Nov 21st 1931

Biggest defeat: 0-10 v Wellington Birmingham League Aug 29th 1920

Record appearances: Bobby McEwan 596 1959-75

Record goalscorer in aggregate: John Inglis 189 1970-77

Record fee received: £27,000 for John Barton to Everton in 1979

DIRECTIONS

**M5 jct 6 (Worcester North),
follow signs to Worcester,
right at first lights, St
Georges Lane is 3rd left.
From South: M5 jct 6
(Worcester) A44 to
Worcester, pass racecourse
and follow A38 (towards
Bromsgrove), ground on
right, 1 mile from Foregate
Street (BR) station.**

HONOURS

Southern League 1979, Div 1 1968 and Div 1 North 1977; Challenge Cup 1940; Champions Cup 1979; Birmingham League 1914, 1925, 1929, 1930; Worcestershire Senior Cup 1908, 1909, 1910, 1911, 1912, 1913, 1914, 1929, 1930, 1933, 1946, 1949, 1956, 1957, 1958, 1959, 1961, 1963, 1965, 1970, 1978, 1980, 1982, 1984, 1988; Birmingham Senior Cup 1976; Staffs Senior Cup 1977; Inter League Champions Cup 1979.

Manager for 1996/97: George Rooney   **Assistant Manager: Graham Selby**

Chairman: Dr M.Sorensen   **Vice Chairman: Mr L.Brown**

Worcester City were formed in 1902 after the amalgamation of two local clubs, Berwick Rangers and Worcester Rovers. The new club played their first competitive match in the Birmingham and District League against reserve sides of such as Aston Villa, Wolves, Birmingham and West Bromwich Albion, winning the title just before the Great War.

From 1918 Worcester became one of the leading teams in the league as the reserve sides pulled out and through the late 20's won the title three times, the last title coming with 113 goals scored and all 17 home matches won. In 1938 they successfully applied to join the Southern League and won the League Cup in 1940 and they remained in, becoming founder members of the new Premier Division in 1959. They tasted relegation in 1967, were promoted within a year but again went down.

Promotion back up took some time but when it arrived in 1977 the Northern Division was won by 15 points. 1979 saw City take the League title outright for the only time and that same season saw them reach the semi-finals of the Welsh Cup and the 2nd Round of the FA Cup.

Their reputation as Cup fighters was established in 1959 when both Liverpool and Millwall were beaten at St George's Lane. They reached the Fourth Round where they lost to Sheffield United in front a record crowd of over 17,000.

The league title meant a place in the Alliance Premier League, where they stayed until 1985 when they returned to the Southern League, where they remain.

The club's first ground was Severn Terrace, the former home of Berwick Rangers, before moving to Thorneloe, former home of Worcester Rovers, a ground which was near Pitchcroft, a road with the same name is there today. The third move came when they played at the Royal Grammar School grounds in Flagge Meadow, still in use and a few hundred yards from the current home. St Georges Lane ground was opened after a public appeal, by the Mayor on Oct 25th 1905.

WORCESTER CITY 1995/96 SEASON

Date	Comp	Rd	Opponent	Att	Score	Scorers
02/09/95	BHL	P	CHELTENHAM TOWN	1212	1-2	Norris
06/09/95	BHL	P	Newport A.F.C.	1407	1-1	Ferguson
16/09/95	BHL	P	RUSHDEN & DIAMONDS	960	0-0	
19/09/95	BHL	P	Stafford Rangers	463	2-0	Norris, Hemstock
23/09/95	BHL	P	Crawley Town	1004	3-1	Norris, Hick, Jackson
30/09/95	BHL	P	BURTON ALBION	978	1-1	Williams
03/10/95	DMC	1(1)	Halesowen Town	441	2-0	Cottrill, Norris
07/10/95	BHL	P	HASTINGS TOWN	723	1-0	Fergusson
14/10/95	BHL	P	Gloucester City	1285	1-2	Norris
21/10/95	BHL	P	CAMBRIDGE CITY	825	2-1	Norris, Ferguson
23/10/95	BHL	P	MERTHYR TYDFIL	1094	4-2	McGrath, Ferguson, Healy, Cottrill
28/10/95	BHL	P	V.S. Rugby	548	0-0	
30/10/95	DMC	1(2)	HALESOWEN TOWN	627	4-1	Norris(2), Williams, Hemstock
04/11/95	FA Trophy	Q2	Clevedon Town	420	4-0	Norris, Ferguson, Jackson, Cottrill
11/11/95	BHL	P	CRAWLEY TOWN	887	2-0	Hicks, Ferguson
13/11/95	BHL	P	NEWPORT A.F.C.	1447	2-0	Norris(2)
18/11/95	BHL	P	Burton Albion	942	0-2	
25/11/95	FA Trophy	Q3	AYLESBURY UNITED	863	3-0	Norris, Fergusson, Williams
02/12/95	BHL	P	GLOUCESTER CITY	1109	1-3	Healey
04/12/95	DMC	2	STOURBRIDGE	305	3-0	Fergusson, Norris(2)
16/12/95	BHL	P	Cheltenham Town	1010	3-1	Norris, Fergusson, Jackson
18/12/95	Birm SC	2	WEST MIDLANDS POLICE	224	3-1	Hemstock(2), Heeley
26/12/95	BHL	P	Halesowen Town	1119	3-3	Norris, Jackson, Williams
06/01/96	BHL	P	Gresley Rovers	677	0-1	
08/01/96	DMC	3	HINCKLEY TOWN	256	2-3	Hemstock, Norris
13/01/96	BHL	P	ILKESTON TOWN	690	4-3	Jackson(2), McGrath, Ferguson
15/01/96	Birm SC	3	Aston Villa	1229	1-2	Hemstock
20/01/96	FA Trophy	1	Bognor Regis Town	524	0-1	
03/02/96	BHL	P	Rushden & Diamonds	2197	0-1	
10/02/96	BHL	P	ATHERSTONE UNITED	588	1-0	Ferguson
17/02/96	BHL	P	CHELMSFORD CITY	743	0-0	
24/02/96	BHL	P	GRESLEY ROVERS	630	3-3	Williams, Fergusson, Wright
26/02/96	Worcs SC	QF	SOLIHULL BOROUGH	262	0-2	
02/03/96	BHL	P	Chelmsford City	710	0-1	
05/03/96	BHL	P	Baldock Town	220	1-0	Wright
09/03/96	BHL	P	Hastings Town	440	0-0	
16/03/96	BHL	P	Gravesend & Northfleet	472	1-0	Scott
18/03/96	BHL	P	SALISBURY CITY	435	2-0	Molloy, McGrath
23/03/96	BHL	P	Dorchester Town	705	2-1	Molloy, Hemstock
25/03/96	BHL	P	SUDBURY TOWN	448	1-1	Hemstock
30/03/96	BHL	P	BALDOCK TOWN	555	0-0	
06/04/96	BHL	P	Atherstone United	326	1-1	Benton
08/04/96	BHL	P	HALESOWEN TOWN	1221	0-1	
13/04/96	BHL	P	V.S. RUGBY	607	4-0	Molloy, Hemstock, Walker, Scott
15/04/96	BHL	P	DORCHESTER TOWN	537	0-1	
20/04/96	BHL	P	Cambridge City	243	2-4	Hemstock, Greenman
27/04/96	BHL	P	Salisbury City	316	1-3	Ferguson
30/04/96	BHL	P	Sudbury Town	263	0-0	
04/05/96	BHL	P	GRAVESEND & NORTHFLEET	702	3-1	Hicks, Ferguson(2)

MARGATE
FOOTBALL CLUB
FOUNDED 1896

CLUB SPONSOR
Westons Dairies

Beazer Homes League

WINSTONLEAD
KENT FOOTBALL LEAGUE

80p

WESTONS DAIRIES

HAVE YOU WON A PAIR OF TICKETS FOR ADMISSION TO THE DREAMLAND CINEMA ? SEE INSIDE FOR LUCKY STICKER

OFFICIAL MATCHDAY PROGRAMME SEASON 1995/96

TODAY WE WELCOME TO HARTSDOWN PARK

FAREHAM TOWN

(Beazer Homes League, Southern Division)

Saturday 27th January 1996
Kick-off 3.00pm

SS PRESS - PRINT & COPY CENTRE
24 High Street, Margate, Kent CT9 2DS (Tel : 01843 299923)

YATE TOWN FC

THE BLUEBELLS

Main Sponsor
Carlsberg Tetley

Beazer Homes League Southern Division

FISHER '93

Wednesday 1st May 1996 7.45 pm

Programme **70p**

Cambridge City Football Club

Beazer Homes League

1995/96 SEASON

Official Match Day Programme
£1

Evening News

Beazer Homes League Premier Division
City v Chelmsford City
Monday 8th April Kick off 3pm

LANCER

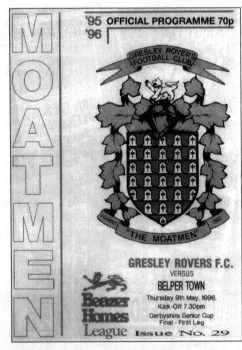

MOATMEN

'95 **OFFICIAL PROGRAMME 70p**
'96

GRESLEY ROVERS FOOTBALL CLUB

"THE MOATMEN"

GRESLEY ROVERS F.C.
VERSUS
BELPER TOWN
Thursday 9th May, 1996.
Kick-Off 7.30pm
Derbyshire Senior Cup
Final - First Leg

Beazer Homes League

ISSUE No. 29

BEDWORTH UNITED

The Oval, Coventry Rd, Bedworth, Warwicks CV12 8NN. Tel: 01203 314302

Secretary: Graham J.Bloxham, 43 Mount Pleasant Rd, Bedworth, Warks. CV12 8EX Tel: 01203 317940

Press officer Alan Robinson, 38 Thirlmere Ave, Nuneaton, Warks. CV11 6HU Tel: 01203 346360

Nickname: The Greenbacks   Capacity: 7,000

Seating: 300   Covered standing: None

Clubhouse on ground: Yes

Record attendance: 5,127 v Nuneaton Borough Southern League 1982

Biggest win: 11-0

Biggest defeat: 1-10

Record appearances: Peter Spacey

Record goalscorer in one season: Peter Spacey

Record goalscorer in total: Peter Spacey

Record fee received: £30,000 from Plymouth Argyle for Richard Landon

DIRECTIONS

M6 Junction 3. Go into Bedworth on the B4113 (Coventry to Bedworth road) and the ground is 200 yards past Bedworth Leisure Centre on this road. Coaches should park at the Leisure Centre. Buses from Coventry and Nuneaton pass the ground.

HONOURS

Birmingham Combination 1949 and 1950; Birmingham Senior Cup 1979, 1981 and 1982; Midland Floodlit Cup 1982 and 1993.

Manager for 1996/97: Dean Thomas   **Assistant Manager: Nicky Platnauer**

Chairman: Alan Robinson   **Vice Chairman: Roy Whitehead**

The first Bedworth Town FC is believed to have been formed in 1895 when several matches were played against local sides. They became founder members of the Nuneaton and District League in 1898 but by 1900 they were gone. Another club, Bedworth Evening Combination School, became the forerunners of the second Town club in 1905. Finishing runners up in the Second Division of the Coventry and North Warwicks League that year, they changed their name to Town on winning promotion and stayed in existence until the early 20's. A third club came on to the scene in 1925 when Collycroft United, formed in 1916, changed their name to Bedworth Town. They became the most successful of the pre-War clubs in the same league, spending one year in the Central Amateur League, before becoming Bedworth Centrals in 1938 and folding in 1940.

The last Town club was formed in 1947 as a semi-pro club and played in the Birmingham Combination, winning the title in 1949 and 1950, losing the Birmingham Senior Cup final. In 1954 the club joined the Birmingham League Northern Section, which was re-titled the West Midland League in 1962. There was little success for Town, and they changed their name to United in 1968. Lights were installed at the Oval in September 1970 and two years later the club were elected into the Southern League, where they were part of the re-formed Premier Division in 1982. In February of that year the non-League world was staggered when a crowd of 5,127 turned up to watch the local derby with Nuneaton Borough which saw them go top of the table.

Sadly after a poor season in 1989, the club were relegated to the Midland Division.

The Oval ground has twice been home to the various Bedworth Clubs. Known originally as the Knob, it subsequently became a Welfare Ground and after the war, when the old British Queen ground near the station was not available, became home again.

BEDWORTH UNITED 1995/96 SEASON

Date	Comp	Round	Opponent	Att	Score	Scorers
19/08/95	BHL	M	Evesham United	175	0-0	
22/08/95	BHL	M	TAMWORTH	511	1-2	Graham
26/08/95	BHL	M	MOOR GREEN	302	0-2	
02/09/95	BHL	M	SOLIHULL BOROUGH	294	5-0	Symonds(3), Graham(2)
05/09/95	BHL	M	Sutton Coldfield Town	168	0-2	
09/09/95	FA Cup	Q1	Boldmere St Michaels	108	2-1	Morrison, Wilkins
16/09/95	BHL	M	ROTHWELL TOWN	292	4-1	Graham, Symonds(2), Wilkins
19/09/95	BHL	M	Tamworth	569	2-1	Morrison, Penny
23/09/95	FA Cup	Q2	Evesham United	223	0-2	
30/09/95	BHL	M	RACING CLUB WARWICK	250	2-1	Thomas, Morrison
03/10/95	DMC	1(1)	Hinckley Town	105	0-1	
07/10/95	BHL	M	Grantham Town	207	1-1	Graham
14/10/95	FA Trophy	Q1	Farsley Celtic	159	1-3	Symonds
21/10/95	BHL	M	PAGET RANGERS	254	1-1	Platnaeur
24/10/95	BHL	M	LEICESTER UNITED	156	2-1	Stackman, Corden
28/10/95	BHL	M	Bilston Town	120	1-0	Symonds
31/10/95	DMC	1(2)	HINCKLEY TOWN	172	0-1	
07/11/95	Mids F'lit	1(1)	Blakenall	73	2-4	Graham(2)
11/11/95	BHL	M	CORBY TOWN	265	3-0	Graham, Platnaeur, Symonds
14/11/95	BHL	M	SUTTON COLDFIELD TOWN	227	3-2	Penny, Platnaeur, Symonds
18/11/95	BHL	M	Moor Green	221	0-0	
25/11/95	BHL	M	Solihull Borough	178	3-1	Thomas, Symonds, Graham
28/11/95	Birm SC	2	BRIERLEY HILL TOWN	139	5-0	Lamb(2), Morrison, Symonds(2)
02/12/95	BHL	M	REDDITCH UNITED	308	5-0	Symonds(2), Penny, Graham(2)
16/12/95	BHL	M	HINCKLEY TOWN	262	3-1	Platnaeur, Thomas, Symonds
01/01/96	BHL	M	Nuneaton Borough	1936	2-1	Graham, Wileman
06/01/96	Birm SC	3	Wednesfield	120	3-0	Platnauer, Wiseman, Morrison
09/01/96	BHL	M	Rothwell Town	250	2-2	Graham(2)
13/01/96	BHL	M	GRANTHAM TOWN	388	2-2	Symonds, Platnaeur
20/01/96	BHL	M	Racing Club Warwick	220	1-2	Clark(og)
23/01/96	BHL	M	BRIDGNORTH TOWN	211	3-0	Symonds(2), Graham
03/02/96	BHL	M	EVESHAM UNITED	255	1-2	Morris
05/02/96	Birm SC	QF	ASTON VILLA	507	1-2	Wilkins
10/02/96	BHL	M	Bury Town	181	1-0	Wilkins
14/02/96	BHL	M	Leicester United	310	1-0	Graham
17/02/96	BHL	M	Stourbridge	185	0-3	
24/02/96	BHL	M	STOURBRIDGE	212	1-1	McGrory
27/02/96	BHL	M	Buckingham Town	85	2-0	Symonds, Graham
02/03/96	BHL	M	BURY TOWN	235	3-2	Thomas, Smith, Beard
09/03/96	BHL	M	Hinckley Town	160	0-0	
16/03/96	BHL	M	King's Lynn	770	0-2	
23/03/96	BHL	M	BUCKINGHAM TOWN	284	1-1	Platnaeur
26/03/96	BHL	M	DUDLEY TOWN	199	3-1	Thomas(2), Symonds
30/03/96	BHL	M	Bridgnorth Town	162	5-0	Symonds, Wileman, Corden(2), Platnaeur
06/04/96	BHL	M	NUNEATON BOROUGH	1540	1-0	Wileman
08/04/96	BHL	M	Dudley Town	200	3-2	Graham, Penny, Beard
10/04/96	Mids F'lit	1(2)	BLAKENALL	72	5-2	Daly(2), Beard, Simmonds, Wilkins
13/04/96	BHL	M	Redditch United	292	0-1	
17/04/96	BHL	M	Corby Town	194	3-2	Wileman, Graham, Smith
20/04/96	BHL	M	KING'S LYNN	701	1-0	Symonds
27/04/96	BHL	M	Paget Rangers	201	1-1	Daly
04/05/96	BHL	M	BILSTON TOWN	335	3-1	Graham, Symonds

BILSTON TOWN

Queen Street, Bilston, WV 14 7EX. Tel: 01902 491498

Secretary: Jeff Calloway, 4 Mervyn Rd, Bradley, West Mids WV14 8DF Tel 01902 681660

Colours: Tangerine and White

Nickname: Steelmen or Boro

Capacity: 4,000

Seating: 350

Covered standing: 350

Clubhouse on ground : Yes

Record attendance: 7,500 v Wolverhampton Wanderers for floodlight opening in 1953, and for competitive match 7,000 v Halifax Town FA Cup 1st Rd 1968

Biggest win: 12-2 v Tipton Town

Biggest defeat: 0-8 v Merthyr Tydfil

DIRECTIONS

M6 junction 10, A454 towards Wolverhampton then pick up A563 towards Bilston and turn left into Beckett Street after a little over a mile, ground at bottom. 3 miles from Wolverhampton (BR), bus 45 from bus station passes ground. Buses 78 and 79 from Birmingham stop within quarter of a mile of ground.

HONOURS

West Midlands League 1961 and 1973, and League Cup 1973

Division Two 1957

Staffs Senior Cup 1958, 1960, 1961, 1962

Birmingham Junior Cup 1896

Wednesbury Charity Cup 1981, 1982, 1983, 1985

Manager for 1996-97: Ian Painter

Bilston Wanderers and Bilston Rovers amalgamated in 1895 to form Bilston United, who played at Prouds Lane, on the present day Villiers Estate, with the changing rooms in the Spread Eagle pub.

Success came quickly and in 1908 United became a Limited Company and in 1921 moved to their present ground in Queen Street. Six years later, sadly the club went bankrupt and the ground was sold to the local Education Committee with the proviso that as long as there was a Town team then they would be allowed to use it for a nominal rent. Within a year the club was re-formed as Bilston FC and joined the Walsall Senior League, playing at Queen Street. They changed their name to Bilston Borough in 1931 but during the Second War they disbanded, and re-formed in 1946 as Bilston FC in the Walsall League.

They were very successful in the early post-War years, winning the league twice, Walsall Senior Cup twice, Walsall Challenge Cup and Express and Star Cup. In 1949 they joined the Birmingham League, which they eventually won in 1961, mostly due to leading goalscorer Ron McDermott who knocked in 78 goals that season, a record which will never be beaten.

They won the Staffs Senior Cup three years running and the Walsall Senior Cup during the next three seasons and reached the FA Cup 1st Round in 1968 when they lost to Halifax. Their best season came in 1972-73 when they won the West Midlands League and Cup double and got to Round 2 of the FA Cup, before losing in a replay to Barnet.

The 80's brought four Wednesbury Charity Cups and promotion to the Southern League in 1985 after finishing runners up to Halesowen Town. Since then Queen Street has been steadily updated and the club enjoyed a run in the FA Vase in 1993 which ended at the quarter final stage.

BILSTON TOWN 1995/96 SEASON

Date	Competition	Round	Opponent	Attendance	Score	Scorers
19/08/95	BHL	M	BURY TOWN	96	2-1	Harnett, Parker
22/08/95	BHL	M	Leicester United	85	1-1	Grant
26/08/95	FA Cup	P	BLAKENALL	131	0-0	
29/08/95	FA Cup	P rep	Blakenall	103	1-2	Jones
02/09/95	BHL	M	Grantham Town	185	1-1	Parker
05/09/95	BHL	M	BRIDGNORTH TOWN	106	1-0	Stokes
16/09/95	BHL	M	CORBY TOWN	122	1-0	Edwards
19/09/95	BHL	M	LEICESTER UNITED	85	3-0	Parker(3)
30/09/95	BHL	M	Dudley Town	191	2-2	Edwards(2)
03/10/95	DMC	1(1)	SUTTON COLDFIELD TOWN	41	3-0	Bannister(og), Berks, Perry
07/10/95	BHL	M	ROTHWELL TOWN	110	3-0	Parker, Grant, Perry
10/10/95	Staffs SC	1	STOURPORT SWIFTS	63	4-1	Perry, Parker(2), Harnett
14/10/95	FA Trophy	Q1	Sutton Coldfield Town	116	1-1	Parker
17/10/95	FA Trophy	Q1 rep	SUTTON COLDFIELD TOWN	85	4-4	Parker(2), Perry, Harnett
21/10/95	BHL	M	Hinckley Town	108	4-2	Ingram, Barnes(2), Brown, Ross(og)
23/10/95	FA Trophy	Q1 rep(2)	SUTTON COLDFIELD TOWN	154	2-1	Harnett, Grant
28/10/95	BHL	M	BEDWORTH UNITED	120	0-1	
31/10/95	DMC	1(2)	Sutton Coldfield Town	41	3-3	Perry, King, Edwards
04/11/95	FA Trophy	Q2	LEICESTER UNITED	100	5-2	Edwards(2), Berks(2), Harnett
07/11/95	BHL	M	SUTTON COLDFIELD TOWN	75	0-1	
11/11/95	BHL	M	EVESHAM UNITED	103	3-1	Perry(2), Edwards
14/11/95	BHL	M	Bridgnorth Town	107	0-1	
18/11/95	BHL	M	SOLIHULL BOROUGH	110	2-1	Edwards, Berks
21/11/95	Staffs SC	2	OLDBURY UNITED	51	4-0	Perry(3), Jones
25/11/95	FA Trophy	Q3	Halesowen Town	601	0-0	
28/11/95	FA Trophy	Q3 rep	HALESOWEN TOWN	307	1-4	Hazlewood
02/12/95	BHL	M	Nuneaton Borough	943	1-2	Edwards
05/12/95	DMC	2	Evesham United	46	2-2	Jones, Harnett
09/12/95	BHL	M	PAGET RANGERS	92	0-2	
12/12/95	BHL	M	Redditch United	80	1-2	Edwards
16/12/95	BHL	M	Rothwell Town	124	2-2	Edwards, Grant
19/12/95	DMC	2 rep	EVESHAM UNITED	25	5-2	Bowater, Perry(3), Jones
23/12/95	BHL	M	MOOR GREEN	155	0-4	
06/01/96	BHL	M	GRANTHAM TOWN	102	3-4	Edwards, Perry(2)
09/01/96	Staffs SC	QF	Macclesfield Town	298	2-1	Jones, Edwards
13/01/96	BHL	M	Bury Town	154	1-0	Edwards
16/01/96	DMC	3	Moor Green	84	1-3	Voice
20/01/96	BHL	M	REDDITCH UNITED	102	2-2	Voice, Edwards
03/02/96	BHL	M	DUDLEY TOWN	127	0-3	
10/02/96	BHL	M	Corby Town	159	1-3	King
17/02/96	BHL	M	TAMWORTH	331	0-3	
24/02/96	BHL	M	NUNEATON BOROUGH	489	0-2	
02/03/96	BHL	M	Evesham United	79	2-3	Edwards(2)
09/03/96	BHL	M	BUCKINGHAM TOWN	53	0-0	
12/03/96	BHL	M	King's Lynn	700	3-1	Williams(3)
16/03/96	BHL	M	Racing Club Warwick	74	2-1	Perry, Ledding
19/03/96	Staffs SC	SF	LEEK TOWN	34	0-1	
23/03/96	BHL	M	Moor Green	233	1-1	Williams
26/03/96	BHL	M	Buckingham Town	80	2-0	Bowater, Parry
30/03/96	BHL	M	STOURBRIDGE	115	3-0	Perry(3)
02/04/96	BHL	M	Sutton Coldfield Town	126	0-1	
06/04/96	BHL	M	Tamworth	407	5-3	Berks, Hazlewood, Perry(2), Voice
08/04/96	BHL	M	RACING CLUB WARWICK	82	1-1	Voice
13/04/96	BHL	M	Solihull Borough	161	0-2	
16/04/96	BHL	M	Stourbridge	129	1-2	Voice
20/04/96	BHL	M	HINCKLEY TOWN	64	4-3	Voice, Hill, Perry, Berks
24/04/96	BHL	M	Paget Rangers	101	0-0	
27/04/96	BHL	M	KING'S LYNN	211	2-0	Berks, Perry
04/05/96	BHL	M	Bedworth United	335	1-3	Perry

CORBY TOWN

Rockingham Triangle Stadium, Rockingham Road, Corby, Northants NN17 2AE

Tel: 01536 406640 or office 401007

Secretary: Roger Abraham, 68 Cornwall Rd, Kettering,
Northants NN16 8PE Tel: 01536 522159

Press officer: Gerry Lucas, 8 Richmond Ave, Kettering,
Tel: 01536 513507

Chairman: Mr T. Howarth, Hamblin Leisure Services,
George St, Corby, NN17 1QE

> ## DIRECTIONS
> **On northern outskirts of town at junction of A6003 and A6116, opposite entrance to Rockingham Castle grounds. One and a half miles from Corby (BR).**

Nickname: The Steelmen   Capacity: 3,000

Seating: 960   Covered standing: No

Clubhouse on ground: Yes

Record attendance: 10,239 v Peterborough Utd FA Cup 3rd Qual Rd 1952 at Occupation Rd

Biggest win: 14-0 v Gainsborough Trinity 1956-57

Biggest defeat: 0-10 v Paget Rangers 1995-96

Record appearances: Derek Walker 600 1978-92

Record goalscorer in one season: David Hofbauer   Record goalscorer in total: David Hofbauer 137 1984-1993

Record fee received: £20,000 for M Murphy to Oxford Utd

HONOURS

United Counties League 1951 and 1952; Northants Senior Cup 1938, 49, 51, 63, 76, 83, Maunsell Cup 1984; Daventry Charity Cup 1994; Midland Floodlit Cup 1975; Evans Halshaw Floodlit Cup 1975; Anglia Floodlit Trophy 1969 and 1972; Wellingborough Charity Cup 1951; Bob Cumming Cup 1986, 87, 88, 89, 93, 94.

Manager for 1996-97: Paul Fitzpatrick   **Assistant Manager: Simon Mason**

Chairman: Tom Howarth   **Vice Chairman: Bip Weatherall**

In the early thirties the village of Corby was transformed by the steel firm of Stewarts and Lloyds. A football team was started and given the firm's name and from this humble beginning grew Corby Town FC, being incorporated and renamed in 1948.

They played in the United Counties League until 1952 when they made their first move by joining the Midland Counties League, finishing runners up to Nottingham Forest Reserves in the first season. After six years they progressed to the Southern League, gaining promotion in 1965. With the various reshuffles within the league they played in the Premier, Division One, Division One North and Midland Division during the 70's and 80's. They first reached the First Round of the FA Cup in 1954 when nearly 7,000 saw them lose to Watford, and a decade later they twice were in the same round, losing to Bristol City and Hartepool United, before going two better, beating Burton Albion and then Luton Town in a replay before losing in the 3rd Round at Plymouth. The Steelmen twice applied for entry to the Football League without polling a vote during their Southern League days.

The original Stewarts and Lloyds team played roughly where the current United Counties side plays today, until the split in ranks meant that Corby moved to Occupation Road, next door. The ground was home until 1985 and was large enough to hold 14,000 at its prime, although the record was a still impressive 10,000+.

On losing the ground to developers, Corby moved to the new £800,000 sports stadium at Rockingham Triangle, leaving Stewarts and Lloyds FC to their own devices.

CORBY TOWN 1995/96 SEASON

Date	Competition	Round	Opponent	Attendance	Score	Scorers
19/08/95	BHL	M	DUDLEY TOWN	203	6-1	Spencer(3), Edwards(2), Clarke
22/08/95	BHL	M	Bury Town	238	2-1	Murphy, Clarke
26/08/95	FA Cup	P	Westfields	122	1-1	Murphy
30/08/95	FA Cup	P rep	WESTFIELDS	217	7-5	King(3), Edwards(2), Luke, Gilzean
02/09/95	BHL	M	Stourbridge	135	0-2	
06/09/95	BHL	M	PAGET RANGERS	230	1-2	King
09/09/95	FA Cup	Q1	Hednesford Town	732	1-3	Spencer
16/09/95	BHL	M	Bilston Town	122	0-1	
20/09/95	BHL	M	BURY TOWN	202	2-2	King, Archer
23/09/95	BHL	M	Sutton Coldfield Town	162	0-4	
30/09/95	BHL	M	MOOR GREEN	253	0-2	
04/10/95	DMC	1(1)	ROTHWELL TOWN	183	2-2	Archer, Edwards
07/10/95	BHL	M	Nuneaton Borough	1075	0-1	
10/10/95	N'hants SC	1	Brackley Town	80	0-1	
14/10/95	BHL	M	Rothwell Town	327	0-1	
24/10/95	BHL	M	Buckingham Town	67	0-5	
28/10/95	BHL	M	TAMWORTH	296	1-0	Harding
31/10/95	DMC	1(2)	Rothwell Town	251	0-1	
04/11/95	FA Trophy	Q2	Purfleet	108	1-6	Spencer
07/11/95	BHL	M	Leicester United	84	2-3	McLeod, Murphy
11/11/95	BHL	M	Bedworth United	265	0-3	
15/11/95	BHL	M	Paget Rangers	115	0-10	
18/11/95	BHL	M	BRIDGNORTH TOWN	205	0-0	
22/11/95	BHL	M	BUCKINGHAM TOWN	182	2-3	Covington(og), Clark
02/12/95	BHL	M	LEICESTER UNITED	142	0-1	
06/12/95	Mids F'lit	1(1)	V.S. Rugby	133	1-2	Murphy
16/12/95	BHL	M	Moor Green	178	0-1	
01/01/96	BHL	M	King's Lynn	1148	0-1	
06/01/96	BHL	M	STOURBRIDGE	110	1-5	Luke
13/01/96	BHL	M	Tamworth	472	0-7	
20/01/96	BHL	M	HINCKLEY TOWN	172	1-1	Spencer
03/02/96	BHL	M	ROTHWELL TOWN	257	0-2	
10/02/96	BHL	M	BILSTON TOWN	159	3-1	Spencer(3)
14/02/96	Mids F'lit	1(2)	V.S. RUGBY	80	2-2	Culpin(2)
17/02/96	BHL	M	Racing Club Warwick	120	4-3	Culpin(2), Fitzpatrick, Spencer
21/02/96	BHL	M	GRANTHAM TOWN	136	2-4	Fitzpatrick, C Tonge
24/02/96	BHL	M	Dudley Town	109	1-1	D Tonge
02/03/96	BHL	M	NUNEATON BOROUGH	602	1-3	Fitzpatrick
09/03/96	BHL	M	Solihull Borough	142	2-0	Rowe, Rowlands
12/03/96	BHL	M	Evesham United	77	1-2	Haines(og)
20/03/96	BHL	M	EVESHAM UNITED	135	0-1	
23/03/96	BHL	M	REDDITCH UNITED	162	1-2	Rowland
30/03/96	BHL	M	SUTTON COLDFIELD TOWN	161	2-2	Spencer, Fitzpatrick
06/04/96	BHL	M	Grantham Town	206	1-4	Rowland
08/04/96	BHL	M	KING'S LYNN	402	1-1	Rowland
13/04/96	BHL	M	Bridgnorth Town	117	3-3	Fitzpatrick(2), McLeod
17/04/96	BHL	M	BEDWORTH UNITED	194	2-3	Rowland, Culpin
20/04/96	BHL	M	RACING CLUB WARWICK	168	4-0	Spencer(2), Fitzpatrick, James
27/04/96	BHL	M	SOLIHULL BOROUGH	222	2-1	Tonge, Harding
30/04/96	BHL	M	Redditch United	193	1-4	
04/05/96	BHL	M	Hinckley Town	135	3-1	Luke(2), Fitzpatrick

DUDLEY TOWN

Halesowen Town FC, The Grove, Old Hawne Lane, Halesowen, West Mids. Tel: 0121 550 2179

Secretary and Press Officer: Tony Turpin, 24 Andrew Drive, Short Heath, Willenhall, West Mids WV12 5PP Tel: 01922 475541

Nickname: The Robins

Ground details as per Halesowen Town FC

Clubhouse on Ground: Yes

Record Attendance: 16,500 at Sports Ground. Rep match to open ground 1932

At Round Oak ground, 2,500 v West Bromwich Albion Friendly 1991

Biggest Win: 8-0 v Banbury Spencer April 1965

Record Goalscorer in one season: Frank Treagust 56 in 1947-48

Record Fee received £25,000 for Gary Piggott from West Bromwich Albion

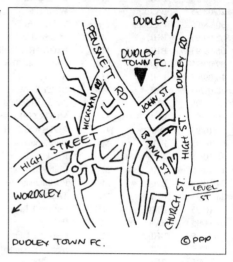

HONOURS

Birmingham Combination 1934; Worcestershire Senior Cup 1946 jt; Camkin Cup 1965; Southern League, Midland Div 1985; Birmingham Senior Cup 1986.

Manager for 1996/7 John Chambers

Assistant Manager: Alan Moore

Chairman: Trevor Lester

Vice Chairman: Philip Edwards

Dudley Town was formed in 1893 and are known as the Robins. Up to 1912, the club played at Shavers End, a couple of miles from Dudley, before moving to the Cricket Ground in the town itself. During the late 1920's and early 30's the Sports Centre Ground was built as a project to provide work for the unemployed, and on completion in 1932, Dudley moved in. To officially open the ground, a crowd of 16,500, the highest recorded attendance, watched the match. For many years Dudley played in the Worcestershire and Birmingham Combinations, later joining what became the West Midlands League, until 1981 when they left to join the Southern League. In the same year new floodlights with a lux value of 480 were installed, a new boardroom built and the huge 1,800 seater grandstand was refurbished to include a VIP area and press box.

The club won the Midland Division title in 1985, gaining promotion, but were devastated a month later, when the ground was closed with immediate effect after a major collapse of the limestone mines beneath the adjacent cricket ground. The club began negotiations with British Steel to purchase the Round Oak ground which was originally built for their employees, and the 8 acre site, which was originally set out for cricket, tennis and bowls, was bought in 1986 and converted into a football ground, whilst Town shared grounds with Stourbridge.

It took until the start of the 1988-89 season for the planning permission to be transferred into reality and the club moved in. It proved to be a relatively short stay, as Town sold the ground for development during last season and moved in with Halesowen Town, whilst the nearby Dell Stadium, currently home to Brierley Hill Town, is developed to Southern League standard.

DUDLEY TOWN 1995/96 SEASON

Date	Comp	Round	Opponent	Att	Score	Scorers
19/08/95	BHL	M	Corby Town	203	1-6	Piggott
23/08/95	BHL	M	NUNEATON BOROUGH	357	0-1	
26/08/95	FA Cup	P	Pelsall Villa	142	1-1	Piggott
28/08/95	FA Cup	P rep	PELSALL VILLA	161	1-0	Hall
02/09/95	BHL	M	Buckingham Town	107	2-0	Piggott, Hall
09/09/95	FA Cup	Q1	Gresley Rovers	541	2-1	Hall(2)
12/09/95	Staffs SC	1	ROCESTER	48	0-1	
16/09/95	BHL	M	SUTTON COLDFIELD TOWN	157	2-1	Hall, Piggott
19/09/95	BHL	M	Nuneaton Borough	1186	4-3	Piggott(3), Hall
23/09/95	FA Cup	Q2	Sandwell Borough	90	1-2	Piggott
30/09/95	BHL	M	BILSTON TOWN	191	2-2	Williams, Piggott
03/10/95	DMC	1(1)	Stourbridge	178	2-4	Harrison, Piggott
07/10/95	BHL	M	HINCKLEY TOWN	135	3-0	Piggott(2), Cooper
10/10/95	Worcs SC	1	Sutton Coldfield Town	75	1-0	Piggott
14/10/95	BHL	M	Evesham United	135	1-1	Brown
16/10/95	Birm SC	1	Cradley Town	112	4-1	Piggott(3), Hall
21/10/95	BHL	M	Leicester United	108	5-0	
24/10/95	BHL	M	Bridgnorth Town	157	2-1	Patrick, Piggott
28/10/95	BHL	M	REDDITCH UNITED	214	2-2	Harrison, Piggott
01/11/95	DMC	1(2)	STOURBRIDGE	246	4-4	Brown, Patrick, Barnes, Piggott
04/11/95	FA Trophy	Q2	Alfreton Town	260	2-2	Piggott, Hall
08/11/95	FA Trophy	Q2 rep	ALFRETON TOWN	183	2-0	Piggott(2)
11/11/95	BHL	M	Tamworth	467	2-3	Hall, Richards
15/11/95	BHL	M	LEICESTER UNITED	124	6-3	Hyde, Cooper (2), Barnes, Hall, Piggott
18/11/95	BHL	M	Paget Rangers	155	0-2	
21/11/95	Birm SC	2	Moor Green	46	3-1	Horne(2), Ingram
25/11/95	FA Trophy	Q3	V.S. RUGBY	283	4-3	Hall(3), Horne
02/12/95	BHL	M	Grantham Town	157	0-2	
09/12/95	BHL	M	ROTHWELL TOWN	127	2-2	Piggott, Brown
16/12/95	BHL	M	King's Lynn	527	1-2	Piggott
18/12/95	Worcs SC	QF	Kidderminster Harriers	370	1-2	Jones
23/12/95	BHL	M	RACING CLUB WARWICK	147	3-3	Hall, Cooper, Piggott
06/01/96	BHL	M	SOLIHULL BOROUGH	178	1-1	Cooper
08/01/96	Birm SC	3	BIRMINGHAM CITY	353	0-3	
13/01/96	BHL	M	Hinckley Town	110	1-1	Hall
20/01/96	FA Trophy	1	HALESOWEN TOWN	769	4-2	Hall, Cooper, Horne, Piggott
03/02/96	BHL	M	Bilston Town	127	3-0	Cooper, Piggott, Hall
13/02/96	FA Trophy	2	MERTHYR TYDFIL	268	1-2	Hall
17/02/96	BHL	M	KING'S LYNN	164	2-2	Hall, Cooper
24/02/96	BHL	M	CORBY TOWN	109	1-1	Hall
28/02/96	BHL	M	BRIDGNORTH TOWN	118	0-0	
02/03/96	BHL	M	Redditch United	240	6-2	Piggott(3), Williams, Cooper, Barnes
06/03/96	BHL	M	Solihull Borough	76	2-4	Barnes(2)
09/03/96	BHL	M	MOOR GREEN	187	2-1	Grant, Piggott
12/03/96	Mids F'lit	QF	V.S. RUGBY	62	0-1	
16/03/96	BHL	M	TAMWORTH	447	1-0	Piggott
20/03/96	BHL	M	BUCKINGHAM TOWN	81	4-2	Piggott(2), Hall, Ingram
23/03/96	BHL	M	Racing Club Warwick	90	0-0	
26/03/96	BHL	M	Bedworth United	199	1-3	Williams
30/03/96	BHL	M	BURY TOWN	132	1-1	Piggott
03/04/96	BHL	M	GRANTHAM TOWN	109	4-1	Piggott, Ingram, Cooper, Cookson
06/04/96	BHL	M	Stourbridge	232	0-1	
08/04/96	BHL	M	BEDWORTH UNITED	200	2-3	Ingram, Piggott
13/04/96	BHL	M	EVESHAM UNITED	142	5-1	Hall(2), Ingram, Piggott(2)
16/04/96	BHL	M	Bury Town	129	3-1	Piggott(2), Hall
20/04/96	BHL	M	Moor Green	233	2-2	Barnes, Cookson
23/04/96	BHL	M	Sutton Coldfield Town	128	1-1	Hall
27/04/96	BHL	M	Rothwell Town	154	1-2	Piggott
01/05/96	BHL	M	STOURBRIDGE	240	2-2	Hall, Cooper
04/05/96	BHL	M	PAGET RANGERS	251	0-0	

EVESHAM UNITED

Common Road, Evesham, Worcestershire, WR11 4PU Tel: 01386 442303

Secretary and Press Officer: Mike Peplow 68, Woodstock Rd, St Johns, Worcester WR2 5NF Tel: 01905 425993

Best contact when confirming fixture. Mike Peplow

Colours: Red, white and black   Nickname:The Robins

Capacity: 2,000   Seating: 350

Covered standing: 250   Clubhouse on ground: Yes

Record attendance: 2,338 v West Bromwich Albion Friendly 1992

DIRECTIONS

From Evesham High Street, turn into Swan Lane, continue down hill between Willmotts factory called Conduit Hill into Common Road, ground 200 yds down on right just before railway bridge. 5 minutes walk from Evesham station.

Biggest win: 11-3 v West Heath Utd

Biggest defeat: 2-7

Record appearances: Sean Cotterill

Record goalscorer in one season: Sid Brain

Record goalscorer in total: Rob Cancy

Record fee paid £1,500 Colin Day from Hayes 1992

Record fee received £ 5,000 for Simon Brain to Cheltenham Town

HONOURS

FA AMATEUR CUP Runners up 1924

Worcestershire Senior Urn 1977 and 1978

Midland Combination 1953, 1955, 1966, 1968, 1969, 1992

Challenge Cup 1954, 1988, 1992, Worcestershire Combination 1953 and 1955

Evesham Hospital Cup 1990, Tony Allden Memorial Cup 1973, 1988, 1992

Manager 1996-97: Nick Jordan   **Assistant Manager: Paul Colicutt**

Chairman: Stuart Reeves   **Vice Chairman: Jim Cockerton**

The original Evesham Town entered the Birmingham Combination in 1926, three years after reaching the FA Amateur Cup Final. The current Evesham club dates from just after the Second War when soldiers returning from action re-formed the club and joined the Worcester League. After some success they moved to the Worcester Combination in 1951, taking the title in 1953. They had five good years before moving up to the Birmingham (West Midlands) League in 1956, rejoining the Midland Comb in 1965, winning the title three times in four years. They took the title a total of six times in all, the last being in 1992 as well as reaching eight League Cup finals, winning three.

1991-92 was a special season, when the club did the League and Cup double and reached the last eight of the FA Vase. It was enough to gain promotion to the Southern League the following season.

United have played at Common Road since 1968, having previously played down on Crown Meadow. When they moved, the stand which was built in 1953, went with them and was re-built on the new ground which is built on an old rubbish tip.

144

EVESHAM UNITED 1995/96 SEASON

Date	Competition	Round	Opponent	Att	Score	Scorers
19/08/95	BHL	M	BEDWORTH UNITED	175	0-0	
22/08/95	BHL	M	Buckingham Town	105	1-3	Jordan
26/08/95	FA Cup	P	Pershore Town	259	1-1	Dixon
29/08/95	FA Cup	P rep	PERSHORE TOWN	206	3-2	Jones, Tipton, Clark
02/09/95	BHL	M	Paget Rangers	110	0-1	
05/09/95	BHL	M	TAMWORTH	200	2-6	Dixon(2)
09/09/95	FA Cup	Q1	Stourbridge	141	2-2	Jones, Cotterill
12/09/95	FA Cup	Q1 rep	STOURBRIDGE	154	3-0	Tipton, Dixon, Yates
16/09/95	BHL	M	Nuneaton Borough	1049	3-6	Yates, Cottrill, Bloomfield
23/09/95	FA Cup	Q2	BEDWORTH UNITED	223	2-0	Judge, Dixon
30/09/95	BHL	M	Stourbridge	164	0-1	
03/10/95	DMC	1(1)	Redditch United	102	0-0	
07/10/95	FA Cup	Q3	Leicester United	169	1-0	Judge
10/10/95	Birm SC	1	Banbury United	80	2-1	Clark, Judd
14/10/95	BHL	M	DUDLEY TOWN	135	1-1	Yates
17/10/95	Worcs SC	1	SOLIHULL BOROUGH	89	2-2	Clark, Tipton
21/10/95	FA Cup	Q4	Nuneaton Borough	1415	1-6	Yates
25/10/95	BHL	M	Solihull Borough	119	0-3	
28/10/95	BHL	M	LEICESTER UNITED	110	3-0	Yates(2), Emms
31/10/95	DMC	1(2)	REDDITCH UNITED	103	3-2	Bloomfield, Judge, Emms
04/11/95	FA Trophy	Q2	ALDERSHOT TOWN	465	0-2	
11/11/95	BHL	M	Bilston Town	103	1-3	Brain
14/11/95	BHL	M	Tamworth	415	2-7	Brain, Tipton
18/11/95	BHL	M	HINCKLEY TOWN	86	5-1	Davis (2), Judge, Dixon, Bloomfield
21/11/95	Birm SC	2	WEDNESFIELD	53	2-3	Tipton, Haines
25/11/95	BHL	M	MOOR GREEN	127	0-5	
29/11/95	Worcs SC	1 rep	Solihull Borough	34	1-2	Clark
02/12/95	BHL	M	Bury Town	142	2-2	Johnstone, Licata
05/12/95	DMC	2	BILSTON TOWN	46	2-2	Bloomfield, Brain
09/12/95	BHL	M	STOURBRIDGE	106	2-1	Johnstone, Licata
16/12/95	BHL	M	Racing Club Warwick	91	4-0	Licata, Johnstone(2), Brain
19/12/95	DMC	2 rep	Bilston Town	25	2-5	Johnstone, Dixon
23/12/95	BHL	M	Grantham Town	161	0-1	
06/01/96	BHL	M	PAGET RANGERS	95	2-2	Cotterill, Johnstone
09/01/96	BHL	M	Bridgnorth Town	117	1-3	Dixon
13/01/96	BHL	M	Moor Green	217	0-1	
03/02/96	BHL	M	Bedworth United	255	2-1	Criddle, Dixon
10/02/96	BHL	M	NUNEATON BOROUGH	460	0-3	
17/02/96	BHL	M	Hinckley Town	68	1-0	Licata
24/02/96	BHL	M	Sutton Coldfield Town	181	0-3	
02/03/96	BHL	M	BILSTON TOWN	79	3-2	Johnstone(3)
12/03/96	BHL	M	CORBY TOWN	77	2-1	Clark, Dixon
16/03/96	BHL	M	ROTHWELL TOWN	77	3-1	Dixon, Johnstone(2)
20/03/96	BHL	M	Corby Town	135	1-0	Pearce
23/03/96	BHL	M	GRANTHAM TOWN	110	4-0	Licata(2), Johnstone, Pearce
26/03/96	BHL	M	KING'S LYNN	137	2-3	Johnstone(2)
30/03/96	BHL	M	King's Lynn	922	0-2	
02/04/96	BHL	M	Rothwell Town	139	1-4	Tipton
06/04/96	BHL	M	BRIDGNORTH TOWN	117	0-3	
08/04/96	BHL	M	Redditch United	278	0-1	
10/04/96	BHL	M	SOLIHULL BOROUGH	91	1-2	Walker
13/04/96	BHL	M	Dudley Town	142	1-5	Pearce
16/04/96	BHL	M	REDDITCH UNITED	103	1-1	Pearce
20/04/96	BHL	M	SUTTON CO FIELD TOWN	106	2-3	Cottrill, Davis
23/04/96	BHL	M	BURY TOWN	80	1-2	Pearce
27/04/96	BHL	M	RACING CLUB WARWICK	104	2-4	Dickson, Bloomfield
30/04/96	BHL	M	BUCKINGHAM TOWN	61	1-4	Dixon
04/05/96	BHL	M	Leicester United	60	2-2	Clark, Jones

GRANTHAM TOWN

South Kesteven Sports Stadium, Trent Rd, Grantham, Lincs. Tel: 01476 62011

Secretary Patrick Nixon, 72 Huntingtower Rd, Grantham, Lincs NG31 7AU Tel: 01476 64408

Nickname: The Gingerbreads

Colours: Black and White stripes

Capacity: 7,500

Seating: 750

Covered standing: 1,250

Clubhouse on ground: Yes

Record attendance: at London Road, 6,578 v Middlesbrough FA Cup 3rd Round 1974

DIRECTIONS

Midway between A1 and A52 on edge of Earlesfield Industrial Estate; from A1 take A607 to Earlesfield Industrial Estate and continue into Trent Road. From Nottingham on A52 turn right into Barrowby gate then into Trent Road. From Boston on A52 follow A607 across two sets of lights to Trent Road.

Biggest win: 13-0 v Rufford Colliery FA Cup 1934

Biggest defeat: 0-16 v Notts County Rovers Midland Amateur Alliance 1892

Record appearances: Chris Gardiner 664

Record goalscorer in aggregate: Jack McCartney 416

HONOURS

Southern League Div 1 North 1973 and 1979

Midland Counties League 1964, 1971, 1972

League Cup 1969 and 1971

Midland Amateur League 1911

Central Alliance League 1925

Lincolnshire Senior A Cup 1954, 1961, 1962

Lincolnshire County Senior Cup 1972 and 1983

Grantham Town FC, known as the Gingerbreads, can trace their history back to 1874.

They joined the Midland Counties League from the Central Alliance in 1925, having previously been members of the Midland Amateur Alliance, but financial problems led to a return in the 50's. After returning to the Midland League again, the championship was won in 1964, 1971 and 1972, losing six games in two years and scoring 216 goals. They then moved to the Southern League Division One North where they won that at the first go in 1973. In the Premier Division they finished runner up to Dartford, but in 1978 they were relegated from the Premier Division, but bounced back again to take the title.

Re-organisation saw the club switch to the Northern Premier League where they finished fourth but in 1985 they were 21st and failed to gain re-election. Eventually they returned to the Southern League Midland Division, where the last two seasons have been a struggle. With the brand new Sports Stadium built to replace London Road, which the club played on from the start. It was a cricket ground long before football was played there, and in the early days, when the club briefly folded, a different club, Grantham Avenue, used the ground. The club re-formed and played for a while on another pitch close to the railway before returning to London Road, which remained home until October 1990.

GRANTHAM TOWN 1995/96 SEASON

Date	Comp	Rnd	Opponent	Att	Score	Scorers
01/08/95	Lincs SC		LINCOLN CITY		1-2	
08/08/95	Lincs SC		BOSTON UNITED		0-2	
19/08/95	BHL	M	REDDITCH UNITED	224	5-3	Ward(2), S Taylor, Stout, Hardwick
22/08/95	BHL	M	Hinckley Town	93	0-2	
26/08/95	FA Cup	P	Shepshed Dynamo	211	1-0	Bullimore
28/08/95	BHL	M	KING'S LYNN	272	0-1	
02/09/95	BHL	M	BILSTON TOWN	185	1-1	Stout
05/09/95	BHL	M	Bury Town	160	4-2	Ward, Dye(2), Taylor
09/09/95	FA Cup	Q1	Rushden & Diamonds	1681	1-4	Ward
16/09/95	BHL	M	Paget Rangers	131	1-0	Taylor
19/09/95	BHL	M	HINCKLEY TOWN	188	0-1	
23/09/95	BHL	M	NUNEATON BOROUGH	543	1-2	Taylor
30/09/95	BHL	M	Tamworth	492	2-3	Watts, Stoutt
03/10/95	DMC	1(1)	ILKESTON TOWN	171	0-3	
07/10/95	BHL	M	BEDWORTH UNITED	207	1-1	Speed
14/10/95	FA Trophy	Q1	Harrogate Town	191	4-1	Leonce, Bullimore, Macek(2)
21/10/95	BHL	M	Stourbridge	103	5-1	Leonce(2), Bullimore, Macek, Hardwick
24/10/95	BHL	M	King's Lynn	728	2-6	Taylor, Leonce
28/10/95	BHL	M	RACING CLUB WARWICK	190	1-1	Hardwick
31/10/95	DMC	1(2)	Ilkeston Town	299	2-2	Parkinson, Ward
04/11/95	FA Trophy	Q2	FARSLEY CELTIC	303	1-3	Parkinson
11/11/95	BHL	M	Solihull Borough	125	2-4	Leonce, Taylor
14/11/95	BHL	M	BURY TOWN	133	3-2	Bullimore, Bogan, Dye
18/11/95	BHL	M	SUTTON COLDFIELD TOWN	189	1-0	Bullimore
25/11/95	BHL	M	Buckingham Town	90	0-1	
02/12/95	BHL	M	DUDLEY TOWN	157	2-0	Speed, Leonce
09/12/95	BHL	M	Bridgnorth Town	95	1-4	Stout
16/12/95	BHL	M	LEICESTER UNITED	158	0-3	
23/12/95	BHL	M	EVESHAM UNITED	161	1-0	Speed
01/01/96	BHL	M	ROTHWELL TOWN	150	0-6	
06/01/96	BHL	M	Bilston Town	102	4-3	Bullimore(2), Piggott, Watts
13/01/96	BHL	M	Bedworth United	388	2-2	Parkinson, Watts
20/01/96	BHL	M	PAGET RANGERS	150	1-3	Piggott
10/02/96	BHL	M	STOURBRIDGE	160	1-3	Hamilton(og)
17/02/96	BHL	M	Nuneaton Borough	1031	0-2	
21/02/96	BHL	M	Corby Town	136	4-2	McDaid, Watts, Bullimore, Taylor
02/03/96	BHL	M	TAMWORTH	315	3-1	Gethfield(2), Rogan
12/03/96	BHL	M	Redditch United	117	1-1	Bullimore
16/03/96	BHL	M	Leicester United	74	1-0	Evans
23/03/96	BHL	M	Evesham United	110	0-4	
30/03/96	BHL	M	MOOR GREEN	165	3-0	Bullimore(2), Parkinson
03/04/96	BHL	M	Dudley Town	109	1-4	Bullimore
06/04/96	BHL	M	CORBY TOWN	206	4-1	Bullimore(3), Speed
08/04/96	BHL	M	Rothwell Town	165	0-3	
13/04/96	BHL	M	Racing Club Warwick	108	2-3	Withers, Bullimore
16/04/96	BHL	M	BUCKINGHAM TOWN	102	2-1	Parkinson, Bogan
20/04/96	BHL	M	SOLIHULL BOROUGH	183	3-4	Bullimore(3)
23/04/96	BHL	M	Moor Green	188	0-1	
27/04/96	BHL	M	BRIDGNORTH TOWN	164	4-1	Speed, Bogan, Taylor, Watts
04/05/96	BHL	M	Sutton Coldfield Town	137	2-0	Macek, Gwyther

HINCKLEY TOWN

Leicester Road Sports Ground, Leicester Road, Hinckley, Leics. Tel: 01455 615062

Secretary Stuart Millidge, 25 Elizabeth Rd,
Hinckley, Leics, LE10 0QY Tel 01455 635808

Colours: Maroon, Sky Blue and White

Nickname: The Town

Capacity: 2,000

Seating: Yes

Covered standing: Yes

Clubhouse on ground: Yes

Record attendance: 2,000 v Real Sociedad Friendly

Competitive game: 1,022 v Nuneaton Boro
Southern League 1991

Biggest win: 10-0 v Kettering Town Res Central
Mids Lge

Biggest defeat: 0-10 v Barry Town Southern League

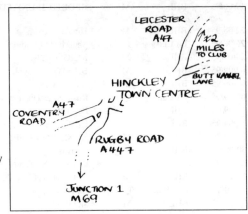

HONOURS

Nuneaton Amateur League Div 3 and Div 2	West Midlands League 1990
Central Midlands League 1987	Leicester Senior League and Cup 1973
Leicestershire Challenge Cup 1990	Leicestershire Senior Cup 1989
Midland Floodlit Cup 1989	

The club was formed in 1958 by a group of ex-Westfield Secondary Modern Schoolboys who named the club Westfield Rovers. They joined the South Leicester League before moving to the Junior Division of the Nuneaton Amateur League. After three highly successful seasons they joined the senior ranks and ran away with the Division Three title, and then Division Two a year later, to reach the top division.

In 1976 the club moved to the current ground at Leicester Road becoming third partners in a sports complex. It was a long way from their previous homes on Westfield Playing Fields and Coventry Road Rec and to celebrate the name was changed to Hinckley Town some four years after a long term ambition was fulfiled when they joined the Leicestershire Senior League. They took the Second Division title in 1973 and were runners up in Division One in 1984, and in 1986 decided to move to the newly formed Supreme Division of the Central Midlands League, and ran away with the title by 7 points.

A year later they were runners up in League and League Cup, but it was a short spell in that league for Town erected floodlights in August 1987 and joined the West Midlands League a year later, from where they won the Leicestershire Senior Cup for the first time. Within two years they were champions of that league which, along with the ground improvements, gave them an entry into the Southern League Midland Division.

The appointment of Frank Worthington as player manager gave the club some impetus but they have yet to make a major impact.

HINCKLEY TOWN 1995/96 SEASON

Date	Comp		Opponent	Att	Score	Scorers
19/08/95	BHL	M	Racing Club Warwick	100	1-2	Percival
22/08/95	BHL	M	GRANTHAM TOWN	93	2-0	Keogh, S Sinden
26/08/95	FA Cup	P	Tamworth	514	1-3	Percival
28/08/95	BHL	M	Moor Green	218	0-2	
02/09/95	BHL	M	SUTTON COLDFIELD TOWN	70	2-1	Percival, Harriman
05/09/95	BHL	M	King's Lynn	761	1-3	Olner
09/09/95	BHL	M	NUNEATON BOROUGH	895	0-3	
16/09/95	BHL	M	Buckingham Town	81	2-1	Harriman, Machin
19/09/95	BHL	M	Grantham Town	188	1-0	McGinty
23/09/95	BHL	M	BURY TOWN	73	1-1	Griffin
30/09/95	BHL	M	ROTHWELL TOWN	95	2-2	Percival(2)
03/10/95	DMC	1(1)	BEDWORTH UNITED	105	1-0	Machin
07/10/95	BHL	M	Dudley Town	135	0-3	
14/10/95	FA Trophy	Q1	Barrow	1119	0-3	
21/10/95	BHL	M	BILSTON TOWN	108	2-4	Percival, McGinty
24/10/95	BHL	M	MOOR GREEN	75	4-3	Sinden(3), Olner
28/10/95	BHL	M	Paget Rangers	131	2-1	Sinden, Percival
31/10/95	DMC	1(2)	Bedworth United	172	1-0	Sinden
11/11/95	BHL	M	Stourbridge	106	1-1	Sinden
14/11/95	BHL	M	KING'S LYNN	114	4-3	Sinden(4)
18/11/95	BHL	M	Evesham United	86	1-5	McGinty
25/11/95	BHL	M	PAGET RANGERS	120	1-2	McGinty
28/11/95	Leics CC	QF	Shepshed Dynamo	115	0-1	
02/12/95	BHL	M	Tamworth	441	2-3	Olner, Percival
05/12/95	DMC	2	Ilkeston Town	106	3-2	Machin, Quinn, Robinson
09/12/95	BHL	M	BUCKINGHAM TOWN	95	0-4	
16/12/95	BHL	M	Bedworth United	262	1-3	Percival
23/12/95	BHL	M	Bridgnorth Town	135	5-2	McGinty, Jameson(2), Percival, Machin
06/01/96	BHL	M	TAMWORTH	321	3-2	Percival, Sinden, McBean
08/01/96	DMC	3	Worcester City	256	3-2	Machin(2), Jameson
13/01/96	BHL	M	DUDLEY TOWN	110	1-1	Jameson
20/01/96	BHL	M	Corby Town	172	1-1	Sinden
03/02/96	BHL	M	Nuneaton Borough	1061	0-1	
10/02/96	BHL	M	Sutton Coldfield Town	151	1-6	Jameson
13/02/96	DMC	QF	MOOR GREEN	60	0-4	
17/02/96	BHL	M	EVESHAM UNITED	68	0-1	
24/02/96	BHL	M	Rothwell Town	196	1-2	Percival
05/03/96	BHL	M	RACING CLUB WARWICK	79	4-1	Jameson, Spencer, Sinden, Emery
09/03/96	BHL	M	BEDWORTH UNITED	160	0-0	
16/03/96	BHL	M	Redditch United	147	2-1	Pugh(og), Percival
19/03/96	BHL	M	LEICESTER UNITED	106	1-0	Olner
23/03/96	BHL	M	BRIDGNORTH TOWN	72	2-0	McBean, Jameson
30/03/96	BHL	M	Solihull Borough	136	0-3	
06/04/96	BHL	M	REDDITCH UNITED	71	1-2	Olner
08/04/96	BHL	M	Leicester United	120	0-1	
13/04/96	BHL	M	STOURBRIDGE	91	1-1	Sinden
18/04/96	Mids F'lit	QF	Redditch United	78	2-1	Robinson, Percival
20/04/96	BHL	M	Bilston Town	64	3-4	Burke(2), Machin
23/04/96	BHL	M	SOLIHULL BOROUGH	50	2-3	Sinden(2)
27/04/96	BHL	M	Bury Town	161	3-1	Beach(og), McBean, Percival
30/04/96	Mids F'lit	SF	V.S. Rugby	141	0-1	
04/05/96	BHL	M	CORBY TOWN	135	1-3	Machin

ILKESTON TOWN

New Manor Ground, Awsworth Rd, Ilkeston, Derbys. Tel: 0115 932 4094

Secretary: Mr Tony Cuthbert, 8 Darwin Rd, Long Eaton, Notts NG10 3NW. Tel: 0115 9731531

Press officer: Mr John Richards 0115 9324848

Other contact Keith Alexander at office 0115 9305622

Colours: Red and white   Nickname: The Robins

Capacity: 3,500   Seating: 270

Covered standing: 1,100   Clubhouse on ground: Yes

Record attendance: At new ground 2,349 v Kidderminster Harriers FA Trophy 3rd Rd 1995

At old ground: 9,800 v Rochdale FA Cup 1st Rd 1951

Biggest win: 14-2 v Codnor Miners Welfare 1947

Biggest defeat: 1-11 v Grantham Town 1948

Record appearances: Terry Swinscoe 377

Record goalscorer in one season: Barry Jepson 62

Record goalscorer in total: Jackie Ward 141

Record fee received: £11,750 for Chris Brookes to Luton Town in 1992

DIRECTIONS

M42 to M1 junction 23A, continue on M1 to junction 26, exit left onto A610 towards Ripley, take 1st exit signed Awsworth and Ilkeston (A6096), continue through Awsworth, right at top of hill into Newtons Lane (signed Cotmanhay & Heanor) — ground half mile on left before canal bridge. Or, A38 to Derby centre, A52 for Nottingham to M5 junction 25, then follow as above from M1 junction 26. Rail to Nottingham or Derby then bus to Ilkeston. Ground about 1 mile from town centre.

HONOURS

Southern League Midland Division 1995; West Midlands League 1994, Division One 1992; League Cup 1994 and Division One League Cup 1992 and 1995; Central Midlands league Cup 1988; Midland League 1968; Central Alliance 1953, 1954, 1955; Derbyshire Senior Cup 1895, 1896, 1897, 1898, 1949, 1953, 1956, 1958, 1963, 1983, 1993.

Manager 1996-97: Keith Alexander   **Assistant Manager: Gary Simpson**

Chairman: Paul Millership

Ilkeston Town were formed in 1945 and were the successors of other Ilkeston sides which played on the Manor Ground, which opened in 1893.

The original club entered the Midland League in 1894, from it winning the Senior Cup four years running. They rejoined the league in 1925 after a break and remained until the War. The new club first played in the Notts and Derby Senior League before moving to the Central Alliance in 1949. It was the start of a golden era as they were champions for four years running which brought in large crowds of close to 4,000 on occasions. In 1951, the record crowd was set for a Cup game with Rochdale, 9,800 cramming in to the Manor, which had much work done to it to enable the game to go ahead.

Four years later 9,592 saw a final qualifying round tie with Peterborough United, then of the Midland League. The Robins joined the Midland League themselves in 1961 and won it in 1968, and three years later they joined the Southern League for the first time, but they struggled financially and returned to the Midland League after two years. In turn that league merged with the Yorkshire League and Town found themselves in the Northern Counties East. After a poor season, they joined the Central Midlands League in 1986 and with new enthusiasm at the club they won the League Cup in 1988 and in 1990, came nearer home by joining the West Midlands League. Ground problems saw the club relegated, and the fine old Manor Ground was sold by the Council with indecent haste, and was soon covered by a supermarket.

Since then the New Manor has developed to Southern League specifications and until last year they had enjoyed immense success, doing the League and Cup double in Division One, and repeating it in the Premier Division which gained them re-entry to the Southern League after 21 years. The first season back saw them crowned as champions, but the move up brought problems and relegation followed last May.

ILKESTON TOWN 1995/96 SEASON

Date	Comp	Round	Opponent	Att	Score	Scorers
19/08/95	BHL	P	WORCESTER CITY	606	2-3	Maddison, P Robinson
22/08/95	BHL	P	Atherstone United	359	3-3	Beckford, Thompson(2)
26/08/95	BHL	P	Chelmsford City	827	0-1	
28/08/95	BHL	P	GRESLEY ROVERS	979	0-0	
02/09/95	BHL	P	DORCHESTER TOWN	654	1-0	D Harbottle
05/09/95	BHL	P	Cheltenham Town	788	0-4	
09/09/95	FA Cup	Q1	Hatfield Main	185	2-0	Campbell, M Harbottle
16/09/95	BHL	P	HALESOWEN TOWN	597	1-3	Maddison
23/09/95	FA Cup	Q2	Matlock Town	759	2-1	M Harbottle, D Harbottle
30/09/95	BHL	P	Merthyr Tydfil	321	1-10	Campbell
03/10/95	DMC	1(1)	Grantham Town	171	3-0	D Harbottle, Randle, Bilby
07/10/95	FA Cup	Q3	Marine	499	0-0	
10/10/95	FA Cup	Q3 rep	MARINE	801	1-2	Thompson
14/10/95	BHL	P	Gravesend & Northfleet	595	1-3	Turner(og)
21/10/95	BHL	P	BALDOCK TOWN	475	3-2	D Harbottle(2), Jackson
24/10/95	BHL	P	Gresley Rovers	637	3-2	M Harbottle(2), Igoe
28/10/95	BHL	P	Cambridge City	276	3-2	M Harbottle(2), Igoe
31/10/95	DMC	1(2)	GRANTHAM TOWN	299	2-2	Jackson(2)
04/11/95	BHL	P	GLOUCESTER CITY	751	1-2	Jackson
11/11/95	BHL	P	Halesowen Town	636	2-3	Baily, Jackson
14/11/95	BHL	P	CHELTENHAM TOWN	610	1-4	M Harbottle
18/11/95	BHL	P	Crawley Town	618	0-1	
25/11/95	FA Trophy	Q3	GAINSBOROUGH TRINITY	626	0-5	
02/12/95	BHL	P	Sudbury Town	349	0-1	
05/12/95	DMC	2	HINCKLEY TOWN	106	2-3	J Close, Jackson
09/12/95	BHL	P	NEWPORT A.F.C.	564	1-1	Campbell
16/12/95	BHL	P	Baldock Town	238	1-1	Close
19/12/95	Evans Hal.	Scorpio	ASHFIELD UNITED	126	2-1	Harbottle, Clarke
23/12/95	BHL	P	Rushden & Diamonds	2312	0-3	
06/01/96	BHL	P	CAMBRIDGE CITY	435	2-2	D Harbottle, M Harbottle
10/01/96	Derbys SC	3	Newhall United	110	0-1	
13/01/96	BHL	P	Worcester City	690	3-4	Campbell, M Harbottle, D Harbottle
17/01/96	Evans Hal.	Scorpio	Alfreton Town	163	1-7	
20/01/96	BHL	P	V.S. Rugby	441	0-4	
03/02/96	BHL	P	Hastings Town	402	1-2	Robinson
10/02/96	BHL	P	STAFFORD RANGERS	430	1-3	Randall
17/02/96	BHL	P	MERTHYR TYDFIL	434	0-1	
24/02/96	BHL	P	Dorchester Town	755	0-3	
02/03/96	BHL	P	HASTINGS TOWN	413	1-0	Jackson
06/03/96	Evans Hal.	Scorpio	Ashfield United	63	0-2	
09/03/96	BHL	P	CRAWLEY TOWN	547	1-4	Bowler
11/03/96	Evans Hal.	Scorpio	ALFRETON TOWN	103	0-2	
16/03/96	BHL	P	SALISBURY CITY	340	2-1	Taylor, Gethfield
19/03/96	BHL	P	ATHERSTONE UNITED	377	1-1	Codner
23/03/96	BHL	P	RUSHDEN & DIAMONDS	1009	1-1	Grayson
27/03/96	BHL	P	Newport A.F.C.	542	3-2	Taylor(2), Grayson
30/03/96	BHL	P	Burton Albion	830	2-1	Clarke, Hallam
06/04/96	BHL	P	V.S. RUGBY	681	1-1	Grayson
08/04/96	BHL	P	Stafford Rangers	665	0-1	
13/04/96	BHL	P	GRAVESEND & NORTHFLEET	598	1-1	Taylor
16/04/96	BHL	P	BURTON ALBION	692	1-0	Grayson
20/04/96	BHL	P	Salisbury City	381	2-0	Carruthers(2)
23/04/96	BHL	P	CHELMSFORD CITY	592	1-1	Taylor
27/04/96	BHL	P	Gloucester City	607	1-3	Taylor
04/05/96	BHL	P	SUDBURY TOWN	534	4-2	Carruthers(3), Hallam

MOOR GREEN

The Moorlands, Sherwood Rd, Hall Green, Birmingham B28 0EX. Tel: 0121 624 2727

Secretary: Martyn Davis, 22 Collingdon Ave, Sheldon, Birmingham, B26 3YL Tel: 0121 694 8405

Club colours: Light and Dark Blue halves

Nickname: The Moors

Capacity: 3,000

Seating: 250

Covered standing: 2,750

Clubhouse on ground: Yes

Record attendance: 5,000 v Romford Amateur Cup 1951

Record goalscorer in one season: Phil Davies 51

Record fee received: £90,000 for Ian Taylor to Port Vale

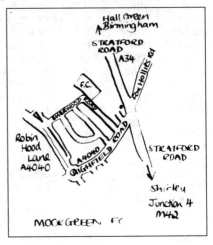

HONOURS

Central Amateur League 1937, 1938, 1939; Verviers Trophy 1933 and 1937; AFA Challenge Cup 1939; AFA Senior Cup 1927 and 1936; Midland Combination 1981 and Div 1 in 1986; President's Cup 1968 and 1979; Midland Comb Challenge Cup 1981; Lord Mayor of Birmingham Charity Cup 1991; Midland Floodlit Cup 1991 and 1992; Tony Allden Trophy 1982; Birmingham Senior Cup 1958; Birmingham Junior Cup 1967; Worcester Junior Cup 1986; Solihull Charity Cup 1986; Smedley Crook Memorial Cup 1988.

Manager 1996-97: Bob Faulkner

Assistant Managers: Barry Powell and Dougie Griffith

Chairman: Geoff Hood

Vice Chairman: Martyn Alcott

Press Officer: Peter Clynes: 0121 745 3262

Moor Green were formed in 1901 when players from Moseley Ashfield Cricket Club began playing football. The first ground was on a part of a farm in Moor Green Lane, but when rent was increased they moved on. A number of grounds were used until 1930 when the current site was acquired. The freehold was bought in 1964 for £6,000. It developed into a substantial ground, but safety regulations led to the enforced demolition of much of the terracing and the pitch was turned 90 degrees and the ground rebuilt. The first 20 years were mostly spent playing friendlies but in 1922 they joined the Birmingham AFA. The title was won in 1936 and the club moved to the Central Amateur League, where they did the hat trick before the War. Also during that time they won the national AFA Senior Cup and went on several tours which culminated in the winning of the Verviers Trophy in Belgium.

After the War, Moors played in the Birmingham Combination and in 1958 they were the first amateur team to win the Birmingham Senior Cup. Before that, in 1951 the record attendance of 5,000 saw a match with Romford. The Birmingham Comb became the West Midlands League and in 1968 the club moved into the largely amateur Midland Comb and club morale improved, winning the league in 1981 by 12 points and moving into the Southern League, having turned professional earlier. 1988 saw promotion and since then they have had cup success and have seen several players move to the full time game, namely Dave Busst and Ian Taylor.

MOOR GREEN 1995/96 SEASON

Date	Comp	Round	Opposition	Att	Score	Scorers
19/08/95	BHL	M	KING'S LYNN	215	0-2	
22/08/95	BHL	M	Redditch United	221	1-1	Agar
26/08/95	BHL	M	Bedworth United	302	2-0	Brogan, Agar
28/08/95	BHL	M	HINCKLEY TOWN	218	2-0	Jones, Davies
02/09/95	BHL	M	NUNEATON BOROUGH	571	0-2	
05/09/95	BHL	M	Stourbridge	141	2-0	Walker, Davies
09/09/95	FA Cup	Q1	Redditch United	210	3-1	Jones(2), Davies
16/09/95	BHL	M	LEICESTER UNITED	231	3-2	Agar, Walker(2)
19/09/95	BHL	M	REDDITCH UNITED	231	3-1	Jones, Smith, Fearon
23/09/95	FA Cup	Q2	Halesowen Town	620	0-1	
26/09/95	Birm SC	1	Sutton Coldfield Town	86	4-2	Smith, Davies, Agar, Jones
30/09/95	BHL	M	Corby Town	253	2-0	Agar, Jones
03/10/95	DMC	1(1)	Racing Club Warwick	120	4-1	Agar, Davies(2), Jones
07/10/95	BHL	M	Paget Rangers	247	2-3	Russell(2)
14/10/95	FA Trophy	Q1	Knowsley United	80	2-3	Frost, Russell
21/10/95	BHL	M	ROTHWELL TOWN	193	1-1	Davies
24/10/95	BHL	M	Hinckley Town	75	3-4	Smith, Davies(2)
28/10/95	BHL	M	Buckingham Town	70	0-2	
31/10/95	DMC	1(2)	RACING CLUB WARWICK	72	4-0	Walker(3), Davies
04/11/95	BHL	M	PAGET RANGERS	213	1-1	Pinner
11/11/95	BHL	M	Bury Town	148	1-0	Gillard
14/11/95	BHL	M	STOURBRIDGE	217	3-0	Bailey, Davies, Agar
18/11/95	BHL	M	BEDWORTH UNITED	221	0-0	
21/11/95	Birm SC	2	DUDLEY TOWN	46	1-3	Davis
25/11/95	BHL	M	Evesham United	127	5-0	Agar, Williams, Davies, Bailey, Walker
02/12/95	BHL	M	BRIDGNORTH TOWN	221	7-0	Walker(5), Agar(2)
05/12/95	DMC	2	Bridgnorth Town	76	0-0	
09/12/95	BHL	M	Leicester United	127	2-0	Davis(2)
12/12/95	DMC	2 rep	BRIDGNORTH TOWN	47	2-1	Davies, Russell
16/12/95	BHL	M	CORBY TOWN	178	1-0	Hamilton
19/12/95	Worcs SC	QF	Bromsgrove Rovers	315	0-5	
23/12/95	BHL	M	Bilston Town	155	4-0	Jones(2), Bailey, Hamilton
26/12/95	BHL	M	SOLIHULL BOROUGH	393	1-1	Bailey
06/01/96	BHL	M	RACING CLUB WARWICK	192	2-2	Agar, Bailey
13/01/96	BHL	M	EVESHAM UNITED	217	1-0	Hayde
16/01/96	DMC	3	BILSTON TOWN	84	3-1	Agar, Hayde, Hamilton
20/01/96	BHL	M	Sutton Coldfield Town	247	5-0	Agar, Davis(2), Jones, Walker
03/02/96	BHL	M	TAMWORTH	543	0-1	
10/02/96	BHL	M	Rothwell Town	191	2-3	Jones, Merchant
13/02/96	DMC	QF	Hinckley Town	60	4-0	Davis(4)
17/02/96	BHL	M	BURY TOWN	228	2-1	Jones, Davies
27/02/96	BHL	M	Racing Club Warwick	140	3-2	Williams, Russell(2)
02/03/96	BHL	M	King's Lynn	840	0-2	
09/03/96	BHL	M	Dudley Town	187	1-2	Cottrill
16/03/96	BHL	M	Nuneaton Borough	937	1-3	Moore
19/03/96	DMC	SF(1)	Nuneaton Borough	528	0-2	
23/03/96	BHL	M	BILSTON TOWN	233	1-1	Merchant
30/03/96	BHL	M	Grantham Town	165	0-3	
02/04/96	DMC	SF(2)	NUNEATON BOROUGH	340	1-1	Davies
06/04/96	BHL	M	SUTTON COLDFIELD TOWN	206	3-0	Davies(2), Moore
08/04/96	BHL	M	Solihull Borough	341	2-0	Davies, Moore
13/04/96	BHL	M	Tamworth	406	5-1	Williams, Moore(2), Cottrill, Jones
20/04/96	BHL	M	DUDLEY TOWN	233	2-2	Moore, Marshall
23/04/96	BHL	M	GRANTHAM TOWN	188	1-0	Moore
27/04/96	BHL	M	BUCKINGHAM TOWN	196	1-2	Davis
04/05/96	BHL	M	Bridgnorth Town	145	3-2	Marshall, Cottrill(2)

PAGET RANGERS

C/O Sutton Coldfield FC, Central Ground, Coles Lane, Sutton Coldfield B72 1NL. Tel: 0121 327 3746

Secretary: Ian Price, 754a Alum Rock Rd, Alum Rock, B'ham B24 Tel: 0121 327 3746

Press Chris Inman, 56 Church St, Whittington, Lichfield WS14 9JH Tel: 01543 433569

Nickname: The P's   Capacity: 2,500

Seating: 200   Covered standing: 500

Colours: Gold and Black   Clubhouse on ground: Yes

Record attendance: 2,000 v Aston Villa. Floodlight opening in 1971 at Springfield Rd

Biggest win: 24- v Evesham Town 1949

Biggest defeat: 1-6 v Sheldon Town 1949

Record appearances: Gary Williams 500+

Record goalscorer in one season: 57 A.Broadhead 1960-61

Record fee received: £10,000 John Gittens to Southampton

HONOURS

Midland Alliance 1995; West Midlands League Cup 1992, Midland Combination 1960, 1961, 1970, 1971; League Cup 1960, 67, 71, 83, 86, Div 1 Cup 1971; Birmingham Junior Cup 1960 and 1970; Lord Mayor of B'ham Charity Cup 1995; Walsall Senior Cup 1986; Tony Allden Memorial Cup 1971, 84, 87; Sutton Coldfield Charity Cup 1958, 60, 66, 68.

Manager for 1996/97: Eddie Caulfield   **Assistant Manager: Paul Edwards**

Chairman: Bob Ruddick   **Vice Chairman: Derek Culling**

Paget Rangers were formed in 1938 and arose when a group of former pupils at Paget Road School combined to form a team. To begin with the club were accepted as members in the Intermediate Division of the Birmingham Youth League. They enjoyed instant success as they won the league at the first attempt and repeated it a year later. Unfortunately the war called a halt to the club's progress, but they eventually moved to the Birmingham Youtha and Boys AFA and in 1949, the Central Amateur League, a year later joining the Worcester Combination. In 1951 they made a bold step forward when they purchased the ground in Springfield Road, Walmley for £550 and set home, where they remained for 42 years.

Throughout the 50's Paget enjoyed a quiet period before their first major success in 1960 when they lifted the league title, League Cup, Birmingham Junior Cup and Sutton Coldfield Charity Cup. They again won the league a year later, but further glory eluded them until 1867 when they again took the League Cup. 1970 saw the title again and runners up in the Cup.

In 1971 Aston Villa provided the opposition for a match to celebrate the switching on of the floodlights, but it was a dozen years before the next trophy came, when the title came in 1983, then again in 1986. A year later the club were transferred to the Southern League, but suffered a disastrous season and were relegated to the West Midlands League. They had a good spell in that league, the best being runners up to Gresley Rovers in 1992, the same season that saw the two teams battle out the League Cup final, which Rangers won. 1993 and 1994 saw two more appearances in the final, both sadly lost. Paget were founder members of the Midland Alliance in 1994, winning the inaugural title in style and gaining promotion again to the Southern League, where last May they finished a creditble fifth. Having lost their Springfield Road home to developers, the club moved in with Sutton Coldfield Town, where they remain.

PAGET RANGERS 1995/96 SEASON

Date	Competition	Round	Opponent	Attendance	Score	Scorers
19/08/95	BHL	M	STOURBRIDGE	110	2-0	Bennett(2)
22/08/95	BHL	M	Bridgnorth Town	128	2-0	Campbell, McDonald
26/08/95	BHL	M	Racing Club Warwick	73	1-1	Scott
02/09/95	BHL	M	EVESHAM UNITED	110	1-0	Clark
06/09/95	BHL	M	Corby Town	230	2-1	Scott, McCarthy
09/09/95	FA Cup	Q1	WEDNESFIELD	85	1-0	Bennett
16/09/95	BHL	M	GRANTHAM TOWN	131	0-1	
20/09/95	BHL	M	BRIDGNORTH TOWN	111	3-2	Clark, Bennett, McDonald
23/09/95	FA Cup	Q2	Leicester United	53	2-3	Bennett, Campbell
30/09/95	BHL	M	Bury Town	161	2-1	Bennett, McDonald
03/10/95	DMC	1(1)	Leicester United	38	3-0	Bennett(2), Campbell
07/10/95	BHL	M	MOOR GREEN	247	3-2	Burroughs, Bennett(2)
11/10/95	Birm SC	1	Lye Town	44	1-1	Tucker
14/10/95	FA Trophy	Q1	Winsford United	183	1-1	Tucker
18/10/95	FA Trophy	Q1 rep	WINSFORD UNITED	124	0-2	
21/10/95	BHL	M	Bedworth United	254	1-1	Scott
24/10/95	Birm SC	1 rep	LYE TOWN	63	1-2	Chawner
28/10/95	BHL	M	HINCKLEY TOWN	131	1-2	McCarthy
01/11/95	DMC	1(2)	LEICESTER UNITED	83	5-3	Campbell, Chawner, Bennett(2), Miller
04/11/95	BHL	M	Moor Green	213	1-1	Burroughs
11/11/95	BHL	M	Rothwell Town	162	2-0	Anifowose(2)
15/11/95	BHL	M	CORBY TOWN	115	10-0	Anifowose(4), Bennett(3), Campbell, Scott
18/11/95	BHL	M	DUDLEY TOWN	155	2-0	Bennett, Campbell
25/11/95	BHL	M	Hinckley Town	120	2-1	Borroughs, Bennett
29/11/95	Birm LMC	1	BOLDMERE ST MICHAELS	106	2-1	McCarthy, Campbell
02/12/95	BHL	M	BUCKINGHAM TOWN	129	1-2	McCarthy
06/12/95	DMC	2	GRESLEY ROVERS	127	2-3	Bennett, McDonald
09/12/95	BHL	M	Bilston Town	92	2-0	Bennett(2)
13/12/95	Staffs SC	2	STOURBRIDGE	65	3-2	Chawner, Bennett, McCarthy
16/12/95	BHL	M	BURY TOWN	102	5-1	Tucker, McCarthy, Anifowose(2), Bennett
23/12/95	BHL	M	King's Lynn	1051	0-2	
06/01/96	BHL	M	Evesham United	95	2-2	Bennett, Scott
13/01/96	BHL	M	NUNEATON BOROUGH	760	2-2	McCarthy, Anifowose
20/01/96	BHL	M	Grantham Town	150	3-1	Bennett(2), Scott
31/01/96	Staffs SC	QF	HEDNESFORD TOWN	102	2-1	Scott, Burroughs
03/02/96	BHL	M	Stourbridge	118	2-3	Bennett(2)
10/02/96	BHL	M	Tamworth	720	1-3	Anifowose
13/02/96	BHL	M	Redditch United	115	0-2	
17/02/96	BHL	M	ROTHWELL TOWN	125	1-0	Burroughs
28/02/96	BHL	M	REDDITCH UNITED	105	0-2	
02/03/96	BHL	M	RACING CLUB WARWICK	115	1-0	Burroughs
09/03/96	BHL	M	Nuneaton Borough	1179	2-0	Tucker, Anifowose
13/03/96	BHL	M	LEICESTER UNITED	81	0-1	
23/03/96	BHL	M	KING'S LYNN	225	0-2	
27/03/96	BHL	M	Solihull Borough	106	1-2	Burroughs
30/03/96	BHL	M	Leicester United	76	1-1	McDonald
02/04/96	Staffs SC	SF	Newcastle Town	56	1-2	Anifowose
04/04/96	Birm LMC	SF	OLDBURY UNITED	55	0-2	
06/04/96	BHL	M	SOLIHULL BOROUGH	143	1-3	McCarthy
08/04/96	BHL	M	Sutton Coldfield United	221	1-0	Burroughs
13/04/96	BHL	M	Buckingham Town	90	4-2	Tucker(3), Rashid
20/04/96	BHL	M	TAMWORTH	345	1-0	Anifowose
24/04/96	BHL	M	BILSTON TOWN	101	0-0	
27/04/96	BHL	M	BEDWORTH UNITED	201	1-1	Anifowose
01/05/96	BHL	M	SUTTON COLDFIELD TOWN	151	3-0	Ling(og), Anifowose, Clark
04/05/96	BHL	M	Dudley Town	251	0-0	

RACING CLUB WARWICK

Townsend Meadow, Hampton Rd, Warwick CV34 6JP. Tel: 01926 495786

Secretary: Patrick Murphy, 20 Dadglow Rd, Bishops Itchington, Leamington Spa, Warws CV33 0TG Tel: 01926 612675

Colours: Gold and Black

Nickname: Racing

Capacity: 1,000

Covered seating: 200

Covered standing: 200

Clubhouse on ground: Yes

Record attendance: 1,000 v Halesowen Town FA Cup 1987

Record appearances: Steve Cooper 600+

Record goalscorer in total: Steve Edgington

DIRECTIONS

On the B4095 Warwick to Redditch Road (via Henley in Arden) next to owners' & trainers' car park of Warwick Racecourse. From M40 jct 15 (one and a half mile) take A429 into Warwick, left into Shakespeare Avenue, straight over island, right at T-junction into Hampton Road, ground 300 yds on left. 2 mile from Warwick BR station.

HONOURS

Midland Combination 1988

Warwick League 1934, 1935, 1936

Birmingham and West Midlands Alliance 1949

Birmingham Senior Cup 1950

Leamington and District League 1938, 1946, 1947, 1948

Leamington Hospital Cup 1938 and 1946

Warwick Cinderella Cup 1936, 1937, 1938, 1939, 1947

TG John Cup 1937

Leamington Junior Cup 1939 and 1947

Racing Club Warwick was founded in 1929 under the name of Saltisford Rovers and they initially spent many years playing in the junior leagues. The club's heyday was from 1947 to 1954 when many trophies were won, including the Birmingham Alliance Senior Cup, where they defeated Birmingham City at St Andrews. The club played in the Warwick League, the Leamington and District League, Warwick Combination, West Midlands League and the Midlands Combination prior to joining the Southern League in 1990. They had been runners up in the previous season, having won it in 1988.

Five people can rightly claim most of the credit for putting Racing Club on the map, Eddie Haines, Pete Walkerm Jack Brown, Jim Wright and Pat Murphy. Eddie has been player, manager and groundsman during his 50 years with the club and Jack Brown had a fine knack of spotting good players. Jim Wright's chairmanship has seen the club progress to the Southern League and Pat Murphy has been at the club for 20 years and performed numerous duties.

Racing Club have carried off a number of trophies over the years including the Warwick Cinderella Cup for four years before the War and the TG John Cup in 1937. Also the Leamington Hospital and Leamington Junior Cups were both won.

The first ground is believed to have been on a pitch next to the Dun Cow pub and that lasted until 1958 when they moved to St Nicholas Park and then Coventry Road, to a ground now covered by Woodlowes Estate. Finally in the early 60's the club moved to a site on part of Warwick racecourse, which became

RACING CLUB WARWICK 1995/96 SEASON

Date	Comp	Rnd	Opponent	Att	Score	Scorers
19/08/95	BHL	M	HINCKLEY TOWN	100	2-1	Jameson, Titterton
22/08/95	BHL	M	Sutton Coldfield Town	146	0-0	
26/08/95	BHL	M	PAGET RANGERS	73	1-1	Titterton
28/08/95	BHL	M	Nuneaton Borough	1010	0-1	
02/09/95	BHL	M	KING'S LYNN	150	2-1	Williams, Parker
05/09/95	BHL	M	Rothwell Town	215	1-2	Daly
09/09/95	FA Cup	Q1	OLDBURY UNITED	108	1-0	Parker
16/09/95	BHL	M	SOLIHULL BOROUGH	104	0-3	
19/09/95	BHL	M	SUTTON COLDFIELD TOWN	70	4-1	Titterton, Clarke, Parker, Bannister(og)
23/09/95	FA Cup	Q2	LONG BUCKBY	159	2-0	Parker, Daly
30/09/95	BHL	M	Bedworth United	250	1-2	Daly
03/10/95	DMC	1(1)	MOOR GREEN	120	1-4	Jameson
07/10/95	FA Cup	Q3	Burton Albion	867	0-2	
14/10/95	FA Trophy	Q1	WARRINGTON TOWN	130	1-0	Parker
17/10/95	Birm SC	1	Halesowen Harriers		2-0	
21/10/95	BHL	M	BRIDGNORTH TOWN	96	2-1	Titterton, O'Neil
24/10/95	BHL	M	NUNEATON BOROUGH	450	2-2	Jameson, Thompson
28/10/95	BHL	M	Grantham Town	190	1-1	Halford
31/10/95	DMC	1(2)	Moor Green	72	0-4	
04/11/95	FA Trophy	Q2	Emley	225	1-2	Jameson
11/11/95	BHL	M	King's Lynn	619	0-2	
18/11/95	BHL	M	TAMWORTH	305	3-7	Halford(2), Clarke
25/11/95	BHL	M	Bridgnorth Town	117	4-2	Parker, Titterton, Rosegreen, O'Neal
28/11/95	BHL	M	ROTHWELL TOWN	117	2-4	Meads(og), Clark
02/12/95	Birm SC	2	Knowle	51	1-2	Findlay
09/12/95	BHL	M	Bury Town	112	5-2	Hubbard(og), O'Neal, Fitzpatrick, Titterton, Rosegreen
16/12/95	BHL	M	EVESHAM UNITED	91	0-4	
23/12/95	BHL	M	Dudley Town	147	3-3	Parker, Clarke, Rosegreen
06/01/96	BHL	M	Moor Green	192	2-2	Clarke, Fitzpatrick
13/01/96	BHL	M	BUCKINGHAM TOWN	110	0-5	
20/01/96	BHL	M	BEDWORTH UNITED	220	2-1	Wallace, Clarke
03/02/96	BHL	M	BURY TOWN	114	4-1	Francis, Daly(2), Wallace
10/02/96	BHL	M	Solihull Borough	125	2-3	Rosegreen, Brown(og)
13/02/96	BHL	M	Buckingham Town	50	2-2	Ross, Rosegreen
17/02/96	BHL	M	CORBY TOWN	120	3-4	Titterton, Clarke, Rosegreen
27/02/96	BHL	M	MOOR GREEN	140	2-3	Daly, Draper
02/03/96	BHL	M	Paget Rangers	115	0-1	
05/03/96	BHL	M	Hinckley Town	79	1-4	Draper
09/03/96	BHL	M	STOURBRIDGE	120	3-5	Draper, Rosegreen, Clark
16/03/96	BHL	M	BILSTON TOWN	74	1-2	Rosegreen
23/03/96	BHL	M	DUDLEY TOWN	90	0-0	
30/03/96	BHL	M	Redditch United	215	1-1	Rosegreen
02/04/96	BHL	M	Stourbridge	122	0-0	
06/04/96	BHL	M	LEICESTER UNITED	110	1-1	Titterton
08/04/96	BHL	M	Bilston Town	82	1-1	Clark
10/04/96	BHL	M	REDDITCH UNITED	150	1-3	Findlay
13/04/96	BHL	M	GRANTHAM TOWN	108	3-2	Finlay(2), Halford
20/04/96	BHL	M	Corby Town	168	0-4	
23/04/96	BHL	M	Leicester United	62	1-1	Finlay
27/04/96	BHL	M	Evesham United	104	4-2	Findlay, Rosegreen(2), Eden
04/05/96	BHL	M	Tamworth	463	0-2	

RAUNDS TOWN

Kiln Park, London Road, Raunds, Northants, NN9 6LD. Tel: 01933 623351

Secretary and Press officer: Mick Jones, 14 Welland Close, Raunds, Northants NN9 6SQ

Tel: 01933 625429

Colours: Red and Black halves

Nickname: The Shopmates

DIRECTIONS

Directions: Take Raunds turning at roundabout on A605 and ground is first left.

Capacity: 3,000   Seating: 250

Covered Standing: 600   Clubhouse on ground: Yes

Record attendance: 1,500 v Crystal Palace for the first game at Kiln Park July 23rd 1991

Biggest win: 11-2 v Brackley Town April 8th 1993 UCL

Biggest defeat: 0-6 V Baldock Town in 1983-84 and Buckingham Town in 1984-85

Record appearances: Possibly Mick Roche 300+

Record goalscorer in one season: Shaun Keeble 45 in 1993-94

Record goalscorer in aggregate: Shaun Keeble 159

HONOURS

United Counties League 1996

Division One 1983

Knock-out Cup 1991

Benevolent Cup 1995

Northants Senior Cup 1991

Northants Junior Cup 1983

Manager for 1996/97: Keith Burt   **Assistant Manager: Glenn Burdett**

Chairman: George Hagan   **Vice Chairman: Peter Scanlon**

Raunds Unity were first formed in 1896 and joined the Northants League, and Raunds Town played until the Great War alongside them. After hostilities they returned to the UCL but finished bottom, and after a one year spell in local football they came back again for another spell until local football again beckoned right up to 1945. A new club was formed in 1946 which again played in the UCL as they have done ever since, moving to Berristers in 1948. Throughout the 50's the club struggled to make an impact on the league and suffered relegation to Division Three in 1979 after many years of strife.

A further change of format for the league coincided with a new manager in Maurice Murphy who took them to third in Division One before winning the championship the following year.

They remained in the top flight until last summer when they were elected to the Southern League.

In 1991 Raunds Town moved from the Berristers which was soon swallowed up by housing and took over a new ground at Kiln Park and they celebrated by making significant progress in the FA Vase, suffering a desperately sad defeat in the semi-final in 1995, losing to Arlesey Town after winning the first leg 3-0. To compound their misery they played a huge backlog of league fixtures, only to lose the title on goal difference.

Their misery did not last long, as last May the club completed the United Counties League championship and with it gained promotion. 1996 sees the club entering a new phase with Southern League football coming to Northamptonshire again, surely one of the fastest rising footballing counties in England.

RAUNDS TOWN 1995/96 SEASON

Date	Competition	Round	Opponent	Score
12/08/95	HSUCL	P	NORTHAMPTON SPENCER	5-1
16/08/95	HSUCL	P	Desborough Town	3-1
19/08/95	HSUCL	P	Mirrlees Blackstone	1-2
23/08/95	HSUCL	P	POTTON UNITED	9-0
26/08/95	FA Cup	P	West Midlands Police	1-1
30/08/95	FA Cup	P rep	WEST MIDLANDS POLICE	3-2
02/09/95	HSUCL	P	Stewarts & Lloyds Corby	2-2
06/09/95	LC	P	HIGHAM TOWN	1-0
09/09/95	FA Cup	Q1	DESBOROUGH TOWN	3-0
12/09/95	HSUCL	P	Spalding United	2-0
16/09/95	HSUCL	P	Long Buckby	2-0
23/09/95	FA Cup	Q2	TELFORD UNITED	1-2
27/09/95	HSUCL	P	ST NEOTS TOWN	4-0
30/09/95	HSUCL	P	BOSTON TOWN	1-1
07/10/95	HSUCL	P	STEWARTS & LLOYDS CORBY	3-0
11/10/95	HSUCL	P	KEMPSTON ROVERS	2-1
14/10/95	HSUCL	P	Stotfold	0-2
21/10/95	HSUCL	P	NEWPORT PAGNELL TOWN	2-1
28/10/95	HSUCL	P	Holbeach United	1-0
01/11/95	HSUCL	P	COGENHOE UNITED	1-2
04/11/95	HSUCL	P	WOOTTON BLUE CROSS	1-1
08/11/95	HSUCL	P	EYNESBURY ROVERS	1-1
11/11/95	HSUCL	P	Newport Pagnell Town	8-0
18/11/95	FA Vase	2	HINCKLEY ATHLETIC	2-2
21/11/95	FA Vase	2 rep	Hinckley Athletic	2-0
25/11/95	HSUCL	P	Potton United	4-0
29/11/95	Daventry	3	NORTHAMPTON SPENCER	4-3
02/12/95	HSUCL	P	SPALDING UNITED	4-1
09/12/95	FA Vase	3	FURNESS	1-1
12/12/95	N'hants SC	QF	Brackley Town	4-0
16/12/95	FA Vase	3 rep	Furness	1-1
03/01/96	FA Vase	3 rep(2)	FURNESS	5-2
06/01/96	HSUCL	P	DESBOROUGH TOWN	1-0
13/01/96	FA Vase	4	TAUNTON TOWN	4-1
20/01/96	HSUCL	P	STAMFORD	1-1
30/01/96	N'hants SC	SF	Rushden & Diamonds	0-1
10/02/96	FA Vase	5	TORPOINT ATHLETIC	2-0
17/02/96	HSUCL	P	BOURNE TOWN	5-0
24/02/96	FA Vase	QF	Mangotsfield United	2-2
27/02/96	HSUCL	P	Eynesbury Rovers	2-2
02/03/96	FA Vase	QF rep	MANGOTSFIELD UNITED	0-1
05/03/96	HSUCL	P	Wootton Blue Cross	4-0
09/03/96	HSUCL	P	HOLBEACH UNITED	5-1
12/03/96	HSUCL	P	Boston Town	1-1
16/03/96	HSUCL	P	Stamford	4-0
23/03/96	HSUCL	P	St Neots Town	0-0
30/03/96	HSUCL	P	Bourne Town	2-0
03/04/96	HSUCL	P	MIRRLEES BLACKSTONE	3-0
06/04/96	HSUCL	P	Cogenhoe United	3-1
08/04/96	HSUCL	P	Wellingborough Town	3-3
13/04/96	HSUCL	P	WELLINGBOROUGH TOWN	5-0
20/04/96	HSUCL	P	Northampton Spencer	7-0
27/04/96	HSUCL	P	Kempston Rovers	2-0
01/05/96	HSUCL	P	STOTFOLD	5-2
04/05/96	HSUCL	P	LONG BUCKBY	2-1
08/05/96	BC	SF	HIGHAM TOWN	2-1
09/05/96	Daventry	SF	COGENHOE UNITED	0-3
15/05/96	BC	F	Stotfold	3-1

REDDITCH UNITED

Valley Stadium, Bromsgrove Rd, Redditch, Worcestershire B97 4RN. Tel: 01527 67450

Secretary: Michael Langfield, 174 Harport Rd, Redditch, Worcs B98 7PE Tel 01527 526603

Colours: All Red

Nickname: The Reds

Capacity: 9,500

Seating: 400

Covered standing 2,000

Clubhouse on ground: Yes

Record attendance: 5,500 v Bromsgrove Rovers West Midlands League 1955

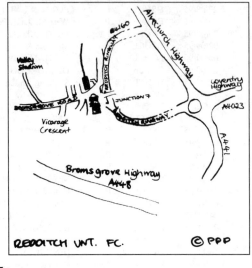

HONOURS

Southern League Div 1 North 1976

Birmingham League (South) 1955

Birmingham Combination 1914, 1933, 1953

Staffs Senior Cup 1991

Birmingham Senior Cup 1925, 1932, 1939, 1977

Worcester Senior Cup 1931, 1975, 1977

Redditch United are one of the oldest established clubs in the Midlands. Redditch Town first played in the Birmingham Combination in 1891 and although the club has been re-formed on at least two occasions, the Reds have recently celebrated their centenary. Their first success came in 1894 when they took the Worcester Senior Cup and four years later they were runners up. In 1914 they won the Combination for the first time and in 1925 they took the Birmingham Senior Cup.

The 30's were much more rewarding and they began with further wins in the Birmingham and Worcestershire Senior Cups and in 1933 they almost pulled off a famous double, winning the Combination and losing the Senior Cup final. Either side of the Second War the club was quiet, but in 1953 they regained the championship, and in 1955 won it again, only failing as runners up in the Senior Cup two years on in 1957. By this time the club had moved into their Valley Stadium home after many years at the works ground on Millborough Road, converting an area of waste ground into a football ground in 1948. They remained in what was then called the West Midlands League until 1972 when after extensive work to upgrade their ground, they were elected to the Southern League. It heralded a successful period which began with a visit to the first round of the FA Cup for the first time, and saw four Worcester Senior Cup finals, two won and two lost. After narrowly missing out on promotion in 1975 they won the championship a year later, losing only twice and scoring over 100 goals.

More ground improvements were made for the eventual and expected entry to the Alliance and despite a poor season they were accepted as founder members, lasting just one season, with a further three years of struggle following on. They were grim times and a new board saw off the threat of liquidation, and saw the club return to the Premier Division in 1986. Sadly in 1989 they went down once again but they did reach the first round of the Cup a year later where they lost to Merthyr Tydfil and also took the Staffs Senior Cup.

Since then there have been other managers come and go, but United survived and last season were comfortably distant from the drop into the Midland Alliance.

REDDITCH UNITED 1995/96 SEASON

Date	Comp	Round	Opponent	Att	Score	Scorers
19/08/95	BHL	M	Grantham Town	224	3-5	McKenzie, S Baker, J Baker
22/08/95	BHL	M	MOOR GREEN	221	1-1	Martin
26/08/95	FA Cup	P	BRIDGNORTH TOWN	153	2-2	Grosvenor, Smith
29/08/95	FA Cup	P rep	Bridgnorth Town	101	4-1	McKenzie(2), Wolsey(2)
02/09/95	BHL	M	LEICESTER UNITED	185	2-3	Baker(2)
05/09/95	BHL	M	Nuneaton Borough	1056	1-4	McKenzie
09/09/95	FA Cup	Q1	MOOR GREEN	210	1-3	Sutton
13/09/95	DMC	P(1)	Solihull Borough	64	4-2	Dyer, Williams, Sutton(2)
16/09/95	BHL	M	TAMWORTH	380	2-3	McKenzie, Smith
19/09/95	BHL	M	Moor Green	231	1-3	Dyer
23/09/95	BHL	M	BRIDGNORTH TOWN	202	0-5	
26/09/95	DMC	P(2)	SOLIHULL BOROUGH	107	2-1	Whittington, Sutton
30/09/95	BHL	M	BUCKINGHAM TOWN	180	0-1	
03/10/95	DMC	1(1)	EVESHAM UNITED	102	0-0	
10/10/95	Worcs SC	1	Stourbridge	147	0-1	
14/10/95	FA Trophy	Q1	Radcliffe Borough	107	1-3	Whittington
17/10/95	Birm SC	1	Oldbury United	78	0-4	
21/10/95	BHL	M	SOLIHULL BOROUGH	183	0-0	
28/10/95	BHL	M	Dudley Town	214	2-2	Brown(og), Whittington
31/10/95	DMC	1(2)	Evesham United	103	2-3	Grosvenor, Sutton
04/11/95	BHL	M	ROTHWELL TOWN	160	0-0	
07/11/95	Mids F'lit	94-95 QF	Tamworth	295	1-2	Mullings
11/11/95	BHL	M	Sutton Coldfield Town	202	0-1	
14/11/95	BHL	M	NUNEATON BOROUGH	385	1-5	Sutton
18/11/95	BHL	M	Bury Town	102	0-2	
25/11/95	BHL	M	STOURBRIDGE	185	1-1	Clifton
02/12/95	BHL	M	Bedworth United	308	0-5	
12/12/95	BHL	M	BILSTON TOWN	80	2-1	Nichols, Mullings
16/12/95	BHL	M	Buckingham Town	90	0-0	
06/01/96	BHL	M	Leicester United	70	4-3	Selby(og), Blain, Laker, Smith
13/01/96	BHL	M	SUTTON COLDFIELD TOWN	236	1-1	Hallam
20/01/96	BHL	M	Bilston Town	102	2-2	Smith, Clifton
23/01/96	Mids F'lit	1(1)	Shepshed Dynamo	61	3-0	Smith(og), Rowlands, Whittington
10/02/96	BHL	M	Bridgnorth Town	145	4-1	Rowlands(2), Laker, Clifton
13/02/96	BHL	M	PAGET RANGERS	115	2-0	Laker, Rowlands
24/02/96	BHL	M	Solihull Borough	171	0-4	
28/02/96	BHL	M	Paget Rangers	105	2-0	Rowlands(2)
02/03/96	BHL	M	DUDLEY TOWN	240	2-6	Laker, Rowlands
05/03/96	BHL	M	KING'S LYNN	128	2-1	Nichols, Hallam
09/03/96	BHL	M	Tamworth	789	2-1	Rowlands, Grosvenor
12/03/96	BHL	M	GRANTHAM TOWN	117	1-1	Grosvenor
16/03/96	BHL	M	HINCKLEY TOWN	147	1-2	Hallam
23/03/96	BHL	M	Corby Town	162	2-1	Wolsey, Nichols
30/03/96	BHL	M	RACING CLUB WARWICK	215	1-1	Rowlands
02/04/96	BHL	M	King's Lynn	1030	0-3	
06/04/96	BHL	M	Hinckley Town	71	2-1	R Smith, Nicholls
08/04/96	BHL	M	EVESHAM UNITED	278	1-0	Clifton
10/04/96	BHL	M	Racing Club Warwick	150	3-1	Nichols, Clifton(2)
13/04/96	BHL	M	BEDWORTH UNITED	292	1-0	Mullings
16/04/96	BHL	M	Evesham United	103	1-1	Wolsey
18/04/96	Mids F'lit	QF	HINCKLEY TOWN	78	1-2	Wolsey
20/04/96	BHL	M	Rothwell Town	172	1-2	Grosvenor
27/04/96	BHL	M	Stourbridge	136	2-1	Grosvenor(2)
30/04/96	BHL	M	CORBY TOWN	193	4-1	Grosvenor(2), Nichols, Mullings
04/05/96	BHL	M	BURY TOWN	265	0-1	

ROTHWELL TOWN

Cecil Street, Rothwell, Northants, NN14 2EZ.Tel: 01536 710694

Secretary: Roger Barratt, 18 Norton Street, Rothwell, Northants NN14 6DL.
Tel: 01536 711244

Press officer and Commercial manager: Peter Bradley 01536 710925

Colours: Blue and White

Nickname: The Bones

Capacity: 3,000

Seating: 270

Covered standing: 1,000

Clubhouse on ground: Yes

Record attendance: 2, 508 v Irthlingborough Diamonds United Counties League 1971

Biggest win: 17-0 v Stamford FA Cup Prelim Replay 1927

Biggest defeat: 1-10 v Coalville Town Leicester Senior League 1949

Record appearance: Gordon Linnett

Record goalscorer: Bert Hanley

Record fee paid: Undisclosed for Andy Wright from Aylesbury Utd i 1992

Record fee received Undisclosed for Matty Watts to Charlton Ath 1990

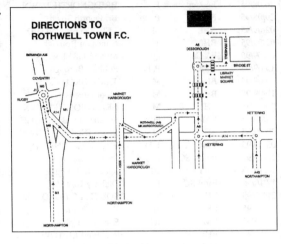

DIRECTIONS TO ROTHWELL TOWN F.C.

HONOURS

United Counties League 1993 and 1994; League Cup 1956, 1971, 1972, 1992, 1993; Division Two League and Cup 1953 and 1954; Benevolent Cup 1993 and 1994; Northants League 1900; Northants Senior Cup 1900, 1924, 1960, 1989, 1996; Kettering Amateur League 1937

Manager 1996-97: Jack Murray　　　　**Assistant Manager: Graham Simmonds**

Chairman: Stuart Andrews　　　　**Vice Chairman: Jeremy Freestone**

Rothwell were founder members of the Northants League in 1895 and were runners up for three seasons before finally taking the title in 1900, for good measure winning the Senior Cup as well.

It was short lived as the club were suspended by the Northants FA and did not finish the season. In 1905 the Bones returned but after two seasons they dropped into the Kettering Combination. It was 1921 before they returned to the Northants League, but there was little to celebrate as the Bones won just one Senior Cup in 12 years, finally dropping into the Kettering Amateur League which they won in 1937.

After the war the club briefly played in the Leicestershire Senior League but in 1950 they helped reform the UCL Division 2. The switch heralded a successful era as they did the League and Cup double in successive seasons, moving into the top division. After just one season they moved to the Central Alliance for five years and they won their third Senior Cup in 1960. Rothwell's return to the UCL in 1965 saw them as runners up and the amateur side of the 70's were twice runners up, Knock-out Cup winners, and Senior Cup winners in 1972. Lean years followed but the last few seasons have been special for the Bones. They won the Senior Cup again in 1989, were Premier Division runners up in 1988, 1990 and 1991, Knock-out Cup winners in 1992 and 1993 and League champions in 1993 and 1994. As well as all that there were two Benevolent Cup wins and a run to the last 16 of the Vase. It culminated in the club joining the Southern League Midland Division where they remain.

ROTHWELL TOWN 1995/96 SEASON

Date	Comp	Rnd	Opponent	Att	Score	Scorers
19/08/95	BHL	M	BRIDGNORTH TOWN	162	4-4	McGuire(2), Lord, Meads
22/08/95	BHL	M	King's Lynn	641	0-2	
26/08/95	FA Cup	P	RUSHALL OLYMPIC	95	2-0	Diver, McDonald
28/08/95	BHL	M	BURY TOWN	215	3-3	McPolin, Lord, Meads
02/09/95	BHL	M	Tamworth	486	2-2	McPolin, Westley
05/09/95	BHL	M	RACING CLUB WARWICK	215	2-1	McDonald, Diver
09/09/95	FA Cup	Q1	Stafford Rangers	306	1-6	Wills
12/09/95	N'hants SC	1	Wellingborough Town	67	3-0	Waite, Stoker(og), Diver
16/09/95	BHL	M	Bedworth United	292	1-4	McPolin
19/09/95	BHL	M	KING'S LYNN	242	1-2	Coe
23/09/95	BHL	M	STOURBRIDGE	168	1-1	Laws
30/09/95	BHL	M	Hinckley Town	95	2-2	McGuire, Wills
04/10/95	DMC	1(1)	Corby Town	183	2-2	McPolin(2)
07/10/95	BHL	M	Bilston Town	110	0-3	
14/10/95	BHL	M	CORBY TOWN	327	1-0	McGuire
17/10/95	BHL	M	Bury Town	107	4-1	McGuire(2), Henry(og), McPolin
21/10/95	BHL	M	Moor Green	193	1-1	Beards
31/10/95	DMC	1(2)	CORBY TOWN	251	1-0	Beards
04/11/95	BHL	M	Redditch United	160	0-0	
11/11/95	BHL	M	PAGET RANGERS	162	0-2	
18/11/95	BHL	M	LEICESTER UNITED	189	5-0	McGuire(2), McPolin, McDonald Diver
25/11/95	FA Trophy	Q3	UXBRIDGE	126	3-2	McGuire(2), Meads
28/11/95	BHL	M	Racing Club Warwick	117	4-2	Meads, McGuire, McDonald, Orton
02/12/95	BHL	M	Stourbridge	107	0-2	
09/12/95	BHL	M	Dudley Town	127	2-2	McGuire(2)
16/12/95	BHL	M	BILSTON TOWN	124	2-2	Lord, McGuire
19/12/95	DMC	2	KING'S LYNN	189	0-1	
23/12/95	BHL	M	Sutton Coldfield Town	139	2-2	Lord, Coe
01/01/96	BHL	M	Grantham Town	150	6-0	Beards(2), McGuire, Westley(2), Calvert
09/01/96	BHL	M	BEDWORTH UNITED	250	2-2	Beards, Orton
13/01/96	BHL	M	Bridgnorth Town	127	3-1	McGuire(2), McDonald
20/01/96	FA Trophy	1	WELLING UNITED	238	2-2	Beards, McGuire
01/02/96	FA Trophy	1 rep	Welling United	312	0-3	
03/02/96	BHL	M	Corby Town	257	2-0	McGuire(2)
10/02/96	BHL	M	MOOR GREEN	191	3-2	Coe, Diver, McGuire
17/02/96	BHL	M	Paget Rangers	125	0-1	
24/02/96	BHL	M	HINCKLEY TOWN	196	2-1	Beards, Lord
27/02/96	N'hants SC	SF	KETTERING TOWN	402	5-0	Lord, McDonald, Beards(2), Wills
02/03/96	BHL	M	BUCKINGHAM TOWN	152	3-1	Beards, Lord, McGuire
05/03/96	BHL	M	TAMWORTH	243	0-1	
12/03/96	BHL	M	SOLIHULL BOROUGH	112	1-4	Beards
16/03/96	BHL	M	Evesham United	77	1-3	Watson
19/03/96	Daventry	QF	NORTHAMPTON O.N. CHENECKS		1-2	
23/03/96	BHL	M	SUTTON COLDFIELD TOWN	145	3-1	Lord, Calvert, Meads
26/03/96	N'hants SC	F	RUSHDEN & DIAMONDS	511	1-0	Beards
30/03/96	BHL	M	Nuneaton Borough	901	0-0	
02/04/96	BHL	M	EVESHAM UNITED	139	4-1	Lord, McGuire(2), Beards
06/04/96	BHL	M	Buckingham Town	80	1-1	Beards
08/04/96	BHL	M	GRANTHAM TOWN	165	3-0	Beards(2), McGuire
13/04/96	BHL	M	Leicester United	110	1-1	McDonald
20/04/96	BHL	M	REDDITCH UNITED	172	2-1	McGuire, Meads
23/04/96	BHL	M	NUNEATON BOROUGH	412	2-0	McGuire(2)
27/04/96	BHL	M	DUDLEY TOWN	154	2-1	Meads, Grant(og)
04/05/96	BHL	M	Solihull Borough	124	1-2	McGuire

SHEPSHED DYNAMO

The Dovecote, Butthole Lane, Shepshed, Leicestershire.

Secretary: Peter Bull, 17 Welland Rd, Barrow upon Soar, Leicester LE12 8NA. Tel: 01509 413338

Colours: Black and white

Nickname: Raiders

Capacity: 5,000

Covered seating: 209

Covered standing: 1,500

Clubhouse on ground: Yes

Record attendance: 1,672

Record appearances: Austin Straker 300

Record goalscorer in total: Jeff Lissaman

DIRECTIONS
M1 junction 23, A512 towards Ashby, right at first lights, right at garage in Forest Street, right into Butthole Lane opposite Black Swan. Five miles from Loughborough (BR).

HONOURS

FA VASE Semi-final 1979

Midland Alliance 1996

Northern Counties East League and Cup 1983

Midland Counties League and Cup 1982

Leicestershire Senior League 1911, 1921, 1979, 1980, 1981

Division Two 1954, 1966, 1978 and Div 2 Cup 1978

Leicestershire Senior Cup 1978, 1980, 1982, 1984, 1985, 1986, 1988

Loughborough Charity Cup 1993

The village of Shepshed, or Sheepshed as it was known in the early days of football, has seen a number of clubs since the first match at Kirkhill in November 1879 when the Institute Athletic played Loughborough Rising Star. The ground was not popular and so the club moved to a field on Charnwood Avenue opposite the police station and in their eight year stay, they changed their name to Shepshed Town. There were two other grounds, in Ashby Road and Little Haw Lane before the turn of the century, when Shepshed Albion took over from the ailing Town. The new club entered the Leicester Senior League in 1908 and began playing at an improved enclosure called the Dovecote. A few years after the Great War, Albion folded and a Parish Church FC used the ground for a while and it was not until after the Second War that another Albion side was formed, which played a season in the Loughborough Alliance before moving to play in the Senior League and they remained there right through to 1981. Divison Two was won three times, but it was in the mid 70's after 100 years of football, that the village finally came to prominence. A sponsorship deal saw the club change its name to Shepshed Charterhouse and wholesale developments occurred at the Dovecote with a clubhouse, stands and floodlights and with it came success with three Senior League titles on the trot and three Senior Cups. It was enough to elevate them into the Southern League in 1983, with a season each in the Midland Counties and Northern Counties East in between, both of which were won and from where they were swopped into the Northern Premier League. Success continued through with an FA Vase semi final and four more Senior Cups. When the sponsorship ended the club reverted to Albion again, but soon a decline set in and the club dropped back into the Midland Combination and subsequently re-formed as Shepshed Dynamos. Last season, with renewed enthusiasm at the Dovecote, Southern League football again returned after the Midland Alliance was won in style.

SHEPSHED DYNAMO 1995/96 SEASON

Date	Competition	Round	Opponent	Score
19/08/95	IEMA		WEST MIDLANDS POLICE	2-0
26/08/95	FA Cup	P	GRANTHAM TOWN	0-1
28/08/95	IEMA		Knypersley Victoria	2-0
09/09/95	IEMA		PERSHORE TOWN	2-2
16/09/95	IEMA		RUSHALL OLYMPIC	3-2
23/09/95	IEMA		Rocester	2-0
30/09/95	FA Vase	Q2	KINGS HEATH	4-0
07/10/95	IEMA		CHASETOWN	1-1
14/10/95	IEMA		Willenhall Town	0-0
21/10/95	IEMA		HALESOWEN HARRIERS	2-0
24/10/95	IWLC	2	SANDWELL BOROUGH	3-3
28/10/95	FA Vase	1	Boston Town	6-2
04/11/95	IEMA		Chasetown	3-3
07/11/95	IEMA		Barwell	0-0
11/11/95	IEMA		Blakenall	3-3
18/11/95	FA Vase	2	Anstey Nomads	1-4
21/11/95	IWLC	2 rep	Sandwell Borough	2-2
25/11/95	Mids TIC	2	RUSHALL OLYMPIC	3-2
28/11/95	Leics CC	QF	HINCKLEY TOWN	1-0
02/12/95	IEMA		Hinckley Athletic	2-0
16/12/95	IEMA		STRATFORD TOWN	2-0
23/12/95	IEMA		Shifnal Town	5-3
06/01/96	IEMA		ROCESTER	7-1
13/01/96	IEMA		Rushall Olympic	2-1
20/01/96	IEMA		OLDBURY UNITED	0-0
23/01/96	Mids F'lit	1(1)	REDDITCH UNITED	0-3
10/02/96	IEMA		BARWELL	1-1
17/02/96	IEMA		Pershore Town	5-0
24/02/96	IEMA		BLAKENALL	4-1
27/02/96	Mids TIC	3	OLDBURY UNITED	1-3
02/03/96	IEMA		Bolehall Swifts	3-1
05/03/96	IEMA		West Midlands Police	1-1
09/03/96	IEMA		BOLDMERE ST MICHAELS	0-0
16/03/96	IEMA		HINCKLEY ATHLETIC	0-2
20/03/96	Leics CC	SF	ST ANDREWS	1-3
23/03/96	IEMA		Boldmere St Michaels	4-1
26/03/96	IEMA		STAPENHILL	2-0
30/03/96	IEMA		Stratford Town	1-2
06/04/96	IEMA		SHIFNAL TOWN	3-2
08/04/96	IEMA		Stapenhill	5-1
13/04/96	IEMA		Sandwell Borough	0-1
16/04/96	IEMA		Oldbury United	6-1
20/04/96	IEMA		SANDWELL BOROUGH	3-0
23/04/96	IEMA		WILLENHALL TOWN	6-1
27/04/96	IEMA		BOLEHALL SWIFTS	4-0
30/04/96	IEMA		Halesowen Harriers	1-5
04/05/96	IEMA		KNYPERSLEY VICTORIA	3-1
01/01/99	Mids F'lit	1(2)	Redditch United	0-0

SOLIHULL BOROUGH

Moor Green FC, The Moorlands, Sherwood Road, Hall Green, B28 0EX. Tel: 0121 624 2727

Club Headquarters: The Borough Club, Tanworth Lane, Shirley, Solihull, West Mids

Tel: 0121 745 6758 FAX: 0121 744 9351

Secretary: John France, 22 Swallows Meadow, Shirley, Solihull, B90 4QB. Tel: 0121 733 6584

Nickname: The Boro   Colours: Red and White

Ground details as per Moor Green FC

Clubhouse on ground: Yes

Record attendance: 1,360 v VS Rugby
FA Cup 1st Round Nov 14th 1991

Biggest win: 6-1 v Hednesford Town (H)
Southern League Midland Div 1991-92

Biggest defeat: 1-7 v VS Rugby (A) Birmingham Senior Cup

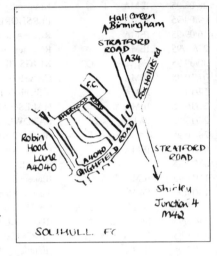

Record appearances: Darrell Houghton

Record goalscorer in one season: Chris Burton   Record goalscorer in aggregate: Chris Burton

Record fee received: £30,000 for Andy Williams from Coventry City

Paid: £5,000 Craig Gillet from Kidderminster Harriers 1994

HONOURS

Southern League Midland Division 1991-92   Merit Cup 1992

Birmingham Senior Cup 1995

Lord Mayor of Birmingham Cup 1992, 1993, 1994

Manager for 1996/97: Paul Dyson   **Press officer: Richard Crawshaw 01564 702746**

Chairman: John Hewitson   **Vice Chairman: Trevor Stevens**

Solihull Borough News-line for all fixtures, news and reports: 0891 664523

Solihull Borough Football Club was formed by a group of friends in the Lincoln Road cafe in Acocks Green, Birmingham, and named Lincoln FC. They played in the old Mercian League before firstly moving to Widney Stadium in 1965, where they eventually moved up into the Midland Combination Division Two, four years later. Although never taking the league title, the club were runners-up twice, the second time in 1991 gaining them promotion to the Southern League.

By then they had sold their ground which stood on prime building land and moved in with Moor Green FC, whilst discussions went ahead to find land for a new ground. Despite the uncertainty, Boro made a great start, winning the Midland Division at the first attempt as well as capturing the Lord Mayor of Birmingham Cup and the Beazer Homes Merit Cup. The success continued in the Premier Division, achieving sixth place in 1993, reaching the 1st Round of the FA Cup.

Since that time the club's protracted pleas for a new ground site have been dismissed by the powers that be, despite the reserves having use of a sports ground in the area which has been suggested but thrown out due to objections from locales. It can only be hoped that the situation improves for the patient supporters and clubmen of Solihull Borough.

FORMER GROUNDS...Widney Stadium was home from 1965 to 1988 and was sold for housing.

SOLIHULL BOROUGH 1995/96 SEASON

Date	Comp		Opponent	Att	Score	Scorers
19/08/95	BHL	M	Tamworth	612	1-1	Coppin
23/08/95	BHL	M	STOURBRIDGE	155	4-0	Coppin(2), Muir, Darling
26/08/95	BHL	M	NUNEATON BOROUGH	381	0-1	
02/09/95	BHL	M	Bedworth United	294	0-5	
06/09/95	BHL	M	BUCKINGHAM TOWN	105	3-2	Dowling(3)
09/09/95	FA Cup	Q1	Chasetown	122	3-1	Hopkins, Muir(2)
13/09/95	DMC	P(1)	REDDITCH UNITED	64	2-4	Love, Downing
16/09/95	BHL	M	Racing Club Warwick	104	3-0	Love, Mulders, Cooper
19/09/95	BHL	M	Stourbridge	132	1-2	Dowling
23/09/95	FA Cup	Q2	Armitage	118	3-2	Muir, Simms, Cooper
26/09/95	DMC	P(2)	Redditch United	107	1-2	Simms
30/09/95	BHL	M	KING'S LYNN	187	2-2	Hopkins, Kurila
07/10/95	FA Cup	Q3	Hednesford Town	1013	2-2	Muir, Dowling
11/10/95	FA Cup	Q3 rep	HEDNESFORD TOWN	421	1-2	Muir
14/10/95	FA Trophy	Q1	Lancaster City	173	0-3	
17/10/95	Worcs SC	1	Evesham United	89	2-2	Dowling, Dyson
21/10/95	BHL	M	Redditch United	183	0-0	
25/10/95	BHL	M	EVESHAM UNITED	119	3-0	Dowling, Palgrave, Muir
28/10/95	BHL	M	BRIDGNORTH TOWN	142	2-2	Palgrave, Kurila
07/11/95	BHL	M	Buckingham Town	70	1-3	Muir
11/11/95	BHL	M	GRANTHAM TOWN	125	4-2	Muir(3), Coppin
18/11/95	BHL	M	Bilston Town	110	1-2	Coppin
21/11/95	Birm LMC	1	Sutton Coldfield Town	36	1-2	Cooper
25/11/95	BHL	M	BEDWORTH UNITED	178	1-3	Palgrave
29/11/95	Worcs SC	1 rep	EVESHAM UNITED	34	2-1	Cappin(2)
02/12/95	Birm SC	2	Coleshill Town	40	3-1	Muir, Cappin, Dowling
09/12/95	BHL	M	TAMWORTH	274	1-3	Coogan
16/12/95	BHL	M	Nuneaton Borough	869	1-2	M Coppin
26/12/95	BHL	M	Moor Green	393	1- 1	Mulders
06/01/96	BHL	M	Dudley Town	178	1-1	Coogan
10/01/96	Birm SC	3	TAMWORTH	133	1-0	Fearon
13/01/96	BHL	M	King's Lynn	1028	0-3	
20/01/96	BHL	M	LEICESTER UNITED	115	1-1	Dowling
03/02/96	BHL	M	Sutton Coldfield Town	165	1-1	Muir
10/02/96	BHL	M	RACING CLUB WARWICK	125	3-2	Muir, Gillett, Latchford
15/02/96	Birm SC	QF	WEST BROMWICH ALBION	102	0-2	
24/02/96	BHL	M	REDDITCH UNITED	171	4-0	Fearon, Palgrave, Dowling, Muir
26/02/96	Worcs SC	QF	Worcester City	262	2-0	Dowling, Sims
02/03/96	BHL	M	Leicester United	59	0-1	
06/03/96	BHL	M	DUDLEY TOWN	76	4-2	Ingram, Hopkins, Dowling, Gillett
09/03/96	BHL	M	CORBY TOWN	142	0-2	
12/03/96	BHL	M	Rothwell Town	112	4-1	Agar(2), Dunn, Dowling
16/03/96	BHL	M	SUTTON COLDFIELD TOWN	118	3-2	Gillett, Coppin, Dowling
19/03/96	BHL	M	Bridgnorth Town	118	4-1	Dowling(2), Coppin(2)
23/03/96	BHL	M	Bury Town	165	0-2	
25/03/96	Worcs SC	SF	BROMSGROVE ROVERS	183	2-2	Dowling, Abel
27/03/96	BHL	M	PAGET RANGERS	106	2-1	Coppin, Simms
30/03/96	BHL	M	HINCKLEY TOWN	136	3-0	Brown(2), Coppin
03/04/96	BHL	M	BURY TOWN	82	1-1	Coppin
06/04/96	BHL	M	Paget Rangers	143	3-1	Muir(3)
08/04/96	BHL	M	MOOR GREEN	341	0-2	
10/04/96	BHL	M	Evesham United	91	2-1	Palgrave, Dowling
13/04/96	BHL	M	BILSTON TOWN	161	2-0	Dowling(2)
16/04/96	Worcs SC	SF rep	Bromsgrove Rovers	524	1-3	Muir
20/04/96	BHL	M	Grantham Town	183	4-3	Dunn, Dowling, Coppin, Muir
23/04/96	BHL	M	Hinckley Town	50	3-2	Coppin, Simms, Beagan
27/04/96	BHL	M	Corby Town	222	1-2	Dowling
04/05/96	BHL	M	ROTHWELL TOWN	124	2-1	Coppin(2)

STAFFORD RANGERS

Marston Road, Stafford, ST16 3BX. Tel: 01785 602430

Secretary: Mr Michael Hughes, 1 Rambleford Way, Parkside, Stafford, ST16 1TW. Tel: 01785 254879

Colours: White and black   Nickname: Boro

Capacity: 6,000   Seating: 400

Covered standing: 3,000   Clubhouse on ground: Yes

Record attendance: 8,536 v Rotherham Utd FA Cup 3rd Rd Jan 1975

Biggest win: 11-0 v Dudley Town FA Cup 1958

Biggest defeat: 0-12 v Burton Town Birmingham League 1930

Record appearances: Jim Sergent

Record goalscorer in total: Mick Cullerton 176

Record fee received: £100,000 for Stan Collymore (Crystal Palace)

Record fee paid: £13,000 for Stephen Butterworth from VS Rugby 1990

DIRECTIONS

From M6 junction 14, A34 (Stone) to roundabout, straight over into Beaconside take third right into Common Road, ground one mile ahead From Town Centre, follow signs for B5066 (Sandon) turn left by Lotus shoe factory. Two miles from railway station.

HONOURS

FA TROPHY WINNERS 1972 AND 1979; RUNNERS UP: 1976; Birmingham Comb 1913; Birmingham League 1926; Northern Premier League 1972 and 1985; Championship Shield 1985; Bob Lord Trophy 1986; Midland Floodlight Cup 1971; Staffs Senior Cup 1955, 1957, 1963, 1972, 1978, 1987, 1992.

It has not been established for sure when Stafford Rangers FC was actually formed as early minute books were destroyed during the Great War. The first reference is in the Staffs Advertiser dated September 30th 1876 when a stranger enquired as to whether there was a team in the town, and Mr A Cotton replied that there was. Later that year, Stafford beat Stone 1-0 at Lammercotes and although never confirmed it is assumed that it was Rangers. Another theory is that Rangers were begun as a bible class in 1877.

The early matches were cup ties and friendlies, playing in the FA Cup 1st Round in 1885 and 1886. They joined the Shropshire League in 1891 and moved to the Birmingham League two years later, only to be voted out after finishing last. In September 1896 they joined the North Staffordshire League and began playing at Marston Road. At the turn of the century they changed leagues again, only to find themselves having to field teams of equal strength in both Birmingham and Cheshire Leagues in 1901. They had one season in Cheshire football before concentrating in Birmingham, but they were demoted to the Combination in 1912 only to win it at the first attempt.

After the Great War they re-joined the Birmingham League, but poor gates and high wages brought problems and they were forced to turn amateur and won the league in 1927 and were twice runners up in four years. The late 30's saw the club fade away sadly and they disbanded during the War, in 1940. Again they reformed after the War, mainly due to the efforts of the supporters. They had six years before re-joining the Cheshire League against the wishes of most and it heralded another barren time for the club.

However, in 1968 came a change of fortune as they won the Cheshire League Cup and a year later were runners up to Skelmersdale and were admitted to the Northern Premier League. Under Roy Chapman, the club won the championship, FA Trophy and Staffs Senior Cup treble in 1972, a remarkable turnaround for the club and three seasons later they reached the Fourth Round of the FA Cup, following wins over Stockport County, Halifax Town and Rotherham United. Rangers were back at Wembley again in 1976 where they lost in extra time to Scarborough, but made up for it in 1979 when their third visit brought success against Kettering Town.

The formation of the Alliance Premier League came when Rangers were on a low ebb and after four difficult seasons they went down to the NPL, only to win it in 1985 and return. The last dozen years have seen more mixed fortunes for Rangers and having having been relegated to the Southern League they then

STAFFORD RANGERS 1995/96 SEASON

Date	Competition	Round	Opponent	Att	Score	Scorers
19/08/95	BHL	P	CAMBRIDGE CITY	550	2-4	Tovey(og), Burndred
21/08/95	BHL	P	Worcester City	775	0-4	
26/08/95	BHL	P	Newport A.F.C.	1279	1-2	Burndred
28/08/95	BHL	P	ATHERSTONE UNITED	522	1-4	O'Toole
02/09/95	BHL	P	Merthyr Tydfil	323	1-3	Mitchell
05/09/95	BHL	P	BURTON ALBION	730	2-3	Mitchell(2)
09/09/95	FA Cup	Q1	ROTHWELL TOWN	306	6-1	Simpson, Rees, Boughey(2), Banks(2)
16/09/95	BHL	P	Salisbury City	379	1-2	Banks
19/09/95	BHL	P	WORCESTER CITY	463	0-2	
23/09/95	FA Cup	Q2	Burton Albion	1014	1-1	Mitchell
26/09/95	FA Cup	Q2 rep	BURTON ALBION	610	2-3	Burton, Banks
30/09/95	BHL	P	V.S. RUGBY	556	1-2	Banks
03/10/95	DMC	1(1)	BRIDGNORTH TOWN	197	0-2	
07/10/95	BHL	P	Baldock Town	281	0-5	
14/10/95	BHL	P	DORCHESTER TOWN	382	0-3	
17/10/95	Staffs SC	1	RUSHALL OLYMPIC		0-2	
21/10/95	BHL	P	Halesowen Town	678	2-2	Boughey, Banks
24/10/95	BHL	P	Atherstone United	263	2-2	Martin, Mitchell
28/10/95	BHL	P	GRESLEY ROVERS	582	3-5	Moore, Mitchell, Banks
31/10/95	DMC	1(2)	Bridgnorth Town	167	2-3	Martin, Kilbane
04/11/95	BHL	P	Rushden & Diamonds	2078	1-5	Haughton
11/11/95	BHL	P	GLOUCESTER CITY	324	3-4	Bywater, Mitchell, Kilbane
14/11/95	BHL	P	Burton Albion	803	1-5	Acton(og)
18/11/95	BHL	P	Cambridge City	257	0-2	
25/11/95	FA Trophy	Q3	TAMWORTH	647	1-1	Bywater
28/11/95	FA Trophy	Q3 rep	Tamworth	741	3-0	Banks, Bertschin, Mitchell
02/12/95	BHL	P	MERTHYR TYDFIL	487	1-2	Mitchell
09/12/95	BHL	P	SALISBURY CITY	433	2-1	Dawson, Mitchell
16/12/95	BHL	P	Gravesend & Northfleet	462	3-0	Mitchell(2), Banks
06/01/96	BHL	P	NEWPORT A.F.C.	634	6-1	Bertschin, Dawson, Mitchell, Hangton, Twigg
13/01/96	BHL	P	Chelmsford City	990	0-1	
20/01/96	FA Trophy	1	GUISELEY	689	1-1	Mitchell
22/01/96	FA Trophy	1 rep	Guiseley	365	1-2	Moore
03/02/96	BHL	P	BALDOCK TOWN	511	0-1	
10/02/96	BHL	P	Ilkeston Town	430	3-1	Boughey(2), Twigg
13/02/96	BHL	P	HALESOWEN TOWN	602	1-0	Mitchell
17/02/96	BHL	P	V.S. Rugby	512	3-0	Banks, Boughey, Twigg
24/02/96	BHL	P	CRAWLEY TOWN	679	3-0	Jennings, Banks(2)
09/03/96	BHL	P	GRAVESEND & NORTHFLEET	635	1-0	Clifford
12/03/96	BHL	P	Gloucester City	435	2-3	Boughey(2)
16/03/96	BHL	P	Hastings Town	451	2-0	Jennings, Boughey
23/03/96	BHL	P	Sudbury Town	347	1-3	Boughey
26/03/96	BHL	P	HASTINGS TOWN	500	1-1	Bywater
30/03/96	BHL	P	CHELTENHAM TOWN	654	0-1	
02/04/96	BHL	P	SUDBURY TOWN	440	0-1	
06/04/96	BHL	P	Gresley Rovers	656	1-1	Mitchell
08/04/96	BHL	P	ILKESTON TOWN	665	1-0	Kilbane
13/04/96	BHL	P	Crawley Town	740	1-2	Bertschin
16/04/96	BHL	P	Cheltenham Town	425	0-4	
20/04/96	BHL	P	CHELMSFORD CITY	460	3-0	Dawson, O'Toole, Mitchell
27/04/96	BHL	P	RUSHDEN & DIAMONDS	1160	0-4	
04/05/96	BHL	P	Dorchester Town	688	2-4	Boughey, Haughton

STOURBRIDGE

War Memorial Athletic Ground, High Street, Amblecote, Stourbridge DY8 4EB.Tel: 01384 394040

Secretary and Press Officer: Hugh Clark, 10 Burnt Oak Drive, Stourbridge, West Midlands DY8 1HL
Tel: 01384 392975

Colours: Red and White stripes

Nickname: The Glassboys

Capacity: 2,000   Seating: 270

Covered standing: 1,100

Clubhouse on ground: Yes

Record attendance: 5,726 v Cardiff City
Welsh Cup Final 1st leg 1974

Record appearances: Ron Page 427 1946-1959

Record goalscorer in one season:
Evran Wright 56 in 1992-93

Record goalscorer in total: Ron Page 269

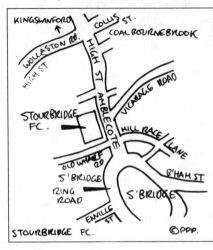

Record fee received: £20,000 for Tony Cunningham (Lincoln City)

HONOURS

WELSH CUP Runners up 1974; Southern League Midland Division 1991; League Cup 1993, Division One North 1974, Merit Cup 1974; Birmingham League 1924; Birmingham Combination 1952; Birmingham Senior Cup 1950, 1959, 1968; Worcester Senior Cup 1905, 1906, 1920, 1922, 1924, 1928, 1950, 1968, 1981; Herefordshire Senior Cup 1955; Camkin President's Cup 1971; Albion Shield 1944; Kidderminster Cup 1888; Keys Cup 1938 and 1963; Dudley Guest Hospital Cup 1892; Worcester Charity Cup 1888; Coronation Cup 1957.

Stourbridge's club shop was one of the first to open in 1972. They occasionally produce a handbook, the last one was in 1994.

Manager 1996-97: Morton Bartlett   **Assistant Manager: Dale Rudge**

Chairman: Morton Bartlett   **Vice Chairman: Nick Pratt**

The Glassboys were founded in 1876 and were originally known as Stourbridge Standard. It was a dozen years before the club took the Worcester and Kidderminster Cups, and by that time the name had shortened to Stourbridge FC. They played in the Birmingham and District League from where they won three Worcester Senior Cups. 1923-24 was one of the best in their history, winning the league by seven points and the Worcester Cup again, but it was just after the War that the club enjoyed their greatest period, winning the Birmingham Combination, and Worcestershire and Herefordshire Cups . In 1954 they returned to the Birmingham League when the Combination folded and in 1971 they moved up to the Southern League, winning Division One North in 1974. Both Chic Bates and Ray Harwood both scored 50 goals that season and were both transferred to Shrewbury Town. Also that season the club reached the final of the Welsh Cup where a record crowd saw the first leg at Amblecote. Through the rest of the 70's and into the 80's the club were quiet and in 1988 a disastrous run ended in relegation although the club were fortunate to be re-elected and under John Chambers, they were revived and took the Midland Division in 1991, only to be denied promotion due to the shared use of the ground with cricket. 1992-93 was ordinary in the league, but the League Cup saw wins over Hednesford Town, Halesowen Town and Rushden and Diamonds before taking the final by beating champions Dover Athletic. Since then the club have reached the Senior Cup final again and are hopeful of overcoming the ground problems to enable them to plan for a higher grade of football in the near future.

STOURBRIDGE 1995/96 SEASON

Date	Comp	Rd	Opponent	Att	Score	Scorers
19/08/95	BHL	M	Paget Rangers	110	0-2	
23/08/95	BHL	M	Solihull Borough	155	0-4	
26/08/95	BHL	M	Sutton Coldfield Town	167	2-3	Davies, Walker
28/08/95	BHL	M	Tamworth	561	2-1	Smith, Clark
02/09/95	BHL	M	CORBY TOWN	135	2-0	Walker, Smith
05/09/95	BHL	M	MOOR GREEN	141	0-2	
09/09/95	FA Cup	Q1	EVESHAM UNITED	141	2-2	Johnson, Smith
12/09/95	FA Cup	Q1 rep	Evesham United	154	0-3	
16/09/95	BHL	M	Bury Town	143	0-1	
19/09/95	BHL	M	SOLIHULL BOROUGH	132	2-1	Johnson, Gardiner
23/09/95	BHL	M	Rothwell Town	168	1-1	Coe(og)
26/09/95	Staffs SC	1	Chasetown	47	1-1	Palmer
30/09/95	BHL	M	EVESHAM UNITED	164	1-0	Walker
03/10/95	DMC	1(1)	DUDLEY TOWN	178	4-2	Smith, Horne(og), Johnson, Jeavons
10/10/95	Worcs SC	1	REDDITCH UNITED	147	1-0	Payne
14/10/95	FA Trophy	Q1	FRICKLEY ATHLETIC	126	1-2	Payne
17/10/95	Birm SC	1	Willenhall Town	93	0-1	
21/10/95	BHL	M	GRANTHAM TOWN	103	1-5	Voice
24/10/95	BHL	M	TAMWORTH	185	3-2	Tomlinson, Johnson, Bastaple
01/11/95	DMC	1(2)	Dudley Town	246	4-4	Johnson(2), Payne, Smith
07/11/95	Staffs SC	1 rep	CHASETOWN	105	4-0	Jeavons, Bastable, Smith, Gardiner
11/11/95	BHL	M	HINCKLEY TOWN	106	1-1	Laker
14/11/95	BHL	M	Moor Green	217	0-3	
18/11/95	BHL	M	KING'S LYNN	133	1-2	Smith
25/11/95	BHL	M	Redditch United	185	1-1	Johnson
02/12/95	BHL	M	ROTHWELL TOWN	107	2-0	Johnson(2)
04/12/95	DMC	2	Worcester City	305	0-3	
09/12/95	BHL	M	Evesham United	106	1-2	Payne
13/12/95	Staffs SC	2	Paget Rangers	65	2-3	Johnson(2)
16/12/95	BHL	M	SUTTON COLDFIELD TOWN	102	0-1	
23/12/95	BHL	M	Nuneaton Borough	975	0-1	
06/01/96	BHL	M	Corby Town	110	5-1	Palmer(3), Johnson, Smith
09/01/96	Worcs SC	QF	HALESOWEN TOWN	421	1-0	Johnson
13/01/96	BHL	M	LEICESTER UNITED	106	1-1	Forrest
20/01/96	BHL	M	BURY TOWN	108	3-2	Palmer(2), Smith
03/02/96	BHL	M	PAGET RANGERS	118	3-2	Band, Palmer(2)
10/02/96	BHL	M	Grantham Town	160	3-1	Walker, Johnson, Palmer
17/02/96	BHL	M	BEDWORTH UNITED	185	3-0	Palmer(3)
24/02/96	BHL	M	Bedworth United	212	1-1	Harnett
02/03/96	Worcs SC	SF	Kidderminster Harriers	750	2-1	Palmer, Smith
05/03/96	BHL	M	Leicester United	39	0-2	
09/03/96	BHL	M	Racing Club Warwick	120	5-3	Smith, R Walker, Palmer(3)
12/03/96	BHL	M	BRIDGNORTH TOWN	126	2-1	Palmer, Harnett
16/03/96	BHL	M	Buckingham Town	80	2-0	Walker, Band
23/03/96	BHL	M	NUNEATON BOROUGH	507	0-1	
30/03/96	BHL	M	Bilston Town	115	0-3	
02/04/96	BHL	M	RACING CLUB WARWICK	122	0-0	
06/04/96	BHL	M	DUDLEY TOWN	232	1-0	Smith
08/04/96	BHL	M	Bridgnorth Town	215	4-2	Harnett, Johnson(2), Yeep
13/04/96	BHL	M	Hinckley Town	91	1-1	Palmer
16/04/96	BHL	M	BILSTON TOWN	129	2-1	Johnson(2)
20/04/96	BHL	M	BUCKINGHAM TOWN	129	0-2	
22/04/96	Worcs SC	F(1)	BROMSGROVE ROVERS	527	2-1	Wood, Trend
27/04/96	BHL	M	REDDITCH UNITED	136	1-2	Palmer
01/05/96	BHL	M	Dudley Town	240	2-2	Johnson(2)
04/05/96	BHL	M	King's Lynn	1688	1-2	Band
09/05/96	Worcs SC	F(2)	Bromsgrove Rovers	987	1-3	Band

SUTTON COLDFIELD TOWN

Central Ground, Coles Lane, Sutton Coldfield, B72 1NL. Tel: 0121 354 2997 or 0121 355 5475

Secretary: Fred Rought, 25 Lebanon Grove, Chase
Terr, Burntwood, Staffs WS7 8BE.Tel: 01543 685029

Nickname: Royals

Colours: Royal Blue and White

Capacity: 4,500

Seating: 200

Covered standing: 500

Clubhouse on ground: Yes

Record attendance: 2,029 v Doncaster Rovers
FA Cup 1st Rd 1980

Record appearances: Eddie Hewitt 465

Record goalscorer in aggregate: Eddie Hewitt 288

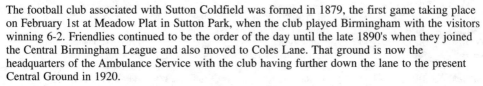

HONOURS

West Midlands League 1980 and League Cup 1981
and 1982; Midland Combination 1978 and 1979 and League Cup 1970; Walsall Senior League
1947; Walsall Senior Cup 1978, 1979, 1980; Sutton Charity Cup 1947, 1966, 1972, 1987, 1990,
1991; Express and Star Cup 1945.

The football club associated with Sutton Coldfield was formed in 1879, the first game taking place
on February 1st at Meadow Plat in Sutton Park, when the club played Birmingham with the visitors
winning 6-2. Friendlies continued to be the order of the day until the late 1890's when they joined
the Central Birmingham League and also moved to Coles Lane. That ground is now the
headquarters of the Ambulance Service with the club having further down the lane to the present
Central Ground in 1920.

Steady progress followed with a number of successes on the league front and in cups, but it is since
the Second War that the club has made major strides. Immediately after the war Town joined the
Walsall Senior League finishing fourth and taking the Express and Star Cup. A year later they won
the title, and a subsequent move to the Birmingham League and then Birmingham Combination saw
the club attracting good gates but little success, probably as a result of their senior status. In 1960
they finished third in the league and reached the semi-final of the Birmingham Senior Cup, but
financial problems saw them disband the reserves and step down into the Worcester Combination
and have a period of consolidation. Things improved and the ground was given floodlights and a
clubhouse, and in 1978 the club won what was then called the Midland Combination plus the
Walsall Senior Cup. Having retained both trophies the following year the decision was taken in
1979 to step up into the West Midland League, which they won immediately as well as taking the
Walsall Cup for the third time on the trot. Another successful season followed in 1981 when the
club reached the 1st Round of the FA Cup, losing to Doncaster Rovers in front of a record crowd of
2,029. Town took the League Cup and a year later won it again, ending runner up to Shifnal in the
league. It was to be the last season in that league for with the re-organisation of the Southern
League saw Town in the Midland Division for 1982.

The club's wildest dreams were to come true as they secured promotion in second spot from
Cheltenham Town. Unfortunately the impetus could not be maintained and they came straight back
again. 1992 saw another great FA Cup run end with an unforgettable day at Bolton Wanderers
where 5,345 saw Sutton go close to forcing a draw.

SUTTON COLDFIELD TOWN 1995/96 SEASON

Date	Competition	Round	Opponent	Attendance	Score	Scorers
19/08/95	BHL	M	Nuneaton Borough	1002	2-1	Swann, Whitehouse
22/08/95	BHL	M	RACING CLUB WARWICK	146	0-0	
26/08/95	BHL	M	STOURBRIDGE	167	3-2	Hunt(2), Whitehouse
02/09/95	BHL	M	Hinckley Town	70	1-2	Ward
05/09/95	BHL	M	BEDWORTH UNITED	168	2-0	Ward, Hunt
09/09/95	FA Cup	Q1	Long Buckby	82	1-2	Manton
16/09/95	BHL	M	Dudley Town	157	1-2	Hunt
19/09/95	BHL	M	Racing Club Warwick	70	1-4	Whitehouse
23/09/95	BHL	M	CORBY TOWN	162	4-0	Ward, Richardson(2), Hunt
26/09/95	Birm SC	1	MOOR GREEN	86	2-4	Hunt, Coogan
30/09/95	BHL	M	LEICESTER UNITED	167	2-2	Stephens(og), Richardson
03/10/95	DMC	1(1)	Bilston Town	41	0-3	
10/10/95	Worcs SC	1	DUDLEY TOWN	75	0-1	
14/10/95	FA Trophy	Q1	BILSTON TOWN	116	1-1	Ward
17/10/95	FA Trophy	Q1 rep	Bilston Town	85	4-4	Swann, Spence, Whitehouse, Richardson
21/10/95	BHL	M	BUCKINGHAM TOWN	152	0-0	
23/10/95	FA Trophy	Q1 rep(2)	Bilston Town	154	1-2	Marshall
28/10/95	BHL	M	Bury Town	158	5-1	Pearson, Coogan, Spence, Swann, Marshall
31/10/95	DMC	1(2)	BILSTON TOWN	41	3-3	Marshall(2), Pearson
04/11/95	BHL	M	BRIDGNORTH TOWN	172	3-0	Ling, Swann, Marshall
07/11/95	BHL	M	Bilston Town	75	1-0	Spence
11/11/95	BHL	M	REDDITCH UNITED	202	1-0	Swann
14/11/95	BHL	M	Bedworth United	227	2-3	Spence, Marshall
18/11/95	BHL	M	Grantham Town	189	0-1	
21/11/95	Birm LMC	1	SOLIHULL BOROUGH	36	2-1	Swan, Richardson
28/11/95	Walsall SC	1	DARLASTON	44	2-0	Swann, Slowey
02/12/95	BHL	M	King's Lynn	590	1-2	Swann
05/12/95	Walsall SC	2	PELSALL VILLA	25	4-2	Swann(3), Ling
09/12/95	BHL	M	NUNEATON BOROUGH	498	0-3	
16/12/95	BHL	M	Stourbridge	102	1-0	Swann
23/12/95	BHL	M	ROTHWELL TOWN	139	2-2	Brown, Dale
13/01/96	BHL	M	Redditch United	236	1-1	Pearson
20/01/96	BHL	M	MOOR GREEN	247	0-5	
03/02/96	BHL	M	SOLIHULL BOROUGH	165	1-1	Wright
10/02/96	BHL	M	HINCKLEY TOWN	151	6-1	Bradley(2), Brown(2), Hadland, Wright
17/02/96	BHL	M	Buckingham Town	88	0-3	
24/02/96	BHL	M	EVESHAM UNITED	181	3-0	Bradley, Radburn, Brown
27/02/96	Walsall SC	QF	NEWCASTLE TOWN	37	0-1	
02/03/96	BHL	M	Bridgnorth Town	118	2-1	Radburn, Brown
07/03/96	Birm LMC	SF	West Midlands Police		3-0	Bradley, Brown, Whitehouse
09/03/96	BHL	M	KING'S LYNN	203	1-4	Radburn
16/03/96	BHL	M	Solihull Borough	118	2-3	Radburn, Brown
19/03/96	BHL	M	TAMWORTH	365	2-0	Richardson, Brown
23/03/96	BHL	M	Rothwell Town	145	1-3	Kodua
26/03/96	BHL	M	Leicester United	54	2-2	Pearson, Brown
30/03/96	BHL	M	Corby Town	161	2-2	Ling, Brown
02/04/96	BHL	M	BILSTON TOWN	126	1-0	Brown
06/04/96	BHL	M	Moor Green	206	0-3	
08/04/96	BHL	M	PAGET RANGERS	221	0-1	
13/04/96	BHL	M	BURY TOWN	151	2-1	Richardson, Brown
20/04/96	BHL	M	Evesham United	106	3-2	Swann(2), Brown
23/04/96	BHL	M	DUDLEY TOWN	128	1-1	Swann
27/04/96	BHL	M	Tamworth	362	0-3	
01/05/96	BHL	M	Paget Rangers	151	0-3	
04/05/96	BHL	M	GRANTHAM TOWN	137	0-2	
07/05/96	Birm LMC	F	OLDBURY UNITED		2-1	

TAMWORTH

The Lamb Ground, Kettlebrook, Tamworth, Staffs B79 7UF Tel: 01827 65798

Secretary: Rod Hadley, 38 Godolphin, Riverside, Tamworth, B79 7UF Tel: 01827 66786

Press officer: Sam Holiday, c/o Tamworth Herald, Aldergate, Tamworth Tel: 01827 60741

Clubline: 0891 446822

Colours: Red and black   Nickname: Lambs

Capacity: 2,500   Seating: 391

Covered standing: 1100

Clubhouse on ground: Yes

Record attendance: 4,920 v Atherstone Birmingham Combination 1948

Biggest win: 14-4 v Holbrook Institute Bass Vase 1934

Biggest defeat: 0-11 v Solihull Birmingham Combination 1940

Record appearances: Dave Seedhouse 869

Record goalscorer in one season: Percy Vials 64 in 1936-37

Record goalscorer in total: Graham Jessop 195

Record fee received £7,500 for Martin Myers to Telford Utd

Record fee paid: £5,000 for Steve Cartwright from Colchester Utd

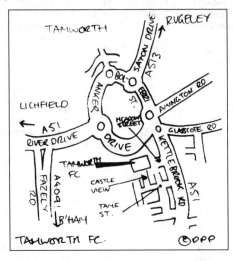

HONOURS

FA VASE WINNERS 1989; West Midlands League 1964, 1966, 1972, 1988, ; Division Two 1956, League Cup 1964, 1966, 1972, 1986, 1988; Birmingham Senior Cup 1961, 1966, 1969; Staffs Senior Cup 1959, 1964, 1966; Camkin Cup 1972.

Club fanzine "Four bleats to the Baah"

Manager 1996-97: Paul Hendrie   **Assistant Manager: Andy Dwyer**

Chairman: Bob Andrews   **Vice Chairman: Tony Reeves**

Tamworth FC were formed in 1933, playing at the Jolly Sailor Ground in the Birmingham Combination. After just one season they moved to the Lamb and have remained there ever since. They stayed in the Comb until 1954 and it was during this period that they reached the Birmingham Senior Cup final. Moving to the Birmingham (West Midlands League) they won the title three times and were runners up twice, took the Senior Cup and Staffs Senior Cup twice. They left the West Midlands in 1972 to move to the Southern League but enjoyed little success before swopping to the Northern Premier League, which saw them struggle against relegation. A move back to the Southern League did not help, for they were relegated to the West Midlands League.

Happily the late eighties saw the finest moment in the club's history as under Graham Smith, the Lambs reached the FA Vase final at Wembley, drawing with Sudbury Town in front of 27,000 and winning the replay at Peterborough United. Surprisingly, a decline set in after that and none of the further success arrived, despite a constant stream of good and well respected managers passing through. In 1995 Tamworth turned to ex-Birmingham City man Paul Hendrie and in the first season the Lambs go to within a point of promotion, but again last season was a disappointment after looking favourites for the title they lost ten in a row to fade away.

TAMWORTH 1995/96 SEASON

Date	Comp	Rd	Opponent	Att	Score	Scorers
19/08/95	BHL	M	SOLIHULL BOROUGH	612	1-1	Mitchell
22/08/95	BHL	M	Bedworth United	511	2-1	Whitehouse, Alsop
26/08/95	FA Cup	P	HINCKLEY TOWN	514	3-1	Smith(2), Mitchell
28/08/95	BHL	M	STOURBRIDGE	561	1-2	Foy
02/09/95	BHL	M	ROTHWELL TOWN	486	2-2	Whitehouse, Bertschin
05/09/95	BHL	M	Evesham United	200	6-2	G Smith, Alsop, Piggon, Whitehouse(2), Christopher
09/09/95	FA Cup	Q1	Bolehall Swifts	803	1-0	Seivwright
12/09/95	Staffs SC	1	LYE TOWN	303	9-3	Seivwright(2), Whitehouse, Howard, Smith, Dean, Christopher(2), Ca
16/09/95	BHL	M	Redditch United	380	3-2	Whitehouse, Howard, Smith
19/09/95	BHL	M	BEDWORTH UNITED	569	1-2	Christopher
23/09/95	FA Cup	Q2	HEDNESFORD TOWN	1138	1-2	Canning
26/09/95	Birm SC	1	Boldmere St Michaels	152	4-1	R Smith, G Smith, Alsop, Christopher
30/09/95	BHL	M	GRANTHAM TOWN	492	3-2	Christopher, Moss, R Smith
03/10/95	DMC	1(1)	Atherstone United	423	3-4	Moss, Howard, Christopher
07/10/95	BHL	M	Bridgnorth Town	308	4-1	Howard, Christopher, Moss, Canning
14/10/95	FA Trophy	Q1	CAERNARFON TOWN	99	0-1	
21/10/95	BHL	M	BURY TOWN	536	3-0	Christopher, Alsop(2)
24/10/95	BHL	M	Stourbridge	185	2-3	Mitchell, Moss
28/10/95	BHL	M	Corby Town	296	0-1	
31/10/95	DMC	1(2)	ATHERSTONE UNITED	617	2-3	Moss, R Smith
04/11/95	FA Trophy	Q2	NETHERFIELD	409	3-1	Alsop, Moss, Canning
07/11/95	Mids F'lit	94-95 QF	REDDITCH UNITED	295	2-1	Moss, Canning
11/11/95	BHL	M	DUDLEY TOWN	467	3-2	Foy, Howard, G Smith
14/11/95	BHL	M	EVESHAM UNITED	415	7-2	G Smith(3), Howard(2),Moss, Christopher
18/11/95	BHL	M	Racing Club Warwick	305	7-3	G Smith(3), Christopher(3), Canning, Whitehouse
21/11/95	BHL	M	King's Lynn	596	3-0	Smith(2), Christopher
25/11/95	FA Trophy	Q3	Stafford Rangers	647	1-1	Canning
28/11/95	FA Trophy	Q3 rep	STAFFORD RANGERS	741	0-3	
02/12/95	BHL	M	HINCKLEY TOWN	441	3-2	Baddams, Whitehouse, Alsop
05/12/95	Birm SC	2	HALESOWEN TOWN	264	1-1	Howard
09/12/95	BHL	M	Solihull Borough	274	3-1	Smith(2), Whitehouse
12/12/95	Birm SC	2 rep	Halesowen Town	275	2-1	Alsop(2)
16/12/95	BHL	M	BRIDGNORTH TOWN	408	4-0	Whitehouse(3), Christopher
23/12/95	BHL	M	Leicester United	263	0-1	
06/01/96	BHL	M	Hinckley Town	321	2-3	Whitehouse, Mitchell
10/01/96	Birm SC	3	Solihull Borough	133	0-1	
13/01/96	BHL	M	CORBY TOWN	472	7-0	Whitehouse(2), Alsop(2), Howard, Wood(og), Dean
20/01/96	BHL	M	KING'S LYNN	845	1-0	Whitehouse
24/01/96	Mids F'lit	1(1)	Leicester United	69	2-0	Howard, G Smith
03/02/96	BHL	M	Moor Green	543	1-0	Christopher
10/02/96	BHL	M	PAGET RANGERS	720	3-1	Tucker(og), Alsop, Moss
17/02/96	BHL	M	Bilston Town	331	3-0	Alsop, Howard(2)
24/02/96	BHL	M	Bury Town	293	1-1	Smith
27/02/96	Staffs SC	2	PORT VALE	347	4-1	Alsop(3), Moss
02/03/96	BHL	M	Grantham Town	315	1-3	Alsop
05/03/96	BHL	M	Rothwell Town	243	1-0	Canning
09/03/96	BHL	M	REDDITCH UNITED	789	1-2	Foy
12/03/96	Staffs SC	QF	NEWCASTLE TOWN	246	0-0	
16/03/96	BHL	M	Dudley Town	447	0-1	
19/03/96	BHL	M	Sutton Coldfield Town	365	0-2	
21/03/96	Staffs SC	QF rep	Newcastle Town	78	1-3	Devery
23/03/96	BHL	M	LEICESTER UNITED	487	2-4	Dunphy, Harbottle
26/03/96	BHL	M	NUNEATON BOROUGH	1635	0-3	
30/03/96	BHL	M	Buckingham Town	230	1-2	Howard
02/04/96	Mids F'lit	1(2)	LEICESTER UNITED	175	6-3	Harbottle(2), Whitehouse, Howard, Baddams, Bennett
06/04/96	BHL	M	BILSTON TOWN	407	3-5	Mann, Alsop, Harbottle
08/04/96	BHL	M	Nuneaton Borough	1388	0-1	
13/04/96	BHL	M	MOOR GREEN	406	1-5	Alsop
20/04/96	BHL	M	Paget Rangers	345	0-1	
23/04/96	BHL	M	BUCKINGHAM TOWN	244	6-0	Baddams(2), Christopher(2), Whitehouse, Foy
27/04/96	BHL	M	SUTTON COLDFIELD TOWN	362	3-0	Bennett(2), Whitehouse
04/05/96	BHL	M	RACING CLUB WARWICK	463	2-0	Whitehouse

VS RUGBY

Butlin Rd, Rugby, Warwicks CV21 3ST. Tel: 01788 543692

Secretary: Trevor Osbourne, 37 Park Leys, Daventry, Northants NN11 4AS Tel 01327 77866

Capacity: 6,000

Seating: 240

Covered standing: 1,000

Clubhouse on ground: Yes

Record attendance: 3,961 v Northampton Town FA Cup 1984

Record appearances: Danny Conway 374

Record goalscorer: Danny Conway 124

Record fee paid: £3,500 for Ian Crawley

Record fee received: £15,000 for Terry Angus to Northampton Town

HONOURS

FA VASE WINNERS 1983

Southern League Mid Div 1987

Midland Floodlit Cup 1985 and 1990

Birmingham Senior Cup 1989 and 1992

Utd Counties Div 3 Cup 1970

Manager for 1996 - 97: Steve Hunt

DIRECTIONS

1 mile walk from station. Ground off Clifton (B54140 on north side of Rugby.

Valley Sports were formed in 1956 and played their first ever competitive game on September 8th of that year. The first seven seasons were spent in the Rugby and District League before transferring to the Coventry and North Warwick League at the start of the 1963-64 season. In 1969 they moved again to Division Three of the United Counties League, where in their first season the Div 3 League Cup was won, the first major trophy.

VS had begun to develop their own ground from what was an allotment and in 1973 they moved in and took over the mantle of top team in the town after the demise of Rugby Town. 1975 saw the move to the West Midlands League where they remained with little great success for eight years, but the appointment of Jimmy Knox as manager in 1981 was the start of a great spell which saw the FA Vase won at Wembley in 1983, the club beating Halesowen Town. It brought entry to the Southern League Midland Division as well as floodlights to the ground and after a spell of consolidation promotion to the Premier Division came. With FA Vase recognition already gained, VS Rugby did the same in the FA Cup, reaching the Second Round in 1987 before losing to Bristol Rovers. Off the field the ground improved with more cover and a turnstile block but on it came a poor spell with relegation just avoided, but the following season saw a vast change with the title in sight until the death.

The early 90's saw success in cups, but Jimmy Knox left the club and after another FA Cup run a slump set in and VS were back in the Midland Division. During a traumatic close season the club were close to going under but they survived and against all odds regained Premiership membership by finishing second.

1995-96 proved to be the worst term in the clubs 40 year history, for they finished rock bottom and once again took their place in the Midland Division.

Date	Comp	Round	Opponent	Att	Score	Scorers
19/08/95	BHL	P	NEWPORT A.F.C.	648	1-3	Green
22/08/95	BHL	P	Baldock Town	352	0-2	
26/08/95	BHL	P	Cheltenham Town	730	0-4	
28/08/95	BHL	P	CAMBRIDGE CITY	338	0-1	
02/09/95	BHL	P	HALESOWEN TOWN	443	0-1	
05/09/95	BHL	P	Rushden & Diamonds	1624	1-6	Owen
09/09/95	FA Cup	Q1	LEICESTER UNITED	307	1-2	Wallace
16/09/95	BHL	P	GRAVESEND & NORTHFLEET	384	0-1	
20/09/95	BHL	P	BALDOCK TOWN	333	0-6	
30/09/95	BHL	P	Stafford Rangers	556	2-1	Mason, Warner
04/10/95	DMC	1(1)	NUNEATON BOROUGH	651	2-4	Martin, Green
14/10/95	BHL	P	CHELMSFORD CITY	454	2-2	Hudson(og), Wood
17/10/95	BHL	P	Burton Albion	518	0-0	
21/10/95	BHL	P	Newport A.F.C.	921	2-5	Green, Warner
24/10/95	BHL	P	Cambridge City	233	1-4	Owen
28/10/95	BHL	P	WORCESTER CITY	548	0-0	
31/10/95	DMC	1(2)	Nuneaton Borough	629	1-2	Martin
04/11/95	BHL	P	Merthyr Tydfil	312	3-2	Martin, Warner, Green
11/11/95	BHL	P	Gresley Rovers	689	0-4	
15/11/95	BHL	P	RUSHDEN & DIAMONDS	741	1-3	Murphy
18/11/95	BHL	P	HASTINGS TOWN	389	1-1	Owen
25/11/95	FA Trophy	Q3	Dudley Town	283	3-4	Murphy, Martin, Green
29/11/95	Birm SC	2	WILLENHALL TOWN	200	3-1	Green, Murphy, Owen
06/12/95	Mids F'lit	1(1)	CORBY TOWN	133	2-1	Furnell(2)
09/12/95	BHL	P	BURTON ALBION	524	3-1	Furnell(3)
16/12/95	BHL	P	Salisbury City	302	0-1	
06/01/96	BHL	P	GLOUCESTER CITY	446	1-2	Owen
10/01/96	Birm SC	3	COVENTRY CITY	417	1-2	Furnell
13/01/96	BHL	P	Hastings Town	530	2-2	Furnell, Murphy
20/01/96	BHL	P	ILKESTON TOWN	441	4-0	Furnell, Hornby, Murphy, Mason
10/02/96	BHL	P	Dorchester Town	660	0-4	
14/02/96	Mids F'lit	1(2)	Corby Town	80	2-2	Green(2)
17/02/96	BHL	P	STAFFORD RANGERS	512	0-3	
24/02/96	BHL	P	Halesowen Town	737	0-0	
27/02/96	BHL	P	Gravesend & Northfleet	426	0-2	
02/03/96	BHL	P	Gloucester City	509	1-1	Yates
09/03/96	BHL	P	ATHERSTONE UNITED	620	3-0	Owen, Green, Yates
12/03/96	Mids F'lit	QF	Dudley Town	62	1-0	Yates
16/03/96	BHL	P	MERTHYR TYDFIL	317	1-2	Green
20/03/96	BHL	P	SALISBURY CITY	250	0-1	
23/03/96	BHL	P	Crawley Town	671	1-3	Owen
26/03/96	BHL	P	Atherstone United	344	1-4	Murphy
30/03/96	BHL	P	SUDBURY TOWN	302	0-2	
06/04/96	BHL	P	Ilkeston Town	681	1-1	Yates
08/04/96	BHL	P	GRESLEY ROVERS	364	1-2	Owen
13/04/96	BHL	P	Worcester City	607	0-4	
16/04/96	BHL	P	Sudbury Town	301	2-3	Warner, Hornby
20/04/96	BHL	P	DORCHESTER TOWN	277	0-0	
24/04/96	BHL	P	CRAWLEY TOWN	220	1-4	Yates
27/04/96	BHL	P	CHELTENHAM TOWN	291	1-1	Yates
30/04/96	Mids F'lit	SF	HINCKLEY TOWN	141	1-0	Murphy
04/05/96	BHL	P	Chelmsford City	722	0-3	

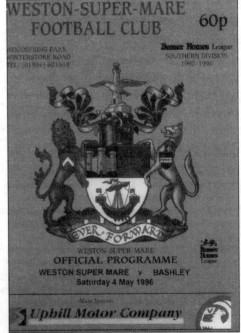

Worcester City F.C.

SUDBURY TOWN
Monday 25th March 1996 Kick-off 7.30pm

OFFICIAL PROGRAMME

£1

BEAZER HOMES LEAGUE PREMIER DIVISION

1066 Country

Main Sponsor:
NEWLITE

Hastings Town F.C

BEAZER HOMES LEAGUE
PREMIER DIVISION

Gloucester City

SOUTHERN FOOTBALL LEAGUE
Beazer Homes League 1894-1996

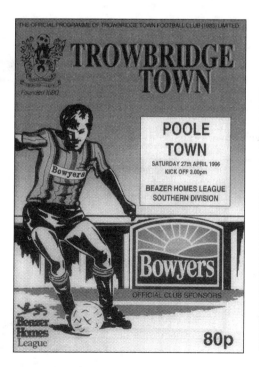

THE OFFICIAL PROGRAMME OF TROWBRIDGE TOWN FOOTBALL CLUB (1983) LIMITED

TROWBRIDGE TOWN

Founded 1880

Bowyers

POOLE TOWN

SATURDAY 27th APRIL 1996
KICK OFF 3.00pm

BEAZER HOMES LEAGUE
SOUTHERN DIVISION

Bowyers

OFFICIAL CLUB SPONSORS

Beazer Homes League

80p

WITNEY TOWN FOOTBALL CLUB

SEASON 1995/96

Unibond League

Saturday 4th May 1996
Beazer Homes League Southern Division
WITNEY TOWN v YATE TOWN
Kick Off : 3.00pm

WINNER
of the
Wirral
Programme
Award 1994/95

CLUB SPONSOR : REGAL (WITNEY) LTD - "THE PERFECT TEAM"   £1

BASHLEY

Bashley Recreation Ground, Bashley Rd, Bashley, Hants BH25 5RY. Tel: 01425 620280 fax 01425 638376

Secretary: Ray Murphy, Flat 10, Richmond Ct, 122 Richmond Park Rd, Bournemouth, Dorset BH8 8TH

Tel: 01202 517607

Press officer: Terry Collett, 52 Ladysmith Close, Purewell, Christchurch, Dorset Tel: 01202 480176

Nickname: The Bash

Colours: Yellow and Black

Capacity: 4,250   Seating: 200

Covered standing: 1,200   Clubhouse on ground: Yes

Record attendance: 3,500 v Emley
FA Vase semi-final 1988

Biggest Win: 21-1 Co-operative
Bournemouth League 1964

Biggest Defeat: 2-20 v Air Speed Bournemouth
League 1957

Record appearances: John Bone

Record goalscorer in total: Colin Cummings

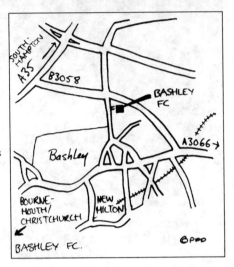

Record fee received: £7,000 for Darren Powell to Weymouth 1996

Record fee paid: £6,000 for Jason Lovell from Wimborne and John Simpkins from Basingstoke Town

HONOURS

FA VASE Semi-final 1988

Hampshire League Div 3 1985

Wessex League 1987, 1988, 1989

Southern League Southern Div 1990

Russell Coates Cup 1989, 1991, 1993

Manager for 1996-97: Andy Bye

Chairman: Jimmy Bartlett   Vice chairman: Frank Whitman

Bashley Football Club was formed in 1947, but in the early years played only friendlies at the Recreation Ground. Their first competitive matches were in the Bournemouth League and for the first ten years the village side struggled. The successful club as it widely known nowadays did not take off until the early 80's when two local businessmen became involved. In 1983 Bash finished third in Division One and a successful application was made to Hampshire League. Under manager Trevor Parker the club were champions of Division Three and after one more year they moved to the Wessex League, where they enjoyed a fine season, pipping RS Southampton to the title. It was retained in 1988, but the exploits in the FA Vase were what caught the public's imagination. Starting in the extra-preliminary round, Bash reached the semi-finals where they played Emley. The home leg brought in a crowd of 3,500, but Emley went through. All this time facilities had been continuing steadily and when the Wessex League was handed feeder status to the Southern League, everyone knew what target was next. That was achieved the following season, along with another good Vase run, as Bash won their third successive title and were taken by the Southern League.

Trevor Parker returned to manage a stunning late run would brought with it the championship and

promotion, their fourth in four seasons. 1990 saw Bash in the Premier Division, but after four years injuries and money problems saw the club relegated. In 1995 Bashley reached the FA Cup 1st Round for the first time and won away at Chesham United, and were given a home tie with Swansea City in Rd 2. After a close match, Bash lost 1-0, just one of 22 cup ties played before Christmas. Last season saw Bash at the bottom half of Division One.

BASHLEY 1995/96 SEASON

Date	Comp		Opponent	Att	Score	Scorers
19/08/95	BHL	S	Sittingbourne	549	2-2	Sales, Lovell
22/08/95	BHL	S	WATERLOOVILLE	230	2-2	Lovell, Powell
26/08/95	BHL	S	ASHFORD TOWN	242	2-0	Powell, Lovell
28/08/95	BHL	S	Havant Town	238	2-1	Powell, Sales
02/09/95	BHL	S	Witney Town	152	1-2	Powell
05/09/95	BHL	S	WEYMOUTH	407	2-3	Lisk, Powell
09/09/95	BHL	S	Fareham Town	150	2-1	Lisk, Sales
13/09/95	Russell CC	1	Havant Town	66	0-2	
16/09/95	BHL	S	FLEET TOWN	172	2-1	Bye, Stagg
19/09/95	BHL	S	Waterlooville	250	2-2	Sales, Powell
23/09/95	BHL	S	TONBRIDGE ANGELS	304	0-2	
26/09/95	Hants SC	1	PAULSGROVE	52	5-1	Morris, Stagg, Johnson(3)
30/09/95	BHL	S	Yate Town	156	3-0	Powell, Bye, Lovell
03/10/95	DMC	1(1)	WEYMOUTH	134	3-0	Lovell(2), Powell
07/10/95	BHL	S	FAREHAM TOWN	241	3-0	Powell, Bye, Lovell
07/10/95	DMC	1(2)	Weymouth	320	0-0	
14/10/95	FA Trophy	Q1	MARGATE	220	1-1	Powell
17/10/95	FA Trophy	Q1 rep	Margate	157	2-1	Dixon(og), Sales
21/10/95	FA Cup	Q4	Newport I.O.W.	1061	1-1	Lovell
24/10/95	FA Cup	Q4 rep	NEWPORT I.O.W.	558	2-3	Lovell, Sales
28/10/95	BHL	S	Fisher	178	3-3	Powell, Sales, Lovell
31/10/95	Hants SC	2	Cove	40	7-1	Lovell(3), Stagg, Sales(2), Record
04/11/95	FA Trophy	Q2	Crawley Town	609	1-0	Powell
18/11/95	BHL	S	FOREST GREEN ROVERS	207	1-2	Sales
25/11/95	FA Trophy	Q3	Wembley	116	0-2	
02/12/95	BHL	S	WESTON-SUPER-MARE	151	1-2	Powell
05/12/95	DMC	2	TROWBRIDGE TOWN	93	1-1	Ferns(og)
09/12/95	BHL	S	Ashford Town	405	4-1	Sales, Fletcher, Shepperd, Bartlett
12/12/95	Hants SC	3	NEWPORT I.O.W.	69	1-0	Sales
16/12/95	BHL	S	YATE TOWN	131	1-2	Powell
23/12/95	BHL	S	MARGATE	142	3-0	Lovell(2), Sales
26/12/95	BHL	S	Newport I.O.W.	464	1-1	Stickler
01/01/96	BHL	S	POOLE TOWN	285	2-0	Sales, Powell
06/01/96	BHL	S	Forest Green Rovers	223	1-2	Record
09/01/96	DMC	2 rep	Trowbridge Town	137	1-2	Sales
13/01/96	BHL	S	ERITH & BELVEDERE	141	2-1	Fletcher, Morris
20/01/96	BHL	S	Fleet Town	123	2-2	Sales(2)
03/02/96	Hants SC	QF	Aerostructures	62	1-0	Powell
10/02/96	BHL	S	CLEVEDON TOWN	192	2-0	Sales, Bartlett
13/02/96	BHL	S	Weymouth	644	0-2	
17/02/96	BHL	S	Braintree Town	164	2-2	Powell, Stagg
24/02/96	BHL	S	Trowbridge Town	311	2-5	Sales(2)
02/03/96	BHL	S	SITTINGBOURNE	171	0-1	
09/03/96	BHL	S	Tonbridge Angels	402	3-2	Powell, Fisher, Sales
13/03/96	Hants SC	SF	WATERLOOVILLE	275	0-1	
16/03/96	BHL	S	CINDERFORD TOWN	138	1-1	Powell
17/03/96	BHL	S	TROWBRIDGE TOWN	215	1-1	Sales
23/03/96	BHL	S	Margate	206	1-2	Fletcher
30/03/96	BHL	S	BRAINTREE TOWN	111	0-1	
02/04/96	BHL	S	Clevedon Town	152	2-1	Morris, Fletcher
06/04/96	BHL	S	Poole Town	402	0-0	
08/04/96	BHL	S	NEWPORT I.O.W.	224	0-1	
13/04/96	BHL	S	Erith & Belvedere	109	1-1	Lovell
16/04/96	BHL	S	HAVANT TOWN	123	2-3	Fletcher, Morris
20/04/96	BHL	S	WITNEY TOWN	183	0-1	
27/04/96	BHL	S	FISHER	211	2-0	Fletcher, Stagg
30/04/96	BHL	S	Cinderford Town	1036	0-3	
04/05/96	BHL	S	Weston-super-Mare	217	0-2	

BUCKINGHAM TOWN

Ford Meadow, Ford Street, Buckingham, Bucks MK18 1AG. Tel: 01280 816257

Secretary:Philip Bettles, c/o Football Club

Colours: All Red

Nickname: The Robins

Capacity: 4,500

Seating: 420

Covered standing: 420

Clubhouse on ground: Yes

Record attendance: 2,451 v Orient
FA Cup 1st Rd 1984

Biggest win: 7-0 Baldock Town (A) 1990

Biggest defeat: 0-8 Poole Town (h) 1990

Record fee paid: £7,000 for
Steve Jenkins from Wealdstone 1992

DIRECTIONS

From town centre take Aylesbury (A413) road and turn right at Phillips Garage after 400yds. By public transport: train to Milton Keynes, then bus to Buckingham.

HONOURS

Southern League South 1991; United Counties League 1984 and 1986, and League Cup 1984; North Bucks League 1925, 1929, 1934, 1936, 1937, 1939, 1949, 1950; Aylesbury and District League 1903; Berks and Bucks Senior Cup 1984; Berks and Bucks Junior Cup 1903 and 1949; Berks and Bucks Minor Cup 1933; Buckingham Senior Charity Cup 1933, 1936, 1938, 1948, 1949, 1950, 1953, 1954, 1955, 1973, 1976, 1977, 1979, 1981, 1984, 1985, 1986, 1987.

Manager 1996-97: Steve Curley

Assistant Manager: John Horsley

Chairman: Gerald Sear

Vice Chairman: Brain Maycock

Press Officer: Vic West

Clubcall line 0891 884431

Town were formed in 1883 and have played at Ford Meadow from the start. They were juniors until 1970, playing in the Aylesbury League and then the North Bucks League before joining the Hellenic League in 1953. They had four years there before moving to the more local South Midlands League until 1974 followed by twelve years in the United Counties where they enjoyed great success, climbing through from the Second to the Premier Division in consecutive seasons, and then taking the title twice in three years. Also in 1984 they took the Berks and Bucks and Buckingham Charity Cups in a wonderful season.

In between the club reached the 1st Rd of the FA Cup where a record gate saw them lose to Orient.

In 1986 they joined the Southern League Midland Division, switching to the South after two years.

The successful side split up, but in 1990 they were placed third before taking the title twelve months later under Phil Lines, only to be denied promotion due to ground grading.

1994 saw Town back in the Midland Division again from where they finished last season above mid-table.

BUCKINGHAM TOWN 1995/96 SEASON

Date	Comp	Rnd	Opponent	Att	Score	Scorers
19/08/95	BHL	M	LEICESTER UNITED	71	3-3	Young(3)
22/08/95	BHL	M	EVESHAM UNITED	105	3-1	Marshall(2), Turnbull
26/08/95	FA Cup	P	Newbury Town	99	0-1	
02/09/95	BHL	M	DUDLEY TOWN	107	0-2	
06/09/95	BHL	M	Solihull Borough	105	2-3	Attfield, Weaver
09/09/95	FA Cup	Q1	Worthing	464	1-1	Hatfield
12/09/95	FA Cup	Q1 rep	WORTHING	84	0-0	
16/09/95	BHL	M	HINCKLEY TOWN	81	1-2	Marshall
18/09/95	FA Cup	Q1 rep(2)	Worthing	277	2-2	Corbett, Mansfield
20/09/95	FA Cup	Q1 rep(3)	WORTHING	100	6-1	Wheeler(3), Attfield, Covington, Lawley
23/09/95	FA Cup	Q2	Thatcham Town	130	1-0	Corbett
30/09/95	BHL	M	Redditch United	180	1-0	Searle
03/10/95	DMC	1(1)	BRAINTREE TOWN	70	1-0	Lawley
07/10/95	FA Cup	Q3	ALDERSHOT TOWN	916	0-1	
14/10/95	FA Trophy	Q1	BRAINTREE TOWN	65	1-1	Covington
17/10/95	FA Trophy	Q1 rep	Braintree Town	103	0-1	
21/10/95	BHL	M	Sutton Coldfield Town	152	0-0	
24/10/95	BHL	M	CORBY TOWN	67	5-0	Young(3), Hamilton, Attfield
28/10/95	BHL	M	MOOR GREEN	70	2-0	Hamilton(2)
31/10/95	DMC	1(2)	Braintree Town	120	0-0	
04/11/95	BHL	M	King's Lynn	787	4-1	Young, Hamilton(2), Wheeler
07/11/95	BHL	M	SOLIHULL BOROUGH	70	3-1	Tubbs, Cooper(og), Wheeler
11/11/95	BHL	M	Bridgnorth Town	95	3-0	Sherlock, Hamilton, Attfield
18/11/95	BHL	M	Nuneaton Borough	1103	1-1	Young
22/11/95	BHL	M	Corby Town	182	3-2	Stephens(og), James(og), Searle
25/11/95	BHL	M	GRANTHAM TOWN	90	1-0	Mansfield
02/12/95	BHL	M	Paget Rangers	129	2-1	Lawley, Covington
05/12/95	DMC	2	CAMBRIDGE CITY	56	1-0	Young
09/12/95	BHL	M	Hinckley Town	95	4-0	Marshall(2), Attfield, Young
16/12/95	BHL	M	REDDITCH UNITED	90	0-0	
06/01/96	BHL	M	KING'S LYNN	170	0-4	
10/01/96	DMC	3	NUNEATON BOROUGH	127	1-3	Brown
13/01/96	BHL	M	Racing Club Warwick	110	5-0	Covington, Mansfield, Brown, Wheeler, Hamilton
20/01/96	BHL	M	BRIDGNORTH TOWN	70	3-0	Hamilton(2), Wilson
23/01/96	B&B SC	1	Abingdon Town	74	1-2	Hamilton
13/02/96	BHL	M	RACING CLUB WARWICK	50	2-2	Wheeler, Hamilton
17/02/96	BHL	M	SUTTON COLDFIELD TOWN	88	3-0	Pearson(og), Marshall, Wilson
24/02/96	BHL	M	Leicester United	59	0-2	
27/02/96	BHL	M	BEDWORTH UNITED	85	0-2	
02/03/96	BHL	M	Rothwell Town	152	1-3	Wilson
09/03/96	BHL	M	Bilston Town	53	0-0	
16/03/96	BHL	M	STOURBRIDGE	80	0-2	
20/03/96	BHL	M	Dudley Town	81	2-4	Allen, Marshall
23/03/96	BHL	M	Bedworth United	284	1-1	Marshall
26/03/96	BHL	M	BILSTON TOWN	80	0-2	
30/03/96	BHL	M	TAMWORTH	230	2-1	Marshall(2)
06/04/96	BHL	M	ROTHWELL TOWN	80	1-1	Marshall
08/04/96	BHL	M	Bury Town	193	1-2	Marshall
10/04/96	BHL	M	BURY TOWN	60	2-2	Goodridge, Sherlock
13/04/96	BHL	M	PAGET RANGERS	90	2-4	Hamilton, Butler
16/04/96	BHL	M	Grantham Town	102	1-2	Marshall
20/04/96	BHL	M	Stourbridge	129	2-0	Marshall, Palmer
23/04/96	BHL	M	Tamworth	244	0-6	
27/04/96	BHL	M	Moor Green	196	2-1	Hamilton, Sherlock
30/04/96	BHL	M	Evesham United	61	4-1	Marshall(2), Hamilton(2)z
04/05/96	BHL	M	NUNEATON BOROUGH	472	2-3	Marshall(2)

CINDERFORD TOWN

The Causeway, Hilldene, Cinderford, Glos. Tel: 01594 822039 or 827147

Secretary: Chris Warren, 9C Tusculum Way, Micheldean, Glos GL17 0HZ Tel 01594 543065

Press officer: Adrian Peacey 01594 823009

Colours: White and black   Nickname: Town

Capacity: 2,500   Seating: 250

Covered standing: 500   Clubhouse on ground: Yes

Record attendance: 4,850 v Minehead 1956-57

Biggest win: 13-0 v Cammills Glos
Northern Senior League 1938-39

Biggest defeat: 0-10 Sutton Coldfield Midland Combination

Record goalscorer in one season: A Goodwin 41

DIRECTIONS

From Gloucester take A40 to Ross-on-Wye, then A48 - Chepstow. In 10 miles turn right at Elton garage onto A4151 signed Cinderford, through Littledean, up steep hill, right at cross-roads, second left into Latimer Road. Ground 5 minutes walk from town centre.

HONOURS

Hellenic League and Cup 1995; Division One 1991; Floodlit Cup 1994 and Division One 1991; Glos Northern Senior League Div 1 1939 and 1961; Glos Senior Amateur Cup North 1950, 1955, 1956, 1969, 1971, 1977; Western League Div 2 1957; Warwickshire Combination and Camkin Cup 1964; West Midlands League Premier Cup 1969; Midland Combination 1982.

Manager 1996-97: Tim Harris   Assistant Manager: Chris Hyde

Chairman: Ashley Saunders   Vice Chairman: Ray Read

"A Season to Remember", a detailed booklet including all press cuttings from 1994-95, Hellenic League treble, is available from the secretary for £2.50 including p & p.

Cinderford Town were formed in 1922 and played in the Gloucester Northern Senior League until 1939 when they joined the Bristol Charity League, which lasted just one game as War broke out and the league was disbanded. They then joined the Western League Second Division, winning it in 1957. It was at the end of that campaign that a record home crowd of 4,850 watched the final game against Minehead. Playing in the higher division, with the travelling required but the club under severe financial pressure and after three years they resigned and went back to the Gloucester Northern League, although within three years they looked north for their football, playing in the Warwickshire Combination, doing the double of league and cup in 1964. The following year they moved to the West Midlands League, which was at the time the highest grade they had ever played at, with such clubs as Kidderminster Harriers, Bromsgrove Rovers and Boston United. Success was never easy but it finally came in 1969 when they drew the League Cup final with Kiddy and shared the trophy. Town returned home to play in the newly formed Gloucester County League in 1970 and stayed for five years, finishing runners up three times, but again looked for a higher class of football and were accepted into the Midland Combination. This time they stayed for 10 years, winning the League Cup in 1983, but again returned to County League football in 1984, until moving to the Hellenic League in 1990.

They were Division One champions in the first season, gaining promotion and when floodlights went up at the Causeway in 1991, they were on the way.

November 1993 saw work begin on a project to level the infamous slope which went 18ft from corner to corner. It was completed in the summer of 1994, and after a year in exile, they returned to begin the most successful season ever. Town won the Hellenic League championship, Premier Division Cup and Hellenic Floodlit Cup and were accepted into the Southern League for 1995-96 season.

They celebrated by reaching the Second Round of the FA Cup and only a replay defeat at Gravesend prevented Town from taking on Aston Villa in the 3rd Round.

Town have played at the Causeway since 1947, having lost their Mousel Barn ground during the war. The early days were spent on a field behind the Royal Oak pub, but having moved to Mousel Barn they closed for the war only to find their equipment gone and the field sold when they returned.

CINDERFORD TOWN 1995/96 SEASON

Date	Comp	Round	Opponent	Att	Score	Scorers
19/08/95	BHL	S	FISHER	220	0-1	
22/08/95	BHL	S	Weston-super-Mare	314	0-2	
26/08/95	BHL	S	SITTINGBOURNE	229	3-2	Hill, Crouch, Harris
28/08/95	BHL	S	Trowbridge Town	350	3-2	Goodwin(3)
02/09/95	BHL	S	Margate	161	1-1	Goodwin
05/09/95	BHL	S	YATE TOWN	220	3-3	Hamilton, Hill(2)
09/09/95	FA Cup	Q1	Tuffley Rovers	124	4-0	Wilton, Hill(3)
16/09/95	BHL	S	Witney Town	161	1-4	Hyde
19/09/95	BHL	S	WESTON-SUPER-MARE	209	1-1	Horlick
23/09/95	FA Cup	Q2	Gloucester City	921	1-0	Harris
30/09/95	BHL	S	WEYMOUTH	201	3-4	Hopkins, Howells(2)
03/10/95	DMC	P(1)	MERTHYR TYDFIL	177	1-4	Thomas
07/10/95	FA Cup	Q3	Forest Green Rovers	335	1-1	Hill
10/10/95	FA Cup	Q3 rep	FOREST GREEN ROVERS	684	1-1	Hill
14/10/95	FA Trophy	Q1	Ruislip Manor	142	1-3	Hamilton
16/10/95	FA Cup	Q3 rep(2)	Forest Green Rovers	671	3-1	Boxall, Price, Hill
21/10/95	FA Cup	Q4	BATH CITY	730	3-2	Hamilton, Hill, Smith
28/10/95	BHL	S	Ashford Town	564	0-4	
31/10/95	Glos NSC	SF	Gloucester City	296	0-2	
04/11/95	BHL	S	POOLE TOWN	201	7-1	Price, Gater(og), Hill(3), Townsend(2)
07/11/95	DMC	P(2)	Merthyr Tydfil	144	3-4	Criddle, Crouch, Beacham
11/11/95	FA Cup	1	BROMSGROVE ROVERS	1850	2-1	Price, Hill
15/11/95	BHL	S	Yate Town	143	1-4	Boxall
18/11/95	BHL	S	ERITH & BELVEDERE	247	3-1	Howells, Price, Campbell
25/11/95	BHL	S	Weymouth	620	0-2	
02/12/95	FA Cup	2	GRAVESEND & NORTHFLEET	2067	1-1	Thomas
09/12/95	BHL	S	Havant Town	106	1-0	Criddle
14/12/95	FA Cup	2 rep	Gravesend & Northfleet	2851	0-3	
16/12/95	BHL	S	NEWPORT I.O.W.	211	2-2	Hill, Campbell
23/12/95	BHL	S	Waterlooville	179	0-3	
01/01/96	BHL	S	Clevedon Town	283	2-2	Hoskins, Thomas
06/01/96	BHL	S	Sittingbourne	597	0-4	
20/01/96	BHL	S	Erith & Belvedere	131	2-2	Hoskins, French
03/02/96	BHL	S	Tonbridge Angels	346	3-0	Thomas, Hill, Peacey
11/02/96	BHL	S	MARGATE	310	3-1	Hill, Wilton, Thomas
17/02/96	BHL	S	HAVANT TOWN	260	1-2	Smith
20/02/96	Glos NSC	SF rematch	Gloucester City	246	2-3	Muckleburg, French
24/02/96	BHL	S	Fisher	120	2-2	Boxall, Quarterly
28/02/96	BHL	S	TROWBRIDGE TOWN	190	2-0	Howells, Boxall
02/03/96	BHL	S	WITNEY TOWN	235	1-0	Thomas
06/03/96	BHL	S	Poole Town	118	4-0	Harris, Powell, Quarterly, Peacey
09/03/96	BHL	S	Fleet Town	120	2-1	Smith, Thomas
16/03/96	BHL	S	Bashley	138	1-1	Smith
23/03/96	BHL	S	WATERLOOVILLE	264	0-4	
30/03/96	BHL	S	Fareham Town	94	1-2	Peacey
06/04/96	BHL	S	CLEVEDON TOWN	227	2-0	Hill, Thomas
09/04/96	BHL	S	Forest Green Rovers	305	1-3	Wilton
13/04/96	BHL	S	ASHFORD TOWN	245	0-1	
14/04/96	BHL	S	BRAINTREE TOWN	235	3-4	Hoskins, Thomas, French
17/04/96	BHL	S	FAREHAM TOWN	170	1-2	French
20/04/96	BHL	S	Newport I.O.W.	369	3-1	Harris, French(2)
23/04/96	BHL	S	FOREST GREEN ROVERS	330	2-1	Thomas, Cheeseman
27/04/96	BHL	S	Braintree Town	151	2-3	Peacey, Thomas
30/04/96	BHL	S	BASHLEY	1036	3-0	Hoskins, Smith, Thomas
02/05/96	BHL	S	TONBRIDGE ANGELS	137	1-2	Wilton
04/05/96	BHL	S	FLEET TOWN	230	3-2	Harris, Hoskins, Wilton

CIRENCESTER TOWN

Smithsfield, Chesterton Lane, Cirencester, Glos Tel: 01285 645783

Secretary: Brian Davis, 97 Golden Farm Rd, Cirencester, Glos GL7 1DG Tel: 01285 654274

Colours: All Blue

Capacity: 2,000

Seating: 150

Covered standing: 100

Clubhouse on ground: Yes

DIRECTIONS

Follow By-pass towards Bristol. The ground is signposted on the left approx quarter of a mile from town. 3 miles from Kemble (BR).

HONOURS

GFA Senior Amateur Cup 1980

GFA Challenge Trophy 1996

Hellenic League 1996 and Div 1 1974

League Cup 1996 and Div I Cup 1991

Manager for 1996-97: Nick Beaverstock.

Cirencester Town were founded before the turn of the century and in those early days played in the Gloucestershire Northern Senior League and the Cheltenham and District League. They remained there until the formation of the Gloucestershire County League, and in that opening season they reached the 2nd Round of the Amateur Cup. It was a short stay before joining the Hellenic League in 1969, where success came quickly, the Division One championship being won in 1971. By the start of the 80's the club were back in Division One and came close to promotion, finishing third in 1981. A lean spell followed , but in 1991 they went up as runners up to Cinderford Town and also took the Division One Challenge Cup.

The strong squad took the Premier Division by storm the next season, leading for months before being pipped by Shortwood United, with another disappointment coming with the loss of the Challenge Trophy final, also against Shortwood. 1995 was a touch disappointing also but dreams came true in 1996 when Cirencester Town walked off with the league title, completing the double by gaining revenge on Shortwood in the League Cup final. To end a spectacular season, the club took the Gloucestershire Challenge Trophy by beating Endsleigh on their own ground at Smithsfield. During the Summer it was confirmed that the club had been accepted into the Southern League for the 1996-97 season.

CIRENCESTER TOWN 1995/96 SEASON

19/08/95	Hellenic	P	BICESTER TOWN	2-0	
22/08/95	Hellenic	P	ENDSLEIGH	1-2	
26/08/95	Hellenic	P	LAMBOURN SPORTS	3-1	
28/08/95	Hellenic	P	Shortwood United	5-2	
02/09/95	Hellenic	P	Almondsbury Town	1-0	
05/09/95	Hellenic	P	Tuffley Rovers	1-3	
09/09/95	PC	1	Kintbury Rangers	4-0	
13/09/95	Hellenic	P	Swindon Supermarine	1-1	
16/09/95	Hellenic	P	Abingdon United	2-1	
23/09/95	Hellenic	P	BANBURY UNITED	5-1	
30/09/95	FA Vase	Q2	OLD GEORGIANS	1-5	
07/10/95	Hellenic	P	FAIRFORD TOWN	2-0	
10/10/95	F'lit Cup	2(1)	SHORTWOOD UNITED	0-1	
14/10/95	PC	2	Fairford Town	3-2	
21/10/95	Glos Tphy	1	Almondsbury Town	6-2	
25/10/95	F'lit Cup	2(2)	Shortwood United	4-0	
04/11/95	Hellenic	P	Kintbury Rangers	1-1	
11/11/95	Hellenic	P	CARTERTON TOWN	2-0	
15/11/95	Hellenic	P	Endsleigh	2-1	
18/11/95	Hellenic	P	Bicester Town	1-0	
22/11/95	Hellenic	P	North Leigh	4-3	
25/11/95	Hellenic	P	BURNHAM	1-0	
02/12/95	Glos Tphy	2	Shortwood United	3-0	
09/12/95	Hellenic	P	Fairford Town	2-0	
16/12/95	Hellenic	P	Lambourn Sports	2-2	
06/01/96	Glos Tphy	QF	FAIRFORD TOWN	3-2	
13/01/96	Hellenic	P	KINTBURY RANGERS	3-0	
20/01/96	Hellenic	P	Brackley Town	1-1	
03/02/96	PC	QF	North Leigh	2-0	
10/02/96	Hellenic	P	Didcot Town	2-0	
17/02/96	Hellenic	P	HIGHWORTH TOWN	2-2	
24/02/96	Hellenic	P	ABINGDON UNITED	3-0	
27/02/96	F'lit Cup	QF(1)	ENDSLEIGH	1-1	
02/03/96	Hellenic	P	Carterton Town	1-0	
05/03/96	Glos Tphy	SF	Winterbourne United	1-0	
09/03/96	Hellenic	P	DIDCOT TOWN	4-0	
13/03/96	F'lit Cup	QF(2)	Endsleigh	1-0	
16/03/96	Hellenic	P	SWINDON SUPERMARINE	1-0	
20/03/96	Hellenic	P	TUFFLEY ROVERS	3-0	
23/03/96	Hellenic	P	Banbury United	2-0	
27/03/96	Hellenic	P	NORTH LEIGH	2-1	
30/03/96	Hellenic	P	Highworth Town	3-0	
03/04/96	F'lit Cup	SF(1)	SWINDON SUPERMARINE	1-3	
06/04/96	PC	SF(1)	BRACKLEY TOWN	1-0	
08/04/96	Hellenic	P	Burnham	0-0	
13/04/96	PC	SF(2)	Brackley Town	3-2	
16/04/96	F'lit Cup	SF(2)	Swindon Supermarine	0-0	
20/04/96	Hellenic	P	ALMONDSBURY TOWN	0-0	
27/04/96	Hellenic	P	BRACKLEY TOWN	2-2	
01/05/96	Hellenic	P	SHORTWOOD UNITED	2-0	
06/05/96	Glos Tphy	F	ENDSLEIGH	2-1	
09/05/96	LC	F	SHORTWOOD UNITED	2-1	

CLEVEDON TOWN

Hand Stadium, Davis Lane, Clevedon.

Secretary: Mike Williams, 34 Robinia Walk, Whitchurch, Bristol, BS14 0SH Tel: 01275 833835

Press officer: Tony Humphries c/o Clevedon Town FC

Nickname: The Seasiders   Capacity: 3,650

Seating: 300   Covered standing: 1,300

Clubhouse on ground: Yes

Record attendance: 2,300 v Billingham Synthonia FA Amateur Cup 1952-53

Biggest win: 18-0 v Dawlish Town Western League 1993

HONOURS

Western League 1993; Somerset Senior Cup 1902, 1905, 1929, 1977.

Manager for 1996/97: Steve Fey

Chairman: Paul Haden

Club shop on ground sells wide selection of programmes and souvenirs.

Exchanges welcome, contact J.Anderson c/o Club

DIRECTIONS

M5 Jct 20 - follow signs for Clevedon Town Sports Complex; first left into Central Way (at island just after motorway), 1st left at mini-r'about into Kenn Road, 2nd left Davis lane; ground half mile on right. Or from Bristol (B3130) left into Court Lane (opposite Clevedon Court), turn right after 1 mile, ground on the left. Nearest BR station: Nailsea & Backwell. Buses from Bristol

Formed in 1880, Clevedon are one of the oldest clubs in the West Country and were founders of the Western League in 1892. Their stay lasted three seasons as they dropped back into local football before re-joining in 1910. Their early years were spent at Dial Hill, still the home of the cricket club, but they moved to a new site next to the Sawmills and the Portishead to Clevedon Light Railway in 1904, the ground then was known as Old Street.

When football resumed after the Great War, Clevedon were in the Bristol and District and Bristol and Suburban Leagues, before the switch to the Somerset Senior in the early thirties. During the Second World War, Clevedon played in theWeston-Super-Mare League until in peacetime they rejoined the Western League, finding success mainly in the Amatuer Cup. The FA Cup also brought some glamour with ties against Mertyr Tydfil in front of 10,000 in Wales and a home tie which set the record crowd at home at the tiem, against Bath City.

Sadly league success did not come and they resigned for financial reasons in 1958 to return to Bristol football where they remained until goingback in 1973 after amalgamating with another local club, Ashtonains, who were already there. The name was changed to Clevedon Town and with professionalism in 1974 Ray Mabbutt, father of Gary Mabbutt, became their first ever paid player.

The new clubhouse and floodlights, at what was then known as Teignmouth Road, was a financial disaster and almost brought about the club's downfall, but they survived and turned for the better when they decided to sell their now, ageing ground for development and moved to a brand new out of town site in Davis Lane.

In the last season at the old ground the club finished runners up to Weston Super Mare, playing the last ever match on April 20th 1992. At the new Hand Stadium, named after the family that have been associated with the club since the last century, Clevedon enjoyed their best season ever, with gates increasing six fold, they were undefeated all season, scoring 137 goals in only 38 matches. It brought entry to the Southern League and although they again survived a financial crisis, the club are well established in the League.

The Hand family are held in great esteem by the club and have been represented by HG Hand who was secretary from 1895 to 1912 and by AW Hand, who took over after the Great War and remained until 1968. The grandson and son of those two, Doug Hand, recently retired after 50 years as Secretary and President, and it is fitting that the new stadium is named after them.

CLEVEDON TOWN 1995/96 SEASON

Date	Comp		Opponent	Att	Score	Scorers
19/08/95	BHL	S	FLEET TOWN	226	0-2	
23/08/95	BHL	S	Yate Town	246	4-1	Morgan(2), Singleton, Walker
26/08/95	FA Cup	P	MANGOTSFIELD UNITED	407	1-5	Walker
02/09/95	BHL	S	Waterlooville	223	1-2	Antonelli
05/09/95	BHL	S	TROWBRIDGE TOWN	292	1-3	Morgan
16/09/95	BHL	S	Erith & Belvedere	118	2-1	Singleton, Morgan
20/09/95	BHL	S	YATE TOWN	207	1-1	Morgan
23/09/95	BHL	S	Poole Town	110	3-0	Singleton(3)
26/09/95	DMC	1(1)	Forest Green Rovers	124	1-2	Walker
30/09/95	BHL	S	TONBRIDGE ANGELS	256	0-2	
07/10/95	BHL	S	Fleet Town	129	2-1	Hogg, Morgan
21/10/95	BHL	S	WITNEY TOWN	239	4-3	Morgan, Yates, Antonelli, Walker
24/10/95	BHL	S	Weymouth	520	4-2	Morgan(3), Yates
28/10/95	BHL	S	Braintree Town	320	0-2	
04/11/95	FA Trophy	Q2	WORCESTER CITY	420	0-4	
07/11/95	DMC	1(2)	FOREST GREEN ROVERS	151	1-3	Yates
11/11/95	BHL	S	FAREHAM TOWN	192	4-1	Adams(2), Webster, Jackson
14/11/95	Som. PC	2	Weston-super-Mare		2-2	Hogg, Antonelli
18/11/95	BHL	S	Sittingbourne	598	1-5	Walker
21/11/95	BHL	S	Trowbridge Town	262	1-1	Rogers
02/12/95	BHL	S	FISHER	272	2-1	Bailey, Jackson
09/12/95	BHL	S	Newport I.O.W.	345	1-3	Walker
16/12/95	BHL	S	MARGATE	185	1-4	Adams
01/01/96	BHL	S	CINDERFORD TOWN	283	2-2	Angle(2)
13/01/96	BHL	S	FOREST GREEN ROVERS	262	1-1	Morgan
20/01/96	BHL	S	Fisher	172	0-3	
24/01/96	BHL	S	Havant Town	105	0-0	
03/02/96	BHL	S	ERITH & BELVEDERE	246	1-2	Yates
10/02/96	BHL	S	Bashley	192	0-2	
17/02/96	BHL	S	NEWPORT I.O.W.	216	5-3	Singleton(2), Yates(2), Hogg
27/02/96	BHL	S	WEYMOUTH	254	2-3	Morgan, Yates
02/03/96	BHL	S	Margate	201	2-1	Jackson, Yates
05/03/96	BHL	S	Witney Town	107	1-2	Yates
09/03/96	BHL	S	POOLE TOWN	237	3-0	Angle, Yates, Singleton
16/03/96	BHL	S	SITTINGBOURNE	218	2-3	Lester, Ward
20/03/96	BHL	S	Fareham Town	78	1-2	Jefferies
23/03/96	BHL	S	Ashford Town	457	1-2	Jackson
30/03/96	BHL	S	HAVANT TOWN	201	2-2	Walker, Morgan
02/04/96	BHL	S	BASHLEY	152	1-2	Lester
06/04/96	BHL	S	Cinderford Town	227	0-2	
08/04/96	BHL	S	WESTON-SUPER-MARE	441	1-2	Walker
13/04/96	BHL	S	BRAINTREE TOWN	243	1-0	Morgan
16/04/96	BHL	S	Weston-super-Mare	310	2-3	Lester, Morgan
20/04/96	BHL	S	Forest Green Rovers	202	2-5	Morgan, Lester
23/04/96	BHL	S	ASHFORD TOWN	157	4-2	Morgan, Angle(2), Yates
27/04/96	BHL	S	WATERLOOVILLE	238	2-0	Yates, Singleton
04/05/96	BHL	S	Tonbridge Angels	419	2-1	Parkinson, Yates

DARTFORD

Erith and Belvedere FC, Park View, Lower Rd, Belvedere, Kent

Nickname: The Darts   Colours: Red and White stripes

Ground info: All as Erith and Belvedere FC

Clubhouse on ground: Yes

Record Attendance: at Watling Street, 11,004 v Leyton Orient FA Cup 1st Rd 1948

Biggest Win: 11-1 v Faversham Town Kent Senior Cup

Biggest Defeat: 0-10 v Guildford City Southern League 1947

DIRECTIONS

From Dartford bridge follow signs for Crayford to Erith and follow A206. Ground half a milefrom Erith Blackwell tunnel: head for Abbey Wood and on to Belvedere. Entrance in Station Road, adjoining Belvedere (BR) station. Bus No. 469.

HONOURS

FA TROPHY: Runners up 1974; Semi-finalists 1987 and 1989; Southern League 1931, 1932, 1974, 1984; Eastern Div 1931, Southern Div 1981; League Cup 1977, 1988, 1989; Championship Shield 1984, 1988, 1989; Kent Senior Cup 1931, 32, 33, 35, 48, 70, 73, 87, 88; Kent Floodlit Cup 1965, 1966, 1971; Kent League Cup 1925; Inter League Challenge Cup 1974.

Formed in 1888 by the Dartford Working Men's Club, the Darts played friendlies for the first six years until having reached the final of the Kent Senior Cup in 1994, the committee entered the club into the newly formed Kent League. They settled in at their home ground, Summers Meadow, until the outbreak of the Great War. After the war a group of businessmen realised the benefit of a properly established club bearing the town's name and with one having access to a site in Watling Street, the club was set up again.

They played the next few seasons in the Kent League before moving to the Southern League Eastern Division in 1926. During that period the title was won on two occasions with four Kent Senior Cup wins in five years. Also in 1936 and 1937 they became the first non-league side to reach the FA Cup 3rd round in successive seasons. The 40's were much quieter, with a Kent Senior Cup win over the famous Bromley to show for their efforts, but at the end of the 50's, with the re-organisation of the Southern League, Dartford joined the Premier Division. It was short lived, for after two seasons they went down, only to bounce back up soon after. It was not until the 70's that a comparative boom arrived, when Ernie Morgan returned to the club to guide them to the title in 1973 as well as the Final of the FA Trophy at Wembley, where they lost Morecambe.

Managers came and went until in 1979 Graham Carr took over and in his first season the club reached the finals of the Southern League Cup and the Kent Senior Cup. Dartford briefly played in the Conference for one season before being relegated, having reached the Trophy semi-final where they lost to Bishop's Stortford, but under John Still the Premier Division was won and Dartford went back to the Conference again, having also reached the League Cup final. Sadly, when Still resigned the club went down again.

1987 saw Peter Taylor's side get to the Trophy semi-final again, this time losing to Burton Albion. They won the Senior Cup and a year later were pipped for the league title by Aylesbury, although again they were consoled by the Senior Cup. In their Centenary season of 1988-89 Dartford won the title again, once again losing out on a Trophy final place for the third time, to Macclesfield on the day of the Hillsborough disaster.

Their bad luck continued a year later, with runners up place to Merthyr Tydfil and after a third place behind Bath City and Dover, Taylor left the club.

Sadly, after sharing their ground with Maidstone United during their brief encounter in the Football League, Watling Street was sold from under their feet and they were made homeless, the ground becoming an estate in a matter of weeks. Since then the club have dropped into the Kent League, ground sharing at Cray Wanderers and latterly Erith and Belvedere, and having finished last season as runner up to Furness on goal difference, the club have returned to the Southern League in triumph.

DARTFORD 1995/96 SEASON

12/08/95	WKL	1	Herne Bay	305	0-0	
16/08/95	WKL	1	BECKENHAM TOWN	350	1-1	
19/08/95	WKL	1	Ramsgate	212	3-1	Robinson, Bowey(2)
23/08/95	WKL	1	CHATHAM TOWN	293	1-0	
26/08/95	FA Cup	P	EGHAM TOWN	123	3-1	Bowey(2), Bance
28/08/95	WKL	1	Folkestone Invicta	311	1-1	Robinson
02/09/95	FA Vase	Q1	STEYNING TOWN	275	2-2	
05/09/95	FA Vase	Q1 rep	Steyning Town	124	4-0	Bennett, Evans, Bristow, Bowie
09/09/95	FA Cup	Q1	Farnborough Town	602	0-1	
12/09/95	WKL	1	CORINTHIAN	266	2-0	
16/09/95	WKL	1	Whitstable Town	275	2-2	Bennett, Bance
23/09/95	WKL	1	Thamesmead Town	283	2-1	Alexander, Bragg
27/09/95	WKL	1	GREENWICH BOROUGH	295	1-0	
30/09/95	FA Vase	Q2	FURNESS	408	1-3	Bennett
07/10/95	WKL	1	Deal Town	322	0-0	
21/10/95	WKLC Cup	1	CRAY WANDERERS	275	0-2	
28/10/95	WKL	1	SHEPPEY UNITED	279	3-0	Fiore, Bragg, Bennett
04/11/95	WKL	1	Hythe United	221	0-0	
11/11/95	WKL	1	Faversham Town	243	4-1	Bowey(2), Dann, Bragg
18/11/95	WKL	1	TUNBRIDGE WELLS	280	3-1	
25/11/95	WKL	1	Canterbury City	169	1-1	Bristow
02/12/95	Kent ST	2	Folkestone Invicta	327	1-0	Bowey
09/12/95	WKL	1	RAMSGATE	306	3-0	Bristow, Alexander, Bennett
16/12/95	WKL	1	Tunbridge Wells	215	5-0	Robinson, Bristow, Bowey, Bennett, Hennessy
26/12/95	WKL	1	FURNESS	571	0-1	
06/01/96	WKL	1	Greenwich Borough	210	0-0	
20/01/96	WKL	1	Beckenham Town	230	0-0	
23/01/96	Kent ST	QF	Whitstable Town		2-1	
03/02/96	WKL	1	HERNE BAY	293	2-0	Fiore, Bowey
10/02/96	WKL	1	Cray Wanderers	319	1-0	Bristow
13/02/96	WKL	1	CROCKENHILL	246	1-0	
17/02/96	WKL	1	Corinthian	271	3-0	Fiore, Coatham, Robinson
24/02/96	WKL	1	WHITSTABLE TOWN	347	2-0	Bristow, Bowey
28/02/96	WKL	1	SLADE GREEN	291	4-1	
02/03/96	WKL	1	Sheppey United	248	3-1	Bowey(2), Bennett
09/03/96	Kent ST	SF	FURNESS	485	1-0	Bowey
12/03/96	WKL	1	Slade Green	306	2-0	
16/03/96	WKL	1	DEAL TOWN	307	1-1	Sawyer
20/03/96	WKL	1	CRAY WANDERERS	259	5-2	
30/03/96	WKL	1	Crockenhill	280	2-0	Alexander(2)
03/04/96	WKL	1	THAMESMEAD TOWN	301	4-3	
06/04/96	WKL	1	FAVERSHAM TOWN	359	2-1	Bowey, Hennessy
10/04/96	WKL	1	CANTERBURY CITY	313	1-0	
13/04/96	Kent ST	F	CHATHAM TOWN	908	3-0	Bowey, Bennett, Bristow
16/04/96	WKL	1	Chatham Town	324	2-0	
20/04/96	WKL	1	FOLKESTONE INVICTA	445	1-0	Bristow
27/04/96	WKL	1	HYTHE UNITED	390	2-1	Bennett, Fiore
02/05/96	WKL	1	Furness	1055	1-1	

ERITH AND BELVEDERE

Park View, Lower Road, Belvedere, Kent DA17 6DF. Tel: 0181 311 4444

Secretary: Kellie Discipline, 30 Chatsworth Rd, Dartford, Kent DA1 5AT Tel 01322 275766

Nickname: The Deres   Colours: Blue and White

Capacity: 1,500,   Seating: 1,000

Covered standing: 500   Clubhouse on ground: Yes

Record attendance: 8,000 v Coventry City
FA Cup 1st Rd 1932

DIRECTIONS

From Dartford bridge follow signs for Crayford to Erith and follow A206. Ground half a mile from Erith Blackwall tunnel: head for Abbey Wood and on to Belvedere. Entrance in Station Road, adjoining Belvedere (BR) station. Bus No. 469.

Biggest win: 16-2 v RAF in Friendly, Sept 4th 1942, or for competitive match, 14-1 v Orpington, Kent Senior Cup Mar 14th 1942, 14-2 v Royal Marines in Kent League April 28th 1933

Biggest defeat: 0-15 v Ashford,
Kent League April 28th 1937

HONOURS

FA AMATEUR CUP: Runners up 1924, 1938; Athenian League Cup 1974 and Memorial Shield 1968; Corinthian League Cup 1948, 1949, 1950; Kent League 1982; London Senior Cup 1945; Kent Amateur Cup 1924, 48, 66, 67, 68, 69, 70; Bromley Hospital Cup 1939; South East Combination and League Cup 1942; Kent Senior Cup 1942; Bromley Hospital Cup 1939; Erith Hospital Cup 1948 and 1950; Essex and Herts Border Combination Cup 1974; Kent Intermediate Cup 1968; Kent Junior Cup 1947 and 1968; South London Alliance 1923; Woolwich Hospital Cup 1949, 52, 53, 65.

Manager for 1996/97: Mike Ackland   **Assistant Manager: David Hutt**

Chairman: John McFadden   **Vice Chairman: R.E. Cowley**

Press Officer: Martin Tarrant c/o Sec.

The 'Deres' were founded in 1922 when they accepted into the Kent League. Success was not long in coming for in 1924 they not only won the Kent Amateur Cup but they were beaten finalists in the FA Amateur Cup, losing to Clapton at New Cross.

The following year saw them in the First Round Proper of the FA Cup but a crowd of over 4,000 saw them lose to Reading. Their only other Cup run of note was in 1933 when after battling through the qualifying rounds they lost to Coventry City, who were challenging for the Division Three South title at the time. The crowd was over 8,000 and that still stands as the ground's attendance record.

In 1938 the club again returned to its best form by reaching the Amateur Cup final again, only to lose to Bromley. They stayed in the Kent League, apart from season 1930-31 in the London League, until the war years when they played in the South East Combination, and in 1942 they did the league and cup double dropping one point and scoring 253 goals in 44 games. In 1945 The Deres became founder members of the Corinthian League, where they won the Memorial Shield three years running from 1947. On the merger of the Delphian, Corinthian and Metropolitan Leagues they became founder members of the Athenian League where they stayed until 1978. During this time they won the Memorial Shield in 1968, the League Cup in 1974 and were league runners up in 1971.

1978 heralded the return to the Kent League for a three year stay, during the last of which they took the title and were beaten finalists in the League Cup. Elected to the Southern League in 1982, Erith have had little success since and the last two seasons have seen them finish last but one in the Southern Division, above only Poole Town last May.

ERITH AND BELVEDERE 1995/96 SEASON

Date	Comp	Round	Opposition	Att	Score	Scorers
19/08/95	BHL	S	WESTON-SUPER-MARE	108	0-0	
22/08/95	BHL	S	Margate	250	0-1	
26/08/95	BHL	S	HAVANT TOWN	77	1-3	Windeatt
28/08/95	BHL	S	Waterlooville	196	0-6	
02/09/95	BHL	S	NEWPORT I.O.W.	119	2-4	Windeatt(2)
06/09/95	BHL	S	Sittingbourne	526	0-1	
09/09/95	FA Cup	Q1	REDHILL	87	4-1	Sesay, Nichols, Windeatt, Humphreys
16/09/95	BHL	S	CLEVEDON TOWN	118	1-2	Windeatt
19/09/95	BHL	S	MARGATE	68	0-2	
23/09/95	FA Cup	Q2	SITTINGBOURNE	247	2-2	Kearns, Ealham
27/09/95	FA Cup	Q2 rep	Sittingbourne	556	1-6	Kearns
30/09/95	BHL	S	Fisher	222	3-4	Ealham, Humphreys, Hake
03/10/95	DMC	1(1)	Fisher	122	0-4	
07/10/95	BHL	S	POOLE TOWN	85	4-1	Donka, Hake, Humphries, Groom
14/10/95	FA Trophy	Q1	BASINGSTOKE TOWN	112	0-6	
18/10/95	Kent SC	1	Sittingbourne	249	3-3	Eeles(og), Carthy, Kearns
21/10/95	BHL	S	Fareham Town	112	1-5	Manchester
28/10/95	BHL	S	Witney Town	123	1-1	N McCarthy
02/11/95	Kent SC	1 rep	SITTINGBOURNE	76	2-5	Jago, Carmo
07/11/95	BHL	S	WATERLOOVILLE	73	1-3	Porter
11/11/95	BHL	S	FISHER	156	1-3	Donka
14/11/95	DMC	1(2)	FISHER	54	0-2	
18/11/95	BHL	S	Cinderford Town	247	1-3	Donka
25/11/95	BHL	S	WITNEY TOWN	112	0-5	
02/12/95	BHL	S	Trowbridge Town	341	0-4	
09/12/95	BHL	S	Weston-super-Mare	190	0-3	
14/12/95	London CC	1	TOOTING & MITCHAM UTD	60	1-6	McCarthy
16/12/95	BHL	S	FOREST GREEN ROVERS	104	0-3	
01/01/96	BHL	S	ASHFORD TOWN	162	2-3	Ealham, Nichols
13/01/96	BHL	S	Bashley	141	1-2	Nicholls
20/01/96	BHL	S	CINDERFORD TOWN	131	2-2	Burns, Williams
03/02/96	BHL	S	Clevedon Town	246	2-1	Burns, Carmo
06/02/96	BHL	S	SITTINGBOURNE	213	0-3	
10/02/96	BHL	S	FAREHAM TOWN	104	3-4	Nichols, Ashworth, Carthy
13/02/96	BHL	S	Fleet Town	134	0-3	
17/02/96	BHL	S	Tonbridge Angels	379	0-1	
27/02/96	BHL	S	Braintree Town	138	0-4	
02/03/96	BHL	S	TONBRIDGE ANGELS	167	0-1	
09/03/96	BHL	S	Havant Town	106	0-1	
19/03/96	BHL	S	WEYMOUTH	71	3-4	Williams(2), Todd
23/03/96	BHL	S	Yate Town	157	0-4	
30/03/96	BHL	S	FLEET TOWN	108	0-3	
03/04/96	BHL	S	Newport I.O.W.	283	0-1	
06/04/96	BHL	S	Ashford Town	558	0-2	
08/04/96	BHL	S	BRAINTREE TOWN	107	1-4	McFee
13/04/96	BHL	S	BASHLEY	109	1-1	McCarthy
16/04/96	BHL	S	YATE TOWN	71	2-1	Carmo, Todd
20/04/96	BHL	S	Weymouth	536	1-3	Bryant
27/04/96	BHL	S	Forest Green Rovers	185	0-2	
30/04/96	BHL	S	Poole Town	113	4-2	Fisher, Liddle, Carthy, McLean
04/05/96	BHL	S	TROWBRIDGE TOWN	157	0-5	

FAREHAM TOWN

Cams Alders, Highfield Avenue, Fareham, Hants PO14 1JA. Tel: 01329 231151

Secretary: Ken Atkins, 4 Cedar Close, Gosport, Hants PO12 4AT Tel: 01705 583049

Nickname: The Town

Colours: Red and Black

Capacity: 5,500

Seating: 450

Covered standing: 500

Clubhouse on ground: Yes

Record attendance: 2,650 v Wimbledon FA Cup 4th Qual Rd 1965

Also 6,035 v Kidderminster Harriers FA Trophy semi-final 2nd Leg 1987 at Southampton FC

Record fee paid: £1,000 for Peter Baxter from Poole Town

Record fee received: £43,000 for David Leworthy to Tottenham Hotspur

> ## DIRECTIONS
> **From Fareham station follow A27 towards Southampton and take second left into Redlands Avenue. Turn right at Redlands Inn then left into Highfields Avenue.**

HONOURS

FA TROPHY: semi-final 1987; Hampshire Senior Cup 1957, 63, 68, 93; Hampshire League 1960, 63, 64, 66, 67, 73, 75; Eastern Division 1925, Div 3 East 1950; Portsmouth Senior Cup 1959, 1964, 1973; Russell Coates Cup 1965, 73, 74, 75, 76, 77; Pickford Cup twice; South West Counties (Pratten) Cup twice.

Fareham Town FC was formed in 1947, following an amalgamation of three clubs in the town. Two of the clubs had histories going back into the last century, but it was felt that the only way to move forward was to join forces. The newly formed club played at their former ground, Bath Lane and initially joined the Portsmouth League before being elected to the Hampshire County League in 1947. By 1954 the club had gained promotion to the First Division and stayed there until 1979, when they were elected to the Southern League.

During that period Fareham won every major Hampshire honour going, including Senior Cup, League Championship, Portsmouth Senior Cup, Russell Coates Cup, Pickford Cup and South West Counties Cup. The reserves and Sunday side have also won trophies including the FA Sunday Cup in 1975.

After finishing 23rd in the second season, they went down, but in 1982 as the league re-formed its Premier Division, they were up again. There was little success and were reprieved in 1986 when RS Southampton pulled out, only to go down in 1989 in 19th place.

In 1987 the club enjoyed a stunning FA Trophy run which saw them reach the two-legged semi-finals before going out to Kidderminster. Having beaten Barnet and Scarborough and drawn 0-0 in the away tie at Aggbrough, Fareham switched the second leg to the Dell and a record crowd of over 6,000 saw them lose 2-0.

In 1995 the club struggled amidst problems on and off the pitch, finishing last but one, and in May this year, they again finished low down, although talk of voluntarily moving to the Wessex League has gone for the time being.

FAREHAM TOWN 1995/96 SEASON

Date	Comp		Opponent	Att	Score	Scorers
19/08/95	BHL	S	TONBRIDGE ANGELS	163	3-3	Anstice, Colbran(og), Odey
22/08/95	BHL	S	Witney Town	172	1-5	Garfin
26/08/95	FA Cup	P	WEYMOUTH	152	1-1	Strowger
29/08/95	FA Cup	P rep	Weymouth	807	2-3	Odey(2)
02/09/95	BHL	S	Weston-super-Mare	264	6-1	Sandry(2), Odey, Semark, Coleman, Anstice
05/09/95	BHL	S	Newport I.O.W.	420	0-1	
09/09/95	BHL	S	BASHLEY	150	1-2	Semark
16/09/95	BHL	S	Trowbridge Town	321	0-5	
20/09/95	BHL	S	WITNEY TOWN	121	3-3	Odey(2), Mottashed
27/09/95	Hants SC	1	MALSHANGER	65	5-4	Odey(2), Mottashed, Wilson, Coleman
30/09/95	BHL	S	WATERLOOVILLE	210	0-3	
04/10/95	DMC	1(1)	FLEET TOWN	75	2-2	Mottashed, Anstice
07/10/95	BHL	S	Bashley	241	0-3	
14/10/95	FA Trophy	Q1	MAIDENHEAD UNITED	90	2-4	Webb, Coleman
21/10/95	BHL	S	ERITH & BELVEDERE	112	5-1	Odey(2), Anstice, Wilson, Webb
25/10/95	BHL	S	Poole Town	102	3-0	Davis, Odey, Strowger
28/10/95	BHL	S	WEYMOUTH	161	1-1	Odey
01/11/95	Hants SC	2	BASINGSTOKE TOWN	104	1-3	Wilson
07/11/95	DMC	1(2)	Fleet Town	104	0-2	
11/11/95	BHL	S	Clevedon Town	192	1-4	Odey
18/11/95	BHL	S	TROWBRIDGE TOWN	157	0-3	
25/11/95	BHL	S	Waterlooville	302	0-1	
02/12/95	BHL	S	Braintree Town	157	0-1	
06/12/95	BHL	S	NEWPORT I.O.W.	84	2-7	Anstice, Odey
09/12/95	BHL	S	SITTINGBOURNE	104	0-2	
13/12/95	BHL	S	POOLE TOWN	77	5-0	Wearn, Fryfield, Odey(3)
16/12/95	BHL	S	Tonbridge Angels	300	8-1	Kirkham, Fryfield(2), Hayes, Odey(3), Williams
01/01/96	BHL	S	HAVANT TOWN	238	1-3	Odey
13/01/96	BHL	S	Yate Town	197	0-2	
20/01/96	BHL	S	ASHFORD TOWN	126	0-3	
03/02/96	BHL	S	WESTON-SUPER-MARE	102	0-3	
10/02/96	BHL	S	Erith & Belvedere	104	4-3	Williams, Darnton, Wearn, Hensman
17/02/96	BHL	S	Weymouth	786	1-2	Odey
02/03/96	BHL	S	Forest Green Rovers	169	5-4	Hensman, Walters, Odey(2), Fyfield
09/03/96	BHL	S	FOREST GREEN ROVERS	133	2-2	Walters, Odey
16/03/96	BHL	S	Fleet Town	97	2-3	Odey, Wearn
20/03/96	BHL	S	CLEVEDON TOWN	78	2-1	Odey(2)
23/03/96	BHL	S	Fisher	185	2-2	Wilson, Odey
30/03/96	BHL	S	CINDERFORD TOWN	94	2-1	Tryon, Odey
03/04/96	BHL	S	FISHER	66	0-2	
06/04/96	BHL	S	Havant Town	231	3-4	Odey(2), Walters
08/04/96	BHL	S	FLEET TOWN	122	0-3	
13/04/96	BHL	S	YATE TOWN	104	2-1	Odey(2)
17/04/96	BHL	S	Cinderford Town	170	2-1	Webb, Howells(og)
20/04/96	BHL	S	Sittingbourne	795	0-3	
21/04/96	BHL	S	Margate	157	0-2	
27/04/96	BHL	S	Ashford Town	688	1-2	Odey
01/05/96	BHL	S	BRAINTREE TOWN	97	1-2	Odey
04/05/96	BHL	S	MARGATE	116	2-1	Odey, Semark
06/05/96	Gosport WM	F	Gosport Borough	150	0-1	

FISHER ATHLETIC (LONDON)

Surrey Docks Stadium, Salter Rd, London SE16. Tel:
0171 252 0590

Nickname: The Fish

Capacity: 5,300

Seating: 400

Covered standing: 4,000

Clubhouse on ground: Yes

Record attendance: 4,283 v Barnet Conference 1991

Biggest win: 6-0 v Bury Town 1993

Biggest defeat: 0-6 v Salisbury 1993

Record appearances: Dennis Sharp 720

Record goalscorer: Paul Shinners 205

DIRECTIONS

Southwark area south of the river on Main Salter road running parallel to the river. Nearest main line station is London Bridge - 3 miles (Waterloo, 5 miles). Nearest underground is Rotherhithe (East London Line) - 7 minute walk. Bus route: P11 and 225 pass the ground

Honours

Southern League 1987 and Southern Division 1983

League Cup 1985 abd Championship Shield 1988

London Spartan League 1981 and 1982 Senior Div `1978

Parthenon League 1962 and League Cup 1964 and 1966

Kent Amateur League 1974 and 1975

London Senior Cup 1985, 1988, 1989

London Intermediate Cup 1960

Kent Senior Cup 1984

Kent Senior Trophy 1982 and 1983

Surrey Intermediate Cup 1962

The story of the club is remarkable. Founded in 1908 to provide sporting facilities for the young people of Bermondsey, the football side competed in various local leagues before folding and re-forming in 1966. Then based at Mitcham, they played initially in the West Kent League before gaining promotion to the Spartan League. In 1982, a second successive championship co-incided with a move to their present home, the purpose built stadium in Surrey Docks.

Fisher won the Southern League Southern Division at the first attempt and two seasons later, in 1987, they were Premier Division champions, edging out Bromsgrove Rovers in the last week of the season. Fisher had gone from minor league football to the Conference, the pinnacle of non-League football, in just 12 years.

During that period much silverware, including the Kent and London Senior Cups and the League Cup went to Surrey Docks, and they also had brief success in the FA Cup, playing Bristol City in 1984 and Bristol City in 1987. Unfortunately Fisher could not carry their success into the Conference and various ownership and managerial changes have led to the club having to struggle on and off the pitch and after four years in the Conference they were back in the Southern League,

FISHER 93 1995/96 SEASON

Date	Comp	Rnd	Opponent	Att	Score	Scorers
19/08/95	BHL	S	Cinderford Town	220	1-0	Donka
22/08/95	BHL	S	Fleet Town	229	2-1	Mehmet
26/08/95	FA Cup	P	MERSTHAM	124	0-0	
29/08/95	FA Cup	P rep	Merstham	175	2-0	Walsh, Falana
02/09/95	BHL	S	FOREST GREEN ROVERS	181	1-1	Francois
05/09/95	BHL	S	Braintree Town	147	1-2	Francois
09/09/95	FA Cup	Q1	LEWES	181	7-0	Falana(3), Walsh(2), Francois, Brooker
16/09/95	BHL	S	POOLE TOWN	172	4-0	Hiscock(2), Walsh, Booker
19/09/95	BHL	S	FLEET TOWN	181	2-2	Nohilly, Walsh
23/09/95	FA Cup	Q2	FARNBOROUGH TOWN	335	1-4	Booker
30/09/95	BHL	S	ERITH & BELVEDERE	222	4-3	Falana(2), Nohilly, Mehmet
03/10/95	DMC	1(1)	ERITH & BELVEDERE	122	4-0	Mehmet(2), Malcolm, Hemley
07/10/95	BHL	S	BRAINTREE TOWN	173	2-2	Booker(2)
10/10/95	BHL	S	Tonbridge Angels	429	1-1	Hanley
14/10/95	FA Trophy	Q1	Salisbury City	319	0-2	
24/10/95	BHL	S	Margate	195	2-2	Booker, Malcolm
28/10/95	BHL	S	BASHLEY	178	3-3	Martin, Walsh, Francois
31/10/95	London CC	1	Barking		1-2	
04/11/95	BHL	S	MARGATE	210	0-2	
07/11/95	Kent SC	1	Tonbridge Angels	266	2-1	Booker(2)
11/11/95	BHL	S	Erith & Belvedere	156	3-1	Hambley(2), Booker
14/11/95	DMC	1(2)	Erith & Belvedere	54	2-0	Booker, Nohilly
18/11/95	BHL	S	Havant Town	93	2-1	Malcolm(2)
25/11/95	BHL	S	ASHFORD TOWN	290	0-0	
02/12/95	BHL	S	Clevedon Town	272	1-2	Malcolm
09/12/95	BHL	S	TONBRIDGE ANGELS	212	0-3	
12/12/95	DMC	2	Tonbridge Angels	192	0-3	
16/12/95	BHL	S	Trowbridge Town	275	1-1	Donka
06/01/96	BHL	S	TROWBRIDGE TOWN	182	1-2	Malcolm
13/01/96	BHL	S	Newport I.O.W.	323	2-4	Donka, Malcolm
20/01/96	BHL	S	CLEVEDON TOWN	172	3-0	Walsh, Quinn, Logan
23/01/96	Kent SC	QF	GRAVESEND & NORTHFLEET	140	2-0	Donka, Quinn
03/02/96	BHL	S	WEYMOUTH	180	1-2	Quinn
10/02/96	BHL	S	Forest Green Rovers	238	2-2	Malcolm(2)
13/02/96	BHL	S	WITNEY TOWN	137	1-0	Malcolm
17/02/96	BHL	S	Ashford Town	489	0-1	
24/02/96	BHL	S	CINDERFORD TOWN	120	2-2	Malcolm(2)
02/03/96	BHL	S	YATE TOWN	144	3-3	Gorman, Hiscock, Brooker
05/03/96	BHL	S	Waterlooville	193	1-0	Hambley
09/03/96	BHL	S	WESTON-SUPER-MARE	151	1-2	Logan
16/03/96	BHL	S	Poole Town	101	1-0	Gorman
23/03/96	BHL	S	FAREHAM TOWN	185	2-2	Hambley, Cort
26/03/96	BHL	S	Weymouth	524	0-2	
30/03/96	BHL	S	Sittingbourne	647	0-3	
03/04/96	BHL	S	Fareham Town	66	2-0	Gorman, Hambley
06/04/96	BHL	S	WATERLOOVILLE	209	3-0	Court, Gorman, Hambley
08/04/96	BHL	S	Witney Town	133	0-1	
11/04/96	Kent SC	SF	CHARLTON ATHLETIC	120	4-8	Collins, Donka, Cort, Logan
13/04/96	BHL	S	HAVANT TOWN	147	0-0	
20/04/96	BHL	S	Weston-super-Mare	171	1-0	Woolfe
23/04/96	BHL	S	SITTINGBOURNE	411	0-2	
27/04/96	BHL	S	Bashley	211	0-2	
01/05/96	BHL	S	Yate Town	110	2-1	Woolfe, Logan
04/05/96	BHL	S	NEWPORT I.O.W.	193	0-1	

FLEET TOWN

Calthorpe Park, Crookham Road, Fleet, Hampshire. Tel: 01252 623804

Secretary: Stephen Hyde, 163 Quilter Rd, Brighton Hill, Basingstoke, Hants RG22 4HE Tel & fax: 01256 59675

Founded: 1890

Nickname: The Tarn   Colours: Dark and Light Blue

Capacity: 2,000   Seating: 220

Covered standing: 250   Clubhouse on ground: Yes

Record attendance: 1,050 v Coventry City Friendly 1994

Biggest win: 15-0 v Petersfield Utd Christmas 1994

Record appearances: Neil Roberts

Record goalscorer in total: Mark Frampton

Record fee paid: £1,500 to Farnborough Town in 1991

DIRECTIONS

M3 Junction 4A. A3013 to Fleet town centre. Pass British Rail station on left. First exit at roundabout. First exit (left) at next roundabout. Up and over railway bridge, straight across small roundabout into Fleet Road. Across traffic lights (EDS building on left). Past shopping centre. Straight across prominent cross roads (traffic lights), with Oaksheaf Pub on far right corner, into Crookham Road. Past Smiths Garage and Fleet Coaches on right. Down small hill. 50 yards after Stanton Drive on the right is entrance to ground and car park.

HONOURS

Wessex League 1995; Aldershot Senior Cup 1993, 1995, 1996; Southern Counties Mid week Cup 1995; Simpsonair Challenge Shield 1993 and 1994.

Manager for 1996/97: Alan Manville   **Assistant manager: Jesse Bone**

Chairman: Anthony Cherry   **Vice chairman: Colin Sturgess**

Press officer and programme editor: Steve Beagley 01252 622112

It is believed that the first team in Fleet was formed well before 1890 by a gentleman called Edwin Edwards.

The football ground and cricket pitch were on the East side of Church Road and spectators could sit on the churchyard railings and watch play. When a house, Woodlands, was built behind the church the occupants objected to the noise so the cricketers and footballers removed their belongings and the goalposts were put up in the meadow bounded on the West side by what is now Birch Avenue. Games could be watched by standing in Fleet Road, now opposite Perkins'.

Fleet moved to their present ground in 1923 where they played in the local Aldershot League until 1953, when they moved to the Basingstoke and District League and a Supporters Club was formed.

It was they in the main that helped to develop the facilities as they were before the recent wholesale changes as Fleet moved into the Southern League. The ground was good enough for the Hampshire League in 1961, and Fleet won Division Three two years later, were relegated after one year but returned again. They won Division Two in 1966 and were in contention for the league itself during the next ten years without actually winning it. They moved on to the Athenian League and then the Combined Counties and suffered a shock when the old stand was razed to the ground in 1991. It proved to be a catalyst which has seen the ground and club raise themselves to build the Calvin Tyrer Stand and re-vamp most of Calthorpe Park, which was presented to the club by Lord Calthorpe. It was subsequently bequeathed to the Council with the proviso that it would always be used by Fleet Town Football Club.

Fleet joined the Wessex League in 1989 and took the title in style in 1995, which enabled the club to take their place in the Southern League Southern Division last season.

FLEET TOWN 1995/96 SEASON

Date	Competition		Opponent	Att.	Score	Scorers
01/08/95	S Co's FC		Oakwood		8-1	
19/08/95	BHL	S	Clevedon Town	226	2-0	J Smith, Hodge
22/08/95	BHL	S	FISHER	229	1-2	Frampton
26/08/95	FA Cup	P	A.F.C. Totton		1-3	
28/08/95	BHL	S	Newport I.O.W.	283	0-1	
02/09/95	BHL	S	POOLE TOWN	153	2-1	Frampton, Rosenior
05/09/95	BHL	S	TONBRIDGE ANGELS	150	1-1	Fealey
16/09/95	BHL	S	Bashley	172	1-2	Frampton
19/09/95	BHL	S	Fisher	181	2-2	Frampton, Rosenior
23/09/95	BHL	S	YATE TOWN	102	3-1	Frampton, Cummins, Rosenior
26/09/95	Hants SC	1	OVERTON UNITED	59	6-1	Frampton(2), Hanley, Thompson(3)
30/09/95	BHL	S	Sittingbourne	646	2-3	Rosenior, Thompson
04/10/95	DMC	1(1)	Fareham Town	75	2-2	Frampton, Thompson
07/10/95	BHL	S	CLEVEDON TOWN	129	1-2	Frampton
10/10/95	S Co's FC	1994-95 F	Sidley United	56	1-0	Ferrett
14/10/95	FA Trophy	Q1	Leyton Pennant	66	1-0	Duffy
21/10/95	BHL	S	Havant Town	122	0-1	
25/10/95	Hants SC	2	BLACKFIELD & LANGLEY	62	4-1	Smith(3), Duffy
28/10/95	BHL	S	Trowbridge Town	303	0-4	
31/10/95	Russell CC	2	CHRISTCHURCH	46	5-4	Smith(2), Hodge, Frampton, Cummins
04/11/95	FA Trophy	Q2	Newport A.F.C.	679	1-2	Smith
07/11/95	DMC	1(2)	FAREHAM TOWN	104	2-0	Bray, Smith
11/11/95	BHL	S	HAVANT TOWN	174	0-3	
14/11/95	BHL	S	Tonbridge Angels	316	2-1	Smith(2)
18/11/95	BHL	S	Weston-super-Mare	230	3-2	Frampton(2), Smith
28/11/95	Aldershot	2	FOUR MARKS	93	9-1	Flaherty, Smith(3), Frampton(4), Jones
02/12/95	BHL	S	Poole Town	76	3-0	Frampton, Smith(2)
05/12/95	DMC	2	Waterlooville	88	0-4	
09/12/95	BHL	S	Margate	200	1-3	Duffy
12/12/95	Hants SC	3	Waterlooville	38	1-2	Duffy
16/12/95	BHL	S	ASHFORD TOWN	117	3-2	Frampton, Fealey
19/12/95	BHL	S	NEWPORT I.O.W.	107	1-1	Flaherty
23/12/95	BHL	S	Forest Green Rovers	201	0-4	
06/01/96	BHL	S	WATERLOOVILLE	204	0-3	
13/01/96	BHL	S	Weymouth	727	1-2	Smith
20/01/96	BHL	S	BASHLEY	123	2-2	Smith, Duffy
23/01/96	Aldershot	QF	Cove	73	4-1	Smith, Frampton(2), Flaherty
30/01/96	Russell CC	QF	Bournemouth		2-4	
03/02/96	BHL	S	Braintree Town	158	0-4	
10/02/96	BHL	S	MARGATE	174	0-4	
13/02/96	BHL	S	ERITH & BELVEDERE	134	3-0	Ealham(og), Frampton, Smith
17/02/96	BHL	S	Yate Town	121	1-3	Smith
24/02/96	BHL	S	WEYMOUTH	379	0-1	
27/02/96	BHL	S	Witney Town	89	1-1	Frampton
02/03/96	BHL	S	Waterlooville	220	0-3	
05/03/96	BHL	S	BRAINTREE TOWN	139	2-4	Pratt, Handley
09/03/96	BHL	S	CINDERFORD TOWN	120	1-2	Pratt
16/03/96	BHL	S	FAREHAM TOWN	97	3-2	Smith(3)
19/03/96	Aldershot	SF	BASS ALTON TOWN	163	5-3	Smith, Handley, Frampton(2), Holloway
23/03/96	BHL	S	FOREST GREEN ROVERS	154	0-3	
30/03/96	BHL	S	Erith & Belvedere	108	3-0	Rowe, Holloway, Jones
06/04/96	BHL	S	WITNEY TOWN	140	1-2	Smith
08/04/96	BHL	S	Fareham Town	122	3-0	Frampton, Smith(2)
13/04/96	BHL	S	SITTINGBOURNE	388	3-1	Smith(2), Thompson
20/04/96	BHL	S	Ashford Town	711	0-1	
27/04/96	BHL	S	WESTON-SUPER-MARE	255	2-1	Rowe, Thompson
30/04/96	BHL	S	TROWBRIDGE TOWN	178	2-1	Frampton(2)
04/05/96	BHL	S	Cinderford Town	230	2-3	Holloway, Thompson
08/05/96	Aldershot	F	Aldershot Town	650	3-1	

FOREST GREEN ROVERS

The Lawn, Nympsfield Rd, Forest Green, Nailsworth, Gloucestershire GL6 0ET. Tel: 01453 834860

Secretary and Managing Director: Colin Peake c/o Club Admin Office, Unit 14, Springfield Business Centre, Stonehouse, Glos, GL10 3SX   Mobile No. 0378 058152

Nickname: Rovers or The Green

Colours: Black and White stripes

Capacity: 3132   Seating: 332

Covered standing: 980   Clubhouse on ground: Yes

Record attendance: 2,200 v Wolverhampton Wanderers Friendly in 1981

Record fee paid or received: £5,000 for Karl Bayliss

DIRECTIONS

4 miles south of Stroud on A46 to Bath. In Nailsworth turn into Spring Hill off mini roundabout and ground is approx 1/2 mile up the hill on the left. Nearest Railway Station is Stroud.

HONOURS

FA VASE WINNERS 1982; Hellenic League 1982; Stroud and Dursley League 1903; Glos Northern Senior League 1938, 1950, 1951; Glos Senior Cup 1985, 1986, 1987; Glos Sen Amateur Cup (North) 1927, 1946, 1972, 1976, 1978; Glos Professional Cup 1985 and 1986.

Manager for 1996/97: Frank Gregan   **Assistant Manager: Tommy Callinan**

Chairman: Trevor Horsley   **Vice Chairman: Doug O'Brien**

Press officer: Heather Cook, "Vraiville", Middle Yard, Kings Stanley, Glos.

01453 823281 (h) 0385 940981 (mobile)

Founded in 1890, the club spent their early years in the Stroud and District League until 1922, when they were founder members of the Gloucestershire Northern Senior League. During their time in the Senior League they were champions in 1938, 1950 and 1951. Then followed a number of seasons where silverware was not forthcoming, although much happened off the pitch, at the Lawn.

On the formation in 1968 of the County League, they, with several of their league colleagues, joined the wider area of competition which included several Bristol based clubs. In 1974, the opportunity arose for a move upwards once again, this time to the Hellenic League. Settling in well, they established a wonderful base by winning the FA Vase at Wembley, beating Rainworth MW in the final. They completed a famous double by taking the league and with it promotion to the Southern League, where they remained members of the Midland Division until transferred to the Southern Division last season.

In 1989, and with the centenary close by, the club name was changed to Stroud FC. The then Board felt that such a move was beneficial at the time but, with hindsight, it proved to the worst decision for the long term future. As a result a new Board was appointed and in late 1991 a resolution was passed to revert to its original name. To ensure ground grading would be adhered to, work commenced in January of 1996 on a new complex which will incorporate underground changing rooms, a 300 seater stand, boardroom, offices, toilets and a press box.

The Lawn was little more than a field with a Hawthorn hedge around it when Forest Green began playing there sometime between the wars. An old tin stand came up from the playing fields further down the hill, and that was all until 1950 when members built the solid looking changing rooms which are about to be made redundant by the new complex.

FOREST GREEN ROVERS 1995/96 SEASON

Date	Competition	Round	Opponent	Att	Score	Scorers
19/08/95	BHL	S	Waterlooville	205	2-1	Bayliss, Johnstone
23/08/95	BHL	S	TROWBRIDGE TOWN	263	2-2	Maynard, Bayliss
26/08/95	FA Cup	P	EXMOUTH TOWN	114	4-0	Ford, Maynard(2), Fitzpatrick
28/08/95	BHL	S	WITNEY TOWN	215	0-0	
02/09/95	BHL	S	Fisher	181	1-1	Kennedy
05/09/95	BHL	S	Weston-super-Mare	240	3-0	Bayliss(2), Johnstone
09/09/95	FA Cup	Q1	MANGOTSFIELD UNITED	179	2-1	Fitzpatrick, Ford
16/09/95	BHL	S	HAVANT TOWN	187	0-1	
19/09/95	BHL	S	Trowbridge Town	306	0-2	
23/09/95	FA Cup	Q2	CHELTENHAM TOWN	544	3-0	Callinan, Kennedy, Banks(og)
26/09/95	DMC	1(1)	CLEVEDON TOWN	124	2-1	Bayliss(2)
30/09/95	BHL	S	Margate	229	1-3	Callinan
03/10/95	Glos NSC	1	GLOUCESTER CITY	215	1-2	Bayliss
07/10/95	FA Cup	Q3	CINDERFORD TOWN	335	1-1	Johnstone
10/10/95	FA Cup	Q3 rep	Cinderford Town	684	1-1	Bayliss
14/10/95	FA Trophy	Q1	SITTINGBOURNE	101	1-2	Johnstone
16/10/95	FA Cup	Q3 rep(2)	CINDERFORD TOWN	671	1-3	Callinan
21/10/95	BHL	S	Braintree Town	152	4-1	Moore, Ford, Skidmore, Johnstone
24/10/95	BHL	S	Witney Town	126	0-1	
28/10/95	BHL	S	TONBRIDGE ANGELS	172	3-0	Johnstone, Saunders, Callinan
04/11/95	BHL	S	Newport I.O.W.	316	1-0	Callinan
07/11/95	DMC	1(2)	Clevedon Town	151	3-1	Callaghan(2), Moore
11/11/95	BHL	S	BRAINTREE TOWN	138	1-1	Bayliss
18/11/95	BHL	S	Bashley	207	2-1	Callinan, Moore
22/11/95	BHL	S	WESTON-SUPER-MARE	167	4-0	Moore, Callinan, Bayliss(2)
25/11/95	BHL	S	SITTINGBOURNE	169	2-0	Skidmore, Moore
02/12/95	BHL	S	Havant Town	91	1-1	Marshall
06/12/95	DMC	2	NEWPORT A.F.C.	185	2-4	Kennedy(2)
09/12/95	BHL	S	WEYMOUTH	187	2-0	Skidmore, Bayliss
16/12/95	BHL	S	Erith & Belvedere	104	3-0	Bayliss, Marshall, Skidmore
23/12/95	BHL	S	FLEET TOWN	201	4-0	Hirons, Bayliss, Maynard, Skidmore
30/12/95	BHL	S	Poole Town	101	2-1	Marshall, Maynard
06/01/96	BHL	S	BASHLEY	223	2-1	Hirons, Bayliss
13/01/96	BHL	S	Clevedon Town	262	1-1	Hirons
20/01/96	BHL	S	MARGATE	174	3-1	Hirons, Callinan, Moore
10/02/96	BHL	S	FISHER	238	2-2	Kennedy, Bayliss
21/02/96	BHL	S	YATE TOWN	147	1-0	Moore
24/02/96	BHL	S	Sittingbourne	750	1-5	Moore
02/03/96	BHL	S	FAREHAM TOWN	169	4-5	Bayliss, New(og), Tomlinson, Maynard
05/03/96	BHL	S	NEWPORT I.O.W.	156	5-2	Scott, Bayliss(2), Marshall, Kennedy
09/03/96	BHL	S	Fareham Town	133	2-2	Callinan, Bayliss
16/03/96	BHL	S	WATERLOOVILLE	206	0-3	
20/03/96	BHL	S	ASHFORD TOWN	131	2-3	Marshall, Moore
23/03/96	BHL	S	Fleet Town	154	3-0	Moore(3)
30/03/96	BHL	S	POOLE TOWN	176	6-0	Moore(2), Callinan(2), Hirons, Sykes
02/04/96	BHL	S	Ashford Town	441	0-3	
06/04/96	BHL	S	Yate Town	209	0-2	
09/04/96	BHL	S	CINDERFORD TOWN	305	3-1	Callinan(2), Kennedy
13/04/96	BHL	S	Tonbridge Angels	423	3-2	Moore, Scott, Kilgour
20/04/96	BHL	S	CLEVEDON TOWN	202	5-2	Moore(3), Scott, Kennedy
23/04/96	BHL	S	Cinderford Town	330	1-2	Sykes
27/04/96	BHL	S	ERITH & BELVEDERE	185	2-0	Sykes, Bayliss
04/05/96	BHL	S	Weymouth	645	1-2	Sykes

HAVANT TOWN

West Leigh Park, Martin Road, West Leigh, Havant PO9 5TH. Tel: 01705 787822

Secretary: Kevin Moore, 68 St Ronans Rd, Southsea, Hants PO4 0PX. Tel: 01705 731530

Colours: Yellow and black

Capacity: 6,000

Seating: 240

Covered standing: 1, 500

Clubhouse on ground: Yes

Record attendance: 3,500 v Wisbech Town
FA Vase quarter-final 1986

DIRECTIONS
Take B2149 to Havant off the A27 (B2149 Petersfield Rd if coming out of Havant). 2nd turning off dual carriageway into Burtons Road then first right into martins road. 1 mile from Havant BR station.

Biggest win: 10-0 v Sholing Sports FA Vase 4th Rd 1986, v Portsmouth RN Wessex League 1991 and v Poole Town Southern League 1995

Biggest defeat: 1-7 v Camberley Town FA Vase 3rd Rd 1989

Record appearances: Tony Plumbley

Record fee paid: £5,750 for John Wilson from Bashley in 1990

Record fee received: £7,000 for Steve Tate of Waterlooville in 1993

HONOURS

FA SUNDAY CUP 1969

Wessex League 1991

Hampshire League Div 3 1973, Div 4 1972,

Russell Coates Cup 1992

Portsmouth Senior Cup 1984, 1985, 1992

Gosport War Memorial Cup 1975, 1992, 1993, 1995.

Havant Town FC are a relatively young club, having been founded as Leigh Park FC in 1958. They joined the Portsmouth League on their original ground, Front Lawn. They moved up to the senior ranks of the Hampshire League in 1971 and won Division Four in 1972 and Division Three a year later as they quickly ascended the league. As the 70's turned into the 80's it became apparent that to progress further they would need to move from what was a roped off pitch and, eventually after over 2 years work where the site was drained and prepared, the club moved in to West Leigh Park in 1983. It was the beginning of a marvellous decade, which began with two Portsmouth Senior Cup wins and a place in the last eight of the FA Vase.

The new ground developed to an extent that the club were invited to join the Wessex League as founder members in 1986. It took just three years for Havant to make their mark, finishing runners up to the all conquering Bashley in 1989, but two years later they went one better and clinched the title.

It was enough for the club and ground to be eligible to move into the Southern League, from where they enjoyed success in the Russell Cotes Cup in 1992, the reserves also taking the Junior and Intermediate Cups and the Portsmouth Senior Cup.

HAVANT TOWN 1995/96 SEASON

Date	Comp	Rnd	Opponent	Att	Score	Scorers
19/08/95	BHL	S	YATE TOWN	196	1-0	Elley
22/08/95	BHL	S	Weymouth	709	2-1	Sherry, Laws(og)
26/08/95	BHL	S	Erith & Belvedere	77	3-1	Elley, Connolly, Boyce
28/08/95	BHL	S	BASHLEY	238	1-2	Sherry
02/09/95	BHL	S	Ashford Town	405	1-1	Green
06/09/95	BHL	S	WITNEY TOWN	103	5-1	Fosbury, Green, Webbe, Boyce, Price
09/09/95	FA Cup	Q1	Basingstoke Town	212	1-2	
13/09/95	Russell CC	1	BASHLEY	66	2-0	
16/09/95	BHL	S	Forest Green Rovers	187	1-0	Connolly
20/09/95	BHL	S	WEYMOUTH	215	2-0	Boyce(2)
30/09/95	BHL	S	NEWPORT I.O.W.	261	0-5	
03/10/95	DMC	1(1)	Dorchester Town	302	0-1	
07/10/95	BHL	S	Tonbridge Angels	482	1-1	Webbe
14/10/95	FA Trophy	Q1	Hastings Town	392	2-2	Boyce(2)
18/10/95	FA Trophy	Q1 rep	HASTINGS TOWN	141	1-0	Connolly
21/10/95	BHL	S	FLEET TOWN	122	1-0	Price
26/10/95	Hants SC	2	Romsey Town		5-0	
28/10/95	BHL	S	MARGATE	131	2-0	Webbe, Lee
31/10/95	DMC	1(2)	DORCHESTER TOWN	65	0-1	
04/11/95	FA Trophy	Q2	Staines Town	207	1-3	Price
11/11/95	BHL	S	Fleet Town	174	3-0	Webb, Dineen, Connolly
14/11/95	BHL	S	Witney Town	142	0-0	
18/11/95	BHL	S	FISHER	93	1-2	Boyce
22/11/95	Russell CC	2	WHITCHURCH UNITED		2-0	
25/11/95	BHL	S	Yate Town	126	1-2	Jones(og)
28/11/95	Hants SC	3	Basingstoke Town	109	0-1	
02/12/95	BHL	S	FOREST GREEN ROVERS	91	1-1	Green
09/12/95	BHL	S	CINDERFORD TOWN	106	0-1	
16/12/95	BHL	S	Sittingbourne	546	1-0	Hards
23/12/95	BHL	S	Trowbridge Town	248	0-0	
26/12/95	BHL	S	WATERLOOVILLE	543	4-2	Wakefield, Webbe, Elley(2)
01/01/96	BHL	S	Fareham Town	238	3-1	Boyce, Jones, Wakefield
06/01/96	BHL	S	ASHFORD TOWN	168	2-1	Boyce(2)
13/01/96	BHL	S	Poole Town	121	3-0	Boyce, Cole, Green
20/01/96	BHL	S	TONBRIDGE ANGELS	132	4-1	Wakefield, Hewitt(2), Green
24/01/96	BHL	S	CLEVEDON TOWN	105	0-0	
27/01/96	BHL	S	BRAINTREE TOWN	177	0-2	
03/02/96	BHL	S	POOLE TOWN	96	7-1	Sherry, Green, Lee(3), Graham, Boyce
10/02/96	BHL	S	Newport I.O.W.	461	2-0	Green, Wakefield
13/02/96	Russell CC	QF	Bemerton Heath Harlequins	32	1-2	
17/02/96	BHL	S	Cinderford Town	260	2-1	Boyce(2)
02/03/96	BHL	S	Braintree Town	175	0-3	
09/03/96	BHL	S	ERITH & BELVEDERE	106	1-0	Price
13/03/96	BHL	S	WESTON-SUPER-MARE	71	3-0	Boyce, Wakefield, Webbe
16/03/96	BHL	S	Weston-super-Mare	204	0-0	
23/03/96	BHL	S	TROWBRIDGE TOWN	209	2-0	Jones, Green
30/03/96	BHL	S	Clevedon Town	201	2-2	Green, Webb
06/04/96	BHL	S	FAREHAM TOWN	231	4-3	Leigh, Wakefield(3)
08/04/96	BHL	S	Waterlooville	529	0-0	
13/04/96	BHL	S	Fisher	147	0-0	
16/04/96	BHL	S	Bashley	123	3-2	Green, Boyce, Lisk(og)
27/04/96	BHL	S	Margate	247	2-3	Wakefield(2)
04/05/96	BHL	S	SITTINGBOURNE	465	2-2	Graham, Price

MARGATE

Hartsdown Park, Hartsdown Rd, Margate, Kent CT9 5QZ. Tel: 01843 291040

Secretary: Ken Tomlinson, 65 Nash Rd, Margate CT9 4BT Tel: 01843 291040

Prog Editor: Keith Smith, 89 All Saints Ave, Westbrook, Margate CT9 5QH Tel: 01843 293220

Club shop: Paul Bates, 49 Arthur Rd, Deal, Kent CT14 9EY Tel: 01304 367257

Commercial office: 01843 864895   Social club: 01843 220411

Nickname: The Gate   Capacity: 6,000, cover on three sides

Seating: 400   Covered standing: Both ends

Clubhouse on ground: Yes

Record attendance: 14,500 v Tottenham Hotspur FA Cup 3rd Rd 1973

Record appearances: Bob Harrop   Record goalscorer in one season: Dennis Randall 66 in 1966-67

Record fee paid: £5,000 for Steve Cuggy from Dover 1994

Record fee received: Undisclosed fee for Martin Buglione to St Johnstone in 1993

HONOURS

Southern League Central Division and Overall champions 1936;Midweek Division champions 1927 and Div 1 1963;Division One South 1978, Southern League Cup 1968;Southern League Champions Cup 1968 ;Kent League Division One 1933, 38, 47, 48; Division Two 1938, 54, 57, 90; Division One League Cup 1936, 48, 54, 69; Kent Senior Cup 1936, 37, 74, 94; Kent Senior Shield 1921, 31, 36, 37, 48, 53, 62, 63; Kent Junior Cup 1902   Kent Floodlight Cup 1963, 67, 76.

Manager for 1996/97: Chris Kinnear   **Assistant Manager: TBA**

Chairman: Keith Piper   **Vice Chairman: Richard Piper**

Press officer: Cliff Egan 01843 864895

Margate have an occasional fanzine entitled `On the Wagon', from Paul Bates

Margate FC was formed in October 1896. They played on various grounds including Northdown Road and Margate College. They joined the Kent League in 1911 and after the Great War turned professional, using grounds at Dreamland Amusement Park and Garlinge. They were runner up in 1928, but heavy debts caused them to fold at the end of that season. It was soon re-formed and moved to Hartsdown Park in 1930. They began a fine run in the FA Cup, beating the likes of Gillingham, QPR, Crystal Palace, Bournemouth and Swansea City. Having won the league in 1933, they joined the Southern League and were runner up in the first season. Margate became the nursery club for Arsenal in 1934, with many Arsenal players turning out for Margate, even playing a home FA Cup tie at Arsenal. This was the club's most successful period for 1936 saw them reach the 3rd Round of the Cup, as well as taking the Southern League championship, Kent Senior Cup, Kent Senior Shield and Kent League Cup. A year later they won the Southern League mid-week section, but heavy debts saw them return to the Kent League in 1937 where they were champions. More debts and the collapse of the Arsenal tie up saw the club fold once more, but again they re-formed soon after for the 1939-40 season, only for war to break out again. When peace returned, so did the club in Kent football again, and they did the double in 1948, under Almer Hall, the old Brighton and Tottenham Hotspur player, who managed for 20 years. In 1959 they joined the expanding Southern League again, taking Division One in 1963, but going down again in 1966. 12 months later they were back again as runner up. In 1971 Bournemouth exacted revenge for an FA Cup defeat in 1961, by beating Margate 11-0 at Dean Court, with Ted Mc Dougall scoring 9 times. The following season they did better, reaching Round 3 before losing to Tottenham Hotspur before a record crowd of 14,500. Relegation was suffered in 1977, which led to the championship of the Southern Division a year later, but yet again they went back down again.

In 1981, the club changed its name to Thanet United in the hope of attracting sponsors from a wider area, but the next three seasons were a nightmare. By 1985 the club had improved to fifth but after another struggle in 1989 a new board was appointed which changed the name back to Margate FC. Since then the club have won the Kent Senior Cup in 1994 and have finished mid-table for the last two seasons.

MARGATE 1995/96 SEASON

Date	Comp	Rnd	Opponent	Att	Score	Scorers
19/08/95	BHL	S	Trowbridge Town	294	1-3	Buglione
22/08/95	BHL	S	ERITH & BELVEDERE	250	1-0	Buglione
26/08/95	BHL	S	WATERLOOVILLE	244	0-1	
02/09/95	BHL	S	CINDERFORD TOWN	161	1-1	Manning
05/09/95	BHL	S	ASHFORD TOWN	373	0-1	
09/09/95	FA Cup	Q1	Corinthian-Casuals	120	5-2	Wickins, Smith, Buglione(2), Weatherly
16/09/95	BHL	S	Weymouth	615	0-2	
19/09/95	BHL	S	Erith & Belvedere	68	2-0	Manning, Buglione
23/09/95	FA Cup	Q2	Walton & Hersham	225	2-2	Handford, Buglione
26/09/95	FA Cup	Q2 rep	WALTON & HERSHAM	189	0-1	
30/09/95	BHL	S	FOREST GREEN ROVERS	229	3-1	Buglione(2), Manning
04/10/95	DMC	1(1)	Sittingbourne	467	3-1	Mannings, Buglione(2)
07/10/95	BHL	S	Weston-super-Mare	165	3-4	Buglione, Smith, Lawrence
14/10/95	FA Trophy	Q1	Bashley	220	1-1	Manning
17/10/95	FA Trophy	Q1 rep	BASHLEY	157	1-2	Pilbeam
21/10/95	BHL	S	WEYMOUTH	206	2-1	Lawrence, Buglione
24/10/95	BHL	S	FISHER	195	2-2	Buglione(2)
28/10/95	BHL	S	Havant Town	131	0-2	
31/10/95	DMC	1(2)	SITTINGBOURNE	154	1-0	Buglione
04/11/95	BHL	S	Fisher	210	2-0	Pilbeam, Smith
07/11/95	Kent SC	1	Gravesend & Northfleet	241	1-2	Gubbins(og)
11/11/95	BHL	S	YATE TOWN	303	2-1	Dixon, Collinson
14/11/95	BHL	S	Ashford Town	499	0-2	
18/11/95	BHL	S	Braintree Town	153	0-3	
25/11/95	BHL	S	NEWPORT I.O.W.	255	2-2	Buglione, Smith
09/12/95	BHL	S	FLEET TOWN	200	3-1	Buglione(3)
12/12/95	DMC	2	Baldock Town	81	0-1	
16/12/95	BHL	S	Clevedon Town	185	4-1	Weatherly, Manning, Buglione, Harris
23/12/95	BHL	S	Bashley	142	0-3	
26/12/95	BHL	S	SITTINGBOURNE	506	1-2	Manning
30/12/95	BHL	S	WITNEY TOWN	256	1-1	Buglione
01/01/96	BHL	S	Tonbridge Angels	423	2-1	Manning, Buglione
06/01/96	BHL	S	POOLE TOWN	206	6-0	Buglione(2), Heritage(2), Smith, Manning
13/01/96	BHL	S	Waterlooville	168	4-0	Smith(2), Buglione(2)
20/01/96	BHL	S	Forest Green Rovers	174	1-3	Manning(og)
10/02/96	BHL	S	Fleet Town	174	4-0	Weatherley, Buglione, Harris(2)
11/02/96	BHL	S	Cinderford Town	310	1-3	Harris
17/02/96	BHL	S	WESTON-SUPER-MARE	238	1-0	Buglione
02/03/96	BHL	S	CLEVEDON TOWN	201	1-2	Harris
09/03/96	BHL	S	Yate Town	168	2-3	Buglione, Harris
16/03/96	BHL	S	BRAINTREE TOWN	184	0-1	
23/03/96	BHL	S	BASHLEY	206	2-1	Buglione(2)
30/03/96	BHL	S	Witney Town	147	2-3	Harris, Manning
06/04/96	BHL	S	TONBRIDGE ANGELS	325	2-2	Heritage, Harris
08/04/96	BHL	S	Sittingbourne	1085	1-3	Manning
13/04/96	BHL	S	Poole Town	112	2-1	Heritage, Buglione
20/04/96	BHL	S	TROWBRIDGE TOWN	229	1-0-	Dixon
21/04/96	BHL	S	FAREHAM TOWN	157	2-0	Buglione(2)
27/04/96	BHL	S	HAVANT TOWN	247	3-2	Buglione(2), Dwyer
30/04/96	BHL	S	Newport I.O.W.	254	0-1	
04/05/96	BHL	S	Fareham Town	116	1-2	Buglione

NEWPORT (I O W)

St George's Park, St George's Way, Newport, IOW PO30 SQH. Tel: 01983 525027

Secretary: C.Cheverton, 127 Westhill Rd, Ryde, IOW PO33 1LW Tel: 01983 567355

Nickname: The Port   Colours: Gold and Blue

Capacity: 5,000   Seating: 300

Covered standing: 1,000   Clubhouse on ground: Yes

Record attendance: 2,217 v Aylesbury Utd FA Cup 1995. At Church Litten 6,000 v Watford FA Cup 1st Round 1956

Biggest win: 14-1 v Thorneycroft Ath Hants League Dec 22nd 1945

Biggest defeat: 2-10 v Basingstoke Hants League Oct 22nd 1968

Record appearances: Jeff Austin 1969-87 540

Record goalscorer in one season: F. Harrison 1929-30 62

Record goalscorer in aggregate: R.Gilfillan 220 1951-57

Record fee paid: £3,000 for S.Ritchie from Bashley May 1991

DIRECTIONS

Roads from all ferry ports lead to Coppins Bridge R'about at eastern extremity of town. Take Swindon/Ventnor exit, proceed to small r-about, St George's way is first exit (straight on), ground immediately visible on the left. Five minute walk from Newport bus station: along Church Litten (past old ground), turn left then right a r-about.

HONOURS

Hampshire League: 1930, 33, 39, 48, 50, 53, 54, 57, 79, 80, 81; Hampshire Senior Cup: 1932, 33, 55, 61, 66, 80, 81; Russell Coates Cup:1978, 79, 80; Pickford Cup: 1948, 49, 50, 53; Isle of Wight Gold Cup: 1930, 36, 38, 40, 45, 46, 47, 49, 53, 54, 56, 58, 66, 68, 71, 72, 73, 74, 75, 76, 78, 79, 81, 87, 88, 90, 92, 93, 94, 96; Hampshire Floodlit Cup 1977 and 1978; Isle of Wight League: 1908, 09, 10, 24; Hampshire Intermediate Cup: 1932; Hampshire Combination Cup: 1939.

Manager for 1996/97: S.Mellor   **Assistant Manager: D.Wakefield**

Chairman: M. Edwards   **Vice Chairman: P. Ranger**

The club's Centenary Book, published in 1988 is still available, from club, cost £3+ p+p

The modern Newport (IOW) Football Club, with its well appointed St George's Park facilities, presents a different picture from that conjured up by the club's origins on January 27th, 1888. The actual date can be established from the original minute book which is still in the club's possession. At that time Newport played on a piece of land known as Well's Field, which later became known as Church Litten. Those early days meant a walk from a local public house, where the players changed, to a field where they had to move the cows before play could commence. Newport became founder members of the Isle of Wight League in 1898 and were champions on four occasions, before becoming members of the Hampshire League in 1927, The club took over the fixtures of the defunct Gosport Albion as their record stood, in mid season, and within three years had won the title. The glory days of the 30's saw further success when the title was twice won again, with the Hampshire Cup won twice also.

Newport reached the 1st Round of the FA Cup for the second time in 1946, before losing to Aldershot. The Church Litten story continued through the next decade as Newport were champions five times as well as taking the Senior Cup again in 1955. It was a golden period for the club, but as the 60's came, then despite more Senior Cup victories, the post War period became just a memory, with the club struggling financially. It reached a crisis when the club were relegated in 1969 for the only time in their history. After regaining the Premiership place with an "all Wight" policy, the club began to prosper again, and the 70's went with the club back on the rails. A hat-trick of titles in 79, 80 and 81, two Senior Cups and a hat-trick of Russell Coates Cups all marked a purple patch for the club. In 1986 they became founder members of the Wessexs League and in 1990 they were promoted to the Southern League as runners up. By that time Church Litten had been sold for a supermarket and moved in to the brand new St George's Park, to coincide with the club Centenary. The facilities are widely admired and in the first six years they have established themselves ready for the next goal, the Premier Division.

NEWPORT (I O W) 1995/96 SEASON

Date	Comp	Round	Opponent	Att	Score	Scorers
19/08/95	BHL	S	WITNEY TOWN	273	0-0	
23/08/95	BHL	S	Poole Town	101	5-0	Leader, Fear(2), Puckett(2)
26/08/95	BHL	S	BRAINTREE TOWN	331	3-0	Hughes, Soares, Fearon
28/08/95	BHL	S	FLEET TOWN	283	1-0	Soares
02/09/95	BHL	S	Erith & Belvedere	119	4-2	Wickens(2), Tagoe(og), Barsdell
05/09/95	BHL	S	FAREHAM TOWN	420	1-0	Soares
09/09/95	FA Cup	Q1	Abingdon Town	168	3-2	Gee, Leader, Wickens
16/09/95	BHL	S	Ashford Town	412	2-4	Fearon, Soares
19/09/95	BHL	S	POOLE TOWN	387	1-0	Puckett
23/09/95	FA Cup	Q2	Salisbury City	412	3-1	Gee, Puckett, Ritchie
30/09/95	BHL	S	Havant Town	261	5-0	Fearon(3), Barsdell(2)
04/10/95	DMC	1(1)	Waterlooville	186	1-0	Barsdell
07/10/95	FA Cup	Q3	Thame United	308	1-1	Fearon
10/10/95	FA Cup	Q3 rep	THAME UNITED	863	3-1	Leader, Bartlett, Soares
14/10/95	FA Trophy	Q1	CHESHAM UNITED	463	1-3	Puckett
17/10/95	Hants SC	2	Gosport Borough	58	5-1	Phillips(2), Fearon(2), Soares
21/10/95	FA Cup	Q4	BASHLEY	1061	1-1	Ritchie
24/10/95	FA Cup	Q4 rep	Bashley	558	3-2	Fearon, Gee, Ritchie
28/10/95	BHL	S	Yate Town	141	0-3	
31/10/95	DMC	1(2)	WATERLOOVILLE	203	1-3	Gee
04/11/95	BHL	S	FOREST GREEN ROVERS	316	0-1	
11/11/95	FA Cup	1	ENFIELD	1818	1-1	Fearon
18/11/95	BHL	S	WATERLOOVILLE	365	2-1	Fearon, K.Hugnes
21/11/95	FA Cup	1 rep	Enfield	2034	1-2	Leader
25/11/95	BHL	S	Margate	255	2-2	Francis(og), Fearon
02/12/95	BHL	S	ASHFORD TOWN	341	2-1	Puckett(2)
06/12/95	BHL	S	Fareham Town	84	7-2	Wickens(2), Puckett(2), Male, Fearon, Wilson(og)
09/12/95	BHL	S	CLEVEDON TOWN	345	3-1	Barsdell, Fearon(2)
12/12/95	Hants SC	3	Bashley	69	0-1	
16/12/95	BHL	S	Cinderford Town	211	2-2	Puckett, Fearon
19/12/95	BHL	S	Fleet Town	107	1-1	Leader
23/12/95	BHL	S	Sittingbourne	675	2-1	Male, Gee
26/12/95	BHL	S	BASHLEY	464	1-1	Gee
30/12/95	BHL	S	TROWBRIDGE TOWN	421	1-3	Fearon
01/01/96	BHL	S	Weymouth	970	1-2	Puckett
06/01/96	BHL	S	Weston-super-Mare	250	0-5	
13/01/96	BHL	S	FISHER	323	4-2	Soares, Puckett, Leader, Fearon
20/01/96	BHL	S	Braintree Town	162	2-1	Fearon, Puckett
30/01/96	IOW SC	QF	WESTLAND AEROSPACE	118	4-1	Wickins(2), Puckett, Soares
10/02/96	BHL	S	HAVANT TOWN	461	0-2	
17/02/96	BHL	S	Clevedon Town	216	3-5	Gee(2), Fearon
27/02/96	BHL	S	Tonbridge Angels	313	2-1	Leader, Fearon
02/03/96	BHL	S	WESTON-SUPER-MARE	309	0-3	
05/03/96	BHL	S	Forest Green Rovers	156	2-5	Leader, Barsdell
09/03/96	BHL	S	Witney Town	130	0-2	
13/03/96	IOW SC	SF	Ryde Sports	275	3-2	Fearon, Male, Puckett
16/03/96	BHL	S	YATE TOWN	251	1-0	Webb
23/03/96	BHL	S	SITTINGBOURNE	385	3-1	Fearon, Barsdell, Puckett
30/03/96	BHL	S	Trowbridge Town	241	2-0	Hughes, Barsdell
03/04/96	BHL	S	ERITH & BELVEDERE	283	1-0	Williams
06/04/96	BHL	S	WEYMOUTH	438	2-0	Soares, Fearon
08/04/96	BHL	S	Bashley	224	1-0	Puckett
13/04/96	BHL	S	Waterlooville	393	1-1	Wollen
20/04/96	BHL	S	CINDERFORD TOWN	369	1-3	Fearon
25/04/96	IOW SC	F	EAST COWES VICTORIA ATH		5-3	
27/04/96	BHL	S	TONBRIDGE ANGELS	290	2-0	Fearon(2)
30/04/96	BHL	S	MARGATE	254	1-0	Gee
04/05/96	BHL	S	Fisher	193	1-0	Gee

ST LEONARDS STAMCROFT

The Firs, Elphinstone Rd, Hastings, East Sussex. Tel: 01424 434755

Secretary: Wynne Mould, 142 Sedlescombe Gardens, St Leonards-on-Sea, East Sussex. Tel: 01424 420244

Commercial Manager: John Huggett

Colours: Blue and white,   Nickname: The Blues

Capacity: 2,500,   Seating: Yes

Covered standing: Yes, Clubhouse on ground Yes

Record attend 1 798 v Tiverton Town FA Vase 4th Rd 1995

Biggest win: 10-1 v Portfield Sussex County League 1993

Biggest defeat: 2-6 v Pagham RUR Charity Cup

Record appearances: Gary Cawkill

Record goalscorer in total: Dean Kewley

DIRECTIONS

Approach Hastings town centre on the A21 from north or A259 from east or west, ground is situated in Elphinstone Road.

HONOURS

Sussex County League 1996, Hastings Invitation Cup 1990

Hastings Intermediate Cup 1980, 1982, 1983, 1986, 1987, 1988

The club originated as a works team when in 1971 the employees of Sussex Turnery And Moulding Company started playing friendlies. In season 1971/72 they were admitted to the Eastbourne & Hastings Football League with the side progressing from Division 5 (East) to the Premier Division where they gained Intermediate status in 1977. In 1976, through auspices of the then club and company Chairman, Stamco F.C. had started playing on its own ground at Pannel Lane in Pett (a village between Hastings and Rye) Following ten years of success at local level, Stamco joined the Southern Counties Combination in 1982, winning the Division Two championship in their first season. After promotion there was a period of success taking the Championship in 1985/86, runners-up the following season and a second Championship in 1988. As a result promotion was gained to the Sussex County League .

At the end of 1991/92 the club narrowly missed promotion ending the season in third place albeit neither side above them was promoted due to inadequate ground facilities. However, in 1992/93 they achieved their goal of promotion to Division One ending the programme as runners-up, only missing out on the championship on the final day of the season. As a consequence of planning restrictions at Pannel Lane, its amenities were not sufficient for promotion, therefore, a long term lease was purchased on "The Firs", the former home of Hastings Town F.C. until they moved next door to the Pilot Field. During the summer of 1993 the laying of a new pitch, installing floodlights and upgrading of the facilities enable Stamco to take their place in Division One for season 1993/94.

The club enjoyed a memorable season in 1994/95 when they ended as runners-up to champions Peacehaven: they also lost 0-1 to Peacehaven in the final of the Sussex R.U.R. Charity Cup. They again received national attention when reaching the last sixteen in the F.A. Vase in their first season of entry: During that Vase run attracted a gate of 1,798 for the 4th round tie with Tiverton Town in one of the most exciting games in Sussex in recent years. The past season was once again successful with Stamco, justifying their position as one of the favourites to take the championship albeit they again finished as runners-up to Peacehaven despite having amassed more points than the previous season's winners. When the top two sides met at The Firs, the champions suffered their only league defeat of the season before a crowd of 1,033.

During the course of the season a sponsorship deal was negotiated with local company Croft Glass and as a result owner Mark Gardiner joined the Club as Chief Executive. At the end of the season that sponsorship deal was extended for a further three years and in recognition of their support their title was incorporated when the club name was changed to reflect its geographical location. With the support of both Croft Glass and Stamco Timber the club was able to carry out the works necessary to meet the Southern League ground criteria for season 1996/97.

ST LEONARDS STAMCROFT 1995/96 SEASON

Date	Competition		Opponent	Att	Score	Scorers
12/08/95	USCL	1	MILE OAK	157	4-2	Scott, Gilligan(3)
16/08/95	USCL	1	HAILSHAM TOWN	384	4-0	Clee(2), Miles(2)
19/08/95	USCL	1	ARUNDEL	238	6-0	Miles(2), Phillips(3), Ramsey
22/08/95	USCL	1	Southwick	105	2-0	Millard(2)
26/08/95	FA Cup	P	Corinthian-Casuals	104	0-3	
30/08/95	USCL	1	RINGMER	329	2-5	Miles, Phillips
02/09/95	USCL	1	Pagham	80	3-4	Miles, Phillips(2)
09/09/95	USCL	1	BURGESS HILL TOWN	223	5-1	Callingham(3), Miles(2)
12/09/95	USCL	1	Crowborough Athletic	78	4-1	Miles, Callingham, Trusson, Phillips
16/09/95	USCL	1	Horsham Y.M.C.A.	106	2-1	Miles, Sallows
20/09/95	USCL	1	OAKWOOD	229	4-0	Gilligan, Callingham(2), Miles
23/09/95	Sussex RUR	1	LANGNEY SPORTS	302	3-1	Willard, Miles, Phillips
30/09/95	USCL	1	Whitehawk	70	1-2	Miles
07/10/95	USCL	1	EASTBOURNE TOWN	240	9-0	Willard(4), Miles(3), Farrier, Own-Goal
14/10/95	USCL	1	Wick	201	1-1	Willard
17/10/95	USCL	1	Hassocks	166	2-1	Miles, Gilligan
21/10/95	LC	2	Saltdean United	112	4-2	Miles(2), Heritage(2)
28/10/95	FA Vase	1	GODALMING & GUILDFORD	485	1-2	Miles
04/11/95	Sussex RUR	2	PEACEHAVEN & TELSCOMBE	287	0-1	
11/11/95	USCL	1	Portfield	53	4-2	Willard, Gatting, Callingham, Miles
15/11/95	USCL	1	Hailsham Town	395	3-1	Callingham, Miles(2)
18/11/95	USCL	1	HASSOCKS	276	6-0	Miles(4), Callingham, Willard
25/11/95	Sussex SC	2	THREE BRIDGES	270	4-0	Miles(3), Farrier
29/11/95	Hastings S	SF	HASTINGS TOWN	240	5-3	Miles(2), Willard(2), Gatting
02/12/95	USCL	1	SOUTHWICK	335	7-0	Miles(2), McDermott(2), Jones, Willard, Sallows
13/12/95	USCL	1	Mile Oak	70	5-0	Tiltman, Heritage(3), Chivers
16/12/95	USCL	1	WHITEHAWK	220	3-1	Willard(2), Phillips
03/01/96	USCL	1	CROWBOROUGH ATHLETIC	228	4-1	Tiltman, Miles(2), Jones
06/01/96	USCL	1	HORSHAM Y.M.C.A.	285	9-0	Tiltman(2), Phillips(2), Ruddy(2),| Miles, Callingham, McDerm
09/01/96	Sussex SC	3	Hastings Town	1418	1-2	Willard
20/01/96	LC	3	Wick	193	2-1	Miles, Millard
03/02/96	USCL	1	Eastbourne Town	312	2-1	Farrier(2)
10/02/96	USCL	1	THREE BRIDGES	228	6-2	Miles(2), Willard(2), Trusson, Own-Goal
17/02/96	LC	QF	Shoreham	145	0-1	
03/03/96	USCL	1	Peacehaven & Telscombe	804	0-2	
09/03/96	USCL	1	WICK	290	4-1	Miles(2), Gatting, Ashworth
12/03/96	USCL	1	Burgess Hill Town	139	1-2	Miles
17/03/96	USCL	1	Shoreham	229	1-1	Flower(og)
23/03/96	USCL	1	PAGHAM	315	4-0	Farrier(2), Ruddy, Gatting
30/03/96	USCL	1	Ringmer	189	1-0	Willard
06/04/96	USCL	1	Three Bridges	222	4-0	Boxall(2), Miles, Farrier
10/04/96	USCL	1	LANGNEY SPORTS	369	3-1	Trusson, Hall, Miles
14/04/96	USCL	1	PEACEHAVEN & TELSCOMBE	1033	2-1	Callingham, Miles
17/04/96	Hastings S	F	Bexhill Town	217	1-1	Boxall
20/04/96	USCL	1	Arundel	145	1-0	Miles
28/04/96	USCL	1	SHOREHAM	485	1-3	Miles
30/04/96	USCL	1	Oakwood	76	8-0	Miles(4), Own-Goal, Boxall(3)
04/05/96	USCL	1	PORTFIELD	219	1-1	Miles
06/05/96	USCL	1	Langney Sports	425	1-0	Ruddy

TONBRIDGE ANGELS

Longmead Stadium, Darenth Avenue, Tonbridge TN10 3JW. Tel: 01732 352417

Secretary: Ken Jarrett, 8 Faraday Ride, Tonbridge TN10 4RL Tel: 01732 351856

Press officer:
S. Piper, 11 Arundel Close, Tonbridge TN9 3UG

Colours: Blue and White

Nickname: Angels

Capacity: 2,500

Seating: 200

Covered standing: 200

Clubhouse on ground: Yes

DIRECTIONS

From Tonbridge BR station, through Hill Street, north up Shipbourne Rd (A2257 Gravesend Road) to 2nd mini-r'bout ('The Pinnacles' pub), left into Darenth Avenue, ground at bottom approx. 1 mile at far side of sports ground car park.

Record attendance: at Longmead 1,483 v Yeovil Town FA Cup 4th qual 1992; at the Angel 8,236 v Aldershot FA Cup 1st Rd 1951

Biggest win: 11-1 v Worthing FA Cup 2nd Qual Rd 1951

Biggest defeat: 2-11 v Folkestone Kent Sen Cup 1949

Record appearances: Mark Gillham 500+

Record goalscorer in one season: Kevin McCurley 40 in 1961-62

Record goalscorer in aggregate: Jimmy Constantine

Record fee received: £4,500 Marcel Gaillard to Portsmouth Feb 1951

HONOURS

Kent Senior Cup 1966 and 1976; Kent Senior Shield 1952, 1956, 1958; Metropolitan League 1953; Professional Cup 1952, 1953, 1957; Kent Floodlit Cup 1964, 1967; Kent League 1993; Kent League Div 1 Cup 1990, 1992; Kent League Div 2 Cup 1993; Charity Shield 1994.

Manager for 1996/97: Bill Roffey

Chairman: Nigel Rimmer

Tonbridge FC, the forerunners of today's club, was formed in 1948 after much discussion and local controversy. They went straight into the Southern League and played the first game on August 21st against Hastings at the old Angel ground. Early success did not come until 1950 when the club reached the First Road of the FA Cup and soon added the Kent Senior Shield and Metropolitan Cup.

The club drew with Aldershot in 1951 which created the ground record of 8,236 and a year later they drew with high flying Norwich City.

In 1975, whilst managed by England World Cup star George Cohen, they won the Senior Cup but sadly went into voluntary liquidation and from the ashes came Tonbridge AFC and they finished the fixtures despite knowing they were to be relegated. At the end of the 70's the landlords, the local council threw the club out after a long wrangle and the Angel Ground, which had staged football and county cricket, was developed. The Angels took their stand with them and moved to a new ground, after playing the final match at the Angel on January 21st 1980. Longmead was ready in August 1980 having been transformed from fields in a matter of months. 1989 saw the club celebrate its 40th birthday, but a disastrous season ended in relegation to the Kent League. Although winning the League Cup twice it took the Angels until 1993 to return to the Southern League.

TONBRIDGE ANGELS 1995/96 SEASON

Date	Comp	Rnd	Opponent	Att	Score	Scorers
19/08/95	BHL	S	Fareham Town	163	3-3	Jarvis, Freeman(2)
22/08/95	BHL	S	BRAINTREE TOWN	472	1-0	Tingley
26/08/95	FA Cup	P	CROYDON ATHLETIC	487	3-1	Mawson(3)
28/08/95	BHL	S	Sittingbourne	749	1-3	Emblen
02/09/95	BHL	S	TROWBRIDGE TOWN	388	3-1	Wilkins(3)
05/09/95	BHL	S	Fleet Town	150	1-1	Coleman
09/09/95	FA Cup	Q1	Ashford Town	732	0-2	
16/09/95	BHL	S	WESTON-SUPER-MARE	416	3-2	Wilkins(2), Forster
19/09/95	BHL	S	Braintree Town	160	2-5	Freeman, Wilkins
23/09/95	BHL	S	Bashley	304	2-0	Emblen, Freeman
30/09/95	BHL	S	Clevedon Town	256	2-0	Wilkins, Forster
03/10/95	DMC	1(1)	ASHFORD TOWN	408	5-3	Mawson, Forster(4)
07/10/95	BHL	S	HAVANT TOWN	482	1-1	Mawson
10/10/95	BHL	S	FISHER	429	1-1	Overton
14/10/95	FA Trophy	Q1	Weymouth	714	0-4	
21/10/95	BHL	S	Waterlooville	205	1-4	Forster
24/10/95	BHL	S	SITTINGBOURNE	588	1-4	Tutton
28/10/95	BHL	S	Forest Green Rovers	172	0-3	
31/10/95	DMC	1(2)	Ashford Town	440	1-1	Forster
07/11/95	Kent SC	1	FISHER	266	1-2	Wilkins
14/11/95	BHL	S	FLEET TOWN	316	1-2	Tingley
18/11/95	BHL	S	WEYMOUTH	356	0-1	
25/11/95	BHL	S	Weston-super-Mare	210	0-2	
02/12/95	BHL	S	WATERLOOVILLE	385	2-2	Forster, Watkins
09/12/95	BHL	S	Fisher	212	3-0	Tingley, Clarke, Mawson
12/12/95	DMC	2	FISHER	192	3-0	Forster(2), Mawson
16/12/95	BHL	S	FAREHAM TOWN	300	1-8	Booth
01/01/96	BHL	S	MARGATE	423	1-2	Wickens(og)
06/01/96	BHL	S	WITNEY TOWN	342	0-0	
16/01/96	DMC	3	Crawley Town	289	0-3	
20/01/96	BHL	S	Havant Town	132	1-4	Mawson
03/02/96	BHL	S	CINDERFORD TOWN	346	0-3	
17/02/96	BHL	S	ERITH & BELVEDERE	379	1-0	Mawson
27/02/96	BHL	S	NEWPORT I.O.W.	313	1-2	Freeman
02/03/96	BHL	S	Erith & Belvedere	167	1-0	Freeman
05/03/96	BHL	S	Trowbridge Town	223	1-1	Mawson
09/03/96	BHL	S	BASHLEY	402	2-3	Forster, Mawson
16/03/96	BHL	S	Weymouth	691	2-1	Wilks, Freeman
19/03/96	BHL	S	Witney Town	89	1-1	Wilkins
23/03/96	BHL	S	Poole Town	140	1-0	Emblen
30/03/96	BHL	S	YATE TOWN	346	3-4	Wilkins, Mawson, Forster
02/04/96	BHL	S	POOLE TOWN	338	5-0	Forster, Wilkins(2), Mawson, Emblen
06/04/96	BHL	S	Margate	325	2-2	Emblen, Freeman
08/04/96	BHL	S	ASHFORD TOWN	761	2-1	Forster, Brenton
13/04/96	BHL	S	FOREST GREEN ROVERS	423	2-3	Wilkins, A Lemoinr
18/04/96	BHL	S	Yate Town	108	0-4	
27/04/96	BHL	S	Newport I.O.W.	290	0-2	
30/04/96	BHL	S	Ashford Town	1036	0-0	
02/05/96	BHL	S	Cinderford Town	137	2-1	Emblen, Watkins
04/05/96	BHL	S	CLEVEDON TOWN	419	1-2	Emblen

TROWBRIDGE TOWN

Frome Road Ground, County Way, Trowbridge, Wilts BA14 0DB. Tel: 01225 752076

Secretary: Colin Elliott, 40 Eastbourne Rd, Trowbridge, Wiltshire, BA14 7KW Tel: 01225 760619

Press officer: Andrew Meadon, C/O Presto Print, Wicker Hill, Trowbridge. Tel: 01225 760565 FAX: 01225 766953

Nickname: The Bees   Capacity: 5,000

Seating: 200   Covered standing: 3,000

Clubhouse on ground: Yes

DIRECTIONS

On entering town, follow inner relief road (County Way) signs towards Frome, ground on left 100 yds past Ship Inn near Bradley Road roundabout. Ground on right if entering from Frome.

Record attendance: 9,009 v Weymouth FA Cup 4th Qual Rd 1949

Biggest win: 17-1 v Yeovil and Petters FC

Biggest defeat: 0-10 v Barnet

Record fee paid or received: £10,000 for Paul Compton (Bournemouth) and Andy Feeley (Leicester City)

HONOURS

Western League 1928, 1930, 1939, 1940, 1947, 1948, 1956; Wiltshire League Div 2: 1912 and 1931; Trowbridge and District League: 1910, 1911, 1920; Wiltshire Senior Cup: 1885, 1896, 1898, 1922, 1926, 193, 1938; Wiltshire Professional Shield: 1946, 1947, 1950, 1969, 1970, 1973, 1993, 1994; Wiltshire Floodlit League Cup: 1992, 1993, 1994; Bristol Charity Cup: 1926; Wiltshire Junior Cup: 1911 and 1913; Trowbridge and District Junior Cup: 1920; Allen Palmer Cup: 924 and 1925; Swanborough Cup: 1934, 1935, 1936; Somerset Senior League: 1931; Western Counties Floodlit League Cup: 1981 and 1986; Coronation Cup: 1993.

Manager for 1996/97: Steve Rutter   **Chairman: Tony Moore**   **Vice Chairman: Chris Belcher**

Trowbridge Town were formed in 1880 by a group of local sportsmen, making them one of the oldest clubs in the south-west, and in 1892 they were founder members of the Western League. There was little of note during the early years until 1912 when Town won the Wiltshire League, Somerset Senior League and Wiltshire Cup in one season. The club's most significant move was in the 1930's when they turned professional, winning the Western League four times either side of the War, finishing second in four other seasons. They remained in that league until 1958 when they were elected to the Southern League, alternating between divisions until 1980 when under Alan Birchenall, the former Charlton, Leicester and England man, they finished 3rd, gaining promotion to the newly formed Alliance Premier League.

They lasted three years before successive relegations saw them back in the Southern Division. A disastrous fire which destroyed the main grandstand in 1985 seemed to herald a run of poor seasons which ended when John Murphy guided the club back to the Premier Division, where they remained until suffering relegation again last year.

The Bees began playing on a pitch at the top of Timbrell Street which was later covered by the County Ground, before moving to Wingfield Road, where John O'Gaunt School is now. The move was not popular and so three years later the Flower Show Field was used. What is now Stallards Rec was also used for Fetes and Funfairs, which again proved unpopular, but they remained until 1923 when they moved to a ground in Bythesea Road, which had banking on three sides and a splendidly ornate wooden stand.

Sadly the council coveted the land and ten years from opening, it was gone to make room for the new County Hall. The stand was transported to Frome Road where it remained until the dreadful fire, which left a chasm which has never been filled.

Trowbridge Town are still hopeful of selling their ground and moving on, but so far have been held up by higher forces.

TROWBRIDGE TOWN 1995/96 SEASON

Date	Comp	Rnd	Opponent	Att	Score	Scorers
19/08/95	BHL	S	MARGATE	294	3-1	Mitchell, Benbow, Cork(og)
23/08/95	BHL	S	Forest Green Rovers	263	2-2	James, Lush
28/08/95	BHL	S	CINDERFORD TOWN	350	2-3	Mitchell, Taylor
02/09/95	BHL	S	Tonbridge Angels	388	1-3	Cole
05/09/95	BHL	S	Clevedon Town	292	3-1	Bowker(og), Ferns(2)
09/09/95	FA Cup	Q1	GOSPORT BOROUGH	282	8-1	James, Thorpe, Ferns, Benbow, Cole, Lush, Watts, Rutter
16/09/95	BHL	S	FAREHAM TOWN	321	5-0	Mitchell(2), Ferns, Anstice(og), James
19/09/95	BHL	S	FOREST GREEN ROVERS	306	2-0	Thorpe, Evans
23/09/95	FA Cup	Q2	Welton Rovers	374	2-1	Mitchell, James
30/09/95	BHL	S	Ashford Town	490	0-1	
03/10/95	DMC	1(1)	YATE TOWN	206	4-1	Benbow, Evans, James, Mitchell
07/10/95	FA Cup	Q3	NEWPORT A.F.C.	623	2-0	Mitchell(2)
10/10/95	Wilts PS	1	Devizes Town	151	2-0	Ferns, Lunt
14/10/95	FA Trophy	Q1	Bury Town	170	2-1	Benbow, James
18/10/95	DMC	1(2)	Yate Town	120	0-2	
21/10/95	FA Cup	Q4	Kingstonian	781	1-3	Benbow
28/10/95	BHL	S	FLEET TOWN	303	4-0	Mitchell, Ferns, Benbow, Evans
04/11/95	FA Trophy	Q2	BISHOP'S STORTFORD	361	1-0	Benbow
11/11/95	BHL	S	WITNEY TOWN	322	0-1	
18/11/95	BHL	S	Fareham Town	157	3-0	Benbow, Own-Goal, Ferns
21/11/95	BHL	S	CLEVEDON TOWN	262	1-1	Mitchell
25/11/95	FA Trophy	Q3	Sutton United	612	1-0	Cole
02/12/95	BHL	S	ERITH & BELVEDERE	341	4-0	Evans, Benbow, Lush, Ferns
05/12/95	DMC	2	Bashley	93	1-1	Conning
09/12/95	BHL	S	Waterlooville	241	2-1	Fishlock, Benbow
16/12/95	BHL	S	FISHER	275	1-1	Cole
23/12/95	BHL	S	HAVANT TOWN	248	0-0	
30/12/95	BHL	S	Newport I.O.W.	421	3-1	Mitchell, Thorpe, Taylor
01/01/96	BHL	S	WESTON-SUPER-MARE	437	1-0	Mitchell
04/01/96	Wilts PS	QF	Melksham Town	320	3-0	Mitchell, Taylor, Culling
06/01/96	BHL	S	Fisher	182	2-1	Rutter, Cole
09/01/96	DMC	2 rep	BASHLEY	137	2-1	Conning, Cole
13/01/96	BHL	S	BRAINTREE TOWN	363	1-5	Mitchell
16/01/96	BHL	S	SITTINGBOURNE	243	3-0	Mitchell(2), Benbow
20/01/96	FA Trophy	1	SUDBURY TOWN	319	2-2	Mitchell, Ferns
23/01/96	FA Trophy	1 rep	Sudbury Town	224	1-1	Lunt
03/02/96	BHL	S	Sittingbourne	629	1-2	Barfoot
05/02/96	FA Trophy	1 rep(2)	SUDBURY TOWN	327	1-1	Rolph(og)
10/02/96	FA Trophy	1 rep(3)	Sudbury Town	368	3-4	Benbow, Stafford(og), Evans
13/02/96	DMC	3	SALISBURY CITY	303	1-1	Evans
17/02/96	BHL	S	Witney Town	213	1-2	Mitchell
21/02/96	DMC	3 rep	Salisbury City	238	1-2	James
24/02/96	BHL	S	BASHLEY	311	5-2	Taylor(3), Lunt, Mitchell
28/02/96	BHL	S	Cinderford Town	190	0-2	
02/03/96	BHL	S	Weymouth	988	1-0	Barfoot
05/03/96	BHL	S	TONBRIDGE ANGELS	223	1-1	Taylor
09/03/96	BHL	S	ASHFORD TOWN	346	1-1	Conning
12/03/96	BHL	S	Braintree Town	152	0-1	
17/03/96	BHL	S	Bashley	215	1-1	Thorpe
23/03/96	BHL	S	Havant Town	209	0-2	
27/03/96	Wilts PS	SF	Salisbury City	168	1-2	Coles
30/03/96	BHL	S	NEWPORT I.O.W.	241	0-2	
06/04/96	BHL	S	Weston-super-Mare	335	5-1	Mitchell, Ferns, Taylor(2), Tagg
08/04/96	BHL	S	YATE TOWN	299	2-2	Mitchell, Cole
10/04/96	BHL	S	Poole Town	105	8-0	Mitchell(4), Tagg, Towler(2), Benbow
13/04/96	BHL	S	WEYMOUTH	342	1-2	Mitchell
16/04/96	BHL	S	WATERLOOVILLE	205	0-2	
20/04/96	BHL	S	Margate	229	0-1	
24/04/96	BHL	S	Yate Town	149	1-2	James
27/04/96	BHL	S	POOLE TOWN	305	9-1	Pearson, Benbow(2), Mitchell(5), Cole
30/04/96	BHL	S	Fleet Town	178	1-2	Mitchell
04/05/96	BHL	S	Erith & Belvedere	157	5-0	Mitchell(4), Cole

WATERLOOVILLE

Jubilee Park, Aston Rd, Waterlooville, PO7 7SZ. Tel: 01705 263867 (Fax) 230732 (Office) 230114

Secretary: Peter Elley, 139 Chichester Rd, North End, Portsmouth PO2 OAQ Tel 01705 665885

Colours: White and navy

Nickname: The Ville

Capacity: 7,000

Seating: 480

Covered standing: 1,500

Clubhouse on ground: Yes

DIRECTIONS

Directions: Turn right off town bypass (B2150) at Asda r'bout. Dual carriage to next island, and return back towards town (ground signposted). Aston Road is first left. Nearest stations; Havant (4 miles), Cosham (5).

Record attendance: 4,500 v Wycombe Wanderers FA Cup 1st Rd 1976

Record fee paid: £6,000 for Steve Tate from Havant in 1993

Record fee received: £6,000 for Dave Boyce to Gravesend and Northfleet in 1993

HONOURS

Southern League Div 1 South 1972

League Cup 1987

Hampshire League Div 2 1960 and 1965

Hampshire Senior Cup 1970, 1973, 1985

Russell Coates Cup 1989

Portsmouth League 1950, 1951, 1952 Div 2 1947, Div 3 1939

Portsmouth Senior Cup 1969 and Portsmouth Victory Cup 1960 and 1970

Waterlooville were formed in October 1902 and began playing on Hart Plain Park in the Waterlooville and District League until moving in 1910 to Stakes Road, former home of Purbrook FC. Some time later they moved in with the Cricket Club until returning to Stakes Road. In 1927 they shared one last year at the cricket ground whilst the new Recreation Ground in Jubilee Road was laid out.

During the next 29 years they rose to the Hampshire League via the Portsmouth League, and during the 60's won promotions as well as the Senior Cup.

In that time the club bought some land a few hundred yards away and after three years of toil and sweat they opened Jubilee Park in September 1957.

Ville were elected to the Southern League in 1971 and opened the 560 seater main stand as well as laying concrete terracing all round the ground, and on the pitch won the title at the first attempt whilst acting as Portsmouth FC's nursery side. They reached the League Cup final twice and were promoted in 1988.

Since then Ville find themselves in the Southern Division again, and last May just missed out on promotion.

WATERLOOVILLE 1995/96 SEASON

Date	Competition	Round	Opponent	Att	Score	Scorers
19/08/95	BHL	S	FOREST GREEN ROVERS	205	1-2	Barnes
22/08/95	BHL	S	Bashley	230	2-2	Thomas, Selby
26/08/95	BHL	S	Margate	244	1-0	Tait
28/08/95	BHL	S	ERITH & BELVEDERE	196	6-0	Selby(3), Murphy, Gilbert, Hore
02/09/95	BHL	S	CLEVEDON TOWN	223	2-1	Hore, James
09/09/95	FA Cup	Q1	CALNE TOWN	223	5-0	Gilbert, Tate, Milkins, Hore, Thomas
16/09/95	BHL	S	BRAINTREE TOWN	236	3-0	Murphy, Tait, Hore
19/09/95	BHL	S	BASHLEY	250	2-2	Hore, Tate
23/09/95	FA Cup	Q2	Weymouth	754	0-1	
30/09/95	BHL	S	Fareham Town	210	3-0	Tate(2), Thomas
04/10/95	DMC	1(1)	NEWPORT I.O.W.	186	0-1	
07/10/95	BHL	S	YATE TOWN	201	1-1	Selby
14/10/95	FA Trophy	Q1	Hendon	179	2-2	Selby(2)
17/10/95	FA Trophy	Q1 rep	HENDON	110	0-1	
21/10/95	BHL	S	TONBRIDGE ANGELS	205	4-1	Murphy, Hore, Thomas, Tate
24/10/95	Hants SC	2	RYDE SPORTS	90	4-0	Murphy, Ingman, Tate, Hore
28/10/95	BHL	S	Sittingbourne	701	2-1	Tate(2)
31/10/95	DMC	1(2)	Newport I.O.W.	203	3-1	Selby, Thomas, Hore
04/11/95	BHL	S	WITNEY TOWN	280	3-2	Tate, Hore, James
07/11/95	BHL	S	Erith & Belvedere	73	3-1	Hore, James, Daley(og)
11/11/95	BHL	S	Weymouth	581	1-2	Thomas
14/11/95	BHL	S	POOLE TOWN	82	8-1	Murphy, Tate(2), Hore, James, Selby(3)
18/11/95	BHL	S	Newport I.O.W.	365	1-2	Tate
25/11/95	BHL	S	FAREHAM TOWN	302	1-0	Tate
02/12/95	BHL	S	Tonbridge Angels	385	2-2	Milkins, Tate
05/12/95	DMC	2	FLEET TOWN	88	4-0	Tate, Hore(2), Selby
09/12/95	BHL	S	TROWBRIDGE TOWN	241	1-2	Selby
12/12/95	Hants SC	3	FLEET TOWN	38	2-1	Selby, Gilbert
16/12/95	BHL	S	Witney Town	122	1-0	Thomas
23/12/95	BHL	S	CINDERFORD TOWN	179	3-0	Gilbert, Tate(2)
26/12/95	BHL	S	Havant Town	543	2-4	Thomas, Molineux
06/01/96	BHL	S	Fleet Town	204	3-0	Burns, Tate, Thomas
10/01/96	DMC	3	Newport A.F.C.	418	0-1	
13/01/96	BHL	S	MARGATE	168	0-4	
23/01/96	Hants SC	QF	ALDERSHOT TOWN	590	3-1	Selby, Parr(og), Milkins
10/02/96	BHL	S	Ashford Town	395	2-3	Milkins, Murphy
17/02/96	BHL	S	SITTINGBOURNE	276	1-0	Milkins
24/02/96	BHL	S	Yate Town	131	3-1	Tate(2), Hore
27/02/96	BHL	S	Weston-super-Mare	205	3-0	Llewellyn(og), Mould, Tate
02/03/96	BHL	S	FLEET TOWN	220	3-0	Tate(2), Milkins
05/03/96	BHL	S	FISHER	193	0-1	
13/03/96	Hants SC	SF	Bashley	275	1-0	Tate
16/03/96	BHL	S	Forest Green Rovers	206	3-0	Clark, Tate, Milkins
20/03/96	BHL	S	Poole Town	85	3-0	Thomas, James, Hore
23/03/96	BHL	S	Cinderford Town	264	4-0	Milkins, Murphy(2), Hore
30/03/96	BHL	S	WESTON-SUPER-MARE	151	3-1	Hore, Tate, Milkins
02/04/96	BHL	S	WEYMOUTH	322	1-0	Murphy
06/04/96	BHL	S	Fisher	209	0-3	
08/04/96	BHL	S	HAVANT TOWN	529	0-0	
13/04/96	BHL	S	NEWPORT I.O.W.	393	1-1	Gilbert
16/04/96	BHL	S	Trowbridge Town	205	2-0	Murphy, Milkins
20/04/96	BHL	S	Braintree Town	209	1-1	Murphy
23/04/96	Hants SC	F	Basingstoke Town	850	0-2	
27/04/96	BHL	S	Clevedon Town	238	0-2	
04/05/96	BHL	S	ASHFORD TOWN	266	1-1	Murphy

WESTON-SUPER-MARE

Woodspring Park, Winterstoke Road, Weston-Super-Mare BS23 2YG. Tel: 01934 621618

Secretary: Keith Refault c/o Football Club

Press officer: Phil Chant c/o Football Club

Nickname: The Seagulls   Capacity: 2, 500

Seating: 254   Covered standing: 400

Clubhouse on ground: Yes

Record attendance: 2,623 v Woking FA Cup 1st Rd Replay Nov 23rd 1993; and at Langford Road 2,500 v Bridgwater Town FA Cup 1st Rd Replay 1961

Biggest win: 11-0 v Paulton Rovers

Biggest defeat: 1-12 v Yeovil Town Res

Record appearances: Harry Thomas 740

Record goalscorer in one season: Matt Lazenby 43

Record goalscorer in aggregate: Matt Lazenby 180

DIRECTIONS

From the north: M5 junction 21, A370 into Weston until junction A371 on left (at Heron Pub). Take A371 over the railway bridge to roundabout, right-hand exit and follow to third roundabout, bear left for 100 yds - club on right.
From south: M5 junction 22, follow Weston signs for approx. 7 miles, right at the first roundabout by the hospital, left at next roundabout, ground is 1 mile on left.

Honours

Somerset Senior League Div 1 1988 and Div 3 1985 (reserves); Somerset Senior Cup 1924 and 1927; Western League 1992; League Cup 1977 and Merit Cup 1977 and 1978.

Manager for 1996/97: Len Ashurst   **Assistant Manager: John Relish**

Chairman: Paul Bliss   **Vice Chairman: Dennis Usher**

Club shop open every match day selling mugs, programmes, pens, scarfs, badges

The current Weston side were formed in 1948, but there have been other clubs in the town which reached prominence long before then. There was a Weston side in the Western League back in 1900 for a couple of years, and again for four years just before the Great War. They won the Somerset Senior Cup in 1924 and 1927.

After the Second War, Borough of Weston-Super-Mare FC joined the Western League again and were ever present from 1948 to 1992 when they won the league and were promoted to the Southern League, playing first in the Midland and then Southern Divisions.

The club have had three grounds to date, beginning at the Great Ground in Locking Road. This was situated opposite Macs Garage and is now covered by housing. It was home for just six years until required for development, whereby the club moved to Langford Road, to a site which was once an old clay pit. A ground was prepared for what they thought would be a year or two, but they stayed for 30, until it was sold and the owners evicted them in 1983. Some 13 years later the site is still there with part of the terracing, pitch posts and clubhouse foundations all just visible amongst the undergrowth and debris.

The club spent most of the 50's in the Western League Second Division, but the first taste of glory came in 1961 when a last minute goal by local rivals Bridgwater Town robbed them of an FA Cup 2nd Round tie with Crystal Palace. During the 70's Weston enjoyed a long spell with Kim Book in charge and his teams won the League Cup, were runners up in the League, and reached the final of the Goldliner Cup. The late 80's saw John Ellener take the club to a Western League title, two Cup finals and promotion to the Southern League. 1994 saw promotion missed by one point but the last two have been a disappointment on the field.

Off it however, Woodspring Park continues to develop, though still in its infancy.

WESTON-SUPER-MARE 1995/96 SEASON

Date	Comp	Round	Opponent	Att	Score	Scorers
19/08/95	BHL	S	Erith & Belvedere	108	0-0	
22/08/95	BHL	S	CINDERFORD TOWN	314	2-0	Willetts, Tapp
26/08/95	FA Cup	P	ST BLAZEY	180	7-0	McLoughlin(4), Cook, Tapp, Elson
28/08/95	BHL	S	Yate Town	301	1-2	Elson
02/09/95	BHL	S	FAREHAM TOWN	264	1-6	McLoughlin
05/09/95	BHL	S	FOREST GREEN ROVERS	240	0-3	
09/09/95	FA Cup	Q1	Falmouth Town	225	1-1	Elson
12/09/95	FA Cup	Q1 rep	FALMOUTH TOWN	250	5-0	Tapp(2), Willetts, McLoughlin, Elson
16/09/95	BHL	S	Tonbridge Angels	416	2-3	Willetts, Cook
19/09/95	BHL	S	Cinderford Town	209	1-1	Tapp
23/09/95	FA Cup	Q2	TIVERTON TOWN	701	1-1	Lindsay
27/09/95	FA Cup	Q2 rep	Tiverton Town	801	0-1	
30/09/95	BHL	S	Braintree Town	194	2-2	Tapp(2)
03/10/95	DMC	1(1)	CHELTENHAM TOWN	195	1-2	Cook
07/10/95	BHL	S	MARGATE	165	4-3	Lindsay, Wotton, Bowering, Stearnes
14/10/95	FA Trophy	Q1	BOGNOR REGIS TOWN	226	2-6	Dylan, Cook
17/10/95	DMC	1(2)	Cheltenham Town	211	2-4	Cook(2)
24/10/95	BHL	S	YATE TOWN	190	6-1	Cook(2), Bowering(2), Rollo(og), Ward
28/10/95	BHL	S	POOLE TOWN	225	7-0	Bowering(2), Penny, McLoughlin(2), Ward, Lindsay
04/11/95	BHL	S	Ashford Town	515	2-2	Bowering, Penny
14/11/95	Som. PC	2	CLEVEDON TOWN		2-2	Bowering(2)
18/11/95	BHL	S	FLEET TOWN	230	2-3	Bowering, McLoughlin
22/11/95	BHL	S	Forest Green Rovers	167	0-4	
25/11/95	BHL	S	TONBRIDGE ANGELS	210	2-0	Penny, Robison
02/12/95	BHL	S	Bashley	151	2-1	Penny, Tapp
09/12/95	BHL	S	ERITH & BELVEDERE	190	3-0	Llewellyn, Penny, Tapp
16/12/95	BHL	S	Poole Town	79	8-1	Holt, Cook(3), Llewellyn, Robison, Penny, Wootton
23/12/95	BHL	S	Weymouth	723	2-2	Llewellyn, Wootton
01/01/96	BHL	S	Trowbridge Town	437	0-1	
06/01/96	BHL	S	NEWPORT I.O.W.	250	5-0	Penny(2), Llewellyn, Tapp(2)
13/01/96	BHL	S	ASHFORD TOWN	249	1-1	Ward
20/01/96	BHL	S	WITNEY TOWN	240	2-2	Penny, Ward
03/02/96	BHL	S	Fareham Town	102	3-0	Tapp(2), McLoughlin
13/02/96	BHL	S	SITTINGBOURNE	220	1-2	Mehew
17/02/96	BHL	S	Margate	238	0-1	
27/02/96	BHL	S	WATERLOOVILLE	205	0-3	
02/03/96	BHL	S	Newport I.O.W.	309	3-0	Holt, Mehew, Tapp
05/03/96	Som. PC	QF	MANGOTSFIELD Utd	235	3-4	Penny(2), McLoughlin
09/03/96	BHL	S	Fisher	151	2-1	Tapp, Penny
13/03/96	BHL	S	Havant Town	71	0-3	
16/03/96	BHL	S	HAVANT TOWN	204	0-0	
20/03/96	BHL	S	Sittingbourne	554	0-2	
23/03/96	BHL	S	WEYMOUTH	325	1-1	Mehew
30/03/96	BHL	S	Waterlooville	151	1-3	McLoughlin
06/04/96	BHL	S	TROWBRIDGE TOWN	335	1-5	McLoughlin
08/04/96	BHL	S	Clevedon Town	441	2-1	Penny, Tapp
13/04/96	BHL	S	Witney Town	141	1-0	McLoughlin
16/04/96	BHL	S	CLEVEDON TOWN	310	3-2	Bowering, Cook(2)
20/04/96	BHL	S	FISHER	171	0-1	
25/04/96	BHL	S	BRAINTREE TOWN	190	2-3	Penny, Mehew
27/04/96	BHL	S	Fleet Town	255	1-2	Tapp
04/05/96	BHL	S	BASHLEY	217	2-0	White, Holt

WEYMOUTH

Wessex Stadium, Radipole Lane, Weymouth, Dorset DT4 OTJ. Tel: 01305 785558

Secretary: Terry Northover, 2 Stoke Road, Wyke Regis, Weymouth, Dorset DT4 9JF Tel 01305 771480

Colours: Claret and sky blue

Nickname: The Terras

Capacity: 10,000

Seating: 900

Covered standing: All sides

Clubhouse on ground: Yes

Record attendance: 4, 995 v Manchester Utd
Ground opening Oct 1987

Record appearances: Tony Hobson 1, 076

Record goalscorer in total: W.Farmer 275

DIRECTIONS

Directions: Arriving from Dorchester on A354, turn right following signs to Granby Industrial Estate at Safeway r'bout — ground on right as you enter estate.

HONOURS

Alliance League Cup 1982

Southern League 1965 and 1966

League Cup 1973

Western League 1923 and Division Two 1934 and 1937

Dorset Senior Cup 1895, 1899, 1900, 1903, 1920, 1923, 1924, 1928, 1932, 1934, 1937, 1948, 1950, 1952, 1954, 1955, 1956, 1957, 1958, 1965, 1985, 1986, 1987, 1991, 1993

Manager for 1996-97: Matthew McGowan.

Known as the Terras' from their original Terra Cotta and blue strip, they were founded in 1890. They began playing on a field in Lodmoor, where they stayed for three years before moving to Westham, changing at the Rock Hotel. They played in local Dorset football where they gained a fine reputation as one of the best amateur sides around and they were admitted to the Western League Division Two in 1907.

By then they had spent ten years on the Recreation Ground in Newstead Road which soon gained a couple of wooden stands with dressing rooms. Weymouth stayed in that league until 1923 when they took the championship, turned professional and joined the Southern League. By then the club had won the Dorset Senior Cup seven times and so a spell with no honours shook them and in 1928 they returned to the Western League. They won Division Two in 1934 and 1937 and were runners up in 1936 and 1938, but the Second World War brought their run to an end.

The ground was requisitioned for the War effort for eight years and in August 1947 with no assets the club was forced to start again in the Western League Division Two. Despite this they again joined the Southern League in 1948 and won the league in 1965 and 1966 under Frank O'Farrell. they had further success in League Cups and with runners up places but in 1987 with the council landlords having sold the Recreation Ground to a supermarket chain, they moved to a brand new stadium, almost on the site of the old Weymouth Speedway Stadium. It was from there that the club began their career in the Alliance Premier League, where they stayed for ten years before suffering relegation for the first time in their history.

Since then the Terras have had some bleak times and were again relegated to the Southern Division where they remain this season.

Date	Competition	Round	Opponent	Attendance	Score	Scorers
19/08/95	BHL	S	Braintree Town	177	1-2	Sheppard
22/08/95	BHL	S	HAVANT TOWN	709	1-2	Laws
26/08/95	FA Cup	P	Fareham Town	152	1-1	Laws
29/08/95	FA Cup	P rep	FAREHAM TOWN	807	3-2	Laws, Limbur, Shephard
02/09/95	BHL	S	SITTINGBOURNE	711	0-3	
05/09/95	BHL	S	Bashley	407	3-2	Housley, Shepperd, Campbell
09/09/95	FA Cup	Q1	Ryde Sports	250	1-1	Shepperd
12/09/95	FA Cup	Q1 rep	RYDE SPORTS	609	2-1	Shepperd(2)
16/09/95	BHL	S	MARGATE	615	2-0	Laws(2)
20/09/95	BHL	S	Havant Town	215	0-2	
23/09/95	FA Cup	Q2	WATERLOOVILLE	754	1-0	Laws
30/09/95	BHL	S	Cinderford Town	201	4-3	Laws(2), Shepherd, Browne
03/10/95	DMC	1(1)	Bashley	134	0-3	
07/10/95	FA Cup	Q3	DORCHESTER TOWN	2527	2-3	Bradford, Hutchinson
07/10/95	DMC	1(2)	BASHLEY	320	0-0	
14/10/95	FA Trophy	Q1	TONBRIDGE ANGELS	714	4-0	Shepherd, Laws(3)
21/10/95	BHL	S	Margate	206	1-2	Shepperd
24/10/95	BHL	S	CLEVEDON TOWN	520	2-4	Shepperd, Sherwood(og)
28/10/95	BHL	S	Fareham Town	161	1-1	Shepperd
31/10/95	Dorset	2	POOLE TOWN	310	5-1	Laws(2), Campbell, Browne, Shepperd
04/11/95	FA Trophy	Q2	Carshalton Athletic	379	1-5	Hutchinson
11/11/95	BHL	S	WATERLOOVILLE	581	2-1	Shepperd, Housley
18/11/95	BHL	S	Tonbridge Angels	356	1-0	Laws
25/11/95	BHL	S	CINDERFORD TOWN	620	2-0	Housley, Browne
28/11/95	Dorset	QF	DORCHESTER TOWN	987	0-2	
02/12/95	BHL	S	Witney Town	172	1-1	Housley
09/12/95	BHL	S	Forest Green Rovers	187	0-2	
16/12/95	BHL	S	BRAINTREE TOWN	547	5-1	Shepperd, Brown, Housley, Laws(2)
23/12/95	BHL	S	WESTON-SUPER-MARE	723	2-2	Housley, Flory
26/12/95	BHL	S	Poole Town	451	4-2	Bradford, Housley, Shepherd, Laws
01/01/96	BHL	S	NEWPORT I.O.W.	970	2-1	Housley, Smith
13/01/96	BHL	S	FLEET TOWN	727	2-1	Browne, Shepherd
20/01/96	BHL	S	YATE TOWN	656	1-0	Housley
03/02/96	BHL	S	Fisher	180	2-1	Laws, Blandford
10/02/96	BHL	S	WITNEY TOWN	714	1-0	Laws
13/02/96	BHL	S	BASHLEY	644	2-0	Housley, Laws
17/02/96	BHL	S	FAREHAM TOWN	786	2-1	Laws(2)
24/02/96	BHL	S	Fleet Town	379	1-0	Laws
27/02/96	BHL	S	Clevedon Town	254	3-2	Hutchinson(2), Laws
02/03/96	BHL	S	TROWBRIDGE TOWN	988	0-1	
09/03/96	BHL	S	Sittingbourne	805	1-2	Bradford
16/03/96	BHL	S	TONBRIDGE ANGELS	691	1-2	Hutchinson
19/03/96	BHL	S	Erith & Belvedere	71	4-3	Waldock, Limber, Brown, Laws
23/03/96	BHL	S	Weston-super-Mare	325	1-1	Limber
26/03/96	BHL	S	FISHER	524	2-0	Laws, Shepherd
30/03/96	BHL	S	ASHFORD TOWN	766	0-2	
02/04/96	BHL	S	Waterlooville	322	0-1	
06/04/96	BHL	S	Newport I.O.W.	438	0-2	
08/04/96	BHL	S	POOLE TOWN	744	6-0	Hutchinson, Waldock, Powell, Shepherd, Bradford, Stephens
13/04/96	BHL	S	Trowbridge Town	342	2-1	Smith, Hutchinson
16/04/96	BHL	S	Ashford Town	587	0-1	
20/04/96	BHL	S	ERITH & BELVEDERE	536	3-1	Powell(2), Shepherd
27/04/96	BHL	S	Yate Town	195	5-1	Laws(2), Hutchinson, Housley, Powell
04/05/96	BHL	S	FOREST GREEN ROVERS	645	2-1	Shepperd, Powell

WITNEY TOWN

Marriotts Stadium, Downs Rd, Curbridge, Witney, Oxon OX8 5LY. Tel: 01993 702549 or 705930

Secretary: Adrian Bircher, 13 Colwell Drive, Witney, Oxon OX8 7NJ. Tel: 01993 700634

Press officer: Jon Adaway, 25 The Fairway, Burnham, Nr Slough, SL1 8DS

Tel: 01628 603612 (h) 01753 676000 (b)

Colours: Yellow and blue

Nickname: The Town or the Blanketmen

Capacity: 3,500   Seating: 350

Covered standing: 2,000 on three sides

Clubhouse on ground: Yes

Record attendance: 3, 500 for ground opener v Aston Villa 1992

For competitive match: 544 v Salisbury FA Cup 4th Qual Rd 1992

At old ground 3,500 Nottingham Forest v West Bromwich Albion Trevor Stokes Benefit

Record appearances: Peter Hutter 405

Record goalscorer in one season: Kenny Clarke

Record goalscorer in total: Kenny Clarke 133

Record fee paid £ 3,000 for Steve Jenkins from Cheltenham Town

Record fee received £3,000 for John Bailey to Worcester City

DIRECTIONS

From West on A40; take B4047 at island past Burford, follow signs for Witney West & N.W. Industrial Estates, through Minster Lovell to West Witney, right into Downs Road, ground on right. From the East on A40, 2nd turn off to Witney and follow signs for South & S.W. Industrial Estates, right at roundabout to traffic lights, left and proceed to roundabout, straight over, signs to West Witney Industrial Estate, left at lights onto B4047, left into Downs Road, ground on right. Nearest BR station is Oxford 12 miles away.

HONOURS

Southern League Div 1 North 1978

Hellenic League 1955, 1958, 1965, 1966, 1967, 1971, 1972, 1973

League Cup 1957, 1964, 1965, 1970, 1972, 1973

Benevolent Cup 1960 and 1964

Oxfordshire Senior League 1929, 1930, 1932, 1952, 1953

Oxfordshire Senior Cup 1895, 1898, 1899, 1953, 1955, 1956, 1959, 1971 jt, 1973, 1995

Manager 1996-97: John Murphy

Assistant Manager: Bob Baird

Chairman: Brian Constable

Vice Chairman: Adrian Dunsby

Formed in 1885 as Witney FC they were almost immediately successful in local circles and within 15 years had won the Senior Cup three times. They played in the County Senior League, and in 1922 they re-formed as Witney Town FC and joined the Oxfordshire Senior League which they won a total of five times. Since the last War the club have steadily moved on, becoming founder members of the Hellenic League in 1953, reigning supreme for 20 years. They won it eight times and were runners up three times more, never once finishing lower then eighth.

The ambitious club joined the Southern League in 1973 and in 1978 won First Division North to gain promotion but, on reorganising following the founding of the Alliance, the club was placed in the Midland Section, gaining promotion when the league was again re-structured in 1982.

The Premier Division was tough and after escaping twice they went down in 1988. By 1992 the club's fortunes had taken another twist when they moved from Marriotts Close to a purpose built stadium in Downs Road, Curbridge. They developed financial difficulties but with a change of personnel they have been overcome and after two near misses for promotion they look forward to 1996-97.

WITNEY TOWN 1995/96 SEASON

13/08/95	Jim Newman	F	Lambourn Sports		1-2	
19/08/95	BHL	S	Newport I.O.W.	273	0-0	
22/08/95	BHL	S	FAREHAM TOWN	172	5-1	Caffel, Hutter(3), Hatswell
26/08/95	FA Cup	P	B.A.T. SPORTS	127	5-0	Nicholls, Hutter(2), Yates, Foster
28/08/95	BHL	S	Forest Green Rovers	215	0-0	
02/09/95	BHL	S	BASHLEY	152	2-1	Nichols(2)
06/09/95	BHL	S	Havant Town	103	1-5	Yates
09/09/95	FA Cup	Q1	Oxford City	376	1-1	Hatswell
12/09/95	FA Cup	Q1 rep	OXFORD CITY	341	3-1	Murphy, Nicholls(2)
16/09/95	BHL	S	CINDERFORD TOWN	161	4-1	Hatswell, Robison, Hutter, Nicholls
20/09/95	BHL	S	Fareham Town	121	3-3	Teggart, Nichols(2)
23/09/95	FA Cup	Q2	Thame United	334	1-1	Foster
26/09/95	FA Cup	Q2 rep	THAME UNITED	273	2-3	Teggart, Murphy
30/09/95	BHL	S	Poole Town	104	3-1	Nicholls, Foster
10/10/95	DMC	1(1)	GLOUCESTER CITY	177	1-0	Hutter
14/10/95	FA Trophy	Q1	Yate Town	156	2-3	Hutter, Taggart
17/10/95	DMC	1(2)	Gloucester City	276	0-3	
21/10/95	BHL	S	Clevedon Town	239	3-4	Nicholls, Ogle, Robison
24/10/95	BHL	S	FOREST GREEN ROVERS	126	1-0	Alder
28/10/95	BHL	S	ERITH & BELVEDERE	123	1-1	Robison
04/11/95	BHL	S	Waterlooville	280	2-3	Nicholls(2)
11/11/95	BHL	S	Trowbridge Town	322	1-0	Caffel
14/11/95	BHL	S	HAVANT TOWN	142	0-0	
18/11/95	BHL	S	POOLE TOWN	133	2-0	Coles, Nicholls
25/11/95	BHL	S	Erith & Belvedere	112	5-0	McGuire(2), Hutter, McNamara, Nichols
02/12/95	BHL	S	WEYMOUTH	172	1-1	McGuire
09/12/95	BHL	S	Yate Town	175	0-3	
16/12/95	BHL	S	WATERLOOVILLE	122	0-1	
30/12/95	BHL	S	Margate	256	1-1	Foster
06/01/96	BHL	S	Tonbridge Angels	342	0-0	
20/01/96	BHL	S	Weston-super-Mare	240	2-2	Hutter, Teggart
10/02/96	BHL	S	Weymouth	714	0-1	
13/02/96	BHL	S	Fisher	137	0-1	
17/02/96	BHL	S	TROWBRIDGE TOWN	213	2-1	McNamara, Nichols
22/02/96	Oxon SC	QF	Carterton Town	80	1-0	Teggart
27/02/96	BHL	S	FLEET TOWN	89	1-1	Teggart
02/03/96	BHL	S	Cinderford Town	235	0-1	
05/03/96	BHL	S	CLEVEDON TOWN	107	2-1	Teggart, Nichols
09/03/96	BHL	S	NEWPORT I.O.W.	130	2-0	Hatswell, Adams
16/03/96	BHL	S	Ashford Town	423	0-2	
19/03/96	BHL	S	TONBRIDGE ANGELS	89	1-1	Hutter
23/03/96	BHL	S	Braintree Town	172	1-2	Waters
30/03/96	BHL	S	MARGATE	147	3-2	Walters(2), Adams
03/04/96	Oxon SC	SF	THAME UNITED	150	0-3	
06/04/96	BHL	S	Fleet Town	140	2-1	Adams(2)
08/04/96	BHL	S	FISHER	133	1-0	Nichols
13/04/96	BHL	S	WESTON-SUPER-MARE	141	0-1	
16/04/96	BHL	S	SITTINGBOURNE	124	0-2	
18/04/96	BHL	S	ASHFORD TOWN	112	1-2	Teggart
20/04/96	BHL	S	Bashley	183	1-0	Walters
27/04/96	BHL	S	Sittingbourne	1072	2-4	Walters(2)
29/04/96	BHL	S	BRAINTREE TOWN	80	2-3	Nichols, Adams
01/05/96	Marriott	F	NORTH LEIGH	100	0-2	
04/05/96	BHL	S	YATE TOWN	111	2-0	Murphy, Adams

YATE TOWN

Lodge Road, Yate, Bristol BS17 5LE. Tel: 01454 228103 or 01454 228972

Secretary and Press officer : Mr Terry Tansley, 1 Tyning Close, Yate, Bristol BS17 5BH. Tel: 01454 324305

Programme Editor: Bob Chester, 30 Queensholm Crescent, Downend, BS16 6LR

Nickname: The Blubells   Capacity: 2,000

Seating: 236   Covered standing: Yes

Clubhouse on ground: Yes

Record attendance: 2,000 for Charity match with Bristol Rovers 1990

Biggest win: 13-3 v Clevedon Bristol Prem Combination 1967-68

Biggest defeat: Not known

Record appearances: Gary Hewlett

Record goalscorer in aggregate: Kevin Thaws

Record fee received: £7,500 for Darren Tilley from York City and £7,500 from Bristol Rovers for Mark Davis

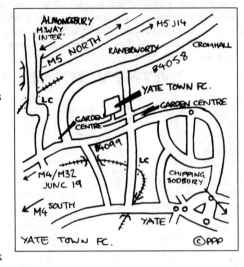

HONOURS

Hellenic League Premier Division 1988 and 1989; South West Counties Vase 1986; Stroud Charity Cup 1977, 1978, 1980, 1983, 1988, 1989; Berkeley Hospital Cup 1974, 1975, 1981; Gloucester Challenge Trophy 1989; GFA Senior Amateur Cup 1978, 1992, 1993 (last two times by reserves); GFA Senior Cup.

Manager for 1996/97: Ian Alexander   **Assistant Manager: Phil Purnell**

Chairman: Mr R Hawkins   **Vice Chairman: Mr A Phillips**

Yate Town FC have their own fanzine, started in 1996 and entitled "In The Net".

They currently share their home with Bristol Rovers Reserves who play their Football Combination games there.

Yate Town FC began life as Yate Rovers in 1906, playing solely in local football. In 1946 they were re-formed and became known as Yate YMCA playing in the Bristol and District League and the Bristol Premier Combination. They were among the founder members of the Gloucestershire County League in 1968 and the following year they changed their name to Yate Town. The club won the Gloucestershire Amateur Cup (South) in 1978 and were beaten finalists in the Challenge Trophy a year later.

Town took a big leap forward in 1983 when they entered the Hellenic League and promotion to the Premier Division was soon achieved when they finished runners up in 1985. More success followed with the South West Counties Vase in 1987, and the following year saw them unbeaten at home in taking the league title. They retained it in 1989 and with it came entry to the Southern League, Southern Division. A finish of 13th in the first year was followed by a switch to the Midland Division in 1991, from where they reached the 5th Round of the FA Vase.

Yate play at Lodge Road, premises they have occupied since 1984, having previously been at Yate Aerodrome until 1954 and a pitch on Newman's Field for a further six years. They then moved to Sunnyside Lane in 1960 and remained there until moving to a new ground in Lodge Road, the reserves continuing to use the old ground. Cover was erected in 1987 and floodlights came a year later. Recent years have not been too good for Yate with just a losing Senior Cup final appearance to show. In 1994 they were spared the drop out of the league by restructuring, but were placed back in the Southern Division again.

YATE TOWN 1995/96 SEASON

Date	Comp	Rd	Opponent	Att	Score	Scorers
19/08/95	BHL	S	Havant Town	196	0-1	
23/08/95	BHL	S	CLEVEDON TOWN	246	1-4	Mortimore
26/08/95	FA Cup	P	Worcester City	595	2-1	Lee(2)
28/08/95	BHL	S	WESTON-SUPER-MARE	301	2-1	Jefferies(2)
02/09/95	BHL	S	BRAINTREE TOWN	157	1-1	Lee
05/09/95	BHL	S	Cinderford Town	220	3-3	Hewlett, Theobald, Lee
09/09/95	FA Cup	Q1	Cheltenham Town	659	0-5	
16/09/95	BHL	S	SITTINGBOURNE	155	2-2	Lee, Hewlett
20/09/95	BHL	S	Clevedon Town	207	1-1	Purnell
23/09/95	BHL	S	Fleet Town	102	1-3	Lee
30/09/95	BHL	S	BASHLEY	156	0-3	
03/10/95	DMC	1(1)	Trowbridge Town	206	1-4	Dempsey
07/10/95	BHL	S	Waterlooville	201	1-1	Hirons
14/10/95	FA Trophy	Q1	WITNEY TOWN	156	3-2	Iddles, Adswell(og), Hirons
18/10/95	DMC	1(2)	TROWBRIDGE TOWN	120	2-0	Lee, Lippiatt
24/10/95	BHL	S	Weston-super-Mare	190	1-6	Dempsey
28/10/95	BHL	S	NEWPORT I.O.W.	141	3-0	Lee, Mehew, Hirons
31/10/95	Glos NSC	SF	Cheltenham Town	131	0-2	
04/11/95	FA Trophy	Q2	HEYBRIDGE SWIFTS	163	1-2	Mehew
11/11/95	BHL	S	Margate	303	1-2	Mehew
15/11/95	BHL	S	CINDERFORD TOWN	143	4-1	Mehew(3), Lippiatt
18/11/95	BHL	S	Ashford Town	554	2-4	Mehew, Iddles
25/11/95	BHL	S	HAVANT TOWN	126	2-1	Mehew(2)
02/12/95	BHL	S	Sittingbourne	547	1-0	Clarke
09/12/95	BHL	S	WITNEY TOWN	175	3-0	Lee, Mehew, Iddles
16/12/95	BHL	S	Bashley	131	2-1	Dempsey, Clarke
06/01/96	BHL	S	Braintree Town	145	· 4-4	Dempsey, Clarke, Mehew(2)
13/01/96	BHL	S	FAREHAM TOWN	197	2-0	Jeffries, Champion(og)
20/01/96	BHL	S	Weymouth	656	0-1	
03/02/96	BHL	S	ASHFORD TOWN	114	0-1	
17/02/96	BHL	S	FLEET TOWN	121	3-1	Freegard(2), Lee
21/02/96	BHL	S	Forest Green Rovers	147	0-1	
24/02/96	BHL	S	WATERLOOVILLE	131	1-3	Freegard
02/03/96	BHL	S	Fisher	144	3-3	Lippiatt, Freegard(2)
09/03/96	BHL	S	MARGATE	168	3-2	Lee(2), Freegard
16/03/96	BHL	S	Newport I.O.W.	251	0-1	
23/03/96	BHL	S	ERITH & BELVEDERE	157	4-0	Freegard(2), Clark, Dempsey
27/03/96	BHL	S	Poole Town	72	8-0	Clarke, Iddles(2), Freegard(3), Theobald, Purnell
30/03/96	BHL	S	Tonbridge Angels	346	4-3	Theobald(2), Clarke(2)
06/04/96	BHL	S	FOREST GREEN ROVERS	209	2-0	Theobald, Iddles
08/04/96	BHL	S	Trowbridge Town	299	2-2	Dempsey, Theobald
13/04/96	BHL	S	Fareham Town	104	1-2	Lee
16/04/96	BHL	S	Erith & Belvedere	71	1-2	Clarke
18/04/96	BHL	S	TONBRIDGE ANGELS	108	4-0	Lee(2), Clarke, Freegard
20/04/96	BHL	S	POOLE TOWN	154	8-0	Dempsey(2), Theobald(2), Freegard(2), Clarke, O'Sullivan
24/04/96	BHL	S	TROWBRIDGE TOWN	149	2-1	Ferns(og), Clarke
27/04/96	BHL	S	WEYMOUTH	195	1-5	O'Sullivan
01/05/96	BHL	S	FISHER	110	1-2	Towler
04/05/96	BHL	S	Witney Town	111	0-2	

Above: Cinderford Town F.C.
Below: Fleet Town F.C.

Above: Gravesend + Northfleet F.C.
Below: Newport A.F.C.

Left: Halesowen Town

Right: Yate Town

Left: Witney Town.

Right: Nuneaton Borough 1996/97 Squad.

JEWSON EASTERN COUNTIES LEAGUE

PREMIER

	P	W	D	L	F	A	PTS
Halstead Town	42	31	8	3	110	50	101
Diss Town	42	29	9	4	94	32	96
Wroxham	42	26	10	6	97	39	88
Stowmarket Town	42	23	7	12	69	47	76
Woodbridge Town	42	22	5	15	73	50	71
Newmarket Town	42	18	13	11	78	58	67
Harwich & P(-19)	42	25	8	9	102	55	64
Felixstowe Town	42	16	11	15	60	57	59
Sudbury Wand.	42	17	8	17	53	58	59
Tiptree United	42	17	8	17	56	67	59
Wisbech Town	42	16	9	17	76	67	57
Soham T Rangers	42	16	9	17	76	78	57
Fakenham Town	42	17	5	20	67	67	56
Lowestoft Town	42	13	14	15	73	59	53
Clacton Town	42	14	10	18	72	84	52
Great Yarm Town	42	11	11	20	34	61	44
Hadleigh United	42	10	9	23	33	85	39
Sudbury T. Res	42	9	11	22	49	86	38
March Town Utd	42	10	7	25	39	67	37
Watton United	42	8	13	21	41	73	37
Haverhill Rovers	42	8	10	24	36	78	34
Cornard United	42	5	7	29	38	108	22

DIVISION ONE

	P	W	D	L	F	A	PTS
Gorleston	32	26	4	2	100	30	82
Warboys Town	32	22	7	3	79	33	73
Ely City	32	19	6	7	82	40	63
Thetford Town	32	20	2	10	72	52	62
Ipswich Wanderers	32	17	8	7	87	41	59
Whitton United	32	15	10	7	67	43	55
Norwich United	32	14	7	11	58	46	49
Mildenhall Town	32	14	5	13	53	61	47
Swaffham Town	32	10	8	14	53	54	38
Brightlings Utd	32	8	11	13	44	61	35
Somersham Town	32	10	5	17	41	62	35
Downham Town	32	9	7	16	46	80	34
Histon	32	8	4	20	54	73	28
King's Lynn Res	32	8	4	20	46	91	28
Stanway Rovers	32	6	9	17	35	67	27
Chatteris Town	32	7	4	21	41	82	25
Bury Town Res	32	6	5	21	54	96	23

Above: Downham Town F.C.
Below: Soham Town Rangers F.C.

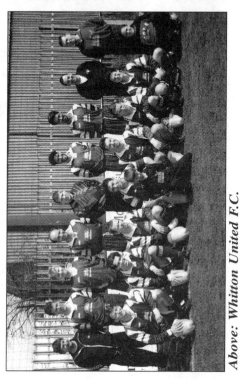

Above: Whitton United F.C.
Below: Wroxham F.C.

BRIGHTLINGSEA UNITED

North Rd, Brightlingsea, Essex. Tel: 01206 304199

Secretary: Harry Beere, 108 Regent Rd, Brightlingsea, Essex CO7 0NZ Tel: 01206 303122

Programme Editor: Mr K. Lay, 18 Francis Street, Brighlingsea, Essex

Colours: Red and white

Nickname: Oystermen

Capacity: 2,000

Seating: 50

Covered standing: 200

Clubhouse on ground: Yes

Record attendance: 1,200 v Colchester Utd Friendly 1968

DIRECTIONS

B1027 Colchester-Clacton, B1029 from Thorrington Cross - follow Church Road into town, left into Spring Road, left into Church Road. Nearest station: Colchester then bus 78 to Brightlingsea.

Honours

Essex Senior League 1989 and 1990

Harry Fisher Memorial Trophy 1990

Essex and Suffolk Border League Prem Div Cup 1972

Harwich Charity Cup 1988

Worthington Evans Cup 1977, 1978, 1979

Manager 1996-97: Frank Thompson

Assistant Manager: Kevin Foskett

Chairman: Graham Steady

Vice Chairman: Michael Cole

Brightlingsea United came about following the amalgamation of two of the numerous clubs that abounded in the town during the early part of the century. The old Town and Athletic clubs joined forces to become Brightlingsea United in 1928. With the help of local benefactors, the present North Road ground was bought for just £400 and by the time the changing rooms, stand and other facilities had been built the outlay was doubled.

The Oystermen are nicknamed the town's main income in the past, and they joined the Essex and Suffolk Border League from the old Tendring Hundred and remained until 1971 when they joined the new Essex Senior League. Throughout most of the 70's and 80's United were annual strugglers until the appointment of Steve Dowman, the former Colchster professional took them to the title in 1989. They retained it a year later and moved up to the Eastern Counties, gaining promotion to the Premier, but when Dowman left things turned sour and they soon went down.

Since then the club have reached the Harwich Charity Cup final and have consolidated in the ECL. in 1989. They retained it a year later and moved up to the Eastern Counties, gaining promotion.

BURY TOWN

Ram Meadow, Cotton Lane, Bury St Edmunds, Suffolk. Tel: 01284 754820

Secretary: Mrs Wendy Turner, 64 Winthrop Rd, Bury St Edmunds, Suffolk IP33 3UF Tel: 01284 753688

Founded: 1872, Nickname: The Blues

Capacity: 3,500, Seating: 300

Covered Standing: 1,500 Clubhouse On Ground:Yes

Record Attend: 2,500 v Enfield FA Cup 3rd Qual Rd 1986

At previous ground 4,710 v King's Lynn 1950

Record Appearance Holder: Doug Tooley

Record Goalscorer In One Season: Doug Tooley 58

Record Goalscorer In Aggregate: Doug Tooley

DIRECTIONS

Leave A45 at sign to central Bury St Edmunds, follow signs to town centre at exit r'bout, 1st exit into Notrthgate Street at next r'bout, left a T junct. (2nd lights) into Mustow Street and left immediately into Cotton Lane - ground 350 yds on right, through Pay & Display car park (n.b. fine for not displaying a 40p ticket is £15) 10 mins walk from station.

Record Fee Paid:£1,500 for Mel Springett from Chelmsford City 1990

Record fee received £ 5,500 for Simon Milton to Ipswich Town

Honours

Suffolk Senior Cup 1937, 1938, 1939, 1945, 1985

Suffolk Premier Cup.1959, 1960, 1961, 1962, 1964, 1965, 1971, 1978

Eastern Counties League. 1964, Metropolitan League.1966,

Manager For 1996-97: Tony Godden, Assistant Manager: Keith Vince

Chairman: Colin Hurley, Vice Chairman: Brian Lafflin

Press and programme: Ron Kent 01284 705765, Club shop manager: Ian Smith 01284 704608

Club sponsors: Greene King

Bury Town play at the Ram Meadow, in Cotton Lane, with their stadium believed to hold 3,500 with covered accommodation for 1,500. They were formed in 1872, being one of the founder members of the Suffolk County FA in 1885. Prior to being Bury Town, they were known as Bury United, and played in the Norfolk and Suffolk Border League. The Blues moved into Senior football when they became founder members of the Eastern Counties League in 1935 and gained their first honour winning the Suffolk Senior Cup in 1937, retaining it for two years. The middle year saw a runners up spot in the league and in 1945 the Senior Cup was won again. 14 years later Bury won the first ever Suffolk Premier Cup, winning it a further three times in a row. This golden period also saw the League Cup in 1962 and the league itself two years later, with the Cup and Premier Cup for good measure. That success prompted the club to join the Metropolitan League and in 1966, another treble saw the League, League Cup and Premier Cup come to Kings Road. The double was won again in 1969, with the club also reaching the First Round of the FA Cup a year earlier in 1968. 3,000 fans saw the tie with Bournemouth and Boscombe Athletic, which ended 0-0.

In 1971 the Premier Cup was won for the eighth time, and it saw the club move into the Southern League for the first time, which proved unsuccessful with the high costs of travel and disappointing results. After five years the Blues returned to the ECL, against popular demand, which was the swansong for the Kings Road ground, as the club moved to the newly built Ram Meadow after 106 years at the old ground.

In 1987 Bury rejoined the Southern League but a series of poor seasons have seen another return to the ECL, following relegation last term.

CAMBRIDGE CITY RESERVES

City Ground, Milton Road

Secretary: Stuart Hamilton, 55 Crowhill, Godmanchester, Huntingdon PE18 8LP, Tel 01480 412266

See entry in Doc Martens Southern League section for information

CHATTERIS TOWN

West Street, Chatteris, Camb. Tel: 01354 692139

Secretary: Jimmy Gill, 3 West End Close, Chatteris, Cambs, PE16 6HW, Tel: 01354 693690

Colours: White and blue,   Nickname: Lillies

Capacity: 2,000,   Seating: 250

Covered standing; 400, Clubhouse on ground: Yes

DIRECTIONS

Entering Chatteris on A141 from Huntingdon turn right into West Street after by-pass roundabout.

Record attendance: 2,000 v March Town Utd
Eastern Counties League 1988

Biggest win: 11-0 v Norwich City A
Eastern Counties League 1968-69

Biggest defeat: 0-11 v Harwich & P 1994-95 and Haverhill Rovers 1989-90

Honours

Eastern Counties League Cup: 1968

Peterborough Premier League: 1964, 1965, 1966

Cambridgeshire Invitation Cup: 1964, 1966, 1968, 1969, 1972, 1974, 1994

Hinchingbrooke Cup 7 times

Cambridge Senior Cup (Challenge) 1952, 1955, 1963, 1964, 1965

Manager for 1996-97: Steven Taylor, Assistant Manager: James Pullan

Chairman: Jimmy Gill, Vice Chairman: Paul Clark

The club was formed in 1920 as Chatteris Town FC and not Chatteris Engineers as is often assumed. They joined the Peterborough League but met with little success until lifting the Cambridgeshire Challenge Cup in 1952 and 1955. Two years later a crowd of well over 1,000 saw an FA Cup tie with Wisbech Town and it was from then and through the 60's that the club enjoyed its finest years, winning the Challenge Cup 3 times and the Peterborough League 3 times.

A new challenge was required and the committee entered the club into the Eastern Counties League, along with Boston and Maldon. The Lillies found it tough going, but 1967-68 was a vast improvement where they won the League Cup, adding the East Anglian Cup a year later. The early seventies saw one or two close calls but it all changed in 1977 when Town finished bottom and for the next four seasons they were in the bottom three. During that decade there was much work off the field and a clubhouse extension was built, followed by floodlights in 1984 at a cost of £14,000. In 1988 the record attendance of 2,000 packed into the ground for the visit of March Town United, when March won 5-0 to collect their only championship to date. Sadly bad times were close by and in 1990 they ended a season without a single win after conceding 208 league goals. However with Sudbury moving on and Norwich United denied promotion, the Lilies were saved, only to finish last again a year later. They again avoided going down but after a number of years of struggle they dropped into Division One.

CLACTON TOWN

Rushgreen Bowl, Rushgreen Rd, Clacton-on-Sea. Tel: 01255 432590

Secretary: Mrs Sandra Harris, 57 Coopers Lane, Clacton-on-Sea Essex CO15 2BY Tel: 01255 476133

Colours: Royal blue

Nickname: Seasiders

Capacity: 2,500

Seating: 200

Covered standing: Yes

Clubhouse on ground: Yes

Record attendance: 3,505 v Romford
FA Cup 1st Qual Rd 1952 at former ground

DIRECTIONS

A133 to Clacton, at roundabout right into St Johns Road, 4th left Cloes Lane, 3rd right Rushgreen Road, ground approximately half mile on right. From B1027 take main Haywick turn off (Jaywick Lane), then 2nd left (after about a mile) into Rushgreen Road. Ground 400 yards. 2 miles from Clacton (BR), buses 3, 5 or 5a to Coopers Lane/Rushgreen Road.

Honours

Essex Junior Cup 1900

Southern League Div 1 1960

Eastern Counties League Cup 1954

Worthington Evans Cup 1957, 1968, 1975

North Essex League Div 2 1900

East Anglian Cup 1947

Clacton Town were formed in 1892 and within three years were playing in the North East Essex League. They won Division Two in 1900 along with the Essex Junior Cup, but the club ceased playing a year later with many players forming Old Clactonians, which became Clacton Town in 1905.

This club had a brief career in the Clacton and District and Harwich and District Leagues until 1911 when they became founder members of the Essex and Suffolk Border League, but after one season they also folded, only to re-form just before the Great War rejoining the Border League.

They subsequently moved to the Ipswich and District League between the wars and then the Eastern Counties in 1935 as founder members. After the War the club turned professional and won the East Anglian Cup, entering the Southern League in 1958, winning the First Division two years later.

Financial problems caught up with Clacton in the early sixties and they moved back to the Eastern Counties League in 1964 where they have twice been runners up.

The club had played since 1906 at the impressive Old Road ground, but the council landlords sold it to to a collection of supermarkets and the club moved, not without some problems, to a new ground in Rushgreen Road in 1987.

CORNARD UNITED

Blackhouse Lane, Great Cornard, Sudbury, Suffolk Tel:01787 376719

Secretary: Richard Powell, 14 North Rise, Gt Cornard, Suffolk CO10 0DE

Tel: 01787 371671

Colours: Blue and White

Nickname: Ards

Capacity: 2,000

Seating; 250

Covered standing: 250

Clubhouse on ground: Yes

Record attendance:509 v Leyton Orient Friendly August 1993

Biggest win: 18-2 v St Peters House Colchester League 1972

Biggest defeat: 4-10 v Finningham Bury League 1968

Record appearances: Malcolm Fisher

Record goalscorer in total: Andy Smiles

DIRECTIONS
Left off roundabout on A134 coming from Ipswich/Colchester into Sudbury, follow signs for Country Park ground is immediately opposite along Blackhouse Lane.

Honours

Eastern Counties League Div 1 1990

Essex and Suffolk Border League and Cup 1989

Suffolk Senior Cup 1990

Cornard are one of the youngest teams in East Anglia, formed 32 years ago, but they have had a remarkable rise to the Eastern Counties League. The Great Cornard based side started life in the Sudbury Sunday League and progressed from there to the Bury St Edmunds League for seven years. They then moved to the Colchester League before moving up to the Essex and Suffolk Border League in 1978.

11 years later they were ready to move into the Eastern Counties League and promotion was won from Division One at the first attempt, with third place in the Premier Division being their top spot to date, in 1992. They followed that with an impressive fourth place, but the last two seasons have seen the club struggle, and in May they were relegated back to Division One, 12 points adrift at the bottom after conceding over 100 goals.

Cornard first played on the local Recreation Ground until 1971 when they gained use of Great Cornard Upper School. They moved to Blackhouse Lane in 1983, where they shared with the cricket team.

To gain acceptance from the ECL the club turned the pitch around 180 degrees and built stands and changing rooms, and floodlights were installed for the Premier Division.

In 1993 the ground attendance record was set when over 500 saw a friendly with Leyton Orient.

DISS TOWN

Brewers Green Lane, Diss, Norfolk, IP22 3DP. Tel: 01379 651223

Secretary Mr R Upson, Bamburgh House, Brewers Green Lane, Diss, Norfolk IP22 3DP

Tel: 01379 642923

Nickname: Tangerines

Colours: Tangerine and Navy

Capacity: 2,500

Seating: 280

Covered standing:500 Clubhouse on ground: Yes

Record Attendance: 1,731 v Atherton LR
FA Vase semi-final 1st leg Mar 1994

Biggest Win: 15-1 v Eastern Coachworks.Centre-forward Ray Button created history by scoring ten times in the match, beating the previous record of nine. Feb 1960

Biggest Defeat: 0-10

Record Appearances: Alan Sheldrake

Record Goalscorer in one Season: Don Whymark and Ray Button 50 goals

DIRECTIONS

Just off B1066 Diss-Thetford Road, near Roydon School. One and a half miles from Diss (BR).

Diss Town FC were formed in 1886 and shared a ground at Roydon Rd with the local cricket club. The first honour came in 1892 when they won the Norfolk Junior Cup, beating Yarmouth in the final, but it was 1925 when they next made a mark, again losing the final. Much of their early football was played in the Norwich and District League and in 1929 they made headlines when holding Ipswich Town to a draw in the FA Cup before losing the replay. Much later, the Anglian Combination was formed and in 1968 Diss won the Division One championship and the Knock-Out Cup. The 70's were very successful, winning the Norfolk Senior Cup and finishing runner up in the Premier Division in 1975 before winning the knock-out cup and finishing runners up in the league a year later. The title finally came in 1977 and again in 1979.

The 80's began with two League Cup victories and ended with them joining the new Division One of the Eastern Counties League and after three near misses, Diss won the championship in 1992, reaching the Norfolk Senior Cup final and the quarter-final of the FA Vase. 1993-94 was without doubt the greatest season in the club's history. Victories over Tring Town, Ford Utd, Torpoint Athletic, King's Lynn, Tiverton Town and Atherton LR brought a final at Wembley against Taunton Town.

In a pulsating final in front of 13,450, Diss took the Vase in extra time after equalising from the penalty spot in the 8th minute of injury time.

Success on the field has led to success off it. In the early 70's Diss planned to buy their own ground with clubhouse and after ten years they bought 7 acres of land in Brewers Green Lane. The clubhouse was opened in 1983 and in 1992 a new stand for 275 was built. Since then the ground has updated even more with Southern League in mind and in May, Town ended another wonderful season by taking the Norfolk Senior Cup, easily beating Wroxham in the final, to add to their runners up medals after finishing behind champions Halstead Town

DOWNHAM TOWN

War Memorial Ground, Lynn Road, Downham Market, Norfolk. Tel: 01366 388424

Secretary Mr Fred Thorne, 6 Maple Rd, Downham Market, Norfolk, PE38 9PY Tel: 01366 382563

Press Officer: Steven Penny, 2 Nene Road, Watlington, Kings Lynn, Norfolk PE33 0TP , Tel: 01553 810392

Colours: All Red with black and white trim

Nickname: Town, previously Saints

Capacity: 1,000   Floodlights: Yes

Seating: None   Covered standing: Yes

Clubhouse on ground: Yes

Record attendance 1,500 for friendly with Norwich City in 1949

Biggest win: 15-0 v Bury Town Res ECL Div 1 1994

DIRECTIONS
One and a quarter miles from Downham Market (BR) - continue to town clock, turn left and ground is three quarters of a mile down Lynn Road.

Honours

Peterborough Senior Cup 1962, 1963, 1964, 1972, 1987

Peterborough League 1963, 1974, 1979, 1987, 1988

Norfolk Senior Cup 1964 and 1966

Isle of Ely Challenge Cup 1986 and 1988

Ely City Invitation Cup 1991

Harper Trophy 1988

West Norfolk Cup 1988

Manager 1996-97: Steve Tyers

Assistant Manager: Harry Yates

Chairman: Mr J.Fish

Vice Chairman: Mr J.Dent

Downham Town is one of the oldest clubs in Norfolk, formed in 1881. They played mainly junior football, in the Kings Lynn area until after the Second War. The Saints, as they were then known, were elected to the Premier Division of the Peterborough League in 1949 and were given senior status. They won a string of honours during the post War period and eventually switched to the Eastern Counties League in 1988, playing in the newly formed Second Division.

Before 1952, the club's teams were all selected by committee, but after appointing George Heagren as manager, they enjoyed their best spell, winning the Peterborough Senior Cup in 1962, retaining it a year later and winning the league title. In 1964 they took the prestigious Norfolk Senior Cup and retained that a year later, and were runners up for a further three seasons.

Tony Chilleystone took over in 1969 and in his reign the club were twice league runners up and Peterborough Senior Cup winners in 1972. Town took the title again in 1974 and 1979 and did the double in 1987, taking it for the last time in their last season before moving up.

ELY CITY

Unwin Sports Ground, Downham Road, Ely, Cambs. Tel: 01353 662035

Secretary Derek Oakey, 37 Fordham Rd, Soham, Cambs, CB7 5AH Tel 01353 722141

Nickname: Robins

Capacity: 1,500

Seating: 150

Covered standing: 200

Clubhouse on ground: Yes

Record attendance: Old Ground 4,260 v Torquay Utd FA Cup 1st Rd 1956

New Ground: 260 v Soham Town Rangers ECL Div 1 April 12th 1993

DIRECTIONS
A10 Ely by-pass turn off for Downham, 3 miles (approx.) from Ely (BR).

Honours

Cambridge Senior Cup 1948

Eastern Counties League Cup 1980

Ely City are the oldest club in Cambridgeshire. They were formed from the original members of a team called Ely St Ethelreda Football and Cricket Club in about 1885. For over 90 years the club played at the Paradise Ground, until they were forced to move in 1986 to a new ground on the outskirts. After being revived following the War the club had some success in the Cups and in 1948 they achieved a double of winning both Senior Cup competitions in the same week.

In 1951 the Robins left the Cambridgeshire League for the Peterborough League and in the first season were runners up in the League Cup. In 1954 they reached the 1st Round of the Amateur Cup which put them in good stead for the FA Cup run in 1956, when a series of wins saw them enter the 1st Round, where a crowd of over 4,000 saw Torquay United win 6-2.

In 1958 the club were elected to the Central Alliance and after a couple of rejections, they were accepted into the Eastern Counties League. The first few seasons were a struggle, but in 1969, under Hugh Barr, the former Linfield, Coventry City and Northern Ireland International, they were runners up in League and Cup.

Since that time the move from the Paradise has seen the new ground named the Unwin Ground, after club President Doug Unwin, and despite improved facilities, the club were relegated from the Premier Division in 1989. 1996 saw the club enjoy a fine season, where they finished third in Division One.

FAKENHAM TOWN

Clipbush Park, Clipbush Lane, Fakenham, Norfolk. Tel: 01328 855859

Secretary: Eric Linnell, 40 Warren Ave, Fakenham,
Norfolk NR21 8NP Tel 01328 855445

Press Sec: John Cushion: Tel 01328 862548

DIRECTIONS
Adjacent to Police Station in Norwich Road.

Fakenham Town have vacated the Barons Hall Lawn and will move into Clipbush Park sometime in October. They will play away games until the ground is ready. Ring press secretary to confirm before travelling.

Colours: Amber and black

Nickname: Ghosts

Capacity: 3,000 approx

Seating: 100 rising eventually to 400

Covered standing 1 side at start, eventually all round ground

Clubhouse on ground: Yes

Record attendance: 1,000 v Norwich City Floodlight opening

Honours

Norfolk Senior Cup 1971, 1973, 1974, 1992, 1995

Anglian Combination Cup 1979

Manager 1996-97: John Waters

Chairman: Tony Fisher

Vice Chairman: Charlie Mitchell

Records indicate that Fakenham Town were formed in 1884 and their first opponents were Lynn Alexander, whom they beat 2-1. They began on a pitch at Hempton Green for the first five years before moving to the Star Meadow in 1889. Those years were spent playing in the North Norfolk League until 1910, by which time they had settled at Barons Hall Lawn. The Ghosts made good progress from there, elevating from the Norwich and District League to the Norfolk and Suffolk between the Wars.

In the 60's Town moved into the Anglian Combination and began a wonderful run through the 70's winning the Norfolk Senior Cup three times. In 1979 they won the League Cup and it was a further eight years without honours before they moved into the Eastern Counties League, just missing promotion three times before finally going up as runners up in 1992, the same year as their fourth Senior Cup win.

Since then the Ghosts have again taken the Senior Cup and fielded former AC Milan and England Striker Luther Blissett for a couple of seasons during the 90's.

Barons Hall Lawn is shared with cricket and funds were raised to build a new clubhouse in 1979 and floodlights in 1987. More recently plans went through for the football club to move into their own ground to enable them to move forward once again.

FELIXSTOWE PORT AND TOWN

Dellwood Avenue, Felixstowe, Suffolk. Tel: 01394 282917

Secretary: Michael Gosling, 23 Vicarage Rd, Felixstowe, Suffolk, IP11 8LR

Tel 01394 279758

Colours: White, blue and gold

Nickname: Seasiders

Capacity: 2,000

Seating: 200

Covered standing None

Clubhouse on ground Yes

Record attendance: 1,500 v Ipswich Town Floodlight opener 1991

DIRECTIONS

A45 to Felixstowe. Turn right at 3rd roundabout then 1st left - ground 100 yards on left. 5 mins from Felixstowe (BR) and town centre.

Honours

Ipswich and District League 1965

Suffolk Senior Cup 1967 and 1975

A new sponsor, change of name and new colours have all transformed Felixstowe Football Club within the past year. Formed in 1890 the club spent much of its time in local football, combining at one stage with Walton United to become Felixstowe United for a while after they both struggled following the Second War. After separating again the Seasiders enjoyed limited success until the mid 60's when they reached the Senior Cup final against Grundisburgh, losing a replay after a 1-1 draw at Portman Road.

The following year saw them take the Ipswich and District League before moving to the Essex and Suffolk Border League in 1966. The first season saw them take the Senior Cup but it was another nine years before they did it again, under manager Dave Ashford. They were twice runners up in the Border League which led to a successful application to the Eastern Counties League in 1976. In 1990 the club installed floodlights which has allowed them to continue in the top flight.

In 1995 the club were joined with Britain's largest container Port and became Felixstowe Port and Town FC. Their current ground is right next door to the old one, and when moving the club switched the old pavilion so that it faced the right way, simply by removing the back and turning the seating round. Although out of use for some while, which caused a problem with the league, everything is now back in shape.

GORLESTON

Emerald Park, Woodfarm Lane, Gorleston, Norfolk. Tel: 01493 602802

Secretary: Mr Arthur Ottley, 60 Peterhouse Ave, Gorleston, Norfolk Tel: 01493 603353

Press & prog editor: Mr Brian Bunn, 71 Harbord Crescent, Great Yarmouth, Norfolk NR 30 3EL Tel: 01493 843114

Colours: All Green,   Nickname: The Greens

Capacity: 4,000,   Seating: 250

DIRECTIONS

On Magdalen Estate - follow signs to Crematorium, turn left and follow road to ground. Five and a half miles from great Yarmouth Vauxhall (BR).

Covered standing: 3, 750, Clubhouse on ground: Yes

Record attendance: 800 v Sudbury Town Res

(4,473 v Leyton Orient
FA Cup 1st Rd Nov 1951 at old ground)

Biggest win: 11-1 v Bury Town Res1995

Biggest defeat: 0-13 v Chelmsford City Res1947

Honours

Norfolk Junior Cup 1907

Great Yarmouth Borough League 1907

Eastern Counties League 1953, 1973, 1980, 1981, League Cup 1956

Norfolk Senior Cup 1922, 1923, 1926, 1928, 1931, 1933, 1936, 1938, 1951, 1953, 1969, 1978, 1984

East Anglian Cup 1953 and 1983, Anglian Combination 1969

Norfolk and Suffolk League 1921, 1926, 1930, 1932, 1933, 1934, 1935

Manager 1996-97: Marty Hubble, Assistant Manager: Steven Foyster, Chairman: Kevin Antcliffe

Club shop sells league and non-League progs plus large range of souvenirs. Metal badge is available £2.50 + 50p p+p.

Match programme voted best in league last season and 14th nationally.

Gorleston FC were formed in 1884, but the early history has gone unrecorded. In 1907 the Greens became founder members of the Great Yarmouth Borough League, winning it at the first attempt and gaining promotion to the Norfolk and Suffolk League and senior status. After the Great War Gorleston became one of the strongest sides in Norfolk, taking the league in 1921 and the Senior Cup a year later. They did the double of league and Senior Cup in 1926 and before the Second War had completed five more titles. They became founder members of the Eastern Counties in 1935 but had little success other than a Senior Cup win over neighbours Great Yarmouth in 1938. In 1951 the club drew national fame when they played Leyton Orient in the FA Cup , drawing 2-2 at their old Recreation Ground, which they had used since the last century. The tie went to three matches before the Greens were defeated but it set them up for the next season which was the best in the club's history. They took the league title, the Norfolk Senior Cup, East Anglian Cup and were runners up in the League Cup. Two years later they won the League Cup again but by then were in financial strife and in 1962 the club moved back to the Norfolk and Suffolk League for a few seasons until joining the Anglian Combination as founder members.1969 saw the revival of fortunes as the title was won along with the Senior Cup and they rejoined the ECL, from where they have enjoyed three championships and several cup triumphs.The club's spiritual home, the Recca, became too expensive to maintain at the start of the eighties and the club built a new purpose built stadium called Emerald Park and moved in in 1981. It so far has not brought too much success, indeed the team was relegated in 1994 but happily they returned as Division One champions in 1996.

GREAT YARMOUTH TOWN

Wellesley Recreation Ground, Wellesley Rd, Great Yarmouth, Norfolk. Tel: 01493 842936

Secretary: Michael Capon, 16 Orchard Way, Fleggburgh, Gt Yarmouth, Norfolk NR29 3AY

Tel: 01493 369530

Nickname: The Bloaters

Capacity: 3,600

Seating: 500

Covered Standing: 1,600

Clubhouse On Ground:Yes

Record Attendance: 8,984 v Crystal Palace
FA Cup 1st Rd 1952

Biggest Win: 13-0 v Cromer Town
FA Cup 1st Qual Rd 1952

DIRECTIONS

Just off Marine Parade, 200 yds north of Britannia Pier. Half a mile from Vauxhall (BR).

Honours

FA VASE: semi-final 1983

Eastern Counties League 1969

League Cup 1938, 1975, 1981

East Anglian Cup

Norfolk Senior Cup

Norfolk Premier Cup

Norfolk and Suffolk League 1914, 1927, 1928

Great Yarmouth Town were formed in 1897 as a result of an amalgamation of the Yarmouth Royal Artillery and the Yarmouth Fearnoughts. In their first season the "Bloaters" won the Norfolk Senior Cup, beating Kings Lynn, the first of 13 wins in the competition. Having played in the Norfolk and Suffolk League, they were founder members of the Eastern Counties League in 1935 and have retained unbroken membership. The first success was in 1938 when they won the League Cup, a feat they have repeated twice, in 1975 and 1981, but to date they have won the league just once, in 1969, finishing runners-up four times. In the FA Cup the club has reached the 4th qualifying round on numerous occasions, and the 1st Round in 1947, when they lost to Shrewsbury Town. In 1952 they reached the 2nd Round and lost to Wrexham, but their finest hour was a year later when a record 8,984 saw Crystal Palace beaten 1-0 at the Wellesley. In 1951 Great Yarmouth won the East Anglian Cup and in 1983 they reached the FA Vase semi-final before losing to VS Rugby.

Yarmouth's Recreation Ground was opened by Mayor HE Buxton at the start of the 1897-98 season, and in 1906 the club's magnificent Grandstand was built, capable of seating over 1,000, and is one of the countries oldest stands, possibly only beaten by the small stand at Wolverton which is currently derelict.

To accommodate more spectators for the Crystal Palace game, fish boxes were arranged around the ground as additional terracing and the nearby racecourse supplied garden seats.

HADLEIGH UNITED

Millfield, Tinkers Lane, off Duke Street, Hadleigh, Suffolk. Tel: 01473 822165

Secretary: Barrie Stokes, 27 Martin Rd, Ipswich, Suffolk, IP2 8BJ

Tel: 01473 688452

Other contacts: Peter Vardon 61 Ann Beaumont Way, Hadleigh, Ipswich, Suffolk 1P7 6SB

Tel: 01473 823835

> ## DIRECTIONS
> Turn off A12 approx. halfway between Ipswich & Hadleigh. Take B1070 & follow signs to Hadleigh, Duke Street is off the High Street - turn left by library.

Colours: White and navy blue

Capacity: 3,000

Seating: 250

Covered standing: 500

Clubhouse on ground: Yes

Record attendance: 518 v Halstead Town FA Vase 1995

Biggest win: 8-1 v Chatteris Town 1995

Biggest defeat: 1-7 v Fakenham Town 1992

Record goalscorer in total: Eric Jennings

Honours

Ipswich and District (Suffolk and Ipswich) League 1954, 1957, 1974, 1977, 1979

League Cup 1977, 1981, 1982, 1987

Suffolk Senior Cup 1969, 1972, 1983

Eastern Counties League 1994

Manager 1996-97: Peter Hutchings

Assistant Manager: Luis Newman

Chairman: Simon King, Vice Chairman: Roger Rush

Press Officer: Terry Adams 01473 729941

Hadleigh United came to prominence in the 1950's, a half a century after their founding in 1892.

For many years they played in the Ipswich and District League, which became the Suffolk and Ipswich League, and their title win in 1954 was the catalyst which saw them move to their current ground, Millfield, which the council had created after the War had seen the area used for manouvres.

Having previously used a variety of farmer's fields around the area, United settled and won the league again in 1957, but it was not until 12 years later that they tasted more success when winning the Suffolk Senior Cup, repeating it in 1972. Throughout the 70's United were never far away from success and they were champions three times before the decade was out, completing the League and Cup double in 1977. It continued into the 80's with Senior Cup and League Cup wins, but they did not take the title again, and joined the Eastern Counties League when it expanded in 1991 and although the first season was a struggle they improved over the next two seasons so that in 1994 they won Division One by five points and reached the League Cup semi-final.

The first two seasons in the top flight have also been a struggle but they have survived and are confident for the new season.

HALSTEAD TOWN

Rosemary Lane, Halstead, Essex. Tel: 01787 472082

Secretary: Mr Steve Webber, 12 Ravens Ave, Halstead, Essex C09 1NZ

Tel: 01787 476959

Colours: White and black

Capacity: 2,000

Seating: 312

Covered standing: 400

Clubhouse on ground Yes

Record attendance: 4,000 v Walthamstow Avenue Essex Senior Cup 1949

DIRECTIONS

A131 Chelmsford to Braintree - follow signs to Halstead. In Halstead, 1st left after Police Station, then 1st right and first left to ground.

Honours

Eastern Counties League 1995 and 1996

Essex Senior Trophy 1995

Essex and Suffolk Border League 1958, 1959, 1978, 1995 (res)

League Cup 1958, 1959, 1974, 1995 (res)

Essex Junior Cup 1902, 1947

Manager for 1996-97: Ian Phillips

Assistant manager: Lee Fish

Chairman: Steve Marzal

Vice Chairman: Martin Fryer

Halstead Town were formed in 1879 and in their early years joined the North Essex League, but the first trophy of note came in 1902 when they won the Essex Junior Cup, beating Chingford 2-0. Around that time the club played in the Halstead League, Haverhill League and North Essex League, playing on various grounds in the town, such as Three Gates, Ravens Meadow, King George V Playing Fields, Courtaulds and Coggeshall Pieces.

After the Second War they won the Junior Cup again and moved to their present ground in Rosemary Lane. The whole project was completed by members and volunteers, with a clubhouse opened in 1949 and the impressive 500 seater stand a year later. Halstead next joined the Essex and Suffolk Border League, and after two runners up spots landed the title in 1958, the double by beating Lakenheath in the two leg League Cup final, 11-4.

There were more league honours before the club joined the Essex Senior League, finishing third twice before in 1988 they moved to the Eastern Counties League Division One, where they were runners up in League and League Cup. From 1992 the club went from strength to strength, winning the Senior Trophy and finishing runners up to Wroxham in the league, but they reversed that result a year later, when taking the title by seven points, and last May retained the Eastern Counties League, completing the double in the process by beating Fakenham in the final at Diss Town.

HARWICH AND PARKESTON

Royal Oak Ground, Main Road, Dovercourt, Harwich. Tel: 01255 503649

Secretary: Mr Andy Schooler, 21 The Vineway, Dovercourt, Harwich, Essex, CO12 4AX Tel: 01255 504590

Colours: White and black stripes, Nickname: Shrimpers

DIRECTIONS

On main road into Dovercourt. 600 yds from Dovercourt (BR).

Capacity: 5,000,   Seating: 350

Covered standing: 1,000, Clubhouse on ground Yes

Record attend: 5,649 v Romford Amateur Cup 4th Rd 1938

Biggest win: 18-0 v Severalls Jan 1936 Essex Senior Cup

Biggest defeat: 1-11 v Norwich City

Record appearances: Possibly Mick Clark 630, Bobby Duffett or Reg Smith

Record goalscorer in one season Tully Day 67

Record goalscorer in total: Tully Day

Record fee paid: £ 2,000 for Paul Smith from Sudbury Town

Honours

FA AMATEUR CUP RUNNERS UP 1899 AND 1953

Eastern Counties League 1936 jt, League Cup 1936 and 1937, Essex County League 1938

Athenian League Div 2 and League Cup 1935, Essex Senior Cup 1899 and 1937

Essex Senior Trophy 1990, AFA Senior Cup 1936 and 1937, Worthington Evans Cup 1981

Manager 1996-97: Colin Hill, Chairman: Paul Revell

Harwich and Parkeston FC were founded in 1877, playing on a number of fields in the early days including the Barrack Field, Phoenix Field and Parkeston. They reached their first final in 1891 when they lost to Clapton in the Essex Senior Cup, but by then they had entered the North Essex League and won it three times in five years. Moran's Meadow was bought in 1898 and acquired on a short lease and the ground, soon known as the Royal Oak, saw Harwich quickly established as one of the biggest clubs in the country as they reached the Amateur Cup final in 1899. They did take the Senior Cup in front of 7,000 spectators but before the Great War the club had slipped back into the pack. In 1934 they joined the Southern Amateur League from the Essex Border League and this sparked off a period of success, where they reached the First Round of the FA Cup. The following year they moved to the Eastern Counties League and did the double and won the FA Senior Cup. That season also saw the record crowd at the Royal Oak of 4,700 against Ipswich Town.

Their great run was ended by the war but not before 5,649 had seen a game with Romford, which broke the ground record again. After the war the team was rebuilt and during the boom time in football the Shrimpers reached the final of the FA Amateur Cup in 1953 where in front of 100,000 people their injury hit side had no answer to Pegasus.

They stayed in the ECL until 1964, reaching three more FA Cup 1st Rounds, before moving to the Athenian League, but although reaching the Premier Division they made no further progress until joining the Isthmian League in 1973. After a good start the impetus slowly went and they returned to the Athenians until they disbanded, before wisely returning to the ECL. In 1990, under Richie Powling, the club won the Harwich Charity Cup and Essex Senior Trophy and in 1991 they reached the last eight of the Vase.

HAVERHILL ROVERS

Hamlet Croft, Haverhill, Suffolk. Tel: 01440 702137

Secretary: Chris Rice, 23 Ovington Place, Haverhill,
Suffolk CB9 0BA

Tel: 01440 712396

Colours: All Red

Nickname: Rovers

Capacity: 3,000

Seating: 250

Covered standing: 250

Clubhouse on ground Yes

Record attendance: 1,578 v Warrington Town
FA Vase Quarter Final 1987

Biggest win: 11-0 v Chatteris Town (a) 1991

Biggest defeat 1-13 v Sudbury Town (a) 1974

Record goalscorer in one season Jim Thompson 44 in 1977-78

<table>
<tr><td>DIRECTIONS</td></tr>
<tr><td>Centre of Haverhill.</td></tr>
</table>

Honours

Eastern Counties League 1979

League Cup 1965

Essex and Suffolk Border League 1963 and 1964

East Anglian Cup 1991

Manager 1996-97: Derek Richardson

Assistant Manager: Paul Gaffan

Chairman: Terry McGerty

Haverhill Rovers were formed in 1886, but their early years are not recorded. They began at Hamlet Croft in 1913, having moved from Seven Acres, an area bordered on two sides by Wratting Road and the old railway line. They joined the East Anglian League in 1909 and between the Wars joined the Essex and Suffolk Border League, but having finished bottom in 1928, resigned. Eight years later they returned and were runners up behind Colchester Casuals in 1947, going one better a year later, and taking the Knock out Cup to complete the double. In 1951 they were runners up behind Stowmarket and in 1963 they took the title again. A year later they joined the Eastern Counties League and won the League Cup, but the 70's came and the club struggled finishing in the bottom three six years running, but in 1978 under Roger Staples they rose to take the title, a crowd of 1,300 seeing the last and deciding game against Chatteris Town.

Since then there have been a number of cup wins but league success has been in short supply. Rovers reached the last eight of the FA Vase in 1987 and the final of the League Cup and the Suffolk Premier Cup, but sadly last May they were relegated for the first time in their history.

243

HISTON

Bridge Rd, Impington, Cambridge. Tel: 01223 232301

Secretary: Gareth Baldwin, Tanglewood, 5 Caxton Lane, Foxton, Cambs CB2 6SR Tel: 01223 872126

Colours: Red and black

Capacity: 2,250

Seating: 250

Covered standing: 200

Clubhouse on ground: Yes

Record attendance 2,400 v Kings Lynn
FA Cup 1948 or 1949

Biggest defeat: Possibly: 1-11 v Aveley 1963 circa

DIRECTIONS

Leave A45 northern Cambridge bypass on B1049 (signposted Histon and Cottenham). Ground half a mile on right. 5 miles from Cambridge (BR). Bus No 104.

Honours

Cambridgeshire Challenge Cup 1928 and 1950

Eastern Counties League Cup 1991

Cambridge Invitation Cup 1978 and 1980

Spartan League Div 1 East 1951

Histon were formed in 1904 as Histon Institute, a title they retained until 1951.

Until 1948, when they moved to the Spartan League, Histon played in the Cambridgeshire League, always in the top section, but without winning any titles until after the War, when as Section A winners they beat Ely City to take the title. They did enjoy success in the Cambridge Challenge Cup in 1928 and 1950 and a year later they won the First Division East of the Spartan League, their last major title.

During the early fifties Histon were a regular visitor to the first round of the Amateur Cup and locally they reached three Cambridge Invitation Cup Finals. They moved to the Delphian League in 1960 but had little success, and when it was merged into an expanding Athenian League, they struggled, losing the first game 11-1 at Aveley. They won just two matches and it got no better, the club wisely pulling out in 1965.

It was around then that the club were forced to moved their pitch forward and across as the town by-pass cut through the site of the old ground and the old stand. Although the ground developed well, it was some time before the team matched it as they had a bleak time in the Eastern Counties League.

There were a couple of Invitation Cup wins but it was not until 1991 that they took the League Cup by beating Wroxham, and the success did not last, for they were relegated to Division One in 1995.

IPSWICH WANDERERS

Humberdoucey Sports Ground, Humberdoucey Lane, Ipswich, Suffolk. Tel: 01473 728581

Secretary: Martin Head, 246 Sidegate Lane, Ipswich, Suffolk 1P4 3DH

Tel: 01473 273811

Press officer Mick Haste 196 Rushmere Rd, Ipswich
Tel 01473 711877

DIRECTIONS

A12 north of Ipswich Rushmere Golf Club. Players Road into Humberdoucey Lane.

Capacity: 2,000

Seating: 50

Covered standing: 500

Floodlights: Yes

Clubhouse on ground: Yes

Record attendance: 700 v Ipswich Town
to open floodlights

Biggest win: 10-1

Honours

Midweek Floodlit League 1996

Manager 1996-97: Alan Dilloway

General manager: Martin Head

Chairman: Alan Haste

Vice chairman: Mick Childs

Wanderers were formed in 1980 as Bramford United, an U14's side who later joined Division 12 of the Ipswich Sunday League. Having gained sponsorship from a local company, they changed their name to Loadwell Ipswich and progressed at some pace winning Divisions 1 and 2 of the Sunday Morning League. In 1987 the Eastern Counties League Division One was formed and Wanderers became members, starting at the current ground in Humberdoucey Lane. A new sponsorship was gained and the club became Lancaster Ipswich briefly, and then Ipswich Wanderers. From there the ground has slowly been upgraded with floodlights, new changing rooms and a small seated stand, enough for the Premier Division.

Chairman Jimmy Barker, who negotiated the sponsorships and was influential in so much of the club's progress, sadly died in November 1994 but he left a fine legacy which carries on this season with Alan Dilloway in charge.

LOWESTOFT TOWN

Crown Meadow, Love Road, Lowestoft, Suffolk. Tel: 01502 573818

Secretary: Terry Lynes, 156 Denmark Rd, Lowestoft,
Suffolk, NR32 2EL Tel: 01502 564034

Colours: Blue and white   Nickname: Blues

Capacity: 4,000   Seating: 466

Covered standing: 500

Clubhouse on ground Yes

Record attendance: 5,000 v Watford
FA Cup 1st Rd Dec 9th 1967

Biggest win: 19-0 v Thetford Town
Eastern Counties League

Record appearances: C.Peck 629

Record goalscorer in total: M.Tooley 383

<table>
<tr><td>DIRECTIONS
Just off A12, 10- mins walk from Lowestoft (BR).</td></tr>
</table>

Honours

Eastern Counties League 1936 jt, 1938, 1963, 1965, 1968, 1970, 1971, 1978,

League Cup 1939, 1955, 1966, 1967, 1969, 1976, 1984

Norfolk and Suffolk League 1898, 1899, 1901, 1902, 1903, 1904, 1929, 1931

Suffolk Premier Cup 1967, 1972, 1975, 1979, 1980

Suffolk Senior Cup 1903, 1923, 1924, 1926, 1932, 1936, 1947, 1948, 1949, 1956

East Anglian Cup 10 times

Lowestoft Town Football Club was founded in 1890, initially adopting the colours of cardinal red and blue. They became founder members of the Norfolk and Suffolk League in 1897 and won the league six times during the first seven years. The odd year out, 1900 saw the Town reach the FA Amateur Cup final before losing to Bishop Auckland. That year they also reached the 3rd qualifying round of the FA Cup, being beaten by Luton from Division Two. After the sixth win in 1904 the club's fortunes went downhill and they won nothing until after the Great War when another wonderful spell saw them win the Suffolk Senior Cup three times in four years and then reach the FA Cup 1st Round in which they lost 10-1 to Watford.

The 1920's saw much activity off the pitch as Crown Meadow, originally owned by the Lowestoft Charity Board became the subject of a compulsory purchase order from the council who wanted the land for housing. After surrendering the lease, the club saw the council change their minds and the outcome was that with a mortgage the ground was bought for £3,150.

By then the club colours had changed three times and they were in blue and white and with the league won for the eighth time and with two more Senior Cup wins they became founder members of the Eastern Counties League. They were joint champions with Harwich and before the War won the title outright and the League Cup.

The 40's and 50's saw more success in League Cup and Senior Cup but it was the 70's and 80's which saw Lowestoft dominate, with eight titles, five League Cups, 2 East Anglian Cups, 5 Suffolk Premier Cups and three visits to the First Round of the FA Cup.

Since those heady days silverware has been more scarce and 1984 saw the League Cup once again come to the Crown Meadow

MALDON TOWN

Wallace Binder Ground, Park Drive, Maldon, Essex. Tel: 01621 853762

Secretary Phil Robinson, 9 Lyndhurst Drive, Bicknacre, Danbury, Essex CM3 4XL Tel: 01245 222633

Colours: Blue and white hoops

Clubhouse on ground Yes

DIRECTIONS

A12 approach to Chelmsford. Don't go into city centre but take the A414 east to Maldon. The club is up Park Drive.

Honours

Mid-Essex League 1949, 1950

Mid-Essex Cup 1950

Essex Senior League 1985

Shield winners 1994

Essex and Suffolk Border League 1966

Essex Intermediate Cup 1953

Tolleshunt D'Arcy Cup 1994

Brightlingsea Charity Cup 1952

Colin Root Memorial Cup 1989, 1990, 1991

Maldon Town were formed after the War in 1946 and played at the Sadds Ground on the Causeway, with their HQ at the Rose and Crown pub. They were runners up in Division Two of the Mid-Essex League in the first year and soon moved home to the Prome and joined the North Essex League, where again they were runners up. The close calls continued in the Essex Junior Cup in 1947, losing a replay to Aveley.

Returning to the Mid-Essex Premier Division, they won the title in 1949 and 1950, as well as the League Cup and the now successful club moved to the Wallace Binder ground in Farnbridge Road

They joined the more senior Essex and Suffolk Border League in 1951 where they were yet again runners up, but they did take the County Intermediate Cup. In 1966, after two intermediate Cup finals and a league title, the club were given senior status and joined the Eastern Counties League in 1966.

After six years they again moved, to the Essex Senior League, where they were champions in 1985, just missing out on the double by losing the League Cup final to Chelmsford City Reserves.

Town moved to the new Wallace Binder ground in 1994 and re-joined the ECL in 1996, having finished fourth behind Romford, Great Wakering and Concord.

MARCH TOWN UNITED

GER Sports Ground, Robin Goodfellows Lane, March, Cambs. Tel: 01354 53073

Secretary: Mr Ray Bennett, 47 Ellingham Ave, March, Cambs, PE15 9TE

Tel: 01354 53271

DIRECTIONS

5 mins from town centre, 10 mins from BR station.

Colours: Yellow and blue stripes

Nickname: Hares

Capacity: 4,000

Seating: 500

Covered standing 2,000

Clubhouse on ground Yes

Record attendance: 7,500 v Kings Lynn FA Cup:1956

Honours

Eastern Counties League 1988

League Cup 1961

United Counties League 1954

Cambridgeshire Invitation Cup1955

East Anglian Cup 1954 jt

At one time the town of March was home to two senior clubs, Town and GER United, but after the War the railway side did not reform and in 1946 Town moved on to their old ground and changed their name to March Town United when becoming a limited company in 1950.

Town were formed around 1885 and initially played on rough grounds on Estover Road, Gaul Drove and Burrowmoor Road, until a landowner, Mr Morton, bequeathed the Avenue Ground for sport in 1923. Town continued there for a year after the War, until moving into the vast and empty GER ground, where they remain.

March GER United were playing on the ground in the early twenties when they bought it from the local Grammar School, after playing for some time at Elm Road. Known then as Shepperson Fields, it regularly hosted bowls, tennis, cycling and until 1960 cricket. The club's heyday was in the mid-fifties when they took the United Counties League, Cambridge Invitation and East Anglian Cups, and had FA Cup runs, one of which saw 7,500 cram in to the ground for a tie with Kings Lynn in 1956. A year earlier the Hares had made the first round before losing to Brentford.

March were founder members of the Isle of Ely League in 1905 and later moved to the Peterborough League, before after the war playing in the United Counties for six years. In 1954 they moved East to the ECL and they have been there ever since.

MILDENHALL TOWN

Recreation Way, Mildenhall, Suffolk. Tel: 01638 713449

Secretary: Brian Hensby, 14 Sanderling Close,
Mildenhall, Suffolk IP28 7LE

Tel: 01638 715772

DIRECTIONS

Next to swimming pool/car, quarter of a mile from town centre.

Colours: Amber and black

Nickname: Town or yellows

Capacity: 2,000

Seating: None

Covered standing: Yes

Clubhouse on ground: Yes

Record attendance: 350 v Norwich City Friendly 1989

Honours

Suffolk Junior Cup 1900

Town are a long established club, formed before the turn of the century. Little is known of the early days, other than that they won the Suffolk Junior Cup in 1900, defeating Southwold RA Volunteers 4-0 in the final. A further 93 years elapsed before their next County success when the reserves won the Cambridgeshire County Junior Cup in 1993, adding the Creake Shield a year later.

Until the 1969-70 season, the club played in the Bury and District League, but seeking pastures new, they joined the Cambridgeshire Premier League, and for many years were consistently high in the league. At the end of the 87-88 season, Mildenhall decided that further progress must be made and were accepted into the Eastern Counties League.

After using pitches in Bridal Way and on Sheldrick's Meadow, the club moved on to the Recreation Ground, which was given to the town during the War by the Bunbury family. Originally the pitch ran at 45 degrees to its current position and was part of a ground shared with cricket, but when the swimming pool was built next door around 1970, the pitch was changed, with the cricket club moving out soon after. Since then the facilities now available have been developed to ECL standards, including the clubhouse, opened in 1992.

NEEDHAM MARKET

Bloomfields Needham Market Tel 01449 721000

Gen Sec: Derek Bloomfield 33 Quinton Rd
Needham Market Tel 01449 720693

Fixture Sec: Ian Croft 30 Macefield Stowmarket
Tel 01449 676517

Colours: Green

Capacity: 1,000

Seating: 250

Covered Standing: No

Clubhouse On Ground: Yes

DIRECTIONS

**Approach from the A14 Bury St
Edmunds-Ipswich road. Take the
turning opposite the A140 turn off
to Norwich (south of Stowmarket)
to Needham Market.**

Honours

Suffolk and Ipswich League Premier Division 1996

Division One 1953

Division Two 1947

Res - Premier Reserve Div 1971 and 72

Intermediate B 1994

Div 3 1986

A Team- Division 8 1984

Mick McNeil Cup 1978 and 1980

Suffolk Junior Cup 1985

Suffolk Senior Cup 1990

Needham Market Football Club was officially formed in 1927 although records show football being played in the late 1890s. They played on Youngs Meadow which was opposite Burlington Garage, then Crowley Park until 1996.

They moved to their new development called Bloomfields which was named after Derek Bloomfield who has served the club for 50 years as player administrator and groundsman. Last season the club won the Suffolk and Ipswich League which coincided with the opening of the new ground and the club were successful in their application to the Eastern Counties League.

The dedicated committee have promotion to the Premier Division as their immediate aim and with improved facilities at their new ground they are very hopeful.

NEWMARKET TOWN

Cricket Field Rd, off New Chieveley Rd, Newmarket, Suffolk. Tel: 01638 663637

Secretary: Eddie Leafhead, 56 Churchill Ct, Newmarket,
Tel: 01638 669503

Other matters: Keith Sheppard, 177 All Saints Rd,
Newmarket Tel: 01638 665878

Press officer Tony Pringle: 30 Windsor Rd, Newmarket
Tel:01638 669438

DIRECTIONS

400 yds from Newmarket (BR) - turn right into Green Road, right at crossroads New Cheveley Road ground at top on left.

Nickname: The Jockeys , Capacity: 1,750

Colours: Yellow and Blue, Seating: 144

Covered standing: 250, Clubhouse on ground: Yes

Record Attendance: 1,700 v Tottenham Hotspur A
April 15th 1949

Biggest Win: 12-0 v Cornard Utd Jan 7th 1995

Biggest Defeat: 0-12 v Biggleswade Mar 30th 1963

Record Appearances: Martin Marris 685

Record Goalscorer In One Season: D Etheridge 45 in 1965-66, Goalscorer in aggregate: D. Etheridge 145

Honours

Cambs Senior League 1920, Cambs Senior Cup: 1920, Cambs Challenge Cup 1926

Bury and District League Div 1 1927, Ipswich and District League 1932, 1933, 1934

Suffolk Senior Cup 1935, Peterborough League 1958, Cambs Invitation Cup 1959

Suffolk Premier Cup 1994, 1995,

Manager For 1996-97: Richard Datson; Assistant Manager: Martin Marris

Chairman: Keith Sheppard, Vice Chairman: Brian Walker

Newmarket Town were formed in 1877, making them one of the oldest clubs in the country.They began life in local football meeting with little success until 1920 when they won the Cambridgeshire Senior League and Senior Cup. They moved to the present Town ground in 1885, the inaugural game being on Wednesday, October 21st against Bury School. The Jockeys, as they were soon to be known, then joined the much stronger Bury and District League, taking the Division One title in 1928, a year after winning the Cambs Challenge Cup for the second time. Natural progression took them to the Ipswich and District League which they won in both 1930 and 1934 before moving on to the United Counties League for three seasons. They won the Suffolk Senior Cup for the only time during that period, in 1935. After the war the club changed direction again, joining the Eastern Counties League. The early days in the league were good, with the club forming an A team, but in 1952 they were rooted at the bottom of the ECL having lost every game and conceding 171 goals. Forced to return to junior football they joined the Peterborough and District League, which they won on goal difference from Ely City. In 1958 they won the Cambs Invitation Cup before returning to the ECL, much stronger than before in 1959, where they have remained ever since.

Their best season was when finishing runners up to Lowestoft Town in 1967, but life was generally a struggle for the Jockeys, finishing last in 1980. They fought a battle to survive in the top division in 1991, only escaping when Braintree moved into the Southern League. The escape heralded a change of fortunes, finishing 7th, 3rd, 3rd, 8th, 6th and 6th in the last six years, winning the Suffolk Premier Cup twice also.The wonderful old wooden grandstand at the Cricket Field finally bit the dust last year with a new one in its place, nearly 70 years after making its debut.

NORWICH UNITED

Plantation Rd, Blofield, Norwich, Norfolk NR13 4PL. Tel: 01603 716963

Secretary: The Secretary, c/o Norwich Utd FC
Plantation Rd, Norwich

Colours: Yellow and blue

Capacity; 3,000

Seating: 100

Covered standing: 1,000

Clubhouse on ground: Yes

Record attendance: 401 v Wroxham ECL 1991

Record appearances: Tim Sayer

DIRECTIONS

Half a mile from Blofield village - coming from Norwich on Yarmouth Road turn left in Blofield at Kings Head pub and follow to Plantation Road (ground on right after bridge over bypass). Half- hour walk Brundall BR (Norwich-Yarmouth line).

Honours

Eastern Counties League Div 1 1991

League Cup 1992

Anglian Combination 1989

Norwich United were founded in 1903 as Poringland and District FC. Their early history is unknown but in the 50's and 60's they competed in the Norwich and District League before joining the Anglian Combination in 1965. They eventually gained senior status in 1982, and continuing success forced a move from Poringland Memorial Playing Field to the Gothic Social Club ground in Heartsease Lane, in 1985. Two seasons later they changed their name to Norwich United and joined the Eastern Counties League in 1989

Their excellent Plantation Park ground, on the A47 ring road, is surrounded by acres of agricultural land and having won the Anglian Combination and then Division One of the ECL, the team broke up and within two years the club were back in Division One.

Before that United won a host of honours, beginning with the Anglian Combination Division Three. They won the Nofolk Junior Cup in 1980 and 1982 and also took the Combination Junior Cup, Bungay Charity Cup and were runners up in the Second Division.

A year later they were runners up in Division One and they took the Senior League Cup in 1984. As the team progressed it reached the Norfolk Senior Cup final in 1986 and 1987 and were runners up in the Anglian Combination a year after that.

It was enough to get into the ECL, where they have had an up and down start.

SOHAM TOWN RANGERS

Julius Martin Lane, Soham, Cambs. Tel: 01353 720732

Secretary Mrs Wendy Gammon, 32 Broad Piece, Soham, Cambs CB7 5EL

Tel: 01353 722139

DIRECTIONS

A142 between Newmarket and Ely - Julius Martins Lane.

Programme Editor Graham Eley, 94 Mereside, Soham, Cambs

Colours: Green and white

Nickname: Town or Rangers

Capacity: 1,500

Seating: 200

Covered standing: 500

Clubhouse on ground: Yes

Record attendance; 3,000 v Pegasus FA Amateur Cup

Honours

Peterborough League 3 times

Joint managers for 1996-97: Richard Goodjohn and Gary Grogan

Chairman: Mr M. Robinson

Vice Chairman: Mr R. Kelly

Soham Town Rangers were formed in 1947 from the amalgamation of Soham Town, formed in 1920, and Soham Rangers, formed in 1919. The club lost their ground after the war when it was required for agriculture and moved to the current ground, where they began in the Cambridgeshire League. 1956 saw a move to the Peterborough League, where in seven years they won the league and the League Cup on two occasions. They then moved into the Eastern Counties but it was relegation that found them in 1989, when they dropped down to the new Division One. In 1991 they regrouped and won the Cambridge Invitation Cup, beating March Town United in the final and in 1993 they regained a place in the top division from where they reached the 4th Round of the FA Vase. Aldershot Town were the opponents and in front of 2,300, they were well beaten.

The ground and facilities are owned entirely by the club, who were proud to host the League Cup final in 1995.

SOMERSHAM TOWN

West End Ground, St Ives Rd, Somersham, Hunts. Tel: 01487 843384

Secretary Mr Norman Burkett, 6 West Leys, St Ives, Cambs PE17 4DS Tel: 01480 464695

Gen Manager: Huntingdon, Cambs PE17 3SX Tel 01480 464411

DIRECTIONS

On A604 St Ives to Somersham on right as you enter town.

John Lyon, Molineux, 1 Asplins Ave, Needingworth

Colours: All Old Gold   Nickname: Westenders

Capacity: 3,000   Seating: None

Covered standing: 750   Clubhouse on ground: Yes

Record attend: 537 v Norwich City Floodlight opener 1991

Biggest win: 9-1 v Bury Town Res

Biggest defeat: 1-11 v Wroxham

Record appearances: Terry Butcher

Record goalscorer in one season: B Doe

Record goalscorer in total: Terry Butcher

Honours

Hunts Senior Cup 1973 and 1994

Peterborough Senior Cup 1973 and 1984

Hinchingbrooke Cup 1934 and 1954

Aubrey Robinson Cup 1984 and 1985

Hunts Junior Cup 1920, 1932, 1936

Hunts Benevolent Cup 1985

Manager 1996-97: Ian Boon

Assistant Manager: Jim Wallace

Chairman: Alan Bailey

Somersham's programme was voted best in league or Division for six years from 1990

The club was formed in December 1893 and played in the local league, although the early history is very vague. After the Second War the club became founder members of the Peterborough and District Premier Division, although they failed to win the title they were runners up on many occasions, the most recent being 1986. At the end of the 1987-88 season they withdrew from that league and entered the Eastern Counties League Division One as founder members. The present ground was bought and the clubhouse opened in 1981 with new changing rooms following four years later. During 1990 railings went in around the pitch and a second stand was added. On March 11th 1991 floodlights were begun and the first match was played in April against Potton in the Hinchingbrooke Cup final.

The club celebrated its Centenary with a Trevor Brooking X1 including Billy Bonds and Frank Lampard playing a match and they ended it by winning the Hunts Senior Cup for only the second time and were runners up in the Hinchingbrooke Cup.

STANWAY ROVERS

Hawthorns, New Farm Rd, Stanway, Colchester, Essex. Tel: 01206 578187

Secretary Alan Brierley, 19 Barley Way, Stanway, Colchester, Essex CO3 5YD Tel: 01206 572439

Colours:Yellow and black

Nickname: Rovers

Capacity: 1,500

Seating: None

Covered standing: 200

Clubhouse on ground: Yes

Record attendance: 156 v Hadleigh ECL 1994

Biggest win: 8-1 v Swaffham Town ECL 1994

Biggest defeat: 0-10 v Sudbury Town ECL Cup

DIRECTIONS

Take turn off marked Stanway off A12. Turn right and go over flyover to Tollgate roundabout, 1st roundabout, 1st right into Villa Road, after 25 yards turn left into Church Road, 200 yards on left into New Farm Road, ground 400 yards on left. Nearest BR station is Colchester North.

Honours

Essex and Suffolk Border League Div 1 1987

Division Two 1981 and 1986

The Stanway Football Club records show that they were formed on July 10th 1956, but newspaper cuttings tell of a Stanway club in the early 1900's. The minute books show that the first meeting was in St Albright's Hall and was chaired by Jack Poole, of the ECFA.

They played their early matches on King George V Playing Fields in Lexden, more commonly known as Clairmont Road, and after moving to the Second Division of the Colchester and East Essex League, they played at Stanway Secondary School, having been promoted to the Premier Division.

The Headmaster, Mr Garnham took the Presidency, an office all Heads' took whilst the club were there, and they enjoyed superb facilities, with fine pitches, a sports hall and a gymnasium.

The club's most successful season was in 1974 when they did a clean sweep in the Colchester League and reached the last eight of the Essex Junior Cup. A year later they reached the final but were beaten by Takeley. That year the first team joined the Border League, Division Two and were promoted and in what was an exciting time for the club, they agreed a long lease with the local authorities for just over 4.5 acres of land on which they eventually built the Hawthorns.

The clubhouse opened in 1982 and after reaching the Intermediate Cup finals of 1990 and 1991, Stanway were given senior status and joined the Eastern Counties League.

STOWMARKET TOWN

Green's Meadow, Bury Rd, Stowmarket. Tel: 01449 612533

Secretary John Doward, Deepland House, Stoupland,
Stowmarket IP14 4DE Tel: 01449 612003

Prog Editor and club shop John Gillingham,
23 Windermere Rd, Stowmarket IP14 1LD
Tel: 01449 674507

Fixture Secretary Christine Gillingham c/o Club

Nickname: The Stow or Gold and Blacks

DIRECTIONS

About 800 yds from Stowmarket BR station - turn right at 1st lights and head out of town over roundabout into Bury Road - ground on right.

Capacity: 2,000, Seating: 200, Covered Standing: 200

Clubhouse On Ground: Yes, Colours: Old Gold and Black

Record Attendance: At Cricket Meadow 3,800 v Romford Amateur Cup Dec 15th 1951

Biggest Win: 7-1 v Chatteris Town

Biggest Defeat: 2-7 v Sudbury Town

Record appearances: Kevin Parris.

Record goalscorer in one season: Stuart Jopling 38

Honours

Ipswich and District League 6 times

Suffolk Junior Cup 1908, Suffolk Senior Cup 1931, 1933, 1934, 1951, 1952, 1958, 1962, 1965

Suffolk Premier Cup 1963, 1986, 1991,

Suffolk Charity Cup 1924 and 1933 and Harwich Charity Cup 1990

Essex and Suffolk Border League 1951, League Cup 1951 and 1952, Battle of Britain Cup 4 times

Manager 1996-97: Trevor Wardlaw: Assistant Manager: Del Aldis

Chairman: Derek Barnard

Press officer: Andrew Horrex, 29 Windermere Rd, Stowmarket TEL: 01449 674184

The club was founded in 1883 and for 101 years played at the Cricket Meadow before moving to its present site at Green's Meadow in 1984. Stow played their formative years in local football and brought off their first championship triumph in 1897 when winning the Ipswich and District League, a feat that was repeated four times before the War. In the early days the club played in both Junior and Senior County Competitions and the Senior Cup final was reached in 1891, but having reached the junior final in 1907, it was won a year later for the only time. After the War the club was quiet until 1922 when they won the league for the sixth and last time, before joining the Essex and Suffolk Border League. Stow were runners up in 1930 and although having little other league success, they won the Senior Cup in three out of four consecutive finals in the thirties. They also won the Charity Cup and made an appearance in the FA Amateur Cup First Round. After the cup successes the club went into decline and actually folded just before the Second War, the ground being taken over by Nobels FC, later to become ICI. They reformed, first as Stowupland Corinthians and then Stowmarket Corinthians before in August 1947 Stowmarket Town was back in business, adopting the gold and black colours which they keep today. In 1950 the club were runners up in the Essex and Suffolk before taking the title a year later. They also won the Senior Cup twice running, as well as the Battle of Britain Cup four times and the Border League Cup twice. Moving to the Eastern Counties League was a different story in 1952, but they survived on a diet of Senior and later Premier Cup triumphs without seriously challenging for the league. In 1984 their quaint and rustic Cricket Meadow finally disappeared under a supermarket after the last game on May 17th and over 400 saw the first game at Green's Meadow the following August.

After Premier Cup win and a short period of financial problems, the club enjoyed a superb season in 1991-92 under Doug Wade. Finishing runners up in the league and the Premier Cup, they did win the Fair Play Award and the reserves took the Border League Cup. Sadly the team parted company with the manager during the next season but they survived and remain in the top flight of the ECL.

SUDBURY WANDERERS

Brundon Lane, Sudbury, Suffolk. Tel: 01787 376213

Secretary: Brian Tatum, 4 Beaconsfield Close, Sudbury, Suffolk CO 10 6JR. Tel: 01787 375840

Colours: All Yellow

Nickname: Wanderers

Capacity: 2,500

Seating: 200

Covered standing: 150

Clubhouse on ground: Yes

Record attendance: 248 v Woodbridge Town Eastern Counties League Div 1 1993

DIRECTIONS
From Sudbury town centre follow Halstead/Chelmsford signs for about 1 mile. Take 1st right after railway bridge at foot of steep hill, and 1st right after sharp lefthand bend.

Honours

Eastern Counties League Div 1 1993

Eassex and Suffolk Border League 1990 and 1991

Suffolk Senior Cup 1991

The Wanderers were formed in 1958 by four men, the late Roy Webber, Brian Tatum, Tootie Eves and Wally Brown. For 18 years the club played at People's Park, often having to clear cow pats and cattle from the pitch before play and with changing rooms some distance away, first at the Black Horse and then at the Horse and Groom.

The first season was spent in the Halstead League, winning the league and cup and they moved on to the Border League but had to wait nearly 20 years before gaining promotion to the top division in 1978.

With the assistance of the Supporters Club, the club's dream of their own ground became a reality as they turned a water meadow into two football pitches, a cricket square, dressing rooms and a bar. On the pitch, although consistent, the club had to wait until 1990 before winning the league, waiting until the last game of the season before doing so. The following season saw Wanderers again take the title and complete another dream by winning the Suffolk Senior Cup in 1991, after twice losing finals.

In 1992 a new dressing room complex was opened and a visitors lounge with new bar was also finished, and more recently floodlights have gone up which allowed the club to compete in the Premier Division which they reached following their Division One championship season in 1993.

Sadly this August sees the club return to Division One following relegation in May.

SUDBURY TOWN RESERVES

Secretary Dave Webb 6 Melford Rd, Sudbury, Tel 01787 372352

See entry in Doc Martens League Premier Division

SWAFFHAM TOWN

Shoemakers Lane, Swaffham, Norfolk. Tel: 01760 722700

Secretary Mr David Ward, 2 Princes St, Swaffham,
Norfolk PE37 7BX Tel 01760 722516

Colours: Black and white stripes

Nickname: Pedlars

Capacity: 2,000

Seating: None

Covered standing: Yes

Clubhouse on ground: Yes

Record attendance: 250 v Downham Town
ECL League Cup 1991

DIRECTIONS

From the north or south take the
A1065 to the town centre. From the
east or west take the A47 to the
town centre. The football club is in
Shoemakers Lane.

Honours

Norfolk Senior Cup twice

Anglian Combination 1990 and Division One 1989

Swaffham Town were formed in 1892 and moved to Shoemakers Lane in 1959, when the new 1.5 acre ground was bought for £250. Today's reserved estimate of the club's value is £350,000, making it a tidy investment and one which hopefully secures the club's future.

The Pedlar's first taste of success came way back in 1894, when they lost the final of the Norfolk Junior Cup to Wymondham Reserves, and it took until 1951 before they made amends, beating RAF Coltishall 1-0.

They following season saw them retain the cup, beating RAF Watton. They could not quite achieve the hat-trick, losing to Norman Old Boys.

In 1974 they club won the Anglian Combination Second Division and built the clubhouse at Shoemakers Lane, thanks to a brewery loan, and further progress was made when the Pedlars joined the Eastern Counties League, where they have remained mostly in the lower half of Division One, although they did reach the semi-final of the Norfolk Senior Cup under manager Mick Simmons.

THETFORD TOWN

Mundford Road, Thetford, Norfolk. Tel: 01842 766120

Secretary: John Wordley, 4 Claxton Close, Thetford,
Norfolk IP24 1BA Tel: 01842 762530

Other matters: M Bailey, 6 Nelson Crescent, Thetford,
Norfolk Tel: 01842 764961

DIRECTIONS
Turn off bypass (A11) at A143 junction - ground 800 yds towards Thetford.

Press officer: Michael Burgess, 14 Ulfkell Road, Thetford, Norfolk

Tel: 01842 764232

Founded: 1882

Nickname: The Town

Capacity: 2,800

Seating: Yes

Covered Standing: Yes

Clubhouse On Ground: Yes

Record Attendance: 391 v Diss Town Norfolk Senior Cup 23rd Jan 1991

Biggest Win: 10-1 v Norwich City A 1964-65

Biggest Defeat: 0-19 v Lowestoft Town 1936-37

Honours

Norfolk and Suffolk League 1955

Norfolk Senior Cup 1948 and 1991

Manager For 1996-97 S. Allen and G. Hughes

Chairman: Michael Bailey

Thetford's recent history has been very grim, with a number of seasons seeing the club finish bottom. However, 1996 saw a vast improvement with the club amongst the top five in Division One. Despite that, it was as recently as 1991 when they won the Norfolk Senior Cup, a year after finishing as runners-up in the league.

The club was formed in 1882, and played in Norfolk and Suffolk local leagues until joining the Eastern Counties in 1935. In two seasons they finished bottom both times, in one match losing 19-0 to Lowestoft. They returned to the Norfolk and Suffolk League, winning the Senior Cup in 1948 and the league in 1955. Eight years later, with several clubs resigning from the ECL, Thetford returned and have remained ever since. The Recreation Ground has been their home since 1905, the club originally having played on pitches at Abbey Heath until 1900 and on meadowland by the river before then. The football pitch is part of a large sports complex and has had floodlights since 1988.

TIPTREE UNITED

Chapel Rd, Tiptree, Essex. Tel: 01621 815213

Secretary: Peter Fidge, 77 Chelmer Rd, Chelmsford,
Essex, CM2 6AA Tel 01245 353667

Colours: Red and black

Nickname: Strawberries

Capacity: 2,500

Seating: 150

Covered standing: 300

Clubhouse on ground: Yes

Record attendance: 1,210 v Tottenham Hotspur
Floodlight opening 1990

DIRECTIONS

**Enter town on B1023 - Chapel Road
is left at second crossroads, ground
200 yds on left. 3 miles from
Kelverdon (BR). Served by eastern
national Colchester to Maldon bus.**

Honours

Essex Senior Trophy 1981

Eastern Counties League 1982

League Cup 1982 and 1985

Harwich Charity Cup 4 times

Manager 1996-97: Steve Sutton

Chairman: Fred Byles

Vice Chairman: Bernie Millgate

Tiptree United were founded back in 1933 and joined the North Essex League before progressing to the Essex and Suffolk Border League, but without success. They joined the Eastern Counties for a while but dropped back and switched to the Essex Senior League, remaining until 1979, when they went back to the ECL, replacing Cambridge United Reserves. They were runners up to Gorleston and a year later took the Essex Senior Trophy for the only time. 1981-82 was the best season to date as manager Edgar Rumney took them to the league and cup double, winning the league by six points from Sudbury Town, and beating Gorleston in the Cup final. To round off a great season they took the Harwich Charity Cup and reached the 3rd Round of the FA Vase.

1983 saw them in the Senior Trophy final and a year later they again enjoyed a run in the Vase. In 1985 and 1986 they won the League Cup, finishing fifth in the league both times, and won the Tollshunt D'arcy and Ipswich Charity Cups, but since them success has been harder to come by.

WARBOYS TOWN

Sports Field, Forge Way, High Street, Warboys, Cambs. Tel: 01487 823483

Secretary: Richard Kelly, Chairman, 5 Medecroft,
Warboys, Huntingdon PE17 2SF

Nickname: The Witches

Capacity: 2,000

Seating: Yes

Covered standing: 200

Clubhouse On Ground: Yes

Record Attendance: v Ramsey Town
Hunts Sen Cup semi-final

DIRECTIONS

Access through Forge Way, half way
along south side of High Street.

Honours

Peterborough Senior Cup 1964

Hunts Senior Cup 1927, 1929, 1932, 1933, 1995

Hunts Scott Gatty Cup 1931

Warboys Town were formed in 1885. They played in the Peterborough and Huntingdon Leagues until 1950 when they switched to the United Counties League. That lasted six years until they returned to the Peterborough League, where they remained until joining the Eastern Counties League in 1988.

The Witches have won the Hunts Senior Cup five times, the last being in 1995 and were runners up in the UCL Division Two in 1955 and the Peterborough Premier League in 1960 and 1962.

Winners of the Hunts Senior Cup in 1927, 1929, 1932 and 1933 the club tried without success for many years to repeat those great days, reaching numerous semi-finals, and eventually they succeeded in 1995, beating Eynesbury.

Part of the land for the field which the club shares with the cricket club was donated by a local farmer and additional land, paid for by public subscription, was laid out and drained in 1946.

Back in 1948 the Supporters Club began the first clubhouse with a War Department hut forming dressing rooms and a tea bar, and floodlights arrived in 1992. Three sides of the pitch were surrounded by a permanent post and rail when the club joined the ECL and there are plans to add another stand in the near future.

WATTON UNITED

Dereham Rd, Watton, Norfolk. Tel: 01953 881281

Secretary: Denis Bealey, 11 Hickling Close, Swaffham, Norfolk, PE37 7SE

Tel: 01760 721869

Colours: All white

DIRECTIONS

On A1075 towards Dereham about half a mile from junction with B1108.

Nickname: Brecklanders

Capacity: 2,000

Seating: 50

Covered standing: 150

Clubhouse on ground: Yes

Record attendance; 1,200 v Norwich City
Floodlight opener 1985

Honours

Anglian Combination 1967, 1968, 1986

League Cup 1967 and 1970

Founded in 1888, Watton United were members of the Dereham and District League until 1950, the year they won their only championship in that league.

The Brecklanders were elected to the East Anglian League and immediately won Division Two in their debut season, and in 1953 they took the League Cup. A year later they were just pipped to the title by Norman Old Boys, which was the last excitement for some years.

By the 1960 season the re-built side had become strong enough to challenge for the title and were just pipped after remaining unbeaten to the last game of the year, but a disastrous second half of the season saw them pipped by Norwich City B.

In 1964 the East Anglian League merged with the Norfolk and Suffolk League to form the Anglian Combination and the first season was a memorable one, as the club won the League and Cup double, beating CEYMS in the final. They retained the title a year later, but it was not until 1970 that they won the League Cup again, beating St Andrews, only to lose the final a year on, to Sheringham.

In 1974 Watton suffered the humiliation of relegation, although they bounced straight back as runners up to Southwold. In 1977 Norwich City were the opposition for the official switching on of the floodlights match which attracted 1,000 people, which is the record crowd at the ground.

In 1986 they successfully applied to join the Eastern Counties League and although reaching the Senior Cup final in 1993, success has been limited.

WHITTON UNITED

King George V Playing Fields, Norwich Rd, Ipswich. Tel: 01473 464030

Secretary: David Gould, 7 Karen Close, Ipswich, Suffolk IP1 4LP

Tel: 01473 253838

Fixture Sec: Mark Woodward, 3 Kempton Rd, Ipswich, IP1 6QY Tel: 01473 742805

Press Secretary: Ian Vernal, 12 Chatsworth Crescent, Ipswich IP2 9BS

Tel: 01473 692359

Colours: Green and white

Capacity: 600 approx

Seating: None

Covered standing: 100

Clubhouse on ground: Yes

Record attendance: 528

DIRECTIONS

Approach Ipswich on either A14 or A12 and stay on these main roads rather than enter the town centre. Whitton is to the north of the urban area (off A14 to Bury St Edmunds) and the ground is on Norwich Road.

Honours

Suffolk Senior Cup 1959, 1960, 1992

Suffolk and Ipswich League 1947, 1948, 1966, 1968, 1993, 1995

Manager 1996-97: Steven Tassell

Assistant Manager: Colin Macrow

Chairman: John Watkins

Vice Chairman: Tommy Woodward

Whitton were formed in 1926 and played in the Ipswich and District League, the forerunner of today's Suffolk and Ipswich League, until 1948. That year the club reached the Senior Cup final for the first time but lost to Lowestoft. The club joined the Border League and during that time won the Senior Cup in 1959 and 1963, beating Bungay both times.

The 1970's saw a decline in Whitton's fortunes and in 1982 they re-entered the Suffolk and Ipswich League and in that momentous first season, all three teams won their Divisions. Since then Whitton have built themselves up to become one of the strongest clubs in the SIL and it was no surprise when after winning Senior Cups and Senior Leagues during the 90's that they entered the Eastern Counties League last year.

The ground has been transformed with floodlights, hard standing, perimeter fencing and a small stand.

WISBECH TOWN

Fenland Park, Lerowe Road, Wisbech, Cambs. Tel: 01945 584176

Secretary: Gavin Stevenson, 4 Main Street, Pymore, Ely, Cambs CB6 2ED Tel: 01353 699260

Nickname: The Fenmen   Club colours: All Red

Capacity: 7,500   Seating 258

Covered standing: 3,000

Clubhouse on ground: Yes

DIRECTIONS

On Lerowe Road, a right turn off the A47 Lynn Road. 20 mins walk from town centre. Irregular bus services to Wisbech from Peterborough or March.

Record attendance: 8,004 v Peterborough United Midland League Aug 25th 1957

Biggest win: 18-1 v Rushden Town 1946

Record appearances: James Brighty 650

Record goalscorer in one season: J. Youles 86 in 1931-32

Record goalscorer in total: B. Titmarsh 246 1931-1937

HONOURS

FA VASE semi-finalists 1985 and 1986

Southern League Div 1 1962

United Counties League 1947, 1948, 1950, 1962 (res), League Cup 1936

Eastern Counties League 1972, 1977, 1991, League Cup 1951, 1971, 1972

Cambridgeshire Invitation Cup 1953, 1956, 1958, 1975, 1976, 1982, 1983, 1992

East Anglian Cup 1988, Peterborough League 1925, 1928, 1929, 1932, 1933

Peterborough Senior Cup 1933, 1977, 1990

The present club was formed in 1920 and was an amalgamation of three clubs which played on Wisbech Park. Initially the club joined both the Peterborough and Lynn Leagues, with Yaxley providing the first ever opposition, some 1,500 witnessing a 1-1 draw. They went on to win the Lynn League and finish ninth in the Peterborough League. The following season the Poppies, as they were then known moved to Rectory Field at Walsoken and in 1922 moved on to Harecroft Road, where they stayed for 25 years. That season they took the Hinchingbrooke Cup, taking the league also five times in eight years. In 1935 they turned pro and a limited company was formed, entering the United Counties League. In their first season, Wisbech won the League Cup and in 1941 were runners up in the East Anglian Cup. After the war, in 1946, they reached the First Round of the FA Cup for the 6th time, where they lost to Ipswich, but they repeated the dose four more times in the 60's. 1946 also saw the highest ever victory, an 18-1 thrashing of Rushden Town and a year later, the year they moved in to Fenland Park, they were champions of the United Counties League. In the next three seasons they were champions twice and runners up, which led to them joining the Eastern Counties League. They finished ninth in the first year and won the League Cup, but at the end of the next term they resigned and joined the Midland League, remaining until the league's demise in 1958 - the season they were runners up and got to the 2nd Round of the Cup. Their record crowd of 8,044 was set during the Midland League days, against Peterborough United in 1957. 1958 saw the Fenmen, as they had become, join the Southern League and under Jesse Pye won Division One in 1962. Sadly in 1965 they were relegated, remaining in Division One until financial problems saw them drop into the Eastern Counties League. In the first season back they were runners up in the league and won the League Cup and a year later they went one better, doing the double. In 1974 they were double runners up, but were champions in 1977, losing the League Cup. In 1985 Wisbech were losing semi-finalists in the FA Vase, beaten by Halesowen Town and were again sadly beaten at the same hurdle a year later, that time by Southall. Town have remained consistently high in the league although last season's eighth was a disappointment.

WOODBRIDGE TOWN

Notcutts Park, Seckford Hall Road, Woodbridge, Suffolk, IP2 1LD. Tel: 01394 385308

Secretary: Ralph Coxall, 5 Orchard Close, Woodbridge, Suffolk, IP12 1LD Tel: 01394 387839

Nickname: Woodpeckers   Capacity: 2,000

Seating: 50   Covered standing: 200

Clubhouse on ground: Yes

Record attendance: 3,000 v Arsenal Floodlight opener Oct 2nd 1990

DIRECTIONS

Turning into Woodbridge off last roundabout from Lowestoft, or 1st roundabout from Ipswich. Take 1st turning left and 1st left again. Drive to ground at end of road on left.

HONOURS

Suffolk Senior Cup 1978, 1994

Suffolk Junior Cup, 1909, 1926, 1971, 1987

Ipswich and District League 1913, 1971, 1987

Suffolk and Ipswich League 1989

Harwich Charity Cup 1994

Churchman Cup 1994

Woodbridge Town Football Club was formed following a meeting held on the 23rd July 1885, and played its first match between its own members, the Hornets and the Wasps, on Farlingaye Hall pitch. The first recorded competitive game was against St Helens of Ipswich in November of that year.

Town were founder members of the Suffolk County FA, whose first priority was the formation of the Challenge Cup, now known as the Suffolk Senior Cup, and Town were the first winners, at Portman Road after two draws.

Eventually they reverted to junior football and in 1909 the County Junior Cup was won. They returned to senior football in the Ipswich and District League, winning it in 1913. Between the Wars they again were given junior status, winning the Junior Cup in 1926, and were senior again a year later where they again played Ipswich in the Senior Cup Final at Portman Road.

The following years saw many changes, one problem being finding a permanent home venue. During the 50's they used five different grounds, including Peterhouse Field and Kingston Playing Field, but it was not until September 1990 that they finally moved to the new Notcutts Park.

The 70's and 80's were very mixed for Town, they won the Ipswich and District League in 1971 and the Junior Cup, which regained them senior status, and in 1978 they won the Senior Cup, beating Crane Sports, but in 1983 they were junior again, doing the double in 1987.

The late 80's saw the Woodpeckers in the Suffolk and Ipswich League, which they won in 1989, and they then took the bold step of moving into the Eastern Counties League, playing at Kingston Field. The new ground was opened with a game against Arsenal which attracted a crowd of over 3,000.

The first two seasons were spent in mid table, but 1994 saw the Senior Cup come to Woodbridge again, as well as being runners up in Division One. The Harwich Charity and Churchman Cups were also won in a remarkable year.

Last season saw the club established in the top division , with the bonus of an appearance in the final of the Suffolk Premier Cup, losing on penalties to Bury Town.

WROXHAM

Trafford Park, Skinners Lane, Wroxham, Norfolk. Tel: 01603 783538

Secretary: Mr Chris Green, 24 Keys Drive, Wroxham, Norfolk, NR12 8SS Tel 01603 783936 (h), 01603 683675 (b)

Chairman: Ray Bayles, 62 Church Close, Sprowston, Norwich, NR7 8QA

Tel 01603 403555 (h) 10603 4437531 (b)

> **DIRECTIONS**
>
> **Arriving from Norwich turn left at Castle PH and keep left to ground. Two and a half miles from Hoveton (BR). Buses 722, 724 and 717.**

Colours: Blue and white   Nickname: Yachtsmen

Capacity: 2,500   Seating: 100

Covered standing: 150   Clubhouse on ground: Yes

Record attendance: 1,011 v Wisbech Town ECL 1993

Biggest win: 15-2 v Thetford Town ECL 1992

Biggest defeat: 1-24 Blofield, Norwich League early 60's.

Record appearances: Mark Halsey

Record goalscorer in one season: Matthew Metcalf

Record goalscorer in total: Jon Rigby

Honours

Eastern Counties League 1992, 1993, 1994, Division One 1989 and League Cup 1993

Norfolk Senior Cup 1993, Norfolk Junior Cup 1975

Anglian Combination 1982, 1983, 1984, 1985, 1988

Anglian Combination Senior Cup 1981, 1983, 1985, 1988

Manager 1996-97: Bruce Cunningham, Assistant Manager: Keith Robson,

Chairman: Ray Bayles, Vice Chairman: Ricky Coulthard

The Yachtsmen were founded in 1892 and in the early days played on Wroxham Park, in colours of pink and black. Initially they played friendlies before joining the East Norfolk League and the Norwich City Junior League. In 1935 they joined the East Anglian League and enjoyed a number of successful seasons until the early fifties when they hit hard times and stepped down to the Norwich and District League where they lost one match 24-0. In 1963 they applied to become founder members of the Anglian Combination and although early years brought little success the 70's saw an upturn in fortunes. Progress was made through the divisions and in 1975 they won the Norfolk Junior Cup, beating Norwich Lad's Club. 1976 saw them take the Division Two title and a year later they won Division One. In 1982 they completed the set by taking the Premier championship, and retained for three more years, also dominating the League Cup.

After another title the club accepted a challenge a year later and entered the new Eastern Counties First Division. They pipped Halstead to take the title and promotion. After a couple of seasons, Wroxham were ready and they took the Eastern Counties League title in 1992, before sweeping all before them a year later. In their Centenary season the club won the league again, and completed the treble with the League Cup and the Norfolk Senior Cup. They completed the hat-trick in style, just missing out on four in a row by coming second to Halstead in 1995. Last season they were third but reached the final of the Norfolk Senior Cup where they lost to Diss Town.

NEWMARKET TOWN F.C.

JEWSON LEAGUE PREMIER DIVISION

SEASON 1995 1996

Suffolk Premier Cup
Winners
1993-94
1994-95

The JOCKEYS

WELCOME to the TOWN GROUND
NEWMARKET TOWN F.C.

Official

50p

Programme

Sat.
6th
April
versus

WOODBRIDGE TOWN

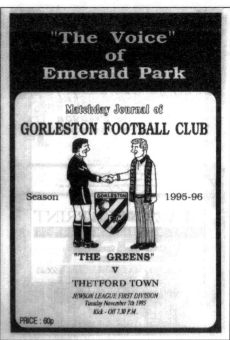

"The Voice"
of
Emerald Park

Matchday Journal of

GORLESTON FOOTBALL CLUB

Season   1995-96

"THE GREENS"
v
THETFORD TOWN

JEWSON LEAGUE FIRST DIVISION
Tuesday November 7th 1995
Kick - Off 7.30 P.M.

PRICE : 60p

SOHAM TOWN RANGERS FOOTBALL CLUB

SEASON 1995-96
OFFICIAL MATCHDAY PROGRAMME

TODAY'S VISITORS

Gt YARMOUTH TOWN FC
PREMIER DIVISION
WED 1st MAY 1996

MAIN CLUB SPONSOR: **CLARK & BUTCHER LTD**

WROXHAM
FOOTBALL CLUB
(FOUNDED 1892)

Welcome to
Trafford Park
Home of
'The Yachtsmen'

Jewson League
Premier Division 95/96

A BARNES PRINT
PRODUCTION
Tel (01362) 860781

Official Club Sponsor
DOLPHIN AUTOS

Interlink Express Midland Alliance

	P	W	D	L	F	A	PTS
Shepshed Dynamo	36	22	10	4	90	37	76
Blakenall	36	19	11	6	60	36	68
Hinckley Athletic	36	21	4	11	78	54	67
Rocester	36	19	9	8	55	50	66
Knypersley Vic	36	18	8	10	73	43	62
Boldmere St M	36	18	5	13	73	51	59
Sandwell Borough	36	17	5	14	56	50	56
Willenhall Town	36	16	7	13	52	62	55
Barwell	36	15	6	15	57	53	51
Oldbury United	36	14	8	14	49	41	50
Rushall Olympic	36	15	5	16	57	65	46
Halesowen Harr	36	13	7	16	54	62	46
Stratford Town	36	12	9	15	56	54	45
Pershore Town	36	12	9	15	58	73	45
West Mids Police	36	11	11	14	49	55	44
Chasetown	36	10	10	16	44	52	40
Shifnal Town	36	8	9	19	38	60	33
Stapenhill	36	5	6	25	38	87	21
Bolehall Swifts	36	5	5	26	30	82	20

Blakenall F.C. League Cup Winners

BARWELL

Kirkby Road, Barwell, Leics. Tel: 01455 843067

Secretary: Shirley Brown, 101 Eskdale Rd, Hinckley, Leics. LE10 0NW. Tel: 01455 619308

Colours: Yellow and green

Nickname: Canaries

Capacity: 2,500

Seating: 140

Covered standing: Yes

Clubhouse on ground: Yes

Record appearances: Kevin Johnson

Record goalscorer in total: Joey Aitchison

Honours

Leicestershire Senior League Cup 1992

DIRECTIONS

M42 junction 10 (Tamworth Services), A5 towards Nuneaton, sharp left signed Market Bosworth after 11 miles (400m after Longshoot Motel), left for Barwell at 3rd island (3 miles), right onto B581 after half mile to Barwell centre (1 mile), turn left opposite Nat West Bank and immediately right into Kirkby Road — entrance to Barwell Sports and Social Club 400m on right. From M69 junction 1 take B4109 towards Hinckley, right at lights after one and a half miles into Brookside, at end after 1 mile left onto Burbage Road, left signed Leicester (A47) at 2nd lights, after Rugby Club take next left for Barwell, half mile to town centre — over mini-roundabout and Kirkby Road is 50 yards on right. BR to Hinckley station — bus station is 200 yards away via Station Road — take Leicester bus and Barwell is 1st village en route (two and a half miles).

Barwell are a new club who were formed by the amalgamation of Hinckley FC and Barwell Athletic in 1992. They won the Midland Combination under the new name in 1993 and were founder members of the Alliance. Barwell Athletic played for many years in the Leicester Senior League with Hinckley FC coming out of the Central Midlands League, where they previously shared the ground of Hinckley Athletic.

Barwell's facilities are part of an impressive sports ground, with a cricket pitch which once staged County matches, a superb indoor bowls centre and clubhouse.

BLAKENALL

The Red Lion Ground, Somerfield Road, Leamore, Walsall. Tel: 01922 405835 or 400600

Secretary: Mr David Birch, 64 Wimperis Way, Great Barr, Birmingham, B43 7DF. Tel: 0121 360 3574

Commercial: Manager, Jeff Husted, at Football ground

Press Officer: Russell Brown, 40 Carisbrooke Rd, Bushbury, Wolverhampton WV10 8AB Tel: 01902 822522

Colours: Red and White,   Nickname: Nall

Capacity: 2,250,   Seating: 250

Covered standing: 50

Clubhouse on ground: Yes

DIRECTIONS

M6 jct 10, follow signs for Walsall centre. At 1st lights turn left (about 200 yds from Motorway junction) into Bloxwich Lane. Keep following this lane to the T-junction and turn right into Leamore Lane, at this island turn left into Somerfield Road. Ground is approx 400yds on the right.

Record attendance: 1,500 v Halesowen Town

Biggest win: 11-0 v Bilston United April 26th 1995

Biggest defeat: 1-7 Oldbury United April 17th 1993

Record fee received £10,000 from Wolves for Darren Simkin

Honours

Midland Football Alliance League Cup 1996

Midland Invitational Cup 1995, West Midlands League 1989, League Cup 1995

Walsall Senior Cup 1964, 1975, 1976, 1977, 1981, 1990, 1996

Midland Combination 1977

Manager for 1996-97: Bob Green, Assistant manager: Brian Taylor

Chairman: Peter Langston, Vice chairman: David Cotterill

Blakenall Football Club was formed in 1946 from a group of regulars based at the New Inns public house in the Leamore district of Walsall. Initially competing in the Bloxwich Combination, they moved to the Saffordshire County League and then the Midland Combination in 1960. It was 1977 before the club won the championship, on goal difference from Bridgnorth Town. `Nall remained in that league until moving across to the West Midlands League, along with Malvern Town and Sutton Coldfield in 1979. Blakenall enjoyed fifteen seasons as members of the Premier Division and have occupied mid-table for most of the tenure, but it all changed in 1988 when Gresley were ousted on the last day, when Nall drew with Chasetown to take the title. As with many winning clubs, they were denied the chance to move to the Southern League by ground grading. 1991 brought more changes to the Red Lion ground, the biggest being the compulsory installation of floodlights, enabling them to stay in the top division. The appointment of Bob Green as manager saw more changes at the club. A finish of 4th in 1994 was a credit but it was just the start as 1994-95 proved to be the best ever. With Pelsall Villa pipping the club to the league title, despite Nall scoring over 100 goals, they took the League Cup for the first time and also won the Invitational Triangular Cup, beating Shifnal on penalties. With extensive ground improvements done, the club were delighted to move up into the Midland Alliance for last season, and another superb effort saw the club end as runners up to Shepshed, and winners of the League Cup, and the Walsall Senior Cup for the seventh time, another wonderful season. The Red Lion Ground dates from the turn of the century and was originally the home of Bloxwich Strollers, who gave up the tenancy in the late 1950's. After the ground had stood empty for a couple of years Blakenall took over the lease and moved in. Before the war the Red Lion boasted an old wooden grandstand which was taken down and put in storage for the war, but the story goes that it never returned but was later used by Walsall Rugby Club. With some irony, Bloxwich Strollers found themselves many years later playing at the Red Lion again, as tenants of Blakenall.

BLOXWICH TOWN

Abbey Park, Glastonbury Crescent, Mossley Estate, Bloxwich, Walsall. Tel: 01922 477640

Secretary: Mr S.Clarke, 10 Sandhill Street, Bloxwich, Walsall, Tel: 01922 492463

Press Sec: Mr K. Edwards 149, Coalpool Lane, Walsall Tel: 01922 723322

Colours: Blue and white

Nickname: Kestrels

Capacity: 2,000

Seating: 200

Covered standing: 200

Clubhouse on ground: Yes

Biggest win: 8-1 in 1995-96

Biggest defeat: 1-9 in 1993-94

Record appearances: Mark Sparrock

Record goalscorer in one season: Robert Wilson

Record goalscorer in total: Tony Eccleston

DIRECTIONS

A34 Walsall-Bloxwich, then west onto A4124. Ground 2-3 miles on right, s.p. Mossley Estate.

Honours

Midland Combination 1996

Challenge Cup 1996

Manager 1996-97: P.Knox

Joint Manager: M.Folland

Chairman: T.Sanghara

Vice Chairman: J.Baines

Formed just 20 years ago as PEEL FC, they began in the Bloxwich Combination, changing to Bloxwich FC two years later. In 1981 they joined the Staffs County League South after winning many honours and they carried on by becoming champions of Division One in the first season, and moving to Abbey Park.

In 1982 they joined the Midland Combination Division One and with improvements to the ground they were allowed into the FA Vase. Promotion came and in 1987 the club reached the final of the Walsall Senior Cup, losing to Boldmere St Mikes. Sadly the club went down the following year only to come straight back up as champions and win the Invitation Cup a year later. The club declined during the early 90's and just stayed in the top division, but during the summer of 1993 they almost folded after a bid for a new ground was turned down. Since then, the club has gone upwards thanks to being saved by two local businessmen. Abbey Park has been transformed and in 1995 they were runners up in the league, a taster for last May when they walked away with the title and were elected into the Midland Alliance.

BOLDMERE ST MICHAELS

Church Rd, Boldmere, Sutton Coldfield. Tel: 0121 373 4435

Secretary Des Green, 4 Blandford Ave, Castle
Bromwich, Birmingham, B36 9HX Tel 0121 747 8404

Colours: Black and white stripes

Nickname: Mikes

Capacity: 2,500

Seating: 100

Covered standing: 100

Clubhouse on ground: Yes

DIRECTIONS

A38 & A5127 from City towards S.Coldfield, left at Yenton lights onto A452 (Chester Road), Church Rd is 6th turning on the right. 400yds from Chester Road (BR).

Honours

FA AMATEUR CUP Semi final 1948

Birmingham AFA Cup 1937

Birmingham AFA Senior Cup 1948

Birmingham Junior Cup 1948

AFA Senior Cup 1948

Central Amateur League 1949

Midland Combination 1986, 1989, 1990

Challenge Cup 1978 and 1990

Tony Allden Memorial Cup 1979, 1989, 1992

Challenge Trophy 1987

Boldmere St Michaels were formed in 1883 as a church youth team playing friendly matches. They progressed into minor local leagues before joining the Birmingham Amateur League. Between the wars the club developed into a strong amateur force and having won the league in 1937 they joined the Central Amateur League for the next season. After the War the club became known nationally when they reached the Amateur Cup semi-final, losing to Barnet at Highbury, but they had by then won the league and AFA Senior Cup. From there they joined the Birmingham and District League, where their amateur status led to some barren times. They replaced their reserve side in the Midland Combination and began a run of 30 years in the league, winning the League Cup in 1978 and the title itself three times in the 80's.

The times were not helped when the clubhouse burnt down in 1970, but it rose again, as did the club who were accepted into the new Alliance in 1994.

BRIDGNORTH TOWN

Crown Meadow, Innage Lane, Bridgnorth, Salop WV16 6PZ. Tel: 01746 762747 or 766064

Secretary: Gordon Thomas, 7 Meadow Cl, Oldbury Wells, Bridgnorth, Salop WV16 5HY Tel 01746 765178

Nickname: The Town

Capacity: 2,000

Colours: Blue and White

Covered seating: 260

Covered standing: 300

Clubhouse on ground: Yes

Record attendance: 1,600 v South Shields FA Vase 5th Rd, 1976

Record appearance holder: Kevin Harris 426

Record goalscorer in one season: Roger Davies

Record goalscorer in aggregate: Roger Davies 157

Record fee received £10,000 for Delwyn Humphreys from Kidderminster Harriers

DIRECTIONS
Follow signs for Shrewsbury (A458) over river bridge on by-pass, turn right for town centre at island, right at T-junction, 1st left into Victoria Rd, right at cross-road, follow road into Innage Lane, ground on left.

HONOURS

Midland Combination 1980, 1983

League Cup 1979

Shropshire Senior Cup 1986

Shropshire County Cup 1971, 1976, 1977, 1979, 1980

Welsh Amateur Cup 1971

Manager for 1996-97: Ian Britton

Chairman: Simon Bromley

Vice chairman: Ian Thomas

Bridgnorth Town has a relatively short history as it was formed in 1946. Prior to that. the club was named St Leonard's Football Club, taking its name from one of the Parish Churches. During the 50's and 60's, the club played in the Kidderminster and District League, winning it just once, and in the late 60's it decided to move up to the Midland Combination and in 15 seasons they were champions twice and runners up twice, also winning the League Cup, before joining the Southern League in 1983. For many seasons as a bordering county side, they played in both the Welsh Senior and Amateur Cups, reaching the third round of the former in the late 70's before losing to Wrexham. In 1971 they won the Welsh Amateur Cup with Roger Davies, who moved to Derby and Leicester, scoring in every round. At County level Town has enjoyed success, the highlight being in 1986, winning the Senior Cup, beating Oswestry Town in the final. The club has also won the Challenge Cup and the Junior Cup, making them one of only two clubs to do so. At the end of 1991-92 season Town were in danger of losing their Southern League status, but after lengthy negotiations with the council landlords, a 260 seater stand was completed to enable them to stay. Sadly, in May after a disastrous season they were relegated to the Midland Alliance.

CHASETOWN

The Scholars, Church Street, Chasetown. Tel: 01543 682222 or 684609

Secretary: Paul Dixon, c/o Chasetown FC

Nickname: The Scholars

Colours: All Blue

Capacity: 2,000

Seating: 120

Covered standing: 250

Clubhouse on ground: Yes

Record Attendance: 659 v Tamworth
FA Cup 2nd Qual Rd 1988

Biggest win: 14-1 v Hanford Walsall Sen Cup 1992

Biggest defeat: 1-8 v Telford Utd Res WML Div One

Record appearances: A Cox 484

Record goalscorer in total: T Dixon 164

DIRECTIONS

Follow Motorways M5, M6 or M42 and follow signs for A5. A5 to White Horse Road/Wharf Lane, left into Church Street at top of hill, ground at end just beyond church. Buses B94 or B95 from Walsall.

Honours

West Midlands League Cup 1990 and 1991

League Div 1 1978

Walsall Senior Cup 1991 and 1993

Since the formation in 1954, Chasetown Football Club have become one of the leading lights in non-League football in the Midland area. From humble beginnings, the club now boasts fine facilities at the Scholars ground. They began as Chase Terrace Old Scholars Youth Club when two men formed a football section at Sankey's Corner. In those days the players were mainly from Chase Terrace Secondary Modern and they first played in the Cannock Youth League. They stayed until 1958 when they moved into the Lichfield and District League, finishing third in the first year. In their three year stay the club were runners up in League and Cup before moving up to the Staffs County League in 1961. From there the club moved into the West Midlands League, changing their name to the familiar Chasetown FC.

They soon established themselves, winning the title once, ending runners up five times and rarely finishing below fourth. They were prevented from moving up due to their home ground, Burntwood Recreation Ground, being unacceptable. The breakthrough came in 1983 when they moved to the Scholars ground, which coincided with promotion.

The first few seasons were a struggle, before in 1991 the club were runners up to Gresley Rovers, winning the League Cup as consolation along with the Walsall Senior Cup. They again were second in 1993, beating Pelsall Villa for the Senior Cup. Chasetown became founder members of the Midland Alliance in 1994.

274

HALESOWEN HARRIERS

Park Road, Halesowen, West Midlands B63 2RG. Tel: 01384 896748

Secretary: Mrs Christine Beasley, 43 Hawne Lane, Halesowen, West Midlands B63 3RN

Press officer: Rob Shinfield, 91 Birch Crescent, Tividale, Warley, B69 1UF Tel : 01384 850819

Colours: White and Blue,   Capacity: 4,000

Seating: 250,   Covered standing: 500

Clubhouse on ground: Yes

Record attendance: 750 v Wolverhampton Wanderers Friendly 1985

Biggest win: 12-1 v Lichfield and Malvern Town , both in 1986

Biggest defeat: 2-8 v Frickley Ath FA Cup in 1992

Record appearances: Chris Mason over 300

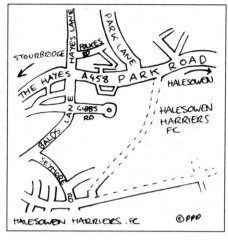

Record goalscorer in one season: Toby Hall over 40

Record goalscorer in total: Nick David over 200

Record fee paid £750 to Oldswinford for Lee Booth in 1991

Manager for 1996-97: Derek Beasley

Assistant manager: Neil Beasley and Colin Gordon, Chairman: Brian Beasley

HONOURS

Sunday Football

Festival League Premier Division 1968, 1970, 1979, 1981 and Div Three 1963

Festival Cup: 1967, 1970, 1971, Presidents Cup: 1970

Senior Cup: 1966, 1967, 1970, 1971, 1979, 1980, Inter Cities Bowl: 1968 and 1969

Oldbury Charity Cup: 1979, Black Country Olympic: 1983, Birmingham Senior Cup: 1982

Saturday Football

West Midlands League Div 2 and Div 2 League Cup 1985, League Div 1: 1986

Halesowen Harriers were formed by current trustee Derek Beasley in 1961 and played 11 friendlies during the first season, the first being on Jan 7th 1962. All games were played away from home as Sunday football at the time was not allowed in Halesowen. In the summer they were admitted to Division Three of the Festival League having acquired a home pitch at Sennelly's Park in Bartley Green. They won the championship and were placed in the Premier Division. In 1965 they moved to Cooksey Lane in Kingstanding where they played until 1969 when they finally moved home, playing on Halesowen Town's ground at the Grove. During their years in the Festival League they won the Premier Division four times and were runners up eight times.In 1984 Harriers made the big step up into Saturday football as they gained permission to Division Two of the West Midlands Regional League. The move coincided with the opening of their new Park Road Ground which club members had hewed out of the hillside themselves. Successive championships of Divisions Two and One followed, elevating them to the Premier in 1996. Eight years of consolidation followed, the best season being 1989 when a third place finish could have meant Southern League football, if not for the lack of floodlights. In 1994 Harriers became founder members of the Midland Alliance and after a sticky start ended as highest scorers, losing the League Cup final to Sandwell Borough Harriers have also had great success in cups, winning the Birmingham Sunday Cup in 1982, reaching the semi-finals of the FA Sunday Cup a year later. As a Saturday team they have won the West Midlands Div 2 League Cup and twice lost the Premier Division League Cup final.

275

HINCKLEY ATHLETIC

Middlefield Lane, Hinckley, Leics Tel: 01455 615012

Secretary: Mr John Colver, 18 Portland Drive, Hinckley, Leics LE10 1SE. Tel: 01455 613936
Press Officer: Mr Andy Gibbs 4 Lupin Close, Burbage, Hinckley, Leics Tel: 01455 233483

Chairman Mick Voce, 60 Brookes Ave, Croft, Leics

Nickname: Robins,   Capacity: 3, 500

Colours: Red and black,   Seating: 320

Covered standing: 1, 000, Clubhouse on ground: Yes

Record Attendance: 5, 410 v Nuneaton Borough Birmingham Comb Boxing Day 1949

Biggest win: 14-0 v Anstey Town Leic Sen Lge Boxing Day 1897, v Croft Rising Star Sept 30th 1899 and also on 27th October 1906, both in Hinckley Hospital Cup

Biggest defeat: 0-20, Record appearances: Steve Markham 455

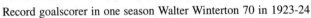

Record goalscorer in one season Walter Winterton 70 in 1923-24

Record fee received £10,000 from Wigan Ath for Mike Love in January 1996

Honours
Leicestershire Senior Cup 1900, 1901, 1910, 1983
Leicestershire Senior League 1897, 1898, 1900, 1908, 1910, 1914
Birmingham Combination 1924 and 1927, Birmingham Senior Cup 1955 jt
Leicestershire Challenge Cup 1958, 1959, 1960, 1961, 1962, 1968

Manager for 1996-97: John Hanna, Assistant Manager: Bill Nally, Vice Chairman: Rob Mayne

A group of young men skipping bible class one Sunday afternoon led to the formation of the present day Hinckley Athletic FC. It was back in the early days of 1889 and all those involved were expelled from the Institute and the football section, and so left without a club they, formed their own. Before the start of the 1889-90 season Hinckley Association was born, initially playing friendlies on the Holywell Ground. The next season saw the club named Hinckley Town and they played friendlies and Cup games until 1894 when they joined the Leicestershire and Northants League, winning the Hinckley Hospital Cup. That league lasted just two years before the Leicester contingent joined the new Senior League. The first season saw Town lose the title by having points deducted but they made amends a year later. It was won again in 1900 and they also beat Football League club Loughborough in the FA Cup. The club made the bold step of entering the Midland League, but financial problems saw them go back to the Senior League in 1903, only to see the problems mount and half way through 1905 they folded, only to re-emerge as Hinckley United. United won the Senior League in 1909 and 1910 and after another win in 1914 they moved to the Birmingham Combination before the Great War. When football resumed they stayed in the Combination and won it in 1924 scoring 130 goals in 34 games. Another championship arrived in 1927, with runners up in 1934, but dark days were ahead and when the Second War came the club were in the doldrumd. When peace returned Hinckley were homeless as the Holywell ground was needed for building and the brewery owners no longer wished it used for sport. Eventually an old dog track in Middlefield Lane was acquired in 1946 and the club changed its name to Hinckley Athletic. They entered the Nuneaton Combination and the South Leicestershire League that year and having secured a ground they were elected back to the Combination in 1947 where they remained until it folded in 1954. A record gate watched a Combination match on Boxing Day 1949. Athletic then joined the Birmingham and District League for 1954-55 where they reached the 2nd Round of the FA Cup and shared the Birmingham Senior Cup. They stayed until 1959 when they replaced Lovells Sports in the Southern League. Under manager Dudley Kernick they began to establish themselves and in 1962 they again reached the FA Cup proper, losing to Queens Park Rangers at the White City. They were promoted but the side broke up and were swiftly relegated again, sadly to eventually drop out of the league in 1967 with more financial problems. Back in the Birmingham League, then called West Midlands League, they struggled, surviving due to some loyal efforts from enthusiasts. Although honours have been rare, the ground has slowly been built up with floodlighting, covered concrete terracing, extended changing rooms and new seats and turnstiles. With the advent of the Midland Alliance Athletic were delighted to be invited in and last May finished fourth.

KNYPERSLEY VICTORIA

Tunstall Road, Knypersley, Stoke-on-Trent, Tel: 01782 522737

Secretary: John A Shenton, 27 Portland Drive, Biddulph, Stoke-o-Trent ST8 6RY Tell: 01782 517962

Colours: Claret and blue stripes

Nickname: The Vics

Capacity: 1,200

Seating: 200

Covered standing: Yes

Clubhouse on ground: Yes

Record attendance: 1,100 v Port Vale Friendly 1989

Biggest win: 10-0 v Clancey Dudley West Mids Lge 1991

Biggest defeat: 0-9 v Meir KA Staffs Senior Lge

Record appearances: M.Gosling 450

Record goalscorer in total: J.Burndred

DIRECTIONS

Directions: M6 Junction 15 join A500, 4th exit, pick up A527, follow through Tunstall, Chell, to Biddulph. Ground is Biddulph, continue through lights, ground on left. Bus 61 Congleton-Tunstall passes ground.

Honours

West Mids Lge Div 1 1993

Staffs Senior Lge 1985

League Cup 1985 and 1986

Staffs FA Vase 1984 and 1987

Sentinel Cup 1987

Leek and Moorlands Lge 1973 and Div 2 1972

Sport has been played at Knypersley since the 1870's when miners from Victoria Colliery wanted to play cricket. Football began in 1933 at the ground although the club folded when the players left to play at Biddulph Moor. Moor themselves disbanded in 1969 and a number of players returned and re-formed the club, playing in the Staffs County League North and the Leek and Moorlands League.

In 1983 former Stoke City star Mike Pejic took the team to a Staffs FA Vase win before he was lured away by Leek Town, but in 1984 the club became founder members of the Staffs Senior League, three years later winning the Staffs FA Vase again. A the end of 1990-91 Vics moved into the West Mids Division 1, winning it in their second season after winning all of the last seven matches. Promotion signalled a further rise in status and after improving the ground they were accepted as founder members of the Midland Alliance in 1994.

OLDBURY UNITED

The Cricketts, York Rd, Rowley Regis, Warley, West Mids. Tel: 0121 559 5564

Secretary: Paul Charnock, 27 Pennyhill Lane, West Bromwich West Mids B71 3RP Tel 0121 588 8369

Colours: Tangerine and black

Nickname: The Blues or the Cricketts

Capacity: 3,000

Covered standing: 500

Seating: 300

Record attendance: 2, 200 v Walsall Wood, Walsall Senior Cup Final 1982

Record win: 10-1 v Blakenall

Record defeat: 1-9 v Moor Green

Record fee received:
£10,000 from Swindon Town for Colin Gordon

DIRECTIONS

Directions: M5 junction 2, follow Blackheath & Halesowen signs, first left at lights and fourth left into York Road (turning before motorway flyover), ground 200 yards on left. One and a half miles from Sandwell & Dudley and Rowley Regis BR stations. Bus 404 from West Bromwich, Oldbury and Blackheath.

Oldbury United were formed in 1958 as Queens Colts, a side comprising of local newspaper boys. After winning the Oldbury League in 1962 they changed their name to Whiteheath United and shortly after merged with Oldbury Town to become Oldbury Utd. They joined the Midland Combination in 1966 and soon after reached the last 16 of the Amateur Cup before losing to Wycombe Wanderers. Six years later they were in the last 16 of the FA Vase before losing to Irthlingborough Diamonds.

1973 saw United buy their own ground, a former quarry that required over £50,000 to build up the club facilities and lay the pitch. The European champions Aston Villa visited the Cricketts in 1982 to switch in the floodlights, a year memorable for winning the Walsall Senior Cup and joining the Southern League. After a promising beginning, relegation came back to the West Midlands League, with runners up places in 1987 and 1988, and a record crowd against Halesowen Town of 1,896 foran FA Cup 4th qualifying round tie.

United's first ever championship came in 1992 when they pipped Chasetown on goal difference and 1996 proved memorable too, with cup final appearances in the Midland Triangular Invitational, Alliance League Cup and Lord Mayor of Birmingham Charity Cups.

PELSALL VILLA

The Bush, Walsall Rd, Heath End, Pelsall. Tel: 01922 692748 or HQ on 682018

Secretary: Gareth Evans, 72 St Pauls Cres, Pelsall
Tel: 01922 693114

Press Officer: Barrie Hill, 12 Argyle Close, Walsall
Tel: 01922 34262

Chairman: Vic Dolphin 29 Field Lane, Pelsall, Walsall
Tel: 01922 682805

Nickname: The Villains, Colours: Red, Black and White

Capacity: 3,000,   Seating: 550

Covered standing: 100

Clubhouse on ground: Yes

Record attendance: 1,800 v Aston Villa
Floodlight opener Nov 1991

Biggest win: 11-0, biggest defeat: 1-7

Record appearances: Kevin Gough

Record goalscorer in one season: Dean Walters

Record goalscorer in total: Dean Walters

DIRECTIONS

M6 jct 7 marked A34 Birmingham. Take A34 towards Walsall to 1st island, turn right (marked Ring Road) cross two islands. At large island at bottom of hill take last exit marked Lichfield, up, hill, cross next island to lights. Continue to next set of lights and turn left (B4154 Pelsall). Go over railway bridge to Old Bush pub on right (next to Pelsall Cricket and Sports Club).

HONOURS

Cannock Charity Cup: 1964, Wednesbury Charity Cup: 1968, 1969, 1973, 1974, 1989, 1990

Staffs Junior Cup: 1969, Stanton Shield: 1974, 1975, Sporting Star Cup: 1977

Rugeley Charity Cup: 1979, Bloxwich Charity Cup: 1982, 1983

Staffs County League Div 1 1984, Edge Cup 1984 West Midlands League Div 1 Cup 1989

Staffs County League Trophy 1990, West Midlands League champions 1995

Premier Div Cup 1996, Midland Triangular Cup 1996

Manager for 1996-97: Reg Priest, Assistant manager: Kevin Gough

Chairman: Vic Dolphin, Vice chairman: Tony Gough

Records from the Walsall Observer show that football was played in the village of Pelsall as long ago as in 1898, which perhaps makes Villa one of the oldest non-League clubs in the country. More recent details show that the club was re-formed in 1961 and although the two World Wars caused a temporary halt to football, it was that reformation that saw the beginning of the club as we know it today. The Bush ground was leased from Bank's Brewery, with changing accommodation in the nearby Red Cow Pub, the club at the time being affiliated to the Staffs FA, competing in the Staffs County League. Some years later, a liaison was formed with the Pelsall Cricket and Sports Clubs, and they gained modern changing rooms and a real HQ. The present management committee came together around 1978 under Chairman Vic Dolphin and new dressing rooms were targeted with the Southern League in mind. The playing surface was improved and the ground fenced in with proper exits and entrances, and in 1982 the club were accepted into the West Midlands Regional League. Two seasons later promotion was gained to Division One, but further development was needed and so a stand to seat 100 was erected at the Bush end and a Directors Box built near to the cricket club. Floodlight plans were unveiled and installed during 1991, with Aston Villa opening them with a match. Success followed under manager Reg Priest in both Cup and Vase and a new 550 seater stand was built in place of the old Bush end stand as Pelsall move into the Midland Alliance.

PERSHORE TOWN

King George Playing Fields, High Street, Pershore Tel: 01386 556902

Secretary: Alan Barnett, 8 Croft Cottages, Cropthorne,
Nr Pershore, Worces. WR10 3LX. Tel: 01386 860243

Match Sec: Mr I Gill 2 Sebright Close, Pershore, Worcs
Tel: 01386 554116

Programme: Mr T.Conway Tel: 01386 554390

Press: Mr C MilwardTel: 01386 555385

Nickname: The Town,   Capacity: 4, 000

Seating: 120,   Covered standing: No

Clubhouse on ground: Yes

Record attendance: 1,356 v Yeading
FA Cup 4th Qual Rd 23rd Oct 1993

Biggest win: 10-0 v Ledbury Town
Robert Biggart Mem Cup semi-final 1992

Biggest defeat: 0-8 v Barwell Midland Floodlit Lge 1996

Record appearances: David Clasen 220

Record goalscorer in one season: Simon Judge 63

Record goalscorer in total: Simon Judge 95

Record fee received: Undisclosed fee for Simon Judge to Worcester City 1993

DIRECTIONS

Directions: M5 Junction 7, A44 to Pershore (8 miles) cross 1st lights in Pershore, at 2nd lights turn left and fold road round into King Georges Way, ground immediately on left

HONOURS

Midland Combination 1994 and Div 2 1990

Worcester Junior Cup 1991

R Biggart Memorial Cup 1991, 1992, 1995

Jack Mould Cup and Alfred Terry Cup 1991

Worcester Senior Urn 1996

Pershore Hospital Cup 1993, 1994, 1996

Managers for 1996-97: Derek Bragg, G.Aldington, Chairman: Mr A.Bradstock

Vice chairman: Mr G.Shepherd and Mr M Goodall

The new club was formed when three teams amalgamated in 1988. Pershore United, Pershore Rec Rovers and Pershore Bullets all became Pershore FC and with help from the council and local businesses the current facilities were installed.

In their first season, the club won Division Two of the Midland Combination by 11 points, and in 1991 they were third in the Division One, gaining promotion in front of Wilmcote. Their best season to date was in 1994 when they won the league and reached the 4th qualifying round of the FA Cup, having beaten Atherstone United along the way. Election as founder members of the Midland Alliance followed but so far the fledgling club has struggled in the lower reaches.

ROCESTER

The Rivers Field, Mill Street, Rocester, Uttoxeter, Staffs Tel: 01889 590463

Secretary: Gilbert Egerton, 23 Eaton Rd, Rocester, Nr Uttoxeter ST14 5LL Tel: 01889 590101

Colours: Amber and black

Nickname: Romans

Capacity: 4,000

Seating: 200

Covered standing: 300

Clubhouse on ground: Yes

Record attendance:1, 026 v Halesowen Town
FA Vase 4th Rd 1987 at Leek Town FC

Record appearances: Peter Swanwick

Record goalscorer in total: Mick Collins

DIRECTIONS
from A50 roundabout adjoining Little Chief restaurant at Uttoxeter take B5030 towards Rocester and Alton Towers, right into Rocester village after 3 miles over narrow bridge, in village centre bear right at sharp left-hand bend into Mill Street, ground 500 yards on left just past former cotton mill.

Honours

Stafford Amateur League Div 3 1953 and Div 1 1955 and 1956

Staffs County League 1971 and League Cup 3 times

Staffs Senior League 1985, 1986, 1987

Staffs FA Vase 1986 and 1988

West Midlands League Div 1 and Cup 1988

Formed in 1876 Rocester initially played friendlies only but later played in local leagues including Ashbourne, Cheadle area leagues, followed by both the Uttoxeter and District and Leek and Moorlands Leagues. In 1952 they joined Division 3 of the Stafford and District Amateur League, winning it scoring 127 goals in 22 games. This led to immediate promotion to the 1st Division which they won in 1955 and 1956.

They moved on to the Staffs County League North until 1984, winning the title in 1971 before joining the Staffs Senior League for three years, all of which saw them crowned as champions. Having also won the Staffs FA Vase they moved to the West Midlands League, having moved to the current ground from the old which was a few yards away in Mill Street.

Success continued with league and cup trophies until they were accepted as founder members of the Midland Alliance in 1994.

RUSHALL OLYMPIC

Dales Lane, off Daw End Lane, Rushall, nr Walsall. Tel: 01922 641021

Secretary: Barry Hall, 10 Miles Meadow Close, New Invention, Willenhall, WV12 5YE Tel 01922 446822

Colours: Amber and black

Nickname: Pics

Capacity: 2,500

Seating: 200

Covered standing: No

Clubhouse on ground: Yes

Record attendance: 2,000 Leeds Utd Old Boys Charity Match 1982

Record appearances: Alan Dawson 400+

Record goalscorer in total: Graham Wiggin

DIRECTIONS

From Rushall centre (A461) take B4154 signed Aldridge. Approx. 1 mile on right, directly opposite Royal Oak public house. In Daw End Lane. Ground on right. Two miles from Walsall (BR) station.

Honours

West Mids Lge Div 1 1980

Walsall Amateur Lge Div 1 1956 and Div 2 1953

Senior Cup 1955 and 1956

Jabez Cliff Cup 1956

Staffs County Lge Div 1 1961, 1962, 1963, 1965, Div 2 1957

Walsall Charity Cup 1953

Walsall Challenge Cup 1955 and 1957

Walsall Memorial Charity Cup from 1956 to 1962

W Preston Challenge Cup 1957, Cannock Charity Cup 1957

Wednesbury Senior Cup 1959, 1960, 1961

Sporting Star Cup 1960, 1961 jt, 1965, 1966, 1968

JW Edge Cup 1963 and 1967, Walsall Senior Cup 1965, Lichfield Charity Cup 1965 and 1967

Manager for 1996-97: Mick Brookes.

Research has showed a football club in Rushall 100 years ago, although football was being played in the village as long ago as 1874 as Walsall FC played their first game against Rushall.

There are few records around, but it is known they were members of the Birmingham Comb between the Wars playing behind the Miners Arms pub. They won the Walsall Amateur League in 1936 but disbanded before the War and re-formed in 1951 returning to the Amateur League Div 2. In 1956 Olympic joined the Staffs County League dominating local football through to 1965. To obtain senior status they moved to a newly developed ground at Daw End after a year at Aston University, and it was opened in 1977, ready for the West Mids League the season after. Promotion soon came and in 1994 became founder members of the Alliance.

SANDWELL BOROUGH

Oldbury Sports Centre, Newbury Lane, Oldbury. Tel: 0121 544 4013

Secretary: Ken Jones, 19 Henn Drive, Princes End,
Tipton, West Midlands. DY4 9NN. Tel: 0121 557 9429

Colours: Green and white stripes

Nickname: Trees

Capacity: 3,000

Seating: 200

Covered standing: 600

Clubhouse on ground: Yes

Record attendance: 950 v Halesowen Town FA Cup 1991

DIRECTIONS

Follow A4123 Birmingham-
Wolverhampton Road, past island at
junction 2 M5, half mile turn left
into Newbury Lane and stadium is
on the right 2 miles from Sandwell
& Dudley (BR).

Honours

Midland Comb President's Cup 1980

Midland Alliance League Cup 1995

The club was formed in 1918 as Smethwick Highfield, playing its early football in the Suburban League in 1926 and won the title seven times, the Lewis Cup 7 times and the Evelyn Cecil Shield five times. During the 20's and 30's the club were a nursery club for West Bromwich Albion.

After the war Smethwick Highfield had two seasons in the Central Amateur League before moving into the Worcester Combination. Through the early 50's the club just missed the title finishing second four times, the last as Smethwick Town and they were also runners up in the Challenge Cup three times. However they did collect a trophy when beating Kenilworth Rangers in the Birmingham Junior Cup in 1956.

They returned to the name Smethwick Highfield in 1963 and in 1972 they were bottom of the league and relegated. They stayed in Division Two for eight years until finishing runners up to Hurley Daw Mill in 1981, having won the Presidents Cup in 1980. The next few years were quiet until merging with Ashtree Rovers from the Kidderminster Sunday League and Moat Farm United, a youth team, which brought another new title, Ashtree Highfield.

By finishing third in the Midland Combination in 1988 they were elected into the Southern League and yet another name change came in 1989 when they took the present title, a season which saw them relegated.

They became founder members of the Midland Alliance in 1994 and took the League Cup at the first attempt. The nickname the Trees comes from a former name. They have played at Newbury Lane since 1981 having moved from the old ground at Londonderry in Smethwick where they played from the start.

SHIFNAL TOWN

Pheonix Park, Coppice Green Lane, Shifnal, Salop Tel: 01952 463667

Secretary: Derek Groucott, 4 Idsall Crescent, Shifnal, Salop TF11 8ES Tel: 01952 402255

Capacity: 3,000

Seating: 104

Covered standing: 300

Clubhouse on ground: No, it is in Newport Road, Shifnal

DIRECTIONS

Directions: M54 junction 3, A41 towards Newport, 1st left for Shifnal (3 miles), in Shifnal take 1st right, and sharp right again up Coppice Green Lane, ground 800 yards on left pass Idsall School. 1 mile from Shifnal BR station.

Record attendance: 1.002 v Bridgnorth Town FA Vase 3rd Rd 1984 at Admirals Park

Biggest win: 10-1 v Malvern Town 1983

Record goalscorer in one season: Steve Kelly 35

HONOURS

West Midlands League 1981 and 1982

Division One 1979

Shropshire Senior Cup 1981, 1991, 1993

Manager for 1996-97: Mervyn Rowe

Shifnal Town FC was formed in 1964 by a group of lads from a youth club, the original name being Shifnal Youth, playing in the Wellington and District League. They climbed through the local leagues, later as Shifnal Juniors and then as Shifnal Town. They moved up to the Shropshire County League in 1969 and within seven years had reached the West Midlands League, where they reached the Premier Division in 1979. 1981 and 82 saw the team take the title against many sides which now grace the Southern League, but in 1985 they received a hammer blow when their Admirals Park ground was sold by the council for housing, making them homeless. They had use of a school pitch, but it meant dropping back into county football for eight years until purchasing a site which has been developed with Southern League in mind. The league was won and a place taken in the Midland Alliance, although last season proved a difficult one with a final place of third bottom.

STAPENHILL

Edge Hill, Maple Grove, Stapenhill, Burton-on-Trent. Tel: 01283 562471

Secretary: David Coulson, The Flat, 171 Calais Rd,
Burton-on-Trent DE 13 0UN. Tel: 01283 516725

Colours: Red and white

Nickname: Swans

Capacity: 2,000

Seating: 50

Covered standing: 200

Clubhouse on ground: Yes

Record attendance: 2,000 v Gresley Rovers
Derbys Senior Cup final 1989

Biggest win: 11-0 v Alcester Town Midland Comb 1993

Biggest defeat: 0-7 v Bridgnorth Town FA Vase

Record appearances: Ian Pearsall

Record goalscorer in total: Brian Beresford 123

DIRECTIONS

Three miles from Burton on A444 Measham Road, turn right (coming from Burton) at Copperhearth Public House into Sycamore Road, Maple Grove is 5th left. 3 miles from Burton-on-Trent (BR) — use buses 22, 23, 38 from opposite station.

Honours

Midland Combination Div 1990

Challenge Cup 1993 and 1994

Leicestershire Senior League 1960, 1987, 1989

League Cup 1988 and 1989

Leicester Senior Cup 1970 and 1987

Formed in 1947 under the name Stapenhill Waterside Community Centre FC they played in the Burton League, winning the title in 1950. The present name was adopted when moving to the Derby and District Senior League, and following title wins in 1953 and 1956 they moved on to the Leicestershire Senior League and were for many years the only club from outside the county to be members.

They won the Senior League in 1960 and again much later in 1987 and 1989, plus the Tebbutt Brown (League Cup). They applied and were elected to the Midland Combination and enjoyed several good seasons winning the Challenge Cup twice and the League Cup. They became founder members of the Midland Alliance in 1994, but have struggled in the new league.

STRATFORD TOWN

Masons Road, off Alcester Rd, Stratford-on-Avon, Warwicks. Tel: 01789 268432

Secretary: Roger Liggins, 17 Hammerton Way, Wellesbourne, Warwicks CV35 9NS Tel: 01789 840755

Press officer: Philip Gardner, 17 Trevelyn Crescent, Stratford-on-Avon CV37 9LL Tel 01789 268432

Colours: Tangerine and black, Nickname: The Town

Capacity: 1,200   Seating: 200

Covered standing: No   Clubhouse on ground: Yes

Record attendance: 1,078 v Aston Villa 1995

Biggest win: 8-2

Biggest defeat: 0-5

Record appearances: Abbey Kelly

Record goalscorer in one season: Richard Landon 44

Record goalscorer in total: Richard Landon 75

DIRECTIONS

Follow Alcester/Worcester A422 signs from Town centre — Masons Road is first right after railway bridge. 400 yards from Stratford-on-Avon (BR) station. Local buses for West Green Drive.

Honours

Midland Comb. 1957 and 1987

Challenge Cup 1987 and 1989

Challenge Vase 1982

Jack Mould Trophy 1982

Tony Allden Memorial Trophy 1987

Birmingham Senior Cup 1963

Records only available since 1971

Manager 1996-97: Stuart Dixon, Assistant Manager: Lenny Derby, Chairman: Gordon Cutler

Stratford Town FC were formed in 1944 and played in the Worcester Comb, winning it as the Midland Combination in 1957. It was the culmination of three seasons where the club scored 313 goals in 102 games. As a result they joined the Birmingham and District League where they were members for three years, but although taking the Birmingham Senior Cup, the league proved too strong and they returned to the Midland Comb in 1970. After five years they moved to have a brief five year spell in the Hellenic League but returned again to the Comb where they were relegated in the first season, but regrouped and were back again, beginning a consistent run which saw them win the title in 1987, under Barry Lynch, as well as the League Cup. An application to the Southern League was turned down as the ground in Masons Road was sadly not acceptable, and so much ground improving went on with changing rooms, a new clubroom and floodlights all being installed. Stratford Town were delighted to be accepted into the Alliance as founder members in 1994, where they finished third in the first season. Last May they were in lower mid-table after a disappointing season.

WEST MIDLANDS POLICE

Tally Ho! Ground, Pershore Rd, Edgbaston, Birmingham B5 7RN. Tel: 0121 472 2944

Secretary: John Black, 57 Grosvenor Close, Sutton Coldfield, West Mids B75 6RP Tel: 0121 308 7673

Colours: Red and black stripes

Capacity: 2,500

Seating: Yes

Covered standing: No

Clubhouse on ground: Yes

Record attendance: 1,072 v Sudbury Town FA Vase quarter-final 1992

Biggest win: 9-3

Biggest defeat: 1-10

DIRECTIONS

Directions: 2 miles south west of city on A441 Pershore Road. Ground is on the left 50 yards past Priory Road lights (Warks County Cricket Ground). 3 mile from Birmingham New Street (BR) — buses 41, 45 & 47 from city.

Honours

Midland Combination 1991

Challenge Cup 1975

Tony Allden Memorial Cup 1976

Worcester Senior Urn 1985, 1991, 1992

National Police Cup 1962, 1963, 1964, 1965, 1967, 1970, 1974, 1975, 1976, 1981, 1988, 1992

Aston Villa Cup 1961, 1965, 1966

Black and White Cup 1955

Birmingham AFA Works League 1962, 1963, 1964

The actual foundation of the club goes back to 1928, when the Birmingham City Police played in the Wednesday League. They continued until 1938, when due to the War, they played only friendlies against other forces and local council sides. In 1946 the club joined the Mercian League, where they stayed until moving into the Birmingham AFA Works League in 1953, where they won the Black and White Cup in 1955. the Aston Villa Cup was won three times and the title itself three years running from 1962 to 1964.

In 1969 they moved to the Midland Combination, and five years later the City Police merged with the West Midlands Constabulary and parts of Coventry and Warwickshire to become the West Midlands Police.

The enlargement meant that there were players available and in the first season the club beat Highfield in the Challenge Cup final.

In 1991 the side at one point went 27 games undefeated, and not surprisingly they were champions of the league and also won the Worcester Senior Urn. There have been many other trophies that have come to the Tally Ho Ground, including 12 Police Cups and with the success, then the ground has also developed to include a superb Headquarters situated a stones throw from Edgbaston Cricket Ground.

WILLENHALL TOWN

Noose Lane, Willenhall, West Midlands WV12 5YE Tel: 01902 605132 or 636586

Secretary: Malcolm Skitt, 52 Longwood Rise,
Willenhall, West Mids Tel: 01902 632557

Prog Editor: Bill Taylor

Nickname: Reds   Capacity: 3, 000

Covered standing: 300, Seating: 250

Clubhouse on ground: Yes

Record attendance: 3,454 v Crewe Alex
FA Cup Rd 1 1981

Biggest win: 11-0

Biggest defeat: 1-6

Record appearances: Gary Matthews

Record goalscorer in total: Gary Matthews

DIRECTIONS

Noose Lane is off the main A454 Walsall to Wolverhampton road. 3 miles from junction 10 (M6) - follow signs for Wolverhampton for 2 miles and turn right into Neachells Lane at 'Neachells' pub, first right into Watery Lane and left at island into Noose Lane - ground 200 yds on left. Two and a half miles from Wolverhampton (BR). Buses 525, 526, 529.

HONOURS

FA VASE RUNNERS UP IN 1981

West Midlands League 1979, Div 1 in 1976 and Premier Div Cup in 1980.

JW Hunt Cup 1974

Manager for 1996-97: Ken Drakeford, Assistant manager: Phil Embery

Chairman: Don Crutchley, Vice Chairman: David Homer

Although football dates back to the 1890's when Willenhall Pickwicks were winners of the Birmingham Junior Cup, the present club were formed in 1953 through the amalgamation of Aston Road Villa and RAF Association. They joined the Wolverhampton League for the first season where they stayed until 1968, and although never taking the title they reached six League Cup finals, without once lifting the cup. 1969 saw them in the Staffs County League and within two years the first trophy was won, the JW Hunt Cup. Willenhall entered the newly formed Staffs Premier League in 1974, where the club went from October to February undefeated. This helped them win the Sporting Star Cup and gain entry to the West Midlands League. During this time they moved to their current Noose Lane base which had been purchased several years earlier, and a stand was bought from Hall Green dog track, the ground opened by Stan Cullis. The first season in the WML saw them gain promotion and reach the League Cup final. Barry Stobart took over as manager in 1978 and he brought the title to Noose Lane as well as overseeing the first FA Vase run, where they lost in the last eight to Whickham. 1980-81 is the most exciting in the club's short history. It began with the erecting of the £20,000 floodlights and ended with an appearance in the FA Vase Final, against Whickham, where an extra time own goal robbed the Reds who lost their goalkeeper early in the game. The following season saw an FA Cup First Round tie with Crewe Alexandra, who posted the record crowd at the ground when winning 1-0, but Willenhall were rewarded with promotion to the Southern League, Midland Division which they won in 1984, scoring 100 goals in the process. During the last ten years Willenhall have struggled to emulate the 70's and in 1991 they returned to the West Midlands League, where they played until becoming founder members of the Alliance in 1994.

FORMER GROUNDS. Spring Lane was home for the first couple of seasons until a move to Memorial Park, close to the current ground. The Reds spent one year at the Marston Sports Ground before moving into Noose Lane.

JEWSON WESSEX LEAGUE

	P	W	D	L	F	A	PTS
Thatcham Town	40	28	8	4	73	27	92
A.F.C. Lymington	40	28	7	5	100	31	91
Ryde Sports	40	25	8	7	92	41	83
Eastleigh	40	21	13	6	83	50	76
Christchurch	40	21	8	11	66	49	71
Wimborne Town	40	20	6	14	85	61	66
Bournemouth	40	17	13	10	85	40	64
Bemerton HH	40	18	8	14	67	63	62
Andover	40	18	7	15	101	70	61
East Cowes Vic	40	17	8	15	60	60	59
Gosport Borough	40	16	9	15	59	58	57
Downton	40	16	6	18	65	73	54
Whitchurch Utd	40	12	13	15	66	76	49
A.F.C. Totton	40	10	13	17	55	66	43
B.A.T. Sports	40	10	12	18	44	58	42
Cowes Sports	40	11	7	22	38	76	40
Portsmouth R N	40	10	8	22	52	84	38
Aerostructures	40	9	10	21	41	71	37
Brockenhurst	40	11	4	25	42	74	37
Petersfield Town	40	8	4	28	53	93	28
Swanage T& H	40	6	4	30	32	138	22

AEROSTRUCTURES SPORTS & SOCIAL

Folland Park, Kings Avenue, Hamble, SO31 4NF Tel: 01703 452173

Secretary: Richard Phippard, 198 Butts Road, Sholing, Soton SO19 1BP Tel: 01703 438413

Chairman: Alistair Tritten, 51 Coach Road, Hamble, Soton, SO31 4LA Tel: 01703 452432

Colours: Maroon and sky blue

DIRECTIONS

Junction 8 of M27, B3397 to Hamble. One and a half miles from Hamble (BR); turn right out of station, proceed for one mile then turn right into Queens Avenue. Ground is 50 yards on the right.

Honours

Hampshire League Division 3 1981

Division 4 1980

Hampshire Intermediate Cup 1980

Southampton Senior Cup 4 times

The club came into being in 1938 and had early success when known as Folland Aircraft, winning both the Hants Senior Cup and Hants League during the War. After the War and up to the 70's they were known as Folland Sports and drifted between County and local football, but in 1979 a more motivated committee appointed Peter Price as manager and they took Division Four in 1980, also winning the Intermediate Cup.

The next season they won Division Three, and after the side broke up it was slowly rebuilt and in 1985 they won the Southampton Senior Cup beating Awbridge. Two years later they won it again and reached Division One after finishing third.

They never did take their place in the top flight as they were elected into the Wessex League, erecting floodlights and a pitch barrier during the summer. Since then they have yet to win more honours and in 1991 they were re-named Aerostructures S&S and soon reached the semi-final of the League Cup, with the reserves winning the Southampton Senior Cup.

AFC LYMINGTON

Sports Ground, Southampton Rd, Lymington, Hants Tel: 01590 671305

Secretary: John Osey, 9 Samphire Close, Lymington, SO41 9LR Tel: 01590 676995

Press Sec/Chairman John Mills, Lydcroft, Brighton Rd, Sway, Lymington, Hants SO41 6EB Tel: 01590 682830

Nickname: The Linnets Colours: Red and Black stripes

Capacity: 3,000   Seating: 200

Covered standing: None, Clubhouse on ground: Yes

DIRECTIONS

M27 Jct 1, follow signs (A337) to Lymington via Lyndhurst and Brockenhurst. ground on left (signposted) 250yds after 2nd set of lights on entering town. 1 mile from Lymington Town BR station.

Record attendance: 2,900 for Charity Game March 1995.

Biggest win: 11-1 v Romsey Town Nov 9th 1992

Biggest defeat: 0-8 v Basingstoke Town April 10th 1990

Record appearances: Glen Limburn 329

Record goalscorer in one season: Darren Pitter 54 in 1995-96

Record goalscorer in total: Darren Pitter 173

Record fee received: £15,000 for Stuart Doling from Doncaster Rovers

Record fee paid: £4,000 for Jimmy Shepherd to Bashley

Honours

As AFC Lymington, Wessex League 1993 and League Cup 1989, Floodlight Cup 1992

Russell Coates Cup 1994, 1995

Lymington Town

Russell Coates Cup 1936, Hampshire League Div 3 1968, Bournemouth Senior Cup 1984

Wellworthy Athletic

Bournemouth Senior Cup 1988, Pickford Cup 1985 and Bournemouth League 1985

Manager for 1996-97: Derek Binns, Assistant manager: Tony Morris,

AFC Lymington was founded in 1988 when the town's two Wessex League clubs Lymington Town and Wellworthy Athletic agreed to amalgamate. A competition was held to find a suitable nickname and the Linnets was immediately popular. Formed in 1876, Lymington Town progressed to become a major Hampshire club during the 30's, winning the Russell Coates Cup in 1936. After the War they dropped through the Hampshire League before winning back their Division One status after 30 years in 1985. Wellworthy Athletic were formed in 1927 and played at various times in the New Forest and Hampshire Leagues. In 1985 they came to prominence by winning the Bournemouth League and gaining promotion to Hampshire Division Three where they finished runners up. Both clubs joined the Wessex League as founder members the following season. Wellworthy did well, reaching the Hampshire Senior Cup semi-final and winning the Bournemouth Senior Cup, but Lymington struggled and failed to win a game in 1987-88. When Wellworthy lost their ground at the end of the season an amalgamation was the obvious solution. John Mills and Paul Mussel were joint managers as the club finished in fifth position and took the League Cup and by 1990 the club had reached the Hampshire Senior Cup final. 1991-92 saw a poor start but the club ended by winning the Floodlight Cup and reaching the final of the Russell Coates Cup as well as finishing runners up in the League to FA Vase finalists Wimborne Town. The following year, the Linnets were mid table in December, but an unbeaten run of 29 games took them to a famous championship win by 2 points. They again lost the Russell Coates but the reserves won the Combination and the Bournemout Senior Cup.

In 1994 the Linnets were third before finally winning the Russell Coates, which they retained a year later as well as winning the League Cup. Last season Linnets were runners up in the League helped by 54 goals from Darren Pitter taking his tally to 107 goals in 108 games.

AFC TOTTON

Testwood Park, Testwood Place, Totton, Southampton Tel: 01703 868981

Secretary: Mrs S Benfield, 35 Fishers Rd, Totton, Soton, SO40 9HW Tel: 01703 865421

Press officer Mr P.Chilcott, 26 Parklands, Stannington Way, Totton, Soton SO40 3QT Tel: 01703 860453

Nickname: The Stags   Capacity: 2 500

Seating: 200   Covered standing: 50

Clubhouse on ground: Yes

DIRECTIONS

From north: M3, M27 west to junction 3, M271 south. From east/west M27 junction 3, M271 south. Turn off roundabout in Totton centre into Library Road, then 1st left and 2nd road. 5 mins walk from Totton station.

Record attendance: 520 v Windsor and Eton FA Cup 4th Qual Rd 1982

Biggest win: 13-2 Hampshire Lge v Cowes Sports

Biggest defeat: 0-8 v Basingstoke Town

Record appearances: D Watley

Record goalscorer in one season W.Curtis

Record goalscorer in total G.Dixon

Honours

New Forest League 3 times, Perkins Charity Cup, Hampshire League Div 1 1982 and 1985

Russell Coates Cup 1982

Southampton Senior Cup, Echo Cup, Mathieson Cup, Eastleigh Sixes (all 1982)

Wessex League Cup 1990,

Manager for 1996-97: Ian Robinson, Assistant manager: P.Wiltshire

Chairman: Mr R Devoy,

Vice Chairman: Mr P.Maiden

Totton Football Club was formed in 1886, and when the Hampshire Football Association was inaugurated, became one of its founder members. The early matches were played at South Testwood Park and when the New Forest League was formed in 1904, Totton were founder members. They won the league on several occasions and were the first holders of the Perkins Charity Cup. After the Great War they entered the Southampton Senior League and the New Forest League and in 1920 moved to the West Division Hants League.

Totton moved to Testwood Park on Dec 30th 1933, where they played Hampshire League football right through to the founding of the Wessex League in 1986, winning the title twice. They had a see-saw existence after the War, being promoted and relegated at regular intervals without making any significant progress.

It was in 1975 that Totton merged with Totton Athletic and during that year floodlights were installed and a clubroom and bar were opened on the ground. The Stags most successful season was in 1981-82 when the League was won as well as the Russell Coates Cup, Hampshire Intermediate Cup, Southampton Senior League, Mathieson and Eastleigh Sixes Trophies.

1990 saw them win the League Cup and the following year they were runners up to Bashley in the Russell Coates Cup, but since then the club have only a semi-final League Cup to show for their efforts.

ANDOVER

Portway Stadium, West Portway Industrial Estate, Andover Tel: 01264 333052

Secretary: Chris Jeremy, 23 Stubbs Court, Artist Way, Andover SP10 3QR Tel 01264 361973 fax 341391

Colours : Red and black   Nickname: The Lions

Capacity: 3 000   Seating: 250

Covered standing: 250, Clubhouse on ground: Yes

Record attendance: 1,100 v Leicester City Ground opening

also 3,484 v Gillingham at Walled Meadow FA Cup 1962

Biggest win: 10-0 v East Cowes Vics 1994-95

Record fee received: £6 000 for Jeremy Stagg to Bashley

Record fee paid: £8,000 for Roger Emms from Newbury

DIRECTIONS

A303 approach to Andover from the western outskirts follow any sign to Portway Industrial estate. Approximately 2 miles from the station.

Honours

Hampshire Senior Cup 1949, 1951, 1956, 1965, Hampshire Junior Cup: 1920

Hampshire Intermediate Cup 1960 and 1961, Andover Open Cup 1987 and 1988

Russell Cotes Cup 1924, 1932, 1938, 1945, 1959, 1961, 1962

Hampshire League 1914, 1925, 1934, 1945, 1949, 1951, 1962

Division 2 1961 and 1962

Salisbury and District League 1895, 1896, 1897, 1900, 1904, 1908, 1913

Pickford's Cup 1951

May League 1899, 1900, 1902, 1908, 1909

Manager 1996-97: Ken Cunningham-Brown

Andover were formed in 1883 and played their first game on October 27th at Stride's Field in Weyhill Rd against Basingstoke Mechanical Engineers. They played in red and black and that tradition is still carried on today. Three years later, in 1886 they took up residence at Walled Meadow and they remained there for 96 years. They joined the newly formed Southern League SW section in 1898 which operated for just one season and after finishing at the foot of the table they returned to the Hampshire League along with many others. Up to the Great War they were members of the North Division winning it in 1914 and upon the restart they remained there until joining the County Division in 1920, winning it in 1925.

Division One of the Hampshire League was formed in 1929 and the Lions stayed there apart from a very brief spell, when they went down for one year. The club won the title in 1934 and during the Second War won another in 1945. Just after it they won two titles and two Hampshire Senior Cups and after one more win in 1962 the club moved to the Western League, finishing runners up in 1970 and 1971. After ten years they again moved up, this time to the Southern League, but life was tough. As the club stumbled, then they sold their old Walled Meadow ground and moved to a brand new stadium on the Portway Industrial Estate.

Costs eventually dictated that the club stepped down the ladder and they joined the Wessex League in 1993. It has proved to be a wise move as the club is again in the move and is looking forward to a new challenge.

B.A.T. SPORTS

B.A. T. Sports Ground, Southern Gardens, Ringwood Road, Totton, Hants Tel: 01703 862143

Secretary: Mick Geddes 136 Regents Park Road, Southampton, Hants SO15 8PD Tel: 01703 325224

Chairman: Rodney Batt, The Belfrey, Southampton Rd, Bartley, Soton SO40 2NA Tel: 01703 812556

Colours: Blue and yellow   Capacity: 2,000   Seating: 150

Covered standing: None   Clubhouse on ground: Yes

Managers for 1996-97: Gary Chant and Derek Dempsey

DIRECTIONS
Into centre of Totton, proceed up Ringwood Road past small roundabout, 2nd left into Southern Gardens. Half mile from Totton (BR), bus X2 (Southampton-Bournemouth).

The club was founded in 1925 as BRAMTOCO FC, as a works team for the British American Tobacco Company. They moved to the sports ground in Totton in 1929, but little success came their way until winning the Southampton Junior A Cup in 1932 and again in 1951. The first league honours came in 1935 in the Southampton Senior League, and in 1950 'Brams' won Junior Division Three and climbed steadily, eventually making the Premier Division in 1970. From there the club joined the Hampshire League and saw their name changed to BAT Sports. They won Division Three in 1975 and Division One in 1988 and 1989, the latter year also bringing the Southampton Senior Cup. The summer of 1989 saw improvements to the ground, with floodlighting, a fixed barrier and a covered area, all to enable them to enter the Wessex League, where they finished third in 1990 and took the Russell Coates Cup. Since then the club have remained in mid-table, although during the last summer there was some doubt as to whether the ground remained acceptable to the league.

BEMERTON HEATH HARLEQUINS

Western Way, Bemerton Heath, Salisbury, Wilts Tel: 01722 331925

Secretary: Andy Hardwick, 2 Ashley Rd, Salisbury, Wilts SP2 7BZ Tel: 01722 333015

Chairman: George Parker, 14 Bedford Rd, Salisbury, Wilts Tel: 01722 334157

Colours: Black and white   Nickname: The Quins   Seating: 155

Covered standing: Yes   Clubhouse on ground: Yes

Record attendance: 1,118 v Aldershot Town FA Cup 1994

Record appearances: Keith Richardson

Honours

Wilts Senior Cup 1993 and Wilts League 3 times as Bemerton Athletic

DIRECTIONS
Turn off A36 Salisbury-Bristol Road at Skew Bridge (right turn if coming out of Salisbury), 1st left into Pembroke Road for half mile, 2nd left along Western Way - ground quarter mile at end. 40 mins walk from Salisbury (BR) station. Bus 351 or 352 from city centre stops at junction of Pembroke Road/Western Way.

Bemerton Heath Harlequins were formed in May 1989 with the amalgamation of three clubs, Bemerton Athletic, Moon FC and Bemerton Boys FC. All three clubs were previously successful in their own right, with Athletic winning the Wiltshire League on three occasions and Moon consistent in the Andover and Salisbury Leagues. Bemerton Boys won several trophies in the Mid Wilts League. The former ground, the Salisbury and South Wilts Sports Ground which was shared with cricket was home until the impressive Westwood Recreation Ground was built. For one year the old cricket ground was transformed with floodlights, perimeter fencing and dug outs, but all that went to the new home, leaving the football pitch as it was since the War. The new club field many teams of all ages, the seniors winning the Wilts Senior Cup in 1993 and the various boys sections all continuing the upward trend.

BOURNEMOUTH

Victoria Park, Namu Rd, Winton, Bournemouth, Dorset Tel: 01202 515123

Secretary: David Hawkins, 12 Bloomfield Ave,
Moordown, Bournemouth Tel: 01202 525914

Chairman: Vic Dominey, 26 Victoria Rd, Parkstone,
Poole, Dorset BH12 3BB Tel: 01202 737859

Nickname: Poppies

Colours: Red and White

Capacity: 3,000

Seating: 250

Covered standing: None

Clubhouse on ground: Yes

Record fee received: £1,500 for Chike Onourah to Wimborne 1993

DIRECTIONS

From the east take A338 to Westbourne and head north to Winton on A347. From the West take A35 into Westbourne and head north to Winton on A347. Any bus to Wimbourne Road, Winton. 2 miles from Bournemouth Central (BR).

Honours

Hampshire League 1913 and 1922

Bournemouth Senior Cup 1967 and 1990

Hampshire Intermediate Cup 1950 and 1970

Founded in 1875, Bournemouth Football Club are one of the oldest clubs in the county and are founder members of the FA, Hampshire FA and the Bournemouth FA. They also became a founder member of the Hampshire League in 1896 and apart from a brief spell at the turn of the century, remained in the league until 1986. The club has had three homes in its history. Firstly a place called East Common, near the railway station, secondly at Dean Park and now at Victoria Park, which was formerly a farmer's field. Bournemouth first tasted County success in 1905 when they won the West Division of the League, a feat which was repeated in 1910, before becoming League champions in 1914. In 1918 the club merged with Bournemouth Wanderers, who prior to the First War were also members of the County League. After the merger they changed their colours from green and white hoops to the now familiar poppy red, hence the nickname.

In 1922 they again won the Hampshire League but just seven years later found themselves at the other end and became a member of the newly formed Division Two. They returned in 1931 as champions but struggled in the few seasons leading up to the Second War.

In 1946 they were back in Division Two, but it took five years before glory came with the Hampshire Intermediate Cup. Twenty years later they won it again and in 1972 following a league organisation, they were promoted only to go straight back down again. In 1986 the Poppies entered the Wessex League and in 1995 after looking favourites, they were pipped at the post by Fleet Town. Last year saw them drop down a little to 8th although they reached the final of the Russell Coates Cup, losing to Downton.

BROCKENHURST

Grigg Lane, Brockenhurst, Hants Tel: 01590 623544

Secretary: Peter Lawford, 22 Fathersfield, Brockenhurst,
Hants Tel: S042 7TH Tel: 01590 623772

Colours: Blue and White squares

Nickname: Badgers

Capacity: 1,200

Seating: 300

Covered standing: 250

Clubhouse on ground: Yes

DIRECTIONS

**From east: M3 junction 3, M271
south. Head west one junction on
A35 (signposted Christchurch) and
then north to Totton on the A36.
From west: M27 junction 2, south on
A36 to Totton.
400 yds from Brockenhurst station,
just off main shopping area.**

Honours

Hampshire League 1976

Division Three 1960

Division Two 1971

Hampshire Intermediate Cup 1962

Bournemouth Senior Cup 1961

Manager 1996-97: Mike Read

Assistant Manager: Paul Ritchie

Chairman: Brian Bidwell

Vice Chairman: Colin Reeves

Brockenhurst Football Club were formed back in 1898 and have had a change of personnel and staff which they hope will lead to a successful centenary season in two years time.

In their early days they played in the New Forest League before eventually switching to the Hampshire League in 1924. They lasted there for two seasons before reverting back to local football, but in 1935 they rejoined the County league only to leave again in 1937.

After the War they again joined the Hampshire League and they remained there until the formation of the Wessex League in 1986.

The first 50 years were spent on a variety of pitches and grounds, the first being behind the Baptist Chapel and then to a field in Wide Lane. From there after the Great War they moved to the Polo Field, now part of Brock College and in the late twenties played on Fathers Field, which is now the site of houses bearing the same name. There were three more rough grounds either side of the War until Grigg Lane was bought in 1950.

So far the club have yet to win a trophy in the Wessex League, but they were successful earlier with the Division Three championship in 1960 and a Bournemouth Senior Cup win a year later. In 1962 they took the Intermediate Cup and after being relegated they bounced back to take the Division Two title in 1971.

In 1974 they were runners up and two years later they took the title.

CHRISTCHURCH

Christchurch Sporting Club, Hurn Bridge, Avon Causeway, Christchurch Tel: 01202 473792

Secretary: Mrs Dawn Page, 87 The Albany, Manor Road, Bournemouth, Dorset BH1 3EJ Tel: 01202 551977

Chairman: Mick Ryan, 48 Highfield Rd, Bournemouth, Dorset BH9 2SG Tel: 01202 518802

Colours: All Royal blue

Nickname: Priory

Capacity: 2,000

Covered standing: Yes

Seating: Yes

DIRECTIONS

A338 from Ringwood, turn off signed Hurn Airport on left. Take Sopley exit at mini roundabout before reaching airport. Ground is immediately on the right. 3 miles from Christchurch (BR).

Honours

Hampshire Junior Cup 1893, 1912, 1921

Hampshire Intermediate Cup 1987

Pickford Cup 1991

Hampshire League Div 2 1938, 1948, 1986

Division Three 1957

Bournemouth Senior Cup 1957, 1960, 1968, 1969, 1970

Page Croft Cup 1995

Founded in 1885, Christchurch Football Club can claim to be one of the pioneers of Hampshire League football, as they were founder members of the Hampshire FA in 1887, following the dissolution of the South Hants and Dorset FA's, and the consequent formation of Dorset County FA.

Their first honours in local football came in 1893, when they won the Hampshire Junior Cup. The team was known then as the 'Can't Whack 'Ems' and they were again winners in 1912 and 1921.

Between the Wars they competed in the Bournemouth and Hampshire Leagues and in 1938 gained promotion to Division One for the first time, having been champions of Division Two.

Like most clubs they have had their ups and downs and subsequently went down to Division Three but climbed back again, winning Division Two again in 1948. They found themselves in Division Three once more later, but have since won it, and Division Two again, and in 1970 were the first club to win the Bournemouth Senior Cup three times in a row.

The club's long association with the Barrack Road Recreation Ground ended at the start of the 1984 season when the Council provided the chance for them top move to the excellent former British Aerospace Ground at Hurn Bridge. They moved up to the Wessex League in 1987 and last season ended in fifth place, equalling their best since the first season.

COWES SPORTS

Westwood Park, Reynolds Close, off Park Road, Cowes, IOW Tel: 01983293793

Secretary: Bill Murray, 53 Park Rd, Cowes, IOW
Tel: 01983 294445

Chairman: Ray Sleep, 100 Upper Moor Green Rd,
Cowes IOW Tel: 01983 293446

Colours: Blue and white stripes Nickname: Yachtsmen

Capacity: 2,000,   Seating: 200

Covered standing: No,   Clubhouse on ground: Yes

Record attendance: 3,000 v Ryde
Hampshire League 1899, at Brooklyn Ground

also 20,544 v Newport IOW Hants Sen Cup Final 1932

DIRECTIONS
From Cowes centre take Park Road. Reynolds Close is a right turn half a mile up the hill.

Honours

Hampshire League 1897, 1927, 1928, 1931, 1937, 1956

Hampshire County League 1909 jt, 1927, 1928, Hampshire League South 1909, 1920,

Division One: 1956, Division Two: 1975,

Cowes Football Club were reported on paper cuttings as having been formed in 1881 although in the Hampshire FA Jubilee brochure, they mention a formation of 1882. It is all immaterial as the club folded in 1899. It was the end of a remarkable era as the club rose to win the Hampshire Junior Cup in 1892 and the Senior Cup in 1897 as well as becoming the first winners of the Hampshire League.

With their well appointed Brooklyn Ground being developed with new stands, dressing rooms and fences and entry into the Southern League, thousands lined the streets to welcome the team home after the Senior Cup win, but with players on wages the finances began to be a problem. Cowes clinched the Southern League Div 2 SW and accepted promotion, but it quickly turned into a nightmare, with internal problems and low gates, along with the rash decision to build another stand causing money worries, and the club went down as quickly as they came up.

Elsewhere Cowes White Star were playing and they eventually changed their name to Cowes FC and moved into Brooklyn Ground. They won the Hampshire Cup in 1906 and in 1920 were double runners up in league and Senior Cup, a year before the Brooklyn Ground was lost, when the landowner reclaimed it to sell for building land. Cowes moved into Westwood Park in 1912 and through the Great War played in the Island League before returning to the Hampshire League in 1920, which they won.

The 20's and 30's were a boom time for the club who regularly featured in Senior Cup and Gold Cup finals racking up a host of successes, and over 20,000 travelled across to the Dell to watch won County Cup final against Newport. After the Second War, Westwood Park was purchased for £665, but despite the success gates began to dwindle and players wages were a constant problem.

The gradual demise manifested itself in 1967 when the club were relegated to Division Two, and although they won the title and came back up in 1975 they were broke and relegated again in 1978 and in serious trouble. In 1980 a junior club merged with Cowes and they became Cowes Sports, but for several years the struggle continued until in the 90's they re-vamped Westwood Park after many years of neglect and joined the Wessex League having won the Hampshire League in 1994.

DOWNTON

Brian Whitehead Sports Ground, Wick Lane, Downton, Wilts Tel: 01725 512162

Secretary: Brian Trent, 21 Fison Walk, Bishopdown, Salisbury, Wilts SP1 3JF Tel: 01722 323097

Chairman: Trevor Halski, 2 Saxonhurst, Downton, Salisbury, Wilts SP5 3JN Tel: 01725 511056

Colours: All Red,   Nickname: Robins

Capacity: 1,600   Seating: 250

Covered standing: None Clubhouse on ground: Yes

DIRECTIONS

A338 south from Salisbury. Turn right into Wick Lane opposite the turn for Downton Village Centre. Ground is 1/4 mile on the left.

Honours

Wiltshire Senior Cup 1980 and 1981

Wiltshire Junior Cup 1950

Bournemouth Senior Cup 1963 and 1980

Bournemouth Senior League 1960, 1961, 1962, 1964, 1965, 1967, 1968

Bournemouth Senior League Cup 1962, 1964, 1967

Hayward Cup 1965

Wessex League Cup 1996

Russell Coates Cup 1996

Manager for 1996-97: Peter Moore

Assistant manager: Eddie Lane

Vice Chairman: Gordon Bacon

In 1905 a general meeting was arranged by the Reverend JH Phillips which resulted in the formation of Downton Football Club, The Robins.

In the early days only friendly matches were played and it was not until 1919 that they entered the Salisbury District League, winning the Norman Court Cup in 1925. Since then they have won that competition a further eight times. At the beginning of the 1948-49 season the club joined the Bournemouth Junior League and in the following campaign won the Wiltshire Junior Cup.

They progressed to the Bournemouth Senior League in 1950 which they won 12 times in 17 years, as well as the Bournemouth Senior Cup twice, the League Cup three times and the Hayward Cup in 1965.

They moved up in 1968 to Division Three of the Hampshire League, but it took 11 years to gain promotion in the year they also won the Wilthire Cup, but 1980-81 was another double year with promotion to Division One and another triumph in the County Cup.

In 1993 Downton were elected to the Wessex League, with last season proving to be the best so far, with the first team and reserves winning their League Cups, plus the Russell Coates Cup.

Downton FC have had a number of grounds over the years, the main pitch was called Barlings and stood opposite the White Horse pub where it was used for over 50 years, although it is now farm land. From there the club moved to Barford Lane from 1952 until the late 60's. It later reverted to agricultural use, although subsequently it became a rugby ground. Next was Long Close Park which was shared with the cricket club and is still in use as such, before moving in 1982 to the current ground.

EAST COWES VICTORIA ATHLETIC

Beatrice Avenue, East Cowes, IOW Tel: 01983 297165

Secretary: Lee Bray, 57 Grange Rd, East Cowes IOW
Tell: 01983 200276

Chairman: Steve Stay 23 Beechcroft Drive, Wooton
IOW Tel: 01983 883357

Press Sec: Alan Green, 6 Greenlands Rd, East Cowes

Colour: Red and white stripes,   Nickname: Vics

Capacity: 2,000,   Seating: 200

Covered standing: 400 Clubhouse on ground: Yes

Record attendance: 2,000 v Poole Town FA Cup 1954

Biggest win: 9-0 v Brading Town 1986-87

Biggest defeat: 0-10 v Andover 1993-94

Record appearances: Joe Reed

DIRECTIONS

From the ferry: Take the lower main road 1 mile from the town centre to Newport or Ryde, near Whippingham Church adjacent to Osborne Middle School.

Honours

Wessex League Cup 1988, Hampshire League Div 1 1986 and 1987

Division 3 1948, 1964, 1972, Isle of Wight Gold Cup 1980, 1982, 1983, 1984, 1985, 1986, 1989

Hampshire Minor Cup 1893

Isle of Wight Division 1 1899, 1900, 1931 jt, 1935, 1936, 1979, 1983, 1987, 1988, 1995

Division 2 1899, 1905, 1907, Division 3 1929 jt, 1933

Isle of Wight Challenge Cup 1900, 01, 02, 20, 48, 51, 52, 53, 81, 85, 88, 91, 92,

Isle of Wight Memorial Cup 1920, 1933, 1983, 1988, 1991

Isle of Wight Charity Cup 1924 and 1926, Isle of Wight Centenary Cup 1990 and 1992

Manager 1996-97: Derek Ohren, Assistant Manager: Dave Barsdell

Chairman: Steve Stay, Vice Chairman: Mick Everett

East Cowes Vics FC was formed in 1888 and were founder members of the Isle of Wight League in 1889. During the first thirty years of their existence, the club scored several firsts in Island football. They won the league in 1899, Challenge Cup in 1901 and Memorial Cup in 1920. Those cups were introduced during those years and Vics were front runners of island football from then on.

Just prior to the Great War, East Cowes entered the Hampshire League but finances dictated that they returned to the Island league. In 1947 they regained senior status and were accepted into Division Three West of the Hampshire League, and were promoted as champions immediately.

Since that time the club spent nine seasons in the Third Division and 18 in the Second, as well as 12 in the top flight. One of the important years in Vic's history was in 1968 when they amalgamated with East Cowes Athletic, a junior side.

Their most successful period came under manager Graham Daish, who built an all island side good enough to win the Hampshire League twice, the first time unbeaten, and they also took the Gold Cup six times whilst under Graham. This success led the club to progress to the Wessex League in 1987, but being strictly amateur they lost players, and were pleased to finish ninth, winning the League Cup beating Romsey Town. It was also a memorable season for the Isle of Wight League side, who won the League, Challenge and Memorial Cups.

EASTLEIGH

Ten Acres, Stoneham Lane, Eastleigh, Hants SO50 9HT Tel: 01703 613361

General Sec: Derik Brooks, 50 Forest Hills Drive, Town Hill Park, Soton SO18 2FW Tel: 01703 557147

Match Sec: Reg Kearslake, 10 Binsey Close, Millbrook, Soton SO16 4AQ Tel: 01703 779545

Press officer: Tommy Whale, 5 Wilmer Rd, Eastleigh, Hants SO50 5EW TEL: 01703 620154

Colours: Blue and White,   Capacity: 4,300

Seating: 190,   Covered standing: 50

Clubhouse on ground: Yes

Record attendance: 2,500 on Sept 30th 1975 v Southampton Friendly

Biggest win: 12-1 v Hythe and Dibden Dec 11th 1948

Biggest defeat: 0-11 v Austin Sports Nov 1st 1947

Record appearances: Ian Knight 611

Record goalscorer in one season Percy Fuccio 54

Record goalscorer in total: Johnny Williams 177

DIRECTIONS

M27 to Junction 5, to roundabout - exit marked Stoneham Lane, ground on left but carry on to roundabout and come back down Stoneham Lane, turning right opposite Concord Club. Ground 400 yds on left. Three quarters of a mile from Southampton Parkway (BR). Bus 48 (Southampton-Winchester) to Stoneham Church stop.

Honours

Hampshire League Div 2 1970, Hants Midweek Floodlit Cup 1979,

 Southampton Senior League 1950

Hants Intermediate Cup 1951 and 1957,

Manager for 1996-97: Roger Sherwood, Chairman: Bruce McLaren

Vice Chairman: Don Broomfield

It all began on Wednesday, May 22nd 1946, when a meeting called by Derik Brooks at Westfield Hall, Swaythling, was attended by fifty people, and Swaythling Athletic was formed. In the early days the club competed in Divisions One and Two of the Southampton Junior League, taking Div 2 in 1948. The first ground used was Southampton Common but before the end of the season they moved to "Westfield", Walnut Avenue, Swaythling where conditions were at first primitive. Cold washing water was collected in buckets with storm lanterns supplying the light. The referee changed in a nearby house.

Conditions improved and after two seasons in the Southampton Senior League West they were promoted in 1950. A year later they were champions of Division Three West and winners of the Hants Intermediate Cup.

The reserves also had success in the league, whilst the first team moved to the Hampshire League Division One in 1955, playing the next ten seasons in either Division One or Two. The most significant development came in 1957, when after much hard work and effort from members, the new ground at Ten Acres was completed. A grandstand was erected in 1971 and floodlights in 1975, with Southampton FC playing a friendly game in front of 2,500 people. The highest place in the Hampshire League was third on three occasions, but in 1980 the club changed its name to Eastleigh FC and became founder members of the Wessex League in 1986. In 1990 the club reached the final of the Russell Coates Cup for the third time and two years later played in the League Cup final, losing in extra time. Last season, Eastleigh's reserves pulled off the Combination title, whilst the first team finished fourth in their division.

GOSPORT BOROUGH

Privett Park, Privett Rd, Gosport, Hants Tel: 01705 583986

Secretary: Brian Cosgrave, 2 Cavanna Close, Rowner, Gosport PO13 0PE Tel: 01329 314117

Colours: Yellow and blue

Nickname: The Boro

Capacity: 4,000

Seating: 350

Covered standing: 100

Clubhouse on ground: Yes

Record attendance: 4,770 v Pegasus FA Amateur Cup 1951

DIRECTIONS

M27 junct, 11 then A32 Fareham to Gosport, at Brockhurst roundabout (after about 3 miles) right into Military Road passing through H.M.S. Sultan, left into Privett Road at next Roundabout, ground 300yds on left signed Privett park Enclosure. 2 miles from Portsmouth Harbour (BR) or Fareham (BR).

Biggest win: 14-0 v Cunliffe Owen Hampshire League Div 1 1945-46

Biggest defeat: 0-9 v Newport, Hants Lge 1948 and Gloucester City Southern League 1990

Record appearances: Tony Mahoney 764

Record goalscorer in total: Richie Coulbert 192

Record fee paid: £6,000 for Sandy Baird from Basingstoke Town in 1990.

Record fee received: £ 30,000 for Gareth Williams to Aston Villa in 1987

Honours

Wessex League Cup 1993

Hampshire League 1946, 1977, 1978

Hampshire Senior Cup 1988

SW Counties Challenge Cup 1978

Gosport War Memorial Cup 1996

Gosport Borough Athletic were formed in 1944 and had a season in the Portsmouth League before joining the Hampshire League. Gates at the ground were good and for an Amateur Cup tie with Pegasus nearly 6,000 crammed in to Privett Park. The ground itself was opened in 1937 and was used by the old Gosport FC in the Hampshire League and has changed little since it was separated from the cricket ground.

Other than a Hampshire League title there was little success, indeed the club won only two FA Cup ties in 10 years before they stopped competing for a decade. The name Athletic was dropped in the early 60's and it was not until 1978 when having won two League titles running, that Gosport moved into the Southern League. It had been a fine spell, topped with an appearance in the last eight of the FA Vase, and in 1985 the club were promoted to the Premier Division in 1983 in fourth place. They were relegated within a season but bounced back as runners up. Sadly in 1991 Borough were relegated again and after a number of disappointing seasons they were forced to drop into the Wessex League. They won the League Cup in 1993 and last year were placed mid-table.

PETERSFIELD TOWN

Love Lane, Petersfield, Tel: 01730 233416

Secretary: Mark Nicoll, 49 Durford Road, Petersfield, Hants GU31 4ER Tel: 01730 300518

Chairman: Geoff Goad, Deer Keepers Cottage, Uppark, Petersfield, Hants Tel: 01705 631485

DIRECTIONS
On A3 circulatory system. 10 mins walk from Petersfield BR station heading towards London.

Colours: Red and black, Capacity: 4,000, Seating: 135

Covered standing: 250, Clubhouse on ground: Yes

Manager for 1996-97: Tony Adams

Petersfield Town Football Club was formed in 1993 following the demise of Petersfield United which had been the principle club since its formation in 1889, and had been playing in its final season of 1992-93.

Hopes were high of an upturn in fortunes of Petersfield football when Peter De Sisto became the club's new Chairman. They were accepted into the Wessex League and former Tottenham and England player Gray Stevens was installed as manager. Unfortunately it proved to be a false dawn and the club failed to prosper. Eventually matters came to a head in 1995 when the Council refused to give a lease on its Love Lane ground, which was the former home of Petersfield Town. They were forced to tender their resignation from the Wessex League at the end of the season and it seemed that senior football was gone in the town. Fortunately an eleventh hour bid to save the club was led by local businessman Geoff Goad and they successfully gained re-election at the AGM.

The Navy Stadium, HMS Temeraire, Burnaby Road, Portsmouth PO21 2HB Tel: 01705 724235

PORTSMOUTH ROYAL NAVY

Secretary: Roy Newman, 8 Kimpton Close, Lee-on-Solent, Hants PO13 8JY Tel: 01705 799198

Chairman: Tony Miklinski, 16 Hoylake Rd, Drayton, Hants PO6 1BH Tel: 01705 327035

Colours: All Royal blue, Nickname: Sailors

Capacity: 1,500, Seating: 500, Covered standing: No

Clubhouse on ground: Yes

DIRECTIONS
From Portsmouth Harbour (BR) turn right onto The Hard, pass under the rail bridge and turn left into Park Road, after approx 200yds take 1st right into Burnaby Road. Entrance to ground via main gate of HMS Temeraire.

Honours

Russell Coates Cup 1968, Basingstoke League Div 2

Hampshire League Div 2 1968, 1978, 1981

Pompey RN are a relatively new club who came into being in 1962 and played in local football before joining the Hampshire League in the mid-60's. Represented solely by serving Navy men, the club used the famous old Victory Stadium from the start until 1987 when they vacated it to move to the Burnaby Road stadium, part of much bigger complex which includes the United Services rugby ground and a County cricket pitch.The club have had some success, winning the Hampshire League Div 2 three times and the Russell Coates Cup but since leaving to join the new Wessex League, they have yet to gain any honours.

ROMSEY TOWN

By-Pass Ground, South Front, Romsey, Hants Tel: 01794 512003

Secretary: Bill Clouder, 15 Malmesbury Rd, Romsey, Hants S051 8FS Tel 01794 518556

Chairman: Derek Edwards, Deer Park Farm, Hursley, Winchester, Tel: 01703 260376

Colours: Yellow and black stripes

Capacity: 2,000

Seating: No

Covered standing: Yes

Clubhouse on ground: Yes

DIRECTIONS
From the west: junction 2 of M27, north on A3090. From the east: junction 3 of M27, north on A3057 through Upton.

Honours

Wessex League 1990

Hants League Div 2 1979 and Div 4 1976

Southampton Junior League 1927

Western Div 1952 and Div 2 1973, Romsey Div 1928

Eastleigh and District League 1923, 1924, 1929

Salisbury and District League 1899

Hampshire Senior Cup 1979

Hampshire Intermediate Cup 1926, 1931, 1978

Hampshire Junior Cup 1901, 1910, 1924

Southampton Senior Cup 1974

Southampton Junior Cup 1923 and 1924

Travers Cup 1930, Warminster Cup 1900

Andover Cup 1896, 1899, Salisbury Cup 1930

Romsey Town were first formed in 1886 and in the early 1900's played in the Eastleigh and Salisbury and District Leagues, winning both before graduating to the Southampton Junior League being founder members of the FA. They won the Southampton FA Junior Cup in 1923 and 1924 and after taking the Intermediate Cup for the second time were elected to the Hampshire League in 1932. They had brief success but gradually fell away during the 50's and in 1964 they were next to bottom of Division Three and found themselves back in Junior Southampton football. After some struggle they won back their place in the Hampshire League in 1975 and by 1979 they had climbed from Division Four to Division One, completing a run of seven promotions in eight years.

They stayed until the Wessex League was formed in 1986 and under Roger Sherwood enjoyed a wonderful run which saw them crowned as champions in 1990 and reaching the fourth qualifying round of the FA Cup a year later. Sadly the team broke up and soon they were back in the Hampshire League, but in the nick of time the club have regrouped and last May they were high enough to be re-elected to the Wessex League behind Moneyfields and Colden Common whose grounds did not comply with the gradings.

RYDE SPORTS

Smallbrook Stadium, Ashey Road, Ryde Tel: 01983 812906

Secretary: Mark Firmin, Smallbrook Stadium, Ryde
Sports FC Tel: 01983 615029 (h)

Chairman: Steve Rann, 8 Birch Gardens, Binstead, Ryde
IOW Tel: 01983 811046

Colours: All Red,   Nickname: The Reds

Capacity: 5000,   Seating: 450

Covered standing: 1000, Clubhouse on ground: Yes

Record attendance: 3,100 v Aston Villa Dec 17th 1990

DIRECTIONS

From the Pier Head follow directions to the Royal Isle of Wight Hospital, carry on past the hospital turning left at the Partlands Hotel - ground is one mile along Ashey Road. Not served by public transport.

Honours

Hants League 1900, 1926, 1990

Div 2 1989 and Div 3 1965

Hants Senior Cup 1900, 1904, 1926, 1935, 1936, 1937, 1938, 1939

Isle of Wight Gold Cup 1927, 1947, 1949, 1956, 1962, 1963, 1964

IOW Senior Challenge Cup 1899, IOW Challenge Cup 1928 and 1981

Portsmouth Senior Cup 1900, 1901, 1906, 1920, 1954, 1967, 1990

IOW Charity Cup 1919, 1920, 1921, 1922, 1945, 1946, 1947

Ryde and District Cup 1990

Westwood Cup 1985

IOW League 1921 and Div 2 1981

Memorial Cup 1994

Manager for 1996-97: Dennis Probee

Assistant managers: Roy Pridham and Tony Newman

Ryde were founder members of the Hampshire League and were one of eight teams that played in that inaugural season in 1896. Although finishing last they soon improved to twice end as runners-up, winning the title in 1900

Hampshire League success returned to the club in 1926 when they again took the title and completed the double by winning the Hants Senior Cup. During the late thirties Ryde enjoyed an unprecedented run winning the Senior Cup five times in a row up to the Second War, and although the league eluded them it was during that period that they reached the First Round proper of the FA Cup, losing to Gillingham.

The first major setback was in 1953 when the club were relegated to Division Two and it was not until 1959 that they returned, only to go straight back down. Things got worse in 1964 with a drop to Division three, which they won a year later. They returned to Division One in 1968 only to again go down to Division Three during the 70's and 80's. Consecutive titles saw Ryde back again in 1990 and admission to the Wessex League was granted the following year.

The club's home for 98 years was Partlands, which they moved to after initially playing at the Isle of Wight College in Appley. Partlands was purchased during the 50's for £2,000 which enabled them to sell for close to £400,000 and finance the move to Smallbrook Stadium, a new multi sports centre where they are today.

THATCHAM TOWN

Waterside Park, Crookham Rd, Thatcham, Berks Tel: 01635 862016

Match Sec: Charles Heaver, 32 Bailey Ave, Thatcham, Berks Tel: 01635 868179

Secretary: John Haines, 10 Southdown Rd, Newbury RG19 3AP Tel: 01635 873934

DIRECTIONS

2 mins walk from Thatcham BR station.

Press Officer: Dave Ware Tel: 10635 861000

Chairman: Phil Holdway, 68 Park Lane, Thatcham, Berks RG18 4JS Tel: 01635 867803

Colours: Blue and white   Capacity: 3, 000

Seating: 295   Covered standing: No

Clubhouse on ground: Yes

Record attend: 1,400 v Aldershot Town in FA Vase 1994

Honours

Wessex League 1996, Wessex League Cup 1991, 1992, 1995

Hellenic League 1975, Division One 1959, 1965, 1973

Premier Div Cup 1975, Benevolent Cup 1964 and 1965

Reading Temperance League Div 2 1906

Reading Town Cup 1936, 1948, 1949, 1950

Newbury Hospital Cup 1924, 1934, 1935, 1990, 1992

Ben Warner Cup 1950 and 1965, Bernard Heath Challenge Cup 1950 and 1952

Hungerford Challenge Cup 1987 and 1992

Berks and Bucks Senior Cup 1975, Berks and Bucks Intermediate Cup 1959

Berks and Bucks Junior Cup 1936

Manager 1996-97: Jim Greenwood, Assistant Manager: Steve Kean

Vice Chairman: Dee Holdway

Thatcham FC was founded in 1894 and played friendlies for two years on The Marsh, Dunstan Green. They then joined the Reading Temperance League where they stayed for 57 years. Steady progress was made winning Div Two in 1906 and between the wars they enjoyed a marvellous spell where in one season alone they won three cups and were runners up in the Reading Premier League as it became. In 1949 Thatcham bought land off Northfield Road and developed what became Lancaster Close. They sold seven acres of the land in the 70's and the funds helped finance a new clubhouse and dressing rooms. In 1953 the Town joined the Hellenic League as founder members and won Division One three times and in 1975 the club had their most successful season, winning the league and Cup and reached the final of the County Cup where they were awarded it by default. 1982 saw them move to the Athenian League and then the Spartan League in 1984. They had a good run in the FA Vase in 1986 and the committee decided to become founder members of the Wessex League. Since then they have had much success, winning the League Cup three times before taking the title last May, from Lymington. In 1993 the club moved from Lancaster Close to a brand new ground close to the railway, built with the Southern League in mind, called Waterside Park, with a capacity for 3,000 and splendid social facilities.

WHITCHURCH UNITED

Longmeadow, Winchester Rd, Whitchurch, Hants Tel: 01256 892493

Secretary: Mr N.Spencer, 54 Winchester Rd, Whitchurch, Hants RG28 7HP Tel: 01256 896895

Chairman: Chris Rowland, 17 Rose Close, Kempshott, Basingstoke, Hants GR22 5FN Tel: 01256 55731

Colours: Red and white

Capacity: 2,000

Seating: 200

Covered standing: No

Clubhouse on ground: Yes

Honours: Hampshire League 1994-95

Manager 1996-97: John Mass

Assistant Manager: Eddie Harper

DIRECTIONS

Approach Whitchurch from north and south on A34. From east and west take A303 and then A34 north. The ground is in Winchester Road.

Whitchurch United, as a Hampshire League club, erected floodlights at their Winchester Road Ground and fulfilled their ambition of promotion to the Wessex League at the end of the season.

In 1993-94 the club made their debut in the FA Vase, losing 1-3 to the then all-conquering Peppard side at Longmeadow. At the end of the 1993-94 season the club found themselves bottom of the Jewson Wessex League and relegated back to County League football.

However, they won the Hamshire League again at the first attempt, in 1994-95, to become the first club to be promoted twice from that league to the Jewson Wessex League.

Whitchurch United's ground is part of an impressive multi-sport facility, though their ground is quite tight, with a sloping pitch. Unusually, midweek matches are staged on Thursdays.

WIMBORNE TOWN

The Cuthbury, Cowgrove Rd, Wimborne, Dorset BH21 2EL Tel: 01202 884821

Secretary: Mark Wallis, 63 Victoria Close, Corfe Mullen, Wimborne, Dorset BH21 3TX Tel: 01202 605089

Nickname: Magpies,

Colours: Black and White stripes

DIRECTIONS
Wimborne to Blandford Road, behind Victoria Hospital.

Capacity: 3,250,　　　　　　　　Seating: 150

Covered standing: 500, Clubhouse on ground: Yes

Record attendance: 3,250 v Bamber Bridge
FA Vase semi-final 2nd Leg 1992

Biggest win: In Wessex League 8-0 v Romsey Town in 192-93 and Eastleigh in 1991-92

Biggest defeat: 2-6 v Thatcham in 1991

Record goalscorer in one season G.Manson 50 in 1980-81

Record fee paid: £5,000 for Jason Lovell to Bashley

Record fee received: £6,000 for Tommy Killick to Dorchester in 1993

also Jason Lovell from Bashley in 1989

Honours

FA VASE Winners 1992

Wessex League 1992 and 1994 and League Cup in 1994

Dorset League Division One 1981 and 1982, Dorset League Division Two 1932, 1935, 1937

Dorset Senior Cup 1981, 1982, 1986, 1992

Mark Frowde Cup 1993 and 1995

Dorset Senior Amateur Cup 1937 and 1964, Dorset Junior Cup 1932 and 1937

Dorset Minor Cup 1913, Dorset Junior Amateur Cup 1935, 1936, 1939

Manager for 1996-97: Alex Pike, Chairman: Mick Sturgess, Vice Chairman: Steve Churchill

The Cuthbury ground is believed to have hosted football since the football club was formed in 1878 and was used by rugby also until used exclusively for football. Wimborne played the first 100 years or so in Dorset League football, where they had some success between the Wars being champions of Division Two three times and runners up once, as well as being runners up in Division One in 1939. They won the Dorset Junior and Senior Amateur Cups during this period, but appear to have had little success from then until the 70's. They were runners up in League and Cup and in 1981 after 103 years, joined the Western League. Although enjoying consistency, with finishes of 4th, 7th, 10th, 4th and 5th, they left the league and joined the Wessex League in 1987. Since that time the club have been put on the national map Having reached the Hampshire Senior Cup semi-final in 1990, the 91-92 season was destined to be the best ever by a very long way. The Wessex League championship was won, as was the Dorset Senior Cup, but after a long run the club reached Wembley in the FA Vase final, having beaten Bamber Bridge in the semi-final, the home tie of which smashed the attendance record. After a wonderful final, Wimborne, inspired by Jamie Sturgess, Tommy Killick and Taffy Richardson, overwhelmed the previous year's winners Guiseley, 5-3, in front of 10,000 fans. Success bred and the club were runners up in the league the following year, going one better and winning it again in 1994, when they completed the League and Cup double. Since then the Mark Froude Cup has been won twice and last May, the Magpies lost the League Cup final to Downton on penalties, at Bemerton Heath.

Left: Andover F.C.

Right: East Cowes Victoria Athletic F.C.

Left: AFC Lymington

WINSTONLEAD KENT LEAGUE

Division One

	P	W	D	L	F	A	PTS
Furness	38	27	8	3	87	19	89
Dartford	38	26	11	1	71	21	89
Chatham Town	38	24	5	9	79	48	77
Herne Bay	38	18	10	10	74	44	64
Deal Town	38	17	13	8	72	52	64
Slade Green	38	17	12	9	66	46	63
Sheppey Utd	38	19	5	14	66	49	62
Whitstable T	38	17	7	14	85	61	58
Thamesmead T	38	17	7	14	59	51	58
Folkestone Inv	38	15	11	12	82	56	56
Greenwich Boro	38	15	7	16	60	66	52
Cray Wands	38	16	5	17	70	70	50
Canterbury C	38	14	6	18	48	59	48
Ramsgate	38	13	6	19	62	81	45
Tunbridge Wells	38	10	10	18	45	64	40
Beckenham T	38	9	9	20	45	60	36
Corinthian	38	9	7	22	53	84	34
Crockenhill	38	8	8	22	51	92	32
Hythe United	38	8	6	24	58	101	30
Faversham Town	38	3	3	32	33	142	12

Division Two

	P	W	D	L	F	A	PTS
Hastings T Res.	36	24	6	4	127	49	84
Furness Res.	36	24	5	7	121	36	77
Dover Ath Res.	36	23	5	8	104	52	74
Tonbridge A Res.	36	22	7	7	108	48	73
Whitstable T Res.	36	22	5	9	107	46	71
Sittingbrne Res.	36	22	4	10	127	57	70
Thamesm T Res.	36	18	6	12	63	48	60
Chatham T Res.	36	15	10	11	56	59	55
Corinthian Res.	36	16	4	16	63	58	52
Folkest Inv Res.	34	15	7	12	69	69	52
Beckenham T Res.	36	15	7	14	62	67	52
Ramsgate Res.	36	14	4	18	79	84	46
Margate Res.	36	10	9	17	57	76	39
Herne Bay Res.	36	12	3	21	49	86	39
Deal Town Res.	36	12	3	21	73	114	39
Canterbury C Res.	36	11	5	20	58	86	38
Crockenhill Res.	36	6	4	26	49	104	22
Faversham T Res.	36	5	3	28	41	138	18
Kent Police	36	2	2	32	28	175	8

BECKENHAM TOWN

Eden Park Avenue, Beckenham, Kent. Tel: 0181 650 1066

Secretary: Peter Parker, 107 Wentworth Rd, Croydon, Surrey CR0 3HZ. Tel: 0181 689 2134

Press Officer: Bob Chilvers, 26 Darwin Rd, Welling, Kent DA16 2EG

Nickname: Becks, Town or Reds

Capacity: 4,000

Seating: 100

Covered standing: None

Floodlights: No, but permission has been sought

Clubhouse on ground: Yes

Biggest win: 7-2 v Kent Police 1993-94

Biggest defeat: 0-6 numerous times

Record appearances: L Fabian 220

Record goalscorer in one season: R Bennett 34 1992-93

DIRECTIONS

M25, A21 to Bromley then follow signs to Beckenham. Ground 1 mile west of town off A214, 2 mins walk from Eden Park (BR) station - trains from London Bridge. Bus 264.

Manager for 1996-97: Kevin Sugrue

Assistant Manager: Bob Chilvers

Records are for Kent League only:

Beckenham Town began life in 1971 rising from Stanhope Rovers, a local junior club operating successfully in the South East Amateur League. They were founded in 1959 at Stanhope Grove, where an earlier Beckenham Town had played until folding in 1969.

Rovers went through the Beckenham and South East London Leagues and became the top team in the area and so it was logical that they should change their name in 1971.

As Beckenham Town, they stayed in the Amateur League gaining Intermediate status and moving back to Stanhope Grove. They were elected to the Metropolitan League in 1973 and on earning senior status in 1975 they moved to the Spartan League, where they played in Senior Div 1. They were promoted in 1978 and reached the final of the League Cup a year later.

In 1980, Beckenham moved to their present ground in Eden Park Avenue, which they obtained with a 25 year lease and on August 16th, Whyteleafe were the visitors for the first ever game in what was to be the penultimate season in that league. Since moving to the Kent League in 1982, major honours have eluded them, although they did reach the League Cup final in 1985. After a couple of poor seasons, the club faced extinction with severe debts, but a new committee and new Chairman saved the day. During the 1990-91 season, the final links with Stanhope Rovers were severed when long serving Secretary Howard Smith stood down.

Beckenham continue to play in the Kent League and are proud of their youth policy which is beginning to bear fruit.

CANTERBURY CITY

Kingsmead Stadium, Kingsmead Rd, Canterbury, Kent CT2 7PH. Tel: 01227 457245

Secretary: Keith Smith, 7 Knight Ave, London Rd Estate, Canterbury CT2 8PZ. Tel: 01227 456116

Press officer: Roy Twyman, 33 Tyndale Park, Herne Bay, Kent CT6 6BS. Tel: 01227 375774

Nickname: The City   Colours: Emerald green and white

Capacity: 5,000   Seating: 200   Covered standing: 200

Clubhouse on ground: Yes

Record attendance: 3,001 v Torquay Utd FA Cup 1st Rd 1964

Biggest win: 10-0 v Deal Town Southern League Jan 30th 65

Biggest defeat: 0-9 v Corby Town Southern League Sept 16th 1963

Record appearances: John Carragher 413

Record goalscorer in one season: Wilf Heathcote 41 in 1948-49

Record goalscorer in total: Wilf Heathcote 113 1948-51

Record fee paid: £2,000 for Graham Knight from Maidstone Utd

Record fee received: £2,000 for Dave Wiltshire to Gillingham

DIRECTIONS

A28 out of city centre into Military Road, left at first roundabout into Tourtel Road, straight over next roundabout into Kingsmead Road - stadium on right opposite Canterbury swimming pool. Half mile from Canterbury West (BR). Bus service 624 or 625 from Canterbury bus station - ask for Kingsmead crossroads.

Honours

Kent League Div 2 Cup 1949 and Div 1 Cup 1950

Kent Senior Cup 1954, Kent Senior Trophy 1980, Kent Intermediate Cup 1974

Kent Messenger Trophy 1975, Frank Norris Memorial Shield 1989

Manager for 1996-97: Martin Farnie   Assistant Manager: Gary Allen

Chairman: Mr L R Gladwis   Vice Chairman: Mr G J Bradley

Canterbury City were the post War successors to the famous Canterbury Waverley and came into being in 1947. Following the War, a local business firm formed their own team known as Brett Sports. Success came quickly and they soon won the Kent Amateur League. A meeting was held between the club and former supporters and officials of the Waverley club and a private limited company with William Brett as Chairman was formed. Brett Sports ground was available and Canterbury City were in business. The new club were accepted into the Kent League and played there until it disbanded, whereupon they moved to the Metropolitan League in 1959. After just one year they joined the Southern League, where the highest finish was in 1966 when coming sixth. After several years of struggle and financial strain, the club resigned and returned to the Kent League in 1993, after 34 years in the Southern League. On appointing 28 year old Darren Hare to the job as manager, he followed his father as player and manager of City thus achieving a unique family double. Hare eventually went to Folkestone to be replaced by Martin Farnie. Over the years the club has won both the Senior Cup and the Senior Trophy as well as a number of cups in the old and new Kent Leagues. The Brett Sports ground had been in existence long before football was first played there in in the early 1900's and was originally known as the Pays Ground. City remained there until 1958 when they moved to the newly built Kingsmead where they remain. In recent years ground improvements have been made at the shared greyhound track. New floodlights have been installed, the main stand has been extended, a new restaurant built and general tidying up taken place, whilst the club remains, although for some time they have been proposing to relocate to a ground nearer the outskirts of the city.

CHATHAM TOWN

Maidstone Road Sports Ground, Maidstone Road, Chatham Kent. Tel: 01634 812194

Secretary: Brian Burcombe, 4 Hallwood Close, Parkwood, Rainham, Kent ME9 9NT.
Tel: 01634 363419

Nickname: Chats,   Colours: Red and Black

Capacity: 5,000   Seating: Yes

Covered standing: Yes   Clubhouse on ground: Yes

Record attendance: 5,000 v Gillingham
Floodlight opening in 1980

DIRECTIONS

M2, A229 Chatham turn-off, follow signs to Chatham, ground one and a half miles on right opposite garage. 1 mile from Chatham (BR).

Honours

FA CUP quarter-final 1889

Kent League 1895, 1904, 05, 25, 27, 72, 74, 77, 80

Kent League Cup 1972 and 1977

Aetolian League 1964, League Cup 1963 and 1964

Benevolent Cup 1964

Thames and Medway Combination 1897, 1904, 1905, 1920, 1924

Kent Badge 1886, 1887, 1888, Kent Senior Shield 1920, Kent Senior Cup 1889, 95, 1905, 11, 19

Eastern Professional Floodlit Cup 1981

The club was formed in 1882 by a group of local traders, with its headquarters in the first of a number of pubs. By 1887 they were based at the Railway Hotel in New Brompton which was within easy reach of the first home ground, high on the Great Lines overlooking Chatham. They played there until 1889, when following a successful run in the FA Cup from the qualifying rounds to the quarter finals, it became apparent that they needed better facilities and above all, an enclosed ground. At this point the club were attracting crowds of up to 16,000 and so the move was made to Alderman Winch's Enclosed Ground, or as it is known today, Maidstone Road Sports Ground.

In 1894 they became founder members of the Southern League and the original Kent League, becoming first winners of the latter. They were also three times winners of the Kent Badge, the forerunner of the Senior Cup and they became the first team to win the Kent and Medway Combination.

Between the Wars the Chats won the Kent Senior Cup and Shield, the Kent League and Chatham Charity Cup within ten years, and reached the 1st Round proper of the FA Cup. Post War the club played in the old Kent League until it was disbanded in 1959, whereupon they moved to the newly formed Aetolian League, enjoying more success, reaching the League Cup final in all five seasons, although winning only one. They were league champions in 1964, and then when the league merged with the London League, they moved on to the stronger Metropolitan League. Although regularly drawing crowds in excess of 1,000 in the 60's, they lost no time in re-joining the Kent League when it reformed in 1968. They won the League on four occasions, doing the double twice in 1972 and 1978, and were double runners up in 1981.

For a brief period they played as Medway FC, but reverted back in 1979 and a year later took the Eastern Professional Floodlit League. In 1983 Chatham rejoined the Southern League for the third time, staying for five years until failing to gain re-election. Chats remain in the Kent League and their Maidstone Road ground, one of the best in the league, may well yet see Southern league football for a fourth time.

CORINTHIAN

Gay Dawn Farm, Valley Rd, Fawkham, Nr Dartford, Kent DA3 8LZ. Tel: 01474 707559

Secretary: David Roff, 79 Edwin St, Gravesend, Kent DA12 1EJ. Tel: 01474 569457

Colours: Green and white hoops

Capacity: 2,000

Seating: Yes

Covered standing: Yes

Clubhouse on ground: Yes

Record attendance: 480 v Tottenham Hotspur Friendly in 1979

Record appearances: Gavin Tovey

Record goalscorer in one season: Lee Annett

Record goalscorer in total: Lee Annett

DIRECTIONS
Junction 3 M25 (Junction 1 M20). A2 off Longfield, take Fawkham Road - ground one mile on left. Or A20 to Fawkham Green then ground one and a half miles on right. One and a quarter miles from Longfield (BR).

Honours

Kent Senior Trophy 1984 and 1987

Kent Intermediate Cup 1990 and 1991

The club was born in 1972 with players of 9 or 10 years of age with the idea of returning fun, sportsmanship and friendship into football. Season 1973-74 saw the first floodlights but it was in friendlies that the club gained a reputation of giving their all, not joining league football until 1985. They went directly into the Southern League on their impressive home and enjoyed a fine first season finishing fifth. In 1988 the club got to the last eight of the FA Vase and won the Kent Senior Cup a year later.

They were relegated to the Kent League in 1991 and have remained there since, last May finishing a lowly fourth from bottom.

CRAY WANDERERS

Oxford Road, Sidcup, Kent. Tel: 0181 3009201

Secretary: Mr Kerry Phillips, Grove Lodge, 15 Watling St, Bexley Heath, Kent DA6 7QJ. Tel: 01322 554108

Club shop and Press: Greg Mann Tel: 0181 318 9604

Colours: Amber and black,   Nickname: Wands

Capacity: 2,000   Seating 106   Covered standing: 300

Clubhouse on ground: Yes,   Floodlights: No

Record attendance: 1,523 v Stamford FA Vase QF 1981

Biggest win: 16-1 v Sidcup September 1892

Biggest defeat: 1-11 v Bromley 1920-21

Record goalscorer in total: Keith Collishaw 272

Record goalscorer in one season: Keith Collishaw 57 in 1956-57

Record appearances: John Dorey 470+

DIRECTIONS

Between Sidcup High Street and Footscray Street; from A20 turn off for Footscray, junction 4, left at lights, Oxford Road is 3rd left. Three quarters of a mile from Sidcup (BR) station - Kentish bus 492 from Dartford and Sidcup station passes top of Oxford Road - 30 mins service on Saturdays.

Honours

London League 1957 and 1958, League Cup 1955, Aetolian League 1963 and League Cup 1964

Greater London League 1966, League Cup 1965 and 1966, Metropolitan League Cup 1971

Met Lge Amateur Cup 1967 and 1968, London Spartan League 1977 and 1978

Kent League 1902, 1981, Division Two 1895, League Cup 1984

Kent Senior Trophy 1993, Kent Amateur Cup 1931, 1963, 1964, 1965

Manager 1996-97: Glenn Cooper   **Assistant Manager: Peter Little**

Chairman: Gary Hillman   **Vice Chairman: Dave Jackson**

Having been formed in 1860, Cray Wanderers FC are the second oldest club in the world. They played their first matches under either code against army and village clubs on a field later to become Star Lane Cemetary next to the railway in St Mary Cray. The club concentrated solely on association rules from around the mid-1880's entering the Kent Junior Cup in 1889 and in 1894 they became founder members of the Kent League and remained there just until 1904 when they switched to the West Kent League, having at one point played in the Southern Suburban League at the same time, as was the fashion at the time. Wanderers moved to a new ground at Fordcroft and took their little wooden stand with them from the Recreation Ground. It was the beginning of troubled times as the club were forced to revert to amateurism, moving back to the Kent League Division Two until the last year before the Great War which was spent in the South Suburban League. The club began again as Cray Old Boys but within a year Wanderers name was back and switched to the London League. The late 20s saw a change in fortunes as the club reached a number of finals and won the Kent Amateur Cup but by the mid 30's the declining league form and financial problems saw them close down for a year, before moving back to the Kent League. Just prior to the Second War the club were stunned when their ground was put up for sale and they were forced out after nearly 40 years. They began playing on Twysdens but soon dropped into the Kent Amateur League as their playing fortunes got worse. The club began the last peacetime season as Sidcup and Footscray FC but War broke out and the season was suspended. The first season back saw them on a field next door to the first home in Derry Downs, called Grassmeade and after one season in the South London Alliance they returned to the Kent Amateur League, but after being thrown off the ground by the owners they found themselves on St Mary Cray Rec for 1948. From then on for the next 20 odd years Cray stumbled from success to near extinction and back and after another couple of ground moves settled at Grassmeade, playing in the London and Aetolian Leagues. both of which brought much success and later the Metropolitan and Spartan Leagues. In 1973 the club once again lost their ground but after much graft, a site at Sidcup Conservative Club in Oxford Rd was made into a home and it remains so with Cray back in Kent League football since 1978.

CROCKENHILL

Wested Meadow, Eynsford Rd, Crockenhill, Kent. Tel: 01322 668275

Secretary: Alan Parkin, 15 Greenside, Swanley, Kent BR8 7ER.
Tel: 01322 663319

Colours: Red and white stripes

Nickname: Crocks

Capacity: 2,000

Seating: 200

Covered standing: No

Clubhouse on ground: Yes

Record attendance: 800 v Maidstone Utd
Kent Amateur Cup 1948

DIRECTIONS

Just off M25 junction 3, B2173 towards Swanley, left after 200 yds into Wested Lane, ground 1 mile on right (Ord. Survey grid Ref: 516669 sheet 177). Just over a mile from Swanley (BR) station - trains from Victoria. Kentish Bus 477 to Crockenhill - at village shops turn left at T-junction - ground 1 mile up narrow lane on left.

Honours

Kent League 1983

Kent Senior Trophy 1981

West Kent Amateur Cup 1957

Sevenoaks Charity Cup 1949

Kent Amateur League 1957

Premier Division 1954

Division One 1949

The present Crockenhill Football Club was founded in 1946 by Mr Cyril Nicholls, although there was an earlier team in the village.They joined the Kent Amateur League where they stayed until switching to the Aetolian League in 1959 having had some success in the various divisions. The Aetolian merged with the London League to become the Greater London League and Crocks stayed there until moving to the Kent League in 1968, when it re-formed. Crock's finest day was without doubt in May 1983 when they were crowned as champions of the league, after a title race only won on the last day with a winner take all match against Hythe Town. A 1-0 win gave them the championship. In 1987 the club came close to another title but were in the end beaten by Greenwich Borough.

Earlier in 1981 Crock won the Kent Senior Trophy beating Slade Green, and before this back in 1975 had reached the final only to lose Sutton Athletic, a junior club.

Crockenhill have played at Wested Meadow from the start and little appears to have changed on what is the epitome of a small country ground.

DEAL TOWN

Charles Sports Ground, St Leonards Rd, Deal Kent. Tel: 01304 375623

Secretary: Mrs Anne Lewis, Silver Hill, Northbourne Rd, Deal, Kent CT14 OLF. Tel: 01304 373918

Colours: Black and white hoops

Nickname: Town

Capacity: 2,000

Seating: 150

Covered standing: 300

Clubhouse on ground: Yes

DIRECTIONS

A258 through Walmer, left into Cornwell Road, continue into Hamilton Road, veer left into Mill Road, follow round to right into Manor Road, right into St Leonards Road, ground 100 yds on right. 1 mile from both Walmer and Deal BR station. Local buses stop near ground.

Record attendance: 4,000 Charity Game 1961

Biggest win: 11-1 v Tunbridge Wells 1993

Biggest defeat: 0-10 v Tunbridge Wells 1986

Record appearances: Alan Barrow 542

Record goalscorer in one season: Joe Brayne 45 1992-93

Record goalscorer in total: Joe Brayne 147

Honours

Kent League 1954, League Cup 1958 and 1982

Greater London League Cup 1969, Kent Senior Trophy 1995

Manager 1996-97: Dave Dadd, Assistant Manager: Eddie Pickford

Chairman: Roy Smith, Vice Chairman: William Bennett

Programme editor: Peter Humphries 01304 367031

Originally known as Deal Cinque Ports FC, the club was formed in 1908, changing its name 12 years later to Deal Town FC. Their first matches were played in the Thanet and East Kent Leagues and in 1909 they joined the Eastern section of the Kent League. They alternated between that and the Amateur League during the inter-War years before joining the Kent League again in 1946, winning it in 1954 and the League Cup in 1958. When the league disbanded in 1959 they became founder members of the Aetolian League.

It lasted until they took the plunge and joined the Southern League, but after three years of desperate struggle, they cut their losses and moved to the Greater London League which had come about following a merger between the London and Aetolian Leagues. Their final move to date came in 1971 when they returned to the Kent League.

The club's only championship to date came in 1954, although they were runners up in 1989 and have won the League Cup twice, losing a third final two years ago to Ramsgate. They have also seen success in the Kent Senior Trophy winning it for the first time in 1995 after three final defeats.

Deal Town have played at the Charles Sports Ground since just after the Great War, when their original field was taken by a hospital. They moved to another site just opposite their current ground and stayed until the Charles Sports Ground was donated to the town and they moved in, enjoying a stipulation that it must always be for the benefit of the young of the town.

FAVERSHAM TOWN

Salters Lane, Faversham, Kent. Tel: 01795 532738

Secretary: R.C.Yorke, 27 Churchill Way, Faversham, Kent ME13 7QX. Tel: 01795 534328

Colours: White and blue

Nickname: Town

Capacity: 2,000

Seating: 350

Covered standing: 1,000

Clubhouse on ground: Yes

Record attendance: 1,400 v Sheppey Utd in 1949

Biggest win: 8-0 v Greenwich Borough Aug 1989

Biggest defeat: 0-9 v Sittingbourne Jan 1982

Record appearances: Bob Mason

Record goalscorer in one season: Tony Rudd 43

DIRECTIONS
On A2 (Canterbury Road) just west of town.

Honours

Kent League 1970, 1971, 1978, 1990

League Cup 1971 and 1991

Kent Senior Trophy 1977, 1978,

Kent Amateur Cup 1957, 1959, 1972, 1973, 1974

Faversham Town FC were formed in 1901 as a junior team, but they quickly gained senior status. Their first ever ground was at Gordon Square in the centre of Faversham and they stayed there until just after the War when they moved to Salters Lane.

They played in the Kent League from 1904 until it disbanded, and like many they switched to the Aetolian League but that was merged and they found themselves in the Metropolitan and then Athenian Leagues before rejoining the new version of the Kent League in 1976. They have a fine record in that league, having won it four times since 1970 plus a runners up spot in 1988. They also have reached three League Cup finals, winning two and four Kent Senior Trophy finals, two of which were won consecutively in 1977 and 1978. They again appeared in consecutive finals in 1988 and 1989 but lost both.

Earlier, Town won five Kent Amateur Cup finals between 1957 and 1974.

In recent times the club has ground shared with the homeless Sheppey Utd but that agreement has now ended and Sheppey are playing at Canterbury City.

FOLKESTONE INVICTA

The New Pavilion, Cheriton Rd, Folkestone, Kent CT19 5RW. Tel: 01303 257461

Secretary: Neil Pilcher, 25 Pavilion Rd, Folkestone, Kent CT19 5RW. Tel: 01303 245066

Colours: Amber and Black

Capacity: 6,000

Seating: 900

Covered standing: 3,000

Floodlights: Yes

Clubhouse on ground: Yes

DIRECTIONS

On the A20 behind Presto foodstore, midway between Folkestone Central and Folkestone West BR stations.

Record attendance: (For Invicta, 1, 211 v Brighton AHA Friendly 1991)

Ground record is 7, 881 Folkestone Town v Margate Kent Senior Cup 1958

Biggest win: Thamesmead Town Res 12-0 1992

Biggest defeat: 1-7 v Crockenhill

HONOURS

Kent League Div 2 and Div 2 League Cup 1992

Kent Intermediate Cup 1992

Manager for 1996-97: Darren Hare

Assistant Manager: Mickey Crowe

Chairman: Tom Guiver

The reputation of the Kent League has been given a boost in recent years by the election of Folkestone Invicta, who were formed in 1936. Their roots are in amateur football, competing in the Kent Amateur League, later the Kent County League. For the majority of their time they played in the shadow of Folkestone Town, but when that club were relegated from the Southern League Premier Division they went into decline and folded mid-way through 1991. At that time Invicta were playing at South Road, nearby Hythe, but events moved quickly and the club took over the Town's old Cheriton Road ground, being elected into the Kent League. As they were still Intermediate, they played in Division Two, but having gained senior status they won the League and Cup double and entered Division One in 1992.

They have reached the Senior Trophy final twice and have established themselves within the league finishing fourth last May.

FURNESS

Green Court Rd, Swanley, Kent BR8 8JG. Tel: 01322 666442

Secretary: Richard Ayling, 22 Houston Rd, London SE23 2RN
Tel 0181 699 1052

Colours: All White

Capacity: 1,500

Seating: 100

Covered standing: No

Clubhouse on ground: Yes

Floodlights: No

DIRECTIONS

From junction of M25 & M20 follow signs for Swanley. Left at Crockenhill turning, then first right after motorway crossing. 500 yards from Swanley (BR).

Record attendance; 1,000 v Dartford, Kent League, 1996

Honours

Kent Junior Cup 1969

South London Alliance League Cup twice

Kent League 1996

Furness FC were formed in 1968 as the football club of Furness Withy Shipping Group from Beckenham. In 1982 the company withdrew its support and the football club relocated, changing the name to Furness.

During the 1990's Danson FC were on the brink of folding and a merger between the two was quickly arranged, as Danson Furness United. However in 1993 they reverted again to Furness FC. The club originally played in the London Shipping League before moving into the South London Alliance and through the years they gradually progressed to the Premier Division and in 1991 they entered sides in both the Spartan League and the Kent League and due to the merger also played in the Kent League itself.

At the start of 1992-93 season Steve Brown took over and the club began to look to dominate, firstly finishing runners up, then third and then runners up again after a nail biting run in with eventual champions Dartford.

Furness now play on the former home of Alma Swanley having moved from Danson's old home at Crook Log, and enjoyed their finest hour in 1995-96 when they held off Dartford in a thrilling title race to lift the Kent League Championship. They also enjoyed a fine run to the last 32 of the FA Carlsberg Vase.

GREENWICH BOROUGH

Harrow Meadow, Eltham Green Rd, Eltham, London SE9. Tel: 0181 850 3098

Secretary: Denise Richmond, 7 Castlecombe Rd, Mottingham,
London SE9 4AU. Tel: 0181 289 8956

Nickname: Boro

Club Colours: All Red

Capacity: 2,000

Seating: 50

Covered standing: None

Floodlights: Yes

Clubhouse on Ground: Yes

Record Attendance: 2,000 v Charlton Athletic Floodlight opener in 1978

> ## DIRECTIONS
> **South Circular (A205)
> to Yorkshire Grey pup
> opposite. 1 mile from
> both Eltham and
> Kidbrooke BR
> stations.**

HONOURS

South London Allliance 1961, 1962, 1963, 1964, 1965, 1966

Kent Junior Cup

London Spartan League 1981

League Cup 1982

Kent League 1987 and 1988

Kent League Cup 1985 and 1987

Kent Senior Trophy 1985

Greenwich Borough were formed in 1928 as Woolwich Borough Council Athletic Club. They played in the Kent Amateur League from 1929 when they gained senior status, but relinquished it as the Amateur League was too strong. They chose to join the South London Alliance and soon progressed to the Premier Division which they went on to win for six consecutive seasons along with the Kent Junior Cup.

They remained there until 1976 when they switched to the London Spartan League before joining the Kent League in 1984. In their first year they made history by becoming the first club to win the Kent League Cup and Kent Senior Trophy in the same season.

Before this they had found success in the Athenian League, winning the Senior Division title in 1981 ahead of Cobham and they then took the League Cup in 1983. Upon joining the Kent League, Boro' quickly found their feet and after final placings of 6th and 7th they achieved back to back championships in 1987 and 1988, also taking the League Cup again.

Before that in 1985 the League Cup and the Kent Senior Trophy were won. Success has eluded the club since then with a mid-table position last May.

HERNE BAY

Winch's Field, Stanley Gardens, Herne Bay, Kent CT6 1SG. Tel: 01227 374156

Secretary: Mr Tommy Sampson, 33 Sharp's Field, Headcorn,
Kent CT6 1SG. Tel: 01622 891784

Fixture Sec: Mr J Bathurst Tel: 01227 363430

Club Historian: Doug Smith: Tel 01227 742182

Colours: Blue and white   Nickname: The Bay

Capacity: 5,000,   Seating: 200

Covered standing: 2,000   Clubhouse on ground: Yes

Record attendance : 2,303 v Margate

DIRECTIONS

Leave A229 at Herne Bay roundabout, 2nd left, 1st left. Half mile from Herne Bay (BR); down Station Approach (half mile), 1st right (Spencer Road), 2nd right.

FA Cup 4th Qual Rd 1970

Biggest win: 15-1 Kent Amateur League March 22nd 1952

Biggest defeat: 0-9 v Hounslow Athenian League 1973-74

Record goalscorer in one season: Eddie Davies 62

Record goalscorer in total: Eddie Davies

Record fee received: £3,000 from Gravesend and Northfleet for Mark Munday in 1994

Honours

Kent League 1992 and 1994, and Division Two 1955

Kent Senior Trophy 1979

Kent Amateur Cup 1958

Aetolian League Div 2 1971 and League Cup 1967

Kent Amateur League Cup 1954 and 1955

Manager 1996-97: Tommy Sampson

Chairman: Michael Todd

Vice Chairman: Bob Gibson

Herne Bay were formed in November 1886 and their first ever match is documented as a 0-6 defeat by East Kent College on December 16th. The team won the East Kent League in 1902 and went on to complete the hat-trick in the next two seasons. Their home matches were played on Mitchell's Enclosure from 1892 for four years until moving to the Victoria Recreation Ground in 1896. They moved to the newly opened Memorial Park ground in 1922. They stayed there, playing in East Kent, Kent Amateur and Thanet Leagues until Winch's Field was acquired in 1951. The site was formerly Winch's Brickyard and it took a year to create a football ground for the club, but they moved in around 1953.

The ground and the club were ready to move up to Kent League and the enjoyed a good spell winning the Division Two League Cup and the Kent Amateur Cup until the league folded and Bay joined the Aetolian league until it was merged into the Ahenian League in 1964. They had success in both leagues before moving to the current Kent League in 1974.

They were League Cup runners up and Kent Senior Trophy winners in 1979, but the 90's saw the finest spell in their history when they twice took the Kent League and were once runners up in the first four years.

HYTHE UNITED

Reachfields, Fort Road, Hythe, Kent. Tel: 01303 264932

Secretary: Anthony Maycock, 86 Dymchurch Rd, Hythe, Kent CT21 6LH Tel: 01303 268346

Colours: Red and white

Capacity: 3,000

Seating: Yes

Covered standing: Yes

Clubhouse on ground: Yes

DIRECTIONS
M20 down towards Folkestone and take the turning for Hythe or approach on A20 from Dover or A259 from Hastings.

Hythe United are a new club, formed from the ashes of the old Hythe Town which collapsed after such a meteoric rise to fame. They play on the same ground having been formed to play in the Kent County League until admitted to the Kent League.

Town were formed in 1910 as an offshoot of Hythe Wednesday which was formed 100 years ago and after playing friendlies the club played in the Folkestone Junior League until joining the Kent Amateur League in 1918. They remained through to the 70's in that league, with few successes other than various Charity Cups and did not come to the fore until winning the league twice in the 70's and taking the Kent Junior Cup in their last year before gaining senior status in 1976.

They moved into Reachfields, an old army training ground, about the same time and joined the Kent League where they were three times runners up before taking the title in 1989. Town were elected to the Southern League during the summer and it was the start of a remarkable season which saw runs in the FA Cup, County Cup and FA Vase, where they got to the semi-finals and won the Floodlight competition at the first attempt. By then the ground was being transformed and the capacity allowed the ground record to be broken twice as the club played 72 matches.

A year later they won the Kent Senior Trophy and Floodlit Cup and reached the Southern League Cup Final and the last eight of the Vase, a season which saw 73 games played. Sadly events off the field saw a rapid decline and in 1992 the club pulled out of the league and folded.

LORDSWOOD

Lordswood Sports and Social Club, Northdane Way, Walderslade, Kent. Tel: 01634 669138

Secretary: Mr Steve Lewis, Sunnybrook, Gorsewood Rd, Hartley, Longfield, Kent. Tel 01474 708233

Colours: Amber and black

Capacity: 1000

Floodlights: No

Seating: 120

Covered standing: No

Manager: for 1996-97 Gary Doe

Assistant manager: Steve Cairns

Chairman: Dave Simms

DIRECTIONS
From M2 near Chatham take junction 3 turning for A2045 (off A229 Chatham to Maidstone) and look for left hand turning to Walderslade.

RAMSGATE

Southwood Stadium, Prices Avenue, Ramsgate, Kent. Tel: 01843 591662

Secretary: Steve Redford c/o Ramsgate FC
(H)01843 596138

Colours: Red and white, Nickname: Rams

Capacity: 3,000, Seating: 150

Covered standing: None, Floodlights: Yes

Clubhouse on ground: Yes

Record attendance: 5,200 v Margate 1956-57

Biggest win: 9-1 v Crockenhill Kent League Cup 1994

Record goalscorer in total: Mick Williamson

Honours

Kent League 1950, 1956, 1957

League Cup 1949, 1993, 1994, 1995

Kent Intermediate Cup 1955

Kent Senior Cup 1964

Thames and Medway Cup 1961

Kent Senior Shield 1961

Kent Floodlit Trophy 1970

Kent Senior Trophy 1988 and 1989

Manager for 1996-97: Jim Ward

Assistant Manager: Paul Jeffcote

Chairman: Richard Lawson BSC (hons)

Vice Chairman: Anthony Payne BSC (hons)

DIRECTIONS

From London on A229, A253 into Ramsgate - left into Netherhill at roundabout, right into Ashburnham Road. Right into Southwood Road. 15 minutes walk from Ramsgate BR station: walk through Warre Recreation Ground, along St Lawrence High Street, left at 'White Horse' follow Southwood Road and turn right into Princes Avenue.

The first recorded club in Ramsgate were called Ramsgate Town who were formed around 1886 and lasted until 1905. Later after the Great War in 1919 Ramsgate FC were in action and for three years Ramsgate Press Wanderers were prominent, followed by Ramsgate Grenville, who used the ground until they folded during the War. Afterwards Ramsgate Athletic took over and were immediately successful in the Kent League winning the League Cup in 1949 and the League in 1950 and 1956. The Rams continued in the Kent League until it folded in 1959, when instead of going into the Aetolian as some did, they moved up into the Southern League. They took the Kent Senior Cup in 1964 after an earlier Senior Shield win and they were League Cup finalists before being promoted in 1972. It was the beginning of the end, for during the 1975-76 season Athletic found themselves in terrible debt and the club was wound up, and they resigned.

At the start of the following season, a new club, Ramsgate FC began playing in the Kent League and since then they have enjoyed cup success, being the only team to win the League Cup three times running, from 1993 to 1995. They also twice took the Senior Trophy back to Southwood Stadium.

SHEPPEY UNITED

Canterbury City FC, Kingsmead Stadium, Kingsmead Rd, Canterbury

Secretary: Barry Bundock, Dunedin, 104 Southsea Ave, Minster, Kent
ME12 2NH
Tel 01795 876025

Colours: Red and white

Nickname: Islanders

**PLEASE SEE CANTERBURY CITY PAGE
FOR GROUND INFORMATION**

DIRECTIONS
As Canterbury City
(see page 313).

Record attendance: 4,000 at Botany Rd v Sittingbourne Kent Sen Trophy 1927

Honours

Kent Lge 1906, 1907, 1928, 1973, 1975, 1979, 1995

League Cup 1976 and 1979

Thames and Medway Comb 1909, 1913, 1923, 1926, 1929, 1956

Kent Amateur Cup 1946 and 1952

Kent Sen Shield 1978

Greater London Lge 1965

Manager 1996-97: John Roseman

Assistant Manager: C Pooley

Chairman: P Sharrock

Vice Chairman: D Whitton

Sheppey were founder members of the Southern League and have had three spells so far. They were formed in 1890 from two Sheerness clubs, Invicta and Victoria and early games were played against Bristol City and Rovers, Portsmouth, Spurs and Southampton. They also helped form the Kent League in 1894, finding success with two titles. After the Great War Sheppey had a good spell in the Kent League and re-entered the Southern League, but finances saw them drop out and revert to amateurism in 1934.

They somehow survived to the War and on returning enjoyed several good seasons although things were hard for amateur clubs. When most of the Kent League professional sides joined the Southern League, it folded and Sheppey joined the Aetolian League which became the Greater London League in 1964. Sheppey turned pro yet again, installed floodlights and won the league, moving immediately to the Metropolitan League. 1972 saw the Islanders return to the new Kent League where the stayed until 1984 when once again they went to the Southern League. In those 12 years the club won the title three times and were runners up twice. With two Kent League Cups it was a great time for the club.

The Southern League membership again was not a success and after 7 years they went down yet again.

In the spring of 1992 Sheppey sold their Botany Road ground and have been sharing with Faversham Town until this season when they have moved in with Canterbury City.

SLADE GREEN

The Small Glen, 35 Moat Lane, Slade Green, Erith, Kent. Tel: 01322 351077

Secretary: Bruce Smith, 15 Gumping Rd, Orpington, Kent BR5 1RX. Tel: 01689 858782

Press Sec: Robert Smith, 6 Selwood Ct, Churchill Close, Dartford, Kent DA1 1QL. Tel: 01322 287982

DIRECTIONS

Off A206 between Erith & Dartford 400 yards from Slade Green BR station. Buses 89 & B13

Nickname: The Green, Capacity: 4,000

Seating: 125, Covered standing: 200

Floodlights: Yes, Clubhouse on ground: Yes

Record attendance: 3,000 v Millwall Friendly July 1992

Biggest win: 13-0 v Asland Social Kent Amateur League 54

Biggest defeat: 1-6 v several times

Record appearances: Colin Dwyer 485

Record goalscorer in one season: Colin Dwyer 33

Record goalscorer in total: Ray Gibbs 86

Honours

Dartford League Cup 1948, Kent Benevolent Cup 1947

Erith Hospitals Cup 1947, 1949, 1954, Kent Amateur League Div 2 1953

Division One 1954, Senior Division 1961

League Cup 1960

West Kent Challenge Shield 1960, West Kent Cup 1966

Kent League Cup 1983, Kent Senior Trophy 1992

Managers for 1996-97: Mickey Watts and Tony Carley

Chairman: Brian Smith

Slade Green Athletic were formed on June 6th 1946 following the amalgamation of three local teams, The Wasps, St Augustines and Southern Railway Sports. The latter also went under the name of Slade Green Loco which gave way to the club's logo of a locomotive. They soon moved to a patch of land named the Glen, (re-named the Small Glen in 1987 in memory of Charlie and Gert Small who had been at the club from the start. It was owned by Edward Stone who later sold it to the club in 1954 for £1,750. The first season saw success in the Kent Benevolent and Erith Hospital Cups, losing the Dartford League Cup, although they won the League Cup a year later. Two further cups came soon after, but they left the Dartford League in 1952 to join the Kent Amateur League, winning Division Two in the first year. A further year saw them promoted to the Senior Division as runaway champions remaining unbeaten and scoring 144 goals. The early 60's saw a host of honours including West Kent Shields and league titles. They moved to the London League briefly where they were runners up in 1969 and in 1970 were elected to the Kent League. They had to wait until 1981 to make their mark, reaching the Kent Senior Trophy final, before losing in a replay but in 1983 their long wait ended with the Kent League Cup. In 1992 they made up for losing the Senior Trophy final by beating Tunbridge Wells. In July 1992 the record crowd was set at the Small Glen when 3,000 saw a friendly with Millwall.

THAMESMEAD TOWN

Bayliss Avenue, Thamesmead, London SE28 8NJ. Tel: 0181 311 4211

Secretary: G A Panting, 97 Sydney Rd, Bexleyheath, Kent
DA6 8HQ. Tel: 0181 303 1350

Nickname: The Meads

Capacity: 400

Seating: 125

Covered standing: None

Floodlights: Yes

Clubhouse on ground: Yes

Record attendance: 400 v Wimbledon 1988

Record appearances: Delroy D'Oyley

HONOURS

Spartan League Div 3 1980

League Cup 1985 and 1987

Intermediate League 1986

Kent Intermediate Cup 1984, 1995

Kent League and Div 2 Cup 1995

Also four promotions and nine trophies whilst Intermediate side

DIRECTIONS

From Abbey Wood (BR) north east along Harrow manor Way, into Crossway at 3rd roundabout, Bayliss Avenue is 3rd right (Bexley bus 272 stops in Crossway near Bayliss Avenue. By road: From Dartford tunnel A2 to London, exit Danson Intercharge and follow signs for Thamesmead and Abbey Wood. from Blackheath tunnel exit on south side and follow signs to Woolwich, to Plumstead and then to Thamesmead.

Thamesmead Town were founded in 1969 and are known as the Meads. Over the years the club has grown to become of the largest in South-East London and Kent. Following the success of the junior and senior teams playing Sunday football, the club joined the Spartan League in 1979, winning many trophies in subsequent years. Following the league's reorganisation, Thamesmead were one of four to gain promotion and they spent four years there before moving to the Kent League in 1991. They have had success, particularly the reserves who won the League and Cup double as well as taking the Intermediate Cup in 1995. The ground is unusual in senior non-League football in that the dressing rooms are reached by crossing a public footpath. The pitch is surrounded by wire fencing which restricts the viewing to one side only.

Bayliss Avenue was opened in 1988 and Wimbledon brought a team down to play a friendly, watched by 400, the record crowd to date.

1995-96 saw the club enjoy a fine FA Vase run in which they won away to holders Arlesey Town. Thamesmead eventually went out to a late goal against the powerful Canvey Island side in the last sixteen, in a match that had to be staged at the nearby Slade Green because of the limited capacity at the Meads.

TUNBRIDGE WELLS

Culverden Stadium, Culverden Down, Tunbridge Wells, Kent. Tel: 01892 520517

Secretary: Peter Wager, 46 Mereworth Rd, Tunbridge Wells TN4 9PL. Tel: 01892 542182

Other contact: Chairman R J Bonny 01892 531898

Nickname: The Wells

Capacity: 3,750

Seating: 300

Covered standing: 500

Floodlights: Yes

Clubhouse on ground: Yes

Record attendance: 967 v Maidstone.

Biggest win: 10-0 v Deal (H) 1986

Biggest defeat: 1-11 v Deal 193

Record appearance holder: A Atkins

Record goalscorer in one season: 42 B Marchant

Record goalscorer in aggregate: John Wingate 150

DIRECTIONS

Leaving town on main Tunbridge road (A26), turn left opposite 'Red Lion' pub — ground half mile. 1 mile from Tunbridge Wells central (BR). Served by Tunbridge Wells-Tonbridge bus — alight at St Johns.

HONOURS

Kent League 1985, League Cup 1975, 1978, 1986, 1988

Manager for 1996-97: Rob Dobereiner   **Assistant manager: Shaun Lovitt**

Chairman: R J Bonny   **Vice chairman: Peter Wager**

Football has been played at Tunbridge Wells since the first town club was formed in 1886. There have been several successors which have come and gone due, in the main to financial troubles. Various clubs have been called Tunbridge Wells Rangers and United and over the years some eight different grounds have been used.

The two decades between the wars were a period of prominence for the Wells, when a number of League clubs were played in FA Cup competition. During this time, Rangers played in the Southern League whilst at other times and in other guises they played in both Kent and London Leagues. Six times in the 30's they reached the first round proper, 1930-31 being the best when beating Kingstonian to get to the 2nd Rd. They repeated it in 1936-37 when beating Bath City but the reward was a trip to Accrington where they lost 1-0. The present club was formed in 1967 by the supporters following the demise of the Southern League club. With determination and spirit they started the club and entered the Kent League in 1968 where they remain today. In their second season the new club were runners up and they waited until 1985 before they were crowned champions. They have also taken the Division one Cup on four occasions.

Culverden Stadium was built in 1962 after the previous ground, the Agricultural Show Ground in Eridge Road, was vacated. Other grounds used by the various clubs have been the Nevil Cricket Ground, a field in Down Lane, Combley Park and Swiss Cottage. Down Lane was the most substantial, with a wooden stand with dressing rooms underneath and a small covered stand opposite. It was home until the War when it was used for the war effort and never used again, although it remains open land and the playing area is still visible. When Culverden Stadium was in the hands of Receivers, it was sold to property developers who could not get planning permission, fortunately and after passing through several hands the Borough Council gained the site and the club have just signed a 30 year lease and installed floodlights.

WHITSTABLE TOWN

Belmont Road, Belmont, Whitstable, Kent. Tel: 01227 266012

Secretary: Mrs Sylvia Davis, 5 Old Bridge Rd, Whitstable, Kent CT5 1RJ. Tel: 01227 265646

Nickname: The Oystermen or The Natives

Colours: Red and White

Capacity: 2,750

Seating: 450

Covered Standing: 500

Floodlights: Yes

Clubhouse on ground: Yes

Record attendance: 2,500 v Gravesend and Northfleet

Biggest win: 18-0 v Greenstreet (h) 1920

Biggest defeat: 0-10 v Sittingbourne

FA Cup 1st Qual 1962

Record appearances: Frank Cox 429 1950-60

Record goalscorer in one season: Barry Godfrey

<table>
<tr><td>

DIRECTIONS

From Thanet Way (A299), left at Tescos roundabout and down Millstrood Road — ground at bottom of road, 400 yards from Whitstable (BR) station. Car Park at Grimshall Road entrance.

</td></tr>
</table>

HONOURS

Kent League Div 2 1928, 1934, 1950, League Cup 1980

Kent Amateur League East 1961, Kent Amateur Cup 1929

Manager for 1996-97: Wayne Godden

Assistant Manager: John Crabbe

Chairman: JC Brownett

Vice Chairman: Peter Dale

Originally founded in 1885 as Whitstable United, their first recorded game in October of that year was against a side from the local college. The Town name can be traced back to 1886 when they played friendlies at Saddleton's Field, but by 1888 a match had already been played at Belmont, against Herne Bay. In 1893 they became Whitstable Swifts and a year later moved to Westmeads in Cromwell Road, and two years on from there they again became Whitstable Town and moved to Joy Lane where they played in the East Kent League from its formation in 1897.

In 1905 the Town suffix was dropped before in 1908 the club moved to their fourth ground, this time in Church Road where they played just one season before moving to Belmont, their present home.

It was then that the club entered the Kent League, which they stayed in until it was disbanded in 1959.

During their time in the league they won Division Two three times as well as the Kent Amateur Cup in 1929. They moved to the Aetolian League for season 1959-60 but the following year saw them in the Kent Amateur League where they won the Eastern Section. From there Whitstable played in the Greater London League and the re-formed Kent League in 1968, once again as Whitstable Town.

WOOLWICH TOWN

Erith Sports Centre Stadium, Avenue Rd, Erith, Kent DA8 3AJ. Tel: 01322 350271

Gen Secretary: Jim Davie, 6 Dashwood Close, Broomfield Rd, Bexleyheath, DA6 7NU.Tel: 0181 306 7068

Press and Programme: Ian Birrell, 21 Windsor Rd, Hornchurch, Essex RM11 1PD. Tel: 01956 291274

Football Sec: John Stancombe 0181 673 4010

Colours: White and navy blue

Nickname: The Dockers

Capacity: 1,450

Uncovered seating: 1,006

Covered standing: Balcony of Leisure Centre

Clubhouse on ground: Yes

Record attendance: 116 v Hillingdon Borough Lon Sen Cup 1st Rd Nov 13th 1995

Biggest win: 7-0 v Craven London Intermediate Cup S/F 1995

Biggest defeat: 0-6 v Tottenham Wine London Spartan Div 1 1994-95

Record appearances: Dean Griffin

Record goalscorer in one season: Junior Crooks 1974-75 (Sunday football)

Record goalscorer in total: Dean Griffin

Honours

Met Sunday League Bartholemew Benn Cup 1960

Met Sunday League Senior Sec 1966, 1971, 1975

Batholemew Bowl 1967 and 1871, Memorial Trophy 1967

SE London Amateur League Div 1 1991

Manager 1996-97: Ian Birrell

Chairman: Albert Putnam

Town were formed in 1959 as a Sunday club and played mostly in the Metropolitan League. In 1989 they briefly changed the name to Woolwich Heathway but soon reverted back. In 1990 they switched to Saturdays in the SE Amateur League, which they won before moving to the London Spartan League. Intermediate status gave them a place in Division One and after much success they gained senior status and moved up to the Premier Division. Until 1991 the club played at Flamingo Park, Charlton, and then shared with Greenwich Borough before moving to the Erith Stadium in October 1995.

In January 1996 they won their appeal to be allowed to cross the pyramid and joined the Kent League for this season.

WINSTONLEAD KENT LEAGUE DIVISION ONE 1995-1996

TUNBRIDGE WELLS

FOOTBALL CLUB

(Affiliated to KCFA)

Chairman: R J Bonny
Secretary: Peter Wager   46 Mereworth Road
Tunbridge Wells, Phone 524182
Treasurer: Shirley Brown
Manager: Mark Higgs
Honours: Kent Snr. Trophy Runners Up 1985/86, 91/92
Kent League Champions 1984/85
Kent League Runners Up 1968/69
Kent League Cup Winners 1974/75, 1977/78
1985/86, 1987/88

40p OFFICIAL PROGRAMME

Culverden Stadium
Telephone: 520517

SLADE GREEN
FOOTBALL CLUB

OFFICIAL MATCHDAY PROGRAMME

FOUNDED 1946

SPONSORED BY KINGSWAY FURNITURE

WINSTONLEAD KENT LEAGUE
DIVISION ONE   AFFILIATED K.C.F.A.

WTFC 1959
WOOLWICH TOWN FOOTBALL CLUB

WOOLWICH
TOWN F.C.
Founded 1959

OPUS

LONDON
SPARTAN LEAGUE
PREMIER DIVISION

Season 1995 - 96
Affiliated to the KCFA & the LFA

Official Match Programme
Sponsored by
OPUS
Air Conditioning (Sales) Ltd

£2

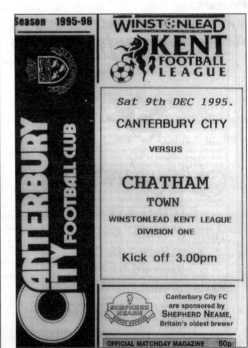

Season 1995-96

CANTERBURY CITY FOOTBALL CLUB

WINST:NLEAD
KENT FOOTBALL LEAGUE

Sat 9th DEC 1995.

CANTERBURY CITY

VERSUS

CHATHAM
TOWN
WINSTONLEAD KENT LEAGUE
DIVISION ONE

Kick off 3.00pm

Canterbury City FC
are sponsored by
SHEPHERD NEAME,
Britain's oldest brewer

OFFICIAL MATCHDAY MAGAZINE   50p

UNIJET SUSSEX COUNTY LEAGUE

DIVISION ONE

	P	W	D	L	F	A	PTS
Peace & Tels	38	32	5	1	133	23	101
Stamco	38	29	3	6	130	38	90
Shoreham	38	25	8	5	91	37	83
Wick	38	23	6	9	95	52	75
Hailsham Town	38	21	10	7	84	48	73
Pagham	38	20	3	15	59	59	63
Arundel	38	19	4	15	80	61	61
Hassocks	38	18	7	13	71	62	61
Langney Sports	38	17	9	12	70	52	60
Ringmer	38	16	6	16	70	59	54
Burgess Hill T	38	14	10	14	66	66	52
Horsham Y.M.C.A.	38	15	7	16	56	75	52
Portfield	38	15	5	18	65	81	50
Eastbourne Town	38	12	4	22	51	89	40
Southwick	38	10	9	19	38	75	39
Whitehawk	38	10	6	22	49	71	36
Mile Oak	38	9	6	23	48	93	33
Three Bridges	38	6	6	26	46	101	24
Oakwood	38	5	2	31	30	113	17
Crowborough	38	4	4	30	40	117	16

DIVISION TWO

	P	W	D	L	F	A	PTS
Saltdean United	34	25	6	3	87	40	81
Selsey	34	24	6	4	113	33	78
Chichester City	34	19	8	7	71	35	65
East Grinstead	34	19	8	7	76	53	65
Redhill	34	15	6	13	67	54	51
Newhaven	34	16	3	15	63	62	51
East Preston	34	13	10	11	63	55	49
Lancing	34	11	10	13	62	70	43
Worthing United	34	10	12	12	67	61	42
Steyning Town	34	11	9	14	61	76	42
Sidley United	34	10	10	14	45	56	40
Bexhill Town	34	11	6	17	65	59	39
Midhurst & E	34	11	6	17	55	69	39
Withdean	34	11	6	17	57	81	39
Littlehampton T	34	8	14	12	48	58	38
Broadbridge H	34	10	7	17	55	82	37
Bosham	34	10	4	20	65	103	34
Eastbourne Utd	34	3	7	24	33	106	16

DIVISION THREE

	P	W	D	L	F	A	PTS
Ifield	30	22	6	2	77	37	72
Crawley Down V	30	22	3	5	83	31	69
Shinewater Ass	30	21	5	4	89	35	68
Sidlesham	30	18	6	6	73	34	60
Franklands Village	30	17	8	5	60	37	59
Lindfield Rangers	30	15	3	12	64	59	48
Forest	30	11	10	9	43	42	43
Hurstpierpoint	30	12	5	13	48	55	41
Haywards H Tn	30	9	8	13	37	50	35
Thomson Athletic	30	9	6	15	44	53	33
Buxted	30	9	5	16	38	57	32
Storrington	30	8	4	18	36	54	28
Seaford Town	30	7	5	18	50	75	26
St Francis Hosp	30	8	1	21	37	74	25
Sun Alliance	30	5	6	19	35	68	21
Lingfield	30	5	3	22	30	83	18

ARUNDEL

Mill Road, Arundel Tel: 01903 882548

Secretary: Doug Feest, 342 Goring Road, Worthing
BN12 4PD Tel: 01903 249276

Chairman: Michael Peters Tel: 01903 505460

Nickname: The Mullets

Formed: 1889   Colours: Red and White

Capacity: 2,200   Seating: 200

Covered standing: 190   Clubhouse on ground: Yes

DIRECTIONS
A27 from Worthing to Arundel town centre, 1st right into Mill Road, ground thru large car park (on right). 1 mile from Arundel. (BR)

Record attendance: 2,200 v Chichester City
Sussex County League 1967-68

Biggest win: 13-0 v Horsham YMCA League 1985

Biggest defeat: 1-9 v East Grinstead 1954-55

Record appearances: Shaun Brennan

Record goalscorer in one season: G.Cogger 42 in 1958-59

Record goalscorer in total: Paul J Bennett 138

Honours

Sussex County League 1958, 1959, 1987

Div 2 Cup: 1977, League Cup 1987

Sussex RUR Cup 1969, 1973, 1979, 1980

West Sussex League 1971, Malcolm Simmonds Cup 1971

Sussex Junior Cup 1908

Manager for 1996-97: Roger Kent   **Assistant Manager: Steve May**

Chairman: Michael Peters   **Vice Chairman: Shaun Brennan**

Arundel Football Club was formed after a meeting held in the local vicarage by a junior curator of Arundel, the Rev PA Butler. The club sought permission to play under Association rules in Arundel Park and it was granted, and so began over 100 years of football in the town.

The first game was on October 17th 1889 and they began playing friendlies. In 1896 the club joined the West Sussex League where they remained until after the War, when the club joined the County League. Honours up to that point are not widely known about, other than a Junior Cup win in 1908, but records show that the club were very successful from there on, winning the league in 1958 and 1959 and taking the RUR Charity Cup in 1969 and 1973.

The club were forced to vacate Mill Road for a while in the sixties whilst the pitch was repaired, but in the 70's the ground was transformed and whilst success came in Division Two and the RUR Cup again, the glory days were in 1987 when the club were again champions of the league, beating Whitehawk by two points.

They clinched the double by taking the League Cup and that remains the last time that the Mulletts have taken a major prize todate.

BEXHILL TOWN

The Polegrove, Brockley Rd, Bexhill-on-Sea Tel: 01424 220732

Hon secretary: Mrs Leigh Quinn, 37 Colebrook Rd,
Bexhill-on-Sea Tel: 01424 214197

Match Secretary: Ian Seaman 7 Langley Close,
Bexhill-on-Sea Tel: 01424 218605

Founded: 1926

Colours: Green and white   Nickname: Green Machine

Clubhouse on ground: Yes

Floodlights: No   Seating: Yes

Covered standing: No   Capacity: 2,000

DIRECTIONS
At Little Common roundabout take 3rd exit to Coden Sea Road, left into Cooden Drive for one and a half miles. Brockley Road on the right. Three quarters of a mile from Bexhill Central (BR).

Honours

Sussex County League 1957, 1966, 1967

Invitation Cup 1956, Sussex RUR Charity Cup 1958 and 1974

Hastings Challenge Cup 1994, Sussex Mid-week Cup 1926

Managers for 1996-97: Glen Sully and Steve Johnson

Chairman: Elwyn Hughes

BOSHAM

Recreation Ground, Walton Lane, Bosham West Sussex Tel: 01243 574011

Secretary: Richard Doncaster 61 Manor Way, Southbourne,
Emsworth, Hants Tel: 01243 375184

Founded: 1901

Colours: Red and white   Nickname: Robins

Seating: None   Floodlights: No

Covered standing: Yes   Capacity: 2,000

DIRECTIONS
Half mile from Bosham (BR) - walk south down station road, over A27 roundabout, left at t-junction, ground entrance 50 yds on left.

Honours

Sussex County League Div 3 League Cup 1985

Sussex Junior Cup 1956

West Sussex League 1978

Division Two 1957

Chichester and District Junior League 1907

Chichester and Bognor League 1912, 1913, League Cup 1912

Chichester and District League 1954 and 1956, Chichester Charity Cup 1956

Manager for 1996-97: Lloyd Fowler

Chairman: Richard Doncaster

BROADBRIDGE HEATH

Broadbridge Heath Sports Centre, Wickhurst Lane, Horsham Tel: 01403 252273

Secretary Andy Crisp, 19 Church Rd, Broadbridge Heath,
Horsham RH12 3LD Tel: 01403 265871

Founded: 1919

Nickname: Bears

Colours: All royal blue

Capacity: 1,300

Seating: 300

Covered standing: No

Clubhouse on ground: Yes

Joint Managers for 1996-97: Tony Beckenham and Kevin Moyse

> ## DIRECTIONS
> **Alongside A24, Horsham north/south bypass.**

BURGESS HILL TOWN

Leylands Park, Burgess Hill, West Sussex, RH15 8AW Tel: 01444 242429

Secretary: Martin Waner, 26 Hamilton Close, Mile Oak,
East Sussex BN41 2WY Tel: 0378 148853 Mobile

Colours: Yellow and black	Nickname: The Hillians
Capacity: 2,000	Seating: Yes
Covered standing: Yes	Clubhouse on ground: Yes

Record attendance: 600 v Carshalton Athletic FA Cup 1981

> ## DIRECTIONS
> **Wivelsfield Station (BR out of Victoria), turn right, first left, ground on right.**

HONOURS

Sussex County League 1976, Division Two 1975

League Cup 1974 and 1980

Mid-Sussex League 1901, 1904, 1940, 1947, 1957

Montgomery Cup 1940 and 1957, Mowatt Cup 1946

Senior Charity Cup 1993

Manager for 1996-97: Alan Pook   Chairman: Jim Collins

Burgess Hill Town were founded in 1882 and were founder members of the Sussex County FA. The early club created a record of winning the prestigious Senior Cup three times in a row , which allowed them to keep the trophy, which languishes in a bank vault. Throughout its formative years, the club were members of the Mid Sussex League, and as founder members they were champions in 1900. The Hillians merged with Worlds End FC in the 60's and with the help of the council, they built their enclosed ground which allowed them entry into the County League. In 1971 they were promoted to Division One, suffering relegation two year later, but in 1974, Hill achieved another unique record, winning the League Cup and the Division Two title in the same season. 1976 saw the Division One title by 6 points. Since that time, success has been modest, in 1980 they took the League Cup again and in 1992, the RUR Cup. Leylands Park was officially opened on April 24th 1971. The club had played on many different fields in its lifetime, including St Johns Park, Janes Lane and Fairfield Road Rec until the Second War. Afterwards they used Janes Lane again, Station Road Meadow, St Wilfred's Road and Fiarfield Road again, changing at the Royal George Inn.

CHICHESTER CITY

Oaklands Park, Chichester Tel: 01243 785978

Hon secretary: John Hutter, 28 Stockbridge Gardens, Donnington, Chichester Tel: 01243 785839

Match Sec: Peter Harding, 28 Exton Rd, Whyke, Chichester Tel: 01243 780137

Colours: White and black   Nickname: Lilywhites

Founded: 1873   Floodlights: Yes   Seating: Yes

Covered standing: Yes   Capacity: 2,500

Record attendance: 2,500 v Dorchester Town FA Cup 4th Qual Rd 1960

Record win: 11-0 v East Grinstead Sussex County League 1968

Record defeat: 0-11 v Bristol City FA Cup 1st Rd 1960

Record fee received: £750 for Tom Peglar to Bognor Regis 1993

Record appearances: Neal Holder, Record goalscorer in total: David Green

DIRECTIONS

Half mile north of city centre adjacent to Festival Theatre. Turn into Northgate car park from Oaklands Way and entrance is beside Tennis and Squash club. 1 mile from Chichester (BR) - walk north through city centre.

Honours

Sussex Senior Cup 1926

Sussex RUR Charity Cup 1961 jt, 1964

Sussex Intermediate Cup 1968

Sussex County League 1960, 1961, 1968, 1973, 1980

Invitation Cup 1948, 1955, 1957, 1964

Division Two League Cup 1985, 1988, 1991

Manager for 1996-97: Adrian Girdler, Chairman: Tony Muncaster

CRAWLEY DOWN VILLAGE

Haven Sportsfield, Hophurst Lane, Crawley Down Tel: 01342 717140

Hon secretary: Stuart Frier, 30 Squires Close, Crawley Down Tel: 01342 714507

Match Secretary: Colin MacCleaster 28 Beech Gardens Crawley Down Tel: 01342 713805

Colours: Red and white

Joint Managers: Graham Standen and Alan Watson

Chairman: Robert Pearce

DIRECTIONS

From the A22, Felbridge, turn onto the A264 signposted Crawley. Turn left into Crawley Down Road. The ground is 2 miles up the hill on the right. Approaching from junction 10 of the M23, along the A264, turn left onto the B2028, signposted Turners Hill. Follow signs to the village until the War Memorial where there is a left turn into Hophurst Lane. The ground is 100 yards up on the left.

CROWBOROUGH ATHLETIC

Alderbrook Recreation Ground, Fermor Rd, Crowborough Tel: 01892 661893

Hon Secretary: Terry Moore, 24 Belvedere Gardens, Crowborough Tel: 01892 654322

Match Secretary: David Mackellow, 38 Eridge Dr, Crowborough Tel: 01892 653122

Colours: White and navy blue

Founded: 1894

Nickname: Crows

Seating: None

Covered standing: 200

Capacity: 1,000

Record attendance: 439 v Stamco Sussex Div 2 1993

DIRECTIONS

Turn east off A26 at Crowborough. Cross traffic lights, through High Street, right into Croft Road, continue into Whitehall Road and Fermor Road, Alderbrook is second left after mini-roundabout.

Honours

Sussex County League Div 2 1993

Division 2 League Cup 1978

Sussex Intermediate Cup 1987

Manager for 1996-97: Tony Atkins

Chairman: Barry Sykes

Crowborough Athletic, nicknamed the Crows, have a long history in local football, having been founded over a hundred years ago. However, it is only in recent years that they have come to the forefront of local football, and they achieved their finest hour in winning the Division Two Championship. In their first season in Division One, the Crows enjoyed a lengthy Vase run, eventually going down 1-4 at home to Corinthian Casuals. The three seasons in the top flight were a continual struggle, finally culminating in relegation last May.

EAST GRINSTEAD

East Court, Holtye Rd, East Grinstead, West Sussex Tel: 01342 325885

Secretary and Press officer Bruce Talbot, 6 Peverel Rd, Ifield,
Crawley Tel: 01293 543809

Hon Secretary: Hugh Roberts 37 Parham Rd, Ifield,
Crawley Tel: 01293 526805

Waspsline: 0891 333 096

Nickname The Wasps

Capacity 2,500

Seating: None

Covered standing: 400

Floodlights: Yes,

Clubhouse on ground: Yes

Record attendance: 2,002 v Lancing Nov 8th 1948

Honours

Sussex Junior Cup 1908

Sussex Invitation Cup 1952

Sussex FA Youth Cup 1986

Mid-Sussex League 1903, 1937, 1948

Div 2 1907 and 1969

Brighton League 1953 Div 2 1969

Mid Sussex Senior Cup 1970, 1972,

DIRECTIONS

A264 Turnbridge Wells road (Moat Road) until mini-roundabout at bottom of Blackwell Hollow, turn immediately right by club sign then 1st left, ground 200yds down lane past rifle club on

Manager for 1996-97: Bryn Marshall

Assistant manager: Paul Short

Chairman: Mark Arnold

East Grinstead badges, programmes, mugs, ties, and caps are available on match days or via post from the secretary.

East Grinstead FC are sponsored by Rydon Group

The club were founder members of the Mid-Sussex League and Sussex County League and also had a spell in the Southern Amateur League before returning to the County League in 1938 where they have remained ever since. The Wasps best years were after the Second War when four figure crowds were the norm. The best finish in the league was third in 1955, and in recent years the club have played in all three divisions, returning to Division One for two seasons. Last year's fourth place was seen as a great improvement.

The Wasps have used East Court since August 26th 1967, when after a long battle to prepare the ground, they were in a position to move in. They had played from the start on the cricket ground in West Street, but between the last game there and the move to East Court, the club were forced to play on a pitch at King George's Field in the town.

EAST PRESTON

Roundstone Recreation Ground, East Preston, West Sussex Tel: 01903 776026

Secretary: Keith Freeman, 41 Ambersham Cres, East Preston Tel: 01903 771158

Colours: White and black

Seating: No

Covered standing: Yes

Honours

Sussex County League Div 3 1984

Division 3 League Cup 1988

West Sussex League 1978, 1981, 1982, 1983

League Cup 1981 and 1983

Vernon Wentworth Cup 1981 and 1990

Worthing League 1968

Benevolent Trophy 1967 and 1969

Worthing Charity Cup 1969

Manager: John Finneran

Chairman: Greg Stanley

> ## DIRECTIONS
> **Take the A280 south from the A27 (between Chichester and Worthing) to the A259 or take the A259 from Worthing to Roundstone Hotel (6 miles). Turn south over the railway crossing, left past Centurion garage and right onto Roundstone Drive.**

EASTBOURNE UNITED

The Oval, Channel View Rd, Eastbourne Tel: 01323 726989

Secretary: Maurice Stevens 21 Brookside Ave, Polegate Tel: 01323 484644

Colours: White and black, Nickname: The U's

Seating: Yes

Covered standing: Yes

Floodlights: Yes

Capacity: 3,000

> ## DIRECTIONS
> **To seafront and turn left. Turn left into Channel View Road at Princess Park and ground 1st right. 2 miles from Eastbourne (BR).**

Honours

Sussex County League 1955

Sussex Senior Cup 1961, 1963, 1964, 1967, 1969

Sussex RUR Charity Cup 1956

Metropolitan League Cup 1961

Athenian League Div 2 1967

Sussex Intermediate Cup 1966 and 1969

EASTBOURNE TOWN

The Saffrons, Compton Place Rd, Eastbourne Tel: 01323 723734

Secretary: Kevin Moore, 27 Chesterton Drive, Seaford, Tel: 01323 897369

Nickname: Bourne

Colours: Yellow and blue

Founded: 1882

Seating: Yes

Covered standing: Yes

Capacity: 3,000

Record attendance: 7,378 v Hastings Utd 1953
FA Cup 2nd Qual Rd

DIRECTIONS

Turn south west off A22
into Grove Road
(opposite BR station).
Ground quarter mile on
right.

Honours

Sussex County League 1977, Sussex RUR Charity Cup 1933, 1948, 1950

Sussex Senior Cup 1890, 1891, 1894, 1895, 1899, 1900, 1901, 1903, 1922, 1932, 1933, 1953

Southern Amateur League twice, AFA Senior Cup 1922, 1925, AFA Invitation Cup 1970

Manager for 1996-97: Rob Thornley

Chairman: Stuart Higgins

HAILSHAM TOWN

The Beaconsfield, Western Rd, Hailsham, East Sussex Tel: 01323 411933

Secretary: Derek York, 59 Anglesey Ave, Hailsham, BN27 3BQ Tel: 01323 848024

Colours: Yellow and green

Capacity: 2,000

Seating: Nil

Covered standing: 250

Clubhouse on ground: Yes

Record attendance: 1,350 v Hungerford Town FA Vase 1989

Record goalscorer in one season: H Stevens 48 in 1995-96

DIRECTIONS

A22 to Arlington Road,
turn east, then left into
South Road - left into
Diplocks Way until
Daltons. Four miles from
Polegate (BR - Brighton-
Eastbourne line); regular
bus service from
Eastbourne.

Honours

Southern Counties Comb 1975

Sussex RUR Charity Cup, Intermediate Cup, Hastings Senior Cup, Sussex Junior Cup,East Sussex League Cup, Hailsham Charity Cup

John O'Hara Cup 1995, Floodlight Cup 1996

Manager 1996-97: Peter Roberts   **Assistant Manager: Chris Marshall**

Chairman: David Challinor   **Vice Chairman: John Green**

Hailsham Town were formed in 1885 and spent their early years in the East Sussex and Southern Combination Leagues. They won the latter in 1975 and six years later they took the County League Division Two, in between taking many other cups.

Since joining Division One they have been steady and despite the lack of league success still attract some of the best crowds in the league. In 1989 they reached the FA Vase 5th Round, a game

HASSOCKS

The Beacon Ground, Brighton Rd, Hassocks, Tel: 01273 842040

Secretary: Robert Preston, 65 Oakhall Park, Burgess Hill, RH15 0DA Tel 01444 245695

Programme Editor: Paul Elphick

Nickname: The Robins

Colours: All Red

Capacity: 2,000

Covered standing: 50

Seating: 50

Clubhouse on ground: Yes

Record attendance: 340 v Bognor Regis
Sussex Senior Cup 1992

DIRECTIONS

Off A273 Pyecombe-
Burgess Hill 300 yds
south of Stonepound
crossroads (B2116) to
Hurstpierpoint or
Hassocks.

HONOURS

Sussex County League Div 3 1992

Southern Counties Comb 1977

League Cup 1980

Brighton, Hove and District 1972

Sussex Intermediate Cup 1975

Managers: Nick Greenwood and Peter Liddell

Chairman: Jim Goodrum Tel: 01273 84384

Vice Chairman: D.Knight Tel: 01273 842023

Hassocks Football Club were founded in 1902 and competed in the Mid-Sussex, Brighton and Southern Counties Combination Leagues before being elected to Division TWO of the County League in 1981.

After pushing for promotion without success, they suffered relegation in 1988, and it was in 1992 that the slow climb back began. They were champions of Division Three in 1992 finishing 10 points ahead of Mile Oak and the same two went up a year later. At that time there was much activity off the field as Hassocks sought to establish a new ground at the Beacon. They had purchased the site some year earlier following a change in the league rules which did not allow them to continue at Adastra Park. After encountering dreadful drainage problems, the club has progressed and floodlights were installed and opened by Chelsea FC in 1995.

342

HORSHAM YMCA

Goring's Mead, Horsham, West Sussex Tel: 01403 252689

Hon Secretary: Robin Bishop, 6 Brook Close, Storrington, Tel: 01903 746332

Match Secretary: Bill Bower, 5 Patching Close, Ifield,
Crawley Tel: 01293 533831

Colours: White and black

Nickname: YM's

Clubhouse on ground: Yes

Seating: 100

Covered standing: 100

Capacity: 1,000

Record attendance: 600+ v Horsham FC in FA Cup

DIRECTIONS

At end of lane at rear of Horsham FC. Half mile from Horsham (BR).

Honours

Sussex County League Div 2 1966, 1983

League Cup 1982

Invitation Cup 1967 and 1968

Manager for 1996-97: John Suter

Chairman: Robert Knight

The YMCA FC was formed in 1898 and played in a local district League before moving to Gorings Mead in the mid 1920's. The first league game on the ground was in September 1929, and they went on to play in the Horsham and District, and Brighton and District League before moving to the Mid-Sussex League. During the 50's the ground developed with dressing rooms and in 1964 a small supporters stand went up.

They were elected to the Sussex County League and won Division Two in 1966 as well as the Invitation Cup twice soon after. They won the Division again in 1983 and were runners up in 1995, sufficient for them to take their place in the top division.

LANCING

Culver Rd, Lancing, West Sussex Tel: 01903 764398

Secretary: John Chisnall, 15 Orchard Way, Lancing, West Sussex BN15 9ED Tel: 01903 763048

Press: John Rea, 73 Lynchmere Ave, North Lancing,
West Sussex BN15 0PB Tel: 01903 521543

Match Sec: Mike Peters 01903 761810

Colours Yellow and blue   Nickname: The Yellows

Capacity: 3,000   Seating: 500

Covered standing: No   Clubhouse on ground: Yes

DIRECTIONS

Third turning left north of Lancing station (BR).

Record attendance: 2,591 v Tooting and Mitcham Nov 1947 at Crowshaw Rec

Biggest win: 10-0 v Peacehaven 1986-87 County League and 11-0 v Lewes Brighton Lge Div 1 1947

Biggest defeat: 3-11 v Bognor Regis Town 1950-51

Record appearances: Dave Menzies 462

Record goalscorer in one season: Adie Chipper 32 1986-87

Record goalscorer in total: Ken Williams 143

Honours

Sussex County Div 2 1958 and 1970, Div 2 League Cup 1982 and 1993

Sussex RUR Charity Cup 1966, Brighton Charity Cup 1984, 1985, 1987

Manager 1996-97: John Bailey

Chairman: John Brown

Vice Chairman: Len Ralph

Lancing FC had its origins in 1938 with a group of youngsters who kicked a ball around on Monks Rec which is next door to the ground today. They were founded in 1941 as an all sports club called Lancing Athletic, but the football split away on joining the County League in 1948, the Athletic suffix fading away in the mid fifties. After the war the club played in the Brighton League, winning the league and cup as well as the Intermediate Cup. They enjoyed a marvellous run to the 4th qualifying round of the Amateur Cup in 1947 and joined the County League when Worthing moved on. In 1952 they moved from Crowshaw Rec to Culver Road and the second game there was a Cup game which ended 6-6 after the club were 6-1 down with 30 minutes left.

Fortunes were mixed and they were relegated in 1957, only to bounce back a year later. 1965 saw a runners up spot behind an all conquering unbeaten Lewes side, but within two years they went down again. The run continued with promotion in 1970 and relegation again in 1972 which was the start of many years in the doldrums until the County FA bought Culver Road, installed lights and a clubhouse and with Lancing there as tenants won the Div 2 Cup with promotion a year later. Once more in 1990 the club were relegated, but they enjoyed a good year in 1993 when winning the Division two Cup and reaching the RUR final. Since then although enjoying sporadic success, Lancing have not managed to return to the top section.

LANGNEY SPORTS

Langney Sports Club, Priory Lane, Langney, Eastbourne, Tel: 01323 766265

Secretary: Myra Stephens, 7B Erica Close, Langney, Eastbourne, BN23 8BG Tel: 01323 755050

Capacity: 3,000   Seating: At planning stage

Covered standing: 600   Clubhouse on ground: Yes

Record attendance: 1,000 v Crystal Palace 1990-91

Biggest win: 10-1 v Haywards Heath 1992

Biggest defeat: 0-8 v Peacehaven in league
and Sheppey Utd in FA Vase, both 1993

Record appearances: Steve Dell 392

Record goalscorer in one season: Nigel Hole 63 1991-92

Record goalscorer in total: Nigel Hole 143

DIRECTIONS

A22 to Polegate, A27 to Stone Cross, right onto B32104 to Langney Shopping Centre, then left and first right. One mile from Pevensey & Westham (BR). Buses from Eastbourne.

Honours

Sussex Intermediate Cup 1986, Sussex County League Cup 1990

Sussex County League Div 2 1988, and Div 3 League and Cup 1987

Eastbourne Charity Cup 1986, 1987, 1996

Manager: Steve Richardson

Chairman: Len Smith

Vice Chairman: Mike Grimer

Press officer: Mike Spooner at club 01323 461003 (B) 01323 849372 (H)

The origins of the club date back to the late 1950's when Langney and Friday Street Youth Club competed in the Under 18 section of the Eastbourne Minor League. Then, as the basis of the team grew too old, they moved into adult football. Langney Football Club were formed in 1964 when they entered the Eastbourne and District League where they played in Division Two. The name was changed to Langney Sports prior to the 1968-69 season, where they were playing on local recreation grounds, before moving to Princes Park on the seafront. Success came and in 1974 they were promoted and gained Intermediate status. The next nine years saw the club win the Eastbourne Challenge Cup and finish runners up in the league four times, finally winning the Eastbourne and Hastings League in 1982.During the 1980's, Sports made startling advancements, having been elected to the Sussex County League in 1983 they moved to their impressive headquarters in Priory Lane and after two fifth places, the club won the Eastbourne and Sussex Intermediate Cups in 1986. The following year they were champions of Division Three, winning the Division Three League Cup and retaining the Eastbourne Cup into the bargain. With promotion came senior status and a year later Division Two was taken by storm, Sports taking the title by 11 points from Bexhill. Division One coincided with the opening of the new pitch on the Priory Lane site, later to add a stand and terracing, before taking the Sussex County League Challenge Cup in 1989. 1991 saw a third place as the club continued to rise, and a year later they were runners up to Peacehaven, reaching the pinnacle for the club by playing Brighton and Hove in the Sussex Senior Cup Final.

Since then there have been more cup successes and near misses and off the pitch a Bowls Hall was opened in 1993, and a new stand, executive boxes, a Presidents Club, admin block, new dressing rooms, club shop, and turnstile access are all part of the continued development.

LITTLEHAMPTON TOWN

The Sportsfield, St Flora's Rd, Littlehampton Tel: 01903 713944

Match secretary: Mark Warren, 5 Dorset Close, Littlehampton Tel: 01903 730114

Hon Secretary: John Savage, 66 Nelson Rd, Worthing,
Tel 01903 502850

Colours: Gold and black

Nickname: Marigolds

Founded: 1894

Seating: 250

Floodlights: Yes

Covered standing: Yes

Capacity: 4,000

Record attendance: 4,000 v Northampton Town FA Cup 1st Rd 1990

Honours

FA VASE Semi-final 1991

Sussex Senior Cup 1974

Sussex County League 1991

Invitation Cup 1953, 1954, 1959 it with Shoreham, 1962,

League Challenge Cup 1976, 1977, 1985, 1991

Manager for 1996-97: Carl Stabler

Chairman: Andy Baumfield

DIRECTIONS
10 minutes walk from Littlehampton station (BR) - turn left along Terminus Rd, continue through High Street and Church Rd to junction with St Flora's Rd (left).

MIDHURST AND EASEBOURNE

Rotherfield Sports Ground, Dodsley Lane, Midhurst, West Sussex Tel: 01730 816557

Secretary: Ted Dummer, 14 Nine Acres, June Lane, Midhurst,
West Sussex GU29 9EP Tel 01730 813887

Press: Rex Lane, Hall Cottage, Stedham, Nr Midhurst West Sussex

Colours: All royal blue

Capacity: 1, 200

Seating: 80

Covered standing: 80

Clubhouse on ground: Yes

Floodlights: No

Record attendance: 300 Gingell Cup 1989

Honours

Sussex County Lge Div 2 Cup 1989, Div 3 1995

Southern Co Combination Div 2 and Challenge Cup 1981

West Sussex League 1968, 1977, 1980 Div 1 1956, 1963 and 1965

Malcolm Simmonds Cup 1960, 1974, 1978, 1980, Bareham Trophy 1971

Sussex Intermediate Cup 1955, 1956, 1957, 1963, 1978

Manager 1996-97: Stuart Groves

Chairman: Pat Perry

Vice Chairman: John Perks

DIRECTIONS
Ground one mile out of Midhurst on London Road (A286) opposite BP Garage. Ample car parking. Buses pass ground every hour.

MILE OAK

Mile Oak Rec, Graham Ave, Mile Oak, Tel: 01273 423854

Hon secretary: Colin Brown 19 The Crescent, Southwick Tel: 01273 591346

Match Secretary: Brian Cash 19 Rowan Ave, Hove
Tel: 01273 777901

Colours: All Tangerine

Nickname: The Oak

Seating: Yes

Covered standing: Yes

DIRECTIONS

From A27 take Mile Oak Road or Locks Hill & Valley Road to Chalky Road, ground 500 yds on right along Graham Avenue which runs up valley from centre of Chalky Road.

Honours

Sussex County League Div 2 1995

Southern Counties Combination 1987

Brighton and District League 1981

Vernon Wentworth Cup 1986

Manager for 1996-97: Tony Gratwicke

Chairman: Geoff Kerly

NEWHAVEN

Fort Rd Recreation Ground, Newhaven Tel: 01273 513940

Secretary: Frank Dixon 39 Southdown Ave, Peacehaven Tel: 01273 585514

Floodlights: Yes

Nickname: Dockers

Seating: Yes

Covered standing: Yes

Clubhouse on ground: Yes

Capacity: 4,000

DIRECTIONS

A275 from Lewes, or A259 coast road, to Newhaven 1-way system. 1 mile from Newhaven Town (BR)

Honours

Sussex County League 1954 and 1974

Division Two 1972 and 1991

Invitation Cup 1949

Sussex RUR Charity Cup 1994

Manager for 1996-97: Martin Langley

OAKWOOD

Oakwood Sports, Tinsley Lane, Three Bridges, Sussex Tel: 01923 515742

Secretary: Gerry Martin, Singlegate, Tinsley Green, Crawley,
Tel: 01293 882400

Colours: Red and black

Nickname: Oaks

Seating: Yes

Covered standing: Yes

Capacity: 2,000

Clubhouse on ground: Yes

DIRECTIONS

From A23 to Gatwick, take 1st set of lights into manor Royal, pass next lights, over roundabout to warehouse marked Canon, turn right signposted Oakwood. last clubhouse down lane. Two miles north of Three Bridges (BR).

Honours

Sussex County League Div 2 League Cup 1990

Division Three 1985

Southern Combination Cup 1985

Managers for 1996-97: Mark Richardson and Paul Crimmen

Chairman: Alf Bridges

Oakwood Football Club were founded in 1962 and were originally known as St Wilfred Youth Wing. They joined the Crawley and District League and became Oakwood FC in 1966, and played on council pitches whilst in the Southern Counties Combination. Later they took over a disused sports ground in Tinsley Lane and began creating a ground good enough for the Sussex County League.

They won Division Three in 1985 having won the Combination Cup the year before, and in 1990 they were runners up in Division Two as well as winning the division's League Cup. Three years later they reached the final of the Sussex Senior Cup, as they established themselves as one of the top clubs in the county.

PAGHAM

Nyetimber Lane, Pagham, West Sussex Tel: 01243 262879

Secretary: Alan Seal, 6 Greenlea Avenue, Pagham
PO21 3LH Te: 01243 262944

Nickname: Lions　　　　　Capacity: 2,000

Covered standing: No　　　Seating: 200

Clubhouse on ground: Yes

Record attendance: 1,200 v Bognor Regis in 1972

Biggest win: 10-1 v Seaford Town
Sussex County Div 2 1970

Biggest defeat: 0-7 v Newport IOW

DIRECTIONS

Turn off A27 Chichester by-pass (signposted A259 Pagham). Ground in village of Nyetimber. Three miles from Bognor (BR). Buses 260 & 240.

Honours

Sussex County League: Div 2 1979 and 1987

League Cup 1989

Division 2 League Cup 1972 and 1986

Sussex RUR Charity Cup 1989

West Sussex League 1966, 1969, 1970

League Cup 1968

Sussex Intermediate Cup 1967

Manager for 1996-97: Graham Peach

Chairman: Graham Peach

Pagham FC were formed in 1903 and competed in the Bognor and District, and Chichester Leagues, before progressing to the West Sussex Intermediate League. They came to prominence in the 60's by taking the title 3 times in five years along with Intermediate and League Cups. In 1970, after several applications, they were finally given senior status and a place in the County League Division Two. Three seasons running the club finished third, just missing promotion and the effect caused a backlash as the fourth season saw them have to apply for re-election. They came again with another third place before taking the title, and two years later, Division One. Another decline followed and they returned to Division Two, before yet two more third places, although they did take the League Cup twice.

It was the start of an astonishing 18 months which began in May 1986, when they were awarded medals as runners up in Division Two after finishing below Wick but above Haywards Heath on goal difference. This included three points awarded to them by the league for a fixture that was called off in contravention of the rules. The County FA overturned the ruling on appeal, thus placing Pagham three points short of promotion. The match was fixed to be played at Wigmore in mid-June and after going 2-0 down amidst amazing scenes they could only draw 2-2 and were deprived of promotion, thus spending another 12 months in Division Two. The club came back and in the next two seasons won Division Two conceding only 11 goals, and then won Division One twice running, the second time by 15 points. The next season saw the League Cup, RUR Cup and Reserve Cup go to Pagham, who installed lights that year.

Southern League ambitions have seen the club state that they are looking to go forward as soon as they are in the position to apply.

PEACEHAVEN AND TELSCOMBE

Piddinghoe Avenue, Peacehaven, East Sussex Tel: 01273 582471

Hon Secretary: Mrs M. Edwards, 87 Ambleside Ave, Peacehaven, East Sussex BN10 7LN Tel:01273 583022

Match Secretary: Fred Parris, 17a Piddinghoe Ave, Peacehaven, Tel: 01273 587279

Colours: All white

Capacity: 3,000

Covered standing: 250

Record attendance 1,420 v Littlehampton Town 1991

Nickname: The Tye

Seating: None

Clubhouse on ground: Yes

Honours

Sussex County League 1979, 1982, 1983, 1992, 1993, 1995, 1996

League Cup 1992 and 1993 and Div 2 Cup 1976

Norman Wingate Trophy 1983, 1992, 1993

Hayden Trophy 1983 and 1993, Division Two Invitation Cup 1970

RUR Charity Cup 1978, 1982, 1993, 1996 Brighton Charity Cup 1992 and 1993

Vernon Wentworth Cup 1992 and 1993

Manager: Peter Edwards

Chairman: Jim Edwards

DIRECTIONS

Arriving from Brighton on A259, cross roundabout and Piddinghoe Avenue is next left after 2nd set of lights - ground at end. From Newhaven Piddinghoe Avenue is first right after first set of lights. Three miles from Newhaven (BR). Peacehaven is served by Brighton to Newhaven and Eastbourne buses.

The club was founded in 1923 following the amalgamation of Peacehaven Rangers (a team of local labourers) and Telscombe Tye (a side made up of jockeys from a local stable). Peacehaven and Telscombe spent their early days in the Lewes League before progressing to the Brighton League, where they enjoyed much success. In 1969, under the management of Bill Parrish, they took the Premier Division undefeated and joined Division Two of the County League. The first season brought some success, with the Division Two League Cup and in the next few seasons they went close to promotion. It was 1976, when under Peter Andrews, Peacehaven won the Division Two League of the Cup and were promoted to Division One behind Selsey.

The progress continued in 1979 as they took the RUR Charity Cup and were runners up in the league, but a year later they finished the job by taking the title for the first time.

In 1981 they were runners up in the RUR and the league, but a year later they enjoyed a memorable year, taking the championship again with ease, and adding the RUR Cup and losing narrowly in the final Sussex Senior Cup.

The championship stayed at Piddinghoe Avenue for the next season, which then signalled a brief quiet spell before under Alan Pook they were runners up in the RUR and the league, exactly as they were under Pook ten years earlier.

The good times returned in the 90's as the league has been won four times so far, with two League Cups, three Norman Wingate Trophies and various other cups as Peacehaven confirm their standing as the club of the decade.

PORTFIELD

Church Rd, Portfield, Chichester, West Sussex Tel: 01243 779875

Match Secretary: Gary Rustell, 102 Churchwood Dr, Tangmere,
Nr Chichester, West Sussex PO20 6GB

Tel: 01243 537978

Hon Secretary: John Dowling, 36 St James Square,
Chichester Tel: 01243 779044

Colours: Amber and black

Nickname: Field

Capacity: 2,000

Seating: Yes

Covered standing: Yes

Clubhouse on ground: Yes

DIRECTIONS

A27 from Arundel to
Chichester, take road to
signposted city centre
then 1st left (Church
Road) after supermarket
roundabout. 1 mile from
Chichester (BR).

Honours

Sussex Co Lge Div 2 1973, 1984,

Div 2 League Cup 1971 and 1973

West Sussex League 1947 and 1949

Junior Cup 1946

Benevolent Cup 1947

Manager for 1996-97: Richie Reynolds

Chairman: Mr T Rustell

Vice Chairman: Mr A Smith

The precise date that Portfield were founded is unknown but a photograph dated 1896 shows a team of villainous characters. During the early years, ever widening gravel workings forced a number of pitches on farm fields, the last being the well known 'Downers', in the 30's and 40's. Again. in advance of the excavators, another move in the early 50's took the 'Field' to a local Recreation Ground until 1958, when Church Road became home. The facilities at the previous grounds were often bleak, an old railway carriage, a timber garage and a groundsmans shed were all used until after 14 years of fund raising the first stage of the clubhouse was finished. A thriving membership enabled it to be extended with separate dressing rooms in 1983.

On the field the club progressed through the Chichester League and West Sussex League to senior status in the County League in 1963. Success has been limited but 1996 sees the club in Division One with a fine ground, testimony to those past members who worked so hard on Church Road.

REDHILL

Kiln Brow, Three Arch Rd, Redhill, Surrey RH1 5AE Tel: 01737 762129

Hon Secretary: Mr Neil Hoad, Braeside,
2b Earlswood Rd, Redhill Tel: 01737 213847

Nickname: The Reds or The Lobsters

Colours: Red and White stripes   Capacity: 2,000

Seating: 150   Covered standing: None

DIRECTIONS

On left hand side of A23, two and a half miles south of Redhill.

Floodlights: Yes   Clubhouse on ground: Yes

Record attendance: 7,000 at Memorial Ground or 1,200 at Kiln Brow Testimonial 1989

Biggest win: 9-0 v Crown and Manor and Little Common

Biggest defeat: 0-8 Stamco (A)

Record appearances: Brian Medlicott 767

Record goalscorer in one season: Steve Turner 32

Record goalscorer in total: Steve Turner 109

Record fee received: £1,500 from Sutton Utd for Steve Turner

Record fee paid: £750 to Sutton Utd for Steve Turner

Honours

FA AMATEUR CUP semi-finalists 1925

East and West Surrey League 1903 and Southern Suburban League West 1912

Athenian League 1925 and 1984, League Cup 1970 and 1971

Gilbert Rice Floodlight Cup 1981, Surrey Senior Cup 1929 and 1966

Southern Counties Combination Cup 1991, Sussex County League Div 2 Cup 1992

Manager for 1996-97: Peter Burdett   **Assistant manager: Dave Gellatley**

Chairman: Eric Lee   **Vice Chairman: Nick Creasey**

Press officer: Ian Austen, 2 Horley Rd, Redhill, Surrey RH1 5AB Tel: 01737 760053

Club shop is sponsored by Merstham Gas, contact S.Mitchell 21 Colebrooke Rd, Redhill, Surrey RH12BL Tel 01737 780634. Redhill Review yearbook is available from club price £2 and the club history "Up the Reds, 100 years of Redhill FC" is also on sale

Redhill Football Club was formed in the autumn of 1894 following a meeting held by prominent local businessmen in the Warwick Hotel. The first match was a friendly against Dorking on a field at Wiggie, lent to the club by the goalkeeper. Two years later the club moved to what is now the Memorial Park and which at the time was an open swamp area before adequate drainage was installed. This was accomplished under the auspices of a Sports Ground Association that lasted until 1919. At first all matches were played on a friendly basis and it was not until 1898 that they entered the South Suburban League followed by others long defunct. They won the East and West Surrey League in 1903 and two years later were runners up in the Surrey Senior Cup. In 1922 the club was accepted into the renown London League and from there they progressed to the Athenian League where they remained until its demise in 1984.

RINGMER

The Caburn, Anchor Field, Ringmer, East Sussex Tel: 01273 812738

Secretary: Alan Lofthouse, Pinewoods, Whitesmith, Ringmer BN8 6JH
Tel: 01825 872343

Colours: Light and dark blue

Capacity: 1,000

Seating: 100

Covered standing: 200

Clubhouse on ground: Yes

Record attendance: 1,200 in FA Cup

DIRECTIONS
Turn into Springett Avenue opposite Ringmer village green. Anchor Field is the first left. Five miles from Lewes (BR).

Honours

Sussex County League 1971 and Division 2 1969

Division 2 Invitation Cup 1967

Sussex Senior Cup 1973

Sussex Junior Cup 1926

Sussex Express Senior Charity Cup 1995

Manager 1996-97: Gary Allen

Assistant Manager: F Weatherall

Chairman: Richard Soan

Vice Chairman: L Howard

Ringmer were founded in 1906 and played their early football in the East Hoathly, Brighton and Lewes and District Leagues. They re-formed after the Great War playing on the Anchor Field, close to the Anchor Inn and used for grazing cattle between matches. After the Second War they began playing in the Lewes League until an influx of players from a disbanded local side persuaded them to move to the Brighton League, from where the club gained strength and eventually moved to a field at the back of the village Post Office, which was offered for use with the option to buy. The club had some success in the Brighton League and eventually were elected to the Sussex County League, at the time when the new ground was slowly being put together.

Promotion came in 1969 and it was the start of memorable spell for Ringmer. In 1970 the club reached the 1st Round of the FA Cup, having beaten Arundel, Chichester City, Bognor Regis and Waterlooville, and were drawn at Colchester United. The following May the club completed a wonderful season by clinching the County League title for the only time to date.

In 1973 they won the Senior Cup and other than some reserve team success, that spelled the end of the era for Ringmer. Since then the Caburn Field has developed into one of the most comfortable and attractive of Sussex's grounds and the club continue to hold a place in the top division

SALTDEAN UNITED

Hill Park, Coombe Vale, Saltdean Tel: 01273 309898

Hon Secretary: Iain Fielding, 40 Rowan Way, Rottingdean,
Brighton Tel: 01273 304995

Match Sec: John Sandison, 114b Sutton Ave, Peacehaven, East
Sussex Tel: 01273 589195

Colours: Red and black

Nickname: Tigers

Seating: 50

Covered standing: No

Capacity: 2,000

DIRECTIONS

A259 coast road east
from Brighton to
Saltdean Lido, left into
Arundel Drive West, and
Saltdean Vale to bridle
path at beginning of
Combe Vale. Club 200
yds along track.

Honours

Sussex County League Div 3 1989

Division Two 1996

Manager for 1996-97: Gerry Green

Chairman: Mick Walker

SELSEY

High Street Ground, Selsey, Chichester, Tel: 01243 603420

Secretary: Denny Lee, 29 Malthouse Cotts,
West Wittering, Chichester Tel: 01243 513788

Colours: Blue and white	Nickname: Blues
Seating: 50	Founded: 1923
Covered standing: Yes	Capacity: 2,250

Record attendance: Not known but believed to be around 800,
for local derbies with Chichester and Portfield in 1950's

DIRECTIONS

B2145 from Chichester
to Selsey, turn right by
Fire Station. Regular
buses from Chichester.

Honours

Sussex County League Div 2 1964 and 1976

Division Two League Cup 1987

Div 2 Invitation Cup 1964, Sussex Intermediate Cup 1959

West Sussex League 1955, 1956, 1958, 1959, 1961

League Cup 1956, 1957, 1958, 1959

Managers for 1996-97: John Davies and Dave Kew

Chairman: Roger Slade

SHOREHAM

Middle Rd, Shoreham-by-Sea, West Sussex Tel: 01273 454261

Secretary: Ms Anne Harper, 66 Willow Cres, Durrington,
Worthing, BN13 2SX Tel: 01903 267672

Colours: Blue and white

Nickname: Musselmen

Capacity: 1,500

Seating: Yes

Covered standing: Yes

Clubhouse on ground: Yes

Record attendance: 1,342 v Wimbledon Floodlight opener

DIRECTIONS

Half mile from Shoreham-by-Sea (BR) - east across level crossing, up Dolphin Road, ground 150 yds on right. Or, A27 to Southlands Hospital - south down Hammy Lane, left at end, ground opposite.

Honours

Sussex County League 1952, 1953, 1978, and Div 2 1962, 1977, 1985, 1994

Division 2 Cup 1975 and 1983

Invitation Cup 1958

Sussex Senior Cup 1901 and 1906

Sussex RUR Charity Cup 1903 and 1906

Vernon Wentworth Cup 1987

Manager 1996-97: Brian Donnelly

Chairman: John Bell

Shoreham FC was formed in 1893 and within six years they had captured the Sussex Senior Cup. A year later they won it again but it was to be over 40 years before their next trophy.

In 1920 the club left the West Sussex League to become founder members of the Sussex County League but it was not until 1935 that they made their presence felt when finishing runners up to Horsham.

They finally took the championship in 1952 and 1953 but in 1961 they were relegated, only to bounce back within a year. Sadly, in 1967 they were again relegated and it was from Division Two that the club played whilst moving from their windswept and sloping Buckingham Park ground, in 1970 to their current home in Middle Road. At first the ground had to be segregated with a canvas sheet but it was eventually fenced off to the required standards. In 1977 they won Division Two and were back in the top flight and the following year were champions again. Soon the ground developed with improved spectator and player facilities and in 1985 a friendly with Brighton marked the opening of the club's clubhouse. A year later Wimbledon visited and switched on the new floodlights, and having suffered another relegation, the club won Division Two once again in 1994.

SIDLEY UNITED

Gullivers, Glovers Lane, Sidley, Bexhill-on-Sea Tel: 01424 217078

Secretary: Tom Hyland, 12 Penland Ct, 56 College Rd,
Bexhill-on-Sea Tel: 01424 217547

Colours: Light and dark blue

Founded: 1906

Nickname: Blues

Seating: None

Covered standing: Yes

Floodlights: No

Capacity: 1,500

DIRECTIONS

From Brighton on A259 to Bexhill bypass traffic lights, left into London Road, continue into Sidley, right into Glovers Lane and 1st left into North Road. One mile from Bexhill (BR).

Honours

Sussex County League Div 2 1959 and 1965

Division Two Invitation Cup 1958

Sussex Intermediate Cup 1948

Sussex Junior Cup 1925

Managers for 1996-97: Mick Day and Paul Haffenden

Chairman: Paul Tidd

Southwick FC

SOUTHWICK

Old Barn Way, Off Manor Hall Way, Southwick, Brighton BN43 4NT Tel: 01273 701010

Press and Programme: Paul Symes 01273 594142

Hon Secretary: Peter Hallett, 10 Hawkins Close, Shoreham-by-Sea, BN43 6TL Tel: 01273 700474

Match Sec: Dave Crowhurst, 32 Solway Ave, Patcham, Brighton Tel: 01273 386655

Colours: Red and black stripes

Nickname: Wickers

Capacity: 3,500

Seating: 220

Covered standing: 1,000

Clubhouse on ground: Yes

DIRECTIONS

Five minutes walk from either Fishergate or Southwick BR stations. By A27 from Brighton take 1st left after 'Southwick' sign to Leisure Centre. Ground adjacent.

Honours

Isthmian Lge Div 2 South 1986

Sussex County Lge 1926, 1928, 1930, 1948, 1969, 1975

League Cup 1978, Div 1 Invitation Cup 1966

Sussex Senior Cup 1897, 1911, 1913, 1925, 1928, 1930, 1931, 1937, 1948, 1968

RUR Charity Cup 1897, 1909, 1911, 1925, 1926, 1928, 1929, 1930, 1938, 1977

West Sussex Lge 1897, 1898, 1909, 1911, Sussex Junior Cup 1892

Manager: Mick Fogden Assistant Manager: Colin Smart

Chairman: Roy Pollard Vice Chairman: Dave Cook

Southwick played competitive football exactly 100 years ago when as founder members of the West Sussex League they took the title, and both Senior and RUR Cups in the same season. They retained the title a year later. They remained enjoying success until two years after the Great War when they became founder members of the County League. The next decade was successful with three titles achieving a Sussex treble twice, and in 1929 they reached the last 16 of the Amateur Cup. After the second War the won both League and Senior Cups and in 1953 decided to seek pastures new and joined the Metropolitan League along with Haywards Heath. It lasted two seasons and by 1960 they were in Division Two of the County League but were promoted as runners up to Sidley in 1965. For the next 20 years the club were consistently near the top although the last win was in 1975 when they also reached the FA Cup 1st Round.

Off the pitch the ground had been given floodlights and with the setting up of the pyramid, the club attempted to go forward again, joining the Combined Counties League in 1984 looking for Isthmian League status. It came, as did the Division Two championship and despite two near misses the team began to slide and they were further hampered by hurricanes which seriously damaged the ground twice in three years.

Serious financial problems saw the club given a choice of returning to Sussex or folding, and taking the sensible option the club took a drop and remain in Division One.

STEYNING TOWN

The Shooting Field, Steyning, West Sussex Tel: 01903 812228

Hon Secretary: Mrs Helen Ellis, 15 Breach Close, Steyning,
West Sussex BN44 3RZ Tel 01903 816495

Nickname: The Reds

Colours: Red and White

Capacity: 2,000

Seating: None

Covered standing: 400

Floodlights: Yes

Clubhouse on ground: Yes

Record attendance: 1,100 v Halesowen Town FA Vase 1985

Biggest win: 15-0 v Battle Rangers in 1968

Biggest defeat: 1-11 v Littlehampton Town in 1991

Record appearances: N Manvell, 793

Record goalscorer in one season: D Deans 42 in 1985-86

Record goalscorer in total: G Salter 100+

Record fee received: £1,000 for Paul Walker to Wokingham in 1989

DIRECTIONS

A27 east then A283 turn off - town centre turning at roundabout, right into Church Street, straight into Church Lane, straight into Shooting Field, ground on left by Grammar School. Bus 10 from Shoreham-on-Sea BR stations stops at end of road.

Honours

Sussex Junior Cup 1902 and 1938

Sussex Senior Cup 1986 and 1989

Sussex County League 1985 and 1986

Sussex League Cup 1978, 1984, 1986

Division Two Invitation Cup 1966

Sussex RUR Charity Cup 1980

Vernon Wentworth Cup 1934

Manager for 1996-97: V Gretton

Chairman: G Matthews

The club were formed in 1892 and spent the first 72 years in local and Intermediate football before joining the Sussex County League Division Two in 1964. They won that division's Invitation Cup a year later and were promoted in 1978. The 80's were by far the club's most successful with Senior Cup triumphs in 1986 and 1989 and consecutive league titles in 1985 and 1986. There were League Cup wins also as well as a marvellous FA Vase run to the quarter finals in 1985.

The club played until 1947 on Hazel's Field before moving to the Shooting Fields, where they remain. The ground was enclosed in the mid-60's in preparation for County League football and has been updated since as the club moved to the Wessex League as founder members in 1986 for two years before changing to the Combined Counties League, returning home to the County League in 1993.

THREE BRIDGES

Jubilee Field, Three Bridges, Crawley, East Sussex Tel: 01293 442000

Secretary: Martin Clarke, 18 Mannings Close, Pound Hill,
Crawley Tel: 01293 883726

Colours: Amber and black

Seating: Yes

Capacity: 3,500

Record attendance: 2,000 v Horsham 1948

Nickname: Bridges

Covered standing: Yes

Clubhouse on ground: Yes

DIRECTIONS
200yds from Three Bridges (BR) - towards Crawley town centre.

Honours

Sussex County League Div 2 1955

Invitation Cup 1971

Division Two Invitation Cup 1963

Sussex RUR Charity Cup 1983

Manager for 1996-97: Steve Dove

Chairman: Alan Bell

WHITEHAWK

Enclosed Ground, East Brighton Park, Brighton Tel: 01273 609736

Hon secretary: John Rosenblatt, 25 Arundel Street,
Brighton Tel: 01273 680322

Match Sec: Fred Moore, 41 Newhaven St, Brighton,
Tel 01273 689433

Colours: All Red

Nickname: Hawks

Covered standing: Yes

Record attendance: 2,100 v Bognor Regis Town
FA Cup 4th Qual Replay 1988

Record appearances: Ken Powell 1,103

Record goalscorer in total: Billy Ford

Clubhouse on ground: Yes

Seating: Yes

Capacity: 3,000

DIRECTIONS
Follow Brighton seafront road towards Newhaven, turn inland (Arundel Road) opposite Marina, 3rd right into Roedean Road, 1st left into Wilson Avenue. Three miles from Brighton (BR), take Newhaven, Eastbourne or Saltdean bus to marina, then as above.

Honours

Sussex County League 1962, 1964, 1984, Division Two 1968 and 1981League Cup 1983 and 1994

Invitation Cup 1961 and 1970, Division Two League Cup 1981, Sussex Senior Cup 1951 and 1962

Sussex RUR Charity Cup 1955, 1959, 1991, Sussex Intermediate Cup 1950

Sussex Junior Cup 1949 and 1952, Brighton Charity Cup 1952, 1960, 1962, 1983, 1988, 1989

Worthing Charity Cup 1983

Manager for 1996-97: Butch Reeves

Chairman: Ken Powell   **Vice Chairman: Mike Grimer**

Press officer: Mike Spooner at club 01323 461003

WICK

Crabtree Park, Coombes Way, Wick, Littlehampton, West Sussex BN17 6PG Tel: 01903 713535

Secretary: Les Hawkins, 30 Lansdowne Rd, Wick, Littlehampton
BN17 6JG Tel: 01903 722765

Match Secretary: Clive Little, 4 Leeward Rd, Littlehampton
Tel: 01903 721962

Colours: Red and black

Nickname: Wickers

Capacity: 2,000

Seating: Yes

Covered standing: Yes

Clubhouse on ground: Yes

Biggest defeat: 0-11 v Lewes Sussex Senior Cup 1965

DIRECTIONS
A27 to Crossbush, left at Howards Hotel, after 1 mile cross level crossing, turn left into Coombes Way next to Locomotive PH - ground at end. One and a half miles from Littlehampton

Honours

Sussex Senior Cup 1993

Sussex County League 1990 and 1994, and Div 2 1982 and 1986

League Cup 1988 and Norman Wingate Trophy 1989 and 1991

Sussex RUR Charity Cup 1990

Sussex Junior Cup 1960

Brighton Charity Cup 1986

Bognor Charity Cup 1977

Manager 1996-97: Jimmy Quinn

Chairman: Norman Cairns

Wick Football Club was formed in 1892 although some believe it was even earlier, and in 1896 they became founder members of the West Sussex Football League. Honours did not arrive until the early 50's when the B side won the Bareham Trophy. They joined the County League in 1964 and for the first six seasons played on the Recreation Ground in Southfields before moving to Crabtree Park.

They made a fine start winning their first eleven matches, but then visited Lewes for a Senior Cup tie and lost 11-0 and from there the season fell to pieces. They then had a poor spell in Division Two, reaching one final, the RUR Cup in 1976. A year later they did take the Bognor Charity Cup

In 1982 things looked up with the side winning the Division Two title and the Merit Award, but again they went down in 1985.

It was then that Barry Wadsworth and Norman Cairns moved across town from Littlehampton as Chairman and manager and from that moment the club took off. They won Division Two and in 1988 won the Challenge Cup, 1989 the Norman Wingate Trophy and in 1990 were League champions, having won the first 13 matches and defeated Peacehaven in the RUR Cup final.

They weren't finished there, for in 1993 the Wickers proudly won the Sussex Senior Cup, beating Oakwood in the final at the Goldstone. The following year they were again champions of the league, were runners up in the Floodlit Cup and shared the Norman Wingate Trophy.

WITHDEAN

Withdean Stadium, Valley Dr, Withdean, Brighton Tel: 01273 551638

Hon secretary: Simon Pattenden 37 Stanmer Park Rd,
Brighton Tel: 01273 507128

Prog Editor Dave Bull, 20 Wilfrid Rd, Hove, East Sussex
BN3 7FL Tel: 01273 412801

DIRECTIONS
Off main London - Brighton road.

Colours: Red and blue   Nickname: The Deans

Capacity: 10,000   Seating: 1,100 in open

Covered standing: 100   Floodlights: No

Clubhouse on ground: Public house

Biggest win: 9-0 v East Preston 1992

Biggest defeat: 0-7 v Peacehaven 1995 and v Saltdean 1996

Record appearances: (over last four seasons, since records kept) Shaun Wilson 132

Record goalscorer in one season: Dave Agnew 25

Record goalscorer in total: Dave Agnew 74

Honours

Sussex County League Div 3 1993

Division Three Cup 1992

Manager 1996-97: Paul Norland   **Assistant Manager: Dave Cole**

Chairman: Phil Bond

WORTHING UNITED

Robert Albon Memorial Ground, Lyons Way, Worthing Tel: 01903 234466

Secretary: Malcolm Gamlen, 11 Westbourne Ave, Worthing Tel:
01903 263655

Colours: Sky blue and white   Floodlights: No

Seating: Yes   Covered standing: Yes

Capacity: 1,000

Record attendance: 180 v Northwood in FA Vase 1992

DIRECTIONS
Ground just to the north of A27. Enter via Superstore.

Honours

Wigmore Athletic

Sussex Junior Cup 1950, Invitation Cup 1960

Sussex County League Challenge Cup 1975

Division Two: 1953, Division Two Invitation Cup 1968

Worthing Utd

Division Three 1990

Manager for 1996-97: Dave Treagus   **Chairman: Len Killpatrick**

OFFICIAL MATCH DAY PROGRAMME

SOUTHWICK FOOTBALL CLUB

Old Barn Way, Southwick. Telephone (0273) 701010

sponsored by

NYNEX

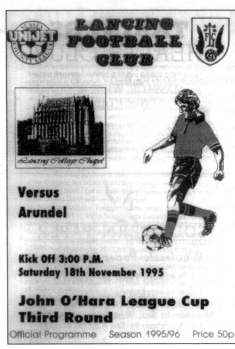

LANCING FOOTBALL CLUB

Lancing College Chapel

**Versus
Arundel**

**Kick Off 3:00 P.M.
Saturday 18th November 1995**

**John O'Hara League Cup
Third Round**

Official Programme   Season 1995/96   Price 50p

Langney Sports

SEASON 1995/96

UNIJET SUSSEX COUNTY LEAGUE DIVISION ONE

v STAMCO

Monday 6th May 1996   Kick Off 3.00

MAIN SPONSOR NOBO
Britain's leading manufacturer of visual
& training aids

In this programme.....
- WELCOME TO STAMCO
- LANGNEY NEWS & VIEWS
- STATISTICS AND REPORTS
- UNIJET LEAGUE UPDATE

60p

Programme No. 28

*Thank you for your support during the past season.....and
it is hoped you will return to Priory Lane in August 1996.*

PRIORY LANE, EASTBOURNE. TEL: 01323 766265

WITHDEAN FOOTBALL CLUB

WITHDEAN STADIUM, BRIGHTON

☎ (0273) 551638

COMPUTER & NETWORK CONSULTANTS LTD.
Main Sponsors to
WITHDEAN F.C.

Official Programme

HELLENIC LEAGUE

Premier Division

	P	W	D	L	F	A	PTS
Cirencester Town	34	24	8	2	69	24	80
Brackley Town	34	19	12	3	60	32	69
Lambourn Sports	34	21	5	8	71	41	68
Tuffley Rovers	34	20	7	7	78	46	67
Burnham	34	20	4	10	66	37	64
Swindon Super	34	20	3	11	82	33	63
Endsleigh	34	16	7	11	56	41	55
North Leigh	34	15	4	15	66	62	49
Carterton Town	34	13	9	12	57	59	48
Abingdon United	34	13	4	17	49	55	43
Fairford Town	34	10	10	14	49	52	40
Almondsbury T	34	10	7	17	53	54	37
Shortwood Utd	34	10	5	19	53	82	35
Kintbury Rangers	34	8	9	17	45	74	33
Banbury United	34	8	6	20	40	66	30
Highworth Town	34	9	3	22	36	80	30
Didcot Town	34	7	7	20	39	88	28
Bicester Town	34	6	4	24	37	80	22

Division One

	P	W	D	L	F	A	PTS
Purton	34	22	6	6	79	40	72
Wantage Town	34	21	8	5	66	34	71
Milton United	34	18	8	8	102	63	62
Hallen	34	16	9	9	75	49	57
Harrow Hill	34	16	9	9	57	38	57
Pegasus Juniors	34	15	7	12	76	62	52
Kidlington	34	13	9	12	73	59	48
Cheltenham Sar	34	14	6	14	71	71	48
Ardley United	34	13	6	15	47	60	45
Wootton Bass T	34	12	9	13	50	64	45
Clanfield	34	9	12	13	54	61	39
Bishops Cleeve	34	10	9	15	50	65	39
Rayners Lane	34	9	11	14	51	66	38
Easington Sports	34	9	10	15	45	64	37
Headington Am	34	10	5	19	51	72	35
Letcombe	34	9	8	17	38	65	35
Yarnton	34	9	6	19	45	84	33
Cirencester United	34	8	8	18	53	66	32

RESERVE Premier Div

	P	W	D	L	F	A	PTS
Endsleigh Res.	26	23	2	1	91	20	71
Swin Super Res.	26	21	2	3	83	27	65.
Almonds T Res.	26	12	8	6	52	33	44
North Leigh Res.	26	12	3	11	60	47	39
Fairford T Res.	26	10	5	11	50	59	35
Brackley T Res.	26	10	3	13	49	53	33
Kintbury R Res.	26	11	0	15	34	61	33
Abingd Utd Res.	26	10	2	14	47	47	32
Bicester T Res.	26	9	4	13	53	63	31
Highworth T Res.	26	9	4	13	40	57	31
Cirenc T Res.	26	9	4	13	34	57	31
Carterton T Res.	26	7	5	14	25	36	26
Didcot T Res.	26	8	2	16	41	68	26
Banbury Utd Res.	26	7	4	15	28	59	25

ABINGDON UNITED

Northcourt Rd, Abingdon, Oxon OX14 1P. Tel: 01235 520255

Secretary: Terry Hutchinson, 41 Austin Place, Abingdon,
Oxon OX14 1LT Tel 01253 559019

Colours: Yellow and blue

Nickname: The U's

Capacity: 2,000

Seating: Yes

Covered standing: Yes

Clubhouse on ground: Yes

Record attendance: 500 v Abingdon Town
Berks and Bucks Senior Cup 1990

Record appearances: D Webb

DIRECTIONS

From north (Oxford) leave A34 at Abingdon north sign and Northcourt Road is 1st major turning after roundabout. From South, East or West leave Abingdon on A4183 and turn left into Northcourt Road after 1 mile. 2 miles from Redley (BR).

Honours

North Berks League 1954

Charity Shield 1953

Hellenic League Div 1 Cup 1966 and 1982

Abingdon United were formed in 1946 when a group of ex-servicemen decided that the town of Abingdon could support two clubs, Abingdon Town having been in existence since the last century.

The initial meeting was called in a pub and the club eventually joined the North Berks League in 1950 and within two seasons had won the Charity Shield. Four seasons later in 1954 they won their first championship and were also runners up in the Challenge Cup. It saw the club set their sight on greater things and in 1958 they were elected to the Hellenic League.

Success was limited and it took until 1966 before Abingdon gained their first trophy, winning the Division One Challenge Cup. A year later they were beaten by Aston Clinton in the final, but it was another 11 years before they tasted success again, when in 1977 they were promoted after finishing third behind Didcot Town and Flackwell Heath.

After three moderate seasons the club dropped back into Division One and with that came a new, more positive approach and with the help of new members they bounced straight back behind Lambourn Sports, adding the Division One Challenge Cup as a bonus.

They were given senior status by the Oxfordshire FA which enabled them to enter the FA Vase and Berks and Bucks Senior Cup, the latter of which has brought two semi-finals and a final, most notably in 1990 when they defeated local rivals Abingdon Town in a fierce encounter.

In the late 80's United proceeded with their ground improvements after completing eight years of negotiations with the council and a small stand was built along with a new entrance. An extension to the clubhouse was completed and after many setbacks, floodlights finally were installed in 1994.

ALMONDSBURY TOWN

Oaklands Park, Almondsbury, Bristol. Tel: 01454 612220

Secretary: David Winstone, 30 Cherington, Yate,
Bristol BS17 4UZ. Tel: 01454 323877

Colours: Sky and navy blue   Nickname: The Almonds

Capacity: 2,000   Seating: No

Covered standing: No   Clubhouse on ground: Yes

Record attendance: for Hellenic Cup final replay,
Newport v Abingdon Utd

Honours

FA VASE RUNNERS UP 1979

SEMI-FINALS 1978

Gloucester County League 1977, 1978, 1980, 1981

GFA Challenge Trophy 1979

Avon Premier Combination 1975

Gloucester Senior Amateur Cup 1988

Hellenic League 1984

League Cup 1984 and 1985

DIRECTIONS

Adjacent to M5 junction 16 - follow A38 Thornbury - ground first left. 4 miles from Bristol Parkway (BR). County bus services to Thornbury, Stroud and Gloucester.

Although there was football in the village of Almondsbury in the late 1800's, there is little known about the club until they began playing in the Bristol and Suburban League after the War. They played on Almondsbury Rec, a pitch now part of the cricket club outfield as it always was, until 1986 when they moved next door to a barriered pitch with porta cabin dressing rooms tucked right next to the M5. It is the ground that can be clearly seen when travelling East bound. This later became home to a new club, Almondsbury FC, from the Suburban League. After many problems internal and financial, they moved another 100 yards or so across the road to a new site behind the motorway traffic HQ.

This ground is unusual in that it has a splendid clubhouse and floodlights, adequate parking but no cover of any kind. The relevant history of Almondsbury Town Football Club begins in 1974 when they merged with a junior club called Greenway Sports who had been successful in local football but without a home ground. The newly formed club Almondsbury Greenway were elected to the Gloucestershire County League and finished runners up. It was a taster as they went on to take the title five times in a row with a runners up spot on the sixth in 1982. During that marvellous spell they reached an FA Vase semi-final in 1978 and went one better in 1979 when they got to Wembley only to be well beaten by Billericay Town in front of 17,500.

In 1982 the club were elected to the Hellenic League and were runners up to Moreton Town in the first season, and reversed it a year later taking the title. Further successes came in the Challenge Cup and the Hungerford Merit Cup and in 1985 they took the Premier Division Cup.

The club then went into decline and it was re-formed more than once with new names, Almondsbury 85 and Almondsbury Picksons, the latter after businessman Colin Pick pulled out of Badminton Picksons to take over at Almondsbury. After the club moved again and built its Oaklands Park ground, they went up as Division One champions, but after a couple of poor seasons with little support the club went into liquidation again and Almondsbury Town was hastily formed to take over in the league. There was a possibility of Woolen Sports FC merging and playing at Almondsbury but that disappeared and more recently the Gloucestershire FA made progress in buying the ground as a County HQ, whilst Almondsbury would remain there as tenants.

BANBURY UNITED

The Stadium, Station Approach, Banbury. Tel: 01295 263354

Secretary: Barry Worsley, c/o Sol Systems Unit 4 Mallorie House,
Beaumont Rd, Banbury Tel: 01295 255536

DIRECTIONS

M40 junction 11,
follows signs for
Banbury then BR
station, turn right
down narrow lane
before entering
station forecourt;
eastern end of town.

Colours: Blue and white   Nickname: The Puritans

Capacity: 6,500   Seating: 50

Covered standing: 500   Clubhouse on ground: Yes

Record attendance: 7,140 v Oxford City FA Cup 3rd Qual Rd 1948

Biggest win: 12-0 v RNAS Culham Oxon Senior Cup 1946

Biggest defeat: 2-11 WBA A Birmingham Comb 1938-39

Record appearances: Dave Mathews

Record goalscorer in one season: Tony Jacques 62 in 73 games 1967-68

Record goalscorer in total: Dick Pike and Tony Jacques both 222

Record fee received: £20,000 from Derby County for Kevin Wilson

Honours

Oxford Senior Cup 1979 and 1988

Oxford Professional Cup 1953 jt, 1973 jt, 1973, 1978, 1980 jt, Oxford Senior Lge 1935 and 1940

Banbury Junior Lge 1934, Oxford and Banbury Charity Cups 1935

Tillottson and Oxford Hospital Cups 1947, Daventry Charity Cup 1989 and 1990

Smiths Memorial Cup 1969 and 1970, Hitchin Centenary Cup 1969

Manager 1996-97: Ian Bowyer

Assistant Manager: Tony Rose

Chairman: Jim Breslin

The club was first formed in 1931 as recreation for workers in the Spencer Corset factory. Known as Spencer Villa they played friendlies on a pitch in Middleton Rd. In 1933 they joined the Banbury Junior League and won Section C, going 10 matches without conceding a goal. The club name was changed to Banbury Spencer in 1934 and moved to the old Brittania Works ground which was renamed Spencer Stadium and is still home today. The first game was in 1935 in the FA Cup against Hayes and that season was spent in the Oxford Senior League where they were champions, also playing in four cup finals. They were elected to the Birmingham Comb for the following year but were forced to wait a year after problems with the Oxford FA. Banbury had a season in the Oxford Senior League at the start of the War, and after it they turned professional. Honours were rare in the 50's and when the Comb folded they moved to the Birmingham League in 1954, but it was the 60's before things changed. As founder members of the West Midlands League in 1962 they reached the FA Cup 1st Round, but the owners were fast losing interest and a group of businessmen bought out shares in the Spencer company and the name changed to Banbury United. They took Deal Town's place in the Southern League in 1966, and wholesale changes were made to the ground, including floodlights. They settled in the new league but as the 80's came so did financial problems and they resigned and went into liquidation in 1984. A last minute deal saved the club and they remained in league, but they were finally relegated in 1990. The Hellenic League beckoned and they were given another blow when the owners gave notice of eviction from what had become a ramshackle ground, but with the club at its lowest ebb, the committee vowed to go on.

Since those times the ground and the club have been turned round and although the tenancy of the ground remains a problem, there is spirit in the club once more.

BICESTER TOWN

Sports Ground, Oxford Rd, Bicester, Oxon. Tel: 01869 241036

Secretary: Philip Allen, 38 Bassett Ave, Bicester,
Oxon OX6 7TZ Tel 01869 252125

Colours: Red and black stripes   Nickname: Foxhunters

Capacity: 2,000   Seating: 120

Covered standing: 100   Clubhouse on ground: Yes

Record attendance: 955 v Portsmouth Floodlight match 1994

Honours

Hellenic League 1981 and 1986

Division One and Div One Cup 1978

Challenge Cup 1986 and 1991

Oxfordshire Junior Cup 1903

Oxfordshire Senior Cup 1904, 1925, Oxfordshire Charity Cup

Banbury and Chipping Norton Charity Cup

Manager 1996-97: Aiden McKay

Assistant Manager: Paul Creed

Chairman: Bill Hammond

Vice Chairman: Ray Honour

DIRECTIONS

From Oxford: past Tescos on outskirts of Bicester - ground on right. From Aylesbury: turn left at first island on outskirts of Bicester onto bypass, right at next island, pass Tescos & ground on right.

Bicester Town were founded in 1874 following an amalgamation of Bicester Harriers and Bicester Rovers, which makes them one of the oldest clubs in the county. They joined the Oxfordshire FA on its inception on January 26th 1884. For a number of seasons they competed at junior level winning the County Junior Shield for the only time in 1903 and the following season, in senior football they won the Oxfordshire Senior League. In the next 20 years honours were scarce, although the 20's saw wins in the Senior and Charity Cups and the Banbury and Chipping Norton Charity Cup.

After the War, Bicester became founder members of the Hellenic League and enjoyed 20 years in the top division before suffering relegation in 1974. Happily it was not long before they bounced back, gaining promotion in 1978, as champions in front of Garrards Athletic. It was a double success as they also took the Challenge Cup and within two years they were again champions of the league, for the first time since 1961.

In 1986 the club won their first Premier Division Challenge Cup and they repeated it in 1991 when beating Bishops Cleeve in the final.

Last year the Foxhunters had a dreadful time but with Cirencester moving on and only Wantage possibly eligible to go up, then they were saved.

The club had a nomadic existence for some time in the early years, playing at the Station Road ground before being offered the use of the cricket field for a few years. They then went to a pitch on Banbury Road owned by a Mr Busby. From there there were other temporary homes in London Road, Station Road again and Oxford Road, where the sports ground was eventually bought for the town and made available for the cricket and football clubs.

BRACKLEY TOWN

St James Park, Churchill Way, Brackley, Northants Tel: 01280 704077

Secretary: Pat Ashby, 17 Manor Rd, Woodford Halse, Daventry, Northants NN1 3QP Tel: 01327 262955

Colours: Red and white

Nickname: Saints

Capacity: 2,000

Seating: 200

Covered standing: 500

Clubhouse on ground: Yes

Record attendance: 780 v Kettering Town Northants Senior Cup 1989

Record goalscorer in total: Paul Warrington

DIRECTIONS

Churchill Way, east off A43, south end of town.

Honours

United Counties League 1989

Division One 1984

Buckingham Charity Cup

Hellenic League Div 1 Cup 1983

Manager 1996-97: Phil Lines

Assistant Manager: Mark Sherlock

Chairman: Kim Golding

Vice Chairman: Rod Bush

Brackley Town were formed in 1890 and played junior football in the Banbury and District League, before becoming members of the North Bucks League.

In 1977 the club moved into senior football, successfully applying for the Hellenic League where they competed in Division Two. After seven years they decided to move across the pyramid and were elected to the United Counties League in 1983. In their first season they were champions and were promoted to the Premier Division, where under the management of Phil Lines they were runners up in 1989. After his departure the team broke up and the club went into decline, finishing bottom three seasons running.

In the summer of 1994, Brackley Town successfully returned to the Hellenic League, where they were put into the top division, and it has proved a success for last season ended with the club second only to Cirencester Town in a strong division.

One honour to come the club's way was an appearance in the Northants Senior Cup final in 1989, where sadly they lost the final.

The club's current ground has only been home since 1974, they having played on several other pitches around the town in the previous 80 years, including Buckingham Rd and Manor Rd.

BURNHAM

The Gore, Wymers Wood Rd, Burnham, Slough SL1 8JG. Tel: 01628 602467

Secretary: Michael Boxall, 39 Tockley Rd, Burnham, Slough SL1 7DQ Tel: 01628 660265

Colours: Blue and white

Nickname: The Blues

Capacity: 2,500

Seating: Yes

Covered standing: No

Clubhouse on ground: Yes

Record attendance: 2,400 v Halesowen Town FA Vase 1983

Biggest win: 18-0 v High Duty Alloys 1971

Biggest defeat: 1-10 Ernest Turner Sports 1964

Record goalscorer in one season Fraser Hughes 65 in 1969-70

DIRECTIONS

North west of village centre, 2 miles from Burnham BR station, 2 miles from M4 Junction 7, 5 miles from M40 Junction 2, 100yds north of Gore cross-roads - fork right into Wymers Wood Rd and ground is immediately on right. Bee line bus 66.

Honours

FA VASE Semi-final 1983

Hellenic League and League Cup 1976

Division One Cup 1972

London Spartan League and League Cup 1985

Founded in 1878, Burnham FC are the second oldest in Buckinghamshire. For many years they played in the South Bucks and East Berks, Great Western Suburban, Windsor, Slough and District, Maidenhead Intermediate, Great Western Combination, Wycombe Combination and Reading Combination Leagues with varying degrees of success before finally settling on the Hellenic League in 1971 for six years after they were granted senior status. Gaining promotion from Division One in 1973 they did the double in 1976.

They were elected to the Athenian League in 1977 and were twice runners up before it folded in 1984. They moved briefly to the Spartan League where they did the league and cup double before in 1985 they were accepted by the Southern League. They had merged with the ailing Hillingdon FC who had lost their Leas Stadium to housing and played in the new league as Burnham and Hillingdon FC. They reverted to the original name two years later.

In 1978 they reached the last eight of the FA Vase and in 1983 went one better before losing a two legged semi-final to Halesowen Town. From 1985 they competed in the FA Trophy although recently on leaving the Southern League to return to the Hellenic League, they once again are in the Vase.

Burnham played on Baldwins Meadow until around 1920 when they moved to the Gore Cricket Ground.

CARTERTON TOWN

Kilkenny Lane, Carterton, Oxfordshire, OX18 3RW. Tel: 01993 842410

Acting Secretary: R Stephens, 40 Shillbrook, Carterton, Oxon Tel 01993 843135

Fixture Secretary: G Yates, 120 Oakfield Rd, Cartertton, Oxon OX18 3QW Tel: 01993 841797

Capacity: 1,000 approx

Seating: 50

Standing: 150

Clubhouse on ground: Yes

Record attendance: 600 v Oxford United Oxon Senior Cup 1993-94

Record goalscorer in aggregate: Tim Dorrington

DIRECTIONS

Enter Swinbrook Road which off the Burford-Carterton road, proceed into Kilkenny Lane (one track road), ground car park 200 yds on left before sharp corner. Hourly buses to Carterton from Oxford.

HONOURS

Oxfordshire Junior Shield: 1986

Witney and District League: 1966

Division 1: 1965 and 1977

Hellenic League Div 1 1990 and 1994

Manager for 1996-97: Andy Sinott

Chairman: Gordon Maxwell

Vice Chairman and Press officer: Paul King Tel: 01993 840412

Originally formed in 1922 as Carterton FC, the club played in the local Witney and District League with their home ground as the recreation ground in the centre of the village.

There was no football during the Second World War, but in 1946 they were re-formed and played on and off in local leagues with limited success. 1972 saw the introduction of Carterton Boys FC and the junior sides flourished to an extent that they took over the running of the men's side and renamed the amalgamated club Carterton Town FC, the name reflecting the growth in population, for it to be recognised as a town, the third largest in West Oxfordshire.

They were offered an area of ground at a peppercorn rent by the council and moved to Kilkenny Lane, the site being derelict. Through dedication and hard work by members temporary floodlights were installed in 1990 and a car-park enlarged. Since then, with the club in the Hellenic League they have won Division One twice, joining the league in 1986.

DIDCOT TOWN

Station Road, Didcot, Oxon. Tel: 01235 813212

Secretary: Norman 'ennett, 75 Churchill Rd, Didcot, Oxon OX11 7BU Tel: 01235 813016

Colours: Red and white

Nickname: Railwaymen

Capacity: 2,000

Seating: 50

Covered standing: 200

Clubhouse on ground: Yes

Record attendance: 2,000 v Wycombe Wanderers
Berks and Bucks Senior Cup 1953

DIRECTIONS
Midway down Station Road, Didcot, on right quarter mile from railway Station towards town centre.

Honours

Hellenic League 1954

League Cup 1966, 1967, 1993

Division One and Div One Cup 1977

Didcot Town were founded in 1907 and are members of the Berks and Bucks Football Association From the start they played in the Berks League before moving up to the part professional Metropolitan League after the War. In 1953 Didcot moved into the newly formed Hellenic League as founder members and other than a short second spell in the Metropolitan League, they have been there ever since.

In their first season Town became the first winners, taking the title from Witney Town and Pressed Steel.

It was another twelve seasons before they tasted success again when in 1966 they took the Premier Division Challenge Cup, retaining it a year later.

After this it was another long ten year stretch before they took the Division One Challenge Cup, having earlier been relegated. In 1987 they were again promoted having finished third behind Bishops Cleeve and Cheltenham Town Res, the latter not being eligible to go up. That year also saw Town win the Challenge Cup for the second time, and they remained in the top division for six years until suffering relegation in 1993.

They then suffered two bad seasons, but off the pitch things had moved on, as part of the ground had been sold for housing, enabling them to move the pitch down a few yards and install floodlights, new drainage and new covered accommodation. The ground was ready for the Premier Division and despite finishing in tenth, the league promoted them on the strength of their facilities, along with Lambourn Sports and Endsleigh.

ENDSLEIGH

Cheltenham Town FC, Whaddon Rd, Cheltenham, Gloucester Tel: 01242 513397

Secretary: Graham Ayres, 7 Oakbrook Drive,
The Reddings, Cheltenham Tel: 01452 548556

Colours: Blue and Gold

Nickname: Super Owls

Capacity: As per Cheltenham Town FC

Clubhouse on ground: Yes

Honours

Gloucester Northern Senior League 1993

Division One 1992

Hellenic League Division One 1994

Manager 1996-97: Gary Leeds

Assistant Manager: Mark Ratcliffe

Chairman: Michael Cocks

Press Officer: Sean Regan 01242 223300 (Business)

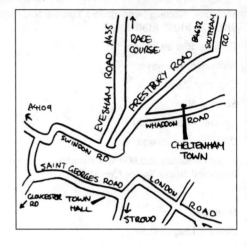

Endsleigh FC and it's founder, the Endsleigh Insurance Company, would not be here today but for the tremendous support and generosity of the late Michael Naylor. Michael was killed in a road accident in Southern France and at the time of his death, he was the Chairman of the company.

His football club have climbed from Sunday morning football to the Premier Division of the Hellenic League in 1996, but it wasn't until 1984 that they moved to Saturdays, starting in Division Five of the Cheltenham Football League and in a remarkable ten years they have seen a meteoric rise through the amateur football world. On their way up they were promoted every season and picked up every league championship apart from the Cheltenham League Division Three in 1988. They moved up to the Northern Senior League Division Two and in 1992 took their place in the County League and entered the Gloucestershire Challenge Cup. That season saw a hectic finish with ten matches in two weeks where the club won them all and were promoted to the Hellenic League Division One.

The following season saw them go 18 matches unbeaten and they clinched the title with a 2-0 win over Ardley United.

To capitalise on the success, several other teams have been formed within the club, whose parent company now sponsor a host of clubs and institutions including Burnley FC, Cheltenham Town FC, Cheltenham and Gloucester College etc.

FAIRFORD TOWN

Cinder Lane, Fairford, Glos. Tel: 01285 712071

Secretary: Michael Cook, Bow Wow, Down Ampney, Cirencester, Glos. GL7 5QU Tel: 01793 751240

Colours: Red and white

Nickname: Town

Capacity: 2,000

Seating: None

Covered standing: Yes

Clubhouse on ground: Yes

Record attendance: 1,500 v Swindon Town Friendly 1992

Record goalscorer in total: Pat Toomey

DIRECTIONS

Entering Fairford on A417 from Lechlade turn left down Cinder Lane 150yds after 40mph sign. From Cirencester on same road, follow through village and turn right down Cinder Lane 400yds after Railway Inn. Buses from Swindon, Lechlade and Cirencester.

Honours

Gloucester Challenge Trophy 1980

Hellenic League Div 1 and Div 1 Cup 1972

Premier Div Cup 1979

Gloucester Junior Cup 1963

Swindon and District League 1965 and 1969

Fairford Town FC was formed in 1891 and for many years played in the Cirencester and District League with varying success. After the War they joined the Swindon and District League and won the title twice in the sixties, taking the Advertiser Cup both years as well. Success was followed by election to the Hellenic League in 1970, only missing promotion on goal average at the first attempt. The following year they did the First Division double, whilst the reserves were runners up in the Swindon League and reached two Cup finals. The success continued through 1973 but in 1974 they suffered relegation back to Division One. Within two years they were back in the top division and progress was made as Town were twice runners up in 1979 and 1980, also winning the Premier Division Cup and the Gloucester Challenge Trophy.

Since then there have been two further runners up spots for Fairford Town who have been consistently there now for well over a decade.

HIGHWORTH TOWN

Elm Recreation Ground, Highworth, Wilts Tel: 01793 766263

Secretary: Fraser Haines, 16 Blandford Mews, Highworth, Swindon,
Wilts SN6 7BQ Tel 01793 861109

Press Sec: Steve Leppard

Colours: Red and white stripes

Nickname: Worthians

Capacity: 2,000

Seating: 50

Covered standing: 200

Clubhouse on ground: Yes

Record attendance: 300 v Swindon Supermarine
Wilts Senior Cup Final 1994

Biggest win: 12-0 v Beeches Arthur Shipway Cup 1992

Biggest defeat: 2-8 v Milton Utd Hellenic League 1987

Record appearances: Rod Haines

Record goalscorer in total: Kevin Higgs

DIRECTIONS

Enter on A361 from
Swindon, past Simpsons
Garage, straight over
island, next sharp left
into Green by Vets
Surgery - ground & car
park 60yds on left next
to Sports Hall.

Honours

Advertiser Cup 1910, 1912, 1948, 1959, 1960, 1968

Cirencester League Division Two 1932

Wiltshire Senior Cup 1964, 1973 and 1996

Hellenic Division One Cup 1989

Arthur Shipway Cup 1989 and 1994

Swindon and District League 1964, 1965, 1966, 1969

Highworth Town celebrated their centenary two seasons ago having been founded in 1893. They began league football in the Swindon and District League before joining the Cirencester League shortly after their outset. In those early days the club were a major force in local football with a great tradition of being a family club. That is still evident today with the Haines family being involved in one way or another.

One of the first successes was in winning the Advertiser Cup, which in those days was the major trophy in the Swindon area. It pulled in big crowds with the finals watched by many hundreds. Highworth won it in 1910 and 1912 but it was 36 years before they won it again. They took it three more times, in 1959, 1960 and 1968, and between those times they also won the Cirencester Division Two in 1932.

Another major honour won by the club is the Wiltshire Senior Cup, which they have now won three times since 1964.

Having moved up to the Wiltshire League earlier, they again moved on to the Hellenic League in the early 80's. It took ten years for them to be promoted but they remain in the top flight although last season's league form was poor, the season livened by their Senior Cup final win.

KINTBURY RANGERS

Recreation Ground, Inkpen Rd, Kintbury Tel: 01488 657001

Secretary: Anthony Plank, 26 Kennet Rd, Kintbury, RG17 9XW Tel: 01488 658460

Nickname: Rangers

Capacity: 1,000

Seating: No

Covered standing: Yes

Clubhouse on ground: Yes

Record attendance: 400 v Newport AFC Hellenic League 1990

Record appearances: Nigel Llewellyn

DIRECTIONS
Turn off A4 (signed Kintbury) between Newbury/Hungerford. 2nd left after level crossing into Inkpen Road, entrance 200yds on right by Jubilee Centre. Half mile from Kintbury (BR).

Honours

North Berks League 1978 and 1982

Berks and Bucks Intermediate Cup 1961

Manager for 1996-97: Darren Angell

Kintbury Rangers were re-formed in 1942 and played in the Newbury and District League until the mid-60s, winning many honours. They were then elected to the Hellenic League where until 1989 they played in Division One, having been promoted in third place behind Cheltenham Town Reserves and Wantage Town. With Reserve sides unable to play in the top division, Town took advantage.

Recent seasons have seen the Recreation Ground improved with refurbished dressing rooms, and floodlights which came from Hounslow's defunct ground.

A disastrous season in 1994-95 saw the club rock bottom, but they were reprieved and last May saw a slight recovery away from the danger area.

LAMBOURN SPORTS

Bockhampton Rd, Lambourn, Berks

Secretary: Clive Bettison, 11 Foxbury, Lambourn, Berks RG17 8PT
Tel: 01488 73537

Club colours: Red and White stripes

Capacity: 1,500   Covered seating: 50

Covered standing: 150   Clubhouse on ground: Yes

Record goalscorer in one season: Stan Fisher

Record goalscorer in total: Stan Fisher

DIRECTIONS

From Lambourn Church take Newbury Street, then 1st right into Station Road, left at T-junction into Bockhampton Road, ground on left.

HONOURS

Berks and Bucks Intermediate Cup 1962 and 1980

Hellenic League Div 1 1980

Berks and Bucks Senior Trophy 1995

Manager 1996-97: Don Rogers

Assistant Manager: Colin Moyle, Chairman: Mr M.Killick, Vice Chairman: Eddie O'Neill

Lambourn FC played its first match on February 1889 and has played continuously since that date. They contested organised friendlies and cup fixtures before joining the Hungerford League in 1909 followed by the Newbury League from 1912 to 1951. For the next ten years they were members of the Swindon and District League, moving to the Hellenic League from 1961 to 1972 and then the North Berks League for 5 years before returning to the Hellenic League in 1977.

Bockhampton Road has been home since 1908 and in 1946 other local sporting organisations joined forces to form Lambourn Sports Club.

During their first spell in the Hellenic League they were runners up in Division One to Botley United, but went one better in the League Cup and they also took the Berks and Bucks Intermediate Cup that season.

In the second spell in 1980 they took the Division One League Cup and the Intermediate Cup again and two years later they were promoted, as champions, beating Abingdon United.

They were sadly later relegated and narrowly missed promotion but in 1995 they went up in third place ahead of Milton United whose ground not meet requirements.

Lambourn Sports gained planning permission to install floodlights and having bought those of Newbury Town, invited Swindon Town to switch them on.

The manager for the last five seasons has been ex-Swindon and Crystal Palace winger Don Rogers, whose career brought him Under 23 and Youth caps as well as a League Cup winners medal for Swindon.

The secretary is Clive Bettison who as player, manager and secretary has been at the club for 35 years. Was given the Berks and Bucks Certificate of Meritorious Service to Football in 1991.

NORTH LEIGH

Eynsham Hall Park Sports Ground, North Leigh, nr Witney, Oxon OX8 6RP

Secretary: Pete Dix, 8 Windmill Close, North Leigh, Witney, OX8 6RP
Tel 01993 881199

Match Sec: R.Kilfoyle, Tel 01993 771852

Programme Editor: J.Fogg, Tel: 01993 881061

Colours: Sky and navy blue

Capacity: 2,000

Seating: 100

Covered standing: No

Clubhouse on ground: Yes

Floodlights: Yes

Record attendance: 700 v Oxford United friendly

Record appearances: Sean King 350+

Record goalscorer in total: John Hill

DIRECTIONS

Ground is situated off A4095 Witney to Woodstock road 3 miles east of Witney. Entrance to ground is 500yds east of Main Park Entrance.

Honours

Witney and District League 1951, 1952, 1953, 1954, 1955, 1956, 1957, 1984, 1986, 1987, 1988, 1989, 1990

Witney and District Senior Cup 1948, 1949, 1950, 1954, 1955, 1956, 1957, 1988

Oxford Junior Shield 1957 and 1984

Oxfordshire Senior Cup 1948, 1952, 1954, 1955, 1957, 1982, 1986, 1987

Marriott Cup and Woodstock Charity Cup 1996

Joint managers: for 1996-97: Adrian Buckingham and Peter Hutter

Chairman: Peter King

Vice Chairman: Brian Sheppard

Press Officer: Barry Norton

North Leigh Football Club was founded in 1908 and played in the Witney and District League for some 80 years, consistently doing well. In a total of 13 championships, their finest spell was in the 1950's when they were champions for seven years on the trot. They had completely dominated the local scene, also taking the League Senior Cup seven times including two hat-tricks and the County Cup which was taken five times before the end of the 50's.

Seven years ago they were elected into the Hellenic League Division One where they had a couple of reasonable seasons before finishing runners up to Tuffley and being promoted in 1993.

Within the last couple of seasons North Leigh have made great strides in improving the facilities at their delightful Eynsham Hall Ground, with the installation of floodlights being the major factor.

Last year the club reached the final of the Oxfordshire Senior Cup where they lost narrowly in extra time to local rivals Witney Town in extra-time.

SHORTWOOD UNITED

Meadow Bank, Shortwood, Nailsworth, Gloucestershire Tel: 01453 833936

Secretary: Mark Webb, 1 The Bungalow, Shortwood, Nailsworth, Glos GL6 0SD Tel: 01453 833204

Colours: All Red   Nickname: The Wood

Capacity: 5,000   Seating: Yes

Covered standing: Yes

Clubhouse on ground: Yes

Record attendance: 1,000 v Forest Green Rovers
FA Vase 5th Rd 1982

Record appearances & Record goalscorer in total: Peter Grant

DIRECTIONS

In Nailsworth turn into Spring Hill then first left. Continue past shop and keep left past "Britannia" (signposted Shortwood) - continue to end for ground. 4 miles from Stroud (BR).

Honours

Tetbury Hospital Cup 1950

Glos North Sen Lge Div 2 1981, Glos North Sen Lge Div 2 Cup 1963

Arthur Shipway Cup 1964, 1965, 1977, 1980, 1981, 1985

Stroud Charity Senior Cup 1965, 1992

Glos County League 1982, Glos FA Challenge Trophy 1984, 1992, 1995

Hellenic League Premier Div 1985, 1992, Hellenic League Div 1 Cup 1984

Anglo-Belgian Challenge Cup 1987

Shortwood United were founded at the turn of the century and played in the Stroud and District League. They remained members before gaining promotion to the Northern Senior League and thence to the Gloucestershire County League in the late 60's. In 1972 Shortwood moved down the lane and bought their Meadow Bank ground from the local council and have slowly developed it ever since. The pitch was gradually improved in what is a very hilly area with little flat surface and a clubhouse and stand were built. In 1989 they completed the installation of floodlights.

On the pitch they had brief success between the Wars winning Division Two of the Stroud League before taking the Division One crown a year later, and much later, in 1968 they were runners up in the Northern Senior League.

United had a superb spell at the start of the 80's when they were twice runners up in the County League before winning the title in 1982 and this saw them move up into the Hellenic League.

They won promotion to the Premier as runners up to Morris Motors and won the Division One Challenge Cup and the Senior Challenge Trophy for the first time in 1984. Success continued a year later with the Hellenic League championship, but they lost the final of the Challenge Cup to Almondsbury.

The late 80's saw two runners up spots, in 1986 to AFC Sharpness and in 1988 to Newport AFC but in 1992 they were champions again when beating Cirencester to the title on the last day after Town had led all season. There was more success in the Challenge Trophy and the Stroud Charity Cup and in 1995 they were again runners up and took the Gloucester Challenge Trophy.

SWINDON SUPERMARINE

Hunts Copse, Highworth Rd, South Marston, Swindon, Wilts. Tel: 01793 824828

Secretary: Eric Stott, 43 Stanier Street, Swindon, Wilts SN1 5QO. Tel: 01793 521301

Colours: White and blue

Capacity: 1,000

Seating: 75

Covered standing: 100

Clubhouse on ground: Yes

Supermarine FC and Swindon Athletic FC merged in 1992

DIRECTIONS

On A361 Swindon/Highworth road, adjoining Marston Industrial Estate. 6 miles from Swindon (BR) - buses in direction of Highworth, Fairford & Lechdale. (Vickers Sports Ground).

Honours

SUPERMARINE

Wiltshire Senior Cup 1986

Hellenic League Challenge Cup 1984

Wilts Combination Senior Div 1976

Swindon and District League Div 3 1956

Dr Elliott Cup 5 times

Faringdon Thursday Cup 3 times

SWINDON ATHLETIC

Wilts Senior Cup 1983, 1987, 1990

Hellenic League Div 1 1986 and 1987

Wilts County League 1983 and 1984 and Senior Division Two 1ª78

Wilts Junior Cup 1977

Swindon Supermarine, members of the Wiltshire FA, were formed in 1991, following the amalgamation of two of Swindon's most respected and successful Hellenic League clubs, who realised that they could achieve their best ambitions through a merger.

Swindon Athletic, formerly Penhill FC until 1989, were formed in 1968 and were previously members of the Wiltshire County League. They won the Wiltshire Junior Cup in 1977 and the Senior Division Two the following year, and success carried through the 80's, where they joined the Hellenic League and won the Wiltshire Senior Cup three times and were promoted to the Premier Division.

Supermarine were founded in 1946 as Vickers Armstrong and played in the Swindon and District League and the Wiltshire League before moving into the Hellenic League. They also were quickly successful there, becoming runners up in 1983 and Wiltshire Cup winners in 1986.

The joint club reached third place in 1995 a year after again reaching the Senior Cup final.

TUFFLEY ROVERS

Glevum Park, Lower Tuffley Lane, Gloucester. Tel: 01452 423402

Secretary: Graham Moody, 50 Giles Cox, Quedgeley, Gloucester, GL2 4YL Tel 01452 724083

Colours: Blue and claret

Capacity: 2,000

Seating: 50

Covered standing: Yes

Floodlights: Yes

Clubhouse on ground: No

Honours

Hellenic League Div 1 and Div 1 Cup 1993

Gloucestershire County League 1991

Gloucestershire Senior Amateur Cup 1988

Stroud League 1973

Glos Northern Senior League Div 1 1988 and Div 2 1980

DIRECTIONS

Follow Gloucester city ring road to roundabout signed M5 south and Bristol, take 4th exit signed Hempstead & city centre, after 200 yds turn right (McDonalds in corner) into Lower Tuffley Lane, ground 400 yds on left.

Tuffley Rovers were founded in 1929 and have always maintained their connection with the Stroud and Gloucester District Leagues. In 1974 the club were promoted into Division Two of the Gloucester Northern Senior League and in 1988 they won Division One. From there they entered the Gloucestershire County League, where they were champions in 1991.

With the championship and facilities which were perfectly acceptable to the Hellenic League, they moved up and were again successful, taking the title as well the Hungerford Cup.

Rovers' Glevum Park ground has come a long way since being converted from waste ground belonging to Gloucester Gas in 1984. The changing room complex was first to go up followed by dug outs and a pitch barrier, and since then floodlights and a stand have gone up, enabling the club to compete in the FA Vase and FA Cup. Previous to the current ground, Rovers played at Beaufort School, and have also used pitches in Stroud Road and Randwick Park, in Tuffley.

WANTAGE TOWN

Alfredian Park, Manor Park, Wantage, Oxon Tel: 01235 764781

Secretary: Nick Morris, 27 Cherbury Green, Grove, Wantage, Oxon.
Tel: 01235 766419

Colours: Green and white

Capacity: 1,500

Seating: 50

Covered standing: 300

Clubhouse on ground: Yes

Record attendance: 496 v Newbury Town in 1954

Biggest win: 11-1 v Amersham Town Hellenic League 1961

Biggest defeat: 0-14 v Thame Utd 1962

Record goalscorer in total: A.Rolls

DIRECTIONS

Take Hungerford Road from Wantage, ground signposted on right opposite recreation ground.

Honours

Hellenic League Division One 1981 and Division One League Cup 1992

Oxfordshire Senior Cup 1983

Berks and Bucks Intermediate Cup 1955

Swindon and District League 1908, 1934, 1953, 1956

Swindon Advertiser Cup 1904, 1908

North Berks Cup 1920, 1921

North Berks League 1922

Managers for 1996-97: Fred Bint and Jon Hawkins

Chairman: Kevin O'Hanlon

Vice Chairman: Tony Woodward

Affiliated to the Berks and Bucks FA in 1892, Wantage celebrated their centenary season in style by winning promotion and the Hellenic Division One Cup. The club's first success came in 1904 with the Swindon Advertiser Cup and they repeated it in 1908 as well as becoming Swindon and District League champions, to the great joy of the town. After the Great War they had a brief spell in the North Berks League, winning the North Berks Cup in 1920 and 1921 and the title itself a year later. From there they moved to the stronger Reading and District League with no success before returning west to the Swindon League where they won the title in 1934.

After the Second War, Wantage enjoyed the 50's, winning the league in 1953 undefeated and again in 1956, whilst a year earlier they won five cups in one season, including the Berks and Bucks Intermediate Cup. Since joining the Hellenic League in 1956, they have spent most of the time in the top division, never winning it but coming third three times. They have also won promotion five times as runners up, including last season, and once as champions in 1981. 1991-92 saw them set an unbeaten record of 32 games which saw them promoted and win the League Cup for Division One.

After demotion in 1994, the installation of floodlights and runners up spot enabled them to take their position in the top flight once again.

Uhlsport UNITED COUNTIES LEAGUE

PREMIER DIVISION

	P	W	D	L	F	A	PTS
Raunds Town	38	26	9	3	111	28	87
Stotfold	38	26	9	3	94	37	87
Desborough T	38	25	4	9	104	56	79
Cogenhoe United	38	21	8	9	84	56	71
Eynesbury Rovers	38	19	9	10	64	39	66
Soalding United	38	19	8	11	62	51	65
Stamford	38	18	10	10	88	56	64
Long Buckby	38	17	10	11	80	63	61
Holbeach United	38	16	12	10	68	45	60
Boston Town	38	15	12	11	74	49	57
Mirrlees Blacks	38	16	9	13	70	71	57
S & L Corby	38	15	8	15	90	77	53
Northampton Sp	38	12	6	20	67	88	42
Woot Blue Cross	38	11	9	18	54	78	42
St Neots Town	38	11	4	23	59	96	37
Potton United	38	9	9	20	46	76	36
Wellingboro T	38	10	6	22	57	88	36
Bourne Town	38	8	9	21	49	103	33
Newport Pagl T	38	4	7	27	37	128	19
Kempston Rovers	38	1	4	33	32	105	7

DIVISION ONE

	P	W	D	L	F	A	PTS
Ford Sps Dav	36	27	5	4	105	42	86
Higham Town	36	27	4	5	94	33	85
Bugbrooke St M	36	25	6	5	91	31	81
Rothwell Cors	36	22	8	6	79	29	74
Olney Town	36	24	2	10	85	47	74
Northampton Van	36	19	8	9	89	63	65
Welling Whits	36	20	4	12	72	35	64
Ramsey Town	36	16	7	13	60	47	55
Burton Park W	36	13	8	15	50	46	47
Yaxley	36	10	12	14	51	67	42
Thrapston Ven	36	12	5	19	64	70	41
Daventry Town	36	12	5	19	55	85	41
Cottingham	36	9	8	19	41	68	35
St Ives Town	36	7	12	17	50	62	33
Blisworth	36	8	8	20	59	103	32
Harrowby United	36	9	3	24	42	115	30
Sharnbrook	36	8	5	23	50	101	29
North O.N Chen	36	6	7	23	38	72	25
Irchester United	36	6	7	23	42	101	25

BLISWORTH

Blisworth Playing Field, Courteenhall Rd, Blisworth, Northants. Tel: 01604 858024

Secretary: Mrs L A Jeyes, 33 Buttmead, Blisworth, Northants, NN7 3DQ Tel: 01604 858750

Match Secretary: Terry Jeyes, same address

Colours: Yellow and green

Capacity: 1,000

Seating: No

Covered standing: No

Clubhouse on ground: Yes

DIRECTIONS

Take the A43 south from junction 15A of M1 (Northampton) and after 1-2 miles turn left into Courteenhall Road, signposted Blisworth.

Honours

Northants Junior Cup 1989

The club was formed in 1897 and has spent most of those years in junior football, playing in the Central Northants Combination and the North Bucks League. First joined the UCL in 1970 for some eight years before not gaining re-election. They returned to the Central Northants and began updating the ground with new dressing rooms and a clubhouse, and Nottingham Forest visited to officially open the new facilities. It all paved the way for a return to the UCL which occurred in 1987. They finished third in a very strong division and in 1989 won the Northants Junior Cup for the first time.

More recent times have seen the club with mixed fortunes, with last May bringing a disappointing season to a close where over 100 goals were conceded.

BOSTON TOWN

The Stadium, Tattershall Rd, Boston, Lincs. Tel: 01205 365470

Secretary: Allan Crick, Daisy Cottage, Shore Rd, Freiston,
Boston, Lincs PE22 0LN. Tel: 01205 760162

Colours: Blue and white stripes

Nickname: Poachers

Capacity: 6,000

Seating: 450

Covered standing: 1,000

Clubhouse on ground: Yes

Record attendance: 2,700 v Boston Utd FA Cup 3rd Qual Rd 1970

Record goalscorer in one season: Carl Smaller 48 1994-95

DIRECTIONS

A52 Grantham — Sleaford, 2nd left into Brothertoft Road, Argyle Street to bridge, immediately over left into Tattershall Road, ground three quarters of a mile on left.

Honours

FA VASE Semi-final 1995

United Counties League 1995

Midland Counties League 1975, 1979, 1981

League Cup 1977

Lincs Senior A Cup 1974, 1980, 1981, 1982, 1990

Lincs Senior B Cup 1966

Central Midlands League 1989

Central Alliance 1966

Lincs League 1965

Boston are a young football club, formed in 1963 by a group of businessmen in an attempt to keep "a decent standard of football in the town." They originally played on the Mayflower Sports ground but a year later moved to the purpose built Tattershall Road stadium, where they remain.

They achieved instant success with the Lincolnshire League won in 1965 and a move to the Central Alliance followed, which was also won easily in 1966, the club remaining unbeaten. In 1968 Boston moved to the Midland League and soon won that too, three times from 1975 to 1981. They also had joy in the FA Cup, reaching the first round in 1977, a few months after the Midland League Cup had been won. When the league merged with the Yorkshire League in 1982, Boston were placed in the Premier Division of the new Northern Counties East and this move saw the beginnings of a slump in fortunes.

Under Bill Brindley, the club were soon back on the up and when they joined the exodus to the Central Midlands League in 1987 they were a force once more within two years, winning the league and County Cup in fine style.

It was the fifth time that they had taken the Cup, but soon they were to change leagues again, entering the United Counties and joining the pyramid and from there the club once again won the Lincs Senior A Cup and have built a marvellous team which not only won the Premier Division of the UCL but which reached the semi-finals of the FA Vase where they lost to Taunton Town.

BOURNE TOWN

Abbey Lawn, Abbey Road, Bourne, Lincs. Tel: 01778 422292

Secretary: Roger Atkins, 106 Stephensons Way, Bourne,
Lincs PE10 9DD Tel: 01778 424882

Match Sec: Geoff McQueen, 9 Ancaster Rd, Bourne,
Lincs PE10 9HL Tel: 01778 394470

Colours: Maroon and sky blue

Nickname: Wakes

Capacity: 3,000

Seating: 300

Covered standing: 750

Clubhouse on ground: Yes

Record attendance: 3,000 v Chelmsford City FA Trophy 1970

Record goalscorer in one season: David Scotley

Record goalscorer in total: David Scotley

DIRECTIONS

In market place take A 151 Spalding Road, ground 500 yards on right. Public transport from Peterborough, Stamford and Grantham.

Honours

United Counties League 1969, 1970, 1972, 1991

Knock-Out Cup 1969

Benevolent Cup 1991

Lincs Senior A Cup 1972

Central Alliance Div 1 South 1960

Peterborough League 1934, 1946, 1947

The Wakes were formed in 1883 and most of their early football was played in the Peterborough League, their best season being in 1934 when they dropped just six points to take the title. After the War the club were too strong for the league, winning it in 1946 and 1947 by dropping just five points in two years.

Wisely, they joined the UCL alongside Spalding and Stamford but it was a different tale with several seasons in the bottom two and rarely venturing above half way. However, finances dictated that they resigned in 1955-56, half way through the season which had the league fixtures in the first half and the League Cup in the second. They had two years in the Peterborough League to regroup and in 1958 joined several other ex-UCL clubs in the Central Alliance, winning Division One South in 1960. Soon they were part of the re-formed Midland League and after four years playing amongst some of the elite, Bourne ironically returned to the UCL due to financial pressures, having left for the same reason.

It was a good move for the Wakes won the title in 1969, 1970 and 1972 as well as the Knock-Out Cup and the Lincs Senior A Cup, under player-manager Terry Bates. Then followed several lean years until 1991 when they took their fourth title and the Benevolent Cup.

Before the Second War, the Wakes played on the cricket ground adjacent to the current home, moving across in 1947.

BUGBROOKE ST MICHAELS

Birds Close, Gayton Rd, Bugbrooke. Tel: 01604 830707

Secretary: Mr R J Geary, 31 Kislingbury Rd, Bugbrooke,
Northampton, NN7 3QG Tel: 01604 831678

Colours: Yellow and blue

Nickname: The Badgers

Capacity: 1,500

Seating: No

Covered standing: Yes

Clubhouse on ground: Yes

Record appearances: Jimmy Nord

Record goalscorer in total: Vince Thomas

DIRECTIONS

A45 Northampton to Daventry road, onto B4525 (Banbury Lane) at Kislingbury, left into Grayton Road, ground on left.

Honours

Northants Junior Cup 1990

Northants Lower Junior Cup 1957, 1977, 1992 (res)

Northants Central Village League 1934, 1935, 1936, 1937, 1938

Central Northants Combination 1968, 1969, 1970, 1971, 1972, 1977, 1986

League Cup 1969, 1970, 1971, 1972

Daventry Charity Cup (twice)

The current side was formed following the closing of the first team in the village, Bugbrooke United, in 1929. They first played in the Northants Central Village League winning it for five seasons from 1934. They became founder members of the Central Northants Combination in 1952 and between 1968 and 1972 they won that league five years running, also completing doubles by winning the League Cup four times.

Elsewhere success has come in the Northants Junior Cup in 1990, the Lower Junior three times and two more titles before leaving for the UCL in 1987. They settled at Birds Close in 1985, having previously used the village school, Campus School and Pilgrims Lane. The club's floodlights were installed in 1991.

BURTON PARK WANDERERS

Latimer Park, Polwell Lane, Burton Latimer, Northants. Tel: 01536 725841

Secretary: David Haynes, 125 Churchill Way, Burton Latimer,
Northants NN15 5RT Tel: 01536 724871

Colours: All Blue

Nickname: The Wanderers

Capacity: 1,000

Seating: Yes

Covered standing: Yes

Clubhouse on ground: Yes

Record attendance: 250 v Rothwell Town May 1989

Floodlights: No

DIRECTIONS

Entering Burton Latimer, turn off A6 Station Rd right into Powell Lane; ground on the right.

Honours

Kettering Amateur League Division Two

UCL Div 3 Knock-out Cup 1969

They first played back in 1960 as Kettering Park Wanderers, playing on Rockingham Park in the town, and on starting league football won Division Two of the Kettering Amateur League in 1961. By 1965 they were in the Premier Division from where they reached two County finals, the reserves winning the Area Cup in 1966.

In 1968 they moved to the UCL 3rd Division winning the Knock-out Cup and finishing third in the league, and a year later they went up as runners up to Long Buckby. Relocation to Burton Latimer in the early 70's saw the present name adopted but success did not come and they were relegated in 1978. The move from the Recreation Ground to Latimer Park was followed by re-election but gradually fortunes changed and in 1989 the club were runners up in Division One to Ramsey Town and lost in the Knock-Out semi-final and Benevolent Cup final. Much work went into improving the ground for Premier status but after two years they again went down.

COGENHOE UNITED

Compton Park, Brafield Rd, Cogenhoe, Northants. Tel: 01604 890521

Secretary: Mick Marriott, 14 Corn Kiln Close, Cogenhoe, Northants NN7 1NX Tel 01604 890043

Match Secretary Derek Wright, 6 Brafield Rd, Cogenhoe, Northants Tel: 01604 890277

Colours: Sky blue and navy

Nickname: Cooks

Capacity: 5,000

Seating: 100

Covered standing: 200

Clubhouse on ground: Yes

Biggest win: 22-0 v Ravensthorpe.
Central Northants Combination Cup 1980

Biggest defeat: 0-6 v Yardley Utd Central Northants Combination 1976-77

Record appearances: Tony Smith

Record goalscorer in total: Tony Smith

Honours

Central Village League Div 2 1952

Daventry Charity Cup 1992

Central Northants Combination 1981, 1983, 1984

Division 2 Cup 1980

Premier Div Cup 1982

Charity Shield 1983 and 1984

DIRECTIONS

Turn off A428 at Brafield-on-the-Green, first turn right to Cogenhoe or A45 to Billing Aquadrome. Carry on, take second Cogenhoe turn on left.

The early days of Cogenhoe United FC were not documented, but friendlies with other village teams such as Brafield, Denton and Yardley Hastings led to membership of the now extinct Central Village League. A variety of pitches including one at Whiston were used until 1950 when the first game against Northampton Yeomanry was played on the village playing field. After modest success the club folded around 1960, before re-forming in 1967. Success was again elusive, but the club was on a good footing with the local pub as an HQ. However, it was not until 1978, when the club were playing in Division Two of the Central Northants Combination that they gained promotion, which coincided with the refurbishment of the old pavilion at the field. Under Brian Foley, Nigel Wagstaff and Stuart Edmunds, who chaired and managed the team, they went from strength to strength in winning thirteen trophies with six runners up awards.

A new ground became a requirement to get into the UCL and 6.5 acres of grassland off Brafield Road was leased and soon a new ground complete with stand saw the club enter the UCL for 1984-85.

The ground was officially opened by Ron Atkinson and promotion was won as runner up to Baker Perkins in 1987. A merger with a youth club and more ground improvements saw the club enter the Premier Division where they remain today.

COTTINGHAM

Berryfield Rd, Cottingham. Tel: 01536 770051

Secretary: Mr V Keefe, 24 Westbury Walk, Corby, Northants NN18 0AE. Tel: 01536 202114

Colours: Yellow and Green stripes

Floodlights: No

Capacity: 1,000

Seating: No

Covered standing: Yes

Clubhouse on ground: Yes

Biggest attendance: 700 for Glen Elliott fund raising match v Queens Park Rangers

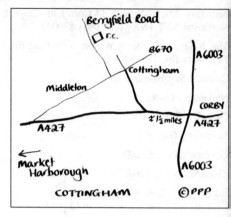

Honours

Kettering Amateur League Division Two 1978

Divison One 1979

United Counties League Division Two 1980

Northants Junior Cup 1984

Desborough Charity Cup 1985

Before joining the UCL Cottingham played in the Market Harborough and Kettering Amateur Leagues, before coming to local attention in 1977, when they went unbeaten in the Amateur League 2nd Division and followed it by taking the Divison One title, also reaching the final of the much sought after Munton Cup.

With new dressing rooms at the ground they set their sights high and after one year in the Premier Division they joined the UCL in 1979.

They won Division Two in their first season and in 1982 were runners up to Newport Pagnell in Division One. 1984 saw them enjoy a wonderful period when they became the first club for nearly 80 years to take the Junior and Lower Junior Cup double, the reserves also gaining promotion in the Reserve Division Two.

1985 saw them narrowly miss out on promotion but they took the Desborough Charity Cup.

DAVENTRY TOWN

Elderstubbs, Staverton Rd, Daventry, Northants. Tel: 01327 706286

Secretary: Cliff Farthing, 45 The Fairway, Daventry,
Northants NN11 4NW Tel 01327 72149

Colours: Black and white stripes

Capacity: 2,000

Seating: Yes

Covered standing: No

Clubhouse on ground: Yes

Record attendance: 350 v Ford Sports in 1991

<table>
<tr><td>DIRECTIONS</td></tr>
<tr><td>Adjacent to A45 by-
pass at top of
Staverton Road
Sports Complex.</td></tr>
</table>

Honours

United Counties League Division One 1990 and 1991

Northants Junior Cup 1931, 1961, 1991

Central Northants Combination Division One 1988

Premier Division and League Cup 1989

Taygold Cup 1989

Daventry Town are 110 years old and in their first 100 years saw limited success in the Rugby and District, Northampton Town and Central Northants Leagues. There were two Junior Cup successes, in 1931 and 1961 and the Centenary year came in the Town League Division Two with the club struggling to stay in business. In 1987 the club was taken over by businessman Willie Barrett and moved to the Central Northants Combination for the next season. Barrett managed the club to the Division Two title and the final of the Lower Junior Cup and a year later Town were undefeated champions of the Premier Division, winning the League Cup and Taygold Cup into the bargain.

They entered the UCL but with the proviso that their Hollow ground was acceptable for one season only, and a new ground was begun at Elderstubbs. Their great run continued with the Division One title, but having been denied promotion on facilities, they won it again a year later, losing just one game.

To round off the season they beat Bugbrooke to take the Junior Cup for the third time, celebrating promotion into the bargain. Daventry became a force, finishing fifth and reaching the Knock-Out Cup final.

Sadly, support and committee members dwindled after the move out to Elderstubbs and after financial problems dogged them they took voluntary demotion to Division One in 1994.

DESBOROUGH TOWN

Waterworks Field, Braybrooke Rd, Desborough, Northants. Tel: 01536 761350

Secretary: John Lee, 85 Breakleys Rd, Desborough,
Northants NN14 2PT Tel: 01536 760002

Colours: Blue and white stripes

Nickname: Ar Tarn

Capacity: 2,200

Seating: 200

Covered standing: 1,000

Clubhouse on ground: Yes

Record attendance: 8,000 v Kettering Town

Biggest win: 14-0 v Nuneaton Res 1924-25

Biggest defeat: 0-12 v Rushden Windmill FA Cup 1912

Record goalscorer in one season: John Marlow 42 in 1965-66

Record fee paid or received: £8,000 for Wakeley Gage from Northampton Town in Oct 1979

Honours

Northants League 1901, 1902, 1907, 1921, 1924, 1925, 1928, (UCL) 1949, 1967

Knock-out Cup 1978

Northants Senior Cup 1911, 1914, 1929, 1952

Manager 1996-97: Willie Kelly

Assistant Manager: Derek Maddox

Chairman: Bryan Walmsley

Vice Chairman: Peter Blissett

> ## DIRECTIONS
> **A6 (Leicester to Kettering), take the turning to Braybrooke at Desborough and the ground is half a mile up Braybrooke Road.**

The forerunner of the club was Desborough Unity who were formed in 1884 and played friendlies before joining the Kettering Combination as founder members in 1895. They were runners up and for the new season became Desborough Town FC where they joined the newly formed Northants League Division One. Although the early history is sketchy, it is known that the club played on a field adjacent to the current ground, changing in pubs in the town up to half a mile away. They established themselves by winning the league twice and were successful right up to the Great War. Between the wars they became one of the finest clubs in the Midlands, with four titles, a Senior Cup and a share in the Maunsell Cup. Also they enjoyed a wonderful FA Cup run, beating the likes of Westwood Works, Wellingborough, Stamford, Waterlows and Peterborough before losing to Doncaster after the first game was abandoned through fog.

It saw the beginning of a slump but after the Second War the club won the title again in 1949, but apart from another win in 1967, there has been no more league success, bar a runners up spot in 1980.

Although the club and ground has kept pace with the league, the 100 year celebrations begin with no silverware on the table, but that may well change this season as the milestone is reached.

EYNESBURY ROVERS

Alfred Hall Memorial Ground, Hall Road, Eynesbury, St Neots, Cambs. Tel: 01480 477449

Secretary: Dereck Irons, 12 Hadleigh Close, Bedford, MK41 8JW.
Tel: 01234 268111

Match Sec: Patrick Worrall, 22 Blea Water, Stukeley Meadows, Huntingdon, Cambs. Tel: 01480 431257

Colours: Royal blue and white stripes

Nickname: Rovers

Capacity: 3,000

Seating: 270

Covered standing: No

Clubhouse on ground: Yes

Record attendance: 5,000 v Fulham 1953 Friendly

DIRECTIONS
Take A428 from A1 (between Bedford and Cambridge) for approximately 1 mile before turning left for St. Neots. Eynesbury is on the south side of St. Neots urban area and the ground is near Ernulf School.

Honours

Bedford and District League Division Two 1927, 1931, 1932

United Counties League Div 1 1977

Hunts Senior Cup 1914, 1947, 1949, 1950, 1951, 1955, 1957, 1970, 1985, 1991, 1992, 1993

Hunts Premier Cup 1951 and 1991

Hinchingbrooke Cup 1947, 1949, 1950, 1951, 1952, 1958, 1967

Cambs Invitation Cup 1962

Hunts Scott Gatty Cup 1936, 1957, 1985, 1990

Hunts Junior Cup 1922 and 1927

Rovers date from 1897 and were an obscure village club in their early years, their only success being the Hunts Senior Cup in 1914. In 1921 they took the Hunts Junior Cup and repeated it in 1927 before winning the Bedford and District League 2nd Division three times in five years. They moved into senior football in 1934. That season saw the club in the South Midlands League Division Two and they were promoted straight away, winning the Hunts Intermediate Cup. They were twice County Cup runners up before the Second War and after it came a move to the United Counties League. Whilst making slow progress in the league, the local cups proved to be very popular and with Hunts Senior and Hinchingbrooke Cup wins in four out of five years they were good times. Over 3,000 saw one final against Histon Institute in 1949 and this success led to a spell in the Eastern Counties League, which came to a sad end in 1961 with just three draws and no wins all season. They returned to the UCL but the next 20 years were a struggle with little success other than one Division One title and two Cups. However, by the 90's the club had picked up considerably and in 1991 they reached the final of the East Anglian Cup, and won the Hunts Senior and Premier Cups and were third in the league.

Rovers first played their football on Priory Park Rec before moving to a field in Cemetary Lane. They played a few games at Shortsands and moved to Hall Lane, then called Mr Walton's Field, in the early 30's.

FORD SPORTS DAVENTRY

Royal Oak Way, Daventry Northants. Tel: 01327 709219

Secretary: Mr D W Hirons, 53 Arnull Crescent,
Daventry, Northants NN11 5AZ Tel 01327 71461

Colours: White and black

Nickname: Motormen

Capacity: 1,000

Seating: Yes

Covered standing: Yes

Clubhouse on ground: Yes

DIRECTIONS

Enter Daventry on A45 or A361 and follow signs for Royal Oak Way.

Honours

United Counties League Div 1 1993, 1996

The Motormen were formed in 1968 and began in the Central Northants Combination, enjoying instant success. They won promotion from Division Two to the Premier in successive seasons whilst the club grew to field three teams. They moved to the present ground in 1972 and in 1977 they joined the UCL, finishing runners up to Timken Duston in 1979. They remained in Division One from then until last May when they took the title and having made vast improvements including erecting a stand which formerly stood at the ground of British Timken, close by. For many years the club struggled to survive but in 1993 they assembled a side which took the Division by storm and pipped Higham to the title.

Last season they did exactly the same, only this time they were granted promotion.

HARROWBY UNITED

Harrowby Fields, Harrowby Lane, Grantham, Lincs. Tel: 01476 590822

Secretary: Mr D Holmes, 33 Kenilworth Rd,
Grantham, Lincs NG31 9TX Tel: 01476 74001

Colours: Blue and white stripes

Floodlights: No

Nickname: Arrows

Capacity: 1,500

Seating: Yes

Covered standing: Yes

Clubhouse on ground: Yes

DIRECTIONS

From A1 take B6403, go past A52 roundabout, pass Ancaster turn and take road to Harrowby. Continue into Grantham, ground on right opposite Cherry Tree public house.

Honours

United Counties League Div 1 1992

Midlands Regional Alliance and League Cup 1990

Lincolnshire League and League Cup 1967

Lincs Senior B Cup 1991 and 1992

Manager 1996-97: Barry Shaw

Harrowby United were formed in 1948 using a lock-up garage as changing rooms at Harrowby Fields. They collected many honours in the Grantham League where stayed for many years before in 1966 moving to the Lincolnshire League, winning the Cup and League double at the first attempt.

From there they changed to the Central Alliance and the East Midlands Regional League, with little success, but following the appointment of Barry Shaw as manager they finished runners up, in what was then re-named the Midlands Regional Alliance. A year later they were unbeaten as they swept to the League and Cup double. They sought a new challenge and finished third in the UCL Division One, before winning the title a year later from Newport Pagnell on goal difference.

Despite Cup wins, the lack of floodlights prevented the club moving up and the side broke up. In 1994 they had a traumatic time as financial problems nearly closed the club, but happily they have survived although still struggling at the wrong end.

HIGHAM TOWN

Vine Hill Drive, Higham Ferrers, Northants. Tel: 01933 353751

Secretary: Chris Ruff, 23 Queensway, Higham Ferrers,
Northants NN10 8BU Tel: 01933 358862

Match Sec: Robin James, 26 Brampton Close,
Eastcotts Rd, Millfield, Bedford, Tel: 01234 305127

Nickname: The Lankies

Colours Sky and Navy Blue

Capacity: 1,000

Seating: None

Covered standing: 100

Floodlights: No

Clubhouse on ground: Yes

DIRECTIONS

From Kettering 1st right on A6
after A45 junction to St Neots.
From Bedford, 3rd left after
entering town on A6 from
Rushden. Higham is served by
London-Bedford-Corby United
Counties Coachlines, and United
Counties local services
Northampton-Raunds and
Bedford-Kettering.

Record attendance: 5,700 v Chesterfield FA Cup Qual Rd 1922

Biggest win: 15-0 v Towcester UCL 1993

Biggest defeat: 3-20 v Kettering Town East Midlands League

Record appearances: Brian Harbour 485

Record goalscorer in one season: Stuart Sinfield 52

Record goalscorer in aggregate: Stuart Sinfield 136

HONOURS

Northants League 1922 and 1923, Northants Senior Cup 1922

Maunsell Premier Cup 1923 and 1934, Northants Junior Cup 1921

Manager for 1996-97: Gary Savage

Assistant manager: Alan Strickland

Chairman: Richard Williams

Vice chairman: Brian Kirk

Planning application has been put in for a new ground for Higham Town FC

The current club started in 1920 with President Billy Brown, a dairy farmer, sparing little expense in ensuring the club were given a good start. After finishing runners up in the Wellingborough League and winning the Junior Cup, the Lankies moved into the Northants League where success followed success.They won the league in 1922 and 1923, along with the Senior and Maunsell Cups, but the highlight was a 12 match FA Cup run which ended at Chesterfield. They were again champions in 1924 and 1927 but in 1934 they took on Northampton Town in the Maunsell Cup final and beat them 2-1. The Cobblers had earlier beaten Football League leaders Huddersfield Town in the FA Cup and this led to the club being called the "Kings of England". Within two years the glory days were forgotten as the professional days quickly became a thing of the past and humiliation took their place. Kettering beat them 20-3 in a league match and following another 12-0 defeat they were suspended and folded. It was 1946 before they re-appeared as an amateur side in the Rushden League, but within four years they were back in the UCL. The lack of facilities at Vine Hill Drive, their home since the 20's has prevented the club from moving on, as four runners up spots in the 90's will testify, but with plans in hand for a move, the Premier Division could be coming soon to the Lankies.

HOLBEACH UNITED

Carters Park, Park Road, Holbeach, Lincs. Tel: 01406 424761

Secretary: John Crunkhorn, The Old Nurseries,
Bakers Corner, High Road, Whaplode, Spalding,
Lincs PE12 6AU. Tel: 01406 422540

Nickname: The Tigers

Capacity: 4,000

Colours: Old Gold and Black stripes

Seating: 200

Covered standing: 450

Clubhouse: Yes

Record attendance: 4,094 v Wisbech 1954

Honours

United Counties League 1990

UCL Knock out Cup 1965 and 1990

Lins Senior A Cup 1984, 1985, 1987

Lins Senior B Cup 1958

DIRECTIONS

Holbeach is just off A17 (King's Lynn to Newark-on-Trent). From A16 and A151 approach take the second left at traffic lights in the two centre and the ground is 220 yds down Park Road on the left.

From the north Park Road is a sharp right turn at the

The Tigers were formed in 1929 and played in the Kings Lynn and Peterborough Leagues pre-war. In 1946 they joined the UCL but took until 1954 before success came with a runners up place. Soon they moved over to the Eastern Counties League for 1955 season where they stayed for seven years competing alongside the A teams of Tottenham, Arsenal, Chelsea and West Ham. There was not surprisingly little joy, with just a Lincs B Cup win in 1958, and in 1962 they moved to the Midland League, but finished last and moved back to the UCL where they remain.

They nearly took the championship in the first season back, but in 1965 they won the Knock-out Cup, beating Desborough 7-1 in the final. Another second place came in 1969, but for the next 20 years it was either good or bad for the Tigers. Two seasons in the bottom four were followed by a second in 1974, then came a barren spell until 1981 when a title was a possibility until a late fade saw them fourth. In 1982 the club reached the FA Cup 1st Round, beating Moor Green and Corby Town, and the tie with Wrexham was switched to Peterborough, where they lost 4-0.

There were a number of Cup wins in the 80's and finally in 1990 the club swept allcomers away to take the treble of UCL championship, Knock-out Cup and Benevolent Cup, also reaching the Senior Cup final.

HUNTINGDON UNITED

Sapley Park, Stoneley Close, Huntingdon. Tel: 01480 417202

Secretary: Stephen Thresh, 41 Maple Drive,
Huntingdon, Cambs PE18 7JE. Tel: 01480 417146

Match Sec: Mrs Sue Cooke, 22 Coronation Ave,
Huntingdon, Cambs PE18 7UA Tel 01480 394385

Colours: Green and Red

Floodlights: No

Capacity: 1,000

Seating: No

Floodlights: No

Covered standing: Yes

Clubhouse on ground: No

DIRECTIONS

Huntingdon is on the
A14 Kettering -
Cambridge road. The A1
and A141 will also take
you into the town
centre for Sapley Park.

Honours

Peterborough League 1975 and 1976

West Anglia League and League Cup 1996

Hunts Junior and Benevolent Cups 1996

Manager 1996-97: Andy Rossi

Assistant Manager: Matt Harwood

Chairman: John Hope

Huntingdon United were formed in 1948 by an amalgamation of two long established clubs, Huntingdon Town and Huntingdon Wanderers. The club progressed via local soccer to join the Central Amateur League before becoming founder members of the UCL first Division in 1950. They stayed for ten undistinguished years before joining the more local Peterborough League, enjoying a good spell in the 70's where they won the title in 1975 and 1976.

They stayed until becoming founder members of the Eastern Counties League Division One in 1988, but withdrew after four years for financial reasons, taking their reserves place in the Huntingdonshire League.

After finishing third and second they again became founder members, this time of the new West Anglian League, finishing runners up to Yaxley in the first season. Last season's side, managed by Andy Rossi, reached new heights. The first team were champions of the league, won the Knock-out Cup, Hunts Junior Cup and the Benevolent Cup, whilst the senior and reserve sides were runners up in the Hamblin Cup and Division One Cup.

This year United will play at Sapley Park, having carried out the necessary improvements, but next season will see them at a purpose built ground provided by the council.

IRCHESTER UNITED

Alfred Street, Irchester, Northants. Tel: 01933 312877

Secretary: Mr P Mayhew, 52 Castle Way, Barton Seagrave,
Northants Tel 01536 518542

Match Sec: Glynn Cotter, 26 Denford Way, Wellingborough,
Northants Tel 01933 402514

Colours: Red and white stripes

Capacity: 1,000

Seating: No

Covered standing: Yes

Floodlights: No

Clubhouse on ground: Yes

DIRECTIONS

Off Rushden Road to Wollaston Road, next to recreation ground.

Honours

Northants League Div 2 1931 and 1932

Northants Junior Cup 1930, 1949, 1976 res

Rushden and District League 1929, 1930, 1933 res, 1934 res, 1936, 1947, 1951, 1952, 1957

Irchester Charity Cup 10 times

Manager 1996-97: Andy Toon

The club was formed back in 1893 as Irchester Excelsior, changing to United two years later. 85 years later there was another name change when the club merged with Wellingborough Eastfield to overcome a player shortage, the name staying for ten years until a return to the more popular United was made.

In the early days the club played on the Boundleys, changing at the working men's club, and the present Alfred Street ground was first used in 1921, although during the war it was used for the war effort and ploughed up, the club using the Recreation Ground until 1952 when they returned. The Romans enjoyed their first success in 1929, with the first of a record nine championships in the Rushden League and it was retained a year later without dropping a point. They also took the Junior Cup for the first time and the Irchester Charity Cup, contested by 20 or so village teams in the area. They won the Charity Cup 10 times until it was abandoned in 1961.

They twice won Division Two of the Northants League in the 30's and had a brief spell in the semi-professional Division One, but returned to the Rushden League in 1936, duly winning it again.

The early post war years were successful with four titles and another Junior Cup and they returned to the UCL, in 1969 winning promotion in 1974.

Since then there have been the odd cup run but Irchester remain in Division One and were wooden spoonists last May.

KEMPSTON ROVERS

Hillgrounds Road, Kempston, Bedford. Tel: 01234 852346

Secretary: Alan Scott, 26 King William Rd, Kempston,
Bedford, MK42 7AT. Tel: 01234 854875

Colours: Red and white stripes

Nickname: Walnut Boys

Capacity: 2,000

Seating: 100

Covered standing: 250

Clubhouse on ground: Yes

Record goalscorer in total: Doug Jack

Record goalscorer in one season: Doug Jack 63 in 1964-65

DIRECTIONS
M1 junction 13, A421 to Kempston, Hillgrounds Road is off the B531 main Kempston-Bedford road. Entrance to Hillgrounds Road is opposite Sainsburys on the B531 - ground can be found just over two miles from Sainsbury's entrance. BR to Bedford Thameslink/Midland then bus No. 103 from Bedford town centre stops outside ground.

Honours

Bedford and District League 1908 and 1909

North Beds Charity Cup 1909

Hinchingbrooke Cup 1926, 1928, 1932

United Counties League 1958, 1974

Division One 1958 and 1986, and Division Two 1956

Knock out Cup 1956, 1958, 1960, 1975, 1977

Beds Senior Cup 1909, 1938, 1977, 1992

Rovers date to 1884 and began league football in the Bedford and District League. They won the title in 1908 and 1909 and took the North Beds Charity and Beds Senior Cups. More success came between the wars with three Hinchingbrooke Cups and a Senior Cup in 1938, after they had lost three successive finals. Rovers moved to the South Midlands League in 1927 but failed to win any honours whilst there.

After the Second War, the club switched to the UCL in 1953 and did the Division Two League and Cup double in 1956, and won the league championship in 1958, and were runners up in 1957 and 1960. Between 1957 and 1961 Rovers played in five successive finals, beating Stewart and Lloyds in 1958 and 1960.

A return to the two division format saw Rovers back in the lower half due to the lack of facilities at Hillgrounds but after putting that right they were promoted only to go straight back down in 1963.

It was 1968 before they were promoted again in second place and in 1973 the club sold their ground to move up the road to a new one and in a glorious first season saw the club take the title losing once and conceding just 16 goals. There were further Cup successes in the late 70's but in 1983 they went down, only to win Division One in 1986. Back in the top division the club began a new era on another new ground on the same road, just a stone's throw away and since then they have won the Senior Cup in 1992 and were runners up a year later and they also reached the Premier Cup final in 1992.

LONG BUCKBY

Station Rd, Long Buckby, Northants. Tel: 01327 842682

Secretary: David Austin, 6 Jubilee Close, Long Buckby,
Northants NN6 6NP. Tel: 01327 843286

Match Sec: Danny Derrig, 8 Manning Rd, Moulton,
Northampton NN3 7XE. Tel: 01604 643037

Colours: All blue

Nickname: Bucks

Capacity: 1,000

Seating: 200

Covered standing: No

Clubhouse on ground: Yes

DIRECTIONS

Near Watford Gap, M1. Long Buckby is on the B5385 off A428 Northampton-Rugby road and off B4036 Daventry - Market Harborough road at Watford. 400 yds from the station (Northampton - Rugby Line).

Record attendance: 750 v Kettering Town Northants Senior Cup Final 1984

Honours

South Northants Area Cup 1938

Rugby and District League 1946, 1947, 1948, 1949, 1950, 1951

Central Northants Combination 1955

Daventry Charity Cup 1972

Northants Junior Cup 1970 and 1971

United Counties League Knock out Cup 1985

Division Two 1971, League and Cup 1972

Division Three 1970

The club began life as Long Buckby Nomads in 1937 and joined the Northampton Town League, winning the South Area Cup in the first year, and after the war they continued winning the Rugby and District League for six consecutive years. A move to the Central Northants Combination saw another title in 1955, but the club's real success began in 1968 when they were admitted to Division Three of the UCL.

In 1970 they won the Division by five points and in 1971 they were four points clear of Higham when taking Division Two. The Station Road ground was not deemed acceptable for the top division but they again were clear of Higham in retaining the title, losing only twice all season. They also took the Knock-out Cup and the Daventry Charity Cup. The Bucks won the Northants Junior Cup in 1970 and 1971 but just missed the hat-trick a year later.

There were two more Knock-out finals in the 70's but in 1984 they reached the Senior Cup final, losing to Kettering. A year later they were runners up in the league but took the Knock-out Cup and since then they have again reached the final.

Buckby have continued to be consistent and in 1993 they relocated to a new pitch just the other side of the old stand, building a new complex away from the cricket pitch and acquiring the old clubhouse from the Berristers, at Raunds, for a tea bar.

MIRRLEES BLACKSTONE

Lincoln Rd, Stamford, Lincs. Tel: 01780 57835

Secretary: Derek Hall, 67 Ringwood, South Bretton,
Peterborough, PE3 9SR. Tel: 01733 332074

Colours: Blue and black stripes

Nickname: Stones

Capacity: 1,000

Seating: 100

Covered standing: Yes

Clubhouse on ground: Yes

Record attendance: 700 v Glinton

Biggest win: 11-0 v Brackley Town 1994

DIRECTIONS

From Stamford, on A1,
head north on A6121
towards Bourne. The
ground is in Lincoln Road,
2nd left past MB works.

Honours

Peterborough and District League 1919

Division Two 1962 and Division One 1976

Stamford and District League 1938

Lincs Senior A Cup 1993

The club's date of formation is unknown but their first recorded success came in 1919 when they dropped just two points in taking the Peterborough League. From there they appear to have returned to junior football as there were many years spent in Stamford and Bourne and District Leagues, with little success other than one Stamford title just before the War. Little was achieved or heard until they moved up again to the Peterborough League and in 1962 they took Division Two. Not until 1976 did they next enjoy success with the Division One title and the impressive facilities at Lincoln Road saw Premier Division football.

They quickly adjusted to the top division and entered the Vase in the late seventies, and in 1984 decided to move up to the UCL. They started well and after enjoying cup runs they were runners up in the First Division in 1988, and were promoted. Floodlights were installed at the ground in 1990, with Aston Villa playing a game to switch them on and in 1993 they took their first Senior honours when beating Bourne Town to win the Senior A Cup.

NEWPORT PAGNELL TOWN

Willen Road Sports Ground, Willen Rd, Newport Pagnell. Tel: 01908 611993

Secretary: John Anderson, 59 Willen Rd, Newport Pagnell,
Bucks. MK16 0DE Tel: 01908 610440

Colours: Green and white stripes

Nickname: Swans

Capacity: 2,000

Seating: 100

Covered standing: No

Clubhouse on ground: Yes

Record goalscorer in total: Alan Higgins 142

DIRECTIONS
Adjacent to A442
Newport Pagnell by-pass.

Honours

United Counties League Div 1 1983

Division One Cup 1978

North Bucks League Div 3 1965

Division 2 and 1 then Premier Div 3 times

Stantonbury Charity Cup 5 times

Joint managers 1996-97: Terry Ashton and Danny Janes

The club was formed in 1963 as a youth team under the title of Newport Pagnell Wanderers. At the time the only other club in the town was Aston Martin Lagonda. The Wanderers first game was on a pitch next to the cricket square on Bury Field Common, with changing rooms at the back of the Cannon pub in Union Street. The next season saw them as champions of the North Bucks League 3rd Division, and with the Car works team folding, many of their players joined the club which embarked on an era of great success.

They won Divisions Two and One before winning the league itself for three years, helped in no small way by Alan Higgins, who in five seasons scored 142 goals. During this period they won two Stantonbury Charity Cups and crowds flocked to the local derbies with the likes of Towcester and Olney

For 1971-72 the club moved to the South Midlands League, using the facilities at the youth club in Wolverton Road, but then in April came the long awaited move to the new Willen Road Sportsground, and with it came a change of name to Newport Pagnell Town FC.

After one year the club switched to the United Counties League, where they won Division One, and the Knock-out Cup. They lasted four years in the top flight but were relegated in 1986. Fortunes improved as the 90's came around and with senior status came promotion to the Premier Division again. Sadly last May saw the end of a traumatic season with Town in last but one place.

NORTHAMPTON O.N. CHENECKS

Old Northamptonians Sports Ground, Billing Road, Northampton. Tel: 01604 34045

Secretary: John Goodger, 74 Beech Avenue, Abington,
Northampton NN3 2JG Tel 01604 717224

Colours: Blue and white

Floodlights: No

Capacity: 1,350

Seating: Yes

Covered standing: Yes

Clubhouse on ground: Yes

DIRECTIONS

South ring road, exit A43 Kettering, left at lights, top of hill, ground 200 yds on right.

Honours

United Counties League Division One 1978 and 1980

Daventry Charity Cup 1985

Manager 1996-97: Neil McAllister

The club was founded as Chenecks FC in 1946, with the intention that Northampton Grammar School Boys would be able to play football rather than rugby, under the guidance of George Lloyd, a well known Coroners sergeant in the Borough police. The unusual name is derived from the school houses, Chipseys, Spencer, Becketts and St Crispin. They played in the Northampton Minor League for Under 17's but as they grew older they progressed to the Town League in 1950, playing at Abington Park.

In 1960 the Old Northamptonians association invited the club to become one of their sports sections, thus they became O.N. Chenecks and relocated to Billing Road. They moved into the UCL in 1969 and despite being unbeaten, they were promoted only as runners up, behind Belsize FC, to Division One. In 1978 they took the title by some 14 points, but they could not go up, despite finishing second a year later and winning the division again a year after that. The senior side won the Daventry Charity Cup in 1985 and the reserves won promotion in 1990, but the best season in recent years was in 1994 when they reached the final of the Junior Cup, losing to Vanaid.

NORTHAMPTON SPENCER

Kingsthorpe Mill, Studland Rd, Kingsthorpe, Northampton NN3 1NF. Tel: 01604 718898

Secretary: Roger Linnell, 53 Muscott Lane, Duston,
Northampton NN5 6HH Tel 01604 471327

Andy Goldsmith, 15 Mealey Close, Rectory Farm,
Northampton Tel 01604 412382

Nickname: Millers   Colours: Yellow and Green

Capacity: 2,000   Seating: 100

Covered standing: 350   Clubhouse on ground: Yes

Record attendance: 800 v Nottingham Forest 1993

Biggest win: 9-3 v Bourne Town 1995-96

DIRECTIONS

Turn off Kingsthorpe Road at traffic lights into Thornton Road, turn right into Studland Road, ground at end.

HONOURS

Pinner Cup 1937

Northants Junior League Div 3 1939, Gorrell Barnes Cup 1947

Northampton Town League 1958, 1960, 1967, Towcester Charity Cup 1960

Daventry Charity Cup 1960, 1966, 1967, 1968, 1969, 1975, 1991

United Counties League Premier Div 1992, Division One 1985

Knock-Out Cup 1989 and 1994, Benevolent Cup 1992

Manager for 1996-97: Gary Sargent, Assistant Manager: Keith Bowen, Chairman: Graham Wrighting

Northampton Spencer FC can trace its history back to 1936 when Spencer School Old Boys FC were born. The team was based on members of the old school team and entered the Northants Lower Junior League. In the early days the club wore black and green quarters and soon saw their first silverware, winning the Pinner Cup in the first season. Just prior to the War they clinched the Division Three title. At the end of hostilities the club was reformed and won the much prized Gorrell Barnes Cup in 1947. In the early 50's they began to struggle and were nearly relegated, but after a couple of poor seasons the fortunes changed for the better. In 1960 they took the Daventry Charity Cup as well as the Northampton Town League title, for the first time in 34 years, winning the Towcester Charity Cup for good measure. By the end of 1967 season, the club had won almost all the trophies on offer and began to look for a new challenge. With the town in United Counties League area, they made an application, but it was turned down and they did not join until 1968, where they finished in runners up spot and were promoted, scoring 123 goals in 36 games. After the first season in the top flight the club moved from Dallington Park to Duston High School, where they played for a year before moving again to the present ground at Kingsthorpe Mill.

Originally it was a private sports ground belonging to Plessey's, but had no proper approach road. The changing rooms were two old church rooms from Long Buckby and were modified and put to use. Over the years the ground has been upgraded, so that after a few mediocre seasons, where relegation was suffered, the Division One championship was won in 1985, and they took their place again.

Gary Sargent took over the club and in 1988 they got to the final of the Knock-Out Cup, but went one better a year later when beating Ramsey Town in the final. In 1991 they finished fifth as well as taking the Daventry Charity Cup and a year later they completed the club's best season, when winning the championship and the Benevolent Cup. 1993 saw another fine campaign end in second place, but it was in the cups that they took the headlines, reaching the Northants Senior Cup Final and winning the Knock-Out Cup beating Raunds Town.

NORTHAMPTON VANAID

Fernie Fields, Moulton, Northampton Tel: 01604 670366

Secretary: Mrs June Loveday, 28 Rickyard Rd, The Arbours,
Northampton NN3 3RR Tel 01604 451356

Match Sec: Tony Loveday, Same address

Colours: Blue and black

Nickname: Vans

Capacity: 700

Floodlights: No

Seating: Yes

Covered standing: Yes

Clubhouse on ground: Yes

> **DIRECTIONS**
> Roundabout at
> Lumbertub pub take
> turn to Moulton, 1st
> right signposted.

Honours

Northants Sunday Cup 1975

UCL Division One 1995

Northants Junior Cup 1995

Northampton Town League 1989 and 1990

Manager 1996-97: Dick Underwood

The club was formed in 1968 as a works team for Sileby Engineering Company, called Sileby Rangers. They began in Sunday football and made rapid progress through the Sunday Alliance to become one of the top sides in the county, winning the Northants Sunday Cup in 1975 with three other final appearances.

In the mid-eighties they moved across to Saturday football and won the Town League twice running with runners up medals in 1991 and 1993, by which point they had become Northampton Vanaid, following a sponsorship deal. They won the Gorell Barnes Cup but lost the Junior Cup and with promotion in mind they began to develop a site in Fernie Fields to UCL standards, and they wasted no time in making an impact, winning the Junior Cup and the UCL Division One and reaching the Benevolent Cup final, but their failure to obtain planning permission for floodlights meant they were unable to move into the Premier Division.

OLNEY TOWN

Recreation Ground, East Street, Olney. Tel: 01234 712227

Secretary: Andrew Baldwin, 49 Midland Rd, Olney,
Bucks. Tel: 01234 711071

Press: Neville Thompson, 62 Dagnall Rd, Olney,
Bucks Tel: 01234 711824

Match Sec: Mick Brown 7 Midland Rd, Olney,
Bucks Tel: 01234 712498

Colours: White and black stripes

Nickname: The Nurserymen

Capacity: 2,000

Seating: None

Covered standing: None

Clubhouse on ground: Yes

Floodlights: No

Biggest win: 17-1 v Little Irchester 1960-61

Biggest defeat: 0-12 v Wellingborough Town Res 1968-69

Record appearances: John Campion

Record goalscorer in one season: 57 Dai Hunt 1974-75

Honours

United Counties League Div 1 1973

Stantonbury Charity Cup 1972

Daventry Charity Cup 1978

Berks and Bucks Intermediate Cup 1993

North Bucks League Div 1 1962, Div 2 1933 and 1964

Rushden and District League 1958 and 1961

Manager 1996-97: Alan Byron

Assistant Manager: Jim King

Chairman: Barry Simons

DIRECTIONS
Enter Olney on A509 from Wellingborough, 100 yds on left enter East Street, ground 200 yds on left.

There was football in the village as early as 1903 and Olney became founder members of the North Bucks League in 1911. They spent the next 50 years in that and the Rushden and District Leagues. There were North Bucks titles in 1933 and 1964 and they followed that with a successful spell in the Rushden League. They reached a number of League Cup finals over the years but sadly managed to lose all of them, but did take the Stantonbury Cup several times. In 1966 Town moved up to the UCL where they enjoyed five years in the top flight, playing two seasons in the FA Cup and winning the Daventry Charity Cup during the late 70's, having won Division One in 1973, but sadly the lack of a stand saw them demoted in 1980, but since then the 80's and brought some success including a Berks and Bucks Intermediate Cup win in 1993.

POTTON UNITED

The Hollow, Biggleswade Rd, Potton. Tel: 01767 261100

Secretary: Derek Inskip, 3 Bellevue Close, Potton, Beds SG19 2QA.
Tel: 01767 260355

Press officer: Bev Westhorp 3, Almond Drive, Gamlingay, Beds
SG19 3NA. Tel: 01767 650722

Nickname: Royals

Capacity: 2,000

Seating: 200

Covered standing: 150

Clubhouse on ground: Yes

Record attendance: 470 v Hastings Town FA Vase 1989

Biggest win: 10-0 twice

Biggest defeat: 0-10 Cambridge Utd FA Cup (h) 1969

Record goalscorer in one season: Ray Seekings 56 1988-89

DIRECTIONS

Outskirts of Potton on Biggleswade Road (B1040). Three and a half miles from Sandy (BR). United Counties buses from Biggleswade.

HONOURS

United Counties League 1987 and 1989

Knock-out Cup 1973, Benevolent Cup 1989, Beds Senior Cup 1948, 1949, 1964, 1976, 1978

Beds Premier Cup 1995, Wallspan Floodlit Cup 1988

Hinchingbrooke Cup 1952, 1985, 1990, 1991, 1992, Hunts Premier Cup 1990, 1992, 1995 jt

Beds Intermediate Cup 1944, Southern Combination Cup 1993

North Beds Charity Cup 1959, 1960, 1966, 1967, 1971, 1972, 1986, 1988, 1990, 1995, 1996

Manager for 1996-97: Ken Davidson

Chairman: Claude Munns

Vice Chairman: Donald Chapman

Potton Utd were formed during the Second World War, in 1943 and quickly made their mark on the limited football scene by winning the Beds Intermediate Cup in 1944. When football returned to normal the club joined the South Midlands League, remaining there until 1955, after they had finished the season as runners up. They resigned to apply for membership of a London based league, but were unsuccessful and so were forced to take a break for one year. They were offered a place in the United Counties League, vacated by Bourne Town, but only in the League Cup competition, and so a year later they moved to the Central Alliance. They finally made it to the United Counties in 1961 and have been in the Premier Division ever since. For many years they were among the 'also rans' of the league until the early 70's when they emerged as one of the most consistent sides before moving on in the late 80's to take the title twice. They also won the League Cup in 1973 and have had success in County Cups as well. The Bedfordshire Senior Cup has gone to the Hollow five times and the neighbouring Huntingdonshire Cup was shared in 1995. With a number of other successes, namely in the North Beds Charity Cup and the Benevolent Cup, Potton have enjoyed many good seasons. One of the best was in 1990, when they reached the fifth round of the FA Vase as well as winning the Hunts Premier Cup, North Beds Charity Cup and the Hinchingbrooke Cup.

The following year they retained the latter two cups, but the last couple of seasons have been disappointing with low positions in the league.

RAMSEY TOWN

Cricketfield Lane, Ramsey, Huntingdon, Cambs. Tel: 01487 814218

Secretary: Mr R.J.Baldwin, 19 Slade Close, Ramsey, Huntingdon, Cambs PE17 1JG. Tel: 01487 814084

Colours: Blue and white

Nickname: The Rams

Floodlights: Yes

Capacity: 1,000

Seating: No

Covered standing: Yes

Clubhouse on ground: Yes

Record appearances: Stuart Kilby

Record goalscorer in total: Jim Barron

DIRECTIONS
100 yds off B1040 Ramsey to Warboys road.

Honours

Hunts Junior Cup 1909

Hunts Senior Cup 1910, 1986, 1990

Hinchingbrooke Cup 1931

Scott Gatty Cup 1948

Peterborough League Division One 1960

Peterborough Senior Cup 1969, 1975, 1976, 1982

United Counties League Div 1 1989

Manager 1996-97: Gary Richardson

Formed in 1880, Ramsey's first notable honours came in 1909 when they lifted the Hunts Junior Cup, following with a Senior Cup success a year later. Between the wars was a barren period other than a Hinchingbrooke Cup win in 1931, while after the Second War in 1948, the Rams won the Scott Gatty Cup in 1948. Until then the club had played in the Huntingdon and Peterborough Leagues, until 1960 when they won the latter's Division One. Although not managing to take the Premier Division title, they did win the Peterborough Senior Cup on four occasions from 1969 to 1982. In 1985 the club took the big step forward by joining the UCL. Although enjoying consistency in Division One, the club facilities have always held them back, but Cups have been fruitful and Town won the Hunts Senior Cup in 1986 and reached the Knock-out Cup final in 1989 having won Division One by 12 points. A year later they narrowly missed a county double by winning the Senior Cup but losing the Premier Cup final.

In 1991 they missed the title in a tight finish with Daventry and lost the 1992 Hunts Senior final, and have since erected floodlights at the Cricketfield which they have used right from the start.

ROTHWELL CORINTHIANS

Seargents Lawn, Desborough Road, Rothwell, Northants. Tel: 01536 418688

Secretary: Bob Clelland, 5 Drake Close, Rothwell, NN14 6DJ. Tel: 01536 710134

Colours: Red and white   Floodlights: No

Seating: Yes   Covered standing: No

Clubhouse on ground: Yes

Honours

East Midlands Alliance 1990 and 1995

DIRECTIONS

From Rothwell on A14 (near Kettering) take the A6 north towards Desborough, on right opposite Greening Road.

Rothwell Corinthians were formed in 1932 as a church youth side and quickly progressed to the Kettering Amateur League, forerunner of today's East Midlands Alliance. They enjoyed a number of spells in the top division with the most recent being in 1984. They were champions in 1990 and 1995, the second title coming when four points ahead of Corby Strip Mills.

Recent years have seen them develop their pleasant Desborough Road ground, now re-named Sergeant's Lawn after the old 18th Century land owner.

Corinthians made an impressive start in the UCL, finishing fourth with 22 wins to their credit.

SHARNBROOK

Lodge Road, Sharnbrook. Tel: 01234 781080

Secretary: Roy Boulton, 19 St Mary's Ave, Rushden, Northants NN10 9EP. Tel 01933 315890

Colours: Claret and royal blue

Capacity: 1,000   Seating: No

Covered standing: Yes   Clubhouse on ground: Yes

Honours

Bedford and District League Division 2 1906

League and League Cup many times

UCL Div 3 Knock-out Cup 1979

Beds Intermediate Cup 1974

DIRECTIONS

Second sign to Sharnbrook from Rushden on A6, under railway bridge, right at t-junction, left past church, right into Lodge Road.

The club were formed around the turn of the century and their first recorded success came in 1906 when they won Division Two of the Bedford League. It was home for many years prior to the club's move up to the UCL in 1968. The most notable seasons were in the fifties and sixties when numerous league and cup successes were enjoyed.

They joined the new Division Three in 1968 and were runners up behind Corby Gainsborough and were promoted until 1978 when they went back down. In 1979 they won the Division League Cup and finished third whilst a year later they were runners up.

County Cup success came in 1974 with the Beds Intermediate Cup and in the early eighties they twice lost in finals although recent years have been unsuccessful.

SPALDING UNITED

Winfrey Avenue, Spalding, Lincs. Tel: 01775 713328

Secretary and Press: J.H. Grimwood, 29 Moons Green, Moulton,
Spalding, Lincs PE12 6QW. Tel: 01406 370698

Nickname: The Tulips   Capacity: 8,000

Seating: 1,000   Covered standing: 2,000

Clubhouse on ground: Yes

Record attendance: 6,973 v Peterborough United FA Cup 1952

Record appearances: Dave Arnold

Record goalscorer in one season: Harry Sharp

Record goalscorer in aggregate: Harry Sharp

DIRECTIONS

Town centre off A16, adjacent to bus station, 250 yards from Spalding (BR) station.

Honours

United Counties League 1955, 1975, 1988

Knock Out Cup 1955 and 1995

Northern Counties East League 1984, Lincs Senior Cup A 1953 and 1988

Lincs Senior Cup B 1951, Lincs Junior Cup 1933 and 1938

Evans Halshaw Floodlit Cup 1990,

Manager for 1996-97: Alan Day,   **Assistant Manager: Phil Ward**

Chairman: Rod Quinton   **Vice Chairman: Graham Chappell**

Spalding United were formed in 1921 but it would appear that football was previously played in the town under the name of Spalding Thursday. Nicknamed the Tulips through the tremendous amount of that flower which are grown in the area, they first played in the Peterborough League until the outbreak of war. They won the Lincs Junior Cup in 1933 and 1938, but after the war they joined the United Counties League which they won in 1955, completing the double with the League Cup. Previously they had won the Senior B Cup and Senior A Cup inside three seasons. Also in 1952 Spalding entertained Peterborough United in the FA Cup before a record crowd of 6,973, and after leading 2-0, Posh equalised and won the replay.

In 1955 the club moved over to the Eastern Counties League, just missing honours on several occasions before joining the Central Alliance for one year and then the new Midland Alliance, which was probably the least successful period, prompting a return to the UCL in 1968. Success came in 1973 as runners up, going one better in 1975, and runners up again in 1976.

From there the Tulips moved again, this time to the Northern Counties East, which they won in 1984, but in 1986 they returned to the UCL where they were again champions a year later. They gained promotion to the Southern League, finishing 6th and 8th in two seasons as well reaching the last eight of the FA Vase, but it was to be the last good season for some while. A loss of major sponsor meant a break up of the team and they finished last. Again it was back to the UCL, but the lack of funds and declining gates saw the club sadly go into liquidation, only for a new man, Rod Quinton to rescue the club. Since then Spalding have settled in the UCL and have reached the Knock-Out Cup final, which they won after penalties, and two 3-3 draws.

The impressive council maintained ground at Sir Halley Stewart Fields was originally known as the Black Swan Field until the 30's, as it was situated behind the pub of the same name. It has always been home, and was presented to the club in 1954 and dedicated to Sir Halley Stewart, a former MP.

ST IVES TOWN

Westwood Road, St Ives. Tel: 01480 463207

Secretary: Mr J Stocker, 23 Townsend Road, Needingworth, St Ives, Huntingdon, PE17 3SE

Tel: 01480 492680

Colours: White and black

Nickname: Saints

Capacity: 5,000

Seating: 130

Covered standing: 300

Floodlights: Yes

Clubhouse on ground: Yes

Record attendance: 400 v Saffron Walden Town FA Vase (at Westwood Rd)

DIRECTIONS

From Huntingdon: A1123 through Houghton, right at 2nd lights into Ramsey Road, after quarter mile turn right opposite Fire Station into Westwood Road.
From A604: Follow Huntingdon signs past 5 roundabouts, left into Ramsey Road.

Honours

Hunts Junior Cup 1901

Hunts Senior Cup 1901, 1912, 1923, 1926, 1930, 1982, 1987, 1988

Cambridgeshire League 1923, 1924, 1925

Scott Gatty Cup 1923, 1924, 1932, 1961

Peterborough League 1938 and Division 3 1978

Division One 1982

St Ives Town, formed in the late 1800's have enjoyed a nomadic existence playing in a variety of leagues, including Cambridgeshire, Peterborough, Central Amateur and UCL leagues.

The club was a force in local Huntingdonshire circles from the turn of the century collecting the Hunts Cup double of Senior and Junior Cups in 1901. It was 1912 before they again took the Senior Cup, but their best years were in the 20's, when playing on Meadow Lane they won trophies galore. The Cambridgeshire League was taken in three consecutive years, with Hunts Senior and Scott Gatty Cup wins, but it came to an end around 1930, when they again took the Senior Cup and had to wait until 1938 for the Peterborough League title. After the War they joined the Central Amateur League but after one season they opted for the more local UCL Second Division. That was not popular either and in 1952 they returned to the Peterborough League. It was 1961 before they took the Scott Gatty Cup and by the late 70's they had slipped to Division Three of the league. However, they won the division in 1978 and by 1982 they were Division One champions. Their impressive Westwood Road ground earned them a Premier place and in 1985 they moved back to the UCL. In the 80's the club enjoyed County success winning the Senior Cup three times and reached the re-launched Premier Cup final in 1989.

Westwood Lane ground was built after the landowners of Meadow Lane decided to sell the lease to ARC who wished to quarry it, and so their old home complete with splendid wooden stand disappeared.

ST NEOTS TOWN

Rowley Park, Cambridge Rd, St Neots, Cambs. Tel: 01480 470012

Secretary: Mrs P. Page, 75 Shakespeare Rd, Eaton Socon,
ISt Neots, Cambs PE19 3HT Tel 01480 215661

Match Secretary: Michael Stokes, Rowley Park,
Cambridge Rd, St Neots PE19 4SN Tel 01159 468866

Colours: Light and dark blue quarters

Nickname: Saints   Capacity: 3,000

Seating: Yes   Covered standing: 250

Clubhouse on ground: Yes

Record attend: 2,000 v Wisbech Town 1966 on old ground

DIRECTIONS

**From west or east A428,
from north or south A1,
through town centre, under
railway bridge, 1st left.**

Honours

Hinchingbrooke Cup 8 times

Scott Gatty Cup 13 times including 1927, 1928, 1929,

United Counties League Cup 1968 and 1969

Central Alliance League Cup 1960, Metropolitan League Professional Cup 1961

Hunts Junior Cup 3 times, Hunts Benevolent Cup 3 times

Beds Charity Cup 6 times, United Counties League 1957, 1968 Premier Div and 1995 Div 1

Fellows Senior Cup 1902, Metropolitan League and Challenge Cup 1950, Braybrooke League 4 times

Hunts Senior Cup 33 times including 1889, 4 more wins before 1900, 02, 24, 28, 36, 37, 38, 39, 54, 56, 58, 59, 60, 61, 62, 63, 64, 65, 66, 67, 68, 69, 81, Beds County League 1933, Fellows Cup 1902

The club dates right back to 1879 and the first honour recorded was in the first Hunts Senior Cup in 1889. Four more victories followed before the turn of the century and they completed the double in 1902 winning the Senior and Fellows Cups. They played at the time in the Biggleswade League, where they were runners up in 1903 and 1922. They changed the club name to St Neots and District in 1924 and won the Senior Cup, moving to the Beds County (later South Midlands) League in 1927. A runners up spot came in 1928 and they won the title in 1933, also winning another Senior Cup and three Scott Gatty Cups.

They first joined the UCL in 1936 and closed off the pre-War period with four Senior Cup wins. After the war they briefly played in the South Midlands League before becoming founder members of the Metropolitan League in 1949, winning the League and Cup double in the first season. However they were on the move again to the UCL in 1951, the Central Alliance in 1956 and back to the Met in 1960. While that was going on they took the Senior Cup in 1954 and 1956 before embarking on a run of 12 successive wins from 1958, believed to be the longest winning run in any competition in senior football.

They were runners up in the Met League in 1961, but lifted the Professional Cup and in 1966 they a re-joined the UCL, from where they reached the FA Cup 1st Round, losing to Walsall.

In 1968 they did the League and Cup double and retained the Cup a year later.

They left once more in 1969 for the Eastern Counties League but were back again in 1973, where they struggled for the next 15 years, suffering relegation in 1982, only to go straight back up as runners up.

In 1981 they won the Senior Cup for the 33rd and last time and in 1988, after winning the Hinchingbrooke Cup they folded, having lost their old Shortsands ground in mid-season as the lease expired. They re-formed a couple of years later and after four successive Hunts League titles they returned to the UCL on the new ground at Rowley Park.

STAMFORD

Wothorpe Road, Stamford, Lincs. Tel: 01780 63079

Secretary: Phil Bee, 3 Launde Gardens, Stamford, Lincs PE9 2RP. Tel: 01780 56665

Match Sec, Press Officer and Programme Editor: Andrew Easom, 36 Queens Walk, Stamford, Lincs PE9 2QE. Tel: 01780 54510

DIRECTIONS

Off A43 Kettering Road, 1 mile east of A1. 200 yards from station.

Colours: Red and white   Nickname: The Daniels

Capacity: 4,000   Seating: 200

Covered standing: 1,000   Clubhouse on ground: Yes

Record attendance: 4,200 v Kettering Town FA Cup 3rd Qualifying Rd 1953

Biggest win: 13-0 Peterborough Utd Reserves UCL 1929-30

Biggest defeat: 0-17 Rothwell Town FA Cup 1928

Record appearances: Kevin Johnson

Record goalscorer in one season: Dick Smith

Record fee received: £2,000 for B. McNamara to Northampton Town

Honours

FA VASE WINNERS 1980, FA VASE RUNNERS UP 1976 and 1984

United Counties League 1976, 78, 80, 81, 1982, Knock-out Cup 1952, 1976, 1980, 1982, 1986

Northants League 1912, Lincs Junior Cup 1949, Lincs Senior A Cup 1979 and 1983

Lincs Senior B Cup 1952 and 1954, Hinchingbrooke Cup twice

William Scarber Memorial Cup 1971, 1983, 1986, 1989, 1995, Stamford Challenge Cup 1990

Manager 1996-97: Steve Evans

Chairman: A.L Twiddy

Vice Chairman: E.W. Warrington

The present Stamford club is believed to have been formed in 1896 although evidence exists to support a club back in 1867. A number of small clubs in the town gathered to form the current club near the end of the century, but the first league action did not come until 1909. Up to then they had already forged a reputation for being cup fighters and they twice won the Hinchingbrooke Cup and in 1908 reached the last 32 of the Amateur Cup. The club turned professional when entering the Northants League and with a strong side it was no surprise when the Daniels won the title in 1912. In the late 1920's the club suffered its biggest defeat, a 17-0 hiding at Rothwell and posted their biggest win, a 13-0 result against Peterborough Utd Reserves. Little happened up to 1939 but after the war they again emerged as a force, winning the Lincs Junior Cup in 1949, the Knock-out Cup in 1952 and the Senior B Cup in 1952 and 1954. After this success the club switched to the Central Alliance and then the Midland League in 1961.

They struggled in that powerful league and in 1972 rejoined the UCL, embarking on a decade of success. After ending a 64 year wait for the title, the club added four more in six years, three Knock-Out Cups and 2 Lincs A Cups, but it was in the FA Vase that fame came to Wothorpe Road. They reached the semi-final in 1975, the first year but a year later, under Norman Rigby, they made it to Wembley only to lose to Billericay. In 1980 they were back again, to win the Vase beating Guisborough and in 1984 they made it three visits, losing this time to Stansted 3-2.

Since then the Daniels have flattered to deceive, but last season finished well above half way.

STEWARTS AND LLOYDS CORBY

Recreation Ground, Occupation Rd, Corby, Northants. Tel: 01536 401497

Secretary: David Foster, 29 Tettenhall Close, Corby,
Northants NN18 9PJ Tel 01536 742358

Colours: Yellow and blue

Nickname: None

Capacity: 1,500

Seating: 100

Covered standing: 200

Clubhouse on ground: Yes

Biggest win: 14-2 v Brackley Town 1992-93

Biggest defeat: 0-8 v Rothwell Town 1993-94

Record appearances: Jim Hamill

Record goalscorer in one season: Joey Martin 48 1992-93

DIRECTIONS

To reach Corby take either the A6003 or A43 from the north and south and the A427 from the west (off A6). The ground is on Occupation Road at the rear of Stewart & Lloyds Leisure Club, next to old Corby Town FC ground.

Honours

Northants Senior Cup 1938 and 1940

Kettering Amateur League 1954

United Counties Div 1 League and League Cup 1974 and 1975

Premier and Div 1 Cup 1987

Manager 1996-97: Elwyn Roberts

Assistant Manager: Stuart Carmichael

Chairman: P L Webb

Vice Chairman: H Nelson and G Hall

Formed in 1935 as a works side for the Iron and Steel firm, they joined the UCL straight away, as the Northants League, and were successful pre-War finishing runners up and twice winning the Northants Senior Cup. In 1948 it was decided to form a town club more representative of the growing community and Corby Town FC was born. Effectively the club split in two with Stewarts playing on in the Kettering Amateur League. In 1954 they won the league having reached the Northants Junior Cup a year earlier and in 1957 they were back in the UCL.

On re-organisation in 1961 they retained a place in the top flight but were relegated in 1966. The 70's saw an upturn in fortunes as they took Division One league and cup doubles, which brought a place in the Premier which they have retained ever since.

Their only honour at senior level has been the Knock-out Cup, which in bizarre fashion the Steelmen played a leg against Spalding who were removed from the competition to allow Irthlingborough in to play a one leg final, which Stewart's won!

In 1989 with the future of the club in doubt, local businessman John Georgiou rescued them, as part of the deal they were re-named Hamlet S & L reflecting the company backing the club. The old name was restored in 1992, and lights were erected in 1993, a year that saw the club play in the FA Cup for the first time since the late 40's.

STOTFOLD

Roker Park, The Green, Stotfold, Herts. Tel: 01462 730765

Secretary: Mr W. Clegg, 12 Common Road, Stotfold,
Hitchin, Herts SG5 4BX. Tel: 01462 730421

Match Sec: Mr C. Kirkham, 43 Mowbray Crescent,
Stotfold, Hitchin, Herts SG5 4DY Tel 01462 732279

Colours: Amber and black   Nickname: Eagles

Capacity: 3,000   Seating: 200

Covered standing: No   Clubhouse on ground: Yes

Record attendance: 1,000 v Letchworth Town in FA Amateur Cup

Record appearances: Dave Chellew 450 to date

Record goalscorer in one season: Roy Boon 51

Record goalscorer in total: Roy Boon

DIRECTIONS

A507 from A1, right at lights, right at T-junction. A507 from Bedford via Shefford, left at lights, right at T-junction.

Honours

Biggleswade and District League 1912

Beds Senior Cup 1965 and 1993

Beds Premier Cup 1982, 1992, 1994

Beds Intermediate Cup 1959

South Midlands League Division One 1954

Premier Division 1981

Challenge Trophy 1982

North Beds Charity Cup 1956, 1957, 1962, 1982, 1988, 1991, 1993

Southern Combination Cup 1995 and 1996

Manager 1996-97: Ian Allinson

Assistant Manager: Gordon Brown

Chairman: John Talbot

Vice Chairman: Tom Peacock

The first record of football in Stotfold is in the Biggleswade Chronicle in September 1904, but it is believed that a club existed before that. In 1906 they played in the Biggleswade League as a junior side, taking the title in 1912, the first season that they used the meadow now known as Roker Park. After the Great War they played at Smith's Meadow as Stotfold Athletic and were runners up in the league and Scott Gatty Cup. 1924 saw them again lose the Scott Gatty Final, before moving into the North Herts League.

After the Second War the club was started up as Stotfold Youth and played at Hitchin Road Rec and in 1951 they joined the South Midland League Division Two and were soon promoted up to the Premier Division, where they remained for 30 years. Despite finishing runners up nine times, they won just one title, in 1981, with a sole Beds Senior Cup win in 1965 to add to it. It was that year that saw Stotfold move back to Roker Park, which was good enough to stage UCL football from 1984. Since then the club have become established and won the Beds Premier Cup in 1992 and the Senior Cup in 1994. Twice in the last three seasons the club have come close to the title, finishing runners up both times.

THRAPSTON TOWN

Chancery Lane, Thrapston. Tel: 01832 732470

Secretary: B Harrison, 23 Springfield Ave Thrapston,
Kettering, Northants NN14 4TJ. Tel: 01832 732150

Match Sec: Mrs A Petts, Draycott House, Loop Rd,
Keyston, Cambs PE18 0RE Tel 01832 710629

Colours: White and blue

Nickname: Venturas

Floodlights: No

Capacity: 1,000

Seating: Yes

Covered standing: No

Clubhouse on ground: Yes

DIRECTIONS

Thrapston is on A14
Huntingdon to Kettering
road where A45 from the
south and A605 from
Peterborough meet.

Honours

Northants Junior Cup 1989

Kettering Amateur League 1971, 1973, 1974, 1977, 1978

Munton Cup four times including 1971 and 1977

Until last May the club were named Thrapston Venturas and were the fourth club from the town to play in the UCL, with United, Engineers and Town all going before them. They all faded when Venturas came on the scene in 1961, playing in the Kettering Amateur League. They quickly worked their way up and gave notice when reaching the final of the Lower Junior Final in 1967, losing to Kings Sutton. In the 70's they dominated the league like no club before or since, winning five titles and four Munton Cups, doing the double twice. The move to the UCL in 1978 gave them a fresh challenge, but so far success has more elusive.

Their best ever season was in 1987 when they challenged for the Division one title before finishing fifth, and since then they have taken the Northants Junior Cup, beating Perkins Sports in a replay in 1989.

Last spring it was decided to rename the club Thrapston Town.

WELLINGBOROUGH TOWN

Dog and Duck Ground, London Road, Wellingborough, Northants. Tel: 01933 223536

Secretary: Mr M Walden, 5 Fernie Way, Wellingborough,
Northants Tel 01933 279561

Nickname: The Doughboys

Formed: 1867 (They are the 6th oldest club in the country)

Capacity: 5,000

Seating: Yes

Covered standing: Yes

Clubhouse on ground: Yes

Record attendance: 4,013 v Kettering Town

Record fee received: £1,200 for Frankie Belfon from Rushden Town

DIRECTIONS
200 yards off A45
bypass, by Dog and
Duck PH. 1 mile from
Wellingborough (BR).

HONOURS

Northants League 1896, 1911, (UCL) 1963 and 1965

Northants League Div 2 1906

Metropolitan League 1970

Northants Senior Cup 1897, 1899, 1900, 1901, 1902, 1903, 1934, 1948, 1950, 1982

Maunsell Cup 1921 and 1922

Northants Junior Cup 1991 Daventry Charity Cup 1995

FA Cup 1st Round 1929, 1966

A local trader, Thomas Slinn, formed Town back in 1867 and they played friendlies until joining the Midland League and later the Southern League, in 1901. They had a number of early homes, including fields in Bassetts Close, Broad Green and Thomas Field before moving to the Dog and Duck ground in readiness for the Southern League. In 1906 a rival club Wellingborough Redwell agreed to an amalgamation, after Town had finished bottom of the league, playing in the Northampton League, now known as the United Counties. The title eluded the club, with a few near misses until the 60's when after finishing runner-up to Wisbech Town reserves, they took the league in 1963. Two years later it was repeated before the club moved on to the Metropolitan League, winning that in 1970. With sights set high they moved back to the Southern League after an absence of 65 years, but it was not a successful period and with ground gradings biting and interest waning, it was back to the UCL in 1989.

The Dog and Duck ground is a fascinating throw back to the old days when facilities were less important. The shape of the ground at once suggests it was once a cricket ground, which indeed it was 40 years ago and the collection of rickety or stark buildings with ancient perimeter fencing gives the place an air of antiquity.

Wellingborough finished last season in the lower reaches of the UCL and have much to do should they at some point wish to return for a third spell in the Southern League.

WELLINGBOROUGH WHITWORTHS

London Rd, Wellingborough. Tel: 01933 227324

Secretary: Mr R Edwards, 15 James Rd, Wellingborough,
Northants, NN8 2LR. Tel: 01933 227765

Colours: Blue and white

Capacity: 700

Seating: No

Covered standing: Yes

Clubhouse on ground: Yes

DIRECTIONS

From north and south A509 or east or west A45 to town centre. Off London Road at Dog & Duck public house.

Honours

Rushden and District League 1976 and 1977

East Midlands Alliance League Cup 1982

Whitworths are a works side who started life in the Rushden and District League and enjoyed little success until their first title in 1976, after a play off with Irthlingborough Diamonds. A year later they dropped only eight points to be champions again, moving into the East Midlands Alliance in 1978. They were there seven years without winning the league, although they reached two League Cup finals, winning one.

In 1985 they entered the UCL having carried out many improvements at their ground, including turning the pitch around, fencing off the playing area and erecting a cover. To date their highest place has been fifth the honours being confined to their reserve side of late.

WOOTTON BLUE CROSS

Weston Park, Bedford Road, Wootton, Beds. Tel: 01234 767662

Secretary: Trevor Templeman, 13 Spring Gardens,
Newport Pagnell, Bucks MK16 0EE. Tel: 01908 843565

Colours: Blue and black

Nickname: Blue Cross

Capacity: 2,000

Seating: Yes

Covered standing: Yes

Clubhouse on ground: Yes

Record attendance: 838 v Luton Town Beds Premier Cup 1988

DIRECTIONS

Four miles south of Bedford on main road through village at rear of Post Office.

Honours

United Counties Div 2 1968 and 1970

Knock-out Cup 1983 and Div 2 Cup 1965

South Midlands League 1948

Beds Senior Cup 1971

Hinchingbrooke Cup

The club is one of the oldest in Bedfordshire having been formed as long ago as 1887. They played their early football in the Bedford and District League which they won twice and didn't step up until after the Second War, when they joined the South Midlands League in 1946. They won the league in the second season and were runners up two years later. They joined the UCL in 1955 and were soon in the top division with teams moving on, but were relegated and it took eight years to return, which heralded a period of great success. In 1965 they won the Divisions Knock out Cup and the Hinchingbrooke Cup, winning the latter a further three times in consecutive years. They won Division Two in 1968 but the lack of facilities stopped them progressing. They repeated the win two years later finishing ten points clear and were promoted.

They have remained in the top flight ever since.

The club played on various pitches including the Recreation Ground, Fishers Field and the Rose and Crown, before playing at Cockfield and finally Weston Road, which they moved to in the early 70's.

Since the 80's they have won the Beds Senior and Knock-out Cups and have finished third in the league, but are yet to take the title.

YAXLEY

Leading Drove, off Holme Road, Yaxley. Tel: 01733 244928

Secretary: Malcolm Larrington, 70 Main Street, Farcet,
Peterborough PE7 3DB Tel 01733 243276

Colours: Yellow and black

Floodlights: Yes

Capacity: 1,000

Seating: Yes

Covered standing: Yes

Clubhouse on ground: Yes

DIRECTIONS
A1, then A15 at Norman Cross up to traffic lights, turn right then immediately right, follow road approx. 1 mile turn right into Holme Road, ground approx. 200 yds on left.

Honours

Hunts Senior Cup 1975, 1976, 1983, 1984

Peterborough League 1977 and 1984

Peterborough Senior Cup 1978 and 1984

Scott Gatty Cup 1993 and 1995

West Anglia League 1995

Hamblin Cup 1995

Manager 1996-97: Dave Willis

Assistant Manager: Dave Eldred

Yaxley were formed around the turn of the century but their rise to prominence started in the 60's when they began working their way through the lower divisions of the Peterborough League. By the mid-70s they were in the top division and for a while were the top team in local circles, winning the title in 1977 and 1984. They also took the Peterborough Senior Cup in 1978 and 1984 and the Hunts Senior Cup four times in nine years.

In 1989 Yaxley joined the Eastern Counties League as founder members of Division One but after three years they were thrown out as their facilities were not up to scratch. They joined the Hunts League and spent the next two years developing their new ground at Holme Road. 18 months ago they moved in, and took the inaugural West Anglia league title, Hamblin Cup, Scott Gatty Cup and Junior Cup, which was enough to see them move to the United Counties League .

PREMIER DIVISION

Taunton Town	34	25	7	2	84	20	82
Tiverton Town	34	25	4	5	101	34	79
Mangotsfield Utd	34	22	7	5	88	23	73
Torrington	34	23	4	7	64	37	73
Brislington	34	17	4	13	60	41	55
Bideford	34	16	7	11	63	47	55
Backwell Utd	34	15	7	12	54	46	52
Paulton Rovers	34	14	10	10	59	53	52
Calne Town	34	14	9	11	41	40	51
Chippenham Tn	34	11	12	11	53	41	45
Bridport	34	13	5	16	51	60	44
Bristol Man Fm	34	11	6	17	55	69	39
Westbury Utd	34	9	9	16	39	53	36
Barnstaple Town	34	10	6	18	81	78	36
Odd Down	34	6	6	22	39	77	24
Elmore	34	6	6	22	30	91	24
Frome Town	34	5	7	22	30	84	22
Crediton Utd	34	3	6	25	18	96	15

DIVISION ONE

Bridgwater Tn	36	29	3	4	93	29	90
Chard Town	36	28	6	2	65	17	90
Keynsham Town	36	22	7	7	69	35	73
Bishop Sutton	36	18	9	9	48	38	63
Clyst Rovers	36	18	7	11	74	52	61
Welton Rovers	36	15	11	10	52	43	56
Devizes Town	36	15	10	11	61	50	55
Dawlish Town	36	14	9	13	56	53	51
Melksham Town	36	13	11	12	59	54	50
Warminster Tn	36	14	6	16	51	57	48
Glastonbury	36	12	10	14	45	54	46
Wellington	36	12	8	16	47	52	44
Pewsey Vale	36	10	6	20	34	71	36
Heavitree Utd	36	9	8	19	64	81	35
Larkhall Ath	36	10	4	22	50	78	34
Amesbury Town	36	7	10	19	37	67	31
Minehead	36	8	7	21	41	73	31
Exmouth Town	36	9	3	24	44	67	30
Ilfracombe Town	36	6	11	19	43	64	29

BACKWELL UNITED

Recreation Ground, Backwell, Avon Tel: 01275 462612

Secretary: Bill Coggins, 34 Westfield Rd, Backwell,
North Somerset BS19 3ND Tel: 01275 463424

Chairman: Richard Cole, 71 Station Rd, Backwell,
North Somerset Tel: 01275 463627

Nickname: Stags

Colours: Red and White

Capacity: 1,500

Seating: 60

Covered standing: 150

Clubhouse on ground: Yes

Record attendance: 487 v Brislington 1994

Biggest win: 8-0 v Dawlish Town (A)
Western League Dec 4th 1993

Biggest defeat: 1-6 v Taunton Town 1995

Record appearances: Wayne Buxton

Record goalscorer in one season: Steve Spalding

Record goalscorer in total: Steve Edmunds

Honours

Somerset Senior League 1978, 1980, 1981, 1982, 1983

League Cup 1983

Div 1 1973

Somerset Senior Cup 1982 and 1990

SW Counties Transformer Cup 1982

Manager for 1996-97: Adrian Britton

Assistant manager: Martin Finn

Chairman: Richard Cole

DIRECTIONS

Near Backwell centre on main A370 Bristol to Weston-super-Mare road. Buses from Bristol or Weston, or 20 mins walk from nailsea & Backwell (BR) station; turn right out of station, right at traffic lights (half miles), ground quarter mile on right just past car sales.

Backwell United Football Club were formed in 1911 and played in various Bristol Leagues, including the Clevedon and District, Bristol Church of England League and Bristol Suburban League, until 1970 when they moved to the Somerset Senior League. After gaining promotion to the Premier Division they went on to win it in 1978, and then a record four times in a row to 1983. They were elected to the Western League in 1983 and stayed in the top half until 1990 when they finished runners up. Sadly, due to a problem with planning permission for floodlights, promotion was refused, but eventually they were given the go ahead and were installed in 1993. Much work has gone on to bring the Recreation Ground up to scratch for promotion was finally gained last year. Prior to the War, United played on very basic pitches around the village and it was not until last year that the Wimpey Minerals Stand was erected opposite the clubhouse, to enable them to go up.

BARNSTAPLE TOWN

Mill Road, Barnstaple, Devon Tel: 01271 43469

Secretary David Cooke, 51 Walnut Way, Barnstaple, North Devon EX32 7RF Tel: 01271 326088

Nickname: Barum,

Seating: 250,

Clubhouse on ground: Yes

Record attendance: 6,200 v Bournemouth

FA Cup 1st Round 1954

Biggest win: 12-1 Tavistock (H)

FA Cup 3rd Qualifying round 1954

Biggest defeat: 1-10 Mangotsfield Utd (A)

Western League Premier Div 1990-91

Record appearances: Trevor Burnell

Record fee received: £6,000 for Ian Doyle from Bristol City in 1978

Capacity: 5,000

Covered standing: 1,000

DIRECTIONS

From M5 junction 26, A361 towards Ilfracombe, in Barnstaple follow A361 Ilfracombe signs, second left after crossing small bridge is Mill Road.

Honours

Western League 1953 and 1980

Devon Professional Cup 1963, 1965, 1968, 1970, 1972, 1973, 1975, 1977,1978,1979, 1980, 1981

Devon St Lukes Cup 1988, Devon Senior Cup 1993, Devon Youth Cup 1949 and 1952

Manager for 1996-97: Phil Lloyd   Assistant Manager: Martin Nicholls

Chairman: Vic Hamilton-Philip

Barnstaple Town were founded in 1904 as Pilton Yeo Vale, becoming founder members of the North Devon League. The first ever match was on October 1st where they were defeated 4-2 by Ilfracombe at Pilton Park. At the end of the season, the club changed its name to Barnstaple Town FC.

They continued in that league, then the Exeter and District and South Western Leagues until joining the Western League in 1948. Five years later the title was won, winning 6-1 on the last day and pipping Street by .001 of a goal. Their second championship was also close, beating Bridport on the last day.

Barum have reached the FA Cup 1st Round proper on four occasions, losing to Folkestone in 1951 and three years later they lost to Bournemouth and Boscombe in front of over 6,000 people, a record which stands today.

The last appearance was in 1972, when they lost to Bilston Town, but in recent times the FA Vase has proved to be a competition to their liking, Barum reaching the 4th round in 1995 before losing to eventual winners Arlesey Town. Mill Road has undergone a transformation in recent years, establishing it as one of Devon's premier grounds. The old chicken run which stretched down one side has been replaced by a new version and a new clubhouse has gone up.

The move to Mill Road is believed to have been around 1936, when the main stand was built into the grass banking surrounding the pitch. Until then a number of grounds had been used, including Town Wharf until the First War, and then Highfield Road in Newport and pitches in Pilton and Rock Parks.

BIDEFORD

The Sports Ground, Kingsley Road, Bideford Devon Tel: 012374 74974

Secretary: Ron Ackland, Korna House, Shebbear,
North Devon EX21 5RU Tel: 01409 281451

Chairman: Jim McElwee, 9 Abbotsham Road, Bideford

Nickname: The Robins

Colours: Red and white　　　Capacity: 6,000

Seating: 120,　　　　　　　Covered standing: 3,000

Clubhouse on ground: Yes

DIRECTIONS
A39 then A361 or A386 south to Bideford - ground on right as you enter the town.

Record attendance: 5,750 v Gloucester City

FA Cup 4th Qual Rd 1949

Biggest win: 16-0 v Soundwell 1950-51

Biggest defeat: 0-10 v Bristol City 1951-52

Record appearances: Derek May 528 League only

Record goalscorer in one season: Tom Robinson 54 in 35 games in 1950-51

Record goalscorer in total: Tom Robinson 259

Record fee received: £15,000 from Stoke City for Peter Griffiths Nov 1980

Honours

Western League 1964, 1971, 1972, 1982, 1983, Div 1 in 1952 and Div 3 in 1950

League Cup 1972 and 1985, Alan Young Cup 1965 and 1970, Merit Cup 1969

Devon Senior Cup 1980, Devon St Lukes Cup 1982, 1984, 1986, 1996

Manager for 1996-97: Pete Buckingham

Bideford AFC are publishing 50 Golden Years, a history of Bideford AFC from 1946 to 1996, and it is available from the Secretary at the club.

Bideford AFC were formed in 1946 as successors to Bideford Town and Bideford Utd. An early Bideford side were one of the founder members of the North Devon League in 1904. The current club joined the Western League in 1949, winning the Division Three Championship by 7 points. That year saw the Robins reach the 4th qualifying round of the FA Cup where the record crowd of 5,750 saw a 1-1 draw with Gloucester City. 1951-52 was a record breaking year when the Division Two title was won with 179 goals in only 36 league games. The 1960's were ushered in by manager Ken Whitfield who played 280 times for the club as they won the league in 1964 and were runners-up three times. They also reached the 1st Round of the Cup, losing to Colchester in a replay. The next title came in 1971, finishing 6 points clear of Andover and a year later they pipped Minehead to retain the trophy. It saw Bideford accepted into the Southern League, which they remained in for just three seasons, one of which was topped by another appearance in the FA Cup 1st Round, the run included a five match epic against Falmouth Town. Financial pressures saw them back in the Western League where they were twice again runners up, but the 80's saw the title won in consecutive years. Recently the title has eluded the club but the St Lukes Cup finally arrived in 1996 when the Robins beat Torrington to break the stranglehold of rivals Tiverton. Bideford have played at the Sports Ground for most of their existence, other than for one season at the Hansen Ground. The Sports Ground was bought by local businessmen just before the War and was shared with the rugby club until the early fifties, when the football club bought a site of their own at the Hansen Ground. It was not a success and after one season the two clubs switched grounds, and both still play at their adopted homes.

BRIDGWATER TOWN

Fairfax Park, Fairfax Road, Bridgwater, Som Tel: 01278 446899 matchdays only

Secretary: Sally Wright, 37 Kidsbury Rd, Bridgwater,
Som Tel: 01278 421189

Colours: Red and white

Nickname: Robins

Capacity: 2,000

Seating: Yes

Covered standing: No

Floodlights: Yes

DIRECTIONS

M5 junction 23, follow signs to Glastonbury (A39), turn right for Bridgwater (A39), turn left for Bridgwater College (Parkway), ground half a mile on right; enter through college. One mile from Bridgwater (BR).

Clubhouse on ground: No, the club use the Sportsman pub two minutes away

Record attendance for new club: 1,112 v Taunton Town Western League Premier Aug 1996

Honours

Somerset Senior Cup 1994, 1995 and 1996

Somerset Senior League 1990 and 1992

Manager for 1996-97: Alan Hooker

Assistant manager: Matt Lazenby

Chairman: Keith Setter

The original Bridgwater Town had a long career in Western and Southern League football, playing on their Castlefield ground until massive financial problems saw them fold in the early 1980's.

Soon after, the new club were formed, starting in Division One of the Somerset Senior League, before gaining promotion and winning the league three times as well as the League Cup and the Somerset Senior Cup. Almost from the start the new club played at a ground next to the College in the town, which was enhanced by a splendid grandstand, the envy of many in the Western League, let alone the Somerset Senior. After much work to provide changing rooms and refreshment rooms on site, the club were elected into the Western League in 1994, finishing sixth before gaining promotion as champions on goal difference from Chard Town last May. With the installation of floodlights, Fairfax Park, in the shade of the imposing new Bridgwater and Albion Rugby ground, moves into another era.

BRIDPORT

St Mary's Field, Bridport, Dorset Tel: 01308 423834

Secretary: Keith Morgan, 95 Orchard Crescent, Bridport,
Dorset Tel: 01308 425113

Colours: Red and black

Nickname: Bees

Seating: Yes

Covered standing: Yes

Capacity: 2,000

Clubhouse on ground: Yes

Record attendance: 1,150 v Exeter City in 1981
at St Mary's Field

Record fee paid: £1,000 for Steve Crabb

Record Fee received : £2,000 for Tommy Henderson

Honours

Western League Cup 1971, 1973, 1978

Merit Cup: 1970, 1972, 1974

Dorset Combination 1986, 1987, 1988

League Cup 1987 and 1988

Dorset Senior Cup 1964, 1970, 1971, 1976, 1979, 1980, 1981, 1988

Dorset Senior Amateur Cup 1949, 1950, 1955, 1957, 1971, 1972

West Dorset Challenge Bowl 1908

Perry Street League 1923

Mark Frowde Cup 1977 and 1989

Manager for 1996-97: Phil Simkin

Chairman: David Fowler

DIRECTIONS
A35 to Bridport. Take West Bay road from town centre, turn right immediately before Palmers Brewery.

BRISLINGTON

Ironmould Lane, Brislington, Bristol Tel: 01179 774030

Secretary: Frank Durbin, 52 Arlington Rd, St Annes,
Bristol BS4 4AJ Tel: 01179 854107

Colours: Red and black

Nickname: Briz

Capacity: 1,000

Seating: 144

Covered standing: 200

Clubhouse on ground: Yes

Record attendance: 422

Record appearances Richard Ollis

DIRECTIONS

Four miles out of Bristol on main A4 to Bath - turn left opposite Garden centre.

Honours

Church of England League U 17 1959

Somerset Intermediate Cup 1962

Gloucestershire Minor Cup 1962

Suburban League Div 6 1962, Div 5 1963, Div 3 1964, Div 2 1965

Bosley Cup 1966, 1972

Somerset League Cup 1977

Somerset Senior League 1989

Somerset Senior Cup 1989, 1991, 1993, 1995

Somerset Premier Cup 1996

Western League Div 1 1995

Fry Club Cup 1990 and 1996

Manager 1996-97: Jamie Patch

Assistant Manager: Dave Payne

Chairman: Paul Bishop

Vice Chairman: Phil Brake

The current Brislington club date to 1956 when as a youth side they played their football in Arnos Park before joining the more senior Suburban League, which brought about a move to Victory Park in the village. It remained home until 1978, the club by then having moved into the Somerset Senior League, but after having gained a new ground, the reserves remained there The new site at the back of the cricket club was a cow field and since then an immense amount of work has gone on to transform it into a ground good enough for Western League Premier Division football.

On winning the Somerset League and Cup they moved up in 1991 and begun building their own dressing rooms and clubhouse, having previously shared with the cricket club.

They soon gained promotion to the top division and last season won the Somerset Senior Cup and were semi-finalists in the Les Phillips (League) Cup. With a final position of 5th it was easily the club's finest year.

BRISTOL MANOR FARM

The Creek, Portway, Bristol Tel: 01179 683571

Secretary: John Coles, 33 Jubilee Cres, Mangotsfield,
Bristol BS7 3BB Tel 01179 563075

Press: Steve Price, 19a Deans Mead, Lawrence Weston,
Bristol BS11 0DX Tel 01179 826952

Colours: Red and Black

Nickname: The Farm

Capacity: 1,500

Seating: 84

Covered standing: 400

Clubhouse on ground: Yes

DIRECTIONS

M5 junction 18 (Avonmouth bridge), follow A4 for Bristol - U-turn on dual carriageway by Bristol & West sports ground and return for half mile on A4 - ground entrance is down narrow lane on left (hidden entrance). Near to Sea Mills station (BR Temple Meads-Severn Beach line).

Record attendance 500 v Portway Western League 1974

Biggest win: 9-0 v Crediton Utd 1995-96

Biggest defeat: 1-8 v Exmouth Town 1985-86

Record appearances: Paul Williams 823

Record goalscorer in one season: Nicky Scarrett 39 in 51 games

Record goalscorer in total: Chris Rex 222 goals in 575 games

Record fee received: £500 for Nicky Dent

Honours

Somerset Senior Div 1, Div 2 and League Cup

Western League Div 1 1983

Gloucester Challenge Trophy 1988

Manager 1996-97: Chris Rex

Assistant Manager: Dave Parsons

Chairman: Fred Wardle

Vice Chairman: Brian Bartlett

The club was formed in 1962 as Bristol Manor Farm Old Boys but was disbanded after one season. They reformed in 1964 and entered Div Six of the Suburban League and by 1967 were in Division One. During the summer of 1966 they applied to use the old Port of Bristol ground and clubhouse, which is home today and is named The Creek. In 1970 the club joined the Somerset Senior League and in 1976 they were joint top only to finish third on goal difference. The following year they were runners up to Radstock Town. 1970saw them enter the Western League and they finished 3rd, but five years later promotion came with just three defeats. In 1986 Mike Fisher retired after 12 years as manager, leaving a fine legacy which saw the Gloucester Challenge Trophy come to the club. Since those times they have held a steady position in the Premier Division.

CALNE TOWN

Bremhill View, Lickhill Rd, North End, Calne Tel: 01249 816716

Secretary: Laurie Drake, 22 Falcon Rd,
Calne SN11 8PL Tel 01249 819186

Nickname: Lilywhites

Colours: White and Black

Capacity: 2,500

Seating: 75

Covered standing: 250

Clubhouse on ground: Yes

DIRECTIONS
**Main A420 Bristol Road or M4
junction 17, A350 to
Chippenham. A4 east,
signposted Malborough. Enter
town, keep left all the way
taking slip road to North End,
off main Swindon Road.**

Record attendance: 1,100 v Swindon Town
Friendly July 1987

Biggest win: 10-0 v Heavitree Utd

Biggest defeat: 2-7 v Liskeard Athletic

Record appearance holder: Gary Swallow 259

Record goalscorer in one season: Peter Horwat 32

Honours

Wiltshire Senior Cup 1913, 1935, 1985

Wiltshire League: 1934

Division Two 1980, Division Three 1986 and Division Four 1982

Ghia Cup 1981 and 1986

Manager for 1996-97: Tom Saunders

Assistant manager: Colin Bush

Chairman: Jeff Evans

Calne Town were founded in 1886, making them one of the oldest clubs in Wiltshire and were originally known as Calne Town until 1920 when the club amalgamated with Harris FC to become Calne and Harris Utd. For 99 years Calne played local Wiltshire football, winning many honours until 1985 when a more ambitious committee was formed with the objective of bringing a higher standard of football to the town. This was achieved when they were accepted into the Western League First Division in 1986.

Via a special package deal organised by the league, Calne erected floodlights at Bremhill View soon after and in 1991 the clubhouse was extended. As runners up the club were promoted in 1993 to the Premier Division but the loss of the manager and many of the players saw them almost relegated again in 1994. Since then the club have held their own in the top division.

Bremhill View has been home since 1967 when the club moved from its original home at Anchor Road which it shared with the town cricket club.

CHARD TOWN

Town Ground, Zembard Lane, Chard, Somerset Tel: 01460 61402

Secretary and Press: Colin Dunford, 27 Manor Gardens,
Ilchester Tel: 01935 841217

Nickname: Robins

Capacity: 1,500

Seating: 60

Covered standing: 200

Clubhouse on ground: Yes

Biggest win: 16-0 v Bath City Colts

Biggest defeat: 0-12 v Bridgwater

Record appearances: Dennis Nicholls

Honours

Somerset Senior League 1950, 1954, 1960, 1968, 1970

Somerset Senior Cup 1953, 1967

Somerset Senior League Cup 1962, 1972, 1977

South-West Counties Cup 1989

Manager for 1996-97: Bob Russell

Assistant manager: Pete Smith

Chairman: Brian Beer

Vice Chairman: John Glentworth

DIRECTIONS

150 yards from the town centre, off Combe Street. 8 miles from Crewkerne BR station.

Chard Town had a brief early spell in the Somerset Senior League before joining the local Perry Street League until 1949. From there they rejoined the Somerset League until moving into the Western League in 1976. They have had two spells in the top division and last season enjoyed a long unbeaten run and were eventually pipped for the championship by Bridgwater Town.

Success came to the club after the war, with championship wins in 1950 and 1954 and the Senior Cup in 1953. Throughout the 60's and 70's the Robins were a force in the league, and within the last dozen years they have been three times runners up in Division One of the Western League.

The club were formed in 1920, and have played on their remarkable sloping Zembard Lane pitch since they moved from their Bonfire Close ground, bringing their old wooden stand with them.

The football pitch was part of a huge sports complex, now segregated but still owned by a brewery and has been a sports ground for 150 years, although the football part was created around the late twenties when Chard moved in.

CHIPPENHAM TOWN

Hardenhuish Park, Bristol Rd, Chippenham, Wilts Tel: 01249 650400

Secretary: Chris Blake, 28 Saddlers Mead, Chippenham,
Wilts SN15 3BP Tel: 01249 658212

Capacity: 4,000

Colours: All Blue

Seating: Yes

Covered standing: Yes

Clubhouse on ground: Yes

Record attendance:
4,800 v Chippenham Utd Western League 1951

Record appearances: Ian Monnery

Record goalscorer in total: Dave Ferris

DIRECTIONS

M4 Junction 17, A350 into Chippenham, follow signs for Trowbridge/Bath until roundabout, left onto A420 into town, ground 400 yds on left. 5 mins walk from railway station on main A420 Bristol Road.

Honours

Western League 1952

Div 1 1981 and Div 2 in 1953

Wiltshire Senior Cup and Shield

Wilts Senior League

Managers for 1996-97: John Freegard and Vic Flippance

Chairman: Malcolm Lyus

Football in Chippenham goes back to 1873 when the first club was formed, although some clubs from that era played under rugby and soccer codes. Town joined the Western League in 1904, but still were forced to pad out the season with friendlies as football developed slowly. The 50's were the most successful time in the town, with two sides, Town and United competing in the Western League alongside Weymouth, Cheltenham and Yeovil. The only title to come to Hardenhuish Park was in 1952 when the club was at its peak, both on and off the pitch.

Progress off the pitch has seen a clubhouse built in 1979 and new changing rooms in 1984, two years before the floodlights arrived. Harnish Park has been home to Town since September 24th 1919, when they moved in, having previously used grounds at Westmead, Lowden, Little George Lane and Malmesbury Road.

ELMORE

Horsdon Park, Tiverton, Devon Tel: 01884 252341

Secretary: Alan Cockram, c/o Elmore FC Tel: 01884 820959

Nickname: Eagles	Colours: Green and White
Capacity: 3,000	Seating: 150
Covered standing: No	Clubhouse on ground: Yes

Record attendance: 1,713 v Tiverton Town
Western League 1995

Biggest win: 17-0

Record appearances: Mark Seatherton

Record goalscorer in one season: Mark Seatherton

Record goalscorer in total: Mark Seatherton

DIRECTIONS

M5 junction 27, A373 towards Tiverton, leave at 1st sign for Tiverton & Business Park, ground 500 yards on right.

Honours

East Devon Senior Cup 1973 and 1976

Western League Cup 1991 and 1995

Devon Senior Cup 1988

Devon Intermediate Cup 1961

Football Express Cup 1961

Exeter and District League 1961

Manager for 1996-97: Neville Crocker

Assistant manager: Robbie Moore

Chairman: Alan Cockram

Vice Chairman: P W Garnsworthy

Formed in 1947, the aim initially was to give its members the opportunity to play a variety of sports. They decided from the start to take the name of the area that the club was based in, rather than incorporate the town name, there already being a Tiverton Town FC.

They began life on a number of fields in the area, the main home being on Ailsabrook Field, just off Blundell Road. They made successful bids to buy part of the old Athletic Field in the town before purchasing the piece of ground called Slaughterhouse Field next to the old railway, in 1958. That proved to be the cornerstone of the club's achievements to date, as they are still based there at what is now known as Hordon Park.

Elmore played in the Tiverton, Exeter and District and South-Western Leagues before finally gaining entry to the Western League in 1978. As a junior club they won numerous trophies but by far the best season, and ultimately the most controversial, was in 1994-95 when Elmore and Tiverton battled out a furious fight at the top of the table, before the Eagles conceded the league but took the League Cup, beating Tivvy in the semi-final and Taunton in the final.

Inevitably the team broke up and last season they escaped the drop with a last day win.

MANGOTSFIELD UNITED

Cossham Street, Mangotsfield, Bristol BS17 3EW Tel: 01179 560119
Secretary: Mr Roger Gray, 105 Chiltern Close, Warmley, Bristol, BS15 5UW Tel: 01179 616523

Club shop manager: Dave Smale, 148 Cotswold Rd, Bedminster, Bristol BS3 4NP Tel: 01179 9878594

Prog Editor: Rob Smale, Tel: 01179 9401926

Nickname: The Field   Colours: Maroon and white

Capacity: 2,500,   Seating: 300

Covered standing: 1000   Clubhouse on ground: Yes

Record attendance: 1,253 v Bath City FA Cup 1974

Record appearances: Geoff Long

Record goalscorer in one season: John Hill 57 in 1968-69

Record goalscorer in total: Geoff Long

Record fee received £300 for Vic Barney from Clevedon Town

Honours

Bristol and District League Div 7 1952, Div 6 1953

Div 4 1954, Div 3 1955, Div 2 1956

Bristol Premier Combination 1969

Western League 1991, League Cup 1974

Somerset Premier Cup 1988

Glos Senior Cup 1969 and 1976, Glos FA Trophy 1985, 1987, 1991, 1994

Hungerford Invitation Cup 1975

Hanham Invitation Charity Cup 1985 and 1986

MANAGER FOR 1996-97: Terry Rowles   **ASSISTANT MANAGER: Andy Perrett**

CHAIRMAN: Richard Davis

DIRECTIONS

M4 junction 19, M32 junction 1; A4174 marked Downend, through lights, over double mini roundabout to Mangotsfield, left by village church onto B4465 signposted Pucklechurch, ground quarter mile on right. From central Bristol take A432 through Fishponds, Staple Hill, to Mangotsfield and turn right by village church onto B4465. From Bath/Keynsham follow A4175, right at island at Willsbridge onto A431, then rejoin A4175 at next island (Cherry Garden Hill) to Bridge Yate, straight over double mini roundabout and take 1st left, right into Carsons Road after 1 mile and follow to Mangotsfield Village & turn right by Church onto B4465.

A club called Mangotsfield were one of the founder members of the Western League in 1892, when it was known as the Bristol and District League. They ended that year with just eight points and continued to struggle against the likes of Warmley and Eastville Rovers. A couple of years later the club left the league.

The modern day club were founded in 1950 and played in a vastly different Bristol and District League until 1967, starting at Division Six and winning successive divisions until elected to the Premier League, which they won in 1969, as well as the Gloucester Senior Amateur Cup. United joined the Western League in 1972 and turned professional a year later, winning the League Cup.

The 80's started on a low note when they were relegated, but they bounced straight back up and have remained at the top flight ever since. Recent years have seen United as a strong club challenging for honours each year and in a superb season in 1990-91 Harold Jarman's side won the League in style, but despite tremendous improvements on the ground which included a 300 seater stand, it was with much sadness that they were rejected by the Southern League.

Last season saw the club go agonisingly close to the FA Vase Final, only beaten in extra time of the semi-final, manager Terry Rowles just failing to emulate his feat with Taunton Town two years earlier. Town have always played at Cossham Street, which until the Western League days was part of the adjoining field until segregated and fenced off as per the league rules.

ODD DOWN

Combe Hay Lane, Odd Down, Bath Tel: 01225 832491

Secretary: Mike Mancini, 36 Caledonian Rd,
East Twerton, Bath BA3 2RD Tel: 01225 423293

Colours: White and black

Capacity: 1,000

Seating: Yes

Covered standing: No

Clubhouse on ground: Yes

Biggest win: 11-1 v Minehead (H) Western League March 19th 1994

Record appearances: Lee Burns and Tony Ridewood

Record goalscorer in total: Joe Motano 89

DIRECTIONS

On main Bath/Exeter road -
leaving Bath turn left into
Coombe Hay Lane opposite
Lamplighters Pub. 40 mins
walk from Bath (BR).

Honours

Western League Div 1 1993

Somerset Senior Cup 1992

Manager for 1996-97: Alan Pridham

Chairman: N Fenwick

Odd Down FC were formed around the turn of the century and have played in both Wiltshire and Somerset Senior Leagues as well as the Bath and District League in earlier days.

Success has been sporadic but in recent years they have captured the Somerset Senior Cup and have been promoted as champions of Division One of the Western League in 1993. To take their rightful place much work had to be done at Combe Hay Lane, with an extension to the stand and floodlights being the main tasks. Combe Hay Lane has been home since the early thirties, when there was one pitch as opposed to the two they have now. The five and a half acre site has undergone a number of changes, having once been the home of Fairway Cricket Club who had a small pavilion where the changing rooms are now. Having previously played on a field at Stirtingate Farm, in Englishcombe Lane and later at the Quarr Ground, covered by Clark's Shoe Factory, they moved to their present home where they changed in a small shack. Milk Churns full of water were brought from the nearby Burnt House Inn to wash with, but after the War a redundant building was installed until the cricket club moved out and the pavilion was taken over.

PAULTON ROVERS

Athletic Ground, Winterfield Rd, Paulton, Somerset Tel: 01761 412907

Secretary Mr John Pool, 111 Charlton Park, Midsomer Norton, Somerset BA3 4BP Tel 01761 415190

DIRECTIONS

Leave A39 at Farrington Gurney (approx 15 miles south of Bristol), follow A362 marked Radstock for two miles, left at junction B3355 to Paulton, ground on right. Bus services from Bristol and Bath.

Colours: White and maroon trim

Nickname: Rovers

Capacity: 3, 000

Seating: Yes

Covered standing: Yes

Clubhouse on ground: Yes

Record attendance: 2, 000 v Crewe Alex FA Cup 1906

Honours

Somerset Senior Cup 1901, 1903, 1904, 1908, 1909, 1910, 1935, 1968, 1969, 1972, 1973, 1975

Somerset Senior League 1901, 1904, 1905, 1971, 1972, 1973, 1974

Manager for 1996-97: John Goss

Chairman: Dave Bissex

Formed in 1881, Paulton Rovers first joined the Western League in 1900. In that time they have had five spells in the league, albeit for three occasions they were missing for only one or two seasons. In that time they have never won the league although they are consistently one of the better sides, their best ever finish being fourth. They have however won the Somerset Senior Cup 12 times and the Senior League 7 times, the last being in 1974, when they re-admitted to the Western League after an absence of 14 years.

Although records are scarce, their best attendance is believed to be the 2,000 which saw them take on Crewe Alexandra in the FA Cup in 1906. Paulton have used a number of pitches around the village, including the Chapel Field and the Cricket Ground, and for a couple of seasons after the War, the Recreation Ground which is still in use. Originally, Winterfield Road ground ran at right angles to its current position, with one of the goals roughly where the clubhouse is now, but in 1967 an old RAF hut was bought as a Social Club, and soon after a more permanent club was built, which meant turning the pitch around.

TAUNTON TOWN

Wordsworth Drive, Taunton, Somerset TA1 2HG Tel: 01823 278191

Secretary: Ton Harr's, C/O Taunton Town FC

Programme Editor: Kerry Miller, Stantons Cottage,
East Lyng, Som. TA3 5AU Tel: 01823 698961

Colours: Sky blue and claret   Nickname: Peacocks

Capacity: 4,000,   Seating: 250

Covered standing: 1, 000,   Clubhouse on ground: Yes

Record attend: 2,960 v Torquay Utd
Western League 1958

Biggest win: 12-0 v Dawlish Town
FA Cup Prel Rd Aug 28th 1993

Biggest defeat: 0-8 v Cheltenham Town
FA Cup 2 Qual Rd Sept 28th 1991

Record appearances: Tony Payne

Record goalscorer in one season: Reg Oram 67

DIRECTIONS

Leave M5 junction 25, follow signs to town centre, at 2nd set of lights turn left into Wordsworth Drive; ground on left. 25 mins walk from Taunton (BR); turn left out of station and follow road right through town centre bearing left into East Reach. Follow road down and turn right into Wordsworth Drive shortly after Victoria pub.

Honours

FA VASE RUNNERS UP 1994

Western League 1969, 1990, 1996

Alan Young Cup 1974 and 1976 (Shared with Falmouth)

Charity Challenge Cup 1950 and 1951

Somerset Senior League 1953

Manager for 1996-97: Russell Musker   **Assistant manager: Derek Fowler**

Chairman: Tom Harris   **Vice Chairman: Tony Rutland**

Taunton Town Football Club were formed in 1947 and quickly established itself as one of the leading clubs in the South-West, winning the Somerset Senior League in 1953. Their progression continued when they joined the Western League which they won in 1969. Seeking a fresh challenge the club entered the Southern League in 1977, where they played until resigning and returning to the Western League in 1983 for financial reasons. They took the title again in 1990, pipping Liskeard Athletic by a single point and under Terry Rowles they had a memorable season, fishing second behind all conquering Tiverton Town and losing the League Cup final to them also. By far the greatest day in the club's history came that year when they reached the FA Vase final at Wembley, which they lost in controversial circumstances to Diss Town to make a hat-trick of runners up spots.

1996 saw new manager Russell Musker steer the side to their third title win, gaining revenge on Tiverton.

Town played on a number of grounds before settling at the current ground which was known as Hamilton Road until it later became Wordsworth Drive. The first few matches were played at the old Police Ground at Mountfields, which still exists as home to Wyvern Club. The next ground was at Ash Meadows, near Taunton Deane Cricket Club followed by Rose Meadows, just down the road from the current ground and now under Bloomfield Close. Victoria Park and Denmans Park in Haines Hill were next for short spells, the latter being graced with two caravans for changing and refreshments. 1954 saw the move to Hamilton Road, which is now on borrowed time, for the club have announced that a new purpose built ground is to be built at Blackbrook within the next two years.

TIVERTON TOWN

Ladysmead, Bolham Road, Tiverton, Devon EX16 8SG Tel: 01884 252397

Secretary: Ramsey Findlay, 35 Park Rd, Tiverton, Devon, EX16 6AY Tel: 01884 252397

Nickname: Tivvy or The Lacemen

Capacity: 3,000

Seating: 300

Covered standing: 700

Clubhouse on ground: Yes

Record attendance

DIRECTIONS

M5 Junction 27, west towards Twerton on A373, continue to end of dual carriageway and turn left at roundabout ground entrance 300 yds on right alongside BP petrol station.

At the Athletic Ground, 2,000 Silverton v Tiverton St Peters Tiverton Charity Cup Final 1921

At the Elms 2,800 v Yeovil and Petters Utd FA Cup Prelim Rd Sept 29th 1934

At Ladysmead v Leyton Orient FA Cup 1st Rd Nov 12th 1994

Biggest win: 15-2 Street Friendly Nov 1st 1930

In competition: 14-1 v University College SW Exeter and District League Feb 11th 1933

Biggest defeat: 0-10 v Dawlish Exeter and District League Dec 27th 1969

Record goalscorer in one season: Kevin Smith 57

Record goalscorer in total: Kevin Smith 250 1990 - to date

Honours

FA VASE FINALISTS 1993

Western League Cup (Les Phillips Cup) 1993, 1994, 1996

Western League 1994, 1995

Tiverton Charity Cup 1923

East Devon League Senior Div 1925, 1926, 1927, 1928

East Devon Senior Cup 1929, 1936, 1938, 1953, 1956, 1961, 1963, 1967,

North Devon League 1932

Plummer Cup 1933, 1935

Exeter and District League 1934, 1965

Hospital Cup 1934, 1939, 1947, 1964, 1980, 1982

Mills Hospital Cup 1937, 1950, Hunt Cup 1949, Coronation Cup 1953

Devon Senior Cup 1956, 1966 jt, Geary Cup 1958, 1966

Sellick Memorial Cup 1966, North Devon Charity Cup 1973

Devon St Lukes Cup 1991, 1992, 1993, 1994, 1995

MANAGER FOR 1996-97: Martyn Rogers,

ASSISTANT MANAGER: Jimmy Giles

CHAIRMAN: Gordon Anderson,

VICE CHAIRMAN: Dave Wright

The History of Tiverton Town Football Club, by Kerry Miller is available from the club price £9.95 + 1.50 pp. Over 160 pages with results, scorers and tables backing up the full story of Tivvy Town.

Tiverton are without question the most successful club in the West country during the last six years, winning two league titles, several County Cups and League Cups and featuring in the FA Vase Final of 1993. However, as their recently published book `The History of Tiverton Town FC' relates, there have been many hard times in the past, and only hard work and determination helped them through the 70's when a return to the Devon and Exeter League was a real possibility. The club was formed in 1913 out of the ashes of the recently folded rugby team and began playing on the Athletic Field as Tiverton Athletic. When the owners of the ground wished to devote it solely to rugby once again, Tivvy moved to another rugby field, in Blundells Road, where they began to develop an enclosed ground, and honours began to come.

Successive seasons as runners-up in the East Devon League saw them promoted to the Premier Division, which they one four years on the trot, and following a series of disputes with that league, they joined the newly formed Saturday section of the Exeter and District League. A fine wooden stand was built and opened at the ground, called the Elms, in 1935 but it was to last but a handful of years, for following the club closing down for the War, the ground was lost and never used again. It is now a lorry park.

As the seasons came and went, Tivvy enjoyed lengthy spells of success, winning the East Devon and Devon Senior Cups on several occasions, after moving to Ladysmead in 1946. Slowly the ground was developed from what was nothing more than a field, and with the Senior Cup double arriving in 1956 they made rapid progress. They remained in the Exeter League, which later became the Devon and Exeter League, until 1973, when they took the gamble of joining the Western League. Tivvy enjoyed a modicum of success in 1977 and 1979, but 1981 saw relegation with only one win. It got worse with 1984 seeing Tivvy at the bottom of the league, but with a new clubhouse and the arrival of a more professional approach, survival was achieved and in 1988 the scoring exploits of Mark Seatherton and Clive Jones saw a third place finish. A year later they went one better and with another 51 goals from Seatherton, they entered the Premier Division.

Since then, a healthy support and strong playing staff has established them as the top non-League club in Devon, and with Southern League football a future possibility, Ladysmead is set to expand.

TORRINGTON

Vicarage Field, School Lane, Great Torrington, Devon Tel: 01805 622853

Secretary: Robert Dymond, Flat 4, 26 South St,
Torrington, Devon EX38 8AA Tel: 01805 623569

Nickname: Torrie or Supergreens

Colours: Green and white hoops

Capacity: 4,000

Seating: Yes

Covered standing: Yes

Clubhouse on ground: Yes

Record appearances: Nigel Reed 450+

Record goalscorer in total Trevor Watkins 254

Record fee received: £3,000 for Dave Walter to Yeovil Town

DIRECTIONS

(From North, Barnstaple, Exeter, South Molton) in town centre turn left by parish church, turn right at swimming pool, ground behind swimming pool. Good parking. Red Bus from Bideford and Barnstaple (nearest BR station). Bus stop 300 yds from ground.

Honours

South-Western League Cup 1981

Devon and Exeter League and Cup double 1974

Senior Division 1973

Hansen Cup 1920

Westward Ho! Cup 1921, 1928

North Devon League 1948

Torridge Cup 1974

Manager for 1996-97: Frank Howarth

Chairman: Robert Dymond

Torrington Football Club was formed in 1908, but there are few records around for that period. The Parish Church ran a team which joined the town club around the same time, but following the Great War the club established itself and were the first to win the Hansen Cup in 1920, beating Bideford 1-0.

A year later they won the Westward Ho! Cup, the final attracting a crowd of over 5,000.

Between the Wars they played in both the North and East Devon Leagues until joining the Exeter and District League after the War, where they were very successful. The 60's were not so good for Torry who were relegated to the North Devon League, but they bounced back in the re-named Devon and Exeter League, winning the league and the Torridge Cup. The following season they did the league and cup double becoming the first club to do so. In 1978 Torry joined the South-Western League, finishing runners up to St Blazey in 1981 and 1983. They gained revenge in the League Cup final of that year.

1984 saw them join the Western League, where promotion was won at the first attempt. The first few years in the top flight were a struggle but 1990-91 saw a change when under John Hore they finished runners up to Mangotsfield United and lost in the League Cup final a year later.

1995 was a different story with Torry finishing bottom but escaping relegation due to the withdrawal of Saltash and Liskeard, but they again bounced back in 95-96 finishing in fourth place.

WESTBURY UNITED

Meadow Lane, Westbury, Wilts. Tel: 01373 823409

Secretary Ernie Barber, 7 Farleigh Close, Westbury,
Wilts BA13 3TF Tel: 01373 822117

Nickname: White Horse Men

Capacity: 2,000

Seating: 150

Covered standing: 200

Clubhouse on ground: Yes

Record attendance: 4,000 v Llanelli FA Cup Rd 1 1937

Record goalscorer in one season: Bill Butler 80 in 1937

Record fee received: £100 for John Atyeo in 1951

DIRECTIONS

In town centre, A350, follow signs for BR station, Meadow Lane on right (club signposted). Ten mins walk from railway station (on main London-South West + South Coast-Bristol lines).

Honours

Western League Div 1 1992

Wilts Senior Cup 1932, 1933, 1948, 1952

Wilts Combination, Wilts League 1935, 1938, 1939, 1950, 1951, 1956

Manager for 1996-97: Peter Tripp

Assistant manager: Chris Selway

Chairman: Phil Alford

Vice Chairman: Bert Back

The club's annual review of the season is now available, £1.50 inc pp

The club started in 1920, when two local sides amalgamated. Westbury Old Comrades had just won promotion to the First Division of the Wiltshire County League and they joined forces with Westbury GWR to form United.

The club struggled through the 20's, but fortunes changed in the years before the War when they won virtually everything there was and reached the First Round of the FA Cup. During that time the club had a forward by the name of Billy Butler who scored 80 goals in one season, including 30 in one month. The club bought and moved to Meadow Lane in 1934, paying £475 for the site and the first game on what was then called the Jubilee Playing Field was against Bristol City, with around 4,000 in attendance. Success came after the War in the Wilts Senior League and Senior Cup, but they did not join the Western League until 1984. Their first honour was in 1989 with the Sportsmanship Trophy, but 1992 finally saw the Division One Championship come to Meadow Lane and with it promotion.

Before the move, Westbury used the ground in Redland Lane, which to this day is still used by junior sides.

AMESBURY TOWN

Amesbury Recreation Ground, Tel: 01980 623489

Secretary: Tony Hinchcliffe, 12 Lanes Close, Amesbury
Tel 01980 624425

Colours: Royal blue,   Floodlights: Yes

Covered standing: Yes,   Seating: No

Clubhouse on ground: Yes,   Capacity: 1,000

DIRECTIONS

Amesbury is nine miles north of Salisbury from where there is an excellent bus service. Turn left at Lloyds Bank, cross bridge, left at road corner into recreation ground.

Honours

Wiltshire League Div One 1960, 1980, 1991, 1992

Wilts Subsidiary Cup 1961

Wilts County League 1980

Wilts Senior Challenge Cup 1984 and 1994

Senior Knock-out Cup 1989, 1990, 1991, 1993

WC Stokes Memorial Cup 1976, 1977, 1978, 1983, 1989

Hospital Cup 1960, 1964, 1977, 1979, 1980, 1987, 1989, 1990

Amesbury Football Club was first established in 1904 where their home matches were played in a field near to Stonehenge. After the Great War the club moved to their present ground off Recreation Road. After many years in the Salisbury and District League, Amesbury moved into the Wiltshire League where they stayed for over 40 years, before taking the bold step of joining the Western League Division One.

The clubhouse at the ground was built in 1967 to replace a couple of huts which were used for training and with the Western League in mind other improvements to the ground have transformed it in a very short space of time.

BISHOP SUTTON

Football Field, Bishop Sutton Tel: 01275 333097

Secretary: Roy Penney, 53 Ridgway Lane, Whitchurch, Bristol Tel: 01275 541392

Colours: All Blue   Floodlights: No

Clubhouse on ground: Yes   Nickname: Bishops

Seating: None,   Covered standing: Yes

Capacity: 1,000

DIRECTIONS

On A368 at rear of Butchers Arms pub - Ground signposted on left entering village from the West.

Record attendance: 400 v Bristol City Res Friendly

Record win: 15-0 v Glastonbury Res in
  Somerset Senior League

Honours

Somerset Senior League Div 1 1984

Division Two 1983, Bristol and Avon League 1981

Division Two 1980, Somerset Junior Cup 1981

Weston Youth League 1978, Chew Valley KO Cup 1984

Manager for 1996-97: Chris Mountford

CLYST ROVERS

Waterslade Park, Clyst Honiton, Devon Tel: 01392 366424

Secretary: Bob Chamberlain, Orchard Cottage,
Clyst St George Tel: 01392 873498

Colours: All blue	Nickname: Rovers
Floodlights: Yes	Founded: 1926
Clubhouse on ground: Yes	Seating: Yes
Covered standing: Yes	Capacity: 2,000

DIRECTIONS
A30 following signs for Exeter Airport. Coming from Exeter take 1st right after airport turning (ground signposted) up narrow 200 yds past Duke of York pub.

Record attendance: 768 v Tiverton Town
St Lukes Cup Final 1993

Record defeat: 0-12 v Torpoint Ath SWL 1990

Record win: 6-0 v Heavitree Utd 1990

Managers: Dean Roberts and Nick Thomas

Chairman: Bob Chamberlain

CREDITON UNITED

Lords Meadow Sports Centre, Crediton, Devon Tel: 01363 774671

Secretary: Tony Sherriff, 17 Churchill Drive, Crediton,
Devon, EX17 2DW Tel: 01363 774002

Colours: Sky and navy blue	Capacity: 2, 000
Seating: Yes	Covered standing: Yes
Clubhouse on ground: Yes	Floodlights: Yes

DIRECTIONS
A337 to Crediton from Exeter, right onto A3072 (signposted Tiverton) at White Hart Hotel, turn right into Commercial Road for Lord's Meadow Industrial Estate - Sports Centre car park 250 metres on left.

Honours

Devon and Exeter League 1988

Senior Div 1 1963 and 1967

Junior Div 3 1949 jt, 1950

East Devon Senior Cup 1934

Okehampton Challenge Cup 1973 and 1975

Whitbread Flowers Cup 1979, Bill Rees Trophy 1987

Joint managers for 1996-97: Bob Calderhead and Rob England

Crediton United have done exceptionally well during the last six years to not only survive but to gain promotion to the Premier Division of the Western League, although sadly last May they returned to Division One. With the toughest of competition around them with Tiverton Town, Elmore and Willand Rovers all close by, it is always a struggle to maintain progress. Crediton United are not the first club from the town, as before the War Jackson's United were prominent as a works team, eventually taking the name of the town in later years. Crediton United were formed after the War and played in the Exeter and District League on the Newcombe Playing Fields, gaining senior status in 1963. The scope for future development was not there, however, and when the Lords Meadow Sports Centre opened in 1976, they moved to play on a fenced off pitch on the site. Since then a clubhouse has been built on the ground, which has two stands and a modern dressing room complex in one corner. Floodlights were installed in time for the club to accept promotion to the Premier Division after they finished third in 1993.

DAWLISH TOWN

Playing Fields, off Sandy Lane, Dawlish, Devon Tel: 01626 863110

Secretary: Graham Jones, 133 Kingsdown Cres, Dawlish, Devon Tel: 01626 866004

Colours: Green and white,   Capacity: 2,000

Seating: Yes,   Covered standing: Yes

Floodlights: Yes,   Clubhouse on ground: Yes

Record attendance: 1,500 v Heavitree Utd
Devon Premier Cup quarter-final

Biggest defeat: 0-18 v Clevedon Town
Western League 1992-93

DIRECTIONS

Approx 1 mile from centre of town, off main Exeter road (A379).

Honours

Western League Cup 1981 and 1984

Devon Premier Cup 1970, 1973, 1981

Devon Senior Cup 1958 and 1968

Devon St Lukes Cup 1983

Founded in 1899, Dawlish played the majority of their football in the Exeter and District League, where they remained, until elected to the Western League in 1973. Having won the Premier Division four times in five years, the last year saw them win everything they entered locally, they finished mid-table, and indeed were third in 1983. They won the League Cup in 1981 and 1984, but relegation came in 1993 with just 8 points all season and a goals against column of 186. Division One was little better until last term when they improved to finish above mid-table.

The Playing Fields in Sandy Lane have been home since around the turn of the century, before which they used pitches at Elm Grove Road and later in Sandy Lane next to Bowerman Sawmills, virtually where the ground is today

DEVIZES TOWN

Nursteed Road, Devizes Tel: 01380 722817

Secretary: Andy Pearce, 66 Avon Rd, Devizes, Wilts Tel: 01380 727625

Colours: Red and white stripes,   Founded: 1883

Clubhouse on ground: Yes,   Floodlights: Yes

Seating: Yes,   Covered standing: None

Capacity: 2,500

DIRECTIONS

Off Nursteed Road (A342 signposted Andover); leaving town ground on right opposite Eastleigh Road.

Honours

Western League 1973

Western League Subsidiary Comp 1963

Merit Cup1976

Amateur Trophy 1969, 70, 71, 72, 73, 74.

Manager for 1996-97: Brian Newlands

EXMOUTH TOWN

King George V Ground, Southern Rd, Exmouth Tel: 01395 263348

Secretary: John Edwards, Lamorna, 5 Pinn Lane, Pinhoe, Exeter Tel: 01392 468633

Formed: 1933

Colours: Blue and white

Nickname: Town or Blues

Seating: Yes

Covered standing: Yes

Floodlights: Yes

Clubhouse on ground: Yes

Capacity: 2,500

Record attendance: 2, 395 v Liverpool Friendly 1987

Record win: 8-1 v Bristol Manor Farm 1986

Record defeat: 0 -10 v Tiverton Town St Lukes Cup 1994

Record appearances: Keith Sprague and Geoff Weeks 410 in Western League

Record goalscorer: Mel Pym 117

DIRECTIONS

On right side of main Exeter to Exmouth road (A376). Half mile from Exmouth (BR) station.

Honours

FA VASE Semi-final 1985

Western League 1984 and 1986

League Cup 1989

Devon Premier Cup 1971 and 1980

St Lukes Cup 1985, 1989, 1990

Devon Senior Cup 1951

East Devon Senior Cup 1951 and 1983

Exmouth Challenge Cup 1965, 1966, 1967, 1969, 1971, 1972, 1974

Manager for 1996-97: Rob Green

Chairman: Paul Marshall

FROME TOWN

Badgers Hill, Berkeley Rd, Frome, Somerset Tel: 01373 453643

Secretary: Mrs Sue Merrill, 56 Nightingale Ave, Frome, Somerset BA11 2UW Tel: 01373 473820

Colours: All Red,   Nickname: Robins

Capacity: 5,000,   Seating: 250

Covered standing: 800, Clubhouse on ground: Yes

DIRECTIONS
Locate 'Vine Tree Inn', Bath Road, ground 100 yds from Inn (1 mile from town centre and Frome BR station).

Record attendance: 8,000 v Leyton Orient, FA Cup 1st Rd 1958

Biggest win: 15-0 v Glastonbury Somerset Senior League 1907

Biggest defeat: 1-11 v Dorchester Town Western League 1958-59

Record goalscorer in total: Dave Allen

Honours

Wiltshire League 1910 and 1911, Western League 1979, Division Two 1920

League Cup 1980 and 1983, Merit Cup 1983, Alan Young Cup 1980

Subsidiary Cup 1960

Somerset Premier Cup 1967, 1969, 1983

Somerset Senior Cup 1933, 1934, 1951

Somerset Senior League 1907, 1909, 1911

Wiltshire Premier League 1963, Western Counties Floodlit Cup 1984

Manager 1996-97: Mike Leeson, Chairman: Colin Skirton

Formed in 1904, little is known about the early years of the club, but they joined the Western League in 1919 and made an immediate impact by winning Division Two. Promotion in those days was not automatic and when the division was disbanded they left the league, to return two years later. After another four year absence from 1927, Frome settled and in the 30's twice won the Somerset Senior Cup. They were placed in Division One when peacetime returned but were relegated, but it was the early 50's when the club saw their most exciting times, as the Senior Cup was won in 1951 again and in 1954 the Robins, under Jock Fairweather reached the 1st Round proper of the FA Cup. Much building work was carried out at the ground to enable them to stage the tie with Leyton Orient and 8,000 packed in to see them bravely lose 3-0.

To cap a superb season they were promoted to Division One as runners up. In 1959 the good times had gone again and the club were relegated to a Division Two which was again disbanded, sending Frome into the Wiltshire League. They were runners up in 1962 and a year later were champions and rejoined the Western League, winning the Somerset Premier Cup in 1967.

After two near misses in the FA Cup the Robins appointed Bob Boyd as manager in 1978 and he guided the club to their only championship win to date. He left for Bath City but returned in 1980 when they were third, but it was Steve D'arcy that took the club to a marvellous season in 1983 when the club won the League Cup and Premier Cup and were runners up in the league to Bideford.

Since then there have been a number of relegation battles, ending with last season's last game heartache.

GLASTONBURY

Abbey Moor Stadium, Godney Road, Glastonbury, Som. Tel: 01458 831460

Secretary: Mrs Lorraine Harmon, Barleys, Bere Lane, Glastonbury Tel: 01458 833221

Press Sec Les Heal 2 Lowerside Rd, Glastonbury, BA6 9BE Tel: 01458 832037

Colours: Gold and black,   Capacity: 2,000

Seating: 80,   Covered standing: 300

DIRECTIONS

At bottom of town centre take Northload Street, go straight over roundabout on new by-pass, first right after crossing bridge, ground immediately on right.

Record attendance 3, 892 v Exeter City
FA Cup 1st Round 1950 at Abbey Lawn

Biggest win: 10-0 v Portland Utd 1948
and Paulton Rovers in 1951, both Western League

Biggest defeat: 0-9 v Wellington Western League 1989

Record appearances Brian Mortimer,
Record goalscorer in total Ted Aldew

Honours

Somerset Professional Cup 1938 and 1949

Somerset Senior Cup 1937, Somerset Charity Cup 1933

Somerset Junior Cup 1912, 1913, 1914

Western League 1949, 1951 and 1970, Weston League Challenge Cup 1966

Somerset Senior League 1950 and 1951

Manager for 1996-97: Dave Sheehan

Chairman: Terry Wolff

Glastonbury FC were founded in 1890 and had an unspectacular early history, primarily in Bristol and District and Suburban League football. They had a brief spell after the Great War, in the Western League, and returned in 1931 where they finished 15th in Division Two. There was some improvement up to the Second War, with a fifth place in the last peace time season, as well as wins in the Somerset Charity, Senior and Professional Cups. After a mid-table position in 1940, the club returned to action in 1946 and a year later began what is to date their golden era.

They were runners up to Trowbridge Town in Division One in 1948 before reversing their fortunes and beating the Wiltshire side by four points twelve months later. In 1950 they came third in a desperate three way finish with Wells City and Poole Town and in 1951 they were champions again, scoring over 100 goals and losing just twice in taking the title from Wells City by five points.

1952 saw the club runners up to Chippenham Town, the last season for some time in which the club challenged.

Their next spell of success came in 1965 when they began a run of 11 seasons where they finished in the top seven, including the title in 1970, again scoring 100 goals in beating Andover by five points. Their picturesque Abbey Park ground, tucked away in the grounds of the Abbey and under the shadow of the Tor, was lost to them in 1980, when they took the agonising decision to leave their home of 60 years and move to the newly built greyhound track at Abbey Moor. Since then, the club have remained in Division One, although they were runners up at the end of a fine season in 1995, the facilities preventing them from moving up to the Premier Division.

HEAVITREE UNITED

Wingfield Park, East Wonford Hill, Exeter, Devon Tel: 01392 73020

Secretary: Keith Gilbert, 9 Dean Street, St Leonards, Exeter, Devon Tel: 01392 438637

Nickname: The Heavies

Colours: Black and Jade,   Capacity: 500

Seating: Yes,   Covered standing: None

Floodlights: No,   Clubhouse on ground: Yes

DIRECTIONS

Leave M5 at Exeter Granada Services, follow signs for City Centre/Heavitree for approx. 3 miles and ground is situated on left at top of East Wonford Hill.

Record attendance: Exeter City Friendly 1989

Biggest win: 6-0 v Ilfracombe Town

Biggest defeat: 0-13 v Larkhall Athletic

Record appearances: Alan Kingdom

Record goalscorer in total: John Laskey

Honours

Exeter and District League 1947 and 1952

Senior Div 2 1957, 1960, 1961, 1968

Devon and Exeter League 1971 and 1977

Devon Senior Cup 1947, 1961, 1971

East Devon Senior Cup 1947, 1971, 1977

Wheaton Trophy 1988

Manager for 1996-97: Steve Riley

Chairman: Denis Bray

Heavitree United were formed in 1885 and played for most of their existence in the Exeter and District League which in the early seventies became the Devon and Exeter League. They had a number of success, winning the title twice after the War as well as Senior Div 2 four times through the 60's.

In 1973 they joined the Western League First Division, where they remain to this day.

Wingfield Park has been home since soon after the War when what was land in part of an estate owned and run by a sport benefactor became available. Until then the club had played on Havitree Park, using various undeveloped pitches.

ILFRACOMBE TOWN

Marlborough Park, Ilfracombe, Devon Tel: 01271 865939

Secretary: Tony Alcock, 2 Worth Rd, Ilfracombe, Devon EX34 9JA Tel: 01271 862686

Press Sec Ron Rose, 18 The Shields, Ilfracombe Tel: 10271 863085

DIRECTIONS
A361 to Ilfracombe, 1st right in town after lights, follow Marlborough Road to top, ground on left.

Colours: All Blue,   Nickname: Bluebirds

Capacity: 3,000,   Seating: 50

Covered standing: 600,   Floodlights: Yes

Clubhouse on ground: Yes

Record attendance: 3,000 v Bristol City
Ground opening October 1924

Biggest win: 10-0 v Chipping Sodbury 1952

Biggest defeat: 1-9 v Falmouth Town FA Vase 1994

Record appearances: Paul Jenkins 410

Record goalscorer in one season Darren Bryant 28

Record goalscorer in total Paul Jenkins 392

Honours

East Devon League 1926, 1929, 1930, North Devon League 1967, 1971, 1982, 1983

Manager 1996-97: Ian Cornish, Assistant Manager: Mark Richards

Chairman: Michael Edmunds, Vice Chairman: Bob Martin

Ilfracombe Football Club were formed in 1902 and played locally until joining the new North Devon League as founder members. The present name was adopted in 1920 and in 1922 they moved to play in the East Devon League, remaining there until it folded and was replaced by the Exeter and District League. The present ground at Marlborough Park was acquired in 1923 and laid out in readiness for the 1924 season. Prior to that the club played on basic fields such as those at Killacleave, close by which was the Grammar School grounds, and Shaftesbury Fields. After the War they returned to the Exeter and District League until 1949 when they joined the Western League, playing in Division Three and winning promotion.

During 1952 they enjoyed their finest FA Cup run when reaching the 4th qualifying round, losing at Llanelli in front of over 8,000 . They were promoted again in 1953 but the rot set in but with little support and relegation, they withdrew from the league in 1959 and returned to the North Devon League. After the club's fourth championship and after some improvements to the old ground, the Bluebirds returned to the Western League in 1984, where they remain.

KEYNSHAM TOWN

Crown Field, Bristol Road, Keynsham Tel: 01179 865877

Secretary: Iain Anderson, 195 Mount Hill Rd, Hanham, Bristol BS15 2SU Tel: 01179 616426

Nickname: The Canaries, Colours: All Yellow

Capacity: 2, 000, Seating: 120, Covered standing: 250

Clubhouse on ground: Yes

Record attendance: 3,000 v Chelsea

For competitive match 2,160 v Saltash in FA Amateur Cup 1952

DIRECTIONS

A4 from Bristol to Bath, ground on left before entering village opposite Crown Inn. Bus service every 30 minutes from Bristol passes ground. 10 minutes walk from Keynsham BR station.

Honours

Somerset Senior Div 1 1978, Somerset Premier Cup 1980 Somerset Senior Cup 1952 and 1958, GFA Junior Cup 192

Manager for 1996-97: Graham Bird, Chairman: Mike Lambern

Keynsham were formed in 1896, but disbanded for the war and were re-formed in 1945, progressing through the Bristol and District, Bristol Premier Combination and Somerset Senior Leagues to the Western League in 1973. They were relegated after three seasons but gained promotion in 1978 as First Division Champions. They were back in Division One when the league was reorganised in 1983. Town have played on the Crown Field since the War, but from the beginning they used a pitch at The Hams, until 1910 when they moved to Gastons. Further pitches in Park Road and Charlton Road followed until the War, when the Crown Field became home. All the previous sites in the town have been built on. Other than Keynsham, both Bath City and Bristol Rovers have played Football Combination games there, and for a while it was the home of American Football, which saw the installation of a temporary stand.

LARKHALL ATHLETIC

Plain Ham, Charlcombe Lane, Larkhall, Bath Tel: 01225 334952

Secretary: Mervyn Liles, 9 Eastbourne Ave, Claremont Ave, Bath Tel: 01225 319427

Nickname: The Larks	Colours: All royal blue
Floodlights: No	Covered standing: Yes
Seating: No	Capacity: 1, 000

Honours

DIRECTIONS

A4 from Bath, 1 mile from city centre turn left into St Saviours Road. In Larkhall square square fork left, and right at junction, road bears into Charlcombe Lane. Ground on right as lane narrows.

Somerset Senior Cup: 1976,

Somerset Senior League. Western League Div 1: 1989.

Div 1 Merit Cup 1983, 1984, 1985, 1986, 1988 jt

The Larks were established just before the Great War and have played in local football and Somerset Senior League until joining the Western League 20 years ago. Their Plain Ham ground is delightfully situated on the side of a valley to the north of Bath and has been home since 1946. Prior to that the club played wherever they could find a plot of land flat enough, until moving to Plain Ham which for a long while had little more than a small hut, until 1964 when a pre-fabricated building was brought over for changing rooms and clubhouse. Honours have been scarce for Larkhall, with possibly their finest hour being the winning of the Somerset Senior Cup in 1976

MELKSHAM TOWN

The Conigre, Melksham, Wilts Tel: 01225 702843

Secretary: Paul Macey, 30 Wellington Square, Bower Hill, Melksham Tel: 01225 706876

Colours: Amber and royal blue   Founded: 1876

Seating: 100   Covered standing: 1,500

Capacity: 3,000   Clubhouse on ground: Yes

Record attendance: 2,821 v Trowbridge Town FA Cup 1957

DIRECTIONS

Just off main square at back of town car park.

Honours

Wiltshire League 1904 and 1994, Western League Div 1 1980

Wiltshire Senior Cup 1904, 1970, 1978

Wiltshire Shield 1981,1982, 1985

Manager for 1996-97: Steve Perrin

Chairman: Mike Perrin

MINEHEAD TOWN

Recreation Ground, Irnham Rd, Minehead Tel: 01643 704989

Secretary Brian Walder, 59 Summerland Drive, Minehead TA24 5BW Tel 01643 706850

Colours: Navy and sky blue, Founded: 1889

Seating: 350, Covered standing: 50, Floodlights: Yes

Clubhouse on ground: Yes

Record attendance: 3,600 v Exeter City FA Cup 2nd Rd 1977

Biggest defeat: 1-11 v Odd Down Western League 1994

DIRECTIONS

Entering town from east on A39 turn right into King Edward Road at Police Station, first left into Alexandra Road and follow signs to car park; ground entrance within. Regular buses to Minehead from Taunton, the nearest railhead.

Honours

Southern League Div 1 South 1976

Western League Div 1 1992, Alan Young Cup 1968 jt

Somerset Premier Cup 1961, 1974, 1977

Manager for 1996-97 Chris Porter

The Minehead club was founded way back in 1889 in a rugby area of Somerset. The early days were spent in the West Somerset and Somerset Senior Leagues although they did have five years in the Western League in the 20's. Minehead rejoined the Western League in 1949 as members of the short lived 3rd Division and they stayed until 1972, during which time they finished 2nd twice, 3rd three times and 4th once, never to win the title. 1972 saw them take the gamble of joining the Southern League and they enjoyed their most successful period to date finishing 1977 in runners up spot behind Wimbledon as they went into the Football League, and twice reaching the 2nd Round of the FA Cup, including a memorable victory over Swansea City at the Vetch. Recent years have been a nightmare for the club which is back in the Western League. Apart from winning the Division One title in 1992, little has gone right and with interest in the town at rock bottom, they were fortunate to survive. A new board has attempted to kick start the club, which has been re-named Minehead Town and 1995-96 season showed signs of progress. However, a further crisis saw the club fold briefly when the new owners conceded defeat, and only a last minute decision by the old manager to keep the club going , and a cash injection from supporters, saved Minehead. The Recreation Ground in Irnham Road has been home since 1899 when it opened, and had a wooden grandstand which only lasted a few years before being destroyed. It was replaced in 1920 and again in 1969.

PEWSEY VALE

Recreation Ground, Ball Road, Pewsey, Wilts Tel: 01672 562990

Secretary: Barbara Flippance, 17 Slater Rd, Pewsey, Wilts Tel: 01672 563665

Colours: White and blue

Floodlights: No

Clubhouse on ground: Yes

Seating: No

Covered standing: Yes

Capacity: 1,000

DIRECTIONS
On entering Pewsey from A345 at the Market Place proceed to end of High Street and turn right into Ball Road, entrance to ground on right opposite pub. BR to Pewsey station.

Honours

Wiltshire County League 1993

WARMINSTER TOWN

Weymouth Street, Warminster, Wilts Tel: 01985 217828

Secretary: Dave Carpenter, 46 Upper Marsh Rd, Warminster, Wilts Tel 01985 212198

Founded: 1878

Colours: Red and black stripes

Nickname: Red and blacks

Seating: Yes

Covered standing: Yes

Clubhouse on ground: Yes

Floodlights: Yes

Capacity: 2, 000

Record attendance: 1,500 for England v Wales Womens International, mid 70's

DIRECTIONS
Take A350 for Weymouth from lights at centre of town - ground on left at brow of hill.

Honours

Wiltshire Senior Cup 1901, 1903, 1911

Wiltshire Premier League 1957

Central Wiltshire League 1909

Manager for 1996-97: Pete Russell

Chairman: Colin Ball

WELLINGTON

Wellington Playing Fields, North Street, Wellington, Somerset TA21 8RY Tel: 01823 664810

Secretary: Mr Tony Brown, 6 Courtland Road, Wellington, Somerset Tel: 01823 662920

Chairman: Mr Selwyn Aspin 38 Howard Rd, Wellington, Somerset Tel: 01823 664520

Press officer: Mr K.Bird, Laburnum Rd, Wellington, Somerset Tel: 01823 666278

DIRECTIONS

At town centre traffic lights turn into North Street then first left by Fire Station into the public car park that adjoins the ground.

Colours: Coral and purple

Capacity: 3,000

Seating: Nil

Covered Standing: 200

Floodlights: Yes

Clubhouse on ground: Yes

Record goalscorer in one season: Robert Cummings

Record goalscorer in total: Ken Jones

Manager for 1996-97: Martin Darby

Assistant Manager: Graham Aspin

Chairman: Selwyn Aspin

The club was formed in 1892 and for many years played in local Taunton and Tiverton Leagues before gaining admission to the Somerset Senior League in 1962. They reached the Western League in 1978, enjoying promotion in 1981 but were relegated to Division One in 1984, where they remain.

Wellington share their ground with the cricket club, which entails having all the facilities along one side. The clubhouse was built in 1973, with a function room three years later, and floodlights were installed in 1986.

The early days were spent playing on various pitches, including fields in Popes Lane, Rockwell Green and Pyles Thorn, before moving to the school pitch at Courtlands Road, which still exists.

In the early fifties the council created the Playing Fields out of the grounds of a private house, and the club moved in around 1954.

WELTON ROVERS

West Clewes, North Road, Midsomer Norton Tel: 01761 412097

Secretary and Press Officer: Geoff Baker, 6 Longfellow
Road, Westfield, Radstock, BA3 3YZ Tel: 01761 413742

Colours: Green and White,   Nickname: Rovers

Capacity: 2,400,   Seating: 350

Covered standing: None,   Floodlights: Yes

Clubhouse on ground: Yes

DIRECTIONS
A367 Bath to Radstock - right at lights at foot of hill onto A362, ground on right.

Record attendance: 2,000 v Bromley FA Amateur Cup in 1963

Record goalscorer in one season: Ian Henderson 53 1965-66

Record goalscorer in total: Ian Henderson

Honours

Western League 1912, 1965, 1966, 1967, 1974.
Division One 1988. Amateur Trophy 1957, 1958, 1959, 1960.
Allan Young Cup 1966, 1967 jt, 1968.
Somerset Senior Cup 1907, 1912, 1913, 1914, 1920, 1925, 1926, 1961, 1962, 1963.
Somerset Junior Cup 1907, 1925, 1931. Somerset Intermediate Cup 1978. City of Wells Cup 1979

Manager for 1996-97: Malcolm Beck   **Chairman: Rae James**

Welton Rovers were formed in 1887 and won the Western League title for the first time in 1912.

Success was not easy to come by and having finished runners up in 1923, failed to notch up any honours until 1957, when Rovers won a trophy for leading amateur club. This feat was repeated for the next three seasons which included a First Division championship in 1960. However, it was the arrival of former Huddersfield Town and Bristol City forward, Arnold Rodgers as manager which heralded a period of unprecedented success in the mid 60's. Three successive League championships in 1965, 66 and 67 followed, with the middle title won with an unbeaten record. Ian Henderson scored 53 times, including 6 hat-tricks and on September 11th, Dorchester Town were beaten 10-0. The following season, Rovers reached the FA Cup 1st Round before losing to Bournemouth and Boscombe Athletic. Despite the constant success, financial problems began to haunt the club and in in 1968 Rodgers departed and there was a mass exodus to Bath City.In 1974 Welton won their fifth championship, under ex-Bristol Rovers player David Stone, but a period of decline followed culminating in relegation at the end of the 81-82 season, It took the club six years to go back up, as First Division champions in 1988, but unfortunately the stay was short lived and in 1992 they went down again.West Clewes is the oldest of the grounds within the old coal mining area of North Somerset, and is believed to have been around since the 1880's. The club bought the ground when they were formed, but in the 20's they experienced much hardship, and sold it to the Miners Welfare. When the mining industry was wound down in that area, the Welfare donated the ground to the council, who now lease it to Welton Rovers.

YEOVIL TOWN RESERVES

Huish Park, Lufton Way, Yeovil, Tel: 01935 23662

Secretary: Jean Cotton, YTFC

Colours: Green and white

GROUND DETAILS AS PER FIRST TEAM IN ICIS LEAGUE SECTION

453

UNIBOND League Tables

PREMIER

	P	W	D	L	F	A	PTS	
Bamber Bridge	42	20	16	6	81	49	76	
Boston United	42	23	6	13	86	59	75	
Hyde United	42	21	11	10	86	51	74	
Barrow	42	20	13	9	69	42	73	
Gainsborough Tri	42	20	13	9	60	41	73	
Blyth Spartans	42	17	13	12	75	61	64	
Accrington Stan	42	17	14	11	62	54	62	(-3)
Emley	42	17	10	15	57	53	61	
Spennymoor U	42	14	18	10	67	61	60	
Guiseley	42	15	14	13	62	57	59	
Bishop Auckland	42	16	11	15	60	55	59	
Marine	42	15	14	13	59	54	59	
Witton Albion	42	17	8	17	60	62	59	
Chorley	42	14	9	19	67	74	48	(-3)
Knowsley United	42	14	6	22	61	89	48	
Winsford United	42	10	16	16	56	79	46	
Leek Town	42	10	15	17	52	55	45	
Colwyn Bay	42	8	21	13	43	57	45	
Frickley Athletic	42	11	14	17	63	87	44	(-3)
Buxton	42	9	11	22	43	72	38	
Droylsden	42	10	8	24	58	100	38	
Matlock Town	42	8	11	23	71	86	35	

DIVISION ONE

	P	W	D	L	F	A	PTS	
Lancaster City	40	24	11	5	79	38	83	
Alfreton Town	40	23	9	8	79	47	78	
Lincoln United	40	22	7	11	80	56	73	
Curzon Ashton	40	20	7	13	73	53	67	
Farsley Celtic	40	19	9	12	66	61	66	
Radcliffe Borough	40	17	13	10	70	48	64	
Eastwood Town	40	18	9	13	60	47	63	
Whitley Bay	40	18	8	14	72	62	62	
Ashton United	40	19	7	14	73	65	60	(-4)
Atherton L.R.	40	15	12	13	60	61	57	
Worksop Town	40	16	8	16	84	90	56	
Gretna	40	13	13	14	75	65	52	
Warrington Town	40	13	10	17	75	72	49	
Leigh R.M.I.	40	14	7	19	53	59	49	
Netherfield	40	13	10	17	64	73	49	
Workington	40	11	12	17	50	62	45	
Bradford Park Ave	40	9	14	17	57	72	41	
Congleton Town	40	11	11	18	36	59	41	(-3)
Great Harwood	40	9	7	24	44	78	33	(-1)
Fleetwood	40	7	10	23	41	81	31	
Harrogate Town	40	7	10	23	54	96	31	

Above: Accrington Stanley F.C.
Below: Blyth Spartans F.C.

Above: Chorley F.C
Below: Boston United F.C.

ACCRINGTON STANLEY

Crown Ground, off Livingstone Road, Accrington, Lancs BB5 5BX. Tel: 01254 383235

Secretary: Philip Terry, 8 Princess St, Colne, Lancs BB8 9AN. TEL: 01282 866768 (h) 01282 864000 (b)

Club shop: John De Maine 01254 383235

Programme Editors: Phil Terry and David Ellis

Colours: Red and white   Nickname: Reds or Stanley

Capacity: 4,000   Seating: 700

Covered standing: 1,650

Clubhouse on ground: Yes

Record attendance: 2,270 v Gateshead

FA Cup 1st Rd 1992

Biggest win: 9-0 v Ashton Town

Lancs Combination 1975-76

Biggest defeat: 1-9 v Runcorn (A)

FA Cup 2nd Qualifying round replay 1985

Record appearances: Chris Grimshaw 352

Record goalscorer in one season: Dave Hargreaves 56, and in total: David Hargreaves 318

Record fee received: £10,000 for Martin Clark from Crewe Alexandra in 1991

Record fee paid: £2,250 for Bernie Hughes from Droylsden

DIRECTIONS

Arriving on A680 from Clayton-le-Moors Livingstone Road is on left 50 yards past Crown Hotel. From M62/M66, through town centre on A860 - Livingstone Road 500 yards on right after Victoria Hospital. One and a half miles from Accrington (BR).

HONOURS

Cheshire County League Div 2 1981

Lancs Combination 1974 and 1978 and Combination Cup 1972, 1973, 1974, 1977

George Watson Trophy 1972, 1974 and 1975 and John Duckworth Trophy 1986, 1992

Manager for 1996-97: Tony Greenwood

Chairman: Eric Whalley   **Press Officer: Brent Peters**

Stanley was formed in 1968 from the cold ashes of the League club, and the new club applied to use Peel Park, the crumbling remains of which still held a main stand which in the long term had led to the club's downfall. Accrington has been home to a number of clubs who have fallen by the wayside, Accrington FC folding exactly 100 years ago to be followed by Stanley Villa who bought the 20,000 capacity Peel Park.They became Accrington Stanley and stayed until their sudden demise in 1962. It was feared that the name would die forever, but fortunately there were sufficient people determined that it should not happen. Their efforts first bore fruit in 1968 when following a meeting in Bold Street WMC, the new Stanley was born, yet it was two years before any football was played. The new club played at the Crown Ground which was used by a works side, joining the Lancs Combination and playing their first game against Formby in 1970 in front of 620 people. There was a link with the old club, in that Terry Tighe, who had played for the old club, was in the team. Success was not long in coming, for Stanley finished runners up in the League, and won the League Cup and Combination Cup a year later. Despite this, Stanley were having terrible problems with the pitch and the following season they made a nostalgic return to Peel Park to play Nelson. The problems were overcome and the club won the Comb Cup for a third time, before taking the league title. In 1975 attempts were made to return to Peel Park, but it was not to be and Stanley carried on at the Crown, where 56 goals from David Hargreaves helped them to runners up again. 1977-78 was the last in the Combination, where they again were champions, and from where David Hargreaves moved to Blackburn Rovers. They joined the Cheshire League and in the second season were runners up in Division Two as well as winning the Shield. Amid great controversy, the club were denied promotion due to their ground problems, and after unsuccessful appeals, went on to win it again, to gain promotion as well as winning the Shield again. On the formation of the North-west Counties League in 1982, Stanley were elected to Division One and in preparation spent £40,000 on the pitch, which had caused them to play several home matches away from the Crown Ground. The first season saw an appearance in the Challenge Trophy final. losing to South Liverpool, and it saw a

quiet spell for the club emerge, until 1987 when floodlights were erected in readiness to go up to the NPL. They left as runners up to Stalybridge Celtic. In 1991, the demise of South Liverpool meant promotion for Stanley, and they have cemented their place since. 1993-94 provided the loyal supporters with more FA Cup thrills when Altrincham were beaten away, before they took on Scunthorpe Utd, played at Turf Moor. Only a late winner denied them further progress. Since then the Crown has undergone another facelift, with £50,000 worth of terracing as well as a new boardroom and Medical Room. The stand has since been trebled in size with major work going on to improve the pitch.

ACCRINGTON STANLEY 1995/96 SEASON

Date	Comp	Round	Opponent	Att	Score	Scorers
19/08/95	NPL	P	Leek Town	367	2-2	Welch, McNally
23/08/95	NPL	P	KNOWSLEY UNITED	472	4-2	Rogerson, McNally, Welch, Rostron
26/08/95	NPL	P	WINSFORD UNITED	475	1-2	Anderson
28/08/95	NPL	P	Barrow	1483	3-0	Anderson, Rawstron, Rogerson
02/09/95	NPL	P	Colwyn Bay	415	2-1	Welch, Rawstron
06/09/95	NPL	P	SPENNYMOOR UNITED	461	0-0	
09/09/95	FA Cup	Q1	OSSETT TOWN	429	2-1	Rogerson, Ormondroyd
12/09/95	NPL	P	Witton Albion	525	2-0	McNally(2)
16/09/95	NPL	P	BUXTON	549	1-0	McNally
19/09/95	NPL	P	Spennymoor United	327	4-3	Anderson, Quick, Thornton(2)
23/09/95	FA Cup	Q2	BRADFORD PARK AVENUE	553	1-2	Grimshaw
30/09/95	NPL	P	Boston United	851	0-4	
04/10/95	NPL	P	BLYTH SPARTANS	446	1-2	Thornton
07/10/95	NPL	P	BOSTON UNITED	484	0-2	
14/10/95	FA Trophy	Q1	BRADFORD PARK AVENUE	415	2-2	Welsh, Thornton
18/10/95	FA Trophy	Q1 rep	Bradford Park Avenue	258	3-2	Walsh, Welch(2)
21/10/95	NPL	P	DROYLSDEN	472	0-2	
24/10/95	LC	2	Barrow	932	4-3	Welch, McNally(2), Rogerson
28/10/95	NPL	P	MATLOCK TOWN	384	2-1	Rawstron, Shaughnessy
04/11/95	FA Trophy	Q2	Atherstone United	422	3-1	Shaughnessy, Mellor, McNally
08/11/95	NPL	P	CHORLEY	483	7-3	Quick, Shaughnessy, McNally(2), Welch(2), Walsh
11/11/95	NPL	P	GUISELEY	602	0-1	
18/11/95	NPL	P	Bishop Auckland	179	2-2	Shaughnessy, Anderson
25/11/95	FA Trophy	Q3	GRESLEY ROVERS	542	2-3	Shaughnessy, Welch
02/12/95	NPL	P	HYDE UNITED	464	1-1	Shaughnessy
05/12/95	LC	3	Colwyn Bay	263	3-2	Welch, Hughes(2)
09/12/95	NPL	P	Gainsborough Trinity	499	1-1	Walsh
13/12/95	NPL	P	BARROW	447	1-1	McNally
16/12/95	NPL	P	WITTON ALBION	409	1-2	Walsh
19/12/95	NPL	P	Marine	324	2-1	Thornton, Quick
01/01/96	NPL	P	MARINE	622	0-0	
06/01/96	NPL	P	Hyde United	512	0-0	
13/01/96	NPL	P	LEEK TOWN	421	0-0	
17/01/96	Lancs ATS	2	RADCLIFFE BOROUGH	276	1-1	Quick
20/01/96	NPL	P	Frickley Athletic	154	1-4	Quick
23/01/96	Lancs ATS	2 rep	Radcliffe Borough	156	1-2	Quick
03/02/96	NPL	P	BISHOP AUCKLAND	415	2-1	Lee(2)
13/02/96	LC	QF	Leek Town	117	0-0	
17/02/96	NPL	P	GAINSBOROUGH TRINITY	404	2-1	McNally, McKenna
24/02/96	NPL	P	Blyth Spartans	541	2-2	McNally, Anderson
28/02/96	LC	QF rep	LEEK TOWN	201	1-3	McNally
02/03/96	NPL	P	EMLEY	361	0-0	
09/03/96	NPL	P	Buxton	217	1-0	Hughes
16/03/96	NPL	P	Droylsden	180	2-1	Thornton(2)
19/03/96	NPL	P	Knowsley United	42	0-1	
23/03/96	NPL	P	FRICKLEY ATHLETIC	348	2-1	Welch, Thornton
26/03/96	NPL	P	Bamber Bridge	512	1-1	Welch
30/03/96	NPL	P	Emley	268	3-1	Rawstron, McKenna, Welch
06/04/96	NPL	P	Winsford United	168	2-2	Quick, Hughes
08/04/96	NPL	P	BAMBER BRIDGE	760	1-2	Thornton
13/04/96	NPL	P	Matlock Town	308	0-2	
20/04/96	NPL	P	COLWYN BAY	535	3-1	Walsh, McNally, Ormerod
23/04/96	NPL	P	Chorley	355	0-0	
27/04/96	NPL	P	Guiseley	507	3-1	Ormerod(2), Thornton

ALFRETON TOWN

Town Ground, North Street, Alfreton, Derbys DE55 7FZ. Tel: 01773 830277

Social Club: Tel 01773 832819 fax: 01773 830277
Secretary: Mr Roger Taylor, 9 Priory Rd, Alfreton, Derbys
DE55 7JT. Tel: 01773 835121

Chairman: Sean Egan, Quarry Cottage, Pentrich Common,
Pentrich, Ripley Derbys. Tel: 01773 832413

Club shop manager: Brian Thorpe. Tel: 01773 836251

Press officer: Chris Tacey, 92 Slough Rd, Sth Normanton,
Alfreton, Derbys DE55 2LE. Tel: 01773 511012

Colours: Red and White   Nickname: The Reds

Capacity: 5,000   Covered seating: 300

Standing: 1,000   Clubhouse on ground: Yes

Record attendance: 5,023 v Matlock Town
Central Alliance 1960

> ## DIRECTIONS
> M1 junction 28 and follow A38
> towards Derby for 1 mile, left
> onto B600, right at main road
> to town centre and after half
> a mile turn left down North
> Street — ground on right. Half
> mile from Alfreton &
> Mansfield Parkway (BR)
> station. Buses 242 & 243
> from both Derby and
> Mansfield.

Biggest win: 15-0 v Loughborough,
Midland League 1969-70

Biggest defeat: 2-9 v Worksop in 1961 and Bridlington in 1992

Record appearance: J.Harrison 560

Record goalscorer in one season: Mick Wadsworth 40

Record goalscorer in one season: Mick Harrison 303

Record fee received: £2,500 for Ricky Greenhough in 1985

HONOURS

Northern Counties East League 1987 and League Cup 1985

Midland Counties League 1970, 1974, 1977 and League Cup 1972, 1973, 1974

Derbyshire Senior Cup 1961, 1970, 1973, 1974, 1982, 1995, Derbyshire Divisional Cup North 1965

Evans Halshaw Floodlit Cup 1988 and 1996, Ladbrokes Gala Cup 1977

Any club shop matters, contact Mark or Brian Thorpe on 01773 836251

Managers for 1996-97: Danny Hague and Paul Mitchell   Vice Chairman: D Gregory

The present Alfreton Town was formed in 1959, thirty years after the collapse of its predecessor of
the same name which survived for only eight seasons. Research shows, however, that the Mid-
Derbyshire town has been represented by a Town club for several other periods in the distant past..
During the late 50's, Alfreton Miners Welfare FC felt strong enough to enter the newly formed
Central Alliance Division Two for the 1958-59 season and at the end of it merged with Alfreton
United to form Alfreton Town. The newly constituted club playing on a new ground in North Street
provided by the council, was admitted directly to the Central Alliance and progressed sufficiently to
gain entry to the Midland Counties League. It was during this time that the record crowd of 5,023
was recorded for the visit of Matlock Town in 1960. After holding the wooden spoon in 1962
Alfreton have seldom looked back and they took the Midland League in 1970 after several near
misses. It was repeated three years later and again in 1977, also winning the League Cup three years
running, with the trophy being presented to the club permanently to mark the feat. In the FA Cup the
club made their mark in 1969 when they reached the 1st Round and took Barrow to three replays
before bowing out. Following the merger of leagues in 1982, Alfreton played for five years in the
Northern Counties East, which they won in 1987, pipping Farsley Celtic, a season which ended with
both clubs elected to the Northern Premier League. 1995 saw Town come agonisingly close to a
promotion place after looking comfortable for so long, but last May finally saw them clinch runners
up spot in Division One to gain promotion. For the third season running they also reached the 1st
Division Cup semi-final and lifted the Floodlit Cup for the 2nd time beating Holbeach in the final.
North Street was provided from new by the Council of the time in 1959, and became home for the
new club. Its early namesake had played virtually next door on the Welfare Ground, but North Street
quickly developed with banking and a stand and has been home ever since, and has also hosted
Rugby League for a while, Mansfield Marksmen using the ground.

ALFRETON TOWN 1995/96 SEASON

19/08/95	NPL	1	WARRINGTON TOWN	203	5-1	Weston, McFadzean, Maybury, Eshelby, Haig
22/08/95	NPL	1	Lincoln United	237	2-0	Maybury, Stafford
26/08/95	FA Cup	P	Radcliffe Borough	118	2-3	Bean(og), McFadzean
28/08/95	NPL	1	WORKSOP TOWN	418	2-2	Dawes, Stafford
02/09/95	NPL	1	ATHERTON L.R.	230	1-2	Dawes
05/09/95	NPL	1	Harrogate Town	270	3-0	Johnson, Megson, Stafford
09/09/95	NPL	1	Gretna	97	0-0	
13/09/95	NPL	1	HARROGATE TOWN	182	2-0	Stafford, Atkinson
16/09/95	NPL	1	Leigh R.M.I.	176	1-1	Stafford
19/09/95	NPL	1	Eastwood Town	290	0-2	
27/09/95	LC	1	LINCOLN UNITED	135	4-0	Hirst, Pickering, Eshelby, Maybury
04/10/95	NPL	1	CURZON ASHTON	181	3-2	Stafford, McFadzean, Haigh
07/10/95	NPL	1	FLEETWOOD	213	1-0	Maybury
11/10/95	NPL	1	Bradford Park Avenue	183	1-1	McFadzean
14/10/95	FA Trophy	Q1	CONGLETON TOWN	202	5-0	Walsh, Stafford, Tibenham(2), Hirst
18/10/95	NPL	1	LINCOLN UNITED	201	2-1	Stafford, McFadzean
21/10/95	NPL	1	Farsley Celtic	164	0-1	
24/10/95	LC	2	Eastwood Town	261	2-3	Stafford, Rush(og)
28/10/95	NPL	1	ASHTON UNITED	235	3-0	McFadzean, Maybury, Johnson
04/11/95	FA Trophy	Q2	DUDLEY TOWN	260	2-2	Hirst, Johnson
08/11/95	FA Trophy	Q2 rep	Dudley Town	183	0-2	
11/11/95	NPL	1	Lancaster City	214	1-1	Stafford
18/11/95	NPL	1	GREAT HARWOOD TOWN	224	4-1	Stafford, Dawes, Johnson, Waller
22/11/95	Evans Hal.	Scorpio	ASHFIELD UNITED	109	2-2	Eshelby, Askey
25/11/95	NPL	1	Congleton Town	141	1-0	Waller
02/12/95	NPL	1	RADCLIFFE BOROUGH	183	1-0	Johnson
09/12/95	NPL	1	FARSLEY CELTIC	184	2-3	Johnson(2)
12/12/95	1C	2	Lincoln United	76	4-1	Stafford(2), McFadzean, Daws
16/12/95	NPL	1	WHITLEY BAY	171	2-3	McFadzean, Stafford
20/12/95	Derbys SC	3	HEANOR TOWN	135	9-1	Johnson, Stafford, Eshelby(3), Askey, McFadzean(2), Walsh
06/01/96	NPL	1	Workington	230	2-1	Johnson, Stafford
10/01/96	PC	1	BOSTON UNITED	188	2-2	McFadzean, Stafford
13/01/96	NPL	1	LANCASTER CITY	333	1-6	Johnson
17/01/96	Evans Hal.	Scorpio	ILKESTON TOWN	163	7-1	Stafford(6), Tibenham
20/01/96	NPL	1	Warrington Town	110	2-2	Pickering, Stafford
03/02/96	NPL	1	GRETNA	195	4-0	Pickering(2), Rickcavage, Stafford
10/02/96	NPL	1	Worksop Town	467	0-2	
14/02/96	1C	QF	ASHTON UNITED	126	3-0	Stafford(2), Walsh
17/02/96	NPL	1	Radcliffe Borough	202	3-1	Stafford, Cheetham, Pickering
24/02/96	NPL	1	CONGLETON TOWN	181	2-1	Eshelby(2)
27/02/96	Derbys SC	QF	Belper Town	404	3-4	Pickering(2), Stafford
02/03/96	NPL	1	Atherton L.R.	126	0-0	
06/03/96	PC	1 rep	Boston United	328	0-4	
09/03/96	NPL	1	LEIGH R.M.I.	140	1-0	Catton
11/03/96	Evans Hal.	Scorpio	Ilkeston Town	103	2-0	Eshelby, McFadzean
16/03/96	NPL	1	Fleetwood	55	2-0	Weston, Hirst
20/03/96	1C	SF(1)	ATHERTON L.R.	130	0-4	
23/03/96	NPL	1	Ashton United	192	1-2	McFadzean
26/03/96	1C	SF(2)	Atherton L.R.	123	2-1	Walsh, Dawes
30/03/96	NPL	1	Great Harwood Town	90	3-1	Weston, Stafford, Eshelby
03/04/96	Evans Hal.	Scorpio	Ashfield United	65	6-2	Cheetham(2), Walsh(2), Stafford, Tibenham
06/04/96	NPL	1	Curzon Ashton	129	1-0	Eshelby
08/04/96	NPL	1	EASTWOOD TOWN	305	2-2	Eshelby, Hirst
10/04/96	Evans Hal.	SF	Belper Town	223	4-1	Dawes(2), Eshelby, Own-Goal
13/04/96	NPL	1	WORKINGTON	205	2-1	Haigh, Walsh
17/04/96	NPL	1	NETHERFIELD	171	4-1	Haigh, Stafford(2), Eshelby
20/04/96	NPL	1	Whitley Bay	187	5-0	Dawes(2), Stafford(2), Maybury
27/04/96	NPL	1	BRADFORD PARK AVE	364	3-2	Stafford(3)
01/05/96	Evans Hal.	F	HOLBEACH UNITED	225	4-0	
04/05/96	NPL	1	Netherfield	188	4-4	Dawes, Stafford, Eshelby, Cheetham

BAMBER BRIDGE

Irongate, Brownedge Rd, Bamber Bridge, Preston, Lancs. Tel: 01772 909690 or 909695 club

Secretary: David Spencer, Bamber Bridge FC
Tel 01772 34355 (h)

Match Sec: Russ Rigby, BBFC 01772 909690 or 909691 fax

Programme Ed: J.Hargreaves Tel: 01772 39682

Colours: White and black   Nickname: Brig

Capacity: 2,400   Seating: 300

Covered standing: 800   Clubhouse on ground: Yes

Record attendance: 2,400 v Czech Republic Friendly 1996

(Competitive game 2,020 v Wimborne Town

FA Vase Semi-final 1st leg 1992

Biggest win: 8-0 v Curzon Ashton NWCL 1994-95

Record appearances: Dave Leaver

Record goalscorer in one season: Andy Whittaker

Record goalscorer in total: Dave Leaver

Record fee received: £16,500 for Tony Black from Wigan Athletic

DIRECTIONS

M6 Junct 29, A6 (Bamber Bridge Bypass) towards Walton le Dale, to r'bout, A6 London Road to next r'bout, 3rd exit signed Bamber Bridge (Brownedge Road) and first right. Ground 100 yds at end of road on left. Just over a mile from Bamber Bridge (BR).

HONOURS

FA VASE Semi-final 1992

Northern Premier League 1996, Northern Premier League Challenge Cup 1995

North-West Counties League Div 2 1992

Preston and District League 1981, 1986, 1997, 1990, Guildhall Cup 1979, 1981, 1985, 1990

Lancs Amateur Shield 1982, Lancastrian Brigade Cup 1977, 1990, 1991, ATS Lancs Trophy 1995

Manager 1996-97: Mick Holgate, Assistant Manager: Mel Gainer

Chairman: Denis Allen, Vice Chairman: Harold Milburn

The origins of Bamber Bridge FC can be traced back to before the Great War, although the present club were re-formed in 1952. They played for 20 years with little success on the King George V Ground in Higher Walton in the Preston and District League, before merging with neighbours Walton-le-Dale. Both clubs were at a low ebb and often exchanged players and so with a joint capital of £211.77p, the new club was born. Negotiations took place with the local council for two pitches and in 1974 there were two sides in the league.In 1976 the first team won the Lytham Medal and in 1979, the first major trophy arrived, with the Guildhall Cup. From there Brig won four Premier Division championships and three more Guildhall Cup finals, the highlight however being the winning of the Lancashire Amateur Shield in 1982. During this period the club were active in fund raising with a view to buying a plot of land in the area and in 1983 the New Town Development Corporation chose a piece of derelict ground at Irongate and within weeks the ground began to develop. The first match was played on the new ground on August 15th 1987 and a year later the clubhouse was opened before a friendly with Preston North End. In 1990 Brig were accepted into the North-West Counties League winning Division Two in 1992. It was the beginning of an astonishing period which saw the club also finish runners up in the Floodlit Cup and more desperately semi-finalists in the FA Vase, losing to Wimborne Town. They shook off the disappointment and were runners up in the League in 1993, gaining promotion to the Northern Premier League.The 1994-95 season brought more success with a runners up spot in Division One which promoted them, the Challenge Cup and ATS Lancs Trophy, a remarkable season. They were not finished there, for last May saw the club as champions of the NPL, denied entry to the Conference as Irongate has not as yet kept pace with the team's exploits.

BAMBER BRIDGE 1995/96 SEASON

12/08/95	S		Marine	354	2-2	McCrae, Mayers
19/08/95	NPL	P	MATLOCK TOWN	378	4-1	Edwards, Senior, Bygale, Corcoram
22/08/95	NPL	P	Marine	406	0-0	
26/08/95	NPL	P	Buxton	298	2-1	Byrne, Allen
28/08/95	NPL	P	CHORLEY	754	2-0	Leaver, McHugh
02/09/95	NPL	P	Witton Albion	623	0-0	
05/09/95	NPL	P	COLWYN BAY	511	5-0	Edwards(3), Senior, Greenwood
09/09/95	FA Cup	Q1	HEANOR TOWN	453	4-1	Byrne, Senior, Greenwood(2)
12/09/95	NPL	P	Barrow	1520	2-0	Allen, Byrne
16/09/95	NPL	P	Gainsborough Trinity	396	3-1	Allen(2), Byrne
19/09/95	NPL	P	WINSFORD UNITED	655	2-0	McHugh, Byrne
23/09/95	FA Cup	Q2	MOSSLEY	583	0-2	
30/09/95	NPL	P	HYDE UNITED	571	3-3	Mayers(2), Senior
03/10/95	NPL	P	BARROW	1238	2-2	Leaver, Brown
07/10/95	NPL	P	Leek Town	293	3-2	Weaver(2), Mayers
10/10/95	NPL	P	Chorley	975	0-0	
14/10/95	NPL	P	BOSTON UNITED	681	1-2	O'Neill
17/10/95	NPL	P	Knowsley United	94	2-2	Mayers, O'Neill
21/10/95	NPL	P	Hyde United	569	3-2	Mayers, Leaver, Burton
24/10/95	LC	2	Workington	194	1-0	Mayers
28/10/95	NPL	P	EMLEY	519	0-1	
04/11/95	NPL	P	BLYTH SPARTANS	464	3-0	Edwards, Leaver(2)
06/11/95	NPL	P	Winsford United	202	4-1	Leaver(2), Senior, Baldwin
11/11/95	NPL	P	Frickley Athletic	152	5-0	Edwards, Leaver(2), Greenwood(2)
18/11/95	NPL	P	BUXTON	495	2-0	Greenwood(2)
21/11/95	PC	1	WARRINGTON TOWN	279	4-1	O'Neill(3), Eaves
25/11/95	FA Trophy	Q3	Burton Albion	964	3-3	Leaver(3)
28/11/95	FA Trophy	Q3 rep	BURTON ALBION	502	2-3	Allen, Edwards
02/12/95	NPL	P	Boston United	1423	3-0	Allen, O'Neill, Leaver
05/12/95	LC	3	LANCASTER CITY	349	0-1	
09/12/95	NPL	P	DROYLSDEN	358	3-2	Eaves, Senior, McHugh
16/12/95	NPL	P	Guiseley	550	0-4	
06/01/96	NPL	P	GAINSBOROUGH TRINITY	531	1-1	Maddock
13/01/96	NPL	P	Blyth Spartans	576	1-1	Edwards
16/01/96	Lancs ATS	2	LANCASTER CITY	380	4-3	Edwards, McHugh, Maddock, Flaherty(og)
20/01/96	NPL	P	LEEK TOWN	424	0-0	
03/02/96	NPL	P	KNOWSLEY UNITED	451	2-2	Chadwick(2)
13/02/96	Lancs ATS	QF	DAISY HILL	220	3-1	Allen, Eaves(2)
17/02/96	NPL	P	Matlock Town	326	1-0	Maddock
20/02/96	PC	QF	RADCLIFFE BOROUGH	303	0-0	
24/02/96	NPL	P	GUISELEY	601	3-1	Chadwick, Leaver(2)
27/02/96	PC	QF rep	Radcliffe Borough	226	2-1	Maddock, Chadwick
02/03/96	NPL	P	Bishop Auckland	184	1-1	Chadwick
09/03/96	NPL	P	Emley	264	1-1	Chadwick
12/03/96	Lancs ATS	SF	CHORLEY	542	3-0	Maddock, Edwards, O'Neill
23/03/96	NPL	P	MARINE	606	4-4	O'Neill, Allen, Mulligan, Maddock
26/03/96	NPL	P	ACCRINGTON STANLEY	512	1-1	Senior
30/03/96	NPL	P	BISHOP AUCKLAND	363	0-2	
02/04/96	PC	SF(1)	Worksop Town	406	0-1	
06/04/96	NPL	P	Colwyn Bay	405	1-1	Leaver
08/04/96	NPL	P	Accrington Stanley	760	2-1	Mulloy(og), Edwards
10/04/96	PC	SF(2)	WORKSOP TOWN	430	2-2	Maddock, Edwards
13/04/96	NPL	P	SPENNYMOOR UNITED	388	2-0	Leaver, Maddock
20/04/96	NPL	P	Droylsden	237	2-1	Allen, O'Neill
24/04/96	Lancs ATS	F	MORECAMBE	1708	0-1	(At Preston North End)
27/04/96	NPL	P	FRICKLEY ATHLETIC	466	2-3	Edwards, O'Neill
30/04/96	NPL	P	Spennymoor United	288	2-4	Petitjean(og), Eaves
04/05/96	NPL	P	WITTON ALBION	589	1-1	Leaver

BARROW

Holker Street, Wilkie Rd, Barrow-in-Furness, Cumbria LA14 5UH. Tel: 01229 820346

Lottery Office: 01229 823061 and Soccerline 0891 884438

Press Officer: Phil Yelland, 6 Tryst Park, Hunter's Tryst, Edinburgh, EH10 7HD Tel: 031 445 1010

Programme Ed: Darren Gardner Tel 01229 833699

Club Shop: Mrs Linda Barker Tel 01229 823061

Secretary: Pat Brewer, Tel 01229 828913 (h)

Colours: Royal Blue and white hoops

Nickname: Bluebirds, Capacity: 4, 550, Seating: 1, 276

Covered standing: 1,300, Clubhouse on ground: Yes

Record attendance: 16, 874 v Swansea Town FA Cup 3rd Rd 1954

Biggest win: 12-0 v Cleator FA Cup 1920

Biggest defeat: 1-10 v Hartlepools Utd Football League Div 4 1959

Record appearances: Colin Cowperthwaite 704

Record goalscorer in total: Colin Cowperthwaite 282 1977 to 1992

> ## DIRECTIONS
> M6 to junction 36, A590 to Barrow, enter Barrow on Park Road and after about 2 miles turn left into Wilkie Rd - ground on right.

HONOURS

FA TROPHY WINNERS 1990

Northern Premier League 1984 and 1989, League Shield 1985, Cumbrian Cup 1983 and 1984

Lancs Senior Cup 1955, Lancs Combination 1921, Lancashire Junior Trophy 1981

Manager 1996-97: Mike Walsh, Chairman: Mr Stephen Vaughan Tel 0151 737 2416

Barrow AFC were formed in 1901 and played their early games in the Lancs Combination on the Strawberry Ground. From there they moved to a new ground at Little Park in Roose and won promotion to Division A. They turned pro in 1908 and a year later moved to Holker Street. After the Great War the club won Division A and were elected to Division Three of the Football League. It held membership for 51 years against a background of financial hardship and geographical isolation, the first nine years bringing four wooden spoons. The 30's brought blessed relief for one year but again before the War the Bluebirds were forced to apply. The immediate post-War years saw relative success in the FA Cup and they secured the services of Billy Gordon, a young forward who went on to score 149 Football League goals, a club record. League re-organisation saw Barrow consigned to Division Four and the return to difficult times, with three re-election campaigns and many heavy defeats. 1963 saw floodlights come to Holker Street and with Don McEvoy in charge the club improved and won promotion to Division Three in 1967. Colin Appleton took over and for a brief spell the club led the division, but his enforced resignation due to ill health saw the beginning of the slump. They were relegated and a year later finished bottom of the Fourth Division. They survived but in 1972 they lost their place after a second vote saw Hereford United elected.The early non-League years were enlivened by Ron Yeats who came as player-manager and guided the club for a while before departing, but in 1977 two brothers Brian and Colin Cowperthwaite joined the club from Netherfield, and Colin went on to break the appearance and goalscoring records for the club over the next dozen years. Barrow joined the Alliance Premier League in 1979 but within four years they were back in the Northern Premier League. March 1986 saw Ray Wilkie take charge and in his second season he reached the FA Trophy semi-finals and in 1989 won the NPL again to return to the newly named Vauxhall Conference. A year later the club were at Wembley for the FA Trophy final and they took it with a fine 3-0 win over Leek Town. Since then the club have once more suffered relegation and have been further hit by the tragic death

of the much loved Ray Wilkie, and the loss of the old main stand which was condemned and eventually replaced.Last season saw the club finish below Bamber Bridge in the league, but neither were able to go up and so Barrow face another season in the NPL.

BARROW 1995/96 SEASON

Date	Comp	Round	Opponent	Att	Score	Scorers
19/08/95	NPL	P	KNOWSLEY UNITED	1124	7-0	Brown, Todhunter, Dodie(3), Hoskin, Murion
22/08/95	NPL	P	Chorley	501	3-2	Todhunter, Parker, Hoskin
26/08/95	NPL	P	COLWYN BAY	1311	1-1	Morton
28/08/95	NPL	P	ACCRINGTON STANLEY	1483	0-3	
02/09/95	NPL	P	Emley	386	2-1	Dobie, Hoskin
05/09/95	NPL	P	Marine	510	2-1	Kennedy, Dobie
09/09/95	FA Cup	Q1	CONSETT	1029	3-0	Brown, Dobie, Kennedy
12/09/95	NPL	P	BAMBER BRIDGE	1520	0-2-	
16/09/95	NPL	P	Matlock Town	406	4-0	Humphreys, Smith(2), Brown
19/09/95	NPL	P	CHORLEY	1513	6-2	Smith(3), Martin(2), Brown
23/09/95	FA Cup	Q2	Gateshead	721	2-2	Parker, Dobie
26/09/95	FA Cup	Q2 rep	GATESHEAD	1908	1-0	Hoskin
30/09/95	NPL	P	FRICKLEY ATHLETIC	1287	1-1	Todhunter
03/10/95	NPL	P	Bamber Bridge	1238	2-2	Hoskin, Dobie
07/10/95	FA Cup	Q3	DURHAM CITY	1413	1-1	Dobie
11/10/95	FA Cup	Q3 rep	Durham City	764	1-0	Todhunter
14/10/95	FA Trophy	Q1	HINCKLEY TOWN	1119	3-0	Morton, Dobie(2)
17/10/95	NPL	P	WITTON ALBION	1490	3-0	Morton(3)
21/10/95	FA Cup	Q4	Winsford United	714	3-0	Brown, Parker, Hoskin
24/10/95	LC	2	ACCRINGTON STANLEY	932	3-4	Smith, Morton(2)
28/10/95	NPL	P	HYDE UNITED	1174	2-1	Wilson, Morton
04/11/95	FA Trophy	Q2	WINSFORD UNITED	1222	0-1	
11/11/95	FA Cup	1	NUNEATON BOROUGH	2869	2-1	Morton, Dobie
18/11/95	NPL	P	SPENNYMOOR UNITED	1176	1-1	Parker
22/11/95	NPL	P	Droylsden	118	4-0	Norton, Dobie, Smith, Parker
25/11/95	NPL	P	Knowsley United	145	2-0	Dobie, Smith
28/11/95	Lancs ATS	1	FLEETWOOD	506	3-1	Morton, Hoskin, Todhunter
02/12/95	FA Cup	2	WIGAN ATHLETIC	3500	0-4	
09/12/95	NPL	P	BOSTON UNITED	1092	2-0	Hoskin, Speak
13/12/95	NPL	P	Accrington Stanley	447	1-1	Dobie
16/12/95	NPL	P	Frickley Athletic	146	0-0	
26/12/95	NPL	P	BLYTH SPARTANS	1665	2-1	Morton, Smith
01/01/96	NPL	P	Hyde United	736	0-0	
06/01/96	NPL	P	Leek Town	324	0-2	
09/01/96	NPL	P	Colwyn Bay	271	1-0	Kenny
13/01/96	NPL	P	GUISELEY	1466	0-2	
16/01/96	Lancs ATS	2	Holker Old Boys	741	2-1	Smith, Kenny
20/01/96	NPL	P	DROYLSDEN	1023	3-3	McDonald, Smith(2)
30/01/96	NPL	P	BISHOP AUCKLAND	982	0-0	
03/02/96	NPL	P	EMLEY	1182	0-0	
14/02/96	Lancs ATS	QF	Southport	321	1-3	Harold
17/02/96	NPL	P	Bishop Auckland	251	2-1	Green(2)
24/02/96	NPL	P	GAINSBOROUGH TRINITY	1216	0-1	
02/03/96	NPL	P	Witton Albion	591	0-1	
09/03/96	NPL	P	LEEK TOWN	1077	1-0	Grimes
16/03/96	NPL	P	Spennymoor United	245	1-1	Humphreys
23/03/96	NPL	P	Gainsborough Trinity	414	0-2	
25/03/96	NPL	P	Winsford United	170	3-4	Green, Foreman(2)
30/03/96	NPL	P	WINSFORD UNITED	953	1-1	Green
06/04/96	NPL	P	MARINE	981	2-0	Ward(og), Green
08/04/96	NPL	P	Blyth Spartans	544	2-1	Humphries, Foreman
13/04/96	NPL	P	Guiseley	380	3-1	Parker, Foreman, Humphries
20/04/96	NPL	P	BUXTON	1093	1-0	Foreman
23/04/96	NPL	P	Buxton	351	0-0	
27/04/96	NPL	P	Boston United	781	1-2	Foreman
04/05/96	NPL	P	MATLOCK TOWN	1139	3-1	Green, McKenna, Hoskin

BISHOP AUCKLAND

Kingsway, Bishop Auckland, Co Durham. Tel: 01388 603686

Secretary: Tony Duffy, 8 Ennerdale Grove, West Auckland, Co Durham DL14 9LN Tel: 01388 833410

Match Sec: Miss Lorna Wilson 28 Grange Ave, Auckland Park, Bishop Auckland, Co Durham Tel: 01388 600129

Programme Editor: Peter Craib Tel 01388 609016

Club shop: Alison Stones & Joanne Russell Tel 01388 607241

Colours: Light and Dark blue   Nickname: Bishops

Capacity: 3,500   Seating: 600

Covered Standing: 1,000   Clubhouse on ground: Yes

Record attendance: 17,000 v Coventry City

FA Cup 2nd Rd Dec 6th 1952

Biggest win: 13-1 v Knaresborough 1911

Biggest defeat: 1-9 v Sunderland Durham Challenge Cup 1904

Record appearances: Bob Hardisty

Record fee received: £9,000 for Dave Laws from Weymouth in 1995

DIRECTIONS

A1 to Scotch corner (or M6 to Bernard Castle) then follow signs to Bishop Auckland. Ground in town centre (rear of Newgate Str). Half mile from station.

HONOURS

FA AMATEUR CUP winners 1896, 1900, 1914, 1921, 1922, 1935, 1939, 1955, 1956, 1958

RUNNERS UP 1902, 1906, 1911, 1915, 1946, 1950, 1951, 1954

Northern League winners 1899, 1901, 1902, 1909, 1910, 1912, 1921, 1931, 1939, 1947, 1950, 1951, 1952, 1954, 1955, 1956, 1967, 1985, 1986

League Cup winners 1950, 1951, 1954, 1955, 1960, 1967, 1976

Durham Challenge Cup 1892, 1899, 1931, 1939, 1952, 1956, 1962, 1967, 1985, 1986, 1988

MANAGER FOR 1996-97: Tony Lee   **ASSISTANT MANAGER: Tony Boylan**

CHAIRMAN: Steve Newcomb   **VICE CHAIRMAN: Charlie Backhouse**

The club was formed by Theology students from Oxford and Cambridge Universities, hence the club colours of light and dark blue. Bishops have always been one of the top non-League clubs in the North-East, being founder members of the Northern League. No other club can match Bishops success in almost a century in the same league. They took the league title 18 times and were equally successful in the Amateur Cup, winning it first in 1896 and going on to take it a further nine times, competing in total in 18 finals and 27 semi-finals.

When the FA ended the competition in favour of the Trophy, the club was presented with a replica in recognition of their achievements. In the 30's the club often fielded a side with 10 Internationals, the last of which was Warren Bradley who later signed for Manchester United and played over 60 League games for them.

One of the best remembered names in the club's history is Bob Hardisty who was in the British team in three Olympics, winning 15 Amateur caps in all.

After their long and illustrious career in the Northern League, Bishops joined the Northern Premier League in 1988, and were promoted as runners-up to Colne Dynamos.

Kingsway has been home to the club since the start, having been a cricket ground for many years before that. The magnificent ornate stand is over 60 years old, but may not see Northern Premier

League football for much longer, as negotiations are in hand to move the club to a purpose built ground elsewhere, the two and a half sided nature of Kingsway not being conducive to the furtherance of the club, despite the fact that 17,000 once saw a game there.

BISHOP AUCKLAND 1995/96 SEASON

19/08/95	NPL	P	Buxton	248	2-1	Morton, Adams
21/08/95	NPL	P	HYDE UNITED	229	1-1	Hyde
26/08/95	NPL	P	Boston United	1015	0-1	
28/08/95	NPL	P	Emley	400	1-1	Adams
02/09/95	NPL	P	Chorley	324	0-2	
04/09/95	NPL	P	BLYTH SPARTANS	559	3-0	Robinson(2), Hyde
09/09/95	FA Cup	Q1	HARROGATE RAILWAY ATH	156	2-1	Robinson(2)
12/09/95	NPL	P	Blyth Spartans	571	0-6	
16/09/95	NPL	P	WINSFORD UNITED	185	1-0	Farrelly(og)
23/09/95	FA Cup	Q2	TOW LAW TOWN	311	2-1	Lobb, McKinlay
25/09/95	NPL	P	FRICKLEY ATHLETIC	133	3-1	Robinson, Adams, Issacs
30/09/95	NPL	P	Leek Town	231	1-0	West
02/10/95	NPL	P	GUISELEY	249	2-2	Hyde(2)
07/10/95	FA Cup	Q3	LANCASTER CITY	298	0-1	
09/10/95	NPL	P	Guiseley	544	0-2	
14/10/95	NPL	P	MARINE	203	0-1	
16/10/95	NPL	P	BUXTON	113	1-1	Hampton
21/10/95	NPL	P	Matlock Town	229	1-1	Hyde
23/10/95	LC	2	SPENNYMOOR UNITED	521	2-2	Carter, Norton
28/10/95	NPL	P	Droylsden	193	4-1	Jewson, Carter(2), Todd
29/10/95	NPL	P	COLWYN BAY	124	1-0	Jewson
31/10/95	Durham CC	1	Esh Winning	93	3-2	Fletcher(2), Waller
04/11/95	NPL	P	WITTON ALBION	208	1-2	Waller
06/11/95	LC	2 rep	Spennymoor United	363	1-3	Milner
11/11/95	NPL	P	MATLOCK TOWN	112	2-3	Fletcher, Sinclair
18/11/95	NPL	P	ACCRINGTON STANLEY	179	2-2	Dobson(2)
25/11/95	FA Trophy	Q3	WITTON ALBION	239	0-0	
28/11/95	FA Trophy	Q3 rep	Witton Albion	461	0-0	
02/12/95	NPL	P	Gainsborough Trinity	378	0-1	
04/12/95	FA Trophy	Q3 rep(2)	WITTON ALBION	222	3-1	Todd, Dobson, Banks
09/12/95	NPL	P	KNOWSLEY UNITED	122	1-2	Jewson
12/12/95	Durham CC	2	West Auckland Town	150	5-1	Dobson(3), Sinclair, Carter
16/12/95	NPL	P	Hyde United	424	1-3	Banks
06/01/96	NPL	P	DROYLSDEN	150	3-2	Ashton(og), Milner(2)
10/01/96	Durham CC	QF	MURTON	74	2-0	Waller(2)
13/01/96	NPL	P	Witton Albion	510	2-1	Dobson, Milner
20/01/96	FA Trophy	1	Bromsgrove Rovers	999	0-1	
30/01/96	NPL	P	Barrow	982	0-0	
03/02/96	NPL	P	Accrington Stanley	415	1-2	Milner
10/02/96	NPL	P	LEEK TOWN	177	1-1	Bayles
17/02/96	NPL	P	BARROW	251	1-2	Dobson
24/02/96	NPL	P	Colwyn Bay	348	3-1	Lobb(2), Dixon
26/02/96	NPL	P	SPENNYMOOR UNITED	346	1-2	Hyde
02/03/96	NPL	P	BAMBER BRIDGE	184	1-1	Dobson
05/03/96	NPL	P	Frickley Athletic	103	3-0	Dobson, Fletcher, Yates(og)
09/03/96	NPL	P	GAINSBOROUGH TRINITY	163	1-1	Carter
16/03/96	NPL	P	Winsford United	120	4-0	Dobson(3), Carter
19/03/96	Durham CC	SF	Durham City	99	0-1	
23/03/96	NPL	P	BOSTON UNITED	163	1-3	Carter
30/03/96	NPL	P	Bamber Bridge	363	2-0	Dobson, Milner
06/04/96	NPL	P	CHORLEY	190	3-1	Milner, Carter, Bayles
08/04/96	NPL	P	Spennymoor United	416	0-1	
13/04/96	NPL	P	EMLEY	173	1-0	Dobson
27/04/96	NPL	P	Knowsley United	44	2-1	Milner, Dixon
04/05/96	NPL	P	Marine	475	2-2	Waller(2)

BLYTH SPARTANS

Croft Park, Blyth, Northumberland. Tel: 01670 352373 office

Secretary: Mr Bob Cotterill, 34 Solingen Estate, Blyth, Northumberland NE24 3ER
Tel: 01670 361057 (h) 01670 716211 (b) 0850 270775 (mobile)

Club shop: Stan Watson, 13 Benwell Grange, Benwell Lane, Newcastle, N15 6RG Tel: 0191 273 9138

Match Secretary: Scott Sawyer Tel 01670 360250 (Best contact when checking fixture)

Nickname: Spartans   Colours: Green and White stripes

Seating 300   Capacity: 6,000 (4,000 safety limit)

Covered standing: 1000   Clubhouse on ground: Yes

Record Attendance: 10,186 at Croft Park (42, 157 at Newcastle Utd for 5th Rd FA Cup replay with Wrexham in Feb 1978)

Biggest win: 18-0 v Gateshead Biggest defeat: 0-10 v Newcastle Utd and Darlington

Record appearances: Eddie Alder 652

Record goalscorer in one season: Johnny Langland

Record goalscorer in total: Brian Slane 224

Record fee received: £30,000 for Les Mutrie from Hull City

DIRECTIONS
Through Tyne tunnel heading north on A19, take Cramlington turn, follow signs for Newsham/Blyth. Right fork at railway gates in Newsham, down Plessey Rd, ground can be seen on left behind chip shop and before Masons Arms. Buses X24, X25, X26, X1 from Newcastle.

HONOURS

FA CUP 5th Rd REPLAY 1978, FA AMATEUR CUP Semi-final 1972

Northern Premier League Div 1 and Div 1 Cup 1995

East Northumberland League 1904, 1906, 1907

Northern League 1973, 1975, 1976, 1980, 1981, 1982, 1983, 1984, 1987, 1988,

League Cup: 1973, 1978, 1979, 1982, 1992

North-Eastern League 1936 and League Cup 1951, 1952, 1953, 1954, 1955

Northumberland League 1904 Northern Alliance 1909 and 1913

Northumberland Senior Cup 1914, 15, 32, 34, 35, 36, 37, 52, 55, 59, 63, 72, 74, 75, 78, 81, 82, 92, 94

Northumberland Minor Cup 1906 Cairns Cup 1906 and 1907

Tynemouth Infirmary Cup 1909, 1910, 1933 Tyne Charity Shield 1914 and 1926 jt

Northumberland Aged Miners Homes Cup 1921 jt Debenhams Cup 1978

JT Cleator Memorial Cup 1982, 1983, 1984, 1988, 1992

Beamish Trophy 1993, 1994, 1995

MANAGER FOR 1996-97: Peter Harrison, ASSISTANT MANAGER: Dereck Bell, ACTING CHAIRMAN: John Broadhead, VICE CHAIRMAN: John Broadhead

Blyth Spartans were formed in September 1899. The name Spartans being suggested by Mr Fred Stoker, the club's first secretary, who thought that by naming the team after the legendary "Spartan Army", the players would give their all as they went into battle on the field.Today the Spartans name is unique in senior non-League football. At first they played friendlies until 1901 when they joined the Northumberland League, the first honour being recorded in 1904 when they took the title, completing a hat-trick by 1907. The following year they joined the Northern Alliance and played there for six seasons, taking the title twice. At the end of the 1908-09 season the club left their Thornton Cottage ground, to move to Croft Park, which was opened on September 1st of that year by Mrs Clark, of Bellister Castle, Haltwhistle. In 1913, Blyth moved to the powerful North Eastern League, joining the ranks of the semi-pros, and they remained there until 1958 when it disbanded. Honours were scarce with only one title, in 1936. They did finish runners up to Newcastle United Reserves in 1923 and took the League Cup twice. Blyth then moved to the Midland League and the Northern Counties, but were unlucky as both leagues folded. In the early 1960's the old North-Eastern League was revived, and Blyth joined but again the

league suffered problems and folded for good. They were at a loss for a suitable semi-pro league and in 1964 reverted to amateur status and joined the Northern League. During 29 years their record was second to none as they took the title 10 times, with five second places, all of which culminated in a place in the Northern Premier League in 1994. The first season up was a great success, with a League and Cup double and promotion to the Premier Division. The club is probably best known for its exploits in the FA Cup which has seen a host of League clubs beaten. Their most famous Cup run was in 1977-78 when they reached the 5th round proper replay with Wrexham after the Welsh had controversially equalised in the dying seconds.

BLYTH SPARTANS 1995/96 SEASON

19/08/95	NPL	P	Gainsborough Trinity	445	0-4	
22/08/95	NPL	P	SPENNYMOOR UNITED	836	3-1	Pyle, Ditchburn, Harkus
26/08/95	NPL	P	LEEK TOWN	510	2-1	Ditchburn, Harkus
28/08/95	NPL	P	Spennymoor United	503	1-2	Hays
02/09/95	NPL	P	MATLOCK TOWN	498	3-0	Harkus(2), Ditchburn
04/09/95	NPL	P	Bishop Auckland	559	0-3	
09/09/95	FA Cup	Q1	GARFORTH TOWN	498	6-0	Pyle(2), Bond, Johnson, Harkus(2)
12/09/95	NPL	P	BISHOP AUCKLAND	571	6-0	Harkus(3), Cooper, Johnson, Bond
16/09/95	NPL	P	Droylsden	183	2-2	Harkus, Cooper
19/09/95	NPL	P	GUISELEY	577	3-3	Bond(2), Harkus
23/09/95	FA Cup	Q2	Billingham Synthonia	246	2-0	Harkus(2)
26/09/95	LC	1	GRETNA	432	2-1	Harkus, Hays
30/09/95	NPL	P	BUXTON	574	1-1	Hayes
04/10/95	NPL	P	Accrington Stanley	446	2-1	Boon, Adams
07/10/95	FA Cup	Q3	BEDLINGTON TERRIERS	648	3-1	Ditchburn, Harkus(2)
10/10/95	NPL	P	FRICKLEY ATHLETIC	553	1-1	Milroy
14/10/95	NPL	P	Witton Albion	502	1-2	Ditchburn
17/10/95	NPL	P	Frickley Athletic	150	2-1	McDonald, Gamble
21/10/95	FA Cup	Q4	GUISELEY	775	2-0	Ditchburn, Pyle
23/10/95	LC	2	Guiseley	466	0-1	
28/10/95	NPL	P	Boston United	1019	0-1	
04/11/95	NPL	P	Bamber Bridge	464	0-3	
11/11/95	FA Cup	1	Bury	3076	2-0	Bond, Ditchburn
18/11/95	NPL	P	Knowsley United	87	0-1	
21/11/95	NPL	P	Emley	193	3-1	Walker, Moat, Raffell
25/11/95	FA Trophy	Q3	GRETNA	453	3-2	McDonald(3)
27/11/95	PC	1	Guiseley	256	0-4	
02/12/95	FA Cup	2	Stockport County	5693	0-2	
09/12/95	NPL	P	CHORLEY	387	3-2	Pyle(3)
16/12/95	NPL	P	Matlock Town	319	3-3	Curry, Proctor, Walker
26/12/95	NPL	P	Barrow	1665	1-2	Bond
06/01/96	NPL	P	Marine	394	0-0	
13/01/96	NPL	P	BAMBER BRIDGE	576	1-1	Moat
20/01/96	FA Trophy	1	Ashton United	535	3-1	Gamble, Proctor(2)
03/02/96	NPL	P	COLWYN BAY	338	2-0	Bond, Young
10/02/96	FA Trophy	2	GRESLEY ROVERS	626	1-2	Young
13/02/96	N'humb SC	QF	MORPETH TOWN	394	5-0	Gamble, Bond(2), Young(2)
17/02/96	NPL	P	Leek Town	251	3-1	Young, Moat, Pyle
24/02/96	NPL	P	ACCRINGTON STANLEY	541	2-2	Pyle, Boon
02/03/96	NPL	P	Winsford United	162	4-2	Bond, Pyle, Walker, Young
09/03/96	NPL	P	WITTON ALBION	497	2-0	Young, Bond
12/03/96	NPL	P	EMLEY	310	0-0	
16/03/96	NPL	P	Chorley	304	4-1	Nicholls(3), Bean
19/03/96	N'humb SC	SF	R.T.M. NEWCASTLE	352	3-2	Young, Pyle, Bond
23/03/96	NPL	P	WINSFORD UNITED	405	3-2	Walker, Young, Pyle
30/03/96	NPL	P	GAINSBOROUGH TRINITY	443	0-0	
02/04/96	NPL	P	DROYLSDEN	445	2-1	Pyle, Young
06/04/96	NPL	P	Guiseley	348	1-1	Young
08/04/96	NPL	P	BARROW	544	1-2	Bond
13/04/96	NPL	P	Buxton	198	1-2	Nicholls
16/04/96	NPL	P	MARINE	336	2-2	Young(2)
20/04/96	NPL	P	KNOWSLEY UNITED	379	4-1	Moat(2), Bond(2)
22/04/96	NPL	P	HYDE UNITED	396	5-1	Raffell(2), Bond, Young, Adams
27/04/96	NPL	P	Colwyn Bay	315	0-0	
28/04/96	NPL	P	Hyde United	396	1-4	Bond
04/05/96	NPL	P	BOSTON UNITED	411	0-3	
08/05/96	N'humb SC	F	NEWCASTLE UNITED RES.	1003	0-3	

BOSTON UNITED

York Street Ground, York Street, Boston, Lincs. Tel: 01205 365524 match days only

Club number: 01205 362967 fax: 01205 354063

General Secretary: John Blackwell, 14-16 Spain Place
Boston PE26 6HN

Tel: 01205 364406 (Gd) 01205 365652 (M) 0860 663299
Club number: 0891 121539

Nickname: The Pilgrims   Colours: Amber and Black

Capacity: 8,771   Seating: 1,826

Covered standing: 6,945

Clubhouse on ground: Yes

Record attendance: 10,086 v Corby Town in 1955 or possibly
11,000 v Derby County
FA Cup replay in 1974

Biggest win: 14-0 v Spilsby Town Grace Swan Cup 1992

Record appearances: Billy Howells 500+

Record goalscorer in one season: Jimmy Rayner 55 in 1966-67

Record goalscorer in total: Chris Cook

Record fee received: £25,000 for Gary Jones from Southend Utd in 1993

Record fee paid: £14,000 for Micky Nuttall from Wycombe Wanderers

> ## DIRECTIONS
> A1 to A17 Sleaford-Boston over rail crossing, bear right at Eagle pub to lights over haven Bridge, thru lights opposite B & Q, right into York Street. Ground just off town centre.

HONOURS

Lincolnshire Senior A Cup 1935, 1936, 1946, 1950, 1955
East Anglian Cup 1961, Central Alliance League and Cup 1962, United Counties League and Cup 966
West Midlands League 1967 and 1968, and League Cup 1968, Eastern Professional Floodlit Cup 1972
Northern Premier League 1973, 1974, 1977, 1978, Non-League Champion of Champions Cup 1973 & 78
NPL Challenge Shield 1974, 1975, 1977, 1978 and NPL Cup 1974 and 1976

MANAGER FOR 1996-97: Greg Fee, ASSISTANT MANAGER: Chris Cook

Acting Chairman: Mr S.Burgess, VICE CHAIRMAN: Mr B.James

It was 1934 before the name Boston United first appeared, but football had been played in the town since the late 19th Century, on the same site as the present York Street stadium. In those early days there were two clubs, Swifts, whose HQ was the Coach and Horses opposite the pitch and Town, who used a different pub, the Indian Queen, as base. That was a good walk away from their ground which was called Main Ridge Ground in those days. Both pitches were end to end in what would be described now as an out of town development. By the 1900's Town boasted a small stand and a roped off pitch. Town played in amber and black stripes whilst Swifts played in claret and pale blue. Both played in the Lincolnshire League and in various cups, but Town entered the FA Cup. Swifts never re-appeared after the Great War, their pitch returning to meadowland and then in the 40's and 50's housing started to appear, so that by the 60's there was no sign of a pitch, with just the players passage in the pub left. The remaining club, then just called Boston, played in the Midland League, but by 1933 they were close to folding until a gentlemen called Ernest Malkinson took over and stayed for over 50 years. They were reformed as Boston Utd and changed to Amber and Black.They found success in 1956 finishing runners up to Peterborough Utd, and in the FA Cup astounded everyone by beating Derby County 6-1 away. Attendances were around the 6,000 mark when they joined the Southern League in 1957 but after three years they resigned and joined the Central Alliance completing a League and Cup double. However, they joined the new Midland League but ran into financial troubles and went amateur in local football until things improved.Unable to gain re-entry they played in the West Midlands League, winning the title before being invited into the new Northern Premier League in 1968. It heralded the start of an eleven year period of success with new records set, winning the league four times, including the treble of League, League Cup and Shield. During this time the Pilgrims beat several Football League clubs in the FA Cup, with the outstanding result being a 0-0 draw with Derby County, 11,000 seeing the replay at York Street. United met a devastating blow in 1977 when the

ground failed to meet the Football League's criteria. The board decided to rebuild virtually the whole ground and new grandstands, floodlights, toilets, refreshment kiosks, turnstiles and terracing transformed the ground, taking ten years to complete.With the financial outlay the playing side suffered, after being founder members of the Alliance Premier League. 1985 was the Golden Anniversary and it was celebrated with a trip to Wembley for the FA Trophy final against champions Wealdstone, although on a day marred by the tragedy of the Bradford Fire, Pilgrims lost 2-1.

BOSTON UNITED 1995/96 SEASON

08/08/95	Lincs SC		Grantham Town		2-0	Fee(2)
19/08/95	NPL	P	WITTON ALBION	1167	1-2	Brook
22/08/95	NPL	P	Emley	331	0-2	
26/08/95	NPL	P	BISHOP AUCKLAND	1015	1-0	Cork
29/08/95	NPL	P	Matlock Town	507	2-0	Varadi, Fee
02/09/95	NPL	P	Droylsden	198	5-2	Hardy, Brook(2), Brolin(2)
06/09/95	NPL	P	FRICKLEY ATHLETIC	870	1-3	Brown
09/09/95	FA Cup	Q1	WISBECH TOWN	983	1-2	Gray
11/09/95	NPL	P	Guiseley	504	2-4	Cook, Circuit
16/09/95	NPL	P	HYDE UNITED	716	0-3	
20/09/95	NPL	P	BUXTON	608	9-3	Price(2), Cook, Chambers, Fee, Circuit, Gray, Grayson, Hardy
23/09/95	NPL	P	DROYLSDEN	706	0-1	
26/09/95	NPL	P	Buxton	210	3-0	Circuit, Grayson(2)
30/09/95	NPL	P	ACCRINGTON STANLEY	851	4-0	Grayson, Gray, Brown, Hardy
03/10/95	NPL	P	Frickley Athletic	194	2-1	Brown(2)
07/10/95	NPL	P	Accrington Stanley	484	2-0	Grayson, Fee
11/10/95	NPL	P	EMLEY	820	1-1	Circuit
14/10/95	NPL	P	Bamber Bridge	681	2-1	Fee, Brown
18/10/95	NPL	P	LEEK TOWN	944	2-2	Cook, Baines
21/10/95	NPL	P	Chorley	331	2-0	Gray, Circuit
24/10/95	LC	2	Worksop Town	483	5-0	Price, Brown(2), Gray(2)
28/10/95	NPL	P	BLYTH SPARTANS	1019	1-0	Brown
04/11/95	NPL	P	Marine	707	4-0	Brown(2), Cook(2)
11/11/95	NPL	P	Winsford United	183	0-1	
18/11/95	NPL	P	MATLOCK TOWN	1008	1-0	Brown
25/11/95	FA Trophy	Q3	Leek Town	370	0-0	
29/11/95	FA Trophy	Q3 rep	LEEK TOWN	819	2-0	Fee(2)
02/12/95	NPL	P	BAMBER BRIDGE	1423	0-3	
06/12/95	Lincs SC	F	GRIMSBY TOWN	353	1-4	Nelson
09/12/95	NPL	P	Barrow	1092	0-2	
16/12/95	NPL	P	MARINE	720	0-1	
19/12/95	LC	3	Guiseley	250	1-1	Nuttell
01/01/96	NPL	P	GAINSBOROUGH TRINITY	1176	1-2	Cook
06/01/96	NPL	P	Knowsley United	42	4-2	Cook(2), Phillips(2)
10/01/96	PC	1	Alfreton Town	188	2-2	Fee(2)
13/01/96	NPL	P	COLWYN BAY	639	0-0	
20/01/96	FA Trophy	1	CHORLEY	808	1-1	Brown
23/01/96	FA Trophy	1 rep	Chorley	294	1-2	Cook
03/02/96	NPL	P	CHORLEY	609	2-1	Gray, Cook
10/02/96	NPL	P	SPENNYMOOR UNITED	648	4-1	Chambers, Fee, Cook, Gray
17/02/96	NPL	P	Colwyn Bay	279	1-3	James
24/02/96	NPL	P	WINSFORD UNITED	611	2-2	Cook, Grayson
28/02/96	LC	3 rep	GUISELEY	268	3-2	Grayson, Cook, Brown
02/03/96	LC	QF	SPENNYMOOR UNITED	424	3-0	Cook, Brown, Gray
06/03/96	PC	1 rep	ALFRETON TOWN	328	4-0	Fee, Grayson(2), Brown
09/03/96	NPL	P	Spennymoor United	237	3-2	Fee, Cook(2)
16/03/96	NPL	P	KNOWSLEY UNITED	618	4-2	Fee, Cook(2), Grayson
20/03/96	PC	QF	WORKSOP TOWN	331	0-2	
23/03/96	NPL	P	Bishop Auckland	163	3-1	Brown, Price, Cook
27/03/96	LC	SF(1)	LEEK TOWN	345	1-2	Circuit
30/03/96	NPL	P	Witton Albion	469	1-1	James
02/04/96	LC	SF(2)	Leek Town	165	0-2	
06/04/96	NPL	P	Hyde United	604	4-2	Munton, Price, Brown(2)
13/04/96	NPL	P	Gainsborough Trinity	854	1-2	Munton
23/04/96	NPL	P	Leek Town	188	2-2	Gray, Ogley(og)
27/04/96	NPL	P	BARROW	781	2-1	Circuit, Brown
02/05/96	NPL	P	GUISELEY	587	4--3	Brown(2), Hardy, Munton
04/05/96	NPL	P	Blyth Spartans	411	3-0	Mason, Munton(2)

BUXTON

Silverlands, Buxton, Derbys Tel: 01298 24733

Secretary: Dave Belfield, 20 Hereford Rd, Buxton, Derbys SK17 9PG Tel: 01298 26033

Programme Editor Andy Sellors: Tel 0374 603837

Club shop manager: David Hughes : Tel 01298 70902

Colours: All white

Nickname: The Bucks

Capacity: 4,000

Seating: 490

Covered standing: 2,500

Clubhouse on ground: Yes

Record attendance: 6,000 v Barrow FA Cup 1st Rd 1962

Record goalscorer in total: Dave Herbert

Record fee received: £16, 500 for Ally Pickering to Rotherham 1989

DIRECTIONS

Within 200 yards of Buxton Market Place, opposite County Police HQ. Half mile from Buxton (BR).

HONOURS

Northern Premier League Cup 1991

Cheshire County League 1973

League Cup 1957, 1958, 1969

Manchester League 1932 and 1960

League Cup 1926 and 1927

Derbyshire Senior Cup 1939, 1945, 1946, 1957, 1960, 1972

Buxton FC was formed in 1877 and in the early days was run for the benefit of the local quarry workers and were originally nicknamed the Quarrymen. They played on the cricket field for some years and eventually entered the Combination and the North Derbyshire and East Cheshire League before being elected to the Manchester League in 1899. It took until 1932 before they took the title, moving to the Cheshire County League for the following season. The reserves remained in the league and won it in 1960, however the first team had to wait until 1973 before becoming champions, having been runners up twice and had the consolation of three League Cup wins. They have also tasted much success in the Derbyshire Senior Cup although it has not been to Silverlands for 23 years.

Since winning the Cheshire League in 1973 success has eluded the club, but despite this, they have adapted to life in the Northern Premier League, taking the President's Cup and winning the League Cup in 1991.

Silverlands is believed to have been first used in 1884 for a match against Bakewell, before which the club used several fields, The Park, then as now the cricket club, a ground at Wyelands, Macclesfield Rd and Cote Heath. Very early in its life, the ground was roped and staked and before the turn of the century there was talk of a stand to encourage ladies to the ground.

The current stand replaced a much older wooden one, in 1965 and although showing signs of being weather beaten, is still an imposing structure.

BUXTON 1995/96 SEASON

Date	Comp	Rnd	Opponent	Att	Score	Scorers
19/08/95	NPL	P	BISHOP AUCKLAND	248	1-2	Bancroft
23/08/95	NPL	P	Droylsden	206	3-1	Bancroft, Lee(2)
26/08/95	NPL	P	BAMBER BRIDGE	298	1-2	Maxwell
28/08/95	NPL	P	Gainsborough Trinity	555	2-2	Heyward, Lee
02/09/95	NPL	P	SPENNYMOOR UNITED	244	1-1	Lee
05/09/95	NPL	P	WITTON ALBION	350	0-4	
09/09/95	FA Cup	Q1	Eastwood Town	229	1-2	Maxwell
16/09/95	NPL	P	Accrington Stanley	549	0-1	
20/09/95	NPL	P	Boston United	608	3-9	Maxwell(2), Wilson
26/09/95	NPL	P	BOSTON UNITED	210	0-3	
30/09/95	NPL	P	Blyth Spartans	574	1-1	Bancroft
03/10/95	NPL	P	DROYLSDEN	203	0-3	
07/10/95	NPL	P	KNOWSLEY UNITED	194	3-2	Holmes, Maxwell, Bainbridge
10/10/95	NPL	P	Leek Town	310	0-0	
14/10/95	NPL	P	HYDE UNITED	350	0-1	
16/10/95	NPL	P	Bishop Auckland	113	1-1	Maxwell
21/10/95	NPL	P	Frickley Athletic	105	2-0	Maxwell, Holmes
24/10/95	LC	2	Leek Town	149	0-1	
28/10/95	NPL	P	MARINE	237	1-3	Hopkinson
04/11/95	NPL	P	Guiseley	431	0-1	
11/11/95	NPL	P	Knowsley United	43	0-2	
18/11/95	NPL	P	Bamber Bridge	495	0-2	
21/11/95	NPL	P	LEEK TOWN	304	1-2	Holmes
25/11/95	FA Trophy	Q3	Matlock Town	516	0-1	
02/12/95	NPL	P	WINSFORD UNITED	165	1-3	Maxwell
09/12/95	NPL	P	Hyde United	394	0-7	
16/12/95	NPL	P	Colwyn Bay	257	1-1	Cunningham
18/12/95	PC	1	Ashton United	151	1-0	Bancroft
06/01/96	NPL	P	Spennymoor United	217	0-0	
09/01/96	Derbys SC	3	Stapenhill		0-0	
13/01/96	NPL	P	FRICKLEY ATHLETIC	188	1-0	Davies
16/01/96	Derbys SC	3 rep	STAPENHILL	84	1-0	Blackwood
20/01/96	NPL	P	Winsford United	189	1-1	Maxwell
13/02/96	Derbys SC	QF	Gresley Rovers	401	0-2	
17/02/96	NPL	P	Chorley	327	1-2	Blackwood
24/02/96	NPL	P	EMLEY	201	1-2	Bancroft
02/03/96	NPL	P	Marine	346	1-1	Brown
04/03/96	PC	QF	Guiseley	126	1-1	Blackwood
09/03/96	NPL	P	ACCRINGTON STANLEY	217	0-1	
16/03/96	NPL	P	Emley	173	1-2	Lowe
19/03/96	PC	QF rep	GUISELEY	97	1-3	Bainbridge
30/03/96	NPL	P	COLWYN BAY	160	0-1	
02/04/96	NPL	P	MATLOCK TOWN	336	3-1	Johnson(2), Lowe
06/04/96	NPL	P	Matlock Town	418	1-0	Fox(og)
08/04/96	NPL	P	GAINSBOROUGH TRIN.	234	1-2	Johnson
13/04/96	NPL	P	BLYTH SPARTANS	198	2-1	Maxwell, Johnson
20/04/96	NPL	P	Barrow	1093	0-1	
23/04/96	NPL	P	BARROW	351	0-0	
27/04/96	NPL	P	Witton Albion	419	3-1	Blackwood, Bancroft, Johnson
30/04/96	NPL	P	GUISELEY	322	0-0	
04/05/96	NPL	P	CHORLEY	437	5-2	Maxwell(2), Blackwood(2), Bancroft

CHORLEY

Victory Park, Duke Street, Chorley, Lancs Tel: 01257 263406 fax: 01257 241625

Secretary: Mick Wearmouth, 6 Avondale Rd, Chorley, Lancs PR7 2ED Tel: 01257 271395

Programme Editor and club shop E.Howe Tel: 01257 263406

Colours: Black and white stripes   Nickname: The Magpies

Capacity: 4,600   Seating: 800

Covered standing: 2,000   Clubhouse on ground: Yes

Record attendance: 9,679 v Darwen 1931-32

Biggest win: 14-1 v Morecambe 1946

Biggest defeat: 3-10 v Skelmersdale Utd 1924

Record appearances: Peter Watson 450

Record goalscorer in one season: Peter Watson 77 in 1960-61

Record goalscorer in total: Peter Watson 372 1959-66

Record fee received: £25,000 David Eatock to Newcastle Utd

DIRECTIONS

M61 jct 6, A6 to Chorley, going past Yarrow Bridge Hotel on Bolton Rd turn left at 1st lights into Pilling Lane, 1st right into Ashley Str, ground 2nd left. From M6; jct 27, follow signs to Chorley, left at lights, continue for two and a half miles on A49, right onto B5251, on entering Chorley turn right into Duke Street 200yds after Plough Hotel. Quarter mile from Chorley (BR).

HONOURS

Northern Premier League 1988

Cheshire County League 1976, 1977, 1982

Lancs Combination 1920, 1923, 1928, 1929, 1933, 1934, 1940, 1946, 1960, 1961, 1964

Division Two: 1961, League Cup: 1925, 1959, 1963 , Lancashire League: 1897 and 1899

Lancashire Alliance: 1893

Lancs Junior Cup 1894, 1909, 1924, 1940, 1946, 1958, 1959, 1961, 1964, 1965, 1976, 1980, 1982, 1983

Manager for 1996-97: Dave Sutton, Assistant Manager: Steve Doyle

Chairman: Jack Kirkland, Vice Chairman: Dennis Benson, Press Officer: Mrs Bowyer, Chorley FC

Chorley FC was originally founded as a rugby club at an inaugural meeting held on October 15th 1875 at the old Anchor Inn in Market Street. In 1883 they converted to Association rules and after a series of friendlies joined their first organised competition, the Lancashire Junior League in 1889.

Since those early days the Magpies have competed in many leagues, including the Lancashire Alliance to 1894, then the Lancashire League until 1903. From there they moved to the Lancs Combination where they remained until 1968. They won a host of trophies, taking the Lancs Comb a total of 11 times and the Junior Cup 14 times. During the early period, Chorley played on Dole Lane before moving to Ranglets Park and St Georges Park, both of which are still just a stone's throw away. They moved to the massive Victory Park in 1920 and enjoyed their success until a catastrophe befell them when their grandstand was razed to the ground following a Christmas match. They recovered and replaced it and remained in the Combination until a spell when they flitted between it, the Northern Premier League and the Cheshire League, all of which culminated in a six year spell in the NPL when the Cheshire League was amalgamated.

They won the NPL in style in 1988 and moved up into the Conference but after two years they were back in the NPL where they remain. More recently much has gone on to raise the profile of the club and with extensive improvements planned for the already impressive Victory Park, things are looking up for Chorley Football Club.

CHORLEY 1995/96 SEASON

Date	Competition	Round	Opponent	Att	Score	Scorers
19/08/95	NPL	P	Frickley Athletic	164	0-1	
22/08/95	NPL	P	BARROW	501	2-3	McDonald, Jardine
26/08/95	NPL	P	GUISELEY	329	1-0	McDonald
28/08/95	NPL	P	Bamber Bridge	754	0-2	
02/09/95	NPL	P	BISHOP AUCKLAND	324	2-0	McDonald, Ross
06/09/95	NPL	P	Knowsley United	152	2-1	McKierney, Leitch
09/09/95	FA Cup	Q1	FARSLEY CELTIC	251	2-2	A McDonald, T McDonald
13/09/95	FA Cup	Q1 rep	Farsley Celtic	221	2-1	McDonald, Ross
16/09/95	NPL	P	Colwyn Bay	386	1-1	McKearney
19/09/95	NPL	P	Barrow	1513	2-6	McKearney, Green
23/09/95	FA Cup	Q2	COLWYN BAY	234	1-2	Leitch
26/09/95	NPL	P	KNOWSLEY UNITED	184	1-0	McDonald
30/09/95	NPL	P	Spennymoor United	326	2-2	McDonald(2)
04/10/95	NPL	P	Witton Albion	583	1-2	Ross
07/10/95	NPL	P	WITTON ALBION	332	4-0	McDonald(2), Ross, McKearney
10/10/95	NPL	P	BAMBER BRIDGE	975	0-0	
14/10/95	FA Trophy	Q1	Atherton L.R.	298	2-1	Leitch, Critchley
21/10/95	NPL	P	BOSTON UNITED	331	0-2	
24/10/95	LC	2	MARINE	262	0-0	
28/10/95	NPL	P	Leek Town	256	0-2	
31/10/95	LC	2 rep	Marine	173	2-4	Ross, McDonald
04/11/95	FA Trophy	Q2	Eastwood Town	86	1-0	McDonald
08/11/95	NPL	P	Accrington Stanley	483	3-7	Pearson, Ross, Emerson
11/11/95	NPL	P	GAINSBOROUGH TRINITY	285	0-6	
18/11/95	NPL	P	Droylsden	130	6-0	Ross(5), Trundle
21/11/95	NPL	P	MARINE	221	1-1	McKearney
25/11/95	FA Trophy	Q3	WINSFORD UNITED	297	3-1	Mayers(2), Leitch
02/12/95	NPL	P	DROYLSDEN	242	6-0	Leitch, Trundle, McKearney, Ross(2), Wright
09/12/95	NPL	P	Blyth Spartans	387	2-3	Ross, Hook
16/12/95	NPL	P	WINSFORD UNITED	221	1-1	Ross
26/12/95	NPL	P	Guiseley	552	3-0	Mayers, Trundle, Ross
09/01/96	NPL	P	Emley	241	3-0	McKearney, Ross(2)
13/01/96	NPL	P	SPENNYMOOR UNITED	278	0-3	
16/01/96	Lancs ATS	2	Atherton L.R.	168	2-1	Elleray(2)
20/01/96	FA Trophy	1	Boston United	808	1-1	Hook
23/01/96	FA Trophy	1 rep	BOSTON UNITED	294	2-1	Trundle, Ross
03/02/96	NPL	P	Boston United	609	1-2	Emerson
13/02/96	FA Trophy	2	GAINSBOROUGH TRINITY	425	2-0	Ross(2)
17/02/96	NPL	P	BUXTON	327	2-1	Trundle, Hook
24/02/96	NPL	P	Marine	401	1-2	Mayers
26/02/96	Lancs ATS	QF	Clitheroe	395	3-2	Worthington, Own-Goal, Ross
02/03/96	FA Trophy	3	Boreham Wood	525	1-1	Leitch
05/03/96	FA Trophy	3 rep	BOREHAM WOOD	833	4-3	Mayers(2), Hook, Ross
09/03/96	NPL	P	Hyde United	603	1-3	Ross
12/03/96	Lancs ATS	SF	Bamber Bridge	542	0-3	
16/03/96	NPL	P	BLYTH SPARTANS	304	1-4	Ross
19/03/96	NPL	P	FRICKLEY ATHLETIC	218	1-1	Wright
23/03/96	FA Trophy	QF	GATESHEAD	1136	3-1	Ross, Mayers, Trundle
30/03/96	NPL	P	LEEK TOWN	326	3-1	Ross(2), McKearney
01/04/96	NPL	P	Winsford United	188	2-0	Trundle(2)
06/04/96	NPL	P	Bishop Auckland	190	1-3	Ross
08/04/96	NPL	P	COLWYN BAY	288	1-1	Hook
13/04/96	FA Trophy	SF(1)	Macclesfield Town	2260	1-3	Hook 25
15/04/96	NPL	P	MATLOCK TOWN	181	3-2	Hook(2), Worthington
20/04/96	FA Trophy	SF(2)	MACCLESFIELD TOWN	3048	1-1	Ross
23/04/96	NPL	P	ACCRINGTON STANLEY	355	0-0	
25/04/96	NPL	P	Gainsborough Trinity	479	0-1	
27/04/96	NPL	P	EMLEY	321	1-0	Ross
29/04/96	NPL	P	Matlock Town	374	3-4	Ross, Hook(2)
30/04/96	NPL	P	HYDE UNITED	348	1-1	Cox(og)
04/05/96	NPL	P	Buxton	437	2-5	McKearney, Hook

EMLEY

Emley Welfare Sports Ground, Emley Huddersfield. Tel: 01924 848398

Secretary: Mr Richard Poulain, 3 Stone Acre Heights, Meltham, Huddersfield HD7 3EF Tel: 01484 851492

Office for match days only 01924 840087 club: 848398

Programme editor: Alan Blackman Tel 01924 403959

Club shop manager: Mrs Linda Sykes Tel 01484 656406

Press officer: Alan Blackman 53 Forge Lane, Liversedge, Wakefield, WF15 7DX Tel 01924 403959

Colours: White and Maroon   Capacity: 3,000

Seating: 250   Covered standing: 750

Clubhouse on ground: Yes

Record attendance: 5,134 v Barking A C 3rd Rd 1969

Also 9,035 v Bolton Wanderers FA Cup 1st Rd 1992, played at Huddersfield Town FC

Biggest win: 12-1 v Boston NCEL 1984-85

Biggest defeat: 0-6 v Shepshed NCEL 1982-83

Record appearances: Ray Dennis 751

Record goalscorer in one season: Mick Pamment 56

Record goalscorer in total: Mick Pamment 305

Record fee received: £10,000 for John Francis to Sheffield Utd in 1988

DIRECTIONS

Follow Huddersfield signs from m1 junction 38, left onto A636 at roundabout, then right after about three quarters of a mile for Emley. From M62 junction 23 to Huddersfield ring-road, follow Wakefield signs for 3 miles, through Lepton, past White Horse pub on left and turn right at top of next hill — just under 3 miles to Emley. Floodlights unmissable in small village. Seven miles from Huddersfield (BR) station — buses to Emley Cross.

HONOURS

FA VASE Runners up 1988 and semi-finalists 1987

Northern Counties East 1988 and 1989

Yorkshire League 1976, 1978, 1980, 1982, League Cup 1970, 1979, 1982

Sheffield and Hallamshire Senior Cup 1976, 1980, 1981, 1984, 1989, 1991, 1992

Huddersfield Challenge Cup 1983, 1984, 1986, Huddersfield League 1966, 1967, 1968, 1969

Manager for 1996-97: Ronnie Glavin, Chairman: Peter Matthews, Vice Chairman: Alan Blackman

Despite the long history of the club, they have only come to prominence since leaving the Huddersfield League in 1969. Early history is unclear, although the Welfare ground was used for sport in the last century. A rugby club was disbanded in 1902 and Emley Clarence FC was born a year later and are believed to have used the Welfare. Before the war Clarence changed their name to Emley Juniors, then Emley United.During the war United played in the Wakefield League, playing home games at Albert Hills, an old cricket ground but following the war United folded and another Emley Juniors were formed using most of the players. The club moved to Chapel Lane, their former home and in 1932 became Emley AFC.The club played on different fields with dressing rooms in the White Horse until August 1957 when the Welfare was re-opened complete with pavilion. The late sixties saw four successive Huddersfield League titles, losing just two matches and it culminated in an Amateur Cup run which saw them reach the last 16, some 5,134 watching the abandoned match with Barking. As the ground improved and a social club opened the club moved on having joined the Yorkshire League and when that merged to form the Northern Counties East in 1982 they moved up. Huddersfield Town opened the new floodlights in 1981, and six years later Emley were in the FA Vase semi-final, where they met St Helens Town and lost, but a year later they made it,

but lost to all conquering Colne Dynamos. That season they were crowned champions but were denied promotion due to ground gradings. The next 12 months saw big changes at the ground with a new stand, offices and a reception area, and when the title was retained, they were promoted to the Northern Premier League. After two seasons they went up as runner up to Whitley Bay and the following year they reached the 1st Round of the FA Cup, playing Bolton Wanderers, at Leeds Road, Huddersfield in front of over 9,000.

EMLEY 1995/96 SEASON

19/08/95	NPL	P	Winsford United	222	4-0	Butterfield, Chapman, Reynolds, Wilson
22/08/95	NPL	P	BOSTON UNITED	331	2-0	Bastock(og), Chapman
26/08/95	NPL	P	Marine	380	1-0	Wilson
28/08/95	NPL	P	BISHOP AUCKLAND	400	1-1	Jones
02/09/95	NPL	P	BARROW	386	1-2	Chapman
05/09/95	NPL	P	Matlock Town	374	1-1	Butterfield
09/09/95	FA Cup	Q1	THACKLEY	186	6-0	Butterfield(3), Chapman, Wilson, Alcide
12/09/95	NPL	P	Spennymoor United	239	0-2	
16/09/95	NPL	P	WITTON ALBION	314	1-0	Chapman
19/09/95	NPL	P	HYDE UNITED	215	1-0	Chapman
23/09/95	FA Cup	Q2	WINSFORD UNITED	253	1-1	Alcide
25/09/95	FA Cup	Q2 rep	Winsford United	248	1-2	Viner
30/09/95	NPL	P	Colwyn Bay	295	0-1	
03/10/95	NPL	P	SPENNYMOOR UNITED	210	0-2	
07/10/95	NPL	P	MATLOCK TOWN	167	3-2	Banks, Viner, Middleton
11/10/95	NPL	P	Boston United	820	1-1	Viner
14/10/95	NPL	P	LEEK TOWN	225	0-1	
17/10/95	NPL	P	GAINSBOROUGH TRINITY	225	1-0	Viner
21/10/95	NPL	P	Leek Town	293	2-2	Soley(og), Constable
24/10/95	LC	2	Harrogate Town	203	2-0	Constable, Viner
28/10/95	NPL	P	Bamber Bridge	519	1-0	Chapman
04/11/95	FA Trophy	Q2	RACING CLUB WARWICK	225	2-1	Chapman, Constable
07/11/95	Sheffield	2	WORKSOP TOWN	175	2-1	Viner, Tonks
11/11/95	NPL	P	DROYLSDEN	196	4-0	Viner(2), Chapman, Bradshaw(og)
18/11/95	NPL	P	Witton Albion	439	1-3	Banks
21/11/95	NPL	P	BLYTH SPARTANS	193	1-3	Alcide
25/11/95	FA Trophy	Q3	GREAT HARWOOD TOWN	224	3-1	Viner, Peltier, Reynolds
02/12/95	NPL	P	GUISELEY	362	2-0	Viner, Lacey
05/12/95	LC	3	Spennymoor United	158	0-5	
09/12/95	Sheffield	3	Frecheville C.A.	106	0-1	
16/12/95	NPL	P	Knowsley United	56	3-1	Banks, McLean(2)
26/12/95	NPL	P	FRICKLEY ATHLETIC	314	5-2	McLean, Graham, Viner, Lacey, Constable
09/01/96	NPL	P	CHORLEY	241	0-3	
13/01/96	NPL	P	KNOWSLEY UNITED	186	1-3	McLean
20/01/96	FA Trophy	1	Morecambe	656	2-2	Graham, Banks
23/01/96	FA Trophy	1 rep	MORECAMBE	412	3-1	David(2), McLean
03/02/96	NPL	P	Barrow	1182	0-0	
10/02/96	FA Trophy	2	GATESHEAD	668	1-2	Banks
17/02/96	NPL	P	WINSFORD UNITED	196	1-1	Graham
24/02/96	NPL	P	Buxton	201	2-1	Banks, Graham
02/03/96	NPL	P	Accrington Stanley	361	0-0	
09/03/96	NPL	P	BAMBER BRIDGE	264	1-1	Graham
12/03/96	NPL	P	Blyth Spartans	310	0-0	
16/03/96	NPL	P	BUXTON	173	2-1	Lacey, McLean
19/03/96	NPL	P	Gainsborough Trinity	378	3-0	David, Viner(2)
30/03/96	NPL	P	ACCRINGTON STANLEY	268	1-3	Banks
03/04/96	NPL	P	Hyde United	333	2-7	Constable, Graham
08/04/96	NPL	P	Frickley Athletic	218	1-2	Graham
13/04/96	NPL	P	Bishop Auckland	173	0-1	
15/04/96	NPL	P	Guiseley	204	1-1	Graham
23/04/96	NPL	P	COLWYN BAY	112	4-1	Reynolds, David, Graham(2)
27/04/96	NPL	P	Chorley	321	0-1	
30/04/96	NPL	P	MARINE	164	2-0	Graham(2)
04/05/96	NPL	P	Droylsden	226	0-3	

FRICKLEY ATHLETIC

Westfield Lane, South Elmsall, Pontefract, Yorks WF9 3LW. Tel: 01977 642460

Secretary: Mr Dennis Fisher, 31 Vicars Ave, South Elmsall,
Pontefract, West Yorks WF9 2LW

Tel 01977 643316

Colours: All Blue

Nickname: The Blues

Capacity: 6,000

Seating: 800

Covered standing: 2,000

Clubhouse on ground: Yes

Record attendance: 6,500 v Rotherham
FA Cup 1st Rd 1971

Record goalscorer in total: K.Whiteley

DIRECTIONS
Follow signs for South
Elmsall from A1 and A638.
left at Superdrug warehouse,
right at T Junction and
immediately left up Westfield
Lane (signposted Frickley
Colliery). Left into Oxford
Road (opposite Westfield
Hotel). ground at bottom on
right. Two miles from South
Elmsall (BR).

HONOURS

Midland Counties League Cup 1976

Sheffield and Hallamshire League Cup 1928, 1957, 1961, 1963, 1967, 1979, 1986, 1988, 1990

Sheffield Association League 1921

Manager for 1996-9l: Mark Dempsey

Assistant manager: Ian Thompson

Chairman: Mike Twiby

Vice Chairman: A Bell

The club was founded in 1910 and played initially in the Sheffield Association before moving into the Yorkshire League. In 1924 they joined the old Midland League where they remained until 1960 when it disbanded. They took the decision to play across the Pennines in the Cheshire County League, until in 1970 they moved back to the newly re-formed Midland Counties League, where four years later they became Frickley Athletic. They were runners up in 1972 and after winning the League Cup in 1976 they were accepted into the Northern Premier League. In 1981 their Westfield Lane ground was given a B grading and after finishing third they took the place of Redditch United in the Alliance Premier League.

In the FA Cup they have reached the First Round six times, and against Rotherham United in 1973 the ground record crowd of 6, 500 was established.

1985-86 saw the club reach the Third Round and make history where they beat a Football League side for the first time, Hartlepool United, 1-0 away in Round Two. Following that success they went on to win the Sheffield Senior Challenge Cup and finish runner up in the Alliance Premier League. A year later there was a complete turn around with early Cup and Trophy exits and relegation back to the NPL.

Since then other than a couple of Sheffield Senior Cup wins, survival has been the main aim for Frickley Athletic Football Club.

FRICKLEY ATHLETIC 1995/96 SEASON

Date	Comp	Round	Opponent	Att	Score	Scorers
19/08/95	NPL	P	CHORLEY	164	1-0	Thompson
23/08/95	NPL	P	GAINSBOROUGH TRINITY	252	3-0	Fuller, Wells, Rayson
26/08/95	NPL	P	Witton Albion	529	0-5	
28/08/95	NPL	P	Guiseley	623	0-3	
02/09/95	NPL	P	MARINE	179	1-1	Wells
06/09/95	NPL	P	Boston United	870	3-1	Canning, Dempsey, Rayson
09/09/95	FA Cup	Q1	PRESCOT	160	0-0	
12/09/95	FA Cup	Q1 rep	Prescot	32	2-2	
16/09/95	NPL	P	Leek Town	262	1-1	Thompson
18/09/95	FA Cup	Q1 rep(2)	Prescot	50	1-0	
23/09/95	FA Cup	Q2	EASTWOOD TOWN	201	2-4	Hatto, Thorpe
25/09/95	NPL	P	Bishop Auckland	133	1-3	Whitehurst
30/09/95	NPL	P	Barrow	1287	1-1	Fuller
03/10/95	NPL	P	BOSTON UNITED	194	1-2	Hatto
07/10/95	NPL	P	DROYLSDEN	105	4-5	Armstrong, Thompson, Hatto, Wells
10/10/95	NPL	P	Blyth Spartans	553	1-1	Thompson
14/10/95	FA Trophy	Q1	Stourbridge	126	2-1	Thorpe, Wells
17/10/95	NPL	P	BLYTH SPARTANS	150	1-2	Armstrong
21/10/95	NPL	P	BUXTON	105	0-2	
25/10/95	LC	2	Bradford Park Avenue	184	1-1	Wells
28/10/95	NPL	P	Knowsley United	140	2-1	Thompson, Armstrong
31/10/95	LC	2 rep	BRADFORD PARK AVENUE	112	3-1	Dickenson, Hatto, Rayson
04/11/95	FA Trophy	Q2	Great Harwood Town	105	2-3	Wells, Rayson
07/11/95	Sheffield	2	Rossington Main	124	8-2	Thorpe(3), Hatto, Rayson(4)
11/11/95	NPL	P	BAMBER BRIDGE	152	0-5	
18/11/95	NPL	P	Marine	366	1-1	Hatto
25/11/95	NPL	P	Droylsden	88	2-2	Rayson(2)
02/12/95	NPL	P	WITTON ALBION	145	1-1	Dempsey(og)
09/12/95	Sheffield	3	The Wetherby Hotel	150	3-1	Armstrong(2), Dickinson
12/12/95	NPL	P	MATLOCK TOWN	116	1-4	Robinson
16/12/95	NPL	P	BARROW	146	0-0	
19/12/95	LC	3	Gainsborough Trinity	368	1-4	Dempsey
26/12/95	NPL	P	Emley	314	2-5	Dickinson, Armstrong
06/01/96	NPL	P	Colwyn Bay	229	3-1	Rayson(2), Thorpe
09/01/96	Sheffield	QF	STOCKSBRIDGE PARK STEELS	151	2-2	Dempsey, Thorpe
13/01/96	NPL	P	Buxton	188	0-1	
16/01/96	Sheffield	QF rep	Stocksbridge Park Steels	150	0-2	
20/01/96	NPL	P	ACCRINGTON STANLEY	154	4-1	Armstrong(2), Yates, Dickinson
03/02/96	NPL	P	Spennymoor United	245	2-2	Rayson(2)
10/02/96	NPL	P	WINSFORD UNITED	112	3-3	Armstrong, Duffty, Dempsey
17/02/96	NPL	P	Hyde United	485	1-4	Thompson
24/02/96	NPL	P	HYDE UNITED	176	3-0	Yates, Duffty(2)
27/02/96	NPL	P	Matlock Town	245	0-6	
05/03/96	NPL	P	BISHOP AUCKLAND	103	0-3	
09/03/96	NPL	P	Winsford United	128	1-4	Thorpe
19/03/96	NPL	P	Chorley	218	1-1	Armstrong
23/03/96	NPL	P	Accrington Stanley	348	1-2	Dickenson
30/03/96	NPL	P	KNOWSLEY UNITED	100	4-3	Hatto, Stubbs(2), Hancock
06/04/96	NPL	P	Gainsborough Trinity	448	2-0	Armstrong, Hatto
08/04/96	NPL	P	EMLEY	218	2-1	Duffty(2)
13/04/96	NPL	P	COLWYN BAY	115	1-1	Kelly
17/04/96	NPL	P	GUISELEY	147	2-2	Hatto, Thorpe
20/04/96	NPL	P	LEEK TOWN	122	1-1	Thorpe
23/04/96	NPL	P	SPENNYMOOR UNITED	109	2-3	Hatto, Taylor
27/04/96	NPL	P	Bamber Bridge	466	3-2	Dempsey(3)

GAINSBOROUGH TRINITY

The Northolme, North Street, Gainsborough, Lincs, DN21 2QN. Tel: 01427 613295 or 615625 club

Secretary: Frank Nicholson, 9 North St, Morton, Gainsborough, Lincs DN21 3AS Tel: 01427 615239

Programme Shop manager: Nigel Tasker

Programme Editor: B. Godley Tel 01427 611612

Colours: Royal Blue and white

Nickname: Blues

Capacity: 7,500

Seating: 238

Covered standing: 5,000

Clubhouse on ground: Yes

Record attendance: 9,760 v Scunthorpe Utd Midland League 1948

Biggest win: 7-0 v Fleetwood 1973-74 and v Gt Harwood 1976-77

Biggest defeat: 0-6 v Emley 1991-92

Record appearances: Monty Brown

Record goalscorer in total: Monty Brown

Record fee received: £20,000 for Tony James to Lincoln City 1988

DIRECTIONS

Ground situated in town centre, 250yds from the Post Office and magistrates court. Two miles from Lea Road (BR).

HONOURS

Northern Premier League Cup 1982

Midland Counties League 1891, 1928, 1949, 1967

Lincs Senior Cup 1890, 1893, 1895, 1898, 1904, 1905, 1907, 1911, 1947, 1948, 1949, 1951, 1958, 1959, 1964

Manager 1996-97: Ernie Moss

Chairman: John Davis

Gainsborough Trinity were formed back in 1873, but did not compete in the Midland League until 1889 where they finished 7th out of 11 clubs. The Northolme ground was originally a cricket ground, and had been since the 1850's, and Trinity used other venues when it was unavailable, such as Pringle Hill and Moreton Terrace. As early as 1884 a crowd of 4,000 saw a Lincolnshire Cup match with Grimsby, and extensive changes were soon made to the ground so as to enable the club to apply to the Football League for membership, which to their surprise was accepted in 1896. The first match was against Newton Heath, who later became Manchester United. Trinity were always hindered by cricketing commitments and eventually after finishing bottom of Division Two in 1912, they resigned and re-joined the Midland League, where they remained until 1968 apart from one season in the Central Alliance. During that period Northolme had ceased to be a cricket ground and had become a well developed football ground which housed a gate of nearly 10,000 for a league match with Scunthorpe just after the War. Trinity won the league that year and took the County Cup three years running, but other than another title in 1967, success has been sporadic.

They entered the Northern Premier League in 1968 and won the League Cup in 1982.

GAINSBOROUGH TRINITY 1995/96 SEASON

Date	Comp	Rnd	Opponent	Att	Score	Scorers
19/08/95	NPL	P	BLYTH SPARTANS	445	4-0	Evans, Matthews, Castledine, Bishop
23/08/95	NPL	P	Frickley Athletic	252	0-3	
26/08/95	NPL	P	Hyde United	319	2-1	Kabia, Castledine
28/08/95	NPL	P	BUXTON	555	2-2	Matthews, Bishop
02/09/95	NPL	P	Winsford United	222	1-1	Matthews
05/09/95	NPL	P	GUISELEY	570	0-2	
09/09/95	FA Cup	Q1	ARNOLD TOWN	385	2-0	Womble, Ellender
13/09/95	NPL	P	Droylsden	94	2-1	Matthews(2)
16/09/95	NPL	P	BAMBER BRIDGE	396	1-3	Matthews
23/09/95	FA Cup	Q2	NANTWICH TOWN	375	5-0	Evans, Kabia(3), Bishop
30/09/95	NPL	P	Knowsley United	74	3-2	Goodacre(2), Kabia
03/10/95	NPL	P	MATLOCK TOWN	510	2-2	Stiles, Fox(og)
07/10/95	FA Cup	Q3	Morecambe	805	2-6	Kabia(2)
10/10/95	NPL	P	Matlock Town	410	2-0	Matthews, Evans
14/10/95	NPL	P	SPENNYMOOR UNITED	417	0-1	
17/10/95	NPL	P	Emley	225	0-1	
21/10/95	NPL	P	KNOWSLEY UNITED	369	2-1	Snodin, Evans
24/10/95	LC	2	Matlock Town	292	1-0	Moore
28/10/95	NPL	P	Witton Albion	455	2-0	Smith, Evans
31/10/95	NPL	P	HYDE UNITED	423	0-0	
04/11/95	NPL	P	LEEK TOWN	416	1-0	Beech
07/11/95	NPL	P	Leek Town	228	0-0	
11/11/95	NPL	P	Chorley	285	6-0	Evans(3), Snodin, Kabia, Smith
25/11/95	FA Trophy	Q3	Ilkeston Town	626	5-0	Ellender, Evans(3), Snodin
28/11/95	PC	1	Worksop Town	500	1-3	Evans
02/12/95	NPL	P	BISHOP AUCKLAND	378	1-0	Morrow
09/12/95	NPL	P	ACCRINGTON STANLEY	499	1-1	Ellender
16/12/95	NPL	P	Spennymoor United	243	1-1	Morrow
19/12/95	LC	3	FRICKLEY ATHLETIC	368	4-1	Morrow(2), Smith, Stiles
01/01/96	NPL	P	Boston United	1176	2-1	Snodin, Morrow
06/01/96	NPL	P	Bamber Bridge	531	1-1	Smith
13/01/96	NPL	P	MARINE	494	1-0	Morrow
20/01/96	FA Trophy	1	NUNEATON BOROUGH	867	4-1	Snodin(3), Morrow
03/02/96	NPL	P	WINSFORD UNITED	464	0-0	
13/02/96	FA Trophy	2	Chorley	425	0-2	
17/02/96	NPL	P	Accrington Stanley	404	1-2	Hardwick
24/02/96	NPL	P	Barrow	1216	1-0	Moore
02/03/96	NPL	P	DROYLSDEN	406	7-1	Smith, Evans(2), Snodin(2), Bishop(2)
05/03/96	LC	QF	WITTON ALBION	420	3-2	Ellender, Evans(2)
09/03/96	NPL	P	Bishop Auckland	163	1-1	Matthews
16/03/96	NPL	P	Marine	335	0-3	
19/03/96	NPL	P	EMLEY	378	0-3	
23/03/96	NPL	P	BARROW	414	2-0	Riley(2)
26/03/96	LC	SF(1)	HYDE UNITED	440	0-2	
30/03/96	NPL	P	Blyth Spartans	443	0-0	
01/04/96	LC	SF(2)	Hyde United	368	0-1	
06/04/96	NPL	P	FRICKLEY ATHLETIC	448	0-2	
08/04/96	NPL	P	Buxton	234	2-1	Evans, Bishop
13/04/96	NPL	P	BOSTON UNITED	854	2-1	Smith, Ellender
16/04/96	NPL	P	Colwyn Bay	246	0-0	
20/04/96	NPL	P	WITTON ALBION	404	1-0	Snodin
25/04/96	NPL	P	CHORLEY	479	1-0	Morrow
30/04/96	NPL	P	COLWYN BAY	464	2-2	Stiles, Lanigan
04/05/96	NPL	P	Guiseley	260	3-1	Morrow, Evans, Bishop

GUISELEY

Nethermoor, Otley Rd, Guiseley, Leeds, LS20 8BT Tel: 01943 872872 club or 873223 office

Secretary: Philip Rogerson, 8 Viewlands Cres, Chevin End, Menston, Ilkley, West Yorks LS29 6BH Tel: 01943 879236

Match Secretary Alan Walker, Reva Bungalow, Goose Lane, Hawksworth, Guiseley LS20 8PL Tel: 01943 875955

Programme Editor: Les Wood Tel 01132 509181

Club shop manager: Johnathan Spinks Tel 01943 878160

Colours: White and Blue   Capacity: 3,000

Seating: 427   Covered standing 1,040

Clubhouse on ground: Yes

Record attendance: 2,486 v Bridlington Town
FA Vase Semi-final 1st leg 1990

HONOURS

FA VASE WINNERS 1991

FA VASE Runners up 1992, FA VASE Semi-final 1990,FA TROPHY Semi-final 1995

Northern Premier League Div 1 1995, Presidents Cup 1995, Division One Cup 1993

Northern Counties East and League Cup 1991, West Riding County Cup 1979, 1980, 1981, 1983, 1994

Yorkshire League Cup 1980, West Riding County Amateur League 1933, 1934, 1935, 1939, 1956

West Yorkshire League Div 1 1961, League Cup 1960 and 1964, Premier Division 1965

Yorkshire League Division Two 1976

Wharfedale Challenge Cup 1907, 33, 41, 47, 55, 56, 59, 61, 62, 63, 64, 65, 66, 67, 68, 87, 89, 93, 94

Wharfedale Invitation Cup 1954, 1956, 1957, 1975, 1976, 1977, 1978

Manager for 1996-97: Steve Richards, Chairman: Gary Douglas

DIRECTIONS

Via M1 to M62 junction 28, follow Leeds road to Leeds ring-road to junction of A65 at Horsforth. At roundabout turn left onto A65 through Rawdon to Guiseley centre. Ground quarter of a mile past traffic lights, on the right entrance on A65 opposite Silver Cross factory. Additional car parking available off Ings Crescent. Five minutes walk from Guiseley (BR/Metro) station.

Guiseley Football Club was formed following the demise of Guisley Celtic, and the new club entered the Wharfedale League four years later, winning it immediately. They moved to the Leeds League and then the West Riding County Amateur Leagues in 1924. The early players were forced to change a mile away in the cellar of the Red Lion Hotel, moving some time later to the Station Hotel, but in 1933 the club acquired a Scout Hut for £10.

This coincided with one of the most successful periods in their history, with a run in 1934 to the 3rd round of the Amateur Cup, where over 2,000 crammed into Nethermoor to watch the locals take on the strong Bournemouth Gasworks Athletic, Guiseley gallantly going down 2-1. They won the league for the first time with the Wharfedale Challenge Cup and the following season the retained the league. 1935 saw them make it three in a row, again reaching the 3rd Round of the Amateur Cup, this time losing to Cambridge Town. Around this time the club acquired for some £50, the old grandstand from Harry Ramsden's Fish Shop, where customers would listen to brass bands. Some 60 plus years later it is still there in good nick. Much later Guisley moved on to the Yorkshire League and in 1973 opened the clubhouse which was shared with the adjacent cricket club. They won the League Cup, defeating rivals Emley in the final and won the County Cup four times in five years, adding an FA Vase quarter-final place to the list of achievements.In 1982, they became founder members of the Northern Counties East, where they did the double in 1991. Since then, both on and off the field, the club has gained nationwide fame, for after reaching the Northern Premier League, winning three titles and cups on the way, they won the FA Vase, after a classic 4-4 draw at Wembley, beating Gresley Rovers in the replay played at Bramall Lane. The following year saw heartbreak with another memorable final, this time against Wimborne Town, where the club lost 5-3 The chances of three appearances in a row was spoiled by Bridlington in the semi-finals the following year, but having moved up to the Trophy, they again went close in 1994, losing the semi-final to Runcorn.

GUISELEY 1995/96 SEASON

Date	Comp	Round	Opponent	Att	Score	Scorers
19/08/95	NPL	P	Droylsden	254	2-1	James(2)
21/08/95	NPL	P	MATLOCK TOWN	355	4-2	Annan, Colville(2), Brockie
26/08/95	NPL	P	Chorley	329	0-1	
28/08/95	NPL	P	FRICKLEY ATHLETIC	623	3-0	Brockie, Colville, Edeson
02/09/95	NPL	P	LEEK TOWN	606	3-1	Brockie(2), Roberts
05/09/95	NPL	P	Gainsborough Trinity	570	2-0	Cook, Richards
09/09/95	FA Cup	Q1	LEIGH R.M.I.	484	3-0	Roberts, Annan, Horsfield
11/09/95	NPL	P	BOSTON UNITED	504	4-2	Flanagan, James, Bottomley, Cook
16/09/95	NPL	P	Knowsley United	112	1-1	Flanagan
19/09/95	NPL	P	Blyth Spartans	577	3-3	James, Horsfield(2)
23/09/95	FA Cup	Q2	LEEK TOWN	507	4-0	Horsfield, Bottomley, Roberts, Cook
25/09/95	NPL	P	SPENNYMOOR UNITED	452	2-2	Flanagan, Roberts
30/09/95	NPL	P	Witton Albion	616	2-3	Roberts, Brockie
02/10/95	NPL	P	Bishop Auckland	249	2-2	Brockie(2)
07/10/95	FA Cup	Q3	MOSSLEY	608	6-1	Brockie, Richards, Horsfield, James, Edeson, Roberts
09/10/95	NPL	P	BISHOP AUCKLAND	544	2-0	Roberts, Edeson
14/10/95	NPL	P	COLWYN BAY	463	1-0	Brockie
17/10/95	NPL	P	Spennymoor United	509	0-0	
21/10/95	FA Cup	Q4	Blyth Spartans	775	0-2	
23/10/95	LC	2	BLYTH SPARTANS	466	1-0	Roberts
28/10/95	NPL	P	WINSFORD UNITED	360	1-1	Roberts
04/11/95	NPL	P	BUXTON	431	1-0	Roberts
07/11/95	W. Riding	1	Goole Town	125	3-0	Horsfield(2), Roberts
11/11/95	NPL	P	Accrington Stanley	602	1-0	James
18/11/95	NPL	P	HYDE UNITED	453	0-1	
21/11/95	NPL	P	Matlock Town	330	0-3	
25/11/95	NPL	P	Colwyn Bay	374	0-0	
27/11/95	PC	1	BLYTH SPARTANS	256	4-0	Hepworth, Taylor(3)
02/12/95	NPL	P	Emley	362	0-2	
04/12/95	W. Riding	2	HATFIELD MAIN	161	3-3	Brockie, Taylor, Cook
09/12/95	NPL	P	Marine	414	1-0	Cook
12/12/95	W. Riding	2 rep	Hatfield Main	72	2-0	Brockie, Roberts
16/12/95	NPL	P	BAMBER BRIDGE	550	4-0	Heald, Taylor(3)
19/12/95	LC	3	BOSTON UNITED	250	1-1	Taylor
26/12/95	NPL	P	CHORLEY	552	0-3	
06/01/96	NPL	P	WITTON ALBION	360	0-1	
13/01/96	NPL	P	Barrow	1466	2-0	Flanagan, Norbury
20/01/96	FA Trophy	1	Stafford Rangers	689	1-1	Norbury
22/01/96	FA Trophy	1 rep	STAFFORD RANGERS	365	2-1	Norbury(2)
10/02/96	FA Trophy	2	ALTRINCHAM	690	4-0	Norbury(2), Cook, Brockie
13/02/96	W. Riding	QF	Thackley	200	2-1	Norbury, Brockie
17/02/96	NPL	P	KNOWSLEY UNITED	450	1-1	Norbury
24/02/96	NPL	P	Bamber Bridge	601	1-3	Roberts
28/02/96	LC	3 rep	Boston United	268	2-3	James, Taylor
02/03/96	FA Trophy	3	GRESLEY ROVERS	790	1-2	Norbury
04/03/96	PC	QF	BUXTON	126	1-1	Taylor
06/03/96	W. Riding	SF	Harrogate Railway Athletic	180	3-1	Norbury(3)
09/03/96	NPL	P	MARINE	380	2-4	Taylor, Atkinson
16/03/96	NPL	P	Leek Town	222	1-1	Taylor
19/03/96	PC	QF rep	Buxton	97	3-1	Cook, James, Flanagan
23/03/96	NPL	P	DROYLSDEN	249	3-0	Taylor, James, Tunnicliffe(og)
28/03/96	PC	SF(1)	Hyde United	241	2-0	James(2)
30/03/96	PC	SF(2)	HYDE UNITED	307	1-1	Hepworth
03/04/96	W. Riding	F	Farsley Celtic	598	0-0	
06/04/96	NPL	P	BLYTH SPARTANS	348	1-1	James
10/04/96	W. Riding	F rep	FARSLEY CELTIC	440	3-2	Roberts, Outhart, Taylor
13/04/96	NPL	P	BARROW	380	1-3	Flanagan
15/04/96	NPL	P	EMLEY	204	1-1	Roberts
17/04/96	NPL	P	Frickley Athletic	147	2-2	James, Roberts
20/04/96	NPL	P	Winsford United	137	2-1	Taylor, Matthews
22/04/96	PC	F(1)	WORKSOP TOWN	470	0-1	
24/04/96	NPL	P	Hyde United	264	1-1	James
27/04/96	NPL	P	ACCRINGTON STANLEY	507	1-3	Matthews
29/04/96	PC	F(2)	Worksop Town	1180	1-3	James
30/04/96	NPL	P	Buxton	322	0-0	
02/05/96	NPL	P	Boston United	587	3-4	Taylor(3)
04/05/96	NPL	P	GAINSBOROUGH TRINITY	260	1-3	Roberts

HYDE UNITED

Ewen Fields, Walker Lane, Hyde, Cheshire SK14 5PL Tel: 0161 368 1031

Secretary Alan Slater, 83 King Edward Rd, Hyde SK14 5JJ Tel: 0161 368 3687

Club shop manager: Joan Slater Tel: 0161 368 3687

Nickname: The Tigers   Colours: Red, White and Black

Capacity: 4,000   Seating: 400

Covered standing: 1,500   Clubhouse on ground: Yes

Record attendance: 9,500 v Nelson FA Cup 1950

Biggest defeat: As Hyde FC 0-26 v Preston FA Cup 1887

Record appearances: Steve Johnson 623

Record goalscorer in total: Peter O'Brien 247

Record fee paid: £8,000 for Jim McCluskie to Mossley 1989

Record fee received: £50,000 for Colin Little from Crewe Alex in 1996

DIRECTIONS

On entering Hyde follow signs for Tameside Leisure Park - in Walker Lane take second car park entrance near Leisure Pool and follow road around to the stadium. Quarter of a mile from Newton (BR).

HONOURS

FA TROPHY semi-finals 1989, 1995, 1996

Northern Premier League Challenge Cup 1986, 1990, 1996

Cheshire County League 1955, 1956, 1982, Cheshire County League Cup 1934, 53, 55, , 73, 82

Cheshire League Challenge Shield 1981 and 1982, Manchester League 1921, 22, 23, 29, 30

Gilchryst Cup 1928, 1929, 1950, 1971, Manchester Senior Cup 1975

Lancs and Cheshire Floodlight Trophy 1955 and 1956

Ashton Challenge Cup 1931, 1932, 1933, 1934, 1940, 1948

Hyde Challenge Cup 1928 and 1929, Reporter Cup 1973, 1974, 1976

Cheshire Senior Cup 1946, 1963, 1970, 1981, 1990, Lancashire Floodlight Trophy 1987 and `1988

Manchester Premier Cup 1994, 1995, 1996,

Manager for 1996-97: Mike McKenzie, Coach: Billy Garton,

Chairman: W D Paterson, Vice Chairman: Alan Slater

Although the present Hyde United club was formed in March 1919, another club, simply called Hyde FC had been in existence since 1885, being best remembered for the thrashing they took when Preston beat them 26-0 in an FA Cup tie at Deepdale in 1887. The new club joined the Manchester League and by 1930 had won the title five times and the Gilchrist Cup twice. They moved on to the Cheshire County League in 1930 and won the League Cup four years later. The decade after World War 2 proved to be the golden years for the club, the Tigers first Cheshire Senior Cup arrived in 1946, being the first of many trophies at Ewen Fields during the next ten years. In 1953 they won the League Cup and followed it by doing the double a year later. 1956 saw them retain the title, and they were runners up for the next three seasons.The 60's saw the club make steady progress and in 1968 they became founder members of the Northern Premier League. However, after only two years they resigned and rejoined the Cheshire League where they were to spend the rest of the decade, winning the League Cup in 1973. In 1981 they were runners up, and went one better a year later, allowing them back into the NPL. The first year back was crowned with 91 league goals and a year later the Tigers were runners up to South Liverpool in the League Cup. In 1987 Hyde took the bold step of installing an artificial surface at Ewen Fields which was re-christened Tameside Stadium. 1987-88 was very successful, finishing runners up in the league again and reaching the semi-final of the FA Trophy and two other semi-finals. The good fortune carried on in 1990 with another Challenge Cup win and a Cheshire Senior Cup triumph. Hyde then went through a difficult period with financial problems, but the last two seasons have again been full of success. 1995 saw Hyde as Manchester Premier Cup winners for the second consecutive time, as well as FA Trophy semi-finalists. Last season saw a return to grass and an astonishing season, where the Tigers again were beaten in the Trophy semi-final, but won the Challenge Cup, and were pipped for runners up in the League. With the Manchester Premier Cup won as well it was a cramped last couple of weeks for the Tigers.

HYDE UNITED 1995/96 SEASON

Date	Competition	Round	Opponent	Att	Score	Scorers
19/08/95	NPL	P	Spennymoor United	321	1-0	Little
21/08/95	NPL	P	Bishop Auckland	229	1-1	Carroll
26/08/95	NPL	P	GAINSBOROUGH TRINITY	319	1-2	Little
28/08/95	NPL	P	Droylsden	286	2-0	Carroll, Owen
02/09/95	NPL	P	Knowsley United	72	1-2	Kimmins
04/09/95	NPL	P	WINSFORD UNITED	274	0-1	
09/09/95	FA Cup	Q1	WINTERTON RANGERS	240	6-0	Esdaille, Kimmins(2), Nolan(2), Carroll
12/09/95	NPL	P	Colwyn Bay	338	3-1	Kimmins(3)
16/09/95	NPL	P	Boston United	716	3-0	Little, Kimmins(2)
19/09/95	NPL	P	Emley	215	0-1	
23/09/95	FA Cup	Q2	Denaby United	185	2-1	Nolan, Little
30/09/95	NPL	P	Bamber Bridge	571	3-3	Kimmins(2), Little
02/10/95	Ches. SC	1	Winsford United	213	4-1	Little(2), Nolan, Carroll
07/10/95	FA Cup	Q3	COLWYN BAY	414	1-2	Kimmins
09/10/95	NPL	P	KNOWSLEY UNITED	249	5-0	Kimmins, Owen, Little(2), Carroll
14/10/95	NPL	P	Buxton	350	1-0	Carroll
16/10/95	NPL	P	COLWYN BAY	286	5-1	Gallagher, Little(2), Carroll, Kimmins
21/10/95	NPL	P	BAMBER BRIDGE	569	2-3	Nolan, Kimmins
23/10/95	LC	2	ASHTON UNITED	466	3-1	Tobin, Nolan, Little
28/10/95	NPL	P	Barrow	1174	1-2	Little
31/10/95	NPL	P	Gainsborough Trinity	423	0-0	
04/11/95	NPL	P	SPENNYMOOR UNITED	462	3-2	Tobin, Kimmins, Nolan
11/11/95	NPL	P	LEEK TOWN	441	3-2	Nolan, Carroll, Owen
18/11/95	NPL	P	Guiseley	453	1-0	Tobin
21/11/95	Ches. SC	QF	Stalybridge Celtic	614	3-0	Nolan(3)
25/11/95	NPL	P	MARINE	561	4-0	Nolan, Switzer, Carroll, Little
02/12/95	NPL	P	Accrington Stanley	464	1-1	Little
09/12/95	NPL	P	BUXTON	394	7-0	Kimmins(2), Little(2), Carroll, Nolan(2)
11/12/95	LC	3	MARINE	330	5-3	Little, Kimmins(2), Carroll(2)
16/12/95	NPL	P	BISHOP AUCKLAND	424	3-1	Owen, Carroll(2)
01/01/96	NPL	P	BARROW	736	0-0	
06/01/96	NPL	P	ACCRINGTON STANLEY	512	0-0	
09/01/96	PC	1	Leek Town	140	2-2	Little, Esdaille
13/01/96	NPL	P	Winsford United	261	4-1	Nolan, Little(2), McCarrick(og)
20/01/96	FA Trophy	1	Marine	467	0-0	
22/01/96	FA Trophy	1 rep	MARINE	416	0-0	
01/02/96	FA Trophy	1 rep(2)	MARINE	374	3-0	Nolan, Carroll, Rooney(og)
03/02/96	NPL	P	Matlock Town	415	3-1	Dowe, Kimmins, Nolan
10/02/96	FA Trophy	2	WELLING UNITED	680	4-1	Kimmins(4)
13/02/96	Manc PC	QF	Maine Road	220	2-1	Esdaille, Carroll
17/02/96	NPL	P	FRICKLEY ATHLETIC	485	4-1	Garton, Carroll(3)
22/02/96	PC	1 rep	LEEK TOWN	285	2-0	Carroll(2)
24/02/96	NPL	P	Frickley Athletic	176	0-3	
26/02/96	Ches. SC	SF(1)	MACCLESFIELD TOWN	716	2-1	Nolan, Carroll
02/03/96	FA Trophy	3	CARSHALTON ATHLETIC	854	3-2	Carroll, Kimmins, Owen
05/03/96	PC	QF	Marine	142	3-0	Nolan(2), Murphy
07/03/96	LC	QF	LANCASTER CITY	231	5-1	Varden(2), Kimmins(2), Nolan
09/03/96	NPL	P	CHORLEY	603	3-1	Varden(2), Murphy
12/03/96	Ches. SC	SF(2)	Macclesfield Town	707	1-1	Varden
16/03/96	NPL	P	Witton Albion	638	1-1	Carroll
18/03/96	Manc PC	SF	RADCLIFFE BOROUGH	320	2-0	Kimmins, Carroll
23/03/96	FA Trophy	QF	STEVENAGE BOROUGH	2012	3-2	Nolan, Kimmins, Carroll
26/03/96	LC	SF(1)	Gainsborough Trinity	440	2-0	Nolan, Kimmins
28/03/96	PC	SF(1)	GUISELEY	241	0-2	
30/03/96	PC	SF(2)	Guiseley	307	1-1	Carroll
01/04/96	LC	SF(2)	GAINSBOROUGH TRINITY	368	1-0	Carroll
03/04/96	NPL	P	EMLEY	333	7-2	Carroll(2), Evans, Kimmins, Nolan, Varden(2)
06/04/96	NPL	P	BOSTON UNITED	604	2-4	Murphy, Carroll
08/04/96	NPL	P	MATLOCK TOWN	508	1-1	Carroll
10/04/96	NPL	P	Marine	333	0-4	
13/04/96	FA Trophy	SF(1)	NORTHWICH VICTORIA	2253	1-2	Varden
15/04/96	NPL	P	WITTON ALBION	367	1-0	Carroll
20/04/96	FA Trophy	SF(2)	Northwich Victoria	2809	0-1	
22/04/96	NPL	P	Blyth Spartans	396	1-5	Evans
24/04/96	NPL	P	GUISELEY	264	1-1	Carroll
26/04/96	NPL	P	DROYLSDEN	491	1-1	Carroll
28/04/96	NPL	P	BLYTH SPARTANS	396	4-1	Nolan, Switzer, Carroll(2)
30/04/96	NPL	P	Chorley	348	1-1	Evans
03/05/96	LC	F	LEEK TOWN	501	1-1	Ogley(og) (won on penalties)
04/05/96	NPL	P	Leek Town	213	1-0	Donnelly
06/05/96	Ches. SC	F	WITTON ALBION	768	1-3	Evans
07/05/96	Manc PC	F	CURZON ASHTON	390	2-2	(at Bolton, won on penalties)

KNOWSLEY UNITED

Alt Park, Endmoor Rd, Huyton, Merseyside L36. Tel: 0151 480 8077 or 480 2529

Secretary: Ken O'Brien c/o The Football Club, 153
Church Rd, Litherland Tel: 0151 474 3808

Match Secretary: Gordon Lonergan 26 Church Way,
Kirkby, Liverpool Tel 0151 546 6563

Programme Editor: J.Pilwick, 87 Butleigh Rd, Huyton,
Merseyside L36 3SW Tel 0151 289 4011

Nickname: The Reds   Colours: Red and Black

Capacity: 3,400   Seating: 300

Covered standing: 800

Clubhouse on ground: Yes

Record attendance: 980 v Everton
Liverpool Senior Cup 1984

Biggest win: 10-1 v Flixton 1991

Biggest defeat: 0-8 v Matlock Town 1995

Record appearances: Joe Barton

DIRECTIONS

Come off M62 at junction 6 onto
M57. Leave at junction 2 (Prescot),
onto Liverpool Road at roundabout,
3rd right at 3rd set of lights into
Seth Powell Way. From Junction 3
(Huyton), go straight across
roundabout onto Huyton link road
(Seth Powell way) and turn right at
lights. From Liverpool; East Prescot
Road-Liverpool Road (6 miles) —
turn left into Seth Powell Way.
Buses 10, 10a, 8, 210 to Page
Moss. Nearest station is Huyton 2
miles away — bus from station to
Page Moss.

Record goalscorer in one season: Jimmy Bell 50

Record goalscorer in total: Jimmy Bell

Record fee received: Undisclosed for Mike Marsh to Liverpool

HONOURS

North West Counties League, Division Three 1985, Division Two 1986

RAAB Karcher Cup 1990, NWCL Champions Cup 1991

Northern Premier League Div 1 1991, Liverpool Senior Cup 1987

MANAGER FOR 1996-97: Peter Orr, CHAIRMAN Peter Orr, VICE CHAIRMAN: Terry Phillips

Knowsley United began life in 1984 as the newly formed Kirkby Town FC and were elected to Division Three of the North West Counties League, winning the title at the first attempt. The following season the same squad clinched Division Two by seven points, but problems with the ground at Simonswood Lane, which would have forced many lesser clubs out of existence, meant that the club had to set up home in the Kirkby Sports Centre for season 1986-87. They finished fourth, plus lifting the prestigious Liverpool Senior Cup by beating a strong Liverpool side at Anfield.

The team had started to grow old together and it was a very young side which finished mid-table a year later. In 1988 the club moved to its present home at Alt Park, the former home of Huyton RLFC, and with the move came the name change to Knowsley Utd. They were runners up in 1989 and 1990, but some consolation was gained by winning the RAAB Karcher Cup and the Champions v Cup winners Cup.

Promotion came in 1991 with striker Jimmy Bell netting 50 times.

In 1993, after an average start in the NPL the club put together a superb run which took them to promotion to the Premier Division. A memorable FA Cup run ended at Goodison Park against Carlisle Utd, but the league form was disappointing. 1994-95 was a testing time for the club. The ground was severely vandalised during the Summer, forcing them to play the first five games away, and once they did return support hit an all time low, with just six gates hitting three figures.

Last season started poorly but a good recovery ensured survival for Knowsley United.

KNOWSLEY UNITED 1995/96 SEASON

Date	Comp		Opponent	Att	Score	Scorers
19/08/95	NPL	P	Barrow	1124	0-7	
23/08/95	NPL	P	Accrington Stanley	472	2-4	Cooper, Jones
26/08/95	NPL	P	Matlock Town	258	0-8	
28/08/95	NPL	P	Colwyn Bay	396	0-0	
02/09/95	NPL	P	HYDE UNITED	72	2-1	Rowlands, Gouldbourne
06/09/95	NPL	P	CHORLEY	152	1-2	Edwards
09/09/95	FA Cup	Q1	BRADFORD PARK AVENUE	74	0-0	
13/09/95	FA Cup	Q1 rep	Bradford Park Avenue	158	2-3	Rowlands(2)
16/09/95	NPL	P	GUISELEY	112	1-1	Wilson
20/09/95	NPL	P	COLWYN BAY	68	1-3	Jones
23/09/95	NPL	P	Witton Albion	436	1-2	Wilson
26/09/95	NPL	P	Chorley	184	0-1	
30/09/95	NPL	P	GAINSBOROUGH TRINITY	74	2-3	Wilson, Harland
03/10/95	NPL	P	Marine	342	1-2	Wilson
07/10/95	NPL	P	Buxton	194	2-3	Wilson(2)
09/10/95	NPL	P	Hyde United	249	0-5	
14/10/95	FA Trophy	Q1	MOOR GREEN	80	3-2	Wilson(2), Jones
17/10/95	NPL	P	BAMBER BRIDGE	94	2-2	Barton, Jones
21/10/95	NPL	P	Gainsborough Trinity	369	1-2	Jones
24/10/95	LC	2	Lancaster City	143	0-2	
28/10/95	NPL	P	FRICKLEY ATHLETIC	140	1-2	Brown
04/11/95	FA Trophy	Q2	Nuneaton Borough	1017	2-3	Wilson(2)
08/11/95	NPL	P	Spennymoor United	276	4-1	Barton, Gouldbourne, Wilson(2)
11/11/95	NPL	P	BUXTON	43	2-0	Johnson, Williams
18/11/95	NPL	P	BLYTH SPARTANS	87	1-0	Clarke
25/11/95	NPL	P	BARROW	145	0-2	
27/11/95	NPL	P	Winsford United	111	1-0	Wilson
09/12/95	NPL	P	Bishop Auckland	122	2-1	Wilson, Jones
12/12/95	L'pool SC	1	SKELMERSDALE UNITED	40	2-0	Barton, Johnston
16/12/95	NPL	P	EMLEY	56	1-3	Wilson
06/01/96	NPL	P	BOSTON UNITED	42	2-4	Wilson(2)
13/01/96	NPL	P	Emley	186	3-1	Wilson(2), Esdaille
20/01/96	NPL	P	SPENNYMOOR UNITED	42	2-0	Kinney, Wilde
23/01/96	NPL	P	WINSFORD UNITED	44	4-1	Harland(2), Wilde(2)
30/01/96	L'pool SC	QF	BOOTLE	38	4-0	
03/02/96	NPL	P	Bamber Bridge	451	2-2	Wilde, Stephens
17/02/96	NPL	P	Guiseley	450	1-1	Wilson
24/02/96	NPL	P	LEEK TOWN	33	3-1	Wilde, Jones, Williams
02/03/96	NPL	P	MATLOCK TOWN	145	1-0	Cowlerton
09/03/96	NPL	P	Droylsden	125	1-5	Wilde
16/03/96	NPL	P	Boston United	618	2-4	Kinney, Wilde
19/03/96	NPL	P	ACCRINGTON STANLEY	42	1-0	Fahy
23/03/96	NPL	P	WITTON ALBION	112	2-2	Congleton, Parker
30/03/96	NPL	P	Frickley Athletic	100	3-4	Wilde, Birchall, Tyrrell
02/04/96	L'pool SC	SF	EVERTON	204	0-2	
08/04/96	NPL	P	DROYLSDEN	66	2-0	Wilde, Williams
13/04/96	NPL	P	Leek Town	177	0-2	
20/04/96	NPL	P	Blyth Spartans	379	1-4	Johnston
25/04/96	NPL	P	MARINE	129	2-1	Barton, Jones
27/04/96	NPL	P	BISHOP AUCKLAND	44	1-2	Barton

CITY OF LANCASTER

Giant Axe, West Road, Lancaster LA1 5PE. Tel: 01524 382238 or 841950

Secretary: Barry Newsham, 104 Willow Lane, Forest Park, Lancaster LA1 5QF. Tel: 01524 35774

Match Secretary: David Hughes, 57 Ullswater Rd, Lancaster LA1 3PS Tel: 01524 68990

Programme Editor: Colin Dyer Tel 01524 382121

Club shop manager: David Crawford

Colours: Blue & white   Nickname: The Dolly Blues

Capacity: 2,500   Seating: 300

Covered standing: 400   Clubhouse on ground: Yes

Record attendance: 7,500 v Carlisle Utd FA Cup in 1936

Biggest win: 8-0 v Leyland Motors 1983-84

Biggest defeat: 0-7 v Newtown NPL 1989-90

Record appearances: Edgar Parkinson 531

DIRECTIONS

From south: M6 junction 33, follow into city, left at lights immediately after Waterstones bookshop, second right, pass railway station on right, follow road down hill, ground first right. From north: M6 jct 34, left on to A683, follow into city on one-way system, pass police station, at next lights by Alexandre pub follow road back down in centre, then follow as from south. 5 mins walk from both bus and rail stations.

HONOURS

Lancashire Combination 1922, 1930, 1935, 1936, Lancashire Combination Cup 1922

Lancashire ATS Trophy 1928, 1929, 1931, 1934, 1952, 1975

Northern Premier League Div 1 and Div 1 Cup 1996, President's Cup 1995

Manager: for 1996-97 Alan Tinsley, Assistant manager: M. Hoyle

Coach: J. Coleman, Chairman: John Bagguley

Managing Director: R.R. Lowman, Commercial Manager: M. Hoyle 01524 382238

Lancaster City Fanzine: The Mad Axeman available from club

Lancaster City FC was founded in 1902 and became members of the Lancashire Combination Football League, playing its first two games at Quay Meadow before moving to the present ground at Giant Axe. In 1921 the club applied for membership of the Football League Third Division North and also became a Limited Company.

The club remained in that league right through to 1970, when they joined the Northern Premier League where they stayed for twelve seasons during which their best pacing was seventh, with a runners up spot in the Challenge Cup. In 1983 the club was re-named City of Lancaster FC and joined the North-West Counties League for a further four seasons, returning to the NPL as founder members of the First Division, in 1987.

The Giant Axe has changed dramatically over the years, being open on one side for many years before being enclosed. It has had a number of stands, at least two of which have burnt down and has had banking built up and then taken down, as needs changed. The name allegedly derives from the shape of the original field, which bordered a railway and held a crowd of 7,500 for an FA Cup tie in 1936.

Honours have been thin on the ground up to last May, when after going close to promotion in 1995, they were champions of Division One of the Northern Premier League. In the early days, City won the Lancashire Combination four times as well as being runners up also four times. They won the League Cup in 1922 and have won the Lancashire ATS Trophy six times. With FA Cup runs to the 2nd Round twice the Dolly Blues have had some success, but last May crowned one of the best years as they took the Division One title by five points from Alfreton Town and completed the double by taking the League Cup.

CITY OF LANCASTER 1995/96 SEASON

Date	Comp	Round	Opponent	Att	Score	Scorers
19/08/95	NPL	1	Bradford Park Avenue	241	3-0	Yeo, Diggle(2)
22/08/95	NPL	1	GRETNA	218	1-0	Bell
26/08/95	NPL	1	CONGLETON TOWN	198	3-0	Shirley, Key, Diggle
02/09/95	NPL	1	ASHTON UNITED	226	2-0	Diggle, Gelling
05/09/95	NPL	1	Workington	320	0-0	
09/09/95	FA Cup	Q1	PICKERING TOWN	208	2-1	Yeo(2)
12/09/95	NPL	1	WORKINGTON	246	2-1	Yeo, Bell
16/09/95	NPL	1	Lincoln United	209	3-1	Bell(2), Borrowdale
19/09/95	NPL	1	Fleetwood	250	1-2	Bell
23/09/95	FA Cup	Q2	PETERLEE NEWTOWN	217	3-0	Diggle(3)
26/09/95	LC	1	FLEETWOOD	154	4-2	Gelling, Diggle(3)
30/09/95	NPL	1	Farsley Celtic	162	1-2	Shirley
03/10/95	NPL	1	LEIGH R.M.I.	202	5-2	Key(2), Diggle, Borrowdale(2)
07/10/95	FA Cup	Q3	Bishop Auckland	298	1-0	Diggle
10/10/95	NPL	1	Gretna	135	3-2	Borrowdale(2), Eatock
14/10/95	FA Trophy	Q1	SOLIHULL BOROUGH	173	3-0	Gelling, Bell, Trainor
17/10/95	NPL	1	GREAT HARWOOD TOWN	205	4-1	Yeo, Diggle, Gelling(2)
21/10/95	FA Cup	Q4	Spennymoor United	621	0-1	
24/10/95	LC	2	KNOWSLEY UNITED	143	2-0	Diggle, Byron
28/10/95	NPL	1	Atherton L.R.	177	1-2	Trainor
31/10/95	NPL	1	FLEETWOOD	220	0-1	
04/11/95	FA Trophy	Q2	Curzon Ashton	278	1-1	Shirley
07/11/95	FA Trophy	Q2 rep	CURZON ASHTON	206	3-0	Bell(2), Shirley
11/11/95	NPL	1	ALFRETON TOWN	214	1-1	Key
18/11/95	NPL	1	Whitley Bay	136	1-0	Diggle
20/11/95	NPL	1	Great Harwood Town	135	1-1	Borrowdale
25/11/95	FA Trophy	Q3	Ashton United	229	1-1	Flanery
28/11/95	FA Trophy	Q3 rep	ASHTON UNITED	228	0-2	
02/12/95	NPL	1	Ashton United	203	1-1	Borrowdale
05/12/95	LC	3	Bamber Bridge	349	1-0	Diggle
09/12/95	NPL	1	BRADFORD PARK AVENUE	278	1-0	Borrowdale
12/12/95	1C	2	FARSLEY CELTIC	115	1-1	Bell
16/12/95	NPL	1	Eastwood Town	120	2-1	Trainor, Shirley
06/01/96	NPL	1	CURZON ASHTON	201	2-1	Shirley, Diggle
10/01/96	1C	2 rep	Farsley Celtic	99	3-1	Shirley(2), Key
13/01/96	NPL	1	Alfreton Town	333	6-1	Key, Borrowdale(2), Shirley, Pickering(og), Bell
16/01/96	Lancs ATS	2	Bamber Bridge	380	3-4	Diggle, Byron, Shirley
20/01/96	NPL	1	HARROGATE TOWN	207	2-1	Borrowdale, Diggle
03/02/96	NPL	1	WORKSOP TOWN	264	3-1	Diggle(3)
10/02/96	NPL	1	ATHERTON L.R.	176	1-0	Diggle
13/02/96	NPL	1	Warrington Town	72	1-1	Diggle
17/02/96	NPL	1	Congleton Town	162	1-1	Byron
20/02/96	1C	QF	WHITLEY BAY	139	2-1	Byron, Diggle
24/02/96	NPL	1	Worksop Town	452	2-0	Nunn(og), Borrowdale
02/03/96	NPL	1	NETHERFIELD	231	2-2	Flannery, Borrowdale
07/03/96	LC	QF	Hyde United	231	1-5	Diggle
09/03/96	NPL	1	Harrogate Town	219	2-2	Diggle, Borrowdale
13/03/96	NPL	1	Leigh R.M.I.	151	1-0	Coleman
16/03/96	NPL	1	WHITLEY BAY	241	3-1	Byram, Coleman, Borrowdale
19/03/96	1C	SF(1)	GREAT HARWOOD TOWN	188	4-1	Diggle(3), Shirley
23/03/96	NPL	1	LINCOLN UNITED	508	2-0	Diggle(2)
25/03/96	1C	SF(2)	Great Harwood Town	116	2-0	Gelling, Trainor
30/03/96	NPL	1	Radcliffe Borough	231	0-0	
06/04/96	NPL	1	WARRINGTON TOWN	330	4-2	Coleman, Shirley(2), Borrowdale
08/04/96	NPL	1	Netherfield	238	2-2	Diggle, Gelling
13/04/96	NPL	1	EASTWOOD TOWN	303	2-2	Coleman(2)
20/04/96	NPL	1	Curzon Ashton	197	3-0	Coleman(3)
23/04/96	1C	F	Atherton L.R.	436	1-0	Coleman (at Bamber Bridge)
27/04/96	NPL	1	RADCLIFFE BOROUGH	503	3-1	Trainor, Coleman(2)
04/05/96	NPL	1	FARSLEY CELTIC	383	1-2	Coleman

LEEK TOWN

Harrison Park, Macclesfield Park, Leek. Tel: 01538 399278 or 383734 club

Secretary: Michael Rowley, 62 London Rd, Chesterton, Newcastle, Staffs SK5 7DY Tel: 01782 562890

Programme Editor: Mike Cope Tel: 01538 384202

Club shop manager Mr R Buxton Tel: 01538 399278

Colours: All Blue,   Nickname: The Blues

Capacity: 3,600   Seating: 625

Covered standing: 3,300   Clubhouse on ground: Yes

Record attendance: 5,312 v Macclesfield Town
FA Cup 2nd Qual Rd 1973

Record appearances: Gary Pearce 447

Record goalscorer in total: Dave Sutton 136

DIRECTIONS

Opposite Courtaults chemical works on A523 Macclesfield to Buxton road half a mile out of Leek heading towards Macclesfield.

HONOURS

FA TROPHY Runners up 1990

Northern Premier League Division One 1990 and League Shield 1991

North-West Counties League and Charity Shield 1985

Cheshire County League and Challenge Shield 1975

Manchester League 1952, 1972, 1973 and League Cup 1973

Staffs County League 1951, 1970, 1971, 1974 Div 2 1962, Staffs Challenge Cup 1974

Leek Post Charity Shield 1947, Leek Cup 1948, 1953, 1971,1972, May Bank Cup 1948, 1951, 1972

Hanley Cup 1949 and 1971

Manager for 1996-97: Phil Wilson, Assistant manager: Peter Ward

Chairman: Lyndon Davies, Vice Chairman: Mike Cope

There was a Leek FC which dated back to 1876, when they played a disputed game with Macclesfield, but the modern club stems from the end of the Second War when a group of locals got together to form Abbey Green Rovers. They graduated from there to Leek Lowe Hamil and played in the Leek and Moorlands League, playing on a field next to the White Lion pub. They moved up to the Staffs County League where they were runners up in 1948 and 1950, but 1951 saw the club take the title without losing a match. From there the club moved up to the Manchester League and changed its name to Leek Town FC. They won the title at the first attempt and also took the Staffs Junior Cup. Within four years they had moved south to join the Birmingham League, but support waned and the club resigned in December 1956, rejoining the Manchester League in August 1957. Finances still proved a problem and they again resigned and joined the Staffs County League again. For some years the club struggled on, having moved to the current ground which was not much more than a field with a hedge, around 1950. Slowly the club and the ground developed and after league titles the club joined the strong Cheshire League in 1973. In their second year they were champions under chairman Geoff Harrison, after whom the ground is now named, Leek were founder members of the NWCL and in 1987 when the NPL formed a second division they were founder members of that too. 1989-90 proved to be a memorable season, as Town were promoted to the Premier Division and reached the final of the FA Trophy, where they lost to Barrow at Wembley. Since then there has been success in various cups, including the FA Cup, and in 1994 they held Wigan Athletic to a 2-2 draw before losing the replay. The season ended with Leek in runners up spot, but they were controversially denied a place in the Conference and found themselves placed in the Southern League instead. They were losing finalists in the League Cup, but the season was a financial disaster and for last year they were back in the NPL where they won the Staffs Senior Cup for the first time and were beaten in the League Cup final.

LEEK TOWN 1995/96 SEASON

Date	Comp	Round	Opponent	Att	Score	Scorers
19/08/95	NPL	P	ACCRINGTON STANLEY	367	2-2	Washington, Sutton
21/08/95	NPL	P	Winsford United	268	0-0	
26/08/95	NPL	P	Blyth Spartans	510	1-2	Sutton
28/08/95	NPL	P	WITTON ALBION	471	2-1	Wheaton(2)
02/09/95	NPL	P	Guiseley	606	1-3	Twigg
05/09/95	NPL	P	DROYLSDEN	221	4-0	Soley(2), Wheaton, Twigg
09/09/95	FA Cup	Q1	CLITHEROE	202	1-1	Twigg
11/09/95	FA Cup	Q1 rep	Clitheroe	237	2-2	Somerville, Soley
16/09/95	NPL	P	FRICKLEY ATHLETIC	262	1-1	Soley
18/09/95	FA Cup	Q1 rep(2)	Clitheroe	258	0-0	
20/09/95	FA Cup	Q1 rep(3)	CLITHEROE	181	1-0	Wheaton
23/09/95	FA Cup	Q2	Guiseley	507	0-4	
26/09/95	NPL	P	Matlock Town	328	1-0	Wheaton
30/09/95	NPL	P	BISHOP AUCKLAND	231	0-1	
02/10/95	Staffs SC	1	STOKE CITY	132	3-2	Soley, Twigg, Brown
07/10/95	NPL	P	BAMBER BRIDGE	293	2-3	Soley, Twigg
10/10/95	NPL	P	BUXTON	310	0-0	
14/10/95	NPL	P	Emley	225	1-0	Somerville
18/10/95	NPL	P	Boston United	944	2-2	Twigg, Fisher
21/10/95	NPL	P	EMLEY	293	2-2	Twigg(2)
24/10/95	LC	2	BUXTON	149	1-0	Soley
28/10/95	NPL	P	CHORLEY	256	2-0	Diskin, Twigg
04/11/95	NPL	P	Gainsborough Trinity	416	0-1	
07/11/95	NPL	P	GAINSBOROUGH TRINITY	228	0-0	
11/11/95	NPL	P	Hyde United	441	2-3	Sutton(2)
14/11/95	Staffs SC	2	Rocester	112	3-2	Leicester, Diskin, Sutton
18/11/95	NPL	P	WINSFORD UNITED	220	5-1	Giblin, Sutton, Leicester, Loughton(2)
21/11/95	NPL	P	Buxton	304	2-1	Sutton, Wheaton
25/11/95	FA Trophy	Q3	BOSTON UNITED	370	0-0	
29/11/95	FA Trophy	Q3 rep	Boston United	819	0-2	
02/12/95	NPL	P	Spennymoor United	232	2-4	Twigg(2)
05/12/95	LC	3	EASTWOOD TOWN	67	4-3	Wheaton(2), Somerville, Soley
09/12/95	NPL	P	COLWYN BAY	186	1-1	Wheaton
16/12/95	NPL	P	Droylsden	124	1-2	Leicester
01/01/96	NPL	P	Witton Albion	607	1-2	Wheaton
06/01/96	NPL	P	BARROW	324	2-0	Soley, Wheaton
09/01/96	PC	1	HYDE UNITED	140	2-2	Soley(2)
13/01/96	NPL	P	Accrington Stanley	421	0-0	
16/01/96	Staffs SC	QF	HALESOWEN HARRIERS	97	3-2	Soley(2), Filson
20/01/96	NPL	P	Bamber Bridge	424	0-0	
10/02/96	NPL	P	Bishop Auckland	177	1-1	Soley
13/02/96	LC	QF	ACCRINGTON STANLEY	117	0-0	
17/02/96	NPL	P	BLYTH SPARTANS	251	1-3	Bauress
22/02/96	PC	1 rep	Hyde United	285	0-2	
24/02/96	NPL	P	Knowsley United	33	1-3	Twigg
28/02/96	LC	QF rep	Accrington Stanley	201	3-1	Twigg(2), Giblin
02/03/96	NPL	P	Colwyn Bay	257	0-0	
09/03/96	NPL	P	Barrow	1077	0-1	
16/03/96	NPL	P	GUISELEY	222	1-1	Giblin
19/03/96	Staffs SC	SF	Bilston Town	34	1-0	Wheaton
23/03/96	NPL	P	MATLOCK TOWN	250	4-2	Leicester, Soley(2), Twigg
27/03/96	LC	SF(1)	Boston United	345	2-1	Twigg, Wheaton
30/03/96	NPL	P	Chorley	326	1-3	Twigg
02/04/96	LC	SF(2)	BOSTON UNITED	165	2-0	Sutton, Leicester
06/04/96	NPL	P	SPENNYMOOR UNITED	212	0-2	
08/04/96	NPL	P	Marine	349	1-2	Batho
13/04/96	NPL	P	KNOWSLEY UNITED	177	2-0	Bates, Batho
16/04/96	Staffs SC	F(1)	Newcastle Town	221	0-1	
20/04/96	NPL	P	Frickley Athletic	122	1-1	Batho
23/04/96	NPL	P	BOSTON UNITED	188	2-2	Twigg, Filson
27/04/96	NPL	P	MARINE	229	0-1	
29/04/96	Staffs SC	F(2)	NEWCASTLE TOWN	204	4-2	Twigg(2), Soley, Bauress
03/05/96	LC	F	Hyde United	501	1-1	Filson (Lost on Penalties)
04/05/96	NPL	P	HYDE UNITED	213	0-1	

MARINE

Rossett Park, College Road, Crosby, Liverpool. Tel: 0151 924 1743 or 924 4046 club

Secretary: John Wildman, 4 Ashbourne Ave, Blundellsands, L23 8TX Tel: 0151 924 5248

Press and Programme: David Wotherspoon, 2 Willow Villas, Mairscough Lane, Downholland, West Lancs

Tel: 0151 520 2253

Club shop manager: Dave Rannard Tel: 0151 474 9848

DIRECTIONS	

DIRECTIONS

College Road is off main Liverpool - Southport road (A565) in Crosby. Ground ten minutes walk from Crosby & Blundellsands (Mersey Rail). Bus No. 92.

Colours: White and black   Nickname: The Mariners

Capacity: 2,500   Seating: 400

Covered standing: 1,500   Clubhouse on ground: Yes

Record attendance: 4,000 v Nigeria Friendly 1949

Biggest win: 14-2 v Rossendale Utd Cheshire Co Lge 1978

Biggest defeat: 2-11 v Shrewsbury Town FA Cup 1995

Record appearances: Peter Smith 952

Record goalscorer in one season: Paul Meachin

Record goalscorer in total: Paul Meachin 200

Record fee paid: £7,000 for John Penman

Record fee received: £16,000 for Brian Ross in 1995

HONOURS

FA AMATEUR CUP Runners up 1932, Semi-finalists 1947

FA TROPHY Semi-finals 1984 and 1992

Northern Premier League 1995, League Cup 1985 and 1992

Cheshire County League 1974, 1976, 1978,

Lancs Combination League Cup 1931, Lancs ATS Trophy 1979, 1988, 1991

Lancs Amateur Cup 1922, 1926, 1931, 1932, 1933, Liverpool Senior Cup 1979, 1985, 1988, 1990, 1995

Liverpool non-League Cup 1969, 1976, 1977, Liverpool Challenge Cup 1943, 1945, 1972

Manager 1996-97: Roly Howard, Assistant Manager: Roger Patience, Chairman: Tom Culshaw

Marine FC, who play at Crosby, seven miles north of Liverpool take their name from a pub a few miles from the ground where they were founded in 1894, as a breakaway club from Waterloo Melville.

In its early days Marine enjoyed enormous success in the local I Zingari League and Liverpool County Combination before moving on just before the Second War to become the only amateur side in the professional Lancashire Combination. They moved on to the Cheshire League and were champions three times in the 70's before joining the Northern Premier League in 1979. They finished twice as runners up in 1986 and 1992 before clinching their first title in 1994. They have also won the League Cup twice in 1985 and 1992. Elsewhere on the cup front they got to the final of the FA Amateur Cup in 1932, losing to Dulwich Hamlet and in the FA Cup they reached the 3rd Round in 1993 losing away to Crewe Alexandra.

They have been in the First Round several times including last year's devastating 11-2 defeat at Shrewsbury Town. In the FA Trophy, the Mariners have twice reached the semi-final although as yet have not reached Wembley.

MARINE 1995/96 SEASON

Date	Comp	Round	Opponent	Att	Score	Scorers
12/08/95	S		BAMBER BRIDGE	354	2-2	Grant, Watson
19/08/95	NPL	P	Colwyn Bay	403	0-0	
22/08/95	NPL	P	BAMBER BRIDGE	406	0-0	
26/08/95	NPL	P	EMLEY	380	0-1	
28/08/95	NPL	P	Winsford United	210	0-1	
02/09/95	NPL	P	Frickley Athletic	179	1-1	Ward
05/09/95	NPL	P	BARROW	510	1-2	Blackhurst
09/09/95	FA Cup	Q1	LOUTH UNITED	259	4-0	McNally, Grant, Gautrey, Atkinson
16/09/95	NPL	P	SPENNYMOOR UNITED	431	2-1	Penman, Rowlands
19/09/95	NPL	P	DROYLSDEN	340	6-1	Rowlands(2), Blackhurst(2), Baines, Watson
23/09/95	FA Cup	Q2	Newcastle Town	313	1-0	Blackhurst
30/09/95	NPL	P	MATLOCK TOWN	420	1-0	Blackhurst
03/10/95	NPL	P	KNOWSLEY UNITED	342	2-1	Blackhurst, Ward
07/10/95	FA Cup	Q3	ILKESTON TOWN	499	0-0	
10/10/95	FA Cup	Q3 rep	Ilkeston Town	801	2-1	Rooney, Blackhurst
14/10/95	NPL	P	Bishop Auckland	203	1-0	Blackhurst
21/10/95	FA Cup	Q4	BRADFORD PARK AVENUE	626	2-0	Grant, Blackhurst
24/10/95	LC	2	Chorley	262	0-0	
28/10/95	NPL	P	Buxton	237	3-1	Penman, Blackhurst(2)
31/10/95	LC	2 rep	CHORLEY	173	4-2	Blackhurst, Withers, Ward, Grant
04/11/95	NPL	P	BOSTON UNITED	707	0-4	
11/11/95	FA Cup	1	Shrewsbury Town	2845	2-11	Penman, Rowlands
18/11/95	NPL	P	FRICKLEY ATHLETIC	366	1-1	Grant
21/11/95	NPL	P	Chorley	221	1-1	Grant
25/11/95	NPL	P	Hyde United	561	0-4	
27/11/95	Lancs ATS	1	Burscough	240	3-3	Withers(2), Blackhurst
02/12/95	NPL	P	Matlock Town	295	3-3	Murray, McNally, Blackhurst
05/12/95	Lancs ATS	1 rep	BURSCOUGH	205	2-0	Murray, Blackhurst
09/12/95	NPL	P	GUISELEY	414	0-1	
11/12/95	LC	3	Hyde United	330	3-5	Murray, Rowlands, Blackhurst
16/12/95	NPL	P	Boston United	720	1-0	Withers
19/12/95	NPL	P	ACCRINGTON STANLEY	324	1-2	Blackhurst
01/01/96	NPL	P	Accrington Stanley	622	0-0	
06/01/96	NPL	P	BLYTH SPARTANS	394	0-0	
09/01/96	PC	1	WITTON ALBION	254	2-0	Gautrey, Withers
13/01/96	NPL	P	Gainsborough Trinity	494	0-1	
16/01/96	Lancs ATS	2	Southport	543	0-1	
20/01/96	FA Trophy	1	HYDE UNITED	467	0-0	
22/01/96	FA Trophy	1 rep	Hyde United	416	0-0	
01/02/96	FA Trophy	1 rep(2)	Hyde United	374	0-3	
10/02/96	NPL	P	Witton Albion	457	0-2	
13/02/96	L'pool SC	QF	ST HELENS TOWN	138	1-0	McNally
17/02/96	NPL	P	WITTON ALBION	453	2-1	Blackhurst, McNally
24/02/96	NPL	P	CHORLEY	401	2-1	Blackhurst, Penman
02/03/96	NPL	P	BUXTON	346	1-1	Draper
05/03/96	PC	QF	HYDE UNITED	142	0-3	
09/03/96	NPL	P	Guiseley	380	4-2	Brennan, Hogarth(og), Blackhurst, Penman
16/03/96	NPL	P	GAINSBOROUGH TRINITY	335	3-0	Proctor, McNally, Blackhurst
23/03/96	NPL	P	Bamber Bridge	606	4-4	Rowlands(2), Lundon, Ward
25/03/96	L'pool SC	SF	TRANMERE ROVERS	273	1-4	Penman
30/03/96	NPL	P	Droylsden	162	1-2	Blackhurst
02/04/96	NPL	P	COLWYN BAY	311	1-1	Blackhurst
06/04/96	NPL	P	Barrow	981	0-2	
08/04/96	NPL	P	LEEK TOWN	349	2-1	Ward, Rowlands
10/04/96	NPL	P	HYDE UNITED	333	4-0	Penman, Rowlands, Blackhurst(2)
16/04/96	NPL	P	Blyth Spartans	336	2-2	Rowlands, Ward
20/04/96	NPL	P	Spennymoor United	255	2-2	Blackhurst, Rowlands
23/04/96	NPL	P	WINSFORD UNITED	336	3-1	Penman(2), Draper
25/04/96	NPL	P	Knowsley United	129	1-2	McNally
27/04/96	NPL	P	Leek Town	229	1-0	Penman
30/04/96	NPL	P	Emley	164	0-2	
04/05/96	NPL	P	BISHOP AUCKLAND	475	2-2	McNally, Rowlands

RUNCORN

Canal Street, Runcorn, Cheshire. Tel: 01928 560076 club 575858

Secretary: Mr Graham Ost, 120 Warrington Rd, Penketh, Cheshire Tel: 01925 722540

Match Secretary: Chris Henshall, 58 Minerva Close, Warrington, Cheshire WA4 2XN Tel: 01925 650311

Club shop manager: Phil Wainwright, Tel 01928 560075

Nickname: The Linnets   Colours: Yellow and Green

Capacity: 4,600   Seating: 441

Covered standing: 1,200   Clubhouse on ground: Yes

Record attendance: 10,111 v Preston North End in FA Cup 39

Biggest win: 11-0 v Congleton

Biggest defeat: 0-8 v South Shields

Record goalscorer in total: Alan Ryan

Record fee received: £80,000 from Nottingham Forest for Ian Woan

DIRECTIONS

From the south: M6. Take the M56 to junction 11. Follow signs for Warrington. along the A56. Turn left at the mini roundabout, signposted Liverpool and Runcorn and continue for 3 miles. Signposted at the slip road Runcorn Old Town. Turn right at the junction and follow the road to the Egerton Arms, turn right and right again to the ground.
From the north : Leave the M62 at Widnes. Carry through Widnes to Runcorn/Widnes bridge. Turn left through the town to Egerton Arms.

HONOURS

FA TROPHY Runners up 1986, 1993, 1994

Alliance Premier League 1982, Championship Shield 1983 and 1986

Bob Lord Trophy 1983 and 1985, Lancs Junior Cup 1920

Cheshire League 1920, 1937, 1939, 1940, 1963

Cheshire Senior Cup 1925, 1936, 1962, 1965, 1968, 1974, 1975, 1985, 1986, 1987, 1988, 1989

Cheshire County Bowl 1938, Northern Premier League 1976, League Challenge Cup 1975, 1980, 1981

Challenge Shield 1981 and 1982

Manager for 1996-97: Derek Brownbill, Chairman: Dr David Robertson

Runcorn AFC were founded in 1918 when a local tannery owner and benefactor acquired Canal Street, and the club became part of the Highfield and Camden Tanneries Recreation Club. The ground had originally been developed for Rugby League and such was its size, that in 1900 some 15,000 crammed in to watch a match. Just before the Great War the pitch was turned around to its current north to south aspect in readiness for association football. Early league matches were in the Lancashire Combination, the club taking the Lancs Junior Cup with a win at Anfield. A year later came the creation of the Cheshire County League and Runcorn joined as founder-members becoming the inaugural champions. Later in 1925 and 1936 they won the Cheshire Senior Cup which was a taster for league success in 1937, 1939 and 1940. The middle season also saw the club beat Aldershot in the FA Cup and reach the 3rd round, only to lose to Preston North End in front of their record crowd. The Linnets were founder members of the Northern Premier League in 1968 and won the league in 1976, but they surpassed all that had gone before in 1981 by winning the treble of League, League Cup and Presidents Cup, achieving promotion to the Alliance into the bargain. The new surroundings posed no problem as Runcorn stormed to the title by seven points and reached Wembley in 1986, losing to Altrincham. Seven years later they were back, losing to Wycombe Wanderers and again a year on, against Woking. Sadly, last season saw the Linnets struggle near the bottom until the trap door opened for them to return back to the Northern Premier League. After a traumatic time which has seen Canal Street suffer fires and closure before being almost completely transformed, Runcorn will be hoping to bounce back in style.

RUNCORN 1995/96 SEASON

Date	Comp		Opponent	Att	Score	Scorers
19/08/95	VC		WELLING UNITED	410	1-3	Finley 8
22/08/95	VC		Morecambe	1425	1-3	Warder 36
26/08/95	VC		Kettering Town	1583	0-4	
28/08/95	VC		SOUTHPORT	708	1-1	Doherty 47
02/09/95	VC		DAGENHAM & REDBRIDGE	461	2-0	Bignall 35 40
05/09/95	VC		Telford United	1008	2-1	Bignall 21 89
09/09/95	VC		SLOUGH TOWN	480	4-3	Bignall 10, Taylor 28, Robertson 43, Dougherty 51
13/09/95	VC		Gateshead	375	0-1	
16/09/95	VC		Woking	1620	1-2	Taylor 2
19/09/95	VC		Southport	1004	1-1	Taylor 34
23/09/95	VC		BATH CITY	519	1-0	Doherty 36
26/09/95	Ches. SC	1	Northwich Victoria	502	1-3	
30/09/95	VC		Bromsgrove Rovers	973	0-2	
07/10/95	VC		HALIFAX TOWN	637	0-1	
14/10/95	VC		Dover Athletic	1277	2-4	Bignall 6, Smith 24
21/10/95	FA Cup	Q4	HALIFAX TOWN	901	2-1	Taylor, Bignall
24/10/95	VC		MACCLESFIELD TOWN	600	0-0	
28/10/95	VC		KETTERING TOWN	569	4-2	Farrington 29 78, Bates 40, Clowes 88
04/11/95	VC		Northwich Victoria	1007	3-4	Bignall 54 75, Taylor 64
11/11/95	FA Cup	1	WIGAN ATHLETIC	2844	1-1	Bignall
18/11/95	VC		Kidderminster Harriers	1879	1-4	Farrington 49
21/11/95	FA Cup	1 rep	Wigan Athletic	3224	2-4	Ruffer, Smith
25/11/95	VC		STEVENAGE BOROUGH	442	0-8	
28/11/95	SCC	2	SOUTHPORT		1-5	
02/12/95	VC		Altrincham	707	2-2	Bignall 2, Doherty 20
09/12/95	VC		WOKING	707	2-3	Bignall 12 63
16/12/95	VC		Halifax Town	834	3-1	Bignall 43(p) 70, Eyre 62
06/01/96	VC		Hednesford Town	1008	0-2	
13/01/96	VC		BROMSGROVE ROVERS	547	0-0	
20/01/96	FA Trophy	1	Macclesfield Town	1401	0-1	
03/02/96	VC		Stevenage Borough	1432	1-4	Taylor 2
10/02/96	VC		KIDDERMIN HARRIERS	475	0-1	
17/02/96	VC		FARNBOROUGH TOWN	429	0-3	
24/02/96	VC		Macclesfield Town	1410	0-1	
27/02/96	VC		GATESHEAD	333	1-1	Bignall 82
05/03/96	VC		ALTRINCHAM	607	0-1	
09/03/96	VC		DOVER ATHLETIC	433	1-3	Bignall 73
16/03/96	VC		Farnborough Town	619	1-0	Taylor 76
19/03/96	VC		Stalybridge Celtic	478	0-2	
23/03/96	VC		HEDNESFORD TOWN	507	2-2	Taylor 42, Eyre 90(p)
30/03/96	VC		Bath City	503	0-3	
06/04/96	VC		Welling United	616	1-1	Taylor 52
08/04/96	VC		MORECAMBE	681	1-3	Eyre 87
16/04/96	VC		STALYBRIDGE CELTIC	352	0-1	
20/04/96	VC		Dagenham & Redbridge	755	3-2	Thomas 16, Clowes 47, Allen 71
23/04/96	VC		NORTHWICH VICTORIA	653	3-4	Allen 14, Ruffer 64, Eyre 82(p)
27/04/96	VC		TELFORD UNITED	401	2-3	Taylor 17, Clowes 67
04/05/96	VC		Slough Town	835	1-0	Allen 64

SPENNYMOOR UNITED

Brewery Field, Spennymoor Co Durham DL16 6UU Tel: 01388 814100 Club / 01388 811934 Grandstand

Secretary: Jim Nutt, 41 Warwick Close, Spennymoor, Co.Durham DL16 6UU Tel: 01388 812179

Chairman: Barry Hindmarch, 7 Green Lane, Spennymoor, Co.Durham DL16 6HD Tel: 01388 815168

Programme and Press: Gary Nunn Tel: 01388 810831

Club shop manager: Peter Fletcher Tel: 01388 814100

Colours: Black and white stripes   Nickname: The Moors

Capacity: 7,500   Seating: 300

Standing: 2,000   Clubhouse on ground: Yes

Record attendance: 7,202 v Bishop Auckland Durham Challenge Cup March 3rd 1957

DIRECTIONS

From South; A1 (M), A167, A688, straight on at mini-r'bout, 3rd exit at next large r'bout (St Andrews church opposite), pass Asda on left, straight on at junction, pass Salvin Arms (Durham Rd), ground 200 yds on left. From A167 North — leave at Croxdale (N.E.S.S. factory), right at cemetery on left— this is Durham Rd — ground half mile on right. Nearest rail station is Durham — buses from there.

Biggest win: 19-0 v Eden Colliery North Eastern League Feb 6th 1937

Biggest defeat: 0-16 v Sunderland A Durham Senior Cup 1902

Record appearances: Ken Banks 600+

Record goalscorer in one season: Doug Humble

Record goalscorer in total: Doug Humble 200

Record fee paid: £3,500 for Don Peattie from Gretna

Record fee received: £20,000 for Mike Heathcote to Sunderland

HONOURS

North Eastern League 1910, 1945, 1946, 1957, League Cup 1929

Northern League 1968, 1972, 1974, 1977, 1978, 1979

League Cup 1966, 1968, 1980, 1981, 1987

Northern Counties East and League Cup double 1993, Northern Premier League Challenge Cup 1994

Durham Challenge Cup 1930, 45, 46, 54, 63, 68, 73, 74, 75, 76, 79, 83, 94, 95, 96

Durham Benevolent Bowl 1927, 1930, 1932, 1948, 1959, 1961, 1994

JR Cleator Cup 1981 and 1987

Manager for 1996-97: Matty Pearson, Assistant manager: David Barton

Chairman: Barry Hindmarch, Vice chairman: John Norman

Spennymoor United were founded in 1904 as an amalgamation of Spennymoor Town and Weardale Ironopolis. The latter were the works team for the then thriving Weardale Iron and Coal Company which was based in the town. They secured use of the Brewery Field in that year, which was previously used by Tudhoe Rugby Club and was once where the Brewery kept its horses. In 1905 they joined the Northern League, but after three years switched to the North Eastern League where they remained for fifty years apart from one season in the Wearside League in 1937 . The league folded in 1957 after Sunderland and Middlesbrough pulled out their reserve sides and after two financially crippling seasons in the Midland League, the club rejoined the ranks of the amateur Northern League. They had little reward in those years, other than a NEL championship in 1910, and two more during the war, but in the Durham Senior Cup and Benevolent Bowl there were eight wins in all during the NEL days. Undoubtedly the proudest moment was in 1937 when the club battled to the FA Cup 3rd Round, where they lost to West Bromwich Albion at the Hawthorns. In 1968, The Moors became the first to do the treble of League, League Cup and Durham Senior Cup, setting a points record with one defeat and five draws. Five more

championships followed with three runners up spots and in 1978 they got to the semi-final of the FA Trophy, losing to Leatherhead. In order to move on towards the Northern Premier League a new grandstand was built at a cost of £250,000 and a new covered terrace was built more recently at the North end. They stepped up into the Northern Counties East and were promoted in 1993 and again went through to the NPL Division One where they lifted the League Cup and won the Durham Challenge Cup. The last two seasons have seen the club retain the County Cup and consolidate in the Premier Division.

SPENNYMOOR UNITED 1995/96 SEASON

19/08/95	NPL	P	HYDE UNITED	321	0-1	
22/08/95	NPL	P	Blyth Spartans	836	1-3	O'Hara
26/08/95	NPL	P	DROYLSDEN	263	2-0	Suddick, Goodrick
28/08/95	NPL	P	BLYTH SPARTANS	503	2-1	Shaw, Skedd
02/09/95	NPL	P	Buxton	244	1-1	Healy
06/09/95	NPL	P	Accrington Stanley	461	0-0	
09/09/95	FA Cup	Q1	GLASSHOUGHTON WELF	247	1-0	Healy
12/09/95	NPL	P	EMLEY	239	2-0	Suddick(2)
16/09/95	NPL	P	Marine	431	1-2	Veart
19/09/95	NPL	P	ACCRINGTON STANLEY	327	3-4	Skedd(2), Healy
23/09/95	FA Cup	Q2	Workington	487	4-2	Skedd, Healy, Shaw, Veart
25/09/95	NPL	P	Guiseley	452	2-2	Veart, Goodrick
30/09/95	NPL	P	CHORLEY	326	2-2	Fleming, Healy
03/10/95	NPL	P	Emley	210	2-0	Shaw, Ludlow
07/10/95	FA Cup	Q3	BILLINGHAM TOWN	337	6-1	Healy(2), Veart, Alderson, Goodrigg, Cowell
10/10/95	NPL	P	WITTON ALBION	357	3-1	Healy, Ludlow, Shaw
14/10/95	NPL	P	Gainsborough Trinity	417	1-0	Healy
17/10/95	NPL	P	GUISELEY	509	0-0	
21/10/95	FA Cup	Q4	LANCASTER CITY	621	1-0	Gorman
23/10/95	LC	2	Bishop Auckland	521	2-2	Saunders, Healy
28/10/95	NPL	P	COLWYN BAY	339	0-0	
31/10/95	Durham CC	1	BIRTLEY TOWN	208	3-2	Alderson(2), Cowell
04/11/95	NPL	P	Hyde United	462	2-3	Ludlow, Healy
06/11/95	LC	2 rep	BISHOP AUCKLAND	363	3-1	Ludlow(2), Gorman
08/11/95	NPL	P	KNOWSLEY UNITED	276	1-4	Healy
11/11/95	FA Cup	1	COLWYN BAY	824	0-1	
18/11/95	NPL	P	Barrow	1176	1-1	Veart
21/11/95	Durham CC	2	South Shields	183	3-0	Ludlow(2), Healy
25/11/95	FA Trophy	Q3	NUNEATON BOROUGH	486	0-2	
02/12/95	NPL	P	LEEK TOWN	232	4-2	Alderson, Veart, Osborne, Ludlow
05/12/95	LC	3	EMLEY	158	5-0	Alderson, Veart, Osbourne(2), Ludlow
09/12/95	NPL	P	Witton Albion	374	2-2	Alderson, Ainsley
16/12/95	NPL	P	GAINSBOROUGH TRINITY	243	1-1	Hinsley
19/12/95	PC	1	Radcliffe Borough	105	2-3	Ainsley, Osbourne
06/01/96	NPL	P	BUXTON	217	0-0	
09/01/96	Durham CC	QF	TOW LAW TOWN	273	2-0	Alderson, Osbourne
13/01/96	NPL	P	Chorley	278	3-0	Veart, O'Hara, Osbourne
20/01/96	NPL	P	Knowsley United	42	0-2	
03/02/96	NPL	P	FRICKLEY ATHLETIC	245	2-2	Healy, Ainsley
10/02/96	NPL	P	Boston United	648	1-4	Alderson
17/02/96	NPL	P	Droylsden	172	1-1	Shaw
24/02/96	NPL	P	MATLOCK TOWN	243	1-1	Skedd
26/02/96	NPL	P	Bishop Auckland	346	2-1	Purvis, Shaw
02/03/96	LC	QF	Boston United	424	0-3	
09/03/96	NPL	P	BOSTON UNITED	237	2-3	Alderson, Innes
16/03/96	NPL	P	BARROW	245	1-1	Alderson
19/03/96	Durham CC	SF	Dunston Federation Brewery	190	1-0	Shaw
23/03/96	NPL	P	Colwyn Bay	280	3-2	Alderson(2), Cowell
30/03/96	NPL	P	Matlock Town	283	1-1	Alderson
06/04/96	NPL	P	Leek Town	212	2-0	Innes, Ogley(og)
08/04/96	NPL	P	BISHOP AUCKLAND	416	1-0	Shaw
13/04/96	NPL	P	Bamber Bridge	388	0-2	
20/04/96	NPL	P	MARINE	255	2-2	Innes, Osbourne
23/04/96	NPL	P	Frickley Athletic	109	3-2	Skedd, Alderson, Healey
27/04/96	NPL	P	WINSFORD UNITED	215	3-3	Healey(2), Shaw
30/04/96	NPL	P	BAMBER BRIDGE	288	4-2	Healy, Ainsley, Cowell, Shaw
04/05/96	NPL	P	Winsford United	110	2-2	Osbourne, Coatsworth
06/05/96	Durham CC	F	Durham City	1950	1-0	Innes

WINSFORD UNITED

Barton Stadium, Wharton, Winsford, Cheshire, CW7 3EU. Tel: 01606 593021 Social Club 01606 861980

Secretary: Peter Warburton, c/o Winsford United FC
Tel: 01606 554295

Assistant Secretary: W A Bayliss, 20 Lower High Street, Winsford, Cheshire Tel: 01606 594346

Programme Editor: Mr A Maylor Tel: 01606 552763

Club shop manager: Mr J McCabe

Colours: Royal Blue and White   Nickname: Blues

Capacity: 6,000   Seating: 250

Covered standing: 5,000   Clubhouse on ground: Yes

Record attendance: 7,000 v Witton Albion 1947

Record appearances: Edward Harrop 400

Record goalscorer in one season: Graham Smith 66

Record fee received: £6,000 for Neville Southall to Bury

DIRECTIONS

From north; M6 junction 19, A556 towards Northwich to Davenham, then A5018 toWinsford. From south; M6 junction 18, A54 through Middlewich to Winsford. Ground quarter mile off main road in Wharton area of town. 1 mile from Winsford (BR).

HONOURS

Cheshire Amateur Cup 1901 and 1903

Cheshire League 1921, Cheshire League Cup 1950, 1956, 1960, 1979, 1980, 1981

Cheshire Senior Cup 1959, 1980, 1993, Cheshire League Challenge Shield 1975

Cheshire League and League Cup double 1977, Edward Case Cup 1980

Mid-Cheshire Senior Cup 1991 and 1993

Northern Premier League Cup 1993, NPL President's Cup 1993

Manager for 1996-97: John Bingham, Chairman: Martin Morgan

Winsford have a long history having been formed back in 1883. In those early days they were called Over Wanderers and played in the Welsh Combination. After a few seasons they changed their name and moved to the current ground which was then known as Great Western Playing Field. Their success saw several of their players taken by League clubs and after a poor spell the club folded. They re-formed in 1913 thanks mainly to Secretary Mr Byrning, but it was short lived as the Great War broke out. They again re-formed with a new committee headed by Mr R.G.Barton, hence Barton Stadium, and they became founder members of the Cheshire League, winning it in the second season. It was to be one of few successes as the club struggled on and off the pitch. Despite suffering during the Second War, the Stadium survived and United became a Limited Company, with the Blues winning the League Cup three times and the Cheshire Senior Cup. The next two decades again saw Winsford struggle, but following a rare FA Cup run to the First Round in 1975 the club returned to winning ways and between 1976 and 1980 they won the Cheshire League and were runners up, and set a record by winning the League Cup four times in five years, including the hat-trick. On top of that there was a Cheshire Senior Cup win in 1980 and an appearance in the last eight of the FA Trophy, in 1978. It was in John Williams' last season that United sold Neville Southall to Bury for £6, 000 with a sell on clause which saw them net £30,000 when he moved to Goodison Park. Once again, after that golden era, the fortunes waned again and after the Cheshire League merged into the North-West Counties League, the club joined Division One of the Northern Premier League in 1987. In 1991 they were bottom, but after appointing Mike McKenzie as manager they lost only four more matches and avoided the drop. The following season saw promotion as runners up with another First Round appearance in the FA Cup, but in 1992-93 the

club cleaned up, winning five trophies, The Northern Premier League Challenge Cup, President's Cup, Cheshire Senior Cup, Mid-Cheshire Senior Cup and NPL Runners-up Cup. They were second to Southport and collected the record amount of points for a team not winning the title.

Sadly the manager was lured into Conference football and the team broke up, but United remain in the Premier Division.

WINSFORD UNITED 1995/96 SEASON

19/08/95	NPL	P	EMLEY	222	0-4	
21/08/95	NPL	P	LEEK TOWN	268	0-0	
26/08/95	NPL	P	Accrington Stanley	475	2-1	T Bishop, J Bishop
28/08/95	NPL	P	MARINE	210	1-0	Russell
02/09/95	NPL	P	GAINSBOROUGH TRINITY	222	1-1	Farrelly
04/09/95	NPL	P	Hyde United	274	1-0	Edwards
09/09/95	FA Cup	Q1	BORROWASH VICTORIA	357	1-0	T Bishop
16/09/95	NPL	P	Bishop Auckland	185	0-1	
19/09/95	NPL	P	Bamber Bridge	655	0-2	
23/09/95	FA Cup	Q2	Emley	253	1-1	Edwards
25/09/95	FA Cup	Q2 rep	EMLEY	248	2-1	McIlroy, Edwards
30/09/95	NPL	P	Droylsden	217	1-1	Talbot
02/10/95	Ches. SC	1	HYDE UNITED	213	1-4	Edwards
07/10/95	FA Cup	Q3	HINCKLEY ATHLETIC	236	3-2	O'Loughlin, Russell, Bishop
10/10/95	NPL	P	Colwyn Bay	276	1-1	Russell
14/10/95	FA Trophy	Q1	PAGET RANGERS	183	1-1	Bishop
18/10/95	FA Trophy	Q1 rep	Paget Rangers	124	2-0	McCarrick, Bishop
21/10/95	FA Cup	Q4	BARROW	714	0-3	
24/10/95	LC	2	Atherton L.R.	82	2-3	Russell, J Bishop
28/10/95	NPL	P	Guiseley	360	1-1	Talbot
04/11/95	FA Trophy	Q2	Barrow	1222	1-0	Russell
06/11/95	NPL	P	BAMBER BRIDGE	202	1-4	Russell
11/11/95	NPL	P	BOSTON UNITED	183	1-0	Farrelly
18/11/95	NPL	P	Leek Town	220	1-5	Edwards
20/11/95	NPL	P	COLWYN BAY	123	1-3	J Bishop
25/11/95	FA Trophy	Q3	Chorley	297	1-3	Bishop
27/11/95	NPL	P	KNOWSLEY UNITED	111	0-1	
02/12/95	NPL	P	Buxton	165	3-1	Dickens, Russell, Farrelly
09/12/95	NPL	P	MATLOCK TOWN	127	3-1	Blundell, Russell(2)
16/12/95	NPL	P	Chorley	221	1-1	O'Loughlin
06/01/96	NPL	P	Matlock Town	325	1-1	Farrelly
13/01/96	NPL	P	HYDE UNITED	261	1-4	Farrelly
20/01/96	NPL	P	BUXTON	189	1-1	McCarrick
23/01/96	NPL	P	Knowsley United	44	1-4	J Bishop
03/02/96	NPL	P	Gainsborough Trinity	464	0-0	
10/02/96	NPL	P	Frickley Athletic	112	3-3	Russell, Talbot, Bishop
17/02/96	NPL	P	Emley	196	1-1	Russell
24/02/96	NPL	P	Boston United	611	2-2	Farrelly, Talbot
28/02/96	Mid-Ches.	SF	Nantwich Town	156	3-1	Farrelly, Russell(2)
02/03/96	NPL	P	BLYTH SPARTANS	162	2-4	Danskin, Russell
09/03/96	NPL	P	FRICKLEY ATHLETIC	128	4-1	Farrelly, O'Loughlin, Danskin, Russell
16/03/96	NPL	P	BISHOP AUCKLAND	120	0-4	
23/03/96	NPL	P	Blyth Spartans	405	2-3	Russell, Farrell
25/03/96	NPL	P	BARROW	170	4-3	Russell(3), Farrelly
30/03/96	NPL	P	Barrow	953	1-1	Russell
01/04/96	NPL	P	CHORLEY	188	0-2	
06/04/96	NPL	P	ACCRINGTON STANLEY	168	2-2	Bishop, German
08/04/96	NPL	P	Witton Albion	513	0-2	
13/04/96	NPL	P	DROYLSDEN	150	3-2	Farrelly, Russell(2)
20/04/96	NPL	P	GUISELEY	137	1-2	Dicken
23/04/96	NPL	P	Marine	336	1-3	Russell
27/04/96	NPL	P	Spennymoor United	215	3-3	O'Loughlin, Danskin, Talbot
29/04/96	NPL	P	WITTON ALBION	160	2-1	German, J Bishop
04/05/96	NPL	P	SPENNYMOOR UNITED	110	2-2	Farrelly, Russell

WITTON ALBION

Wincham Park, Chapel Street, Wincham, Northwich, Cheshire CW9 6DA.
Tel: 01606 43008 or 47117 club

Secretary: David M.Leather, 34 Grosvenor Avenue, Hartford, Northwich, Cheshire Tel: 01606 76488

Assistant Match Sec: Ken Payne, 23 Northfield Drive, Biddulph, Stoke-on-Trent Staffs Tel: 01782 518433

Programme Editor: Phil Chadwick Tel: 01606 44845

Commercial Manager: Mrs Jackie Birks 01538 381209

Colours: Red and White stripes

Nickname: Albion or the Albs

Capacity: 4,394   Seating: 646

Covered standing: 1,629   Uncovered 2,119

Clubhouse on ground: Yes

Record attendance: 3,940 v Kidderminster Harriers FA Trophy semi-final

Record appearances: John Goryl

Record goalscorer in one season: Frank Fidler

Record goalscorer in total: Frank Fidler

Record fee paid: £12,500 for John McCluskie

DIRECTIONS

M6 junction 19. Follow A556 towards Northwich, after 3 miles turn into A559 at beginning of dual carriageway, after three-quarters of a mile turn left opposite Black Greyhound Inn and grounds is half a mile on the left immediately after crossing Canal Bridge.

HONOURS

FA TROPHY Finalists 1992

Semi finalists 1991 and 1993

Cheshire League 1897, Lancs Combination Div 2 1914

Cheshire County League 1949, 1950, 1954, Cheshire League Cup 1954 and 1976

Northern Premier League 1991, Cheshire Senior Cup 1902, 22, 28, 39, 48, 56, 61, 78, 95, 96

NPL Presidents Cup 1990 and 1995

Manager for 1996-97: Russ Perkins (Temporrary)

Chairman: D. Lloyd, Vice chairman: S. Marlor

Witton Albion was established initially in 1887 and reformed in 1890. Their name evolved from the main parish in the town of Northwich. Their ground at Wincham is situated just out of town but for 79 years they resided at the well appointed Central Ground where during the late forties and fifties crowds of over 5,000 were commonplace. They were halcyon days as the club carried off many Cheshire County League honours and regularly reached the First Round of the FA Cup.

Success was then limited until the late Seventies when they made it to the Northern Premier League, where in the first season they missed the title by one point. Later in May 1987 the management team of Stan Allan and John Davidson twice led the team to a third place but it came good in 1991 as Albion took the title and promotion to the Conference. As a bonus the team made it to the semi-final of the FA Trophy, and repeated it before finally making it to Wembley for the 1992, where they lost a bitterly fought contest against Colchester United.

For three years Witton played at the highest level but were unable to progress and relegation was the end result, although since the club has staved off a major financial problem and has taken the Cheshire Senior

Cup for the past two seasons as well as the President's Cup. Witton played their very early football on a pitch at the back of Witton Vicarage before moving to a ground called Penny Lane, just off Middlewich Road. In 1910 they were offered a plot of land for rent with the agreement that they fenced it off. They bought the ground in 1921 for £750 and six years later the Central Ground began to be developed. It remained home until the last game against Frickley Athletic in 1989.

WITTON ALBION 1995/96 SEASON

19/08/95	NPL	P	Boston United	1167	2-1	Thomas, Cowley
22/08/95	NPL	P	COLWYN BAY	621	2-3	Camden(2)
26/08/95	NPL	P	FRICKLEY ATHLETIC	529	5-0	Rose(2), Thomas, Byrne, Camden
28/08/95	NPL	P	Leek Town	471	1-2	Thomas
02/09/95	NPL	P	BAMBER BRIDGE	623	0-0	
05/09/95	NPL	P	Buxton	350	4-0	Thomas, Rose, Stannard, Cowley
12/09/95	NPL	P	ACCRINGTON STANLEY	525	0-2	
16/09/95	NPL	P	Emley	314	0-1	
19/09/95	NPL	P	MATLOCK TOWN	439	3-2	Thomas(3)
23/09/95	NPL	P	KNOWSLEY UNITED	436	2-1	Thomas, Camden
26/09/95	NPL	P	Colwyn Bay	323	1-1	Rose
30/09/95	NPL	P	GUISELEY	616	3-2	Camden, Rodwell, Thomas
04/10/95	NPL	P	CHORLEY	583	2-1	Camden, Thomas
07/10/95	NPL	P	Chorley	332	0-4	
10/10/95	NPL	P	Spennymoor United	357	1-3	Thomas
14/10/95	NPL	P	BLYTH SPARTANS	502	2-1	Camden(2)
17/10/95	NPL	P	Barrow	1490	0-3	
21/10/95	FA Cup	Q4	MORECAMBE	931	3-2	Cowley, Watson(2)
24/10/95	LC	2	LEIGH R.M.I.	305	2-2	Camden(2)
28/10/95	NPL	P	GAINSBOROUGH TRINITY	455	0-2	
01/11/95	LC	2 rep	Leigh R.M.I.	72	3-0	Pritchard, Watson, McAulay
04/11/95	NPL	P	Bishop Auckland	208	2-1	Watson, McNeilis
11/11/95	FA Cup	1	Telford United	1277	1-2	Watson
18/11/95	NPL	P	EMLEY	439	3-1	Cowley, McNeilis, Watson
21/11/95	Ches. SC	QF	NORTHWICH VICTORIA	1006	2-0	Cowley, McAuley
25/11/95	FA Trophy	Q3	Bishop Auckland	239	0-0	
28/11/95	FA Trophy	Q3 rep	BISHOP AUCKLAND	461	0-0	
02/12/95	NPL	P	Frickley Athletic	145	1-1	Pritchard
04/12/95	FA Trophy	Q3 rep(2)	Bishop Auckland	222	1-3	Watson
09/12/95	NPL	P	SPENNYMOOR UNITED	374	2-2	Watson(2)
16/12/95	NPL	P	Accrington Stanley	409	2-1	Pritchard, Brenchley
19/12/95	LC	3	Atherton L.R,	183	5-2	Watson(4), Jones
01/01/96	NPL	P	LEEK TOWN	607	2-1	Horsfield, Watson
06/01/96	NPL	P	Guiseley	360	1-0	Taylor
09/01/96	PC	1	Marine	254	0-2	
13/01/96	NPL	P	BISHOP AUCKLAND	510	1-2	Brenchley
10/02/96	NPL	P	MARINE	457	2-0	Watson, Whalley
17/02/96	NPL	P	Marine	453	1-2	Taylor
20/02/96	Ches. SC	SF(1)	ALTRINCHAM	460	1-1	Watson
24/02/96	NPL	P	DROYLSDEN	399	2-1	McNeilis, Horsfield
27/02/96	Mid-Ches.	SF	NORTHWICH VICTORIA	667	3-2	
02/03/96	NPL	P	BARROW	591	1-0	McNeilis
05/03/96	LC	QF	Gainsborough Trinity	420	2-3	Watson(2)
09/03/96	NPL	P	Blyth Spartans	497	0-2	
12/03/96	Ches. SC	SF(2)	Altrincham	481	2-1	McDonald(2)
16/03/96	NPL	P	HYDE UNITED	638	1-1	Watson
19/03/96	NPL	P	Matlock Town	237	2-5	Whalley, Horsfield
23/03/96	NPL	P	Knowsley United	112	2-2	McDonald, Watson
30/03/96	NPL	P	BOSTON UNITED	469	1-1	Watson
06/04/96	NPL	P	Droylsden	167	1-2	Horsfield
08/04/96	NPL	P	WINSFORD UNITED	513	2-0	Watson(2)
15/04/96	NPL	P	Hyde United	367	0-1	
20/04/96	NPL	P	Gainsborough Trinity	404	0-1	
27/04/96	NPL	P	BUXTON	419	1-3	Watson
29/04/96	NPL	P	Winsford United	160	1-2	McDonald
04/05/96	NPL	P	Bamber Bridge	589	1-1	Watson
06/05/96	Ches. SC	F	Hyde United	768	3-1	Watson, Stannard(2)
						(Played at Altrincham)

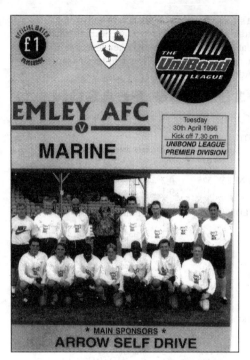

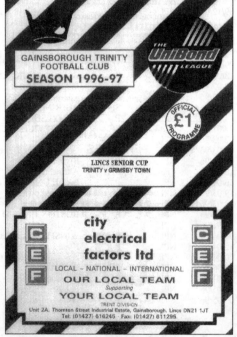

BAMBER BRIDGE FOOTBALL CLUB

UNIBOND LEAGUE
Premier Division Champions 95/96

Versus -
CZECH
REPUBLIC

BAXI PARTNERSHIP

PRICE £1
Official Match Programme
June 6th '96

THE UniBond LEAGUE

⚽ CURZON ⚽ ASHTON F.C.

Season 1995/96
Price 60p

Saturday 6th April 1996
v Alfreton Town
Unibond League Division One

THE UniBond LEAGUE

Main Sponsors

BYFORD Computer Services

pm Communications

CORAL TRAVEL

CURZON ASHTON F.C.

NATIONAL PARK · KATHERINE STREET · ASHTON-U-LYNE

LEIGH R.M.I. F.C.
HILTON PARK
SEASON 1995-96

Main Club Sponsor:
WREKIN CIRCUITS LTD.

OFFICIAL PROGRAMME

80p

THE UniBond LEAGUE

Wednesday 13th March 1996
LEIGH R.M.I. v LANCASTER CITY
The Unibond League, First Division
Kick Off 7.30 p.m.

MATLOCK TOWN FOOTBALL CLUB

MONDAY 5th AUGUST 1996

MATLOCK TOWN
v
CHESTERFIELD

CLUB SPONSORS
Panasonic
at
WESTON'S of WIRKSWORTH

THE UniBond LEAGUE

OFFICIAL PROGRAMME 80p

ASHTON UNITED

Hurst Cross, Surrey Street, Ashton-u-Lyne, Lancs OL6 8DY. Tel: 0161 339 4158 or 0161 330 1511

Secretary: Carolyne Slater, 1 Crossway Rd, Sneyd Green, Stoke-on-Trent, ST6 2ND. Tel: 01782 858280

Other matters: Terry Liversidge, Belgrave Mill, Fitton Hill Rd, Oldham, Lancs

Best contact when confirming a fixture

Simon Axford 0161 330 1511 or 0161 339 4158 Tel and fax

Programme Editor: Debbie Quaile Tel 01457 834208

Club shop manager: Ken and Steve Lee Tel: 0161 330 9800

Press officer: John Milne, 1 Westminster Ave, Ashton-u-Lyne: 0161 330 6860

Colours: Red and white halves, Nickname: Robins

Capacity: 2,700 local authority licensing, Seating: 250

Covered standing: 800, Clubhouse on ground: Yes

Record attendance: 7,474 v Halifax Town FA Cup 1st Rd 1952

Biggest win: 11-3 v Stalybridge Celtic, Biggest defeat: 1-11 v Wellington Town

Record appearances: Micky Boyle 367, Record goalscorer in one season: Stuart Dimond

Record goalscorer in total: Barney Daniels

Record fee paid £9,000 for Andy Whittaker from Netherfield 1994

Record Fee received £15,000 for Karl Marginson from Rotherham in 1993

DIRECTIONS

Directions: M62 jct 20, A627 (M) to Oldham, keep in righthand two lanes, leave at Ashton sign after 2 miles passing Belgrade Hotel, take A627 at next island, keep in left lane and take slip road signed Ashton-under-Lyme, at island follow Stalybridge/Park Road sign, go straight ahead for 3 miles to ground at Hurst Cross. BR to Charles Street (Ashton), or Stalybridge. Buses 331, 332, 337, 408 (Ashton-Stalybridge) all pass ground.

HONOURS

Northern Premier League Division One Cup 1995

Manchester Senior Cup 1885, 1914, 1976, 1978, Manchester League 1912

Lancs Combination Div 2 1961 and League Cup 1963, Manchester Premier Cup 1980, 1983, 1993

North West Counties League and Challenge Cup 1992, Division Two 1988, Floodlit League 1991, Challenge Shield 1993, Manchester Challenge Shield 1936, 1939, 1950, 1954

Manchester Intermediate Cup 1959, 1963, 1966, Manchester Junior Cup 1895, 1911, 1912, 1933

Manager 1996-97: Phil Staley, Assistant Manager: Benny Phillips

Chairman: Terry Styring, Vice Chairman: John Milne

The club was originally formed as Hurst FC in 1878, playing at Rose Hill in friendlies and cup matches They had early success in 1882 by reaching the FA Cup 2nd Rd and in 1885 won the first Manchester Senior Cup. The first league football was in the Manchester League in 1909, when they moved to Hurst Cross. During the four years, Alderman Kenworthy, a local benefactor, provided funds for stands and further improvements and in 1912 the club were champions and moved to the Lancs Combination. Apart from the odd cup, success eluded the club, who joined the Cheshire County League in 1923. After the War, they returned to the Lancs Comb and changed their name to Ashton United and began playing in red and white, acquiring the nickname The Robins. One player whose brief career at the club was ended by the War was Dixie Dean, who had played just four matches. Another former Evertonian and ex-England player began his career at Hurst Cross. Alan Ball played several matches as a 15 year old in 1960 when his father managed the club, before joining Blackpool as an apprentice. In 1953, Ashton reached the 1st Rd of the Cup and were the

first non-League side in the North West to install floodlights, but the sixties were unsettled as the club moved from the Lancs Combination to the Cheshire League and also had a brief spell in the Midland Counties. They did however, take the Combination Div 2 and Cup double in 1962, but eventually settled in the Cheshire League until the North West Counties League was formed in 1982. They tried unsuccessfully to join the Northern Premier League but went on to take the Division Two crown, however the old ground at Hurst Cross was by then a forlorn sight, and needed extensive work. A local businessman, Terry Liversidge changed the club fortunes, as they became a Limited Company and the ground was transformed with two new stands and concrete terracing.The new style club won four trophies in 1992, the League and Cup double, Challenge Shield and Manchester Premier Cup, and promotion was achieved.

ASHTON UNITED 1995/96 SEASON

19/08/95	NPL	1	FARSLEY CELTIC	180	2-1	Evans, Kirkham
22/08/95	NPL	1	Warrington Town	104	2-2	Kirkham(2)
26/08/95	FA Cup	P	Hinckley Athletic	218	1-1	Evans
28/08/95	NPL	1	CURZON ASHTON	315	1-4	Thompson
30/08/95	FA Cup	P rep	HINCKLEY ATHLETIC	170	2-4	Kirkham(2)
02/09/95	NPL	1	Lancaster City	226	0-2	
09/09/95	NPL	1	FLEETWOOD	177	3-0	Jordan, Williams(2)
16/09/95	NPL	1	Netherfield	174	1-1	Thompson
18/09/95	NPL	1	BRADFORD PARK AVENUE	283	0-1	
23/09/95	NPL	1	Leigh R.M.I.	185	4-1	Jones(2), Kirkham, Jordan
30/09/95	NPL	1	WORKINGTON	192	3-1	Jordan, Williams, Jones
03/10/95	LC	1	Warrington Town	50	2-1	Jordan, Hagan
07/10/95	NPL	1	Lincoln United	173	1-2	Whittaker
09/10/95	NPL	1	ATHERTON L.R.	202	2-1	Evans, Thompson
14/10/95	NPL	1	Gretna	95	2-3	Williams, Hagan
21/10/95	NPL	1	WHITLEY BAY	171	2-3	Evans(2)
23/10/95	LC	2	Hyde United	466	1-3	Gayle
28/10/95	NPL	1	Alfreton Town	235	0-3	
31/10/95	NPL	1	Radcliffe Borough	139	1-1	Channon(og)
07/11/95	Manc PC	1	Maine Road	132	0-1	
11/11/95	NPL	1	Harrogate Town	188	4-0	Clowes, Turner, Evans, Robinson
13/11/95	NPL	1	WARRINGTON TOWN	167	3-1	Evans, Turner, Harrison
18/11/95	NPL	1	Workington	239	2-2	Harrison, Washington
20/11/95	NPL	1	CONGLETON TOWN	123	2-0	Williams, Harrison
25/11/95	FA Trophy	Q3	LANCASTER CITY	229	1-1	Clowes
28/11/95	FA Trophy	Q3 rep	Lancaster City	228	2-0	Turner, Whittaker
02/12/95	NPL	1	LANCASTER CITY	203	1-1	Washington
09/12/95	NPL	1	Whitley Bay	115	1-5	Turner
11/12/95	1C	2	CURZON ASHTON	171	1-1	Robinson
16/12/95	NPL	1	WORKSOP TOWN	133	1-2	Clowes
18/12/95	PC	1	BUXTON	151	0-1	
06/01/96	NPL	1	Farsley Celtic	97	4-2	Evans, Marginson, Jordan, German
09/01/96	1C	2 rep	Curzon Ashton	206	2-0	Evans, Turner
13/01/96	NPL	1	EASTWOOD TOWN	185	2-1	Marginson, Jones
20/01/96	FA Trophy	1	BLYTH SPARTANS	535	1-3	Whittaker
10/02/96	NPL	1	Great Harwood Town	123	3-2	Jordan, Bell, Williams
14/02/96	1C	QF	Alfreton Town	126	0-3	
17/02/96	NPL	1	NETHERFIELD	168	5-0	Bell(3), Evans, Marginson
24/02/96	NPL	1	Eastwood Town	130	1-2	Bell
02/03/96	NPL	1	Curzon Ashton	275	2-4	Bell(2)
09/03/96	NPL	1	GRETNA	140	2-1	Bell, Williams
16/03/96	NPL	1	Atherton L.R.	123	2-1	Bell, Wolstenholme
23/03/96	NPL	1	ALFRETON TOWN	192	2-1	Bell, Jordan
30/03/96	NPL	1	HARROGATE TOWN	155	1-4	McPhillips
02/04/96	NPL	1	Congleton Town	142	0-3	
06/04/96	NPL	1	Fleetwood	114	1-0	Thompson
08/04/96	NPL	1	GREAT HARWOOD TOWN	122	1-2	McPhillips
13/04/96	NPL	1	LEIGH R.M.I.	150	3-2	Bierne, McPillips, Clowes
15/04/96	NPL	1	RADCLIFFE BOROUGH	165	1-1	McPhillips
20/04/96	NPL	1	Bradford Park Avenue	169	1-0	McPhillips
01/05/96	NPL	1	Worksop Town	266	3-1	McPhillips, Clowes, Wilson
04/05/96	NPL	1	LINCOLN UNITED	135	1-1	Wilson

ATHERTON LABURNUM ROVERS

Crilly Park, Spa Road, Atherton, Greater Manchester. Tel: 01942 883950

Secretary: Steve Hartle 32 Greensmith Way,
Westhoughton, Bolton BL5 3LR. Tel: 01942 840906

Programme Editor: Mr P Jones Tel: 01942 895305

Club shop manager: Mrs C Pottinger Tel 01942 875304

Colours: Yellow and blue

Nickname: L.R

Capacity: 3,000

Seating: 250

Covered standing: Three sections

Clubhouse on ground: Yes

Record attendance: 1,856 v Aldershot Tn

FA Vase quarter-final replay 1994

DIRECTIONS

Directions: M61 to Jct 5, follow signs for Westhoughton, left onto A6, right onto A579 (Newbrook Rd/Bolton Rd) over the railway bridge, right into Upton Rd passing Atherton Central Station, left into Springfield Rd and left again into Hillside Rd into Spa Rd and ground.

HONOURS

FA VASE Semi-finals 1995

North West Counties League 1993 and 1995

Champions Cup 1993

Manager for 1996-97: David Morris

Chairman: Mr D Halliwell

Laburnum Rovers were a successful youth team and they carried that success into senior football, joining the Leigh League, playing their home games at Hag Ford. From there they moved to the Bolton Combination and soon a farmers field next to Laburnum Mill became available. The club began to develop the ground on a long lease and Crilly Park is the outcome. Progress has been tremendous with an enclosing wall, clubhouse and changing rooms, with two stands added in later times as the Northern Premier League beckoned. They joined the Cheshire League in 1980 and due to a league stipulation, they changed their name to Atherton Laburnum Rovers. With the merger of the Cheshire League into the North West Counties the facilities enabled them to start in Division One.

The 90's have proved to be a highly productive time for Rovers, for they reached the top division and won the championship in 1993 as well as the Champions Cup and two years later took the title again, only to suffer the heartache of an FA Vase semi-final defeat. Having drawn the tie with Diss Town over two legs, they were leading the replay at VS Rugby with 10 minutes to go, only to lose 2-1.

Their second championship in 1995 saw them promoted to the Northern Premier League where last May they finished in mid-table.

ATHERTON LABURNUM ROVERS 1995/96 SEASON

Date	Comp	Rd	Opponent	Att	Score	Scorers
19/08/95	NPL	1	NETHERFIELD	107	2-4	Feeley(2)
22/08/95	NPL	1	Radcliffe Borough	153	2-4	Dunn, McDonald
26/08/95	FA Cup	P	Eccleshill United	37	2-3	Dunn, Feeley
28/08/95	NPL	1	LEIGH R.M.I.	178	3-1	Simm(2), McDonald
02/09/95	NPL	1	Alfreton Town	230	2-1	Cryer, Dunn
05/09/95	NPL	1	Warrington Town	110	2-1	Dunn, McDonald
12/09/95	NPL	1	RADCLIFFE BOROUGH	129	1-1	McDonald
16/09/95	NPL	1	Whitley Bay	175	1-1	McDonald
23/09/95	NPL	1	GREAT HARWOOD TOWN	127	2-2	Dunn(2)
30/09/95	NPL	1	Worksop Town	318	3-1	Cryer, McDonald, Dunn
03/10/95	NPL	1	FLEETWOOD	135	1-0	McDonald
07/10/95	NPL	1	HARROGATE TOWN	147	0-2	
09/10/95	NPL	1	Ashton United	202	1-2	McDonald
14/10/95	FA Trophy	Q1	CHORLEY	298	1-2	Cryer
17/10/95	NPL	1	CURZON ASHTON	98	2-2	Cryer, Dunn
24/10/95	LC	2	WINSFORD UNITED	82	3-2	Cryer, Stewart, Blundell(og)
28/10/95	NPL	1	LANCASTER CITY	177	2-1	McDonald, Pemberton
31/10/95	NPL	1	Curzon Ashton	102	3-2	Pemberton, Cryer, Quigg
04/11/95	NPL	1	Harrogate Town	193	1-3	Cryer
07/11/95	1C	1	CONGLETON TOWN	111	3-1	McDonald, Dunn, Burrows
11/11/95	NPL	1	Great Harwood Town	110	0-2	
18/11/95	NPL	1	Lincoln United	175	0-2	
25/11/95	NPL	1	WORKSOP TOWN	125	4-1	Dunn, McDonald(2), Burrows
28/11/95	Lancs ATS	1	BACUP BOROUGH	144	7-0	McDonald(3), Dunn(2), Christie, Burrows
02/12/95	NPL	1	CONGLETON TOWN	123	2-1	Kelly, Dunn
09/12/95	NPL	1	Fleetwood	83	2-2	Pemberton, Southern
12/12/95	1C	2	Warrington Town	66	1-0	Quigg
16/12/95	NPL	1	WORKINGTON	117	0-0	
06/01/96	NPL	1	Gretna	83	0-0	
13/01/96	NPL	1	WHITLEY BAY	95	2-1	Dunn, Cryer
16/01/96	Lancs ATS	2	CHORLEY	168	1-2	Pemberton
20/01/96	NPL	1	LINCOLN UNITED	126	0-1	
10/02/96	NPL	1	Lancaster City	176	0-1	
13/02/96	1C	QF	Workington	229	3-2	Cryer, Iley, Dunn
17/02/96	NPL	1	BRADFORD PARK AVENUE	176	3-1	Cryer(2), McDonald
21/02/96	NPL	1	Leigh R.M.I.	202	1-3	McDonald
24/02/96	NPL	1	Netherfield	109	4-2	Dunn, Cryer, McDonald, Stewart
02/03/96	NPL	1	ALFRETON TOWN	126	0-0	
09/03/96	NPL	1	EASTWOOD TOWN	143	2-1	Southern, Cryer
16/03/96	NPL	1	ASHTON UNITED	123	1-2	Iley
20/03/96	1C	SF(1)	Alfreton Town	130	4-0	Cryer, Quigg, Bennett, Stewart
23/03/96	NPL	1	Eastwood Town	115	0-1	
26/03/96	1C	SF(2)	ALFRETON TOWN	123	1-2	Cryer
30/03/96	NPL	1	FARSLEY CELTIC	98	1-1	Dunn
03/04/96	NPL	1	Bradford Park Avenue	155	2-2	Dunn(2)
06/04/96	NPL	1	GRETNA	124	1-1	Gavin
08/04/96	NPL	1	Congleton Town	156	1-4	Gavin
13/04/96	NPL	1	WARRINGTON TOWN	115	2-1	Dunn, Gavin
17/04/96	NPL	1	Farsley Celtic	72	3-3	Cryer(2), Brooks
20/04/96	NPL	1	Workington	210	1-0	Brooks
23/04/96	1C	F	LANCASTER CITY	436	0-1	(at Bamber Bridge)

BRADFORD PARK AVENUE

Horsfall Stadium, Horsfall Playing Fields, Halifax Road, Bradford BD6. Tel: 01274 604578

Secretary: Alan Hirst, 24 Quarryfields, Mirfield, West Yorkshire WF14 0NT Tel: 01924 480349

Press and Programme: Tim Clapham, 5 Glen View Grove, Nab Wood, Shipley, West Yorks Tel: 01274 598130

Comm Sec and Club shop: Garry Sawyer Tel: 01274 607780

Colours: White and green, Nickname: Avenue

Capacity: 3,000, Seating: 1,247

Covered standing: None, Clubhouse on ground: No

Record attendance: 34,429 v Leeds 1930's at Park Avenue

Biggest win: 11-0 FA Cup in 1908-09

Biggest defeat: 0-7 v Barnsley 1910-11 and

Accrington Stanley in 1955-56

Record appearances: Tommy Farr 542

Record goalscorer in one season: Kevin Hector 44 1965-66

Record goalscorer in total: Len Shackleton 171 1940-46

Record fee received: £34,000 from Derby County for Kevin Hector in 1966

HONOURS

Football League Division Two runners up 1914, Division Three North 1928,

Yorkshire League 1921 and 1923, Midland League 1932, North West Counties League and Challenge Trophy 1995, West Riding Senior Cup 1911, 1913, 1925, 1927, 1932, 1936, 1951, 1953, 1963

West Riding County Cup 1929 and 1991

Manager 1996-97: Dave Heeley,Chairman: Mike Firth

When Bradford Park Avenue folded in 1974, it looked as though that was the end for one of Yorkshire's best loved clubs. However, thanks to many dedicated people the name lives on and they are making a good job of re-establishing the club on the football map.

Soccer first took over from rugby at Park Avenue in 1907 and the club joined the Southern League, with election to the Fotball League Division Two coming a year later. Just prior to the Great War the club reached Division One. In 1920 the club's main benefactor Mr Harry Briggs died, and it coincided with a rapid decline which saw Avenue relegated in straight seasons to Division Three. It took six years to get back to Division Two where they remained until 1950, when relegation and subsequently re-organisation dumped them into the Fourth.

1961 saw the team promoted but by 1963 they were back in the 4th, where they remained until after four successive re-elections they were voted out of the League, and duly became members of the Northern Premier League. At the end of the 1970-71 season they had stopped the rot and in 1973 they finished fifth but serious financial problems saw the sale of Park Avenue. They moved across the city to ground share with Bradford City for the following season, but support dwindled and form deteriorated. A final placing of 21st preceded their resignation. In 1988 a team was entered in the West Riding County Amateur League to build on the foundations laid by a Sunday outfit formed when the original club perished. They won promotion but immediately resigned and switched to the Central Midlands League, playing home matches at McLaren Field, home of Bramley RLFC. After

one mediocre season they switched again, opting for the North West Counties where rapid progress has been made throughout the 90's. In 1993 they moved rugby grounds, to use Batley's Mount Pleasant ground and they moved into Horsfall Stadium, back in Bradford, for the start of this season. In 1995 they secured the NWCL title and were promoted to the Northern Premier League, where they found things hard going, finishing fifth from bottom.

However, the new ground back in the city may well launch the club on another title bid.

BRADFORD PARK AVENUE 1995/96 SEASON

Date	Comp	Round	Opponent	Att	Score	Scorers
19/08/95	NPL	1	LANCASTER CITY	241	0-3	
22/08/95	NPL	1	Worksop Town	460	1-4	Mumby
26/08/95	FA Cup	P	Armthorpe Welfare	85	1-1	Craven
30/08/95	FA Cup	P rep	ARMTHORPE WELFARE	148	1-0	Daykin
02/09/95	NPL	1	WORKINGTON	155	3-0	Brown, Brandon, Annan
05/09/95	NPL	1	Lincoln United	246	2-5	Mumby, Annan
09/09/95	FA Cup	Q1	Knowsley United	74	0-0	
13/09/95	FA Cup	Q1 rep	KNOWSLEY UNITED	158	3-2	A Brown, M Brown, Roberts
16/09/95	NPL	1	GRETNA	151	2-2	Roberts, Craven
18/09/95	NPL	1	Ashton United	283	1-0	Craven
23/09/95	FA Cup	Q2	Accrington Stanley	553	2-1	Marshall, Roberts
27/09/95	LC	1	FARSLEY CELTIC	177	2-0	Brown(2)
30/09/95	NPL	1	Curzon Ashton	205	1-0	Marshall
03/10/95	NPL	1	Whitley Bay	134	1-2	Craven
07/10/95	FA Cup	Q3	CURZON ASHTON	202	2-1	Brown, Craven
11/10/95	NPL	1	ALFRETON TOWN	183	1-1	Edmonds
14/10/95	FA Trophy	Q1	Accrington Stanley	415	2-2	Annan(2)
18/10/95	FA Trophy	Q1 rep	ACCRINGTON STANLEY	258	2-3	Annan, Morris
21/10/95	FA Cup	Q4	Marine	626	0-2	
25/10/95	LC	2	FRICKLEY ATHLETIC	184	1-1	Marshall
27/10/95	NPL	1	Radcliffe Borough	211	0-3	
31/10/95	LC	2 rep	Frickley Athletic	112	1-3	Daykin
04/11/95	NPL	1	Congleton Town	136	2-1	Marshall, Price
07/11/95	1C	1	Lincoln United	108	0-2	
11/11/95	NPL	1	LEIGH R.M.I.	163	3-1	Marshall, Higgins, Craven
18/11/95	NPL	1	Fleetwood	186	2-3	Price, Roberts
22/11/95	NPL	1	EASTWOOD TOWN	133	2-2	Brown, Rae
25/11/95	NPL	1	WARRINGTON TOWN	156	1-0	Roberts
28/11/95	NPL	1	Harrogate Town	225	2-1	Brierley, Price
02/12/95	NPL	1	Netherfield	186	0-0	
06/12/95	W. Riding	2	OSSETT ALBION	101	3-1	Craven, Sullivan, Brandon
09/12/95	NPL	1	Lancaster City	278	0-1	
15/12/95	NPL	1	RADCLIFFE BOROUGH	169	2-2	Pearson, Price
26/12/95	NPL	1	Eastwood Town	182	1-0	Browne
06/01/96	NPL	1	Leigh R.M.I.	161	0-1	
13/01/96	NPL	1	HARROGATE TOWN	228	1-1	Pearson
20/01/96	NPL	1	Workington	251	2-3	Craven, Hoy
24/01/96	NPL	1	FARSLEY CELTIC	152	1-1	Roberts
03/02/96	NPL	1	GREAT HARWOOD TOWN	161	1-3	Brierley
13/02/96	W. Riding	QF	Glasshoughton Welfare	100	2-0	Brierley, Jackson
17/02/96	NPL	1	Atherton L.R.	176	1-3	Sharpe
24/02/96	NPL	1	FLEETWOOD	172	2-2	Benn, Sharpe
02/03/96	NPL	1	Gretna	93	1-1	Sharpe
09/03/96	NPL	1	CURZON ASHTON	175	2-3	Brierley, Sharpe
16/03/96	NPL	1	Great Harwood Town	120	3-1	Gabbiadini(2), Sharpe
20/03/96	W. Riding	SF	Farsley Celtic	173	0-1	
23/03/96	NPL	1	WORKSOP TOWN	187	4-4	Sharpe, Gabbiadini(2), Annan
27/03/96	NPL	1	LINCOLN UNITED	176	2-3	Boyle, Brierley
30/03/96	NPL	1	Warrington Town	103	1-1	Marginson
03/04/96	NPL	1	ATHERTON L.R.	155	2-2	Brandell, Gabbiadini
08/04/96	NPL	1	Farsley Celtic	188	3-3	Price, Brierley, Hoyle
10/04/96	NPL	1	CONGLETON TOWN	171	0-0	
13/04/96	NPL	1	NETHERFIELD	147	0-2	
20/04/96	NPL	1	ASHTON UNITED	169	0-1	
27/04/96	NPL	1	Alfreton Town	364	2-3	Brandon, Benn
04/05/96	NPL	1	WHITLEY BAY	198	2-3	Brown, Gabbiadini

CONGLETON TOWN

Booth Street Ground, Crescent Rd, Congleton, Cheshire Tel: 01260 274460

Secretary David Wilcock, 4 Maxwell Rd, Congleton, CW12 3HY Tel: 01260 276347

Programme Editor: Paul Marshall, 26 Astbury Lane Ends, Congleton, Cheshire Tel: 01260 272249

Club shop manager: Robert Fletcher Tel 01260 278151

Colours: White and black

Nickname: Humbugs or the Bears

Capacity: 5,000

Seating: 250

Covered standing: 1,200, Clubhouse on ground Yes

Record attendance: 7,000 v Macclesfield Town 1954

Biggest win: 10-0 v Audley 1887-88

Record appearances: Ray Clack 600+

Record goalscorer in total: Mick Biddle 150+

DIRECTIONS

On approach to Congleton via Clayton bypass take second right after fire station, into Booth Street. Two miles from Congleton (BR).

Manager for 1996-97: Nigel Deeley, Chairman: Paul Marshall

HONOURS

Cheshire County League Div 2 1982

Mid-Cheshire League 1974, 1976, 1978

League Cup 1972

Cheshire Senior Cup 1921 and 1938

Events which led to the formation of Congleton Town FC began with the St James Alexandra club which played in the town in the 1880's. When they disbanded a new club, St James North Street School was formed and amalgamated with another club called Messrs Pointers Joiners Shop FC. They played on West Heath before houses were built, and they then became Congleton Hornets.

Hornets played at Willow Street, a famed ground in the town, in the South Cheshire League during the 1890's, the club record win coming during this era, a 10-0 win over Audley.

Hornets were succeeded by Congleton Town FC, which was formed in 1901 and played in the Crewe and District League, moving to the Staffordshire League in 1905. After the Great War, in 1920, they moved up to the Cheshire County League, where they were runners up and took the Cheshire Senior Cup. They were again runners up before enduring a lean spell which lasted until 1938 when they won the Senior Cup again.

There was little joy for the club after the War, and right through to 1972, when the club, by then in the Mid-Cheshire League almost did the league and cup double, but three titles were won in five years together with the League Cup and Cheshire Saturday Cup.

As founder members of the North West Counties League in 1982 they played out three seasons in mid-table but in 1987 they joined the Northern Premier League, the highlight of the 1989-90 season being a run to the FA Cup 1st Round where they lost to Crewe Alexandra.

Booth Street has undergone major changes in recent years and although honours have not come, the future looks far more rosy.

CONGLETON TOWN 1995/96 SEASON

Date	Competition	Round	Opponent	Att	Score	Scorers
19/08/95	NPL	1	GREAT HARWOOD TOWN	109	0-0	
22/08/95	NPL	1	Curzon Ashton	115	0-0	
26/08/95	NPL	1	Lancaster City	198	0-3	
28/08/95	NPL	1	RADCLIFFE BOROUGH	167	1-4	McKinlay
02/09/95	NPL	1	GRETNA	980	1-1	Williams, Faulkner, McKinley
16/09/95	NPL	1	Workington	327	0-2	
19/09/95	NPL	1	Lincoln United	186	1-1	Gavin
23/09/95	FA Cup	Q2	HINCKLEY ATHLETIC	203	1-1	Wallis
26/09/95	FA Cup	Q2 rep	Hinckley Athletic	213	0-1	
30/09/95	NPL	1	Fleetwood	158	2-0	McKinley, Adams
03/10/95	Ches. SC	1	STALYBRIDGE CELTIC	146	2-6	McKinley, Dickin
10/10/95	LC	1	WORKSOP TOWN	145	1-3	Gavin
14/10/95	FA Trophy	Q1	Alfreton Town	202	0-5	
21/10/95	NPL	1	LINCOLN UNITED	115	0-2	
28/10/95	NPL	1	Harrogate Town	196	1-1	Wallace
04/11/95	NPL	1	BRADFORD PARK AVENUE	136	1-2	Wallace
07/11/95	1C	1	Atherton L.R.	111	1-3	Williams
11/11/95	NPL	1	WHITLEY BAY	92	2-1	Gavin, Adams
14/11/95	NPL	1	EASTWOOD TOWN	144	1-1	Gavin
18/11/95	NPL	1	Leigh R.M.I.	153	1-1	Faulkner
20/11/95	NPL	1	Ashton United	123	0-2	
25/11/95	NPL	1	ALFRETON TOWN	141	0-1	
28/11/95	NPL	1	CURZON ASHTON	107	1-1	Roberts
02/12/95	NPL	1	Atherton L.R.	123	1-2	Powell
05/12/95	Mid-Ches.	1	MIDDLEWICH ATHLETIC		3-2	
09/12/95	NPL	1	NETHERFIELD	82	1-1	Williams
16/12/95	NPL	1	FARSLEY CELTIC	95	0-1	
06/01/96	NPL	1	Worksop Town	278	0-6	
13/01/96	NPL	1	WARRINGTON TOWN	124	0-4	
20/01/96	NPL	1	Farsley Celtic	92	2-0	Roberts, Williams
23/01/96	Mid-Ches.	QF	NANTWICH TOWN		2-2	(lost on penalties)
17/02/96	NPL	1	LANCASTER CITY	162	1-1	Roberts
24/02/96	NPL	1	Alfreton Town	181	1-2	Roberts
02/03/96	NPL	1	Great Harwood Town	85	2-1	Williams(2)
09/03/96	NPL	1	WORKSOP TOWN	134	0-2	
16/03/96	NPL	1	Radcliffe Borough	169	2-1	McIlroy, Williams
23/03/96	NPL	1	LEIGH R.M.I.	104	1-0	Roberts
30/03/96	NPL	1	Gretna	71	1-2	Roberts
02/04/96	NPL	1	ASHTON UNITED	142	3-0	Washington, Roberts(2)
06/04/96	NPL	1	Eastwood Town	103	0-3	
08/04/96	NPL	1	ATHERTON L.R.	156	4-1	Roberts(3), Washington
10/04/96	NPL	1	Bradford Park Avenue	171	0-0	
13/04/96	NPL	1	HARROGATE TOWN	153	2-1	Weston, Washington
16/04/96	NPL	1	Warrington Town	85	1-4	Washington
20/04/96	NPL	1	Netherfield	105	0-3	
23/04/96	NPL	1	FLEETWOOD	134	1-0	Moore
27/04/96	NPL	1	Whitley Bay	163	2-1	Moore, Williams
04/05/96	NPL	1	WORKINGTON	158	0-0	

CURZON ASHTON

National Park, Katherine Street, Ashton-Under-Lyne. Tel: 0161 330 6033

Secretary: Mr Alun Jones, 36 Forrest Rd, Denton, Manchester, M34 7RL Tel 0161 336 8004

Club Fax: 0161 330 6445

Chairman and Press: Stuart Kay, 64 The Avenue, Sale, Cheshire Tel: 0161 976 1644

> **DIRECTIONS**
>
> Behind Ashton police station off Manchester Rd (A635), Ashton-under-Lyne, one and a half miles from Ashton-under-Lyne (BR).

Shop Manager: Roy Howe: Tel 0161 220 8345

Programme Editor: Barry Thorpe Tel 0161 799 5964

Nickname: Curzon,   Capacity: 5,000

Seating: 350,   Covered standing: 300

Clubhouse on ground: Yes

Record attendance: 1,800 v Stamford

FA Vase semi-final 1980

Biggest win: 7-0 Ashton United

Biggest defeat: 0-7 v Bamber Bridge

Record appearances: Alan Sykes 600+

Record goalscorer in one season: Malcolm O'Connor

Record goalscorer in total: Alan Sykes

Record feepaid or received: £3,000 for Keith Evans

HONOURS

Manchester Amateur League Div 1 1964 and 1966

Div 3 1965 and Aggregate Cup 1981, Manchester Intermediate Cup 1972, 1973, 1974,

Manchester Premier Cup 1982, 1984, 1986, 1987, Ashton Challenge Cup 1965 and 1968

Manchester League and Gilgryst League Cup 1978, Murray Shield 1971

Manager for 1996-97: Terry McLean

Curzon Ashton was formed in 1963 with the amalgamation of two clubs, Curzon Road Methodists and Ashton Amateurism FC. They joined the Manchester Amateur League and immediately won the title race and were runners up in the first three years.

They then joined the Manchester League, taking a string of honours, including the Manchester Intermediate Cup three times. In 1974 they finished second in Div 1 of the league and runner up in the Premier 12 months later, also losing the Gilgryst Cup final two years running. In 1978 the club did the league and cup double and moved up to become founder members of the Cheshire County League Division Two, going up at the first attempt.The first season in the top flight was celebrated by becoming the first north west club to reach the FA Vase semi-final, losing to Stamford, but the home leg crowd of 1,800 was a record which still stands.

Curzon have picked up the Manchester Premier Cup five times since the 80's, and were accepted as founder members of the North West Counties League in 1982. They erected floodlights with the intention of going for the league title and Northern Premier League but it was from a relegation position that they took their place, where they remain. The `Nash' has been around since before the Great War, originally owned by a church who sold it to the National Gasoil and Engine Company. Dukinfield Town used the ground at some point until Curzon took over.

CURZON ASHTON 1995/96 SEASON

Date	Competition	Round	Opponent	Att	Score	Scorers
22/08/95	NPL	1	CONGLETON TOWN	115	0-0	
28/08/95	NPL	1	Ashton United	315	4-1	Pickering, Street, O'Connor, Schofield
02/09/95	NPL	1	HARROGATE TOWN	78	2-1	Schofield, O'Connor
05/09/95	NPL	1	LEIGH R.M.I.	101	2-1	McCrory, Ashton
09/09/95	FA Cup	Q1	Crook Town	118	1-1	Schofield
12/09/95	FA Cup	Q1 rep	CROOK TOWN	108	3-1	O'Connor, Schofield(2)
16/09/95	NPL	1	FLEETWOOD	126	1-1	O'Connor
20/09/95	NPL	1	Farsley Celtic	131	1-1	O'Connor
23/09/95	FA Cup	Q2	Trafford	108	2-1	Cook, Street
25/09/95	LC	1	EASTWOOD TOWN	109	1-2	O'Connor
30/09/95	NPL	1	BRADFORD PARK AVENUE	205	0-1	
04/10/95	NPL	1	Alfreton Town	181	2-3	O'Connor(2)
07/10/95	FA Cup	Q3	Bradford Park Avenue	202	1-2	Pickering
11/10/95	NPL	1	WARRINGTON TOWN	121	2-1	O'Connor, McAuley
14/10/95	FA Trophy	Q1	WORKSOP TOWN	170	4-3	Schofield(2), Burns, Street
17/10/95	NPL	1	Atherton L.R.	98	2-2	McCrory, Lee
21/10/95	NPL	1	Worksop Town	281	3-0	Schofield, O'Connor, Street
28/10/95	NPL	1	GREAT HARWOOD TOWN	108	4-1	Lee(2), Nestor, O'Connor
31/10/95	NPL	1	ATHERTON L.R.	102	2-3	O'Connor, Cook
04/11/95	FA Trophy	Q2	LANCASTER CITY	278	1-1	O'Connor
07/11/95	FA Trophy	Q2 rep	Lancaster City	206	0-3	
11/11/95	NPL	1	Workington	238	1-0	O'Connor
14/11/95	Manc PC	1	MOSSLEY	221	2-1	O'Connor, Pickering
18/11/95	NPL	1	NETHERFIELD	106	2-1	Nestor(2)
22/11/95	1C	1	Leigh R.M.I.	136	1-0	Heavey
25/11/95	NPL	1	Harrogate Town	182	4-2	Heavey, Street, O'Connor(2)
28/11/95	NPL	1	Congleton Town	107	1-1	Noon(og)
02/12/95	NPL	1	Eastwood Town	92	3-2	Heavey(2), Schofield
09/12/95	NPL	1	EASTWOOD TOWN	111	0-0	
11/12/95	1C	2	Ashton United	171	1-1	Heavey
16/12/95	NPL	1	Leigh R.M.I.	139	0-1	
06/01/96	NPL	1	Lancaster City	201	1-2	Heavey
09/01/96	1C	2 rep	ASHTON UNITED	206	0-2	
13/01/96	NPL	1	GRETNA	110	2-2	Heavey, O'Connor
20/01/96	NPL	1	Whitley Bay	120	2-3	O'Connor(2)
23/01/96	Manc PC	QF	OLDHAM TOWN	59	2-1	O'Connor(2)
03/02/96	NPL	1	Warrington Town	136	2-0	Heavey, Cook
17/02/96	NPL	1	Gretna	66	2-0	Armstrong(og), Finlay
24/02/96	NPL	1	LINCOLN UNITED	128	1-2	Heavey
02/03/96	NPL	1	ASHTON UNITED	275	4-2	Pickering, Nestor, O'Connor, Heavey
09/03/96	NPL	1	Bradford Park Avenue	175	3-2	Warder, Cook, Heavey
16/03/96	NPL	1	FARSLEY CELTIC	107	1-0	Schofield
19/03/96	Manc PC	SF	TRAFFORD	79	6-2	Ashton, Heavey(3), Nestor, Schofield
23/03/96	NPL	1	Netherfield	141	0-1	
26/03/96	NPL	1	WORKINGTON	102	3-0	O'Connor, Wardle, Pickering
02/04/96	NPL	1	RADCLIFFE BOROUGH	127	1-2	Heavey
06/04/96	NPL	1	ALFRETON TOWN	129	0-1	
08/04/96	NPL	1	Lincoln United	293	4-1	O'Connor(3), Heavey
13/04/96	NPL	1	Great Harwood Town	123	4-3	O'Connor(2), Heavey, Pickering
16/04/96	NPL	1	WHITLEY BAY	220	1-3	Heavey
20/04/96	NPL	1	LANCASTER CITY	197	0-3	
27/04/96	NPL	1	Fleetwood	72	2-1	O'Connor(2)
30/04/96	NPL	1	Radcliffe Borough	162	1-2	Heavey
04/05/96	NPL	1	WORKSOP TOWN	120	3-0	Nestor, O'Connor, Lee
07/05/96	Manc PC	F	Hyde United	390	2-2	Randles(2), (Lost on pens) (Played at Bolton)

DROYLSDEN

Butchers Arms Ground,Market Street, Droylsden, Manchester. Tel: 0161 370 1426

Secretary: Bernard King, 22 Hart Street, Droylsden, Manchester M43 7AW Tel: 0161 285 5232

Programme Editor: John Schofield Tel 0161 223 5643

Colours: Red and white, Nickname: The Bloods

Capacity: 3,500, Seating: 450 New stand currently being built

Covered standing: 2,000

Clubhouse on ground: Yes

Record attendance: 4,250 v Grimsby Town FA Cup 1st Rd 76

Biggest win: 13-2 v Lucas Sports Club

Record goalscorer in one season: E.Gillibrand 78 1931-32

DIRECTIONS

4 miles east of Manchester via A662 Ashton New Road, behind Butchers Arms Hotel.

HONOURS

Northern Premier League Div 1 Cup 1988

North West Counties Division 2 Cup 1987

Cheshire County League Cup 1978, Manchester League 1931 and 1933, League Cup 1924 and 1934

Manchester Premier Cup 1981, Manchester Senior Cup 1973, 1976, 1979

Manchester Intermediate Cup1960, 1965, 1970, Manchester Challenge Shield 1947

Manager 1996-97: Tommy Lawton, Chairman: Dave Pace

Vice Chairman: Roy Day, Commercial Manager: Ray Lee

By 1890 there were as many as six football clubs in Droylsden, including Amateurs, Albion, Celtic, Villa, Ramblers and Wesleyans. The Town club were formed in 1892 on a pitch next to the bowling green behind the Butchers Arms, and friendlies were played. They joined the Manchester and District Alliance, but between then and 1909 they disbanded and re-formed four times, as one time playing and winning the Hooley Hill and District League. Finally they emerged in the Ashton and District League in 1909 and after the Great War they stepped up into the Manchester League and reached the final of the Manchester Junior Cup, losing to Hyde but winning the cup a year later. The Bloods shared the title with Buxton in 1931 but were outright winners a year later. In 1936 they entered the Lancashire Combination and signed a deal as a nursery club for Manchester City, and this continued until the Second War.

On the resumption they were invited to join the Cheshire League, but after finishing runners up they hit a bad spell and finished bottom, whereupon they were further hit when the Brewery landlords sold the ground to Belle Vue Football Club. After a meeting it was decided that both clubs would share the ground. Belle Vue changed their name to Droylsden United, and carried on in the Lancs Comb, although Droylsden FC were voted out of the Cheshire League and went back to the Manchester League.

They moved out of the Butchers Arms ground and began playing at Moorside Trotting stadium, where they were well supported, until the council bought the Butchers Arms and developed it by turning the pitch around and building terraces and stands. They also called the two clubs together, and they amalgamated and began, as Droylsden FC, in the Lancs Combination.

They remained there until 1968, when they joined the Cheshire League, from where they enjoyed much cup success, reaching the FA Cup 1st Round in 1976, playing Grimsby Town in front of 4,500 people. Two seasons later they beat Rochdale at Scottland before losing in the Second Round

to Altrincham. When the North-West Counties League was formed in 1982, they joined and won Division Two, and were elected as founder members of the Northern Premier League's Division One, where they won the League Cup and were soon promoted as runners up behind Leek Town.

Since then the club has battled against set backs such as the loss of their social club and main stand through fire, and vandalism, but after dropping back to Division One, the club and the ground are on the up once more with a new club and stand.

DROYLSDEN 1995/96 SEASON

Date	Comp	Rnd	Opponent	Att	Score	Scorers
19/08/95	NPL	P	GUISELEY	254	1-2	Doody
23/08/95	NPL	P	BUXTON	206	1-3	Evans
26/08/95	NPL	P	Spennymoor United	263	0-2	
28/08/95	NPL	P	HYDE UNITED	286	0-2	
02/09/95	NPL	P	BOSTON UNITED	198	2-5	Evans, Lowe
05/09/95	NPL	P	Leek Town	221	0-4	
09/09/95	FA Cup	Q1	Nantwich Town	84	0-3	
13/09/95	NPL	P	GAINSBOROUGH TRINITY	94	1-2	Ashton
16/09/95	NPL	P	BLYTH SPARTANS	183	2-2	Bradshaw(2)
19/09/95	NPL	P	Marine	340	1-6	Lowe
23/09/95	NPL	P	Boston United	706	1-0	Pannett
26/09/95	LC	1	Radcliffe Borough	94	3-0	Bradshaw, Evans, Blain
30/09/95	NPL	P	WINSFORD UNITED	217	1-1	Bradsman
03/10/95	NPL	P	Buxton	203	3-0	Evans(2), Blain
07/10/95	NPL	P	Frickley Athletic	105	5-4	Bradshaw, Evans(2), Pennett, Heath
14/10/95	FA Trophy	Q1	MATLOCK TOWN	173	0-3	
17/10/95	NPL	P	Matlock Town	247	2-2	Heaton(2)
21/10/95	NPL	P	Accrington Stanley	472	2-0	Ashton, Evans
28/10/95	NPL	P	BISHOP AUCKLAND	193	1-4	Blain
31/10/95	Manc PC	1	FLIXTON	93	2-4	Bradshaw, Pannett
04/11/95	LC	2	Colwyn Bay	280	1-3	Evans
11/11/95	NPL	P	Emley	196	0-4	
18/11/95	NPL	P	CHORLEY	130	0-6	
22/11/95	NPL	P	BARROW	118	0-4	
25/11/95	NPL	P	FRICKLEY ATHLETIC	88	2-2	Evans(2)
02/12/95	NPL	P	Chorley	242	0-6	
09/12/95	NPL	P	Bamber Bridge	358	2-3	Evans, Bradshaw
16/12/95	NPL	P	LEEK TOWN	124	2-1	Wood, Evans
06/01/96	NPL	P	Bishop Auckland	150	2-3	Heaton, Blain
13/01/96	NPL	P	MATLOCK TOWN	165	3-0	McKinlay, Evans, Wood
20/01/96	NPL	P	Barrow	1023	3-3	Ashton, Tunnicliffe, Evans
10/02/96	NPL	P	Colwyn Bay	283	0-0	
17/02/96	NPL	P	SPENNYMOOR UNITED	172	1-1	Weston
24/02/96	NPL	P	Witton Albion	399	1-2	Pannett
28/02/96	NPL	P	COLWYN BAY	229	0-1	
02/03/96	NPL	P	Gainsborough Trinity	406	1-7	Pannett
09/03/96	NPL	P	KNOWSLEY UNITED	125	5-1	Tobin, Evans(3), Ribus
16/03/96	NPL	P	ACCRINGTON STANLEY	180	1-2	Evans
23/03/96	NPL	P	Guiseley	249	0-3	
30/03/96	NPL	P	MARINE	162	2-1	Pannett, Evans
02/04/96	NPL	P	Blyth Spartans	445	1-2	Evans
06/04/96	NPL	P	WITTON ALBION	167	2-1	Evans, Hall
08/04/96	NPL	P	Knowsley United	66	0-2	
13/04/96	NPL	P	Winsford United	150	2-3	Evans, Cooke
20/04/96	NPL	P	BAMBER BRIDGE	237	1-2	Hall
26/04/96	NPL	P	Hyde United	491	1-1	Evans
04/05/96	NPL	P	EMLEY	226	3-0	Lattie, Heaton, Hall

EASTWOOD TOWN

Coronation Park, Eastwood, Notts. Tel: 01773 715823 Fax: 712301

Secretary: Paddy Farrell, 7 Primrose Rise, Newthorpe, Nottingham, NG16 2BB Tel: 01773 715500

Club shop manager: Mr Ron Storer Tel: 0115 938 5239

Colours: Black and white stripes,

Nickname: The Badgers

Capacity: 5,900, Seating: 200

Covered standing: 1,290, Clubhouse on ground: Yes

Record attendance: 2,723 v Enfield FA Amateur Cup 1965

Biggest win: 26-0

Biggest defeat: 1-7

Record appearances: Arthur Rowley 800 + 1955-1976

Record goalscorer in one season: Brian Richardson

Record goalscorer in total: Martin Wright

Record fee received: £72,000 for Richard Liburd to Middlesbrough 1993

DIRECTIONS

From North — M1 junction 27 then follow Heanor signs via Brinsley to lights in Eastwood. Turn left then first right after Fire Station — ground entrance on Chenton Street. From South — M1 jct 26, A610 to Ripley, leave at 1st exit (B6010), follow to Eastwoods, left at lights, first left at 'Man In Space' — ground entrance on Chenton Street. Nearest rail station is Langley Mill. Buses every 10 mins (R11, R12 or R13) from Victoria Centre, Nottingham, journey time 40 mins.

HONOURS

Midland Counties League 1976 and League Cup 1978 and 1980

Central Alliance 1964

Notts Alliance 1957 and League Cup 1956

Notts Senior Cup 1976, 1978, 1979, 1980, 1983, 1984, 1989, 1990, 1992

East Midlands Regional League 1968 and 1969

Midland Regional Alliance 1987 and 1989

Evans Halshaw Cup 1994

Manager 1996-97: Bryan Chambers, Assistant Manager: Jim McGowan

Chairman: George Belshaw, Vice Chairman: Richard James

The club was founded in 1953 after the local Eastwood Collieries side had disbanded. Town started their football life on August 29th with a 4-1 win over Bilsthorpe Colliery in the Notts Alliance Division One and finished the season as runners up. They came close many times during the next ten years but only won the title once, sharing it with Gedling Colliery in 1957.

In 1961 they moved to the Central Alliance and they were champions in 1964 and runners up a year later, moving on to the East Midlands Regional League where they were runners up in 1969. It was during this period that the club enjoyed some stiring runs in the Amateur Cup, one match against Enfield pulling in a record crowd of 2, 723. They turned professional and joined the Midland Counties League in 1971, staying until it merged to become the NCEL in 1982.

They were successful times with one championship, two second places, two League Cups and the first of nine Notts Senior Cup wins. In 1987 the Northern Premier League set up a second division and Eastwood Town became founder members. Coronation Park is the club's only home, although the first pitch was a few yards behind the bottom goal within the same complex and is now a bowling green, although the banking can still be seen.

Recently the club have profited from astute moves in the transfer market, with four players joining Football League clubs, netting well over £120,000.

EASTWOOD TOWN 1995/96 SEASON

Date	Comp	Rnd	Opponent	Att	Score	Scorers
19/08/95	NPL	1	WHITLEY BAY	98	0-2	
23/08/95	NPL	1	Farsley Celtic	159	1-2	Brocklehurst
26/08/95	FA Cup	P	Chadderton	96	1-0	N Illman
28/08/95	NPL	1	LINCOLN UNITED	124	4-2	N Illman(2), Knapper, Clarke
02/09/95	NPL	1	Fleetwood	132	2-2	Knapper, Clarke
05/09/95	NPL	1	WORKSOP TOWN	232	2-3	Clarke, Browne
09/09/95	FA Cup	Q1	BUXTON	229	2-1	Marsh, Illman
16/09/95	NPL	1	GREAT HARWOOD TOWN	109	1-0	Clarke
19/09/95	NPL	1	ALFRETON TOWN	290	2-0	Illman, Connolly
23/09/95	FA Cup	Q2	Frickley Athletic	201	4-2	Illman, Brown(2), Knapper
25/09/95	LC	1	Curzon Ashton	109	2-1	Browne, Richardson
30/09/95	NPL	1	WARRINGTON TOWN	126	2-1	Illman(2)
07/10/95	FA Cup	Q3	Northwich Victoria	742	0-0	
10/10/95	FA Cup	Q3 rep	NORTHWICH VICTORIA	640	1-2	Illman
10/10/95	Notts SC	1	Hucknall Town	301	1-3	Connelly
14/10/95	NPL	1	Netherfield	167	4-1	Illman(2), Henson, Knapper
21/10/95	NPL	1	Great Harwood Town	81	0-1	
24/10/95	LC	2	ALFRETON TOWN	261	3-2	Marsh, Illman(2)
28/10/95	NPL	1	Gretna	101	2-0	Illman, Knapper
31/10/95	NPL	1	HARROGATE TOWN	119	1-1	Illman
04/11/95	FA Trophy	Q2	CHORLEY	86	0-1	
08/11/95	1C	1	Farsley Celtic	119	1-2	Smith(og)
11/11/95	NPL	1	RADCLIFFE BOROUGH	116	2-1	Browne, Illman
13/11/95	Evans Hal.	Fiesta	Blidworth Welfare		3-0	
14/11/95	NPL	1	Congleton Town	144	1-1	N Illman
18/11/95	NPL	1	Warrington Town	80	0-2	
22/11/95	NPL	1	Bradford Park Avenue	133	2-2	N Illman, Marsh
25/11/95	NPL	1	WORKINGTON	172	2-1	N Illman(2)
28/11/95	NPL	1	FARSLEY CELTIC	119	1-2	Knapper
02/12/95	NPL	1	CURZON ASHTON	92	2-3	Richardson, Browne
05/12/95	LC	3	Leek Town	67	3-4	Illman, Barnes, Flint
09/12/95	NPL	1	Curzon Ashton	111	0-0	
16/12/95	NPL	1	LANCASTER CITY	120	1-2	Brown
19/12/95	Evans Hal.	Fiesta	BLIDWORTH WELFARE		0-0	
26/12/95	NPL	1	BRADFORD PARK AVENUE	182	0-1	
06/01/96	NPL	1	NETHERFIELD	82	1-0	Knapper
09/01/96	Evans Hal.	Fiesta	Arnold Town		2-1	
13/01/96	NPL	1	Ashton United	185	1-2	Richardson
20/01/96	NPL	1	FLEETWOOD	98	3-0	Richardson(2), Browne
23/01/96	Evans Hal.	Fiesta	ARNOLD TOWN		1-1	
03/02/96	NPL	1	Harrogate Town	198	3-1	Barnes, Knapper(2)
10/02/96	NPL	1	LEIGH R.M.I.	94	1-0	Richardson
17/02/96	NPL	1	Workington	192	2-1	Richardson, Barnes
24/02/96	NPL	1	ASHTON UNITED	130	2-1	Marsh, Illman
02/03/96	NPL	1	Lincoln United	196	0-2	
09/03/96	NPL	1	Atherton L.R.	143	1-2	Connolly
16/03/96	NPL	1	Leigh R.M.I.	136	0-1	
23/03/96	NPL	1	ATHERTON L.R.	115	1-0	Richardson
30/03/96	NPL	1	Whitley Bay	147	0-0	
06/04/96	NPL	1	CONGLETON TOWN	103	3-0	Hoy, Place, Tucker
08/04/96	NPL	1	Alfreton Town	305	2-2	Ghislanzoni, Heath
10/04/96	Evans Hal.	SF	HOLBEACH UNITED		0-2	
13/04/96	NPL	1	Lancaster City	303	2-2	Hoy(2)
16/04/96	NPL	1	Worksop Town	283	2-1	Browne, Hoy
20/04/96	NPL	1	GRETNA	129	3-1	Ingall(2), Connolly
23/04/96	NPL	1	Radcliffe Borough	130	1-1	Hoy

FARSLEY CELTIC

Throstle Nest, Newlands, Farsley, Pudsey, Leeds LS28 5BE Tel: 0113 256 1517 club 0113 257 1058 fax

Secretary: Mrs Margaret Lobley, 29 Springbank Rd, Farsley, Leeds LS28 5LS Tel: 0113 257 5675

Programme Editor: Keith Huggins Tel: 0113 274 3254

Club shop manager: Mr B Falkingham Tel: 0113 255 0749

Colours: Sky and navy blue stripes

Nickname: Villagers

Capacity: 4,000

Seating: 430

Covered standing: 1,000

Clubhouse on ground: Yes

Record attendance: 11,000 (At Elland Rd, Leeds v Tranmere Rovers FA Cup 1st Rd 1974)

HONOURS

West Riding County Cup 1958, 1960, 1967, 1971, 1984, 1988, 1995

Yorkshire League   1960 and 1969, and Div 2 in 1952

League Cup 1963, 1964, 1967

DIRECTIONS

From North East: A1 south to Wetherby, A58 to Leeds, at 1st island (approx 8 miles) take 3rd exit (A6120 ring-rd), follow Bradford signs to 12th r'bout (approx 12 miles) — 1st exit (B6157 Stanningley). From M62 jct 26, M606 (Bradford) to r'bout, 4th exit (A6177 passing Rooley lane — Sticker lane passing Morrisons store on left to lights (approx 3 miles) — right onto A647 (Leeds) to 2nd r'bout, 2nd exit (B6157 Stanningley). Continue 800 yds passing Police & Stations on left. Turn left down New Street at Tradex Warehouse before turning right into Newlands. Ground at bottom of road. 1 mile from New Pudsey (BR).

Manager for 1996-97: Martin Haresign

Assistant manager: Jim Mackay

Chairman: John Palmer

Vice Chairman: Paul Robinson

Formed in 1908 by a group of local lads in the village, Farsley Celtic played for many years on various pitches including ones in Red Lane and Calverley Lane. Early football was played in the Leeds Red Triangle League and later the West Riding County Amateur before the War.

When football resumed, the club bought the current ground from the council and in 1949 joined the Yorkshire League, which they won in 1960 and 1969, taking the League Cup in 1964 and 1967.

1974 saw by far the club's finest run in the FA Cup when they beat four Yorkshire sides to reach Round one for the only time. Their home tie with Tranmere Rovers was switched to Elland Road, Leeds and is the only time they have played a League club in the Cup.

In 1982 when the Yorkshire and Midland Leagues merged, the Northern Counties East became home and in 1985 they were promoted to the Premier Division. Two years later they were runners up and after installing floodlights they were invited to join the newly formed 1st Division of the Northern Premier League in 1987.

That season saw the best Vase run, when they reached the last eight before going out to eventual winners Colne Dynamoes.

FARSLEY CELTIC 1995/96 SEASON

Date	Comp	Rd	Opponent	Att	Score	Scorers
19/08/95	NPL	1	Ashton United	180	1-2	Allen
23/08/95	NPL	1	EASTWOOD TOWN	159	2-1	Freeman, Drury
26/08/95	FA Cup	P	OLDHAM TOWN	103	2-2	Whellans(2)
29/08/95	FA Cup	P rep	Oldham Town	75	2-0	Sharp, Cawthorne
02/09/95	NPL	1	WARRINGTON TOWN	113	1-0	Carrington
05/09/95	NPL	1	Whitley Bay	203	2-5	Carrington, Allen
09/09/95	FA Cup	Q1	Chorley	251	2-2	Carrington, Whellans
13/09/95	FA Cup	Q1 rep	CHORLEY	221	1-2	Wallace
20/09/95	NPL	1	CURZON ASHTON	131	1-1	Whellans
23/09/95	NPL	1	WHITLEY BAY	124	1-0	Green
27/09/95	LC	1	Bradford Park Avenue	177	0-2	
30/09/95	NPL	1	LANCASTER CITY	162	2-1	Whellans, Carrington
07/10/95	NPL	1	Leigh R.M.I.	165	0-0	
10/10/95	NPL	1	Lincoln United	260	0-0	
14/10/95	FA Trophy	Q1	BEDWORTH UNITED	159	3-1	Green, Whellans, Turner
21/10/95	NPL	1	ALFRETON TOWN	164	1-0	Whellans
28/10/95	NPL	1	FLEETWOOD	97	0-2	
01/11/95	NPL	1	WORKSOP TOWN	124	2-2	Green, Allen
04/11/95	FA Trophy	Q2	Grantham Town	303	3-1	Freeman, Whellans(2)
08/11/95	1C	1	EASTWOOD TOWN	119	2-1	Allen(2)
11/11/95	NPL	1	Netherfield	183	3-1	Carrington, Allen, Morris
21/11/95	NPL	1	Harrogate Town	184	6-1	McClelland, Whellans(3), Carrington
25/11/95	FA Trophy	Q3	Radcliffe Borough	155	1-3	Armitage
28/11/95	NPL	1	Eastwood Town	119	2-1	Carrington, Allen
02/12/95	NPL	1	GRETNA	82	0-2	
06/12/95	W. Riding	2	HARROGATE TOWN	76	3-2	Allen(2), Whellans
09/12/95	NPL	1	Alfreton Town	184	3-2	Allen, Green, Whellans
12/12/95	1C	2	Lancaster City	115	1-1	Learoyd
16/12/95	NPL	1	Congleton Town	95	1-0	Whellans
06/01/96	NPL	1	ASHTON UNITED	97	2-4	Whellans, Green
10/01/96	1C	2 rep	LANCASTER CITY	99	1-3	Carrington
13/01/96	NPL	1	Radcliffe Borough	152	0-2	
20/01/96	NPL	1	CONGLETON TOWN	92	0-2	
24/01/96	NPL	1	Bradford Park Avenue	152	1-1	Whellans
03/02/96	NPL	1	Workington	215	1-2	Freeman
14/02/96	W. Riding	QF	HALIFAX TOWN	211	1-0	Whellans
17/02/96	NPL	1	Fleetwood	86	3-1	Green, Allen, Carrington
24/02/96	NPL	1	Warrington Town	84	1-5	Carrington
02/03/96	NPL	1	WORKINGTON	83	3-0	Carrington, Whellans(2)
09/03/96	NPL	1	GREAT HARWOOD TOWN	81	1-0	Whellans
16/03/96	NPL	1	Curzon Ashton	107	0-1	
20/03/96	W. Riding	SF	BRADFORD PARK AVENUE	173	1-0	Whellans
23/03/96	NPL	1	RADCLIFFE BOROUGH	88	4-1	Whellans, Carrington, Allen, Waterfield
30/03/96	NPL	1	Atherton L.R.	98	1-1	Whellans
03/04/96	W. Riding	F	GUISELEY	598	0-0	
06/04/96	NPL	1	Great Harwood Town	117	3-0	Whellans, Adams, Chapman
08/04/96	NPL	1	BRADFORD PARK AVENUE	188	3-3	Little, Diamond, Allen
10/04/96	W. Riding	F rep	Guiseley	440	2-3	Green, Allen
13/04/96	NPL	1	Gretna	70	1-7	Whellans
15/04/96	NPL	1	HARROGATE TOWN	98	2-2	Craven, Adams
17/04/96	NPL	1	ATHERTON L.R.	72	3-3	Allen(2), Waterfield
20/04/96	NPL	1	Worksop Town	258	0-1	
24/04/96	NPL	1	NETHERFIELD	57	3-1	Little, Green(2)
27/04/96	NPL	1	LEIGH R.M.I.	58	2-1	Waterfield, Allen
01/05/96	NPL	1	LINCOLN UNITED	73	2-1	Waterfield, Whellans
04/05/96	NPL	1	Lancaster City	383	2-1	Whellans, Allen

FLIXTON

Valley Road, Flixton, Manchester M31 2RQ. Tel: 0161 747 7757 or 748 2903 club

Secretary: John A Fradley, 3 Hawthorn Rd, Stretford, Manchester M32 8WE Tel: 0161 865 0418

Colours: Blue and white stripes

Nickname: Valley Roaders

Capacity: 2,000

Seating: 250

Covered standing: 650

Clubhouse on ground: Yes

Record attendance: 1,540 v Brigg Town

FA Vase semi-final 2nd leg 1996

Biggest win: 10-2 v Irlam Town 1994

Biggest defeat: 1-10 v Knowsley Utd 1990-91

Record appearances: John Mitchell

Record goalscorer in one season: John Mitchell

Record goalscorer in total: John Mitchell

DIRECTIONS

M63 junction 3, B5214 (signed Urmston), follow Trafford General Hospital signs, at 4th roundabout take 3rd exit (Woodbridge Road), ground at top. One and a quarter miles from Flixton BR station (trains from Manchester Oxford Road) - turn right out of station onto Flixton Road, left after quarter mile into Woodsend Road, at roundabout after quarter mile take 2nd exit into Woodbrirdge Road - ground at top. Take any bus from Manchester Piccadilly bus station to Flixton and alight at Flixton Red Lion.

HONOURS

FA VASE Semi-final 1996

North West Counties League 1996, Division Two 1995

Manchester League Div 1 1978, Lancs Amateur Cup 1980

Manchester Challenge Trophy 1984,

Manager 1996-97: Dalton Steele, Assistant Manager: Steve Smythe

Chairman: Alan Edge, Vice Chairman: Peter Dentith

Formed in 1960, Flixton AFC began playing amateur football in the South Manchester and Wythenshawe League. Three years in 1963 the club joined the Lancashire and Cheshire League winning Division Three.

Ten years later they joined the Manchester League and moved to Valley Road, which they soon improved by building changing rooms and a clubhouse. Further work brought the ground in line with North West Counties requirements and in the first season they were runners up in Division Three, losing the title by one point. That year also saw them reach the final of the Manchester Premier Cup and the semi-final of the Divisional Cup. In the second season, another runners up place was enough for promotion again.

As the club and ground progressed, then lights were installed in 1989. The last two seasons have been remarkable for the Valley Roaders, who took the Division Two championship in 1995 as well as reaching the final of the Lamot Pils Trophy. The massive new £500,000 clubhouse was opened and in 1996 they were crowned champions of the North West Counties League, and had the sadness of losing at home in the second leg of the FA Vase semi- final to Brigg Town. They also reached the Challenge Cup final but were given the ultimate consolation by being accepted into the Northern Premier League for this season.

FLIXTON 1995/96 SEASON

Date	Comp	Rd	Opponent	Score
19/08/95	NWCL	1	St Helens Town	0-0
22/08/95	NWCL	1	SKELMERSDALE UNITED	3-0
26/08/95	FA Cup	P	Leigh R.M.I.	0-2
28/08/95	NWCL	1	GLOSSOP NORTH END	3-0
02/09/95	NWCL	1	Prescot	0-2
05/09/95	NWCL	1	Bootle	3-2
09/09/95	NWCL	1	SALFORD CITY	3-1
12/09/95	NWCL	1	HOLKER OLD BOYS	5-0
16/09/95	NWCL	1	Maine Road	3-1
19/09/95	NWCL	1	Blackpool Rovers	2-1
23/09/95	NWCL	1	DARWEN	1-0
26/09/95	NWCL	1	CHADDERTON	4-0
30/09/95	FA Vase	Q2	POULTON VICTORIA	2-1
03/10/95	FT	1(1)	ATHERTON COLLIERIES	5-0
07/10/95	NWCL	1	PRESCOT	2-2
10/10/95	NWCL	1	Salford City	1-1
14/10/95	NWCL	1	MOSSLEY	1-2
17/10/95	FT	1(2)	Atherton Collieries	0-0
21/10/95	NWCL	1	Burscough	1-0
24/10/95	NWCL	1	NEWCASTLE TOWN	3-3
28/10/95	FA Vase	1	GLOSSOP NORTH END	3-0
31/10/95	Manc PC	1	Droylsden	4-2
04/11/95	NWCL	1	CLITHEROE	1-0
07/11/95	NWCL	1	Holker Old Boys	1-1
11/11/95	LC	2	ROSSENDALE UNITED	2-1
18/11/95	FA Vase	2	HUCKNALL TOWN	5-1
21/11/95	FT	2	Glossop North End	1-4
25/11/95	NWCL	1	Darwen	0-0
02/12/95	NWCL	1	Chadderton	3-2
09/12/95	FA Vase	3	Winterton Rangers	4-0
12/12/95	NWCL	1	Eastwood Hanley	1-1
16/12/95	NWCL	1	Skelmersdale United	2-1
23/12/95	NWCL	1	BLACKPOOL ROVERS	2-0
06/01/96	NWCL	1	ROSSENDALE UNITED	5-0
13/01/96	FA Vase	4	DUNSTON FED BREW	2-0
20/01/96	LC	3	Tetley Walker	3-1
23/01/96	NWCL	1	PENRITH	4-0
30/01/96	Manc PC	QF	Trafford	3-1
03/02/96	FA Vase	5	BARWELL	3-1
17/02/96	NWCL	1	MAINE ROAD	2-0
24/02/96	FA Vase	QF	CANVEY ISLAND	3-0
02/03/96	NWCL	1	Clitheroe	0-1
05/03/96	NWCL	1	Trafford	1-2
09/03/96	LC	QF	TRAFFORD	2-0
16/03/96	FA Vase	SF(1)	Brigg Town	0-0
19/03/96	NWCL	1	KIDSGROVE ATHLETIC	3-1
23/03/96	FA Vase	SF(2)	BRIGG TOWN	0-1
26/03/96	NWCL	1	NANTWICH TOWN	2-1
30/03/96	NWCL	1	Penrith	1-2
02/04/96	NWCL	1	Mossley	1-1
06/04/96	LC	SF(1)	Newcastle Town	0-0
08/04/96	NWCL	1	Rossendale United	3-1
13/04/96	LC	SF(2)	NEWCASTLE TOWN	3-0
16/04/96	NWCL	1	Kidsgrove Athletic	5-0
18/04/96	NWCL	1	BOOTLE	2-0
20/04/96	NWCL	1	EASTWOOD HANLEY	4-0
23/04/96	NWCL	1	BURSCOUGH	2-0
25/04/96	LC	F	Burscough	0-1
27/04/96	NWCL	1	Glossop North End	2-0
30/04/96	NWCL	1	ST HELENS TOWN	1-0
02/05/96	NWCL	1	Newcastle Town	1-0
04/05/96	NWCL	1	Nantwich Town	0-1
06/05/96	NWCL	1	TRAFFORD	1-0
17/05/96	Shield		BURSCOUGH	0-1

GREAT HARWOOD TOWN

The Showground, Wood Street, Great Harwood, Lancs. Tel: 01254 883913

Secretary: Mr R. Smith, 56 Gladstone St, Great Harwood, Blackburn BB6 7NH Tel: 01405 877908

Nickname: The Robins

Colours All Red

Capacity: 2,500

Seating: 200

Covered standing: 800

Clubhouse on ground: Yes

Record atten: 5,397 v Manchester United in 1980

Biggest win: 7-0 v Farsley Celtic NPL 1992-93

Biggest defeat: 1-8 v Caernarvon Town NPL 1994-95

Record appearances: Peter Smith

Record goalscorer in one season: Peter Smith

Record goalscorer in total: Peter Smith

DIRECTIONS

M66 from Manchester to Haslingden exit, A680 through Baxenden, Accrington to Clayton-le-Moors, left at the Hyndburn Bridge Hotel into Hyndburn Road and right into Wood Street to ground. Or M6 jct 31, Clitheroe/Skipton Road to Trafalgar Hotel, A677 to Blackburn, left at Moat House Hotel and follow ring-road to M65 junction, A678 to Rishton, left at lights (B6536) to Gt Harwood, right at Town Gate into Queen Street, follow signs for Lomax Square, left into Park Rd, right into Balfour Street to ground. 3 miles from Rishton (BR), 6 miles from Blackburn (BR). Various buses from Heyes Lane & Park Road to Blackburn & Accrington.

HONOURS

North-West Counties League Div 2 1991

Lancs FA ATS Trophy 1991,

Lamot Pils Trophy 1990

Tennants Floodlit Trophy 1991

Manager for 1996-97: Martin Eatough

Assistant manager: Dave Sargent

Chairman: William Holden

Vice chairman: Mark Smith

Great Harwood Town FC began life as Great Harwood Wellington Football Club back in the mid-sixties, when a group of friends started a team at their local pub. The club enjoyed tremendous success and dominated the Blackburn Combination for a number of years, before stepping up into the West Lancs League where the success continued. Great Harwood FC from the Northern Premier League had fallen on hard times and had sadly folded in 1978, and this gave "Welli" as they were commonly known, the opportunity to progress further by moving 50 yards from Lydon House Field to the Showground. Membership of the Lancs Combination immediately followed and in so doing, kept senior football alive in the town. Changing their name to Town, they became founder members of the North-West Counties League and plodded on until nearly going out of the league in 1988. The club then went through a radical change and success followed. The first success was in 1990 with the Lamot Pils Trophy, but the next season was the peak. They became Champions of the Division Two by a record margin, losing only two games and reached the quarter-finals of the FA Vase. In addition they reached the ATS Lancashire Trophy where they lost to Marine in the final. 1990-91 was again outstanding, winning the ATS Trophy at Bolton against Southport. Then at Wigan the club took the Tennants Trophy, beating Bamber Bridge. In the league, after leading for

most of the season, they were pipped at the post by Ashton United. After much graft and ground improvements, the club were admitted to the Northern Premier League and more recently they reached the final of the Division One Cup only to lose to Blyth Spartans over two legs.

In 1992 the club introduced its Great Harwood Town Football Club in the Community project with the object of involving local people within the club. There is now a Junior Robins section as well as all year round coaching, which has led to four junior clubs in local leagues.

GREAT HARWOOD TOWN 1995/96 SEASON

Date	Comp	Rd	Opponent	Att	Score	Scorers
19/08/95	NPL	1	Congleton Town	109	0-0	
21/08/95	NPL	1	FLEETWOOD	150	2-1	Rasul, G Smith
26/08/95	FA Cup	P	Goole Town	99	2-2	G Smith, Baker
31/08/95	FA Cup	P rep	GOOLE TOWN	112	3-2	Baker, P Smith(2)
02/09/95	NPL	1	LINCOLN UNITED	108	0-1	
05/09/95	NPL	1	Netherfield	193	1-3	Baker
09/09/95	FA Cup	Q1	Matlock Town	290	2-5	Baker(2)
11/09/95	NPL	1	GRETNA	93	1-1	Baker
16/09/95	NPL	1	Eastwood Town	109	0-1	
18/09/95	NPL	1	WARRINGTON TOWN	106	0-5	
23/09/95	NPL	1	Atherton L.R.	127	2-2	Burswell, Baker
27/09/95	LC	1	Leigh R.M.I.	145	4-6	Burswell(2), Baker(2)
30/09/95	NPL	1	WHITLEY BAY	102	2-0	Smith, Baker
03/10/95	NPL	1	Workington	276	0-0	
07/10/95	NPL	1	Worksop Town	307	2-3	Hamilton, Brookes(og)
09/10/95	NPL	1	NETHERFIELD	120	0-2	
17/10/95	NPL	1	Lancaster City	205	1-4	Smith
21/10/95	NPL	1	EASTWOOD TOWN	81	1-0	Baker
28/10/95	NPL	1	Curzon Ashton	108	1-4	Raywood
04/11/95	FA Trophy	Q2	FRICKLEY ATHLETIC	105	3-2	Baker(2), Smith
11/11/95	NPL	1	ATHERTON L.R.	110	2-0	Raywood, Mooney
18/11/95	NPL	1	Alfreton Town	224	1-4	Saunders
20/11/95	NPL	1	LANCASTER CITY	135	1-1	Mooney
25/11/95	FA Trophy	Q3	Emley	224	1-3	Smith
28/11/95	Lancs ATS	1	Radcliffe Borough	105	1-3	Baker
02/12/95	NPL	1	Lincoln United	165	1-3	Lang
09/12/95	NPL	1	Harrogate Town	146	2-3	Whitehead, Raywood
12/12/95	1C	2	Radcliffe Borough	103	1-0	Mooney
01/01/96	NPL	1	RADCLIFFE BOROUGH	107	0-4	
06/01/96	NPL	1	Warrington Town	72	1-1	Baker
13/01/96	NPL	1	LEIGH R.M.I.	102	0-2	
20/01/96	NPL	1	WORKSOP TOWN	109	1-2	Whalley
03/02/96	NPL	1	Bradford Park Avenue	161	3-1	Baker, Whitehead, Wilkins
10/02/96	NPL	1	ASHTON UNITED	123	2-3	Raywood, Strange
13/02/96	1C	QF	Worksop Town	230	1-1	Keys
17/02/96	NPL	1	HARROGATE TOWN	117	2-3	Sanders, Grunshaw
19/02/96	1C	QF rep	WORKSOP TOWN	70	2-1	Wilkins, Grunshaw
24/02/96	NPL	1	Whitley Bay	203	1-1	Whitehead
02/03/96	NPL	1	CONGLETON TOWN	85	1-2	Coulson(og)
09/03/96	NPL	1	Farsley Celtic	81	0-1	
16/03/96	NPL	1	BRADFORD PARK AVENUE	120	1-3	Diamond
19/03/96	1C	SF(1)	Lancaster City	188	1-4	Whitehead
25/03/96	1C	SF(2)	LANCASTER CITY	116	0-2	
30/03/96	NPL	1	ALFRETON TOWN	90	1-3	Haywood
03/04/96	NPL	1	Leigh R.M.I.	133	1-3	Whalley
06/04/96	NPL	1	FARSLEY CELTIC	117	0-3	
08/04/96	NPL	1	Ashton United	122	2-1	Baker, Whalley
13/04/96	NPL	1	CURZON ASHTON	123	3-4	Baker(2), Burshell
15/04/96	NPL	1	WORKINGTON	120	1-0	Whitehead
20/04/96	NPL	1	Fleetwood	140	2-1	Whalley, Bursdell
23/04/96	NPL	1	Gretna	82	2-0	Whalley, Baker
04/05/96	NPL	1	Radcliffe Borough	217	0-2	

GRETNA

Raydale Park, Dominion Road, Gretna, Dumfriesshire. Tel: 01461 337602

Secretary: Ron McGregor, Brackenhurst, Lochmaben, Lockerbie, DG11 1QA. Tel: 01387 811820

Nickname: Black and Whites

Capacity: 2,200

Seating: 385

Covered standing: 800

Clubhouse on ground: Yes

Record goalscorer: 2,307 v Rochdale

FA Cup Rd one 16th November 1992

Record appearances: William Cross

Record goalscorer: Denis Smith .

HONOURS

Northern League 1991 and 1992

League Cup 1991

Cumberland Senior Cup 9 times

JR Cleator Cup 1990, 1991, 1992

Craven Cup 1992

Carlisle and District League 28 times

Charity Shield 25 times

League Cup 20 times

Benevolent Cup 15 times

Gretna are the only Scottish club in English senior non-league football and were formed at a public meeting in July 1946 by two gentlemen from Queen of the South FC. They played just one season in the Dumfries Junior League before joining the Carlisle and District League in 1947. It was the beginning of a long and often victorious campaign of border raids which made the Scots one of the most prominent teams in Cumbria. In 1951 the club entered the newly formed Cumberland League, which was established to bring together the best from East and West of the County but it folded after just one season. Reverting to the Carlisle League they were champions a total of 28 times before finally moving up to the Northern League in 1982.

Many years earlier with interest increasing Gretna built a clubhouse in 1957 which was extended, but a new one replaced it in 1971. Six years earlier Raydale Park was the scene of Greyhound racing which continued for 18 years. To enter the Northern League, over £100,000 was spent on floodlights, a stand and a perimeter wall and promotion came straight away, as did the Cumberland Cup. After finishing runners-up to Billingham Synners in 1990, Gretna won the league two years running, gaining entry to the Northern Premier League, where they remain.

Date	Comp	Rnd	Opponent	Att	Score	Scorers
19/08/95	NPL	1	LINCOLN UNITED	105	3-3	Walker, Armstrong(2)
22/08/95	NPL	1	Lancaster City	218	0-1	
26/08/95	FA Cup	P	Guisborough Town	101	0-1	
28/08/95	NPL	1	NETHERFIELD	85	1-4	Walker
02/09/95	NPL	1	Congleton Town	98	1-0	McDonald
05/09/95	NPL	1	FLEETWOOD	80	7-1	Wilkinson, Walsh, Potts, Armstrong, McDonald, Townsley(2)
09/09/95	NPL	1	ALFRETON TOWN	97	0-0	
11/09/95	NPL	1	Great Harwood Town	93	1-1	Robson
16/09/95	NPL	1	Bradford Park Avenue	151	2-2	Armstrong, Walker
19/09/95	NPL	1	WORKINGTON	235	1-1	McDonald
23/09/95	NPL	1	RADCLIFFE BOROUGH	90	1-0	Walker
26/09/95	LC	1	Blyth Spartans	432	1-2	Robson
30/09/95	NPL	1	LEIGH R.M.I.	90	3-1	Forbes(2), Walker
03/10/95	NPL	1	Netherfield	157	2-2	Walsh, Walker
07/10/95	NPL	1	Whitley Bay	238	1-1	Walker
10/10/95	NPL	1	LANCASTER CITY	135	2-3	D Armstrong, L Armstrong
14/10/95	NPL	1	ASHTON UNITED	95	3-2	Jones, Townsley, D Armstrong
21/10/95	NPL	1	Leigh R.M.I.	132	3-1	Walker(2), Forbes
28/10/95	NPL	1	EASTWOOD TOWN	101	0-2	
04/11/95	Cumberland	2	CARLISLE GILLFORD PARK	85	3-2	D Armstrong, Walker, Bird
11/11/95	NPL	1	Worksop Town	282	2-4	Townsley(2)
18/11/95	NPL	1	HARROGATE TOWN	86	4-1	Walker(2), Forbes, Townsley
25/11/95	FA Trophy	Q3	Blyth Spartans	453	2-3	Townsley(2)
29/11/95	Cumberland	3	WORKINGTON	63	1-0	Irwin
02/12/95	NPL	1	Farsley Celtic	82	2-0	Irwin, Walker
09/12/95	NPL	1	WORKSOP TOWN	90	6-0	Forbes(3), Townsley(2), Walker
12/12/95	1C	2	WHITLEY BAY	70	1-2	Forbes
16/12/95	NPL	1	Harrogate Town	110	5-0	Mulholland, Walker(3), Walsh
06/01/96	NPL	1	ATHERTON L.R.	83	0-0	
13/01/96	NPL	1	Curzon Ashton	110	2-2	Townsley, Robson
23/01/96	Cumberland	QF	Workington	206	1-2	Irwin
03/02/96	NPL	1	Alfreton Town	195	0-4	
17/02/96	NPL	1	CURZON ASHTON	66	0-2	
24/02/96	NPL	1	Radcliffe Borough	148	1-1	Townsley
02/03/96	NPL	1	BRADFORD PARK AVENUE	93	1-1	Forbes
09/03/96	NPL	1	Ashton United	140	1-2	Bird
16/03/96	NPL	1	Lincoln United	162	0-2	
23/03/96	NPL	1	WARRINGTON TOWN	70	1-3	Walsh
26/03/96	NPL	1	Fleetwood	60	1-2	Walker
30/03/96	NPL	1	CONGLETON TOWN	71	2-1	Monaghan, Bird
02/04/96	NPL	1	Workington	213	2-2	Townsley(2)
06/04/96	NPL	1	Atherton L.R.	124	1-1	Bird
08/04/96	NPL	1	WHITLEY BAY	89	1-3	Walker
13/04/96	NPL	1	FARSLEY CELTIC	70	7-1	Townsley(2), Monaghan, Potts, Bird(2), Walker
20/04/96	NPL	1	Eastwood Town	129	1-3	Walker
23/04/96	NPL	1	GREAT HARWOOD TOWN	82	0-2	
27/04/96	NPL	1	Warrington Town	126	4-3	Townsley(2), Walsh, Bird

HARROGATE TOWN

Wetherby Road, Harrogate, North Yorkshire HG1 4JX. Tel: 01423 883671 Fax: 01423 703101

General Secretary: Roy Dalby, 123a Dene Park, Harrogate, HG1 4JX Tel: 01423 567973

General Manager: Alan Smith 31 Church Avenue, Harrogate HG1 4HG Tel: 01423 522056

Match Secretary: Steve Lawrence 160 Forest Lane, Harrogate HG2 2EE Tel: 01423 880871

Programme Editor: Bob Head Tel: 01423 523735

Club shop: Colin Grunwell Tel 01423 871850

Colours: Yellow and black, Nickname: The Sulpherites

Capacity: 3,500, Seating: 500

Covered standing: 300, Clubhouse on ground: Yes

> ## DIRECTIONS
> from Leeds turn right at traffic lights (Appleyard's) into Hookstone Road, continue to Woodlands Hotel (traffic lights) turn left into Wetherby Road, ground on the right. From Harrowgate (BR), turn left and left again, cross road (Odeon Cinema), proceed for about 400 yds to main road, cross over to The Stray (open land) using footpath which leads to Wetherby Rd, ground 200 yds on left.

Record attendance: 3,208 v Starbeck LNER Whitworth Cup Final 1948

Biggest win: 11-1 v Winsford Utd, Biggest defeat: 0-7 v Hyde Utd

Record appearances: Geoff Lunn, Record goalscorer in one season: Steve French

HONOURS

Northern Premier League Division One Cup 1990

Yorkshire League Div 1 1927 and Division Two 1982

West Riding County Cup 1925, 1927, 1963, 1973, West Riding Challenge Cup 1925 and 1927

Manager 1996-97: Mick Doig, Chairman: George Dunnington

Harrogate FC was formed in 1919, their ground being in Starbeck Lane, but after only one season there, the club was given notice to leave by the Harrogate Corporation, the land being needed for housing, it now being covered by St Andrews Estate.

A Limited Company was formed in 1920 and they bought 6 acres of land in Wetherby Lane at a very acceptable price. They raised £3,000 by issuing 3,000 £1 shares and the ground was officially opened by the Mayor of Harrogate on August 28th 1920.

From 1919 to 1921 the club played in the Yorkshire League and they moved to try their luck in the Midland League, but it lasted one season before they went back to Yorkshire football. They took the West Riding Challenge Cup in 1925 and 1927, when they were Division One champions.

In 1931 they took the unwise decision to move north and play in the Northern League. It proved a disastrous season, as they were next to bottom and folded, selling the ground to the council. In their wisdom they hired out the ground to anybody who wanted it and both Yorkshire Amateur and Leeds United A team used it.

Another club, Harrogate Hotspurs came into being in 1936 and began in the local league until it was suspended by the war. They began again in the West Yorkshire League and stayed until 1950 when they changed their name to Harrogate Town and joined the Yorkshire League.The ensuing years saw County Cup and Division Two honours and when the league and the Midland League were merged in 1982, Town found themselves in the Northern Counties East.

Town were then invited into the new First Division of the Northern Premier League and have since won the Challenge Cup.

HARROGATE TOWN 1995/96 SEASON

19/08/95	NPL	1	LEIGH R.M.I.	201	1-2	Elliott
22/08/95	NPL	1	Whitley Bay	200	1-1	Greenhough
26/08/95	NPL	1	Warrington Town	105	2-2	Elliott, Falk
02/09/95	NPL	1	Curzon Ashton	78	1-2	Clarkson
05/09/95	NPL	1	ALFRETON TOWN	270	0-3	
09/09/95	FA Cup	Q1	BEDLINGTON TERRIERS	183	1-2	Walmsley
13/09/95	NPL	1	Alfreton Town	182	0-2	
16/09/95	NPL	1	Radcliffe Borough	129	0-1	
19/09/95	NPL	1	WHITLEY BAY	208	2-3	Cameron(og), Greenhough
23/09/95	NPL	1	NETHERFIELD	184	4-6	Liddle, Wright, McDaid, Elliott
26/09/95	LC	1	Whitley Bay	121	2-1	Switheringale, Elliott
30/09/95	NPL	1	Netherfield	120	0-0	
03/10/95	NPL	1	LINCOLN UNITED	213	2-5	Wright, Hutchinson
07/10/95	NPL	1	Atherton L.R.	147	2-0	McDaid, Wright
14/10/95	FA Trophy	Q1	GRANTHAM TOWN	191	1-4	Greenough
21/10/95	NPL	1	Fleetwood	206	2-1	Greenhough(2)
24/10/95	LC	2	EMLEY	203	0-2	
28/10/95	NPL	1	CONGLETON TOWN	196	1-1	Liddle
31/10/95	NPL	1	Eastwood Town	119	1-1	Greenhough
04/11/95	NPL	1	ATHERTON L.R.	193	3-1	Barker, Greenhough, Wright
11/11/95	NPL	1	ASHTON UNITED	188	0-4	
18/11/95	NPL	1	Gretna	86	1-4	Hutchinson
21/11/95	NPL	1	FARSLEY CELTIC	184	1-6	Elliott
25/11/95	NPL	1	CURZON ASHTON	182	2-4	Williams(og), McDaid
28/11/95	NPL	1	BRADFORD PARK AVENUE	225	1-2	Liddle
02/12/95	NPL	1	Workington	223	0-2	
06/12/95	W. Riding	2	Farsley Celtic	76	2-3	Pidgeon, Wright
09/12/95	NPL	1	GREAT HARWOOD TOWN	146	3-2	Elliott, Pidgeon, Liddle
12/12/95	1C	2	Worksop Town	191	1-5	McDaid
16/12/95	NPL	1	GRETNA	110	0-5	
06/01/96	NPL	1	RADCLIFFE BOROUGH	144	2-2	Elliott, Liddle
13/01/96	NPL	1	Bradford Park Avenue	228	1-1	Egan
20/01/96	NPL	1	Lancaster City	207	1-2	Regan
03/02/96	NPL	1	EASTWOOD TOWN	198	1-3	Watkinson
10/02/96	NPL	1	Lincoln United	197	0-5	
17/02/96	NPL	1	Great Harwood Town	117	3-2	Lormor, Watkinson, McDaid
24/02/96	NPL	1	WORKINGTON	210	0-3	
02/03/96	NPL	1	Leigh R.M.I.	130	0-2	
09/03/96	NPL	1	LANCASTER CITY	219	2-2	Ward, Pidgeon
23/03/96	NPL	1	FLEETWOOD	159	2-2	Rogan(2)
30/03/96	NPL	1	Ashton United	155	4-1	Dutton, Greenhough, McDaid, Ward
06/04/96	NPL	1	WORKSOP TOWN	213	3-2	Ward, Regan, Watkinson
08/04/96	NPL	1	Worksop Town	307	1-2	Elliott
13/04/96	NPL	1	Congleton Town	153	1-2	Smitherdale
15/04/96	NPL	1	Farsley Celtic	98	2-2	Pidgeon, Sellars
20/04/96	NPL	1	WARRINGTON TOWN	206	1-3	Watkinson

LEIGH RMI

Hilton Park, Kirkhall Lane, Leigh, Lancs. Tel: 01942 743743

Secretary: Alan Robinson, 55 Janice Drive, Fulwood, Preston, Lancs Tel: 01772 719266

Colours: Red and white stripes   Nickname: Railwaymen

Capacity: 10,000   Seating: 4,000

Covered standing: 4,000   Clubhouse on ground: Yes

Record attendance: 4,500 at Grundy Hill

Record fee received: £5,000 for Tony McDonald to Chorley

HONOURS

Premier Inter League Cup 1988

Cheshire County League and Challenge Shield 1979

Lancs Combination 1958

League Cup 1929, 1954, 1957, 1966

West Lancs League 1911 and 1912

Lancs Junior Cup 1925 and 1930

Lancs Floodlit Trophy 1985

Lancs FA Cup 1985

Manager for 1996-97: Steve Waywell

Assistant Manager: Kevin Booth

Chairman: Chris Healey

Vice Chairman: Alan Leach

The club was first formed in 1896 when the Railway Mechanics Institute in the town began playing on a pitch at what was known as the old Racecourse. They were known as the Lancs and Yorks Railway FC before becoming RMI in 1896, and around the turn of the century the club moved to Grundy Hill. Joiners from the railway works helped construct the first buildings on the ground, as they played in the Lancs Alliance and Lancs League, before joining the West Lancs League, which they won in 1911 and 1912. They had one year in the Lancs Combination before joining again and playing through to the Second War, finishing as runners up in 1930 and twice winning the Lancs Junior Cup.

They had a further 22 years in that league, with success in league and cup before moving to the stronger Cheshire League in 1968, where they won the league and Championship Shield in 1969. It was absorbed into the North-West Counties League in 1982 and after a brief stay they again moved up to the Northern Premier League.

1991 saw Horwich reach the last eight of the FA Trophy, but with the old ground beginning to show its age and the spectre of gradings looming, the RMI took the decision to move from the town they had played in for 100 years and move to Hilton Park, home of Leigh RLFC. Changing the club name to Leigh RMI they have struggled and were relegated to Division One, but with a ground capable of holding 10,000 there is every chance of expansion.

LEIGH RMI 1995/96 SEASON

Date	Competition	Round	Opponent	Att	Score	Scorers
19/08/95	NPL	1	Harrogate Town	201	2-1	Monk, Shaw
26/08/95	FA Cup	P	FLIXTON	60	2-0	Diamond, Briffa
28/08/95	NPL	1	Atherton L.R.	178	1-3	Birch
02/09/95	NPL	1	WHITLEY BAY	144	0-1	
05/09/95	NPL	1	Curzon Ashton	101	1-2	Schofield
09/09/95	FA Cup	Q1	Guiseley	484	0-3	
16/09/95	NPL	1	ALFRETON TOWN	176	1-1	Shaw
19/09/95	NPL	1	Worksop Town	316	1-1	McCarty
23/09/95	NPL	1	ASHTON UNITED	185	1-4	Fahey
27/09/95	LC	1	GREAT HARWOOD TOWN	145	6-4	Booth, Monk(3), Shaw(2)
30/09/95	NPL	1	Gretna	90	1-3	Shaw
03/10/95	NPL	1	Lancaster City	202	2-5	Birch, Walmsley
07/10/95	NPL	1	FARSLEY CELTIC	165	0-0	
11/10/95	NPL	1	WORKINGTON	165	4-2	Shaw(3), Birch
14/10/95	FA Trophy	Q1	Bridgnorth Town	90	1-1	Walmesley
17/10/95	FA Trophy	Q1 rep	BRIDGNORTH TOWN	51	7-0	Lewis(2), Arnold, Walters, Senior, Shaw, McCarty
21/10/95	NPL	1	GRETNA	132	1-3	Schofield
24/10/95	LC	2	Witton Albion	305	2-2	Shaw, Orrell
28/10/95	NPL	1	Netherfield	121	0-1	
01/11/95	LC	2 rep	WITTON ALBION	72	0-3	
04/11/95	FA Trophy	Q2	MATLOCK TOWN	90	0-2	
11/11/95	NPL	1	Bradford Park Avenue	163	1-3	Shaw
18/11/95	NPL	1	CONGLETON TOWN	153	1-1	Diamond
22/11/95	1C	1	CURZON ASHTON	136	0-1	
25/11/95	NPL	1	LINCOLN UNITED	137	2-0	Briffa, Diamond
29/11/95	Lancs ATS	1	ATHERTON COLLIERIES	129	1-0	Birch
02/12/95	NPL	1	Fleetwood	85	4-0	Shaw(2), Kirkham, Walmsley
06/12/95	NPL	1	WARRINGTON TOWN	153	2-2	Birch, Briffa
09/12/95	NPL	1	Warrington Town	109	1-0	Shaw
16/12/95	NPL	1	CURZON ASHTON	139	1-0	Walmsley
06/01/96	NPL	1	BRADFORD PARK AVENUE	161	1-0	Shaw
13/01/96	NPL	1	Great Harwood Town	102	2-0	Edwards, Smyth
16/01/96	Lancs ATS	2	Morecambe	266	0-2	
20/01/96	NPL	1	NETHERFIELD	144	1-4	Wheeler
03/02/96	NPL	1	Whitley Bay	129	1-3	Birch
10/02/96	NPL	1	Eastwood Town	94	0-1	
17/02/96	NPL	1	WORKSOP TOWN	150	1-1	Shaw
21/02/96	NPL	1	ATHERTON L.R.	202	3-1	Schofield, Shaw, Briffa
28/02/96	NPL	1	FLEETWOOD	149	2-0	Shaw, Wheeler
02/03/96	NPL	1	HARROGATE TOWN	130	2-0	Shaw, Edwards
09/03/96	NPL	1	Alfreton Town	140	0-1	
13/03/96	NPL	1	LANCASTER CITY	151	0-1	
16/03/96	NPL	1	EASTWOOD TOWN	136	1-0	Wheeler
23/03/96	NPL	1	Congleton Town	104	0-1	
30/03/96	NPL	1	Lincoln United	174	1-3	Carter(og)
03/04/96	NPL	1	GREAT HARWOOD TOWN	133	3-1	Briffa, Shaw, Kirkham
06/04/96	NPL	1	Radcliffe Borough	207	1-3	Charlton
08/04/96	NPL	1	Workington	208	3-0	Leishman, Wheeler, Briffa
13/04/96	NPL	1	Ashton United	150	2-3	Leishman, Briffa
20/04/96	NPL	1	RADCLIFFE BOROUGH	158	1-1	Kirkham
27/04/96	NPL	1	Farsley Celtic	58	1-2	Briffa

LINCOLN UNITED

Ashby Avenue, Hartsholme, Lincoln. Tel: 01522 690674

Secretary: Steve Eastmead, 23 Woodvale Ave,
Doddington Park, Lincoln LN6 3RD Tel 01522 885112

Colours: All white   Nickname: United

Capacity: 2,714   Seating: 400

Covered standing: 1,484   Clubhouse on ground:
Yes

Record attendance: 1,200 v Crook Town
FA Amateur Cup 1968

Biggest win: 12-1 v Pontefract Colleries 1995

Biggest defeat: 0-7 v Heanor Town 1989

Record appearances: Brian Davies 439

Record goalscorer in total: Terry Nelson 189

HONOURS

Northern Counties East 1995

Northern Counties East Div 1 1993

Division One South 1983 and Div 2 1986

President's Cup 1995

Yorkshire League 1971 and 1974

League Cup 1971

Lincs League 1964

Lincs Senior A Cup 1973 and 1986, Lincs Senior B Cup 1964 and 1970

Central Midlands League 1992, Wakefield Cup 1991

Lincs Intermediate Cup 1968, 1969, 1970, 1971, 1972, 1973, 1981

DIRECTIONS

From Newark A46 onto Lincoln relief road (A446), right at 2nd roundabout for Birchwood (Skellingthorpe Road), go for 1 mile passing lake and Country Park, 1st right 10 yds after 30 mph sign into Ashby Avenue, ground entrance 200 yds, opposite Old Peoples home. From north proceed along A57 via Saxilby until reaching A46 Lincoln relief road - continue on this and turn left at roundabout signed Birchwood then above. 3 miles from Lincoln central (BR).

Lincoln Amateurs were formed just prior to the Second War and joined the Lincolnshire League in 1945. The one season was spent on a basic field near the Skew Bridge before they began using the Co-op Ground in Skellingthorpe Road. They remained in local football until 1967, having much earlier dropped the Amateurs tag when signing an ex-professional player, and then moved up to the Yorkshire League, moving in with Hartsholme Cricket Club, where they played, erecting a small stand along one side.

They had one Lincolnshire League title to their name, in 1964, and added to it when taking the Yorkshire League and Cup double in 1971. It was the start of a spell of success, as they took the County A Cup in 1973, the year that they won the Intermediate Cup for the sixth year on the trot. They were champions again in 1974 and when the league was merged in 1982, they joined the NCEL, moving next door to a corporation pitch and taking the stand with them.

With security gained the club built up the Ashby Avenue ground and as Division One South champions in 1983 and a re-structured Division Two champions in 1986, they took their place amongst the top clubs.

With the ground up to Northern Premier League standards, United took the NCEL title in 1995 and were promoted to the NPL Division One, and the run continued last season when United were runners up to Lancaster City.

LINCOLN UNITED 1995/96 SEASON

Date	Comp	Rnd	Opponent	Att	Score	Scorers
19/08/95	NPL	1	Gretna	105	3-3	Rookyard, Carter, Ranshaw
22/08/95	NPL	1	ALFRETON TOWN	237	0-2	
26/08/95	FA Cup	P	STOCKSBRG PARK STEELS	164	3-2	Simmons(2), Rookyard
28/08/95	NPL	1	Eastwood Town	124	2-4	Simmons, Creane
02/09/95	NPL	1	Great Harwood Town	108	1-0	Trotter
05/09/95	NPL	1	BRADFORD PARK AVE	246	5-2	Simmons(3), Creane, Rookyard
09/09/95	FA Cup	Q1	Eccleshill United	73	3-2	Rookyard(2), Ranshaw
12/09/95	NPL	1	Worksop Town	455	4-2	Simmons(3), Ranshaw
16/09/95	NPL	1	LANCASTER CITY	209	1-3	Simmons
19/09/95	NPL	1	CONGLETON TOWN	186	1-1	Wright
23/09/95	FA Cup	Q2	NORTHWICH VICTORIA	354	1-4	Rookyard
27/09/95	LC	1	Alfreton Town	135	0-4	
30/09/95	NPL	1	RADCLIFFE BOROUGH	176	2-1	Rookyard, Cudworth(og)
03/10/95	NPL	1	Harrogate Town	213	5-2	Wright, Williams(2), Carter, Rookyard
07/10/95	NPL	1	ASHTON UNITED	173	2-1	Wright, Williams
10/10/95	NPL	1	FARSLEY CELTIC	260	0-0	
14/10/95	FA Trophy	Q1	Atherstone United	278	1-2	Barker
18/10/95	NPL	1	Alfreton Town	201	1-2	Wingatt
21/10/95	NPL	1	Congleton Town	115	2-0	Ranshaw, Williams
28/10/95	NPL	1	WARRINGTON TOWN	221	1-0	Williams
31/10/95	Lincs `A'	QF	WINTERTON RANGERS	82	4-0	Simmons, Ranshaw, Carter, Rookyard
04/11/95	NPL	1	Warrington Town	104	2-4	Ranshaw(2)
07/11/95	1C	1	BRADFORD PARK AVE	108	2-0	Simmons, Rookyard
18/11/95	NPL	1	ATHERTON L.R.	175	2-0	Rookyard, Simmons
25/11/95	NPL	1	Leigh R.M.I.	137	0-2	
02/12/95	NPL	1	GREAT HARWOOD TOWN	165	3-1	Rookyard, Ranshaw(2)
09/12/95	NPL	1	Radcliffe Borough	142	1-3	Simmons
12/12/95	1C	2	ALFRETON TOWN	76	1-4	Ranshaw
16/12/95	NPL	1	FLEETWOOD	94	2-2	Simmons(2)
01/01/96	NPL	1	WORKSOP TOWN	263	4-1	Wright, Simmons, Ranshaw(2)
13/01/96	NPL	1	WORKINGTON	230	4-0	Lake, Frecklington, Ranshaw(2)
20/01/96	NPL	1	Atherton L.R.	126	1-0	Ranshaw
10/02/96	NPL	1	HARROGATE TOWN	197	5-0	Trotter, Simmons(2), Leonce, Frecklington
13/02/96	Lincs `A'	SF	BRIGG TOWN	96	4-0	Leonce(2), Simmons(2)
24/02/96	NPL	1	Curzon Ashton	128	2-1	Nestor(og), Carter
02/03/96	NPL	1	EASTWOOD TOWN	196	2-0	Simmons, Trotter
09/03/96	NPL	1	Workington	217	2-1	Ranshaw, Smith
16/03/96	NPL	1	GRETNA	162	2-0	Ranshaw(2)
23/03/96	NPL	1	Lancaster City	508	0-2	
27/03/96	NPL	1	Bradford Park Avenue	176	3-2	Bailey, Simmons(2)
30/03/96	NPL	1	LEIGH R.M.I.	174	3-1	Ranshaw, Kirkham(og), Simmons
02/04/96	NPL	1	WHITLEY BAY	183	4-3	Frecklington, Williams, Simmons, Whittle
06/04/96	NPL	1	Netherfield	116	0-0	
08/04/96	NPL	1	CURZON ASHTON	293	1-4	Carter
13/04/96	NPL	1	Fleetwood	73	1-1	Simmons
16/04/96	Lincs `A'	F	BOSTON TOWN	195	2-1	Simmons(2)
23/04/96	NPL	1	Whitley Bay	132	0-2	
27/04/96	NPL	1	NETHERFIELD	150	4-0	Womble, Williams(2), Frecklington
01/05/96	NPL	1	Farsley Celtic	73	1-2	Simmons
04/05/96	NPL	1	Ashton United	135	1-1	Bailey

MATLOCK TOWN

Causeway Lane, Matlock, Derbys. Tel: 01629 583866 or 55362

Secretary: Keith Brown, 1 Malvern Gardens, Matlock, Derbys DE4 3JH. Tel: 01629 584231

Match Secretary: Ian Richardson, 14 Allen Hill, Matlock, Derbys DE4 3LR Tel: 01629 56042

DIRECTIONS

On A615, 500 yds from town centre and Matlock (BR).

Club shop: Sue Tomlinson Tel 01629 583866

Commercial manager: Tom Wright

Colours: Royal blue and white, Nickname: The Gladiators

Capacity: 1,000 Safety Act ruling. Formerly 7,500

Seating: 200   Covered standing: 500

Clubhouse on ground: Yes

Record attendance: 5, 123 v Burton Albion FA Trophy 1975

HONOURS

FA TROPHY WINNERS 1975

Northern Premier League Cup 1978 and Challenge Shield 1979

Midland Counties League 1962 and 1969

Central Alliance North 1960 and 1961

Division Two League and Cup 1960 League Cup 1961

Derbyshire Senior Cup 1975, 1977, 1978, 1984, 1985, 1992

Derbyshire Divisional Cup North 1962

Evans Halshaw Floodlit Cup 1989 and 1991

Anglo-Italian non-League Cup 1979

Manager 1996-97: Imre Varadi, Assistant Manager: Charlie Williamson

Chairman: Don Carr, Press Officer: Ian Richardson

Matlock Football Club is believed to have been formed in the late 1870's, probably playing friendly matches before joining the Derbyshire League, where they were champions in 1891 and 1892. They had a brief spell in the Midland League, where in 1902-03 they lost every game, scoring nine goals and conceding 130. They then played in various leagues until the Second War, including the Central Combination, Derby Senior League and Central Alliance, before the club was closed. Matlock Town was re-formed in 1946 and joined the Chesterfield and District League, and later the Central Alliance, which they won in 1960, taking promotion to the Midland Counties League. During that season the club reached the first round of the FA Cup and they went on to take the Midland Counties at the first attempt. Seven years later they were champions again and they joined the Northern Premier League, where they have remained ever since.

The 70's saw the most successful period in the club's history, under the management of Peter Swan, where they won the FA Trophy at Wembley beating favourites Scarborough 4-0. Three Fenoughty brothers, Tom, Mick and Nick all played to become the first trio of brothers to play at Wembley.

They reached the first round of the Cup twice more, playing Wigan Athletic and Blackburn Rovers, but the highlight came in 1977 when Town beat Mansfield 5-2 at Field Mill, before losing to Carlisle United in Round Three. The 80's were quieter, with a runners up place to Barrow in 1984 and several Senior Cup finals, but since then league form has been a problem and it culminated in relegation to Division One last May.

MATLOCK TOWN 1995/96 SEASON

Date	Competition	Round	Opponent	Att	Score	Scorers
19/08/95	NPL	P	Bamber Bridge	378	1-4	Burton
21/08/95	NPL	P	Guiseley	355	2-4	Evans(2)
26/08/95	NPL	P	KNOWSLEY UNITED	258	8-0	Sheppard, Tilly, Evans, Newey(2), Culley(2), Burton"
29/08/95	NPL	P	BOSTON UNITED	507	0-2	
02/09/95	NPL	P	Blyth Spartans	498	0-3	
05/09/95	NPL	P	EMLEY	374	1-1	Burton
09/09/95	FA Cup	Q1	GREAT HARWOOD TOWN	290	5-2	Tilly, Burton, Culley, Taylor, Allen
16/09/95	NPL	P	BARROW	406	0-4	
19/09/95	NPL	P	Witton Albion	439	2-3	Tilly(2)
23/09/95	FA Cup	Q2	ILKESTON TOWN	759	1-2	Evans
26/09/95	NPL	P	LEEK TOWN	328	0-1	
30/09/95	NPL	P	Marine	420	0-1	
03/10/95	NPL	P	Gainsborough Trinity	510	2-2	Cully, Evans
07/10/95	NPL	P	Emley	167	2-3	Cully, Kerry
10/10/95	NPL	P	GAINSBOROUGH TRINITY	410	0-2	
14/10/95	FA Trophy	Q1	Droylsden	173	3-0	Tilly, Culley, Cheetham
17/10/95	NPL	P	DROYLSDEN	247	2-2	Hanbury, Cheetham
21/10/95	NPL	P	BISHOP AUCKLAND	229	1-1	Tilly
24/10/95	LC	2	GAINSBOROUGH TRINITY	292	0-1	
28/10/95	NPL	P	Accrington Stanley	384	1-2	Culley
04/11/95	FA Trophy	Q2	Leigh R.M.I.	90	2-0	Burton, Cheetham
11/11/95	NPL	P	Bishop Auckland	112	3-2	Varadi, Cheetham(2)
18/11/95	NPL	P	Boston United	1008	0-1	
21/11/95	NPL	P	GUISELEY	330	3-0	Cheetham, Culley, Evans
25/11/95	FA Trophy	Q3	BUXTON	516	1-0	Evans
02/12/95	NPL	P	MARINE	295	3-3	Evans, Cheetham, Varadi
09/12/95	NPL	P	Winsford United	127	1-3	Cheetham
12/12/95	NPL	P	Frickley Athletic	116	4-1	Culley(2), Cheetham, Varadi
16/12/95	NPL	P	BLYTH SPARTANS	319	3-3	Cheetham, Taylor, Tilly
06/01/96	NPL	P	WINSFORD UNITED	325	1-1	Cheetham
13/01/96	NPL	P	Droylsden	165	0-3	
16/01/96	Derbys SC	3	SANDIACRE TOWN	214	8-2	Cheetham(3), Cully, Taylor, Flynn, Varadi(2)
20/01/96	FA Trophy	1	Radcliffe Borough	241	2-3	Varadi, Cully
03/02/96	NPL	P	HYDE UNITED	415	1-3	Culley
10/02/96	Derbys SC	QF	Graham Street Prims	141	0-1	
17/02/96	NPL	P	BAMBER BRIDGE	326	0-1	
24/02/96	NPL	P	Spennymoor United	243	1-1	Reed
27/02/96	NPL	P	FRICKLEY ATHLETIC	245	6-0	Taylor(3), Culley(2), Evans
02/03/96	NPL	P	Knowsley United	145	0-1	
09/03/96	NPL	P	COLWYN BAY	336	1-4	Taylor
16/03/96	NPL	P	Colwyn Bay	251	3-3	Varadi(2), Burton
19/03/96	NPL	P	WITTON ALBION	237	5-2	Varadi(3), Culley(2)
23/03/96	NPL	P	Leek Town	250	2-4	Varadi(2)
30/03/96	NPL	P	SPENNYMOOR UNITED	283	1-1	Evans
02/04/96	NPL	P	Buxton	336	1-3	Culley
06/04/96	NPL	P	BUXTON	418	0-1	
08/04/96	NPL	P	Hyde United	508	1-1	Tilly
13/04/96	NPL	P	ACCRINGTON STANLEY	308	2-0	Taylor, Culley
15/04/96	NPL	P	Chorley	181	2-3	Varadi, Mills
29/04/96	NPL	P	CHORLEY	374	4-3	Culley(2), Wake, Taylor
04/05/96	NPL	P	Barrow	1139	1-3	Varadi

NETHERFIELD

Parkside Road, Kendal, Cumbria. Tel: 01539 727472 (office) 722469 (club)

Secretary: Andrew Roe, 4 Lowther Park, Kendal, Cumbria. LA9 6RS Tel: 01539 731680

Match Secretary Craig Campbell, 34 High Sparrowmire, Kendal, Cumbria LA9 5PD Tel: 01539 725557

Programme Editor: Peter Savage, 46 Hayclose Rd, Kendal, Cumbria LA9 7NE Tel 01539 726488

Colours: White and black　　Nickname: The Field

Capacity: 2,490　　　　　Seating: 250

Covered standing: 500　　Clubhouse on ground: Yes

Record attendance: 5,184 v Grimsby Town FA Cup 1st Rd 1955

Biggest win: 11-0 Great Harwood March 22nd 1947

Biggest defeat: 0-10 v Stalybridge Celtic Sept 1st 1984

Record goalscorer in total: Tom Brownlee

Record goalscorer in one season: Tom Brownlee

Record fee received: £10, 250 for Andy Milner

HONOURS

Lancs Combination 1949 and 1965

League Cup 1956 and 1961

Westmorland Senior Cup 1925, 1932, 1933, 1936, 1947, 1948, 1964, 1966, 1972, 1987, 1989, 1991

Manager for 1996-97: Steve Edmondson

Assistant manager: Bruce Richardson

Chairman: Ian Needham

DIRECTIONS

M6 junction 36, follow signs for Kendal (South), right at lights, left at roundabout to shoe factory - Parkside Road on right opposite factory main offices - ground 400 yds. One and a half miles from Oxenholme (BR) station bus service to shoe factory.

Netherfield Football Club came about through a young Londoner, Robert Miller-Somervell, who moved north and began a shoemaking business near Nether Bridge in Kendal. The company grew and they bought a whole property called Netherfield. In 1920 a football team was formed within the company and it was given the name of the factory, and they played with a large K on their shirts, the company's mark which was first used to prevent leather being returned as inferior.

They began in the Westmoreland and North Lancashire Leagues and after the Second War made the big leap to the Lancashire Combination, winning their first title in 1949, no mean feat as it was one of the strongest leagues outside the Football League itself. In 1965 the first and reserve teams did the double by both winning their divisions with Chorley runner up both times. 1968 was the last season in the Combination as it made way for the Northern Premier League, of which Netherfield were founder members.

After 15 years the club dropped into the North-West Counties League, but when the NPL expanded to two divisions, Parkside was sufficiently well developed to allow the club in.

Despite their long history, Netherfield have little other than Westmorland Cup victories to show for the last 30 years but they have overcome a spell where only the demise of other clubs saved them and remain in the NPL First Division.

NETHERFIELD 1995/96 SEASON

Date	Comp	Rnd	Opponent	Att	Score	Scorers
19/08/95	NPL	1	Atherton L.R.	107	4-2	Close, McCullough, Byron, Whittaker
22/08/95	NPL	1	WORKINGTON	242	1-1	Whittaker
26/08/95	FA Cup	P	EVENWOOD TOWN	116	9-0	Livingstone,Close(2), Whittaker(3),McCullough, Chaplow,Fleming
28/08/95	NPL	1	Gretna	85	4-1	Livingston, Smith, Whittaker, Fleming
05/09/95	NPL	1	GREAT HARWOOD TOWN	193	3-1	Watt(2), Fleming
09/09/95	FA Cup	Q1	PETERLEE NEWTOWN	128	2-4	Smith, Close
12/09/95	NPL	1	Fleetwood	80	2-1	Smith, Whittaker
16/09/95	NPL	1	ASHTON UNITED	174	1-1	Hodgson
19/09/95	NPL	1	RADCLIFFE BOROUGH	182	0-2	
23/09/95	NPL	1	Harrogate Town	184	6-4	Watt, Fleming(3), Close, Bickerstaffe
26/09/95	LC	1	Workington	211	2-3	Close, Watt
30/09/95	NPL	1	HARROGATE TOWN	120	0-0	
03/10/95	NPL	1	GRETNA	157	2-2	Watt(2)
07/10/95	NPL	1	Radcliffe Borough	119	2-1	Hodgson, Watt
09/10/95	NPL	1	Great Harwood Town	120	2-0	Haigh, Fleming
14/10/95	NPL	1	EASTWOOD TOWN	167	1-4	Fleming
17/10/95	NPL	1	FLEETWOOD	120	0-3	
21/10/95	NPL	1	Warrington Town	93	6-3	Fleming, Sang(3), Close, McCullough
28/10/95	NPL	1	LEIGH R.M.I.	121	1-0	Burrows
04/11/95	FA Trophy	Q2	Tamworth	409	1-3	Close
11/11/95	NPL	1	FARSLEY CELTIC	183	1-3	Sang
18/11/95	NPL	1	Curzon Ashton	106	1-2	Brown
25/11/95	NPL	1	Whitley Bay	108	1-2	Whitehead
02/12/95	NPL	1	BRADFORD PARK AVENUE	186	0-0	
09/12/95	NPL	1	Congleton Town	82	1-1	Watt
12/12/95	1C	2	Workington	165	2-4	Hodgson, Barron
16/12/95	NPL	1	WARRINGTON TOWN	161	0-1	
06/01/96	NPL	1	Eastwood Town	82	0-1	
13/01/96	NPL	1	WORKSOP TOWN	124	0-2	
20/01/96	NPL	1	Leigh R.M.I.	144	4-1	Watt, Emmett(2), Wallace
17/02/96	NPL	1	Ashton United	168	0-5	
24/02/96	NPL	1	ATHERTON L.R.	109	2-4	Houseley(2)
02/03/96	NPL	1	Lancaster City	231	2-2	Emmett, Renwick
16/03/96	NPL	1	Worksop Town	231	2-3	Watt, Emmett
19/03/96	NPL	1	WHITLEY BAY	104	1-2	Emmett
23/03/96	NPL	1	CURZON ASHTON	141	1-0	Emmett
30/03/96	NPL	1	Workington	207	0-1	
06/04/96	NPL	1	LINCOLN UNITED	116	0-0	
08/04/96	NPL	1	LANCASTER CITY	238	2-2	Emmett, Watt
13/04/96	NPL	1	Bradford Park Avenue	147	2-0	Watt, Emmett
17/04/96	NPL	1	Alfreton Town	171	1-4	Houseley
20/04/96	NPL	1	CONGLETON TOWN	105	3-0	Emmett, Houseley, Yeo
24/04/96	NPL	1	Farsley Celtic	57	1-3	Emmett
27/04/96	NPL	1	Lincoln United	150	0-4	
04/05/96	NPL	1	ALFRETON TOWN	188	4-4	Brown, McCullough, Blamire, Renwick

RADCLIFFE BOROUGH

Stainton Park, Pilkington Rd, Radcliffe, Lancs M26 0PE. Tel: 0161 724 8346 office 724 5937 club

Secretary: David Murgatroyd, 62 Croston Rd, Lostock Hall, Preston Tel: 01772 314768

Comp Sec: Graham Fielding, 93 Callender St, Ramsbottom, Bury BL0 9DU

Programme Editor: David Johnston Tel: 0772 495306

Club house: Ronnie Doyle c/o The Boro Club

Colours: All Blue

Nickname: Boro

Capacity: 3,000

Seating: 350

Covered standing: 1,000

Clubhouse on ground: Yes

Record attendance: 1,468 v Caernarvon Town NWCL 1983

Biggest win: 8-1 v Sutton Town 1987

Biggest defeat: 0-11 v Witton Albion 1978

Record appearances: Gary Howarth 127

Record goalscorer in one season: Peter Coyne 28 in 1992-93

Record fee received: £5,000 for Kevin Hulme from Bury

Record fee paid: £5,000 to Buxton for Gary Walker 1991

DIRECTIONS

M62 junction 17 - follow signs for Whitefield and Bury then A665 to Radcliffe. Through town centre, turn right into Unsworth Street (opposite Turf Hotel), ground half mile on left, Colshaw Close Easy. Half a mile from Radcliffe (BR).

HONOURS

North West Counties League 1985

Division Two 1983

Manchester League Cup 1959 jt

Manager 1996-97: Kevin Glendon

Assistant Manager: Jimmy Golder

Chairman: Bernard Manning Jnr

Vice Chairman: Ronnie Doyle

Radcliffe Borough were formed in 1949 by Mr Jack Pickford and joined the South East Lancs League.

After a short period they progressed through the Manchester League to the Lancs Combination in 1963. Their best season in that league was in 1971 winning the League Cup and finishing third. Two years later they successfully applied to join the Cheshire County League and were subsequently founder members of the North West Counties League when it was formed through the merger of their two previous leagues.

The first season ended in triumph, when they pipped Carnarvon Town to the Division Two title in front of a record crowd of 1,468. As members of the First Division they joined the exodus to the new First Division of the Northern Premier League where they remain.

RADCLIFFE BOROUGH 1995/96 SEASON

Date	Comp	Rnd	Opposition	Att	Score	Scorers
19/08/95	NPL	1	Workington	273	1-1	Graham
22/08/95	NPL	1	ATHERTON L.R.	153	4-2	Edwards, Lunt, Graham(2)
26/08/95	FA Cup	P	ALFRETON TOWN	118	3-2	Graham, Connor, Lunt
28/08/95	NPL	1	Congleton Town	167	4-1	Channon, Brennan, Connor(2)
02/09/95	NPL	1	Worksop Town	439	2-2	Graham, Lunt
09/09/95	FA Cup	Q1	Worksop Town	357	0-4	
12/09/95	NPL	1	Atherton L.R.	129	1-1	Lunt
16/09/95	NPL	1	HARROGATE TOWN	129	1-0	Lunt
19/09/95	NPL	1	Netherfield	182	2-0	Connor, Lunt
23/09/95	NPL	1	Gretna	90	0-1	
26/09/95	LC	1	DROYLSDEN	94	0-3	
30/09/95	NPL	1	Lincoln United	176	1-2	Connor
07/10/95	NPL	1	NETHERFIELD	119	1-2	Brennan
10/10/95	NPL	1	Fleetwood	139	0-1	
14/10/95	FA Trophy	Q1	REDDITCH UNITED	107	3-1	Whittle, Brown, Strange
17/10/95	NPL	1	Warrington Town	68	1-1	Whittle
21/10/95	NPL	1	WORKINGTON	115	4-1	Graham, Connor(2), George(og)
27/10/95	NPL	1	BRADFORD PARK AVENUE	211	3-0	Whittle, Graham, Brennan
31/10/95	NPL	1	ASHTON UNITED	139	1-1	Lunt
04/11/95	FA Trophy	Q2	FLEETWOOD	136	2-0	Brennan, Lunt
11/11/95	NPL	1	Eastwood Town	116	1-2	Graham
15/11/95	Manc PC	1	GLOSSOP NORTH END	101	2-1	McCrae, Graham
18/11/95	NPL	1	WORKSOP TOWN	152	5-1	Whittle, Brennan(2), Lunt(2)
25/11/95	FA Trophy	Q3	FARSLEY CELTIC	155	3-1	Graham, McCrae(2)
28/11/95	Lancs ATS	1	GREAT HARWOOD TOWN	105	3-1	Lunt, McCrae(2)
02/12/95	NPL	1	Alfreton Town	183	0-1	
09/12/95	NPL	1	LINCOLN UNITED	142	3-1	Connor, McCrae, Lunt
12/12/95	1C	2	GREAT HARWOOD TOWN	103	0-1	
15/12/95	NPL	1	Bradford Park Avenue	169	2-2	Connor, Lunt
19/12/95	PC	1	SPENNYMOOR UNITED	105	3-2	McCrae(2), Connor
01/01/96	NPL	1	Great Harwood Town	107	4-0	McCrae, Phillips, Whittle, Kilner
06/01/96	NPL	1	Harrogate Town	144	2-2	McCrae(2)
13/01/96	NPL	1	FARSLEY CELTIC	152	2-0	Lunt(2)
17/01/96	Lancs ATS	2	Accrington Stanley	276	1-1	Kilner
20/01/96	FA Trophy	1	MATLOCK TOWN	241	3-2	McCrae(3)
23/01/96	Lancs ATS	2 rep	ACCRINGTON STANLEY	156	2-1	Kilner, Brennan
10/02/96	FA Trophy	2	Bognor Regis Town	539	3-1	Lunt(2), Kilner
13/02/96	Lancs ATS	QF	Morecambe	318	0-3	
17/02/96	NPL	1	ALFRETON TOWN	202	1-3	Lunt
20/02/96	PC	QF	Bamber Bridge	303	0-0	
24/02/96	NPL	1	GRETNA	148	1-1	Lunt
27/02/96	PC	QF rep	BAMBER BRIDGE	226	1-2	Graham
02/03/96	FA Trophy	3	GATESHEAD	716	1-2	Lunt
05/03/96	Manc PC	QF	Salford City	47	4-0	Cordner(og), Lunt(2), Graham
09/03/96	NPL	1	Whitley Bay	186	1-1	Burke(og)
16/03/96	NPL	1	CONGLETON TOWN	169	1-2	McCrae
18/03/96	Manc PC	SF	Hyde United	320	0-2	
23/03/96	NPL	1	Farsley Celtic	88	1-4	Graham
26/03/96	NPL	1	WARRINGTON TOWN	127	3-1	McCrae(3)
30/03/96	NPL	1	LANCASTER CITY	231	0-0	
02/04/96	NPL	1	Curzon Ashton	127	2-1	Brennan, Lunt
06/04/96	NPL	1	LEIGH R.M.I.	207	3-1	Lunt(2), Haddon
08/04/96	NPL	1	FLEETWOOD	187	3-2	McCrae, Lunt, Bunn
13/04/96	NPL	1	WHITLEY BAY	177	1-0	Whittle
15/04/96	NPL	1	Ashton United	165	1-1	Lunt
20/04/96	NPL	1	Leigh R.M.I.	158	1-1	Bunn
23/04/96	NPL	1	EASTWOOD TOWN	130	1-1	Place(og)
27/04/96	NPL	1	Lancaster City	503	1-3	Lunt
30/04/96	NPL	1	CURZON ASHTON	162	2-1	Connor, Lunt
04/05/96	NPL	1	GREAT HARWOOD TOWN	217	2-0	Bunn(2)

STOCKSBRIDGE PARK STEELS

Bracken Moor Lane, Stocksbridge, Sheffield. Tel: 0114 288 2045

Secretary: Michael Grimmer, 48 Hole House Lane, Stocksbridge, Sheffield S30 5BP. Tel: 0114 288 6470

Programme and club shop Edwin O'Sullivan Tel: 0114 288 4218

Nickname: Steels

Colours: Yellow and Blue

Capacity: 3,500

Seating: 450

Covered standing: 600

Clubhouse on ground: Yes

Record attendance: 2,000 v Sheffield Wednesday Floodlight opener Oct 1991

Record fee received: £15,000 for Lee Mills to Sheffield Wednesday

DIRECTIONS

M1 junction 35a from south, 36 from north, A616 to Stocksbridge (A6102 from Sheffield - on arriving at Stocksbridge turn left into Nanny Hill under the Clock Tower and continue up the hill for about 500 yds - ground on left.

HONOURS

Northern Counties East Div 1 1992, Sheffield and Hallamshire Senior Cup 1952, 1993

Yorkshire League 1952, 1955, 1956, 1957, 1958, 1962, 1963

Div 2 in 1951 and 1965 and Div 3 in 1971 and 1975, League Cup in 1962

Manager for 1996-97: Michael Horne, Chairman: Alan Bethel

The first club to be formed in Stocksbridge was The Foresters who played in the Hatchard League until 1902. They reached the League Cup semi-final in 1900 but lost to Kiveton Park in front of 3,000 spectators. Foresters then joined the Sheffield Minor League where they remained until 1914, where it is believed they folded. Stocksbridge Church FC date to 1890 and were members of the Sheffield Sunday School League, moving to the Minor League and then the Sheffield Amateur League. They won the league in successive seasons in 1929 and 1930 but appeared to fold in 1932 when Stocksbridge Works Social Services took over their ground. The Works were formed in 1908 and played in the Sheffield Amateur, Works and Drake Leagues before rejoining the Amateur League in 1932, where they stayed until 1947 when they moved to the stronger Sheffield Association. After two years they gained membership of the Yorkshire League, winning the title seven times in the 50's, including four in succession, and were presented with a plaque to commemorate the feat. They also won the Sheffield and Hallamshire Cup, reaching a number of other finals. Around the mid-60's the club began to go into decline, dropping to Division Three of the Yorkshire League until finding themselves in the lower reaches of the Northern Counties East.

Oxley Park FC was formed in 1945, playing in the Penistone League and the Friendlies League in 1953. They were promoted in six successive seasons before moving to the Sports and Athletic League where they again won promotions and the title. In 1970 Park joined the Hatchard League and after a couple of ordinary seasons the league amalgamated with the County Senior League in 1983, where three promotions soon came. The two clubs merged in 1986 to become Stocksbridge Park Steels, but there was no immediate success on the field, although there was much work behind the scenes. Many improvements were made , including floodlights, a social club and new dressing rooms, with new stands following later as the Northern Premier League loomed.In 1992 the club were champions of Division One and a year later the club took the County Cup for the first time in over 40 years. After finishing third in 1995, the club were shocked to be turned down by the NPL, but with a runners up place in May, promotion was secured at long last.

STOCKSBRIDGE PARK STEELS 1995/96 SEASON

19/08/95	NCEL	P	Glasshoughton Welfare	0-0
22/08/95	NCEL	P	Liversedge	2-1
26/08/95	FA Cup	P	Lincoln United	2-3
28/08/95	NCEL	P	Hatfield Main	3-0
02/09/95	NCEL	P	Hucknall Town	1-2
05/09/95	NCEL	P	SHEFFIELD	0-0
09/09/95	NCEL	P	MALTBY MINERS WELFARE	1-1
12/09/95	NCEL	P	Arnold Town	1-1
16/09/95	NCEL	P	Armthorpe Welfare	1-1
19/09/95	NCEL	P	THACKLEY	3-3
23/09/95	NCEL	P	OSSETT ALBION	0-0
30/09/95	NCEL	P	Sheffield	2-1
07/10/95	NCEL	P	GOOLE TOWN	2-3
14/10/95	NCEL	P	PICKERING TOWN	3-3
17/10/95	NCEL	P	BRIGG TOWN	2-0
21/10/95	NCEL	P	Ashfield United	1-0
24/10/95	PC	2	BRODSWORTH MINERS	3-1
28/10/95	FA Vase	1	Brigg Town	1-2
04/11/95	NCEL	P	Brigg Town	0-5
15/11/95	PC	3	Brigg Town	1-3
25/11/95	NCEL	P	OSSETT TOWN	3-4
28/11/95	LC	2	Louth United	5-0
02/12/95	NCEL	P	Pickering Town	6-1
06/12/95	Sheffield	3	Denaby United	3-2
09/12/95	NCEL	P	HATFIELD MAIN	2-0
13/12/95	LC	3	HALL ROAD RANGERS	5-1
16/12/95	NCEL	P	Thackley	1-1
23/12/95	NCEL	P	LIVERSEDGE	3-0
06/01/96	NCEL	P	DENABY UNITED	2-0
09/01/96	Sheffield	QF	Frickley Athletic	2-2
13/01/96	NCEL	P	Ossett Town	1-0
16/01/96	Sheffield	QF rep	FRICKLEY ATHLETIC	2-0
20/01/96	NCEL	P	GLASSHOUGHTON	0-1
10/02/96	NCEL	P	Ossett Albion	3-1
17/02/96	NCEL	P	ARNOLD TOWN	4-2
20/02/96	Sheffield	SF(1)	Maltby Miners Welfare	1-1
24/02/96	NCEL	P	Goole Town	2-1
27/02/96	Sheffield	SF(2)	MALTBY MINERS WELFARE	4-2
02/03/96	NCEL	P	North Ferriby United	1-0
05/03/96	LC	QF	ARNOLD TOWN	3-0
09/03/96	NCEL	P	ASHFIELD UNITED	2-1
16/03/96	NCEL	P	Denaby United	1-0
23/03/96	NCEL	P	BELPER TOWN	1-0
26/03/96	LC	SF	OSSETT ALBION	1-2
30/03/96	NCEL	P	Hallam	0-2
02/04/96	NCEL	P	NORTH FERRIBY UNITED	0-0
06/04/96	NCEL	P	ARMTHORPE WELFARE	1-0
08/04/96	NCEL	P	Maltby Miners Welfare	1-0
13/04/96	NCEL	P	Belper Town	0-1
16/04/96	Sheffield	F	GRIMETHORPE MINERS	1-0
20/04/96	NCEL	P	HUCKNALL TOWN	1-0
25/04/96	NCEL	P	HALLAM	2-0

WARRINGTON TOWN

Cantilever Park, Loushers Lane, Latchford, Warrington, Cheshire WA4 2RS. Tel: 01925 631932 club 653044 office

Secretary: Ian Dick, 53Arlington Drive, Penketh, Warrington WA5 2QG Tel: 01925 724421

Prog Editor: Rick Barker, Tel 01925 604101

Colours: Yellow and blue

Nickname: The Town

Capacity: 2,500

Seating: 300

Covered standing: 500

Clubhouse on ground: Yes

Record attendance: 3,000 v Halesowen Town
FA Vase semi-final 1st leg 1986

Biggest win: 14-0 Crosfields Depot Cup 1951-52

Biggest defeat: 0-10 Eastwood Mid-Cheshire Challenge Cup 1967-68

Record goalscorer in one season: L.Arnold 60

DIRECTIONS

M6 junction 20, then A50 towards Warrington. After 2 miles turn left immediately after swing bridge into Station Road, ground 600yds on left. From town centre travel 1 mile south on A49, left at lights into Loushers Lane, ground quarter mile on right. 2 miles from Warrington Bank Quay (BR).

HONOURS

FA VASE Runners up 1987

FA VASE Semi-final 1986

North West Counties League 1990, League Cup 1986, 1988, 1989

Mid-Cheshire League 1961, League Cup 1955 and 1956, Altrincham Amateur Cup 1955,

Manager for 1996-97: Alan Lord, Chairman: Stephen Plant

Warrington Town were only formed in 1949, starting out as Stockton Heath FC in the Warrington and District League. 1952 saw them move to the Mid-Cheshire League and when the ex-Portsmouth star Freddie Worrall was appointed manager, his 13 years in charge brought the title in 1960, three League Cups and three Cheshire Amateur Cup finals. Freddie, who sadly died in 1979, saw many players from that era go on to the Football League including World Cup star Roger Hunt who moved to Liverpool.

In 1956 they moved to the present ground in Common Lane, which was much later re-named Cantilever Park and in 1962 they were re-named Warrington Town FC.

Town stayed in that league until 1978 when they joined the Cheshire County League and when it was merged in to form the North West Counties League they found themselves in the 3rd Division. It was the start of a fine era, for promotion was won immediately and within three seasons they were in the top flight. In 1990 they celebrated the championship and were promoted to the Northern Premier League.

Without question, the club's finest hour to date was in 1987, when after the heartbreak of losing a semi-final a year earlier to Halesowen Town they went one better and beat Collier Row to reach Wembley.

In an epic final they eventually lost to St Helens Town 3-2.

Since those great days Town have remained in the Northern Premier League Division One and in 1994 only missed promotion on the last day when losing at home to Workington. There have been a number of managerial changes and some internal problems but the club hope to improve on last May's finish of below mid-table.

WARRINGTON TOWN 1995/96 SEASON

19/08/95	NPL	1	Alfreton Town	203	1-5	Glass
22/08/95	NPL	1	ASHTON UNITED	104	2-2	O'Callaghan, Heavey
26/08/95	NPL	1	HARROGATE TOWN	105	2-2	O'Callaghan(2)
02/09/95	NPL	1	Farsley Celtic	113	0-1	
05/09/95	NPL	1	ATHERTON L.R.	110	1-2	O'Callaghan
09/09/95	FA Cup	Q1	TRAFFORD	87	2-2	O'Callaghan(2)
12/09/95	FA Cup	Q1 rep	Trafford	118	3-4	Heavey, O'Callaghan, Diamond
16/09/95	NPL	1	WORKSOP TOWN	123	3-2	O'Callaghan, Helme, Heavey
18/09/95	NPL	1	Great Harwood Town	106	5-0	Lawrenson, Heavey, Johnson, O'Callaghan(2)
23/09/95	NPL	1	FLEETWOOD	124	3-3	Heavey, Lawrenson, Glass
26/09/95	Ches. SC	1	NANTWICH TOWN	85	6-1	O'Callaghan(3), Brady(2), Lawrenson
30/09/95	NPL	1	Eastwood Town	126	1-2	Heavey
03/10/95	LC	1	ASHTON UNITED	50	1-2	Heavey
07/10/95	NPL	1	Workington	243	2-2	Diamond, Heavey
11/10/95	NPL	1	Curzon Ashton	121	1-2	O'Callaghan
14/10/95	FA Trophy	Q1	Racing Club Warwick	130	0-1	
17/10/95	NPL	1	RADCLIFFE BOROUGH	68	1-1	Edwards
21/10/95	NPL	1	NETHERFIELD	93	3-6	O'Callaghan, Boardman, Glass
28/10/95	NPL	1	Lincoln United	221	0-1	
04/11/95	NPL	1	LINCOLN UNITED	104	4-2	O'Callaghan(2), Atkinson, Glass
13/11/95	NPL	1	Ashton United	167	1-3	O'Callaghan
18/11/95	NPL	1	EASTWOOD TOWN	80	2-0	Atkinson(2)
21/11/95	PC	1	Bamber Bridge	279	1-4	O'Callaghan
25/11/95	NPL	1	Bradford Park Avenue	156	0-1	
28/11/95	Ches. SC	QF	Altrincham	273	0-4	
02/12/95	NPL	1	WHITLEY BAY	70	2-1	O'Callaghan, Atkinson
06/12/95	NPL	1	Leigh R.M.I.	153	2-2	O'Callaghan, Murphy
09/12/95	NPL	1	LEIGH R.M.I.	109	0-1	
12/12/95	1C	2	ATHERTON L.R.	66	0-1	
16/12/95	NPL	1	Netherfield	161	1-0	Dodd
06/01/96	NPL	1	GREAT HARWOOD TOWN	72	1-1	Murphy
13/01/96	NPL	1	Congleton Town	124	4-0	O'Callaghan(3), Atkinson
20/01/96	NPL	1	ALFRETON TOWN	110	2-2	Rudge, Birch
03/02/96	NPL	1	CURZON ASHTON	136	0-2	
13/02/96	NPL	1	LANCASTER CITY	72	1-1	O'Callaghan
17/02/96	NPL	1	Whitley Bay	213	1-2	Atkinson
24/02/96	NPL	1	FARSLEY CELTIC	84	5-1	Glass(2), Atkinson, O'Callaghan(2)
02/03/96	NPL	1	Worksop Town	283	3-2	Oxton, O'Callaghan(2)
09/03/96	NPL	1	Fleetwood	77	1-0	Birch
16/03/96	NPL	1	WORKINGTON	84	2-3	O'Callaghan, Atkinson
23/03/96	NPL	1	Gretna	70	3-1	Birch(2), Atkinson
26/03/96	NPL	1	Radcliffe Borough	127	1-3	Birch
30/03/96	NPL	1	BRADFORD PARK AVENUE	103	1-1	O'Callaghan
06/04/96	NPL	1	Lancaster City	330	2-4	Atkinson, Payne
13/04/96	NPL	1	Atherton L.R.	115	1-2	O'Callaghan
16/04/96	NPL	1	CONGLETON TOWN	85	4-1	O'Callaghan(2), Owen, Glass
20/04/96	NPL	1	Harrogate Town	206	3-1	O'Callaghan(2), Atkinson
27/04/96	NPL	1	GRETNA	126	3-4	Atkinson, Birch, O'Callaghan

WHITLEY BAY

Hillheads Park, Hillheads Rd, Whitley Bay Tyne and Wear Tel: 0191 251 3680 club 252 9570 matchday office and fax

Secretary: Ian Fitzgerald, 116 Claremont Rd, Whitley Bay, NE26 3TX Tel 0191 252 0419

Ass Secretary: Derek Breakwell, 27 Kings Rd, Whitley Bay, NE26 3BD Tel: 0191 252 7940

Prog Editor: Lynn Bone

Club shop manager: David McCall,

Colours: Blue and white stripes

Nickname: The Bay   Capacity: 4, 500

Seating: 450   Covered standing: 650

Clubhouse on ground: Yes

Record attendance: 7,301 v Hendon Amateur Cup 1965

Biggest win: 12-0 v Shildon 1961

Biggest defeat: 1-8 v Bishop Auckland 1979

Record appearances: Bill Chater 640

Record goalscorer in one season: Billy Wright 51 in 1964-65

Record goalscorer in total: Billy Wright 307

Record fee received: £ 10,000 for Kevin Todd from Berwick Rangers

DIRECTIONS

1 mile walk from bus station — leave St Pauls Church southward, turn right at r'bout, ground 3rd left at rear of ice rink. Whitley Bay (25 mins from Newcastle) or Monkseaton metro stations, both 1 mile.

HONOURS

FA AMATEUR CUP Semi-finals 1966 and 1969

Northern League 1965 and 1966, Challenge Cup 1965 and 1971

Northern Premier League Div 1 1991, Division One League Cup 1989 and 1991

Northumberland Senior Cup 1953, 1961, 1964, 1965, 1968, 1969, 1970, 1971, 1973, 1987

Manager 1996-97: Ken Parker, Assistant Manager: Paddy Lowery

Chairman: Mike Robinson, Vice Chairman: Peter Siddle

There was a football team in the town at the turn of the century, but the current club date to 1950 and were known as Whitley Bay Athletic. For five years they played in the Northern Alliance, winning it once and the League Cup twice, as well as becoming the first amateur club to win the Northumberland Cup for 60 years. In 1955 they joined the powerful North Eastern League but for three seasons they struggled at the foot of the table, and so a limited company was formed, the Athletic tag was dropped and they moved to the Northern League in 1958. During the next decade they took the title twice and the League Cup in 1965. They won the Senior Cup six times and reached two Amateur Cup semi-finals and four quarter finals, without making it to Wembley. The 70's saw more success in League and League Cup but the demise of amateur football caused the club nose dive so that they were forced to apply for re-election in 1979. The late 80's saw a fine period under Bobby Graham, where league form picked up and the Senior Cup was won. The following season, 1987-88 was the last in the Northern League and after a fine campaign the Northern Premier League accepted them. Soon the club were to enjoy a memorable FA Cup run, starting at the preliminary round and reaching the 3rd Round after beating Preston North End.

A year later they did the Division One league and cup double and were promoted, but after one season in mid-table they were relegated amongst serious financial problems. Last season started well but after a management change tailed off, although the top eight finish was encouraging.

WHITLEY BAY 1995/96 SEASON

Date	Comp	Rnd	Opponent	Att	Score	Scorers
19/08/95	NPL	1	Eastwood Town	98	2-0	Bell, Pearson
22/08/95	NPL	1	HARROGATE TOWN	200	1-1	Pearson
26/08/95	FA Cup	P	EASINGTON COLLIERY	142	3-0	Pearson, King(2)
02/09/95	NPL	1	Leigh R.M.I.	144	1-0	Thompson
05/09/95	NPL	1	FARSLEY CELTIC	203	5-2	Bell, Blower(3), Barker
09/09/95	FA Cup	Q1	WORKINGTON	277	1-2	Barker
16/09/95	NPL	1	ATHERTON L.R.	175	1-1	Greenwood
19/09/95	NPL	1	Harrogate Town	208	3-2	Pearson, Cameron, Bell
23/09/95	NPL	1	Farsley Celtic	124	0-1	
26/09/95	LC	1	HARROGATE TOWN	121	1-2	King
30/09/95	NPL	1	Great Harwood Town	102	0-2	
03/10/95	NPL	1	BRADFORD PARK AVENUE	134	2-1	Moat, Fell
07/10/95	NPL	1	GRETNA	238	1-1	Blower
14/10/95	FA Trophy	Q1	Fleetwood	119	1-2	Bell
17/10/95	NPL	1	WORKSOP TOWN	122	3-3	Moat, King(2)
21/10/95	NPL	1	Ashton United	171	3-2	Coxall, Cameron(2)
04/11/95	NPL	1	Worksop Town	285	2-6	Moat(2)
07/11/95	N'humb SC	1	MORPETH TOWN	139	2-4	Cameron, Moat
11/11/95	NPL	1	Congleton Town	92	1-2	Moat
18/11/95	NPL	1	LANCASTER CITY	136	0-1	
25/11/95	NPL	1	NETHERFIELD	108	2-1	Blower, Cameron
02/12/95	NPL	1	Warrington Town	70	1-2	Blower
09/12/95	NPL	1	ASHTON UNITED	115	5-1	Blower, Houlden, Wilson, King(2)
12/12/95	1C	2	Gretna	70	2-1	Blower, Houlden
16/12/95	NPL	1	Alfreton Town	171	3-2	Wilson(2), Cullen
06/01/96	NPL	1	FLEETWOOD	136	6-0	Wilson, Cameron(2), Houlden(2), McKenzie
13/01/96	NPL	1	Atherton L.R.	95	1-2	Forster
20/01/96	NPL	1	CURZON ASHTON	120	3-2	Warder(og), Pearson, Wilson
03/02/96	NPL	1	LEIGH R.M.I.	129	3-1	Cullen, McDonald, Ludlow
17/02/96	NPL	1	WARRINGTON TOWN	213	2-1	Cameron, McDonald
20/02/96	1C	QF	Lancaster City	139	1-2	Cullen
24/02/96	NPL	1	GREAT HARWOOD TOWN	203	1-1	Blower
02/03/96	NPL	1	Fleetwood	58	0-0	
09/03/96	NPL	1	RADCLIFFE BOROUGH	186	1-1	Blower
16/03/96	NPL	1	Lancaster City	241	1-3	Cullen
19/03/96	NPL	1	Netherfield	104	2-1	Blower, Ludlow
23/03/96	NPL	1	Workington	205	0-1	
30/03/96	NPL	1	EASTWOOD TOWN	147	0-0	
02/04/96	NPL	1	Lincoln United	183	3-4	Cameron, Cawley, Snowdon
06/04/96	NPL	1	WORKINGTON	189	1-2	Cawley
08/04/96	NPL	1	Gretna	89	3-1	Cawley, Snowdon, Blower
13/04/96	NPL	1	Radcliffe Borough	177	0-1	
16/04/96	NPL	1	Curzon Ashton	220	3-1	Pearson, Cawley, Blower
20/04/96	NPL	1	ALFRETON TOWN	187	0-5	
23/04/96	NPL	1	LINCOLN UNITED	132	2-0	Blower, Cullen
27/04/96	NPL	1	CONGLETON TOWN	163	1-2	Blower
04/05/96	NPL	1	Bradford Park Avenue	198	3-2	Blower, Greenwood, Snowdon

WORKINGTON

Borough Park, Workington, Cumbria, CA14 2DT Tel: 01900 602871 fax: 605208

Secretary: Tom Robson, 12 Derwent Bank, Seaton, Workington, Cumbria CA14 1EE Tel: 01900 605208

Match secretary, Press and Programme: Steve Durham, 10 Grant Drive, Bleach Green, Whitehaven, Cumbria CA28 6JS Tel: 01946 61380

Best contact when confirming a fixture: Steve Durham

Club shop manager: Keith Lister

Nickname: The Reds   Colours: Red and White

Capacity: 2,500   Seating: 300,

Covered standing: 800   Clubhouse on ground: Yes

DIRECTIONS

A66 into town, right at 'T' junction, follow A596 for three quarters of a mile - ground is then visible and signposted. Ground is to north of town centre quarter of a mile from Workington (BR) station and half mile from bus station in town centre.

Record attendance: 21,000 v Manchester Utd FA Cup 3rd Rd 1958

Biggest win: 17-1 v Cockermouth Crusaders Jan 19th 1901

Biggest defeat: 0-9 v Chorley (a) 1987-88 NPL

Record appearances: Bobby Brown 419

Record goalscorer in one season: Jack Thom 65 in 1928-29

Record goalscorer in total: Billy Charlton 193

Record fee received: £33,000 for Ian McDonald from Liverpool in 1974

HONOURS

Cumberland County Cup 1887, 1888, 1889, 1890, 1891, 1896, 1897, 1898, 1899, 1907, 1908, 1910, 1925, 1935, 1937, 1938, 1950, 1954, 1968, 1986, 1996

North Eastern Challenge Cup 1935 and 1937, NPL Presidents Cup 1984

Manager for 1996-97: Wayne Harrison, Assistant manager: Keith Hunton

Chairman: Jackie Donald, Vice chairman: Colin Doorbar

The club was formed in 1884 with the first game being played on January 12th , a team from Wigton providing the opposition for a 0-0 draw. There was no league as such in those early days with matches played merely on a friendly basis until the introduction of the Cumberland Cup in 1885. In 1890 the club became founder members of the Cumberland Association League where they remained until 1894. A seven year spell in the Cumberland Senior League followed and whilst there a 17-1 victory was posted over Cockermouth Crusaders, a record for the club. The Reds joined the Lancashire League in 1901, for just two seasons before returning to Cumberland football for a year. From 1904 to 1910 the club played in the Lancashire Combination but to attempt to economise, it was decided to switch to the North Eastern League, but the club disbanded in 1911, going into voluntary liquidation. After a ten year break, Workington AFC was reborn in 1921 and was elected to the North Eastern League again and after some 18 years, success came with a runner up placing in a season which saw a 18 match unbeaten run. There had been some success in the Challenge Cup, however, with wins in 1935 and 1937 and a final place in 1938. On 8 occasions the team scored 100 or more goals with 147 in 1933-34 being exceptional. The complete record in the North Eastern League is P 923 W 454 D 150 L 319 For 2205 Against 1667 Pts 1058.Saturday August 18th 1951 remains a significant date in the clubs history, when Reds made their Football League debut at Halifax Town. Life was a struggle in the early years, but promotion to Division Three was a high point, with failure to gain re-election an obvious low one, when only 4 games were won and 102 goals conceded. The full record in the Football League reads P 1194 W 385 D 310 L 499 For 1525 Against 1810 Pts 1080 . In the League Cup Reds developed a proud record, twice progressing to the quarter-final stage. In 1964 West Ham beat Reds at Upton Park while Chelsea were held at Borough Park, but won the replay a year later. Before that tie, Workington had beaten Blackburn Rovers and Norwich City. In the FA Cup the best season was 1933-34 when, as a non-League side, Reds reached the 4th Round. In 1958 Manchester United were the visitors for an FA Cup game, just prior to the Munich disaster, and over 21,000 saw the match, a record crowd. On losing FL status, Reds joined the Northern Premier League, and in 1983 finished 7th, the best finish to date. Reds lifted the Presidents Cup by beating Marine, but relegation to the newly formed Division One was

inevitable in 1988, where they remain. Many famous faces have managed Workington over the years, including Bill Shankley, Joe Harvey, Ken Furphy, Keith Burkinshaw, John McNamee, and Alan Ashman, while Bobby Johnstone, Barry Endean, Wayne Harrison and Mick Heaton are some of the well known non-League men.

WORKINGTON 1995/96 SEASON

Date	Comp		Opponent	Att	Score	Scorers
19/08/95	NPL	1	RADCLIFFE BOROUGH	273	1-1	Holliday
22/08/95	NPL	1	Netherfield	242	1-1	Henderson
26/08/95	FA Cup	P	HEBBURN	253	8-1	Kilburn, Henderson(2), Corrie(3), Halliday, Wilson
28/08/95	NPL	1	Fleetwood	188	1-1	Henderson
02/09/95	NPL	1	Bradford Park Avenue	155	0-3	
05/09/95	NPL	1	LANCASTER CITY	320	0-0	
09/09/95	FA Cup	Q1	Whitley Bay	277	2-1	Henderson, Milburn
12/09/95	NPL	1	Lancaster City	246	1-2	Henderson
16/09/95	NPL	1	CONGLETON TOWN	327	2-0	Milburn, Wilson
19/09/95	NPL	1	Gretna	235	1-1	Rowntree
23/09/95	FA Cup	Q2	SPENNYMOOR UNITED	487	2-4	Henderson, Rowntree
26/09/95	LC	1	NETHERFIELD	211	3-2	Gibson(og), Henderson, Wright
30/09/95	NPL	1	Ashton United	192	1-3	Henderson
03/10/95	NPL	1	GREAT HARWOOD TOWN	276	0-0	
07/10/95	NPL	1	WARRINGTON TOWN	243	2-2	Parry, Henderson
11/10/95	NPL	1	Leigh R.M.I.	165	2-4	Messenger, Walmsley(og)
14/10/95	FA Trophy	Q1	LEICESTER UNITED	286	1-1	Henderson
17/10/95	FA Trophy	Q1 rep	Leicester United	125	0-5	
21/10/95	NPL	1	Radcliffe Borough	115	1-4	Wright
24/10/95	LC	2	BAMBER BRIDGE	194	0-1	
28/10/95	NPL	1	WORKSOP TOWN	237	6-2	Caton(2), Wilson, Corrie, Henderson, Holliday
04/11/95	Cumberland	2	Abbeytown	140	5-0	Rowntree, Holliday, Henderson, Wright
07/11/95	1C	1	Fleetwood	85	2-2	Henderson, Williamson
11/11/95	NPL	1	CURZON ASHTON	238	0-1	
18/11/95	NPL	1	ASHTON UNITED	239	2-2	Corrie, Rowntree
21/11/95	1C	1 rep	FLEETWOOD	193	3-0	Williamson, Rowntree, Henderson
25/11/95	NPL	1	Eastwood Town	172	1-2	Rowntree
29/11/95	Cumberland	3	Gretna	63	0-1	
02/12/95	NPL	1	HARROGATE TOWN	223	2-0	Corrie, Wright
09/12/95	Cumberland	3	Whitehaven Amateurs	165	3-0	Holliday, Rowntree, Wright
12/12/95	1C	2	NETHERFIELD	165	4-2	Henderson, Milburn, Rowntree, Taylor
16/12/95	NPL	1	Atherton L.R.	117	0-0	
06/01/96	NPL	1	ALFRETON TOWN	230	1-2	Wright
13/01/96	NPL	1	Lincoln United	230	0-4	
20/01/96	NPL	1	BRADFORD PARK AVENUE	251	3-2	Taylor, Rowntree, Wilson
23/01/96	Cumberland	QF	GRETNA	206	2-1	Milburn, Henderson
03/02/96	NPL	1	FARSLEY CELTIC	215	2-1	White, Henderson
13/02/96	1C	QF	ATHERTON L.R.	229	2-3	Messenger, Caton
17/02/96	NPL	1	EASTWOOD TOWN	192	1-2	Flint(og)
18/02/96	Cumberland	SF	Keswick	540	3-1	Messenger, Milburn, Caton
24/02/96	NPL	1	Harrogate Town	210	3-0	Dustin(2), Williamson
02/03/96	NPL	1	Farsley Celtic	83	0-3	
09/03/96	NPL	1	LINCOLN UNITED	217	1-2	Suddick
12/03/96	NPL	1	FLEETWOOD	137	3-0	Henderson, Wright(2)
16/03/96	NPL	1	Warrington Town	84	3-2	Gilmour(2), Suddick
23/03/96	NPL	1	WHITLEY BAY	205	1-0	Fyfe
26/03/96	NPL	1	Curzon Ashton	102	0-3	
30/03/96	NPL	1	NETHERFIELD	207	1-0	Gilmour
02/04/96	NPL	1	GRETNA	213	2-2	Henderson, Holliday
06/04/96	NPL	1	Whitley Bay	189	2-1	Milburn, Taylor
08/04/96	NPL	1	LEIGH R.M.I.	208	0-3	
13/04/96	NPL	1	Alfreton Town	205	1-2	Henderson
15/04/96	NPL	1	Great Harwood Town	120	0-1	
20/04/96	NPL	1	ATHERTON L.R.	210	0-1	
27/04/96	NPL	1	Worksop Town	227	2-2	Caton(2)
01/05/96	Cumberland	F	CLEATOR MOOR CELTIC	397	4-1	Rowntree(2), Dustin(2)
04/05/96	NPL	1	Congleton Town	158	0-0	

WORKSOP TOWN

Babbage Way, Sandy Lane, Worksop, Notts S80 1UJ. Tel: 01909 501911 fax 01909 487934

Secretary: Keith Illett, 2 Mount Ave, Worsop, Notts 01909 487934

Prog Editor: Mel Bradley Tel 01909 500491

Club shop manager: Steve Jarvis Tel 01623 792047

Colours: Amber and Black   Nickname: Tigers

Capacity: 2,500   Seating: 360

Covered standing: 1,000   Clubhouse on ground: Yes

DIRECTIONS

M1 jct 31 (from north) jct 30 (from south), follow Worksop signs, join A57 and follow signs for Sandy Lane Industrial Estate - ground on left. 5 mins walk from station.

Record attendance: At Central Ave 8,171 v Chesterfield FA Cup 1925

And at Sandy Lane: 1,503 v Sheffield Utd Friendly

Biggest win: 20-0 v Staveley Derbyshire League Sept 1st 1894

Biggest defeat: 0-12 v Alfreton Town 1970-71

Record appearances: Kenny Clark 347

Record goalscorer in one season: Dickie Everett 64

Record goalscorer in total: Kenny Clark 251

Record fee paid: £10,000 for Martin Hardy from Boston Utd 1987

HONOURS

NPL President's Cup 1986 and 1996

Midland Counties League 1922, 1966, 1973

Sheffield Association League 1899 and 1949

Sheffield and Hallamshire Senior Cup 1924, 1953, 1955, 1966, 1970, 1973, 1982, 1985, 1995

Mansfield Charity Cup 1923, Wharncliffe League 1916

Manager for 1996-97: Tommy Spencer, Assistant manager: John Stokes

Chairman: Rick Knowles,Vice chairman: John Shuker

Worksop Town FC are now back home and established in their new ground after a turbulent time which threatened to see the club go out of existence. After losing their ground, the Tigers spent a period in exile at Gainsborough Trinity. They had played at Central Avenue, a ground in the middle of town, but redevelopment to create an extra car park for shoppers caused the football part of the shared cricket ground to disappear and made Tigers homeless at the end of the 1988-89 season. They were also relegated from the Premier Division of the Northern Premier League. The next season they fought to preserve their Division One status, but that was followed by two title challenges where they finished third on both occasions. In addition they reached the Sheffield Senior Cup final three times and the Division One Cup final once.

The club's Sandy Lane home is in fact their fourth ground in a very long history which goes back to 1861, only four seasons after Sheffield FC. The glory years for the Tigers were the 1920's when several League teams were beaten in the FA Cup. Spurs were held to a draw at White Hart Lane and the Midland League title was won in 1922. Those days saw gates of 3-4,000 and some 8,171 packed into Central Avenue to see an FA Cup tie with Chesterfield in 1925.

The mid-60's also saw great sides and after taking the Midland League again, they were founder members of the Northern Premier League in 1968. Since then honours have been less frequent, but

there was a President's Cup to celebrate in 1986 and several more Senior Cup successes.

With the development of Sandy Lane continuing gradually, the club is stabilising and last season they finished mid-table in Division One although they tasted success by winning the President's Cup, beating Guiseley in the final.

WORKSOP TOWN 1995/96 SEASON

Date	Comp	Round	Opponent	Att	Score	Scorers
19/08/95	NPL	1	Fleetwood	141	4-1	Harris, Clark, Whitehead, Barnard
22/08/95	NPL	1	BRADFORD PARK AVENUE	460	4-1	Harris(2), Whitehead, Howard
26/08/95	FA Cup	P	Belper Town	261	3-2	Howard, Harris, Clark
28/08/95	NPL	1	Alfreton Town	418	2-2	Howard, Clark
02/09/95	NPL	1	RADCLIFFE BOROUGH	439	2-2	Howard, Whitehouse
05/09/95	NPL	1	Eastwood Town	232	3-2	Harris(2), Campbell
09/09/95	FA Cup	Q1	RADCLIFFE BOROUGH	357	4-0	Harris(3), Campbell
12/09/95	NPL	1	LINCOLN UNITED	455	2-4	Clark, Harris
16/09/95	NPL	1	Warrington Town	123	2-3	Higginbotham, Harris
19/09/95	NPL	1	LEIGH R.M.I.	316	1-1	Campbell
23/09/95	FA Cup	Q2	MORECAMBE	529	2-3	Clark(2)
30/09/95	NPL	1	ATHERTON L.R.	318	1-3	Whitehead
07/10/95	NPL	1	GREAT HARWOOD TOWN	307	3-2	Whitehead, Harris, Clark
10/10/95	LC	1	Congleton Town	145	3-1	Howard, Clark, Whitehead
14/10/95	FA Trophy	Q1	Curzon Ashton	170	3-4	Brookes, Howard, Clark
17/10/95	NPL	1	Whitley Bay	122	3-3	Clark(2), Starkey
21/10/95	NPL	1	CURZON ASHTON	281	0-3	
24/10/95	LC	2	BOSTON UNITED	483	0-5	
28/10/95	NPL	1	Workington	237	2-6	Clark, Howard
01/11/95	NPL	1	Farsley Celtic	124	2-2	Clark, Campbell
04/11/95	NPL	1	WHITLEY BAY	285	6-2	Clark(2), Harris, Howard, Whitehead, Campbell
07/11/95	Sheffield	2	Emley	175	1-2	Brookes
11/11/95	NPL	1	GRETNA	282	4-2	Clark(2), Campbell, Harris
18/11/95	NPL	1	Radcliffe Borough	152	1-5	Clark
25/11/95	NPL	1	Atherton L.R.	125	1-4	Howard
28/11/95	PC	1	GAINSBOROUGH TRINITY	500	3-1	Clark, Starkey, Howard
09/12/95	NPL	1	Gretna	90	0-6	
12/12/95	1C	2	HARROGATE TOWN	191	5-1	Campbell(2), Watkinson(og), Clark, Harris
16/12/95	NPL	1	Ashton United	133	2-1	Campbell, Clark
01/01/96	NPL	1	Lincoln United	263	1-4	Clark
06/01/96	NPL	1	CONGLETON TOWN	278	6-0	Campbell(2), Rookyard, Clark(2), Howard
13/01/96	NPL	1	Netherfield	124	2-0	Rookyard(2)
20/01/96	NPL	1	Great Harwood Town	109	2-1	Clark, Rookyard
03/02/96	NPL	1	Lancaster City	264	1-3	Rookyard
10/02/96	NPL	1	ALFRETON TOWN	467	2-0	Campbell, Clark
13/02/96	1C	QF	GREAT HARWOOD TOWN	230	1-1	Harris
17/02/96	NPL	1	Leigh R.M.I.	150	1-1	Clark
19/02/96	1C	QF rep	Great Harwood Town	70	1-2	Clark
24/02/96	NPL	1	LANCASTER CITY	452	0-2	
02/03/96	NPL	1	WARRINGTON TOWN	283	2-3	Rookyard(2)
09/03/96	NPL	1	Congleton Town	134	2-0	Clark, Rookyard
16/03/96	NPL	1	NETHERFIELD	231	3-2	Rookyard, Howard, Clark
20/03/96	PC	QF	Boston United	331	2-0	Clark(2)
23/03/96	NPL	1	Bradford Park Avenue	187	4-4	Whitehead, Clark, Rookyard(2)
30/03/96	NPL	1	FLEETWOOD	274	4-1	Rookyard(2), Clark, Campbell
02/04/96	PC	SF(1)	BAMBER BRIDGE	406	1-0	Rookyard
06/04/96	NPL	1	Harrogate Town	213	2-3	Clark, Howard
08/04/96	NPL	1	HARROGATE TOWN	307	2-1	Dwyer, Thorpe
10/04/96	PC	SF(2)	Bamber Bridge	430	2-2	Rookyard, Clark
16/04/96	NPL	1	EASTWOOD TOWN	283	1-2	Howard
20/04/96	NPL	1	FARSLEY CELTIC	258	1-0	Howard
22/04/96	PC	F(1)	Guiseley	470	1-0	Rookyard
27/04/96	NPL	1	WORKINGTON	227	2-2	Scott, Whitehead
29/04/96	PC	F(2)	GUISELEY	1180	3-1	Brookes, Clark, Rookyard
01/05/96	NPL	1	ASHTON UNITED	266	1-3	Starkey
04/05/96	NPL	1	Curzon Ashton	120	0-3	

The UniBond League
Premier Division
ACCRINGTON STANLEY v
FRICKLEY ATHLETIC
SATURDAY,
23rd MARCH, 1996
KICK-OFF 3.00 p.m.
Match & Ball Sponsor
A. J. ENGINEERING

Michael Jackson
PAPER LIMITED

PRICE : ONE POUND

Mon
22nd April 1996
MATCH DATE

BLYTH
SPARTANS
AFC

OFFICIAL MATCH DAY PROGRAMME
UNIBOND PREMIER LEAGUE 1995/96 SEASON

UNIBOND DIVISION ONE CHAMPIONS &
UNIFILLA CUP WINNERS 94/95

MEMBERS
OF THE
FOOTBALL ASSOCIATION
NORTHUMBERLAND FOOTBALL ASSOCIATION

PROGRAMME 80P

TODAYS OPPONENTS
Premier Division
Hyde Utd
No. 28

The Salt of the Earth

WINSFORD
UTD FC

WINSFORD UNITED F.C.
BARTON STADIUM KINGSWAY WINSFORD CHESHIRE

WORKINGTON A.F.C.

1995 - 1996
Programme 70p

UNIBOND LEAGUE
First Division
WORKINGTON
v
BRADFORD PARK AVENUE
Saturday 20th January 1996
Kick-Off 3.00 pm

THE **BIG**
BREAKFAST

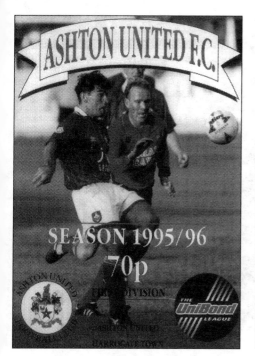

ASHTON UNITED F.C.

SEASON 1995/96

70p

FIRST DIVISION

ASHTON UNITED
HARROGATE TOWN

BISHOP AUCKLAND FOOTBALL CLUB

Founded 1886 1995 - 1996

KINGSWAY GROUND
BISHOP AUCKLAND
CO. DURHAM
DL14 7JN
Tel: (01388) 604403

Bishops Club Call
0891 664497 updated daily

EMLEY F.C.
Saturday 13th April 1996

UNIBOND LEAGUE
PREMIER DIVISION
CHORLEY v
ACCRINGTON
STANLEY
SAT. 27th JAN.
1996
Kick-Off 3.00 p.m.
Match Sponsor
MATTHEW BROWN
Matchball Sponsor
THE MASONS ARMS

COLOROLL

THE MAGPIES

OFFICIAL CLUB SPONSOR

OFFICIAL MATCH PROGRAMME
PRICE £1.00

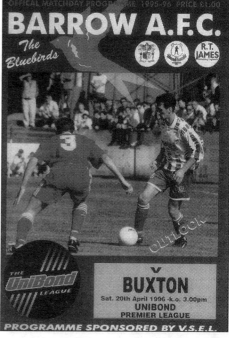

BARROW A.F.C.

The Bluebirds

OFFICIAL MATCHDAY PROGRAMME 1995-96 PRICE £1.00

v
BUXTON
Sat. 20th April 1996 -k.o. 3.00pm
UNIBOND
PREMIER LEAGUE

PROGRAMME SPONSORED BY V.S.E.L.

Above: Spennymoor United win the Durham Senior Cup

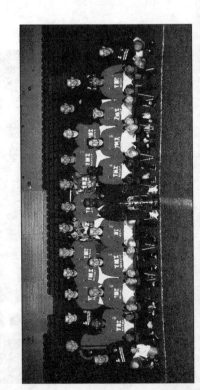

Above: Hyde United F.C.
Below: Workington F.C.

The Original Stan The Man

You know how footballers usually write boring books about their boring lives to cash in while they're famous.

Stan Bowles didn't.

But Stan The Man was one of the few who really had a story to tell.

Rangers' superbly gifted number 10 made the headlines as much for his off the field exploits, as he did for his outrageous talents on it.

His autobiography is a roller-coaster ride through fame, addiction and wrongful arrests.

How does a trip to a burger-bar lead to a charge of attempted armed robbery? How does a pre-season friendly end with a gun being held to your head? And how can a super-fit athlete chalk-up the lowest ever score in TV's *Superstars*?!

Stan The Man explains it all.

This unmissable autobiography will, at times, be hard to believe but even harder to put down.

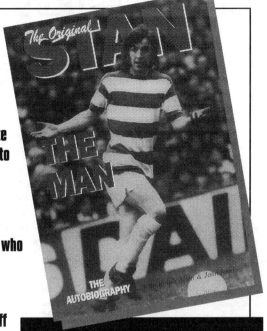

If you like reading about high-life, low-life and football, you'll love this.

NORTH WEST COUNTIES LEAGUE

DIVISION ONE

	P	W	D	L	F	A	PTS
Flixton	42	28	8	6	85	30	92
Newcastle Town	42	26	7	9	88	42	85
Trafford	42	26	5	11	89	45	83
Mossley	42	24	8	10	87	59	80
Burscough	42	23	8	11	77	40	77
Bootle	42	23	5	14	74	55	74
Clitheroe	42	20	12	10	63	44	72
St Helens Town	42	19	13	10	71	53	70
Nantwich Town	42	20	7	15	64	59	67
Prescot	42	17	11	14	70	66	62
Holker Old Boys	42	19	4	19	77	72	61
Glossop North E	42	15	15	12	55	48	60
Kidsgrove Ath	42	15	9	18	61	64	54
Eastwood Hanley	42	12	15	15	60	57	51
Maine Road	42	12	14	16	60	71	50
Chadderton	42	14	8	20	52	69	50
Blackpool Rov	42	11	9	22	49	74	42
Penrith	42	9	12	21	57	69	39
Darwen	42	9	10	23	57	77	37
Salford City	42	10	5	27	49	93	35
Rossendale Utd	42	6	10	26	32	114	28
Skelmersdale Utd	42	5	3	34	45	121	18

DIVISION TWO

	P	W	D	L	F	A	PTS
Vauxhall G.M.	34	28	4	2	112	25	88
Atherton Colls	34	25	5	4	90	44	80
Tetley Walker	34	22	7	5	76	35	73
Castleton Gabs	34	19	5	10	77	52	62
Nelson	34	17	9	8	78	55	60
Cheadle Town	34	17	5	12	67	49	56
Haslingden	34	15	9	10	69	45	54
Maghull	34	16	3	15	55	42	51
Oldham Town	34	14	8	12	75	74	50
Middlewich Ath	34	12	7	15	45	74	43
Daisy Hill	34	12	4	18	46	66	40
Ramsbottom Utd	34	11	6	17	60	65	39
Formby	34	10	7	17	59	76	37
Stantondale	34	11	4	19	47	75	37
Blackpool Mechs	34	8	8	18	56	74	32
Ashton Town	34	8	3	23	53	102	27
Squires Gate	34	5	7	22	37	82	22
Bacup Borough	34	4	3	27	35	102	15

ATHERTON COLLIERIES

Alder House, Alder Street, Atherton, Gt Manchester Tel: 01942 884649

Secretary: Colin Jones, 12 Prescot Ave, Atherton, M46 9LN Tel: 01942 879614

Chairman: Steve Payne, 209 Newbrook Rd, Atherton Tel: 01942 887241

Nickname: The Colls   Capacity: 3,500

Colours: Black and Red stripes   Seating: 200

Covered standing: 800

Floodlights: Yes

Clubhouse on ground: Yes

Record attendance: 3,300 unknown opponents in Lancs Comb 1920's

DIRECTIONS

M61 junction 5, follow sign for Westhoughton, left onto A6, right onto A579 (Newbrook Road/Bolton Road) into Atherton. (From M61 junction 4, left, right onto A6 after 80 yds, left down Newbrook Road at 1st lights). At lights next to Atherton town hall turn left into High Street, 2nd left into Alder Street to ground. Quarter mile from Atherton Central (BR).

HONOURS

North-West Counties Div 3 1987

Bridge Shield 1986

Lancs Junior Shield 1920, 1923, 1942, 1946, 1957, 1965

Managers for 1996-97: Steve Walton and Alan Lamb, Chairman: Steve Paine

Press officer: Frank Anderton, 109 Douglas Street, Atherton

Atherton Collieries FC was founded in 1916, in the dark days of the Great War, by enthusiastic miners from six pits then operative within the old urban district of Atherton. Since then the club has sometimes survived, sometimes flourished, in many senior non-league competitions in the North-West. They are believed to have started in the Bolton Combination in 1920 and staying until after the Second War, when they joined the Lancs Combination for two years. Returning to the Bolton League, they had another spell of 20 years before trying the Lancs Comb again until 1978. For four years until the new league was created by amalgamation, they played in the Cheshire League, but have remained in the NWCL ever since.

During the 20's, two Colliers joined Bolton Wanderers and won six FA Cup medals, but Atherton Colls were renown in Lancashire and won the Lancs FA Shield four times by 1964. They were often challenging in the old Lancashire Combination and became founder members of the North-West Counties League in 1982. They have since won the Bridge Shield in 1986, the Third Division championship in 1987 and were runners up in the Lamot Pils Trophy in 1992. Last May saw the club enjoy a highlight when finishing runner up to Vauxhall GM in Division Two, gaining promotion.

With the demise in mining in the town and with growing unemployment, finance became a nightmare, but ground improvements continued and floodlights are now in place at Alder House.

The ground is by far the oldest in the area, having been a Welfare ground since the club were formed in 1916. When the pits were nationalised, the ground was given to the town, having been built along with the impressive Community Centre at the entrance, by the mining owners, Fletcher Burrows.

BLACKPOOL (WREN) ROVERS FC

Bruce Park, School Rd, Marton, Blackpool, Lancs Tel: 01253 760570

Secretary: Paul Kimberley, 34 Priory Gate, South Shore, Blackpool, Lancs FY4 2QE Tel: 01253 349853

Colours: All Red

Capacity: 1,000

Seating: Yes

Covered standing: Yes

Floodlights: Yes

Clubhouse on ground: Yes

Record attendance: 1,011 v Manchester City for floodlight opener Oct 1991

DIRECTIONS

M6 to M55, leave at Jct 4, left onto A583, sharp right at 1st lights (Whitehall Road), follow signs for Airport. Ground approx 1.5 miles on right. 6 miles from Blackpool North (BR).

HONOURS

West Lancs League 1970 and 1971

League Cup 1971 and 1972

Lancs FA Shield 1969 and 1971

Lancs Combination and Cup double 1979 and League 1981

Bridge Shield 1977

Wren Rovers were formed in 1931 as a youth team, and although disbanding during the war, they reformed and joined the Blackpool Amateur League. In 1959 they were instrumental in reviving the then defunct West Lancashire League, winning the championship in 1970 and 1971. During those two exceptional years they won the Lancashire FA Challenge Shield twice and for 1971 were elected to the Lancashire Combination, where some years later, in 1978, they were runners up in both league and cup only to go one better a year later and complete the double successfully. Another title was won in 1981, before the league was amalgamated into the new North-West Counties League, where Rovers were placed in the Second Division. Only a lack of facilities stopped the club being promoted until after work was completed, the club finished runners up to Great Harwood and were promoted.

Soon after, the club merged with Boston Rovers which brought with it the funds for more ground improvements, along with a new clubhouse and floodlights. Wren also added the town name to their own to give themselves a stronger identity.

Wren's Bruce Park ground lies next door to that of Squires Gate and just a few yards from another North-West Counties League club, Blackpool Mechanics. At one time the Squires Gate and Wrens were separated by nothing more than a rope, but gradually the ground was enclosed and improved, although for a brief period they were forced to play on the former Blackpool Borough Rugby League ground.

BOOTLE

Bucks Park, Northern Perimeter Rd, Netherton, Merseyside L30 7PT

Tel: 0151 526 1850 Clubhouse and
Tel: 0151 527 1851 Ground on matchdays only

Secretary: Paul Carr, 58 Orchard Hey, Old Roan, Bootle, Merseyside L30 8RY Tel: 0151 474 0153

Chairman: Frank Doran, 39 Galloway Rd, Waterloo, Merseyside, L22 4QX Tel: 0151 526 1850

Colours: All Royal blue

Nickname: Bucks

Capacity: 5,000

Seating: 400

Covered standing: 1,000

Clubhouse on ground: Yes

Floodlights: Yes

Record attendance: 750 v Carshalton Athletic FA Trophy 2nd Rd 1981

Biggest win: 9-1 v Glossop NWCL 1986

Biggest defeat: 1-8 v Accrington Stanley NWCL 1983

Record appearances: Peter Cumiskey

DIRECTIONS

At the end of the M57 and M58 follow the signs to Bootle/All Docks. Turn right at the next lights by Police Station. Entrance is 150 yds on the right. 300 yds from Old Roan Station.
Bus 55 (150 yds from ground) 302 341 345 350 (350 yds).

HONOURS

Liverpool Challenge Cup 1965, 1976, 1979

Liverpool Amateur Cup 1966, 1968, 1974

Lancashire Amateur Cup: 1970

Liverpool Combination: 1965, 1966, 1968, 1969, 1970, 1971, 1972, 1973, 1974

Lancashire Combination: 1976 and 1977

George Mahon Cup: 1967, 1968, 1969, 1970, 1973, 1974

Cheshire League Div 2 1979

Tennants Floodlit Trophy 1994

BURSCOUGH

Victoria Park, Mart Lane, Burscough, Lancs. L40 0SD TEL: 01704 893237

Secretary and Press: Stan Strickland, 109 Redgate, Ormskirk, Lancs. L39 3NW Tel: and Fax 01695 574722

Fixture details and match results on answerphone at ground 01704 893237

Nickname: The Linnets

Capacity: 2,500

Seating: 250

Covered standing: 1,000

Floodlights: Yes

Clubhouse on ground: Yes

DIRECTIONS
M6 jct 27, follow signs through Parbold A5209, right into Junction Lane (signed Burscough & Martin Mere) to lights, right onto A59 from Ormskirk to Burscough Village, 2nd left over canal bridge into Mart Lane to ground. Half a mile from Burscough Bridge BR station (Wigan-Southport line). Slightly further from Burscough Junction (Ormskirk-Preston line).

Record attendance: 4,798 v Wigan Athletic FA Cup 3rd Qual Rd 1950

Biggest win: 10-0 v Crompton Recs Liverpool Co. Comb 1948-49, v Nelson Lancashire Comb 1968-69

Biggest defeat: 0-9 v Earlstown Liverpool Co.Comb 1948-49

Record goalscorer in one season: Johnny Vincent 60 in 1953-54

Record fee received: reported £10,000 for Gary Martindale from Bolton Wanderers

HONOURS

Lancashire Junior Cup 1948, 1950, 1967, Liverpool Challenge Cup 1948, 1951, 1955

George Mahon Cup 1948, Liverpool County Combination 1950 and Division Two 1954 and 1968

Lancashire Combination 1956 and 1970 and Division Two 1954

Liverpool Senior non-League Cup 1956 and 1972; Lord Wavertree Cup 1968

Cheshire County League Challenge Cup 1975

North-West Counties League 1983 and League Cup 1993 and 1996

Champions v Cup winners Trophy 1983 and 1996; Bill Tyrer Memorial Trophy 1990

Manager for 1996-97: John Davidson

Assistant manager: Peter King

Chairman: Frank Parr

Vice chairman: Stuart Heaps

Green Village Heroes, the Story of Burscough Football Club, has recently been published by the club. Written and researched by club secretary Stan Strickland and local journalist John Yates, it is over 300 pages long, with over 120 photos and covers the roots of the present club right back to 1880. There is a complete match by match record including tables, scorers and honours. Available from the club, price 11.95.

Formed in 1946, Burscough FC started life in the Liverpool County Combination and in only their second season they achieved a unique treble, winning the Lancashire Junior Cup, George Mahon Cup and Liverpool Challenge Cup. Two years later they again claimed the Junior Cup and also won the Challenge Cup again. In 1953 they joined the Lancashire Combination and won the Division Two title, with the championship following in 1956. Three years later another milestone was reached when Burscough got to the FA Cup 1st Round for the first time, where they played Crewe Alaxandra at Victoria Park in front of 4,200 spectators.

In 1967 they won the Junior Cup and in 1970 they were again league champions, moving on to the Cheshire County League, finishing runners up to Rossendale United. The following season they won the Liverpool non-League Senior Cup and in 1975, the League Cup. Having reached the 1st Round of the Cup a further three times, the Linnets entered the North-West Counties League in 1982 as founder members and were the first ever champions. 1990 saw relegation but two years on they were back, winning the League Cup. The last few seasons have been the most eventful in the club's history. In 1993 they lost the Liverpool Senior Cup Final to neighbours Southport, but on a memorable night at Bury FC, the League Cup was won, 2-1 against Nantwich Town. Then on March 24th 1994 Bolton Wanderers signed Gary Martindale and Rochdale signed Kevin Formby, both for substantial fees. In the close season Rochdale were back to snap up Alex Russell. These signings helped in no small way, as a further area of cover for 500 was erected soon after.

Prior to the War, a different club, Burscough Rangers used the Victoria Ground, until they folded in 1935. It was originally used for cricket from the turn of the century, but for a while during the Great War it reverted to agriculture. Burscough Rangers and Burscough Vics subsequently used it until the current club moved in after the war and bought it around 1951.

CHADDERTON

Andrew Street, Chadderton, Oldham Tel: 0161 624 9733

Secretary: Ron Manton, 24 Whitegate Lane, Chadderton, Oldham Tel: 0161 620 0368

Chairman: H.Mayall, 14 Norley Close, Chadderton, Oldham, Tel: 0161 626 4178

Colours: Red and white

Nickname: Chaddy

Capacity: 2,000

Seating: 150

Covered standing: 200

Floodlights: Yes

Clubhouse on ground: Yes

Record attendance: 1,500 v Guinness Exports 1969 and v Oldham Ath. pre-season friendly 1991

Record goalscorer in one season: David Kershaw

Record Appearances: Billy Elwell 750+ 1964-1990

DIRECTIONS

M62 Jct 20. A627 (M) to Oldham. Motorway then becomes dual carriageway. Turn left at first major traffic lights A669 (Middleton Road), then first left opposite 'Harlequin' P.H. into Burnley Street - Andrew Street 2nd left. 1 mile from Oldham Werneth (BR), buses 458 & 459 (Oldham-Manchester) stop at the Harlequin.

HONOURS

Oldham Amateur League Cup 1955

Manchester Amateur League 1963

North Division 1956

Manchester County Challenge Trophy 1972

Manchester League Div 1 1967, Division 2 1965

Gilgryst Cup 1970

Murray Shield 1966

Alfred Pettit and Hulme Celtic Cup 1962

Manager 1996-97: Dick McKay

Assistant Manager: Joe Royal

Chairman: H.Mayall

Vice Chairman: D.Glynn

CLITHEROE

Shawbridge, Clitheroe, Lancs Tel: 01200 423344

Secretary and Press: Colin Wilson, 4 Moss St, Clitheroe, Lancs BB7 1DP Tel: 01200 24370

Chairman: Steve Rush, 24 Mearley Syke, Pendle Park, Clitheroe, BB7 1JG Tel: 01200 442456

Nickname: The Blues

Club colours: Blue and White stripes

DIRECTIONS

M6 jct 31, A59 to Clitheroe (17 miles), at 4th roundabout left into Pendle Road, after 1 mile ground is just before 'The Bridge Inn' on the right. 11 miles from Blackburn BR station.

Capacity: 2,000   Seating: 400

Covered standing: 1,400   Clubhouse on ground: Yes

Record attendance: 2,086 v Mangotsfield
FA Vase semi-final 1996

Biggest win: 9-1   Biggest defeat: 1-8

Record appearance holder: Lindsay Wallace 640

Record goalscorer in one season: Don Francis 71

Record goalscorer in total: Don Francis

HONOURS

FA VASE runners up 1996

Lancs Comb 1980, League Cup 1935, Lancs Challenge Trophy 1893 and 1985

North-West Counties League Div 3 in 1984, Div 2 in 1985 and Div 1 in 1986, East Lancs Floodlit Trophy 1995

Managers 1996-97: Gary Butcher and Dennis Underwood, Vice Chairman John Hosty

In May, Clitheroe had their finest hour when they appeared in the FA Vase final at Wembley. Tremendous publicity was given with television and radio, plus nationwide coverage by the press, and over 3,000 made the trip.

Clitheroe FC was formed after a meeting at the Swan Hotel between a group of local businessmen. The new club was called Clitheroe Central and they immediately entered the Blackburn and District League. Their first match was played on November 17th at the new pitch on Ribble Hill Commons, the first opponents being Blackburn Rovers. In early 1900, Clitheroe joined the Lancashire Combination and dropped Central from the name. They disbanded during the Great War but re-formed in 1920 and rejoined the Comb six years later, remaining until 1982 when the North-West Counties League was formed. The club moved to Shawbridge in 1925. A lot of hard work went into making the sheep meadow ready for football, but over the years it suffered terribly from waterlogging. The club survived at least two financial crises until a new 16 man committee was formed to rescue the side and the ground. On the pitch they have twice won the County Cup, in 1893 and 1985, with the Combination Cup only coming to the club once, in 1935.The club enjoyed the best period in its history in the early 80's when they won the Third, Second and First Division titles in successive years, but 1996 saw everything surpassed when Clitheroe won a spine tingling semi-final in extra time of the FA Vase match with Mangotsfield to reach Wembley. Although beaten in the final, it was a fine reward for some sterling work to rescue the club a few years ago.

DARWEN

Anchor Ground, Anchor Road, Darwen, Lancs BB3 0BB Tel: 01254 705627

Secretary: Lynn Atkinson, 58 Harwood St, Darwen BB3 1PD Tel: 01254 761755

Chairman: Mrs K.Marah, 40 Anchorsholme Lane East, Cleveleys Tel: 01253 852426

Colours: Red and white

Capacity: 4,000

Seating: 250

Covered standing: 2,000

Clubhouse on ground: Yes

Record attendance: 9,000 v Luton Town FA Cup 1909

DIRECTIONS

A666 Blackburn/Bolton road, 1 mile north of Darwen town centre, turn right at Anchor Hotel, ground 100 yds on left. One and a half miles from Darwen (BR), bus 51 to Anchor Hotel.

HONOURS

FA CUP SEMI-FINAL 1881

Lancashire League 1902

Lancashire Combination 1931, 1932, 1973, 1975

Lancs Junior Cup 1973

George Watson Trophy 1973

NWCL League Cup 1983

Lancashire Floodlight Trophy 1990

Darwen's glory days date to well over 100 years ago, when they reached the Football League and got to the semi-finals of the FA Cup, and so their mere survival to still be playing senior non-League football is a tribute in itself. The club were formed in 1875 and eventually joined the Football Alliance in 1889, playing at Barley Bank, which had a basic wooden grandstand which remained until the club left the ground and the Football League in 1899. They had reached that lofty height in 1891 and were promoted to Division One in 1893, but were forced to drop into the Lancashire League, when they lost the ground and were embroiled in a court case with an ex-player which saw the club forced to sell the dressing tents and railings from Barley Bank.

Members started from scratch at the Anchor Ground and a new stand went up, legend has it from the remains of the old one, and Darwen continued for four years until switching to the Lancashire Combination, where they stayed until 1975.

They won the Lancs League title in 1902, but their next dominant spell came in the 30's, when they took the Combination in successive years, also twice winning the League Cup.

Throughout this time the ground was developed, especially in 1932 when Darwen's FA Cup tie at Arsenal generated enough funds to cover the near 'Gracie Fields End', and at one stage the Anchor had three large stands, capable of holding close to 10,000 people, indeed over 9,000 saw an FA Cup tie with Luton Town in the early days.

In 1975 Darwen did the League and Cup double in the Combination, and joined the stronger Cheshire League for seven years, and when that was absorbed into the North-West Counties League they were founder members, where their only honour to date is the League Cup in 1983.

EASTWOOD HANLEY

C/O Newcastle Town FC, Lyme Valley Stadium, Lilleshall Rd, Clayton, Newcastle-u-Lyne

Tel: 01762 662351 or 662350

Secretary: John Reid, 2 Northam Rd, Sneyd Green,
Stoke-on-Trent ST1 6DA Tel: 01782 279062

DIRECTIONS
As Newcastle Town (see page 566).

Colours: Blue and white halves

Nickname: Blues

Ground details: As per Newcastle Town FC

Clubhouse on ground: Yes

Record attendance: 5,000 v Stoke City in 1978

Biggest win: 11-2 v Manchester University

Biggest defeat: 1-9 v Alvechurch

Record appearances: Mick Astley 1968-1978

Record goalscorer in one season: A.Tunstall 84 in 1963-64

Record fee received: £ 1,800 for Mick Bates to Leek Town

HONOURS

Staffs County League and Cup 1965

Gylchrist Cup 1968

Sentinel Cup 1968, 1969, 1988

Staffs FA Vase 1982, Staffs Senior Cup 1986

Manager 1996-97: Jimmy Wallace, Assistant Manager: Chris Hagan

Chairman: Les Wagg, Vice Chairman: Geoff Eccleston

Eastwood Hanley were formed in 1946 and celebrated their 50th anniversary on May 17th this year. They began in local leagues before moving to the Mid-Cheshire and then Manchester Leagues, before in 1968 moving across to the West Midlands League, where they remained for ten seasons. They then went back up country and joined the Cheshire County League in 1978 until it was merged to form the North West Counties League in 1982. Eastwood were founder members and were runners up in Division Two gaining promotion in 1984. Progress up the pyramid came in 1987 when an expanding Northern Premier League accepted them into the First Division and they spent three years there before being relegated back to the NWCL.

Hanley have had a little Cup success, with the Staffs Senior Cup in 1986 following wins in the Sentinel Cup and the Staffs FA Vase. Earlier the club did the County League and Cup double.

The Hanley part of the club name was added to contrast it with Eastwood Town from Nottinghamshire. Their Trent Mill ground was subject to continual and prolonged acts of vandalism and after losing the dressing rooms to an arson attack, the club conceded defeat and were given a lifeline when Kidsgrove Athletic agreed to a groundshare for two years. This season they have moved in with Newcastle Town whilst they size up the possibilities of moving back home at some point.

GLOSSOP NORTH END

Surrey Street, Glossop, Derbyshire Tel: 01457 855469

Secretary: Peter Hammond, 15 Longmoor Rd, Glossop,
Derbyshire SK13 9NH Tel: 01457 863852

Chairman: P.Heginbotham 19 Grange Rd, Bramhall,
Stockport, Cheshire SK7 3BD Tel: 0161 439 3932

Colours: Blue and white

Nickname: Hillmen

Capacity: 1,500

Seating: 250

Covered standing: 300

Clubhouse on ground: Yes

Record attendance: 10,736 v Preston North End
FA Cup 1914

HONOURS

FA CUP QUARTER-FINAL 1909

FOOTBALL LEAGUE DIV 2 Runners up 1899

FA AMATEUR CUP Quarter-final 1909

Lamot Pils Trophy 1991

Manchester League 1928

Gilgryst Cup 1923, 1930, 1935, 1975

DIRECTIONS

A57 (Manchester-Sheffield) to
Glossop town centre, turn into
Shrewsbury Street, follow to top of
the hill, left at t-junction for ground.
700 yds from Glossop (BR). Buses
236 & 237 from Manchester.

Manager for 1996-97: Syd White

Glossop North End were founded in 1886 and began playing friendlies. They entered the North
Cheshire League in 1890 and turned professional in 1894. Four years later after applying three
times, they were accepted into the Football League and won promotion in their first season. They
had just one year in Division One, finishing bottom, with a best win of 3-0 over Nottingham Forest
and they stayed in Division Two until finishing bottom of that, in 1915, whereupon they were not
elected.

Their Chairman and benefactor through those times was Sir Samuel Hill Wood who later became
Chairman of Arsenal FC. They ceased playing from 1916 to 1919 but were re-formed by Sir
Oswald Partington MP, who played in the 1890's. They joined the Lancashire Combination and the
Manchester League , winning the latter in 1928, and the Gilgryst Cup three times, adding a fourth
in 1949.

They moved from the old League ground in North Road to the present ground in Surrey Street in
1955 and since then have played in the Cheshire League before becoming founder-members of the
NWCL.

In 1991, after a financial problem the club almost folded, when the then chairman sold their ground
to the Council and left them with huge debts, but a new board took over, and reverting to their old
name of Glossop North End, which was abandoned in the 1890's, they were saved. Floodlights were
erected and improvements done to enable the club to take their place in Division One.

HOLKER OLD BOYS

Rakesmoor Lane, Hawcoat, Barrow-in-Furness, Cumbria Tel: 01229 828176

Secretary: Allan Wilson, 56 Fairfield Lane, Barrow-in-Furness, Cumbria Tel: 01229 822983

Chairman: R. Moffatt, 5 Highlands Ave, Barrow-in-Furness, Cumbria Tel: 01229 823747

Colours: Green and white hoops

Nickname: Cobs

Capacity: 2,500

Seating: 220

Covered standing: 300

Clubhouse on ground: Yes

Record attendance: 1, 240 v Barrow Lancs ATS Cup 1995-96

Biggest win: 12-0

Record appearances: Derek Biddle and Peter McKenna

DIRECTIONS

M6 junction 36, A590 to Barrow-in-Furness, on entering Barrow, continue across roundabout, 2nd right (Dalton Lane) to top of road, right into Rakesmoor Lane, ground on right.

HONOURS

West Lancs League 1987

Lancs Junior Shield 1989 and 1991

Manager 1996-97: John Goodwin

Assistant Manager: Kevin Proctor

Vice Chairman: Ray Sharpe

Programme Editor: Ian Elliott

Operating in the shadow of Barrow, undoubtedly one of the biggest non-league clubs in the country, Holker Old Boys have done magnificently to consolidate in the North West Counties League, as the amount of travelling it entails is immense. The first step up the long ladder for the club, which was founded in 1936, came in 1970 when they progressed from the Furness Premier League to the West Lancs League. Promotion to the North West Counties League was accepted in 1991, and Holker Old Boys finished in fifteenth place in each of their first two seasons in Division Two. However, third place, and with it promotion, was achieved in 1993-94. Holker finished fourteenth in their first season in the top flight, and eleventh last time. They are expected to improve further this season following an impressive recruitment drive, which has included the capture of ex-Barrow favourite Stuart Todhunter.

KIDSGROVE ATHLETIC

Clough Hall, Hollinwood Road, Kidsgrove, Stoke-on-Trent Tel: 01782 784582

Secretary: David Stringer, 66 Chatterley Dr, Kidsgrove, Stoke-on-Trent Tel: 01782 785407

Chairman: P C Stonier, 30 Windmill Ave, Kidsgrove, Stoke-on-Trent Tel: 01782 772331

Colours: Blue and white

Capacity: 4,500

Seating: 250

Covered standing: 500

Clubhouse on ground: Yes

Record attendance: 620 v Crewe Alexandra Friendly July 1995

Record win: 23-0 v Cross Heath WMC Staffs Junior Cup Oct 1965

Record defeat: 2-7 v Glossop NE NWCL 1993-94

DIRECTIONS

M6 junction 16, A500 towards Stoke, 2nd junction onto A34 towards Manchester, turn right at 1st set of lights into Cedar Avenue. 2nd right into Lower Ash Road, and 3rd left into Hollinwood Road to ground.

HONOURS

Mid-Cheshire League 1971, 1979, 1987, 1988

League Cup 1968, 1970, 1986

Staffs County FA Vase 1988 and 1990

Sentinel Cup 1967, 1977, 1985

Leek Cup 1985, Hanley Cup 1986

Manager for 1996-97: Peter Bartley

Assistant manager: Wayne Smith

Chairman: Phil Stonier

Vice Chairman: Harry Thomas

The present Kidsgrove Athletic were formed in 1952, after breaking away from Kidsgrove Town whose history goes back to the turn of the century. Athletic joined the Burslem and Tunstall League and after spells playing at Bathpool Park and Vickers and Goodwins, they moved to the current home at Clough Hall in 1958. A year later they reached the Sentinel Cup final and a year after that became Division Two champions. After winning Division One in 1963 they joined the Staffs County League, winning that Division Two at the first attempt. Two years later they were League champions and carried off the Hanley Cup and the Staffs Challenge Cup. In 1967 Athletic joined the Mid-Cheshire League, winning the League Cup in 1968 and the title itself in 1971. Two further championships and three League Cups followed and in 1979 they became the first winners of the Staffs FA Vase, winning it again ten years later.

In 1990 the club moved up to the North-West Counties League, where they remain in Division One, currently sharing their ground with Eastwood Hanley.

MAINE ROAD

Manchester FA group, Brantingham Rd, Chorlton-Cum-Hardy, Manchester M14 Tel: 0161 862 9619

Secretary: Kevin Hunter, 157 Aston Ave, Fallowfield, Manchester M14 7HN Tel: 0161 226 9937

Press: Mr P. Ramsden, 216 Fog Lane, Didsbury, Manchester M20 6EL Tel: 0161 448 1659

Chairman: R. Meredith, The Firs, Carr Wood Rd, Bramhall, Stockport, Cheshire Tel 0161 486 1892

Nickname: The Blues

Capacity: 2,000   Seating: 200

Covered standing: 700   Clubhouse on ground: Yes

Record attendance: 875 v Altrincham FA Cup 1990

Biggest win: 15-1 v Little Hulton Sept 2nd 1986

Biggest defeat: 0-6 Old Altrinchamians Sept 22nd 1979

Record appearances: Robin Gibson 382

Record goalscorer in one season Steve Burns 59 1982-83

Record goalscorer in aggregate John Wright 140

HONOURS

Manchester Premier League 1983, 1984, 1985, 1986

Div 1 1974 and Div 2 1973 and 1986, Gilgryst Cup 1983 and 1984

Murray Shield 1973 and 1974, Manchester Premier Cup 1988

Challenge Cup 1983, 1985, 1986, 1987

Intermediate Cup 1976 and 1977, Manchester Amateur Cup 1973

NWCL Div 2 1990, Altrincham Senior Cup 1986 and 1987

Manager: D. Barber, Assistant Manager: C. Nicholson

DIRECTIONS

M63 Junction 7, A56 towards city centre, right onto A5145, onto A6010 to Chorlton, through lights (ignore pedestrian lights), left at next lights into Withington Road, left into Brantingham Road, ground 400 yds on left. Manchester A-Z ref. 100/6B. 2 miles from Stretford (Metrolink(tram)), 3 miles from Piccadilly and Victoria (BR). Buses 85, 102, 103, 168, 188, 276, 277.

The club was formed in 1955 as City Supporters Rusholme, when the former Chairman and a few friends formed a team, who after a few friendlies, played in the Rusholme Sunday League.

In the late 60's they moved to the Manchester Amateur Sunday League, moving headquarters to the newly-built Maine Road Social Club, hence the current name.

In 1972 both sides won their leagues, plus the Manchester Sunday Cup, and the success prompted a change to Saturday football in the form of the Manchester League.

Success followed and after several years of moving grounds, they moved to their present home in Brantingham Road in 1980. After a lean spell the Manchester League was won in in 1984, the first of four consecutive titles. Manchester County FA built their new complex at the ground during the late 80's, and Maine Road were accepted into the North-West Counties League. The second season ended a runners up, but promotion was denied due to ground grading, but it came in 1990, with the Second Division Championship. 1988 proved to be a watermark for the club, as when they beat Irlam Town in the Premier Cup it meant that the club had won all five County Cups.

The club's previous grounds were mostly undeveloped and included Hough End Playing Fields, until 1973, Ward Street OB for two years and the Tootal Sports Ground until 1979, when they played at Leasfield.

MOSSLEY

Seel Park, Market Street, Mossley, Lancashire Tel: 01457 832369 or 836104 Social

Secretary: Andrew Fenna, 254 Fairfield Rd, Droylsden, Manchester M43 6AN Tel: 0161 370 0508

Chairman: F.P.Whelan Tel: 01942 879804

Colours: White and black

Nickname: Lilywhites

Capacity: 4,500

Seating: 200

Covered standing: 1,500

Clubhouse on ground: Yes

Record attendance: 7,000 v Stalybridge Celtic 1950

Record fee received: £25,000 for Eamon O'Keefe 1979

DIRECTIONS

Off M62, from west via Oldham, Lees and Grotton, from east via Saddleworth. From M1 or Sheffield via Stalybridge then Mossley. Half mile from Mossley (BR), buses 153 from Manchester, 343 from Oldham or 350 from Ashton.

HONOURS

FA TROPHY Runners up 1980

Northern Premier League 1979 and 1980

League Cup 1979 and 1989

Challenge Shield 1989

Cheshire County League Cup 1921 and 1961

Manchester Premier Cup 1989 and 1991

Manchester Intermediate Cup 1961, 1967, 1968

Manchester Challenge Shield 1915, 1934, 1938, 1949

Reporter Floodlit Cup 1975 and 1989

Mossley were formed in 1903 as Park Villa and initially played in the Ashton League but after one season they changed their name to Mossley Juniors and in 1909 became Mossley FC. They moved to the Lancashire League, then the Lancs Combination and in 1919 were founder members of the Cheshire County League.

After more than 50 years the Lilywhites were elected to the Northern Premier League in 1972. They grew to be a formidable force, winning the league two years running in 1979 and 1980, followed by three runners up spots. During this time the club had its proudest moment when they reached the final of the FA Trophy at Wembley after beating Altrincham, Blyth Spartans and Boston United. Sadly they lost the final to Dagenham 2-1, but Granada TV filmed the day for posterity. Their great run ended abruptly in 1984 when they were forced to re-apply after finishing bottom, and since then it has been a struggle as Hyde United and Stalybridge have become the more powerful sides in the area. In 1989 saw a brief revival with the League Cup and Manchester Premier Cup won, but relegation to Division One was unavoidable and after a number of managerial changes, the club dropped into the North West Counties League two years ago.

NANTWICH TOWN

Jackson Avenue, off London Rd, Nantwich, Cheshire Tel: 01270 624098

Secretary: Arthur Birtwistle, 26 Kinloch Close, Crewe, Tel 01270 258751

Chairman: Roy Tilley, 20 Prince Edward St, Nantwich, Cheshire Tel: 01270 627827

Nickname: The Dabbers   Capacity: 1,500

Colours: Black and white stripes   Seating: 150

Covered standing: 400   Clubhouse on ground: Yes

DIRECTIONS

M6 Junction 16, A500 for Nantwich (about 8 miles), continue on A52 over railway crossing (London Road), first right into Jackson Avenue. From Chester take A51. 3 miles from Crewe (BR).

Record attendance: at Jackson Avenue, 2,750 v Altrincham Cheshire Senior Cup 1967 and at Kingsley Fields, 5,121 v Winsford Utd, Cheshire Senior Cup replay 1920

Record fee paid: £ 4,000 to Stafford Rangers - D.Dawson

Record fee received: £ 2,500 for Paul Mayman to Northwich Vics

HONOURS

Cheshire County League 1981, Cheshire Senior Cup 1933 and 1976

Cheshire Junior Cup 1896, Crewe and District Cup 1898, 1899, 1902, 1962

Crewe Amateur Combination 1947, Mid-Cheshire League 1964

League Cup 1962 and 1964, Cheshire Amateur Cup 1964

Mid-Cheshire Cup 1949, North West Counties League Cup 1995

General Manager: Clive Jackson, 1st Team Coach: Dave Pullar

Director of Coaching: John Brydon, Programme Editors Che Kerin and Dave Jodrell

Programme was voted Best in NWCL in 1992

Founded in 1884 as Nantwich FC, (the Town was not added until 1973), the club spent its early years participating in a variety of local leagues including the Shropshire, and then Crewe and District before moving to the Manchester League and Lancashire and Cheshire Combinations. After World War 1 they became founder members of the Cheshire County League and although never dominating the league, they won the Senior Cup, beating ICI in front of 8,000 fans at the Drill Field. After the Second War the Dabbers were again founder members, this time of the Mid-Cheshire League in which they completed the treble of League, League Cup and Cheshire Amateur Cup in 1963 under Alan Ball Senior. With the leading Cheshire clubs vacating the County League in 1968, Nantwich went back in and success came in 1976 when the dabbers beat Runcorn 5-4 in the Senior Cup final at Gresty Road. Probably the club's finest hour came in May 1981 when a four figure crowd saw them clinch the County League by beating runners up Hyde United. It led to the club being part of the new North-West Counties League, sadly finishing bottom in the first season and dropping to Division Two where they stayed until 1986, when they dropped to Division Three, but happily they bounced back and have since reached the League Cup final. Nantwich played at the current ground from the start, when it was known as London Road, but during the Great War it had been used for growing oats and so for 1919 they played at the cricket ground in Kingsley Fields, erecting a wooden stand for 500. A record crowd of over 5,000 once saw a Senior Cup replay with Winsford, but problems with the cricket square led them to move to London Road in 1921. Again after the Second War the club could not use London Road and so played on Barony Park, but even that was not ready and so a few Crewe Combination games were played at the Grammar School. Eventually with the help of a loan, the club bought the London Road ground for £750, where they remain today. In 1995 Andy Locke scored the fastest hat-trick in the history of the FA Cup, in 2 minutes 20 seconds, against Droylsden.

NEWCASTLE TOWN

Lyme Valley Parkway, Lilleshall Rd, Clayton, Newcastle-under-Lyne, Staffs
Tel: 01782 662351 Social club: 01782 662350
Secretary: John Cotton, 293 Weston Rd, Weston Coyney,
Staffs ST3 6HA Tel: 01782 333445
Commercial manager: Paul Robinson
Chairman: J.W.Walker, Green View, 15 Napples Dr,
Westlands, Newcastle-u-Lyne Tel 01782 617412
Press officer: Ray Tatton

DIRECTIONS
M6 junction 15, A500 for Stoke, left at roundabout A519 for Newcastle, right at 2nd roundabout into Stafford Avenue, 1st left into Tittensor Road to ground 3 miles from Stoke-on-Trent (BR).

Nickname: Castle   Colours: Royal blue and red
Capacity: 4,000   Seating: 300
Covered Standing: 1,000   Clubhouse on ground.: Yes
Record attendance.: 3,586 v Stoke City Friendly August 1991
Biggest win: 8-0 v Skelmersdale Utd (a) 1995-96
Biggest defeat: 0-5 v Eastwood Hanley (a)
Record appearance: Phil Butler 249 NWCL only
Record goalscorer in one season: John Burndred 39 1995-96
Record goalscorer in aggregate: Shaun Wade 80 NWCL only
Record fee Andy Holmes (Leek Town)

HONOURS
Newcastle Town and Parkway Clayton, North West Counties Div 2 Trophy 1992
Floodlit Trophy 1993 and 1996, Walsall Senior Cup 1994 and 1995
Mid Cheshire League Div 1 1986 and Div 2 1983 and 1991, League Cup 1985
Midland Sunday Cup 1986 and 1987, Potteries Sunday League and Cup 1985 and 1986
Staffs FA Vase 1980, Staffs FA Sunday Cup 1980, Leek Cup 1988, Sentinel Sunday Cup 1985
Manager: Glyn Chamberlain, Assistant Manager: Trevor Brissett
Chairman: John Walker, Vice Chairman: Ken Walshaw
Town's programme was voted NWCL Programme of the Year last season

From a humble beginning in 1964 as a Sunday side, the club has developed to their current status in the North-West Counties League. Their 3,000 capacity stadium has been given the necessary grading to move on should they be able to. The club emerged in its current format from a merger of two clubs, Parkway Clayton and Newcastle Town in 1986. The merged clubs were runners up in the Mid-Cheshire League in their first season moving into the North-West Counties League in 1987 with the reserves in the Mid-Cheshire Division Two. They were runners up in Division One gaining promotion as well as winning the Lamot Pils Trophy, and the club enjoyed a run to the 5th Round of the FA Vase the same year. Many other honours have come their way in a short space of time including the Walsall Senior Cup.

Parkway Clayton FC were formed in 1964 as Parkway Hanley, playing Sunday football in Hanley Park. They changed their name when they moved to Northwood Lane and switched to Saturdays with much success. Newcastle Town were a re-formation of Clayton Park in 1980, also playing at Northwood Lane. They played in the Staffs County League for two years before joining the Mid-Cheshire League. They moved to Lilleshall Road and the ground has developed with the club and for this season new perimeter fencing, turnstile blocks, a secretaries office, players entrance, physio room, kit room, press box and directors lounge will be added to comply with requirements for the Northern Premier League.

The club's Lyme Valley Parkway ground has an interesting history, having been built during the 50's as part of a much larger complex involving rugby and cricket. The banked track around the pitch was redundant for some time as a former velodrome and the whole area was used by Stoke City as a training ground.

Last season saw the club enjoy runs in the Staffs Senior, Walsall Senior and Staffs Floodlight Cups, all of which ended in the semi-finals, but they were winners of the Floodlit Trophy.

PENRITH

Southend Road Ground, Penrith, Cumbria, Tel: 01768 863212 match days only

Secretary: D. Johnson, Greenacre, 2, Bridge Lane, Penrith CA11 8JB Tel: 01768 862994

Chairman: As above

Colours: Blue and white

Nickname: Blues

Capacity: 2,500

Seating: 200

Covered standing: 1,000

Clubhouse on ground: Yes

Record attendance: 4,000 v West Auckland 1961

Biggest win: 13-2 v Parton Utd

Biggest defeat: 0-13 v Bishop Auckland

Record appearances: Ray Thornton

Record goalscorer in total: Charles Short

DIRECTIONS

M6 junction 40, onto dual carriageway to Appleby & Scotch Corner, turn off at next roundabout approx half a mile into Penrith, follow A6 into town, take 1st left for ground. Three quarters of a mile from Penrith (BR).

HONOURS

Cumberland Senior Cup 1947, 1948, 1951, 1961, 1962, 1963, 1964, 1965, 1966, 1971, 1973, 1975, 1981

Manager 1996-97: Geoff Byers

Vice Chairman: M.Robson

Press Officer: Mr J.Bell 01768 863898

Penrith FC was founded in 1894 and first played in local leagues including the Carlisle and District, which they won a number of times. Just after the Second War they joined the Northern League where they stayed until 1982. In the 30 odd years they were runners up once and were twice beaten in League Cup finals.

In 1981-82 they reached the First Round of the FA Cup, beating Chester at Penrith. They lost 3-0 at Doncaster Rovers in the next round in what was their last season in the Northern League. They moved to the newly formed North West Counties League as founder members and in 1984 they were runners up to Stalybridge Celtic and three years later joined the newly formed Northern Premier League Div 1. After two seasons they returned relegated to the NWCL where their only success was in taking the Floodlit Trophy.

PRESCOT CABLES

Hoghton Road, Sutton, St Helens, (ST HELENS TOWN FC) Tel: 01744 817225

Secretary: Dot Lace, 20 Cable Rd, Prescot,
Tel 0151 426 6440

Chairman: Ted Mercer, 2 Alness Drive, Rainhill,
Merseyside Tel: 0151 426 1794

DIRECTIONS

As St. Helens Town (see page 571).

Nickname: The Tigers

Club colours: Gold and Black

Record attendance: 8,122 v Ashton National 1932

Ground information as for St Helens Town FC

HONOURS

Lancashire Combination 1957

League Cup 1948

Cheshire County League 1979

Division Two 1977

Mid-Cheshire League 1977

Liverpool Non-League Cup 1952, 1953, 1959, 1961

Liverpool Challenge Cup 1928, 1929, 1930, 1949, 1962, 1978

Lancs Intermediate Cup 1896

George Mahon Cup 1924, 1926, 1927, 1937

Lord Wavertree Cup 1966

Prescot AFC was formed in 1884 when the 30 year old local cricket club decided to form a football club to give themselves something to do in the winter. After playing friendlies they decoded on something more serious by entering the Liverpool and District League and the Liverpool Cup. Progress was so good that they entered the FA Cup in 1891, a home game against Crewe Alexandra attracting a crowd of 3,000 to the old Slacky Brow ground on the Warrington Road, where the team played before moving to Hope Street in 1906.

The new ground was known as the Athletic Ground and consequently the club was renamed Prescot Athletic FC. They entered the Liverpool County Combination and after the Great War discarded the Athletic tag to become known as Prescot AFC as it is today, now for the third time in its history.

In 1928 the local expanding cable company became interested in the welfare of the club and donated a magnificent 1,000 seater stand, which lasted until tragically destroyed by fire in 1960. Due to this interest Prescot Cables was created with team colours becoming amber and black, as the first insulated cable drawn at Prescot was covered with amber and black paper. In 1928 they joined the Lancashire Combination, which they enjoyed for 50 years apart from three seasons in the 30's when they played in the Cheshire County League. In 1929 the club made a bold attempt to join the Football League North, together with four other hopefuls. All applicants failed although Mansfield Town got in two years later.

In 1975, under the name of Prescot Town, they were voted out of the Lancs Combination and joined the Mid-Cheshire League which they won at the first attempt. Two years later the name Prescot Cables was re-taken and they joined the Cheshire County League again until 1982 when they were founder members of the North West Counties League. On becoming a Limited Company in 1990 they reverted once again to Prescot AFC.

Since then the club have suffered a traumatic time and were forced to move from Hope Street when a new Rugby League club took over, and they played the 1995-96 season at Knowsley, moving to St Helens during this summer.

ROSSENDALE UNITED

Dark Lane, Newchurch, Rawtenstall, Rossendale, Lancs Tel: 01706 215119

Secretary Brian Melia, 4 Brow Edge, Newchurch,
Rossendale, Lancs. BB4 7TT Tel 01706 212634 (h) and fax

Chairman: Jack Feber, 82 Woodside Cres, Rossendale,
Lancs BB4 7UG Tel 01706 214 977

Nickname: The Stags   Colours: Blue and White

Capacity: 4,000   Seating: 400

Covered standing: 500   Clubhouse on ground: Yes

Record attendance: 3,400 v Shrewsbury Town FA Cup
1975 also 12,000 v Bolton Wanderers at Bury FC

Biggest win: 10-0 v Wigan Rovers Lancs Comb 1969-70

Biggest defeat: 0-14 v Morecambe Lancs Comb. 1967-68

Record appearances: Johnny Clarke 770 1947 to 1965

Record goalscorer in one season: Bob Scott 72 1959-60

Record goalscorer in aggregate: Bob Scott 223

Record fee received £1,500 for Dave O'Neill from Huddersfield Town

Record fee paid £3,000 to Buxton for Jimmy Clarke 1992

DIRECTIONS

M66, then A682 to Rawtenstall, keep left around roundabout past library until Bishop Blaize pub, right into Newchurch Road (past market), after a mile turn right into Staghills Road - through estate to ground (half mile). Buses 32 or 33 from Rawtenstall (to Todmorden, Edgenride or Burnley) stop at ground.

HONOURS

North-West Counties League 1989 and League Cup 1994

Lancs Combination 1927, Div 2 in 1957 and League Cup 1929

Cheshire County League 1971 and League Cup 1974

Lancs Junior Cup (ATS Trophy) 1912 and 1973, Central Lancs League 1900

Lancs Floodlit Cup 1971, 1972, 1974

Rossendale United were formed in 1898 and joined the Lancashire Combination after only one season in the Lancashire League. Their first success was the league title, followed by the Combination Cup two years later. However the only further success until leaving the league in 1970 was a Second Division title in 1957. Their move to the Cheshire League heralded the most successful years in the club's history under the management of Les Rigby and Alan Kirkham. They won the Cheshire League once, were runners up twice and between 1970 and 1975 had won the Lancashire Junior Cup, the Floodlight Trophy, the Cheshire League Cup and the Ashworth Cup twice. They also got to the 2nd Round proper of the FA Cup in 1972, losing to Bolton Wanderers. In 1975 they got to the 1st Round, losing to Shrewsbury Town, but this was to be the last success for some time as they ran into difficulties over a ground lease, culminating in a lengthy legal battle to stay at Dark Lane. They kept the ground and were promoted to the North West Counties League, and after getting to the FA Vase 5th round a year earlier, they lost the title on goal difference to Colne Dynamoes. A year later they went one better in winning the league in style with 22 games without defeat, again reaching the FA Vase 5th Round. From 1989 to 1993 United played in the Northern Premier League, but with little success and in 1993, after the worst season in the club's history, they were relegated back to the NWCL. The last two seasons have been a struggle and in May, after finishing last but one, they were relegated to Division Two.

Dark Lane has been a sports ground since the last century, when a rugby team played there. In 1890, many players had changed to the association code and Myrtle Grove FC changed their name to Rossendale United and began playing there. They disbanded in 1897 and the current club were formed on July 6th 1898, with the first match at Dark Lane on September 3rd against Oswaldtwistle Rovers FC.

SALFORD CITY

Moor Lane, Kersal, Salford, Manchester Tel: 0161 792 6287

Secretary: Stephen Blake, 71 Blandford Rd, Salford, M6 6BD Tel: 0161 737 0922

Chairman: H.Brearley, 77 Doveleys Rd, Salford, Manchester Tel: 0161 792 6287

Colours: Tangerine and black

Nickname: Ammies

Capacity: 8,000

Seating: 260

Covered standing: 600

Clubhouse on ground: Yes

Record attendance: 3,000 v Whickham FA Vase 1981

DIRECTIONS

M62 junction 17, A56 Bury New Road to Manchester, continue through 4 sets of lights, right into Moor Lane, 1st left into Neville Road to ground. 4 miles from Manchester Victoria (BR). Buses 96, 139, 94, 95 to Moor Lane.

HONOURS

Lancashire Amateur Cup 1973, 1975, 1977

Manchester Senior Cup 1974, 1975, 1976, 1977

Manchester Challenge Cup 1974, 1975, 1976

Manchester League 1975, 1976, 1977, 1979

Division One 1969

Open Trophy: 1976

Manager 1996-97: Alan Kershaw

Assistant Manager: Graham Taylor

The club was formed in 1940 as Salford Central, and they progressed steadily through local leagues until stepping into the Manchester League in 1963 and changing their name to Salford Amateurs. The 'Ammies' as they had become known became force in the early 70's, winning the Lancs Amateur Cup three times and in one season seven trophies were won. The prestigious Manchester Challenge Trophy was also claimed in 1975 and 1976 with the Champion of Champions Cup in 1978.

In 1979 the club took on the challenge of restoring the current ground, which was derelict and abandoned having previously been a rugby ground. It was restored and passed ready for entry into Cheshire League football in 1980. A year later Salford enjoyed a run in the FA Vase which saw Whickham visit, a match seen by 3,000 people, a club record. When the NWCL was formed in 1982 the ground was again acceptable and the club joined as founder members, moving up to the First Division when the NPL expanded and took many leading clubs.

In 1989 Salford played at Old Trafford in the Premier Cup final and installed lights at Moor Lane. They also lost the Amateurs tag and entered the FA Cup for the first time in 1990, although in the league they struggled and were relegated. Re-structuring of the league saw Salford back in the top flight and another name change saw them as Salford City FC.

ST HELENS TOWN

Hoghton Rd, Sutton, St Helens, Merseyside WA9 3HU Tel: 01744 817225 or 812721 Social club

Secretary: W.J. Noctor, 95 Sutton Park Drive, Marshalls Cr, St Helens, M'side WA9 3TR Tel: 01744 816182

Chairman and Press officer: J.Barratt, 4 Grant Close, St Helens, Merseyside WA10 2HG Tel: 01744 735703

Colours: Blue and white stripes   Nickname: Town

Capacity: 4,400   Seating: 250

Covered standing: 275   Clubhouse on ground: Yes

Record attendance: 4,000 v Manchester City (Bert Trautmann transfer match) 1950

Biggest win: 10-4 v Everton 'B' 1954

Biggest defeat: 1-8 v Liverpool Reserves 1961

Record appearances: Alan Wellens

Record goalscorer in one season: Mervyn Bull 47 1972-73

Record goalscorer in total: Steve Pennington

Record fee received: £2,800 for Bryan Griffiths from Wigan Ath. Nov 1988

DIRECTIONS

M62 junction 7, at roundabout take 5th exit (St Helens linkroad, A570) for 3 miles, at 3rd roundabout take exit for Sutton, at next roundabout take 1st exit to lights, follow road to right, down Robins Lane, straight on to Station Road, at crossroads (station on right) straight across into Leonard Street, right at t-junction, ground on right. Buses 121, 122, 5D, 41, 6 to St Helens Junction.

HONOURS

FA VASE WINNERS 1987, George Mahon Cup 1949

Lancs Combination 1972 and Div 2 1951, Bass Charrington Cup 1974

Manager 1996-97: Jim McBride, Assistant Manager: B.Howard, Chairman: J.Barrett

The current club is the second to bear the name as the original set up was founded in 1903 and played at the old Greyhound Stadium until folding in 1923. They were re-formed in 1946 when businessmen bought Hoghton Road and the early years were a boom time as they joined the Lancs League Div 2 which they won in 1951. They switched between Div's 1 and 2 until the league reduced in the late 60's, and in 1972 the club won the league for the only time along with the Bass Charrington Cup in the same year. In 1974 they switched to the Cheshire County League where they remained until it was absorbed into the new North-West Counties League in 1982. They avoided relegation and improved to reach the last qualifying round of the Cup in 1985, but all that paled into insignificance in 1987 when the club went all the way to Wembley and beat Warrington Town in the FA Vase final.As is so often the case, the side soon broke up, but Saints finished third in the league in 1989, their highest placing. In 1994 success came again with the Challenge Cup final reached at Gigg Lane, although beaten by Rossendale Utd, and the same year saw Liverpool FC play a Liverpool Senior Cup match in front of 1, 000 plus. 1995 saw the club again finish third, behind Clitheroe and Bradford PA and last season, with resources stretched due to ground improvements, they were a creditable 8th.This season sees the Golden Jubilee of the club and also sees Prescot Cables AFC ground sharing after moving from Alt Park last May.

Hoghton Road has been home from the start, having once been used by Sutton Cricket Club and an RAF building was brought across from Haydock as an HQ. For one year the ground was up for sale and the club played on City Road, formed home of Pilkington's Rugby League side, but returned and began developing the ground which later saw greyhound racing and Rugby League in the shape of Runcorn Highfield.

TRAFFORD

Shawe View, Pennybridge Lane, Flixton, Urmston, Manchester M41 5DL Tel: 0161 747 1727

Secretary: Graham Foxall 62 Grosvenor Rd, Urmston, Manchester M41 5AQ Tel: 0161 746 9726

Chairman: Mr J.Ackerley, 23 Lowood Ave, Davyhulme, Manchester M41 8GD Tel: 0161 748 7014

Nickname.The North

Capacity: 2,500

Seating: 222

Covered standing: 500

Clubhouse on ground: Yes

DIRECTIONS

M63 junction 4, B5158 towards Urmston, 1st exit at island, right into Moorside Road at next lights, 2nd exit at next island, sharp left at next lights, 1st right into Pennybridge Lane (next to Bird-in-the-Hand pub), car park 100 yds on left - ground adjacent.

Biggest win: 10-0 v Haslingden St Mary's Lancs Amateur Shield Oct 12th 1991

Biggest defeat: 0-6 v Oldham Town NWCL Div 2 March 13th 1993

HONOURS

Lamot Pils Trophy 1994

Manager for 1996/97: David Law

North Trafford FC was formed in the summer of 1990 when football enthusiasts got together to form and develop a club of their own after many years experience with others. They acquired the use of the Shawe View pitch and dressing rooms which they shared with Trafford Borough Rugby League Club. In June they suffered an initial set back when their application to join the Mid-Cheshire League was turned down and for a while the only alternative was to merge with another club, however, due to a late withdrawal, the league invited them to fill the vacancy, thus putting the club on the first rung of the non-League pyramid.

Success came at once with runners up spot and promotion, but more significantly the club was given exclusive use of the ground when the Rugby Club disbanded their reserve side. A 30 year lease was secured and the club began a series of ground developments.

On the field the success continued and in 1992 a plan was started to get the club into the North West Counties League and after much toil the dream came true at the league AGM, with the club voted to Division 2. Promotion and the Lamot Pils Cup came in 1994, and with floodlights and a new stand in place, it was Division One football. In the 94-5 season, Trafford, as they were now known, reached the League Cup Final, played at Gigg Lane, Bury, and the Manchester Premier Cup Final, played at Boundary Park, Oldham.

Their Shawe View home has a fascination pedigree, having many years ago been the training ground of Manchester City FC in the late 50's. It has since been home at various times to Salford RLFC reserves, Altrincham Reserves and later Urmston Town, in the Manchester League. It lay overgrown and unused until North Trafford resurrected it.

VAUXHALL G M

Vauxhall Sports Ground, Rivacre Rd, Hooton, Ellesmere Port, Sth Wirral

Tel: 0151 328 1114 or club 0151 327 2115

Secretary: Stephen McInerney, 12 Merton Rd, Gt Sutton, Ellesmere Port, L66 2SW Tel: 0151 356 0941

Press Sec: Alan Bartley 5 Marlborough Rd, New Brighton, Wirral L45 1JE Tel 0151 639 3955

Chairman: A.J.Woodley 10 Cleveland Drive, Little Sutton, Sth Wirral Tel: 0850 757133

DIRECTIONS

Junction 5 of M53, south on A41. Turn into Hooton Green at Hooton crossroads, left at the t-junction, right at the next t-junction and the ground is 100 yds on the right.

Colours: All white   Nickname: The Motormen

Capacity: 3,250   Seating: 250

Covered standing: 800   Clubhouse on ground: Yes

Record attendance: 1,500 v English FA X1 1987

Biggest win: 12-2 v Blackpool Mechs 1995-96

Biggest defeat: 0-4 v Macclesfield Town 1995-96

Record appearances: Carl Nesbitt

Record goalscorer in one season: Graham Stamper 34

Record goalscorer in total: Graham Stamper

HONOURS

North-West Counties Div 2 1989 and 1996

Challenge Cup 1991

Manager 1996-97: Paul Rowlands

Assistant Manager: Archie Lloyd

Chairman: Tony Woodley

Vice Chairman: Len Jones

When Vauxhall Motors opened a new plant in Ellesmere Port it soon formed a football section. In the early days they played on company land at Hooton Park, but the company eventually bought land at Riveacre Road adjoining the clubhouse and after much toil, an enclosed football ground was completed.

It was opened by Bobby Robson, who brought a team of ex-Internationals to play a friendly.

The first season in the North West Counties League was in 1987 and they finished seventh, but a year later the club lost just one game in clinching the Division Two title, at home to Wren Rovers.

The long unbeaten run continued in the First Division until the end of September, and they ended the season fourth. Since then the club have reached the Challenge Cup final, where they beat Darwen at Bury, but as soon as they had arrived, they went, and left the league to drop into the West Cheshire League. They have returned and last season took the Division Two by a clear eight points from Atherton Collieries.

MAGHULL
FOOTBALL CLUB

FOUNDED 1921
GROUND : HALL LANE, MAGHULL

OFFICIAL PROGRAMME

MAGHULL F.C.

FOUNDED 1921

THE NORTH WEST
COUNTIES
FOOTBALL
LEAGUE

Price 50p

BURSCOUGH
Football Club
Victoria Park Burscough

est 1946

B.A.F.C

Official Sponsors

crown
COMPUTER PRODUCTS

1995/6

THE NORTH WEST COUNTIES LEAGUE DIVISION ONE

OFFICIAL MATCH DAY PROGRAMME

PROGRAMME SPONSORED BY
Rectella
INTERNATIONAL LIMITED

1877

N.W.C.F.L

THE BLUES REVIEW

CLITHEROE F.C

CLITHEROE · F·C

PROGRAMME ISSUE 95/96:35

Northwest Counties League
Division One
Saturday
27th April 1996
K.O 3.00 pm
MATCH SPONSOR
Science in Sport

REFEREE
MR. B.COWARD
BLACKPOOL
LINESMEN
Mr. A.CHRISTY
BLACKPOOL
Mr. J.J.SIMPSON
CARNFORTH

50p

The
WOODER'S
REVIEW

The Official Matchday Programme of
Garswood United Football Club 1995-96

CHAMPIONS!

GREEN INSULATION
MID-CHESHIRE LEAGUE DIVISION 1

Garswood United
v
CHEADLE HEATH

Saturday 20th April 1996 Kick Off
3.00pm

Today's Match Sponsor
ST. HELENS THEATRE ROYAL

1994-95
Lancashire Amateur
Cup Winners

Mid-Cheshire League
Cup Winners

Wigan Cup Winners

Liverpool County FA
Challenge Cup Finalists

Mid-Cheshire League
Programme of the Year

Main
Sponsors
MATTHEW BROWN

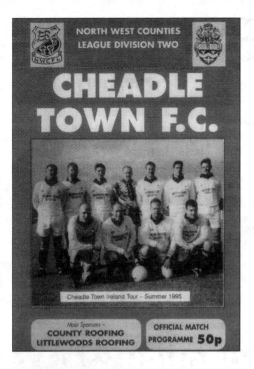

NORTH WEST COUNTIES
LEAGUE DIVISION TWO

CHEADLE TOWN F.C.

Cheadle Town Ireland Tour – Summer 1995

Main Sponsors –
COUNTY ROOFING
LITTLEWOODS ROOFING

OFFICIAL MATCH
PROGRAMME **50p**

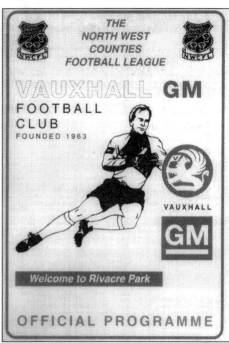

THE
NORTH WEST
COUNTIES
FOOTBALL LEAGUE

VAUXHALL **GM**
FOOTBALL CLUB
FOUNDED 1963

VAUXHALL

GM

Welcome to Rivacre Park

OFFICIAL PROGRAMME

SEASON
1995-1996

ST. HELENS TOWN

Members
of the
NORTH
WEST
COUNTIES
FOOTBALL
LEAGUE

MATCHDAY
50p
PROGRAMME

Hoghton Road
REVIEW

MATCHDAY PROGRAMME OF ST. HELENS TOWN AFC

Wednesday 28th February 1996, Kick Off 7.30pm
TOWN v MAINE ROAD
North West Counties League Division One

Main Sponsors
OGDENS TRAVEL

EASTWOOD
(Hanley)
FOOTBALL CLUB

North West Counties
Football League
DIVISION
ONE

PROGRAMME 50p.

ASHTON TOWN

Edge Green Street, Ashton-in-Makerfield, Wigan Tel: 01942 510677

Secretary: Chris Ashcroft, 8 Mason Close, Ashton-in-Makerfield, WN4 8SD Tel: 01942 203247

Chairman: G.Messer, 8 Diane Rd, Ashton-in-Makerfield, WN4 8SY Tel: 01942 203401

Formed: 1965

Colours: Red with white trim

Floodlights: No

Record attendance: 600 v Accrington Stanley 1976-77

DIRECTIONS

M6 junction 23, A49 to Ashton in M. Right at lights onto A58 towards Bolton. After 3/4 mile turn right at 'Rams Head' P.H. into Golbourne Road. After 200 yds right into Edge Green Street. Ground at end.

BACUP BOROUGH

West View, Cowtoot Lane, Blackthorn, Bacup, Lancs Tel: 01706 878655

Secretary: Frank Manning, 38 Acre Avenue, Stacksteads, Bacup OL13 0HN Tel: 01706 877460

Chairman: W.Heywood, 2 Church Street, Colne, Lancashire BB8 0LG Tel: 01282 863520

Colours: Black and white stripes

Nickname: The Boro

Capacity: 3,000

Seating: 500

Covered standing: 500

Clubhouse on ground: Yes

Record attendance: 4,980 v Nelson 1947

Record goalscorer in total: Jimmy Clarke

DIRECTIONS

From M62, M66 into A681 through Rawtenstall to Bacup centre, left onto A671 towards Burnley, after approx 300 yds right (immediately before Irwell Inn) climbing Cooper Street, right into Blackthorn Lane then first left into Cowtoot Lane to ground.

Honours

Lancashire Junior Cup 1911

Lancashire Combination 1947

BLACKPOOL MECHANICS

Jepson Way, Common Edge Rd, Blackpool, FY4 5DY Tel: 01253 761721

Secretary: William Singleton C/O BMFC
Tel: 01253 768105 (h)

Chairman: Henry Baldwin, 5 Ribble Rd, Blackpool, Lancs FY1 4AA Tel: 01253 20926

Colours: Green and yellow

Nickname: Mechs

Capacity: 2,000

Seating: 250

Covered standing: 1,500

Clubhouse on ground: Yes

Record attendance: 1,200 v Morecambe in Lancs Combination 1968

DIRECTIONS

M6 to M55, follow Airport signs. Left at roundabout along (Preston New Road) to lights, right into Whitehall Road, becomes School Road, to lights. Straight over main road and follow signs for Blackpool Mechanics F.C. to ground. Rail to Blackpool North - then bus 11c from Talbot Road bus station (next to rail station) and alight at Shovels Hotel, Common Edge Road.

Honours

North-West Counties League Div 3 1986; Lancs FA Shield 1958, 1961
West Lancs League 1961, 1962; Lancs Combination Bridge Shield 1973
George Watson Trophy 1976; Fylde and District League 1954 and 1957
Division Two 1951 and League Cup 1953 and 1958; Bannister Cup 1953 and 1957
Evening KO Cup 1962 Richardson Cup 1961 and 1962; Blackpool Co-op Medal 1955 and 1961
Manager for 1996-97 Steve Swallow

CASTLETON GABRIELS

Butterworth Park, Chadwick Lane, off Heywood Rd, Castleton, Rochdale Tel: 01706 527103

Secretary: David Lord, 34 Fairway, Castleton, Rochdale OL11 3BU Tel: 01706 522719

Colours: Blue and black stripes

Nickname: Gabs

Capacity: 1,500

Floodlights: Yes

Seating: 250

Covered standing: 250

Clubhouse on ground: Yes

Record attendance: 650 v Rochdale Pre-season friendly v Rochdale in 1991

for competitive match 450 v Bamber Bridge
Lancs Shield 1987

Biggest win: 8-0 v Squires Gate NWCL Div 2 1994

Biggest defeat: 1-10 v Blackpool Mechs NWCL Div 2 1995

DIRECTIONS

M62 junction 20, A6272M to roundabout. Left towards Castleton (A664 Edinburgh Way) to next roundabout, keeping Tesco Superstore to the left, take 1st exit to next roundabout, take 2nd exit into Manchester Road (A664), after just under miles turn right at 'Top House' P.H. into Heywood Road, to end and ground on right.

Honours

Manchester League and Murray Shield 1987

CHEADLE TOWN

Park Road Stadium, Park Road, Cheadle, Stockport SK8 2AN Tel: 0161 428 2510

Secretary: Susan Burton, 2 Lavington Ave, Cheadle, Stockport Tel: 0161 491 0823

Chairman: Chris Davies 33 Grasmere Ave, Heaton Chapel, Stockport Tel: 0161 432 7699

Press: Stuart Crawford c/o Football Ground

Colours: White and navy blue   Capacity: 3,000

Seating: 250   Covered standing: None

Clubhouse on ground: Yes

Record attendance: 1, 700 v Stockport County August 1994

Biggest win: 7-1 v Blackpool Mechs NWCL Div 1 Oct 1993

Record appearances: John McArdle

Record goalscorer in one season: Peter Tilley

Record goalscorer in total: Peter Tilley

DIRECTIONS

M63 junction 11, follow signs towards Cheadle, Park Road half mile on left. 1 mile from Gatley (BE), buses from Stockport.

Honours

Manchester Under 21 Lge 1968; Manchester Sunday League Premier Div 1970 Harry Goodwin Cup 1971 and Supp Shield 1975; Manchester Amateur Cup 1980 Derbyshire Cup 1981; Manchester League Div 1 1980

Manager 1996-97: Peter Blundell   Vice Chairman: Clive Williams

The club was founded in 1961 as Grasmere Rovers, an under 16 team in the Manchester Sunday League. They won the league in 1970 and became open age the year after and joined the Manchester League which heralded a marvellous era with Manchester Amateur Cup, Derbyshire Cup, and Manchester Challenge Cup finals reached. After ground sharing with Hyde United and Glossop, the club moved to Park Road in 1983 changing their name and since then the stadium, which has been a training ground for Manchester City in the past, was developed to a standard good enough for the NMCL.

Cheadle Town have been great ambassadors for the game, travelling the world under the banner of Manchester FC and playing in such stadia as the Azteca in Mexico and the Maracana in Rio.

In February 1995 a Manchester United X1 visited and opened the new floodlights and two years ago the record crowd assembled for a pre season friendly against Stockport County.

COLNE

Colne Dynamoes Stadium, Holt House, Colne, Lancs Tel: 01282 862545

Secretary: Jean Moore, 5 Haverholt Close, Colne BB8 9SN Tel: 01282 868857

Chairman: D.Blacklock, 7 Linton Gardens, Barrowford, Nelson Tel: 01282 696340

Colours: All Red

Floodlights: Yes

Covered standing: Yes

Seating: Yes

Clubhouse on ground: Yes

Colne FC are a new club, founded in the summer of 1996

DIRECTIONS

Approach from M65 junction 14. Colne is signposted. Alternative main roads in are A682, A56 and A6068.

DAISY HILL

Secretary Robert Naylor, 8 Bailey Fold, Westhoughton, Bolton BL5 3HH Tel: 01942 813720

Press: Jimmy Hilton, 43 Amber Gardens, Hindley, Wigan Tel: 01942 253114

Chairman: M.Ford, 30 Whitsundale, Westhoughton, Bolton BL5 3LQ Tel: 01942 819654

Treasurer Geoff Hughes, 141 Mornington Rd, Bolton Tel: 01204 494403

Colours: All royal blue   Capacity: 2,000

Floodlights: No   Seating: 200

Covered standing: 250   Clubhouse on ground: Yes

DIRECTIONS

M61 junction 5, A58 (Syndale Way/Park Road) for 1.5 miles, left into Leigh Road (B5235) for 1 mile, right fork into village then left. Straight forward between Church and School into St James Street. Ground 250 yds on the left. Half mile from Daisy Hill (BR).

Record attendance 2,000 v Horwich RMI Westhoughton Charity Cup final 1980

Record appearances: Alan Roscoe 450
Record goalscorer in total: Alan Roscoe 300

Honours

Lancs Amateur Shield 1962, 1972, 1987, Bolton Combination Div 1 1963

Premier Division 1973, 1976, 1978, Premier Cup 1960, 1962 1972, 1973 Division One Cup 1958

Westhoughton League and Tonge Cup 1922 and 1924

League Challenge Cup 1953, Wigan and District League 1897

Westhoughton Charity Cup 1902, 1924, 1925, 1957

Bolton Infirmary Cup 1932, Bolton Hospital Cup 1986, Atherton Charity Cup 1994

Westhoughton Medals Comp 1954, Chorley FC Amateur Cup 1964, Hindley Green Medals Comp 1922

Manager 1996-97: Jimmy Hilton

Assistant Manager: Tony Riley

Chairman: Mark Ford

The village of Daisy Hill first saw football in 1894, when records were first kept and the first known honours were exactly 100 years ago when the Wigan League was won along with the Westhoughton Cup, undefeated. The ground used then is not known, but New Sirs was used during the Great War when the club played in the Leigh Sunday School League. Between the Wars the Westhoughton League was strong and many honours were won then. Unfortunately little is known of the club until after the War when the club reformed in 1951, playing on St James Street cricket ground until the landlords offered New Sirs back to the club in 1957. The lease was a major boost for the club whose success prompted the move to the Bolton Combination and began the building of one of the best teams in the area, the Lancs Amateur Shield and Under 18's Youth Cup amongst the honours.

In 1967 a building was purchased and converted into dressing rooms and in 1978 they were accepted into the Lancs Combination. With the advent of the pyramid the league was amalgamated and the club became founder members of the North West Counties League, which meant new dressing rooms and a social club for the ground.

FORMBY

Brows Lane, Formby, Merseyside L37 4AB Tel: 01704 833505

Secretary: Paul Lawler, 13 Sefton Rd, Formby, Merseyside L37 2JG Tel 01704 878409

Chairman: C.Welsh, 38 Greenloons Walk, Formby, L37 2LE Tel: 01704 877414

Formed: 1920

Colours: Yellow and blue

Nickname: Squirrels

Seating: 200

Covered standing: 300

Floodlights: No

Capacity: 2,000

Clubhouse on ground: No

Biggest win: 11-1 v Earle 1952

Biggest defeat: 0-10 v Irlam Town 1986

Record attendance: 2,500 v Oldham Athletic FA Cup 1973

Record fee received: £1,000 from Chorley for Geoff Twentyman

DIRECTIONS

A565 Liverpool-Southport, turn for Formby at lights opposite Do-It-All DIY into Altcar Road, fork left at junction to roundabout (opposite Blundell Arms Hotel), take 2nd exit then sharp left into Dike Street, 1st right into Elbow Lane, ground entrance 50 yds on left. Half a mile from Formby (BR), buses from Formby & Southport stations.

Honours

Liverpool Combination 1949

Liverpool Senior Cup 1978

Liverpool Challenge Cup 1964

Liverpool Amateur Cup: 1930, 1947, 1948, 1949

Lamot Pils Trophy 1995

Lancashire Amateur Cup 1935

Formby, a club with a proud history, have struggled since they were last relegated from the first division of the North West Counties League in 1988. However, the club are tipped for success again this season, and have new tenants in Division Two rivals Stantondale, who have moved in at Brows Lane.

GARSWOOD UNITED

Simms Lane Ends, Garswood Rd, Garswood, Nr Wigan Tel: 01744 892258

Secretary: Mr J.Anelay, 128 Victoria Rd, Garswood, Wigan

Press and Prog Editor: John Richards 45 Elm House, Egerton Rd, Prescot L34 3LZ

Tel: 0151 430 9378 (h) 01942 275224 (a)

Chairman: Roy Jones, 155 Victoria Rd, Garswood, Nr Wigan Tel: 01942 744869

DIRECTIONS

From M6 north take junction 25, B5207 and Garswood is signposted. From M6 south take junction 24. Head a short distance on A58 and then turn right to Garswood.

Colours: Blue and white stripes   Nickname: The Wooders

Capacity: 1,000   Seating: 40

Covered standing: 300   Clubhouse on ground: Yes

Record attendance: 480 v Manchester United Vets.

Biggest win: 22-0 v Waterloo Dock 1969,

Biggest defeat: 2-5 v Grove Utd in 1994

Record appearances: Nobby Jones 465

Record goalscorer in one season Fred Blueitt 70

Record goalscorer in total Nobby Jones 134

Honours

Griffiths Trophy 1971, Worral Cup 1972, Burtonwood Cup 1973

Chadwick Cup 1974, Ford Cup 1975,

Dodds Shield, Guardian Cup and Jubilee Cup 1977

Memorial Shield 1978, Lord Wavertree Cup 2nd Div 1979

Liverpool Junior Cup 1st Div 1980

Davenport Cup 1987 and 1988, Mid-Cheshire Challenge Cup 1989

Mid-Cheshire League Div 2 1990, Himsworth and Rynads Cups 1990

Lancs FA Amateur Cup 1995, Mid-Cheshire League Cup 1995

Mid-Cheshire League 1996, Liverpool Challenge Cup 1996, Wigan Cup 1996

Manager 1996-97: Alan Aspinall, Assistant Manager: Frank Melia, Vice Chairman: John Richards

Garswood United were formed in 1968 and played on the local Recreation ground before moving to the now defunct RAF camp at Haydock. This is now a major housing development and the club moved again to a derelict site in Simms Lane in 1973. The land was levelled and top soil spread and with much work and a sports grant the ground has developed to North West Counties standards.

Last season saw the side win the Mid-Cheshire League by nine points after a previous season where they won everything they entered, including the Lancs Amateur Cup and League Cup. United have linked up with the community and have a 5,000 circulation newsletter which is distributed each month. They have enjoyed much success since their formation in 1968 and have a host of Cup credits to their name. This season their efforts have been rewarded with a place in the North West Counties League

HASLINGDEN

Ewood Bridge, Manchester Rd, Haslingden, Lancs BB4 6JY Tel: 01706 217814

Secretary: Len Chenery, 83 Belgrave Rd, Darwen, Lancs Tel: 01254 704518 (h) 0585 908898 (mobile)

Chairman Brian Horsbrough at club during day and evening

Nickname: Hassy

Colours: Tangerine and Black   Capacity: 1,500

Seating: 50   Covered Standing: 200

Floodlights: Yes   Clubhouse on ground: Yes

Record Attendance: 551 v Blackburn Rovers 1993

Biggest Win: 13-0 v Squires Gate

Record goalscorer in one season and in aggregate: Jimmy Clarke

Honours

West Lancs Div 2 1981; President's Cup 1972, 1981, 1993; North-West Counties League Div 2 1994

DIRECTIONS

From South: M66 Blackburn/Clitheroe exit, left at roundabout past Woolpack Hotel, sharp left at bottom of hill - ground 100 yds on right. From North: M6 junction 31, A59 to Blackburn, take ring-road at Moat House Hotel and follow signs to M65, leave M65 at junction 8 and follow signs for Bury, follow dual carriageway for about 5 miles and leave at Todmorden exit, right at lights, straight across roundabout by Woolpack Hotel, then follow as above.

Manager for 1996-97: Steve Parry; Assistant manager: Jimmy Clarke

Chairman: Brian Horsbrough; Vice Chairman: Bill Wade

In the period from 1905 to 1910 there was a Haslingden Football Club who were members of the Lancashire Combination Division Two. In 1911 they won the championship and remained there until returning to Division Two in 1913. After the War it did not reappear and it was 1969 before a club formed and in 1972 they had won the West Lancashire President's Cup. It was to be the only success until the 1980-81 side did the League and Cup double after a tremendous season which regularly saw crowds of 300 at Ewood Bridge. There then followed more lean years until 1993 when the club were runners up to Leyland by just one goal. Revenge was sweet in the President's Cup final as they beat Leylands at Turf Moor.

Following a re-development of the ground Haslingden were elected to the North-West Counties League Division Two and in 1994 they took the title by some nine points, promotion sadly being refused due to ground gradings.

LEEK CSOB

Harrison Park, Leek Town FC, Macclesfield Rd, Leek Tel: 01538 383734

Secretary: Stan Lockett, 5 Fitzherbert Close, Swynnerton, Stone, Staffs ST15 0PQ Tel: 01782 796551

Chairman: K.J. Hill, 11 Springfield Drive, Leek, Staffs ST13 Tel: 01538 371859

Founded: 1945

Colours: Red and white

Ground details as Leek Town F.C.

DIRECTIONS

Opposite Courtaults chemical works on A523 Macclesfield to Buxton road half a mile out of Leek heading towards Macclesfield.

Honours

Refuge Midland League 1996

League Cup 1995 and 1996

Leek Cup 1995 and 1996

Charity Shield 1996

Sportsline Challenge Cup 1996

MAGHULL

Old Hall Field, Hall Lane, Maghull, Merseyside L31 3DY Tel: 0151 526 7320

Secretary: Danny Sherlock, 14 Alexander Drive, Lydiate, Merseyside Tel: 0151 526 7320

Press Secretary: Andy Boyd, 53 Grosvenor Rd, Maghull, Merseyside Tel: 0151 526 2715

Colours: Blue and Red stripes

Nickname: The Blues

Capacity: 2,000

DIRECTIONS

M57 or M58 to end (Switch Island). A59 towards Preston (Northway) to lights at Hall Lane, turn right following signs for Maghull Station. Ground 200yds on the left. Half mile from Maghull (Merseyrail).

Seating: None   Covered standing: 200

Floodlights: No   Clubhouse on ground: Yes

Record Attendance: 500 v Marine
Liverpool Challenge Cup 1982

Biggest win: 8-1 v Westhoughton Town 1994

Biggest defeat: 1-7 v Clitheroe 1983

Record appearance holder.: Bobby Prince

Record goalscorer in one season: Lee Cooper

Record goalscorer in total: Bobby Prince

Honours

North-West Counties League Div 2 1993

Liverpool County Amateur Cup 1935 and 1963

Liverpool County Challenge Cup 1980, 1986, 1994

Lancashire Amateur Cup 1949 and 1958

Lancashire Combination Challenge Cup 1978

Liverpool County Combination 1967

Liverpool I Zingari League 1934, 1955, 1956

League Cup: 1935 and 1947

Manager for 1996/97: Frank O'Brien,   **Assistant Manager: Ritchie Hughes**

Chairman Les Jacques,   **Vice Chairman: Gerry Fisher**

Maghull celebrates its 75th anniversary this year. Since its inception in 1921 it has progressed through the ranks of local non-League football via the powerful Liverpool County Combination, the now extinct Lancashire Combination, and the Cheshire County League and was a founder member of the North-West Counties League.

Maghull have played at the Old Hall Field since the early fifties having previously used a ground at Days Lane High School with other matches played at Pimbley Rec.

MIDDLEWICH ATHLETIC

Seddon Street, Middlewich, Cheshire Tel: 01606 835842

Secretary: Bryan Longley, 16 Northway, Holmes Chapel, Cheshire, CW4 7EF Tel: 01477 537310

Chairman: J. McAteer, 32 Poplar Drive, Middlewich, Cheshire Tel: 01606 833946

Re-formed: 1988

Colours: Red and white

Floodlights: No

DIRECTIONS

M6 to junction 18, A54 Middlewich to traffic lights, forward to the end of dual carriageway, right into Pepper Street/Webbs Lane, second left Seddon Street, ground on the right.

Honours

Crewe and District Premier League 1990

Crewe FA Cup 1990

Mid-Cheshire FA Cup 1994 and 1996

NELSON

Victoria Park, Lomeshaye Way, Nelson, Lancashire Tel: 01282 613820

Secretary: Cyril King, 1 Grange Ave, Barrowford, Nelson, BB9 8AN Tel: 01282 695578

Chairman: Ken Broom, 6 Broadness Drive, Nelson, BB9 0SP Tel: 01282 601359

Colours: Blue and white stripes

Nickname: Blues

Seating: Yes

Covered standing: Yes

Record attendance: 15,000 in Football League at old Seedhill Ground

DIRECTIONS

M65 junction 13, first left onto the A6068, 2nd left onto the B6249 for Nelson. Take the 2nd right, signposted Lomeshaye Village, to the ground.

Honours

Lancashire League 1896, 1955

Lancs Junior Cup 1908 and 1955

Lancs Combination 1950 and 1952

Lancs Combination Cup 1950, 1951, 1960

Bridge Shield 1976 and 1982

George Watson Trophy 1979

OLDHAM TOWN

Whitebank Stadium, Whitebank Rd, Hollins, Oldham OL8 3JH Tel: 0161 624 2689

Secretary: Graham Shuttleworth,
42 Southgate Rd, Chadderton, Oldham
OL9 9PT Tel: 0161 682 1137

Chairman: K.Hughes, c/o Oldham Town FC

Colours: All Royal blue

Floodlights: Yes

Covered standing: Yes

Record attendance: 452 Halifax Town
FA Cup 1st qualifying round 1996

DIRECTIONS

M62 jct 18, M66 to Heaton Park
right on to A576, left at 2nd lights
on to A6104, following Victoria Ave
on to Hollinwood Ave. under bridge
to T-junction, right then 1st left at
Roxy Cinema follow Hollins Road for
one and a half miles to Fire Station,
left on to Elm Rd and follow to next
left, Whitebank Rd on left.

RAMSBOTTOM UNITED

Riverside Ground, Acre Bottom, Ramsbottom Tel: 01706 822799 (Cricket club)

Secretary: John Maher, 75 Ramsbottom Rd, Hawkshaw,
Bury, BL8 4JS Tel: 01204 852742

Chairman: H.Williams, 35 Nuttall Lane, Ramsbottom
Tel 01706 822799

Colours: Blue and white

Founded: 1966

Record attendance: 264 v Accrington Stanley Friendly 1995

DIRECTIONS

M66 junction 1, A56 towards
Ramsbottom, left down Bury New
Road after 1 mile, left again
immediately after Rover Bridge.

Honours

Bolton Combination 1977 and 1987

Div 1 1973

Manchester League Div 1 and Div 1 Cup 1991

Gilgryst Cup 1995

NWCL Div 2 Trophy 1996

SKELMERSDALE UNITED

White Moss Park, White Moss Rd, Skelmersdale, Lancs Tel: 01695 722123

Secretary: Ken Hilton, 34 Mill Lane, Burscough, Ormskirk, Lancs, L40 5TJ Tel: 01704 894504

Chairman: Dave Tomlinson, 64 Clipsey Cres, Haydock WA11 0UH Tel: 01744 24419

Nickname: Skemmers   Capacity: 10,000

Club colours: Blue and White   Seating: 250

DIRECTIONS

M58 junction 3, at 2nd roundabout take 3rd exit towards Skelmersdale, continue for approx 1 mile, ground on the right. 4 miles from Ormskirk (BR).

Covered standing: 1,000

Floodlights: Yes

Clubhouse on ground: Yes

Record attendance: 7,500 v Slough Town
FA Amateur Cup 1967

Record fee received:
£10,000 for Russell Payne from Liverpool 1990

Honours

FA AMATEUR CUP 1971 and **Runners up** in 1967

Cheshire County League 1969 and 1970, Jubilee Cup 1970

Liverpool County Combination 1911, 1914, 1915, 1920, 1939, 1940, 1946, 1951, 1952, 1954

Lancashire Combination Div 2 1956

Liverpool Challenge Cup 1912, 1914, 1920, 1921, 1939, 1940, 1946, 1947

Lancashire Amateur Shield 1908

George Mahon Cup 1925, 1935, 1940, 1952, 1955, Lancashire Floodlit Cup 1970

Lancashire Junior Cup 1915, 1970, 1971, Ashworth Cup 1970

Barassi Anglo-Italian Cup 1971, Liverpool non-League Cup 1974 and 1975

Skelmersdale United was founded in 1882 by a group of local miners and played on a pitch at the top of Sandy Lane in old Skelmersdale. They moved to the present ground in 1958, and it has a capacity of 10,000 with seating for 250. United's first major success was in 1967 when they reached the final of the Amateur Cup at Wembley. They played a draw after extra time with Enfield, but sadly lost the replay at Maine Road. Happily, four years later they were back, this time lifting the Cup after beating Dagenham 4-1, including a hat-trick by Ted Dickin. Since 1968 Skem have played in the first round proper of the FA Cup twice, losing to Scunthorpe and Chesterfield.

Prior to the formation of the North West Counties League, Skem played in the Liverpool County Combination, the Lancashire Combination, and Cheshire County League before joining the Northern Premier League in 1971. Their roll of honour also includes Cheshire League titles, Barassi Anglo Italian Cup and North West Counties League Cups, as well in earlier times the Lancashire Junior Cup. Last season saw the club suffer both on and off the pitch and they were sadly relegated to Division Two

SQUIRES GATE

School Rd, Marton, Blackpool, Lancs Tel: 01253 798584

Secretary: John Maguire, 2 Squires Ct, Cairn Grove, Blackpool FY4 2RA Tel: 01253 348512

Chairman: P.Mack, 211 Palatine Rd, Blackpool Tel 01253 300405

Colours: Royal blue and black

Floodlights: No   Formed : 1948

Seating: Yes   Covered standing: Yes

Record attendance: 600 v Everton July 1995

Honours

West Lancs League Div 2 1981

Richardson Cup 1987

DIRECTIONS

M6 to M55 junction 4, left onto A583, right at 1st lights (Whitehall Rd) follow signs for airport. Ground approx one and a half miles on right.

STANTONDALE

Formby FC, Brows Lane, Formby, Merseyside L37 2LE Tel: 01704 833505

Secretary: Alan Hardaker, 89 Park Lane, Netherton, Merseyside L30 1QB Tel: 0151 521 6313

Chairman: Roy Grundy, 15 Stand Park Ave, Netherton, Liverpool L30 3SA Tel: 0151 521 8277

Colours: Green and white

Formed: 1986

DIRECTIONS AND GROUND INFO AS PER FORMBY FC

Honours

Liverpool Combination Div 1 1991

Division 2 1988

Liverpool Junior Cup 1991

Liverpool Challenge Cup 1992

McEwans Lager Cup 1992

Lamot Pils Trophy 1993

DIRECTIONS

A565 Liverpool-Southport, turn for Formby at lights opposite Do-It-All DIY into Altcar Road, fork left at junction to roundabout (opposite Blundell Arms Hotel), take 2nd exit then sharp left into Dike Street, 1st right into Elbow Lane, ground entrance 50 yds on left. Half a mile from Formby (BR), buses from Formby & Southport stations.

TETLEY WALKER

Tetley Walker Sports and Social Club, Long Lane, Warrington Tel: 01925 634904

Secretary: Brian Gleave, 8 Cossack Ave, Warrington Tel: 01925 659559

Chairman: R. Fisher, 53 Shakespeare Grove, Orford, Warrington Tel: 01925 631112

Colours: Red and blue   Nickname: Walkers   Seating: 40

Covered standing: 150   Floodlights: No

Record attendance: 108 v St Helens Town 1995

Record Win: 10-1 v Grappenhall Sports Guardian Cup 1993

Honours

Guardian Cup 1985, 1986, 1994; Warrington and District League 1987 and 1994; Jubilee Cup 1994

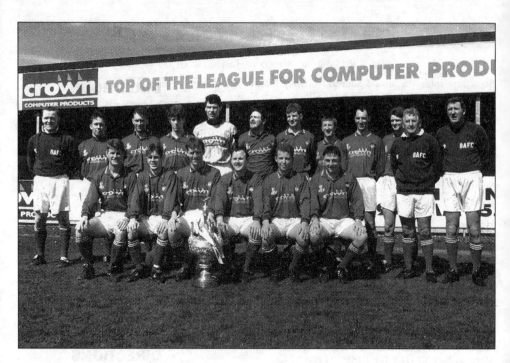

Above: Burscough F.C.

Below: Clitheroe F.C.

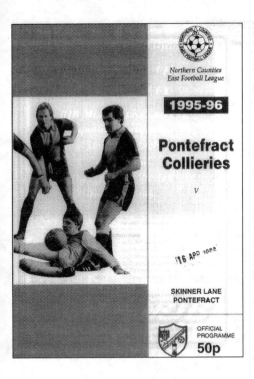

Northern Counties
East Football League

1995-96

Pontefract
Collieries

v

'16 APD 1996

SKINNER LANE
PONTEFRACT

OFFICIAL
PROGRAMME
50p

DENABY UNITED F C

Ben Bailey Homes

United
Review

1895/6 Centenary Season 1995/6
Match Programme

Wednesday 24th April
v BELPER TOWN
NCEL
Prem Div
50p

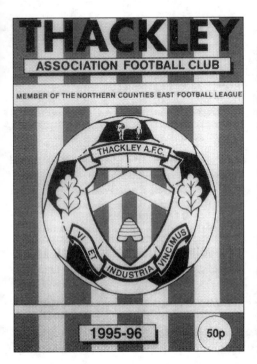

THACKLEY
ASSOCIATION FOOTBALL CLUB

MEMBER OF THE NORTHERN COUNTIES EAST FOOTBALL LEAGUE

THACKLEY A.F.C.

VI ET INDUSTRIA VINCIMUS

1995-96 | **50p**

BELPER TOWN
FOOTBALL CLUB

B|FC   *Season 1995-96*

GRAHAM
STREET PRIMS
Derbyshire Senior Cup
Semi-Final

2nd April 1996
Kick off 7.30pm

OFFICIAL
MATCHDAY
PROGRAMME
60p

PREMIER DIVISION

	P	W	D	L	F	A	PTS
Hatfield Main	38	22	9	7	77	45	75
Stocksbridge P. S.	38	21	10	7	59	36	73
North Ferriby U.	38	21	9	8	78	33	72
Belper Town	38	20	10	8	66	39	70
Thackley	38	20	9	9	60	40	69
Denaby United	38	19	5	14	63	56	62
Brigg Town	38	17	8	13	65	50	59
Ashfield United	38	17	5	16	56	50	56
Liversedge	38	16	7	15	52	49	55
Ossett Albion	38	13	12	13	56	55	51
Armthorpe Welfare	38	13	11	14	53	47	50
Pickering Town	38	14	5	19	73	86	47
Goole Town	38	13	8	17	53	74	47
Arnold Town	38	13	7	18	51	57	46
Ossett Town	38	12	9	17	48	61	45
Hucknall Town	38	12	6	20	52	67	42
Hallam	38	11	7	20	41	68	40
Glasshoughton W.	38	10	9	19	45	62	39
Maltby M. W.	38	11	5	22	58	83	38
Sheffield	38	6	7	25	46	94	25

DIVISION ONE

	P	W	D	L	F	A	PTS
Selby Town	30	19	6	5	79	34	63
Pontefract Coll	30	19	6	5	76	33	63
Garforth Town	30	18	7	5	63	27	61
Yorkshire Amateur	30	18	6	6	51	30	60
Hall Road Rangers	30	17	5	8	65	34	56
Eccleshill United	30	18	1	11	74	53	55
Borrowash Victoria	30	13	5	12	59	46	44
Harrogate R. Ath.	30	12	5	13	48	52	41
Winterton Rangers	30	11	6	13	44	51	39
Rossington Main	30	10	7	13	43	55	37
Worsborough Bri.	30	9	5	16	48	60	32
Louth United	30	8	7	15	54	66	31
Blidworth Welfare	30	9	3	18	47	83	30
Tadcaster Albion	30	6	5	19	25	61	23
Parkgate	30	6	4	20	36	81	22
Brodsworth M. W.	30	2	12	16	23	69	18

ARMTHORPE WELFARE

Welfare Ground, Church St, Armthorpe. Tel: 01302 833674 (welfare) 01302 831247 (club)

Secretary: Mrs M Cottam, Roydean, Whiphill Lane, Armthorpe, Doncaster DN3 3JP Tel 01302 832514

Prog. Editor: Sharon Morgan, 68 Woodlea Grove, Armthorpe, Doncaster DN3 3JP Tel 01302 834475

Colours: White and navy blue

Nickname: Wellie

Capacity: 2,500

Seating: 200

Covered standing: 200

Clubhouse on ground: Yes

Record attendance: 2,000 v Doncaster Rovers Charity match 1986

Record appearances: Gary Leighton

Record goalscorer in total: Martin Johnson

DIRECTIONS

From north: Turn left at main roundabout in centre of Doncaster, straight across next roundabout on to Wheatley Hall Road. Right at Mines Rescue Station, go to top of hill on to Armthorpe Road. From south: M18 Junction 4, on to A630, left at roundabout then proceed to next roundabout and turn right. Ground 400 yds on left behind Plough Inn. Two and a half miles from Doncaster (BR). Buses A2, A3 & 181 pass ground.

Honours

Northern Counties East Central Div 1 1985

Doncaster District Lge 1983, Div 1 1982, Div 2 1980, Div 3 1979

League Cup 1980, 1981, 1982, 1983

Challenge Cup 1983

West Riding Challenge Cup 1982 and 1983

Goole and Thorne Cup 1983

The original Welfare FC were formed in 1926 and disbanded in 1974. A new club took the name in 1976 and swept all before them in the Doncaster and District League rising through four divisions with a host of trophies before taking promotion to the Northern Counties East in their newly formed Div 1 Central.

Their success was built around striker Martin Johnson and Peter Camm and it was enough to gain promotion to the Premier Division whilst the old Welfare ground was given an overhaul.

The following season they were runners up to Emley and a year later lost the League Cup final to the all conquering North Shields.

During the last few years floodlights have been erected and a new stand and enclosing wall have gone up in long term preparation for the Northern Premier League.

ARNOLD TOWN

King George V Recreation Ground, Gedling Rd, Arnold, Notts NG5 6NQ. Tel: 01159 815390

Secretary: Steve Shout, 11 Newholm Drive, Silverdale, Nottingham NG11 7FR Tel: 01159 263660

Supporters Club Secretary Martin Williams 86 Burgass Rd, Thorneywood, Nottm Tel: 01159 598759

Press officer Andrew Walker, 57 Sunnyside Rd, Chilwell, Nottm NG9 4FG Tel: 01159 229749

Confirm Fixture Rob Hornby 01159 456549

Colours: Yellow and blue stripes, Nickname: Eagles

Capacity: 3,400

Seating: 150

Covered standing: 950, Clubhouse on ground: Yes

Record attendance: 3,390 v Bristol Rovers FA Cup 1967

Biggest win: 10-1 v Denaby Utd
Northern Counties East 1994

Biggest defeat: 0-5 v Lincoln Utd and North Ferriby Utd

Record appearances: Neil Waters 229

Record goalscorer in one season: Chris Freestone 41

Record goalscorer in total: Peter Fletcher 98

Record fee received: £15,000 for Chris Freestone to Middlesbrough 1994

DIRECTIONS

From North M1 junction 26, B6004 (Stockhill Lane) 3 miles to A60 (White Hart pub on left), right at A60, immediate left (St Albans Road), through lights by Sainsburys, left at rear of Sainsburys, ground on right adjacent to market. From A1(M)/A614/A60 to lights (White Hart on right), 1st left through lights, St Albans Road then as above. From Nottm ring-road left into A60, right into Nottingham Road after quarter mile to lights at Sainsburys, right then as above. Four miles from Nottingham Midland BR station. Buses 53, 55, 59 pass ground, buses 25, 26, 40, 56, 57, 58 within 100 yds.

Honours

Northern Counties East President's Cup 1995, Division One 1994

Central Midlands League Supreme Div 1993, Wakefield Cup 1990, Notts Senior Cup 1993, ARNOLD FC

Central Midlands League Cup 1988, Northern Counties East Premier Division 1986

Midland League Cup 1975, Central Alliance Premier 1963, Notts Senior Cup 1961, 65, 66, 69, 71

ARNOLD KINGSWELL Midland League Div 1 1980

Managers for 1996-97: Ray O'Brien and Iain McCulloch

Assistant Manager: John Adams, Chairman: David Law

Independent magazine 'Arnold Who?' available 50p + SAE from Mark Butler, 27 Dunvegan Drive, Rise Park, Nottm NG5 5DX.

An Arnold Town handbook will be available from mid-August, 50p + sae same address

Arnold Town FC was formed in 1989 following a merger of Arnold FC, (originally Arnold St Marys in 1928) and Arnold Kingswell (founded in 1962).

Arnold FC were having success on the pitch but could not attract sponsorship or committee members, whilst Kingswell had the opposite problem. With both clubs stagnating, an amalgamation was agreed upon.

Town adopted the yellow of the Saints and the blue of the Kings as the club colours and the home of Arnold FC was a natural choice. The club was re-structured and after 10 years a clubhouse was opened which was to become a focal point. In the next six seasons a great deal of success came their way, including a Wakefield Cup win and two final defeats in the League and Senior Cups.

Ex-International Ray O'Brien took over in 1991 and within two seasons they were champions of the Central Midlands League Supreme Division and Notts Senior Cup winners. A switch to the Northern Counties East saw another title win and the Presidents Cup was also won.

ASHFIELD UNITED

Lowmoor Rd, Kirkby-in-Ashfield, Notts. Tel: 01623 752181

Secretary: Frank Grainger, Hawthorn Cott, New St, South Normanton, Derbys DE55 2BS Tel 01773 510066

Prog Editor Peter Bough, 45 Bonser Gardens, Sutton-in-Ashfield, Notts NG17 1DT Tel 01623 511374

Colours: Claret and Blue, Nickname: The Snipes

Capacity: 8,000,   Seating: 250

Covered standing: 250

Clubhouse on ground: Yes

Record attendance:
At Priestic Rd, 6,000 v Peterborough Utd 1958

DIRECTIONS
M1 junction 28, A38 towards Mansfield, at 4th lights turn right onto B6021 (s.p. Kirkby-in-Ashfield). After half mile turn right at lights into Lowmoor Road immediately after crossing railway lines. Ground half mile on left next to Lowmoor Inn. Nearest rail station is Alfreton & Mansfield Parkway - 3 miles.

At Avenue Gd, 8,000 v Reading FA Cup 1933, at Lowmoor Rd, 1,562 Floodlight opener v Leeds Utd 1980

Honours

Notts Senior Cup 1909, 13, 14, 24, 56, 58, 60, 62, 63, 64, 68, 70, 72, 73, 74, 75, 77

Notts and District League 1906 and 1907, Derby Senior League 1931, 1932, 1933

Central Alliance 1951, Northern Counties East League Cup 1986 and 1996

Mansfield Charity Cup 1893, 1906, 1924, Sutton Charity Cup 1930, 1931, 1932

Byron Cup 1931 and 1932

Manager for 1996-97: Bud Evans, Assistant manager: Dave Moxon

Chairman: Roy Gregory JP 65 Kingsley Ave, Mansfield Woodhouse, Notts Tel: 01623 633578

Vice chairman: Roy Link OBE, Press officer: Peter Bough

Ashfield Utd were founded, as Sutton Town, in 1885 and played their first games at the rear of the Dog and Duck pub. Colours at the time were red caps, black jerseys, white pants and black socks. After playing friendly matches for a few seasons, Sutton joined the Notts and District League in 1890 and won the league in successive seasons in 1906 and 1907. The first ever honours however were in 1893 when they took the Mansfield Charity Cup. By the time they were in the Derbyshire League they had made the first of many moves and were playing at the New Cross ground, sharing with the long defunct cricket club. The most successful period in the club's history came between the Wars, and particularly between 1929 and 1934 when they won the Derbyshire Senior Cup three seasons in a row, reached the Second Round of the FA Cup and won six local cups. By this time matches were being played on the Avenue ground behind the Potmakers Arms on Mansfield Road which also had a greyhound track which was in use until around 20 years ago when the site was developed. After the War the club was revived and spent ten seasons in the Central Alliance before stepping up into the Midland League. A new ground was built at Priestic Road and crowds of 5,000 or more came to see the like of Peterborough United, North Shields Ashington and Scarborough. Unfortunately the ground, adjacent to the town centre, was never owned by the club and the landlord sold it to a property developer, and a superstore now covers the site. The club almost folded as a result, but East Kirkby Miners Welfare came to the rescue and the club took over their ground, at the time an undeveloped recreation ground in Kirkby-in-Ashfield. When the Midland League joined forces with the Yorkshire League the club became founder members of the Northern Counties East League, winning the League Cup in 1986. They moved up to the Northern Premier League, but struggled and returned to the NCEL in 1989 In 1992 the club agreed a package deal with Ashfield District Council to help redevelop the ground, which included a name change to Ashfield United. Although supporters opposed it, the FA sanctioned it, although during last season there was rumour that the club was considering reverting again to Sutton Town. What is for sure is that the club will be moving to a new ground in June 1997, to be built to Conference standards at Huthwaite Road, and to be part of a new sports complex.

BELPER TOWN

Christchurch Meadow, Bridge St, Belper. Tel: 01773 825549

Secretary: David Laughlin, Lorne Cott, 1 Hagg Lane, Fritchley, Belper, Derbys DE56 2HJ

Tel: 01773 856556 (h) 01332 347141 ext 2381 (b) 0585 949713 (m)

Chairman: Phil Varney Tel: 01773 824680 (h) 01773 821211

Press Sec: Nigel Oldrini Tel 01332 882677

Nickname: The Nailers, Colours: Gold and black

Capacity: 2,640   Seating: 200

Covered standing: 1,000, Clubhouse on ground: Yes

Record attendance: 3,600 v Ilkeston Town in 1951

Biggest win: 15-2 v Nottm Forest A 1956

Biggest defeat: 0-12 v Goole Town 1965

Record appearances: Gil Rhodes

Record goalscorer in one season: Gordon Warrington 64

Record goalscorer in total: Mick Lakin 231

Record fee received: £700 for Brian Hall from Mansfield Town in 1959

DIRECTIONS

From M1 North, Junction 28 onto A38 towards Derby, turn off at A610 (s.p. Ripley/Nottingham), then 4 exit at roundabout towards Ambergate. At junction with A6 (Hurt Arms Hotel) left to Belper. Ground on right past traffic lights. 400 yards from Belper (BR).

Honours

Midland Counties Lge 1980, Central Alliance Lge 1959, Northern Counties East 1985

Derbys Senior Cup 1959, 1961, 1963, 1980,

Manager for 1996-97: Martin Rowe, Assistant manager: Eddie Green

Chairman: Philip Varney, 19 Derwent View, Milford, Nr Belper, Derbys Tel 01773 824680

Belper Town's unusual nickname "The Nailers", came about because of the nail making which began in Belper in the middle ages, when it was the site of a hunting lodge for John of Gaunt.

The huntsmen needed nails for the horse shoes and the trade grew. In the players entrance there is a plaque made of 17th Century nails which were discovered when the foundations were being excavated for the dressing rooms. Like the industry, Belper Town has faded away in the past, originally formed in 1883, they folded three times through lack of finance. They re-formed for the fourth time in 1951 and it was in that year that they enjoyed their record attendance when 3,600 watched a match with Ilkeston Town. Regular four figure crowds were commonplace in those days In 1957 they joined the Central Alliance League but the 1958-59 season was a turning point as the Nailers outshone wealthy Heanor and Ilkeston to win the league and Derbyshire Senior Cup. Three years later they were invited to join the revamped Midland Counties League although major ground improvements were required. Three times they finished bottom, the last time in 1979, and only goodwill from member clubs saved them from obscurity once again. The club responded in magnificent style by winning the League in the next season as well as the Senior Cup again.

When, in 1982 the league merged into the Northern Counties East, Belper moved on and in 1985 won the championship under Harry Bethell. That coincided with the arrival of ex-England and Derby striker Kevin Hector who scored over 20 goals and laid on countless others.

In 1995 Belper enjoyed a magnificent FA Vase run, with victories over South Shields, Falmouth Town and Met Police before losing the two-legged semi-final to Oxford City, having won the first leg at Christchurch Meadow in front of 2,000 people. Last season saw the club finish in fourth place.

BLIDWORTH WELFARE

Welfare Ground, Blidworth, Notts. Tel: 01623 793361

Secretary: Paul Deakin, 8 Birks Rd, Mansfield, Notts NG19 6JU. Tel: 01623 453812

Match Sec: Bill Deakin, 220 Brick Kiln Lane, Mansfield, Notts NG19 6LR. Tel 01623 29033

Prog Editor: Andy Brown 18 Teignmouth Ave, Mansfield, Notts NG18 3JQ Tel: 0585 728761

Colours: Orange and black

Nickname: Hawks

Capacity: 3,000

Seating: 200

Covered standing: 500

Clubhouse on ground: Yes

Record attendance: 400 v Shirebrook Colliery 1990

Biggest win: 6-0 v Harworth CI 1992

Biggest defeat: 0-11 v Sheffield Aurora Central Mids Lge 1991

Record appearances: Dave Colley

Record goalscorer in one season:

Record goalscorer in total: Andy Locker

DIRECTIONS

On B6020, Rainsworth side of Blidworth. From M1 junction 27 take A608 to Kirby and Annesley Woodhouse, at lights follow A611 to Kirby then take B6020 through Ravenshead to Blidworth - through village and ground at top of hill on right. From A1 follow A614 and A617 to Rainworth, left at lights then 1st right on to B6020 to Blidworth - ground on left at top of hill. Served by Mansfield-Nottingham buses.

Manager 1996-97: Andy Brown

Assistant manager: John Miller

Chairman: Richard Paterson, 258 Southwell Rd West, Mansfield Notts Tel 01623 27470

Blidworth Welfare were reformed in 1980 and joined the Notts Alliance for two years until moving to the NCEL. In 1986 they left to join the Central Midlands League and finished third in the Supreme Division in 1993. They applied for a return to the NCEL and were accepted and although losing their first home match 0-7 they survived.

Their Welfare Ground is tucked away below the remains of the Miners Welfare itself and has a capacity of 3,000.

BORROWASH VICTORIA

Asterdale Sports Centre, Borrowash Rd, Spondon, Derbys. Tel: 01332 669688 or 668656

Secretary: Ian Collins, 30 Margreave Rd, Chaddesden, Derby DE21 6JD. Tel: 01332 739437

Press officer: David Dooley, 50 Balmoral Drive, Bramcote Hills, Notts NG9 3FU

Ass Sec: Trevor Daeffler 89 Priorway Ave, Borrowash, Derbys DE72 3HX Tel: 01332 661380

Colours: Red and white stripes

Nickname: The Vics,   Capacity: 5,000

Seating: 250,   Covered standing: 250

Clubhouse on ground: Yes

Record attendance: 2,600 v Nottm Forest
Floodlight opener Oct 1985

Biggest win: 13-0 v Derby South End Oct 1963

Biggest defeat: 0-6 v Belper Town Colts Nov 1963

Record appearances: D.Dickenson 650 1963-1985

Record goalscorer in one season: P.Acklam 37 in 1984-85

Record goalscorer in total: T.Keogh 175 1972-1983

DIRECTIONS

M1 junction 25, A52 towards Derby, 3rd left off bypass into Borrowash Road, ground 400 yds on left. 2 miles from Spondon (BR). Nottingham to Derby buses pass nearby.

Honours

Derby Combination 1978 and League Cup 1969 and 1976

Northern Counties East Div 1 South 1984

Midland Counties Div 1 and Div 1 Cup 1981

Derbys Divisional Cup 1974

Manager 1996-97: Peter McGurk

Assistant Manager: Graham Walker, Chairman: Ian Anderson, Vice Chairman: Peter Erwin

Borrowash Victoria Amateur FC was originally formed in 1911, taking its name from one of the village roads and playing in a field in Draycott Road. Twice reformed between the Wars, it reappeared in 1952 in the Derby Sunday Schools and Welfare League for four years before disbanding. The present club started in 1963 when it took the place of Borrowash Youth FC. Since then they have progressed through the Derby Comb, Central Alliance, East Midlands Regional League, Midland Counties and Northern Counties East, joining the Central Midlands Supreme Division as founder members in 1986.

Playing at Deans Drive from the start, the club moved to Spondon Leisure Centre in 1984 from where two years later, Vics and others moved to the Central Midlands, only to return last season.

The club has gained many honours in its 30 years including three championships, three league cups and numerous other final and semi-finals.

A major highlight was in 1986 when Brian Clough brought a full Nottingham Forest first team down to open the new lights and dressing rooms, which attracted a crowd of 2,000. Derby County paid a similar visit in 1987 as part of the 75th anniversary of the original club.

BRIGG TOWN

Hawthorns, Hawthorn Avenue, Brigg , North Lincs DN20 8PG. Tel: 01652 652767 or 651605

Secretary: Robert Taylor, Highfield House, Barton Rd, Wrawby, Brigg DN20 8SH

Te: 01652 652284 (h) 01724 402749 (b)

Match Sec: John Martin, Kingfisher Lodge, The Old Stackyard, Brigg Rd, Wrawby, Brigg DN20 8RO Tel 01652 654526

Nickname: The Zebras,

Capacity: 4,000

Seating: 250

Covered standing: 2 stands

Clubhouse on ground: Yes

Record attendance: 2,000 v Boston Utd at Brocklesby Ox FA Cup 1954

Biggest win: 15-2 v Holbeach 1952

Biggest defeat: 0-9 v Barton Town Lincs Senior B Cup

Record appearances: Dave Hutchinson and Timmy Bowers

Record goalscorers in one season: Hutchinson and Bowers both averaged over 60 a season

Record goalscorer in total: Timmy Bowers

Record fee received: £2,000 for Paul Emson to Derby Co. 1971

> ## DIRECTIONS
> **From M180 Scunthorpe East, A18 through Brigg leaving on Wrawby Road, left into East Parade/Woodbine Avenue, follow houses in right into Hawthorn Avenue. One mile from brigg (BR).**

Honours

FA Vase Winners 1996

Lincolnshire League 1950, 1954, 1974, 1976., Div 1 1970, 1971, 1972,

League Cup 1950, 1966, 1969, 1970, 1973, Midland Counties League and Cup 1978

Lincs Senior Cup A 1976, 1977, 1995, Lincs Senior Cup B 1955, 1957, 1967, 1969, 1985

Manager for 1996-97: Ralph Clayton, Coach: John Kaye

Chairman: David Crowder, Vice Chairman: John Martin

More than a century has passed in North Lincolnshire before Brigg Town have finally found fame. Only four clubs are older than the Zebras, who were formed in 1864. Brigg was clearly a major centre for football and when the Lincolnshire FA was formed in 1881, four sides from the town made up the original complement of 16. Much of the early football remains a mystery although they were runners up in the first two County Cups in 1882 and 1883. They played for many years in the Lindsay League at the Old Manor House Ground in Station Road before moving onto the Brocklesby Ox ground, just behind the pub.

From there they were founder members of the Lincolnshire Senior League and won the title, as well as winning five League Cups to 1973. They were elected to the Midland Counties League in 1976 which they won in 1978 and when they were offered the chance to join the Northern Counties East in 1982, they jumped at it, although at first they were placed in Division One as the Hawthorns ground was not up to the required standard. In 1985 they were promoted and have been in the top flight ever since

The previous 130 odd years paled into insignificance last May, when the club came from nowhere to reach the Wembley final of the FA Vase, where they crushed Clitheroe in a one-sided match.

BRODSWORTH MINERS WELFARE

Welfare Ground, Woodlands, Nr Doncaster. Tel: 01302 728380

Secretary: Robert Beswick, 45 High St, Bolton-on-Dearne Rotherham S63 8LH Tel 01709 892489

Match Sec: John Muldowny, 24 Askern Rd, Carcroft, Doncaster DN6 7AQ Tel 01302 721274

Colours: Green and yellow stripes

Nickname: Brody

Capacity: 3,000

Floodlights: Yes

Seating: No

Covered standing: Yes

Clubhouse on ground: Yes

DIRECTIONS

Adjacent to the old Great North Road (A638), 3 miles north of Doncaster at Woodlands. Ground entrance approx 30 yds into Welfare Road. Left turn into car park. Regular bus service from North Bridge Bus Station, Doncaster.

Honours

Yorkshire Lge 1925

Doncaster Lge 1985 and League Cup 1986

Division Two and Div 2 League Cup 1979

Sheffield Junior Cup 1984

Mexborough Montagu Cup 1992 and 1993

Manager 1996-97: Neil Brandon

Chairman: Barry Hogg, 2 Church Lane, Adwick-le-Street, Doncaster DN6 7AQ Tel 01302 722501

Brodsworth were founded in 1912 and played in the Sheffield Association until moving into the strong Doncaster Amateur League for one season. In 1921 they joined the Yorkshire League and their only major success came in the 1924-25 season when they took the title. They had short spells in both the Doncaster Senior and Sheffield League's before leaving the Yorkshire League for good in 1976. They started at the bottom of the Doncaster League the following year and fought their way up to the Premier Division and ultimately the Northern Counties East. They won the Donny League in 1985 and the League Cup in 1986, after doing the league and cup double in Division Two in 1979.

Recent seasons have seen the old Welfare club struggle and last season saw them rooted to the bottom of Division One.

DENABY UNITED

Tickhill Square, Denaby Main, Doncaster. Tel: 01709 864042

Secretary: Mrs B. Norton, Ravenscarr Close, Denaby Main, Doncaster DN12 4HJ Tel 01709 867606

Match Sec: Derek Mower 60 Windmill Cres, Mexborough, S.Yorks S64 0EB Tel 01709 588360

Prog Editor: David Green, 1 Lime Tree Walk, Denaby Main, Doncaster DN12 4TE. Tel: 01709 862319

Colours: Red, white and black, Capacity: 6,000

Seating: 250,

Covered standing: 300

Clubhouse on ground: Yes

Record attendance: 3,801 v Oldham Athletic. FA Cup 1st Rd Nov 15th 1958

Biggest win: 20-0 v Shirebrook Colliery Central Alliance 1960-61

Biggest defeat: 0-11 v Grantham Jan 1957

Record fee paid: £300 for Kevin Deakin from Mossley 1984

Record fee received: £3,500 from Exeter City for Jon Brown in 1990

DIRECTIONS

From Conisbrough take first left in Denaby along Wadworth Street. From Mexborough take first right after Reresby Arms, left on to Bolton Street then left on to Wheatley Street. Rail to Conisbrough.

Honours

Yorkshire League Cup 1972, Sheffield and Hallamshire Senior Cup 1933, 1936, 1987

Sheffield Association League 1941, Mexborough Montegue Cup 1915

Manager for 1996-97: David Lloyd, Assistant Manager: Dennis Hobson

Chairman: Brian Beckett,   Vice Chairman: David Hough

Denaby's programme was voted best of the season in the league by the Wirral club in 1994 and 1995. Club shop is open all matchdays.

Formed in 1895 as the focal point of the mining village of Denaby Main, United are determined to carry on despite the decimation of the mining industry. Although the club's very early days were spent in local football, the decision was soon made to take the club higher, and so, in season 1902-03 they were elected to the Midland League after finishing runners up in the Sheffield Association League. The Midland League at the time was one of the top competitions and often provided the Football League with new clubs. Although United never won the title, they finished runner up to Sheffield Wednesday Reserves in 1908. In 1913, shortly after moving to Tickhill Square, they failed to gain re-election and were forced to rejoin the Sheffield League. The exile lasted seven years until they returned, and remained until the league folded in 1960. They had one season in the Central Alliance before the Midland League reformed, but in 1965 they were again refused re-election, moving to the Yorkshire League Division 2. In 1967 they were runners up and promoted, and the following season they were runners up to Bridlington Trinity. 1972 saw the League Cup won, but from then the club began to go into decline. In 1982, the league was merged into the Northern Counties East, and they gained promotion as runners up once again, to the Premier Division where they remain.

Denaby United's record crowd of 3,801 was set on November 15th 1958, when Oldham Athletic visited Tickhill Square in the FA Cup. In 1989 the floodlighting was finally completed after three years work and Sheffield United played a game during the following year to officially open them. United moved to Tickhill Square in 1912 to a pitch which had a side to side slope which was eliminated in 1921. The grandstand which remains today was transported from the previous ground at Denaby Lane Rec. They first played on the Red Rose ground, but when moving to Tickhill Square took the old stand complete with changing rooms. A further stand, the footings of which can still be seen on the far side of the ground, was transported from Hellaby Greyhound Stadium in 1928.

ECCLESHILL UNITED

Plumpton Park, Kingsway, Wrose, Bradford BD2 1PN. Tel: 01274 615739

Secretary: Ian Gardiner, Falt 3, 20 Cunliffe Terrace, Bradford BD8 7AS. Tel: 01274 226052

Match Sec: Keith Firth, 98 Low Ash Drive, Wrose, Shipley, BD18 1JH. Tel: 01274 592608

Prog Editor: John Burgess, Victoria Hotel, 192 Saltaire Rd, Shipley BD18 3JF. Tel: 01274 585642

Colours: Blue and white stripes

Nickname: Eagles

Capacity: 2,225

Seating: 225

Covered standing: No

Clubhouse on ground: Yes

DIRECTIONS

M62 junction 26 onto M606, right on Bradford Ring Road A6177, left onto A650 for Bradford at 2nd roundabout. A650 Bradford Inner Ring Road onto Canal Road, branch right opposite Woodhouse Builders Merchants into Kings Road, fork right after 30mph sign to junction with Wrose Road, across junction - continuation of Kings Road, 1st left onto Kingsway - ground 200 yds on right. 2 miles from Bradford (BR). Buses 686 or 687 for Wrose.

Record attendance: 600 v Bradford City in 1990

Biggest win: 7-1 v Yorkshire Main, NCEL Div 2 1986 and Winterton Rangers NCEL 1994

Biggest defeat: 0-6 Rossington Main NCEL Cup 1993 and Gt Harwood FA Cup 1991

Honours

Bradford Amateur League Cup 1962

Bradford Senior Cup 1985 and 1986

West Riding Co Amateur Lge 1977

Manager 1996-97: Ray Price

Chairman: Keith Firth

Vice Chairman: Peter Smith

There was an Eccleshill Utd prior to the Second War but this disbanded when most of the players signed up, but it re-formed in 1948 and began playing on Eccleshill Recreation Ground, which is now covered by a housing estate. Kings Park was the next stop, then Myers Lane, with a local pub providing the dressing rooms. In 1963 the club purchased some land at Plumpton Park and after much toil it was opened and has been steadily developed ever since.

United moved up from the Bradford Amateur to the West Riding League and applied to join the NCEL, but fell short of ground gradings. They ground shared with another club, Phoenix Park, who had lost their ground and after a year they disbanded and United moved into the NCEL.

With terracing, floodlights and seats for over 200, they are on their way to a Northern Premier League ground of the future.

On the pitch honours have mainly come in the 80's, with a Division Two runners up spot in 1987, and two Bradford Senior Cups in 1985 and 1986.

GARFORTH TOWN

Brierlands Lane, Aberford Rd, Garforth, Leeds LS25 2AA. Tel: 0113 286 4083

Secretary: Paul Bracewell, 24 Coupland Rd, Garforth, Leeds LS25 1AD. Tel: 0113 2863314

Prog Editor: Kevin Strangeway, 3 Poplar Ave, Garforth, Leeds LS25. Tel: 0113 286 6500

Chairman: Stephen Hayle, 17 Richmondfield Lane, Barwick, Leeds LS15 4HB. Tel: 0113 281 2548

Colours: Red and black, Nickname: The Miners or Town

Capacity: 2,000,

Seating: None

Floodlights: Yes, Covered standing: Yes, plus new stand

Clubhouse on ground: Yes

Record attendance: 817 v Leeds Utd Friendly 1987

Biggest win: 7-0 Immingham Town NCEL 1991-92

Biggest defeat: 1-7 v Lincoln Utd NCEL 1992-93

Record appearances: Philip Matthews 1982-1993

Record goalscorer in total: Vinnie Archer

DIRECTIONS

From south/east/north A642 from A1 to Garforth, ground one and a half miles on left over brow of hill. From south west, M62 junction 30, A642 to Garforth (A63 to Garforth from Leeds), through Garforth on A642, ground on right 1 mile on from lights just past junior school and Indian restaurant. Buses 18 and 83 from Leeds, alight at East Garforth Post Office - ground 500 yds on right walking away from Garforth. By rail to Garforth (Leeds-York) line - cross over bridge to Safeways side and ground just under 1 mile down road.

Honours

Barkston Ash Senior Cup 1981, 1985, 1986, 1987, 1993

Manager 1996-97: Dave Parker, Chairman: Stephen Hayle.

Garforth Town Football Club was originally formed as the Miners Arms FC in 1964 and they spent the early years in the Elmet Sunday League and the Leeds Combination, playing on a pitch in Swillington.

Following several successful years they moved to Saturday football, joining the West Yorkshire League in 1974 and acquiring their own ground on a reclaimed rubbish tip in Brierlands Lane.

In 1977 they applied to join the Yorkshire League, and on being informed that pub teams could not compete, changed their name to Garforth Miners and were elected in time to start in Division Three in 1978.

They were runners up in 1980 but became founder members of the NCEL in 1982, changing their name to Garforth Town in 1985.

Although league success has been thin on the ground, they have enjoyed themselves in cups, reaching the last eight of the FA Vase in 1987. The 90's saw both Whitby Town and Ashton United beaten in the FA Cup and some six Barkston Ash Senior Cup wins have come their way.

GLAPWELL

Hall Corner, Park Ave, Glapwell, Chesterfield, Derbys S44 5NG. Tel: 01623 812213

Secretary: Ms Lynn Winterton, 17 Park Ave, Glapwell, Chesterfield, Derbys S44 5PZ. Tel: 01623 810043

Prog Editor: Paul Winterton: Same address

Chairman: Ellen Caton, 1 The Hill, Glapwell, Chesterfield, Derbys S44 5LX Tel 01246 854648

Colours: Black and white stripes

Capacity: 1,000   Seating: No

Covered standing 200

Clubhouse on ground: Yes

Record attendance: 800+ v Chesterfield Friendly 1996

Record appearances: Stephen Brown

Record goalscorer in one season: Peter Murcott (60+ league goals in two seasons)

Record goalscorer in total: Dave Waller

Biggest win: 13-0 v Cote Heath   Biggest defeat: 1-7 v Louth United

Honours

Central Midlands Lge 1995, Floodlit Cup 1995

Manager 1996-97: Graham Gladwin, Assistant Manager: David Cunnington

Chairman: Ellen Caton, Vice Chairman: David Brunt

> ## DIRECTIONS
> A617 towards Mansfield from M1 junction 29, left at Young Inn after 2 miles, ground 100 yds on right. From Mansfield on A617, right at Glapwell crossroads after 5 miles, ground 100 yds on right.

GLASSHOUGHTON WELFARE

Welfare Ground, Leeds Rd, Glasshoughton, Castleford. Tel: 01977 518981

Secretary: Eric Jones, Marrica, Westfields Ave, Cutsyke, Castleford, WF10 5JJ. Tel: 01977 556257

Colours: Blue and white stripes

Capacity: 2,000

Seating: None

Covered standing: 250

Clubhouse on ground: Yes

Record attendance: 300 v Bradford City floodlight opener 1990

Honours

West Riding County Cup 1994

> ## DIRECTIONS
> M62, junction 31 or 32 towards Castleford. From exit 32 the road comes into Glasshoughton. From exit 31 turn right at second roundabout at Whitwood Technical College. Ground is on the left in Leeds Road. Carpark is next to the ground. 1 mile from Castleford. (BR)

The club began in 1964 as a works team called Anson Sports, playing in the Castleford Sunday League. The change to Saturday football saw them in the West Yorkshire League, when they used a number of pitches including Allerton Bywater. In 1974 an approach was made to Glasshoughton Colliery to make use of the name of the old Welfare Football Club and to play on the old Leeds Road Welfare Ground. They joined the Northern Counties East in 1985 finishing fourth in Division Three, and promotion was gained through ground grading in 1990 and again in 1991, taking them into the Premier Division where they finished last, only to survive through yet another league shuffle. The first major honour came in 1994 with the West Riding Senior Cup.

HALL ROAD RANGERS

Dene Park, Dene Close, Beverley Rd, Dunswell, Nr Hull. Tel: 01482 850101

Secretary: Peter Smurthwaite, 52 Bricknell Ave, Hull HU5 4JT. Tel: 01482 441421 (h) 211132 (b)

Prog Editor: Brendon Smurthwaite, Same address

Chairman: Roberts Smailes, 7 Cotterdale, Sutton Park, Hull HU7 4AA. Tel: 01482 821354

Colours: Blue and white hoops,

Capacity: 1,200,   Seating: 50

Covered standing: 750, Clubhouse on ground: Yes

Record attendance: 400 v Manchester City   August 1993

Record appearances: G.James

Record goalscorer in one season: G.James

Record goalscorer in total: G.James

DIRECTIONS

Hull-Beverley road (A1079 and A1174). Dunswell is first village from the Hull boundary. Entrance to ground on A1174 is 20 yds past large roundabout and opposite Dunswell Village road sign. Four and a half miles from Hull (BR).

Honours

NCEL Div 2 1991

Yorkshire Lge Div 3 1973 and 1980

East Riding Senior Cup 1973 and 1994

Manager 1996-97: Pete Smith

Assistant Manager: Pete Smurthwaite

Chairman: Bob Smailes

Press Officer: Brendon Smurthwaite

Hall Road Rangers were formed in 1959 for a group of schoolboys. They had no ball, no kit and no ground and played away friendlies which were lost heavily.

The next season saw them in the now familiar blue and white hoops and having rented a ground on Inglemire Lane, they entered the Hull Boys Sunday League. After five straight defeats they went the rest of the season unbeaten and were runners up in the league and won the Intermediate Cup.

1963 saw them win the double, and they also played in the Saturday version, a year later completing a clean sweep of two doubles, along with the Dr Lilley Cup.

It also meant that Rangers senior team were in the East Riding County League, and they won the League Senior Cup, with the junior sides also bringing in silverware. In 1965 the success continued as they won the league and Intermediate Cup, and following this spell the club moved up again to the Yorkshire League, which they won twice before it was absorbed into the new Northern Counties East League, which they won in 1991.

HALLAM

Sandygate Rd, Crosspool, Sheffield 10. Tel: 0114 230 9484

Secretary: Gordon Holland, 34 Standon Cres,
Sheffield S9 1PP. Te: 0114 249 0428

Press & Prog: Mark Radford, 98 Wheldrake Rd,
Sheffield, S5 6UE. Tel: 0114 249 7287

Other matters: J.Creswick 0114 230 2409

Colours: Blue and white, Nickname: The Countrymen

Capacity: 1,000,   Seating: 180

Covered standing: 100   Clubhouse on ground: No

Record attendance: 2,000 v Hendon
FA Amateur Cup 1959

Biggest win: 7-0 v Hatfield Main 1993

Biggest defeat: 0-7 v Hatfield Main 1988-89

Record appearances: P.Ellis 500+

Record goalscorer in one season A.Stainrod 46

DIRECTIONS

A57 Sheffield to Glossop Road, left at Crosspool shopping area signed 'Lodge Moor' on to Sandygate Road. Ground half mile on left opposite Plough Inn. 51 bus from Crucible Theatre.

Honours

Sheffield Senior Cup 1951, 1962, 1965, 1968

Youdan Cup 1867 (first ever cup competition)

Yorkshire League Div 2 1961

Manager 1996-97: K.Johnson, Assistant Manager: A.Jackson

Chairman: A. Scanlan, Vice Chairman: P.Fuller

In 1804 the landlord of the Plough Inn allowed his field to be used for cricket and by the 1850's the club was so popular that it had 300 members, many familiar with football which had started in Sheffield in 1957.

They formed Hallam FC and the first match against Sheffield took place on Boxing Day. The club founder and captain, John Charles Shaw became President of the FA and was instrumental in laying the new rules down.

In 1867 Hallam won what is believed to be the first ever cup, the Youdan Cup, named after Thomas Youdan a local football enthusiast. With the advent of professionalism Hallam could not hope to compete and were content with their place in amateur football, with occasional success in league and cup. In 1925 over 2,000 saw Hallam beat Bishop Auckland in the Amateur Cup which was the last big crowd until the club lost its ground in the 30's because the landlord of the time preferred another club. The club maintained registration and returned after the War.

By rapid promotion Hallam reached the top non-league of the area and one match in the Amateur Cup against Dulwich Hamlet was switched to Hillsborough where over 13,000 watched the game.

Hallam's history since then has been quiet and has been researched by club member John Steele. It shows the club playing in the Yorkshire League until it merged to form the Northern Counties East League.

The historic Sandygate is now secure until 2088 for the club's five sides and the future is brighter now than at any time.

HARROGATE RAILWAY ATHLETIC

Station View, Starbeck, Harrogate. Tel: 01423 885539

Secretary: W.Douglas Oldfield, 80 Stonefall Ave,
Harrogate, N.Yorks HG2 7NP. Tel: 01423 540786

Prog Editor: Craig Dinsdale, 21 Devonshire Way,
Harrogate, N.Yorks. Tel: 01423 521815 (h) 872778 (b)

Colours: Red and green, Nickname: The Rail

Capacity: 3,000, Seating: None

Covered standing: Yes, Clubhouse on ground: Yes

Record attendance: 1,400 in FA Amateur Cup
in 1962 v Billingham Synthonia

DIRECTIONS

A59 Harrogate to Knaresborough road. After approx 1.5 miles turn left just before railway level crossing. Ground is 150 yds up the lane. Adjacent to Starbeck (BR). Served by any Harrogate to Knaresborough bus.

Honours

NCEL League Cup 1987, NCEL Div2 North 1984

Harrogate Charity Cup

Harrogate Whitworths Cup, West Yorks League Cup 1953

Manager 1996-97: Tony Vincent

General Manager: Graham Shepherd

Assistant Manager: Paul Williams

Chairman: Dennis Bentley

Harrogate Railway was founded in 1935, with the railway workers from the local engine yard at Starbeck forming a side to play in the Harrogate and District League. It was not until after the Second War, however, that the club began to move up, and in 1946 the club reached the British Railways National Cup final, the success of which prompted them to begin a search for their own ground. They stayed at Station View, when the LNER agreed to lend the club £1,500 to purchase the site. The workers had 1d per week deducted from their wages to repay the debt. They did not have to wait long before their faith was repaid for both teams won their championships, with the first team winning all 24 matches and scoring 150 goals in the process.

They left the local league and joined the West Yorkshire League and in 1953 won the League Cup and became giantkillers, beating Penrith and West Auckland on their way to reaching the last eight of the Amateur Cup. In 1955 they moved up to the Yorkshire League and won Division Two in 1959.

Around that time the Railway Works at Starbeck was closed and many locals left to find work elsewhere. The club struggled from then on through the 50's and 60's and in 1970 returned to the Harrogate League. After five years of stabilising they returned to the Yorkshire League which became the NCEL. In 1984 they won the Second Division North and in 1987 they took the League Cup and were promoted to the Premier Division. They also reached the West Ridng County Cup final where they lost to Goole Town 2-1.

More recently the old ground has had floodlights installed as the Railwaymen continue in Division One, having suffered relegation.

HATFIELD MAIN

Dunscroft Welfare, Dunscroft, Doncaster, S.Yorks. Tel: 01302 841326

Secretary: Bruce Hatton, 92 Ingram Rd, Dunscroft, Doncaster DN7 4JE. Tel: 01302 841648

Chairman: Arthur Jones, 26 Hampton Rd, Dunscroft, Doncaster DN7 4AJ. Tel: 01302 843338

Prog Editor: Anthony Ingram, 78 Grange Ave, Hatfield, Doncaster, DN7 6RD Tel 01302 842795

Colours: All Red

Nickname: The Main

Capacity: 4,000

Seating: Yes

Covered standing: Yes

Clubhouse on ground: Yes

Record attendance: 1,000 v Leeds Utd Arthur Jones Testimonial and 750 v Bishop Auckland FA Amateur Cup

Record appearances: Lal Dutt

DIRECTIONS

From Doncaster (A18) Scunthorpe Road to Dunsville, left at Flarepath Hotel down Broadway. Ground half mile on right. Half mile from Stamforth & Hatfield (BR). Buses ever fifteen minutes from Doncaster.

Honours

NCEL Div 1 1995

West Riding Senior Cup 1962 & 1963

Hatfield Main FC were formed in 1936 as a representation of the local mining industry and their early days were spent in the Doncaster and District League before moving up to the Yorkshire League in 1955.

They were runners up in Division Two in 1964 and having been promoted were runners up in Division One in 1966. There has been silverware via the West Riding Cup, in 1962 and 1963, and when the NCEL was formed following the merger, the club became founder members. In 1989 the club were runners up in the league but the team soon split up and they were relegated a year later. After a few barren years they went close to regaining their spot, and were champions in 1995, moving up to take the Premier Division title last season by two points from Stocksbridge Park Steels. Sadly they were not in a position to go up and Steels were promoted above them.

HUCKNALL TOWN

Watnall Rd, Hucknall, Notts NG15 7LP. Tel: 0115 956 1253

Secretary: Brian Scothern, 95 Brookfield Ave, Shortwood Est, Hucknall, Notts NG15 6FF

Tel: 0115 956 3151

Press and Prog editor: Simon Matters, 199 Nottingham Rd, Hucknall, Notts NG15 7QB

Tel: 0115 956 1336 (h), 0115 974 1383 (b) 0378 172877 (m)

Nickname: Town,   Capacity: 2,500

Seating: 240,   Covered standing: 1,000

Clubhouse on ground: Yes

Record atten: 1,302 v Macclesfield Town FA Cup 92

Honours

Notts Junior Cup 1963

Bulwell and District League and Cup double twice

Notts Alliance Div 2 1971, Notts Alliance Div 1 1973, 1981, 1987

Senior Division 1977, 1978, 1988, 1989, Intermediate Cup 1973, 1979, 1980, 1981, 1984

League Cup 1979, Notts FA Intermediate Cup 1988

Central Midlands League Supreme Division 1990 and 1991, League Cup 1990, 1991, 1992

Northern Counties East League Cup 1994, Notts Senior Cup 1985 and 1991

Manager for 1996-97: John Ramshaw, Chairman: John Coleman

Vice Chairman: John Beharall

> ## DIRECTIONS
> M1 junction 27, A608 to lights, right onto A611 to Hucknall, right at roundabout (new bypass), over next roundabout, right at next roundabout into Watnall Road - ground entrance on right. From M1 junction 26 follow Nottm signs to lights on island, left onto A610, right at Three Ponds pub onto B600 towards Watnall, 200 yds past Queens Head turn right signed Hucknall, follow over morotway and past Rolls Royce - ground on left. 7 miles from Nottingham (BR) station - bus 344.

The 1995-96 season, the club's 50th was the fourth that the club had competed in the Northern Counties East, where they picked up the League Cup in 1994.

Their rapid rise from a Colliery side has been impressive. Founded in 1945 the club did not enjoy success until 1963 when taking the Notts Junior Cup as a Central Alliance club. Upon re-joining the Bulwell and District League in 1964, Town won the League and Cup double two seasons running. A move to the Notts Spartan League saw them claim runners up spot in the second season and in 1970 they moved up to the Notts Alliance. Wasting no time, the club won Division Two in 1971 and went on to take the Division One and Cup double 12 months later. A further promotion to the Senior League brought the title in 1976 and 1977 with the League Cup in 1979.

There were several more titles in the 80's which heralded a run of FA Vase success, reaching the last 16 on three occasions. The closure of the Colliery in 1988 marked the beginning of the success story. Many clubs would have gone under, but Hucknall changed their name from Colliery Welfare to Town and began to build up their ground. They entered the Central Midlands League in 1989, doing the League and Cup double and repeating it a year later. In 1992 they retained the League Cup again and were runners up in the league and following the league entering the pyramid, the club joined the Northern Counties East, earning promotion in 1993 and the League Cup in 1994.

Hucknall have been at Watnall Road since moving from the Welfare Ground in Wigwam Lane in the 50's, when it was needed for tipping. The ground was laid out parallel to the road with the changing rooms at the Pit Baths across the road where the petrol station is now. In recent times there have been plans suggested for a change of ground, but for the time being it looks as though the club are staying put having invested much money and toil into gaining the necessary gradings.

LIVERSEDGE

Clayborn Ground, Quaker Lane, Hightown Rd, Cleckheaton. Tel: 01274 862108

Secretary: Michael Balmforth, 7 Reform St, Gomersal, Cleckheaton, BD19 5NP. Tel: 01274 862123

Chairman: Robert Gawthorpe, 23 Clayborn View, Hightown Rd, Cleckheaton BD19 5NP. Tel: 01274 879055

Colours: All Blue

Nickname: Sedge

Capacity: 2,000

Seating: 250

Covered standing: 300

Clubhouse on ground: Yes

DIRECTIONS

M62 junction 26, A638 into Cleckheaton, right at lights on corner of Memorial Park, through next lights & under railway bridge, 1st left (Hightown Road) and Quaker Lane is approx quarter mile on left and leads to ground. From M1 junction 40, A638 through Dewsbury and Heckmondwike to Cleckheaton, left at Memorial Park lights then as above. Buses 218 & 220 (Leeds-Huddersfield) pass top of Quaker Lane.

Honours

West Riding County Challenge Cup 1949, 1952, 1970

West Riding County Cup 1990

West Riding County Amateur League 1924, 1926, 1928, 1965, 1966, 1969

League Cup 1958 and 1965

Spen Valley League and League Cup 1949

Manager 1996-97: Paul Murphy

Assistant Manage: Tony Passmore

Chairman: Bob Gawthorpe

Liversedge were founded in 1910 from the old Liversedge Rugby Club which was a member of the Northern Union which preceded the Rugby League. They were one of a number of clubs which switched codes around that time and they joined the West Riding County Amateur League just after the Great War, winning the title three times in five years.

The long association with the league was maintained until the early 70's when they applied to the Yorkshire League, where they won promotion straight away. Whilst not winning trophies, there was some success as they reached the top division before it was amalgamated into the new Northern Counties East League in 1982. The early years saw Sedge struggle on and off the pitch but in 1989 they were promoted to Division One and only the lack of floodlights stopped them going up a year later. Lights were installed in 1991 and they went up in third place and won the West Riding County Cup for the first time in their history.

LOUTH UNITED

Park Ave, Louth, Lincs LN11 8BX. Tel: 01507 607351

Secretary: Albany Jordan, 20d Upgate, Louth, Lincs
LN11 9ET. Tel: 01507 600694

Chairman: George Horton, 56 Spire Rd, Louth, Lincs
LN11 8SL. Tel: 01507 606578

DIRECTIONS
A16 to Louth market place, exit via
Eastgate/Eastfield Road to 1st
junction, past Fire Station.

Colours: Royal blue and white stripes, Nickname: Lions

Capacity: 4,000,   Seating: No

Covered standing: Yes, Clubhouse on ground: Yes

Record attendance: 3,200 v Derby County Friendly 1990

Record appearances: Gary Smith 476

Record goalscorer in one season: Peter Rawcliffe

Record goalscorer in total: Alan Cooper

Record fee received £10,000 for Martyn Chalk to Derby Co. 1990

Honours

Lincolnshire League 1973, 1986, 1987

Division One 1958, 1967, 1968

Challenge Cup 1974 and 1987

Charity Cup 1956, 1957, 1968

Supplementary Cup 1986

Lincs Senior A Cup 1978

Manager 1996-97: Steve Newby, Assistant Manager: Nigel Fanthorpe

Training advisor: David Cole, Chairman: George Horton

Vice Chairman: Andrew Silvester, Press Officer: Albany Jordan

Commercial Manager: John Gardiner c/o Football Club

The present Louth United was formed in 1947 after an amalgamation of Louth Town and Louth Nats.

It was the formation of the Lincolnshire League that prompted the merger with United becoming founder members. They remained until the mid-70's before joining the Midland Counties for a spell until financial problems saw them return to the Lincolnshire league.

Since then the club has been on a sounder footing and in 1987 accepted an offer to join the Supreme Division of the Central Midlands League. Louth United FC own the 7 acres of land at Park Avenue which was bought by public subscription. Recent success includes winning the Lincs League in 1986 and 1987, as well as the Supplementary Cup and Challenge Cup.

MALTBY MAIN

Muglet Lane, Maltby,. Tel: 01709 812462

Secretary: Nick Dunhill, 10 Conrad Drive, Maltby,
Rotherham, S66 8RS. Tel: 01709 815676

Chairman: Graham McCormick 41 Parkstone Crescent,
Hellaby, Rotherham, S66 8HG Tel 01709 546154

Colours: White and black

Nickname: Miners

Capacity: 2,000

Seating: Yes

Covered standing: Yes

Clubhouse on ground: Yes

Record attendance: 1,500 v Sheffield Wed in friendly 1992, 940 v Thackley Yorkshire League Cup 1978

Record appearances: Russ Evans

Record goalscorer in total: Russ Evans

DIRECTIONS

Exit M18 junction with A631. Two miles into Maltby, right at crossroads at Queens Hotel corner onto B6427. Ground is 3/4 mile on left. Bus 101 from Rotherham stops at ground.

Honours

Sheffield and Hallamshire Sen Cup 1978

NCEL Presidents Cup 1993

Mexborough Montague Cup 1977, 1981, 1991

Wharncliffe Cup 1981

Manager 1996-97: Dave McCarthy

Assistant Managers: Simon Dwyer and Kenny Geelan

Vice Chairman: Mick Richardson

Reformed as recently as 1972, Maltby have made tremendous progress in their time.

Having had one year in the Sheffield County Senior League they joined the Yorkshire League in 1973 and were runners up in the first season. By the time the league was absorbed into the new Northern Counties East in 1982, they had risen to the the top, but played the last season in Division Two having been relegated.

They were put in Division One South until the league went to three divisions with Maltby in the Central Division, but when they again changed things Maltby were placed in Division Two. They made it to the top division in 1990 and in 1993 they won the Presidents Cup.

Much work has gone on to enclose the football ground from the rest of what was the Welfare Ground, where the original club played as Maltby Main. After 24 years as the Miners Welfare, the club again are known as Maltby Main.

NORTH FERRIBY UNITED

Grange Lane, Church Rd, North Ferriby, East Yorkshire HU14 3AA.Tel: 01482 634601

Secretary: Stephen Tather, 16 Peasholme, Heads Lane, Hessle, East Yorkshire HU13 OHY

Tel: (h) 01482 642046 (b) 01482 581090

Prog Editor: Mr Jeff Frank, Coach House, West End, Swanland, E. Yorks HU14 3PE. Tel: 01482 633387

Chairman: Les Hare, 235 Hull Road, Anlaby Common, Hull HU4 7RY. Tel: 01482 564285

Press Officer: Roy Wallis, 54 Wolfreton Rd, Anlaby, East Yorkshire HU10 6QT

Tel: 01482 657721 (H) 01482 586144 (B)

DIRECTIONS	
Main Leeds-Hull road A63 or M62, North Ferriby is 8 miles west of Hull. Into North Ferriby, through village past the Duke of Cumberland Hotel, right down Church Road, ground half mile on left. One mile from North Ferriby (BR).	

Nickname: United,   Capacity: 2,500

Seating: 250,   Covered standing: 500

Clubhouse on ground: Yes, Colours: Green & white

Record attendance: 1,800 v Tamworth FA Vase semi-final 2nd Leg 1989

Biggest win: 9-2

Biggest defeat: 1-7 v North Shields NCEL 1991

Record appearances: Richard Womble

Record goalscorer in one season: Mark Tennison 43

Record goalscorer in total: Mark Tennison

Record fee received: £60,000 for Dean Windass to HullCity

Honours

FA VASE semi-final 1989

Yorkshire League Division Two 1971, Yorkshire League Cup   1975

East Riding Senior Cup 1971, 77, 78, 79, 91, Northern Counties East Div 1 1986

President's Cup 1991

Manager for 1996-97: Tim Hotte, Assistant Manager: Brian France

Chairman: Les Hare, Vice chairman: Brian Sievewright

In 1984, North Ferriby produced a Golden Jubilee Handbook to celebrate their first 50 years.

North Ferriby United were formed in 1934 when some of the best players in the area decided to form a team for the village. They first competed in the local East Riding Church League and in 1938 they won the Division One championship. Post-War re-formation saw them join the East Riding Amateur League and they were fairly successful during this period, the highlight being when they reached the last qualifying round of the Amateur Cup in 1949-50. In 1969 Ferriby gained a more senior status when they joined the Yorkshire League Division Two, and the following season went on to win the championship and the East Riding Senior Cup. In 1975 they won the Yorkshire League Cup and finished runners up to Emley a year later. During the 70's, United won the Senior Cup three times and broke new ground by reaching the 3rd qualifying round of the FA Cup, losing away to Boston Utd. In 1982 they joined the new Northern Counties East, in Division One North where they finished runners up, but were denied promotion due to ground grading problems. Three years later they were champions and were promoted and reached the 4th Round of the FA Vase, a year later going one better, losing to Farsley Celtic.1988-89 was the highlight of the club's history to date when they progressed to the FA Vase semi-final, winning the First Leg at Tamworth. Over 1,800 saw the return when they were defeated with just ten minutes left. Ferriby continued to prosper, winning the Presidents Cup over two legs against Guisley and then winning the East Riding Cup again, finishing runners up in the League Cup. On promotion to the Yorkshire League in 1969, United built a ground suitable for that competition, after playing on the nearby Playing Fields and having to erect trainers boxes, post and rail, goals and nets before each game, whilst building continued. Post and rails from the defunct Hull Brunswick ground were used at Grange Road, which opened in 1970.

OSSETT ALBION

Dimple Wells, Ossett Tel: 01924 273618 Club or 280450 matchdays only

Secretary: David R Chambers, 109 South Parade, Ossett, Wakefield WF5 0BE. Tel: 01924 276004

Also try Andrew Lightfoot 01924 276898

Chairman: Neville Wigglesworth, 41 Greenfield Ave, Ossett, Wakefield WF5 0ER. Tel 01924 273618

Colours: Old Gold and black,   Nickname: Albion

Capacity: 3,000,   Seating: Yes

Covered standing: Yes, Clubhouse on ground: Yes

Record attendance: 1, 200 v Leeds Utd
Floodlight opener1986

DIRECTIONS

M1 junction 40. Take Wakefield road, right at Post House Hotel down Queens Drive. At end right then second left down Southdale Road. At end right, then first left down Dimple Wells (cars only). Coaches take second left following the road for 200 yds bearing left twice. Four miles from both Wakefield and Dewsbury BR stations. Buses 116 and 117.

Biggest win: 12-0 British Ropes Yorks Lge Div 2 1959

Biggest defeat: 2-11 v Swillington West Yorks Lge 1956

Record appearances: Peter Eaton 800+ in 22 years

Record goalscorer in one season: John Balmer 44

Record goalscorer in total: John Balmer

Honours

Yorkshire League 1975

League Cup 1976 and 1977, Division Two 1979 and 1981

NCEL Div 1 1987 and League Cup 1984, West Yorks Lge 1954 and 1956

Division Two and League Cup 1953, West Riding County Cup 1965, 1966, 1968

Wheatley Cup 1957 and 1959

Manager 1996-97: Jimmy Martin, Assistant Manager: Peter Eaton

Chairman: Neville Wigglesworth, Vice Chairman: Stewart Garside

Ossett Albion was formed in 1944 as a junior team, a rarity in that they were formed during the War.

The first fixture was on September 16th against Batley St Mary's.

After a couple of seasons at junior level they were successful in the Heavy Woollen League and Cup competition. It was not long before the club were elected to the West Riding County Amateur League for a year before joining the West Yorkshire League for seven years, winning the Division Two League and Cup double in 1953, and the League itself in 1954 and 1956. They joined the Yorkshire League in 1957 and enjoyed a run of success taking Division Two twice and the title in 1975, also winning consecutive League Cups and County Cups.In those early days the club were nomadic, having played at Manor Road School Playing Fields, Church Street Recreation Ground, Netttleton's Field, Luther Ingram's Field in Kingsway Deneside and Fern House, which they shared with Ossett Town. They made their last move in 1956, and at Queens Terrace they have developed from being part of a cricket ground to a fully enclosed football pitch and in recent years much work has gone on at the Dimple Wells ground, which was until fairly recently part of the cricket ground, but with segregation, floodlights, new dressing rooms and additional cover, it has been transformed. In 1980 the club was rocked by internal problems and it ended with relegation, but the ship was steadied and since the formation of the NCEL the club has won the League Cup in 1984 and the Division One championship in 1987. Premier Division football proved a struggle but they came through and reached the League Cup final and the last 16 of the FA Vase, under Jimmy Martin.

OSSETT TOWN

Ingfield, Prospect Rd, Ossett, Wakefield, WF5 8AN Tel: 01924 272960

Secretary: Frank Lloyd, 27 Park Close, Mapplewell, Barnsley, S75 6BY Tel 01226 382415

Chairman: Graham Firth, 4 Tumbling Close, Ossett, Wakefield, WF5 0QX Tel: 01924 279049

Prog Editor: Tony Timlin, 4 Belgrave St, Ossett, Wakefield WF5 0AD Tel 01924 277384

Colours: All Red,   Capacity: 4, 000

Seating: 360,   Covered standing: 650

Clubhouse on ground: Yes

DIRECTIONS

M1 junction 40, B6129 to Ossett, left into Dale Street, left again at lights opposite bus station on ring road, ground on left. Nearest stations Dewsbury or Wakefield Westgate - both three miles from. Buses 116, 117, 126 and 127 from Wakefield, buses 116, 126 and 127 from Dewsbury, buses 117, 118 or 216 from Leeds.

Record attendance: 2,600 v Manchester Utd Friendly 1988

Biggest win: 12-0 v Wombwell 1959-60

Biggest defeat: 0-7 v Easington Colliery FA Vase 1983

Record appearances: Frank Lloyd

Record goalscorer in one season: Don Scarlett 60+, Record goalscorer in total Don Scarlett

Record fee received: £1,350 for Derek Blackburn to Swansea in 1957

Honours

West Riding Senior Cup 1948, West Riding County Cup 1959 and 1982

Northern Counties East Div 2 1989 and League Cup 1980

Manager for 1996-97: Trevor Best, Assistant manager: Paul Murphy

Chairman: Graham Firth, Vice Chairman: Bruce Saul

A new fanzine is to be published 'Red Mist', details from Tony Timlin, 4 Belgrave St, Ossett, Wakefield, WF5 0AD

Ossett Town were formed in 1936 by Mr John Carter and friends at a meeting in the Cock and Bottle pub in Ossett. They played on a pitch behind the Fern House Working Mens Club on Wakefield Road, whilst their first league matches were in the Leeds League, re-named the West Yorkshire League in 1939. During the War, they transferred to the more local Heavy Woollen League, when the Army commandeered Fern House, meaning the club moved to a pitch in Back Lane. In 1945, Ossett Town joined the Yorkshire League and won the West Riding Senior Cup three years later, but apart from two League Cup finals in 1954 and 1958, there was a lack of silverware. Despite this the club attracted attendances of 1,000 plus and the Supporters Club thrived. Astute transfers in the late 50's meant that they could buy the Ingfield site, where they currently play. In 1959 the won the Senior Cup again, only to be relegated the same season. Promotion was won at the first attempt, but in 1962 they went down again and their fortunes declined during the 60's to a point where attendances dropped to 30. In 1970, they were founder members of the new Third Division, and won promotion but once again in 1975 they were relegated again. Yet again they went back up at the first attempt and in 1977 missed out on Division One by one goal. They finally returned in 1978, but two years later went down yet again. 1981-82 was the last ever season of the Yorkshire League, and Ossett were runners up to Harrogate Town, also winning the County Cup, beating Bradley Rangers 2-0. In 1982 they joined the Northern Counties East, ending after reshuffles in Division Two. With a strong squad they won the league under Micky Bullock in 1989, where the FA Vase Fifth Round was reached . The League Cup was also won and in the first season in the top flight, they were eighth. Since then the club has had a quiet period, but Ingfield has vastly improved. New changing rooms were acquired from Denby Grange Colliery, the pitch was relaid, a 5-a-side pitch laid down and floodlights erected in 1990.

PARKGATE

Roundwood Sports Complex, Green Lane, Rawmarsh, Rotherham S62 6LA. Tel: 01790 826600

Secretary: Bruce Bickerdike, 2 Cardew Close, Rawmarsh, Rotherham, S62 6LB.
Tel: 01709 522305 Fax: 01709 528583

Chairman: Albert Dudill, 27 Nether Haugh, Wentworth, Rotherham S62 7RZ. Tel: 01709 524533

Press and programme Stuart Bisby, 21 Trueman Green, Maltby, Rotherham S66 8QR

Tel: 01709 817524 fax: 01709 528583

Nickname: The Steelmen

Capacity: 3,000

Seating: 100

Covered standing 300

Floodlights: Yes

Clubhouse on ground: Yes

Honours

Rotherham Charity Cup

Manager for 1996-97: Glyn Kenny

Assistant manager: John Mason

Vice chairman: Leslie Taylor

> ## DIRECTIONS
> **From Rotherham A633 to Rawmarsh. From Doncaster A630 to Conisborough, then A6023 through Swinton to Rawmarsh. Ground at Green Lane - right from Rotherham, left from Conisborough at the Crown Inn. Ground 800 yds on right.**

The club was formed in September 1969 from the Steelworks Wire Department, and were four times winners of the National Wire Drawers Cup. Joined Division Two of the Hatchard League and in 1971 joined the Sheffield and Hallamshire Senior League, where the reserves still are, which is now known as the County Senior League. In 1973 the club moved into the Yorkshire League as BSC Parkgate FC and when that league was incorporated into the Northern Counties East, they were part of it. They have since been known as RES Parkgate, although they are known simply as Parkgate FC.

PICKERING TOWN

Recreation Club, Mill Lane (Off Malton Rd), Pickering, North Yorks. Tel: 01751 473317

Secretary Alan Brenkley, 32 The Chase, Norton, Malton, N.Yorks YO17 9AS. Tel: 01653 692743

Chairman Anthony Dunning, 13 Mill Lane, Pickering, N.Yorks YO18 8DJ Tel 01751 473697

DIRECTIONS
A169 from Malton, 1st left past Police Station and B.P. garage into Mill Lane, ground 300 yds on right.

Nickname: The Pikes

Founded: 1888

Capacity: 2,000

Seating: 100

Covered standing: 500

Clubhouse on ground: Yes

Record attendance: 1,412 v Notts Co Friendly 1991

Honours

Recent honours only Yorkshire League Div 3 1974

Northern Counties East Div 2 1988

North Riding County Cup 1991

Manager for 1996-97: Michael Hodgson

Assistant manager: Bob Scaife

Vice chairman: Keith Stamper

The club celebrated its 100th birthday in 1988, Bobby Robson, the England manager presenting the club with the FA Scroll of Honour.

For the first eighty odd years the Pikes played in Beckett, York and District and Scarborough and District League football until moving up to the 3rd Division of the Yorkshire League in 1972. They were champions the following season, gaining promotion to Division Two where they finished runners-up, reaching Division One. They became founder members of the Northern Counties (East) in 1982, winning Division Two in 1988.

The Pikes won the North Riding County FA Cup in 1991 for the very first time in their history and a year later finished second in Division One, finally reaching the Premier Division, losing out to Spennymoor United in the race for the championship on the last day of the season.

Over the past ten seasons the club has made vast improvements to their picturesque ground, including installing floodlights and a covered area for 300 people. Last season was a modest one, finishing in mid-table.

FORMER GROUNDS

Pickering have been at Mill Lane since 1920, where they shared the ground with cricket and bowls. In the early days a field was used at Westgate Back, players often changing behind a hedge. After moving to Mill Lane a small pavilion was erected and in 1956 supporters built a new stand of steel and corrugated sheeting.

PONTEFRACT COLLIERIES

Skinner Lane, Pontefract, West Yorks. Tel: 01977 600818

Secretary: Alan Slater, 1 Northland View, Pontefract, WF8 1HS. Tel: 01977 600966

Match Secretary, Programme Editor and Press Officer:

Alan Dean, 1 Scawthorpe Close, Pontefract WF8 2HT Tel: 01977 796091

Chairman Mike Norman, Ashville Lodge, 10 High Ash Drive, Leeds LS17 8QY. Tel: 0113 266 4900

Nickname: The Colls,

Capacity: 1,200

Seating: 400,

Covered standing: 400

A new 220 seater stand is expected to be ready for the start of this season.

Clubhouse on ground: Yes

Record attendance: 1,000 v Hull City Friendly in 1985

Biggest defeat: 0-12 v Lincoln Utd 1994-95

Record appearances: John Brown

Record goalscorer in one season: Gary Cygan

Record goalscorer in total: John Williams

DIRECTIONS

M62 junction 32 towards Pontefract. Left at traffic lights opposite Racecourse entrance (travelling through Pontefract follow Racecourse/Leeds signs to traffic lights and turn right) - ground past Territorial Army unit. 1 mile from Monkhill (BR). All Leeds and Castleford buses stop near ground.

Honours

Castleford Cup: 1983 and 1994, Embleton Cup: 1983, 1994, 1996

Northern Counties East Floodlit Cup 1988 and 1989

NCEL Div 1 1984, Division Two North: 1983

Yorkshire League Div 3 1982

Manager for 1996-97: Jim Kenyon, Assistant Manager: Frank Maclachlan

Chairman: Mike Norman, Vice Chairman: George Jackson

Pontefract Collieries FC was formed in 1958 from the remnants of the former Pontefract United. The club quickly gained success in the West Yorkshire League but the most notable achievement was winning the West Riding Challenge Cup in 1972.

Season 1979-80 saw them join the Yorkshire League where they missed promotion by one place in the first season, but in 1982 they became founder-members of the new Northern Counties East League, where they gained promotion in 1985. Since then a number of honours have come their way and last May they completed a memorable season, finishing runners up to Selby Town on goal difference of two goals.

However the Wilkinson Sword, and Embleton Cups were won.

ROSSINGTON MAIN

Welfare Ground, Oxford Street, Rossington, Doncaster. Tel: 01302 865524

Secretary: Gerald Parsons, 15 Seaton Gardens,
Rossington, Doncaster DN11 0XA. Tel: 01302 867542

Chairman: Stephen Tagg, Clematis Cott, 52 High St,
Collingham, Newark NG23 7LB. Tel: 01636 892833

Colours: All White

Nickname: Colliery

Seating: 200

Covered standing: 300

Floodlights: Yes

Clubhouse on ground: Yes, Welfare Ground

Record attendance: approx 2,000 Leeds Utd 1991 opening new stand

Record appearances: Darren Phipps

DIRECTIONS

Enter Rossington and go over the railway crossings. Pass the Welfare Club on right, Oxford Street is next right - ground is at bottom. 8 miles from Doncaster (BR).

Honours

Central Midlands Premier Division and League Cup 1985

Manager 1996-97: Dave Ridley

Assistant Manager: Louis Ossell

The team was originally formed in 1926 to provide Colliery workers with a game of football and was called Rossington Main FC. When the mines were nationalised the club changed its name to Rossington Miners Welfare and has only reverted within the last ten years.

The present day club came through the Doncaster Senior League into the Central Midlands League during the early 80's and did the League and League Cup double in 1985. As a result they were invited to join the newly formed Supreme Division. Despite its considerable success, the club were forced to make significant ground improvements and new dressing rooms and a stand was completed in 1991, and with other work done the ground was ready for the club to move into the NCEL.

SELBY TOWN

Richard Street, Scott Rd, Selby, YO8 0BS. Tel: 01757 210900

Secretary: Keith Tiplady, 58a St Mary's Ave, Hemingbrough, Selby N.Yorks YO8 7YY
Tel 01757 638219

Match Sec: Paul Atkin, 6 The Link, Carlton, Nr Goole, E.Yorks DN14 9QE. Tel: 01405 861829

Chairman: Barrie Wilkes, Milton Lodge, Wistow Gt, Cawood, Nr Selby, YO8 0UT Tel 01757 268319

Prog Editor Mark Fairweather, 48 Baffam Gardens, Brayton, Selby YO8 9AZ Tel 01757 705376

Colours: Red and white,

DIRECTIONS

From Leeds, left at main traffic lights in Selby Town down Scott Road, then 1st left into Richard Street. From Doncaster go straight across main traffic lights into Scott Road then 1st left. From York at main traffic lights into Scott Road, and 1st left. 1 mile from Selby Railway Station.

Nickname: Robins

Capacity: 3,000, Seating: 225, Covered standing: 300, Clubhouse on ground: Yes

Record attendance: 6, 500 v Bradford PA FA Cup 1st Rd 1953

Biggest win: 14-1 v Altofts WRC 1935

Biggest defeat: 0-14 v Bradford Park Ave Res Yorkshire League 1928

Record goalscorer in total: Graham Shepherd 163 1963-1982

Honours

Yorkshire League 1933, 1935, 1936, 1953, 1954, League Cup 1938, 1954, 1955, 1963

West Riding Senior Cup 1938, West Riding County Cup 1928 and 1949

West Riding Challenge Cup 1935 and 1936, Northern Counties East Div 1 1996

Manager 1996-97: Barry Walker and Tony Carter, Chairman: Barry Wilkes

Vice Chairman: Ken Hambrett

Selby Town were formed in 1919 and were the first senior club in the town since before the Great War. After one year in the York and District League they became founder members of the Yorkshire League in 1920, and were the only club to play every season in the league's history. The club's best days came either side of the Second War. The 30's saw them win the league three times with a League Cup and three West Riding Cups and in the 50's there were two more titles and two League Cups. It also saw the best FA Cup performances reaching the First Round on four occasions.

Other than a runners up place in Division Two of the Northern Counties League there has been little to cheer about since then, the club having been founder members when the Yorkshire and Midland Leagues merged in 1982. Apart from one short spell at a temporary home in the 20's, Selby have only had two homes. The first was at the James Street Recreation Ground, known locally as the Bowling Green, which was council owned and was a notorious mud heap, and the current ground which became home in the early 1950's. At one time the purpose built ground could hold 10,000 but it deteriorated and has only recently been refurbished and is looking better than for for many years.

On the field there have been improvements for in 1995 the club put together an unbeaten run of 14 games to finish third and last year they were Division One champions, also having runs in three major cup competitions.

SHEFFIELD

Owlerton Stadium, Penistone Rd, Owlerton Green, Sheffield S6 2DE. Tel: 0114 234 3074 fax 0114 233 3631

Secretary: Stephen Hall, 24 Crofton Ave, Sheffield S6 1WF. Tel: 0114234 4553

Chairman: Peter Beal, 46 Crawford Rd, Norton Lees, Sheffield S8 9BU Tel 0114 258 6186

Prog Editor: Terry Langford, 1 Fife Gardens, Wincobank, Sheffield. Tel: 0114 296 7022

Colours: Red and black quarters

Nickname: The Club

Capacity: 2,000   Seating: Yes

Covered standing: Yes   Clubhouse on ground: Yes

Record attendance: 2,000 v Barton Rovers
FA Vase semi-final 1977

DIRECTIONS

Adjacent to Hillsborough Stadium, home of Sheffield Wednesday FC.

Honours

FA AMATEUR CUP WINNERS 1904

FA VASE Runners up 1977

NCEL League Cup 1995

Division One 1989 and 1991

Yorkshire Lge Div 2 1977

Sheffield Football Club is the oldest football club in the world, having been established on the 24th October 1857. Two Army Officers, Colonel Nathaniel Creswick and Major William Priest, both stationed at Sheffield Barracks, who had the idea of developing the game and drew up a code as well as laid down regulations for running the club. By 1862 15 clubs had been formed in Sheffield but Sheffield FC were dominant up to the advent of professionalism. In 1872 England played Scotland in the first ever International and Sheffield's JC Clegg was capped by England. He went on to become a League referee, officiated in the Cup finals in 1882 and 1892 and became President of the FA.

As the game became more popular, professional players were introduced and Sheffield fought against it and their stand coincided with the club's decline. Throughout the years they have often only just managed to survive. They managed to remain within the Yorkshire League right through to its amalgamation into the NCEL, but with little success after the glory days of the turn of the century when they won the Amateur Cup, beating Ealing FC at Bradford.

Nearly 75 years later the club were back in the limelights as they reached Wembley in the FA Vase Final and held Billericay Town to a 1-1 draw before losing the replay at Nottingham Forest. More recently they were champions of Division One of the NCEL in 1989 and 1991 and in 1994 won the Sheffield Senior Cup beating Worksop in the final.

Sheffield played a few early matches at Bramall Lane and later moved to Abbeydale Park which is now a multi sports complex. Having been overtaken by league gradings they moved in 1989 to a n old athletics track next door to Hillsborough, but due to the lack of floodlighting they moved again to the awesome 25,000 capacity Don Valley Stadium in 1991.

From there they moved in 1994 to the Owlerton Greyhound Stadium where they remain.

TADCASTER ALBION

The Park, Ings Lane, Tadcaster LS24 9AY. Tel: 01937 834119

Secretary: Mrs A. Burnett, 5 Beech Grove House,
Ouston Lane, Tadcaster, N Yorks LS24 8DP

Tel: and fax: 01937 832802

Match Sec: Howard Clarke, 1 Auster Bank Crescent,
Tadcaster, N.Yorks LS24 8AY. Tel: 01937 833521

Chairman: Michael R.Burnett, address as Secretary

Colours: Red and navy halves

Nickname: Brewers

Founded: 1926

Capacity: 2,000

Seating: No

Floodlights: Yes

Covered standing: Yes

Clubhouse on ground: Yes

Record attendance: 1,000 v Winterton Rangers FA Vase 1977

Biggest win: (NCEL) 7-1 v Immingham Town 1993-94

Biggest defeat: (NCEL) 2-10 v Thackley 1984-85

DIRECTIONS

From West Riding and South Yorks, turn right off A659 at John Smith's Brewery Clock. From East Riding turn left off A659 after passing over river bridge and pelican crossing (New Street).

Manager 1996-97: Bob Hunter

Assistant Manager: Rob Hunter

Vice Chairman: Jack Tomkinson

Tadcaster Albion are not surprisingly nicknamed the Brewers, and were formed in 1926. They play at The Park in Ings Lane, which has an estimated capacity of around 1,500, some 500 above the record gate which saw the club play Winterton Rangers in the FA Vase in 1977.

They played in York and District and Harrogate and District Leagues before joining the Yorkshire League and subsequently the NCEL.

THACKLEY

Dennyfield, Ainsbury Ave, Thackley, Bradford, West Yorks. Tel: 01274 615571

Secretary: Stewart Willingham, 3 Kirklands Close, Baildon, Shipley, West Yorks. Tel: 01274 598589

Colours: Red and White,

Capacity: 2,000

Seating: 250 seater stand is expected to be ready by end of this season

Covered standing: 200

Clubhouse on ground: Yes

Record attendance: 1,500 v Leeds Utd Friendly 84

Record goalscorer in one season:
Stuart Taylor 48 in 1993-94

DIRECTIONS

On main Leeds/Keighley A657 road, turn off at Thackley corner which is 2 miles from Shipley traffic lights and 1 mile from Greengates lights. Ainsbury Avenue bears to the right 200 yds down the hill. Ground is 200 yds along Ainsbury Avenue on the right. 3 miles from Bradford Interchange (BR), one and a half miles from Shipley (BR). Buses to Thackley corner (400 yds).

Honours

Bradford Mutual Sunday School League 4 times, League Cup 3 times

Bradford Amateur League 5 times, League Cup twice

West Riding County Cup 1974 and 1975

Bradford Senior Cup 1939, 1950, 1956, 1958, 1959, 1960, 1966, 1967, 1979, 1988, 1995

West Riding County Amateur League 1958, 1959, 1960

Challenge Cup 1964 and 1967

Yorkshire League Div 2 1974

West Yorkshire League 1967

Managers for 1996-97: John Boyle and Colin Smith, Chairman: John Myers

Club shop is open on match days selling programmes, badges, hats and mugs.

Contact 30 Park Avenue, Thackley, Bradford, West Yorks BD10 0RJ

Thackley AFC was founded in 1930 as Thackley Wesleyans and joined the Bradford Mutual Sunday School League. Between 1930 and 1938, when they moved into the Bradford Amateur League, they won the league four times and the league cup three times.

On entry to the Amateur League, the Wesleyans suffix was dropped and Thackley AFC firmly established itself between 1938 and 1952, when they joined the West Riding County Amateur League, by taking the title five times and the League Cup twice. They moved to the present ground in Dennyfield during that spell, in 1948. Continuing to be successful, they won the West Riding League three times in a row in the late 50's before joining the West Yorkshire League in 1966 and winning it a year later, transferring again to the stronger Yorkshire League in 1968.

They stayed in that league until it merged into the new Northern Counties East.

Other honours include the West Riding County Cup, Challenge Cup and Bradford and District Senior Cup, which they have won on eleven occasions. One of their best achievements was in 1981 when they purchased the land on which the ground is situated, from the Metropolitan Council and during the last few years the club have built new dressing rooms and refurbished the clubhouse at Dennyfield.

WINTERTON RANGERS

54 West Street, Winterton, Scunthorpe. Tel: 01724 732628

Secretary: Gerald Spencer, 2 Dale Pk Ave, Winterton, Scunthorpe, Lincs DN15 9UY Tel: 01724 732039

Prog Editor: Mark Fowler 3 Teanby Drive, Winterton, Scunthorpe, Lincs. Tel: 01724 734570

Colours: White and navy blue

Nickname: Rangers

Capacity: 3,000

Seating: 200

Covered standing: No

Clubhouse on ground: Yes

Record attendance: 1,200 v Sheffield Utd Floodlight opener 1978

Record fee received: £5,000 for Henry Smith to Leeds Utd 1979

Honours

Lincs Junior Cup 1948 and 1962

Lincs Senior B Cup 1970

Yorkshire Lge 1972, 1977, 1979

League Cup 1981

NCEL Div 2 1990

Scunthorpe and District League and Cup many times

Manager 1996-97: Martin Jacklin

Chairman: Derek Waterfall

Vice Chairman: Alf Smith

DIRECTIONS

From Scunthorpe take A1077 Barton-on-Humber road for 5 miles. On entering Winterton take second right (Eastgate), third left (Northlands Road) and first right (West Street). Ground 200 yds on left.

Winterton Rangers were founded in 1934 and were originally an intermediate side before becoming founder members of the Scunthorpe and District League following the War. They were successful and won a number of trophies before moving on to the Lincolnshire League. By then they had settled at West Street having moved there from a field in Watery Lane in 1950, but within five years they had joined the Yorkshire League. The next decade saw the club develop into a major force and they took the title on three occasions, as well reaching the 4th qualifying round of the FA Cup and the last eight of the FA Vase.

In 1982 they became founded members of the NCEL, but it was sad time as the club folded within two seasons with financial problems. They re-entered the league in 1986 and after several poor seasons won Division Two in 1990 and went straight to the Premier Division. Sadly the club went back down in 1994 where they remain.

WORSBROUGH BRIDGE MW & ATHLETIC

Park Road, Worsbrough Bridge, Barnsley, S70 5LJ. Tel: 01226 284452

Secretary: Garry Wiggan, 9 Pantry Well,
Worsbrough Dale, Barnsley, South Yorks S70 4SW

Tel: 01226 247023 (h) 01226 733200 (b)

Prog Editor: Roy Lunn, 55 Vernon Rd, Worsbrough,
Barnsley S70 5HQ. Tel: 01226 293582

Colours: All Red

Capacity: 1,000

Seating: 200

Covered standing: No

Clubhouse on ground: Yes

Record attendance: 2,300 v Blyth Spartans FA Amateur Cup 1971

Biggest win: 23-0 Jump WMC Barnsley League Late 50's

Record appearances: Billy Pickering

Record goalscorer in total: Frank Briscoe

DIRECTIONS

On the A61 Barnsley-Sheffield road two miles south of Barnsley, 2 miles from M1 junction 36 opposite Blackburns Bridge. Two and a half miles from Barnsley (BR). Yorkshire Traction run buses every 10 mins through Worsbrough bridge.

Honours

County Senior League 1966 and 1970

League Cup 1970

Barnsley League 1953, 1959, 1960

League Cup 1957, 1959, 1960, 1961

Beckett Cup 1954, 1957, 1958

Joint managers for 1996-97: Alan Billingham and Dave Bowman

Chairman: John Wright

Worsborough Bridge Miners Welfare and Athletic Club were formed back in 1923 and were originally known as Worsbrough Bridge St James, the name of the local church parish. They reformed in 1947 as the Athletic Club, playing football and cricket and a partnership enabled them to develop the ground and the facilities. In 1962 they joined the Sheffield and Hallamshire Senior League before moving into Division Three of the Yorkshire League. They quickly climbed the divisions and enjoyed some success in the Amateur Cup, their record crowd of 1, 500 coming against Blyth Spartans. Financial backing from the Welfare scheme ended in the early 90's with the winding down of the industry, but the club have continued to improve facilities with floodlights being installed in 1993.

Despite finishing in a promotion spot last year the club were unable to take their place in the higher league due to ground grading and last season saw the backlash with a disappointing below mid-table finish.

YORKSHIRE AMATEUR

Bracken Edge, Sycamore Avenue, Leeds LS8 4DZ. Tel: 0113 262 4093

Secretary: Brian Whaley, 50 Moseley Wood Walk, Leeds LS16 7HG Tel: 0113 267 9806

Prog editor: Chas Sharman, 44 Roxholme Place, Leeds LS7 4JQ. Tel: 0113 293 8894

Nickname: The Ammers,   Capacity: 1,550

Colours: White and Blue,   Seating: No

Covered standing: Yes, Floodlights: Yes

Clubhouse on ground: Yes

Record attendance: 4,000 v Wimbledon FA Amateur Cup quarter-final in 1932

DIRECTIONS

From South M1 to Leeds, then A58 Wetherby Road to Fforde Green Hotel, left at lights and proceed to Sycamore Avenue (on right). From east A1 to Boot & Shoe Inn then to Shaftesbury Hotel, turn right into Harehills Lane, then to Sycamore Avenue. Two and a half miles from Leeds (BR). Buses 2, 3 & 20 from Briggate to Harehills Avenue.

Honours

FA Amateur Cup semi-final 1932

Yorkshire League Div 1: 1932

Yorkshire League Div 2: 1959

Yorkshire League Div 3: 1978

League Cup 1933

West Riding County FA Cup 1954, 1961, 1972, West Riding Challenge Cup: 1931, 1934, 1946

Leeds Senior Cup: 1931, Leeds Hospital Charity Cup: 1993

Oxford Charity Cup: 1993, Embleton Cup: 1993

Manager for 1996-97: Kevin Smith, Assistant manager: Brian Richardson

Chairman: William Ellis

The club was founded in November 1918 but began playing a year later. It played friendly matches at Elland Road following the demise of Leeds City FC on orders from the League. In 1920 the club sold the lease for Elland Road to the newly formed Leeds United AFC for £250. The aim of the club was to compete as a major force in amateur Football against professional teams in the north of England. It was a founder member of the Yorkshire League, enjoying considerable success up to the Second World War. Honours included the championship, League Cup, West Riding County Cup, Leeds FA Cup and numerous Charity Cups. The club produced a number of leading amateur Internationals, reaching the semi-final of the Amateur Cup in 1932. That year the club moved to Bracken Edge, where the record crowd stands at 4,000 for the Amateur Cup quarter final tie with Wimbledon. The post War years saw a decline in fortunes with occasional success in the lower levels of the Yorkshire League along with County Cup wins, reaching the 1st Round proper of the FA Cup on two occasions. By the late 70's, Yorkshire Amateur was at a low ebb and a youth policy was started with the formation of Yorkshire Amateur Juniors. This has produced rich dividends in recent years with a number of players moving on to full time football.

The last five years have seen an upturn on and off the pitch, with the ground re-developed and floodlights installed. The team have enjoyed some success in the NCEL and the reserves have won the Leeds Senior Cup and Reserve League Cup.

Above: Hallam F.C.

Below: Belper Town F.C.

Federation Brewery Northern

Billingham Syn.	38	24	8	6	78	34	80	
Bedlington Terriers	38	22	12	4	90	37	78	
Durham City	38	24	6	8	85	35	78	
Tow Law Town	38	23	9	6	82	43	78	
Whitby Town	38	21	7	10	100	59	70	
Guisborough Town	38	20	8	10	80	54	68	
Dunston Fed.Bre.	38	20	8	10	75	52	68	
West Auck. T.	38	19	5	14	66	57	62	
Crook Town	38	17	9	12	59	41	60	
Consett	38	17	7	14	76	64	58	
Stockton	38	16	8	14	88	71	56	
Shildon	38	16	3	19	74	74	51	
Seaham Red Star	38	13	11	14	62	66	50	
Murton	38	12	11	15	57	53	47	
R.T.M. Newcastle	38	13	7	18	68	58	46	
Chester-le-St. T.	38	11	9	18	72	78	42	
Whickham	38	11	8	19	43	77	41	
Peterlee Newtown	38	5	4	29	40	96	19	
Eppleton Coll. W.	38	2	3	33	26	153	9	
Ferryhill Athletic	38	0	5	33	27	146	5	
Morpeth Town	36	27	5	4	104	40	86	
South Shields	36	25	4	7	89	34	79	
Easington Colliery	36	23	7	6	86	40	76	
Shotton Comrades	36	22	7	7	74	42	73	
Northallerton	36	18	9	9	70	43	63	
Ashington	36	18	9	9	66	48	63	
Billingham Town	36	18	6	12	72	51	60	
Evenwood Town	36	16	8	12	73	61	56	
Prudhoe Town	36	17	4	15	75	69	55	
Brandon United	36	16	6	14	59	55	54	
Esh Winning	36	13	7	16	80	75	46	
Hebburn	36	13	5	18	50	58	44	
Washington	36	14	4	18	71	74	43	(-3)
Horden Coll Wel.	36	13	3	20	65	75	42	
Willington	36	11	8	17	53	75	41	
Alnwick Town	36	10	6	20	47	65	36	
Ryhope Com. Ass.	36	6	5	25	41	82	23	
Norton&Stock.Anc	36	6	5	25	53	120	17	(-6)
Darlington Clel.Soc	36	0	4	32	33	151	4	

ALNWICK TOWN

St James Park, Alnwick, Northumberland Tel: 01665 603162

Secretary: Robert Miller, 13 Kiln Lonnen, Shilbottle, Northumberland Tel 01665 575937

Colours: Black and white stripes

Seating: 100

Covered standing: 100

Capacity: 2,500

Record attendance: 600 v Bedlington Terriers Northern Alliance 1971

DIRECTIONS

35 miles north of Newcastle on A1, take the slip road to Alnwick, then first left. At roundabout turn left, ground is then on your left.

Honours

Northern Alliance 1938, 1963, 1964, 1966, 1968, 1969, 1970, 1971, 1972

Challenge Cup: 1962, 1966, 1968, 1969, 1971

Subsidiary Cup: 1981

Northumberland Amateur Cup 1972

Durham Central League Cup 1965

Benevolent Bowl 1987

North Northumberland League 1899

Alnwick Town were the most northerly based team to enter the FA competitions until Gretna came along. They play at the North-East's other St James Park and have done since 1900.

Football began in the area in the 1870's, and Alnwick United Services were going in 1879 and before the FA was formed they played in Northumberland and Durham cups. In 1900 Alnwick United Juniors were formed and moved to St James Park under a lease owned by the Duke of Northumberland. The name was changed to Alnwick Town but went back to United before the Great War, when they were in the North Northumberland League. In 1923 they also entered the East Northumberland League and in 1936 they became Town again, entering the Northern Alliance. The club's best years were between 1960 and 1972 when they collected 29 trophies, including the Durham Central League Cup in the one season that the Alliance did not operate. After several unsuccessful applications, Town finally got into the new Second Division in 1982 and since then much work has gone on at the ground, including new lights switched on in 1987 by Newcastle United. A year or so later the club were promoted as runners up, although they are currently back in Division Two.

ASHINGTON

Portland Park, Ashington NE63 9XG Tel: 01670 811991

Secretary Alan Hayton, 21, Chillingham Crescent,
Ashington, Northumberland NE63 8BQ
Tel: 01670 815958

Club secretary Brian Mitcheson, 35, Nursery Park,
Ashington Tel: 01670 813070

DIRECTIONS

200 yds north at traffic lights in centre of town.

Colours: Black and White Stripes

Nickname: The Colliers   Capacity: 4,000

Seating: 350   Covered standing: 2,200

Clubhouse on ground: Yes

Record attendance: 13,199 v Rochdale
FA Cup 2nd Rd Dec 9th 1950

Record appearances: Brian Pringle

Record goalscorer in one season: Bobby Cummings

Record goalscorer in total: Bobby Cummings

Record fee received: £2,500 for Tony Lowery to WBA in 1981

Honours

FA AMATEUR CUP semi-final 1974

Northumberland Senior Cup 1921, 1933, 1939, 1950, 1956, 1957, 1962, 1967, 1980

Northumberland Challenge Bowl 1913, 22, 23, 24, 26, 34, Midland League 1959

Northern Alliance 1914,

Manager for 1996-97: Keith Grant, Assistant manager: Colin Stocks

Press officer: Brian Bennett, 14 St Andrews Terrace, Ashington

Club badges and the club fanzine "The Pit Pony Express" are available at 70p +pp from Mr N.S.Thomas 14 Kenilworth Rd, Ashington, Northumberland NE63 8AS Tel 01670 851617

Ashington Football Club was formed in 1883 and for almost a decade, played only friendly matches until they joined the Northern Alliance for the 1892 season. They ceased activities however, after only one season until they joined the East Northumberland League, for five years. They rejoined the Alliance in 1902 until the Great War and just after had a couple of seasons in the North Eastern League, before launching themselves into the Football League in 1921. They were elected to the new Third Division North where they stayed until 1929, when they finished bottom and failed to gain re-election.The Colliers then reverted to the North Eastern League where they played until 1958, winning the League Cup during the War. They spent two ill fated seasons in the Midland League, plus two more in the Northern Counties League and a further two back in the North Eastern League, until 1964.After spending 1964-65 in the Wearside League, Ashington joined the North Regional League and the Northern Premier League for the 1969 season, before after leading the table, they slipped back to bottom place, and found themselves in the Northern League in 1970. The league introduced a Second Division in 1982 and after two seasons the Colliers were relegated and have been in Division Two ever since.For the first 25 years Ashington played their home games at Ashington Recreation Ground before moving to Station Road. However, a year later, the club moved to Portland Park, which remains home. Greyhound racing, Speedway and Stock Car racing have all been held at the stadium over the years, a meeting of the latter resulting in the main stand being destroyed by fire in 1971. The dressing rooms were situated in the stand, and so until a new one was built, players changed in Ashington YMCA. Possibly one of Ashington's finest feats was reaching the semi-final of the Amateur Cup in 1974. After a 0-0 draw the Colliers lost 3-0 to Bishops Stortford in the replay.

BEDLINGTON TERRIERS

Welfare Park, Park Road, Bedlington, Northumberland Tel: 01670 825485

Secretary and Press Eric Young 6 Millbank Place, Bedlington, Northumberland Tel: 01670 82919

Nickname: The Terriers

Colours: Red and black stripes

Capacity: 2,500

Seating: 150

Covered standing: 200

Clubhouse on ground: Yes

Record attendance: 1,200

Biggest win: 10-0 (H) 9-0 (A)

Biggest defeat: 0-8 (A)

Record goalscorer in one season: Cameron Boon 24

Record goalscorer in total: Steve Boon

DIRECTIONS

Into Bedlington, turn left at 'Northumberland Arms' on Front Street, then second right, ground on right.

Honours

NFA Minor Cup 1954 and 1981

Northern Alliance 1967

League Cup 1958, 1967, 1970, 1982

Tyneside Amateur League 1980

Northern League Division Two 1994

Manager for 1996-97: Keith Perry

Assistant manager: Steve Locker

Chairman: Dave Perry

Vice Chairman: Carole Cavens

Though Bedlington teams can be traced back to the early 1900's, the present club was formed in 1949 as Bedlington Mechanics. Town, United and Colliery Welfare were subsequent suffixes.

Mechanics joined the Northern Combination in 1949, winning the title five seasons later and in 1955 they joined the Northern Alliance where they remained until disbanding in 1963, with a League Cup victory under their belt. Reformed in 1965 as Bedlington Colliery Welfare, the club moved from their West Sleekburn headquarters to its present location at Doctor Pit Welfare, again in the Alliance. Bedlington won the League and Cup double in 1967 and the League Cup again three years later, but left at the end of the 1970-71 season. As Bedlington United the club played in several minor leagues until 1979, when re-named Bedlington Town, they joined the Tyneside Amateur League.

After a successful campaign they were re-elected to the Northern Alliance the following season, as Bedlington Terriers, beating Darlington CB in the League Cup final at St James Park in 1982. Then came the Northern League and after the heady days of 1986 came upheaval. With the appointment of Keith Perry as manager success came soon. Their brilliant campaign in 1993-94 brought them the Second Division title and last year after a titanic struggle, Terriers clinched runner up spot in the league behind Billingham Synners.

BILLINGHAM SYNTHONIA

Central Avenue. Billingham, Cleveland Tel: 01642 532348

Secretary: Graham Craggs, 2 Ribble Close, Billingham, Cleveland, TS22 5NT Tel: 01642 535856

Nickname: The Synners

Colours: Green and white

Capacity: 1,970

Seating: 370

Covered standing: No

Clubhouse on ground: Yes

Record attendance: 4,200 v Bishop Auckland Sept 6th 1958

Record appearance holder: Andy Harbron

Record goalscorer in aggregate: Tony Hetherington

DIRECTIONS

Turn off A19 onto A1027 signposted Billingham, Norton (this applies from either north or south), continue straight on along Central Avenue, ground on left opposite office block. By rail: ground 1 mile along Cowpen Lane from Billingham (BR).

Honours

Northern League 1957, 1989, 1990, 1996

League Cup 1952, 1988, 1990

Teeside League 1937

League Cup 1935 and 1939

Durham Challenge Cup 1989 and 1991

North Riding Senior Cup 1967, 1972 and 1979

North Riding Amateur Cup 1939, 1957, 1963, 1964

The club have always been connected with ICI Billingham, mercifully changing their name from Billingham Synthetic Ammonia FC, one of the company's main products. They were formed in 1923 and played in the Teeside League until the War. In 1945 they replaced the disbanded Billingham South, with whom they were unconnected, in the Northern League and have been members ever since. Synners won the League Cup in 1952 and 1988, plus the championship in 1957 and 1989, with the North Riding Senior Cup three times. Cup football has been fruitful for the club who have reached the FA Cup 1st Round on a number of occasions, as well as the FA Trophy quarter-final more recently.

They left their original Belasis Lane ground in 1958 to make way for an office block, moving across the road to the impressive Central Avenue stadium with its 2,000 seater stand and running track. It was opened by Lord Derby on September 6th before a match with Bishop Auckland, watched by 4,200 spectators, a record which has never been broken. Soon afterwards the ground was used for a England B athletics meeting.

Last May, Synners came out on top of a gripping title race by winning it by two points from Bedlington Terriers, Durham City and Tow Law Town, all on 78 points. Unfortunately their ground is not suitable for the Northern Premier League.

BILLINGHAM TOWN

Bedford Terrace, Billingham, Cleveland Tel: 01642 560043

Secretary: Tom Donnelly, 36 Cumberland Crescent, Billingham, Cleveland TS23 1AY Tel: 01642 555332

Colours: Blue and white stripes

Nickname: The Social

Capacity: 3,000

Seating: Yes

Covered standing: No

Clubhouse on ground: Yes

Record attendance: 1,500 v Manchester City FA Youth Cup 1985

Record appearances: Darren Marsh

Record goalscorer in total: Paul Rowntree

DIRECTIONS

Leave A19 on A1027 (signed Billingham). Turn left at 3rd roundabout, over bridge 1st left, then 1st left again to ground.

Honours

Teesside League 1978 and 1982

Durham Amateur Cup 1977 and 1978

Stockton and District League champions 3 times

Town are much the younger of the two Billingham sides in the Northern League and in their time have seen a number of players go on to the League stage, the most famous being Gary Pallister at Middlesbrough and Manchester United. They began in 1968 as Billingham Social in the Stockton League and became Town on moving to the Northern League in 1982.

The first ground, in Mill Lane, had such a slope across it that the top of the corner flag was level with the cross bar, but in 1974 Social joined the Teesside League and moved to Bedford Terrace.

Eight years and two championships later the club began raising money to build a ground to NPL standards and this they did, joining the Second Division and gaining promotion in 1985. They returned a year later, but went up again in 1988, the year that they lost to Synners in an all Billingham Durham Challenge Cup Final, played at Hartlepool.

BRANDON UNITED

Welfare Ground, Rear of Commercial Street, Brandon, Co.Durham Tel: 0191 378 2957

Secretary: Brian Richardson, 108 Brauncespath Estate,
New Brancepeth, Durham DH7 7JF

Tel: 0191 373 1304

DIRECTIONS

A690 - 3 miles west of Durham City.
Buses 49 & 49a from Durham.

Nickname: United   Capacity: 3,000

Seating: 200   Covered standing: 400

Floodlights: Yes

Clubhouse on ground: Yes

Record attendance: 2,500 FA Sunday Cup semi-final 1976

Biggest win: 11-0 Stobswood

Biggest defeat: 0-9 Murton

Record appearances: Derek Charlton

Record goalscorer in one season: Tommy Holden 55

Honours

Durham and District Sunday League

Div 3 1969, Div 2 1970, Div 1 1974, 1975, 1976, 1977

FA Sunday Cup 1976

Durham Sunday FA Cup 1974, 1976, 1977

Staffieri Cup 1976

Northern Alliance 1978 and 1979

League Cup 1978

Sunderland Shipowners Cup 1982

Northern League Div 2 1985

Manager for 1996-97: John Carey   **Assistant manager: Roli Bell**

Chairman: Neil Scott   **Vice chairman: Joe Cutmore**

The club started life in the late sixties as a Sunday League outfit called Rostrons, named after the local waste paper company where most of the founders worked. Success came soon winning the Durham Sunday League Division Three in 1969. The following years saw them Div 2 champions two seasons running, plus League Cup finalists. In 1973 they were runners up in Division One. The following year they changed their name to Brandon United and they had four more years of success as a Sunday club, winning the league four times and the Durham Sunday FA Cup three times. In 1977 they switched to Saturday football, joining the Northern Alliance which they won in the first two years. In 1980 they moved to the Northern Amateur League before joining the Wearside League and soon after, the Second Division of the Northern League, winning promotion to Division One. Sadly the club took a backward step in 1994, and last May United finished mid-table

Brandon took over the old Welfare Ground from the Brandon C Pit, which had passed over to the council and in their time developed a stand, clubhouse and floodlights to gain the facilities good enough to maintain Northern League membership.

CHESTER-LE-STREET TOWN

Moor Park, Points North, Chester Moor, Chester-le-Street Tel: 0191 388 3363

Secretary: Mel yn Atkinson, 1 St Mary's Close,
Chester-le-Street, Co Durham Tel: 0191 388 3664

Nickname: The Cestrians

Capacity: 2,000

Seating: 200

Covered standing: 600

Clubhouse on ground: Yes

Record attendance: 473 v Barrow FA Cup 1984

also 3,000 Sunderland v Newcastle Bradford appeal match

Biggest win: 8-0 v Billingham Town
FA Vase Prel Rd Oct 6th 1984

Biggest defeat: 1-7 v Curzon Ashton
FA Vase 3rd Rd Dec 12th 1992

Record appearances: Brian Wray 148

Record Goalscorer in total: Colin Howey

DIRECTIONS

Ground lies approx. 2 miles south of town on A167 (C.-le-S. to Durham Road). Regular buses from C.-le-S. and Durham pass ground. Railway station 2 miles distant in town centre.

Honours

Northern League Div 2 1984

Wearside League 1981

Monkwearmouth Cup 1981 and 1982

also Washington League and Cup and Durham Minor Cup

The club was founded in 1972 when a group of enthusiasts got together in a local public house and formed a football club which was called Chester-Le-Street Garden Farm after the pub itself. They entered the Newcastle City Amateur League that same year and played on a pitch in Low Fell, Gateshead, as there were none in the town itself. However, after one season they were allotted a pitch at the Riverside which was to be home until 1977. In 1975 the Cestrians joined the Washington League, winning the league, the Durham Minor Cup and the Washington AM Cup. By then flourishing, Garden Farm moved to Sacriston Welfare ground and were admitted to the Wearside League in 1977, changing their name to Chester-Le-Street Town FC the following year. Over the next few years the championship once and the Monkwearmouth Cup twice, came to the club. In 1980 they moved to their present home at Chester Moor Park. It had only dressing rooms and a perimeter fence and so far over £100,000 has been spent on bringing it up to Northern League standards, so that there is now a 200 seater stand, covered terracing for 500, uncovered terracing and floodlights.

Town joined the Northern League in 1983 and won Division Two at the first attempt, gaining promotion, but after a number of successful seasons, they were relegated, but have bounced back since.

CONSETT

Belle Vue Park, Ashdale Rd, Consett Tel: 01207 503788

Secretary: Ian Hamilton, 29 Grange St, Delves Lane, Consett, DH8 7AG Tel: 01207 509366

Nickname: The Steelmen   Colours: Red and black

Capacity: 4,000   Seated: 400

Covered standing: 1,000   Clubhouse on ground: Yes

Record attendance: 7,000 v Sunderland Res
First match on ground 1950

Record fee received £ Undisclosed for Gary Best and Tommy Lumley

Record fee paid: £ Undisclosed for Gary Best

DIRECTIONS

Quarter of mile north of town centre - along Medomsley Road, left down Ashdale Road, ground 100m yards on left. Follow signs for Sports Centre and Baths. Buses 745, 711 & 772 from Newcastle. 719, 765 from Durham. Follow signs for Sports Centre and Baths, about 800 yards from town centre.

Honours

Northern League Division 2 1989, Northern League Cup 1995

North Eastern League 1940, Division 2 1927, League Cup 1951 jt and 1954

Durham Challenge Cup 1948, 1950, 1959, 1961, 1969

Northern Counties League 1962, Sunderland Shipowners Cup 1968

Monkwearmouth Charity Cup 1968

Formed as Consett Celtic, the club played local football until joining the Northern Alliance League in 1919. Seven years later they switched to the North-Eastern League, winning promotion from the 2nd Division in the first season. From 1935 to 1937, the Steelmen spent two further seasons in the Northern Alliance before returning to the semi-professional North-Eastern League until its demise in 1958. In that time the title was won in 1940 and the League Cup in 1951 and 1954.

After a couple of years in the Midland League, Consett became founder members of the Northern Counties League in 1960, winning the championship in 1962 before deciding to move back to the re-formed North-Eastern League only to see it fold again two years later. They then joined the Wearside League, finishing runners-up in 1969 and 1970, when they moved up to the Northern League. Since then their best placing was in 1977 when they finished tied with Spennymoor, losing the play-off 3-0. Relegation came in 1988 when they won just five games, however they made a swift and triumphant return a year later taking Division Two by nine points, clinching it with an 8-0 win at Willington. They were also unbeaten at home in all competitions with only Ashington scraping a draw.

Consett have been losing finalists in the League Cup on three occasions, against Blyth Spartans in 1979, losing 4-3, Spennymoor United in 1981, 2-0 and again to Blyth in 1992, 1-0. Against this they have won the Durham Challenge Cup five times and have reached the First Round of the FA Cup once, back in 1958, losing at Doncaster Rovers.

FORMER GROUNDS...Consett played on the Vicarage Field until 1948 when it was needed for an ironworks extension. They spent two years at Leadgate's Eden Colliery Ground whilst Belle Vue Park was being built. Almost all the work was voluntary, in between pit shifts, and fund raising brought in £5,000 to pay for materials. Sunderland Reserves attracted a crowd of 7,000 for the first game in 1950

EPPLETON C.W.

Eppleton Welfare Park, Park View, Hetton-le-Hole, Tyne and Wear Tel: 0191 526 1048

Secretary: A Tate, 2 Fletcher St, Newbottle,
Houghton-le-Spring, Tyne and Wear Tel 0191 594 3927

Founded: 1929

Colours: White and blue

Former Leagues: Wearside, and Houghton and District

Nickname: Welfare

Seating: 250

Record attendance:
1,250 Monkwearmouth Charity Cup final 1988

DIRECTIONS
Situated behind Front Street Post Office & directly behind Hetton swimming baths, Hetton-le-Hole on A182. Buses 194, 535, 231, X5, X94 in Front Street. 8 miles from Durham BR station: buses 154 and 254 from Durham.

Honours

Wearside League 1991 and 1992

League Cup 1975, 1979, 1988

Sunderland Shipowners Cup 1948, 1986, 1991

Monkwearmouth Charity Cup 1990, 1991, 1992

Durham Challenge Cup 1990

Eppleton's recent history has been quite remarkable. During the first two season's of the decade they totally dominated Wearside League Football claiming the Division One Championship in both 1990-91 and 1991-92. The Monkwearmouth Charity Cup was also lifted on both these occasions, and the Sunderland Shipowners Cup in 1990-91. Elevation to the Northern League was granted for 1992-93, and promotion to the First Division was won at the first attempt. However, by now the club had peaked and they were relegated last season collecting just nine points and conceding over 150 goals.

Remarkably, they avoided bottom spot despite this horrible record, homeless Ferryhill Athletic amassing just five points. Eppleton Colliery Welfare were founded in 1929, incorporating local side Natcobos in the early seventies. They have played most of their football in the Wearside League.

CROOK TOWN

Millfield Ground, West Road, Crook, Co Durham, Tel: 01388 762959

Sec and Press Alan Stewart, The Wardens Flat, 47
Grasmere Grove, Crook, Co Durham Tel 01388 763425

Nickname: Black and Ambers   Capacity: 3,500

Seating: 400   Covered standing: 300

Clubhouse on ground: Yes

Record attendance 17,500 v Walton and Hersham
FA Amateur Cup Feb 24th 1952

DIRECTIONS
400 yds west of town centre on Wolsingham Road (A698). Nearest BR station is Bishop Auckland. Buses 1A & 1B from Bishop Auckland or X46 & X47 from Durham.

Biggest win: 12-0 v South Bank twice, on 5th April 1958 at home and 12th April 1958 away

Biggest defeat: 0-11 v Bishop Auckland (a) Nov 17th 1938

Record appearances: Jimmy McMillan 505 1952-1968

Record goalscorer in one season: Colin Cook 72 in 1931-32

Record goalscorer in total: Ronnie Thompson 118 1952-66

Honours

FA AMATEUR CUP WINNERS 1901, 1954, 1959, 1962, 1964

FA AMATEUR CUP Semi-finalists 1949, 1958, 1960

Northern League 1915, 1927, 1953, 1959, 1963, League Cup 1937, 1946, 1961

Durham Challenge Cup 1927, 1932, 1955, 1960, Durham Benev Bowl 1914, 1920, 1922, 1926, 1955

Crook Town FC was formed in 1889 as a result of an amalgamation of Crook FC and Crook Excelsior FC. They played friendlies and cup matches until 1894 when they joined the Auckland and District League. Two years later Crook were accepted into the Northern League. The club's first honour came in 1901 when they took the Amateur Cup after a replay against Kings Lynn at Ipswich. Just before the war the club made the first of three trips to Spain and one of the players of the time never came back, instead he played for Barcelona and married a local girl. Eventually Jack Greenwell managed the national team before coaching all over the world. The 1920's saw success in League and Cup before disaster struck in 1928 when found guilty of illegal payments to players. They were suspended, but the club was re-constituted and spent a season in the Durham Central League, before returning to the Northern League. A year later they turned pro in the powerful North Eastern League. It was a torrid time, but they won the County Cup and reached the Third Round of the FA Cup, but after finishing bottom in 1936 they reverted to amateurism and went back to the Northern League. Crook played through the war in War Leagues, and it was in 1943 that the club amalgamated with two clubs, Peases West Welfare FC and Hole-in-the-Wall Colliery FC to form Crook Colliery Welfare FC. That name survived until 1949 when after a thrilling run to the Amateur Cup semi-final, it reverted to Crook Town.The 50's and 60's were glory days for Crook as between 1953 and 1966 the league was won three times with five runners up spots. The League Cup, Durham Challenge Cup and Bowl were all won, but overshadowed by four visits to Wembley in ten years when the Amateur Cup was won each time, in 1954, 1959, 1962 and 1964. The first final was watched by 100,000 against Bishop Auckland with 90,000 seeing the two replays at Newcastle and Middlesbrough. Barnet, Hounslow and Enfield were all beaten in subsequent finals as Crook attempted to take the mantle from Bishops. The 70's were less inspired until 1977 when they reached the FA Cup First Round, the last 16 of the FA Trophy and finished fourth in the league. Again fortunes declined and through the 80's it became a battle for survival, relegation to Division Two coming in 1989. Crook came close to folding in the early 90's until new officials and sponsors breathed new life into the club and the ground, gaining promotion again in 1995.

Crook have played on the Millfield Ground since forming, apart from two years in the mid 1880's. Initially it was the home of Crook Rugby Club and the football club shared until moving to the Bankfoot Sports Ground at Peases West. The rugby club went under soon after and the club bought the ground and have remained ever since. Millfield is a cavernous ground which still has the atmospheric feel about it which brings thoughts of crowds of 17,000+ in the 50's.

DUNSTON FEDERATION BREWERY

Federation Park, Wellington Rd, Dunston, Gateshead Tel: 0191 493 2935

Secretary: Bill Montague, 12 Dundee Close, Chapel House, Newcastle, NE5 1JJ Tel: 0191 267 2250

Colours: All Blue   Nickname: The Fed

Capacity: 2,000   Seating: Yes

Covered standing: Yes

Clubhouse on ground: Yes

DIRECTIONS

Dunston/Whickham exit off A1(M), ground 400 yds north along Dunston Road on left. 1 mile from Dunston or Metrocentre stations. Numerous buses from Gateshead & Metrocentre stop outside ground.

Record attendance:
1,550 for 1988 Sunderland Shipowners Cup Final

Biggest win: 11-0 v Willington Northern League Div 2 1993

Biggest defeat: 1-6 v Billingham Synthonia Division One 1994-95

Record appearances: Paul Dixon

Record goalscorer in total: Paul King

Honours

Northern Amateur League and Cup double 1978

League Cup 1979, and League Shield 1979 and 1980

Gateshead Charity Cup 1978 and 1981

Durham Minor Cup 1980

Durham County Trophy 1982

Northern Combination League 1987

League Cup 1984 and 1987

Sunderland Shipowners Cup 1988

Wearside League 1989, 1990 and League Cup 1991

Northern League Div 2 1993

The club was formed in 1975 under the name of Whickham Sports and began in the Northern Amateur League. They played on a public park at Dunston and were elected to the Northern Combination in 1980. Their move to new headquarters brought a name change to Dunston Mechanics, as they moved onto what was to become Federation Park. The re-location of the brewery from Newcastle to Dunston saw them gain major sponsorship for the first time and this resulted in the club name changing once more. They progressed rapidly with a long term lease on the ground bringing stability and giving an incentive to make improvements on and off the pitch.

In 1987 the first season in the Wearside League ended in a record crowd of over 1, 500 watching Fed narrowly beat neighbours Whickham in the Shipowners Cup and they finished as champions in the next two seasons, winning the League Cup and being runner up the year after.

Their exploits brought entry to the Northern League in 1991 and two seasons later as champions of Division Two, Feds were promoted.

DURHAM CITY

New Ferens Park, Belmont, Durham Tel: 0191 386 9616

Secretary: Brian Last, 5 Belle Vue Rd, Ashbrooke, Sunderland, SR2 7SQ Tel: 0191 528 5808

Nickname: City

Colours: Yellow and blue

Capacity: 3,000

Seating: 200

Covered standing: No

Clubhouse on ground: Yes

Record attendance: 7,000 v Tranmere Rovers FA Cup 2nd Rd Nov 7th 1957

Record appearance holder: Joe Raine 552

Honours

Northern League 1994

Durham Benevolent Bowl 1956

Durham Challenge Cup 1972

DIRECTIONS

The ground is situated in Belmont outside the City.

Durham City AFC has a long and creditable history and is one of only two clubs operating in the Northern League which can boast of having previously been members of the Football League, the others being Ashington. The club was first inaugurated in 1918-19 and for that season only operated in the old Victory League which was formed to celebrate the end of the War. Subsequently the team was admitted to the North-Eastern League where they stayed for two seasons before joining Division Three North of the Football League.The club operated in that league until 1928 when they failed to gain re-election, and immediately joined the North-Eastern League for ten years, when due to financial problems, they disbanded.

For a short period during the following season the club, having changed to Durham AFC, became members of the Wearside League but were again disbanded in November, and it was not until 1950 that they re-formed, again playing in the Wearside League.

Two years later they entered the Northern League, where they remain to this day.

Since it was originally formed, it has occupied five grounds. The first being Garden House Park, almost where County Hall stands now, where they stayed for one season before moving to Kepier Heughs, a large field near to the old Ferens Park ground. They stayed there for four years before moving to Holliday Park, named after the former Mayor of the City, which was a greyhound stadium next to the large gasometer along Framwellgate Waterside and saw League football.

When the club re-formed they acquired Ferens Park, named after Alderman Ferens who was President of the club and bought the land. The final move to Belmont came this year after Ferens Park was sold for development.

EASINGTON COLLIERY

Easington Colliery Welfare Ground, Colliery Welfare Park, Easington, Co Durham Tel: 0191 527 3047

Secretary: Alan Purvis, 12 Wark Crescent, Jarrow, Tyne and Wear NE32 4SH Tel 0191 489 6930

Colours: Green and white stripes

Nickname: The Colliery

Capacity: 2,500

Seating: 50

Covered standing: 400

Clubhouse on ground: Yes

Record attendance: 4,500 v Tranmere Rovers FA Cup 1st Rd 1955

Biggest win: 7-0 v Ashington (H) Northern League 1994

Biggest defeat: 2-8 v Blyth Spartans (A) Northern League 1988

Record appearances: D Howard

Record goalscorer in aggregate: D.Howard

Honours

Wearside League 1930, 1932, 1933, 1948, 1949

League Cup 1933, 1946, 1962

Monkwearmouth Cup 1931, 1948, 1976

Sunderland Shipowners Cup 1975 and 1980

> ## DIRECTIONS
>
> **A19 (Middlesbrough-Newcastle) take the Easington, Houghton Le Spring turn-off. B1284 through Easington until the Black Diamond pub. Turn right at this zebra crossing to the Colliery Welfare Park.**

Formed in 1913 as Easington Colliery Welfare, the club got off to a slow start before any honours came, but in the early thirties they began to dominate the Wearside League winning three championships and two cup finals. Sadly they were forced to disband in 1937 but reformed two years later and again won the league twice with three more cup finals. In 1955 Easington's biggest day came when a crowd of over 4,500 saw them lose 1-0 to Tranmere Rovers in the First Round of the FA Cup, the only time they have reached that far.

In 1964 the team again disbanded, but were playing again in 1973. A new era was just around the corner and in 1980, the Welfare amalgamated with Easington Rangers from the Houghton and District League to become Easington Colliery AFC.

The new club wanted to play at a higher level and quickly plans were made to progress, but as the new stand was incomplete they were rejected by the Northern League, however in 1985 they made it to Division Two and soon made their presence felt, winning promotion scoring over 100 goals. The following year saw them consolidate as well as reach the League Cup, only to lose to Spennymoor Utd. In 1988 Bishop Auckland beat them in the County Cup final, and since then they have suffered ups and downs, suffering relegation but bouncing straight back, only to go down yet again in 1993.

The Welfare Park ground has been home since 1913 and has seen many changes over the years, especially since 1985 with the new stand and floodlights two years later. The terracing and hardstanding were completed in 1982.

ESH WINNING

West Terrace, Waterhouses, Durham Tel: 0191 373 3872

Secretary: Robin Hinds, 158 Norburn Park, Witton Gilbert, Durham Tel: 0191 371 0204

Nickname: Esh   Colours: Green and Yellow

Capacity: 2,000   Seating: 160

Covered standing: None   Floodlights: Yes

Clubhouse on ground: Yes

Record attendance: 1,500 v Liverpool Fantail
FA Sunday Cup 1982

Biggest win: 11-0

Biggest defeat: 0-8 v Dunston Feds Northern League

Record appearances: P. Hewitson

Record goalscorer in one season: Paul Ward

Record goalscorer in total: Paul Ward

DIRECTIONS

From the A167 through Durham take the B6302 west through Ushaw Moor to Esh Winning. The ground is 1 mile on at Waterhouses.

Honours

Durham Sunday League 1979 and 1980, Stafferi Cup 1975, Guards Cup 1973

North Durham Youth League 1995,

Manager for 1996-97: Charlie Gott,   Chairman: Mr C. A. Ryan   Vice Chairman: Mr W. Hall

Press officer: Mr I. Fish, 6 The Wynds, Esh Winning, Durham

No North-East football fan could forget Sunderland's Raich Carter of Middlesbrough's George Camsell, both England Internationals, and few would remember that they both played for Esh Winning. At least another two dozen from the club or the surrounding Deerness Valley have joined Football League clubs.But despite it there have been times when Esh, twice disbanded, have struggled. Formed in 1889 as Esh Winning Rangers, the club played minor football until joining the Northern League in 1912, winning the championship at the first attempt along with the Benevolent Bowl.

The name Rangers was dropped from the title in 1913, but after the Great War came the biggest day in the club's history, when a 5,000 crowd assembled at the Stags Head Recreation Ground to see Esh play mighty Bishop Auckland in the quarter final of the Amateur Cup, only to see them lose 5-4 after extra time.

The depression days between the Wars were a real struggle and in October 1934 the club disbanded, West Auckland taking over the fixtures.

Revived in 1945 in the Durham Central League they again had to disband when a local man took over the rent of the Stags Head and gave them 24 hours notice to quit and remove the goalposts. Ironically, the same man later became secretary. In 1967 with the pending closure of nearby Waterhouses Colliery and the vacating of Welfare Grounds, enthusiastic locals formed a Durham Sunday League 3rd Division team called Esh Winning and eventually bought the ground from the Coal Board. Promoted in 1971, they won the Guards Cup in 1972 and Division Two the following year. In 1974 they won the Stafferi Cup, two years later the Guards Cup again and in 1978 the First Division title, and were finalists in the County Cup. A crowd of 1,500 watched the match with Liverpool Fantail in the National Cup.

They were champions again in 1980, before turning to Saturday football and joining the Northern Alliance. Three years later they were elected to the Northern League Second Division and now boast new changing rooms, a grandstand, floodlights and a floodlit fives court.

EVENWOOD TOWN

Welfare Ground, Stones End, Evenwood, Co Durham Tel: 01388 832281

Secretary: Jim Coates, 19 Wellgarth, Evenwood, Co Durham Tel: 01388 833035

Colours: Blue

DIRECTIONS

The ground is in the centre of the village by the Sports and Leisure

Nickname: The Wood

Seating: Yes

Covered standing: Yes

Capacity: 3, 500

Clubhouse on ground: Yes

Record attendance: 9,000 v Bishop Auckland FA Amateur Cup 1931

Honours

Northern League 1949, 1970, 1971

League Cup 1936

Durham Challenge Cup 1970

Durham Amateur Cup 1929

Evenwood FC were formed in 1890 and played in a host of different leagues before entry at the fourth attempt to the Northern League. They began in the Barnard Castle and District League for one year in 1893 before reverting to a year of friendlies, then after a year in the Auckland and District League they joined the Wear Valley League for three seasons. From 1899 to 1903 it was back to friendlies before another year in the Auckland League and two in the Wear Valley.

From there they played in the Gauntless Valley League followed by a year of friendlies, before once again joining the Auckland League where they remained until 1923. They left to play friendlies for a season and had another in the Wear Valley before yet two more seasons of friendlies from 1925.

Moving across they joined the South Durham League for just one season before their next spell in the Auckland League in 1928.

During all of this the club changed its name to Evenwood Crusaders in 1911 and in 1924, when the football ground was taken over by the Welfare, they became Evenwood Town. Town survived the trauma of having their dressing rooms and pavilion burnt down in 1953 and went on to record successive championships in 1970 and 1971, also taking the Durham Challenge Cup.

FERRYHILL ATHLETIC

C/O Brandon United FC, Welfare Ground, rear of Commercial St, Brandon Tel: 01740 651937

Secretary: Eric Burton, 12 West End Villas, Crook, Co
Durham DL15 9PE Tel 01388 762026

Colours: Amber and black

DIRECTIONS

**A690 - 3 miles west of Durham City.
Buses 49 & 49a from Durham.**

Nickname: Latics

ALL GROUND DETAILS AS PER BRANDON UTD FC

Record attendance: 13,000 v Bishop Auckland
FA Amateur Cup

Record win: 18-0 v Skinningrove Works
FA Cup 1st Qual Rd 1953

Honours

Northern League 1938, 1948, 1958

Durham Challenge Cup 1924 and 1971

Benevolent Bowl 1954, 1957, 1962

Durham Amateur Cup 1922

Ferryhill Athletic FC were formed in 1921 by a breakaway group from Dean Bank Villa FC, who continued to play locally. That year the club bought their impressive Darlington Road ground from a local farmer and joined the Palatine League, eventually winning it and the Durham Amateur Cup.

The Latics joined the Northern League in 1923, where they were runners up to Tow Law, and completed a fine season by winning the Durham Challenge Cup, beating Cockfield in the final. The following night they lost to Cockfield in the first League Cup final.

A year before the Second War, Ferryhill won the Northern League, and again in 1948, and ten years later they won it for a final time. Since then success has been sporadic, with a quarter-final place in the Amateur Cup in 1964 as a highlight, although the junior side had a fine spell in the 80's with a number of trophies.

In 1988 the club completed new dressing rooms and installed floodlights as they aimed high again, but sadly events overtook the club and they were forced to move out of their ground in 1994, and it now lays derelict and forlorn, the club playing at Brandon United this season.

GUISBOROUGH TOWN

King George V Ground Howlbeck Rd, Guisborough, Cleveland Tel: 01287 636925

Secretary: Keith Smeltzer, 55 Thames Ave, Guisborough, Cleveland Tel: 01827 638993

Colours: Red and white stripes

Nickname: Priorymen

Seating: 150

Covered standing: 400

Capacity: 3,500

Record attendance: 3,112 v Hungerford Town
FA Vase Semi-final 1980

Record appearances: Mark Davis 323

Record goalscorer in total: Mark Davis 551

DIRECTIONS

From west: bear left at 2nd set of lights, left into Howlbeck Road after quarter mile, ground at end. Buses from Middlesbrough.

Honours

FA VASE Runners up 1980

Northern League Cup 1988

Northern Alliance 1980

League Cup 1979

North Riding Senior Cup 1990, 1991, 1992, 1993, 1995,

Football in Guisborough dates back over 110 years to the days of Red Rose FC and Belmont FC. There were several others around by 1910, including Brigantes who played at Guisborough Hall by permission of Lady Gisborough and who won the North Riding Junior Cup. The first Guisborough Town were formed in 1945, winning the Teesside League and then the Cleveland League before Guisborough Boys Club took over in 1947, building a club house in Belmangate, and in 1953 Blackett Hutton FC were formed and they played on a new ground behind the local foundry, until 1972. From there the Priorymen of Guisborough Town were born and it is they who are the current flag bearers for the town, after being formed following a public meeting called by the Urban District Council. After much success in the Middlesbrough and District and South Bank Leagues, they joined the Northern Alliance in 1977, and within three years they had reached Wembley, losing to Stamford FC in the FA Vase final. Town moved into the Midland League which was incorporated into the Northern Counties East, and following pressure from supporters they joined the Northern League in 1985.

The King George V Ground has been substantially improved over the years and Town have enjoyed success most often in the North Riding Senior Cup in recent years.

HEBBURN

Victoria Road West, Hebburn, Tyne and Wear Tel: 0191 483 5101

Secretary: Tom Derrick, 63 Staneway, Felling, Gateshead, Tel: 0191 442 1563

Colours: Yellow and sky blue

Nickname: Hornets

Seating: 150

Covered standing: 400

Capacity: 2,000

Clubhouse on ground: Yes

Record attendance: 503 v Darwen FA Cup 1991

Record goalscorer in total: Keith Carter

DIRECTIONS

On the main road through the town about 1 mile from railway station. Hebburn lies on the Metroline - excellent bus service from Heworth Metro.

Honours

Shields Gazette Cup 1992

Wearside League 1967

Monkwearmouth Charity Cup 1969

Durham Challenge Cup 1943 and 1992

Tyneside League 1939

Northern Combination 1944

Gateshead Charity Cup 1936 and 1938

Palmer Hospital Cup 1928

Hebburn Aged Miners Cup 1936

Hebburn Homes Cup 1943

Hebburn Infirmary Cup 1936, 1937, 1938, 1939

Reyrolles FC were formed in 1912 and entered the Jarrow and District Junior League until the Great War curtailed football in the area. They had three years in the South Shields Combination before moving to the Tyneside Combination in 1922. They remained there until the second War, winning the final peacetime title as well as gaining success in a number of local cups during the 30's.

They played through the Second War in the Northern Combination and then the North-Eastern League, winning the former in 1944 and the Durham Challenge Cup a year earlier. On resumption of open football after the war they again joined the Comb and remained there until having just one year back in the North-Eastern League. From there they joined the Wearside League, which they won in 1967, and they stayed until elected to the Northern League in 1989, as Hebburn, having earlier become Hebburn Reyrolles.

HORDEN COLLIERY WELFARE

Welfare Ground. Park Road, Horden, Peterlee Co Durham Tel: 0191 586 8802

Secretary: Robert Ord Wood, 29 Morpeth St, Horden, Peterlee, Co Durham Tel 0191 586 8802

Nickname: Colliers, Colours: Red

Capacity: 4,000, Seating: 300

Covered standing: 200, Clubhouse on ground: Yes

Record attendance: 8,000 FA Cup 2nd Round 1939

DIRECTIONS

A19 to Peterlee, signposted from there.

Honours

Warside League 1912, 1913, 1914, 1934, 1965, 1968, 1970, 1971, 1972, 1973, League Cup 1934 and 1950

Sunderland Shipowners Cup 1966 and 1973

Monkwearmouth Cup 1913, 1924, 1933, 1970, 1973

Northern League Cup 1984

Durham Challenge Cup 1936, 1964, 1981, 1982

North Eastern League 1938 and 1964

The club was formed in 1908 as Horden Athletic in the Wearside League and became Colliery Welfare in 1928. They also played in the North Eastern League from 1935 and the Midland Counties and Northern Counties Leagues for two years apiece from 1958 before rejoining the Wearside League in 1963, and finally moving to the Northern League in 1975. Their Wearside League days were most fruitful, as they took the title ten times, taking a host of cups as well. Either side of the War, Horden gained a reputation as FA Cup fighters and reached the Second Round in 1939, before reaching Round One in 1948, 1952, 1953 and the last time, 1981, when they drew Blackpool at home, but were forced to play at Hartleppol.

1973 was one of the best seasons in their history when they completed the treble of Sunderland Shipowners Cup, Waerside League and Monkwearmouth Cup. They finished runners up in 1980 and 1983 and won the League Cup a year later, but were sadly relegated twelve months later and have struggled ever since.

The Welfare Park football ground is still a huge, brooding place, part of an even bigger complex which catered for the miners until the pit closed in the mid-Eighties. In recent years it has been given a facelift and a social club built on the ground.

JARROW ROOFING BOLDON CA

Boldon Sports Club, New Road, Boldon Colliery, Tyne and Wear Tel: 0191 519 1391

Secretary: R.McLoughlin, 8 Kitchener Terrace, Jarrow, Tyne and Wear Tel: 0191 489 9825

Colours: All Blue, Nickname: Roofing

Seating: 150, Covered standing: 800, Capacity: 3,500

Record appearances: Kevin Gibson

Honours

Bill Dixon Cup 1991, Mid-Tyne League 1988, Monkwearmouth Cup 1995

MORPETH TOWN

Craik Park, Morpeth Common, Morpeth, Northumberland Tel: 01670 513785

Secretary: Joe Hobin, 23 Princes Gardens, Malvins Close, Blyth, NE24 5HJ Tel 01670 360820

Colours: Yellow and black

Covered standing: No

Seating: 100

DIRECTIONS

Morpeth signs off A1 onto A197, take B6524, right at Milford sign, right after 1 mile into ground next to Morpeth Common.

Honours

Northumberland Senior Cup 1886 jt and 1903

Northumberland Benevolent Bowl 1979 and 1986

Northern League Division Two 1996

Northern Alliance League 1903, 1984, 1994

League Cup 1939 and 1986

Subsidiary Cup 1987

Northumberland Aged Miners Cup 1936, 1937, 1938, 1988

Manager for 1996-97: Peter Feenan

Football in Morpeth was established in 1880, Morpeth Harriers being the most prominent team. Town have carried on their tradition of wearing black and white stripes. Harriers played on a field to the north of Dogger Bank and in 1886 they held Shankhouse to a draw in the Northumberland Senior Cup and so it was shared. The mid 1890's saw the amalgamation of Morpeth FC and Morpeth United to form the new Harriers, which won the East Northumberland League in 1890. Thirteen years later the club lifted both the Senior Cup and the Northern Alliance. Six years later, after the club lifted the Benevolent Bowl, Morpeth Town FC were formed with the club playing at the rear of the Stobhill Cricket Club, their headquarters being at the Phoenix Hotel.

In the 20's there is evidence that some matches were played at Grange House Field before moving to Storey Park in 1954. From 1920 to 1954 there were success, chiefly in the Aged Miners Cup, which was won three years running. Much later, the 1980's were a very profitable time for the club, Northern Alliance runners up in 1982 and champions in 1984, runners up again in 1985 and double winners in 1986.

Again in 1994 two trophies were won, the same season that saw the club move to their new Craik Park ground. It was this that prompted the club's move into the Northern League in 1994 where they made an impact by winning Division Two last May.

MURTON

Recreation Park, Church Lane, Murton, Co Durham Tel: 0191 517 0814

Secretary: John Gardner, 74 Winds Lonnen, Murton, Seaham, Co Durham Tel 0191 526 3449

Colours: All white with red trim

Nickname: Gnashers

Seating: 100

Covered standing: 300

Capacity: 3,500

Record attendance: 3,500 v Spennymoor Utd Durham Challenge Cup 1951

Record appearances: Robert Welch 500+   1962 to 1978

DIRECTIONS

Exit A19 onto B1285 heading west into Murton - Church Lane on left opposite catholic church.

Honours

Northern League Div 2   1990

Wearside League 1929, 1937, 1960

League Cup 1959 and 1971

Sunderland Shipowners Cup 1960, 1970, 1971

Monkwearmouth Charity Cup 1922, 1929, 1935, 1936, 1964, 1971, 1988

Durham Challenge Cup 1993

Durham Junior Cup 1951

Murton FC play on what was the Colliery Welfare Ground and were associated with the Coal Industry for 70 years, only dropping the Colliery Welfare tag when entering the Northern League in 1988.

They were formed in 1912 and played on a ground called Fatten Pasture until moving to the Welfare Ground in 1928. From there they were twice Wearside League champions before the War. On the resumption of football they joined the North-Eastern League, but after struggling returned to the Wearside League in 1951. Nine year later they were champions again and they repeated it a decade later.

The ground in its heyday was impressive, with a small stand which was once moved 80 yards overnight with pulleys and ropes, and had dressing rooms built underneath.

The club's most recent success came in 1988 when they took the Monkwearmouth Charity Cup for the seventh time, and in 1993 when they won the Durham Challenge Cup for the only time.

R.T.M. NEWCASTLE

Wheatsheaf Sports Ground, Woolsington, Newcastle-Upon-Tyne Tel: 0191 286 0425

Secretary: Jim Anderson, 7 Whitbeck Rd, Stayford, Newcastle-Upon-Tyne Tel: 0191 243 1025

Colours: Blue and white stripes   Nickname: Star

Seating: 300   Covered standing: Yes

Capacity: 2,000

Record attendance: 1,800 v Almondsbury Greenway FA Vase semi-final 1978

Record appearances: Ian Crumplin

Record goalscorer in total: Ian Crumplin

DIRECTIONS

From Newcastle central station follow the airport signs for 7 miles on the A167. This road becomes the A696 after crossing the A1 and the ground is next to the Wheatsheaf Hotel on the left, approximately 800 yards before the airport.
Callerton Parkway metro station is 400 yards from the ground.

Honours

FA VASE WINNERS 1978

FA VASE Semi-final: 1982

Northern League Division Two 1986

League Cup 1986

Wearside League 1974, 1976, 1983, 1984, 1985

League Cup 1977, 1980, 1981, 1983, 1984

Sunderland Shipowners Cup 1983 and 1985

Monkwearmouth Charity Cup 1975, 1980, 1983, 1989

Northern Combination 1963 and 1969

League Cup 1967 and 1972

Northumberland Senior Cup 1977, 1983, 1986, 1988

JR Cleator Cup 1987

Blue Star FC were founded in 1932 and until 1986 when they entered the Second Division of the Northern League, had the proud record of always winning the league in the first season. They began in the Newcastle and District Trades League which became the Newcastle Business Houses League, where they remained until the War. In 1946 they started up again in the Tyneside Amateur League, and in 1962 moved to the Northern Combination. They were champions and repeated the feat in 1969, also winning the League Cup twice and the Minor Cup.

In 1973 they moved up to the Wearside League and they took the title five times in twelve seasons, including a hat-trick from 1983 to 1985. They also won the League Cup five times, Monkwearmouth Cup three times and the Shipowners Cup twice, doing the grand slam in 1983. Their finest hour came in 1978, when they reached the final of the FA Vase at Wembley, where they beat Barton Rovers. They got to the semi-final again in 1982, but went out, and their next glory time was in 1984 when they reached the First Round of the FA Cup. In 1985 Blue Star won Division Two scoring 133 goals and winning all but two games, plus the League and County Cups, and in the first year in Division One finished fourth.

Since then the club have embarked on a number of ground improvements and have twice changed their name, to Newcastle Blue Star in 1986 and to RTM Newcastle in 1994, in line with the club's main sponsors.

NORTHALLERTON

Ainderby Rd, Romanby, Northallerton, Yorks DL7 8BJ Tel: 01609 772418

Secretary: Peter Coulson, 3 Manor Green, Romanby, Northallerton, N.Yorks DL7 8BA Tel: 01609 779354

Press officer Ian Bolland, 90 Bullamoor Rd, Northallerton, North Yorks

Colours: Black and white stripes Nickname: Town

Capacity: 3,000   Seating: 150

Covered standing: 500   Clubhouse on ground: Yes

DIRECTIONS

Leave A1 at Leeming Bar (A684) follow signs to Northallerton, approaching town take B1333 signed Romanby - ground 250 yds on left. Three quarters of a mile from Northallerton BR station - local bus from town centre (one and a half miles) passes ground.

Record attendance: 671 v Farnborough Town FA Trophy 1993

Biggest win: 7-0 v Farnborough Town FA Trophy

Biggest defeat: 1-9 v Chester-le-Street Northern League

Record appearances: Lee Wasden

Record goalscorer in one season: John Woods

Record goalscorer in total: John Woods

Honours

Northern League Cup 1994

Harrogate League, Richmond Cup, Bedale Cup, Millbank Cup, Orde Powlett Cup

Harrogate Invitation Cup and Alverton Trophy.

Joint managers 1996-97: John Woods and Michael Sell

Chairman: Dennis Cope

Vice Chairman: Ralph Alderson

A football club has existed in the town since the 1890's and has been known variously as Northallerton, Northallerton Alliance, Northallerton Town and Northallerton 1994.

The exact date of formation is uncertain but The Eliot Bowl was played for in 1895 and carries the name of the club as the first winners. The early years saw them playing in the Allertonshire League, and from there they moved to the Vale of Mowbray, Ripon and District, Darlington and District, North Yorkshire and Harrogate Leagues before their status saw them in the Teeside League.

They entered the Northern League in 1982, with the ground having been transformed with new changing rooms, floodlights, fencing and a stand. North Yorks Council bought the clubs Bluestone Ground in 1974 and the club moved out to Ainderby Road. Two pitches with a clubhouse and a car park were opened in August 1976 and more improvements were added in 1985. A 150 seater stand was built in 1990 as promotion to the First Division came. They reached the North Riding Cup Final in 1984 and won the League Cup in 1994 but in recent times the club has suffered severe financial problems which culminated with the new club name soon after.

NORTON & STOCKTON ANCIENTS

Station Rd, Norton, Stockton-on-Tees, Cleveland TS20 2TQ Tel: 01642 530203

Secretary: Steven Clarkson, 4 South Way, Norton,
Stockton-on-Tees, Cleveland Tel 01642 534524

Nickname: Ancients, Capacity: 2, 000, Seating: 200

Covered standing: Yes, Clubhouse 150 yards away

Record attendance: 1,430 v Middlesbrough Friendly 1988

DIRECTIONS

Norton village 2 miles from Stockton centre, turn into Station Road on outskirts of village.

Honours

Northern League Cup 1982

Manager: Andy Boynton

Norton and Stockton Ancients are a club of two distinct eras, Norton being the new with Stockton, like their nickname `The Ancients', is the old. Norton came into being in 1959, establishing themselves in the Teeside League until taking the opportunity of being part of the new Northern League Division Two in 1982. Success was rapid and unexpected with the League Cup won in the first year, beating Whitby Town in the final. 12 months later the club reached the Durham Challenge Cup Final, losing 2-1 to Coundon.Immediately prior to joining the League they amalgamated with Stockton Ancients when the remaining assets of Stockton Football and Athletic Club were transferred to the Cricket Club Trust. The ground at Norton is part of a large complex shared by other sports with full time professional ground staff.

Eden Lane, Peterlee, Co Durham Tel: 0191 586 3004

PETERLEE NEWTOWN

Secretary: Danny Cassidy, 23 Melbury Street, Seaham
Co Durham Tel 0191 581 4591

Colours: Sky and navy blue   Nickname: Newtowners

Seating: 50   Covered standing: 200

Capacity: 6,000   Clubhouse on ground: Yes

Record attendance: 1,500 v Whitby Town
FA Cup 4th qual Rd 1984

Record appearances: Keith Bendelow 200+

DIRECTIONS

From town centre Fire Station, turn left into Edenhill Road, then right into Robson Avenue. Left at the next junction and ground is on the right.

Honours

Northern League Div 2 1983

Floodlit League 1981 and 1982

League Cup 1981

Peterlee Newton FC were formed in 1976, having been backed by the local council who installed them on Eden Lane playing fields. They joined the Northern Alliance, where they were always challenging near the top in their three seasons, before joining the Wearside League, from where they won the mid-week Floodlit League twice. They moved into the Northern League Second Division in 1982, where a run of 26 matches unbeaten brought the championship and promotion, the season finishing with a close battle in the Durham Challenge Cup final against Spennymoor United.

PRUDHOE TOWN

Kimberley Park, Broomhouse Road, Prudhoe, Northumberland NE42 5EH Tel: 01661 835900

Brian Tulip, 12 Orchard Close, Prudhoe, Northumberland, Tel: 01661 833169

Nickname: Citizens

Colours: Purple and Jade

Capacity: 3,000

DIRECTIONS

Approach Prudhoe along A695, turn right at 'Falcon' Inn, 200 yds down Eastwood Road turn left into Broomhouse Road, ground on right.

Seating: 150

Covered standing: Yes

Clubhouse on ground: Yes

Biggest attendance 2,500 v Blyth Spartans Northumberland Senior Cup 1981

Hexham and District League and Cup 1969

Newcastle and District League 1970 and 1971

League Cup 1970

Charity Shield 1970 and 1971

Northern Combination 1980

Northern Amateur League 1972

Clayton Charity Cup 1969

Northumberland Minor Cup 1979

Northumberland Benevolent Bowl 1980

Heddon Homes Charity Cup 1982

The club was formed in 1959 by as group of enthusiasts from nearby Ovington, playing on a farmer's field behind the Social Club and taking the village name. For ten years they played in the Hexham and District League. In 1968 the club moved it's HQ to the West Wylam Inn and its pitch to Eastwood Park in Prudhoe, to become Prudhoe East End. As well as improving the ground, the club sought a better standard of football and joined the Newcastle and District League from 1969 to 1971, the Northern Amateur League in 1971-72 and then the Northern Combination from 1972 to 1984.

A further four seasons were spent in the Northern Alliance , with two runners up spots, before they achieved their ambition of election to the Northern League in 1988. Their new ground at Kimberley Park, which had been a council rubbish dump, underwent a remarkable transformation with the development of the clubhouse, dressing rooms, floodlights and covered seating. Success soon followed with promotion to the First Division, with the club changing the name to Prudhoe Town, but relegation was suffered in 1995.

RYHOPE COMMUNITY ASSOCIATION

Meadow Park, off Stockton Rd, Ryhope, Tyne and Wear Tel: 0191 523 6555

Secretary Robert Lewins, 7 Belsay Gardens,
St Gabriels Est, Sunderland Tel: 0191 514 1725

Nickname: Ryes

Colours: Red and white stripes

Capacity: 2,000

Seating: 150

Covered standing: 100

Clubhouse on ground: Yes

Record attendance: 2,000 v Newcastle Utd
Friendly 1982

Record appearances: Paul Carr

Record goalscorer in one season: Ian Lawson

Record fee received: £2,000 for Kevin Todd from Newcastle United in 1983

DIRECTIONS

From Sunderland follow signs for A19 south - ground adjacent to Cherry Knowle Hospitals in Ryhope.

Honours

Northern Alliance League Cup 1981

Northern League Division Two 1984

Banks Youth League and Cup double 1993

Ryhope Youth Club first came into existence playing friendly games on what was known as the Store Field, behind the local Co-op. On reaching 18, the team moved into senior football and joined the Seaham and Houghton and District Leagues, playing all fixtures away. The following year saw them move to the Colliery Welfare Ground, changing their name to the Ryhope Community, where they enjoyed almost unequalled success, winning 18 cups and several league titles.

Rejected several times by the Wearside League because another Ryhope side were already in it, they joined the Northern Alliance in 1978, winning the Challenge Cup at St James Park in their third season. Ryhope were league runners-up that season but were playing on the local Comprehensive ground until persuading the council to lease them some land, whereupon Meadow Park was under way. Help came from the Sunderland, and Tyne and Wear Councils as well as the Sports Council, but by far the greatest contribution came from the members themselves. The result is an enclosed sports ground with a 200 seater grandstand, clubhouse and floodlights.

In 1982 the club were founder members of the Northern League Division Two, gaining promotion two years later, until losing their place in 1988.

SEAHAM RED STAR

Seaham Town Park, Stockton Rd, Seaham, Co Durham Tel: 0191 581 2540

Secretary: John McBeth, 29 Frederick St, Seaham, Co Durham Tel: 0191 581 5712

Colours: Red and white stripes

Nickname: The Star

Seating: 60

Covered standing: 200

Capacity: 4,000

Clubhouse on ground: Nearby

Record attendance: 1, 500 approx v Guisborough in Wearside League

Record appearances: Mick Whitfield

Record goalscorer in total: Tom Henderson   211 in 276 games

Record goalscorer in one season: Tom Henderson   62 in 1978-79

DIRECTIONS

Approach Seaham by the A19. Take the B1404 Seaham slip road at the Seaton Junction and turn left at the top. Turn right at the set of traffic lights and first left past the school into the ground.

Honours

Phillips Floodlight Trophy 1979

Durham Challenge Cup 1980

Wearside League and League Cup 1982

Northern League Cup 1993

Manager for 1996-97: Dave Callaghan

Seaham Red Star were formed as a Sunday side in 1973, and within 15 years were in the Northern League. They quickly switched to Saturdays and joined the Houghton and District League, and in 1974 moved up to the Northern Alliance. After two years on the Deneside Recreation ground the club moved to Vane Tempest Colliery Welfare, where they stayed for two years until moving to their present ground in 1978. Part of the deal was that they changed their name, and were thenceforth known by the somewhat cumbersome title of Seaham Colliery Welfare Red Star. There had been a Seaham CW years previously which used the ground, but they were then the main club and they won the Phillips tournament in Birmingham, which brought them £10,000 worth of lighting for the ground, which coincided with the move to the Wearside League in 1979. They won the League and Cup double in 1982 and were elected to the Northern League a year later, where despite the miners strike which paralysed the community, many improvements were made to the ground which was taken over by the council in 1987 and renamed Town Park.

Red Star then reverted to their original name and won the League Cup in 1993, and despite a fire which destroyed their clubhouse, they have fought back and remain in the top flight of the Northern League.

SHILDON

Dean Street, Shildon, Co Durham Tel: 01388 773877

Secretary: John Armitage, 22 Hambleton Ct, Byerley Park, Newton Aycliffe, Co Durham Tel: 01325 316322

Colours: Red and white

Nickname: Railwaymen

Seating: 400

Covered standing: 100

Capacity: 4,000

Record attendance: 13,000 Leeholme v Perkinsville Schools match 1920,

or 11,000 v Ferryhill Ath Durham Senior Cup 1922

Record appearances: Bryan Dale

Record goalscorer in one season: Jack Downing 61 in 1936-37

Record win: 13-1 v Tow Law Town Northern League 1934

Record defeat : 0-12 v Whitley Bay Northern League 1961

DIRECTIONS

Approach Bishop Auckland from the A1(M) along the A689 from the south or along the A688 from the north. The A688 and A68 lead in from the Barnard Castle direction and Consett area respectively. Take the B6282 south from Bishop Auckland centre towards Shildon. The ground is one mile from the BR station and 300 yards from Darlington-Bishop Auckland bus stop (Hippodrome stop).

Honours

Northern League 1934, 1935, 1936, 1937, 1940

League Cup: 1934, 1935, 1938, 1939, 1953

Durham Challenge Cup 1908, 1926, 1972

Benevolent Bowl: 1925

Durham Amateur Cup 1902 and 1903

Formed in 1890, as Shildon Town, they played friendlies until joining the Auckland League in 1892. Within a further two years they had combined with Shildon Rangers and Shildon Heroes to become Shildon United and they played in the Wear Valley League before entering the Northern League Second Division in 1897.

United disbanded in 1900 due to severe financial problems along with the league, but soon reformed as Shildon Athletic, playing on Dean Street which was then known as South Durham Athletic ground and had a cycle track around it. When Stockton St John dropped out of the Northern League they were in again.

Shildon moved into the semi-professional North Eastern League in 1907, and stayed until once again moving back to the Northern League in 1932, by which time they had dropped the Athletic tag.

Just before the War, the club reached the quarter final of the Amateur Cup, as they dominated local football, winning the league five times and coming second twice, all within eight years.

They were relegated to Division One in 1987, but since then have fought back again without threatening to repeat the astonishing feats of the pre-War days.

SHOTTON COMRADES

Shotton Recreational Ground, Station Rd, Shotton Colliery, Co Durham, Tel - 0191 526 2859

Secretary: Mr W.Banks, 6 Syston Close, Chilton Moor, Fencehouses, Houghton-le-Spring, Co Durham

Tel - 0191 385 5361

Club colours: Black and White halves

Nickname   The Coms

Capacity   1,700

Floodlights   No

Covered seating   80

Covered standing   400

Clubhouse on ground   Yes

Biggest win: 8-0   v   Bedlington Terriers 1992

Biggest defeat: 1-7 at Brandon Utd in FA Cup 1991

Record appearance Holder: J.Cudlip

Record goalscorer in one season: Keith Willets 50

| **DIRECTIONS** |
| A19 to Peterlee to Shotton, right at War Mem, t-junction, follow round 800yds, ground on right. |

Honours

Houghton and District League 1979

Hetton Charity Cup 1979

Peterlee Sunday League 1976 and Div 2 1975

Northern League Div 2 Cup 1996

Craven Cup   1996

Manager: B.Huntingdon, Chairman: J.Maddison, Vice Chairman: T.Robinson

Shooton were formed by one man, Tim Tuttle, in 1973, when a group of players had become too old for junior football at the successful Shotton Juniors club. Originally a Sunday club, they played in the Peterlee Sunday League in 1975 winning promotion and finishing runners up in three cups. The following year they were Division One champions. In 1976 they switched to Saturdays and after two seasons in the Houghton League were runners up as well reaching the Hetton Charity Cup final. 1978-79 was the most successful, taking the title unbeaten along with the Hetton Cup and finishing runners up in the League Cup. At the end of 1979-80 season the club moved into the Northern Alliance League and senior football and after four seasons moved up to the Northern League where they remain.

The last two seasons have seen the club reach the Division Two League Cup final, winning it last May.

SOUTH SHIELDS

Filtrona Park, Shaftesbury Ave, Simonside Ind Est, South Shields Tel: 0191 427 9839

Secretary: David Fall, 50 Basil Way, Holder House Estate, South Shields, Tel 0191 426 2135

Colours: Claret and Blue

Nickname: The Mariners

Capacity: 2,000

Seating: 200

Covered standing: 200

Record attendance: 1,400 v Hartlepool Town Sunderland Shipowners Cup final 1993

DIRECTIONS

A1(M), A194(M) to S. Shields, A194 town centre road for 5 miles, ignore A1300 (Sunderland & coast) turn left at next lights beside Co-op store into Simonside Ind. Est. (Shaftesbury Avenue), ground at bottom on right.

Honours

Northern Alliance 1975 and 1976

Wearside League 1977 and `1993

Monkwearmouth Charity Cup 1987

Sunderland Shipowners Cup 1993

Durham Challenge Cup 1977

Manager For 1996-7: Bobby Graham

The present South Shields FC was formed in 1974 when the existing club, which had competed in the Northern Premier League, moved to Gateshead. They were elected to the Northern Alliance, winning the league and the following year was just as successful with the Mariners again taking the league as well as enjoying a run in the FA Vase. Election to the Wearside League came next where again the club made a remarkable start, with the league and Durham Challenge Cup won.

At this time the club's ground was in Jack Clarke Park, a council owned ground which was not suitable for development. Numerous applications were made for a new ground, without success until the summer of 1992 when the club obtained the Filtrona Sports Ground. The first season was very exciting as the Mariners won the Wearside League and the Sunderland Shipowners Cup, the final of which was played at Filtrona Park in front of over 1,400 people. Since then the ground has been transformed with hardstanding, floodlights and a covered area, plus new function suites and changing rooms. The Wearside League was again won in 1995, during which they club reached the final of the Durham Challenge Cup, losing in a replay to Spennymoor United in front of 1,500. It brought admittance to the Northern League Division Two, where they gained promotion behind winners Morpeth Town.

STOCKTON

Teesdale Park, Acklam Rd, Thornaby, Stockton-on-Tees TS17 8TZ Tel: 01642 606803

Secretary: Peter Morris, 20 Wheatear Lane, Ingleby,
Barwick, Stockton, Cleveland Tel 01642 209718

Colours: Red and black stripes

Capacity: 5,000

Covered standing: 200

Seating: 150

Clubhouse on ground: Yes, within complex

Record attendance: 3,000 v Middlesbrough
Friendly 1986

Biggest win: 10-0 v Evenwood (h)
Northern League 1991-92

Record appearances: Micheal Watson

Honours

Northern League Div 2 1988 and 1992

North Riding County Cup 1986

DIRECTIONS

A19 to Thornaby turn off, ground half mile on right. One mile from Thornaby BR station. Any Stockton-Middlesbrough bus - stop at Acklam Road, Thornaby.

The original Stockton Football and Athletic Club was formed in 1882, becoming one of the Country's leading amateur sides and winning many honours in its 50 years as Northern League members. 30 seasons in other leagues followed until due to financial problems the club was disbanded in 1975 and the historic Victoria Ground was sold for housing.

The new club was formed in 1980 when a successful Stockton and District side, Stockton Cricket Club FC, changed its name. Stockton FC were elected to the Wearside League in 1980 spending two seasons at Grangefield Youth and Community Centre before moving to the Tilery Recreation Ground. In 1983 they reached the Sunderland Shipowners Cup Final and a year later took the major step of moving to Teesdale Park in Thornaby, which they secured on a long lease. This was the formed home of Head Wrightson Sports club which covers over 15 acres overlooking the old Teesside Park Race Course.

In 1984 the club converted the cricket and tennis areas into a football pitch and despite finishing bottom of the Wearside League, were elected to the Northern League in 1985. They finished seventh in the first two seasons and then won the North Riding Cup, taking the Second Division championship in 1988. They embarked on a ground development scheme which saw £50,000 spent on refurbishing the clubhouse, and £26,000 on floodlights and terracing and £20,000. Sadly disaster struck in 1989 when vandals destroyed the dressing rooms and stand with fire, and these were eventually replaced. Recently there have been mixed fortunes, winning Division Two again in 1992 but going down in 1994, only to go up again a year later.

TOW LAW TOWN

Ironworks Road, Tow Law, Co Durham Tel: 01388 731443

Secretary: Bernard Fairbairn, 3 Coppice Walk,
Mowden Park, Darlington, Co Durham
Tel: 01325 350743

Colours: Black and white stripes

Nickname: Lawyers

Seating: 200

Covered standing: 300

Capacity: 6,000

Record attendance: 5,500 v Mansfield Town
FA Cup 1967

DIRECTIONS

Tow Law is on the A68. From the A1(M) junction 3 travel north through West Auckland and Fir Tree. The ground is off Tow Law High Street. From the north on the A68 Tow Law is about 8 miles south of Consett.

Honours

Rothmans National Cup 1977

Northern League 1924, 1925, 1995

League Cup 1974

Durham Challenge Cup 1896

Durham Amateur Cup 1893

Managers for 1996-97: Warren Pearson and Andy Sinclair

Tow Law were formed in 1890 and two years later were founder members of the Auckland and District League. They won the Durham Amateur and Challenge Cups and entered the Northern League until 1900 when they joined the South Durham Alliance in 1900. Five years later they were in the Crook and District League before either side of the Great War, when they had two further spells in Auckland football.

The club's first home was in Church Lane, but in 1892 during the miners strike, men volunteered to build a new ground, which was improved and rebuilt during the next strike in 1921.

The Lawyers were Northern League champions in 1924 and 1925 but in the main they have gained their success in cups, none more so than as recently as December 1967, when having reached the First Round of the FA Cup, they hammered Mansfield Town 5-1.

Last year the club won the Northern League for only the third time and brought back the trophy to what is regarded as the highest, and definitely the coldest, non-League football ground in England.

WASHINGTON

Albany Park. Spout Lane, Concord, Washington, Tel: 0191 417 7779

Secretary: George Abbott, 14 Grosvenor Street, Southwick, Sunderland Tel 0191 549 1384

Nickname: The Mechanics

Colours: All Red

Capacity: 3,000

Seating: 50

Covered standing: Yes

Floodlights: Yes

Record attendance: 3,800 v Bradford PA FA Cup 1970

DIRECTIONS

Ground situated behind the cinema opposite bus station.

Washington Football Club was formed in 1947, before the New Town was thought of. They were known as Washington Colliery Mechanics, based at `F' Pit. Playing on the Miners Welfare Ground and then later at Usworth Colliery Welfare, the club joined the Washington League in 1949, winning it seven times along with the Durham Minor Cup twice.

In 1967 they joined the Northern Alliance, staying just one year before admitted to the Wearside League, where they played with little success for 20 years. The club had already made improvements to Albany Park, part of another Welfare Ground, when it was elected to the Northern League Division Two in 1988. A new £100,000 clubhouse was built but sadly it was victim of an arson attack in 1991, which meant the club played at Ryhope CA for a season. The floodlights were installed having come from the Wearside Colliery once it had closed and were open for business in 1995

WEST AUCKLAND TOWN

Darlington Rd Ground, West Auckland, Co Durham Tel: 01388 834403

Secretary: Allen Bayles, 11 Edith Terrace, West Auckland, Co Durham Tel: 01388 833783

Colours: Black and Amber

Nickname: West

Capacity: 3,000

Seating: 250

Covered standing: Yes

Clubhouse on ground: No, working men's club in town

Record attendance: 6,000 v Dulwich Hamlet FA Amateur Cup 1959

Record win: 11-0 in Durham Challenge Cup

DIRECTIONS

Approach West Auckland by the A68 or the A688. The ground is on the A68 on the edge of the village. The bus route is via Bishop Auckland from Newcastle or Darlington.

Honours

FA AMATEUR CUP Runners up 1961

Northern League 1960 and 1961

Division Two 1991

League Cup 1959 and 1963

Durham Challenge Cup 1965

Benevolent Bowl 1963

Thomas Lipton Trophy 1909 and 1911

West Auckland Town have never been as big as their neighbours, the Bishops, but they will be forever associated with the first World Cup, the Thomas Lipton Trophy, which they won in the Turin Stadium in 1909 and 1911, whilst a Northern League side. They beat FC Winterhour 2-0 and the famous Juventus 6-1, to bring home the magnificent trophy which was housed in the working men's club until stolen a few years back. The club began in the Auckland and District League in 1893 before moving to the Wear Valley and then South Durham Leagues. In 1905 they transferred to the Mid-Durham League for three years before joining the Northern League. Sadly the European journeys had taken their toll financially and the club folded in 1912, only to re-form in 1914 to play in cup matches.

In 1919 they were known as Auckland St Helens United, for one season, and after one season in the Northern League they went nomadic with spells in the Palatine League for four years, Auckland League for three, a year in the South Durham League, another five in the Auckland and District from 1928, the Gauntless Valley League for a season in 1933, and then back to Auckland again for a year until they replaced Esh Winning in the Northern League. They have remained there ever since, winning the title twice at the end of the 50's.

Their ground has been home since the 1890's, and the stand was bought with the gains from the Wembley final appearance.

WHICKHAM

Glebe Ground, Rectory Lane, Whickham, Tyne and Wear Tel: 0191 420 0186

Secretary: Harry Hodgson, 18 Deepdale Close,
Whickham, Tyne and Wear Tel 0191 488 2493

Colours: Black and white stripes

Seating: 100

Covered standing: Yes

Capacity: 2,000

Record attendance: 3,165 v Windsor and Eton
FA Vase semi-final 1981

DIRECTIONS

A692 (Consett) from A69. Left at roundabout signed Consett/Whickham. Up hill and right at mini roundabout. Continue along and turn left into Rectory Lane (by Lloyds Bank) for about 500 yds, clubhouse on right.

Honours

FA VASE WINNERS 1981

FA VASE Semi-finals 1979 and 1984

Wearside League 1978 and 1988

League Cup 1987

Monkwearmouth Charity Cup 1977 and 1979

Sunderland Shipowners Cup 1978 and 1981

Northern Combination 1970, 1973, 1974

League Cup 1961 and 1974

Vaux Challenge Cup 1981

Whickham FC were formed in 1944, as Axwell Park Colliery Welfare, known locally as the Home Guard team. They played after the War in the now defunct Derwent Valley League, changing in 1955 to the Northern Combination. Two years later, whilst the Coal Board improved their ground, they played in the Tyneside Amateur League, but returned to the Combination in 1959 whilst groundsharing with Watergate Colliery Welfare FC.

They changed their name to Whickham in 1962, and after winning the league three times and the Cup twice they switched to the Wearside League in 1974. Much more success followed in various cups and the league championship was taken twice, with the highlight undoubtedly being the club's run to the FA Vase final in 1981, when 12,000 saw them win in extra time over Willenhall Town. The club also reached the semi-final in 1979 and 1984, and on gaining promotion to the Northern League, built a new stand, changing rooms and toilets to comply with league rules.

Recently after a period in the doldrums the club has enjoyed promotion to the top division.

WHITBY TOWN

Turnbull Ground, Upgang Lane, Whitby   Tel: 01947 603193

Secretary Charles Woodward, 6 Westlands Ave, Whitby,
North Yorks YO21 3DZ Tel 01947 602312

Nickname: The Seasiders   Capacity: 4, 000

Seating: 200   Covered standing: 400

Clubhouse on ground: Yes

Record Attendance: 4,500 v Scarborough
North Riding Senior Cup April 18th 1965

Biggest win: 11-2 v Cargo Fleet Works 1950

Biggest defeat: 3-13 v Willington March 24th 1928

Record appearances: Derek Hampton 414

Record goalscorer in one season: Paul Pitman 60

Record goalscorer in total: Paul Pitman 284 to date

DIRECTIONS

Approach Whitby on the A171 or the A169. Take the A174 north from the town centre towards Sandsend. The ground is on the offside in Upgang Lane.

Honours

FA AMATEUR CUP runner-up 1965

Northern League 1993, League Cup 1929, 1964, 1970, 1977, 1985, 1996

Rothmans Knockout Cup 1976 and 1978

North Riding Senior Cup 1965, 1968, 1983, 1990

J R Cleator Cup 1985 and 1993

Mickey Skinner Trophy 1984, 1985, 1988, 1989, 1991, 1993

Rothmans National KO Cup 1976 and 1978

North Riding Benevolent Cup 1993

Manager: Harry A Dunn, Assistant Manager: Steve Harland

Chairman: Graham Manser

Whilst the first traceable evidence of football in Whitby was a report of a friendly played by Whitby Church Temperance in 1880, there are hints that a Whitby team was in existence earlier than the first published fixture list in 1882.Whitby FC joined the Northern League for the first time in 1893 only to return to the Cleveland Amateur League two years later, They regained their Northern League status in 1899, winning the second Division the same year. Once again the expense of travel forced them out, this time to the Cleveland Alliance, until reverting to friendlies, a move which led to relative obscurity. After the Great War, clubs in the town were reformed and Whitby Whitehall Swifts were the senior side, playing in the Scarborough and District League, with Whitby Town in the same league. The two rivals met in 1926 and after much discussion two clubs amalgamated as Whitby United. A successful application to the Northern League was made in 1926 and the club, who changed their name to Whitby Town in 1946, have remained there ever since, finishing runners up five times before finally winning the league in 1993.

The club reached its peak in the early sixties, getting to the Amateur Cup quarter-finals in 1964 before going all the way to Wembley the following year, losing to Hendon. In addition to the league, the League Cup has been won five times with the Rothmans Knockout Cup won twice in the 70's. In 1983 they reached the Second Round of the FA Cup, beating Halifax Town at the Shay before losing to Wigan and in the same season Whitby reached the FA Trophy last eight. In 1993 the club finally won the league but were denied the chance to move into the Northern Premier League by circumstances beyond their control.

The early club played its football on Stakesby Fields, moving to Upgang Lane for the Northern League. This was adjacent to todays ground at 45 degree angle. Upgang Lane was used by a number of clubs who shared it with the cricket club until 1926, when a local benefactor saved the site by buying it and having purchased the field next door, levelled it, and while Whitby played at Stakesby Road for two years, prepared the Turnbull Ground, named after him, for use. It was opened on August 31st 1929

WILLINGTON

Hall Lane, Hall Lane Estate, Willington, Co Durham Tel: 01388 746221

Secretary: Bob Nicholls, 34 Stephenson Crescent, Willington, Co Durham Tel: 01388 745297

Capacity: 2,680

Colours: Royal blue and white

Seating: 400

Covered standing: None

Clubhouse on ground: No, but two mins away at back of ground

Record attendance: 10,000 v Bromley FA Amateur Cup Jan 24th 1953

Biggest win: 13-3 v Whitby (H) in 1928

Biggest defeat: 0-11 v Dunston (H) Sept 5th 1992

Record appearances: Gordon Brown

Record goalscorer in one season: Tommy Holden

Record goalscorer in total: John Taylor 1955-69

DIRECTIONS

Willington is on A690 seven miles west of Durham City and 2 miles east of Crook. Off main through road at 'The Black Horse' Tavern corner turn into Commercial Street, then into Hall Lane after 100 yds. Northern Bus Co. operates a service through Willington from Crook or Durham City. Bond Bros Bus Transport operates a service from Bishop Auckland.

HONOURS

FA AMATEUR CUP WINNERS 1950

Runners up 1939 and semi-finalists 1928

Northern League 1914, 1926, 1930,

League Cup 1925, 1926, 1928, 1931, 1932, 1949, 1957, 1975

Durham Benevolent Bowl 1949, 1951, 1958

Manager for 1996-97: Malcolm Smith

Assistant Manager: Kevin Stonehouse

Chairman: Desmond Ayre

Vice chairman: Bob Nicholls

Willington Temperance, the present club's forerunners, were formed in 1906 as an Auckland and District League side based at the Temperance Club and playing on the West End ground. In 1911 they changed to Willington AFC and were elected to the Northern League and moved to their present Hall Lane ground. They won the championship in 1914 and again in 1926 and 1930, lifting the League Cup eight times between 1925 and 1975.

Out of many memorable occasions in the club's history, one milestone is the 1939 FA Amateur Cup final at Roker Park when Willington lost an amazing game 3-0 after extra time to Bishop Auckland, who had Bob Paisley playing for them. Also the 10,000 record crowd which packed in to watch a 2-1 Amateur Cup win over Bromley in 1953 and the 5,000 which saw Blackburn Rovers held 0-0 in the FA Cup 1st Round in 1973.

But the zenith was the 1950 Amateur Cup final v Bishops at Wembley, where over 88,000 saw Eddie Taylor inspire Willington to a 4-0 win.

In 1983 Willington were relegated to the Second Division where success has been elusive although a number of well known names have held positions within the club, Alan Durban, Malcolm Allison, Tony McAndrew and John Hope are just some.

ICIS FOOTBALL LEAGUE

PREMIER DIVISION

	P	W	D	L	F	A	Pts
Hayes	42	24	14	4	76	32	86
Enfield	42	26	8	8	68	35	86
Boreham Wood	42	24	11	7	69	29	83
Yeovil Town	42	23	11	8	69	51	80
Dulwich H	42	23	11	8	85	59	80
Carshalton	42	22	8	12	68	49	74
St albans C	42	20	12	10	70	41	72
Kingstonian	42	20	11	11	62	38	71
Harrow B	42	19	10	13	70	66	67
Sutton U	42	17	14	11	71	56	65
Aylesbury U	42	17	12	13	71	57	63
Bishops St	42	16	9	17	61	62	57
Yeading	42	11	14	17	48	60	47
Hendon	42	12	10	20	52	65	46
Chertsey T	42	13	6	23	45	71	45
Purfleet	42	12	8	22	48	67	44
Grays Ath	42	11	11	20	43	63	44
Hitchin T	42	10	10	22	41	74	40
Bromley	42	10	7	25	52	91	37
Molesey	42	9	9	24	46	81	36
Walton & H	42	9	7	26	42	79	34
Worthing	42	4	7	31	42	106	19

DIVISION 1

Oxford C	42	28	7	7	98	60	91
Heybridge S	42	27	7	8	97	43	88
Staines T	42	23	11	8	82	59	80
Leyton pen	42	22	7	13	77	57	73
Aldershot	42	21	9	12	81	46	72
Billericay T	42	19	9	14	58	58	66
Bognor	42	18	11	13	71	53	65
Marlow	42	19	5	18	72	75	62
Basingstoke	42	16	13	13	70	60	61
Uxbridge	42	16	12	14	46	49	60
Wokingham	42	16	10	16	62	65	58
Chesham U	42	15	12	15	51	38	57
Thame U	42	14	13	15	64	75	55
Maidenhead	42	12	14	16	50	63	50
Whyteleafe	42	12	13	17	71	81	49
Abingdon T	42	13	9	20	63	80	48
Barton R	42	12	10	20	69	87	46
Berkhamsted	42	11	11	20	52	68	44
Tooting & M	42	11	10	21	45	64	43
Ruislip manor	42	11	9	22	55	77	42
Wembley	42	11	8	23	49	66	41
Barking	42	4	11	26	35	90	24

DIVISION 2

Canvey Is	40	25	12	3	91	36	87
Croydon	40	25	6	9	78	42	81
Hampton	40	23	10	7	74	44	79
Banstead	40	21	11	8	72	36	74
Collier Row	40	21	11	8	73	41	74
Wivenhoe T	40	21	8	11	82	57	71
Met police	40	18	10	12	57	45	64
Bedford	40	18	10	12	67	59	64
Bracknell	40	18	8	14	69	50	62
Edgware	40	16	9	15	72	57	67
Tilbury	40	12	11	17	52	52	47
Ware	40	13	8	19	55	80	47
Chalfont	40	11	13	16	58	63	46
Leatherhead	40	12	10	18	71	77	46
Saffron W	40	11	12	17	56	58	45
Cheshunt	40	10	12	18	56	90	42
Hemel H	40	10	10	20	46	62	40
Egham	40	12	3	25	42	74	39
Witham	40	8	10	22	35	68	34
Hungerford	40	9	7	24	44	79	34
Dorking	40	8	5	27	44	104	29

DIVISION 3

Horsham	40	29	5	6	95	40	92
Leighton T	40	28	5	7	95	34	89
Windsor	40	27	6	7	107	46	87
Wealdstone	40	23	8	9	104	39	77
Harlow T	40	22	10	8	85	62	76
Northwood	40	20	9	11	76	56	69
Epson	40	18	14	8	95	57	68
Kingsbury	40	15	16	9	61	48	61
Eastthur	40	17	8	15	61	60	59
Aveley	40	16	10	14	62	53	58
Wingate	40	16	7	17	74	70	55
Lewes	40	14	7	19	56	72	49
Flackwell H	40	14	5	21	60	84	46
Hornchurch	40	11	8	21	55	77	41
Harefield U	40	11	7	22	49	89	40
Tring T	40	10	8	22	40	78	38
Camberley T	40	9	9	22	45	81	36
Hertford T	40	10	5	25	72	103	35
Cove	40	8	12	22	37	89	34
Clapton	40	9	6	25	48	89	33
Southall	40	9	5	26	33	104	32

AYLESBURY UNITED

The Stadium, Buckingham Rd, Aylesbury HP20 2AQ Tel; 01296 436350 or 436525

Secretary: Tony Graham, c/o Football Club

Club colours: Green and White

Nickname: The Ducks

Capacity: 4,500

Covered seating: 400

Covered standing: 1,000

Clubhouse on ground: Yes

DIRECTIONS

Directions: On A413 to Buckingham, just off ring road opposite Horse & Jockey PH. Arriving from Buckingham ground is on left — from all other directions follow Buckingham signs and ground on right. Half hour walk from Aylesbury rail and bus stations.

Record attendance: 6,000 v England X1 and at Turnfurlong Lane 7,500 v Watford FA Cup 1st Rd 1951

Record appearance holder: Cliff Hercules

Record goalscorer in total: Cliff Hercules

Record fee paid: £ 15,000 for Glen Donegal from Northampton in 1990

Record fee received £ 35,000 for Glen Donegal to Maidstone Utd in 1991

Honours

Southern League 1988

Delphian League 1954

Delphian League Cup 1960

Spartan League 1909

West Division 1929

Division One 1939

Berks and Bucks Senior Cup 1914 and 1986

Isthmian League Cup 1995

Known around football as the Ducks, Aylesbury United Football Club were formed in 1897 on the merger of the Printing Works and Night School Football Clubs. Early seasons were spent in the Bucks Contiguous, and South Eastern Leagues until playing at the Printing Works Ground, they joined the Spartan League in 1907. They had success almost at once, winning it in 1909 and they subsequently won the West Division in 1929 and Division One in 1939, after being runners up in 1935.

That year the club moved to the sports stadium in Wendover Road, later known as Turnfurlong Lane, and in 1951 they had a dozen year spell in the Delphian League, finishing as runners up in 1953 and going one better a year later. They took the League Cup in 1960 and in 1963 it was incorporated into the Athenian League. United had little success for the next ten years or so, but still joined the Southern League, becoming semi-professional in 1976. Crowds were often around 1,000 and for some while the Ducks were a force, and won the Southern League in 1988. By then they had moved into their purpose built new ground on Buckingham Road which was opened by an England X1 which attracted 6,000 to the ground. The sojourn into the Alliance Premier lasted one year and they were relegated to the Isthmian League, where they remain.

Date	Competition	Round	Opponent	Att	Score	Scorers
12/08/95	IFL	P	Dulwich Hamlet	324	0-1	
19/08/95	IFL	P	YEOVIL TOWN	812	3-1	Pluckrose, Bashir, Danzey
23/08/95	IFL	P	Harrow Borough	417	3-3	Williams, Caesar, Hercules
26/08/95	IFL	P	Molesey	450	4-1	Shea, Hobbs, Caesar, Bashir
29/08/95	IFL	P	BROMLEY	703	3-0	Pluckrose, Caesar, Danzey
02/09/95	IFL	P	WALTON & HERSHAM	713	0-0	
05/09/95	GIC	1	MAIDENHEAD UNITED		3-0	
12/09/95	CS		Enfield	422	2-1	Caesar(2)
16/09/95	IFL	P	YEADING	875	1-1	Caesar
23/09/95	IFL	P	Hitchin Town	418	3-0	Hercules, Pluckrose, Hobbs
30/09/95	IFL	P	Sutton United	653	3-2	Cobb, Hercules, Maynard
03/10/95	IFL	P	Chertsey Town	434	3-0	Shea, Cobb, Hercules
07/10/95	IFL	P	BOREHAM WOOD	855	1-3	Caesar
14/10/95	IFL	P	KINGSTONIAN	739	0-2	
21/10/95	FA Cup	Q4	STEVENAGE BOROUGH	1480	1-3	Pluckrose
28/10/95	IFL	P	GRAYS ATHLETIC	490	2-2	Caesar, Cubb
31/10/95	GIC	2	Chesham United		3-2	
07/11/95	CC	1	Chesham United		3-2	
18/11/95	IFL	P	St Albans City	695	0-2	
25/11/95	FA Trophy	Q3	Worcester City	863	0-3	
28/11/95	CC	2	PURFLEET		0-1	
02/12/95	IFL	P	Hayes	393	1-0	Caesar
09/12/95	IFL	P	WORTHING	778	1-1	Crown
16/12/95	IFL	P	Purfleet	156	2-1	Hayward, Crown
03/01/96	IFL	P	BISHOP'S STORTFORD	451	0-0	
06/01/96	IFL	P	Walton & Hersham	266	1-2	Crown
09/01/96	IFL	P	ST ALBANS CITY	421	1-1	Davies
13/01/96	IFL	P	HARROW BOROUGH	531	2-0	Heard, Caesar
15/01/96	B&B SC	1	Wycombe Wanderers		2-1	
03/02/96	IFL	P	Bromley	264	3-0	Caesar(2), Davies
10/02/96	IFL	P	SUTTON UNITED	606	4-1	Davies(2), Crown, Sullivan
13/02/96	GIC	3	CARSHALTON ATHLETIC		3-1	
17/02/96	IFL	P	Yeading	181	0-0	
24/02/96	IFL	P	Grays Athletic	274	0-2	
27/02/96	B&B SC	QF	Thatcham Town	143	2-0	
02/03/96	IFL	P	CHERTSEY TOWN	501	2-0	Hayward, Caesar
05/03/96	GIC	QF	CROYDON		2-1	
09/03/96	IFL	P	HITCHIN TOWN	503	2-1	Haworth, Cobb
12/03/96	IFL	P	HENDON	346	1-0	Pluckrose
16/03/96	IFL	P	Boreham Wood	324	2-2	Newson, Davies
19/03/96	B&B SC	SF	Maidenhead United		0-0	
23/03/96	IFL	P	Kingstonian	598	1-1	Caesar
26/03/96	B&B SC	SF rep	MAIDENHEAD UNITED		4-0	
28/03/96	GIC	SF(1)	KINGSTONIAN		1-3	
30/03/96	IFL	P	CARSHALTON ATHLETIC	469	0-1	
02/04/96	GIC	SF(2)	Kingstonian	292	1-2	Caesar
04/04/96	IFL	P	DULWICH HAMLET	424	0-3	
06/04/96	IFL	P	Bishop's Stortford	308	6-3	Smart, Danzey, Cobb, Haworth, Pluckrose, Caesar
08/04/96	IFL	P	ENFIELD	859	2-3	Cobb(2)
13/04/96	IFL	P	Hendon	253	2-4	Davies, Newson
16/04/96	IFL	P	Yeovil Town	2008	2-3	Pluckrose, Davies
20/04/96	IFL	P	HAYES	809	1-3	Caesar
23/04/96	IFL	P	MOLESEY	259	1-1	Hayward
27/04/96	IFL	P	Worthing	89	3-1	Haworth(2), Caesar
30/04/96	IFL	P	Enfield	1344	3-3	Shea, Haworth, Newson
02/05/96	IFL	P	Carshalton Athletic	236	1-3	Bashir
04/05/96	IFL	P	PURFLEET	402	1-0	Shea
06/05/96	B&B SC	F	WOKINGHAM TOWN		0-1	

BISHOP'S STORTFORD

George Wilson Stadium, Rhodes Ave, Bishop's Stortford CM23 3JN.Tel: 01279 654140

Secretary: Graeme Auger, 58 Braziers Quay, Bishop's Stortford, Herts CM23 3YW Tel 01279 465998

Office Tel: 01279 656538 daytime

Press Officer: Edward Stalley, 48 Prestwick Dr, Bish Stortford CM23 5ES Tel 01279 658536

Nickname: Blues, Colours: Blue and White stripes

Capacity: 4,500, Seating: 270

Covered Standing: 1,800, Clubhouse on ground: Yes

Record Attendance: 6,000 v Peterborough Utd
FA Cup 2nd Rd in 1972 and v Middlesbrough
FA Cup 3rd Rd replay 1983.

Biggest win: 11-0: Nettleswell and Burntmill
Herts Junior Cup 1911 and Tufnell Pk 1954-55

Biggest defeat: 0-13 v Cheshunt Herts Senior Cup 1926

Record appreances: Phil Hopkins 543

Record ,goalscorer in total: Jimmy Badcock 123

Record fee received: £10,000 for Carl Hoddle to Leyton Orient 1989

DIRECTIONS

M11 junction 11, A120 towards town centre, right at crossroads into London Road (A1184), right at mini-roundabout and cross railway bridge, right at next island (by garage). Rhodes Avenue is 2nd left (5-10 mins from M11). By rail: BR West Anglia Line (London Liverpool Street - Cambridge) cross BR car park from main station entrance, over footbridge, through 'Maltings' area and 2nd left into South Road, pass Rhodes Centre, Rhodes Avenue 1st right (5-10 mins walk from station).

Honours

FA TROPHY Winner 1981, FA AMATEUR CUP Winner 1974, Isthmian League Div 1 1981 and 1995

League Cup 1989, Full Members Cup 1991, Premier Inter-League Cup 1990, Athenian League 1970, Div 1 1966, Delphian League 1955, Spartan League Div 2 East 1932, London Senior Cup 1974

Herts Senior Cup 1933, 1959, 1960, 1964, 1971, 1973, 1974, 1976, 1987, East Anglian Cup 1982

Herts Charity Cup 1963, 1966, 1974, 1982, 1983, 1985, 1988, Herts Charity Shield 1955, Eastern Floodlit Cup 1985, Essex Floodlit Cup 1968, East Herts League 1920, Stansted and District League 1920

Essex and Herts Border Combination 1882 and 1889

Manager for 1996-97: Dave Edwards, Assistant manager: Ray Wickenden

Chairman: Gordon Lawrence, Vice Chairman: Mick Hancock

Bishop's Stortford Football Club was formed on January 28th 1874 at the Chequers Hotel in the town. League football came in the 1890's through the East Herts, Stansted and District, Saffron Walden, Herts and Essex Border and Herts County Leagues. The highlights between 1889 and 1929 were two double seasons in 1913 and 1920, before in 1929 the club moved to the Spartan League Div 2 East. They won the trophy a year later, with promotion and celebrated by winning the Herts Senior Cup for the first time. After the war, when the club played mainly friendlies against service units, they were back in the re-formed Spartan League, where they stayed until the Delphian League was formed in 1951. They made steady progress and the league was won from Dagenham in 1955, but it was not until 1963 that the next real excitement came around, as they reached the quarter-final of the Amateur Cup, losing to Isthmian League champions Wimbledon at Plough Lane in front of 9,000 spectators. The mid-60's were the most exciting period in the history of Stortford, for in three years, the club, having moved to the expanded Athenian League, were runners up in Division Two, champions of Division One and runners up in the Premier. They were to take the title in 1970, and despite finishing 12th the following year, their application to the Isthmian League was successful. The early 70's were again hugely successful with six cup final victories in four seasons, the pinnacle being reached in the Centenary season when they took the Amateur Cup was won at Wembley Stadium, Ilford being beaten 4-1 in the last ever final.

The rest of the decade was quiet with only a Herts Senior Cup win in 1976, but a year later they suffered relegation for only the second time ever. Since then the club has see-sawed between Divisions as they attempt to move forward again.

BISHOP'S STORTFORD 1995/96 SEASON

Date	Comp		Opponent	Att	Score	Scorers
15/08/95	Herts CC 1		Boreham Wood	183	0-2	
19/08/95	IFL	P	SUTTON UNITED	384	1-3	Cooper
2/08/95	IFL	P	Dulwich Hamlet	260	1-4	Burns
26/08/95	IFL	P	Walton & Hersham	215	2-0	Walker, Parkyn
02/09/95	IFL	P	BROMLEY	386	1-1	Braithwaite
05/09/95	LC	1	Edgware Town	137	2-0	Hollamby (2)
09/09/96	FA Cup	Q1	BOSTON TOWN	352	2-2	Cooper, Hollamby
12/09/95	FA Cup	Q1rep	Boston Town	183	2-5	Hollamby (2)
16/09/95	IFL	P	WORTHING	242	0-0	
23/09/95	IFL	P	Yeovil Town	1629	3-1	Hollamby,Braithwaite,Walker
26/09/95	IFL	P	PURFLEET	189	1-1	Walker
30/09/95	IFL	P	Hendon	183	1-1	Jordan
03/10/95	E. Filt	Gp10	HAVERHILL ROVERS	154	3-0	Braithwaite,Moore Cooper
07/10/95	IFL	P	Molesey	120	1-2	Hollamby
14/10/95	FA Trophy	Q1	Abingdon Town	182	1-1	Braithwaite
17/10/95	FA Trophy	Q1rep	ABINGDON TOWN	208	5-1	Hollamby(2), Forbes, Parkyn, Parratt
21/10/95	IFL	P	Grays Athletic	205	2-0	Braithwaite, Walker
28/10/95	IFL	P	ENFIELD	879	0-1	
31/10/95	LC	2	STAINES TOWN	192	3-1	Barnaby, Parkyn, Braithwaite
04/11/95	FA Trophy	Q2	Trowbridge Town	361	0-1	
07/11/95	E. Flit	Gp 10	Haverhill Rovers	62	0-3	
11/11/95	IFL	P	ST ALBANS CITY	487	3-2	Adekola, Walker, Jordan
14/11/95	E. Flit	Gp 10	WARE	195	3-1	Paxton, Adekola (2)
18/11/95	IFL	P	KINGSTONIAN	422	2-3	Adekola (2)
21/11/95	CC	2	HITCHIN TOWN	201	3-0	Adekola, Own-Goal, Cooper
25/11/95	IFL	P	WALTON & HERSHAM	308	2- 0	Adekola (2)
02/12/95	IFL	P	BOREHAM WOOD	360	0-2	
05/12/95	Herts SC 2		BERKHAMSTED TOWN	80	2-0	Walker, Cooper
09/12/95	IFL	P	Harrow Borough	221	0-0	
12/12/95	LC	3	Hitchin Town	121	1-4	Walker
16/12/95	IFL	P	YEADING	202	3-1	Walker (2) Cooper
23/12/95	IFL	P	Bromley	208	2-0	Claridge, Edmonds
03/01/96	IFL	P	Aylesbury United	451	0-0	
06/01/96	IFL	P	YEOVIL TOWN	466	2-2	Jackman, Walker
13/01/96	IFL	P	DULWICH HAMLET	408	1-2	Edmonds
16/01/96	CC	3	Yeading	71	1-0	Edmonds
20/01/96	IFL	P	Sutton United	469	1-2	Walker
30/01/96	Herts SC QF		Hitchin Town	192	1-4	Edmonds
03/02/96	IFL	P	Purfleet	173	2-1	Hollamby, Parkyn
06/02/96	E. Flit	Gp 10	Ware	125	4-0	Parratt, Conroy(2), Wardley
10/02/96	IFL	P	HENDON	323	3-1	Hollamby, Shuttlewood, Conroy
13/02/96	E. Flit	1	Aveley	66	2-1	Roberts(2)
17/02/96	IFL	P	Worthing	321	1-0	Conroy
24/02/96	IFL	P	Enfield	773	1-0	Shuttlewood
27/02/96	CC	QF	Billericay Town	202	2-0	Claridge, Wardley
02/03/96	IFL	P	GRAYS ATHLETIC	306	2-0	Parratt, Cooper
05/03/96	IFL	P	Hayes	243	1-3	Wardley
09/03/96	IFL	P	Chertsey Town	317	0-3	
16/03/96	IFL	P	MOLESEY	264	4-0	Cooper(2), Roberts, Wardley
19/03/96	IFL	P	Carshalton Athletic	251	0-2	
23/03/96	IFL	P	HAYES	427	1-2	Shuttlewood
26/03/96	CC	SF	Boreham Wood	182	1-4	Parratt
30/03/96	IFL	P	St Albans City	603	0-3	
02/04/96	IFL	P	HITCHIN TOWN	265	2-2	Conroy, Cooper
06/04/96	IFL	P	AYLESBURY UNITED	308	3-6	Shuttlewood (2), Walker
08/04/96	IFL	P	Hitchin Town	436	1-1	Roberts
10/04/96	E. Flit	QF	Ashford Town	253	2-0	Conroy, Walker
13/04/96	IFL	P	CARSHALTON ATHLETIC	340	0-2	
16/04/96	IFL	P	Kingstonian	259	1-2	Claridge
20/04/96	IFL	P	Boreham Wood	432	1-0	Parratt
23/04/96	IFL	P	CHERTSEY TOWN	246	3-1	Cooper,Conroy(2)
27/04/96	CC	P	HARROW BOROUGH	285	2-3	Roberts, Conroy
04/05/96	IFL	P	Yeading	148	4-2	Cooper(2), Walker, Forbes

669

BOREHAM WOOD

Meadow Park, Broughinge Rd, Boreham Wood, Herts WD6 5AL. Tel: 0181 953 5097

Secretary: Bob Nicholson, 56 Newcombe Rd, Shenley, Radlett, Herts WD7 9 EJ Tel: 0181 953 5097

Press officer: John D Gill, 295 Bilton Rd, Greenford, Middx UB6 7HH

Best contact when confirming a fixture
Dennis Pobjoy: 0181 207 7982

Club Shop: Dell Ward 0181 363 7345 (h)

Capacity: 4,502   Colours: White and Black

Seating: 500   Covered standing: 1,568

Clubhouse on ground: Yes

Record attend: 2,500 v St Alban Amateur Cup 1971

Record appearances holder: Steve Waller 575

Record goalscorer in total: Micky Jackson 208

DIRECTIONS

A1 towards London from M25, 1st turn off for Boreham Wood, head for town centre, into Brook Road at roundabout before town centre, Broughinge Road is 1st left. 1 mile from Elstree & Boreham Wood station (Thameslink), then bus 292 or 107 to Red Lion (5 mins walk).

Honours

Isthmian League Div 1 1995, Isthmian League Div 2 1977

Herts Senior Cup 1972, Herts Charity Cup 1967, 1984, 1986, 1989, 1990

London Senior Cup 1990, Parthenon League 1956, Fred Budden Trophy 1991

Neale Trophy 1970, Mithras Cup 1977

Manager for 1996-97: Bob Makin, Assistant manager: Alan Carrington, Chairman: Phil Wallace

Boreham Wood Football Club was formed in 1948 following the amalgamation of Boreham Rovers and Royal Retournez FC's. They progressed through the Mid-Herts and into the Parthenon League, where they finished runners up three times and champions once. They moved up to the Spartan League where they were runners up in 1964 and 1965 before again moving up, to the Athenian League. They made rapid progress and won the Premier Division by a mile in 1974, from where they entered the Isthmian League.

It took three seasons before they were crowned champions of Division Two by some 16 points. After five seasons in the Premier Division the club were relegated for the first time ever in 1982.

In 1995 a strong Wood took Division One by an incredible 22 points as well as reaching the Herts Charity and Carlsberg Cup finals, and the semi-final of the London Challenge Cup.

In County football, Boreham Wood have won the Senior Cup, Charity Shield, Junior Cup, Intermediate Cup and the Charity Cup over the years and having finished third in a tight championship race last May. Broughinge Road, which has been given the nod of approval, could well be staging Conference matches in the near future.

From the start, Wood played on Eldon Avenue, a well developed ground which was home until 1963 when it was built on as part of the expansion of the Elstree Studios. They moved to Broughinge Road, now called Meadow Park, in 1963.

BOREHAM WOOD 1995/96 SEASON

Date	Competition	Round	Opponent	Att	Score	Scorers
15/08/95	Herts CC	1	BISHOP'S STORTFORD	183	2-0	P Ferry, Joyce
19/08/95	IFL	P	YEADING	245	1-1	Harrigan
23/08/95	IFL	P	Molesey	125	2-1	Liburd, Joyce
26/08/95	IFL	P	Hendon	252	1-1	D Samuels
02/09/95	IFL	P	SUTTON UNITED	427	0-1	
04/09/95	GIC	1	Purfleet	127	1-0	A Samuels
09/09/95	FA Cup	Q1	CHALFONT ST PETER	151	1-0	Joyce
16/09/95	IFL	P	BROMLEY	252	3-1	Stein, Prutton, Nisbet
19/09/95	IFL	P	Enfield	777	2-0	Joyce(2)
23/09/95	FA Cup	Q2	STAINES TOWN	314	0-1	
26/09/95	IFL	P	HARROW BOROUGH	224	3-2	Liburd, Ashenden, Joyce
30/09/95	IFL	P	Yeovil Town	1283	1-0	T Samuels
07/10/95	IFL	P	Aylesbury United	855	3-1	Stein, Samuels, Heffer
14/10/95	IFL	P	GRAYS ATHLETIC	315	2-0	Joyce, Heffer
24/10/95	London CC	1	Leyton Pennant	101	5-5	Stein, Joyce, Own-Goal, Prutton, A Samuels
28/10/95	IFL	P	KINGSTONIAN	522	0-0	
31/10/95	GIC	2	Bromley	101	3-3	
04/11/95	IFL	P	Hitchin Town	511	2-1	Stein(2)
06/11/95	IFL	P	Purfleet	174	0-1	
11/11/95	IFL	P	CARSHALTON ATHLETIC	552	2-3	Joyce, Samuels
14/11/95	GIC	2 rep	BROMLEY	119	1-0	Own-Goal
18/11/95	IFL	P	Chertsey Town	283	3-0	Hatchett, T Samuels, Joyce
21/11/95	IFL	P	HAYES	308	0-0	
25/11/95	FA Trophy	Q3	HEYBRIDGE SWIFTS	204	3-0	Samuels, Joyce(2)
28/11/95	CC	2	BARKING	93	3-1	Joyce, Nisbet, Stein
30/11/95	London CC	1 rep	LEYTON PENNANT	88	2-3	Gammons, A Samuels
02/12/95	IFL	P	Bishop's Stortford	360	2-0	Nisbet(2)
12/12/95	Herts CC	SF	St Albans City	85	0-2	
12/12/95	Herts SC	2	Royston Town	23	2-0	Stein, Nisbet
16/12/95	IFL	P	Worthing	339	2-0	Stein, Prutton
19/12/95	GIC	3	Aldershot Town	954	0-1	
23/12/95	IFL	P	PURFLEET	302	2-1	Hatchett, Stein
01/01/96	IFL	P	DULWICH HAMLET	586	2-2	A Samuels, Nisbet
06/01/96	IFL	P	Sutton United	521	3-0	T Samuels(2), Stein
13/01/96	IFL	P	MOLESEY	292	0-1	
20/01/96	FA Trophy	1	Cambridge City	287	2-1	Gentle(2)
23/01/96	CC	3	Heybridge Swifts	116	2-0	Heffer, Joyce
03/02/96	IFL	P	Harrow Borough	276	1-1	Gentle
06/02/96	Herts CC	QF	BALDOCK TOWN		9-1	
10/02/96	FA Trophy	2	DOVER ATHLETIC	506	2-1	Harrigan, Gentle
13/02/96	IFL	P	WALTON & HERSHAM	247	1-1	Gentle
17/02/96	IFL	P	Bromley	231	1-0	Daly
24/02/96	IFL	P	Kingstonian	523	0-1	
27/02/96	CC	QF	LEYTON PENNANT	102	5-1	Miles(3), Shaw, Nisbet
02/03/96	FA Trophy	3	CHORLEY	525	1-1	Prutton
05/03/96	FA Trophy	3 rep	Chorley	833	3-4	Heffernan, Hatchett, Fox
12/03/96	Herts SC	QF	BARNET	227	2-3	Liburd, A Samuels
16/03/96	IFL	P	AYLESBURY UNITED	324	2-2	Hatchett, Harrigan
19/03/96	IFL	P	ENFIELD	507	4-1	Stein(2), A Samuels(2)
23/03/96	IFL	P	Carshalton Athletic	373	0-0	
26/03/96	CC	SF	BISHOP'S STORTFORD	182	4-1	Fox(2), Miles, Nisbet
30/03/96	IFL	P	HITCHIN TOWN	348	1-0	Heffernan
02/04/96	IFL	P	St Albans City	727	0-0	
06/04/96	IFL	P	Dulwich Hamlet	402	2-0	A Samuels, Shaw
08/04/96	IFL	P	ST ALBANS CITY	821	2-0	A Samuels, Shaw
10/04/96	IFL	P	Yeading	262	3-0	T Samuels, Prutton, Liburd
13/04/96	IFL	P	Hayes	707	1-1	Liburd
16/04/96	IFL	P	CHERTSEY TOWN	263	2-0	Liburd, Fox
20/04/96	IFL	P	BISHOP'S STORTFORD	432	0-1	
23/04/96	IFL	P	HENDON	307	4-0	Stein, A Samuels(2), Gammons
25/04/96	IFL	P	Grays Athletic	196	2-1	A Samuels, Risley(og)
27/04/96	IFL	P	Walton & Hersham	202	4-0	T Samuels, Stein(2), Prutton
30/04/96	IFL	P	YEOVIL TOWN	784	0-2	
04/05/96	IFL	P	WORTHING	428	3-1	Liburd, Stein(2)
07/05/96	CC	F	SUTTON UNITED	612	2-2	Liburd, Stein (at Purfleet. Lost on penalties)

BROMLEY

Hayes Lane, Bromley, Kent BR2 9EF.Tel: 0181 460 5291

Secretary and Press Officer: Ron McLean, 60 Fawkham Ave, New Barn, Kent DA3 7HE

Match Secretary John Fiorini, 43 Bromley Common, Bromley, Kent BR2 9LS

Tel (h) 0171 736 3435 (b) 0181 460 9013

Capacity: 8,500   Seating: 2,000

Covered standing: 2,000

Clubhouse on ground: Yes

Record attendance: 12,000 v Nigeria Friendly 1950

Record appearance holder: George Brown

Record goalscorer in one season: George Brown

Record goalscorer in total: George Brown 570

Record fee received: £50,000 for Jon Goodman from Millwall 1990

DIRECTIONS

Directions: 1 mile from Bromley South (BR). Buses 316, 146 and 119 pass ground. Junction 4 off M25, then A21 towards London.

Honours

FA AMATEUR CUP 1911, 1938, 1949

Isthmian League 1909, 1910, 1954, 1961, Athenian League 1923, 1949, 1951

London League Div 2 1897 Spartan League 1908, London Senior Cup 1910, 1946, 1951

Kent Senior Cup 1950, 1977, 1992, Kent Amateur Cup 1908, 1932, 1936, 1937, 1939, 1947, 1949, 1951, 1953, 1954, 1955, 1960, London Challenge Cup 1996

Manager: George Wakeling, Chairman: Glyn Beveley, Vice Chairman: Eddie Davies

Bromley Football Club spent its first season playing mainly friendlies against local opposition before in 1893 they entered the South London League, which they won, along with the Kent Junior Cup.They entered various leagues in the early years, including the South London League from 1894, the Southern League for two years until 1896, the London League for two years and the Kent League for one, before another two years in the London League. From there it was four seasons in the West Kent League, three in the South Suburban, one in the Spartan, three in the Isthmian and another three in the Kent League ! On resumption after the Great War, Bromley's wanderings were over, staying in the Athenian League until 1952 when they rejoined the Isthmians. Despite the changes there were successes amongst the failures during the early years, winning the London, Spartan and Isthmian League's as well as various cups, including the Amateur Cup in 1911. They won the Athenian League in 1922 but then suffered a barren spell until 1932 which heralded a spell of success where the Kent Amateur Cup was won five times, and the biggest cup of all, the FA Amateur Cup was again won when Erith and Belvedere were defeated. The post-War years were possibly the finest, with Bromley by then playing on the Hayes Lane ground which they had purchased, establishing themselves as one of the very best amateur clubs in the country. A third FA Amateur Cup win arrived in the first Wembley final in front of 96,000 people against Romford and the success continued in Athenian League and cups. The 60's saw Bromley again go through a quiet spell and indeed having turned professional the next trophy did not arrive until 1977 when they won the Kent Senior Cup. After a yo-yo couple of years the club were shattered when a massive fire destroyed the premises at Hayes Lane, leaving Bromley to play all their matches away. The stand and changing rooms were rebuilt and having survived relegation by the skin of their teeth last year, they will look to the future with more optimism.

FORMER GROUNDS

The first season was spent at the Queensmead Rec before transferring to Glebe Road where they stayed for seven years until the site was required for housing. It had an entrance off Station Road and boasted a pavilion each for the footballers and cricketers. The next move was 100 yards away to Plaistow Cricket Club, until 1904 when the site was again needed. After talks with local landowners, a site was given to the various sports clubs and opened in September 1904, lasting until 1938. A new road bisected the ground, which was partly built on by the council, the clubs having again moved just down the road to the present stadium which was already in advanced stages of being built.

BROMLEY 1995/96 SEASON

Date	Competition	Round	Opponent	Attendance	Score	Scorers
12/08/95	IFL	P	HAYES	419	0-1	
19/08/95	IFL	P	Grays Athletic	251	3-0	Francis(2), Sharman
22/08/95	IFL	P	KINGSTONIAN	664	1-1	Rawlings
26/08/95	IFL	P	CARSHALTON ATHLETIC	637	1-2	Quail
29/08/95	IFL	P	Aylesbury United	703	0-3	
02/09/95	IFL	P	Bishop's Stortford	386	1-1	J Francis
05/09/95	GIC	1	Harefield United		3-0	
09/09/95	FA Cup	Q1	HERNE BAY	338	3-1	Coles, Quail, Francis
16/09/95	IFL	P	Boreham Wood	252	1-3	Quail
23/09/95	FA Cup	Q2	Welling United	722	2-2	Francis, Quail
26/09/95	FA Cup	Q2 rep	WELLING UNITED	451	3-3	Brown(2), Francis
30/09/95	IFL	P	HITCHIN TOWN	310	0-2	
02/10/95	FA Cup	Q2 rep(2)	Welling United	701	2-1	Adedeji, Brown
07/10/95	FA Cup	Q3	SITTINGBOURNE	692	1-1	Keen
11/10/95	FA Cup	Q3 rep	Sittingbourne	1030	2-3	J Francis, Silk
14/10/95	IFL	P	MOLESEY	326	1-3	Brown
21/10/95	IFL	P	Hendon	234	0-2	
28/10/95	IFL	P	YEOVIL TOWN	357	1-5	Coles
31/10/95	GIC	2	BOREHAM WOOD	101	3-3	Joyce, A Samuels, D Samuels
04/11/95	IFL	P	Enfield	1006	0-5	
07/11/95	CC	1	Aldershot Town	1193	0-3	
11/11/95	IFL	P	YEADING	285	1-0	Dennis
14/11/95	GIC	2 rep	Boreham Wood	119	0-1	
18/11/95	IFL	P	Walton & Hersham	238	1-3	Dennis
25/11/95	FA Trophy	Q3	OXFORD CITY	250	1-1	Cherry
28/11/95	FA Trophy	Q3 rep	Oxford City	248	2-3	Coles, Cherry
02/12/95	IFL	P	Worthing	417	2-2	Richards(2)
05/12/95	London CC	1	Dulwich Hamlet		2-1	
16/12/95	IFL	P	St Albans City	485	0-5	
23/12/95	IFL	P	BISHOP'S STORTFORD	208	0-2	
26/12/95	IFL	P	Dulwich Hamlet	706	1-4	Coles
06/01/96	IFL	P	Hayes	267	1-5	Antoine
09/01/96	Kent SC	1	MILLWALL		4-1	
13/01/96	IFL	P	Kingstonian	602	1-0	Richards
20/01/96	IFL	P	GRAYS ATHLETIC	264	2-2	Cherry, Brown
31/01/96	IFL	P	Harrow Borough	206	3-1	Coles, Cherry, Samuels
03/02/96	IFL	P	AYLESBURY UNITED	264	0-3	
10/02/96	IFL	P	Hitchin Town	373	1-2	Dennington
13/02/96	Kent SC	QF	Gillingham		1-1	(lost on penalties)
17/02/96	IFL	P	BOREHAM WOOD	231	0-1	
24/02/96	IFL	P	Yeovil Town	1869	3-4	Bunter, Brown, Silk
27/02/96	IFL	P	PURFLEET	254	0-2	
02/03/96	IFL	P	HENDON	259	2-5	Wordsworth(2)
05/03/96	IFL	P	SUTTON UNITED	361	2-3	Wordsworth, Silk
09/03/96	IFL	P	Molesey	120	2-3	Campfield, Coles
16/03/96	IFL	P	HARROW BOROUGH	204	5-1	Wordsworth(3), Coles, Tomkins
19/03/96	IFL	P	CHERTSEY TOWN	201	3-3	Wordsworth, Tompkins, Antoine
23/03/96	IFL	P	Yeading	183	0-3	
26/03/96	IFL	P	WALTON & HERSHAM	202	3-2	Dennington, Brown, Wordsworth
30/03/96	IFL	P	ENFIELD	469	0-1	
06/04/96	IFL	P	Chertsey Town	316	2-0	Tompkins, Dennington
08/04/96	IFL	P	DULWICH HAMLET	584	0-2	
13/04/96	IFL	P	Sutton United	627	3-1	Brown, Tompkins, Dennington
16/04/96	IFL	P	ST ALBANS CITY	298	1-0	Tompkins
20/04/96	IFL	P	WORTHING	401	3-2	Tompkins(2), Uvieghara
22/04/96	IFL	P	Carshalton Athletic	365	0-0	
27/04/96	IFL	P	Purfleet	268	1-1	Wordsworth
01/05/96	London CC	F	Leyton Pennant	486	3-2	(played at Millwall F.C.)

CARSHALTON ATHLETIC

War Memorial Sports Ground, Colston Avenue, Carshalton SM5 2PW. Tel: 0181 770 3692

Social Club: 0181 642 8658

Press Sec: Clive Allard Tel: 01959 540002

Secretary: Billy Miller, 94 Craddocks Ave, Ashtead, Surrey: Tel 01372 272992

Match Secretary: Vic Thompson, 11 Poulton Ave, Sutton, Surrey SM1 3PZ Tel: 0181 644 6402

Programme Ed: Robert Wooldridge

Colours: Maroon and White, Nickname: The Robins

Capacity: 4,000   Seating: 350

Covered standing: 2,000   Clubhouse on ground: Yes

Record atten: 7,800 v Wimbledon London Senior Cup

Biggest win: 14-0 v Sutton Utd Res Boxing Day 1913

Biggest defeat: 0-11 v Southall April 1963

Record appearances: Jon Warden

Record goalscorer in one season, record goalscorer in total and record fee paid: £2,000 to Farnboro for Jimmy Bolton

Record Fee Received: Undisclosed for Ian Cox

DIRECTIONS

Directions: Turn right out of Carshalton BR Station, and Colston Avenue is first left. Entrance 150 yards on right. London Transport bus 151 from Morden to Wrythe Green Lane.

Honours

Corinthian League 1953 and 1954, Surrey Senior Cup 1989, 1990, 1992

London Challenge Cup 1992, Surrey Senior Shield 1977

Southern Combination Cup 1960, London Senior Cup 1961, 1965, 1982, 1989

Manager For 1996-97: Tony Jennings

Mill Lane Mission were formed in 1903 and changed their name to Carshalton Athletic in the summer of 1907, continuing to play in the Croydon and District League. Carshalton St Andrews FC were formed in 1897 and the two clubs amalgamated in 1908 and played in the Southern Suburban League. From 1907 to the war the club used pitches in the Wrythe Recreation Ground and for one year after a pitch at Culver Park was used. The Memorial Ground was built after the War and Carshalton moved in and played the first game on New Years Day 1921 against Thornhill. Successive promotions saw them in the First Division. Two league titles and various local and County cups were won and in 1922 they were founder members of the Surrey Senior League. After just one season, where they were runners up in League and Charity Cup, they moved to the London League, gaining promotion after three seasons.

After the Second War Athletic joined the Corinthian League which they won in 1953 and 1954 and by 1956 they had been elected to the Athenian League, reaching the Surrey Senior Cup Final in 1958. They stayed without winning the league until 1973 when they became founder members of the new Isthmian League Division Two. They struggled for a while but in 1977 they reached the Premier Division, also winning the Surrey Senior Shield. In 1989 Carshalton won their first major honour in years when they beat Woking in the Surrey Senior Cup Final. It was the first ever win and ended Sutton's domination. They retained the cup a year later and in 1990-91 they enjoyed the longest season in their history, playing 71 games, in the process reaching the AC Delco and London Challenge Cup Finals and the semi-finals of the Surrey Senior and Premier Inter-League Cup. The AC Delco was lost and the London Challenge was held over, although it was eventually won. In 1992 they won the County Cup for the third time, and since then the club has been consistently in the running for honours, last season finishing sixth in a very strong league.

CARSHALTON ATHLETIC 1995/96

19/08/95	IFL	P	MOLESEY	352	4-0	Hazel(2), Bassey, Ndah(og)
22/08/95	IFL	P	Yeading	170	3-1	Underwood, Vines, Salako
26/08/95	IFL	P	Bromley	637	2-1	Lunn, Vines
29/08/95	IFL	P	Enfield	834	0-4	
02/09/95	IFL	P	HENDON	501	1-1	Vines
05/09/95	GIC	1	Wembley		3-1	
09/09/95	FA Cup	Q1	SHEPPEY UNITED	289	3-1	Salako, Underwood, Vines
12/09/95	IFL	P	Walton & Hersham	245	1-0	Ugbah
16/09/95	IFL	P	PURFLEET	404	3-1	Bassey, Vines, Ugbah
23/09/95	FA Cup	Q2	WINDSOR & ETON	360	4-3	Vines(2), Hazell, Salako
25/09/95	IFL	P	YEOVIL TOWN	641	2-1	Salako(2)
30/09/95	IFL	P	Harrow Borough	279	1-0	Lunn
07/10/95	FA Cup	Q3	Gravesend & Northfleet	685	1-2	Salako
09/10/95	IFL	P	KINGSTONIAN	843	0-3	
14/10/95	FA Trophy	Q1	DULWICH HAMLET		1-1	Hanlan
17/10/95	FA Trophy	Q1 rep	Dulwich Hamlet	292	1-1	Saunders
21/10/95	IFL	P	Worthing	531	3-2	Vines, Salako, Ugbah
23/10/95	FA Trophy	Q1 rep(2)	Dulwich Hamlet	301	2-1	Bowyer, Vines
28/10/95	IFL	P	HITCHIN TOWN	389	1-1	Salako
30/10/95	GIC	2	BOGNOR REGIS TOWN		2-0	Salako(2)
04/11/95	FA Trophy	Q2	WEYMOUTH	379	5-1	Vines(3), Salako(2)
11/11/95	IFL	P	Boreham Wood	552	3-2	Salako(2), Vines
18/11/95	IFL	P	Dulwich Hamlet	457	1-2	Salako
25/11/95	FA Trophy	Q3	BRAINTREE TOWN	309	1-1	Vines
28/11/95	FA Trophy	Q3 rep	Braintree Town	260	5-0	Bishop(og), Vines, Robson, Salako, Brady
02/12/95	IFL	P	St Albans City	702	0-3	
09/12/95	IFL	P	CHERTSEY TOWN	376	3-1	Vines, Salako, Underwood
11/12/95	Surrey SC	1	KINGSTONIAN		1-1	
16/12/95	IFL	P	Hayes	283	2-1	Saunders, Clark
19/12/95	Surrey SC	1 rep	Kingstonian		2-1	
23/12/95	IFL	P	WALTON & HERSHAM	429	5-2	Ugbah, Hanlon(2), Salako, Vines
01/01/96	IFL	P	ST ALBANS CITY	603	1-1	Hanlon
06/01/96	IFL	P	Hendon	246	0-0	
08/01/96	CC	2	YEOVIL TOWN	346	2-1	
13/01/96	IFL	P	YEADING	372	2-0	Vines, Ugbah
15/01/96	CC	3	THAME UNITED		4-0	
20/01/96	FA Trophy	1	WOKING	1485	3-1	Salako, Vines, Ugbah
23/01/96	Surrey SC	QF	Corinthian-Casuals		3-2	Hazel, Vines, Underwood
03/02/96	IFL	P	Yeovil Town	1920	1-2	Salako
10/02/96	FA Trophy	2	NEWPORT A.F.C.	682	2-1	Salako, Ugbah
13/02/96	GIC	3	Aylesbury United		1-3	
17/02/96	IFL	P	Purfleet	210	1-2	Robson
24/02/96	IFL	P	Hitchin Town	384	5-2	Hazel, Vines, Salako(3)
27/02/96	Surrey SC	SF	Tooting & Mitcham United		2-4	
02/03/96	FA Trophy	3	Hyde United	854	2-3	Clark(2)
09/03/96	IFL	P	Kingstonian	707	1-2	Salako
12/03/96	IFL	P	Sutton United	784	1-2	Vines
14/03/96	CC	QF	Kingstonian		3-2	
16/03/96	IFL	P	GRAYS ATHLETIC	313	3-1	Vines, Salako(2)
19/03/96	IFL	P	BISHOP'S STORTFORD	251	2-0	Vines(2)
23/03/96	IFL	P	BOREHAM WOOD	373	0-0	
26/03/96	CC	SF	Sutton United	719	1-1	Vines
30/03/96	IFL	P	Aylesbury United	469	1-0	Vines
01/04/96	CC	SF rep	SUTTON UNITED	565	1-4	Ugbah
04/04/96	IFL	P	HARROW BOROUGH	283	0-1	
08/04/96	IFL	P	SUTTON UNITED	794	1-2	Daly
13/04/96	IFL	P	Bishop's Stortford	340	2-0	Saunders, Daly
15/04/96	IFL	P	Grays Athletic	179	0-1	
17/04/96	IFL	P	Molesey	180	1-0	Salako
20/04/96	IFL	P	ENFIELD	823	1-1	Hazel
22/04/96	IFL	P	BROMLEY	365	0-0	
25/04/96	IFL	P	WORTHING	248	4-0	Saunders, May, Salako(2)
27/04/96	IFL	P	Chertsey Town	416	1-0	Kingsford
29/04/96	IFL	P	DULWICH HAMLET	365	2-2	May, Saunders
02/05/96	IFL	P	AYLESBURY UNITED	236	3-1	Salako, May, Vines
04/05/96	IFL	P	HAYES	1025	0-3	

CHERTSEY TOWN

Alwyns Lane, Chertsey, Surrey, KT16 9DW. Tel: 01932 561774

Secretary: Chris Gay, 23 Richmond Close, Frimley, Camberley, Surrey GU16 5NR. Tel: 01932 56174

Capacity: 3,000, Nickname: The Curfew

Colours: Blue and White stripes, Seating: 250

Covered standing: 1,000, Clubhouse on ground: Yes

DIRECTIONS

Alwyns Lane is off Windsor Street at north end of shopping centre. 10 mins walk from Chertsey (BR). London Country bus.

Record attendance: 2,150 v Aldershot Town Isthmian League Dec 4th 1993

Biggest win: 10-1 v Clapton (H) Isthmian League 1992

Biggest defeat. 1-12 v Bromley (H) FA Cup Prelim Rd 1982

Record goalscorer in one season: Alan Brown 54 1962-63

Record goalscorer in total: Alan Brown 202

Record fee received: £67,500 for Lee Charles August 1995

Honours

Isthmian League Cup 1994

Associate Members Trophy 1994, Surrey Senior League 1960, 1962, 1963, League Cup 1960 & 1962

Combined Counties Concourse Trophy 1986

Manager for 1996-97: Allan Cockram, Assistant Managers: Stuart Cash and Simon Webber

Chairman: David Raynor, Vice Chairman: Chris Mason

Organised football was evident in Chertsey well over a century ago but county affiliation did not take place immediately. The official founding of the club was in 1890 when matches were played in the West Surrey League. The first success came in 1897 when they won the Surrey Junior Cup, but they then spent some 50 undistinguished years in junior and intermediate football. Chertsey played at various locations, Willow Walk, Free Prea Road and Chilsey Green before moving into Alwyns Lane in 1929 to a ground donated by Sir Edward Stern for use as a football ground to the premier club in the parish. Next door the cricket club were similarly looked after. The main stand dates from the mid-fifties and more recently the ground has been vastly improved to gain the necessary grading. Immediately after the War, Chertsey Town as they became in 1950, entered the Surrey Senior League but it was not until ten years later that success came in the form of three league titles and three League Cup wins, in four years. They were unable to move to the preferred Corinthian League, so against the wishes of many, turned professional and joined the Metropolitan League. They enjoyed three seasons, but the costs were too high and so after one year in the Greater London League they moved into the Spartan League in 1967.

For two decades the club ticked over, briefly emerging as runners up in League and Cup to the all conquering Farnborough Town, but steadily they began to rise through the Spartan and Athenians, to the Isthmian League Division Two South in 1984. They were relegated at once to the Combined Counties but bounced back. During the last dozen years, the club has been to Division Three and risen to the Premier, has reached the last eight of the FA Vase and won the League Cup, Carlsberg Trophy and League Charity Shield.

CHERTSEY TOWN 1995/96 SEASON

Date	Comp	Round	Opponent	Att	Score	Scorers
12/08/95	IFL	P	Yeading	356	3-1	Harrak, Nabil, Tucker
19/08/95	IFL	P	WALTON & HERSHAM	603	1-3	Dawber
21/08/95	IFL	P	Purfleet	238	3-1	Dawber, Walton, Hippolyte
26/08/95	IFL	P	Worthing	540	2-1	Walton, Tucker
29/08/95	IFL	P	SUTTON UNITED	638	1-1	Hippolyte
02/09/95	IFL	P	YEOVIL TOWN	766	1-3	Sparks
05/09/95	GIC	1	Aldershot Town	1388	2-3	Argrave, Tucker
09/09/95	FA Cup	Q1	SHOREHAM	272	2-2	Own-Goal, Hippolyte
12/09/95	FA Cup	Q1 rep	Shoreham	236	3-1	Nabil(2), Argrave
16/09/95	IFL	P	HENDON	366	3-1	Argrave(2), Sparks
23/09/95	FA Cup	Q2	Tooting & Mitcham United	253	2-2	Walton, Argrave
26/09/95	FA Cup	Q2 rep	TOOTING & MITCHAM	327	1-2	Harrak
30/09/95	IFL	P	Dulwich Hamlet	380	0-0	
03/10/95	IFL	P	AYLESBURY UNITED	434	0-3	
07/10/95	IFL	P	ENFIELD	726	0-3	
14/10/95	FA Trophy	Q1	POOLE TOWN	326	9-0	Watson(og),Argrave(2),Sparks(2), Hippolyte,Walken, Savage(2)
24/10/95	IFL	P	HAYES	603	1-3	Savage
28/10/95	IFL	P	St Albans City	551	0-2	
04/11/95	FA Trophy	Q2	CHESHAM UNITED	518	2-2	Cash(2)
07/11/95	FA Trophy	Q2 rep	Chesham United	397	3-2	Harper, Hippolyte, Tucker
11/11/95	IFL	P	Harrow Borough	365	1-3	Pucker
14/11/95	IFL	P	Hitchin Town	291	0-2	
18/11/95	IFL	P	BOREHAM WOOD	283	0-3	
21/11/95	CC	1	YEOVIL TOWN	215	0-2	
25/11/95	FA Trophy	Q3	PURFLEET	266	0-1	
02/12/95	IFL	P	GRAYS ATHLETIC	292	2-0	Walton, Hippolyte
09/12/95	IFL	P	Carshalton Athletic	376	1-3	Tucker
14/12/95	Surrey SC	1	Egham Town		4-2	
16/12/95	IFL	P	MOLESEY	280	3-0	Argrave(2), Pratt
23/12/95	IFL	P	Yeovil Town	2417	0-1	
26/12/95	IFL	P	KINGSTONIAN	518	2-1	Argrave(2)
06/01/96	IFL	P	YEADING	342	1-1	Tucker
13/01/96	IFL	P	PURFLEET	389	2-1	Argrave, Nicholls
20/01/96	IFL	P	Walton & Hersham	409	1-0	Tucker
27/01/96	Surrey SC	QF	TOOTING & MITCHAM UN		1-3	
03/02/96	IFL	P	Sutton United	512	1-2	Argrave
10/02/96	IFL	P	DULWICH HAMLET	449	0-1	
17/02/96	IFL	P	Hendon	262	0-0	
24/02/96	IFL	P	ST ALBANS CITY	418	1-2	Nabri
02/03/96	IFL	P	Aylesbury United	501	0-2	
09/03/96	IFL	P	BISHOP'S STORTFORD	317	3-0	Kelly, Tucker, Furnell
12/03/96	IFL	P	WORTHING	260	2-1	Argrave, Sparks
16/03/96	IFL	P	Enfield	611	0-0	
19/03/96	IFL	P	Bromley	201	3-3	Argrave, Tucker, Chester
23/03/96	IFL	P	HARROW BOROUGH	337	1-6	Walton
30/03/96	IFL	P	Hayes	507	0-4	
06/04/96	IFL	P	BROMLEY	316	0-2	
08/04/96	IFL	P	Kingstonian	422	2-0	Hippolyte, Riley(og)
13/04/96	IFL	P	HITCHIN TOWN	361	2-1	Sparks, Hippolyte
16/04/96	IFL	P	Boreham Wood	263	0-2	
20/04/96	IFL	P	Grays Athletic	239	1-2	Hippolyte
23/04/96	IFL	P	Bishop's Stortford	246	1-3	Hippolyte
27/04/96	IFL	P	CARSHALTON ATHLETIC	416	0-1	
04/05/96	IFL	P	Molesey	220	0-2	

DAGENHAM & REDBRIDGE

Victoria Rd, Dagenham RM10 7XL. Tel: 0181 592 7194
Fax: 0181 593 7227

Club Secretary: Derek Almond
c/o Dagenham and Redbridge FC

Best contact: when confirming fixture
Steve Thompson: 0181 592 1549

Club colours: All Red   Nickname: Daggers

Capacity: 5,500   Seating: 800

Covered standing: 2,500

Clubhouse on ground: Yes

DIRECTIONS

On A112 between A12 & A13. Buses 103 & 174 or, exit Dagenham East tube station, turn left and after approximately 500 yards take 5th turning left into Victoria Road.

All records relate to new club

Record attendance: 5,300 v Leyton Orient in FA Cup 1st Rd Nov 14th 1992

Biggest win: 8-1 v Woking in Conference April 19th 94

Biggest defeat 0-5 v Stalybridge Celtic, Northwich Vics and Slough Town, all in Conference

Record appearances: Paul Watts 174

Record goalscor: Paul Cavell 47

Record goalscorer in total: Paul Cavell

Record fee paid £30,000 for Paul Cavell and Paul Richardson from Boston United

Honours

None as new club

Manager 1996-97: Ted Hardy, Assistant Manager: Dennis Moore, Chairman: Dave Andrews

Press Officer: Steve Warren

Dagenham and Redbridge Football Club was formed on the 1st July 1992, replacing the former Redbridge Forest and Dagenham Football Clubs. The amalgamation provided a sound base for the club to build for the future, and part of the progression has been in ground improvements with total refurbishment and upgrading of lights.

The club had a very successful first season, finishing third in the Conference, semi-finalists in the League Cup and reaching the FA Cup 1st Round, where they lost 5-4 in front of the SKY cameras and 5,300 fans. Seven players from the squad were picked for the England semi-pro team that season. The following season saw them lose in the final qualifying round of the FA Cup to Cambridge City and Woking knocked them out of the Trophy, and at the end of a season which saw Juan Mequel De Souza sign for Birmingham City for a five figure fee, manager John Still left to take over at Peterborough United.

In 1994 the Daggers suffered a catalogue of injuries and never recovered from a poor start, finishing 15th, having had little success in the Cups. Despite the lack of success the crowds remained at just under the 1,000 mark.

After another poor start, to season 1995-96, the club parted company with Dave Cusack and former Northampton Town manager Graham Carr took over, but he too could not stop the side and with the club out of all the cups and bottom of the Conference, he parted company to be replaced by Ted Hardy. The inevitable drop to the Isthmian League occurred and the new Daggers look forward to a new challenge and returning to the top level.

DAGENHAM & REDBRIDGE 1995/96 SEASON

Date	Comp	Opponent	Att	Score	Scorers
19/08/95	VC	Stalybridge Celtic	547	1-2	Haag 2
21/08/95	VC	FARNBOROUGH TOWN	758	2-2	Conner 28, Haag 34
26/08/95	VC	ALTRINCHAM	662	1-0	Shipp 84
28/08/95	VC	Macclesfield Town	1172	1-3	Shipp 37
02/09/95	VC	Runcorn	461	0-2	
04/09/95	VC	HEDNESFORD TOWN	837	1-2	Greene 68
09/09/95	FA Cup Q1	HORNCHURCH	539	4-0	McDonough, Greene, Broom, Haag
12/09/95	VC	Bromsgrove Rovers	728	0-2	
16/09/95	VC	MORECAMBE	834	2-2	Tomlinson 37(og), Haag 90(p)
18/09/95	SCC 1(1)	SLOUGH TOWN	403	0-3	
23/09/95	FA Cup Q2	Berkhamsted Town	292	2-1	Haag(2)
26/09/95	VC	Farnborough Town	494	0-2	
30/09/95	VC	NORTHWICH VICTORIA	646	0-3	
03/10/95	SCC 1(2)	Slough Town	456	0-3	
07/10/95	FA Cup Q3	PURFLEET	718	1-1	Dyer
09/10/95	FA Cup Q3 rep	Purfleet	683	1-2	Haag
14/10/95	VC	Gateshead	587	0-2	
28/10/95	VC	KIDDERMINSTER	756	4-2	Matthews 10 28, Wilson 35 Dyer 43
31/10/95	VC	Dover Athletic	1164	1-0	Hughes 76
04/11/95	VC	Kettering Town	1616	0-2	
11/11/95	VC	GATESHEAD	712	0-4	
18/11/95	VC	HALIFAX TOWN	701	1-1	Bennett 1
20/11/95	VC	SLOUGH TOWN	712	1-3	Prindiville 34
25/11/95	VC	Telford United	711	0-0	
02/12/95	VC	WELLING UNITED	805	1-1	Bennett 65
04/12/95	Essex SC 2	LEYTON ORIENT	298	1-3	Crookes
09/12/95	VC	DOVER ATHLETIC	862	3-0	Worthington 27, Aldridge 50, Barry 87
11/12/95	VC	STEVENAGE BOROUGH	762	1-2	Taylor 56
16/12/95	VC	Southport	904	1-2	Taylor 54
26/12/95	VC	Woking	2874	2-2	Worthington 37 90
30/12/95	VC	BROMSGROVE ROVERS	1020	2-2	Worthington 34, Taylor 80
01/01/96	VC	WOKING	1358	0-0	
06/01/96	VC	Halifax Town	729	0-3	
13/01/96	VC	SOUTHPORT	964	1-2	Prindiville 22
20/01/96	FA Trophy 1	Stevenage Borough	1348	2-3	Stringfellow, Prindiville
03/02/96	VC	Kidderminster Harriers	1439	1-5	Worthington 83
10/02/96	VC	Morecambe	787	2-2	Taylor 6, Stringfellow 28
17/02/96	VC	STALYBRIDGE CELTIC	706	4-1	Stringfellow 17, Derry 36 50, Worthington 47
24/02/96	VC	Northwich Victoria	727	0-1	
09/03/96	VC	Slough Town	912	0-5	
16/03/96	VC	TELFORD UNITED	668	1-1	Stringfellow 18
23/03/96	VC	Welling United	623	0-0	
25/03/96	VC	BATH CITY	695	0-1	
06/04/96	VC	KETTERING TOWN	730	1-2	Prindiville 75
08/04/96	VC	Bath City	541	2-0	Stringfellow 12, Crooks 43
13/04/96	VC	Hednesford Town	946	0-0	
20/04/96	VC	RUNCORN	755	2-3	Stringfellow 40(p) 90
27/04/96	VC	MACCLESFIELD TOWN	660	3-0	Tinson 12(og), Broom 64, Stringfellow 67(p)
29/04/96	VC	Stevenage Borough	2379	0-1	
04/05/96	VC	Altrincham	748	1-3	Prindiville 79

DULWICH HAMLET

Champion Hill Stadium, Dog Kennel Hill, London SE22 8BD.Tel: 0171 274 8707

Secretary: Paul Hobdell, c/o Dulwich Hamlet FC

Nickname: Hamlet   Capacity: 3, 000

Seating: 500   Covered standing: 500

Clubhouse on ground: Yes

Record attendance: 20,744 Kingstonian v Stockton Amateur Cup Final 1933

Biggest win: 10-1 v West Norwood 1920-21

Biggest defeat.: 1-10 v Hendon 1963-64

Record appearance: Reg Merritt 571 1950-1966

Record goalscorer in one season:
Edgar Kail 53 in 1925-26

Record goalscorer in total: Edgar Kail 427 1919-1933

DIRECTIONS

Directions: East Dulwich station, 200 yds. Denmark Hill station, 10 mins walk. Herne Hill station then bus 37 stops near ground. Also buses 40 & 176 from Elephant & Castle, 1875 from Victoria, 484 from Camberwell.

Honours

FA AMATEUR CUP 1920, 1932, 1934, 1937

Isthmian League 1920, 1926, 1933, 1949 Div 1 1978

London Senior Cup 1925, 1939, 1950, 1984

Surrey Senior Cup 1905, 06, 09, 10, 20, 23, 25, 28, 34, 37, 47, 50, 58, 59, 74, 75

London Charity Cup 1911 jt, 1920, 1921, 1923, 1924 jt, 1926, 1928, 1929, 1931 jt, 1948, 1957, 1958

Surrey Senior Shield 1973, Surrey Centenary Shield 1978

South of the Thames Cup 1957, 1958, 1959, 1960,

Southern Combination Cup 1974

There can be few clubs in non-League football with a more illustrious past than Dulwich Hamlet. Now just over 100 years old, the club name still evokes memories of that golden age between the wars when Hamlet were giants of the amateur game. Success has been more elusive since then, but a recent development at Champion Hill of a new stadium has rekindled enthusiasm amongst the club faithful who are looking to recapture some former glory. It all began in 1893 when Lorraine Wilson was handed the princely sum of 1s 8d by a couple of young lads and asked to start a football club. He tackled the task with relish and over the next 30 years helped to build Hamlet into a powerful force. Life in the early days was tough. The original ground in Woodwards Road had no changing rooms and on matchdays players walked through the streets of Dulwich to the pitch carrying the goalposts, crossbars and corner flags with them. Dulwich joined the Camberwell League in 1894 and won the B Division the following year. Achieving senior status in 1900 they went from strength to strength and in 1907 gained election to the Isthmian League where they have remained ever since. Their progress continued between the wars when as the finest undisputed amateur side in the country, they won the Amateur Cup four times, winning many other cups also with such Internationals as Edgar Kail. In 1947 the club were runners up in the league, going one better a year later and a dozen years later were again runners up, although never again winning the league. They then went through a lean patch and apart from three good seasons in the 70's, it did not improve greatly and they were relegated. Happily the Division One title was won at the first attempt and they bounced back, only to struggle again through the 80's. In 1989 they again went down, but three years later a nine game winning run saw them promoted. Last season was a triumph, as despite being turned down by the Conference half way through the term, they

challenged for the title right to the end, only to finish fifth in a strong league. Dulwich were able to celebrate their centenary by playing in a new stadium, built on the same site as the famous old ground which was opened in 1931 and for many years was the Mecca of amateur football. Numerous Internationals and Amateur Cup matches were played there including the final in 1933 which attracted a crowd of 20,744. Sadly the old ground fell into disrepair over the years and in order to satisfy safety regulations several alterations were made. Finally in 1991 it was demolished as part of Sainsbury's development of the area, and the new Hamlet ground was created.

DULWICH HAMLET 1995/96 SEASON

12/08/95	IFL	P	AYLESBURY UNITED	324	1-0	Odegbami
19/08/95	IFL	P	Hayes	327	2-2	Whitmarsh, Lillington
22/08/95	IFL	P	BISHOP'S STORTFORD	260	4-1	Whitmarsh(2), Kerrins(2)
26/08/95	IFL	P	ST ALBANS CITY	385	3-1	Akers, Whitmarsh(2)
29/08/95	IFL	P	Hitchin Town	281	3-1	Whitmarsh, Odegbami, Akers
02/09/95	IFL	P	Grays Athletic	270	4-1	Odegbami(2), Whitmarsh, Lillington
05/09/95	GIC	1	Flackwell Heath		3-1	Kamara(2), Gartell
09/09/95	FA Cup	Q1	SOUTHWICK	298	7-1	Odegami(2), Whitmarsh(2), Akers, Murphy, Lillington
16/09/95	IFL	P	Enfield	939	0-1	
23/09/95	FA Cup	Q2	CHATHAM TOWN	293	2-1	Allen, Odegbami
30/09/95	IFL	P	CHERTSEY TOWN	380	0-0	
07/10/95	FA Cup	Q3	Bognor Regis Town	780	2-4	Whitmarsh, Akers
10/10/95	IFL	P	Walton & Hersham	232	2-0	Lillington, Odegbami
14/10/95	FA Trophy	Q1	Carshalton Athletic		1-1	Whitmarsh
17/10/95	FA Trophy	Q1 rep	CARSHALTON ATHLETIC	292	1-1	Lillington
21/10/95	IFL	P	Molesey	190	2-1	Lewington, Odegbami
23/10/95	FA Trophy	Q1 rep(2)	CARSHALTON ATHLETIC	301	1-2	Anderson
28/10/95	IFL	P	WORTHING	296	4-1	Whitmarsh(3), Odegbami
04/11/95	IFL	P	Sutton United	697	1-1	Akers
07/11/95	GIC	2	Barton Rovers		1-0	
11/11/95	IFL	P	PURFLEET	261	1-1	Odegbami
18/11/95	IFL	P	CARSHALTON ATHLETIC	457	2-1	Edwards, Allen
21/11/95	CC	2	Thame United		0-3	
25/11/95	IFL	P	Yeovil Town	1960	3-5	Whitmarsh, Anderson(2)
02/12/95	IFL	P	YEADING	289	3-0	Holness(2), Allen
05/12/95	London CC	1	BROMLEY		1-2	
12/12/95	GIC	3	Heybridge Swifts		2-3	
16/12/95	IFL	P	HARROW BOROUGH	262	3-2	Whitmarsh, Lillington, Odegbami
26/12/95	IFL	P	BROMLEY	706	4-1	Whitmarsh, Patullo, Odegbami(2)
01/01/96	IFL	P	Boreham Wood	586	2-2	Whitmarsh, Lillington
06/01/96	IFL	P	GRAYS ATHLETIC	320	3-5	Lillington(2), Holness
13/01/96	IFL	P	Bishop's Stortford	408	2-1	Whitmarsh(2)
20/01/96	IFL	P	HENDON	417	1-0	Odegbami
03/02/96	IFL	P	HITCHIN TOWN	411	3-3	Whitmarsh(2), Lillington
10/02/96	IFL	P	Chertsey Town	449	1-0	Lillington
17/02/96	IFL	P	ENFIELD	1604	1-1	Whitmarsh
24/02/96	IFL	P	Worthing	370	3-1	Lillington(2), Gartel
02/03/96	IFL	P	MOLESEY	414	2-0	Kerrins, Holness
09/03/96	IFL	P	WALTON & HERSHAM	442	1-1	Whitmarsh
12/03/96	IFL	P	St Albans City	751	1-4	Kerrins
16/03/96	IFL	P	Hendon	301	2-1	Allen, Bartley
19/03/96	IFL	P	HAYES	448	1-1	Akers
23/03/96	IFL	P	Purfleet	293	1-3	Allen
30/03/96	IFL	P	SUTTON UNITED	559	2-2	Whitmarsh, Bartley
04/04/96	IFL	P	Aylesbury United	424	3-0	Whitmarsh, Akers, Lillington
06/04/96	IFL	P	BOREHAM WOOD	402	0-2	
08/04/96	IFL	P	Bromley	584	2-0	Hewitt, Akers
13/04/96	IFL	P	YEOVIL TOWN	1289	2-1	Anderson, Lillington
18/04/96	IFL	P	Kingstonian	418	2-0	Holness, Whitmarsh
20/04/96	IFL	P	Yeading	260	3-5	Hewitt, Lillington(2)
27/04/96	IFL	P	KINGSTONIAN	629	1-3	Lillington
29/04/96	IFL	P	Carshalton Athletic	365	2-2	Whitmarsh(2)
04/05/96	IFL	P	Harrow Borough	276	2-1	Holness, Anderson

ENFIELD

The Stadium, Southbury Rd, Enfield, Middx EN1 1YQ. Tel: 0181 292 0665

Secretary:Alan Diment, 30 Apple Grove, Enfield, Middx EN1 3DD. Tel: 0181 363 6317

Colours: White and Blue, Nickname: The E's

Capacity: 8,500   Seating: 800

Covered standing: 3,500, Clubhouse on ground: Yes

DIRECTIONS

Directions: At junction of A10 & A110. 800 yards from Southbury Road station. Buses from town centre.

Record attendance: 10,000 v Tottenham Hotspur Oct 10th 1962 Floodlight opener

Record appearances: Steve King 617

Record goalscorer in one season:Tommy Lawrence 49 in 1959-60

Record goalscorer in total:
Tommy Lawrence 191

Record fee paid: For Gary Abbott

Record fee received: For Paul Furlong

Honours

FA TROPHY WINNERS 1982 and 1988

FA AMATEUR CUP WINNERS 1967 and 1970, RUNNERS UP 1964 and 1972

Alliance Premier League 1983 and 1986, Isthmian League 1968 1969, 1970, 1976, 1977, 1978, 1980, League Cup 1979 and 1980, Athenian League 1962 and 1963, London League Div 1 1912; Middlesex Senior Cup 1914, 1947, 1962, 1966, 1969, 1970, 1971, 1978, 1979, 1980, 1981, 1989, 1991; London Senior Cup 1935, 1961, 1967, 1972, 1973, 1976, Middlesex League West 1910; European Amateur Cup 1970

Manager 1996-97: George Borg

Founded in 1893 as Enfield Spartans, they played friendlies until entering the Tottenham and District Junior Alliance, playing at Bailey Fields, but when joining the North Middlesex League they moved to the larger Tuckers Field. The club became Enfield FC in 1900 and moved again to Cherry Orchard Lane where they won the league twice running losing just one game. They then became a senior club in the stronger London League, making progress until winning Division One and gaining promotion. In 1912 they were invited to join the Athenian League as founder members and in the last season before the Great War they won the Middlesex Senior Cup. On the resumption they spent a season each in the Middlesex and London Leagues before returning to the Athenians in 1921, where they remained until 1963.The most successful season between the wars was in 1935 when they were second in the league and reached the final of the Amateur Cup, also winning the London Senior Cup for the first time. Enfield moved to the current stadium in 1936 and after playing through the war they again joined the Athenians which they won in 1962 winning every home game. They repeated the feat a year later and as a result they were invited in to the Isthmian League in 1963. Since then they have dominated the league, winning the title seven times and only failing to challenge for it twice in all that time. For the 1981 season Enfield joined the Alliance Premier League and having finished runners up in the first season they won the title a year later on the last day. They won it again in 1986 and applied to join the Football League unsuccessfully and after a further spell they were sadly relegated in 1990, but have since gone close to returning , finishing runners up in the last two seasons. Enfield have an impressive cup pedigree also, twice winning the Amateur Cup and FA Trophy as well as enjoying numerous FA Cup runs over the years.

ENFIELD 1995/96 SEASON

Date	Comp	Round	Opponent	Att	Score	Scorers
12/08/95	IFL	P	Molesey	405	4-1	Terry, Gentle, Abbott, Raffington(og)
19/08/95	IFL	P	HENDON	802	2-0	Nolan, Abbott
22/08/95	IFL	P	Sutton United	613	4-2	Abbott(3), Sayer
26/08/95	IFL	P	Purfleet	517	1-1	Abbott
29/08/95	IFL	P	CARSHALTON ATHLETIC	834	4-0	Sayer(2), Abbott, Kerr
02/09/95	IFL	P	HARROW BOROUGH	890	3-0	Richardson, Abbott, Gentle
05/09/95	GIC	1	LEYTON PENNANT	279	4-2	Flemming(2), Abbott, Turner
09/09/95	IFL	P	Yeading	432	1-1	Sayer
12/09/95	CS		AYLESBURY UNITED	422	1-2	Flemming
16/09/95	IFL	P	DULWICH HAMLET	939	1-0	Terry
19/09/95	IFL	P	BOREHAM WOOD	777	0-2	
30/09/95	IFL	P	Worthing	627	1-0	Abbott
03/10/95	IFL	P	WALTON & HERSHAM	603	4-0	Abbott(2), Terry, Flemming
07/10/95	IFL	P	Chertsey Town	726	3-0	Sayer, Richardson(2)
10/10/95	IFL	P	St Albans City	1102	0-1	
14/10/95	IFL	P	HAYES	1023	1-1	Kerr
28/10/95	IFL	P	Bishop's Stortford	879	1-0	Gentle
31/10/95	GIC	2	Worthing	266	4-1	Abbott(2), Gentle(2)
04/11/95	IFL	P	BROMLEY	1006	5-0	Sayer(2), Nolan, Adams, Gentle
11/11/95	FA Cup	1	Newport I.O.W.	1818	1-1	Abbott
18/11/95	IFL	P	GRAYS ATHLETIC	731	3-0	Abbott, Gentle, Sayer
21/11/95	FA Cup	1 rep	NEWPORT I.O.W.	2034	2-1	Abbott(2)
25/11/95	IFL	P	Kingstonian	940	1-0	Sayer
02/12/95	FA Cup	2	WOKING	3477	1-1	Gentle
09/12/95	IFL	P	Hitchin Town	611	0-1	
12/12/95	FA Cup	2 rep	Woking	2253	1-2	Abbott (played at Wycombe Wanderers F.C.)
16/12/95	IFL	P	YEOVIL TOWN	1177	2-1	Ridout, Flemming
19/12/95	CC	2	YEADING		1-2	
23/12/95	IFL	P	Harrow Borough	603	1-3	Nolan
06/01/96	IFL	P	MOLESEY	765	2-0	Abbott(2)
13/01/96	IFL	P	SUTTON UNITED	823	0-2	
20/01/96	FA Trophy	1	Hayes	502	0-0	
23/01/96	FA Trophy	1 rep	HAYES	436	2-2	Abbott, Carstairs
29/01/96	FA Trophy	1 rep(2)	HAYES	398	2-2	Abbott, Carstairs
01/02/96	FA Trophy	1 rep(3)	Hayes	369	0-2	
03/02/96	IFL	P	Walton & Hersham	451	1-0	Abbott
10/02/96	IFL	P	WORTHING	714	5-1	Grazioli(3), Moran, Turner
13/02/96	Middx SC	QF	STAINES TOWN		3-2	
17/02/96	IFL	P	Dulwich Hamlet	1604	1-1	Terry
24/02/96	IFL	P	BISHOP'S STORTFORD	773	0-1	
27/02/96	GIC	3	KINGSTONIAN		2-2	
05/03/96	GIC	3 rep	Kingstonian		0-3	
09/03/96	IFL	P	Hayes	625	1-3	Richardson
12/03/96	IFL	P	Grays Athletic	305	3-0	Abbott(2), Richardson
13/03/96	Middx SC	SF	Hampton		1-3	
16/03/96	IFL	P	CHERTSEY TOWN	611	0-0	
19/03/96	IFL	P	Boreham Wood	507	1-4	Abbott
23/03/96	IFL	P	ST ALBANS CITY	1006	2-2	Carstairs, Terry
26/03/96	IFL	P	Hendon	346	1-0	Blackford
30/03/96	IFL	P	Bromley	469	1-0	Sayer
06/04/96	IFL	P	YEADING	806	2-0	Edwards, Richardson
08/04/96	IFL	P	Aylesbury United	859	3-2	Richardson(2), Gentle
13/04/96	IFL	P	KINGSTONIAN	904	2-1	Underwood, Richardson
16/04/96	IFL	P	PURFLEET	744	3-0	Terry, Abbott, West
20/04/96	IFL	P	Carshalton Athletic	823	1-1	West
27/04/96	IFL	P	HITCHIN TOWN	982	3-0	Terry, Abbott, West
30/04/96	IFL	P	AYLESBURY UNITED	1344	3-3	Richardson, Moran, Terry

GRAYS ATHLETIC

Recreation Ground, Bridge Rd, Grays RM17 6BZ. Tel: 01375 391649

Secretary: Jeff Saxton, 216 Thundersley Pk Rd, South Benfleet, Essex SS7 1HP. Tel: 01268 756964

Press Officer: Gordon Norman Tel 04024 51733

Nickname: The Blues, Colours: Royal Blue and White

Capacity: 4,500   Seating: 300

Covered standing 1,200   Clubhouse on ground: Yes

Record attendance: 9,500 v Chelmsford City
FA Cup 4th Qual 1959

Record appearance: Phil Salmons 601

Record Goalscorer in total Harry Brand 269
from 1944 to 1952

DIRECTIONS

Directions: Seven minutes walk from Grays station — turn right round one-way system, right into Clarence Road, and at end into Bridge Road. Bus No. 370. By road — A13 towards Southend from London, take Grays exit and follow signs to town centre, keep left on one-way system, continue up hill for about half a mile, turn right into Bridge Road, ground half mile on right.

Record fee received: Undisclosed for Tony Witter to Crystal Palace and Dwight Marshall to Plymouth

Record fee paid: Undisclosed for Ian Durant from Canvey Island

Honours.

Isthmian League Div 2 South 1985 and League Cup 1992

Corinthian League 1946 and League Cup 1946 and 1947

Memorial Shield 1946, 1947, 1978, 1980

London League 1922, 1927, 1930 and League Cup 1937

Essex Senior Cup 1915, 1921, 1923, 1945, 1957, 1988, 1993, 1995

East Anglian Cup 1945, Essex Thamesside Trophy 1948, 1979, 1981, 1988, 1989, 1991

Essex Elizabethan Trophy 1977 Claridge Trophy 1988 and 1989

Mithras Cup 1980 Essex Intermediate Cup 1957, 1959, 1960

Essex Junior Cup 1920 Fred Budden Trophy 1987

Hornchurch Charity Cup 1979 and 1987

Stan Veness Memorial Trophy 1988, 1989, 1990, 1991, 1992, 1993, 1994, 1995, 1996 jt

Managers for 1996-97: Jeff and Fred Saxton, Assistant manager: Vince Craven

Club shop: Bill Grove or Dave Smith: 01375 377753 or 391649 club

Grays were founded in 1890 and have played at the Rec in Bridge Road since 1894. Their early seasons were in local football until becoming founder members of the Athenian League in 1912, playing for two years before moving to the London League, where they won the Amateur Division in 1915, along with the Essex Senior Cup. In the 20's the club were formidable winning the Senior Cup twice with three other finals. They also took the London League Premier Division three times with three more second places, before moving into the Kent League for two years. Lapsing in the 30's they were strong again after the War, winning the Essex Senior and East Anglian Cups in 1945. A further decade of success came as they entered the new Corinthian League with three runners up places and five Senior Cup finals, one of which was won. Rejoining the Athenian League, Grays were not at the forefront during the 60'a and 70's other than with the odd cup appearance and a battle with the Trustees and owners of the ground did not end until Mr Ron Billings, the club Patron, bought the ground in 1981. They were promoted to the Isthmian League in 1982 but just before the end of the season, the club was stunned when the 400 seater stand and dressing rooms were destroyed by fire. Again the Patron built a new complex with

dressing rooms and after a fine FA Cup run in 1984, they won Division Two South. In the third season in Division One they had possibly their most successful season winning promotion to the Premier Division and taking the Senior Cup for the first time in 31 years and the Thamesside Trophy. Another FA Cup run ended at the 1st round at Bath City and the third season at the top flight saw a final sixth position, a position equalled in 1993.

A Centenary history , "Grays Athletic, the First Hundred Years" was published in 1990 and is still available from the club at £5.95 + £1 pp

GRAYS ATHLETIC 1995/96 SEASON

Date	Comp	Rnd	Opponent	Att	Score	Scorers
12/08/95	IFL	P	Worthing	461	1-1	Wallace
19/08/95	IFL	P	BROMLEY	251	0-3	
22/08/95	IFL	P	Walton & Hersham	239	4-1	Wilson(2), Heffer, Cherry
26/08/95	IFL	P	Yeovil Town	1668	0-1	
29/08/95	IFL	P	YEADING	167	0-0	
02/09/95	IFL	P	DULWICH HAMLET	270	1-4	Walker
05/09/95	GIC	1	Hayes	109	1-0	Heffer
09/09/95	FA Cup	Q1	WEALDSTONE	291	2-2	
12/09/95	FA Cup	Q1 rep	Wealdstone	209	3-4	Cherry, Heffer, Wilson
16/09/95	IFL	P	HARROW BOROUGH	168	0-2	
30/09/95	IFL	P	Molesey	115	0-0	
03/10/95	IFL	P	Kingstonian	332	0-1	
14/10/95	IFL	P	Boreham Wood	315	0-2	
21/10/95	IFL	P	BISHOP'S STORTFORD	205	0-2	
28/10/95	IFL	P	Aylesbury United	490	2-2	Rupert, Ray
04/11/95	IFL	P	ST ALBANS CITY	212	0-3	
14/11/95	GIC	2	Aldershot Town	1177	1-2	Walker
18/11/95	IFL	P	Enfield	731	0-3	
26/11/95	FA Trophy	Q3	Newport A.F.C.	679	0-1	
02/12/95	IFL	P	Chertsey Town	292	0-2	
05/12/95	Essex SC	2	Harwich & Parkeston	80	3-2	Penn, Cox, Own-Goal
12/12/95	CC	2	BILLERICAY TOWN	102	1-2	D Roberts
16/12/95	IFL	P	Sutton United	392	0-0	
23/12/95	IFL	P	WORTHING	215	6-0	Ray(2), Lawrence(2), D Gentle, McIntyre
02/01/96	IFL	P	HAYES	226	3-3	Gentle(2), Sammons
06/01/96	IFL	P	Dulwich Hamlet	320	5-3	Gentle(2), Ray, Deleon, Lawrence
09/01/96	Essex SC	3	FORD UNITED	106	3-2	Risley, Gentle, Wallace
13/01/96	IFL	P	WALTON & HERSHAM	264	3-1	Mitchell, Penn, D Gentle
20/01/96	IFL	P	Bromley	264	2-2	Goldstone(2)
30/01/96	Essex TST	2	ROMFORD	118	3-0	Penn, Mitchell, Deleon
03/02/96	IFL	P	Yeading	104	1-0	Mitchell
06/02/96	Essex SC	QF	WITHAM TOWN	85	4-0	Penn(2), Tripp, Wallace
10/02/96	IFL	P	MOLESEY	255	1-0	Penn
13/02/96	IFL	P	HITCHIN TOWN	197	1-0	Mitchell
17/02/96	IFL	P	Harrow Borough	250	0-3	
24/02/96	IFL	P	AYLESBURY UNITED	274	2-0	Lawrence, Southon
27/02/96	IFL	P	HENDON	217	0-0	
02/03/96	IFL	P	Bishop's Stortford	306	0-2	
04/03/96	IFL	P	Purfleet	231	0-1	
12/03/96	IFL	P	ENFIELD	305	0-3	
16/03/96	IFL	P	Carshalton Athletic	313	1-3	Southon
19/03/96	Essex SC	SF	BILLERICAY TOWN		0-2	
23/03/96	IFL	P	Hitchin Town	369	0-1	
26/03/96	IFL	P	YEOVIL TOWN	251	0-2	
30/03/96	IFL	P	KINGSTONIAN	261	1-1	Gentle
06/04/96	IFL	P	Hayes	583	1-5	Gentle
08/04/96	IFL	P	PURFLEET	341	2-0	Southon, Alexander
11/04/96	Essex TST	QF	GREAT WAKERING		2-1	Ashenden, Gentle
13/04/96	IFL	P	St Albans City	441	1-1	Southon
15/04/96	IFL	P	CARSHALTON ATHLETIC	179	1-0	Gonzague
20/04/96	IFL	P	CHERTSEY TOWN	239	2-1	Gonzague, D Gentle
25/04/96	IFL	P	BOREHAM WOOD	196	1-2	Charles
27/04/96	IFL	P	Hendon	239	0-0	
04/05/96	IFL	P	SUTTON UNITED	318	1-2	Alexander
06/05/96	Essex TST	SF	CANVEY ISLAND		0-2	

HARROW BOROUGH

Earlsmead, Carlyon Avenue, South Harrow, Middx HA2 8SS. Tel: 0181 422 5221

Secretary and Press Officer: Peter Rogers, 21 Ludlow Close, South Harrow, Middlesex, HA2 8SR

Tel: 0181 248 8003 (h) 0171 601 5732 (b)

Colours: Red and White Nickname: The Boro

Capacity: 3,070 Seating: 350

Covered standing: 1,000 Clubhouse on ground: Yes

Record attend: 3,000 v Wealdstone FA Cup 1st Qual Rd 1946

DIRECTIONS

Underground to Northolt (Central Line) then 140 or 282 bus, or to South Harrow (Piccadilly Line) then 114 or H10. By road leave A40 at Target PH towards Northolt station (A312 north), left at lights, right at next island, ground 5th turning on right.

Biggest win: 13-0 v Handley Page (A) Middx Sen Lge Oct 18th 1941

Biggest defeat: 0-8 (Five times) Wood Green Town (A) Middx Lge Sept 14th 1940. Met Police (A) Spartan Lge Feb 2nd 1952, Brigg Sports (A) Spartan Lge Oct 31st 1953, Hertford Town (A) April 24th 1953, Hendon (A) Middx Sen Cup March 15th 1965

Record appearances: Les Currell 582

Record goalscorer in one season: Dave Pearce 46   Record goalscorer in total: Dave Pearce 153

Record fee received: £15,000 from Chelsea for Chris Hutchings

Honours

FA TROPHY SEMI-FINAL 1983

Isthmian League 1984, Spartan League Div 2 West 1939

Middx Senior Cup 1983 and 1993, Middx Charity Cup 1980 and 1993

Manager for 1996-97: Harry Manoe, Assistant Manager: Cliff Rapley, Chairman: Jim Ripley

Roxonian FC was formed in the summer of 1933, They spent their first season in the Harrow and District League, playing home games on a ground in Northolt Road, where they finished second in Division 1. They were quickly accepted into the Spartan League which coincided with a move to Earlsmead. In 1938 Roxonian finished as runners-up in Division Two West, but went one better a year later, as Harrow Town, their new name. Through the War Harrow played in the West Middlesex Combination and the Middlesex Senior League before moving back to the Spartan League in peacetime. They were runners up in 1958, and that enabled Town to move to the Delphian League for five seasons, until league mergers saw them in Division Two of the Athenian League in 1963.

They missed the title on goal average, but relegation came in 1967, as did the change of name to Harrow Borough. They were bleak times, with a move to junior football a distinct possibility, but a deal to sell the club's second pitch for the development of a school and those funds saw the rebirth of the club and the ground, with lights and terracing. Boro were elected to the Isthmian League in 1975 and four years later were in the Premier Division.The early 80's saw Borough's most successful spell ever, with the Middlesex Charity Cup being won in 1980 and the Senior Cup three years later. However, 1983 saw the heartbreak of Borough reaching the semi-finals of the Trophy, losing to Telford in extra time after taking an away lead in the first leg.

The Golden Jubilee season was celebrated by reaching the Second Round of the FA Cup, when the club hosted Newport County and to cap the season, they won the league by 17 points. Manager Micky Tomkys oversaw those successes, but on his retirement the club went into decline until George Borg's reign saw the Senior and Charity Cups come back to Earlsmead in 1993. The most recent seasons have seen former player Harry Manoe in charge alongside Cliff Rapley and they guided the club to 8th last May.

HARROW BOROUGH 1995/96 SEASON

Date	Comp	Rd	Opponent	Att	Score	Scorers
06/08/95	Harrow SC	F	Wealdstone		3-1	Xavier(2), Metcalfe
19/08/95	IFL	P	Hitchin Town	304	5-1	Xavier(2), Jones(2), Egbe
23/08/95	IFL	P	AYLESBURY UNITED	417	3-3	Xavier(3)
26/08/95	IFL	P	KINGSTONIAN	338	2-1	Jones, Xavier
02/09/95	IFL	P	Enfield	890	0-3	
05/09/95	GIC	1	Chesham United		1-4	Biggins
09/09/95	FA Cup	Q1	LEATHERHEAD	198	2-1	Jones, Davies
13/09/95	IFL	P	ST ALBANS CITY	324	0-0	
16/09/95	IFL	P	Grays Athletic	168	2-0	Xavier, Davies
23/09/95	FA Cup	Q2	Bracknell Town		1-2	Endersby
26/09/95	IFL	P	Boreham Wood	224	2-3	Xavier(2)
30/09/95	IFL	P	CARSHALTON ATHLETIC	279	0-1	
10/10/95	IFL	P	Yeading	189	2-1	Hurlock(2)
14/10/95	FA Trophy	Q1	MARLOW	244	1-1	Clarke
17/10/95	FA Trophy	Q1 rep	Marlow	261	4-1	Hurlock, Seabrook, Clarke, Xavier
24/10/95	IFL	P	Sutton United	452	0-4	
28/10/95	IFL	P	MOLESEY	198	3-1	Ndah(og), Xavier, Metcalfe
04/11/95	FA Trophy	Q2	Braintree Town	203	0-4	
07/11/95	CC	1	Uxbridge	117	0-1	
11/11/95	IFL	P	CHERTSEY TOWN	365	3-1	Xavier(3)
18/11/95	IFL	P	Hendon	273	2-0	Endersby(2)
02/12/95	IFL	P	Walton & Hersham	247	2-1	Xavier(2)
09/12/95	IFL	P	BISHOP'S STORTFORD	221	0-0	
13/12/95	IFL	P	PURFLEET	107	2-2	Endersby, James
16/12/95	IFL	P	Dulwich Hamlet	262	2-3	Endersby, Xavier
23/12/95	IFL	P	ENFIELD	603	3-1	Fraser(2), Endersby
01/01/96	IFL	P	WORTHING	360	3-1	Dkoku(2), Endersby
06/01/96	IFL	P	St Albans City	620	2-0	Ekoku, Endersby
10/01/96	Middx SC	2	WEMBLEY		2-2	
13/01/96	IFL	P	Aylesbury United	531	0-2	
20/01/96	IFL	P	HITCHIN TOWN	276	1-2	Fraser
23/01/96	Middx SC	2 rep	Wembley		3-2	
31/01/96	IFL	P	BROMLEY	206	1-3	Hurlock
03/02/96	IFL	P	BOREHAM WOOD	276	1-1	Stein(og)
10/02/96	IFL	P	Yeovil Town	1942	0-0	
14/02/96	Middx SC	QF	UXBRIDGE	110	2-2	
17/02/96	IFL	P	GRAYS ATHLETIC	250	3-0	Endersby, Hurlock(2)
24/02/96	IFL	P	Molesey	120	0-0	
27/02/96	Middx SC	QF rep	Uxbridge	138	1-0	
02/03/96	IFL	P	SUTTON UNITED	339	0-0	
09/03/96	IFL	P	YEADING	256	4-1	Xavier(3), Endersby
12/03/96	Middx SC	SF	Hayes		1-2	
16/03/96	IFL	P	Bromley	204	1-5	Fishington
23/03/96	IFL	P	Chertsey Town	337	6-1	Fishenden, Xavier(4), Endersby
26/03/96	IFL	P	Kingstonian	302	1-0	Xavier
30/03/96	IFL	P	YEOVIL TOWN	489	0-1	
04/04/96	IFL	P	Carshalton Athletic	283	1-0	James
06/04/96	IFL	P	Worthing	338	2-1	Ekoku, Xavier
13/04/96	IFL	P	Purfleet	162	1-0	Xavier
17/04/96	IFL	P	HENDON	253	2-2	Clarke, Hurlock
20/04/96	IFL	P	WALTON & HERSHAM	237	2-3	Xavier, Clarke
23/04/96	IFL	P	Hayes	716	1-2	Bensted
27/04/96	IFL	P	Bishop's Stortford	285	3-2	Xavier, Fraser, Fishenden
01/05/96	IFL	P	HAYES	1212	1-1	Xavier
04/05/96	IFL	P	DULWICH HAMLET	276	1-2	Marshall

HENDON

Claremont Rd, London NW2 1AE. Tel: 0181 201 9494

Secretary: Graham Etchell, c/o Hendon FC.

Nickname: The Dons or The Greens.

Colours: Green and White halves

Capacity: 3,026, Seating 329, Covered standing: 601

Clubhouse on ground: Yes

Record attendance: 9,000 v Northampton Town
FA Cup Rd 1 1952

Biggest win: 13-1 v Wingate (H)
Middlesex Senior Cup Feb 2nd 1957

Biggest defeat: 2-11 v Walthamstow Ave
Athenian League Nov 9th 1935

DIRECTIONS

From Brent Cross tube station (Northern Line) to the east take first left and flyover on North Circular. Claremont Road is then left at 3rd mini roundabout. From Golders Green station (Northern Line) take bus 226 or 102. From Cricklewood main line station, turn left out of station and Claremont Road is first left - ground half mile down on right. Buses 102, 210, 226 and C11 pass ground.

Record appearances: Bill Fisher 787

Record goalscorer in total: Freddie Evans 176 1929-35

Record fee paid: £5,000 twice

Record fee received: £30,000 for Ian Dowie to Luton Town

Honours

FA AMATEUR CUP WINNERS 1960, 1965, 1972

Runners Up 1955, 1966

European Amateur Champions 1972

Isthmian League 1965 and 1973, League Cup 1977, Full Members Cup 1994

Middlesex League 1913 and 1914, Athenian League 1953, 1956, 1961

Finchley and District League 1911, London Senior Cup 1964 and 1969

Middlesex Senior Cup 1934, 1939, 1956, 1958, 1960, 1965, 1967, 1972, 1973, 1974, 1986

Middlesex Charity Cup 1922, 27, 36, 45, 46, 47, 48, 54, 57, 76, 77, 79, 85, 88

London Intermediate Cup 1965, 1973, 1976, 1980

Middlesex Intermediate Cup 1965, 1967, 1973, Suburban League 1993

Manager for 1996-97: Neil Price, Assistant Manager, Richard Parkin

Chairman: Ivor Arbiter, Chief Executive, John Wheeldon

Press Officer: David Ballheimer 0181 455 0030 (H)

Fanzine "The Sleeping Giant" Editor 88 Ravenscroft Ave, Wembley, Middx HA9 9TG

Hendon were founded in 1908 as Christ Church Hampstead FC and in their first season won the Finchley Football League Division 3. They started the second season with a new name, Hampstead Town, and again finished champions. A year later they completed the hat-trick. Their first home was the National Athletic Ground which had also been used by Queens Park Rangers and stood behind Kensal Rise Station. They remained there until 1912 when the club moved to the Avenue Ground in Cricklewood Lane where they stayed until 1926 when they moved to Claremont Road, by which time they had joined the Athenian League. The ground was officially opened on September 18th in that year, the same year that the word `Town' was dropped from the name. Seven years later the club registered as Golders Green FC, but it was not until May 1946 that they became Hendon FC.

Elected to the Isthmian League in 1963, Hendon have been in the top division ever since, maintaining a record of never having been relegated in their entire history. Runners up to Wimbledon in the first season, they were

champions the following year, winning it again and coming second three times during the next ten years. Hendon played at Wembley in the Amateur Cup 5 times, winning it on three occasions, one of which was in front of 100,000 people against Bishop Auckland. Elsewhere the European Amateur Cup was won in 1972 and a total of 12 Middlesex Charity Cups, 11 Middlesex Senior Cups and 2 London Senior Cups have been won.

The three highest capped England players at amateur level were from Hendon, Rod Haider with 65 caps, John Swannell with 61 and Mike Pinner with 52.

HENDON 1995/96 SEASON

Date	Comp	Round	Opponent	Att	Score	Scorers
19/08/95	IFL	P	Enfield	802	0-2	
22/08/95	IFL	P	HAYES	262	0-2	
26/08/95	IFL	P	BOREHAM WOOD	252	1-1	Haynes
29/08/95	IFL	P	St Albans City	425	1-3	Hunter
02/09/95	IFL	P	Carshalton Athletic	501	1-1	Haynes
05/09/95	GIC	1	Yeovil Town	1092	3-1	McKimm, Haynes, James
09/09/95	FA Cup	Q1	FLACKWELL HEATH	156	8-0	Haynes(3), Pike, Sweetman, Gallagher(2), McKimm
16/09/95	IFL	P	Chertsey Town	366	1-3	Clarke
23/09/95	FA Cup	Q2	Clapton	158	3-2	Haynes, Gallagher, Stephenson
30/09/95	IFL	P	BISHOP'S STORTFORD	183	1-1	Haynes
07/10/95	FA Cup	Q3	HAYES	376	0-3	
10/10/95	IFL	P	SUTTON UNITED	275	0-4	
14/10/95	FA Trophy	Q1	WATERLOOVILLE	179	2-2	Haynes, Stephenson
17/10/95	FA Trophy	Q1 rep	Waterlooville	110	1-0	Gallagher
21/10/95	IFL	P	BROMLEY	234	2-0	Gallagher, Haynes
28/10/95	IFL	P	Purfleet	169	3-2	Matthews(og), Gallagher, Stephenson
31/10/95	GIC	2	CROYDON		0-1	
04/11/95	FA Trophy	Q2	GRAVESEND & NORTH	291	3-0	Deadman(2), Fiore
11/11/95	IFL	P	Walton & Hersham	267	0-1	
14/11/95	Middx SC	1	RUISLIP MANOR		2-5	Pike, Fiori
18/11/95	IFL	P	HARROW BOROUGH	273	0-2	
21/11/95	CC	1	ST ALBANS CITY		3-4	Dowson(3)
25/11/95	FA Trophy	Q3	Cambridge City	234	0-2	
02/12/95	IFL	P	MOLESEY	197	2-0	Haynes, Turner
16/12/95	IFL	P	KINGSTONIAN	278	0-3	
19/12/95	IFL	P	HITCHIN TOWN	182	1-2	Dawber
26/12/95	IFL	P	YEADING	241	1-1	Fiori
01/01/96	IFL	P	Yeovil Town	2306	1-4	Price
06/01/96	IFL	P	CARSHALTON ATHLETIC	246	0-0	
13/01/96	IFL	P	Hayes	347	1-3	Banton
20/01/96	IFL	P	Dulwich Hamlet	417	0-1	
03/02/96	IFL	P	ST ALBANS CITY	357	1-2	Bolton
10/02/96	IFL	P	Bishop's Stortford	323	1-3	Bolton
17/02/96	IFL	P	CHERTSEY TOWN	262	0-0	
24/02/96	IFL	P	PURFLEET	227	2-4	Price, Banton
27/02/96	IFL	P	Grays Athletic	217	0-0	
02/03/96	IFL	P	Bromley	259	5-2	Stephenson, Coles(og), Clarke, Duffield, Banton
05/03/96	IFL	P	Hitchin Town	209	1-0	Hobbs
09/03/96	IFL	P	Sutton United	529	3-2	Duffield, Banton(2)
12/03/96	IFL	P	Aylesbury United	346	0-1	
16/03/96	IFL	P	DULWICH HAMLET	301	1-2	Banton
23/03/96	IFL	P	WALTON & HERSHAM	225	4-0	Banton(2), Dawber(2)
26/03/96	IFL	P	ENFIELD	346	0-1	
30/03/96	IFL	P	Worthing	336	5-0	Banton, Dawber(3), Stephenson
02/04/96	IFL	P	Yeading	202	0-0	
06/04/96	IFL	P	YEOVIL TOWN	443	1-3	Duffield
09/04/96	IFL	P	WORTHING	249	3-0	Duffield, Dawber, Driscoll
13/04/96	IFL	P	AYLESBURY UNITED	253	4-2	Banton, Clarke, Powell, Dawber
17/04/96	IFL	P	Harrow Borough	253	2-2	Banton(2)
20/04/96	IFL	P	Molesey	190	2-1	Dawber, Price
23/04/96	IFL	P	Boreham Wood	307	0-4	
27/04/96	IFL	P	GRAYS ATHLETIC	239	0-0	
04/05/96	IFL	P	Kingstonian	421	1-0	Stephenson

HEYBRIDGE SWIFTS

Scraley Rd, Heybridge, Maldon, Essex. Tel: 01621 852978

Secretary: Dennis Fenn, 31 Saxon Way, Maldon, Essex CM9 5JN Tel: 01621 854798

Nickname: Swifts, Colours: Black and White stripes

Capacity: 3,000   Seating: 450

Covered standing: 600   Clubhouse on ground: Yes

Record attendance: 915 v Nuneaton Borough FA Cup 4th Qual Rd 1994

Record appearance holder: H.Askew 500+

Record goalscorer in total: J.Lamb 115

DIRECTIONS

Leave Maldon on main road to Colchester, pass through Heybridge then turn right at sign to Tolleshunt Major (Scraley Road). Ground on right. Six miles from nearest station (Witham). By bus via Chelmsford.

Honours

Isthmian League Div 2 North 1990

Essex Senior Trophy 1982

Essex Senior League 1982, 1983, 1984

League Cup 1983

JT Clarke Cup 1983

The origins of the Swifts date back as far as 1880, and initially friendly matches and then local league games were played. The first club colours were blue and white hoops, which were then switched to white and green before settling on the distinguished black and white stripes in 1893. In the late 50's a switch was made to quarters, but the stripes came back after a few years and have remained. In those formative years, matches were played at the Plains, near Heybridge Hall on the east side of the village. In the 1890's a move was made to the Bentall's Field in Colchester Road, where they remained in 1964 when a company take over forced them off the ground and nearly caused them to fold. For a few seasons, whilst looking for land for a new home, fixtures were played at John Sadd's playing field, until the late 60's when Scraley Road site was bought as a carrot field. Much hard work and sweat has gone into making the ground what it is today, with a capacity now around 4,000.

The black and whites first league match was in 1895 in the North Essex League and this was to be the arena for a number of seasons, before the switch was made to the Chelmsford and District League. After the Great War football was played in the Essex and Suffolk Border League until 1925 when they went back to the North Essex League. Five years later they went back again, and took the title and the Essex Junior Cup.

The Swifts re-formed in 1946 winning the North Essex League a year later and after a spell in the South Essex League, Swifts again went back to the Essex and Suffolk, until 1971. They took a bold step and joined the new Essex Senior League where they found the rise in standards difficult for ten years or more, but things changed in the 80's with a hat-trick of championships from 1982, and wins in the Essex Trophy and Senior League Cup.

The move up to the Isthmian League came in 1984 and after five good seasons, they finally won Division 2 North in 1990. Division One was a struggle for two seasons, but last May Swifts capped a great season by finishing second behind Oxford City, thus gaining promotion to the Premier Division, their highest ever place in football.

HEYBRIDGE SWIFTS 1995/96 SEASON

Date	Comp	Rnd	Opponent	Score	Scorers
12/08/95	IFL	1	Aldershot Town	1-1	
19/08/95	IFL	1	MARLOW	3-1	
22/08/95	IFL	1	Barking	2-1	Pollard(2)
28/08/95	IFL	1	BOGNOR REGIS TOWN	5-1	
02/09/95	IFL	1	BILLERICAY TOWN	3-2	
05/09/95	GIC	1	Whyteleafe	2-1	
09/09/95	FA Cup	Q1	Diss Town	2-0	
12/09/95	IFL	1	Basingstoke Town	3-1	Adcock(2), Jones
16/09/95	IFL	1	UXBRIDGE	4-0	
19/09/95	E. F'lit	Gp 5	MALDON TOWN	2-0	
23/09/95	FA Cup	Q2	Sudbury Town	1-2	Rolfe
30/09/95	IFL	1	Tooting & Mitcham United	1-0	Caldon
03/10/95	E. F'lit	Gp 5	Maldon Town	2-1	Caldon, Rolfe
07/10/95	IFL	1	Wokingham Town	0-1	
10/10/95	E. F'lit	Gp 5	HARWICH & PARKESTON	3-0	
17/10/95	IFL	1	MAIDENHEAD UNITED	1-1	Springett
21/10/95	IFL	1	THAME UNITED	5-1	Adcock(2), Jones, Caldon, Game
24/10/95	E. Anglian	1	Burnham Ramblers	3-0	
28/10/95	IFL	1	Wembley	3-0	Pollard, Springett, Jones
31/10/95	GIC	2	BILLERICAY TOWN	4-3	
04/11/95	FA Trophy	Q2	Yate Town	2-1	Rolfe, Weeks(og)
11/11/95	IFL	1	Berkhamsted Town	2-1	Adcock, Vickers
18/11/95	IFL	1	Barton Rovers	4-1	Bain, Caldon, Matthews, Adcock
25/11/95	FA Trophy	Q3	Boreham Wood	0-3	
28/11/95	CC	1	Barton Rovers	1-0	
02/12/95	IFL	1	Chesham United	1-1	Caldon
09/12/95	IFL	1	ABINGDON TOWN	3-0	Jones, Adcock, Vickers
12/12/95	GIC	3	DULWICH HAMLET	3-2	
16/12/95	IFL	1	Whyteleafe	1-4	
19/12/95	CC	2	UXBRIDGE	3-1	
01/01/96	IFL	1	RUISLIP MANOR	3-0	Cook, Caldon, Springett
06/01/96	IFL	1	Billericay Town	0-2	
09/01/96	Essex SC	3	Halstead Town	3-0	
13/01/96	IFL	1	BARKING	7-0	Matthews(3), Caldon(3), Jones
20/01/96	IFL	1	Marlow	0-1	
23/01/96	CC	3	BOREHAM WOOD	0-2	
03/02/96	IFL	1	Bognor Regis Town	3-1	Matthew, Bain, Caldon
06/02/96	IFL	1	STAINES TOWN	3-0	Caldon(2), Bain
08/02/96	E. Anglian	2	Aveley	2-3	
10/02/96	IFL	1	TOOTING & MITCHAM UNI	1-2	Pollard
13/02/96	Essex SC	QF	BILLERICAY TOWN	1-3	
15/02/96	E. F'lit	Gp 5	Harwich & Parkeston	0-1	
17/02/96	IFL	1	Uxbridge	0-1	
24/02/96	IFL	1	WEMBLEY	4-1	Bain(2), Springett, Caldon
02/03/96	IFL	1	Thame United	1-1	Cook
05/03/96	IFL	1	Leyton Pennant	1-0	Springett
09/03/96	IFL	1	Maidenhead United	4-1	Caldon(2), Pollard, Springett
12/03/96	GIC	QF	KINGSTONIAN	2-2	
16/03/96	IFL	1	WOKINGHAM TOWN	2-0	Springett, Pollard
19/03/96	IFL	1	ALDERSHOT TOWN	2-0	Jones, Caldon
21/03/96	GIC	QF rep	Kingstonian	0-2	
23/03/96	IFL	1	BERKHAMSTED TOWN	4-2	Jones, Caldon, Pollard, Matthews
30/03/96	IFL	1	Oxford City	3-4	McDonough, Martin(og), Matthews
02/04/96	IFL	1	BARTON ROVERS	3-1	Matthews(2), Adcock
06/04/96	IFL	1	Ruislip Manor	2-1	Hewes, Matthews
08/04/96	IFL	1	LEYTON PENNANT	0-0	
13/04/96	IFL	1	Staines Town	2-2	Adcock, Springett
16/04/96	IFL	1	OXFORD CITY	2-2	Matthews, Clanfield
20/04/96	IFL	1	CHESHAM UNITED	2-0	Matthews, Adcock
27/04/96	IFL	1	Abingdon Town	1-3	Vickers
02/05/96	IFL	1	BASINGSTOKE TOWN	3-1	Matthews, Springett, Pollard
04/05/96	IFL	1	WHYTELEAFE	2-0	

HITCHIN TOWN

Top Field, Fishponds Rd, Hitchin, SG5 1NU. Tel: 01462 459028 matchdays only

Secretary: Roger Austin, 22 St Katherines Close, Ickleford, Herts SG5 3XS Tel 01462 452811

Nickname: The Canaries, Colours: Yellow and Green

Capacity: 4,000   Seating: 500

Covered standing: 1,250   Clubhouse on ground: Yes

DIRECTIONS

On A505 near town centre opposite large green. 1 mile from Hitchin (BR).

Record attendance: 7,878 v Wycombe Wanderers FA Amateur Cup 1956

Record appearances: Paul Giggle

Record goalscorer in one season.Eddie Armitage 84 1931-32

Record goalscorer in total: Paul Giggle

Record fee received: £5,750 for Steve Conroy to Kingstonian in 1990

Record fee paid: £2,000 for Ray Seekings from Potton Utd in 1989

Manager For 1996-97: Andy Melvin.

Honours

FA AMATEUR CUP semi-finals 1961 and 1963

Isthmian League Division One 1993, Spartan League 1935

AFA Senior Cup 1931

Herts Senior Cup 1895, 96, 98, 1900, 03, 05, 10, 31, 32, 34, 38, 39, 41, 43, 62, 70, 75, 76, 1977

London Senior Cup 1970, East Anglian Cup 1973

Herts Charity Cup 1902, 03,05, 10, 31, 32, 34, 38, 39, 41, 43, 62, 70, 75, 76, 77, 78, 79, 80

Herts Intermediate Cup 1940, 1947, 1949, 1957, 1961, 1962, 1968, 1969

Woolwich Trophy 1983, Televised Sport International Cup 1989 and 1991

Southern Combination Senior Floodlit Cup 1991

Hitchin Town are the oldest of the Isthmian League club members, having come into being originally in 1865 and were one of the founder members of the Football Association, paying £25 towards the first FA Cup.

Hitchin were widely regarded as Hertfordshire's senior club at the turn of the century and soon were playing Brighton, Watford, Woolwich Arsenal and Tottenham in the old South East Counties League. They more than held their own for a handful of seasons before financial problems forced them to return to amateur status in the Spartan League. Eighteen months later they went under when finances got worse and the club's grandstand at Top Field was destroyed by fire. Hitchin Blue Cross FC kept the ball rolling after the Great War, but they too folded in 1927, prompting a re-forming of Town. They were immediately elected back to the Spartan League, reaching the top in 1935, on goal average from Met Police. In 1939 they were elected to the Athenian League, but after netting 21 goals in three games, war broke out, breaking up one of the club's finest ever sides.

They returned to the league after the war, but never set the world alight until 1963, when following the installation of floodlights and two Amateur Cup semi-final appearances, they were elected to the Isthmian League. In 1969 runners up spot was achieved, that being the nearest the Canaries have got to the title, but the 70's saw some stirring deeds in Cups. In 1971 the much sought after London Senior Cup was won and two years later they reached the Second Round of the FA Cup, which they equalled three years later. The 80's by contrast were lean times with a number of relegation battles ending in 1988 when they went down. It took five years to go back, when winning Division One in

a tense finish. The team broke up in 1994 but the season still saw a marvellous FA Cup run which saw Hereford United beaten 4-2 in a replay at Top Field.

Hitchin have played at Top Field since 1871, after playing a more unorganised game at Payne's Park in the town. The ground has undergone a number of changes but still retains areas of its unusual wooden terracing.

HITCHIN TOWN 1995/96 SEASON

Date	Comp	Rnd	Opponent	Att	Score	Scorers
15/08/95	Herts CC	QF	Stevenage Borough	818	0-3	
19/08/95	IFL	P	HARROW BOROUGH	304	1-5	Burke
26/08/95	IFL	P	Yeading	160	0-2	
29/08/95	IFL	P	DULWICH HAMLET	281	1-3	Williams
02/09/95	IFL	P	WORTHING	250	2-2	McMenamin, Ryan
09/09/95	IFL	P	Yeovil Town	1739	1-1	Williams
12/09/95	GIC	1	CANVEY ISLAND	185	4-1	Conroy(2), Scott, Burke
16/09/95	IFL	P	MOLESEY	292	0-1	
23/09/95	IFL	P	AYLESBURY UNITED	418	0-3	
30/09/95	IFL	P	Bromley	310	2-0	Williams, Roberts
07/10/95	IFL	P	Kingstonian	524	1-0	Burns
21/10/95	FA Cup	Q4	ST ALBANS CITY	1147	2-1	Burns, Williams
24/10/95	IFL	P	ST ALBANS CITY	443	0-0	
28/10/95	IFL	P	Carshalton Athletic	389	1-1	Williams
31/10/95	GIC	2	Sutton United	229	1-0	Williams
04/11/95	IFL	P	BOREHAM WOOD	511	1-2	Covington
11/11/95	FA Cup	1	BRISTOL ROVERS	3101	2-1	Conroy, Burns
14/11/95	IFL	P	CHERTSEY TOWN	291	2-0	Burns, Gillard
18/11/95	IFL	P	Hayes	303	1-1	Ryan
21/11/95	CC	2	Bishop's Stortford	201	0-3	
25/11/95	FA Trophy	Q3	BOGNOR REGIS TOWN	394	1-2	Gillard
02/12/95	FA Cup	2	Gillingham	7142	0-3	
05/12/95	Herts SC	2	Hertford Town	60	6-0	Conroy(3), Issott(2), Roberts
09/12/95	IFL	P	ENFIELD	611	1-0	Williams
12/12/95	GIC	3	BISHOP'S STORTFORD	121	4-1	Williams, Roberts(2), Cooper
16/12/95	IFL	P	Walton & Hersham	186	1-4	Roberts
19/12/95	IFL	P	Hendon	182	2-1	Brett, Roberts
02/01/96	IFL	P	SUTTON UNITED	303	1-0	Roberts
06/01/96	IFL	P	Worthing	353	0-2	
13/01/96	IFL	P	YEOVIL TOWN	523	1-2	Conroy
20/01/96	IFL	P	Harrow Borough	276	2-1	Clarke(2)
23/01/96	GIC	QF	Wokingham Town	110	3-2	
30/01/96	Herts SC	QF	BISHOP'S STORTFORD	192	4-1	G Williams(2), Burke, Own-Goal
03/02/96	IFL	P	Dulwich Hamlet	411	3-3	Williams(3)
10/02/96	IFL	P	BROMLEY	373	2-1	Clark, Williams
13/02/96	IFL	P	Grays Athletic	197	0-1	
17/02/96	IFL	P	Molesey	142	1-2	Williams
21/02/96	IFL	P	HAYES	164	1-3	Stevens(og)
24/02/96	IFL	P	CARSHALTON ATHLETIC	384	2-5	Clark, Parker
27/02/96	GIC	SF(1)	ALDERSHOT TOWN	664	0-1	
02/03/96	IFL	P	St Albans City	626	1-5	McMenamin
05/03/96	IFL	P	HENDON	209	0-1	
09/03/96	IFL	P	Aylesbury United	503	1-2	Clark
12/03/96	GIC	SF(2)	Aldershot Town	1965	0-2	
16/03/96	IFL	P	KINGSTONIAN	365	1-1	Clark
18/03/96	IFL	P	Purfleet	156	1-1	Parker
23/03/96	IFL	P	GRAYS ATHLETIC	369	1-0	Parker
30/03/96	IFL	P	Boreham Wood	348	0-1	
02/04/96	IFL	P	Bishop's Stortford	265	2-2	Burke, Williams
06/04/96	IFL	P	Sutton United	490	0-4	
08/04/96	IFL	P	BISHOP'S STORTFORD	436	1-1	Parker
13/04/96	IFL	P	Chertsey Town	361	1-2	McMenamin
16/04/96	IFL	P	YEADING	201	0-3	
20/04/96	IFL	P	PURFLEET	299	2-0	Dunlop, Gillard
27/04/96	IFL	P	Enfield	982	0-3	
04/05/96	IFL	P	WALTON & HERSHAM	331	0-2	

KINGSTONIAN

Kingsmeadow Stadium, Kingston Rd, Kingston-on-Thames, Surrey KT1 3PBTel: 0181 547 3335

Secretary: Mr Chris Kelly, c/o Football Club

Colours: Red and White hoops

Nickname: K's   Capacity: 9,000

Seating: 690   Covered standing: 3,500

Clubhouse on ground: Yes

Record attendance: On old ground
11,000 v Bishop Auckland Amateur Cup 1955

On new ground: 4, 582 v Chelsea Friendly July 22nd 1995

DIRECTIONS

From town centre - Cambridge Road on to Kingston Road (A2043) to Malden Road. From A3, turn off at New Malden and turn left on to A2043 - ground 1 mile on left. Half mile from Norbiton (BR), one mile from Kingston (BR). Bus 131 passes the ground.

Biggest win: 15-1 v Delft in friendly Sept 5th 1951. For competitive game 10-0 v Hitchin Tn March 1966

Biggest defeat: 0-11 v Ilford Isthmian League Feb 1937

Record appearances: Mickey Preston 555

Record goalscorer in total: Johnny Whig 295

Record fee paid £10,000 for Richard Cherry from Redbridge Forest

Record fee received £10,000 for David Harlow from Farnborough Town

Honours

FA AMATEUR CUP 1933

RUNNERS UP 1960

Isthmian League 1934 and 1937, Athenian League 1924 and 1926, London Senior Cup 1963, 1965, 1987

Surrey Senior Cup 1926, 1931, 1932, 1935, 1939, 1952, 1963, 1964, 1967

The Kingstonian Football Club was formed in 1885 as Kingston and Surbiton YMCA FC, playing the first match on November 28th of that year. In April 1887 the name was changed to Saxons (Kingston YMCA) , in April 1890 to Kingston Wanderers FC and in September 1893 to Kingston-on-Thames FC. The first honours arrived 100 years ago when they became the first ever champions of the Kingston and District League and they subsequently entered the East and West Surrey League, winning it as the West Surrey League in 1906. In May 1908 a number of committee men broke away to form Old Kingstonians FC but after the Great War the two clubs merged again to form Kingstonian FC, joining the Athenian League. The club rented the ground, but at the end of the first season Leyland Motors FC secured the tenancy and after some discussion the two clubs ground shared, although unsuccessfully. Eventually K's bought a plot of land to develop. After a worrying period the club won the league in 1924 and 1926, and in 1929 joined the Isthmian League, winning it in 1934 and 1937, after taking the FA Amateur Cup for the only time in 1933 when they beat Stockton in a replay at Darlington. After the Second War, K's had little success until 1956 when beaten semi-finalists and then 1960 when they again reached the final, losing at Wembley to Hendon. The 60's were better with Surrey and London Senior Cup wins and good positions in the league, but the 70's were the opposite, struggling to avoid relegation until the inevitable happened in 1979. Happily promotion came in 1985 behind Farnborough Town and in 1986 they won the London Senior Cup, the first trophy for 20 years. 1988 marked the end of football at Kingston Road as the ground was sold for development, and K's played virtually all the next season at Hampton FC before moving on to their brand new Kingsmeadow Stadium. Since then the club has enjoyed consistency in the top division and has beaten Brighton and Hove in the FA Cup, in 1994 and won the League Cup, demolishing Aldershot Town last May.

KINGSTONIAN 1995/96 SEASON

Date	Comp	Round	Opponent	Att	Score	Scorers
19/08/95	IFL	P	WORTHING	389	1-1	Wiggins
22/08/95	IFL	P	Bromley	664	1-1	Warden
26/08/95	IFL	P	Harrow Borough	338	1-2	Bolton
29/08/95	IFL	P	MOLESEY	394	1-1	Riley
02/09/95	IFL	P	PURFLEET	397	1-1	Bolton
05/09/95	GIC	1	ABINGDON TOWN		2-1	
09/09/95	IFL	P	Sutton United	944	1-0	Bolton
16/09/95	IFL	P	YEOVIL TOWN	642	2-2	Bowyer, Jasper
23/09/95	IFL	P	SUTTON UNITED	747	2-2	Bowyer, Broderick
30/09/95	IFL	P	Yeading	281	2-0	Stevens, Wingfield
03/10/95	IFL	P	GRAYS ATHLETIC	332	1-0	Brooker
07/10/95	IFL	P	HITCHIN TOWN	524	0-1	
09/10/95	IFL	P	Carshalton Athletic	843	3-0	Warden, Luckett, Barton
14/10/95	IFL	P	Aylesbury United	739	2-0	Brooker, Wingfield
21/10/95	FA Cup	Q4	TROWBRIDGE TOWN	781	3-1	Warden, Nebbeling, Fisher
28/10/95	IFL	P	Boreham Wood	522	0-0	
31/10/95	IFL	P	HAYES	432	1-0	Luckett
11/11/95	FA Cup	1	WISBECH TOWN	1396	5-1	Wingfield(2), Riley, Warden, Akuamoah
14/11/95	GIC	2	Barking		6-0	
18/11/95	IFL	P	Bishop's Stortford	422	3-2	Warden(2), Wringfield
22/11/95	CC	1	Molesey		3-0	
25/11/95	IFL	P	ENFIELD	940	0-1	
03/12/95	FA Cup	2	PLYMOUTH ARGYLE	2961	1-2	Warden
11/12/95	Surrey SC	1	Carshalton Athletic		1-1	
16/12/95	IFL	P	Hendon	278	3-0	Warden, Brooker, Fisher
19/12/95	Surrey SC	1 rep	CARSHALTON ATHLETIC		1-2	
26/12/95	IFL	P	Chertsey Town	518	1-2	Riley
02/01/96	IFL	P	WALTON & HERSHAM	402	1-0	Jones
06/01/96	IFL	P	Purfleet	248	3-1	Bolton, Brooker(2)
09/01/96	CC	2	Walton & Hersham		3-1	
13/01/96	IFL	P	BROMLEY	602	0-1	
16/01/96	CC	3	OXFORD CITY		5-3	
20/01/96	FA Trophy	1	Wembley	214	1-2	Bolton
23/01/96	IFL	P	Worthing	334	5-0	Stevens, Luckett(2), Akuamoah(2)
03/02/96	IFL	P	Molesey	310	2-0	Nebelling, Akuamoah
10/02/96	IFL	P	YEADING	419	3-1	Jasper, Warmington, Warden
17/02/96	IFL	P	Yeovil Town	1953	1-1	Warden
24/02/96	IFL	P	BOREHAM WOOD	523	1-0	Annon
27/02/96	GIC	3	Enfield		2-2	
02/03/96	IFL	P	Hayes	431	1-2	Warden
05/03/96	GIC	3 rep	ENFIELD		3-0	
09/03/96	IFL	P	CARSHALTON ATHLETIC	707	2-1	Warden, Nebbling
12/03/96	GIC	QF	Heybridge Swifts		2-2	
14/03/96	CC	QF	CARSHALTON ATHLETIC		2-3	
16/03/96	IFL	P	Hitchin Town	365	1-1	Warden
19/03/96	IFL	P	St Albans City	469	2-1	Warden, Jones
21/03/96	GIC	QF rep	HEYBRIDGE SWIFTS		2-0	
23/03/96	IFL	P	AYLESBURY UNITED	598	1-1	Danzey(og)
26/03/96	IFL	P	HARROW BOROUGH	302	0-1	
28/03/96	GIC	SF(1)	Aylesbury United		3-1	
30/03/96	IFL	P	Grays Athletic	261	1-1	Warden
02/04/96	GIC	SF(2)	AYLESBURY UNITED	292	2-1	M Jones, Luckett
06/04/96	IFL	P	Walton & Hersham	402	2-0	M Jones, Warden
08/04/96	IFL	P	CHERTSEY TOWN	422	0-2	
13/04/96	IFL	P	Enfield	904	1-2	Barton
16/04/96	IFL	P	BISHOP'S STORTFORD	259	2-1	D Jones, Warden
18/04/96	IFL	P	DULWICH HAMLET	418	0-2	
20/04/96	IFL	P	ST ALBANS CITY	501	4-1	Bolton(4)
27/04/96	IFL	P	Dulwich Hamlet	629	3-1	Bolton(3)
04/05/96	IFL	P	HENDON	421	0-1	
06/05/96	GIC	F	Aldershot Town	3511	4-1	Bolton(2), Akuamoah, Jasper

OXFORD CITY

Court Place Farm, Marsh Lane, Marston, Oxford. Tel: 01865 744493

Secretary: John Shepperd 20 Howe Close, Wheatley, Oxford OX33 1SS Tel: 01865 872181

Colours: Blue and White hoops, Nickname: City

Capacity: 3,000   Seating: 300

Covered standing: 500   Clubhouse on ground: Yes

Record attendance: 9,500 v Leytonstone
FA Amateur Cup 1950 (at old ground)

DIRECTIONS

Directions: From London M40/A40, ring-road to North, take 1st slip road, follow signs to John Radcliffe hospital, ground on left after leaving flyover. From the North same ring-road.

Biggest win: 9-0 Harlow Town Isthmian League 1976

Biggest defeat: 0-8 Wycombe Wanderers Isthmian League date not known

Record appearances: John Woodley

Record goalscorer in one season: John Woodley

Record goalscorer in total: John Woodley

Record fee paid £3,000 for Steve Adams from Woking

Honours

FA AMATEUR CUP WINNERS 1906

RUNNERS UP 1903, 1913

FA VASE RUNNER UP 1995

South Midlands League 1993, Isthmian League Div 1 1996, Oxfordshire Senior Cup 27 times

Manager 1996-97: Andy Thomas, Assistant Manager: Alan Thorne, Chairman: M. Woodley

Oxford City were formed in 1882 and in 1906 they won the FA Amateur Cup. A year later they joined the Isthmian League and until 1950 were the top club in the City of Oxford. Since their formation they have won the Oxford Senior Cup 28 times, the Benevolent Cup 18 times and the Oxford Charity Cup 9 times.

In December 1979 the club became a limited company and in the following year Bobby Moore was appointed manager with Harry Redknapp as his assistant. Unfortunately that year saw City relegated to Division One. They remained there until they were forced to resign from the league when Brasenose College, owners of the White House Ground, terminated their lease due to a contravention in the terms and the club vacated in May 1988.

An enthusiastic band of supporters continued to meet after the Directors resigned and eventually City entered a youth side in the County Youth League in 1989. A year later the club were elected into the South Midlands League First Division, playing under Peter Foley at Cuttesloe Park. They were quickly promoted and shared Pressed Steel's ground at Roman Way and won the Premier Division in style. A new ground had become an urgent priority and with the help of the local council and other contributors a site was made available and in a race against a league deadline, the ground was opened in time to join the Isthmian League.

The first season saw the club promoted in third place, winning their last five matches and in 1995, they reached Division One and got to the final of the FA Vase, where they lost to the all conquering Arlesey Town in the Wembley final. The run continued last season when the club were promoted to the top flight as champions of Division One.

OXFORD CITY 1995/96 SEASON

Date	Competition	Round	Opponent	Score	Scorers
19/08/95	IFL	1	BASINGSTOKE TOWN	3-2	
22/08/95	GIC	P	Horsham	6-3	
26/08/95	IFL	1	Chesham United	2-0	
29/08/95	IFL	1	MARLOW	1-6	Kemp
02/09/95	IFL	1	RUISLIP MANOR	2-2	
05/09/95	GIC	1	Staines Town	1-3	
09/09/95	FA Cup	Q1	WITNEY TOWN	1-1	Thomas
12/09/95	FA Cup	Q1 rep	Witney Town	1-3	S Fontaine
16/09/95	IFL	1	TOOTING & MITCHAM UNI	3-1	
30/09/95	IFL	1	Barking	3-2	Douglas, Herbert, Charles
07/10/95	IFL	1	Maidenhead United	2-0	Herbert, Martin
10/10/95	IFL	1	BERKHAMSTED TOWN	1-0	Brown
14/10/95	IFL	1	Aldershot Town	2-0	Fontaine, Hewitson
21/10/95	IFL	1	Abingdon Town	2-4	S Fontaine, Charles
28/10/95	IFL	1	WOKINGHAM TOWN	2-0	K Douglas(2)
04/11/95	FA Trophy	Q2	Walton & Hersham	0-0	
07/11/95	FA Trophy	Q2 rep	WALTON & HERSHAM	5-2	Herbert(2), Thomas, Morrisey, S Fontaine
11/11/95	IFL	1	WEMBLEY	5-1	McCleary(2), Kemp, Herbert, Martin
18/11/95	IFL	1	Staines Town	2-0	Martin, Thomas
21/11/95	IFL	1	Uxbridge	2-2	Herbert, McCluskey(og)
25/11/95	FA Trophy	Q3	Bromley	1-1	Thomas
28/11/95	FA Trophy	Q3 rep	BROMLEY	3-2	Charles, Morrisey, Brown
02/12/95	IFL	1	Leyton Pennant	3-1	McLeary(3)
09/12/95	IFL	1	WHYTELEAFE	2-0	McCleary, Charles
12/12/95	CC	2	BASINGSTOKE TOWN	1-0	
16/12/95	IFL	1	Billericay Town	0-1	
23/12/95	IFL	1	CHESHAM UNITED	1-0	McCleary
03/01/96	IFL	1	BOGNOR REGIS TOWN	1-0	Hewitson
06/01/96	IFL	1	Ruislip Manor	5-4	McLeary(2), Muttock, S Fontaine, Martin
13/01/96	IFL	1	UXBRIDGE	1-0	Martin
16/01/96	CC	3	Kingstonian	3-5	
20/01/96	FA Trophy	1	MERTHYR TYDFIL	1-2	Herbert
28/01/96	IFL	1	ALDERSHOT TOWN	1-3	S Fontaine
03/02/96	IFL	1	Marlow	4-2	S Fontaine(2), C Fontaine, Thomas
10/02/96	IFL	1	BARKING	1-0	Herbert
14/02/96	Oxon SC	QF	NORTH LEIGH	3-1	
28/02/96	Oxon SC	SF	BICESTER TOWN	2-1	
02/03/96	IFL	1	ABINGDON TOWN	3-3	McCleary, Thomas, S Fontaine
09/03/96	IFL	1	Berkhamsted Town	3-2	McCleary(2), Thomas
12/03/96	IFL	1	BARTON ROVERS	3-0	McCleary, Smith, Pierson
16/03/96	IFL	1	MAIDENHEAD UNITED	2-2	Smith, Herbert
19/03/96	IFL	1	Tooting & Mitcham United	3-1	McCleary, Greig, S Fontaine
23/03/96	IFL	1	Wembley	2-0	Muttock, S Fontaine
26/03/96	IFL	1	Basingstoke Town	1-3	Lee
30/03/96	IFL	1	HEYBRIDGE SWIFTS	4-3	S Fontaine(2), McCleary(2)
06/04/96	IFL	1	Bognor Regis Town	1-3	McCleary
08/04/96	IFL	1	THAME UNITED	5-0	McCleary(3), Pearson, Herbert
13/04/96	IFL	1	Barton Rovers	0-1	
16/04/96	IFL	1	Heybridge Swifts	2-2	McCleary, Morrisey
20/04/96	IFL	1	LEYTON PENNANT	2-2	S Fontaine(2)
23/04/96	IFL	1	STAINES TOWN	1-1	Herbert
25/04/96	IFL	1	Thame United	2-0	Herbert, C Fontaine
27/04/96	IFL	1	Whyteleafe	5-3	Thomas, Herbert, Phillips, Bloxham, Smart(og)
30/04/96	IFL	1	Wokingham Town	4-2	S Fontaine(2), Smith, McCleary
04/05/96	IFL	1	BILLERICAY TOWN	4-1	
08/05/96	Oxon SC	F	Thame United	2-1	

PURFLEET

Thurrock Hotel, Ship Lane, Grays, Essex .Tel: 01708 868901

Secretary`: Norman Posner, 1 Chase House Gardens, Hornchurch, Essex RM11 2PJ Tel 01708 458301

Colours: Green and Yellow

Nickname: Fleet

Capacity: 4,500

Seating: 300

Covered standing: 1,000

Clubhouse on ground : Yes

Record atendance: 950 v West Ham United in friendly in 1989

Biggest win: 10-0 v Stansted (H) 1986-87

Biggest defeat: 0-5 v Kingsbury Town (H) League 1989-90

Record appearances: Colin McBride 234

Record goalscorer in one season: Terry Bellamy 59

DIRECTIONS

M25 or A13 to Dartford tunnel roundabout. Ground is fifty yards on right down Ship Lane. Nearest station is Purfleet, two miles from ground.

Honours

Isthmian League Div 2 1992

Associate Members Trophy 1992

Essex Senior League 1988

League Cup 1987 and 1988

Stanford Charity Cup 1988

Purfleet Football Club was founded as recently as April 1985 which makes it one of the youngest senior clubs in the country. The first competitive game was on August 24th that year against Canvey Island Reserves in Division One of the Essex Senior League, a 3-0 win.

The club ground forms part of the Thurrock Hotel and Oasis Leisure Centre, and at first consisted of two pitches with dressing rooms in the main building, but with that set up they could only play as juniors. Midway through the season the pitch was turned round to give just one pitch and the dressing rooms were begun, in order to become self-contained. The end of the first season saw a third place and senior status and with planning permission for floodlights and a grandstand the club was up and running. Application to the Isthmian League was made and by winning the League and Cup double they were accepted in June 1988, with the stand having been finished in time for the new season. They finished as runners up to Harlow in Division Two North and were promoted, but relegation followed. 1990-91 saw a run in the FA Vase to the last 32 and the final placing of 7th ensured a place in the new Division Two the following August. That was the start of the finest season in their short history, Champions of Isthmian League Division Two and the winners of the Loctite Trophy. Terracing was laid down at the Ship Lane end giving cover for 600, which brought an A grading and in 1994, by finishing second to Bishops Stortford they were promoted again, to the Premier Division.

PURFLEET 1995/96 SEASON

Date	Comp	Round	Opponent	Att	Score	Scorers
19/08/95	IFL	P	St Albans City	492	0-3	
21/08/95	IFL	P	CHERTSEY TOWN	238	1-3	Bourne
26/08/95	IFL	P	ENFIELD	517	1-1	Crown
02/09/95	IFL	P	Kingstonian	397	1-1	Riley
04/09/95	GIC	1	BOREHAM WOOD	127	0-1	
09/09/95	FA Cup	Q1	FELIXSTOWE TOWN	105	4-0	
16/09/95	IFL	P	Carshalton Athletic	404	1-3	Jeyes
23/09/95	FA Cup	Q2	CHESHAM UNITED	220	3-1	Rees, Crown, Matthews
26/09/95	IFL	P	Bishop's Stortford	189	1-1	Crown
30/09/95	IFL	P	HAYES	181	0-0	
07/10/95	FA Cup	Q3	Dagenham & Redbridge	718	1-1	McFarlane
09/10/95	FA Cup	Q3 rep	DAGENHAM & REDBRI	683	2-1	Bourne, Jeyes
14/10/95	FA Trophy	Q1	Berkhamsted Town	98	2-1	
17/10/95	IFL	P	Yeading	110	1-3	McFarlane
21/10/95	FA Cup	Q4	RUSHDEN & DIAMONDS	650	1-1	Crown
24/10/95	FA Cup	Q4 rep	Rushden & Diamonds	2850	1-3	Donovan
28/10/95	IFL	P	HENDON	169	2-3	Crown(2)
04/11/95	FA Trophy	Q2	CORBY TOWN	108	6-1	Crown(3), Jeyes(2), Bates, Comer
06/11/95	IFL	P	BOREHAM WOOD	174	1-0	Southon
11/11/95	IFL	P	Dulwich Hamlet	261	1-1	Goldstone
13/11/95	CC	1	HAYES	58	2-0	
18/11/95	IFL	P	YEOVIL TOWN	302	0-3	
25/11/95	FA Trophy	Q3	Chertsey Town	266	1-0	Bourne
28/11/95	CC	2	Aylesbury United		1-0	
13/12/95	IFL	P	Harrow Borough	107	2-2	Rees(2)
16/12/95	IFL	P	AYLESBURY UNITED	156	1-2	Rees
19/12/95	Essex TST	2	Billericay Town		2-0	
23/12/95	IFL	P	Boreham Wood	302	1-2	Nesling
01/01/96	IFL	P	Molesey	180	3-2	Bourne, Deadman, Jeyes
06/01/96	IFL	P	KINGSTONIAN	248	1-3	Deadman
09/01/96	Essex SC	3	Collier Row		1-0	
13/01/96	IFL	P	Chertsey Town	389	1-2	Brown
20/01/96	FA Trophy	1	Rushden & Diamonds	1906	1-0	Jeyes
23/01/96	CC	3	Leyton Pennant		1-5	
30/01/96	IFL	P	Sutton United	334	0-1	
03/02/96	IFL	P	BISHOP'S STORTFORD	173	1-2	Rees
05/02/96	Essex SC	QF	SOUTHEND UNITED		2-4	
10/02/96	FA Trophy	2	Macclesfield Town	1003	1-2	Locke(og)
12/02/96	IFL	P	ST ALBANS CITY	163	0-1	
17/02/96	IFL	P	CARSHALTON ATHLETIC	210	2-1	Bourne, Portway
19/02/96	IFL	P	WORTHING	102	3-1	Portway(2), Cobb
24/02/96	IFL	P	Hendon	227	4-2	Donovan, Bourne, Cobb(2)
27/02/96	IFL	P	Bromley	254	2-0	Cobb, Bourne
02/03/96	IFL	P	YEADING	123	1-2	Portway
04/03/96	IFL	P	GRAYS ATHLETIC	231	1-0	Jeyes
09/03/96	IFL	P	Worthing	275	2-1	Portway(2)
11/03/96	IFL	P	WALTON & HERSHAM	127	2-1	Portway(2)
16/03/96	IFL	P	SUTTON UNITED	262	2-1	Portway(2)
18/03/96	IFL	P	HITCHIN TOWN	156	1-1	Cobb
23/03/96	IFL	P	DULWICH HAMLET	293	3-1	Cobb, Portway(2)
26/03/96	IFL	P	Hayes	371	1-2	Rees
30/03/96	IFL	P	Walton & Hersham	170	2-1	Ross, Deadman
02/04/96	IFL	P	Yeovil Town	2267	1-2	Cobb
06/04/96	IFL	P	MOLESEY	129	0-2	
08/04/96	IFL	P	Grays Athletic	341	0-2	
13/04/96	IFL	P	HARROW BOROUGH	162	0-1	
16/04/96	IFL	P	Enfield	744	0-3	
20/04/96	IFL	P	Hitchin Town	299	0-2	
23/04/96	Essex TST	QF	Leyton Pennant		2-6	
27/04/96	IFL	P	BROMLEY	268	1-1	Deadman
04/05/96	IFL	P	Aylesbury United	402	0-1	

ST ALBANS CITY

Clarence Park, York Rd, St Albans, Herts AL1 4DP. Tel: 01727 866819/864296

CLUBLINE: 0891 664354

Secretary: Steve Trulock, 42 Heath Rd, St Albans, Herts AL1 4QW
Tel: 01727 834920

Commercial Manager Graham McDougall c/o SAFC

Press Officer: Dave Tavener 43 Startpoint, Downs Rd, Luton, Beds
LU1 1XW Tel 01582 401487

Fixture Secretary: Steve Eames: Tel 01582 620521

Club shop: Terry Edwards 01727 833685

Nickname: The Saints, Colours: Blue and Yellow

Capacity: 4, 500, Seating: 904, Covered standing: 1, 000

Clubhouse: Yes

Record attendance 9,757 v Ferryhill Ath Amateur Cup
Feb 27th 1926

Biggest win 14-0 v Aylesbury Utd Spartan League
Oct 19th 1910

Biggest defeat 0-11 v Wimbledon Isthmian League Nov 9th 1947

Record appearance holder: Phil Wood 1,017, 1963 to 1984

Record goalscorer in one season Steve Clark 56

Record goalscorer in total Billy Minter 356 1920-1932

Record fee paid: £4,500 for Steve Clark from Wivenhoe 1991

Record fee received: £92,000 for Dean Austin to Tottenham Hotspur

Honours

FA AMATEUR CUP semi-finals 1923, 1925, 1926, 1970,
 Isthmian League 1924, 1927, 1928 and Div 1 1986

Athenian League 1921 and 1922, Spartan League 1912 and East Div 1910

Herts County League 1910 and West Div 1909

London Senior Cup 1971, AFA Senior Cup 1934, East Anglian Cup 1993

Herts Sen Cup 1925, 29, 35, 44, 47, 51, 55, 56, 57, 66, 68, 69, Herts Sen Trophy 1987

Herts Charity Cup 1910, 13, 21, 22, 23, 24,925, 26, 29, 39, 41, 42, 51, 53, 54, 56, 57, 58, 67, 69,
70, 71, 72, 87, 93

Mithras Cup 1965 and 1972, Wycombe Floodlit Cup 1969 and 1970

St Albans Hospital Cup 1946, Hitchin Centenary Cup 1971

Victory Cup 1926 and 1928, Liege Cup 1927, Billy Minter Invitational Cup 1991, 1992, 1993

Herts Charity Shield 1925, 1932, 1938, London Challenge Cup 1995

Manager for 1996-97: Alan Randall, Assistant manager: Mick Gilchrist

Founded on April 13th 1908, St Albans City are the third longest serving continuous members of the Isthmian
League, having moved up from the Athenians in 1923. Their first season, 1908-09 saw them in the Herts County
League and the Spartan League, winning the former. The following season, City won the Herts League again
and were runners-up in the Spartan, also winning the Charity Cup for the first of many times. Before the Great
War City won the Spartan League, seven of the players losing their lives in the conflict, and after one peacetime
season, they joined the Athenians and after two championships and one runner-up place, they were elected into
the Isthmian League, winning the title at the first attempt. By 1928, St Albans were established as one of the
leading clubs in the country, having won two more championships. The 20's were the golden age for the club,
when amongst others, they fielded England Amateur International Billy Minter, who once scored seven times in
an FA Cup tie at Dulwich, but still lost 8-7 in near darkness after extra time. The decade saw City reach three
Amateur Cup semi-finals, without once reaching the final. The next two decades were quiet for the club, who
did not threaten to win the league again until 1955, when they were runners up. Since increasing divisions, the
Isthmian League has seen City twice relegated, but the 90's saw them come back with a bang.

DIRECTIONS
Turn left out of St Albans
station - Clarence Park
200 yds ahead across
Hatfield Road. By road
from M25 roundabouts and
one larger island, through
two sets of lights and right
at island at far end of city
centre (St Peters Street)
into Hatfield Road, over 1
mini roundabout, left at
2nd lights into Clarence
Road, ground on left. from
M25 (anticlockwise), jct 22
onto A1081 towards city
centre, 3rd exit at 2nd
island, through two lights,
right at island just before
Odeon into Alma Road,
right at lights, straight
through next 2 sets (road
bends considerably) into
Clarence Road, ground on
left.

ST ALBANS CITY 1995/96 SEASON

Date	Competition	Round	Opponent	Att	Score	Scorers
04/08/95	W Minter T	94-95	Saffron Walden Town	106	1-1	Wilkinson
12/08/95	Herts CC	QF	WARE	128	4-2	Clarke, Clark, Blake, Attrell
19/08/95	IFL	P	PURFLEET	492	3-0	Howell, Daly, Clarke
22/08/95	IFL	P	Worthing	562	5-1	Daly, Clark(2), Attrell(2)
26/08/95	IFL	P	Dulwich Hamlet	385	1-3	Clark
29/08/95	IFL	P	HENDON	425	3-1	Clark, Daly, Procobi(og)
02/09/95	IFL	P	YEADING	456	0-1	
05/09/95	GIC	1	WORTHING	162	2-3	Clark(2)
09/09/95	FA Cup	Q1	BARTON ROVERS	407	4-1	Clark, Blackman, Howell, Blake
13/09/95	IFL	P	Harrow Borough	324	0-0	
16/09/95	IFL	P	SUTTON UNITED	651	2-2	Gurney, Blake
19/09/95	E. Anglian	1	ROMFORD	155	2-0	Duffield, Howell
23/09/95	FA Cup	Q2	Woodbridge Town	292	1-1	Howell
26/09/95	FA Cup	Q2 rep	WOODBRIDGE TOWN	358	2-0	Howell, Gurney
30/09/95	IFL	P	Walton & Hersham	281	2-1	Attrell, Duffield
07/10/95	FA Cup	Q3	ROMFORD	648	3-1	Clark, Daly, Duffield
10/10/95	IFL	P	ENFIELD	1102	1-0	Clark
14/10/95	IFL	P	YEOVIL TOWN	853	2-2	Blake, Clark
21/10/95	FA Cup	Q4	Hitchin Town	1147	1-2	Mudd
24/10/95	IFL	P	Hitchin Town	443	0-0	
28/10/95	IFL	P	CHERTSEY TOWN	551	2-0	Clark, Howell
31/10/95	E. F'lit	Gp 2	Sawbridgeworth Town		1-1	
04/11/95	IFL	P	Grays Athletic	212	3-0	Howell, Clark(2)
08/11/95	London CC	1	Collier Row		1-2	
11/11/95	IFL	P	Bishop's Stortford	487	2-3	Howell, Clark
14/11/95	E. F'lit	Gp 2	SAWBRIDGEWORTH TOWN		2-2	
18/11/95	IFL	P	AYLESBURY UNITED	695	2-0	Clark, Biggins
21/11/95	CC	1	Hendon		4-3	
25/11/95	FA Trophy	Q3	THAME UNITED	456	4-2	Daly(2), Driscoll, Howells
28/11/95	CC	2	RUISLIP MANOR		1-2	
02/12/95	IFL	P	CARSHALTON ATHLETIC	702	3-0	Gurney, Howells, Biggins
05/12/95	Herts SC	2	Barnet		0-3	
12/12/95	Herts CC	SF	BOREHAM WOOD	85	2-0	
16/12/95	IFL	P	BROMLEY	485	5-0	Biggins(3), Howell, Clark
19/12/95	IFL	P	Hayes	238	0-0	
23/12/95	IFL	P	Yeading	245	1-2	Clarke
01/01/96	IFL	P	Carshalton Athletic	603	1-1	Coleman
06/01/96	IFL	P	HARROW BOROUGH	620	0-2	
09/01/96	IFL	P	Aylesbury United	421	1-1	Clark
13/01/96	IFL	P	WORTHING	503	2-0	Coleman, Biggins
20/01/96	FA Trophy	1	Kettering Town	1577	1-1	Clark
23/01/96	FA Trophy	1 rep	KETTERING TOWN	705	2-3	Howell, Gurney
30/01/96	E. Anglian	2	Harpenden Town	65	2-1	
03/02/96	IFL	P	Hendon	357	2-1	Clark, Blake
10/02/96	IFL	P	WALTON & HERSHAM	454	3-0	Clark, Peters(2)
12/02/96	IFL	P	Purfleet	163	1-0	Clark
14/02/96	E. F'lit	Gp 2	CHELMSFORD CITY		0-2	
17/02/96	IFL	P	Sutton United	640	1-0	Blake
24/02/96	IFL	P	Chertsey Town	418	2-1	Peters, Clark
26/02/96	E. Anglian	3	BARKING	78	1-0	
28/02/96	IFL	P	Molesey	190	1-1	Blake
02/03/96	IFL	P	HITCHIN TOWN	626	5-1	Blake(2), Biggins, Gurney(2)
06/03/96	E. F'lit	Gp 2	Chelmsford City		3-3-	
09/03/96	IFL	P	Yeovil Town	2758	1-1	Cockram
12/03/96	IFL	P	DULWICH HAMLET	751	4-1	Cockram, Biggins, Blackman, Clark
16/03/96	IFL	P	HAYES	765	0-3	
19/03/96	IFL	P	KINGSTONIAN	469	1-2	Biggins
23/03/96	IFL	P	Enfield	1006	2-2	Cockram, Peters
30/03/96	IFL	P	BISHOP'S STORTFORD	603	3-0	Cockram, Howell, Blake
02/04/96	IFL	P	BOREHAM WOOD	727	0-0	
06/04/96	E. Anglian	QF	SOHAM TOWN RANGERS	194	1-0	
08/04/96	IFL	P	Boreham Wood	821	0-2	
13/04/96	IFL	P	GRAYS ATHLETIC	441	1-1	Peters
16/04/96	IFL	P	Bromley	298	0-1	
18/04/96	E. Anglian	SF	Braintree Town	152	0-2	
20/04/96	IFL	P	Kingstonian	501	1-4	Peters
27/04/96	IFL	P	MOLESEY	378	1-0	Martin
10/08/96	Herts CC	F	STEVENAGE BOROUGH		2-4	

STAINES TOWN

FIRST TEAM Chertsey Town FC, Alwyns Lane, Chertsey.

Please see Chertsey FC for information

RESERVES, YOUTHS AND FRIENDLIES
at Wheatsheaf Ground until further notice

DIRECTIONS
As Chertsey Town (see page 676).

Secretary Steve Parsons 3 Birch Green, Staines, Middx TW18 4HA Tel: 01784 450420

Prog Co-Editor: Stuart Moore 42 Cranford Ave,Stanwell, Middx TW19 7AH

Match Sec: Mick Burrell 39 Newtown Rd New Denham, Assis Sec: Paul Carter, 69 Conway Rd, Hounslow, Middx

Nickname: The Swans, Colours: All White

Seating, Covered standing, Clubhouse on ground
all as Chertsey Town FC

Record attendance: 2,750 v Banco Di Roma in
Barrasi Cup, 1975

Biggest win: 14-0 v Croydon (A) Isthmian League Div 1 March 19th 1994

Biggest defeat: 1-18 v Wycombe Wanderers (A) GWS League Dec 27th 1909

Record appearances: Dickie Watmore 840

Record goalscorer in one season.: Alex Garland 50+

Record goalscorer in total..Alan Gregory 122 or possibly Neville Warner

Record fee paid: Undisclosed for Richard Teale from Slough Town

Record fee received: Undisclosed for Scott Taylor to Millwall

Honours

Isthmian League Div 1 1975, 1989 and Div 2 1975

Athenian League Div 2 1972, Spartan League 1960, Spartan League Cup 1969

Great Western Sub League Div 2 1921, West London Alliance Div 1 1900

West London League Div 1 1901, West Middlesex League 1905

Middlesex Senior Cup 1975, 1976, 1977, 1988, 1990, 1995

Middlesex Senior Charity Cup 1995, Middlesex Junior Cup 1901 and 1904, Barrassi Cup 1976

Southern Combination Cup 1965, 1967, 1969, 1995, West Middlesex Cup 1924

Staines Cottage Hospital Cup 1925, Middlesex/Merthyr Charity Shield 1991

Isthmian League Full Members Cup 1995

Manager for 1996-97: Chris Wainwright, Assistant manager: Keith Bristow

Chairman: Alan Boon, Vice Chairman: Ken Williams

The origins of the club are very difficult to unravel, with a number of clubs, namely St Peter's Institute, Staines FC, Staines Albany, Staines Lagonda, and Staines Lammas all prominent at one time or another. It is known that the Institute played at Edgell Road, near the church, with at the turn of the century Staines FC using the Lammas, sometimes known as Ashby Recreation Ground, in Wraysbury Road. There was possibly another ground, near Shortwood Common, but between the Wars they had a ground in Mill Mead, near the Lino Sports Ground. Despite sharing with Staines Athletic for a while in the early 30's the rent proved too much and the stand was sold and the ground was lost. In 1951, Wheatsheaf Park was opened which has remained home ever since.

Several local leagues have been competed for, including the West London Alliance, West Middlesex League, and Great Western Suburban League, where the best finish was runner up in 1912, but just prior to the Great War they moved to the Western Combination. The Projectile and Lagonda clubs used different works leagues during the War, but after Lagonda played in the Hounslow and District before reverting to the Great Western Suburban League and later Spartan League, as Staines Town. In 1942 Staines Vale, the new name for the amalgamation of Town with a number of junior clubs, played in the Middlesex Senior League which became the Parthenon and two years later they were founder members of the Hellenic League, where they finished second in 1956. After a further two years, Town, as they were then called, joined the Spartan League, winning that in 1960 after 11 years the club advanced again, this time to

the Athenian League, winning Division Two at the first attempt with a record points tally. Election to the Isthmian League came next, where they were champions of Division One. During the last few years the club has gone up and down, but 1996 saw them return to the top after finishing third behind Oxford City and Heybridge Swifts. This season will see them ground share with Chertsey Town as the Wheatsheaf Ground receives a well deserved overhaul..

STAINES TOWN 1995/96 SEASON

12/08/95	IFL	1	Basingstoke Town	0-5	
19/08/95	IFL	1	WHYTELEAFE	2-2	
26/08/95	IFL	1	Billericay Town	1-2	
02/09/95	IFL	1	BARKING	2-2	
05/09/95	GIC	1	OXFORD CITY	3-1	
09/09/95	FA Cup	Q1	Hampton	2-1	
13/09/95	IFL	1	Chesham United	0-2	
16/09/95	IFL	1	ALDERSHOT TOWN	3-2	
23/09/95	FA Cup	Q2	Boreham Wood	1-0	Wheatley
30/09/95	IFL	1	Bognor Regis Town	1-3	Williams
07/10/95	FA Cup	Q3	Stevenage Borough	0-2	
10/10/95	IFL	1	RUISLIP MANOR	3-3	Anderson, Beeks, O'Shea
14/10/95	FA Trophy	Q1	WOKINGHAM TOWN	2-1	Bygrave, Beeks
17/10/95	IFL	1	Leyton Pennant	3-1	Lucas, O'Shea, Grainger
21/10/95	IFL	1	MAIDENHEAD UNITED	2-1	Beeks, Williams
28/10/95	IFL	1	Thame United	2-1	Anderson, Grainger
31/10/95	GIC	2	Bishop's Stortford	1-3	
04/11/95	FA Trophy	Q2	HAVANT TOWN	3-1	Reilly, Williams, Grainger
11/11/95	IFL	1	Marlow	3-2	Grainger, Evans, Reilly
14/11/95	S Comb Cup	1	Croydon Athletic	0-2	
18/11/95	IFL	1	OXFORD CITY	0-2	
21/11/95	CC	1	WALTON & HERSHAM	0-1	
25/11/95	FA Trophy	Q3	Molesey	2-2	Reilly, Grainger
28/11/95	FA Trophy	Q3 rep	MOLESEY	5-0	Beeks(3), Williams(2)
02/12/95	IFL	1	BERKHAMSTED TOWN	2-1	Grainger, Williams
09/12/95	IFL	1	Wembley	1-0	Beeks
16/12/95	IFL	1	UXBRIDGE	3-1	Anderson(2), Livey
02/01/96	IFL	1	Tooting & Mitcham United	1-1	Anderson
06/01/96	IFL	1	BASINGSTOKE TOWN	3-1	Evans(2), Beeks
09/01/96	Middx SC	2	RUISLIP MANOR	1-0	
13/01/96	IFL	1	CHESHAM UNITED	3-3	Evans(2), Beeks
16/01/96	IFL	1	BARTON ROVERS	3-2	McNally(og), Beeks, Anderson
20/01/96	FA Trophy	1	Gloucester City	0-5	
25/01/96	Middx CC	3	EDGWARE TOWN	0-0	
30/01/96	IFL	1	ABINGDON TOWN	6-0	Evans, Beeks(2), Williams(2), Anderson
03/02/96	IFL	1	Ruislip Manor	2-0	Evans(2)
06/02/96	IFL	1	Heybridge Swifts	0-3	
13/02/96	Middx SC	QF	Enfield	2-3	
17/02/96	IFL	1	Aldershot Town	3-3	Grainger, Beeks, Walters
24/02/96	IFL	1	THAME UNITED	1-1	Evans
02/03/96	IFL	1	Maidenhead United	0-1	
09/03/96	IFL	1	LEYTON PENNANT	1-2	P Lucas
16/03/96	IFL	1	Abingdon Town	2-0	Evans, O'Shea
19/03/96	IFL	1	WOKINGHAM TOWN	2-1	Williams, Evans
23/03/96	IFL	1	MARLOW	3-1	Anderson, Livey, Evans
26/03/96	IFL	1	Barking	2-1	Gasson, Evans
30/03/96	IFL	1	Barton Rovers	2-0	Gasson, Grainger
02/04/96	IFL	1	BILLERICAY TOWN	4-1	Evans, Beeks, Grainger, Anderson
06/04/96	IFL	1	TOOTING & MITCHAM UNI	2-1	Beeks(2)
08/04/96	IFL	1	Wokingham Town	3-0	Livey, Evans, Grainger
13/04/96	IFL	1	HEYBRIDGE SWIFTS	2-2	Beeks(2)
16/04/96	IFL	1	Whyteleafe	2-0	Beeks, Evans
20/04/96	IFL	1	Berkhamsted Town	2-1	Casson, Bartlett(og)
23/04/96	IFL	1	Oxford City	1-1	Gasson
27/04/96	IFL	1	WEMBLEY	1-0	Anderson
30/04/96	IFL	1	BOGNOR REGIS TOWN	2-2	Beeks, Pentland
02/05/96	Middx CC	SF	HAMPTON	2-3	
04/05/96	IFL	1	Uxbridge	1-1	

SUTTON UNITED

Borough Sports Ground, Gander Green Lane, Sutton, Surrey SM1 2EY.,Tel: 0181 644 5120/ 4440
Secretary: Brian Williams, 49 Panmure Rd, Sydenham,
London Tel 0181 699 2721 (h) 0181 644 5120 (b)
Press Sec: Tony Dolbear, 81 The Drive, Beckenham, Kent
BR3 1EF Tel: 0171 782 8644 (b)

Nickname: The U's   Colours: Amber and Chocolate
Capacity: 6,200   Seating: 800
Covered standing: 1,000   Clubhouse on ground: Yes
Record attendance: 14,000 v Leeds Utd
FA Cup 4th Rd Jan 21st 1970
Biggest win: 11-1 v Clapton 1966 and Leatherhead 1982
Biggest defeat: 0-13 v Barking 1925
Record appearances: Larry Pritchard 781
Record goalscorer in one season: Charlie Vaughan 68
Record goalscorer in total: Paul McKinnon 279
Record fee received: £100,000 for Efan Ekoku

DIRECTIONS

Gander Green Lane runs
between A232 (Cheam Road -
turn by Sutton Cricket Club)
and A217 (Oldfields Road - turn
at 'Gander' PH lights). Ground
opposite 'The Plough' 50 yards
from West Sutton BR station.
Bus 413 passes ground.

Honours

FA TROPHY runners up 1981, FA AMATEUR CUP runners up 1963 and 1969
Isthmian League 1967, 1985, 1986, League Cup 1983, 1984, 1986
Loctite Cup 1992, Carlton Cup 1996, Athenian League 1928, 46, 58, League Cup 1946, 56, 62, 63
Anglo-Italian Semi-Pro Cup 1979, London Senior Cup 1958 & 1982
London Charity Cup 1970,
Surrey Senior Cup 1946, 65, 68, 70, 80, 83, 84, 85, 86, 87, 88, 93,
Surrey Senior Charity Shield 1934, 1937, 1938
Surrey Intermediate Charity Shield 1932, Dylon Charity Shield 1984, Bob Lord Trophy 1991

Manager for 1996-97: John Rains, Assistant manager: Tony Rains, Chairman: Bruce Elliiott
Supporters magazine, Touchliner, price 50p is available from the club

Sutton United came into being in 1898 after a meeting held at the Robin Hood Hotel between two local clubs, Sutton
Association and Sutton Guild Rovers. The early years were chequered, and fluctuating fortunes were met in junior
leagues before the club earned senior status. The move to the Borough Sports Ground in Gander Green Lane, a gift to
the people of the town in 1913, helped cement the club's standing and in 1928 they won their first major honour, the
Athenian League.The 1930's were difficult times and Sutton's future was threatened at one time, but a door to door
collection helped pull them back from the brink of extinction, and from there they grew again in stature. Either side of
the Second War, the U's were one of the top amateur sides in the country, winning the Athenian League again in 1946
and finishing second twelve months later. There was then little success until the late 50's when a third title was
coupled with their first ever London Senior Cup in 1958. George Smith arrived as manager, followed by Sid
Cann, and this led to the first ever appearance at Wembley, when they lost to Wimbledon in the Amateur Cup Final.
Also that year, the U's moved up to the Isthmian League, winning it in 1967 and finishing runners up a year later.
1969 saw another final at Wembley, where sadly they again lost, this time to North Shields. It set the club for their
famous FA Cup run to the 4th Round, where they played Leeds United at Gander Green Lane When that side broke up
the club entered a quiet spell until 1977, when the appointment of Keith Blunt saw a new era. In 1979 Sutton were the
first and only winners of the Anglo-Italian semi-pro tournament and in 1981 they reached Wembley for the third time,
this time in the FA Trophy, where a late Bishop's Stortford goal again beat them. Barrie Williams eventually took over
and he led the side through another famous period, where they set a record by winning the Surrey Senior Cup six
years on the trot as well as taking the league in 1985 and 1986. Having turned it down once, they opted to go into the
Vauxhall Conference, from where they earned a reputation as Cup fighters, for in 1987-88 they beat Aldershot and
Peterborough United, and a year later wins over Dagenham and Aylesbury saw them in the 3rd Round, where a
Matthew Hanlon goal famously beat Coventry City. A year later Sutton lost their Conference place despite winning the
League Cup, and were relegated for the first time in their history, but in the first season back in the Isthmian League
they won the Loctite Cup and were third in the league. 1993 saw the Surrey Senior Cup arrive again as Sutton
continued in the Isthmian League.

FORMER GROUNDS

Sutton Association played on a pitch at Western Road, whilst Guild Rovers played at Manor Lane. Both grounds were retained which enabled them to field two sides, but this lasted one season as Western Road was not available. Manor Lane was home until moves to Rose Hill, Fairfield in Collingham and London Road, prior to using a ground called `The Find', in Grove Road. The Adult School Sports Ground had been opened in 1912, used by the school themselves, but after the Great War Sutton moved in to what is now known as the Borough Sports Ground.

SUTTON UNITED 1995/96 SEASON

Date	Comp	Rnd	Opponent	Att	Score	Scorers
19/08/95	IFL	P	Bishop's Stortford	384	3-1	Feltham(2), Vansittart
22/08/95	IFL	P	ENFIELD	613	2-4	Feltham, Dennis
26/08/95	IFL	P	HAYES	611	2-2	Feltham(2)
29/08/95	IFL	P	Chertsey Town	638	1-1	Vansittart
02/09/95	IFL	P	Boreham Wood	427	1-0	Golley
05/09/95	GIC	1	TRING TOWN	263	2-0	Shepherd, Lempierre
09/09/95	IFL	P	KINGSTONIAN	944	0-1	
16/09/95	IFL	P	St Albans City	651	2-2	Vansittart(2)
23/09/95	IFL	P	Kingstonian	747	2-2	Vansittart, Feltham
30/09/95	IFL	P	AYLESBURY UNITED	653	2-3	Vansittart, Hynes
07/10/95	IFL	P	Worthing	575	2-5	Vansittart, Feltham
10/10/95	IFL	P	Hendon	275	4-0	Costello, Vansittart, Payne(2)
14/10/95	IFL	P	Yeading	260	2-2	Feltham, Vansittart
21/10/95	FA Cup	Q4	CRAWLEY TOWN	1637	4-1	Hynes(2), Feltham(2)
24/10/95	IFL	P	HARROW BOROUGH	452	4-0	Feltham(2), Hynes, Vansittart
28/10/95	IFL	P	Walton & Hersham	445	1-1	Feltham
31/10/95	GIC	2	HITCHIN TOWN	229	0-1	
04/11/95	IFL	P	DULWICH HAMLET	697	1-1	Watson
11/11/95	FA Cup	1	Kidderminster Harriers	2513	2-2	Hynes, Vansittart
18/11/95	IFL	P	MOLESEY	494	2-0	Hynes, Dack
21/11/95	FA Cup	1 rep	KIDDERMIN HARRIERS	1804	1-1	Payne (won on penalties)
25/11/95	FA Trophy	Q3	TROWBRIDGE TOWN	612	0-1	
02/12/95	FA Cup	2	Hereford United	2908	0-2	
12/12/95	Surrey SC	1	Tooting & Mitcham United	132	1-2	Payne
16/12/95	IFL	P	GRAYS ATHLETIC	392	0-0	
19/12/95	CC	2	ABINGDON TOWN	166	3-0	Hynes, Payne, Watson
02/01/96	IFL	P	Hitchin Town	303	0-1	
06/01/96	IFL	P	BOREHAM WOOD	521	0-3	
09/01/96	CC	3	Tooting & Mitcham United	201	3-1	Dack, Feltham, Own-Goal
13/01/96	IFL	P	Enfield	823	2-0	Hynes, Feltham
17/01/96	IFL	P	Molesey	275	5-0	Dennis, Feltham, Hynes, Green, Dack
20/01/96	IFL	P	BISHOP'S STORTFORD	469	2-1	Hynes, Payne
30/01/96	IFL	P	PURFLEET	334	1-0	Hynes
03/02/96	IFL	P	CHERTSEY TOWN	512	2-1	Golley, Feltham
10/02/96	IFL	P	Aylesbury United	606	1-4	Hynes
17/02/96	IFL	P	ST ALBANS CITY	640	0-1	
21/02/96	CC	QF	Bognor Regis Town	280	2-1	Dennis, Hynes
24/02/96	IFL	P	WALTON & HERSHAM	483	2-1	Hynes(2)
27/02/96	IFL	P	YEOVIL TOWN	537	1-1	Green
02/03/96	IFL	P	Harrow Borough	339	0-0	
05/03/96	IFL	P	Bromley	361	3-2	Dennis, Hynes, Dack
09/03/96	IFL	P	HENDON	529	2-3	Feltham, Hynes
12/03/96	IFL	P	CARSHALTON ATHLETIC	784	2-1	Watson, Hynes
16/03/96	IFL	P	Purfleet	262	1-2	Golley
23/03/96	IFL	P	WORTHING	461	3-1	Feltham(2), Dack
26/03/96	CC	SF	CARSHALTON ATHLETIC	719	1-1	Feltham
30/03/96	IFL	P	Dulwich Hamlet	559	2-2	Hynes, Feltham
01/04/96	CC	SF rep	Carshalton Athletic	565	4-1	Hynes(2), Costello, Feltham
06/04/96	IFL	P	HITCHIN TOWN	490	4-0	Feltham, Payne(2), Bone(og)
08/04/96	IFL	P	Carshalton Athletic	794	2-1	Dack(2)
13/04/96	IFL	P	BROMLEY	627	1-3	Feltham
16/04/96	IFL	P	Hayes	516	0-0	
20/04/96	IFL	P	Yeovil Town	2818	0-0	
27/04/96	IFL	P	YEADING	455	2-2	Feltham, Hynes
04/05/96	IFL	P	Grays Athletic	318	2-1	Vansittart, Hynes
07/05/96	CC	F	Boreham Wood	612	2-2	Dack, Green (at Purfleet. Won on penalties)

YEADING

The Warren, Beaconsfield Rd, Hayes, Middx. Tel: 0181 848 7362/7369 Fax: 0181 561 2222

Secretary: Peter Bickers, 140 Hercies Rd, Hillingdon, Middx Tel UB10 9ND Tel 01895 811061

Colours: Red and Black stripes   Nickname: The Dinc

Capacity: 3,500   Seating: 250

Covered standing: 1,500   Clubhouse on ground: Yes

Record attend: 3,000 v Hythe Tn FA Vase semi-final 1990

Record appearance holder.: Norman Frape

Record goalscorer in total: Dave Burt 327

Record fee received £45,000 for Andrew Impey to QPR

DIRECTIONS

Two miles from Hayes (BR) - take Uxbridge Road and turn right towards Southall, right into Springfield Road and then left into Beaconsfield Road. Bus 207 stops half mile from ground.

Honours

FA VASE WINNERS 1990

Isthmian League Div 2 South 1990

Spartan League 1987

League Cup: 1986 and 1987

Middlesex Senior League 1972, 1973, 1975, 1976, 1982, 1984

League Cup 1973, 1976, 1980, 1981, 1982, 1983, South West Middlesex League 1970 and 1971

Middlesex Senior Cup 1990 and 1992, Middlesex Premier Cup 1981

Middlesex Intermediate Cup 1971, 72, 75, 76, 78, Middlesex Junior Cup 1969, 71, 72, 75

Uxbridge League 1967

Originally formed in the late 1950's as Yeading Youth Club, they became Yeading FC in 1965. The early days were spent in the now extinct Hayes and District Youth League and the old Uxbridge League.

They left the Uxbridge League as champions in 1967 to join the South West Middlesex League which they twice won, also taking the coveted Middlesex Junior Cup for the first time.

In 1971 they won both the Junior and Intermediate Cups, the first of five times that they won the latter.

In 1973 the two sides did a clean sweep of all four trophies in the Middlesex League and in all won the League and League Cup six times each. Another landmark was winning the first ever Premier Cup in 1981 and in 1984, after moving in to their long awaited new home, they were given senior status and joined the Spartan League, winning promotion immediately.

Yeading continued their march and were unbeaten league and Cup double winners a year later, the first in the league history. It was rounded off by the club entering the Isthmian League for the 1987-88 season. The first two seasons were quiet, but in 1990 after an epic run, the club reached the final of the FA Vase at Wembley. The 0-0 scoreline meant a replay at Elland Road, where they beat Bridlington 1-0. It rounded off another magnificent season in which they took the Division Two South title and reached the final of the Senior Cup.

1991 saw another near miss in the Senior Cup, losing the final to Enfield but a year later Yeading became the first club to take all four County Cups at junior and senior level when they won the Senior Cup after beating Wembley. By then promotion had been secured to the Premier Division and although the first two seasons were a struggle, Yeading are immensely proud of their history.

YEADING 1995/96 SEASON

Date	Comp	Round	Opponent	Att	Score	Scorers
12/08/95	IFL	P	CHERTSEY TOWN	356	1-3	Dicker
19/08/95	IFL	P	Boreham Wood	245	1-1	Bowder
22/08/95	IFL	P	CARSHALTON ATHLETIC	170	1-3	McGrath
26/08/95	IFL	P	HITCHIN TOWN	160	2-0	Cordery, Graham
29/08/95	IFL	P	Grays Athletic	167	0-0	
02/09/95	IFL	P	St Albans City	456	1-0	Bowder
05/09/95	GIC	1	BOGNOR REGIS TOWN		0-3	
09/09/95	IFL	P	ENFIELD	432	1-1	Graham
16/09/95	IFL	P	Aylesbury United	875	1-1	Graham
30/09/95	IFL	P	KINGSTONIAN	281	0-2	
07/10/95	IFL	P	Yeovil Town	1281	0-2	
10/10/95	IFL	P	HARROW BOROUGH	189	1-2	Gell
14/10/95	IFL	P	SUTTON UNITED	260	2-2	McGrath(2)
17/10/95	IFL	P	PURFLEET	110	3-1	Evans, Horne(og), Wallace
21/10/95	FA Cup	Q4	SLOUGH TOWN	473	0-2	
28/10/95	IFL	P	Hayes	437	0-0	
04/11/95	IFL	P	MOLESEY	155	2-2	Gell, Cordery
07/11/95	CC	1	Berkhamsted Town		3-0	
11/11/95	IFL	P	Bromley	285	0-1	
18/11/95	IFL	P	Worthing	210	1-2	Graham
25/11/95	FA Trophy	Q3	Chelmsford City	828	1-2	Graham
02/12/95	IFL	P	Dulwich Hamlet	289	0-3	
16/12/95	IFL	P	Bishop's Stortford	202	1-3	Gell
19/12/95	CC	2	Enfield		2-1	
23/12/95	IFL	P	ST ALBANS CITY	245	2-1	Houghton, Carter
26/12/95	IFL	P	Hendon	241	1-1	Gell
06/01/96	IFL	P	Chertsey Town	342	1-1	McGrath
09/01/96	Middx SC	2	Uxbridge	98	1-2	
13/01/96	IFL	P	Carshalton Athletic	372	0-2	
16/01/96	CC	3	BISHOP'S STORTFORD	71	0-1	
20/01/96	IFL	P	WORTHING	120	1-0	Fitzgerald
03/02/96	IFL	P	GRAYS ATHLETIC	104	0-1	
10/02/96	IFL	P	Kingstonian	419	1-3	McGrath
17/02/96	IFL	P	AYLESBURY UNITED	181	0-0	
24/02/96	IFL	P	HAYES	403	0-1	
02/03/96	IFL	P	Purfleet	123	2-1	Allen(2)
09/03/96	IFL	P	Harrow Borough	256	1-4	Ripley
16/03/96	IFL	P	YEOVIL TOWN	403	1-1	Ripley
23/03/96	IFL	P	BROMLEY	183	3-0	Kellman, Carter, Ripley
30/03/96	IFL	P	Molesey	110	2-1	Carter, Roddis
02/04/96	IFL	P	HENDON	202	0-0	
06/04/96	IFL	P	Enfield	806	0-2	
10/04/96	IFL	P	BOREHAM WOOD	262	0-3	
13/04/96	IFL	P	Walton & Hersham	185	0-0	
16/04/96	IFL	P	Hitchin Town	201	3-0	Kellman, Gell, Carter
20/04/96	IFL	P	DULWICH HAMLET	260	5-3	Roddis(2), Kellman(2), Graham
23/04/96	IFL	P	WALTON & HERSHAM	136	3-0	Witter, Kellman(2)
27/04/96	IFL	P	Sutton United	455	2-2	Graham, Witter
04/05/96	IFL	P	BISHOP'S STORTFORD	148	2-4	Sewell, Kellman

YEOVIL TOWN

Huish Park, Lufton Way, Yeovil, Somerset BA22 8YF. Tel: 01935 23662 fax: 01935 73956

Secretary: Jean Cottam c/o Football Club

Colours: Green and White   Nickname: The Glovers

Capacity: 8,720   Seating: 5,212

Covered standing: None

Record attendance: 8,612 v Arsenal
FA Cup 3rd Round Jan 2nd 1993

old ground, 17,200 v Sunderland FA Cup 4th Round 1949

Record appearance holder: L.Harris

Record goalscorer in total: Dave Taylor 285 1960-69

Record fee paid £15,000 for Joe Jackson
from Worcester City in 1990

Record fee received £75,000 for Mark Shail to Bristol City

DIRECTIONS

Directions: Leave A303 at Cartgate roundabout and take A3088 signposted Yeovil. Take first exit at next roundabout and first exit again at next roundabout into Lufton Way. Railway Station — Yeovil Pen Mill (Bristol. Westbury to Weymouth) 2.5 miles from ground. Yeovil Junction (Waterloo — Exeter — 4 miles). Bus service — from both stations on Saturday — matchdays.

Honours

Southern League 1955, 1964, 1971, Southern League Cup 1949, 1955, 1961, 1966

Isthmian League 1988, Isthmian League Cup 1988

Bob Lord Trophy 1990

Manager for 1996-97: Graham Roberts

Originally founded in 1897 as Yeovil Casuals, they played on a ground at Pen Mill, between the hotel and the station, taking the name Town in 1908. Petters Utd were also founded around this time, playing in Brickyard Lane, and the two clubs merged in 1914. After the War, Pen Mill continued in use, with its 300 seater stand, the players changing in the hotel, but a second attempt to buy the Huish Athletic Ground was successful and they moved in, along with their stand, in 1920.

The club joined the Southern League in 1922, where apart from a brief spell in the Western League, they remained until 1979. 1924, 1932 and 1935 saw the club finish runners up but it was not until after the War that success came with a vengeance, the Southern League Cup being won in 1948, and as Yeovil Town again, they embarked on the now world famous FA Cup run which saw them beat Sunderland at the Huish in front of 17,200 in the 4th Round. The 5th Round saw them lose at Old Trafford in front of 81,565 people. Since then the Glovers have reached the First Round over 40 times.

The Southern League championship and Cup double followed in 1955, with further cup wins in 1961 and 1966, and the title was won again in 1965 and 1971. Yeovil entered the Alliance Premier League in 1979 where they found life difficult. After a six year spell they were relegated to the Isthmian League, where they were runners-up two years running, doing the league and cup double a year later, 1988.

Returning to what was then called the GM Vauxhall Conference, Yeovil finished fourth in 1993 but after skirting relegation three years ago, they went down again to the Isthmian League, where they remain.

Yeovil Town's former Huish ground was possibly the most famous non-League ground in the country, with its sloping pitch and splendid facilities, and it was an emotional time when it was sold for a Tesco supermarket, and the club moved to the newly built Huish Park in 1990.

YEOVIL TOWN 1995/96 SEASON

19/08/95	IFL	P	Aylesbury United	812	1-3	St Hilaire
26/08/95	IFL	P	GRAYS ATHLETIC	1668	1-0	St Hilaire
28/08/95	IFL	P	WALTON & HERSHAM	1530	4-1	Patmore(4)
02/09/95	IFL	P	Chertsey Town	766	3-1	St Hilaire(3)
05/09/95	GIC	1	HENDON	1092	1-3	Groves
09/09/95	IFL	P	HITCHIN TOWN	1739	1-1	Patmore
16/09/95	IFL	P	Kingstonian	642	2-2	Engwell, St Hilaire
23/09/95	IFL	P	BISHOP'S STORTFORD	1629	1-3	Whale
25/09/95	IFL	P	Carshalton Athletic	641	1-2	St Hilaire
30/09/95	IFL	P	BOREHAM WOOD	1283	0-1	
07/10/95	IFL	P	YEADING	1281	2-0	Patmore, Whale
14/10/95	IFL	P	St Albans City	853	2-2	Browne, Patmore
17/10/95	Som. PC	1	Chard Town	495	2-0	Burton, Patmore
21/10/95	FA Cup	Q4	Farnborough Town	1409	1-2	Patmore
28/10/95	IFL	P	Bromley	357	5-1	Patmore(2), Dillon, St Hilaire, Burton
04/11/95	IFL	P	WORTHING	1602	3-1	Grazioli, Patmore, Dillon
11/11/95	IFL	P	Molesey	300	3-2	Seymour, Grazioli(2)
15/11/95	Som. PC	2	Brislington	175	1-2	Doherty
18/11/95	IFL	P	Purfleet	302	3-0	Grazioli(2), Patmore
21/11/95	CC	1	Chertsey Town	215	2-0	Patmore, Grazioli
25/11/95	IFL	P	DULWICH HAMLET	1960	5-3	Patmore(2), Kemp, Grazioli, Browne
09/12/95	IFL	P	HAYES	2025	3-0	Grazioli(2), Seymour
16/12/95	IFL	P	Enfield	1177	1-2	Patmore
23/12/95	IFL	P	CHERTSEY TOWN	2417	1-0	Burton
26/12/95	IFL	P	Worthing	561	2-3	Grazioli, Patmore
01/01/96	IFL	P	HENDON	2306	4-1	Grazioli(2), St Hilaire, Patmore
06/01/96	IFL	P	Bishop's Stortford	466	2-2	Grazioli(2)
08/01/96	CC	2	Carshalton Athletic	346	1-2	Birkby
13/01/96	IFL	P	Hitchin Town	523	2-1	Grazioli(2)
21/01/96	FA Trophy	1	Bath City	2225	1-1	Patmore
23/01/96	FA Trophy	1 rep	BATH CITY	2731	2-3	Whale(2)
03/02/96	IFL	P	CARSHALTON ATHLETIC	1920	2-1	Whale, Birkby
10/02/96	IFL	P	HARROW BOROUGH	1942	0-0	
17/02/96	IFL	P	KINGSTONIAN	1953	1-1	Birkby
24/02/96	IFL	P	BROMLEY	1869	4-3	Braybrook, Whale, St Hilaire, Patmore
27/02/96	IFL	P	Sutton United	537	1-1	Whale
02/03/96	IFL	P	Walton & Hersham	406	3-1	Engwell, Seymour, Birkby
09/03/96	IFL	P	ST ALBANS CITY	2758	1-1	Seymour
16/03/96	IFL	P	Yeading	403	1-1	Whale
23/03/96	IFL	P	MOLESEY	1870	3-2	Patmore(2), St Hilaire
26/03/96	IFL	P	Grays Athletic	251	2-0	Alexander(og), Birkby
30/03/96	IFL	P	Harrow Borough	489	1-0	Patmore
02/04/96	IFL	P	PURFLEET	2267	2-1	Patmore, Birkby
06/04/96	IFL	P	Hendon	443	3-1	Nugent, Patmore(2)
13/04/96	IFL	P	Dulwich Hamlet	1289	1-2	Birkby
16/04/96	IFL	P	AYLESBURY UNITED	2008	3-2	Lynch, Birkby, Laidlaw
20/04/96	IFL	P	SUTTON UNITED	2818	0-0	
27/04/96	IFL	P	Hayes	1537	1-1	Roberts
30/04/96	IFL	P	Boreham Wood	784	2-0	Stein(og), Laidlaw
04/05/96	IFL	P	ENFIELD	3804	0-1	

Above: Barton Rovers F.C.
Below: Hampton F.C.

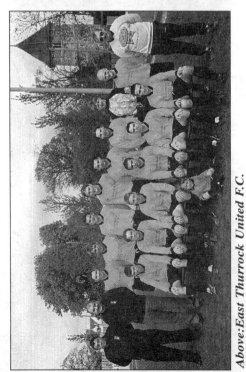

Above: East Thurrock United F.C.
Below: Braintree Town F.C.

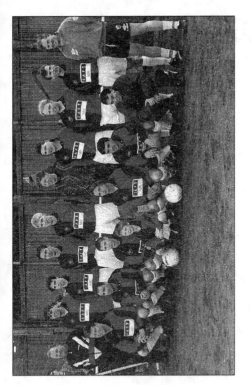

Above: Harrow Borough F.C.
Below: Bracknell Town F.C.

Below: Heybridge Swifts celebrate

ABINGDON TOWN

Culham Road, Abingdon OX14 3BT Tel 01235 555566 bdroom and press box 521684 ground

Secretary: Ted Quail, 107 Park Lane, Thatcham, Berks RG18 3BZ Tel 01635 868967

Colours: Yellow and Green Nickname: Over The Bridge

Capacity: 3,000   Seating: Yes

Covered standing: Yes   Clubhouse on ground: Yes

DIRECTIONS
On A415 road to Dorchester-on-Thames half a mile south of town centre. Nearest rail stations is Culham. Main line: Didcot Parkway or Oxford. Bus service from Didcot and London.

Record Attendance: 1,400 v Oxford City FA Cup 2nd Qual Rd Replay 1960 in modern times although crowds of several thousand were common in the 20's and 30's

Record appearance holder: John Harvey-Lynch

Honours

Berks and Bucks Senior Cup 1959

Isthmian League Div 2 South 1991

London Spartan League 1989

Hellenic League 1957, 1959, 1960, 1987, League Cup 1958, 1971, 1982

Division One and Div One League Cup 1976, Oxford and District League 1899, 1900, 1901

Reading and District League 1948, Berks and Bucks Junior Cup 1907

Abingdon Centenary Cup 1959, Joan Lee Memorial Cup 1970, 1971, 1987

Town were formed in 1870 and are one of the oldest clubs in the country, being second oldest within the Berks and Bucks FA. In the early years, only friendly matches were played but before the turn of the century they joined the Oxford and District League. In 1899 they amalgamated with local side St Michael's and the Town suffix was dropped, not to reappear until 1920. At this time Leagues were changed quickly and before 1910, The Berks and Bucks, West Berkshire and Reading Temperance Leagues had all been competed for. In 1909 the club moved to the new North Berks League, staying until the late 1920's when moving to the Reading and District League. In the 1930's the club purchased the Culham Road ground for £300 from the Morrell Brewing family. The ground already had a stand, built in 1928, but it was burned down soon after the war and a replacement built. In 1950 after some success post-War, they joined the Spartan League, but success did not come and so in 1953 they became founder members of the Hellenic League. The late 50's brought three titles and a League Cup as well as a win in the Berks and Bucks Cup over Aylesbury Utd in 1959. In all the club spent 35 years in the Hellenic League, being relegated twice but bouncing back each time. They switched to the Isthmian side of the pyramid by playing a year in the Spartan League, taking the title and gaining promotion to the Isthmians.

They took the Division Two South title in the first year and remain in Division One where they just avoided relegation last May.

ABINGDON TOWN 1995/96 SEASON

Date	Comp	Rnd	Opponent	Score	Scorers
19/08/95	IFL	1	ALDERSHOT TOWN	1-2	
21/08/95	IFL	1	Ruislip Manor	0-1	
26/08/95	FA Cup	P	ANDOVER	3-2	
30/08/95	IFL	1	WHYTELEAFE	1-3	McNamara
02/09/95	IFL	1	MARLOW	3-4	
05/09/95	GIC	1	Kingstonian	1-2	
09/09/95	FA Cup	Q1	NEWPORT I.O.W.	2-3	Shepperd, Farrington
16/09/95	IFL	1	BOGNOR REGIS TOWN	1-2	
23/09/95	IFL	1	BARTON ROVERS	4-2	Lee(2), Shepherd, Giamattei
30/09/95	IFL	1	Billericay Town	3-1	Hickey, Forinton, Jenkins
07/10/95	IFL	1	Berkhamsted Town	2-4	Lee, Whitehead
10/10/95	IFL	1	Uxbridge	1-1	Forinton
14/10/95	FA Trophy	Q1	BISHOP'S STORTFORD	1-1	Harvey-Lynch
17/10/95	FA Trophy	Q1 rep	Bishop's Stortford	1-5	Whitehead
21/10/95	IFL	1	OXFORD CITY	4-2	Rayson(4)
24/10/95	IFL	1	Chesham United	0-4	
28/10/95	IFL	1	Leyton Pennant	2-0	Lee, Jenkins
11/11/95	IFL	1	Thame United	1-1	Lee
18/11/95	IFL	1	BERKHAMSTED TOWN	2-0	McCumce, Lee
25/11/95	IFL	1	Wokingham Town	4-3	Jenkins(3), Harvey-Lynch
02/12/95	IFL	1	WEMBLEY	0-2	
09/12/95	IFL	1	Heybridge Swifts	0-3	
16/12/95	IFL	1	BARKING	4-0	Rayson, Jenkins, Denton, Whitehead
19/12/95	CC	2	Sutton United	0-3	
23/12/95	IFL	1	Marlow	1-2	Denton
06/01/96	IFL	1	UXBRIDGE	0-2	
09/01/96	IFL	1	Basingstoke Town	0-0	
13/01/96	IFL	1	RUISLIP MANOR	2-2	Denton, Wood
20/01/96	IFL	1	Aldershot Town	1-5	Rayson
23/01/96	B&B SC	1	BUCKINGHAM TOWN	2-1	Thornton, Denton
30/01/96	IFL	1	Staines Town	0-6	
03/02/96	IFL	1	Whyteleafe	2-4	Harvey-Lynch, Denton
10/02/96	IFL	1	BILLERICAY TOWN	1-2	Rayson
17/02/96	IFL	1	Bognor Regis Town	0-2	
24/02/96	IFL	1	LEYTON PENNANT	2-2	McCance, Lee
02/03/96	IFL	1	Oxford City	3-3	Lee(2), Denton
06/03/96	IFL	1	CHESHAM UNITED	0-0	
09/03/96	IFL	1	Barton Rovers	1-0	Lee
16/03/96	IFL	1	STAINES TOWN	0-2	
23/03/96	IFL	1	THAME UNITED	1-2	Watts
30/03/96	IFL	1	Tooting & Mitcham United	0-1	
06/04/96	IFL	1	BASINGSTOKE TOWN	1-0	Dodds
08/04/96	IFL	1	Maidenhead United	0-4	
13/04/96	IFL	1	WOKINGHAM TOWN	3-1	Forinton(3)
17/04/96	IFL	1	TOOTING & MITCHAM UTD	2-1	Jenkins, Harvey-Lynch
20/04/96	IFL	1	Wembley	1-1	Denton
27/04/96	IFL	1	HEYBRIDGE SWIFTS	3-1	Jenkins(2), Rayson
01/05/96	IFL	1	MAIDENHEAD UNITED	1-1	Forinton
04/05/96	IFL	1	Barking	5-1	

ALDERSHOT TOWN

Recreation Ground, High Street, Aldershot, Hants. GU11 1TW Tel: 01252 20211

Secretary: Graham Brookland, c/o Football Club offices

Colours: Red and Blue   Capacity: 7,500

Seating: 1,800   Covered standing: 5,050

Clubhouse on ground: Yes

Record Attendance: 5,961 v Farnborough Town
Hants Senior Cup semi-final Mar 16th 1993

Ground Record, 19,138 Aldershot v Carlisle Utd
FA Cup 4th Rd Replay 1970

Biggest win: 7-0 Gosport Borough (H)
FA Vase Prel Rd Oct 2nd 1993

Biggest defeat: 1-5 Gloucester City FA Trophy 1995

Record appearances: Mark Butler 219

Record goalscorer in one season: Mark Butler 35 1993-94

Record goalscorer in total: Mark Butler 131

Record fee paid: £5,000 Paul Chambers from Basingstoke Town 1994

Record fee received: £3,000 Daren O'Neill from Kingstonian July 1994

Honours

Isthmian League Div 3 1993

Simpsonair Trophy 1993

Skol Invitation Trophy 1993

Manager for 1996-97: Steve Wigley, Assistant manager: Paul Shrubb, Chairman: Terry Owens

Press Officer: Nick Fryer, 23 Barnwood Close, Guildford, Surrey GU2 6GG Tel: 01483 244280

Aldershot Town FC Supporters Club issue a handbook each year and there is also available from the club "The Rise and Rise of Football in Aldershot" plus videos of the first four seasons.

Club phoneline: 0891 446834

Sponsors: DATRONTECH

> ### DIRECTIONS
> **Ground situated on eastern end of High Street next to large multi-storey B.T. building. From M3 (jct 4) take A325 to Aldershot. After five miles at roundabout take 1st exit marked town centre (A323) into Wellington Avenue. At Burger King roundabout take 2nd exit into High Street - ground on left, large car park adjacent. 5 mins walk from Aldershot (BR).**

Aldershot Town were formed from the ashes of the old Football League club in 1992 and in a short space of time have gained two promotions to reach Division One of the Isthmian League, only missing out two years ago on goal difference. The media attention which surrounded the sad demise of Aldershot FC turned to happier things as the new club arose. With the superb facilities at the Recreation Ground at their disposal, the Shots lifted the championship by 18 points, averaging over 2,000 to their home games where they were unbeaten. The biggest attendance was the 5,961 that watched the match with Conference neighbours Farnborough Town in the Hampshire Senior Cup semi-final. The success continued in 1993-94 when third place secured promotion to Division One. Attendances continued to impress with 4,000 reached three times and they also reached the quarter finals of the FA Vase, losing to Atherton LR after two replays. The club began 1994-95 by lifting the Arlington Gold Cup and made a solid start in the league only to lose out on goal difference on the last day. They entered the FA Cup and Trophy for the first time that season, and last May the club finished a slightly disappointing fifth in Division One, although they reached the League Cup final, losing to Kingstonian.

ALDERSHOT TOWN 1995/96 SEASON

Date	Comp	Rnd	Opponent	Att	Score	Scorers
12/08/95	IFL	1	HEYBRIDGE SWIFTS	1652	1-1	Butler
19/08/95	IFL	1	Abingdon Town	812	2-1	Young, Butler
26/08/95	FA Cup	P	SELSEY	1644	5-0	Young, Holmes, Butler(2), Janson
29/08/95	IFL	1	RUISLIP MANOR	1542	0-1	
02/09/95	IFL	1	Wembley	561	2-1	Holmes, Eriemo
05/09/95	GIC	1	CHERTSEY TOWN	1388	3-2	Cleeve, Humphrey, Butler
09/09/95	FA Cup	Q1	PAGHAM	1614	4-0	Butler(2), Holmes, Young
16/09/95	IFL	1	Staines Town	835	2-3	Cleeve(2)
23/09/95	FA Cup	Q2	Wokingham Town	1469	2-1	Young(2)
30/09/95	IFL	1	LEYTON PENNANT	1562	4-1	Butler(3), Young
03/10/95	IFL	1	Thame United	545	2-2	Butler, Parr
07/10/95	FA Cup	Q3	Buckingham Town	916	1-0	Butler
14/10/95	IFL	1	OXFORD CITY	1818	0-2	
21/10/95	FA Cup	Q4	Ashford Town	2016	0-2	
28/10/95	IFL	1	Chesham United	1016	0-1	
31/10/95	Hants SC	2	EAST COWES VICTORIA	831	5-0	Young(3), Osgood, Butler
04/11/95	FA Trophy	Q2	Evesham United	465	2-0	Osgood, Young
07/11/95	CC	1	BROMLEY	1193	3-0	Osgood, Wood, Sugrue
11/11/95	IFL	1	Whyteleafe	675	6-0	Butler(3), Wood, Osgood, Sugrue
14/11/95	GIC	2	GRAYS ATHLETIC	1177	2-1	Butler, Sugrue
18/11/95	IFL	1	MARLOW	1688	2-3	Chambers(2)
21/11/95	IFL	1	BARTON ROVERS	1180	6-2	Butler(3), Holmes, Anderson, Osgood
25/11/95	FA Trophy	Q3	Gloucester City	1041	1-5	Sugrue
02/12/95	IFL	1	UXBRIDGE	1486	4-0	Wood(3), Sugrue
05/12/95	CC	2	MAIDENHEAD UNITED	899	3-1	Osgood, Wood, Butler
09/12/95	IFL	1	Berkhamsted Town	771	0-0	
16/12/95	IFL	1	WOKINGHAM TOWN	1486	2-2	Butler(2)
19/12/95	GIC	3	BOREHAM WOOD	954	1-0	Own-Goal
26/12/95	IFL	1	BASINGSTOKE TOWN	2019	1-1	Butler
01/01/96	IFL	1	Barking	402	4-0	Horton, Wood, Butler, Sugrue
03/01/96	Hants SC	3	Eastleigh	319	3-2	
06/01/96	IFL	1	WEMBLEY	1575	0-3	
09/01/96	CC	3	BOGNOR REGIS TOWN	1054	2-2	Horton(2) (lost on penalties)
13/01/96	IFL	1	Barton Rovers	435	3-0	Wood(2), Hunt(og)
20/01/96	IFL	1	ABINGDON TOWN	1398	5-1	Head, Wood, Chewins, Eriemo, Butler
23/01/96	Hants SC	QF	Waterlooville	590	1-3	Head
28/01/96	IFL	1	Oxford City	703	3-1	Head(2), Sugrue
30/01/96	GIC	QF	BASINGSTOKE TOWN	1273	1-0	Humphrey
03/02/96	IFL	1	THAME UNITED	1635	1-0	Sugrue
10/02/96	IFL	1	Leyton Pennant	525	0-1	
13/02/96	IFL	1	TOOTING & MITCHAM UN	1529	3-1	Wood(2), Horton
17/02/96	IFL	1	STAINES TOWN	2034	3-3	Parr, Butler, Horton
24/02/96	IFL	1	CHESHAM UNITED	1655	1-0	Horton
27/02/96	GIC	SF(1)	Hitchin Town	664	1-0	Humphrey
02/03/96	IFL	1	Tooting & Mitcham United	628	2-0	Butcher, Chambers
05/03/96	IFL	1	Maidenhead United	702	1-1	Butler
09/03/96	IFL	1	Ruislip Manor	840	2-1	Parr, Head
12/03/96	GIC	SF(2)	HITCHIN TOWN	1965	2-0	Cleeve, Head
16/03/96	IFL	1	BOGNOR REGIS TOWN	2078	1-1	Wood
19/03/96	IFL	1	Heybridge Swifts	506	0-2	
23/03/96	IFL	1	WHYTELEAFE	1697	3-0	Davenport(og), Holmes, Butler
25/03/96	IFL	1	Bognor Regis Town	996	0-0	
30/03/96	IFL	1	Billericay Town	635	2-1	Horton(2)
02/04/96	IFL	1	Marlow	868	3-0	Parr, Head(2)
06/04/96	IFL	1	BARKING	2141	5-1	Chambers, Butler, Head, Cleeve, Anderson
08/04/96	IFL	1	Basingstoke Town	1588	1-4	Butler
13/04/96	IFL	1	MAIDENHEAD UNITED	1751	0-1	
20/04/96	IFL	1	Uxbridge	554	2-0	Parr, Nunn
27/04/96	IFL	1	BERKHAMSTED TOWN	1433	2-1	Butler, Jeffrey(og)
30/04/96	IFL	1	BILLERICAY TOWN	1349	0-1	
04/05/96	IFL	1	Wokingham Town	759	0-1	
06/05/96	GIC	F	KINGSTONIAN	3511	1-4	Holmes
08/05/96	A'shot SC	F	FLEET TOWN	650	1-3	

BARTON ROVERS

Sharpenhoe Rd, Barton-Le-Clay, Bedford, MK45 4SD Tel: 01582 882607

Secretary: Owen Clark, 108 Manor Rd, Barton-le-Clay, Beds MK45 4NS Tel 01582 882398

Press Sec: Nick Rhodes 32 Windsor Rd, Barton-le-Clay Beds MK45 4LX Tel: 01582 881865

Colours: All Blue   Nickname: Rovers

Capacity: 4,000   Seating: 150

Covered standing: 1,000   Clubhouse on ground: Yes

DIRECTIONS

Directions: M1 Junction 12, from London exit turn right, take second right through Harlington and Sharpenhoe. Ground on right entering village. 4 and a half miles from Harlington (BR), good bus service from Luton.

Record attendance: 1,900 v Nuneaton Borough FA Cup 4th Qualifying Rd 1976

Biggest win: 17-1 v Flitwick Ath. South Mids Lge 1956

Biggest defeat: 1-11 v Leighton United South Mids Lge 1963

Record appearances: Bill Goodyear 475 1982-93

Record goalscorer in one season: Bill Horsler, 62 in 26 league games 1954-55

Record goalscorer in total: Richard Camp 138 1989 to date

Record fee paid £1, 000 for Bill Baldry in 1980 from Hitchin Town

Record fee received £1,000 for Bill Baldry to Bishop's Stortford 1981

Honours

FA VASE Runners up 1978, FA VASE Semi-final 1977 and 1982

South Midlands League 1971, 72, 73, 75, 76, 77, 78, 79, Division One 1965, Division Two 1955

League Shield 1958, 61, 69, 72, 75, 78, 79, Challenge Trophy 1972, 1975, 1978, 1979

Beds Senior Cup 1972, 1973, 1981, 1982, 1990, Beds Premier Cup 1996

Beds Intermediate Cup 1954, Luton and District League Div 3 1948

North Beds Charity Cup 1973, 1975, 1977, 1978, 1980, 1981

Manager 1996-97: Gordon Taylor, Assistant Manager: Paul Burgess

Chairman: Steve Harris, Vice Chairman: Trevor Capon

Barton Rovers were formed in the village of Barton-le-Clay in 1898 and played in inter village football for the first 50 years until 1946, when they reformed after the war and joined the Luton and District League. Progress was such that in 1954 they moved into the South Midlands League, having won Division 3 in 1948 and reached the Premier Division in 1950, never finishing below fourth. In their first season the club were champions of Division Two and a year later runners up in Division One which took them into the Premier Division where they made little impact for nearly a decade. Former Leicester City and Luton Town defender Barry Reed won promotion back to the Premier after two years in Division One . From there until they left the league in 1979, Rovers enjoyed one of the most remarkable runs in any senior football in this country. They finished no lower than third the first five years, being runners up in 1968, and then completed a hat-trick of titles from 1971 to 1973. After a third position in 1974, Rovers went on to take the title five times in succession, losing just eight games in those five years. The final season ended in a flourish with the Challenge Trophy, Reserve Division title and Reserve Challenge Trophy, the only time it has been achieved. Three years earlier the club reached the FA Vase quarter finals before losing to Farnborough Town and a year later they went one better with a semi-final against Sheffield. Finally in 1978 Rovers reached the Wembley final and in front over 16,000 they narrowly lost to Newcastle Blue Star.

Since then the Rovers have joined the Isthmians and enjoyed another race run to the semi-final in 1982. A revival after a number of quiet years has seen promotion take them to Division 1.

BARTON ROVERS 1995/96 SEASON

Date	Comp	Rnd	Opposition	Score	Scorers
19/08/95	IFL	1	BOGNOR REGIS TOWN	0-5	
23/08/95	GIC	P	Epsom & Ewell	3-2	Camp(2), Doyle
26/08/95	FA Cup	P	Brimsdown Rovers	2-0	Doyle, R Smith
29/08/95	IFL	1	BILLERICAY TOWN	1-1	Camp
02/09/95	IFL	1	UXBRIDGE	1-1	Hamilton
05/09/95	GIC	1	Dorking	5-1	R Smith(2), Warner, Olney, Golds
09/09/95	FA Cup	Q1	St Albans City	1-4	Olney
11/09/95	IFL	1	Ruislip Manor	1-3	Quarman
16/09/95	IFL	1	WHYTELEAFE	4-0	Warner, McNally, R Smith(2)
23/09/95	IFL	1	Abingdon Town	2-4	Golds, R Smith
30/09/95	IFL	1	Chesham United	0-4	
10/10/95	IFL	1	Tooting & Mitcham United	0-0	
14/10/95	FA Trophy	Q1	CRAWLEY TOWN	1-3	Doyle
21/10/95	IFL	1	Wokingham Town	1-1	Warner
24/10/95	Beds SC	1	Stotfold	4-2	Golds(2), Sullivan, Camp
28/10/95	IFL	1	BASINGSTOKE TOWN	1-2	Huntley
07/11/95	GIC	2	DULWICH HAMLET	0-1	
11/11/95	IFL	1	LEYTON PENNANT	2-2	Guile, Warner
18/11/95	IFL	1	HEYBRIDGE SWIFTS	1-4	Guile
21/11/95	IFL	1	Aldershot Town	2-6	Guile(2)
28/11/95	CC	1	HEYBRIDGE SWIFTS	0-1	
02/12/95	IFL	1	MAIDENHEAD UNITED	4-0	Doyle(2), Camp, Smith
09/12/95	IFL	1	Barking	4-1	Guile(2), Camp, R Smith
12/12/95	IFL	1	THAME UNITED	3-3	Guile, Camp, Neufville
16/12/95	IFL	1	WEMBLEY	5-1	Guile(2), Smith, Doyle, Neufville
18/12/95	Beds PC	QF	LUTON TOWN	2-1	Guile, Camp
23/12/95	IFL	1	Uxbridge	2-3	Camp, Guile
06/01/96	IFL	1	TOOTING & MITCHAM UTD	2-0	Golds, Warner
13/01/96	IFL	1	ALDERSHOT TOWN	0-3	
16/01/96	IFL	1	Staines Town	2-3	Warner, Guile
23/01/96	IFL	1	RUISLIP MANOR	1-0	Guile
03/02/96	Beds SC	QF	Totternhoe	3-1	Camp(2), Guile
10/02/96	IFL	1	CHESHAM UNITED	0-0	
17/02/96	IFL	1	Whyteleafe	3-3	Neufville, Guile, Warner
24/02/96	IFL	1	Basingstoke Town	1-3	Guile
02/03/96	IFL	1	WOKINGHAM TOWN	2-2	Guile(2)
06/03/96	Beds SC	SF	Arlesey Town	2-0	Own-Goal, Guile
09/03/96	IFL	1	ABINGDON TOWN	0-1	
12/03/96	IFL	1	Oxford City	0-3	
16/03/96	IFL	1	Thame United	1-3	Guile
19/03/96	Beds PC	SF	SHILLINGTON	2-1	Own-Goal, Camp
23/03/96	IFL	1	Leyton Pennant	2-4	Camp, Yates
26/03/96	IFL	1	MARLOW	2-1	Golds, Guile
30/03/96	IFL	1	STAINES TOWN	0-2	
02/04/96	IFL	1	Heybridge Swifts	1-3	Guile
06/04/96	IFL	1	BERKHAMSTED TOWN	5-2	Cunniff, D Turner(2), Golds(2)
08/04/96	IFL	1	Marlow	0-2	
13/04/96	IFL	1	OXFORD CITY	1-0	Timson
15/04/96	IFL	1	Bognor Regis Town	0-3	
20/04/96	IFL	1	Maidenhead United	4-3	Doyle, Golds, Guile, Timson
24/04/96	IFL	1	Billericay Town	6-1	Timson(3), Guile(2), Yates
27/04/96	IFL	1	BARKING	0-0	
30/04/96	IFL	1	Berkhamsted Town	2-1	Doyle, McNally
02/05/96	Beds PC	F(1)	Bedford Town	0-0	
04/05/96	IFL	1	Wembley	0-3	
06/05/96	Beds SC	F	Bedford Town	0-1	
10/05/96	Beds PC	F(2)	BEDFORD TOWN	1-0	

BASINGSTOKE TOWN

Camrose Ground, Western Way, Basingstoke, RG24 6H Tel: 01256 464353 or 25063

Secretary: Richard Trodd, 5 Lehar Close, Brighton Hill, Basingstoke, Hants RG22 4HT Tel 01256 413076

Press Sec: John Grey c/o The Camrose Ground

Colours: Blue and gold stripes

Nickname: Stoke or Blues   Capacity: 6,000

Covered seating: 651   Covered standing: 1,500

Clubhouse on ground: Yes

Record attendance: 4,091 v Northampton Town
FA Cup 1st Rd 1971

Biggest win: 10-0 v Chichester City (h)
FA Cup 1st Qual Rd Sept 1966

Biggest defeat: 0-8 v Aylesbury United
Southern League April 1979

Record appearance holder: Billy Coombs

Record fee paid: £4,750 v Steve Ingham Gosport Borough

Record fee received: £6,750 for Steve Ingham from Bashley

DIRECTIONS

Exit 6 off M3 and follow A30 west, ground off Winchester Road. Two miles from bus and rail stations.

Honours

Southern League Southern Division 1986, Hants League 1968, 1970, 1971

North Division 1912 and 1920, Hants Senior Cup 1971, 1990, 1996

Manager for 1996-97: Ernie Howe, Assistant manager: Steve Richardson, Chairman: David Knight

Basingstoke Town were founded in 1896 and can trace their origins back through the 1880's to the amalgamation of two teams, Basingstoke Albion and Aldsworth United. In 1901 they entered the Hampshire League and a few years later a merger took place with another local team, North Hants Ironworks. The first notable success came in 1920 when the club won the Hampshire League Division Two. Town had played at Castle Field from the start, but were offered a piece of land by Lord Camrose, off Winchester Road, with a 99 year lease and they began to develop it. The last game at Castle Fields was in October 1945, whereupon the club played for a while at West Ham Park, home of Thorneycroft Athletic before playing their first game at the Winchester Road ground, as it was called, on December 1st 1945, against Southampton Borough Police. Castle Fields is still used for sport, as the home of Basingstoke CC's lower X1's, and Fairfield School use it for football. The first real successful period for the club started in 1968 when the Division One title was won, and repeated two years later. In 1971 they won the Senior Cup and boyed up, were promoted to the Southern League, finishing 8th. In that season the club reached the 1st Round of the FA Cup, losing to Northampton Town in front of a record crowd. It was 1985 before the Southern Division championship was won, but just one season was played in the top Division before the club were asked to move across the Pyramid to the Isthmian League. Having spent a large sum on ground improvements, they struggled on the field and were relegated, although a change of management saw them bounce straight back. 1989 saw Town reach the 2nd Round of the Cup, just losing a battle with Torquay United, and although they finished the league in 8th, they took the Hampshire Senior Cup again, hammering Lymington 8-0 in the process. Recently the club has struggled again and was relegated to Division One and last May finished 9th although they had the bonus of only their third Hampshire Senior Cup win.

BASINGSTOKE TOWN 1995/96 SEASON

12/08/95	IFL	1	STAINES TOWN	5-0	
19/08/95	IFL	1	Oxford City	2-3	
22/08/95	IFL	1	WEMBLEY	2-0	Deigham, Richardson
26/08/95	FA Cup	P	Westbury United	2-2	Coombs, Deighan
29/08/95	FA Cup	P rep	WESTBURY UNITED	5-1	Biggs, Terry(2), Mancey, Coombs
02/09/95	IFL	1	Thame United	0-1	
06/09/95	GIC	1	Molesey	1-0	
09/09/95	FA Cup	Q1	HAVANT TOWN	2-1	
12/09/95	IFL	1	HEYBRIDGE SWIFTS	1-3	Coombs
16/09/95	IFL	1	Maidenhead United	0-0	
23/09/95	FA Cup	Q2	Dorchester Town	0-2	
30/09/95	IFL	1	WOKINGHAM TOWN	0-2	
03/10/95	Hants SC	1	PIRELLI GENERAL	8-0	
07/10/95	IFL	1	Barking	2-2	Biggs, Harris
14/10/95	FA Trophy	Q1	Erith & Belvedere	6-0	Stairs(2), Coombs(4)
21/10/95	IFL	1	CHESHAM UNITED	2-1	Biggs, Coombs
28/10/95	IFL	1	Barton Rovers	2-1	Terry, Stairs
01/11/95	Hants SC	2	Fareham Town	3-1	Harris, Mitchell, Coombs
04/11/95	FA Trophy	Q2	UXBRIDGE	0-2	
07/11/95	CC	1	WHYTELEAFE	4-1	
11/11/95	IFL	1	Tooting & Mitcham United	3-1	Coombes(2), Stairs
18/11/95	IFL	1	Billericay Town	2-2	Staines, Terry
21/11/95	GIC	2	RUISLIP MANOR	2-2	
25/11/95	IFL	1	WHYTELEAFE	2-2	Coombes(2)
28/11/95	Hants SC	3	HAVANT TOWN	1-0	Morley
04/12/95	GIC	2 rep	Ruislip Manor	3-2	
09/12/95	IFL	1	RUISLIP MANOR	1-1	Coombes
12/12/95	CC	2	Oxford City	0-1	
16/12/95	IFL	1	Leyton Pennant	1-3	
19/12/95	GIC	3	MARLOW	6-0	
23/12/95	IFL	1	THAME UNITED	3-3	Coombes(2), Dark(og)
26/12/95	IFL	1	Aldershot Town	1-1	Mitchell
06/01/96	IFL	1	Staines Town	1-3	Coombs
09/01/96	IFL	1	ABINGDON TOWN	0-0	
13/01/96	IFL	1	Wembley	2-0	Cooms, Terry
20/01/96	IFL	1	UXBRIDGE	0-1	
27/01/96	Hants SC	QF	D.C.A. BASINGSTOKE	4-1	
30/01/96	GIC	QF	Aldershot Town	0-1	
03/02/96	IFL	1	BERKHAMSTED TOWN	1-1	Mundee
10/02/96	IFL	1	Wokingham Town	3-3	Coombes(2), Mitchell
14/02/96	IFL	1	Bognor Regis Town	1-4	Coombes
17/02/96	IFL	1	MAIDENHEAD UNITED	2-2	Manley, Coombes
24/02/96	IFL	1	BARTON ROVERS	3-1	Mancey, Coombs(2)
02/03/96	IFL	1	Chesham United	2-2	Norris, Mancey
06/03/96	Hants SC	SF	Bournemouth	3-1	
09/03/96	IFL	1	Marlow	3-3	Mancey, Mitchell, Mund
16/03/96	IFL	1	BARKING	1-0	Coombes
19/03/96	IFL	1	Berkhamsted Town	3-0	Terry, Coombs(2)
23/03/96	IFL	1	TOOTING & MITCHAM UNITED	0-2	Green, Mancey
26/03/96	IFL	1	OXFORD CITY	3-1	Coombs(2), Mitchell
30/03/96	IFL	1	Uxbridge	1-0	Mancey
06/04/96	IFL	1	Abingdon Town	0-1	
08/04/96	IFL	1	ALDERSHOT TOWN	4-1	Coombes, Stairs, Mancey, Mitchell
13/04/96	IFL	1	Whyteleafe	0-2	
16/04/96	IFL	1	BILLERICAY TOWN	2-1	Mancey, Coombs
20/04/96	IFL	1	BOGNOR REGIS TOWN	4-2	Mitchell(2), Biggs, Mancey
23/04/96	Hants SC	F	WATERLOOVILLE	2-0	
27/04/96	IFL	1	Ruislip Manor	0-1	
30/04/96	IFL	1	MARLOW	0-1	
02/05/96	IFL	1	Heybridge Swifts	1-3	Green
04/05/96	IFL	1	LEYTON PENNANT	2-1	

BERKHAMSTED TOWN

Broadwater, Lower Kings Rd, Berkhamsted, Herts, HP4 2AA Tel: 01442 862815

Secretary: Mrs Christine Sims, 18 Chiltern Park Avenue, Berkhamsted, Herts Tel 01442 873413

Colours: White & Black, Nickname: Lilywhites or Berko

Capacity: 2,000   Seating: 120

Covered standing: 200   Clubhouse on ground: Yes

DIRECTIONS
Adjacent to Berkhamsted station (Euston-Birmingham line). A41 to Berkhamsted town centre traffic lights, left into Lower Kings Road.

Record attendance: 1,163 Barnet
FA Cup 3rd Qualifying Rd 1987

Honours

Herts Senior Cup: 1953

London Spartan League 1980 (Div 2 1927)

Herts Charity Shield: 1974, 1980, 1985, 1991 Joint in 1951

Aubrey Cup: 1953, St Mary's Cup: 12 times,
Apsley Senior Charity Cup: 9 times

Wallspan Southern Combination: 1985, Floodlit Cup: 1985

In 1895 the first Berkhamsted Town side was formed which brought the 100 year celebrations last season. That club lasted until 1906, and it was not until after the Great War that the current side was formed as Berkhamsted Comrades, playing at Lower Kings Road. The name was dropped three years later when they joined the Spartan League.

In 1951 Berko became founder members of the Delphian League which included Aylesbury, Bishop's Stortford, Dagenham and Slough and in that first season the Herts Charity Shield was shared with Stevenage Borough. 1953 saw their greatest triumph to date when they took the Herts Senior Cup, beating St Albans City 4-2 at Barnet in front of over 2,500 people.

1963 saw a major league reconstruction with the Athenian League forming a Division Two from the Delphian clubs. It was a poor time for the club, who dropped down to the Spartan League in 1966. They took the title in 1980, which was part of a treble of League, Charity Shield and St Mary's Cup.

Three years later the Lower Kings Road ground was sold, flats built on the old pitch and the club moved 100 yards sideways into the old cricket pavilion which had been part of the same complex. New dressing rooms and a stand were built which earned the club an immediate return to the Athenian League. Lights were installed and with the Isthmian League expanding they were welcomed in, where they have enjoyed promotion through regionalisation and then by finishing third in 1993, winning the last 14 league matches

FORMER GROUNDS

Berko used the impressive Lower Kings Road ground from 1919 until 1983, but before that the earlier club had used a ground previously used by the Sunnyside Club, called the Sunnyside Enclosure, situated near the church of the same name. The new club used part of the cricket pitch, with a large wooden stand, complete with dressing rooms, which was built in 1924. A small area of terracing was laid in the late 40's and much later a clubhouse was added, all now under a development of flats.

BERKHAMSTED TOWN 1995/96 SEASON

12/08/95	Herts CC	1	Baldock Town	0-2	
19/08/95	IFL	1	TOOTING & MITCHAM UN	0-1	
22/08/95	IFL	1	Whyteleafe	1-1	Coles
26/08/95	FA Cup	P	Biggleswade Town	4-0	
02/09/95	IFL	1	BOGNOR REGIS TOWN	0-2	
09/09/95	FA Cup	Q1	HILLINGDON BOROUGH	3-2	
12/09/95	IFL	1	Billericay Town	0-3	
16/09/95	IFL	1	MARLOW	1-1	
23/09/95	FA Cup	Q2	DAGENHAM & REDBRIDGE	1-2	Cosby
26/09/95	GIC	1	KINGSBURY TOWN	1-2	
30/09/95	IFL	1	Uxbridge	2-1	Rutherford, Lawford
07/10/95	IFL	1	ABINGDON TOWN	4-2	Nightingale, Lawford, S Butler, Rutherford
10/10/95	IFL	1	Oxford City	0-1	
14/10/95	FA Trophy	Q1	PURFLEET	1-2	
21/10/95	IFL	1	LEYTON PENNANT	1-1	Lawford
28/10/95	IFL	1	Maidenhead United	2-0	Butler, Lawford
04/11/95	IFL	1	Wokingham Town	2-1	Lawford(2)
07/11/95	CC	1	YEADING	0-3	
11/11/95	IFL	1	HEYBRIDGE SWIFTS	1-2	Lawford
18/11/95	IFL	1	Abingdon Town	0-2	
21/11/95	IFL	1	Barking	2-1	Lawford, Rutherford
28/11/95	IFL	1	WEMBLEY	1-0	Lawford
02/12/95	IFL	1	Staines Town	1-2	Lawford
05/12/95	Herts SC	2	Bishop's Stortford	0-2	
09/12/95	IFL	1	ALDERSHOT TOWN	0-0	
16/12/95	IFL	1	Ruislip Manor	3-2	Lawford, Butler, Rutherford
23/12/95	IFL	1	BILLERICAY TOWN	2-0	Winks, Lawford
26/12/95	IFL	1	Chesham United	1-0	Lawford
06/01/96	IFL	1	Bognor Regis Town	1-1	Lawford
13/01/96	IFL	1	WHYTELEAFE	1-1	Lawford
20/01/96	IFL	1	Tooting & Mitcham United	2-3	Harthill, Lawford
03/02/96	IFL	1	Basingstoke Town	1-1	Nightingale
13/02/96	IFL	1	THAME UNITED	4-1	Winks, Nightingale, Lawford(2)
17/02/96	IFL	1	Marlow	1-1	Lawford
02/03/96	IFL	1	Leyton Pennant	1-3	Lawford
09/03/96	IFL	1	OXFORD CITY	2-3	Lowe, Rutherford
12/03/96	IFL	1	BARKING	0-1	
16/03/96	IFL	1	Wembley	0-2	
19/03/96	IFL	1	BASINGSTOKE TOWN	0-3	
23/03/96	IFL	1	Heybridge Swifts	2-4	Rutherford(2)
30/03/96	IFL	1	WOKINGHAM TOWN	2-1	D Butler, S Butler
06/04/96	IFL	1	Barton Rovers	2-5	Lowe, S Butler
08/04/96	IFL	1	CHESHAM UNITED	0-1	
13/04/96	IFL	1	Thame United	2-2	Winks, Nightingale
16/04/96	IFL	1	MAIDENHEAD UNITED	2-2	Issott, Coles
20/04/96	IFL	1	STAINES TOWN	1-2	Harthill
23/04/96	IFL	1	UXBRIDGE	1-3	D Butler
27/04/96	IFL	1	Aldershot Town	1-2	Nightingale
30/04/96	IFL	1	BARTON ROVERS	1-2	Harthill
04/05/96	IFL	1	RUISLIP MANOR	1-1	

BILLERICAY TOWN

New Lodge, Blunts Wall Road, Billericay, CM12 9SA Tel: 01277 652188: Ansaphone 01277 655177

Secretary: Len Dewson, 14 Graham Close, Billericay, Essex CM12 0QW, Tel: 01277 622375

Nickname: Town or Blues   Colours: All Royal Blue

Capacity: 3,500   Seating: 238

Covered standing: 850   Clubhouse on ground: Yes

Record attendance 3,841 v West Ham United Floodlight opener

and for a competitive match 3,193 v Farnborough Town FA Vase semi-final 1st Leg Mar 13th 1976

Biggest win: 11-0 Stansted (A) Essex Sen. May 5th 1976

Biggest defeat: 3-10 v Chelmsford City Essex Sen Cup Jan 4th 1993

Record appearances: John Pullen 418

Record goalscorer in one season: Fred Clayden 49 in 53 games, 1977-78, Record goalscorer in total: Fred Clayden 273

Record fee received: £22,500 + increments for Steve Jones to West Ham Utd in 1992

DIRECTIONS

From Shenfield (A129) turn right at 1st lights then 2nd right,. From Basildon (A129) proceed over 1st lights in town, then left at next lights and 2nd right. Half mile from Billericay (BR station London Liverpool Street-Southend line). Ground 5 miles from buses 222, 251, 357, 255, 551.

Honours

FA VASE WINNERS 1976, 1977, 1979

Essex Senior League 1973, 1975, 1976, League Cup 1972, 1973, 1974, 1977 and Challenge Cup 1973

Isthmian League Div 2 1980, Athenian League 1978 and 1979, and League Cup 1978

Essex Senior Cup 1976 and Essex Senior Trophy 1978, 1980 and 1995 (res)

Essex Thamesside Trophy 1987 and 1992,

Essex Floodlit Trophy 1978 and Phillips Floodlit Trophy 1977, Rothman's Merit Award 1978

Best contact when confirming a fixture: Townline 0891 101980

Manager for 1996-97: John Kendall. Assistant manager. Ken Varne, Chairman: Rod Moore.

Press Officer: Phil Heady, 9 Lampern Cres, Billericay CM12 0FE, Tel: 01277 626560 (h)

CLUB MAIN SPONSOR: IMATION "Borne of 3M Innovation"

Billericay Town Football Club was formed in 1880 and joined the Romford and District League in 1890, where they remained until 1914. After the Great War they entered the Mid-Essex League where they stayed until 1947. They then joined the Southern Essex Combination, where they played until 1966 when becoming founder members of the Essex Olympian League. Five years later they were again founder members, this time of the Essex Senior League and their six year stay saw them win three titles and finish runners up twice. In addition they won the League Cup four times, losing in one final.They moved up to the Athenian League in 1977, doing the League and Cup double immediately, retaining the title the following year and entering the Isthmian League in 1979. During this period Billericay experienced phenomenal success in the FA Vase, becoming the only club to win it three times, in 1976 where they beat Stamford, in 1977 beating Sheffield in a replay and in 1979 when they crushed Almondsbury Greenway 4-1.Town's first season as an Isthmian saw them take the Div 2 title by 17 points and a year later they were in the Premier Division, having finished runner-up to Bishop's Stortford. They spent five years in the Premier before the good times ran out and they went down, and two years later they were in Division Two again. In 1992, an unbeaten 15 match run gained them promotion in third place, and they remain in Division One where they ended the season in sixth place last May.Billericay played at the Archer Ground in Laindon until 1971 when they moved to New Lodge, which at the time had two pitches separated by a cricket square and was used by Outwell Common FC. For Town's big games, including the Vase matches, temporary terracing was shipped in from the County Ground at Chelmsford, which allowed crowds approaching 4,000 to cram in on occasions.

BILLERICAY TOWN 1995/96 SEASON

Date	Comp	Round	Opponent	Score	Scorers
19/08/95	IFL	1	Wokingham Town	0-3	
26/08/95	IFL	1	STAINES TOWN	2-1	Battram, Payne
29/08/95	IFL	1	Barton Rovers	1-1	Howard
02/09/95	IFL	1	Heybridge Swifts	2-3	Caines, Payne
05/09/95	GIC	1	HAMPTON	3-1	Roser, Evans, Caines
09/09/95	FA Cup	Q1	AVELEY	2-0	Battram, Own-Goal
12/09/95	IFL	1	BERKHAMSTED TOWN	3-0	Payne, Evans, Barry
16/09/95	IFL	1	Leyton Pennant	2-1	Evans, Payne
23/09/95	FA Cup	Q2	GREAT YARMOUTH TOWN	2-0	Howard, Keune
30/09/95	IFL	1	ABINGDON TOWN	1-3	Prue
07/10/95	FA Cup	Q3	Chelmsford City	1-1	Collins
10/10/95	FA Cup	Q3 rep	CHELMSFORD CITY	2-1	Evans, Roser
14/10/95	FA Trophy	Q1	WEMBLEY	0-4	
17/10/95	IFL	1	Chesham United	1-0	Payne
21/10/95	FA Cup	Q4	WISBECH TOWN	1-1	Prue
24/10/95	FA Cup	Q4 rep	Wisbech Town	0-2	
28/10/95	IFL	1	Bognor Regis Town	0-4	
31/10/95	GIC	2	Heybridge Swifts	3-4	Howard, Battram(2)
11/11/95	IFL	1	RUISLIP MANOR	4-1	Howard, Battram, Gutzmore(2)
14/11/95	IFL	1	WHYTELEAFE	1-1	Payne
18/11/95	IFL	1	BASINGSTOKE TOWN	2-2	Gutzmore(2)
21/11/95	Essex SC	2	Wivenhoe Town	3-3	Gutzmore, Payne, Berry
28/11/95	Essex SC	2 rep	WIVENHOE TOWN	2-1	Battram, Gutzmore
02/12/95	IFL	1	TOOTING & MITCHAM UNI	1-0	Gutzmore
05/12/95	IFL	1	WEMBLEY	0-1	
09/12/95	IFL	1	Maidenhead United	2-2	Howard, Gutzmore
12/12/95	CC	2	Grays Athletic	2-1	Battram, Payne
16/12/95	IFL	1	OXFORD CITY	1-0	Gutzmore
19/12/95	Essex TST	2	PURFLEET	0-2	
23/12/95	IFL	1	Berkhamsted Town	0-2	
02/01/96	Essex SC	3	Leyton Pennant	2-3	Waters, Gutzmore
06/01/96	IFL	1	HEYBRIDGE SWIFTS	2-0	Battram, Gutzmore
13/01/96	IFL	1	Thame United	1-0	Jacques
15/01/96	CC	3	Ruislip Manor	4-1	Shirt(2), Battram, Gutzmore
20/01/96	IFL	1	WOKINGHAM TOWN	0-0	
30/01/96	IFL	1	Uxbridge	1-0	Gutzmore
10/02/96	IFL	1	Abingdon Town	2-1	Battram, Waters
13/02/96	Essex SC	QF	Heybridge Swifts	3-1	Battram, Gutzmore(2)
17/02/96	IFL	1	LEYTON PENNANT	0-3	
24/02/96	IFL	1	BOGNOR REGIS TOWN	3-1	Shirt, Sinfield, Gutzmore
27/02/96	CC	QF	BISHOP'S STORTFORD	0-2	
02/03/96	IFL	1	Wembley	2-2	Gutzmore, Sinfield
05/03/96	IFL	1	Marlow	4-1	Battram, Gutzmore, Leach(og), Sinfield
09/03/96	IFL	1	CHESHAM UNITED	2-0	Battram, Jacques
12/03/96	IFL	1	THAME UNITED	1-2	Gutzmore
16/03/96	IFL	1	Whyteleafe	1-2	Battram
19/03/96	Essex SC	SF	Grays Athletic	2-0	Gutzmore(2)
23/03/96	IFL	1	Ruislip Manor	2-2	Loomes, Shirt
30/03/96	IFL	1	ALDERSHOT TOWN	1-2	Gutzmore
02/04/96	IFL	1	Staines Town	1-4	Gutzmore
06/04/96	IFL	1	MARLOW	2-0	Payne, Sinfield
08/04/96	IFL	1	Barking	1-0	Sinfield
11/04/96	IFL	1	BARKING	3-0	Gutzmore(3)
13/04/96	IFL	1	UXBRIDGE	0-0	
16/04/96	IFL	1	Basingstoke Town	1-2	Payne
20/04/96	IFL	1	Tooting & Mitcham United	1-0	Gutzmore
22/04/96	Essex SC	F	BRAINTREE TOWN	1-2	Battram (played at Dagenham & Redbridge F.C.)
24/04/96	IFL	1	BARTON ROVERS	1-6	Barry
27/04/96	IFL	1	MAIDENHEAD UNITED	1-1	Evans
30/04/96	IFL	1	Aldershot Town	1-0	Barry
04/05/96	IFL	1	Oxford City	1-4	

BOGNOR REGIS TOWN

Nyewood Lane, Bognor Regis, PO21 2TY .Tel: 01243 822325

Secretary: Paul Harwood, c/o Football Club
Tel: 01243 587554 (h)

Nickname: The Rocks   Colours: White and Green

Capacity: 6,000   Seating: 250

Covered standing: 3,000   Clubhouse on ground: Yes

DIRECTIONS

West along seafront from pier, past Aldwick shopping centre, and right into Nyewood Lane.

Record Attendance: 3,642 v Swansea City
FA Cup 1st Rd Replay 1984

Record appearances: Mick Pullen

Record goalscorer in total: Kevin Clements

Record fee received: £10,500 John Crumplin and Geoff Cooper to Brighton AHA in 1987 and also for Simon Rodger to Crystal Palace in 1989

Honours

Isthmian League Cup 1987

Sussex County League 1949 and 1972

West Sussex League 1921, 1922, 1923, 1924, 1925, West Sussex Junior League 1911 and 1914

Sussex Senior Cup 1955, 1956, 1980, 1981, 1982, 19823, 1984, 1987

Sussex Professional Cup 1974, Sussex RUR Cup 1972

Sussex Intermediate Cup 1953, Littlehampton Hospital Cup 1930 and 1934

Bognor Charity Cup 1929, 1931, 1933, 1938, 1948, 1959, 1972, 1973

Gosport War Memorial Cup 1982 and 1983

Manager for 1996-97: Jack Pearce

Bognor FC was formed in 1883, and their early years were spent mainly playing friendly matches until they joined the West Sussex League in 1896. They enjoyed a certain amount of success in that league, winning it five years in succession in the twenties. As a result they joined the Brighton and Hove District League in 1926 for one year, until being accepted into the Sussex County League where they remained until 1972.

They had mixed fortunes in the league, winning the championship in 1949, but relegation to Division Two in 1969 signalled a new era, gaining promotion immediately before taking the Premier title the following year. This prompted them to join the Southern League and it took some while for the Rocks to settle at that level, but in 1981 they were runners-up in both League and League Cup. They switched to the Isthmian the following season where they were promoted, again as runners-up, to the Premier Division, where they remained until relegated two years ago.

Bognor won the Sussex Senior Cup for the first time in 1955, and created a record by winning it five years on the trot from 1980 to 1984. In other cups they have also made their mark, winning the AC Delco Cup in 1987, but more importantly they have made the Second Round of the FA Cup on two occasions, beating Swansea City in a replay at Nyewood Lane in 1984.

Bognor FC became Bognor Regis after King George V visited the town whilst convalescing in 1935, and decreed that the name could be used, and they have used their superb ground for around 80 years, since moving from playing on various farmers fields at the west end of the town.

BOGNOR REGIS TOWN 1995/96 SEASON

Date	Comp	Rnd	Opponent	Score	Scorers
19/08/95	IFL	1	Barton Rovers	5-0	Miles, Kilpatrick, R Pearce, Beazeley, More
23/08/95	IFL	1	LEYTON PENNANT	3-2	R Pearce, P Pullen, Lewis
26/08/95	FA Cup	P	WHITEHAWK	4-3	D Pearce(2), Rutherford, Bermingham
28/08/95	IFL	1	Heybridge Swifts	1-5	Miles
02/09/95	IFL	1	Berkhamsted Town	2-0	Cormack, Miles
05/09/95	GIC	1	Yeading	3-0	Cormack, Rutherford, Rice
09/09/95	FA Cup	Q1	Dover Athletic	2-1	Miles, Rice
16/09/95	IFL	1	Abingdon Town	2-1	Miles(2)
23/09/95	FA Cup	Q2	Banstead Athletic	3-0	Cormack(2), Rutherford
30/09/95	IFL	1	STAINES TOWN	3-1	Cormack, Eastland, Marriner
07/10/95	FA Cup	Q3	DULWICH HAMLET	4-2	Birmingham, Rice, Rutherford(2)
14/10/95	FA Trophy	Q1	Weston-super-Mare	6-2	Birmingham(3), Rice, D Pearce, Rutherford
17/10/95	IFL	1	Whyteleafe	4-2	D Pearce, Rice, Cormack, Miles
21/10/95	FA Cup	Q4	Tiverton Town	4-1	Miles(3), Rice
28/10/95	IFL	1	BILLERICAY TOWN	4-0	Miles(2), Cormack, Birmingham
30/10/95	GIC	2	Carshalton Athletic	0-2	
04/11/95	FA Trophy	Q2	SITTINGBOURNE	2-2	Cormack, Rutherford
08/11/95	FA Trophy	Q2 rep	Sittingbourne	2-1	D Pearce, Eastland
11/11/95	FA Cup	1	ASHFORD TOWN	1-1	Birmingham
18/11/95	IFL	1	WEMBLEY	1-1	Rice
21/11/95	FA Cup	1 rep	Ashford Town	1-0	Pearce
25/11/95	FA Trophy	Q3	Hitchin Town	2-1	Miles(2)
02/12/95	FA Cup	2	Peterborough United	0-4	
06/12/95	Sussex SC	2	SIDLEY UNITED	5-1	Miles(4), P Pullen
09/12/95	IFL	1	Wokingham Town	5-0	Miles(2), Cormack, Rice,Birmingham
13/12/95	CC	2	WORTHING	6-0	Matthews, Beazeley, Rice, Ford(2), Cormack
16/12/95	IFL	1	MARLOW	0-1	
18/12/95	IFL	1	CHESHAM UNITED	3-0	Eastwood, Wood, D Pearce
03/01/96	IFL	1	Oxford City	0-1	
06/01/96	IFL	1	BERKHAMSTED TOWN	1-1	Rutherford
09/01/96	CC	3	Aldershot Town	2-2	Rutherford, Wood (won on penalties)
13/01/96	IFL	1	Leyton Pennant	2-3	Eastland, Miles
15/01/96	Sussex SC	3	Brighton & Hove Albion	3-2	Cormack(2), Pearce
20/01/96	FA Trophy	1	WORCESTER CITY	1-0	Cormack
23/01/96	IFL	1	Uxbridge	0-0	
31/01/96	IFL	1	Ruislip Manor	0-2	
03/02/96	IFL	1	HEYBRIDGE SWIFTS	1-3	Birmingham
06/02/96	Sussex SC	QF	Langney Sports	1-2	M Pullen
10/02/96	FA Trophy	2	RADCLIFFE BOROUGH	1-3	Cormack
14/02/96	IFL	1	BASINGSTOKE TOWN	4-1	Birmingham, Cormack, Rutherford, Eastland
17/02/96	IFL	1	ABINGDON TOWN	2-0	Ford, Miles
21/02/96	CC	QF	SUTTON UNITED	1-2	Cormack
24/02/96	IFL	1	Billericay Town	1-3	Miles
27/02/96	IFL	1	Thame United	3-2	D Pearce, R Pearce, Miles
02/03/96	IFL	1	UXBRIDGE	0-2	
05/03/96	IFL	1	Barking	1-1	Stephens
09/03/96	IFL	1	WHYTELEAFE	2-2	Cormack, Eastland
12/03/96	IFL	1	Maidenhead United	1-0	P Pullen
16/03/96	IFL	1	Aldershot Town	1-1	Miles
18/03/96	IFL	1	THAME UNITED	0-1	
23/03/96	IFL	1	Chesham United	1-0	Pullen
25/03/96	IFL	1	ALDERSHOT TOWN	0-0	
30/03/96	IFL	1	RUISLIP MANOR	1-1	D Pearce
02/04/96	IFL	1	Wembley	1-2	R Pearce
06/04/96	IFL	1	OXFORD CITY	3-1	Birmingham, R Pearce, Eastland
08/04/96	IFL	1	Tooting & Mitcham United	0-1	
13/04/96	IFL	1	BARKING	1-1	Miles
15/04/96	IFL	1	BARTON ROVERS	3-0	Miles, Eastland, Cormack
20/04/96	IFL	1	Basingstoke Town	2-4	Miles, Clements
22/04/96	IFL	1	MAIDENHEAD UNITED	0-0	
27/04/96	IFL	1	WOKINGHAM TOWN	2-0	Miles, Birmingham
30/04/96	IFL	1	Staines Town	2-2	D Pearce, Reed
02/05/96	IFL	1	TOOTING & MITCHAM UNI	3-2	Miles, P Pullen, Eastland
04/05/96	IFL	1	Marlow	0-3	

CANVEY ISLAND

Park Lane, Canvey Island. Tel: 01268 682991

Secretary: Mrs Frances Roche, 56 Harvest Rd, Canvey Island, Essex SS8 9RP Tel 01268 698586

Colours: Yellow

Nickname: Gulls

Capacity: 2,500

Seating: Yes

Covered standing: Yes

Clubhouse on ground: Yes

Record attendance: 3,250 v Tiverton Town FA Vase semi-final 1993

DIRECTIONS

A130 from A13 or A127 at Sadlers Farm roundabout, 1 mile through town centre, first on right past old bus garage. Bus 3 or 151 from Benfleet (BR) to stop after Admiral Jellicoe (PH).

Honours

FA VASE Semi-final 1993

Essex Senior League 1987 and 1993

League Cup 1984 and 1993

Harry Fisher Memorial Trophy 1994

Essex Thamesside Trophy 1994

Greater London League 1968 and 1969

Isthmian League Div 2 1996

Associate Members (Carlton Trophy) 1996

Manager For 1996-97: Jeff King

Canvey were formed in 1926, competing in the Southend and District League and playing at Furtherwick School. They later played at the Paddocks and at King George V Playing Fields before moving to their present ground. At the time of the terrible floods in the east of the country in 1953 when so many lost their lives, they were playing in the Thurrock and Thameside League, but all club records were lost. They entered the Parthenon League in 1957, winning it a year later and progressed to the Metropolitan League where they did the League and Cup double in 1968 and 1969.

Joining the Essex Senior League in 1974 they had to wait before success came in 1979 with a runners up place and 1980 with a League Cup win. It was 1987 before they finally took the title but they soon had financial problems and the club was totally re-organised in 1991.

A change of personnel saw changes made and floodlights were installed as manager Jeff King embarked on a marvellous run which is continuing still. Having taken the Essex League and Cup double in 1993 they were to suffer a semi-final defeat in the FA Vase, losing to Tiverton Town, but the next season saw the club win the Harry Fisher Trophy, reach the final of the Senior Trophy and win the Thameside Trophy, with their third place good enough to get them into the Isthmian League. As runners up to Collier Row in the first season they were again promoted, reaching the last eight of the Vase before losing to Oxford City and last May they took the Division Two title by a street from Croydon.

CANVEY ISLAND 1995/96 SEASON

Date	Competition	Round	Opponent	Score	Notes
19/08/95	IFL	2	Egham Town	4-0	
23/08/95	LC	P	Collier Row	0-0	
26/08/95	FA Cup	P	Wroxham	0-0	
29/08/95	FA Cup	P rep	WROXHAM	3-1	
02/09/95	IFL	2	Hampton	0-0	
05/09/95	LC	P rep	COLLIER ROW	0-2	
09/09/95	FA Cup	Q1	Cambridge City	3-2	
12/09/95	LC	1	Hitchin Town	1-4	
16/09/95	IFL	2	Edgware Town	1-1	
19/09/95	IFL	2	Metropolitan Police	1-1	
23/09/95	FA Cup	Q2	BRAINTREE TOWN	2-0	
26/09/95	IFL	2	SAFFRON WALDEN TOWN	1-0	
30/09/95	IFL	2	BANSTEAD ATHLETIC	1-0	
03/10/95	IFL	2	BEDFORD TOWN	2-2	
07/10/95	FA Cup	Q3	King's Lynn	0-1	
10/10/95	E. F'lit	Gp 7	SOUTHEND MANOR	2-0	
14/10/95	IFL	2	WITHAM TOWN	2-0	
17/10/95	IFL	2	LEATHERHEAD	1-1	
21/10/95	FA Cup	Q4	HEDNESFORD TOWN	2-0	
24/10/95	E. F'lit	Gp 7	Southend Manor	5-0	
28/10/95	IFL	2	HEMEL HEMPSTEAD	1-0	
31/10/95	E. F'lit	Gp 7	CONCORD RANGERS	2-2	
04/11/95	IFL	2	Tilbury	5-0	
12/11/95	FA Cup	1	BRIGHTON & HOVE ALB	2-2	
14/11/95	IFL	2	WIVENHOE TOWN	3-3	
21/11/95	FA Cup	1 rep	Brighton & Hove Albion	1-4	
25/11/95	IFL	2	Cheshunt	0-0	
28/11/95	Essex SC	2	Southend United	0-6	
02/12/95	IFL	2	CHALFONT ST PETER	2-0	
12/12/95	Essex TST	1	East Thurrock United	2-1	
16/12/95	IFL	2	DORKING	4-0	
19/12/95	Carlton	2	COLLIER ROW	3-2	
23/12/95	IFL	2	Bedford Town	7-1	
01/01/96	IFL	2	Bracknell Town	1-2	
06/01/96	IFL	2	HAMPTON	3-3	
20/01/96	IFL	2	EGHAM TOWN	5-1	
23/01/96	IFL	2	WARE	4-1	
30/01/96	Carlton	3	CLAPTON	1-0	
06/02/96	E. F'lit	Gp 7	Concord Rangers	1-1	
10/02/96	IFL	2	Banstead Athletic	3-0	
12/02/96	IFL	2	Croydon	2-0	
17/02/96	IFL	2	EDGWARE TOWN	2-0	
05/03/96	Carlton	QF	Wivenhoe Town	3-1	
09/03/96	IFL	2	Witham Town	0-0	
12/03/96	IFL	2	Leatherhead	4-2	
16/03/96	IFL	2	HUNGERFORD TOWN	3-0	
21/03/96	Essex TST	2	Basildon United	3-1	
23/03/96	IFL	2	Ware	0-1	
26/03/96	Carlton	SF	HUNGERFORD TOWN	1-1	
28/03/96	E. F'lit	QF	Romford	1-6	
30/03/96	IFL	2	TILBURY	3-2	
02/04/96	IFL	2	METROPOLITAN POLICE	2-0	
06/04/96	IFL	2	BRACKNELL TOWN	0-0	
08/04/96	IFL	2	Collier Row	3-1	
11/04/96	Carlton	SF rep	Hungerford Town	2-1	
13/04/96	IFL	2	CHESHUNT	1-1	
16/04/96	Essex TST	QF	CONCORD RANGERS	1-0	
18/04/96	IFL	2	Hemel Hempstead	2-0	
20/04/96	IFL	2	Chalfont St Peter	2-1	
23/04/96	IFL	2	Saffron Walden Town	4-1	
25/04/96	IFL	2	Hungerford Town	5-2	
27/04/96	IFL	2	CROYDON	0-0	
30/04/96	IFL	2	COLLIER ROW	2-1	
02/05/96	IFL	2	Wivenhoe Town	2-6	
04/05/96	IFL	2	Dorking	3-2	
06/05/96	Essex TST	SF	Grays Athletic	2-0	
09/05/96	Carlton	F	BANSTEAD ATHLETIC	2-1	(At Aveley)
12/05/96	Essex TST	F	WITHAM TOWN	5-0	

CHESHAM UNITED

Meadow Park, Amy Lane, Amersham Rd, Chesham HP5 1NE.Tel: 01494 783964 - 791608
Fax 0891 884580 match info service

Secretary: Ron Campion, Burslee, Chiltern Rd,
Ballinger, Bucks, HP16 9LH Tel 01494 837494

Colours: Claret and Blue   Nickname: The Generals

Capacity: 5,000   Seating: 224

Covered standing: 1,000   Clubhouse on ground: Yes

Record attendance: 5,000 v Cambridge Utd
FA Cup 3rd Rd Dec 5th 1979

Record appearance Holder: Martin Baguley 600+

Record goalscorer in one season: John Willis

DIRECTIONS

**M25 junction 18, A404 to
Amersham, A416 to Chesham —
go down to r'bout at foot of
Amersham Hill, then sharp left. 10
mins walk from Chesham station
(Metropolitan Line).**

Honours

FA AMATEUR CUP Runners up 1968

Isthmian League 1993

Division One 1991 and Div 2 North 1987

Charity Shield 1995, Athenian League Div 1 Cup 1964 and 1969

Corinthian League Cup 1961, Spartan League 1922, 1923, 1925, 1933

Berks and Bucks Senior Cup 1922, 1926, 1929, 1934, 1948, 1951, 1965, 1967, 1976, 1993

Chesham United were formed, as Chesham FC around 1878. They later added the suffix Town and when the club merged with Chesham Generals during the Great War, they created Chesham United. Town were founder members of the Southern League in 1894 and the Athenian League in 1912, whilst the Generals also played in the Spartan League from 1909 to 1914, winning it in their last season. The combined club had much success between the Wars winning Div One three times and the Premier Division in 1933. It was a boom time for the club who played initially on the cricket ground next door to the Meadow ground before moving up after the Great War and taking their wooden stand with them.

In 1947 they joined the new Corinthian League and in 1963 moved to the Athenian League where they twice won the League Cup. The late 60's were without question the most exciting time that the club has enjoyed, twice taking the Berks and Bucks Senior Cup before battling as rank outsiders through over a dozen matches to reach the FA Amateur Cup final at Wembley against Leytonstone. They were saddened to miss a penalty and lose 1-0 in front of 55,000 people. It was the beginning of a quiet period until, firstly they played Brentford in the FA Cup in 1976 and then enjoyed another remarkable run in 1979, which saw them beat the likes of Bedford Town, Merthyr Tydfil and Minehead before hosting Cambridge Utd at the Meadow. A record crowd of 5,000 saw them bow out. In preparing the ground for the match, officials cleared a grassed area behind the top goal to discover terracing that nobody knew existed! It was hastily cleared to add to the capacity.

They suffered a major set back in 1983 when the marvellous old grandstand burned down and they were forced to play at other grounds during re-building, and it heralded some bleak times for the club, as in 1986 the receivers were called in, and a group emerged who rescued the club who had gone down to Division Two of the Isthmian League. The Div 2 North title was soon won and in 1991 they won Division One to take their place in the top flight.

Since those times under George Borg there have sadly been more financial problems and United were again relegated and last season saw them in mid table.

CHESHAM UNITED 1995/96 SEASON

Date	Comp		Opponent	Score	Scorers
19/08/95	IFL	1	Thame United	2-1	
26/08/95	IFL	1	OXFORD CITY	0-2	
02/09/95	IFL	1	Wokingham Town	2-3	
05/09/95	GIC	1	HARROW BOROUGH	4-1	
09/09/95	FA Cup	Q1	Edgware Town	1-0	
13/09/95	IFL	1	STAINES TOWN	2-0	Heffernan, Cooper
16/09/95	IFL	1	Wembley	2-0	
19/09/95	IFL	1	Leyton Pennant	2-2	McKay, Heffernan
23/09/95	FA Cup	Q2	Purfleet	1-3	Beckett
30/09/95	IFL	1	BARTON ROVERS	4-0	Kerr, Heffernan, Barnes, McKay
07/10/95	IFL	1	Ruislip Manor	0-1	
14/10/95	FA Trophy	Q1	Newport I.O.W.	3-1	Cordice, Heffernan(2)
17/10/95	IFL	1	BILLERICAY TOWN	0-1	
21/10/95	IFL	1	Basingstoke Town	1-2	Heffernan
24/10/95	IFL	1	ABINGDON TOWN	4-0	Heffernan(4)
28/10/95	IFL	1	ALDERSHOT TOWN	1-0	Gleeson
31/10/95	GIC	2	AYLESBURY UNITED	2-3	
04/11/95	FA Trophy	Q2	Chertsey Town	2-2	Davies(2)
07/11/95	FA Trophy	Q2 rep	CHERTSEY TOWN	2-3	Heffernan, Beckett
07/11/95	CC	1	AYLESBURY UNITED	2-3	
18/11/95	IFL	1	BARKING	1-1	Spurr
21/11/95	IFL	1	WHYTELEAFE	2-2	Heffernan, Spurr
25/11/95	IFL	1	Marlow	2-1	Leach(og), Davies
02/12/95	IFL	1	HEYBRIDGE SWIFTS	1-1	Davies
09/12/95	IFL	1	Tooting & Mitcham United	1-1	Heffernan
16/12/95	IFL	1	MAIDENHEAD UNITED	1-0	Pickett
18/12/95	IFL	1	Bognor Regis Town	0-3	
23/12/95	IFL	1	Oxford City	0-1	
26/12/95	IFL	1	BERKHAMSTED TOWN	0-1	
01/01/96	IFL	1	Uxbridge	0-0	
06/01/96	IFL	1	WOKINGHAM TOWN	2-0	Murnagh, Lay
13/01/96	IFL	1	Staines Town	3-3	Cordice, Norman, Beckett
20/01/96	IFL	1	THAME UNITED	0-0	
23/01/96	B&B SC	1	HUNGERFORD TOWN	0-2	
03/02/96	IFL	1	LEYTON PENNANT	0-1	
10/02/96	IFL	1	Barton Rovers	0-0	
17/02/96	IFL	1	WEMBLEY	3-0	Lay(3)
24/02/96	IFL	1	Aldershot Town	0-1	
02/03/96	IFL	1	BASINGSTOKE TOWN	2-2	Spurr, Williams
06/03/96	IFL	1	Abingdon Town	0-0	
09/03/96	IFL	1	Billericay Town	0-2	
16/03/96	IFL	1	RUISLIP MANOR	3-2	Benning(2), Nolan
23/03/96	IFL	1	BOGNOR REGIS TOWN	0-1	
30/03/96	IFL	1	Whyteleafe	4-3	Ross(2), Lawford, Dodman(og)
02/04/96	IFL	1	Barking	2-0	Ross, McKay
06/04/96	IFL	1	UXBRIDGE	1-0	Lawford
08/04/96	IFL	1	Berkhamsted Town	1-0	Lawford
13/04/96	IFL	1	MARLOW	1-1	Lawford
20/04/96	IFL	1	Heybridge Swifts	0-2	
27/04/96	IFL	1	TOOTING & MITCHAM UNI-	1-2	Lawford
04/05/96	IFL	1	Maidenhead United	0-1	

CROYDON

Croydon Sports Arena, Albert Rd, South Norwood, SE25 4QL. Tel: 0181 654 3462

Secretary: Mrs J.Jarvie, 2 Spa Close, South Norwood, London SE25 6DS.Tel: 0181 771 3242

Colours: Sky Blue

Capacity: 8,000

Seating: 450

Covered standing: Yes

Clubhouse on ground: Yes

Record attendance: 1,600 v Dorking Surrey Senior League Charity Cup final 1954

Record appearance Holder: Alec Jackson 400+

DIRECTIONS

Train to East Croydon or Norwood Junction, then bus 12 to either Belmont or Dundee Road. Walk down either — ground at bottom. 5 minutes walk from Woodside (BR).

Honours

Surrey Senior Cup 1982

Surrey Premier Cup 1987

Spartan League 1964

Athenian League Div 2 1966

Surrey Senior League Cup 1961

Charity Cup 1954 and 1963

Manager for 1996-97: Ken Jarvie

Croydon are one of the youngest sides in the Isthmian having been formed as Croydon Amateurs in 1953.

They joined the Surrey Senior League and in the first season reached the finals of the Challenge and Charity Cups, the second in front of 1,600 people at the Croydon Arena. During the next nine seasons they won both cups and during that period were helped by a certain Peter Bonetti who went on to play for England in the World Cup. In 1963 Croydon were elected to the Spartan League where they had one season, winning the league and scoring 123 goals in 34 games. They stepped into the Athenian League and won Division Two, but it was a little quick for they went straight back down again. The early 70's saw the club win two promotions to reach the Premier Division of the league.

In 1974 they were elected to the recently formed 2nd Division of the Isthmian League and the name Amateurs was dropped, and in 1975-76 they went through unbeaten in 42 matches, but still were second to Tilbury! During their time at the top, the club reached London and Surrey Senior Cup finals and League Cup finals and had their best finish when fourth behind Sutton in 1986.

Since those heady days the club has endured no end of turmoil with their ground closed for re development, arson attacks on the club house and a crisis when the club was forced to draft in a pub side to complete the fixtures, with the resulting goals against record being shattered.

To the credit of all concerned, they made a triumphant return last year by being promoted as runners up in Division Two.

CROYDON 1995/96 SEASON

19/08/95	IFL	2	CHESHUNT	3-2
21/08/95	LC	P	CAMBERLEY TOWN	4-0
26/08/95	FA Cup	P	DORKING	5-2
04/09/95	LC	1	WITHAM TOWN	3-0
09/09/95	FA Cup	Q1	HASTINGS TOWN	2-3
16/09/95	IFL	2	WIVENHOE TOWN	1-2
18/09/95	IFL	2	HEMEL HEMPSTEAD	2-0
23/09/95	IFL	2	Ware	2-2
26/09/95	IFL	2	Tilbury	0-2
02/10/95	IFL	2	CHALFONT ST PETER	4-0
07/10/95	IFL	2	Hampton	3-5
09/10/95	Surrey SC	Q2	CAMBERLEY TOWN	0-1
14/10/95	IFL	2	SAFFRON WALDEN TOWN	2-0
21/10/95	IFL	2	Metropolitan Police	0-1
23/10/95	IFL	2	BRACKNELL TOWN	2-1
31/10/95	LC	2	Hendon	1-0
04/11/95	IFL	2	Dorking	3-0
07/11/95	Carlton	1	Chalfont St Peter	0-1
11/11/95	IFL	2	BEDFORD TOWN	4-1
18/11/95	IFL	2	Egham Town	3-2
25/11/95	IFL	2	EDGWARE TOWN	0-1
27/11/95	LC	3	WALTON & HERSHAM	2-1
02/12/95	IFL	2	Leatherhead	2-2
16/12/95	IFL	2	Hungerford Town	3-0
19/12/95	London CC	1	Metropolitan Police	1-2
23/12/95	IFL	2	TILBURY	2-1
01/01/96	IFL	2	WITHAM TOWN	2-0
06/01/96	IFL	2	Hemel Hempstead	0-0
20/01/96	IFL	2	Cheshunt	5-0
22/01/96	IFL	2	COLLIER ROW	1-3
30/01/96	IFL	2	Banstead Athletic	0-1
03/02/96	IFL	2	Chalfont St Peter	1-0
12/02/96	IFL	2	CANVEY ISLAND	0-2
17/02/96	IFL	2	Wivenhoe Town	4-3
29/02/96	IFL	2	Bracknell Town	2-0
02/03/96	IFL	2	METROPOLITAN POLICE	4-1
05/03/96	LC	QF	Aylesbury United	1-2
09/03/96	IFL	2	Saffron Walden Town	3-2
13/03/96	IFL	2	Collier Row	2-1
16/03/96	IFL	2	HAMPTON	1-0
23/03/96	IFL	2	Bedford Town	0-2
25/03/96	IFL	2	EGHAM TOWN	1-0
30/03/96	IFL	2	DORKING	2-1
06/04/96	IFL	2	Witham Town	0-0
08/04/96	IFL	2	BANSTEAD ATHLETIC	0-0
13/04/96	IFL	2	Edgware Town	4-1
15/04/96	IFL	2	WARE	5-2
20/04/96	IFL	2	LEATHERHEAD	2-1
27/04/96	IFL	2	Canvey Island	0-0
04/05/96	IFL	2	HUNGERFORD TOWN	3-0

HAMPTON

The Beveree Stadium, Beaver Close, off Station Road, Hampton TW12 2BX. Tel: 0181 979 2456

Secretary: Adrian Mann, 30 Burniston Ct, Manor Rd, Wallington, Surrey SM6 0AD Tel 0181 773 0858

General Secretary: Alan Clark, 9 Bramley Close, Whitton, Twickenham, Middx Tel: 0181 898 3744

Nickname: The Beavers   Colours, Red and Blue

Capacity: 3,000   Seating: 220

Covered standing: 600   Clubhouse on ground: Yes

Record attendance: Not known

Biggest win: 11-1 v Eastbourne Utd
Isthmian League Div 2 South 1991-92

Biggest defeat: 0-13 v Hounslow Town 1962-63

Record appearances: Tim Hollands

Record goalscorer in one season: Syd Carter

Record goalscorer in total: Peter Allen

Record fee received: £2,500 for Ricky Walkes by APOP (Cyprus) 1989

Honours

Middlesex Charity Cup 1970 and 1996

Spartan League 1965, 1966, 1967, 1970 and League Cup 1965, 1966, 1967, 1968

Surrey Senior League 1964

Southern Combination Cup 1969, 72, 77, 82, 84, 86

DIRECTIONS

5 minutes walk along Station Road from Hampton (BR) — half hourly service from London Waterloo via Clapham Junction, Wimbledon & Kingston. Buses 111 (Hampton-Heathrow) & 216 (Kingston-Staines) stop in Station Road. 726 (Dartford-Kingston-Windsor) & 267 (Hammersmith-Hampton Court) stop in nearby Church Street. By road; A3 out of London, fork left (signed Staines/Esher/Sandown Park) onto A243, A309 Staines exit to Hampton Ct at Scilly Isles' roundabout after Hampton Ct Bridge onto A308, after 1 mile right into Church Street (A311), left after White Hart after 200 yards into High Street, Station Road on right just before junction with A308. From M25; junction 12, M3 towards London, junction 1 for the A308 (Sunbury) and turn right under Motorway onto A308 for Kingston & Hampton, continue past racecourse, left into Hampton High Street, just after waterworks (on right), Station Road 1st left.

Club or Beaverline on: 0891 122922

Manager for 1996-97: Chick Botley, Assistant manager: Barry Barnes

Chairman: Robert Hayes,Vice chairman: Ken Gazzard

PRESS OFFICER: Les Rance, 5 Lyndhurst Ave, Whitton, Twickenham TW2 6BG TEL : 0181 287 4682

Hampton were formed in 1920 following a meeting involving four local clubs. They spent the early years in the South-West Middlesex and Kingston and District Leagues before stepping up into Senior football and returning to their home at the Beveree which had been taken over by Twickenham FC following a dubious plot involving that club's chairman. After 26 years in the SWML the club joined the Surrey Senior League, winning it in 1964. Success came also in Middx Senior and Surrey Senior Cups, which helped gain promotion to the Spartan League, which heralded the start of the Beaver's best era to date, with four championships and four consecutive League Cup victories. They never finished lower than fourth, and twice reached the final of the Middlesex Charity Cup, beating Uxbridge in 1970. A sign of the club's rise to power was the switching on of the first floodlights in 1967, when a Spartan League X1 played an England Amateur X1, but they were constantly rebuffed by the Athenian League until 1971 finishing runners-up to Ruislip Manor in 1973. Only playing in the Athenians for two seasons, they however reached their first ever Senior final, losing to Hendon in the Middlesex Senior Cup. Since joining the Isthmian League, the highest placing has been fifth in the First Division, when they also reached the semi-final of the League Cup. Since then the club have suffered relegation but happily 1996 saw them return to Division One. In 1987 Beavers were beaten by rivals Kingstonian in the London Senior Cup, yet within months the clubs had agreed a ground sharing scheme at the Beveree whilst the K's new ground was being built. At the end of 1989-90 season, the club suffered relegation for the first time in its history, and two days later lost to Chelsea in the Middlesex Charity Cup final. They were unable to halt the slide and when

the two regions were formed into a third division, Hampton dropped down, for just one season, as more club movements saw them promoted again. In 1995 the club celebrated its 75th anniversary, where they lost in the final of the Charity Cup again, this time to Wembley. However last May saw the Beavers beat Tilbury on the last day to clinch promotion in third place. To cap a fine season they reached both Middlesex Cup finals, beating Enfield in the Senior Cup after extra time and losing the Charity Cup to Hayes, also after extra time.

HAMPTON 1995/96 SEASON

22/08/95	LC	P	Leighton Town	2-1	
26/08/95	FA Cup	P	Haverhill Rovers	1-0	
02/09/95	IFL	2	CANVEY ISLAND	0-0	
05/09/95	LC	1	Billericay Town	1-3	
09/09/95	FA Cup	Q1	STAINES TOWN	1-2	
16/09/95	IFL	2	CHESHUNT	2-2	
19/09/95	IFL	2	WIVENHOE TOWN	2-0	
23/09/95	IFL	2	Collier Row	1-0	
26/09/95	IFL	2	Hemel Hempstead	3-3	
07/10/95	IFL	2	CROYDON	5-3	
10/10/95	S Comb Cup	1	EGHAM TOWN	1-0	
14/10/95	IFL	2	Dorking	1-3	
17/10/95	IFL	2	Chalfont St Peter	0-2	
21/10/95	IFL	2	Egham Town	2-0	
24/10/95	London CC	1	Uxbridge	2-0	
04/11/95	IFL	2	Bedford Town	1-1	
07/11/95	Middx SC	1	Bedfont	2-0	
11/11/95	IFL	2	BRACKNELL TOWN	1-0	
25/11/95	IFL	2	WARE	3-1	
28/11/95	IFL	2	Witham Town	1-0	
02/12/95	IFL	2	Edgware Town	2-4	
05/12/95	Carlton	2	Cove	4-0	
23/12/95	IFL	2	WITHAM TOWN	2-1	
02/01/96	IFL	2	LEATHERHEAD	3-3	
06/01/96	IFL	2	Canvey Island	3-3	
09/01/96	Middx SC	2	EDGWARE TOWN	2-1	
16/01/96	London CC	QF	Metropolitan Police	3-1	
27/01/96	IFL	2	COLLIER ROW	0-0	
03/02/96	IFL	2	METROPOLITAN POLICE	2-0	
10/02/96	IFL	2	HEMEL HEMPSTEAD	2-3	
13/02/96	Middx SC	QF	Hillingdon Borough	6-1	
15/02/96	Carlton	3	Hungerford Town	0-1	
17/02/96	IFL	2	Cheshunt	3-0	
18/02/96	S Comb Cup	QF	CROYDON ATHLETIC	1-2	
24/02/96	IFL	2	Saffron Walden Town	0-1	
27/02/96	IFL	2	CHALFONT ST PETER	1-0	
02/03/96	IFL	2	EGHAM TOWN	1-0	
05/03/96	IFL	2	Tilbury	3-0	
09/03/96	IFL	2	DORKING	2-1	
11/03/96	IFL	2	Banstead Athletic	1-1	
13/03/96	Middx SC	SF	ENFIELD	3-1	
16/03/96	IFL	2	Croydon	0-1	
19/03/96	IFL	2	Metropolitan Police	2-0	
23/03/96	IFL	2	Bracknell Town	5-3	
26/03/96	IFL	2	SAFFRON WALDEN TOWN	1-1	
30/03/96	IFL	2	BEDFORD TOWN	3-0	
02/04/96	IFL	2	BANSTEAD ATHLETIC	5-4	
06/04/96	IFL	2	Leatherhead	2-1	
08/04/96	Middx SC	F	HAYES	2-3	(At Yeading FC)
11/04/96	London CC	SF	Leyton Pennant	1-2	
13/04/96	IFL	2	Ware	0-1	
16/04/96	IFL	2	HUNGERFORD TOWN	1-0	
20/04/96	IFL	2	EDGWARE TOWN	1-0	
23/04/96	IFL	2	Wivenhoe Town	2-0	
27/04/96	IFL	2	Hungerford Town	1-1	
02/05/96	Middx CC	SF	Staines Town	3-2	
04/05/96	IFL	2	TILBURY	4-0	
10/05/96	Middx CC	F	RUISLIP MANOR	3-2	(At Edgware Town FC)

LEYTON PENNANT

Wadham Lodge, Kitchener Rd, Walthamstow, E17. Tel: 0181 527 2444

Secretary: Andy Perkins, 4 Chestnut Drive, Wanstead, E11 2TA Tel: 0181 530 4551 (h) 0181 520 3587 (b)

Match Secretary: Ian Ansell, 120 Limes Ave, Limes Farm, Chigwell, Essex 1G7 5LX

Tel: 0181 500 9778 (h) 0181 527 5544 ext 6228 (b)

Nickname: Lilywhites

Colours: White and Navy Blue

Capacity: Not Known

Seating: 200

Covered Standing: 600

Clubhouse on ground: Yes

DIRECTIONS

North circular to Crooked Billet, turn into Chingford Road, then into Brookscroft Road, first on left.

Record attendance: 550 at Wadham Lodge. Recent times at Leyton FC 500 v Whickham FA Vase quarter final in 1984, although many more watched Leyton in the fifties when they reached the Amateur Cup final which was seen by 100,000.

Biggest win: (New Club) 6-2 v Purfleet April 1996

Biggest Defeat: 1-5 v Boreham Wood Feb 1996

Honours

Walthamstow Pennant FC

London Spartan League 1991 and League Cup 1989 and 1991

South-West Essex League 1973

Junior Cup 1969, Intermediate Cup, 1970 and Senior Cup 1971

London Junior Cup 1975

Metropolitan London League 1975, Metropolitan Inter League Cup 1979

Spartan Senior Cup 1989, Spartan League and League Cup 1991

Leyton FC

FA AMATEUR CUP WINNERS 1927, 1928

RUNNERS UP 1929, 1934, 1937, 1952

Walthamstow Charity Cup 1892, 1897

Isthmian League Div 2 North 198

London Senior Cup 1904

London Charity Cup 1935 and 1937

London League 1924, 1925, 1926 and League Cup 1957

Athenian League 1929, 1966, 1967, 1977, 1982

Essex Senior Cup 1897,1898, 1900,1901,1903,1930,1931, 1935

Essex Thameside Trophy 1965, 1967, 1982

Leyton and District Alliance 1893 and 1895

South Essex League 1896, 1897, 1900, Essex Junior Cup 1894.

Manager for 1996/97: Paul Taylor   **Chairman: John Stacey**

Press officer: Charlie Ward, Lynian House, Ivy Lane, Shutford, Oxfordshire OX15 6PD. Tel: 01295 780639

Fanzine: Own Goal is available from the club who are also on World wide Web page - http:// dspace.dial.pipex.com/town/square/gh32

LEYTON PENNANT 1995/96 SEASON

Date	Competition	Round	Opponent	Score	Scorers
19/08/95	IFL	1	RUISLIP MANOR	1-2	Staunton
23/08/95	IFL	1	Bognor Regis Town	2-3	O'Neill, Barnett
26/08/95	FA Cup	P	CLACTON TOWN	2-2	Flint. Own-Goal
29/08/95	FA Cup	P rep	Clacton Town	4-0	Popplewell(2), Barnett, O'Neill
02/09/95	IFL	1	TOOTING & MITCHAM	4-1	Day, Salmon, Flint, O'Neill
05/09/95	LC	1	Enfield	2-4	Popplewell, Day
09/09/95	FA Cup	Q1	Arlesey Town	0-3	
12/09/95	IFL	1	Whyteleafe	3-1	Day, Read, Edwards
16/09/95	IFL	1	BILLERICAY TOWN	1-2	B Read
19/09/95	IFL	1	CHESHAM UNITED	2-2	Thomas, Barley
23/09/95	IFL	1	Barking	2-1	M Cole, Barnett
30/09/95	IFL	1	Aldershot Town	1-4	Thomas
07/10/95	IFL	1	Uxbridge	0-1	
14/10/95	FA Trophy	Q1	FLEET TOWN	0-1	
17/10/95	IFL	1	STAINES TOWN	1-3	Drake
21/10/95	IFL	1	Berkhamsted Town	1-1	Cole
24/10/95	London CC	1	BOREHAM WOOD	5-5	B Read, Staunton(2), Gerraghty, Barnett
28/10/95	IFL		ABINGDON TOWN	0-2	
11/11/95	IFL	1	Barton Rovers	2-2	Read, Popplewell
18/11/95	IFL	1	WOKINGHAM TOWN	1-1	Barnett
21/11/95	CC	2	Wembley	3-2	
30/11/95	London CC	1 rep	Boreham Wood	3-2	Cole, Edwards. Own-Goal
02/12/95	IFL	1	OXFORD CITY	1-3	M Cole
05/12/95	Essex SC	2	SAFFRON WALDEN TOWN	2-1	
09/12/95	IFL	1	Marlow	1-2	M Cole
16/12/95	IFL	1	BASINGSTOKE TOWN	3-1	Barnett, Pratt, T Read
19/12/95	IFL	1	THAME UNITED	1-0	M Cole
23/12/95	IFL	1	Tooting & Mitcham United	3-2	M Cole, T Cole, Frampton(og)
02/01/96	Essex SC	3	BILLERICAY TOWN	3-2	
06/01/96	IFL	1	BARKING	3-0	Pratt, Garrity, A Read
13/01/96	IFL	1	BOGNOR REGIS TOWN	3-2	McLeod, M Cole, Barnett
20/01/96	IFL	1	Ruislip Manor	1-0	M Cole
23/01/96	IFL	3	PURFLEET	5-1	
31/01/96	London CC	QF	COLLIER ROW	3-3	
03/02/96	IFL	1	Chesham United	1-0	Salmon
10/02/96	IFL	1	ALDERSHOT TOWN	1-0	Flint
13/02/96	IFL	1	Maidenhead United	2-0	Creighton(og), Read
17/02/96	IFL	1	Billericay Town	3-0	Flint, Garretty, Gordon
24/02/96	IFL	1	Abingdon Town	2-2	P Read, T Read
27/02/96	CC	QF	Boreham Wood	1-5	
02/03/96	IFL	1	BERKHAMSTED TOWN	3-1	M Cole(2), T Read
05/03/96	IFL	1	HEYBRIDGE SWIFTS	0-1	
09/03/96	IFL	1	Staines Town	2-1	Flint, T Cole
11/03/96	London CC	QF rep	Collier Row	2-1	
16/03/96	IFL	1	UXBRIDGE	2-1	Salmon, McCluskey(og)
19/03/96	IFL	1	WHYTELEAFE	4-0	Barnett(2), Flint(2)
23/03/96	IFL	1	BARTON ROVERS	4-2	Gerarthey(2), A Read, Barnett
26/03/96	IFL	1	Wokingham Town	1-0	B Read
30/03/96	IFL	1	Thame United	0-2	
06/04/96	IFL	1	MAIDENHEAD UNITED	5-1	Barnett, Scott, Sapita, A Read(2)
08/04/96	IFL	1	Heybridge Swifts	0-0	
11/04/96	London CC	SF	HAMPTON	2-1	
13/04/96	IFL	1	WEMBLEY	4-2	A Read(3), Sapiro
20/04/96	IFL	1	Oxford City	2-2	Gerraghty, Cole
23/04/96	IFL	1	Wembley	1-0	B Read
27/04/96	IFL	1	MARLOW	2-4	Cole, Barnett
01/05/96	London CC	F	BROMLEY	2-3	(At Millwall)
04/05/96	IFL	1	Basingstoke Town	1-2	

Leyton Pennant FC was formed in May 1995 following the merger of Leyton FC and Walthamstow Pennant FC. The latter were formed in 1966 and played in the South-West Essex League until 1974, having won the league a year previously. They won the Junior Cup in 1969, the Intermediate Cup in 1970 and the Senior Cup in 1971 to complete a marvellous treble. They moved up to the London Metropolitan League after this where they stayed until the Spartan League took over. Pennant won the league in 1991 doing the double, and became Walthamstow Pennant. Their excellent Wadham Lodge ground is very new, as until recently the club played on what is now the second pitch on the complex.

Leyton FC are a much older and famous club, founded in 1868, making it the oldest senior club in London. The first club folded after briefly appearing in the FA Cup, in 1880 but reformed as Matlock Swifts in 1889. They won the Walthamstow Charity Cup in 1892 and the Essex Junior Cup two years later. They won the London Junior Cup in 1894 and having become Leyton FC, gained senior status and joined the South Essex League. It was a successful time as the Senior Cup, London Senior Cup and league title were all won.

In 1897 the club turned professional and in 1905 joined the Southern, South Eastern and United Leagues as well as fielding a side in the London League. Leyton got to the last 16 of the Cup in 1910, but disaster struck when they finished bottom of the First Division and were placed in Division Two, which consisted almost entirely of Welsh sides, and so they resigned. After the Great War the club again became Amateur and via the Middlesex and South Essex Leagues joined the London League in 1921 where they won a hat-trick of titles. In 1927 they won the coveted FA Amateur Cup for the first time and retained it a year later against Cockfield, at Middlesbrough.

Leyton joined the Athenian League in 1927, won it in 1929 and again in 1930. Honours continued through the 30's, with three Essex Senior Cups, two London Charity Cups and two more Amateur Cup finals. At the time the club were playing at Osborne Road, but despite signing a lease in 1930 the council gave the ground to Clapton Orient, who play there today, although it is better known as Brisbane Road. Walthamstow Avenue allowed the club to ground share until they acquired the Hare and Hounds Ground.

Leyton were runners up in the London Senior Cup in 1938 and the Essex Senior in 1940, and in six seasons after the war the club lost six more finals as well as losing the 1952 Amateur Cup final at Wembley to neighbours Walthamstow Avenue in front of 100,000 people. After a lean spell success returned in the 60's. They were Athenian League runners up in 1965 and champions in the next two seasons, but a dramatic slump saw successive relegations with Leyton playing in Division Two in 1970.

Financial problems almost forced the club to fold in 1975 but they were saved by a merger with Jewish club Wingate FC. In 1976 the ground freehold was purchased and and it was named Wingate-Leyton Stadium. There was a set back when the clubhouse was destroyed by fire, but the club now called Leyton-Wingate FC were Division One champions. Despite the win, they remained in the Athenian League until having won it again, they were promoted automatically. The debut season in the Isthmian League saw them score 111 goals but finish fourth, but they were to go up in 1985 as champions of Division Two North.

Playing in Division One they reached the FA Cup 1st Round, losing to Swansea City and got to the last eight of the FA Vase. Promotion to the top flight came in 1987 as runners up to Leytonstone and Ilford, when a last minute winner in the last game took them up. They spent four seasons at the top, before going down to Division one again in 1991.

The Wingate name was dropped in 1992 when Finchley FC joined forces with the Wingate side that had continued in the South Midlands League. Wingate had played briefly at Summers Lane when their original ground was taken for an extension to the M1, but they had acquired a ground at Arkley which was unsuitable for senior football. The club then merged with Leyton, enabling the youth football to continue at Arkley. Wingate later joined the Herts County and South Midlands Leagues, from where they merged with Finchley.

After many financial and ground problems, Leyton FC left the Hare and Hounds in 1995 and merged with Walthamstow Pennant, from where they enjoyed a fine season, ending in fourth place.

The dressing room block at Wingate's ground at Arkley, where Wingate FC enjoyed a brief spell in the South Midlands League before merging with Finchley.

MAIDENHEAD UNITED

York Road, Maidenhead, Berks SL6 1SQ. Tel: 01628 24739

Secretary: Roy Bannister, 24 Queensway, Maidenhead Berks SL6 7SDF. Tel: 01628 35369

Colours: Black and white stripes

Nickname: The Magpies   Capacity: 3,000

Seating: 220   Covered standing: 900

Clubhouse on ground: Yes

Record attendance: 7,920 v Southall
FA Amateur Cup quarter-final Mar 7th 1936.

Biggest win: 14-1 v Buckingham Town
FA Amateur Cup Sept 6th 1952

Biggest defeat: 0-14 v Chesham United (A)
Spartan League Mar 31st 1923

Record appearances: Bert Randall 532 1950-1964

Record goalscorer in one season: Jack Palethorpe 66 1929-30

Record goalscorer in total: George Copas 270 1924-35

DIRECTIONS

From Maidenhead BR station proceed eastwards down Bell Street - ground 300 yds along. From bus station, southwards down bridge Avenue to York Road, turn right, ground 200 yds on left. Large car park opposite ground entrance in York Road.

Honours

FA AMATEUR CUP semi-final 1936

FA CUP QUARTER-FINALS 1873, 1874, 1875, Spartan League 1927, 1933, 1934

Corinthian League 1958, 1961,

Memorial Shield 1957, 1962, Mithras Cup 1963 and 1967, Neale Cup 1949, 1958, 1961

Great Western Suburban League 1920, Great Western Combination 1949

Berks and Bucks Senior Cup 1895, 96, 1907, 12, 28, 30, 31, 32, 39, 46, 56, 57, 61, 63, 66, 70

Berks and Bucks Benevolent Cup 1931, 1937, 1940, 1959, 1961

Reading Senior Cup 1956 and 1959

Maidenhead can trace their beginnings back to 1869, which makes them one of the oldest clubs in the world. They spent their early years playing friendlies in a field on the banks of the Thames before moving to York Road to share with the Cricket Club. They were one of the original entrants to the FA Cup and since 1871 have missed only one year of entry. They reached the quarter-finals in 1874, 1875 and 1880, after getting to the semi-final in 1873, although that match was originally a quarter-final. Maidenhead FC had an unsuccessful period in the Southern League, against the likes of Tottenham, Brentford, Fulham and Southampton and so joined the Great Western Suburban League in 1904, winning it in 1920. After the Great War, the club merged with another senior amateur club, Maidenhead Norfolkians, who played at the now landscaped Kidwells Park and the new club were briefly known as Town before reverting to United. In 1922 they moved into the Spartan League and in seven seasons from 1926 won the title three times and were runners up twice. 1936 saw United reach the semi-finals of the Amateur Cup, where they lost to Ilford, at West Ham, in front of over 18,000 spectators. The round before saw 2,000 locked out of the match with Southall, as the ground record of 7,600 was set. Most of them watched the game from the railway.

This success saw sweeping changes at York Road which had remained unchanged for 40 years. Two stands were built and the banking around the ground was terraced, much of which has now been replaced.

After the Second War United entered the Corinthian League, winning it three times and finishing second twice, also reaching the Shield final six times. 1963 saw a move to the Athenians following rejection by the Southern League and it spelled the end of the glory days, although the odd Amateur and FA Cup runs brought in the crowds. After ten years, Maidenhead moved up again, this time to the Isthmian League, where they stayed in what is now Division One, before suffering relegation in 1987. It was a terrible time for the club, whose ground also suffered an arson attack which destroyed the wonderful 60 year old grandstand, changing rooms and offices. The club languished until 1991 when they were promoted, losing the championship to Abingdon Town on the last day. Last season saw the club finish in relative safety in Division One.

MAIDENHEAD UNITED 1995/96 SEASON

19/08/95	IFL	1	BARKING	0-2	
22/08/95	IFL	1	Marlow	0-3	
26/08/95	FA Cup	P	Thame United	0-4	
29/08/95	IFL	1	TOOTING & MITCHAM UNITED	2-2	Smith, Houston
02/09/95	IFL	1	WHYTELEAFE	2-1	
05/09/95	GIC	1	Aylesbury United	0-3	
16/09/95	IFL	1	BASINGSTOKE TOWN	0-0	
30/09/95	IFL	1	Ruislip Manor	1-0	McKinnon
07/10/95	IFL	1	OXFORD CITY	0-2	
14/10/95	FA Trophy	Q1	Fareham Town	4-2	Pritchard, Pratt, Creighton, Tate
17/10/95	IFL	1	Heybridge Swifts	1-1	McNamee
21/10/95	IFL	1	Staines Town	1-2	Pratt
28/10/95	IFL	1	BERKHAMSTED TOWN	0-2	
31/10/95	IFL	1	Uxbridge	0-0	
04/11/95	FA Trophy	Q2	THAME UNITED	0-5	
11/11/95	IFL	1	WOKINGHAM TOWN	0-3	
18/11/95	IFL	1	Thame United	5-2	Norman(2), Harrison, Dadson, Brown
02/12/95	IFL	1	Barton Rovers	0-4	
05/12/95	CC	2	Aldershot Town	1-3	
09/12/95	IFL	1	BILLERICAY TOWN	2-2	Gold, M Harrison
12/12/95	IFL	1	Wembley	1-0	Norman
16/12/95	IFL	1	Chesham United	0-1	
06/01/96	IFL	1	Whyteleafe	1-2	A Smith
13/01/96	IFL	1	MARLOW	4-1	McKinnon, Smith, Dadson(2)
16/01/96	B&B SC	1	BRACKNELL TOWN	1-0	
20/01/96	IFL	1	Barking	1-1	Dadson
30/01/96	IFL	1	THAME UNITED	2-1	McKinnon, Hanratty
03/02/96	IFL	1	Tooting & Mitcham United	1-1	Attrell
10/02/96	IFL	1	RUISLIP MANOR	2-1	Smith, Attrell
13/02/96	IFL	1	LEYTON PENNANT	0-2	
17/02/96	IFL	1	Basingstoke Town	2-2	Attrell, Dadson
02/03/96	IFL	1	STAINES TOWN	1-0	Dadson
05/03/96	IFL	1	ALDERSHOT TOWN	1-1	Houston
09/03/96	IFL	1	HEYBRIDGE SWIFTS	1-4	Smith
12/03/96	IFL	1	BOGNOR REGIS TOWN	0-1	
16/03/96	IFL	1	Oxford City	2-2	Dadson, Houston
19/03/96	B&B SC	SF	AYLESBURY UNITED	0-0	
23/03/96	IFL	1	Wokingham Town	1-2	Norman
26/03/96	B&B SC	SF rep	Aylesbury United	0-4	
30/03/96	IFL	1	WEMBLEY	1-0	Dadson
02/04/96	IFL	1	UXBRIDGE	1-2	Small
06/04/96	IFL	1	Leyton Pennant	1-5	Norman
08/04/96	IFL	1	ABINGDON TOWN	4-0	M Harrison, McKinnon, Creighton(2)
13/04/96	IFL	1	Aldershot Town	1-0	Croxford
16/04/96	IFL	1	Berkhamsted Town	2-2	Norman, Harland(og)
20/04/96	IFL	1	BARTON ROVERS	3-4	M Harrison, Smith, Creighton
22/04/96	IFL	1	Bognor Regis Town	0-0	
27/04/96	IFL	1	Billericay Town	1-1	Smith
01/05/96	IFL	1	Abingdon Town	1-1	Creighton
04/05/96	IFL	1	CHESHAM UNITED	1-0	

MARLOW

Alfred Davis Memorial Ground, Oak Tree Road, Marlow, Bucks SL7 3ED. Tel: 01628 483970

Secretary: Paul Burdell, 69 Wycombe Rd, Marlow, Bucks SL7 3HZ. Tel: 01628 48372

Press officer: Terry Staines, 49 Sunnycroft, Downley, High Wycombe, Bucks HP13 5UR Tel 01494 531580

Nickname: The Blues   Capacity: 3,000

Seating: 250   Covered standing: 600

Clubhouse on ground: Yes

DIRECTIONS

A404 to Marlow (from M4 or M40), then A4135 towards town centre. Turn right into Maple Rise (by ESSO garage), ground in road opposite (Oak Tree Road). Half mile from Marlow (BR) station. Quarter of mile from Chapel Street bus stops.

Record attendance: 8,000 Slough Town v Wycombe Wanderers Berks and Bucks Senior Cup Final 1972. For Marlow game 2,700 v Plymouth Argyle FA Cup 1st Rd 1993

Record appearances: Mick McKeown 500+

Record goalscorer in one season: Kevin Stone 31

Record fee received: £8,000 for David Lay

Honours

Isthmian League: 1988

Spartan League: Div 1 1938, Div 2 West 1930

Berks and Bucks Sen Cup: 1881, 83, 85, 86, 88, 89, 90, 94. 97, 99, 1900, 91, 94

Manager for 1996-97: Graham Wilkins, Assistant manager: Steve Roberts

Chairman: Terry Staines, Vice Chairman: Michael Watson

Founded in 1870, Marlow are one of the oldest clubs in the country. In the last century, then known as Great Marlow, they were a major force in the game and were one of the original entrants to the first FA Cup competition in 1971, contributing a share of the £25 which bought the first trophy. In 1882 they were semi-finalists, losing to the eventual winners Old Etonians, 5-0 at the Oval. Two Amateur Cup semi-finals and a succession of Berks and Bucks Cup wins were amongst many honours during that golden period.

In 1894 Marlow rejected an invitation to join the Southern League, preferring to remain amateur, and Tottenham Hotspur joined in their place.

Up to 1919 the club played at Crown Meadow, now the Riley Recreation Ground, and an enforced move to Star Meadow meant demotion from the Great Western Suburban League to the Reading League as the new ground was unfenced with no facilities. Hon Secretary Alfred Davis appealed for funds to purchase a new headquarters, but sadly he died before the official opening of the new ground, which is named in his memory. The picturesque grandstand was built six years later to celebrate their revival and the Spartan League Division Two championship.

Apart from a war-time break, Marlow stayed in the Spartan League until 1965 when they joined the Athenians, securing promotion in 1971. They moved up to the Isthmians fourteen years later, and under Mike Keen, the former Queens Park Rangers and Watford player, began a rapid rise, reaching the Premier Division and taking the championship.

Keen eventually left the club, and Dave Russell took them to a Berks and Bucks Cup win and FA Cup ties against West Bromwich Albion, Plymouth Argyle and most famous of all, a 3rd Round tie at White Hart Lane against Tottenham Hotspur in front of 27,000 spectators.

Since those heady days the club has sadly suffered relegation to Division One, but continue to enjoy one of the best kept grounds anywhere in non-League football.

MARLOW 1995/96 SEASON

Date	Comp	Rd	Opponent	Att	Score	Scorers
19/08/95	IFL	1	Heybridge Swifts	116	1-3	Clarke
22/08/95	IFL	1	MAIDENHEAD UNITED	504	3-0	Clarke, McDonnell(2)
26/08/95	IFL	1	WOKINGHAM TOWN	330	1-1	McDonnell
29/08/95	IFL	1	Oxford City	272	6-1	Floyd, McDonnell(4), Regan
02/09/95	IFL	1	Abingdon Town	192	4-3	Watkins, Phillips, Clarke, McDonnell
05/09/95	GIC	1	HEMEL HEMPSTEAD	168	2-1	Goodall, Walsh
16/09/95	IFL	1	Berkhamsted Town	173	1-1	Clarke
23/09/95	IFL	1	WHYTELEAFE	210	2-0	Rhoades-Brown, Wiltshire
30/09/95	IFL	1	WEMBLEY	274	0-2	
14/10/95	FA Trophy	Q1	Harrow Borough	244	1-1	Watkins
17/10/95	FA Trophy	Q1 rep	HARROW BOROUGH	261	1-4	Ferguson
21/10/95	FA Cup	Q4	Gravesend & Northfleet	814	1-1	Gubbins(og)
24/10/95	FA Cup	Q4 rep	GRAVESEND & NTHFLEET	814	3-3	Clark, McDonnell(2)
28/10/95	IFL	1	UXBRIDGE	203	2-3	Rhoades-Brown, Regan
30/10/95	FA Cup	Q4 rep(2)	Gravesend & Northfleet	1346	0-4	
04/11/95	IFL	1	Barking	127	0-2	
07/11/95	GIC	2	Leatherhead	54	2-0	Wiltshire, Regan
11/11/95	IFL	1	STAINES TOWN	260	2-3	Wallbridge, McDonnell
14/11/95	CC	1	Thame United	162	1-4	Own-Goal
18/11/95	IFL	1	Aldershot Town	1688	3-2	McDonnell(2), Clarke
25/11/95	IFL	1	CHESHAM UNITED	504	1-2	Ferguson
28/11/95	IFL	1	THAME UNITED	202	4-6	McDonnell(2), Clarke, Floyd
02/12/95	IFL	1	Whyteleafe	76	1-3	McDonnell
05/12/95	IFL	1	TOOTING & MITCHAM	125	3-1	Clarke(2), Pedley
09/12/95	IFL	1	LEYTON PENNANT	208	2-1	Rhoades-Brown, McDonnell
16/12/95	IFL	1	Bognor Regis Town	362	1-0	Leach
19/12/95	GIC	3	Basingstoke Town	75	0-6	
23/12/95	IFL	1	ABINGDON TOWN	230	2-1	McDonnell, Harvey-Lynch(og)
06/01/96	IFL	1	Thame United	195	3-0	Clarke, Watkins(2)
13/01/96	IFL	1	Maidenhead United	285	1-4	Rhoades-Brown
16/01/96	B&B SC	1	THATCHAM TOWN	94	0-2	
20/01/96	IFL	1	HEYBRIDGE SWIFTS	274	1-0	Rhodes-Brown
03/02/96	IFL	1	OXFORD CITY	310	2-4	Clarke, McDonnell
17/02/96	IFL	1	BERKHAMSTED TOWN	195	1-1	Rhoades-Brown
24/02/96	IFL	1	Uxbridge	134	0-4	
02/03/96	IFL	1	RUISLIP MANOR	124	3-2	McDonnell(2), Goodall
05/03/96	IFL	1	BILLERICAY TOWN	154	1-4	Floyd
09/03/96	IFL	1	BASINGSTOKE TOWN	278	3-3	Goodall, McDonnell, Pritchard
12/03/96	IFL	1	Wokingham Town	165	0-2	
16/03/96	IFL	1	Tooting & Mitcham United	91	0-2	
23/03/96	IFL	1	Staines Town	294	1-3	O'Donnell
26/03/96	IFL	1	Barton Rovers	62	1-2	Wiltshire
30/03/96	IFL	1	BARKING	120	2-0	Goodall, Floyd
02/04/96	IFL	1	ALDERSHOT TOWN	868	0-3	
06/04/96	IFL	1	Billericay Town	171	0-2	
08/04/96	IFL	1	BARTON ROVERS	214	2-0	Rhoades-Brown, Wiltshire
13/04/96	IFL	1	Chesham United	484	1-1	Rhodes-Brown
16/04/96	IFL	1	Wembley	74	2-1	McDonnell(2)
22/04/96	IFL	1	Ruislip Manor	95	1-0	McDonnell
27/04/96	IFL	1	Leyton Pennant	108	4-2	Pitchard(2), Ayres, McDonnell
30/04/96	IFL	1	Basingstoke Town	147	1-0	Williams
04/05/96	IFL	1	BOGNOR REGIS TOWN		3-0	

MOLESEY

412 Walton Road, West Molesey, Surrey KT8 0JG. Tel: 0181 979 4823

Secretary: Martyn Cole, 1 Elmtree Ave, Esher, Surrey
KT10 8JG Tel: 0181 398 1751

Nickname: The Moles

Capacity: 4,000

Seating: 400

Covered standing: 600

Clubhouse on ground: Yes

Record attendance: 1,255 v Sutton Utd
Surrey Senior Cup semi-final 1966

Record appearances: Frank Hanley 453

Record goalscorer in total: Micheal Rose 130

DIRECTIONS

**A3 from London to Hook, then
A309 to Marquis of Granby pub,
right to Hampton Court station,
turn right for West Molesey,
ground one mile on left.**

Honours

Surrey Senior League 1958

Charity Cup 1957

Spartan League Cup 1961

Southern Combination Cup 1991 and 1994

The current Molesey FC came into being in 1953 when Molesey St Pauls United changed their name. However, it is thought that the area has been represented by a football club since 1898. A side named Molesey and St Paul United won the Surrey Minor Cup in 1913 and the following season won the Surrey Junior Cup. A club called Molesey FC won its first county honours with a 3-0 win over Brighton Railway in the 1921 Surrey Junior Cup final and in the same year they took the Junior Charity Cup.

They won it a further three times, but after the war they reached the Intermediate Charity Cup final.

Molesey St Pauls United were formed in 1950, and as Molesey they joined the Surrey Intermediate League, moving to the Surrey Senior League in 1956. In the first season they won the League Charity Cup and a year later took the title. They moved on to the Spartan League in 1959 along with Bletchley Town and they remained there until 1973. Although never winning the league they were runners up and also won the League Cup in 1962, losing three other finals. In 1966, Molesey reached the Senior Cup semi-final and faced Sutton United in front of 1,255 which is still a record for the club.

Floodlights were installed in 1971 and the club joined the Athenian League Division Two in 1973, and for a few seasons enjoyed some success in the new FA Vase until joining the Isthmian League in 1977. The Isthmians expanded again in 1984 which saw Molesey placed in Division Two South.

However, the club were deep in debt and the committee at the time attempted to sell the ground and relocate but members angrily turned the proposal down. A new committee cleared the debts and soon the club were up to Division One finishing runners up to Yeading. With Tony Dunne managing the side in 1992 the club got to the Loctite Cup semi-final. The following year was a great success with a 17 match unbeaten run which took the club to the Premier Division for the first time, also reaching the League Cup final against Marlow. Having just escaped relegation in 1995, it was with sadness that the club conceded defeat to the ground gradings long before the final outcome and so start 1996-97 back in Division One.

MOLESEY 1995/96 SEASON

Date	Comp	Rnd	Opponent	Att	Score	Scorers
12/08/95	IFL	P	ENFIELD	405	1-4	Burton
19/08/95	IFL	P	Carshalton Athletic	352	0-4	
23/08/95	IFL	P	BOREHAM WOOD	125	1-2	George
26/08/95	IFL	P	AYLESBURY UNITED	450	1-4	Burton
29/08/95	IFL	P	Kingstonian	394	1-1	Smart
02/09/95	IFL	P	Hayes	318	0-2	
06/09/95	GIC	1	BASINGSTOKE TOWN		0-1	
09/09/95	FA Cup	Q1	WHITSTABLE TOWN	130	4-1	Smart, Burton, McCoy, Lewis
16/09/95	IFL	P	Hitchin Town	292	1-0	Underdown
23/09/95	FA Cup	Q2	GRAVESEND & NTHFLEET	295	0-6	
30/09/95	IFL	P	GRAYS ATHLETIC	115	0-0	
07/10/95	IFL	P	BISHOP'S STORTFORD	120	2-1	Lewis, Smart
10/10/95	S Comb Cup	1	Cove	99	0-1	
14/10/95	IFL	P	Bromley	326	3-1	Tutt, Lewis, Gnaye
21/10/95	IFL	P	DULWICH HAMLET	190	1-2	Swift
28/10/95	IFL	P	Harrow Borough	198	1-3	Swift
04/11/95	IFL	P	Yeading	155	2-2	Gnaye(2)
11/11/95	IFL	P	YEOVIL TOWN	300	2-3	Swift, Smart
18/11/95	IFL	P	Sutton United	494	0-2	
22/11/95	CC	1	KINGSTONIAN		0-3	
25/11/95	FA Trophy	Q3	STAINES TOWN	150	2-2	Lewis, Swift
28/11/95	FA Trophy	Q3 rep	Staines Town	208	0-5	
02/12/95	IFL	P	Hendon	197	0-2	
13/12/95	Surrey SC	1	LEATHERHEAD		3-1	
16/12/95	IFL	P	Chertsey Town	280	0-3	
23/12/95	IFL	P	HAYES	200	0-2	
01/01/96	IFL	P	PURFLEET	180	2-3	Kellman, McCoy
06/01/96	IFL	P	Enfield	765	0-2	
13/01/96	IFL	P	Boreham Wood	292	1-0	Raffington
17/01/96	IFL	P	SUTTON UNITED	275	0-5	
23/01/96	Surrey SC	QF	Woking		1-8	
03/02/96	IFL	P	KINGSTONIAN	310	0-2	
10/02/96	IFL	P	Grays Athletic	255	0-1	
17/02/96	IFL	P	HITCHIN TOWN	142	2-1	McKinn, Bates
18/02/96	S Comb Cup	QF	ASHFORD TOWN (MIDDX)	99	0-1	
24/02/96	IFL	P	HARROW BOROUGH	120	0-0	
28/02/96	IFL	P	ST ALBANS CITY	190	1-1	Ndah
02/03/96	IFL	P	Dulwich Hamlet	414	0-2	
09/03/96	IFL	P	BROMLEY	120	3-2	Bates(2), McKimm
16/03/96	IFL	P	Bishop's Stortford	264	0-4	
19/03/96	IFL	P	Walton & Hersham	212	3-3	McCoy, Bates, McKimm
23/03/96	IFL	P	Yeovil Town	1870	2-3	McCoy, McKimm
30/03/96	IFL	P	YEADING	110	1-2	McKinnon
03/04/96	IFL	P	WORTHING	130	3-1	Bates(3)
06/04/96	IFL	P	Purfleet	129	2-0	Bates, McCoy
08/04/96	IFL	P	WALTON & HERSHAM	240	2-2	Bates, McCoy
13/04/96	IFL	P	Worthing	304	4-4	Bates, McCoy(3)
17/04/96	IFL	P	CARSHALTON ATHLETIC	180	0-1	
20/04/96	IFL	P	HENDON	190	1-2	Ndah
23/04/96	IFL	P	Aylesbury United	259	1-1	Bates
27/04/96	IFL	P	St Albans City	378	0-1	
04/05/96	IFL	P	CHERTSEY TOWN	220	2-0	Gallagher, McKimm

THAME UNITED

Windmill Road, Thame, Oxon OX9 2 DR. Tel: 01844 213017

Secretary: Paul Smith, 18 Musgrave Rd, Chinnor Oxon
Tel OX9 4PL Tel 01844 354133

Nickname: United

Colours: Black and White

Capacity: 2,500

Seating: 230

Covered standing: 400

Clubhouse on ground: Yes

Record attendance: 1,035 v Aldershot Town Isthmian League Div 2 April 4th 1994

Biggest win: 9-0 v Bracknell Town 31st October 1992

Biggest defeat: 2-11 Hungerford Town
FA Cup Prelim Rd 1984

Record appearances: Steve Mayhew

DIRECTIONS
Into Nelson Street from Market Square 3 miles from Haddenham & Thame Parkway (BR). Nearest bus stop at Town Hall (half mile away).

Honours

Oxfordshire Senior Cup 1895, 1906, 1909, 1910, 1976, 1981, 1993

Oxfordshire Intermediate Cup 1977, 1979 1992

Hellenic League 1962 and 1970

Premier Div Cup (4 times)

South Midlands League 1991

Isthmian League Division 2 1995

The club was formed in 1883 which makes it one of Oxfordshire's oldest clubs. The early years were spent in Oxfordshire Leagues and in 1906, 1909 and 1910 Thame won the Senior Cup, taking the Senior League five times in 25 years. A switch to the Hellenic League then brought further success culminating in the championship in 1962 and 1970 as well as three runners-up spots.

After winning the Senior Cup twice in 1976 and 1981 the club went through a barren spell in the mid-eighties before crossing the pyramid to try their luck in the South Midlands League in 1988. Consecutive runners-up spots followed before the title was finally won in 1991 under the guidance of Bob Pratley. It led to the club being accepted into the Isthmian League in 1991 and after a season of consolidation promotion was gained after finishing behind Aldershot Town. That season also saw the Oxon Senior Cup come to the Windmill Ground.

1994-95 proved to be one of the best in the club's history, with the new £750,000 development transforming the ground into one of the most well appointed in the league. On the field they went from strength to strength winning Div 2 by 11 points.

THAME UNITED 1995/96 SEASON

19/08/95	IFL	1	CHESHAM UNITED	1-2	Mott
22/08/95	GIC	P	CHALFONT ST PETER	0-1	
26/08/95	FA Cup	P	MAIDENHEAD UNITED	4-0	Barresi(2), Cooper, Mason
02/09/95	IFL	1	BASINGSTOKE TOWN	1-0	Mason
09/09/95	FA Cup	Q1	A.F.C. TOTTON	1-1	Cooper
14/09/95	FA Cup	Q1 rep	A.F.C. Totton	4-0	Gascoyne(2), Mott(2)
16/09/95	IFL	1	RUISLIP MANOR	2-0	Gascoyne, Rodney
23/09/95	FA Cup	Q2	WITNEY TOWN	1-1	Mason
26/09/95	FA Cup	Q2 rep	Witney Town	3-2	Mott, Mason, Rodney
30/09/95	IFL	1	Whyteleafe	2-1	Mott, Cooper
03/10/95	IFL	1	ALDERSHOT TOWN	2-2	Mason, Webb
07/10/95	FA Cup	Q3	NEWPORT I.O.W.	1-1	Mott
10/10/95	FA Cup	Q3 rep	Newport I.O.W.	1-3	Mott
14/10/95	FA Trophy	Q1	Worthing	1-1	Barresi
17/10/95	FA Trophy	Q1 rep	WORTHING	2-0	Baptiste, Lonergan
21/10/95	IFL	1	Heybridge Swifts	1-5	Webb
28/10/95	IFL	1	STAINES TOWN	1-2	Webb
04/11/95	FA Trophy	Q2	Maidenhead United	5-0	Cooper, Webb, Mott(2), Baptiste
11/11/95	IFL	1	ABINGDON TOWN	1-1	Mott
14/11/95	CC	1	MARLOW	4-1	
18/11/95	IFL	1	MAIDENHEAD UNITED	2-5	Shildrick, Webb
21/11/95	CC	2	DULWICH HAMLET	3-0	
25/11/95	FA Trophy	Q3	St Albans City	2-4	Shildrick, Barresi
28/11/95	IFL	1	Marlow	6-4	Cox(2), Mott, Mason(3)
02/12/95	IFL	1	WOKINGHAM TOWN	4-3	Mott(2), Shildrick(2)
09/12/95	IFL	1	Uxbridge	2-2	Shildrick, Mason
12/12/95	IFL	1	Barton Rovers	3-3	Baptiste(2), Orlando
16/12/95	IFL	1	TOOTING & MITCHAM	0-0	
19/12/95	IFL	1	Leyton Pennant	0-1	
23/12/95	IFL	1	Basingstoke Town	3-3	Mott(2), Cooper
01/01/96	IFL	1	Wembley	2-2	Barresi, Shildrick
06/01/96	IFL	1	MARLOW	0-3	
13/01/96	IFL	1	BILLERICAY TOWN	0-1	
15/01/96	CC	3	Carshalton Athletic	0-4	
20/01/96	IFL	1	Chesham United	0-0	
23/01/96	IFL	1	BARKING	1-1	Mason
30/01/96	IFL	1	Maidenhead United	1-2	Mott
03/02/96	IFL	1	Aldershot Town	0-1	
10/02/96	IFL	1	WHYTELEAFE	1-1	Shildrick
13/02/96	IFL	1	Berkhamsted Town	1-4	Hamilton
17/02/96	IFL	1	Ruislip Manor	3-2	Tolerbey, Shildrick, Webb
24/02/96	IFL	1	Staines Town	1-1	
27/02/96	IFL	1	BOGNOR REGIS TOWN	2-3	McCoy, Shildrick
02/03/96	IFL	1	HEYBRIDGE SWIFTS	1-1	Orlando
05/03/96	Oxon SC	QF	BANBURY UNITED	7-0	
09/03/96	IFL	1	Barking	4-1	Cooper(2), Mason, McCoy
12/03/96	IFL	1	Billericay Town	2-1	Webb, Shildrick
16/03/96	IFL	1	BARTON ROVERS	3-1	Shildrick, Mason, Baptiste
18/03/96	IFL	1	Bognor Regis Town	1-0	Shildrick
23/03/96	IFL	1	Abingdon Town	2-1	Cooper, Webb
30/03/96	IFL	1	LEYTON PENNANT	2-0	McCoy, Baptiste
03/04/96	Oxon SC	SF	Witney Town	3-0	McCoy, Shildrick(2)
06/04/96	IFL	1	WEMBLEY	1-0	Rourke
08/04/96	IFL	1	Oxford City	0-5	
13/04/96	IFL	1	BERKHAMSTED TOWN	2-2	Orlando, Baptiste
20/04/96	IFL	1	Wokingham Town	0-2	
25/04/96	IFL	1	OXFORD CITY	0-2	
27/04/96	IFL	1	UXBRIDGE	3-1	Southam(2), Mason
04/05/96	IFL	1	Tooting & Mitcham United	0-1	
08/05/96	Oxon SC	F	OXFORD CITY	1-2	

TOOTING AND MITCHAM UNITED

Sandy Lane, Mitcham, Surrey CR4 2HD. Tel: 0181 648 3248

Secretary: Les Roberts, 91 Fernlea Rd, Mitcham, Surrey CR4 2HG Tel 0181 646 5275

Nickname: The Terrors, Capacity: 8, 000

Colours: Black and White stripes   Seating: 1,990

Covered standing: None   Clubhouse on ground:
Yes

DIRECTIONS

Tooting (BR) quarter mile. Sandy Lane is off Streatham Road near Swan Hotel.

Record attendance: 17,500 v Queens Park Rangers
FA Cup Rd 2 1956

Biggest win: 11-0 v Welton Rovers
FA Amateur Cup 1962-63

Biggest defeat: 1-8 v Kingstonian Surrey Senior Cup 1967 and Redbridge Forest, Loctite Cup 1991

Record appearances: Danny Godwin 470

Record goalscorer in total: Alan Ives 92 1972-78

Record fee paid: £9,000 for Dave Flint from Enfield

Record Fee Received: £10,000 for Herbie Smith to Luton Town

Honours

Isthmian League 1958 and 1960, Isthmian Full Members Cup 1993

Athenian League 1950 and 1955, Surrey Senior Cup 1938, 1944, 1945, 1953, 1960, 1976, 1977, 1978

London Senior Cup 1943, 1949, 1959, 1960, South of the Thames Cup 1970

Surrey Senior Shield 1952, 1961, 1962, 1966

Tooting and Mitcham United were formed in 1932 when two long standing and established clubs, Tooting Town (1919) and Mitcham Wanderers (1912), decided to amalgamate. The new United played in the London League before eventual election to the Athenian League in 1938 just prior to the War. They were champions in 1950 and 1955 and a year later joined the Isthmian League. They became one of the strongest clubs around during that era as the title was won in 1958 and 1960 and a number of FA and Amateur Cup runs were recorded. Following that period of success they then went through a long spell in the mid-table area of what is now the Premier Division, until 1984 when they were fortunate to escape the drop because of Staines Town's ground grading problems. Unfortunately the drop came in 1989 and although being in the top eight for the next five years, last May saw them just escape relegation to Division Two.

Tooting have a fine record in the FA Cup where they reached the 3rd Round proper in 1959, only losing a replay to Nottingham Forest who went on to win the Cup. In 1976 they improved on that when reaching Round Four before bowing out to Bradford City.

Prior to the merger in 1932, there had been a number of clubs in the Tooting area, most of whom have a connection in some way to today's club. Tooting Graveney was formed in 1887 and played on Figges Marsh and Tooting Bec and Tooting St Johns also amalgamated and proved strong. After the war with none of the old guard around to re-float the clubs, the natural progression was to form Tooting Town who played at Tyrrell Poultry Farm. Mitcham Wanderers first played on Cranmer Green and then Park Place and Streatham Lane and when the merger came, with both clubs in the same league, it was logical to move to Sandy Lane which was an unfenced agricultural field when first bought. A stand was quickly built and later enlarged and the huge area was terraced so much that in the 50's regular five figure crowds would flock to the ground. Since then Sandy Lane has changed little, but along with the club itself has suffered in recent times.

TOOTING AND MITCHAM UNITED 1995/96 SEASON

Date	Comp	Rd	Opponent	Score	Scorers
19/08/95	IFL	1	Berkhamsted Town	1-0	
22/08/95	IFL	1	WOKINGHAM TOWN	1-2	Fowler
25/08/95	FA Cup	P	Epsom & Ewell	4-0	
29/08/95	IFL	1	Maidenhead United	2-2	Tompkins, James
02/09/95	IFL	1	Leyton Pennant	1-4	
05/09/95	GIC	1	WEALDSTONE	4-3	
09/09/95	FA Cup	Q1	PEACEHAVEN & TELSCOM	0-0	
12/09/95	FA Cup	Q1 rep	Peacehaven & Telscombe	1-0	Tompkins
16/09/95	IFL	1	Oxford City	1-3	
23/09/95	FA Cup	Q2	CHERTSEY TOWN	2-2	Gabriel, Tompkins
26/09/95	FA Cup	Q2 rep	Chertsey Town	2-1	Blake(og), Tompkins
30/09/95	IFL	1	HEYBRIDGE SWIFTS	0-1	
07/10/95	FA Cup	Q3	ASHFORD TOWN	0-1	
10/10/95	IFL	1	BARTON ROVERS	0-0	
14/10/95	FA Trophy	Q1	Whyteleafe	2-1	Rootes, Cooper
17/10/95	IFL	1	UXBRIDGE	1-0	Spence
21/10/95	IFL	1	WEMBLEY	1-1	Bealey
28/10/95	IFL	1	BARKING	5-1	Tompkins(3), Gritt, Cooper
04/11/95	FA Trophy	Q2	BALDOCK TOWN	2-1	Rootes(2)
07/11/95	GIC	2	Bedford Town	2-3	
11/11/95	IFL	1	BASINGSTOKE TOWN	1-3	Loughlan
18/11/95	IFL	1	Whyteleafe	2-0	Loughlin, Dennington
25/11/95	FA Trophy	Q3	Sudbury Town	0-2	
25/11/95	Surrey SC	Q4	Horley Town	4-1	
28/11/95	CC	2	WOKINGHAM TOWN	4-3	
02/12/95	IFL	1	Billericay Town	0-1	
05/12/95	IFL	1	Marlow	1-3	
09/12/95	IFL	1	CHESHAM UNITED	1-1	Gritt
12/12/95	Surrey SC	1	SUTTON UNITED	2-1	
14/12/95	London CC	1	Erith & Belvedere	6-1	Tomkins(3), Gabriel, Loughlin
16/12/95	IFL	1	Thame United	0-0	
23/12/95	IFL	1	LEYTON PENNANT	2-3	Rootes(2)
02/01/96	IFL	1	STAINES TOWN	1-1	Tompkins
06/01/96	IFL	1	Barton Rovers	0-2	
09/01/96	CC	3	SUTTON UNITED	1-3	
13/01/96	IFL	1	Wokingham Town	1-2	Taylor
20/01/96	IFL	1	BERKHAMSTED TOWN	3-2	James, Myatt, Tompkins
27/01/96	Surrey SC	QF	Chertsey Town	3-1	
03/02/96	IFL	1	MAIDENHEAD UNITED	1-1	Jellow
10/02/96	IFL	1	Heybridge Swifts	2-1	Gellow(2)
13/02/96	IFL	1	Aldershot Town	1-3	Tompkins
15/02/96	London CC	QF	WELLING UNITED	2-1	
24/02/96	IFL	1	Barking	1-1	Tompkins
27/02/96	Surrey SC	SF	CARSHALTON ATHLETIC	4-2	
02/03/96	IFL	1	ALDERSHOT TOWN	0-2	
09/03/96	IFL	1	Uxbridge	1-1	Taylor
12/03/96	IFL	1	WHYTELEAFE	0-5	
16/03/96	IFL	1	MARLOW	2-0	Fowler, James
19/03/96	IFL	1	OXFORD CITY	1-3	Fowler
23/03/96	IFL	1	Basingstoke Town	0-2	
26/03/96	IFL	1	Wembley	0-1	
30/03/96	IFL	1	ABINGDON TOWN	1-0	Loughlin
06/04/96	IFL	1	Staines Town	1-2	Carruth
08/04/96	IFL	1	BOGNOR REGIS TOWN	1-0	Loughlin
13/04/96	IFL	1	Ruislip Manor	1-2	Dwyer
17/04/96	IFL	1	Abingdon Town	1-2	Gabriel
20/04/96	IFL	1	BILLERICAY TOWN	0-1	
23/04/96	Surrey SC	F	Woking	0-2	
27/04/96	IFL	1	Chesham United	2-1	Loughlin, Fowler
30/04/96	IFL	1	RUISLIP MANOR	1-1	Petruzziello
02/05/96	IFL	1	Bognor Regis Town	2-3	Kempton, Rootes
04/05/96	IFL	1	THAME UNITED	1-0	

UXBRIDGE

Honeycroft, Horton Road, West Drayton, Middx UB7 8HX. Tel: 01895 443557

Information Line: 01895 445830

Secretary: Graham Hiseman, 96 New Peachey Lane, Cowley, Uxbridge, Middx UB8 3SY Tel: 01895 237195

Press Officer: Andy Peart, Tel 01895 444686

Commercial Manager: Trevor Birch 0181 561 1789

Programme Editors Andy Peart and Roy Green

Nickname: The Reds, Colours: Red and white

Capacity: 4,500   Seating: 201

Covered standing: 480   Clubhouse on ground: Yes

> ## DIRECTIONS
> From West Drayton (BR) turn right and then 1st left (Horton Road). Ground 1 mile on left. From Uxbridge (LT) take 222, U3 or U5 bus to West Drayton station, then follow as above. By road, ground 1 mile north of M4 junction 4 taking road to Uxbridge and leaving by first junction and turning left into Horton Road — ground 600 yards on right.

Biggest win: 12-1 v Civil Service FA Amateur Cup 1949

Biggest defeat: 1-9 v Erith and Belvedere Corinthian Shield 1952

Biggest attendance: 1,000 v Arsenal Floodlight opening 1981

Record appearances: Roger Nicholls 1054

Record goalscorer in total: Danny Needham 125

Club shop sells programmes, mugs, badges, ties, etc . Contact club secretary

Honours

FA AMATEUR CUP runners up 1898

London Challenge Cup 1994, Corinthian League 1960, Memorial Shield 1951 and 1953

Middlesex Senior Cup 1894, 1896, 1951, Middlesex Senior Charity Cup 1908, 1913, 1936, 1982

Middlesex Premier Cup 1996,

Manager for 1996-97: George Talbot, Coach: Micky Nicks, Chairman: Alan Holloway

Vice Chairman: Tom Barnard, Treasurer: David Tucker

Uxbridge Football Club was founded in 1871, and is one of the oldest clubs in the south of England. In those days they wore white, before reverting to red in 1880. The first ten years were very successful, with the Heron brothers gaining full International caps for England, and Uxbridge joined the Southern League in 1894 and four years later reached the final of the Amateur Cup, losing to Middlesbrough at Crystal Palace. Despite this, the club almost folded with a deficit of £130 at the turn of the century.

In 1906 they moved to the Great Western Combination and remained members until moving to the RAF Stadium in the town, when they moved to the Athenian League for one season, before rejoining the Combination. Now known as Uxbridge Town, they had a further spell in the Athenians until moving to the Spartan League for one year, Combination again and thence to the London League towards the end of the War. In 1948 Uxbridge moved to Honeycroft, a ground in Cleveland Road which was home until 1978, when it became part of Brunel University, playing in the Corinthian League. They took the title in 1960 and when it merged with the Athenians they were back again, in 1963. The first Honeycroft lasted until 1978, when it was sold and the current ground begun. Some £170,000 was spent on developments and Arsenal opened the floodlights two years later. They reached the Isthmian League in 1982, and were promoted in 1985 to Division One, where they remain.

The RAF Stadium is still very much alive and well and used by the forces, but the first Honeycroft sadly is no more, the two stands disappearing in 1978 under the extension of the University.

UXBRIDGE 1995/96 SEASON

Date	Competition	Round	Opponent	Att	Score	Scorers
19/08/95	IFL	1	Wembley		2-0	Hanratty, Latty
26/08/95	FA Cup	P	KEMPSTON ROVERS	98	4-0	Gill(2), Sam, Latty
29/08/95	IFL	1	Wokingham Town	201	1-3	Ryder
02/09/95	IFL	1	Barton Rovers		1-1	Gill
05/09/95	GIC	1	BARKING	70	0-1	
09/09/95	FA Cup	Q1	Northwood	143	5-0	Crawford, Downes, Latty, Gill, Hanratty
16/09/95	IFL	1	Heybridge Swifts	203	0-4	
23/09/95	FA Cup	Q2	STEVENAGE BOROUGH	460	0-1	
30/09/95	IFL	1	BERKHAMSTED TOWN	90	1-2	Gill
07/10/95	IFL	1	LEYTON PENNANT	98	1-0	King
10/10/95	IFL	1	ABINGDON TOWN	116	1-1	Gill
14/10/95	FA Trophy	Q1	King's Lynn	833	2-1	Downes, Ryder
17/10/95	IFL	1	Tooting & Mitcham United		0-1	
24/10/95	London CC	1	HAMPTON	88	0-2	
28/10/95	IFL	1	Marlow	203	3-2	Gill(2), Hanratty
31/10/95	IFL	1	MAIDENHEAD UNITED	93	0-0	
04/11/95	FA Trophy	Q2	Basingstoke Town	165	2-0	Sam, Gill
07/11/95	CC	1	HARROW BOROUGH	117	1-0	Ryder
11/11/95	IFL	1	BARKING	114	1-0	Gill
18/11/95	IFL	1	Ruislip Manor		1-0	Ryder
21/11/95	IFL	1	OXFORD CITY	114	2-2	Toms, McCluskey
25/11/95	FA Trophy	Q3	Rothwell Town	126	2-3	King, Gill
02/12/95	IFL	1	Aldershot Town	1486	0-4	
09/12/95	IFL	1	THAME UNITED	80	2-2	Gill, Bamford
16/12/95	IFL	1	Staines Town		1-3	Bamford
19/12/95	CC	2	Heybridge Swifts	110	1-3	Ryder
23/12/95	IFL	1	BARTON ROVERS	103	3-2	Yeardley, Toms, Cleary
01/01/96	IFL	1	CHESHAM UNITED	250	0-0	
06/01/96	IFL	1	Abingdon Town	116	2-0	Gill, Perry
09/01/96	Middx SC	2	YEADING	98	2-1	Ryder, Gill
13/01/96	IFL	1	Oxford City	203	0-1	
16/01/96	Middx CC	3	ASHFORD TOWN (MDDX)	65	0-1	
20/01/96	IFL	1	Basingstoke Town		1-0	Yeardley
23/01/96	IFL	1	BOGNOR REGIS TOWN	101	0-0	
30/01/96	IFL	1	BILLERICAY TOWN	116	0-1	
03/02/96	IFL	1	WOKINGHAM TOWN	116	1-1	Gill
14/02/96	Middx SC	QF	Harrow Borough	110	2-2	Own-Goal, Ryder
17/02/96	IFL	1	HEYBRIDGE SWIFTS	112	1-0	Toms
24/02/96	IFL	1	MARLOW	134	4-0	Yeardley(2), Ryder, Downes
27/02/96	Middx SC	QF rep	HARROW BOROUGH	138	0-1	
02/03/96	IFL	1	Bognor Regis Town	329	2-0	Yeardley, Gill
05/03/96	IFL	1	Whyteleafe		1-1	Yeardley
09/03/96	IFL	1	TOOTING & MITCHAM UNI	116	1-1	Frampton(og)
12/03/96	IFL	1	WEMBLEY	60	0-4	
16/03/96	IFL	1	Leyton Pennant		1-2	Toms
23/03/96	IFL	1	Barking		2-0	Gill, Toms
30/03/96	IFL	1	BASINGSTOKE TOWN	114	0-1	
02/04/96	IFL	1	Maidenhead United	99	2-1	Gill(2)
06/04/96	IFL	1	Chesham United	249	0-1	
08/04/96	IFL	1	WHYTELEAFE	100	1-0	Latty
13/04/96	IFL	1	Billericay Town		0-0	
16/04/96	IFL	1	RUISLIP MANOR	231	2-1	Bamford, Latty
20/04/96	IFL	1	ALDERSHOT TOWN	554	0-2	
23/04/96	IFL	1	Berkhamsted Town		3-1	Yeardley, Toms, Regan
27/04/96	IFL	1	Thame United		1-3	Gill
04/05/96	IFL	1	STAINES TOWN		1-1	

WALTON AND HERSHAM

Sports Ground, Stompond Lane, Walton-On-Thames. Tel: 01932 244967

Secretary: Mark Massingham, 7b Sidney Rd, Walton-on-Thames, Surrey KT12 2NB Tel: 01932 885814

Press officer: Brian Freeman, 40 Fordwater Rd, Chertsey, Surrey KT16 8HL Tel: 01932 560738

Colours: Red and White   Nickname: The Swans

Capacity: 6,500, Seating: 500, Covered standing: 2,500

Clubhouse on ground: Yes

Record attendance: 10,000 v Crook Town

FA Amateur Cup quarter-final replay March 1st 1952

Biggest win: 14-1 v Guildford Pinks

Surrey Senior League Oct 5th 1935

Biggest defeat: 0-15 v Dorking Surrey Senior League Dec 7th 1929

Record appearances: Dave Worby 450+

Record goalscorer in one season:
Brian Jenkins 55 in 1960-61

DIRECTIONS
From North: Over Walton bridge & along New Zealand Avenue. down 1-way street and up A244 Hersham Road - ground 2nd right. From Esher: Down Lammas Lane then Esher Road, straight over 1st roundabout, 4th exit at next roundabout (West Grove) 2nd left at end of Hersham Road and Stompond Lane is half mile on left. Ten minutes walk from Walton-on-Thames (BR). Bus 218 passes ground.

Record goalscorer in total For Walton FC George Hoyle 230, For Hersham FC, Fred Richardson 53, and for Walton and Hersham, Reg Sentance 210

Honours

WALTON UTD, Kingston and District League

WALTON-ON-THAMES FC, West Surrey League 1911, SW Middx League 1913

Surrey Senior League Charity Cup 1931, 1936 and 1937, Surrey Senior League 1937

London League Challenge Cup 1938

WALTON AND HERSHAM FC

FA AMATEUR CUP WINNERS 1973, FA AMATUER CUP Semi-finals 1953 and 1959

Corinthian League 1947, 1948, 1949, Surrey Senior Cup 1948, 51, 61, 62, 71, 73,

Surrey Combination Cup 1950, Surrey Charity Shield 1952

Premier Midweek League 1969, 1970, 1971, 1972, Athenian League 1969

Southern Combination Cup 1989, 1990, 1992, Manager for 1996-97: Dave Russell

Assistant manager: Laurie Craker, Chairman: Theo Paphitis, Vice Chairman: Alan Smith

" History - The Centenary of Walton and Hersham FC" by Kerry Miller is now available from the club.

Walton celebrate their 100th anniversary this year and 50 years since the amalgamation of Walton and Hersham Football Clubs in 1946. There were a number of Walton sides 100 years ago, with Walton Juniors, Walton United and Walton FC all appearing to either come together or step aside for the new club. There was also a Hersham club which came and went before the Great War and was formed again in the 20's. The two clubs twice came close to merging but resisted to become the bitterest of rivals, playing in the Surrey Senior League to large crowds. Hersham always played their football on a pitch within the grounds of Mole House, which was undeveloped until just before the War, when a hastily put up stand lasted only a couple of seasons, before the ground was taken over by troops and never used again. Later the site disappeared under a new by-pass.

Walton had a number of grounds, starting on Elm Grove Rec which still exists, before using a number of other sites, the most famous being at Mount Felix, near the river, now covered by housing. From there the club moved to Terrace Road and Cottimore Lane before a rough site on the corner of Stompond Lane became available. It was prepared and the club moved in around 1933 and have been there ever since. The early years of the new club were very successful with a hat-trick of Corinthian League wins elevating them to the Athenian League where they finished runners-up. It was the peak of the Amateur Cup's importance as a national competition and the Swans were twice to reach the semi-finals, where they lost at London grounds in front of huge crowds. 1952 saw the record crowd at the ground, of 10,000 which saw the Amateur Cup match with Crook Town, but despite the attention the club went into decline until the arrival of Allen Batsford as manager. In a seven year spell his sides were Athenian League champions, Surrey Senior Cup winners twice and runners up in the Isthmian

League. They also took the Premier Mid-week League three times and knocked Exeter City out of the FA Cup. But the big prize was in 1973 when in front of 41,000, the Swans took the Amateur Cup by beating Slough Town with a last minute goal by Roger Connell. A few months later Brighton drew at Stompond Lane in the FA Cup, but were given a shock when beaten 4-0 on their own ground in the replay. That was to be the final fling for that team which broke up when Batsford went to Wimbledon, and within a year they had been relegated. Barren years followed when more than once the club were a whisker away from going under, but they survived and waited until 1994, when under the managership of ex-FA Cup finalist Neil Price, they were promoted. With work going on to secure a new ground in another part of the town, the club had high hopes for last season but a nightmare run saw them relegated back to Division One.

WALTON AND HERSHAM 1995/96 SEASON

19/08/95	IFL	P	Chertsey Town	603	3-1	Croxford(2), D Thomas
22/08/95	IFL	P	GRAYS ATHLETIC	239	1-4	Brodrick
26/08/95	IFL	P	BISHOP'S STORTFORD	215	0-2	
28/08/95	IFL	P	Yeovil Town	1530	1-4	Croxford
02/09/95	IFL	P	Aylesbury United	713	0-0	
05/09/95	GIC	1	CHALFONT ST PETER	129	2-2	Brodrick, Swift
09/09/95	FA Cup	Q1	CAMBERLEY TOWN	164	4-0	Gasson(2), Mitchell, D Thomas
12/09/95	IFL	P	CARSHALTON ATHLETIC	245	0-1	
16/09/95	IFL	P	Hayes	293	0-2	
19/09/95	GIC	1 rep	Chalfont St Peter	65	5-3	Banton(2), Swift(2), Davidson
23/09/95	FA Cup	Q2	MARGATE	225	2-2	Banton, Brodrick
26/09/95	FA Cup	Q2 rep	Margate	189	1-0	Everitt
30/09/95	IFL	P	ST ALBANS CITY	281	1-2	Worley
03/10/95	IFL	P	Enfield	603	0-4	
07/10/95	FA Cup	Q3	Farnborough Town	761	2-3	Callaghan, Mitchell
10/10/95	IFL	P	DULWICH HAMLET	232	0-2	
24/10/95	S Comb Cup	1	Leatherhead		0-5	
28/10/95	IFL	P	SUTTON UNITED	445	1-1	Mitchell
04/11/95	FA Trophy	Q2	OXFORD CITY	201	0-0	
07/11/95	GIC	2	Kingsbury Town	85	1-1	Callaghan
07/11/95	FA Trophy	Q2 rep	Oxford City	196	2-5	Banton, Taylor
11/11/95	IFL	P	HENDON	267	1-0	Brodrick
14/11/95	GIC	2 rep	KINGSBURY TOWN	120	3-1	Hutchinson, Flack(2)
18/11/95	IFL	P	BROMLEY	238	3-1	Hutchinson, Barton, Brodrick
21/11/95	CC	1	Staines Town	305	1-0	Hutchinson
25/11/95	IFL	P	Bishop's Stortford	308	0-2	
27/11/95	GIC	3	Croydon	125	1-2	Brodrick
02/12/95	IFL	P	HARROW BOROUGH	247	1-2	Mitchell
14/12/95	Surrey SC	1	CRYSTAL PALACE		0-3	
16/12/95	IFL	P	HITCHIN TOWN	186	4-1	Hutchinson(4)
23/12/95	IFL	P	Carshalton Athletic	429	2-5	Edwards, Hutchinson
02/01/96	IFL	P	Kingstonian	402	0-1	
06/01/96	IFL	P	AYLESBURY UNITED	266	2-1	Brindou, Brodrick
09/01/96	CC	2	KINGSTONIAN		1-3	
13/01/96	IFL	P	Grays Athletic	264	1-3	Hutchinson
20/01/96	IFL	P	CHERTSEY TOWN	409	0-1	
03/02/96	IFL	P	ENFIELD	451	0-1	
10/02/96	IFL	P	St Albans City	454	0-3	
13/02/96	IFL	P	Boreham Wood	247	1-1	Mason
17/02/96	IFL	P	HAYES	302	0-1	
24/02/96	IFL	P	Sutton United	483	1-2	Mitchell
02/03/96	IFL	P	YEOVIL TOWN	406	1-3	Edwards
05/03/96	IFL	P	Worthing	223	2-0	Hutchinson, Edwards
09/03/96	IFL	P	Dulwich Hamlet	442	1-1	Smart
11/03/96	IFL	P	Purfleet	127	1-2	Mitchell
16/03/96	IFL	P	WORTHING	203	1-0	Smart
19/03/96	IFL	P	MOLESEY	212	3-3	Westley, Lay, Byrne
23/03/96	IFL	P	Hendon	225	0-4	
26/03/96	IFL	P	Bromley	202	2-3	Smart, Lay
30/03/96	IFL	P	PURFLEET	170	1-2	Norman
06/04/96	IFL	P	KINGSTONIAN	402	0-2	
08/04/96	IFL	P	Molesey	240	2-2	Taylor, Hutchinson
13/04/96	IFL	P	YEADING	185	0-0	
20/04/96	IFL	P	Harrow Borough	237	3-2	Taylor, Sayer, Byrne
23/04/96	IFL	P	Yeading	136	0-3	
27/04/96	IFL	P	BOREHAM WOOD	202	0-4	
04/05/96	IFL	P	Hitchin Town	331	2-0	Hutchinson, Smart

WHYTELEAFE

15 Church Rd, Whyteleafe, Surrey. Tel: 0181 660 5491 or Bd room 0181 645 0422

Secretary: Mr I A Robertson, 253 Godstone Rd, Whyteleafe, Surrey Tel: 01883 622096

Colours: Green and White, Nickname: The Leafe

Capacity: 3,500   Seating: 150,

Covered standing: 450,

Clubhouse on ground: Yes

DIRECTIONS

Five minutes walk from Whyteleafe (BR) — turn left from station and left into Church Road.

Record attendance: 861 in League and 2,500 non-competitive

Record fee received: £25,000 for Steve Milton from Fulham FC in 1989

Honours

Thornton Heath and District League 1952

Edenbridge Charity Cup: 1952, Caterham and Purley Hospital Charity Cup 1952

Caterham and Edenbridge League Div 3, Surrey County Intermediate League East Div 1

Borough of Croydon Charity Cup, Surrey Senior League 1969

Surrey Senior League Charity Cup 1972, East Surrey Charity Cup: 1980

Southern Counties Floodlit Cup 1996

Manager for 1996-97: Lee Richardson, Assistant manager: Bernie Donnelly

Press officer: Peter Stimpson, 01883 348310 or Warren Filmer, 42 Church Rd, Kenley, Surrey CR8 5DU Tel: 0181 660 3255

The club was re-formed in 1946 as Whyteleafe FC, having previously been known as Whyteleafe Albion. They commenced junior football as members of the Caterham and Edenbridge League, Thornton Heath and District and Croydon Leagues. Season 1951-52 was the most successful, being Thornton Heath League champions, winners of two Charity Cups and runners up in the Surrey County Junior Cup and League Cup. In 1954 they progressed to the County Intermediate League (Eastern) and were Div 1 champions in 1955-56. 1958 saw the transition to senior status and entry into the Surrey Senior League, meaning a move from New Barn Lane School as it was inadequate for senior football. The club purchased 4 acres of farmland in Church Rd and many hours of voluntary work was required from committee men to raise funds to purchase the ground and change it into a pitch, as well as convert the existing farm buildings into a clubhouse with bar and dressing rooms. The original scheme was to include a cricket table and running track but these did not materialise.

They began playing there in 1959 and the club's next success came in 1969, as Surrey Senior League champions, losing the League Cup final to Bracknell. In the 70's the floodlit training area and stand were built and in 1975 after 17 happy years they moved into the Spartan League, where the best they achieved was third on two occasions. In 1981 the club joined the Athenian League, soon after installing floodlights, with new dressing rooms being provided, enabling the clubhouse to be extended. They reached the 5th Round of the FA Vase in 1981 and three years later, when the Athenians merged into the Isthmian League, Whyteleafe found themselves in Division Two South.

In 1986 former Crystal Palace player Steve Kember joined the club as manager and gained promotion to Division One as runner up to Dorking. Steve resigned in 1993 and Lee Richardson, a popular and long serving former player has taken over. In recent times the ground has been improved with new toilets, tea bar, physio room, surrounding wall and covered standing behind the goal, with another 100 new seats in the stand.

WHYTELEAFE 1995/96 SEASON

Date	Competition		Opponent	Score	Scorers
12/08/95	GIC	1	WEMBLEY	2-0	
19/08/95	GIC	1	Staines Town	2-2	
22/08/95	GIC	1	BERKHAMSTED TOWN	1-1	Pearson
26/08/95	FA Cup	P	Chatham Town	1-3	Pearson
30/08/95	GIC	1	Abingdon Town	3-1	Thompson, Weeks, Pearson
02/09/95	GIC	1	Maidenhead United	1-2	
05/09/95	LC	1	HEYBRIDGE SWIFTS	1-2	
12/09/95	GIC	1	LEYTON PENNANT	1-3	Pearson
16/09/95	GIC	1	Barton Rovers	0-4	
23/09/95	GIC	1	Marlow	0-2	
27/09/95	S Co's FC	1 (1)	Hailsham Town	4-1	Milton(2), Boorman, Fowler
30/09/95	GIC	1	THAME UNITED	1-2	Fowler
14/10/95	FA Trophy	Q1	TOOTING & MITCHAM	1-2	Jones
17/10/95	GIC	1	BOGNOR REGIS TOWN	2-4	Sheridan(2)
21/10/95	GIC	1	Barking	2-2	Fowler, Sheridan
28/10/95	GIC	1	RUISLIP MANOR	8-3	Milton(3), Lunn(2), Deman(2)
07/11/95	CC	1	Basingstoke Town	1-4	
11/11/95	GIC	1	ALDERSHOT TOWN	0-6	
14/11/95	GIC	1	Billericay Town	1-1	Pearson
18/11/95	GIC	1	Tooting & Mitcham	0-2	
21/11/95	GIC	1	Chesham United	2-2	Paterson, Pearson
25/11/95	GIC	1	Basingstoke Town	2-2	Pearson, Milton
02/12/95	GIC	1	MARLOW	3-1	M Jones(2), Pearson
09/12/95	GIC	1	Oxford City	0-2	
16/12/95	GIC	1	HEYBRIDGE SWIFTS	4-1	Pearson(3), Howland
19/12/95	Surrey SC	1	Corinthian-Casuals	0-1	
02/01/96	GIC	1	Wokingham Town	1-1	Pearson
06/01/96	GIC	1	MAIDENHEAD UNITED	2-1	Davenport, Pearson
13/01/96	GIC	1	Berkhamsted Town	1-1	Pearson
03/02/96	GIC	1	ABINGDON TOWN	4-2	Dodman, Howland, Jones, Yetzes
10/02/96	GIC	1	Thame United	1-1	Milton
17/02/96	GIC	1	BARTON ROVERS	3-3	Davenport, Jones, Pearson
02/03/96	GIC	1	BARKING	2-0	Fisher, Dickson
05/03/96	GIC	1	UXBRIDGE	1-1	Pearson
09/03/96	GIC	1	Bognor Regis Town	2-2	Fisher, Howard
12/03/96	GIC	1	Tooting & Mitcham	5-0	Fisher, Pearson(2), Milton, Richards
16/03/96	GIC	1	BILLERICAY TOWN	2-1	M Kember, Wilgoss
19/03/96	GIC	1	Leyton Pennant	0-4	
23/03/96	GIC	1	Aldershot Town	0-3	
30/03/96	GIC	1	CHESHAM UNITED	3-4	Milton, Yetzes(2)
01/04/96	GIC	1	Ruislip Manor	1-0	Yetzes
06/04/96	GIC	1	WOKINGHAM TOWN	1-2	Pearson
08/04/96	GIC	1	Uxbridge	0-1	
13/04/96	GIC	1	BASINGSTOKE TOWN	2-0	Pearson(2)
16/04/96	GIC	1	STAINES TOWN	0-2	
27/04/96	GIC	1	OXFORD CITY	3-5	Richards, Fisher, Dickson
30/04/96	GIC	1	Wembley	2-2	Milton(2)
04/05/96	Gic	1	Heybridge Swifts	0-2	

WOKINGHAM TOWN

Town Ground, Finchampstead Rd, Wokingham, Berks RG11 2NR. Tel: 01734 780253

Secretary: John Aulsberry, 8 Paice Green, Wokingham, RG 40 1YN Tel: 01189 790441

Nickname: The Town,   Colours: Amber and Black

Capacity: 3,500   Seating: 300

Covered standing: 1,000,   Clubhouse on ground: Yes

Record attendance: 3,473 v Norton Woodseats
FA Amateur Cup 1958

Record appearances: David Cox 533

Record goalscorer in one season: Steve Darlington 41

Record goalscorer in aggregate:
Dave Pearce 79

Record fee paid: £5,000 for Freddie Hyatt
from Burnham in 1990

Record fee received: £ 25,000 for Mark Harris to Crystal Palace in 1988

DIRECTIONS

Half mile from town centre on A321, (signed Camberley & Sandhurst) Finchampstead Road - walk down Denmark Street to swimming pool and straight on into Finchampstead Road. Half a mile from Wokingham (BR) - turn right out of station, walk along Wellington Road to swimming pool, right into Finchampstead Road, - ground entrance on right immediately after railway bridge.

Honours

FA Trophy semi-final 1988

Isthmian League Div 1 1982

Berks and Bucks Senior Cup 1969, 1983, 1985, 1996, Berks and Bucks Intermediate Cup 1953

Ascot and District League 1912, 1913, Camberley Hospital Cup 1913

Joint Managers for 1996-97: Derek Cottrell and Wayne Wanklyn, Chairman: Peter Walsh

Wokingham Town was founded in 1875, making them the fourth oldest club in Berkshire. They originally played on a ground in Oxford Road, before moving to the cricket ground in Wellington Road and then in 1896 to Langborough Road before settling at Finchampstead Road in 1906. They entered the Ascot and District League before merging with the reserve side of Wokingham Athletic in 1910 and soon became champions, also winning the Camberley Hospital Cup. After the war a dispute between club and league led to them joining the Reading Temperance League, from where they reached the semi-final of the Reading Town Cup and the final of the Berks and Bucks Junior Cup. In 1928 the league was won for a second time and the club purchased the Finchampstead Road ground. The grandstand which is still in use today was opened in April 1939. In 1953 they reached the final of the Intermediate Cup which prompted the move into senior football, when they joined the Metropolitan League. After three years they transferred to the Delphian League from where they had a wonderful Amateur Cup run in 1958, playing 14 games before losing to Crook Town in the last eight. An earlier tie against Norton Woodseats attracted 3,473, a record crowd. After one more season the club joined the Corinthian League, where they lost two Memorial Shield finals. Town started the 63-64 season in the new Athenian League Division One, but it was 1969 before success came, in the shape of the Berks and Bucks Senior Cup, beating Slough Town. They remained in that division until 1973 when they were invited to be founder members of the Isthmian League Division Two. They finished the season last but gradually improved until the championship was won in 1982. Since then the highest position gained was fourth in 1985 although in 1988 they were in the running before a fixture pile up killed their chances. It was that season which saw Town beaten in a two leg FA Trophy semi-final by Telford United, the 2nd leg attracting over 2,500 spectators. There have been other cup runs in recent years, the County Cup was won in 1983 and 1985 and the AC Delco League Cup semi-final semi-final was reached in 1988. The clubs best chance of winning the title came in 1990 when a win over Hendon and a Slough Town defeat would have clinched it, although it wasn't to be. Major alterations were made to the ground in 1990, with the wooden terrace replaced and the new covered stand built. The work meant that the club played some matches at Elm Park, Reading. The next two seasons were a struggle and in 1993 after early cup exits and a relegation battle just went their way. The reprieve only lasted until 1995, for only six wins out of 42 games doomed the club. Last May saw the club in mid-table as they consolidated their position.

WOKINGHAM TOWN 1995/96 SEASON

Date	Competition	Round	Opponent	Att	Score	Scorers
12/08/95	IFL	1	Ruislip Manor	215	2-1	Darlington(2)
19/08/95	IFL	1	BILLERICAY TOWN	205	3-0	Prior(2), Darlington
22/08/95	IFL	1	Tooting & Mitcham United	235	2-1	Darlington(2)
26/08/95	IFL	1	Marlow	330	1-1	Newbery
29/08/95	IFL	1	UXBRIDGE	201	3-1	Darlington, Devereux, Newbery
02/09/95	IFL	1	CHESHAM UNITED	401	3-2	Darlington(2), Newbery
09/09/95	FA Cup	Q1	RINGMER	226	3-1	Potter, Nwaokolo, Darlington
16/09/95	IFL	1	BARKING	315	1-1	Prior
19/09/95	GIC	1	Bracknell Town	254	53	Darlington, Newbery, French, Devereux, Christie
23/09/95	FA Cup	Q2	ALDERSHOT TOWN	1469	1-2	Darlington
30/09/95	IFL	1	Basingstoke Town	320	2-0	Newbery, Crouch
03/10/95	IFL	1	Wembley	81	1-3	Darlington
07/10/95	IFL	1	HEYBRIDGE SWIFTS	347	1-0	Lockyer
14/10/95	FA Trophy	Q1	Staines Town	244	1-2	Darlington
21/10/95	IFL	1	BARTON ROVERS	274	1-1	Prior
23/10/95	S Comb Cup	1	FELTHAM		0-2	
28/10/95	IFL	1	Oxford City	289	0-2	
31/10/95	GIC	2	BANSTEAD ATHLETIC	114	0-3	
04/11/95	IFL	1	BERKHAMSTED TOWN	276	1-2	Darlington
11/11/95	IFL	1	Maidenhead United	259	3-0	Prior, Darlington, Nwaokolo
18/11/95	IFL	1	Leyton Pennant	110	1-1	Wooler
25/11/95	IFL	1	ABINGDON TOWN	276	3-4	Duncan, Line, Christie
28/11/95	CC	2	Tooting & Mitcham United	104	3-4	Newbery(2), Darlington
02/12/95	IFL	1	Thame United	169	3-4	Darlington, Newbery, Christie
09/12/95	IFL	1	BOGNOR REGIS TOWN	209	0-5	
12/12/95	GIC	3	Bedford Town	118	2-1	Darlington, Newbery
16/12/95	IFL	1	Aldershot Town	1486	2-2	Newbery, Nwaokolo
02/01/96	IFL	1	WHYTELEAFE	165	1-1	Darlington
06/01/96	IFL	1	Chesham United	346	0-2	
13/01/96	IFL	1	TOOTING & MITCHAM UTD	267	2-1	Darlington, Newbery
16/01/96	B&B SC	1	Burnham	125	5-1	Darlington(3), Newbery(2)
20/01/96	IFL	1	Billericay Town	231	0-0	
23/01/96	GIC	QF	HITCHIN TOWN	110	2-3	Darlington(2)
03/02/96	IFL	1	Uxbridge	116	1-1	McCluskey(og)
10/02/96	IFL	1	BASINGSTOKE TOWN	308	3-3	Newbery, Gribben, Darlington
17/02/96	IFL	1	Barking	95	3-1	Darlington(3)
28/02/96	B&B SC	QF	HUNGERFORD TOWN	77	3-0	Savage, Prior, Potter
02/03/96	IFL	1	Barton Rovers	125	2-2	Darlington(2)
05/03/96	IFL	1	RUISLIP MANOR	114	0-1	
09/03/96	IFL	1	WEMBLEY	166	3-1	Darlington(2), Walkington
12/03/96	IFL	1	MARLOW	165	2-0	Darlington(2)
16/03/96	IFL	1	Heybridge Swifts	215	0-2	
19/03/96	IFL	1	Staines Town	252	1-2	Savage
23/03/96	IFL	1	MAIDENHEAD UNITED	263	2-1	Prior, Darlington
26/03/96	IFL	1	LEYTON PENNANT	176	0-1	
30/03/96	IFL	1	Berkhamsted Town	165	1-2	Darlington
03/04/96	B&B SC	SF	Reading	377	2-0	Prior, Darlington
06/04/96	IFL	1	Whyteleafe	140	2-1	Potter, Christie
08/04/96	IFL	1	STAINES TOWN	286	0-3	
13/04/96	IFL	1	Abingdon Town	163	1-3	Prior
20/04/96	IFL	1	THAME UNITED	202	2-0	Walkington, Prior
27/04/96	IFL	1	Bognor Regis Town	242	0-2	
30/04/96	IFL	1	OXFORD CITY		2-4	Darlington, Duncan
04/05/96	IFL	1	ALDERSHOT TOWN	759	1-0	
06/05/96	B&B SC	F	Aylesbury United		1-0	

WORTHING

Woodside Road, Worthing, West Sussex BN14 7HQ. Tel: 01903 239575

Secretary: Paul Damper, 19 Fletcher Rd, Worthing, West Sussex BN14 7HQ Tel: 01903 210290

Match Sec: Don Read, 53 West Way, Lancing Tel: 01903 751237

Gen Manager: Ray Smith, c/o club

Nickname: The Rebels   Colours: Red and White

Capacity: 4,500   Seating: 450

Covered standing: 1,000   Clubhouse on ground: Yes

DIRECTIONS

Follow A24 to town, at end of Broadwater Road having gone over railway bridge, take first right into Teville Road, take right into South Farm Road, second left into Pavilion Road, Woodside Road is first right. Half a mile from Worthing (BR).

Record attendance: 4,500 v Depot Batt Royal Eng. Amateur Cup quarter final replay 1908

Biggest win: 25-0 v Littlehampton Tn
West Sussex League 1911-12

Biggest defeat: 0-14 v Southwick (A)
Sussex County League 1946-47

Record appearances: Geoff Raynsford

Record goalscorer in one season: Bill Wren 61 in 1938-39

Record goalscorer in total: Micky Edmonds 275

Record fee paid: £1,000 for Steve Guille from Bognor Regis

Record fee received: £7,500 for Tim Read from Woking

Honours

Isthmian League Div 1 1983 and Div 2 1982 and 1993

Athenian Memorial Shield 1964

Sussex Senior Cup 1893, 1904, 08, 14, 20, 23, 27, 29, 35, 40, 45, 47, 52, 57, 59, 61, 75, 77, 78

Sussex RUR Charity Cup 1904, 07, 08, 10, 14, 20, 23, 27, 34, 42, 45, 49, 53, 54

Sussex County League 1921, 1922, 1927, 1929, 1931, 1934, 1939, 1940,

West Sussex League 1899, 1904, 1907, 1908, 1910, 1913, 1914

Brighton Charity Cup 1930, 1931, 1935, 1963, 1970, 1971, 1974, 1981, 1982

Worthing Charity Cup 1912, 1926, 1927, 1931, 1933, 1934, 1935, 1938, 1939, 1965

AFA Invitation Cup 1964, 1969, 1974, 1976

Manager for 1996-97: Gary Chivers

Chairman: Beau Reynolds, Vice: Chairman Ray Smith

Press Officer Morty Hollis c/o Worthing FC

Worthing Football Club was founded in 1886 and throughout its history has been the most successful non-League club in Sussex. In 1893 the first of 20 wins in the Sussex Senior Cup was achieved, with the league championship also won that year. They won the Sussex Charity Cup 13 times between 1904 and 1954, the Brighton Charity Cup 9 times and the Worthing Charity Cup 10 times. In 1908 Worthing reached the quarter finals of the FA Amateur Cup where they drew with the eventual winners, Depot Battalion Royal Engineers, losing the replay in front of 4,500 spectators. Worthing collected six more championships before becoming founder members of the County League in 1919-20, racking up a further 7 titles in 20 years. They also reached the First Round of the FA Cup in 1936, losing to Yeovil and Petters United. After the War, the club joined the Corinthian League, but were not so successful during the 50's and it was not until 1964, after they joined the Athenian League, that promotion was achieved. There were a number of minor cup triumphs during the 60's and 70's until the club joined the Isthmian League in 1977, playing in the newly formed Second Division. The appointment of former Fulham player Barry Lloyd signalled an upturn in fortunes, for the Div 2 title was won in

1982, on the back of 53 goals from striker Mick Edmonds followed by promotion a year later with a Cup run to the Second Round as well. 1984 and 1985 both saw the Rebels finish runners-up in the league, but on Lloyds departure the club were relegated to Division One, with 1991 ending with another drop to Division Two. Gerry Armstrong, the Northern Ireland International returned the club to Division One in 1993, and under John Robson the club climbed back to the Premier Division in 1995, only to finish bottom last May and go down again. Worthing are believed to have always played at Woodside Road, although the pitch was at a different angle in the early days. A generous benefactor donated the land to the club in the last century and at one time they owned much around it, but it has been slowly sold off.

WORTHING 1995/96 SEASON

12/08/95	IFL	P	GRAYS ATHLETIC	461	1-1	Brown
19/08/95	IFL	P	Kingstonian	389	1-1	Thomas
22/08/95	IFL	P	ST ALBANS CITY	562	1-5	Gysami
26/08/95	IFL	P	CHERTSEY TOWN	540	1-2	Riley
02/09/95	IFL	P	Hitchin Town	250	2-2	Joseph, Gyami
05/09/95	GIC	1	St Albans City	162	3-2	
09/09/95	FA Cup	Q1	BUCKINGHAM TOWN	464	1-1	Joseph
12/09/95	FA Cup	Q1 rep	Buckingham Town	84	0-0	
16/09/95	IFL	P	Bishop's Stortford	242	0-0	
18/09/95	FA Cup	Q1 rep(2)	BUCKINGHAM TOWN	277	2-2	Moss, Hack
20/09/95	FA Cup	Q1 rep(3)	Buckingham Town	100	1-6	Riley
30/09/95	IFL	P	ENFIELD	627	0-1	
03/10/95	IFL	P	Hayes	240	0-2	
07/10/95	IFL	P	SUTTON UNITED	575	5-2	Moss, Joseph(2), Maynard(2)
14/10/95	FA Trophy	Q1	THAME UNITED	372	1-1	Moss
17/10/95	FA Trophy	Q1 rep	Thame United	152	0-2	
21/10/95	IFL	P	CARSHALTON ATHLETIC	531	2-3	Joseph, Riley
28/10/95	IFL	P	Dulwich Hamlet	296	1-4	Moss
31/10/95	GIC	2	ENFIELD	266	1-4	
04/11/95	IFL	P	Yeovil Town	1602	1-3	Shuttlewood
18/11/95	IFL	P	YEADING	210	2-1	Moss, Cordery(og)
25/11/95	Sussex SC	2	OAKWOOD		7-0	
02/12/95	IFL	P	BROMLEY	417	2-2	Moss, Maynard
09/12/95	IFL	P	Aylesbury United	778	1-1	Thwaites
13/12/95	CC	2	Bognor Regis Town	300	0-6	
16/12/95	IFL	P	BOREHAM WOOD	339	0-2	
23/12/95	IFL	P	Grays Athletic	215	0-6	
26/12/95	IFL	P	YEOVIL TOWN	561	3-2	Poulton(2), Brown
01/01/96	IFL	P	Harrow Borough	360	1-3	Oliva
06/01/96	IFL	P	HITCHIN TOWN	353	2-0	Dineen, Carter
13/01/96	IFL	P	St Albans City	503	0-2	
16/01/96	Sussex SC	3	Pagham	103	2-1	Joseph, Robson
20/01/96	IFL	P	Yeading	120	0-1	
23/01/96	IFL	P	KINGSTONIAN	334	0-5	
03/02/96	IFL	P	HAYES	305	0-3	
05/02/96	Sussex SC	QF	CRAWLEY TOWN	314	1-4	Thwaites
10/02/96	IFL	P	Enfield	714	1-5	Harris
17/02/96	IFL	P	BISHOP'S STORTFORD	321	0-1	
19/02/96	IFL	P	Purfleet	102	1-3	Harris
24/02/96	IFL	P	DULWICH HAMLET	370	1-3	Okenia
05/03/96	IFL	P	WALTON & HERSHAM	223	0-2	
09/03/96	IFL	P	PURFLEET	275	1-2	Riley
12/03/96	IFL	P	Chertsey Town	260	1-2	Okenia
16/03/96	IFL	P	Walton & Hersham	203	0-1	
23/03/96	IFL	P	Sutton United	461	1-3	Oliva
30/03/96	IFL	P	HENDON	336	0-5	
03/04/96	IFL	P	Molesey	130	1-3	Southam
06/04/96	IFL	P	HARROW BOROUGH	338	1-2	Johnson
09/04/96	IFL	P	Hendon	249	0-3	
13/04/96	IFL	P	MOLESEY	304	4-4	Tiltman, Harris, Johnson, Joseph
20/04/96	IFL	P	Bromley	401	2-3	Tiltman, Riley
25/04/96	IFL	P	Carshalton Athletic	248	0-4	
27/04/96	IFL	P	AYLESBURY UNITED	89	1-3	Harris
04/05/96	IFL	P	Boreham Wood	428	1-3	Joyce(og)

Above: Northwood F.C.
Below: Oxford City F.C.

Above: St Albans City F.C.
Below: Uxbridge F.C.

Above: Wokingham Town action

Right: Dagenham & Redbridge

Left: Chertsey Town

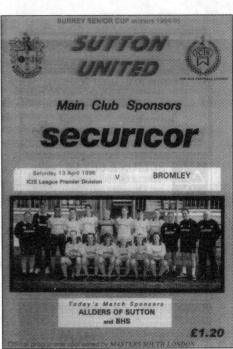

BANSTEAD ATHLETIC

..Merland Rise, Tadworth, Surrey RT20 5JG Tel 01737 350982

Sec. Gordon T.ylor, 116 Kingston Avenue, North Cheam, Surrey SM3 9UF Tel 0181 641 2957

Press Officer: Colin Darby 5 Brookfield Ave, Sutton, Surrey SM1 3QW: Tel 0181 643 5437

Nickname: The A's

Colours: Amber and Black

Capacity: 3,000:   Seating 250

Covered standing: 800

Clubhouse on ground: Yes

Record attendance: 1,300 v Leatherhead
FA Amateur Cup 1953

Biggest win: 12-0 v Reigate Priory

Biggest defeat: 0-10 v St Albans City

Record appearances: Dennis Wall

Record goalscorer in one season: Harry Clark

Record goalscorer in total: Harry Clark

DIRECTIONS

Follow signs to Tattenham Corner (Epsom racecourse), then to Bansteads Sports Centre. The ground is adjacent to the swimming pool. Half a mile from Tattenham Corner (BR). Bus 420 from Sutton stops outside ground. Also buses 406 & 727 from Epsom.

HONOURS

Epsom and Ewell League and Cup 1945, Sutton Hospital Cup 1946, Surrey Intermediate Cup 1947 and 1955, Surrey Intermediate League 1948 and 1949, Surrey Senior League 1951, 1952, 1953, 1954, 1957, 1965, League Challenge Cup 1958 and League Charity Cup 1953 and 1959

Surrey FA Shield 1956, East Surrey Charity Cup 1960, 1967, 1977, 1978, Athenian League Cup 1981 and 1982,

MANAGER FOR 1996-97: Bob Langford,   CHAIRMAN: Terry Malloy

One of the few clubs to be founded during the Second War, Banstead began in 1944 as Banstead Juniors. They played in the Epsom and Ewell League at Tattenham Way Rec. In their first season they won the League Cup and were league runners up, joining the Sutton and District League after just one season.

Within a year they were in the Surrey Intermediate League and during 1947 they changed the club name to Banstead Athletic FC. The first two seasons in the new league saw the club win the title twice and the Intermediate Cup. After five successful years they were given senior status and moved into the Surrey Senior League for 1949-50. It marked the start of a decade of honours as within a year they were runners up to Leatherhead. In 1950 the club moved to Merland Rise and celebrated by winning the league by 11 points from Dorking. Harry Clark had topped a hundred goals in the previous year and followed with a mere 81 in 26 games. They won the title for the next three seasons before slowing down until 1957, although they were runners up four times. To add to the list, they won six County competitions. The success slowed and from 1959 to 1964 was a barren time with just the East Surrey Charity Cup, but under Gordon Taylor the title was won again in 1965. Owing to the problem with short leases on the ground, they were unable to expand but as soon as a long lease was available the club joined the Spartan League in 1965. The first two seasons saw Banstead lose the League Cup final to Hampton and they failed to challenge for the league itself until 1978 when they became runners up of what was then the London Spartan League. They joined the Athenian League in 1979 and won the League Cup in 1981 and 1982, losing the final in 1983. With the demise of the Athenians the club moved up to the Isthmian League Division Two South in 1984.

During 1990 the club faced a crisis when the board resigned over a disagreement with the council over leasing and for a while the club was in danger, however it was settled and new floodlights and an upgraded clubhouse were soon in place. 1993 saw the club's best ever run in national cups, when they reached the last eight of the FA Vase. For the 93-94 season Banstead were joined at Merland Rise by Epsom and Ewell whose ground had been sold and between them they have brought the ground to within the league's grading.

BARKING

Mayesbrook Park, Lodge Avenue, Dagenham RM8 2JR, Tel: 0181 595 6511

Secretary: Roger Chilvers, 50 Harrow Rd, Barking,
Essex IG11 7RA Tel: 0181 591 5313

Nickname: The Blues   Colours: Blue and White

Capacity: 2,500   Seating: 200

Covered standing: 600   Clubhouse on ground: Yes

DIRECTIONS

Come off A13 on A1153 (Lodge Avenue), and ground 1 mile on left. Bus 162 from Barking station. Nearest tube station is Beacontree.

Record attendance: 1,972 v Aldershot in FA Cup Rd 2 1978

Biggest win: 10-2 v Chelmsford City
FA Trophy Nov 11th 1978

Biggest defeat: 0-8 v Marlow date unknown

Record appearances: Bob Makin 566

Record goalscorer in one season: Jeff Wood

Record goalscorer in total: Micky Guyton 135

Record fee paid or received: £6,000 for Alan Hull from Orient in 1987

Honours

FA AMATEUR CUP Runners up 1927, Isthmian League 1979, Athenian League 1935

London League 1921 Div 1 A 1910, South Essex League Div 1 1899 Div 2 1901, 1902, 1905, 1906

London Senior Cup 1912, 1921, 1927, 1979, Essex Senior Cup 1895, 1896, 1920, 46, 63, 70, 90

Dylon Shield 1980, London Intermediate Cup 1986

PROGRAMME EDITOR Peter Pendle 01992 578286, MANAGER FOR 1996-97: Paul Downes, Chairman: Stephen Ward, Press officer Terry Horgan, 50 South Park Terrace, Ilford, Essex

Barking FC were originally formed as Barking Rovers in 1880, playing their home matches at Vicarage Fields. They shared the ground with a cricket club, but following damage to the square they were forced to move to Eastbury Fields. Shortly after the move the club folded and Barking Woodville were formed. Their first success was in 1896 when they beat Woodford in the Essex Senior Cup Final, whilst the reserves took the Junior version. They played in the London League for two years but they too disbanded in 1898. At the turn of the century, Barking Working Lads Institute formed a football club, playing in the South Essex Leagueat Vicarage Fields. They reached the Junior Cup final and were Division Two champions, and a year later took the London Junior Cup. After the Great War they were elected to the London League, from where they won the Essex Senior and West Ham Charity Cups. By then they had changed to Barking Town FC where they had success in London League and Senior Cup and the success continued in 1922 as they reached the semi-finals of the Amateur Cup. The success rubbed off when the Athenian League accepted them in 1923. 1926-27 was one of the club's best ever seasons, as they reached the Amateur Cup final, losing to Leyton, and also reached the final of the Essex Senior Cup, where Ilford won 2-1. However they did take home the London Senior Cup that season. 1927 saw Barking play the first of four consecutive Senior Cup finals, which were all sadly lost, but during the pre war years the name was shortened and the Athenian League title won. The club played through the War and in 1950 and 1952 twice reached the Amateur Cup semi-finals, before joining the Isthmians in 1953. Little further success came and in 1973 the club were forced to leave Vicarage Fields for a new ground in Mayesbrook Park. In 1978-79 the club surprised all when they took the Isthmian League championship and the London Senior Cup, and got to Round Two of the FA Cup. It was to be the last real success so far, for relegation came to Division One in 1991 and last May Barking dropped to Division Two. Vicarage Field was left to go to pot for many years until comparatively recently it was levelled and is now developed.

BEDFORD TOWN

The New Eyrie, Meadow Lane, Cardington, Bedford MK44 3SB Tel: 01234 838448

Secretary: Barry Stephenson, 9 Aspen Ave, Putnoe, Bedford MK41 8BX. Tel: 01234 342276

Nickname: Eagles

Capacity: 3,000, Covered seating: 150

Covered Standing: 500

Clubhouse on ground: Yes

Record attendance: 3,000 v Peterborough Utd, opening of ground Aug 6th 1993

At Allen Park, 1,227 v Bedford Utd SML 1991

Record crowd for old Bedford Town FC at Eyrie was 18,407 v Everton FA Cup 4th Round Feb 12th 1966

Biggest win: 9-0 v Ickleford, Biggest defeat: 1-7 v Canvey Island, Record appearances, goalscorer in one season and goalscorer in total: Jason Reed

Record fee received: (previous club) Bill Garner to Southend Utd in 1969, £15,000

DIRECTIONS

On A603 Bedford to Sandy Road. Come off A1 at Sandy following signs to Bedford - ground on right. From Bedford take Cardington Road out of town signposted Biddleswade and Sandy. An 'Eagles Special' bus picks up at various points in town and arrives at ground twenty minutes before kick-off, leaving fifteen minutes after game.

Honours

FA TROPHY semi-final 1975, South Midlands League 1995, Div 1 in 1993, Floodlit Cup 1995, Hinchingbrooke Cup 1994 and 1995, Beds Senior Cup 1995 and 1996, **Previous club** , Southern League 1959 and Div 1 1970, United Counties League 1931, 1933, 1934,

Manager for 1996/97: Mick Foster: Assistant Manager: Neal Rodney

Chairman: David Donnelly   Vice chairman: John Lang

Bedford Town Football Club was founded in 1908 and played in the Northants League, which became the United Counties League, until the War, when they joined the Southern League in 1945.

They became a limited company in 1950 and a year later the ex-Fulham and Arsenal forward Ronnie Rooke was appointed manager. Through the 50's and early 60's Town gained a fine reputation as FA Cup battlers and beat a host of League clubs, including Watford, Norwich City, Newcastle Utd, Exeter City, Brighton and Hove Albion and Oxford United, the finest day being in February 1966, when over 18,000 crammed into the Eyrie to watch a 4th round tie with Everton. The Eagles were runners up in the league in 1957 and 1958 before taking the title a year later. Twice they reached the 4th Round FA Cup but soon relegation followed and a decade of fluctuating fortunes began which terminated after a long period of decline, when the lease on the magnificent Eyrie Ground was terminated and the club folded in 1982.

Happily they re-formed and in 1993 they were champions of the South Midlands League Division One, gaining promotion to the Premier which they won a year later. The outstanding amount of hard work done by members and officials alike to bring the New Eyrie up to date, paid off in style when the Eagles entered the Isthmian League Division Three, which they were promoted from in third place in 1995.

Much has been written elsewhere about the old Eyrie, which had a capacity of close to 20,000, but the new club began in more modest surroundings at Allen Park and Queens Park before moving in to the current ground, the site of which has been extended recently to create a new home for Bedford United FC.

BRACKNELL TOWN

Larges Lane, Bracknell, Berks RG12 9AN.Tel: 01344 412349 or 300933

Sec: Cliff McFadden, 15 Goodways Drive, Bracknell, Berks, RG12 9AU Tel - 01344 640349

Colours: Red and White stripes

Nickname: Robins

Capacity: 2,500

Seating: 190

Covered standing: 400

Clubhouse on ground: yes

Record attendance: 2,500 v Newquay FA Amateur Cup 1971

Biggest win: 9-0 v Flackwell Heath

Biggest defeat: 0-9 Thame Utd and Royston

Record appearances: Justin Day

Record goalscorer in one season: Mickey Havermans

Record goalscorer in total: Justin Day

Honours

Surrey Senior League 1970

Surrey Senior League Cup 1969 and 1970

Isthmian League Div 3 1995

Manager 1996-97: Brian Broome

Assistant Manager: Chris Hodge

Chairman: Dave Mihell

Vice Chairman: Paul Broome

Press Officer: Bob Scully, c/o Football Club

> ## DIRECTIONS
> **Off A329 just before Met Office roundabout by Bracknell College, ground 200 yards. From Bracknell (BR)/bus station — right out of station, follow path over bridge, left down steps and follow cycle path ahead, after 300 yards follow curve over footbridge, right and follow lane to end, left and ground on left after bend.**

Bracknell Town were formed in 1896 and played in local league football until 1959, when elected to the Great Western League where they stayed for four seasons. In 1963 they moved to the Surrey Senior League, winning the League Cup in 1969 and doing the double a year later, prompting them to move to the Spartan League. They won that League Cup in 1975 and 12 months later they were runners up in League and Cup to Farnborough Town. After more success in League and Cup, they were admitted to the Athenian League in 1984, finishing runners up in the second year, and gaining promotion. A year later they missed moving to the Premier League by one point. 1987-88 was a complete contrast as they were nearly relegated but sadly the following term saw them go down to Division Two South. With the league restructure, Town played 1991-92 in Division Three, which they won in style in 1994 under Nicky Collier and Ken Wilson.

Last season saw the club embroiled in several cup runs which saw them reach the 4th qualifier of the FA Cup, meaning a fixture backlog which saw a final ninth position.

CHALFONT ST PETER

The Playing Fields, Amersham Rd, Chalfont St Peter SL9 7BQ. Tel: 01753 885797

Secretary: Mal Keenan, 41 Cedar Avenue, Hazlemere, Nr High Wycombe, Bucks Tel: 01494 718332

Nickname: Saints

Colours: Red and green

Capacity: 2,500

Seating: 250

Covered standing: 150

Clubhouse on ground: Yes

Record attendance: 2,500 v Watford for Benefit match in 1985

Record appearance: Colin Davies

Record fee paid: £750 for Steve Church March 1989

DIRECTIONS

A413 from Uxbridge (London) to Chalfont. Turn left 100 yards after second major roundabout (between Ambulance station and Community Centre). Two miles from Gerrards Cross (BR), regular buses from Slough.

Honours

Isthmian League Div 2 1988

Athenian League Cup 1977 and 1983

London Spartan League Div 2 1976

Berks and Bucks Intermediate Cup 1953

Berks and Bucks Benevolent Cup 1965

Manager for 1996-97: Kevin Stone

Coach: Graham Bressington

Chairman: Ray Franks

The club was formed in 1926 but made little progress in its early years, playing in Berks, Bucks and Middlesex junior football, until accepted into the Great Western Combination in 1948.

The first silverware came in 1953 when they won the Berks and Bucks Intermediate Cup, and admission to the Parthenon League soon followed which gave them senior status. Although never taking the title they did well enough to be promoted to the Spartan League, via the London League, in 1962. It was an unspectacular period, livened only by winning the last ever Berks and Bucks Benevolent Cup, when they beat Athenian champions Slough Town 2-0 in the final watched by 2,000 spectators. Poor support saw the club slump in the early 70's, but a move into the Athenian League saw them improve to become the first Division Two side to win the League Cup by beating Epsom in the final. It was repeated in 1983, beating Banstead at Edgware. The following season saw another upward move, to the Isthmian League, following a nail biting last day where they lost the title to Redhill. The first four seasons in Division Two saw Saints in the top eight each year and they finally won the title in 1988 after a battle with Met Police and Dorking.

1993 and 1994 saw the club struggle and relegation came and since then with stringent ground grading and poor gates, life has been a struggle for Chalfont.

CHESHUNT

The Stadium, Theobalds Lane, Cheshunt, Herts.Tel: 01992 626752

Secretary: Richard Cotterell, 46 Friends Ave, Cheshunt, Herts EN8 8LX Tel 01992 634796

Press Officer: Neil Harrison, 137 Russells Ride, Cheshunt, Herts EN8 8UD Tel 01992 423678

Colours: Yellow and Blue

Nickname: Ambers

Capacity: 2,500, Seating: 285

Covered standing: 600, Clubhouse on ground: Yes

Record attendance: 7,000 v Bromley London Senior Cup in 1947

Biggest win: 11-1 v Hastings United London League 1949 (First game on new ground)

Biggest defeat: 1-9 v Wolverton Town Isthmian League 1987

Record fee paid: £250 for Tony Tilbrook, Borehamwood 1988

Record fee received £1, 500 for Andy Prutton, Dartford 1989

DIRECTIONS

M25 to junction 25, A10 north towards Hertford past ground on right, turn back towards London at first traffic lights to enter. 400 yards from Theobalds Grove BR station — turn left and left again for ground. Buses 279, 242, 715 and 310 to Theobalds Grove station.

Honours

Athenian League 1976 and Division One 1968, League Cup 1975 and 1976,

Spartan League 1963 and League Cup 1964 and 1993

London League 1950, Division One 1948 and 1949. Division One Cup 1947

Park Royal Cup 1947, Herts Senior Cup, 1924, Herts Charity Cup 1901, 1906W, Herts Charity Shield 1947, 1966, Herts Senior Centenary Trophy 1992, East Anglian Cup 1975, Mithras Cup 1970

London Charity Cup 1974

Manager 1996-97: John Ward, Assistant Manager: Ernie Ford

Chairman: George Norman, Vice Chairman: Paul Cully

Cheshunt Football Club was founded in 1946 by the late Roy Bailey, the club's former President and they successfully applied for membership of the London League. In the first season they were runners up and won the Herts Charity Shield, Herts Junior Cup and two other local competitions. They went on to complete a hat-trick of titles although the best achievement was winning the Herts Senior Cup in 1949.

They moved up to the Premier Division which they won at first try and went on to reach the last eight of the Amateur Cup and the final of the Senior Cup. After that amazing start to life the club moved on to the Delphian League, back to the London League and then the Aetolian League before the Athenian League, where they were runners up in Division Two in 1966.

The club merged with the strong Cheshunt Youth FC in 1975, and the senior side won the Premier Division in 1976 having won Division One in 1968, and as a result were invited to join the Isthmian League the following season. They reached Division One in 1982 but having reached the last eight of the FA Vase they were relegated back to Division Two North. The decline continued unabated and they found themselves in the Spartan League in 1986, and after two near misses the club revived in 1992 winning the League Cup and scraping into third place behind Brimsdown and Casuals to move back into the Isthmian League.

COLLIER ROW & ROMFORD

Sungate, Collier Row Rd, Collier Row, Romford, Essex. Tel: 01708 722766

Secretary: Mrs Anne Rogers, 11 Witham Rd, Dagenham, Essex RM10 8JL Tel 0181 593 2182

Press Sec: Dave Fletcher, c/o 3rd Floor sport, 245 Blackfriars Rd, London SE1 9UX Tel 0171 922 7126 (b)

Colours: Yellow and blue

Nickname: The Boro

Capacity: 2,000

Seating: 200

Covered standing: 200

Clubhouse on ground: Yes

Record attendance: 412 v East Ham Utd Essex Senior League 1992

Biggest win: 9-0 v Hullbridge Essex Senior League 1995

Biggest defeat: 0-5 v Lowestoft Town FA Vase 1994 and v Halstead 1993

Record appearances: Micky Ross

Record goalscorer in one season: Micky Ross: 26 in 1994-95

Record goalscorer in total: Micky Ross

Honours

As Collier Row

FA VASE semi-final 1987

Spartan League 1984 and 1986

Senior Division 1983

As Romford

Essex Senior League and League Cup 1996

Manager 1996-97: Don McGovern

Assistant Manager: Alan Marson

Chairman: Bradley Goodwin

Vice Chairman: Steve Gardener

Collier Row and Romford FC was formed during the summer of 1996 by an amalgamation of the two clubs, Row who were in the Isthmian League and Romford from the Essex Senior League.

> ### DIRECTIONS
> **A12 from London, left at Moby Dick (PH) traffic lights, right at next roundabout, ground entrance signposted 200 yards on right. London bus 247 passes ground.**

DORKING

Meadowbank, Mill Lane, Dorking, Surrey RH4 1DX. Tel: 01306 884112

Secretary: David Short, 29 Bennett Close, Cobham,
Surrey KT11 1AH Tel 01932 866496

Commercial Manager: Mrs Anne Eames 0181 645 3651

Chairman: Jack Collins The Villa, Old London Rd,
Mickleham, Surrey KT11 1AH Tel 01372 375004

Programme Ed: Paul Mason 01737 222921

Club Shop: Harry Tyler: 01306 886174

Colours: Green and White hoops

Nickname: The Chicks   Capacity: 3,600

Seating: 200   Covered standing: 800

Clubhouse on ground: Yes

Record attendance: 4,500 v Folkestone Tn
FA Cup 1st Qual Rd 1955

Biggest win: 15-0 v Walton Surrey Senior League 1929

Record appearances: Steve Lunn

Record goalscorer in one season: Neil Goodman 64 in 1955-56

DIRECTIONS

Mill Lane is off Dorking High Street next to Woolworths and Marks & Spencers opposite the White Horse pub. Fork right in Mill Lane past the Malthouse pub. Half mile from both Dorking and Deepdene (BR) stations.

Honours

Isthmian League Div 2 South 1989

Surrey Senior Shield 1959 and 1960, Surrey Senior League 1929, 1930, 1955, 1956

Gilbert Rice Floodlit Cup 1988, Surrey Intermediate Cup 1957

Southern Combination Challenge Cup 1993

Manager 1996-97: Terry Eames, Assistant Manager: Steve Osgood

Chairman: Jack Collins, Vice Chairman: Ray Collins, Press Officer: Brian Bletso: 0171 972 9720

Dorking's origins are vague, but it is known that they were founded in 1880, with only Reigate Priory having seniority in the county. Having played in local football, the Chicks came to prominence in 1910 when they fought their way through to the final of the Surrey Senior Shield where they lost to Kingstonian, and after the Great War they became founder members of the Surey Senior League in 1922, playing at Pixham Lane. They were held up by the strong Farnham Breweries and Epsom Town sides, but were not to be denied as the title was won in 1929 and 1930. Either side of the Second War was a lean period for the club but in 1949 they took both the League Cup and League Charity Cup and in 1953, their move to a new purpose built council owned ground at Meadowbank, saw league success begin with a runners up spot and then two titles and several League and Charity Cup final appearances.

In 1956 the Chicks moved to the Corinthian League and although not winning the league they won two Surrey Senior Shields and reached a third final. In 1963 they moved to the Athenian League when it merged the Corinthian and Delphian Leagues, but it proved to be the start of another barren spell which eventually led to a hasty amalgamation with Guildford City in 1974. The new club, Guildford and Dorking United played briefly in the Southern League at Meadowbank before it too went under, and Dorking Town were formed in 1977. They completed the old club's fixtures before joining the Surrey Senior League in 1977. After a year they joined the Athenian League and soon after, as Dorking FC, they were in the Isthmian League for 1981.The Chicks won Division Two South in 1989 and the Senior Cup in 1990, and for a while looked to be developing into a strong club once again, a feeling backed up by an FA Cup run in 1992 which saw them narrowly beaten by Plymouth Argyle. It proved to be the last big occasion to date, as internal turmoil has spread on to the pitch and after successive relegations the Chicks would have started this season in Division Three, but for the resignation of members during the summer.

EDGWARE TOWN

White Lion Ground, High Street, Edgware, Middx. HA8 6BS. Tel: 0181 952 6799

Secretary: Barry Boreham, 28 St Brides Ave, Edgware, Middlesex HA8 6BS Tel 0181 952 1685

Colours: All Red

Nickname: Wares

Capacity: 3,500   Seating: 240

Covered Standing: 600, Clubhouse on ground: Yes

Record attendance: 8,500 v Wealdstone FA Cup 1947

Record appearances: John Mangan

DIRECTIONS

Turn left out of Edgware tube station (Northern Line), turn left again at crossroads and ground 300 yards on right in Edgware High Street behind White Lion pub. Buses 32, 288 and 142.

Honours

Isthmian League Div 3 1992

London Spartan League 1988 and 1990
League Cup 1988

Corinthian League Memorial Shield 1953 and 1962

Middlesex Senior League 1941, 1942, 1943, 1944, 1945

Middlesex Senior Cup 1948

Manager for 1996-97: Jim McLeish

Assistant manager: Peter Grant

Chairman: Michael Flynn

Press Officer: Tom Hooks c/o Secretary

Originally emanating from junior club William Moss and Sons Sports and Social Club, Town have played on the White Lion Ground, previously the home for many years of Edgware Rugby Club, since its formation in 1939. Plans were immediately disrupted by the outbreak of war, but the Great Western Combination was formed and subsequently the Middlesex Senior was also formed in 1940, which Edgware joined and won five years running between 1941 and 1945. They also won the Middlesex Senior Cup in 1947 and were runners up in the London Senior Cup the same season. Admission to the Corinthian League in 1951 meant that Edgware were competing in a higher standard of football, and success eluded them until 1954 when they were runners up, although they did win the League's Memorial Shield in 1953, winning it again in 1962, the last time it was played for. At the end of the 1962-63 season there was an amalgamation of Athenian, Corinthian and Delphian Leagues and Edgware were placed in Division One alongside the likes of Dagenham, Enfield, Barnet, Wealdstone and Finchley. They were promoted to the Premier in 1965, and in 1970 changed the club name to Edgware FC, but since an appearance in a Middlesex Senior Cup final in 1974, success has been limited. They were runners up in 1982, but with the League folding and clubs reorganising, Edgware were put into the Spartan League where in 1988 they did the double of League and Cup in the most successful season ever, having gone back to the name Edgware Town again.

In 1990 they won the league once again and were successful in joining the Isthmian League, where they won Division Three and reached the last 16 of the FA Vase. They also beat Brentford in the Middlesex Senior Cup semi-final, losing to Chelsea in the final. A good run in the same competition in 1994 again saw them lose in the final, this time to Staines Town.

EGHAM TOWN

Tempest Road, Pooley Green, Egham, Surrey TW20 9DW. Tel: 01784 435226

Secretary: Chris Thompson, 138a Thorpe Lea Rd, Egham, Surrey TW20 8BL

Tel: 01784 463562, Pager 0881 830702

Press Secretary: Mark Ferguson (b) 01784 463481

Colours: Blue and White

Nickname: Sarnies, Swans or the Town

Capacity: 5,635

Seating: 335

Covered standing: 2,100

Clubhouse on ground: Yes

Record: attendance: 2,000 v Select X1 in 1981

Biggest win: 10-1 v Camberley in 1982-83

Biggest defeat: 0-10 v Fisher Ath Parthenon League 1965

Record appearances: Dave Jones 850+

Record goalscorer in one season: Mark Butler 50 in 1991-92

Record goalscorer in total: Mark Butler

Record fee paid: £3,000 for Mark Butler in 1990

Record fee received: £4,000 for Mark Butler to Wycombe Wanderers

DIRECTIONS

M25 junction 13, follow signs to Egham, under M25 at roundabout, left to end, left at mini-roundabout, over railway crossing, left to end (Pooley Green Road), right, ground on right after 'Compasses' and 'Robin Hood' pubs. Bus 441 from Staines to Pooley Green. Forty minutes walk from Egham (BR) station.

Honours

Surrey Intermediate Charity Cup 1920, 1921, 1927

Surrey Intermediate League 1921

North-west Surrey Charity Cup 1921

Surrey Senior League and League Charity Cup 1923

Spartan League 1972

Athenian League Division Two 1975

Manager for 1996-97: Eric Howard

Chairman: Patrick Bennett

Vice Chairman: Peter Barnes

Egham Town, the original senior club in the town, were formed in 1896 and competed in the Hounslow and District League. Along with many others, it folded during the Great War but reformed in 1919, moving headquarters to the Forester's Arms from the Anglers Rest near Runnymede, playing at Manorcroft Road. They became very strong in local football, with two final appearances in their first season in the Surrey Intermediate League, 1919. Both finals were against Farnham United Breweries, winning the Intermediate but losing the Challenge Cup. The following season the club dropped just one point in taking the league, conceding just 7 goals, they retained the Intermediate Cup and also won the North-West Surrey Charity Cup. Leading scorer Jimmy Riddle bagged 42 goals out of a total of 126.

In 1922 Egham were founder members and inaugural champions of the Surrey Senior League ahead of Carshalton whom they beat in the final of the Senior Charity Cup. Four years later the club were again on the move, this time to Vicarage Crescent and they had two more finals to celebrate, losing the Senior League Challenge Cup but winning the Intermediate Cup again. It was a dress rehearsal for the following year when Egham were runners up in both Senior League and Senior League Cup.

This success continued into the 30's when they reached the 1st Round of the FA Cup and were rewarded with election to the Spartan League. It was much harder and they returned to the County just three years later.

With the Second War the club disbanded again, but this time they stayed dormant for 24 years. The ground was sold to meet debts and other commitments and the monies held in trust. Due to the age of the Trustees it was decided to use the money to good purpose and a new pavilion was built for Englefield Green.

The next momentous date was December 9th 1963 when 100 people gathered in the Literary Institute to ressurect the team for the town. With a public collection raising £7, 6/- Egham Town Football Club was started. The council were persuaded to give the club Tempest Road ground and the first season was spent in the Parthenon League before returning to the Senior League and then two years on, the Spartan League. After a poor start the league was won in 1972, and within two years the new club had joined the Athenians, winning Division Two and then finishing second in Division One, in the first two seasons. The third and last season saw them ninth, but it was enough to get into the Isthmian League Division Two.

Several poor seasons followed, with only an FA Vase run to get excited about. 1991 saw an upturn as Chris Wainwright's side got to the 4th qualifying round of the Cup before losing to Telford. That year saw a third place with 100 goals scored and a year later Mark Butler netted 50 goals in all to set a new record. They also got to two finals, the Loctite Trophy where they lost to Purfleet and the Surrey Senior Cup where Carshalton Athletic beat them.

HEMEL HEMPSTEAD

Vauxhall Ground, Adeyfield Rd, Hemel Hempstead, HP2 4HW. Tel: 01442 259777

Secretary: Mrs Vivienne Herbert, 2 Montgomery Ave, Adeyfield, Hemel Hempstead, Herts, HP2 4HD. Tel: 01442 395633

DIRECTIONS

Euston to Hemel Hempstead Station. H2 or H3 bus to Windmill Road, Longlands.

Colours: All Red   Nickname: Hemel

Capacity: 3,000   Seating: 100

Covered standing: Yes   Clubhouse on ground: Yes

Record attendance: 2,000 v Watford 1985 Friendly
at Crabtree Lane: 3,500 v Tooting & M. FA Amateur Cup 1962

Record appearances: John Wallace 1012

Record goalscorer in total: Dai Price

Honours

Herts Senior Cup 1906, 1908, 1909, 1926, 1962, 1966, 1992; Herts Charity Cup 1926, 1935, 1952, 1964, 1977, 1983; Spartan League 1934; Herts Intermediate Cup 1955, 1966, 1984; West Herts St Marys Cup 1971, 1976, 1983, 1986, 1991, 1992, 1994.

Hemel Hempstead Football Club was founded in 1885 as Apsley F.C and originally played their football in the West Herts League. At the time the Club enjoyed only moderate league success, but did achieve a run of County Senior Cup victories in the first decade of the 1900's, capturing the trophy in 1906, 1908 and retaining it in 1909.

In 1921 the Club made the move to the Spartan League. However, once again they had to look to the County Cups for their honours, winning the Senior cup for the fourth time in 1926 and also, for the first time, the Charity Cup in the same season. League success finally came in 1934 when they won the Spartan League Division One Championship. The Charity Cup was again won in 1935 and 1952. In between these wins the club changed its name to Hemel Hempstead Town, as well as becoming associate members of the Football Association in 1935.

A major step came in 1952 when they joined the Delphian League and became full members of the Football Association. They stayed for eleven years, but unfortunately without any major success. However, in 1962 the senior side reached the first round of the FA Amateur Cup for the first time ever. Although they lost 1-3 to Tooting & Mitcham, the match was played in front of a crowd of 3,500 spectators. The following season the Club joined the newly formed Athenian League. Once more with a change of league came a County cup success, with the Club winning the Charity Cup once again. In 1965 they gained promotion to the Premier Division and following several seasons in the Premier Division, the Club was relegated in 1969.

In 1972 they amalgamated with Hemel Hempstead United from the South Midlands League and changed names to become the present Hemel Hempstead FC. Also, the Club moved ground to the current ground in Vauxhall Road and enjoyed success in the West Herts St Mary's Cup competition in 1971, 1976 and 1977. In 1977 the Club joined the expanded Isthmian League, where they have remained since, and during that season they won the Herts Charity Shield, while the following year they went on to win the Middlesex Border League Cup. In the 1980's the Club won the Herts Charity Shield in 1984 and the West Herts St Mary's Cup in 1982, 1983 and 1986.

The 1990's started with another St Mary's Cup victory and then in 1992 the Club reached the final of the Herts Senior Cup where they lost 4-1 to Barnet FC. In November 1992 the Club was rocked by a damaging fire which destroyed the clubhouse and changing rooms, and they were forced to rearrange several matches away.

In 1993/94 the club again won the St Mary's Cup, and at the same time underwent a major change in club officials and personnel both on and off the pitch. During the 1995/96 season, the team was managed by Steve Ringrose and through the Club's strong youth policy, was able to develop a team which comfortably finished 11 points clear of the bottom position. Furthermore, they reached the Herts County Cup Final and the St Mary's Cup Final both of which they lost by a single goal.

HORSHAM

Queen Street, Horsham, West Sussex RH13 5AD. Tel: 01403 65787

Secretary: Frank King, 51 Laughton Rd, Horsham, West Sussex, RH12 4EJ Tel 01403 264647

Colours: Yellow and Green

Nickname: Hornets

Capacity: 4,300

Seating: 300

Covered standing: 1,800

Clubhouse on ground : Yes

Record attendance: 8,000 v Swindon Town FA Cup November 1966

DIRECTIONS

From Brighton Road proceed into Queen Street towards town centre — ground entrance opposite Queens Head. 10 minutes walk from Horsham (BR) station; along North Street past Arts Centre, fork left, left at lights, ground opposite Queens Head. Buses 107, 137, 2, 283 to Horsham Carfax then thru East Street under Iron Bridge and turn left.

Honours

Sussex Senior Cup 1934, 1939, 1950, 1954, 1972, 1974, 1976

Sussex RUR Cup 1900, 1931, 32, 34 jt, 35, 36, 37, 38 jt, 46, 49 jt, 51, 52, 57

Sussex County League 1932, 1933, 1935, 1936, 1937, 1938, 1947, League Cup 1946 and 1947

Metropolitan League 1952

Athenian League Div 1 1973 and Div 2 in 1969

Sussex Floodlit Cup 1973

Isthmian League Div 3 1996

Manager for 1996-97: Mark Dunk, Chairman: Frank King

Founded in 1885, three years before the first professional league, Horsham Football Club was soon to rise to become one of the strongest clubs in the county, dominating the local scene for close on 20 years. Playing in the West Sussex Senior League from its inception in 1896 and taking the championship four times, the club moved on to the Sussex County League in 1926 and enjoyed a great period of success.

The league was first won in 1932 after successive near misses and the title was retained in 1933, 1935, 1936, 1937 and 1938 with the team regularly topping 100 goals in a season. After the War Horsham won the first post War title and then went close in the next four years. Crowds at Queen Street reached upwards of 5,000, mostly during the Amateur Cup runs. During this heyday the Sussex Senior Cup was won four times and the RUR Cup 13 times, as well a number of minor trophies.

By 1951 Horsham FC had grown too big for the county scene and joined the Metropolitan League, which they won at the first attempt, though for a further five years they struggled and in 1957 joined the Corinthian League until it merged into a bigger Athenian League. The club was placed in Division 1, from where they were relegated after two season. Three years later they were back, having taken the Division Two title and a new successful period dawned with wins in Senior and Floodlight Cups.

In 1973 they were elected to the Isthmian League Division Two, to which they returned in May, after taking the Division Three title.

HUNGERFORD TOWN

Town Ground, Bulpit Lane, Hungerford, RG17 0AY. Tel: (club) 01488 682939 (boardroom) 684597

Secretary: Ken Holmes, 10 Bulpit Lane, Hungerford, Berks RG17 0AU Tel 01488 683846

Colours: White and Blue

Nickname: Crusaders

Capacity: 3,000

Seating: 150

Covered standing: 300

Clubhouse on ground: Yes

Record attendance: 1,684 v Sudbury Town
FA Vase semi-final 1989

Record appearances: Dean Bailey 400+

Record goalscorer in total: Ian Farr 268

Record fee paid £4,000 for Joe Scott from Yeovil Town

Record fee received £3,500 for Joe Scott to Barnstaple

DIRECTIONS

M4 junction 14 to A4, right and left at Bear Hotel, through town centre on A338, left into Priory Road, second left into Bulpit Lane, over crossroads, ground on left. Three quarters of a mile from Hungerford BR station.

Honours

FA VASE Semi-final 1978, 1980, 1989

Berks and Bucks Senior Cup 1982

Hellenic League Div 1 1971

Premier Div Cup 1978 and Div 1 Cup 1971

Benevolent Cup 1961

Hungerford Town were formed in 1886 and competed at Intermediate level in the Newbury and District and Swindon and District Leagues before their senior status saw them enter the Hellenic League in 1958. They won the Benevolent Cup two years later but it was another ten years before further success came with the Division One League and Cup double. the 70's were a memorable time for Town, for the ground began to develop with new dressing rooms, a new clubhouse, stand and floodlights, and on the pitch the club reached the Berks and Bucks Senior Cup final for the first time. A further appearance when losing to Slough Town in a replay, was enough to gain the club election to the Isthmian League in 1978, after winning the League Cup and reaching the semi-final of the FA Vase, eventually losing to Barton Rovers in a replay at Harrow Borough.

After another Senior Cup final defeat, the club again got to the Vase semi-final, sadly losing this time to Guisborough from the Northern Alliance, also having the heartbreak of just missing promotion. They did however get to the First Round of the FA Cup where they lost to Slough Town. After two more third places, Town finally won some silverware, by taking the Senior Cup when beating Wycombe Wanderers, but once again in 1985 promotion was narrowly missed. In 1989 after a period of rebuilding, Hungerford reached their third semi-final in the Vase, but once again they were denied, by Sudbury Town after a disastrous second leg.

Since then the club has survived in Division Two without going close to emulating the etams of the 70's and 80's

LEATHERHEAD

Fetcham Grove, Guildford Rd, Leatherhead, Surrey KT22 9AS.Tel: 01372 360151

Secretary: Mike Bailey, c/o LFC

Commercial Manager: Keith Wenham,
189 Rangefield Rd, Bromley, Kent Tel 0181 461 1369

Colours: Green and White

Nickname: Tanners

Capacity: 3,400   Seating: 550

Covered standing: 800   Clubhouse on ground Yes

Record attendance: 5,500 v Wimbledon in 1976

Record appearances: Dave Reid

Record win: 13-1 v Leyland Motors

Record goalscorer in total: Fred Stenning

Record fee received: Undisclosed for John Hunphrey to Millwall

DIRECTIONS

M25 junction 9 to Leatherhead; follow signs to Leisure Centre, ground adjacent. Half mile from Leatherhead (BR). London Country Buses 479 and 408 — ground opposite bus garage.

Honours

FA AMATEUR CUP Semi-final 1971 and 1974

FA TROPHY Runners up 1978

Isthmian League Cup 1978

Corinthian League 1963, Athenian League Division One 1964

Surrey Senior Cup 1969, Surrey Senior League 1947, 1948, 1949, 1950

League Cup 1950 and Charity Cup 1947 and 1950, East Surrey Charity Cup 1969

Surrey Senior Shield 1969

Manager 1996-97: Mike Bailey, Assistant Manager: Terry Quick, Chairman: Keith Wenham

Leatherhead Football Club was founded in 1946 and elected to the Surrey Senior League where they were immediately successful, winning four successive championships. They then had one year in the Metropolitan League before becoming founder members of the Delphian League in 1951. Progression to the Corinthian League followed in 1958 and the Tanners were crowned champions in 1963. They were incorporated into the new Athenian League Division One and won promotion. There were two Surrey Senior League finals in 1965 and 1967 before in 1969 they did a unique treble by winning the Surrey Senior Cup, Senior Shield and Intermediate Cup. Soon they were making headlines in the Amateur Cup, reaching the semi-final in 1971 and 1974, either side of their election to the Isthmian League.

In 1975 the club were nationally known as they reached the Fourth Round of the FA Cup, beating Bishop's Stortford, Colchester United and Brighton and Hove Albion, which gave them a home tie with Leicester City. It was switched to Filbert Street and although taking a 2-0 lead Leicester hit back to win.

Later that year they reached the London and Surrey Senior Cup finals, losing both which began a heartbreaking series of cup final losses which only ended in 1990.

The long awaited Wembley appearance came in the Trophy in 1978 but they lost to Altrincham and also lost the London Senior and Isthmian League Cup finals that season.

It was the last of the great sides to date, for since then Tanners have struggled to make an impact on the league and are currently in Division Two, with former Wolves and England man Mike Bailey in charge, also acting as the club General Manager.

LEIGHTON TOWN

Bell Close, Lake Street, Leighton Buzzard, Beds. Tel: 01525 373311

Secretary: Alec Irvine, 12 Rowley Furrows, Linslade, Beds LU7 7SH Tel 01525 376475

Colours: Red and White

Nickname: Reds

Capacity: 2,500

Seating: 155

Covered standing: 750

Clubhouse on ground: Yes

Record attendance: 1,522 v Aldershot Town Isthmian Div 3 1993

Honours

South Midlands League 1967 and 1992
League Cup 1991 O'Brien Trophy 1991

Beds Senior Cup 1927, 1968, 1969, 1970, 1993

Bucks Charity Cup 1995

Spartan League Division Two 1924 and 1928

Leighton Town were at one time known as Leighton United and were mainly involved in local leagues in their early days, winning the Leighton and District League on several occasions. They were original members of the South Midlands League in 1922, when it was known as the Bedfordshire County League, until 1923 when they moved to the Spartan League until 1952, where after the 20's the club had little if any real success. They were back in the South Midlands League in 1966, when they were bottom, but a year later they were champions at last, celebrating by going back into the Spartan League. The late 60's saw the Senior Cup hat-trick at Bell Close, but the team broke up and again Leighton went into decline.

A brief move to the United Counties League was a failure and they moved back to the South Midlands League, where they waited until 1991 before tasting success with the Challenge Trophy. and the Premier Division Cup. The following season was the best ever, with the Premier Division won and a place in the Isthmian League assured. Since then they have been promoted as runners up in May this year.

METROPOLITAN POLICE

Imber Court, East Molesey. Tel: 0181 398 7358

Secretary: Tony Brooking, 15 Westmoreland Ave, Hornchurch, Essex RM11 2EJ.Tel: 01708 450715

Assistant Sec DS Neil Eames Tel: 0181 287 0773

Press Sec: Cliff Travis, 33 Minsterley Ave, Shepperton, Middx TW17 8QS. Tel: 01932 782215

Commercial Manager: Roger Dobson Tel: 01753 544911

Nickname: Blues

Colours: All Blue

Capacity: 3,000   Seating: 294

Covered standing: 1,000   Clubhouse on ground: Yes

Record attendance: 4,500 v Kingstonian FA Cup 1934

Biggest win: 10-1 v Tilbury 1995

Biggest defeat: 1-11 v Wimbledon 1956

Record appearances, goalscorer in one season, and record goalscorer in total: Mario Russo

DIRECTIONS

From London: A3 then A309 to Scilly Isles roundabout, right into Hampton Court Way, left at 1st roundabout into Imber Court Road — ground faces in 300 yards. From M25 junction 10: A3 towards London for 1 mile, A307 through Cobham, left immediately after Sandown Park into Station Road — ground 1 mile on left. Half mile from either Thames Ditton or Esher BR stations.

Honours

Spartan League 1929, 1930, 1937, 1939, 1946, 1954, 1955, League Cup 1960

Middlesex Senior Cup 1928, Surrey Senior Cup 1933

Surrey Charity Shield 1939

Metropolitan League Cup 1969

Metropolitan Amateur Cup 1969 and 1970

Herts and Middlesex Combination 1940

Isthmian League, Carlsberg Trophy 1995

90 years after Sir Robert Peel founded the Met Police, their own football club was formed and played friendlies until joining the Spartan League in 1928. Apart from the war years they remained there until 1960. During that time the club were champions eight times and runners up once, also winning the League Cup. In 1960, eager to enhance their status, the club joined the Metropolitan League, winning that League Cup in 1969. Two years later they took a bold step forward when they were accepted into the Southern League, playing in Division One South. In 1977 they moved to the Isthmian League as founder members of the new Division Two and finished runners up, gaining promotion. 1985, however, saw them finish third from bottom and were back in Division Two South. Ironically, that season they fought their way to the First Round of the FA Cup, where they met Dartford, shown on Match of the Day. A crop of injuries ruined the season.

In 1987 the Mets surrendered the title to Chalfont St Peter, when they drew their last three games 0-0, where scoring one goal would have given them the title. However, they were promoted only to be in Division Two again when the league was re-structured. Cup success has largely eluded the club, winning the Surrey Senior Cup just once in 1933 and the Charity Shield in 1939. Before that when the club ground was at Hendon, they won the Middlesex Senior Cup.

The Mets home ground is in Imber Court, at East Molesey. It has been in existence since 1919 with the main clubhouse opened a year later. The football section has vastly improved over the years to the point where it is acknowledged as one of the best grounds in the league.

TILBURY

Chadfields, St Chads Rd, Tilbury, Essex RM18 8NL. Tel: 01375 843093

Secretary and Press officer:
Lloyd Brown, 52 Lionel Oxley House, New Road,
Grays, Essex RM17 6PP Tel 01375 377427

Colours: Black and White Stripes

Nickname: The Dockers

Capacity: 6,000

Seating 450

Covered standing: 1,500

Clubhouse on ground: Yes

Record attendance: 5,500 v Gorleston
FA Cup 4th Qual Rd Nov 19th 1949

Biggest win: 17-0 v No 9 Com Royal Artill. (h) South
Essex League Oct 4th 1902

Biggest defeat: 1-10 v Maidstone Utd (A) Corinthian
League Sept 4th 1962

Record appearances: Nicky Smith 452

Record goalscorer in total: Ross Livermore 305 in 282 games 1958-1966

DIRECTIONS

BR from Fenchurch Street to Tilbury Town then bus 377 or 20 mins walk - right out of station, walk along Left Hand Road fork to town centre traffic lights, left into St Chads Road, Chadfields 1 mile on left. By road: M25 (junction 30 or 31) - A13 Southend bound, Tilbury Docks turn off after 4 miles, Chadwell St Mary turns off (left) after another one and a half miles, left again after 400 metres, right at roundabout (signed Tilbury), right into St Chad's Road after half mile, 12st right into Chadfields for ground.

Honours

Isthmian League Div 1 1976 and Div 1 Cup 1975

Athenian League 1969 and Div 2 1964

London League 1959, 1960, 1961, 1962 and League Cup 1959, 1961, 1962

Delphian League 1968, Essex Senior Cup 1961, 1964, 1973, 1975

Essex Professional Cup 1976, Mithras Cup 1973, 1975, 1976, 1978, 1979

Essex Elizabethan Trophy 1964 and 1969

Essex Floodlit Cup 1969, Essex Junior Cup 1909 and 1925

South Essex League 1925, Stanford Charity Cup 1963 and 1993

Grays and District League many times , Neale Trophy 1966

Manager for 1996-97 Paul Armstrong

Assistant manager: Shaun McCann

Chairman: Robin Nash

Vice chairman: Tony Harvey

Tilbury Football Club was officially founded in January 1900, but didn't begin playing in league competition until entering the Grays and District League in 1901, winning the title in the first two years. From 1902 they followed the pattern of the day in local football, and played in two leagues, also competing in the South Essex League. They won the Junior Cup in 1909 but with Grays United having played in Southern League football nearby until 1906, the support for Tilbury was poor. In 1912 playing was suspended while the committee established a financial base and after the Great War, in 1919, they resumed in the larger South Essex League. Champions in 1925, they also won the Junior Cup again and were invited to play in the Senior Cup, gaining senior status two years later. During the summer of 1927 the club were rejected by several leagues until they finally agreed to join the Kent League, where they stayed for four years until moving to the London League. The Dockers helped found the wartime South Essex Combination but when their ground was taken over by anti-aircraft guns, they disbanded.

They resumed in the London League in 1946 and were immediately successful. Three times in four years they were runners up, having also reached the quarter final of the Amateur Cup in 1947. The best performance was saved for the FA Cup where they got to the First Round in 1949, when 29,000 saw them play Notts County at Meadow Lane.

In 1950 they joined the Corinthian League, but after seven unsuccessful years they returned in 1957, finishing third before taking the title four years on the trot. 1961 saw the Essex Senior Cup won for the first time, and 1962 saw them play just one season in the Delphian League before moving to Division Two of the Athenian League and winning the title. Five years later they were champions of the league and after another four years, they were elected to the Isthmian League, winning the League Cup and gaining promotion in three years. The proudest moment in the club's history came in 1977, when after starting in the extra preliminary round, they fought through to the Third Round Proper, where they played Stoke City at the Victoria Ground, in front of 16,000. Amid financial crisis, the club were relegated with debts of £60,000 two seasons later, which meant a new committee and a new fight to save the club, which happily survived. On the field the 80's were unhappy with two relegations finding them in Division Three. Since then they have climbed back to Division Two and have embarked on a series of improvements at St Chads Road with a view to the all important A grading.

Before the Great War, Tilbury played at the Green and Silley Weir Sports Ground, but between the Wars they played next door to their current ground, at the Orient Field, virtually rent free, but after it and the greyhound track next door were taken over in the War, the agreement ended when the club director who owned the field, stipulated that if they wanted to continue there, they would have to act as a nursery side to a League club. The greyhound track was badly derelict and after much work to clear the banks and build a stand, it reopened and has been the home of Tilbury FC ever since.

WARE

Wodson Park, Wadesmill Road, Ware, Herts SG12 0HZ. Tel: 01920 463247

Secretary: Cecil Hudson, 6 Portland Place, Hertford Heath, Herts SG13 7RR Tel: 01992 581862

Fix Secretary Ian Bush, 42 Burnett Square, Hertford, Herts SG14 2HD Tel: 01992 587334

Colours: Blue and white stripes

Nickname: Blues

Capacity: 3,300

Seating: 300

Covered standing: 500

Clubhouse on ground: Yes

Record attendance: 3,800 v Hendon FA Amateur Cup 1957

Biggest win: 10-1 v Wood Green Town

Biggest defeat: 0-11 v Barnet

Record appearances: Gary Riddle 654

Record goalscorer in one season: George Dearman 98 in 1926-27

Record goalscorer in total: Mo Hibbert 229

Honours

Herts Senior Cup 1899, 1904, 1907, 1922, 1954

Herts Charity Shield 1927, 1953, 1957, 1959, 1963, 1986

Spartan League 1953 Div 1 Sec B 1952 and Div 2 Sec A in 1927

Athenian League Div 2 Cup 1966, 1973

East Anglian Cup 1974

Herts County League 1909, 1922

East Herts League 1905, 1907 and League Cup in 1907

Perry Cup 1927, 1929, 1938, 1952, 1953, 1954, 1956

Dunkels Cup 1953

Rolleston Cup 1940 and 1952

Manager for 1996-97: John Godleman

Coach: Dermot Drummy

Chairman: Walter Luck

Ware FC are one of the oldest clubs in Hertfordshire, having been founded in 1892. For a spell they played in the Middlesex League, but after that their fixture list consisted of local sides in the Herts County League. Having been honoured to host the Herts Senior Cup Final in 1891, they reached the final themselves eight years later, beating Hitchin. They won it again in 1904 and in 1909 the first league honours came. Ware and St Albans won their respective East and West divisions with Ware winning the play-off match. The situation was reversed a year later. 1922 saw the Senior Cup and the Senior League both won, which was their last season before entering the Spartan League, which they were members of until 1955, although honours were few. In 1927 the clubs individual scoring record was set when George Dearman netted 98 times in winning the Division Two B crown.

1952 and 1953 saw the Division One and Premier Division titles in succession and a year later the Herts Senior Cup was won for the last time. When Cheshunt moved to the London League in 1955 a vacancy arose in the Delphian League and they remained there until 1963 when it merged with the Athenians. The 60's are best remembered for the club's epic FA Cup run, after a number of near misses, when they drew Luton Town in the First Round. With an hour gone the scores were level, but Luton eventually overpowered the Blues to win 6-1. They moved into the Isthmian League in 1975 following the disbanding of the Athenian Premier Division and have moved around as that league has changed over the years.

Buryfield was home to the club since 1926. The club's first ground was at Presdales, a field owned by a Mr Cox, who was invited to be President. The next ground was along Hoe Lane, at Highfields, now home of Hertford Rugby Club. They erected a pavilion but were soon forced to move to Canons Park, roughly where Canons Road is now. In 1902 Ware moved to London Road, to a ground now buried under an Industrial Estate, which remained home until 1921, when the Lower Park at Presdales became available after Canons Park was sold.

Three years later came another move to Pages Field, an unsatisfactory ground with no facilities which is now under Fanshawe Crescent and thence to Park Road in 1926, the ground used previously by Ware Engineers.

The owners of the ground gave notice to the club that they wished to convert the site into a car park and so work began on Wodson Park, which opened in 1995, thus consigning Buryfields to history after over 70 years.

WEMBLEY

Vale Farm, Watford Rd, Sudbury, Wembley HA0 4UR. Tel: 0181 908 8149

Secretary: Mrs Jean Gumm, 14 Woodfield Ave, North Wembley HA0 3NR Tel 0181 908 3353

Match Sec: Mrs Ann Lewin, 12 Perkin Close, Wembley, Middx HA0 3NR Tel 0181 904 4673

Nickname: The Lions   Capacity: 3,500

Colours: Red and White

Seating: 250   Covered standing: 1,000

Clubhouse on ground: Yes

Record attendance: 2,654 v Wealdstone
FA Amateur Cup 1952-53

Biggest win: 11-1 v Hermes London Senior Cup 1963

Biggest defeat: 1-16 v Chelsea London Challenge Cup 1959-60

Record appearances: Spud Murphy 505 1978-1988

Record goalscorer in aggregate: Bill Handrahan 110 1946-52

Record fee received £10,000 for Gary Roberts to Brentford

DIRECTIONS

Sudbury Town (tube) 400 yards, or 10 minutes walk from North Wembley (BR) station. Buses 18, 92, 245 & 182.

Honours

Middlesex Senior Cup 1984 and 1987, Middlesex League 1948 and League Cup 1947

Middlesex Charity Cup 1968 jt, 1981 jt, 1983, 1987, 1995, Middlesex Invitation Cup 1957

Spartan League Div 1 West: 1951 and Dunkel Trophy 1951 jt

Manager for 1996-97: Glen Charles, Assistant manager: Paul Shields and John Walsh

Chairman: Brian Gumm, Vice Chairman: Eric Stringer

Press Officer: Richard Markiewicz, 16 Meadow Way, Wembley, Middx Tel 0181 902 0541

Wembley FC was formed in 1946 following an amalgamation of two clubs, Sudbury Ratepayers Association and Sudbury Rangers. Nicknamed the Lions, they found a home at Vale Farm and have remained there ever since. They joined the Middlesex League and won the championship in 1948, before moving on to the Spartan League in 1950. They stayed for two years, clinching the Western Division in 1951 before becoming founder members of the Delphian League. In 1956 they finished runner up in the League and also reached the finals of the Middlesex and London Senior Cups and so were invited to join the Corinthian League, subsequently spending £1,000 on cover at the ground. Following a quiet period, the club moved to the Athenians in 1963, which had absorbed both the clubs previous two leagues, and were placed in the middle division where they won promotion in 1968

Floodlights were installed but seasons went by without success, and with the league declining they were unable to break into the Isthmian League, but after building new dressing rooms and finishing runners up in 1975, they were invited into the second division.

Success has come in Cups, the FA Cup 1st Round was reached in 1980 and the Middlesex Charity Cup was won in 1983, followed by the Senior Cup and then the Cup double a year after. They almost repeated the feat the following year, but the loss was tempered by the fact that the Charity Cup final was played at Wembley Stadium. Despite the club's decline on the field and the loss of the wooden grandstand to fire, Vale Farm has undergone much work in recent years, although on the field the club were relegated in May to Division Two.

WITHAM TOWN

Spa Road, Witham, Essex CM8 1UN. Tel: 01376 511198

Secretary: Reg Wright, 28 Mersey Rd, Witham, Essex CM8 1LJ Tel: 01376 512990

Other: Arthur Marshall, 335, Rickstones Rd, Rivenhall, Witham, Essex CM8 3HH Tel 01376 515816

Nickname: The Town

Colours: Red and Black Stripes   Capacity: 2,500

Seating: 150   Covered standing: 300

Clubhouse on ground: Yes

Record attendance: 800 v Billericay Town
Essex Senior League 1976

Biggest win: 7-0 v Banstead Ath 1995

Biggest defeat: 0-9 v Collier Row 1996

Record appearances: Keith Dent

Record goalscorer in one season: Steve Tilson

DIRECTIONS

From Witham BR (network S.E) station; through pub car park and follow road to Faulkbourne, at main roundabout turn left and ground is on the right. By road: Off A12 at Witham sign left at 1st lights (Spinks Lane), right at end of road follow road under railway bridge - ground 100 yds on left.

Honours

Essex Senior League 1971 and 1986, Essex Senior Trophy 1986

Manager for 1996-97: Spencer Pratten, Chairman: Arthur Marshall

Vice chairman: Reg Wright

Witham Town have club badges available this season, price £2.50 each

Although the current Witham team was only formed after the War in 1947, they were a reformation of previous Witham teams who had enjoyed success in junior football including winning the Braintree and District League twice. The club was twice disbanded, in 1914 and again in the early 30's, when interest waned, but not before they had enjoyed many successes in Braintree and District League and Essex Shield matches. In 1948 they re-formed and became founder members and champions of the Chelsford and Mid-Essex League Div 2. as well as winning the Tiptree Charity Cup and Tolleshunt D'Arcy Cup. The following season the club moved to Crittall's Ground in The Park, as founder members of the Mid-Essex League Premier Division and soon a thriving supporters club was formed. In 1958 they stepped up to Intermediate level and joined the Essex and Suffolk Border League and again were successful, winning the league and cup during the next few years.

Town moved to their present headquarters in 1975, three years after they had become founder members of the Essex Senior League, winning the championship at their first attempt. In 1986 they did it again, also taking the Senior Trophy, beating Heybridge Swifts in the final. The following season saw them embark on a FA Vase mission which finished in the Fifth Round with a home defeat by Falmouth Town, having beaten Great Yarmouth, Bury Town, Harefield United and Yeading on route.

This was enough to gain Witham election to the Isthmian League and they finished the first season in 7th place. However, within two years they had finished one off the bottom, with relegated Letchworth the only team below them. With a sixth place behind Stevenage Borough in 1991, they were high enough to survive the regionalisation changes.

On reformation, Witham moved to play in the Park, home of Crittall Athletic, where they stayed until a six year search for land finally brought them to Spa Road, which took a further five years to make ready.

WIVENHOE TOWN

Broad Lane Ground, Elmstead Rd, Wivenhoe, Essex CO7 7HA. Tel: 01206 825380

Secretary: Mike Boyle, 15 Daniell Drive, Colchester, Essex CO2 9EZ Tel: 01206 573223

Colours: All Blue   Nickname: The Dragons

Capacity: 2,876   Seating: 226

Covered standing: 1,300   Clubhouse on ground: Yes

DIRECTIONS

Coming out of Colchester towards Clacton take first turning (right) towards Wivenhoe, first left and ground clearly visible on right at crossroads. 1 mile from Wivenhoe (BR).

Record attendance: 1,912 v Runcorn FA Trop 1st Rd 1990

Biggest win: 18-0 v Nayland

Biggest defeat: 0-8 v Carshalton Ath Isthmian Lge 1993

Record appearances: Keith Bain 536

Record goalscorer in total: Paul Harrison 258 in 350 appearances

Record fee received: £ 5,875 for Bobby Mayes to Redbridge Forest

Honours

Isthmian League Div 1 1990 and Div 2 North 1988

Harry Fisher Trophy 1984 and 1986

Essex and Suffolk Border League 1979, Div 1 in 1973 and Div 2 in 1972

Colchester and East Essex League 1953 and 1956

Div 1 1960 and 1970, League Cup 1952, 1953, 1955, 1956, Challenge Cup 1953

Brightlingsea Lge Div 1 1936, 1937, 1948, League Cup 1937, 1938,1948, Challenge Cup 1937

Essex Senior Trophy 1988, Amos Charity Cup 1937, 1938, 1952, 1953, 1954, 1955, 1956

Stokes Cup 1949, 1953, 1954, Wivenhoe Charity Cup 1953, 1969, 1974

Crystal Mono Cup 1969, 1979, 1980, 1981, 1982, Sidney James Memorial Trophy 1970

Tolleshunt D'Arcy Mem Cup 1972, 1973, 1974, Walton Charity Cup 1974 and 1979

Coggeshall Brotherhood Cup 1981, Worthington Evans Cup 1981, Woodbridge Challenge Cup 1992

Manager for 1996-97: Steve Dowman, Assistant Manager: Sean Bailey, Chairman: Dave Whymark

The club was originally formed as Wivenhoe Rangers in 1925 by students from Colchester Grammar School but did not enter a league until 1927 when they became members of the Brightlingsea and District League.

Their first championship came in 1936 and the following season they scored 280 goals in 38 matches, winning four trophies. The early fifties were also successful in the Colchester and East Essex Premier Division, with a host of trophies, but the club went into a decline in the late 50's, suffering relegation and slipping into Division Two during the 60's. The turning point came in 1969 with promotion and the following season they won Division One and were back at the top. By then, after playing on various fields, they were at the Essex University and in 1971 they stepped up to the Border League, and two successive championships saw them at the top of that league. The club name was changed to Wivenhoe Town and in 1977 the club purchased a carrot field for £2, 500 and with the aid of grants began building the ground. They gained senior status and joined the Essex Senior League.The first few years were spent at or near the top, with two runners ups and more Cups and after a FA Vase run to the 5th Round and another runners up spot they moved up to the Isthmian League Division Two North after more improvements to the ground. Later they took the Essex Senior Trophy and the league Div 2 North, and reached the Premier Division, but in 1994 after a struggle and a financial crisis, they went down, only to find the owner of the ground wishing to sell, and threatening to evict the club. Not surprisingly with finances concentrated on buying the ground, the playing side suffered and they find them

STAINES TOWN F.C.

CARLSBERG CUP WINNERS 1994/95

The ICIS Football League
Division One - Season 1995-96

Official Matchday Magazine

WOKINGHAM TOWN F.C.

SPONSORED BY
HIGGS & HILL

V OXFORD CITY
ICIS LEAGUE DIVISION 1
Tuesday 30th April 1996
Kick-Off 7-45pm

SEASON 1995-96 OFFICIAL PROGRAMME £1.00

St.Albans CITY

TELE CENTIAL

St. Albans City v Coventry City
Friendly Match, Tuesday 30 July 1996, Kick off 7.30pm
Match Sponsor The Herts Advertiser, Matchball Sponsor Canada Life
Official Programme £1.30

Dagenham & Redbridge FC

Sponsored by
The Barking & Dagenham Post

VAUXHALL CONFERENCE

KIDDERMINSTER HARRIERS
Vauxhall Conference
Saturday 28th October 1995 KO 3pm
Official Programme £1.30
Match Sponsors
TROJAN SERVICES (ESSEX) LTD

AVELEY

Mill Field, Mill Road, Aveley, Essex RM15 4TR Tel 01708 865940

Secretary: Ken Sutliff, 9 Westlyn Close, Rainham, Essex RM13 9JP Tel 01708 555271

Nickname: The Millers,

Colours: Royal Blue & White

Capacity: 5,000,   Seating: 400

Covered standing: Yes

Clubhouse on ground: Yes

Record attendance: 3,741 v Slough Town
FA Amateur Cup Feb 1971

Biggest win: 11-1 v Histon Aug 24th 1963

Biggest defeat: 0-8 v Leyton Orient
Thameside Trophy April 1995

Record appearances: Ken Riley 422 in Junior football and Paul Franklin 313 in Senior football

Record goalscorer in aggregate: Jotty Wilks 214

DIRECTIONS

London — Southend A13, turn into Sandy Lane at Aveley. Rainham or Purfleet BR stations then bus No. 723 to the ground.

Honours

Isthmian League Cup 1990

London League 1952 and 1955 and League Cup 1954, Delphian League Cup 1962

Athenian League 1971, Essex Junior Cup 1948 and 1949

Essex Thameside Trophy 1980, Hornchurch Charity Cup 1982

East Anglian Cup 1989

Aveley Football Club was formed in 1927 and played with success in several local leagues until 1939, when activities were suspended for the war years. In 1946 they re-formed and played in the Thurrock Combination, winning the Essex Junior Cup in 1948 and 1949. This prompted the Essex FA to grant senior status for 1949-50 and they were elEcted to the London League Division Two. 12 months later they were promoted to Division One after becoming champions. The following season saw the club purchase the present Mill Field ground, and were immediately nicknamed the Millers. They enjoyed further success in the London League, winning the League Cup in 1953, the league title in 1955 and finishing runners up in 1957.

From there they moved to the Delphian League, again finishing runners up and winning the League Cup in 1952. At the end of the next campaign, the league was absorbed into the expanded Athenian League and Aveley joined Division Two. 1964 saw full FA membership granted, but the next milestone was not until 1969 when they finished runners up and thus were promoted. 1970-71 was equally successful with the Millers reaching the 1st Round of the FA Cup and the quarter-final of the Amateur Cup, as well as winning the Division One title and promotion to the Premier Division.

Aveley were elected to the Isthmian League in 1973 and stayed without success until relegated to Division Two North in 1986. Happily they were again promoted in 1990 following a runners up spot.

After a fourth spot in 1991 Aveley suffered the worst two seasons in their history, where in successive seasons they finished bottom of their division. Financial restraints and the loss of players and managers took its toll and the club have yet to fully recover from it and are now in Division Three.

BRAINTREE TOWN

Cressing Road Stadium, Clockhouse Way, Braintree, Essex .Tel: 01376 345617

Secretary: Tom Woodley, 19a Bailey Bridge Rd, Braintree, Essex CM7 5TT Tel 01376 326234

Club shop: Jon Weaver 28 Drake Gardens, Braintree, Essex Tel: 01376 347920

Press officer: Ron Webb, Connaught Gardens,

Braintree, Essex Tel: 01376 325338

Nickname: The Iron

Capacity: 4,000

Seating: 292

Covered standing: 1,000

Clubhouse on ground: Yes

> ## DIRECTIONS
> **From all routes use Braintree by-pass and turn into Braintree at the McDonalds r'bout following signs for East Braintree Industrial Estates - floodlights visible on left half mile into town behind 'The Sportsman' snooker entrance is next left in Clockhouse Way, then left again. 1 mile from Braintree & Bocking (BR). Bus 353 from Witham or town centre stops at 'The Sportsman' Town centre is twenty minutes walk.**

Record attendance: 6,000 v Saffron Walden v Rainham Essex Junior Cup Final 1926

4,000 for Braintree match v Tottenham
Charity Match in 1952

Biggest win: 15-3 v Hopes(Birmingham) Friendly Jan 28th 1939

12-0 v Thetford Town ECL 1935-36

Biggest defeat: 0-14 v Chelmsford City A North Essex League Feb 10th 1923

Record appearances: Paul Young 524 1966-77

Record goalscorer in one season Cecil Purkiss 55 in 1927-28

Record goalscorer in total Chris Guy 211 1983-90

Record fee paid £3,000 for Matt Metcalfe to Sudbury Town 1995

Record fee received £10,000 for Matt Metcalfe to Brentford and John Cheesewright to Colchester Utd

Honours

North Essex League 1906, 1911, 1912; Essex Senior Cup 1996; Eastern Counties League 1937, 1984, 1985 and League Cup 1988; London League Cup 1948 jt, 1949, 1952 , Metropolitan League Cup 1970; East Anglian Cup 1947, 1969 and 1996, Essex Senior Trophy 1987; Essex and Suffolk Border League 1936, 1937, 1938, 1960, 1985; Division 2A West 1923 and 1924, League Cup 1960; North Essex League 1906, 1911, 1912, RAFA Cup 1957; Greater London Benevolent Cup 1966, Worthington Evans Cup 1963 jt, 1972, 1976; Eastern Floodlit Cup 1986, Anglian Floodlit League 1970; Braintree and Witham Times Charity Cup 1985; Maldon Town International Tournament 1971, Braintree Trades Cup 1905 and 1906; Braintree Hospital Cup 1928, Halstead Hospital Cup 1927 and 1928; Chelmsford Hospital Cup 1927, Sudbury Charity Cup 1984; Tolleshunt D'arcy Cup 1992, 1993, 1995, 1996.

Manager for 1996-97: Keith Martin

Assistant Manager: Tony Hall

Chairman: George Rosling

Vice Chairman: Ivan Kibble

"Our Flag's Been To Wembley" fanzine available £1 from Jon Weaver, see above.

A Centenary history and an 80 page illustrated book on the history of Cressing Road ground will soon be available. Club shop sells Groundtastic magazine.

Founded in 1898 as Manor Works FC, the club has always been to the forefront of football in Braintree. Soon to celebrate their centenary, The Iron got the nickname through being associated with Crittalls metal window company for over 80 years. As the business extended so did the football club which changed its name to Crittall Athletic in 1921 before opening the present Cressing Road ground in 1923 and gaining senior status.

Moving on from local North Essex and Essex and Suffolk Border Leagues, Iron joined the Spartan League in 1928. The companies policy of employing men from Wales and the North benefited the football Club in the depression days, providing them with jobs and housing and as a result the club rose to a high amateur level.

Crowds of 2,000 were common at Cressing Road and with great enthusiasm the club stepped up to the Eastern Counties League in 1935. During this time the Iron took 1,000 supporters in a special train to see them beat Ipswich Town in the Amateur Cup and some 15,000 saw them play an Amateur Cup match at Champion Hill against Dulwich Hamlet. Apart from a single post war season in the Essex County League, the club switched between London League and Eastern Counties and as interest faded, down to the Border League. Gates went to virtually nil as the team soldiered on with young local players, but a revival was attempted by joining the Greater London and then Metropolitan Leagues, and despite floodlighting and attractive opposition, it was still a struggle. A return to the Eastern Counties in 1970 did not work, and by then the company interest and subsidy had gone and to try to attract finance the Town name had been added to the club title, to make Braintree and Crittall Athletic in 1968. Following a take over, the ground was sold to the council, but the club were allowed to stay, although by then the facilities were well below those of a senior club. All links with the company finally ended in the 1981 and the present title was adopted.

From then the club took off, with a new clubhouse and vastly improved facilities, better players returned and with two Eastern Counties League championships plus several cups, they went from strength to strength both on and off the field. In 1991 they joined the Southern League and although the ground has now been thoroughly modernised, at the end of the 1995-96 season, the club resigned from the Southern League due to the continued travelling problems and applied for membership across the pyramid, in the Isthmian League. Although turned down, the FA saw sense and sanctioned the move, so that The Iron play in Division Three of the Isthmian League in 1996.

Before moving to Cressing Road, the club played firstly on Fair Field, just behind the Town Hall and Library until 1903, when they moved to Spaldings Meadow in Panfield Lane, which had a wooden stand which was erected every year for the Agricultural Show. Cressing Road was opened on August 25th 1923 in front of 6,000 people who attended the Annual Sports Day.

CAMBERLEY TOWN

Krooner Park, Krooner Rd, off Frimley Rd, Camberley, Surrey GU15 2QP.Tel: 01276 63592

Secretary: David Slater, 33 Blythwood Ave, Frimley , Camberley, Surrey Tel: 01276 23096

Colours: Red and White

Nickname: Town, Reds or Krooners

Capacity: 3,000

Seating: 200

Covered standing: 200

Clubhouse on ground: Yes

DIRECTIONS

M3 junction 4, follow signs to Frimley, follow B3411 towards Camberley, ground on left opposite 'The Standard'

Record attendance 2,066 v Aldershot Town Isthmian Lge 1992 (3,500 Crystal Pal, Friendly 1974)

Biggest win: 15-0 v Royal Engineers Friendly 1919

Biggest defeat: 0-11 v Abingdon Tn Isthmian Lg 1990

Record appearances: Brian Ives

Honours

Surrey Senior League1931, 1932, 1933, League Charity Cup 1938 and 1952

Surrey Senior Cup 1979

West Surrey League 1914, Ascot and District League 1904,

Surrey Junior Cup 1898, 1910

Aldershot Senior League 1913

Southern Combination Cup 1981

Camberley and Yorktown FC were formed in 1896 and joined the Ascot and District League, winning the Surrey Junior Cup in 1898 and the League in 1904. They won the cup again in 1910 and then moved to the East and West Surrey League, where they were champions in 1914, before becoming founder members of the Surrey Senior League in 1922.

They won that three years running from 1931 and in 1936 reached their first ever Senior Cup final, losing to Wimbledon. Cup success came in 1938 with the Senior League Charity Cup.

After the War the club shortened its name to Camberley FC when they merged with Camberley Wanderers and were second behind Leatherhead in 1948 and in 1963 were runners up to Chertsey, before joining the Spartan League in 1973. By then they had become Camberley Town and after two years they joined the Athenian League, timing it right, as it was shortly weakened by an exodus to the expanding Isthmians, of which Town were one. It was a fine spell for the club who were promoted and got to the Senior Cup final, beating Leatherhead and taking it for the only time.

It was their last success for some while as successive relegations saw them drop back into the Athenian League, but luck was on their side and the league was swallowed up by the Isthmians and the Krooners were back in again.

Since then the club has had modest success, reaching the last eight of the FA Vase in 1986, but a fire which destroyed the main stand in 1990 rocked the club, but to their credit they rebuilt and although still in Division Three, have hopes of moving up again.

CLAPTON

The Old Spotted Dog, Upton Lane, Forest Gate, London E7 9NP. Tel: 0181 472 0822

Secretary and press: Steven Walters, 10 Buttfield Close, Dagenham, Essex RM10 8TJ Tel 0181 596 0424

Other matters: Iain Holloway, 22 Gean Ct, Langthorne Rd, Leytonstone, E11 4HT Tel 0181 555 6639

Nickname: The Tons

DIRECTIONS
BR to Forest Gate, tube to Plaistow (District Line), or bus 278 passes ground. Officials entrance in Upton Lane, spectator's in Disraeli Rd.

Capacity: 2, 000   Seating: 100

Covered standing: 150   Clubhouse on ground Yes

Record attendance: 12,000 v Tottenham Hotspur FA Cup 1898-99

Biggest defeat: 0-14 v Nottingham Forest FA Cup 1890

Record appearance holder: Dave Fahy

Honours

FA AMATEUR CUP WINNERS 1907, 1909, 1915, 1924, 1925

Isthmian League.1911 and 1923

Essex Thameside Trophy, London Senior Cup, London Charity Cup, Essex Senior Cup

Middlesex Senior Cup, Essex Senior Trophy, London Challenge Cup, AFA Invitation Snr Cup

Manager for 1996-97: Lyndon Lynch, Ass Manager: John Simmonds, Chairman: Ken Harris

Clapton Football Club is steeped in history, having been founded back in 1877 as Downs FC, changing their name after one season and playing mainly friendly games. They moved to the Old Spotted Dog ground in 1888 and took just one year before winning the London Senior Cup, beating Casuals 4-2. In 1890 Clapton became the first touring English club to play abroad when they beat a Belgian X1 in Antwerp, 8-1.

Clapton helped set up the Southern League in 1892 and were one of the original entrants for the Amateur Cup a year later. From 1899 to 1905 they appeared in every final of the prestigious London Charity Cup and during that last year they were founder members of the Isthmian League, along with Casuals, Ilford, Civil Service, Ealing Association and London Caledonians. When Ilford resigned in 1979 it left Clapton as the sole survivors.

Prior to that, Clapton played in the first of six appearances in the Amateur Cup final, losing to West Hartlepool at Shepherds Bush, but the next five were all wins against Stockton in 1907, Eston United in 1909, Bishop Auckland in 1915, Erith and Belvedere in 1924 and Southall a year later. They also won the Isthmian League twice and finished second on four occasions after the Great War.

By the mid-Thirties success was harder to come by and support dwindled after the Second War with amateurism slowly dying on its feet. They slipped down the expanding Isthmian League during the 70's and 80's, but they bounced back in 1983 winning Division Two and taking the Essex Senior Cup a year later.

FORMER GROUNDS.. Clapton have been at the Old Spotted Dog since 1888, before which they played on an enclosed ground at Elm Farm. Originally the current ground was used by St Barts Hospital, but a successful negotiation with the owner saw them move in. At that time it was rural with an entrance in Upton Lane to the ground which was shared with cricket up to the Great War.

EAST THURROCK UNITED

Rookery Hill, Corringham, Essex. Tel: (club) 01375 644166 (boardroom) 641009

Secretary: Malcolm Harris 14 Colne Valley, Upminster, Essex RM14 1QA Tel 017082 28818

Colours: Amber and Black

Nickname: The Rocks

Capacity: 2,500   Seating: 160

Covered standing: 200, Clubhouse on ground: Yes

Record attendance: 947 v Trevor Brooking X1 May 1987

Biggest win: 7-0 v Coggeshall 1984

Biggest defeat: 0-9 v Eton Manor 1981

Record appearances: Glen Case 600+

Record goalscorer in one season: Graham Stewart 32

Record goalscorer in total: Graham Stewart 102

Record fee received: £2,000 for Greg Berry

DIRECTIONS

A13 London-Southend, take 1014 at Stanford-le-Hope for two and a half miles - ground on the left. Two miles from Stanford-le-Hope and Basildon BR stations.

Honours

Metropolitan League Div 2 1973

Essex Senior League Cup 1989 and 1992

Harry Fisher Memorial Trophy 1984 and 1991

Manager for 1996-97: Tommy Lee, Assistant Manager: Ian Bodley

Chairman: Brian Grover, Vice Chairman: Harry Caine

The club was founded in 1969 by a group of enthusiasts who felt that the expanding area around Stanford-le-Hope and Corringham should have a senior football club. The club were formed as part of the successful Corringham Sunday side, but the first hurdle was finding a suitable ground. It proved a formidable task and the first season was played in the Southern Essex Combination at Corringham Rec. After one season they moved up to Intermediate status in the Greater London League, and played at the Billet ground, enjoying a fine spell. They won Division Two, and then Division One, at once applying for senior status.

For a while the club played at Grays Athletic and a further move into the Senior Division Two of the Metropolitan League and they carried off their third championship in a row, but dissolutioned with the lack of home a ground, many important figures were lost to the club and they began to struggle badly, as first the Billet and then Tilbury FC were used was home grounds. In 1979 the club joined the Essex Senior League and moved to the Thames Board Mills Ground in Purfleet, but just as the club reached its lowest ebb, a site in Corringham became available. With loans an eight acre site was bought and the current ground began to take shape.

On 25th August 1984 the first game took place, as Coggeshall were beaten 7-0.

In 1989 the Rocks reached the 5th Round of the Vase and two years later they took the League Cup but lost the Senior Trophy to Ford United in the final.

They were promoted to the Isthmian League in 1992, and are slowly acclimatising as well as keeping pace with the ground requirements needed to stay afloat.

EPSOM & EWELL

Banstead Ath FC, Merland Rise, Tadworth, Surrey KT20 5JG. Tel: 01372 729817

Secretary:David Wilson, 33 Delaporte Close, Epsom,
Surrey KT17 4AF Tel 01372 729817

Nickname: E's

Colours: All yellow

All ground details as per Banstead Athletic FC

Clubhouse on ground: Yes

Record attendance: 5,000 v Kingstonian
FA Cup 2nd Qual Rd Oct 15th 1949

Record goalscorer in total: Tommy Tuite

DIRECTIONS
Follow signs to Tattenham Corner (Epsom racecourse), then to Banstead Sports Centre. The ground is adjacent to the swimming pool. Half a mile from Tattenham Corner (BR). Bus 420 from Sutton stops outside ground. Also buses 406 & 727 from Epsom.

Honours

FA VASE runner up 1975

London League 1928

Corinthian League Mem Shield 1960

Isthmian League Div 2 1978

Surrey Senior League 1926, 1927, 1975

Charity Cup 1927

Surrey Senior Cup 1981, Surrey Senior Shield 1933, 1955, Surrey Intermediate Cup 1930, Surrey Intermediate Charity Cup 1958, Southern Combination Cup 1980

The club was formed as Epsom FC back in 1917 and gained Senior status playing in the South Suburban League with some success early on. It prompted a move to the Surrey Senior League which they won twice between the Wars. They then joined the strong London League which they won in 1928 being runners-up on five other occasions. Epsom reached the First Round of the FA Cup in 1933 where they lost to Clapton Orient, having beaten three Isthmian League sides along the way. On the outbreak of War, the club temporarily disbanded, letting their ground to Epsom Town FC, but in 1945 they reclaimed West Street and played again in the London League.

In 1949, they moved up to the Corinthian League, which proved a stronger league for they never finished higher than third, although there was some success in Cups. 1960 saw the amalgamation of Epsom with Ewell and Stoneleigh FC, to become the club as it is today, and as Epsom and Ewell they joined the Athenian League in 1963. It was a barren time for the new club and after a number of bleak seasons they dropped back into the Surrey Senior League. It was the start of a remarkable upturn in fortunes which saw two League Cup wins and a runners up spot preceded by the championship itself in 1975. Again the Athenian League accepted them but more importantly the second year saw Epsom and Ewell create history by appearing in the very first FA Vase Final at Wembley, losing 2-1 to Hoddesdon Town. Success continued in 1977, with new lights installed, the club joined the Isthmian League Division Two. In 1981 they won the Surrey Senior Cup for the only time, and having reached the Premier Division they then hit another barren spell which currently sees them in Division Three.

Horton Lane in Epsom was home to the club before they moved to West Street in 1926. The ground had a large grandstand from early on and remained home until it was sold to Wimpey Homes and is now covered by housing. Epsom and Ewell moved in with Banstead Athletic whilst negotiating for a new ground in the town.

FLACKWELL HEATH

Wilks Park, Heath End Rd, Flackwell Heath, High Wycombe, Bucks. Tel: 01628 523892

Secretary: Mrs C Hobbs, 23 Southfield Rd, Flackwell Heath, Bucks HP10 9BT 01628 521051

Press Officer: Donna Marie Burton, 'The Crown', Sydenham, nr Chinnor, Oxon Tel 01844 351634

Colours: Red and White

Nickname: Heathens

Capacity: 2,000   Seating: 150

Covered standing: 150   Clubhouse on ground : Yes

Record attendance: 4,500 v Oxford Utd Charity match 1986 700 v Aldershot Isthmian Lge 1992)

Biggest win: 6-0 v Clapton and v Petersfield

Biggest defeat: 0-10 v Hendon FA Cup 1995

Record appearances: Tony Wood

Record goalscorer in one season: Ray Edwards

Record goalscorer in total: Tony Wood

Record fee paid: £500

DIRECTIONS

M40 junction 4, follow A404 towards High Wycombe, 1st turning into Daws Hill Lane, continue for 2 miles until you see signs for the club, left into Magpie Lane, ground at rear of Magpie (PH). Bus 301 either from bus station or High Street near bottom of Crendon Street which comes from BR station. Ask for Oakland Way.

Honours

Great Western Combination 1958 and 1963

Wycombe League Premier Div 6 times, Division One 8 times

Berks and Bucks Intermediate Cup 1976

Reading Senior Cup 1976, Wycombe Senior Cup 1976

Manager 1996-97: Terry Glynn, Assistant Manager: Geoff Turner

Chairman: Terry Glynn

Flackwell Heath Football Club was formed in 1907 and initially competed in the local Wycombe League with much success. They were Division One champions eight times and Premier Division champions 6 times.

Their success stretched to eleven victories in the Wycombe Senior Cup and in 1950 the club joined the Great Western Combination, where they were champions twice before the league folded in 1956. They reverted to the Wycombe League until in 1977 after winning the Berks and Bucks Intermediate Cup, Reading Cup, Wycombe Cup and Wycombe League all in the same season. They were accepted by the Hellenic League and won promotion to the Premier Division where they remained until moving to the Athenian League in 1982. Two years later the league folded and the majority of the clubs moved to the expanding Isthmian League Division Two North, which became Division Three.

Season 1992-93 saw the Heathens best run in the Berks and Bucks Senior Cup when having defeated Wycombe Wanderers, Buckingham Town and Aylesbury United they eventually lost the semi-final to Chesham United.

794

HARLOW TOWN

Harlow Sports Centre, Hammerskjold Rd, Harlow CM20 2JF. Tel: 01279 445319

Secretary: Mr Ron Bruce, 12 Priory Ct, Harlow, Essex Tel: 01279 300585

Press and Prog Editor Phil Tuson, 84 Orchard Croft, Harlow, Essex Tel 01279 416743

DIRECTIONS
Near town centre, 10 minutes walk from Harlow (BR) station.

Nickname: Hawks

Colours: Blue and Black stripes   Capacity: 10,000

Covered standing: 500 - 400 being erected Seating: 300

Clubhouse on ground: Yes

Record Attendance: 9,723 v Leicester City
FA Cup 1980

Biggest win: 12-0 v Hertford Ath East Herts League 1929

Biggest defeat: 0-11 v Ware Spartan League 1948

Record appearances: Norman Gladwin 646 1949-70

Record goalscorer in one season: Jeff Wood 45 in 1988-89

Honours

Isthmian League Div 1 1979 and Div 2 North 1989; Athenian League Div 1 1972; East Anglian Cup 1990; Essex Senior Cup 1979; London League Challenge Cup 1960; Spartan League Cup 1953; Epping Hospital Cup 1947, 1948, 1949; Fred Budden Trophy 1989 and 1990.

Manager for 1996-97: David Greene   **Assistant manager: Steve Carey**

Chairman: Mr J Taylor   **Vice Chairman: Mr R Young**

Harlow Town Football Club were formed way back in 1879, playing their first match against Saffron Walden. In the early years they played mainly in Stansted and District, and East Herts Leagues, finally moving to senior football in 1932, when it joined the Spartan League Div 2 East. After five years the club was granted status and played in the FA Cup and Essex Senior Cup for the first time. At the time Harlow had the smallest population of all the Senior Cup clubs, a far cry from today's 80,000+.

They re-formed after the war and re-joined the Spartan League the following season, winning the Div 1 Cup in 1953. A year later they switched leagues to the more demanding London League, where they played six seasons, winning the League Cup in 1960. In August of that year the club moved away from the old town to a new stadium at the Harlow Sports Centre, having played at the Green Man Field since 1922 and a ground called The Marigolds before that. The new facilities brought a further switch in leagues, this time to the Delphians, but after two years there was a three division Athenian League. Harlow won promotion first time, but several seasons of mediocrity were spent before the Division One title was lifted, the club's first ever, and after one year in the top flight, they were invited in by the Isthmian League. Things took off in 1978-79 under Ian Wolstenholme. Division One was taken by 14 points and the Essex Senior Cup was also won. The next year was dominated by an incredible FA Cup run which saw the club go from the Preliminary Round to the 4th Round proper, beating the likes of Southend Utd and Leicester City before losing 4-3 at Watford on Match of the Day. Cup form was good in the next years, but poor league form saw relegation come in 1982, but promotion back to the Premier at the first attempt was achieved, only for financial problems to cause the club to plummet through two divisions. The Div 2 North title was won in 1989 and the East Anglian Cup a year later, and they even got to the 1st Round of the cup again, but again, financial problems had seen the collapse of a new ground scheme and in 1992 the club were suspended by the league, the Sportscentre having been closed. The Isthmian's gave the club a year to sort itself out, which it has, albeit in Division Three, but a fifth place last season bodes well for the future.

HERTFORD TOWN

Hertingfordbury Park, West Street, Hertford. Tel: 01992 583716

Secretary: Stephen Hedley, 28 Cherry Tree Green,
Hertford SG14 2HP Tel: 01992 587011

Colours: All Royal Blue

Nickname: The Blues

Capacity: 6,500

Seating: 200

Covered standing: 1,000

Clubhouse on ground: Yes

Record attendance: 5,000 v Kingstonian
FA Amateur Cup Rd 2 1956

Record appearances: Rob Burns

DIRECTIONS

**Rail to Hertford Nth (from Moorgate)
or Hertford east (Liverpool Street);
both 15 minutes walk. Green Line
bus to town centre then 10 minutes
walk. By road; off bypass heading
east, turn off at Ford garage.**

Honours

Herts Charity Cup 1973

Herts Senior Cup 1967

Hertford Charity Shield 1920, 1921, 1936, 1950, 1956, 1960

Eastern Counties League Cup 1973

East Anglian Cup 1963 and 1970

Hertford Town began life as Port Vale Rovers and won the Herts Junior Cup in 1901. They were permitted to change their name to Hertford FC soon after, and in 1908 merged with Blue Cross, becoming Hertford Town, playing on the current ground at Hertingfordbury Park. They won the East Herts League and joined forces with Horns FC to play in the Herts Senior League. After the Great War they began playing in the Spartan League, from where they reached the Herts Senior Cup final in 1934, losing to Hitchin Town. Just prior to the Second War they were promoted to the Premier Division, but were denied the chance, and when football began again they were not so strong and finished bottom. As the ground was not available the club did not play for a year but in 1949 they returned to the Spartan League and won Division One East in 1950.

After two runners up places they enjoyed their best ever spell in the Delphian League, winning the title twice and finishing second in the other two seasons. Two County Cup finals and an East Anglian final were achieved before the Delphians merged with the Athenians, and Hertford gained promotion in the first season. In 1972 the club moved over to the Eastern Counties League for one year before joining the new Isthmian Second Division, and after narrowly missing promotion they found themselves in Division Two North.

The last few seasons have been a struggle not helped by a fire which destroyed the club house, but it has been replaced and although finishing low down last May, Town still have hopes to climb the league.

HORNCHURCH

The Stadium, Bridge Ave, Upminster, Essex RM14 2LX.Tel: 01402 220080

Secretary: Edward Harris, 13 Claremont Gardens, Upminster, Essex RM14 1DW Tel 01708 227891

Nickname: The Urchins

Colours: Red and White

Capacity: 3,500

Seating: 300

Covered standing: 350

Clubhouse on ground: Yes

Record attendance: 3,000 v Chelmsford City FA Cup 1966

DIRECTIONS

Ten minutes walk from Upminster Station. Or, take tube to Upminster Bridge, turn right outside station, second right into Bridge Avenue and ground is 200 yards on the right. By car, Bridge Avenue is off A124 between Hornchurch and Upminster.

Honours

Athenian League 1967

Romford League

Essex Thameside Trophy 1985

Hornchurch Football Club were formed in 1923 as Upminster Wanderers FC and played on the local Recreation Ground. They were elected to the Romford League two years later, winning the Second Division in the first season. They then joined the Spartan League shortly before the Second World War, playing in Division Two East, before joining Division One East after the war. In 1952 they were promoted to the Premier Division and a year later were elected to the Delphian League.

Soon after the move they became Hornchurch and Upminster, and it was around then that the move to the present ground at Upminster Bridge was made. In 1959 the Urchins once again changed leagues, moving to the Athenians, dropping Upminster from the name, becoming Hornchurch FC.

In 1967 the club won the Division One championship and had its best ever FA Cup run, reaching the 4th qualifying round, but a year later they were back in Division One, returning again in 1971. The first FA Vase competition saw the Urchins reach the 5th Rd before losing to finalists Epsom and Ewell, but a year later they were elected to the Isthmian League, experiencing relegation and promotion inside 4 years.

The Essex Thamesside Trophy was won in 1985, beating Grays Athletic, but a year later they were relegated again and when the league re-organised they were placed in Division Three where they remain.

KINGSBURY TOWN

Silver Jubilee Park, Townsend Lane, Kingsbury, London NW9 0DE. Tel: 0181 205 1645 (club)

Secretary: Dave Thomas, 9 Hillview Gardens,
Kingsbury, London NW9 0TE Tel 0181 205 2047

Nickname: Kings

Colours: Royal Blue and White

Capacity: 4,000

Seating: 150

Covered standing: 200

Clubhouse on ground: Yes

Record attendance: 1,300 v Wealdstone
FA Amateur Cup 1971

Biggest win: 8-0 v Eastbourne Utd
Isthmian League 1991-92

Record appearances: Mick Coffey

Honours

Parthenon League 1952

League Charity Cup 1953 and 1954

Middlesex Senior Charity Cup 1954

Middlesex Charity Cup 1986

Middlesex League Charity Cup 1945, 1946, 1947

Willesden and District League Div 2 1935

DIRECTIONS
Underground to Kingsbury, cross road and take bus 183 to Townsend Lane (2 miles) — ground in far left-hand corner of Silver Jubilee Park.

Kingsbury Town were originally founded in 1919, becoming Davis Sports in 1927 and Kingsbury 584 FC before the current title was taken on. In the first season it finished runners up in the Willesden and District League, and further success came in 1935 with the Division Two title. Five years later they were promoted to the Senior Division.

In 1943 they were elected to the Middlesex Senior League where they won the Charity Cup three years running. Membership of the Parthenon League followed with the league and League Cup both won. In that year Kingsbury moved to Silver Jubilee Park. In 1959 they joined the Spartan League and stayed until 1976 when it and the Metropolitan League merged to form the London Spartan League. After one year in the new league they left to join the Athenians, but it was a poor move and in 1978 they were back with the Spartans. Three seasons later, Kingsbury tried again in the Athenians. With the expansion of the Isthmians, Kingsbury took their chance in Divison Two North, gaining promotion and winning the Middlesex Charity Cup, in 1986. Another couple of final appearances came in the late 80's, but after two relegations they find themselves in Division Three in 1996.

LEWES

The Dripping Pan, Mountfield Rd, Lewes BN7 1XN. Tel: 01273 472822

Secretary: John Lewis, Marshlands, Kingston Rd, Lewes, BN7 3NB. Tel: 01273 472822

Nickname: The Rooks

Capacity: 2,600

Seating: 400   Covered standing: No

Clubhouse on ground: Yes

Record attendance: 2,500 v Newhaven Sussex County League Boxing Day 1947

Record appearance holder: Dave Packham 401

Record fee received: £2,500 for Grant Horscroft to Brighton AHA in 1987

DIRECTIONS

Two minute walk from Lewes Rail Station — turn left out of station and left into Mountfield Road. Ground 100 yards on right.

Honours

Athenian League Div 1 1970 and Div 2 in 1968

Sussex County League 1965 and League Cup 1940, Mid-Sussex League 1911 and 1914

Sussex Senior Cup 1965, 1971, 1985, Sussex RUR Charity Cup 1962, 1963, 1965

Gilbert Rice Floodlit Cup 1983 and 1989, Neale Trophy 1969

Sussex Floodlit Cup 1977, Southern Counties Combination Div 1 1981

Manager for 1996-97: Terry Parris

Lewes Football Club play at the Dripping Pan, a ground with an estimated capacity of 5,000. The unusual name of the ground originates from the days when Monks used to pan for salt in the nearby river with the adjacent ground being known as the Priory. On September 23rd 1885, a group of enthusiasts from the ancient town of Lewes, met at the Royal Oak and formed the club. The colours at first were green but they soon switched to red and black. Their first taste of competitive football came when they joined the Mid-Sussex League. The Rooks, as they were popularly known, had a quiet period before winning the league in 1911 and again in 1914. After the Great War the County League was formed and they became founder members in 1920. They were runners up in 1925, 1934 and 1959, but had to wait until 1962 before winning the RUR Charity Cup, finishing second for the fourth time in the league a year later. 1964-65 was to prove very successful, as they won the championship, the Sussex Senior Cup, and the RUR Charity Cup to complete a clean sweep.

After 25 years in the league during which time the record attendance of 2,500 was set up for a game with Newhaven in 1947, they joined the Athenian League Division Two in 1965. The division was won in 1968 by pipping Aylesbury and in 1970 they again were promoted after winning Division One on goal average from Boreham Wood. In 1971 the Senior Cup was won again, but had to wait until 1977 for the next victory, in the Floodlight Cup. In 1977 the club were successful in moving to the Isthmian League Division Two, finishing runners up in 1980 and gaining promotion as well as reaching the Senior Cup final. 1986 saw another Senior Cup final appearance, at last breaking Bognor's dominance and taking the Cup.

The 90's have been a different story, as a slump saw them relegated for the first time ever in 1991, although they bounced straight back as runner up to Purfleet. 1992-93 proved to be a turning point, sadly, as they again went down as a cash crisis hit the club, ending in a mass exodus of players. Worse was to come as another drop took them into Division Three, where they remain.

New!

COMPREHENSIVELY COVERING SEMI-PRO FOOTE

Non-League

monthl

Only £25 for one year!

Keep ahead of the crowd by subscribing today to **Non-League Monthly**, the exciting new magazine for non-League enthusiasts that's taking supporters by storm.

Subscriptions are now available, and represent a significant cost saving against our news-stand price of £2.25 a copy.

- Complete your collection by ordering every back-issue, still available at **£3 each**
- Delivered direct to your door - postage and packing is **FREE!**
- Subscribe for two years and save **FIVE POUNDS!**
- Life-time subscription available for only **£100**

Send completed coupons, (photocopies are acceptable) to:

**NLM Subscriptions
Portman Media Ltd
65a Osborne Road
Southsea
Hampshire PO5 3LS**

For enquiries or overseas rates, **telephone 01705 825522** or **facsimile 01705 829988**

NLM PRIORITY SUBSCRIPTION ORDER FORM

Please tick the appropriate boxes:

☐ Send me **NLM** for one year, for only **£25.00**
☐ Send me **NLM** for two years, for only **£45.00**
☐ Send me **NLM** for life for only **£100.00**
☐ Send me details about **NLM BACK ISSUES**

I enclose a cheque or Postal Order for £_____ made payable to:
Portman Media Limited,
or please debit my: Access/Mastercard ☐ Visa ☐
Card Number: ☐☐☐☐☐ ☐☐☐☐☐ ☐☐☐☐☐ ☐☐☐☐☐
Signature: _____ **Expiry Date:** ☐☐☐ ☐

Name: _____
Address: _____
Address: _____ Postcode: _____

Non-League Football Yearbook

CREDIT CARD HOTLIN 01705 425000

800

NORTHWOOD

Northwood Park, Chestnut Avenue, Northwood, Middlesex. Tel: 01923 827148

Secretary: Steve Williams, 35 Evelyn Drive, Hatch End, Pinner, Middx Tel: 0181 428 1533

Match Sec: Alan Evans, 46 Webster Gardens, Ealing, W5 5ND
Tel: 0181 566 2880 (h) 0181 758 5318 (b)

Programme Editor Alan Evans

Colours: All Red

Capacity: 2,330

Covered standing: 450

Nickname: The Woods

Seating: 120

Clubhouse on ground: Yes

Record attendance: 1,412 v Chelsea in July 1995

Biggest win: 15-0 v Dateline (h) Middx Intermediate Cup 1973

Bigest defeat: 0-8 v Bedfont (h) Middx League 1975

Record appearances: Norman Heslop 320 1973-1982

Record goalscorer in one season: Martin Ellis 55 in 1978-79

Record goalscorer in total: Martin Ellis 168 1976-1984

DIRECTIONS

A404 (Pinner-Rickmansworth) — Chestnut Avenue on left by large grey iron railway bridge and shell petrol station. Third of a mile from Northwood Hills station (Metropolitan Line) — turn right out of station to roundabout, left into Pinner Road, left into Chestnut Avenue by Shell petrol station after 300 yards. Buses 282 and H11 to Northwood Hills.

Honours

Isthmian Assoc Members Cup 1993; Spartan League 1992; Spartan League Cup 1990 and 1992; Middlesex Intermediate Cup 1979; Middlesex Premier Cup 1995; Hellenic League Div 1 1979; Hellenic League Div 1 Cup 1979; Middlesex League 1978; Middlesex League Challenge Cup 1975, 1977, 1978; Middlesex Junior Cup 1947, 1948, 1949; Harrow and Wembley League 1932, 1933, 1934, 1935, 1936, 1937, 1947, 1948, 1949.

Manager for 1996-97: Steve Emmanuel

Assistant manager: Terry Benning

Chairman: Andy Johnson

Vice Chairman: Geoff Foster

Northwood's programme has been given the "Best programme in non-League football award" in 1996. They won the award in 1994 and were runners up in 1993 and 1995

Northwood Football Club was formed in the early 1900's although the exact date has never been established. There is a photograph of a team in existence in 1907 but it is quite likely that they were formed before this date.

The club has had a long and varied existence but it is only during the past decade or so that they have taken off, bringing the Spartan League championship. In 1931 they joined the Harrow and Wembley League, winning the Premier Division from 1932 right through to 1937. After the War they were champions again from 1947 to 1949, also winning the Middlesex Junior Cup in those three years. However the success on the park was not matched by the facilities off it and they began a decline which stretched through the fifties and early sixties, with the tide not turning until the late 60's. They were elected to the Middlesex Senior League in 1969 and were runners-up two years later and in the following years they won the League Cup five times and the League itself once, in 1978, completing a double which saw them elected to the Hellenic League.

With help from the London Borough of Hillingdon they developed the present pitch and soon they were promoted as champions and Cup winners of Division One. Floodlights were erected and senior status gained in 1981. Due to increased travelling, Northwood switched to the Spartan League in 1984, from where with considerable ground improvements they were accepted by the Isthmian League, winning the Associate Members Trophy first time.

SOUTHALL

Tring Town FC, Pendley Sports Centre, Cow Lane, Tring. Tel: 01442 823075

Secretary: Mrs Maria Smith, 22 Barchester Rd, Harrow Weald, Middx Tel 0181 933 9699

Club colours: Red and White stripes

Nickname: Fowlers

ALL GROUND DETAILS AS PER TRING TOWN FC

Record attendance: 17,000 v Watford FA Cup 1935 at Western Rd

Record appearances: Hamid Harrak

Record goalscorer in total Steve Fraser

Record fee received: £5,000 for Alan Devonshire

DIRECTIONS

One mile from Tring centre on the A41 — direct connection to M25 (junction 20) via new A41 bypass. One and a half miles from Tring (BR).
Numerous buses from the station plus Watford-Aylesbury routes serve ground.

Honours

FA AMATEUR CUP Runners up 1925

SEMI-FINAL 1926, 1953

FA VASE Runners up 1986

Great Western Suburban League 1913

Athenian League 1927,

Middlesex Senior Cup 1908, 1911, 1912, 1913, 1923, 1924, 1925, 1927, 1937, 1945, 1954, 1955

Middlesex Charity Cup 1911, 1912, 1914, 1923 jt, 1924 jt, 1928, 1937, 1952, 1969, 1984

Southall Football Club was founded in 1871 and their early years were spent playing friendlies before joining the Southern League in 1896. They struggled on until 1905 as amateurs until joining the Great Western Suburban League, of which they were champions in 1913 and the Herts and Middlesex League prior to moving to the Athenian League in 1919. They won both the Senior and Charity Cups in 1924 and a year later reached the Amateur Cup final. The success continued with another semi-final and another league title and when the bulk of the strong Park Royal club moved in with Southall, their already imposing Western Road ground became large enough to hold 20,000, as players and members built stands and terraces. Southall enjoyed an FA Cup run in 1936 which took them to the 3rd round , where they lost to Watford in front of the ground's record crowd which estimates put at 20,000.

After the War there was more success with another Amateur Cup semi-final in 1953 and the 12th Middlesex Senior Cup, but then a barren spell followed until in 1973 they switched to the Isthmian League, and with Ron Noades as Chairman they were runners up in Division Two.

In 1985-86 a strong squad reached the Middlesex Senior Cup final, but surpassed some of the great teams of the past by reaching the FA Vase final at Wembley, where 18,000 saw the club lose to Halesowen Town.

Sadly the whole team and management left the club soon after and with juniors and reserves they plummeted to the bottom of the league.

It has been a battle since then, for the club moved out of Western Road in 1992 and shared with Harefield United and latterly Tring Town, and they still await a new ground as the huge old stadium is dismantled and lost for good.

TRING TOWN

Pendley Sports Centre, Cow Lane, Tring, Herts HP23 5NS. Tel: 01442 823075

Secretary: Ian Bradding, 5 Eight Acres, Tring Herts, HP23 5DB Tel: 01442 381461

Press Sec: Alan Lee, 16 Havenside, Little Wakering, Essex Tel: 01702 216063

Best contact when confirming fixture Martin Jones (at club)

Colours: Red and White Nickname: Tee's

Capacity: 2,000 Seating: 150

Covered standing: 250, Clubhouse on ground: Yes

Record attendance: 2,000 Aylesbury Utd v Slough Town FA Cup 1st Rd Replay 1986

Biggest win: 8-1 v Willesden Isthmian League 1977

Biggest defeat: 1-11 v Epsom and Ewell Isthmian League 1996

Record appearances, goalscorer in total: Gary Harthill

DIRECTIONS

One mile from Tring centre on A41 — direct connection to M25 (junction 20) via new A41 bypass. One and a half miles from Tring (BR), Numerous buses from station and Watford-Aylesbury routes serve ground.

Honours

Great Western Combination 1951 and 1952

Spartan League 1968

Herts Charity Shield 1969

Manager 1996-97: John Arnold, Assistant Manager: Micky Connolly, Chairman: Martin Jones

Tring Town were founded in 1889 and played mostly in junior leagues until joining the Great Western Combination just after the Second War. They moved to their current ground, which was built on land owned by Showjumping commentator Dorian Williams, just after the War and won successive titles and were elected to the Spartan League in 1953, winning promotion at the first attempt, as runners up to Letchworth Town. They struggled at the higher level but under manager Gordon Todd they enjoyed a championship season in 1968 and just failed to retain it a year later. They were consoled by winning the Herts Charity Shield, which they almost won again in 1972, losing the final, but a barren spell then came along on the pitch.

The building of the present clubhouse by members and friends was the springboard for the club's entry into the Athenian League and the erection of floodlights, which were used for the first time for the visit of West Ham United which attracted a record crowd of 3, 500. After a successful 1976-77 season where the club reached the Fifth Round of the Vase, the final of the Charity Shield and were runners up in Division Two of the league, they joined the exodus to the Isthmian League, from where they reached the Herts Senior Cup final where they lost 2-1 to Watford, and won the Charity Shield.

The next few years were disappointing although in 1989 the club led the league at the New Year only to finish third, but with crippling financial problems the club went to pieces and between February 1990 and April 1991 did not win a game.

Since then they have attempted to stabilise in Division Three but the summer saw more problems with rumours of the club's demise. Happily that is not the case and they remain in the Isthmian League.

WEALDSTONE

White Lion Ground, Edgware Town FC, High Street, Edgware, Middx. HA85QA

Tel: 0181 381 1671 fax: 0181 381 1672

Secretary: Steve Hibberd, 17 Brancaster Rd, Newbury Park, Essex IG2 7ER

Tel: 0181 597 7534 (h) 01702 345739 (b)

Match secretary: Alan Couch, 31 Jersey Avenue, Stanmore, Middlesex HA7 2JG Tel 0181 907 4421

DIRECTIONS

Turn left out of Edgware tube station (Northern Line), turn left again at crossroads and the ground is 300 yards on right in Edgware High Street behind White Lion pub. Buses 32, 288 and 142.

Nickname: Stones

Colours: Blue and White

Capacity: 3,300   Seating: 250

Covered standing: 800   Clubhouse on ground: Yes

Record attendance: 13,504 v Leytonstone
FA Amateur Cup 4th Rd Replay March 5th 1949 at Lower Mead

Biggest win: 22-0 v 12th London Regiment (The Rangers) FA Amateur Cup Oct 13th 1923

Biggest defeat: 0-14 v Edgware Town London Senior Cup Dec 9th 1944

Record appearances: Charlie Townsend 514 1957-68 and 70-71

Record goalscorer in one season: George Duck 62 1973-74

Record goalscorer in total: George Duck 251 1972-79

Record fee paid: £15,000 to Barnet for David Gipp, August 1990

Record fee received: £25,000 from Coventry City for David Pearce, Nov 1983 with an additional £55,000 when he was transferred to Nottm Forest in 1985

Honours

Athenian League 1952

FA AMATEUR CUP WINNERS 1966

Southern League Div 1 South 1974

Southern Division 1982

League Cup 1982

GM Vauxhall Conference 1985

FA TROPHY WINNERS 1985

Manager for 1996-97: Gordon Bartlett

Assistant Manager: Leo Morris, Chairman: Paul Rumens, Vice Chairman: Nick Dugard

Press officer: Graham Sharpe, 10 The Lawns, Hatch End, Pinner, Middx UB10 0RG

TEL: 0836 235188 (Mobile)

The Stones fanzine "The Elmslie Ender" is published regularly and is available through the club or at the club shop on match days

Wealdstone Football Club was founded in 1900 and began life in the Willesden and

District League. They were the league champions in 1905 and 1913 before they closed down for the duration of the Great War. They had been playing home matches on a pitch at College Farm, in Locket Road, Wealdstone, moving in 1910 to Belmont Road for 12 years either side of the War.

When football got underway once again in 1919 they joined the London League and the Middlesex Senior League. A new ground at Lower Mead was ready for the start of the 1922 season and the club had hoped to compete in the Athenian League but the application was rejected, however a further application to the Spartan League was accepted. Although Wealdstone never won that league they did record their biggest wins whilst members, A 22-0 victory over the 12th London Regiment (The Rangers) in an FA Amateur Cup tie in 1923 was followed three years later by a 16-2 Spartan League win over Hertford Town, both matches played at Lower Mead. In 1928 Wealdstone were accepted into the Athenian League, replacing Summerstown, the club's grandstand coming from that ground, and during the 1929-30 season the Middlesex Senior and Charity Cups were won for the first time.

Since then they have won the Senior Cup a further ten times and the Charity Cup eight times.

In December 1944, Stones suffered their heaviest ever defeat, going down 14-0 to Edgware Town in a London Senior Cup tie. On a happier note, in 1946 they were involved in the first televised match, the BBC showing part of the Athenian League match with Barnet. They also took part in the first two live FA Cup ties in 1949, against Edgware and Colchester United.

Stones won the league in 1952, before leaving to join the Isthmians in 1964. Two years later success came when they won the Amateur Cup at Wembley, beating Hendon 3-1. It was the only win, for they turned pro in 1971, joining the Southern League, where they won the Southern Division in 1974. Five years later they were one of the founder members of the Alliance Premier League. After tasting European football in the Anglo-Italian Cup, they were relegated in 1981 for the first time ever, but a year later a jubilant club won all five trophies on offer to return to the Alliance. They then created history in 1985 by becoming the first side to do the ultimate double, of Conference title and FA Trophy. It proved to be the peak for the club, for since then they have suffered from two relegations and a ground sale deal that went badly wrong, when Lower Mead was sold for development and the company acting on their behalf went bust. To add to the woe, Stones entered an agreement to share Vicarage Road with Watford FC which cost a further £2,000,000, the club playing just 58 matches there. The next two seasons were spent at Yeading FC but at the end of the 1994-95 season, the club resigned from the Southern League and entered Division Three of the Isthmian League, which they had left in 1971. At the same time they left Yeading to move in with Edgware Town, which has improved attendances for the club, who still harbour dreams of again having their own ground.

WINGATE AND FINCHLEY

Abrahams Stadium, Summers Lane, Finchley. Tel: 0181 446 2217

Secretary: Richard Cooper, 14 Parkfield, Chorleywood, Herts WD3 5AY Tel 01923 284243

Colours: Blue and white

Nickname: Blues

Capacity: 8,500   Seating: 500

Covered standing: 500   Clubhouse on ground: Yes

Record attendance Finchley v Bishop Auckland Amateur Cup 1950

Biggest win: 9-0 Wingate v Sarratt Herts Co Lge Div 1 1985

Biggest defeat: 0-5 v Tudor Corinthians Herts Co Lge 1985

Record appearances: Marc Morris 587 1975-93

Record goalscorer in total: Marc Morris 578

DIRECTIONS

North Circular (A406) to junction with High Road Finchley (A1000), go north and Summers Lane is 200 yards on right — parking for 80 cars. Tube to East Finchley Station (Northern Line) and then 263 bus to Summers Lane. Buses 263 and 17.

Honours

FINCHLEY FC

London Senior Cup 1933, 1952, 1953

Athenian Lge 1954 and Challenge Cup 1947

Middx Senior Cup 1929, 1944, 1952, London Charity Cup

London Lge 1937, Div 2 1907 jt, League Cup 1935

Park Royal Cup 1938

WINGATE FC

Middx Lge twice and Lge Cup, London Lge Cup

Athenian Lge Div 2 1970

Herts Co Lge Div 1 1985 and Aubrey Cup 1986

Herts Intermediate Cup 1985

Herts Senior Trophy 1987

Wingate and Finchley FC was formed in 1991, being the merger of Wingate FC, formed in 1946 and Finchley from 1874. The objective of the club is to field amateur teams to play with the intent of fostering goodwill between Jewish and non-Jewish players. The merger came when Finchley, in common with many old and famous clubs, faced increasing problems and with Summers Lane becoming dilapidated and facing mounting debts, they were in danger. Wingate also had problems, although playing on an excellent pitch at Arkley the ground was limited. The two clubs went back to 1973 when Finchley came to their assistance when the old ground was swallowed up by the M1 extension at Hall Lane Hendon.

The stadium was refurbished at a cost of £400,000 and the old Finchley club plus the relatively young Wingate can look forward with confidence.

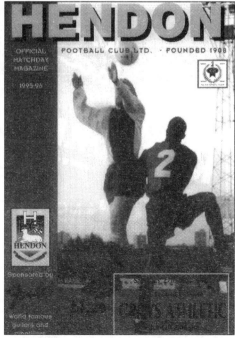

ESSEX SENIOR LEAGUE

PREMIER DIVISION

	P	W	D	L	F	A	PTS
Romford	28	23	2	3	91	27	71
Gt Wake Rovers	28	20	4	4	67	28	64
Concord Rangs	28	20	3	5	67	31	63
Maldon Town	28	16	4	8	87	47	52
Ford United	28	14	6	8	59	53	48
Sawbrdgewrth T	28	13	5	10	59	43	44
Stansted	28	12	8	8	47	34	44
Southend Manor	28	12	7	9	50	49	43
Burnham Rambs	28	13	3	12	63	48	42
Brentwood	28	13	2	13	56	53	41
Basildon United	28	5	8	15	31	52	23
Bowers United	28	5	6	17	28	57	21
Eton Manor	28	4	6	18	32	72	18
Hullbridge Sports	28	4	5	19	30	88	17
East Ham United	28	0	3	25	18	103	3

RESERVE DIVISION

	P	W	D	L	F	A	PTS
Canvey Is Res.	18	13	3	2	42	14	42
Brentwood Res.	18	12	2	4	44	23	38
Burnham R Res.	18	8	3	7	33	27	27
Gt Wake R Res.	18	8	2	8	40	36	26
Basildon Utd Res.	18	7	3	8	21	24	24
Sawbr'wth T Res.	18	7	3	8	34	43	24
Southend M Res.	18	6	3	9	36	40	21
Eton Manor Res.	18	6	3	9	28	40	21
Bowers Utd Res.	18	5	5	8	22	36	20
Hullbridge Sp Res.	18	2	5	11	26	43	11

BASILDON UNITED

Gardiners Close, Gardiners Lane, Basildon SS14 3AW. Tel: 01268 520268

Colours: Amber and black,   Nickname: Bees

Capacity: 2,000,   Seating: 400

Covered standing: 1,000,   Clubhouse on ground: Yes

Record attendance: 4,000 v West Ham United
1st game on ground August 1970

DIRECTIONS

A176 off Southend arterial (A127), left at roundabout into Cranes Farm Road, proceed to end of dual carriageway, left at lights, Gardiners Close is 1st left (Football Club signed). Two and a half miles from Basildon Railway Station.

Honours

Isthmian League Div 2 1983. Essex Senior League 1977, 1978, 1979, 1980, 1995. League Cup 1978 and 1995. Essex Senior Trophy 1979

Nicknamed the Bees, Basildon United came into being in 1967, previously operating as Armada Sports, who were a junior club who were formed years earlier. In 1967 the re-named club joined the Grays and Thurrock League and in 1970 they took the mighty step of gaining senior status from the Essex FA, whereupon they joined the Senior League. It was not long before they won honours and from 1977 to 1980 they won four straight titles which prompted them to move to the Athenian League. In addition they were runners up twice and won the League Cup and Senior Trophy. They were runners up to Windsor and Eton in their one season before being promoted to the Isthmian League Division Two and as they progressed in 1980, they made it to the last eight of the FA Vase before losing a replay with Irthlingborough Diamonds 6-4. After three seasons, United were promoted as champions pipping St Albans on the last day of the season, but they found life a lot harder and were relegated, and after two further seasons, the league de-regionalised Division Two which was the killer blow. United could not justify the extra travelling and they resigned and moved back to the Essex Senior League. Basildon have only been on their ground since 1970, having previously played on the Gun Ground in Pitsea and in Grosvenor Park, before West Ham United came down to open Gardiners Close. Although they remain, for some time there has been talk of a new ground on the edge of town.

BOWERS UNITED

Crown Avenue, off Kenneth Rd, Pitsea, Basildon, Essex. Tel: 01268 452068

Secretary: Ernie Brown, 92 Quilters Straight, Basildon, Essex SS14 2SJ Tel 01268 521201

Colours: Red and black stripes

Capacity: 2,000   Seating: Yes

Covered standing: No   Clubhouse on ground: Yes

Record attendance: 1, 800 v Billericay Town FA Vase

DIRECTIONS

Turn into Rectory Road from Old London Road (B1464) at Pitsea Broadway into Kenneth Road, right at top into Crown Avenue. One and a quarter miles from Pitsea (BR). Bus 523 to Rectory Road, Bowers Guild.

Honours
Thurrock and Thameside Combination 1959
Essex Senior League 1981 Division One Cup 1991 Harry Fisher Memorial Trophy 1992

After the War years, many new sports clubs sprang up, one being Bowers United who began playing at the Gun Meadow in Pitsea. As members of the Thurrock and Thameside Combination they established their roots in the game, and after winning the league in 1959 they moved up to the Essex Olympian League. Their prowess as a competitive and well organised club brought with their move to Crown Avenue the chance to gain senior status which allowed them to join the Essex Senior League. Since then they have gained several trophies including the league title in 1981 and runners up spot in 1984 and showed what could be achieved when 1,800 turned up for the FA Vase match against Billericay Town a few years ago.

BRENTWOOD

Brentwood Centre, Doddinghurst Rd, Brentwood, Essex. Tel: 01277 210464

Secretary: Colin Harris, 56 Viking Way, Brentwood, Essex CM15 9HY. Tel: 01277 219564

Fixtures Sec: Ken Hobbs, 53 Larchwood Gardens, Brentwood, Essex CM15. Tel: 01277 210935

Colours: Blue and white stripes

Nickname: Blues

Capacity: 2,000

Seating: No

Covered standing: Yes

Clubhouse on ground: Yes

Floodlights: No

Record attendance: 407 v Romford Essex Senior League 1996

Record appearances: John Taylor

Record goalscorer in one season: Noel Cullen

Honours

Olympian League Cup 1968

Essex Intermediate Cup 1977

Essex League Cup 1976, 1979, 1991

Manager 1996-97: Derek Stittle

Assistant: Ian McGowan

Chairman: Kevin O'Neill

Press Officer: Ken Hobbs

DIRECTIONS

Junction 28 off the M25. Take the A12 north, signposted Brentwood and Chelmsford. The ground is in Doddinghurst

The current Brentwood club have no connection with Brentwood Town FC who were wound up in controversial circumstances in 1970. They were formed in 1955 as Manor Athletic and played at King George's Playing Fields in Hartswood, moving to Larkins in 1957. They were in the Romford and District League until 1961 when they moved to the South Essex Combination and then the London and Essex Border League.

In 1967 they were on the move again to the Essex Olympian League where they won the League Cup before being runners up four years in a row.

Following the demise of Brentwood Town, Manor Athletic found themselves the most senior club in the district and changed to Brentwood Athletic, dropping the Athletic in 1972. Two years later the club joined the Essex Senior League, and despite losing senior status for a season they stayed in the league and won the Intermediate Cup.

Brentwood have been of the most consistent sides in the league, being runners up four times and League Cup winners three times. In 1992 the Larkins lost its senior status and the club moved in with East Thurrock, but the club is happily now ensconced at the Brentwood Centre.

BURNHAM RAMBLERS

Leslie Field, Springfield Rd, Burnham-On-Crouch, Essex CM0 8UA. Tel: 01621 784383

Secretary: Gordon Brasted, 6 Ramblers Way, Burnham-on-Crouch Essex CM0 8LR. Tel: 01621 782785

Fixture Secretary Peter Pask, 7 Maple Ave, Maldon, Essex CM9 7BP

Colours: all Royal Blue   Nickname: Ramblers

Capacity: 2,000   Seating: 200

Covered standing: 100   Floodlights: Yes

Clubhouse on ground: Yes

Record attendance: 1,500

Record appearances: Tony Wilkin

Record goalscorer in one season: Frank Tunbridge in 1931

Record goalscorer in total: Frank Tunbridge

DIRECTIONS
North west of village centre, 2 miles from Burnham BR station, 2 miles from M4 junction 7, 5 miles from M40 junction 2, 100yds north of Gore cross-roads - fork right into Wymers Wood Rd and ground is immediately on right. Bee line bus 66.

Honours

Essex Olympian League 1966

Mid Essex League:

North Essex League

Manager for 1996-97: Colin Wallington

Assistant manager: Grant Gordon

Chairman: Gordon Brasted

Vice chairman: Ron Hatcher

Press officer: Ron Bush, 124 Station Rd, Burnham, Essex Tel: 0162 783706

The first recorded football activity in Burnham came in 1895, and from this, in 1900, Burnham Ramblers were formed. For the first 27 years they played on four different grounds before settling down at Wick Road in 1927. This ground was gradually improved upon and extended over the years and after many successful seasons as firstly a junior, and then Intermediate club, they reached senior status in 1985.

During all those years Ramblers played in a number of leagues and had many championships to show for it. As a junior club they reached the Junior Cup semi-final on three occasions, but went one better as an Intermediate, reaching the final in 1981. In 1989 the club had its most successful season to date, reaching the last 16 of the FA Vase before losing to Bury Town. The club's biggest venture came to fruition in 1987, when after many years of planning and negotiation, the construction of the complex at Leslie Field was completed, moving away from Wick Road after 60 years.

It comprises three pitches, a training pitch, and a two storey clubhouse with stand and inside is a lounge, function room and bar. The Ramblers have four Saturday adult sides and a Vets team, seven boys' sides and a women's team.

CONCORD RANGERS

Thames Road, Canvey Island, Essex. Tel: 01268 682991

Secretary: Mrs Carol McKenna, 285 Link Road, Canvey Island, Essex SS8 9YU Tel 01268 515048

Colours: Yellow and blue

Capacity: 1,500

Seating: No

Covered standing: Yes

Clubhouse on ground: Yes

Record attendance: 1,500 v Lee Chapel North FA Sunday Cup 1990

Biggest win: 7-0 v Bowers Utd ESL 1993

DIRECTIONS

Football Club is signposted in Canvey Island.

Honours

Essex Intermediate Div 2 League and Cup

Southend Alliance

Manager for 1996-97: Colin McBride

Chairman: Grant Bignall

Vice Chairman: Rob Fletcher

Concord Rangers play just around the corner from Canvey Island FC, but are rapidly emerging from the shadow of the neighbouring "Giants". Having captured players of the calibre of Tony Mahony (ex-Fulham and Brentford) from their neighbours, Concord are expected to make a strong challenge this season for the Essex Senior League title and ICIS League status. Rangers are a comparatively young side, having been founded as recently as 1967. They started life in the Southend Alliance before progressing to the Essex Intermediate League before leaving to join the Senior League in 1991.

EAST HAM UNITED

Ferndale Sports Ground, East Ham Manorway, Beckton E6 4NG. Tel: 0171 476 5514

Secretary: Rueben Gane, 108 Beccles Drive, Barking
Tel: 0181 594 7861

Club Photographer: Gavin Ellis-Neville

Programme Editor: Roland Clooge

Nickname: The Hammers   Capacity: 2,500

Seating: 150   Covered standing: 100

Floodlights: Yes

Clubhouse on ground: Yes

Record attendance: 2,400 v Sutton United Amateur Cup November 1953

also 5,666 v West Ham Friendly at
Terrance McMillan Stadium Feb 1976

Biggest win: 9-1

Biggest defeat: 0-10

Record appearances: Ken Bowhill 1962-1982

Record goalscorer in one season: Dave Norris

Record goalscorer in total: Dave Norris

DIRECTIONS

East Ham Manorway - Cyprus Place - Beckton off A13 Newham Way from east or west. Nearest tube is East Ham then bus 101 to ground.

Honours

Metropolitan League 1977, Essex Senior Trophy 1977

Greater London League Cup 1970, London Junior Cup 1947

Bob Murrant Memorial Trophy 1995, Carpathian Charity Cup 1995

Manager for 1996-97: Rueben Gane, Assistant manager: Cornel Dobbs

Chairman: Edward Watmough, Vice chairman: Sandra Gane

The club have their own rock group 'Stereolab' and Fanzines are..'At home with the other Hammers', and 'Rueben's hero was Albert Foan'

East Ham United were originally formed in 1890 and played in the South Essex League. Another side in the league at the time were Thames Ironworks, later to become West Ham United. East Ham joined the Spartan League in 1909, remaining members until 1913, but records show that the club continued until the Great War. It was 1933 before the club re-appeared, as Storey Athletic. The club had originally played at Whitebarn Lane, but Storey began at Tillets Farm until moving to Ferndale after the war. They won the London League in 1953 and a record crowd of 2,400 crammed in to Ferndale to watch an Amateur Cup tie with Sutton United in 1953.

Storey changed their name to East Ham United in August 1955 and played in the Spartan League, Metropolitan League and the Greater London League, winning the latter in 1970, before joining the Essex Senior League in 1978. A year earlier the club had reached the quarter-final of the FA Vase and taking the Essex Senior Trophy. The Hammers have often formed strong links with West Ham and many ex-players have benn used as coaches, namely Malcolm Allison, Frank Lampard and Peter Braybrook. Others such as David Webb and the late Harry Cripps have spent time at the club.

ETON MANOR

Mile End Stadium, Rhodeswell Rd, Poplar, London

Secretary George Whiting, 20 Old South, Fairstead Estate, Kings Lynn, Norfolk PE30 4RN
Tel: 01553 773866

Colours: Sky and navy blue   Nickname: The Manor

Clubhouse on ground: Yes

Record attendance: 600 v Leyton Orient for floodlight opener at Roding Lane

DIRECTIONS
From Blackwall Tunnel turn left into East India Road. Follow to Commercial Road, turn right into Burdett Road and ground is on the left.

Honours
London League 1934, 1938, 1953, 1954. League Cup 1956. Greater London League 1965. Essex Intermediate League 1965

Eton Manor were founded in 1901 and according to some sources, were known as Wilderness Leyton. They were granted senior status in 1933 upon which they joined the then strong London League. They gathered four league titles and a League Cup win before moving on to the Aetolian League in 1959, which became the Greater London League on merger with the London League. In 1969 they played in the Metropolitan London League, another merger where they stayed until joining the Essex Senior League in 1975. Since joining the club have found silverware hard to come by and a number of ground changes have not helped.

FORD UNITED

Ford Sports and Social Club, Rush Green Rd, Romford, Essex. Tel: 01708 745678

Secretary: Michael Ewen, 215 Rush Green Rd, Rush Green, Romford, Essex RM7 0JR. Tel: 01708 724178

Nickname: Motormen   Colours: All Blue   Capacity: 2, 500

Seating: 800   Floodlights: Yes

Clubhouse on ground: Yes   Record appearances: Roger Bond

DIRECTIONS
On the A124 (Rush Green Road) on left going towards Hornchurch. 2 miles from Romford (BR). Buses 173, 175, 87, 106, 23.

Honours
FA AMATEUR CUP semi-final 1954 (as Brigg Sports). London Senior Cup 1956, 1957, 1995. Essex Senior Trophy 1991 and 1992. Essex Senior Cup 1940, 1950, 1951, 1952. Spartan League 1950, 1951, 1956, 1957, 1958. London League 1937 and 1939. Essex Elizabethan Cup 1960, 1961, 1971. Greater London League 1971. Essex Senior League 1992. League Cup 1986

Ford United were formed in 1958 from the amalgamation of Ford Sports and Brigg Sports, both of whom were formed in 1934. Although Ford found success difficult to attain, Brigg Sports won many honours right up to the merger, reaching the semi-final of the Amateur Cup in 1954, losing to Bishop Auckland 2-1 in front of 58,000 people at St James Park. The new Ford United entered the equally new Aetolian League in 1959 and were the first champions. The following year they were runners up in the League Cup and in 1962 took the league again. During this prolific period they won the Essex Elizabethan Cup twice and reached the Essex Senior Cup final, losing to Tilbury. Towards the end of the 60's the club's fortunes were on the wane and with the demise of the Aetolian League, United joined the Greater London League, being Cup winners in 1970 and League champions in 1971. Several young players have gone from United to make the grade, including Mike Flanagan, Jim Stannard, Nick Hammond, Laurie Abrahams and Doug Barton, whereas a number of ex-pros have turned out, such as John Dunn and Peter Braybrook. The club returned to success in 1992, by then in the Essex Senior League, winning the title and the Essex Senior Trophy twice.

GREAT WAKERING ROVERS

Burroughs Park, Little Wakering Hall Lane, Great Wakering, Southend on Sea, Essex. Tel: 01702 217812

Secretary: Roger Sampson, 37 Lee Lotts, Gt Wakering, Southend-on-Sea, Essex SS3 0HA Tel 01702 218794

Colours: Green and white　　Nickname: Rovers

Capacity: 1,500　　Seating: No　Covered standing: Yes

Floodlights: Yes　　Clubhouse on ground: Yes

Record attendance: 500 v Leyton Orient, friendly in 1992

Biggest win: 9-0 v Stansted 1993

Biggest defeat: 3-6 v Maldon Vale, Essex Senior League 1994

DIRECTIONS
4a bus from Shoeburyness (BR), 4a or 4b from Southend - alight at British legion in Great Wakering alongside which runs Little Wakering Hall Lane. A127 past Southend signposted Great Wakering. In Great Wakering, half mile past large Esso garage along High Street is Little Wakering Hall Lane, ground 250 yds along on left.

Honours
Essex Intermediate Cup 1992, Essex Intermediate League Div 2 1992. Division Three 1991 and League Cup 1992, Southend Charity Shield 1991 and 1992. Essex Senior League 1995

Manager 1996-97: Kevin Maddocks and Edie Nash, Assistant: Manager

Chairman: Mr F G Smith, Vice Chairman: Mr M P Beadle

Press Officer: Nobby Johnson: 01702 611964

HULLBRIDGE SPORTS

Lower Road, Hullbridge, Essex SS5 6BJ. Tel: 01702 230420

Secretary: Bob Cheesewright, 85 Bardfield Way, Rayleigh, Essex SS6 9HE. Tel: 01268 782937

Colours: Blue and white stripes　Capacity: 1, 000

Floodlights: No　　Seating: No

Covered standing: Yes　　Clubhouse on ground: Yes

DIRECTIONS
Turn into Rawreth Lane from A130 (left if arriving from Chelmsford), down to mini roundabout, left, across next mini roundabout, up hill, ground signed on right just past garage.

Honours
Essex Intermediate League Senior Div Cup 1988.
Southend and District League Div 1 1966, Div 2 1952, Div 3 1957. French Cup 1952

Manager 1996-97: John Bacon

Assistant Manager: John Gilbert

Chairman: Martin Hardy. Vice Chairman: Alan Smith

Hullbridge Sports were formed in 1945 by local residents who wanted to play football between themselves and in 1947 the council purchased a piece of land by the River Crouch for a recreational park, where a football pitch was laid. They started in the Chelmsford and Mid-Essex League and after one year joined the Southend and District League Division Three where they stayed until 1982 two Southend Leagues merged to form the Alliance. The club gained honours in league and cup before joining the Essex Intermediate League in 1984 where they were promoted in the first season and won the League Cup in 1988. Back in the 60's the club expanded into other sports and by the late 70's they were negotiating to buy their own ground. In 1980 they set about transforming 16.5 acres into a sports complex with clubhouse, and later after improving the ground itself the club gained senior status and joined the Senior League in 1989.

ILFORD

Cricklefield Stadium, Ilford. Tel: 0181 514 0019

Secretary: Michael Roberts, 168 Dawlish Dr, Ilford,
Essex IG3 9EG Tel 0181 599 2384 (h) 0171 280 6675 (b)

Fixtures Sec: Clifford Nowell, 16 Boleyn Gardens,
Dagenham, Essex RM10 9TU. Tel: 0181 252 2116

Press Sec: Mick Foley, 24 Breamore Rd, Seven Kings,
IG3 9NB. Tel: 0181 599 8950

Colours: Blue and white hoops   Capacity: 7,000

Covered standing: None   Seating: 220

Clubhouse on ground: No   Floodlights: Yes

DIRECTIONS
Approach on the North Circular Road, A406, and take the A118 exit away from the city centre, Ilford Hill. Turn right at the end of the road into Chapel Road, A123. Turn left at the roundabout continuing along Winston Way, A118. Go straight over the next roundabout and follow signs for A1083, Green Lane. Cricklefield Stadium is on the left after Pelham Road.

**Managers for 1996-97: Mick Foley and Mickey Hunt. Assistant manager: Phil Douglas.
Chairman: George Hogarth. Vice chairman: Alan Gray**

The new Ilford have waged a long war with the Redbridge Council for many years to try to obtain a ground for the re-formed club. Senior status finally arrived after their ninth application to use the Cricklefields Stadium was granted despite fierce opposition. Thousands of phone calls, letters and bi-monthly bulletins later, and after 57 different committee members, Mick Foley and father Peter have at last succeeded having been there from the start.

The club estimate that it has cost in the region of £11,000 top campaign for the ground. The club gained a lottery award to extend the pitch which the council had shortened and to erect new dressing rooms.

SAFFRON WALDEN TOWN

Catons Lane, Saffron Walden, Essex CB10 2DU. Tel: 01799 522789

Secretary: Mr Harry Harvey, 1 New Willow Cott,
Langley, Saffron Walden, Essex CB11 4RU
Tel: 01799 550615

Colours: Red and black   Nickname: Bloods

Capacity: 5,000   Seating: 500

Covered standing: 1,000   Clubhouse on ground: Yes

DIRECTIONS
In Saffron Walden High Street turn into Castle Street, left a T-junction, 1st left by Victoria Pub.

Record attendance: 6,000 v Rainham Ath Essex Junior Cup Final 1926 (at Crittalls FC)

Record appearances: Les Page 700+

Record goalscorer in total: John Tipputt

Honours

Essex Senior League 1974
Eastern Counties League 1983
Spartan League East Div 2 1937. Essex Senior Trophy 1983, 1984, 1985. Eastern Floodlit Competition 1992. Essex Junior Cup 1897. Stansted and District League 1908, 1909, 1910, 1912, 1921, 1923, 1924. Haverhill and District League 1909, 1923, 1924, 1930, 1934. Herts and Essex Border League 1927. Haverhill Charity Cup 1937, Halstead Charity Cup 1935. Saffron Walden Rotary Cup 1939, 1940, 1946

Manager 1996-97: Phil Hopkins   **Chairman: Paul Diggins**

Vice Chairman: P. Walker   **Programme Editor: Russell Scott**

SAWBRIDGEWORTH TOWN

Crofters End, West Road, Sawbridgeworth, Herts. Tel: 01279 722039

Secretary: Mr Gary Bennett, 21 Sayesbury Rd, Sawbridgeworth, Herts Tel 01279 830306

Nickname: The Robins　　Capacity: 1,500

Seating: No　　Covered standing: Yes

Floodlights: Yes　　Clubhouse on ground: Yes

Record attendance: 610 v Bishops Stortford

DIRECTIONS
Three quarters of a mile from station; up Station Road then West Road.

HONOURS
Essex Olympian League 1972
Herts Senior Trophy 1991 and 1994
Harry Fisher Memorial Cup 1988
Herts Charity Shield 1993
Ullesford Charity Cup 1993

In 1897, Sawbridgeworth Cricket Club members decided to form a football team and they played regular friendly matches at Pishiobury Park. The first competitive matches can be traced back to 1902 when the team played in the Stortford and District League. By then they had moved to Great Hyde Hall with the headquarters at the Railway Hotel, nearby. They later played in the East Herts League, again moving this time to a field next to the Hand and Crown pub, where they changed in an upstairs room. It was a very popular venue and was regularly used for local cup finals, and it lasted until 1930 when they moved to Cambridge Road, where they play today, although the entrance is now in Crofters End which was originally allotments. In 1975, when the clubhouse was first built, the council decreed that the Cambridge Road entrance should be pedestrian only and so the new entrance was built. On the field, just after the War, Sawbridgeworth were granted senior status and played in the Spartan League, with little success and after a spell in junior football they became founder members of the Essex Olympian League. 1976 saw them again gain senior status where they joined the Essex Senior League. 1993 and 94 saw the Robins lose in the League Cup final, but they have since lifted it, beating Stansted and have also finished second in the league, losing to Great Wakering on goal difference.

SOUTHEND MANOR

Southchurch Park Arena, Lifstan Way, Southend-on-Sea. Tel: 1702 615577

Secretary: Dave Kittle, 15 Seymour Rd, Hadleigh, Essex SS7 2HB Tel 01702 559581

Colours: Yellow and red　　Nickname: The Manor

Capacity: 2,000　　Seating: Yes

Covered standing: Yes　　Clubhouse on ground: Yes

DIRECTIONS
A127 then A1159 for 1 mile turn right at second roundabout at Rusty Bucket PH, due south for 1 mile - ground on right near sea front.

Record attendance: 1,521 v Southend

Floodlight opener 1991

Honours
Southend Borough Combination 1972, 1974, 1979, 1980, 1981, 1982. Southend and District Alliance 1984 and 1985. League Cup 1983. Essex Senior Trophy 1993. Essex Intermediate Cup 1979. Essex Senior League 1991. Division One 1988 and Division One South 1987. Div 1 League Cup 1988. Challenge Cup 1990. Harry Fisher Memorial Trophy 1991, 1993

STANSTED

Hargrave Park, Cambridge Rd, Stansted, Essex. Tel: 01279 812897

Secretary: Mrs D. Murnane, Apple Tree House, Fullers
End, Elsenham, Bishops Stortford, Herts CM22 6DU
Tel: 01279 815404

Colours: Blue and black stripes

Capacity: 2,000

Seating: 200

Covered standing: Yes

Clubhouse on ground: Yes

Record attendance: 828 v Whickham FA Vase 1984

Biggest win: 5-1 v Coggeshall Town Essex Sen Lge 1984

DIRECTIONS

**B1383 north of Bishops Stortford on
west side of Cambridge Road.
Stansted (BR) - 1/2 mile.**

Honours

FA VASE WINNERS 1984

Essex Senior League and Cup 1984

Harry Fisher Memorial Trophy 1983 and 1985

East Anglian Cup 1984

Eastern Floodlit Cup 1984

Stansted Challenge Cup 1914 and 1922

East Herts League 1935

West Essex Border Charity Cup 1935

The club was formed in 1902 and soon established itself on Greens Meadow until moving to the current ground in 1937. They won the local Challenge Cup in 1914 and 1922 and in 1935 took both the East Herts League and the West Essex Border Charity Cup.

After the War they had spells in the Spartan, London and Herts County Leagues before joining the Essex Senior League as founder members.

The early 80's saw a most successful era, with the building of the new clubhouse followed by wins in the Harry Fisher Cup and the installing of floodlights. 1983-84 saw Stansted go all the way to Wembley in the FA Vase, beating Stamford in the final. They also took the East Anglian Cup, Essex League Challenge Cup and Eastern Floodlit Cup. After winning the Harry Fisher Cup again the team broke up and since then they have not gained much success, other than a League Cup and another Harry Fisher Cup win.

Premier Division

	P	W	D	L	F	A	PTS
St Margaretsbury	30	18	7	5	51	29	61
Hillingdon Borough	30	16	9	5	54	28	57
Brimsdown Rovers	30	15	9	6	55	36	54
Corinthian-Casuals	30	15	6	9	49	30	51
Cockfosters	30	14	7	9	61	43	49
Tottenham Omada	30	13	6	11	67	53	45
Croydon Athletic	30	13	6	11	50	51	45
Barkingside	30	11	6	13	48	46	39
Tufnell Park	30	11	4	15	38	55	37
Brook House	30	9	9	12	29	38	36
Hanwell Town	30	10	6	14	41	60	36
Woolwich Town	30	9	7	14	42	48	34
Waltham Abbey	30	8	10	12	27	45	34
Beaconsfield	30	8	6	16	42	56	30
Willesden (Hawk)	30	7	8	15	37	44	29
Amersham Town	30	6	8	16	29	58	26

AMERSHAM TOWN

Spratleys Meadow, School Lane, Old Amersham, Bucks Tel: 01494 727428

Secretary: Richard Phillips, 16 Cameron Rd, Chesham, Bucks Tel: 01494 784469

Match Sec: David Rake, 12 Stokes Lane, Haddenham, Bucks Tel: 01844 290176

Colours: Black and white stripes

Seating: None

Covered standing: None

Floodlights: No

Capacity: 1,500

Record attendance: 2,000 v Aston Villa Centenary match (at Chesham Utd) 1990

DIRECTIONS

A413 London to Aylesbury road, right into Mill Lane at end of Amersham old town, left into School Lane at top of Hill Lane, ground on left 300 yds past school. 1 mile from Amersham Station - BR & underground Metropolitan Line.

Honours

Hellenic League 1964 and Division One 1963

League Cup 1954, St Marys Cup 1990, Berks and Bucks Junior Cup 1900, 1914, 1923

Wycombe Challenge Cup 1924, Wycombe and District Combination 1903

Aylesbury and District League 1909, 1910, 1911, 1920

Southern Section 1908, Chesham League 1920

Amersham Town were formed on October 10th 1890, at the Crown Hotel, and they began playing on Barn Meadow, owned by the Brewery head and situated at the back of the High Street. They played friendlies and entered the Junior Cup in 1892, but soon ran into financial trouble. They joined the Aylesbury and District League in 1896 and two years later merged with Amersham Rovers, who handed over match balls, goal posts and money, and in 1900 they entered the Wycombe Combination, which they won and five years later took the Aylesbury League title, Southern section. They went on to take the title three more times before the war, plus the Junior Cup in 1914. They won both Chesham and Aylesbury Leagues on resumption and in 1920 moved to Spratley's Meadow, joining the Great Western Suburban League, coming runners up in Division Two and winning the Junior Cup again.

After the Second War, Amersham took advantage of their fine facilities by joining the Spartan League, where they finished fifth in 1953 and left to join what was to be called the Coronation League, but became the Hellenic League, as founder members. They won the League Cup in 1954 and the Division One title, and had a season in the London League before returning to the Hellenic, which they won in 1964, and were runners up in the next two seasons.

The 70's saw the slow decline of the club and they returned to the Spartan League, where they found themselves in Senior Divison Two. They installed floodlights and won promotion and were runners up in 1980, reaching the Senior Cup semi-final, but that was to be the last real success so far.

In 1990 they were devastated when a huge storm demolished their old grandstand, and with the floodlights now only good enough for training, Spratley's Meadow is back to how it was many years ago.

BARKINGSIDE

Oakside, Station Rd, Barkingside, Ilford, Essex Tel: 0181 550 3611

Secretary: Norman Ingram, 45, Cheneys Rd,
Leytonstone, E11 3LL
Tel: 0181 555 1447 (h) 0181 532 9397 (b)

Club colours: Blue and White hoops

Nickname: The Side

Capacity: 2,000

Covered seating: 60

Floodlights: Yes

Covered standing: 60

Clubhouse on ground: Yes

Record attendance: 957 v Arsenal Res in London League 1957

DIRECTIONS

From London A12 Eastern Avenue to Green Gate, left into Hurns Road to Barkingside, right into Craven Gardens, right again Carlton Drive leading to Station Road, under bridge and ground entrance on right. Adjacent to Barkingside station (Central Line), 3 miles from Ilford station (BR). Bus 169 to Craven Gardens.

Honours

London League Cup 1956

Ilford Festival Cup 1952

Romford Charity Cup 1952

Greater London League 1965

Spartan League Harry Sunderland Shield 1984

Manager 1996-97: C. Edwards

Assistant Manager: W. Roche

Chairman: K. Harris

Barkingside FC were formed in 1898. Played in Ilford League on ground opposite State Cinema in High Street. Shared championship after War but disbanded in 1923 due to lack of support, but resumed in 1925 as Barkingside Boys Guild in Ilford Minor League. Changed to Barkingside Old Boys and then dropped OB's tag in the thirties. Club played at Barkingside Recreation Ground for 25 years before moving to the current ground in 1957. After War in the Ilford League they moved to South Essex League and were runners up before joining the Walthamstow League and then the London League in 1950. The club won the League Cup in 1956 and were twice runners up before joining the Greater London League in 1964, winning promotion in 1966, but were relegated. The club entered the Spartan League in 1976 and were soon promoted, although they went straight down again. They took the Harry Sunderland Shield in 1984 and in 1986 they were promoted again, where they remain, finishing runners up to Walthamstow Pennant in 1991.

BEACONSFIELD SYCOB

Holloways Park, Beaconsfield, Bucks Tel: 01494 676868

Secretary Ken Barratt, 31 Stockley End, Abingdon, Oxon OX14 2HF Tel: 01235 526832

Colours: Red and white quarters

Nickname: The Rams

Capacity: 2,000

DIRECTIONS

M40 (Junction 2), 1st exit to A355. Club 100 yds on right. One and a half miles from Beaconsfield (BR). Bus 441 Slough-High Wycombe.

Seating: Stand for 300 being erected

Covered standing: 60

Clubhouse on ground: Yes

Record attendance: v Windsor and Eton Berks and Bucks Senior Cup

Biggest win: 6-0 v Hanwell Town (a) 1995

Biggest defeat: 0-5 v Hillingdon Borough 1996

Record goalscorer in one season Tony Thompson

Manager: Simon Delahunty

Assistant Manager: Stephen Norman

Chairman: Fred Deanus

Vice Chairman: Kelvin Beck

Beaconsfield SYCOB was formed in 1994 following a merger of Slough YCOB and Beaconsfield United.

United were also formed from an amalgamation of a Boy Scouts club and Beaconsfield FC, who played on White Hart Meadow before the Great War. They played in the Wycombe and Maidenhead Leagues until 1979, when gaining higher status they joined the Spartan League Intermediate Section.

They won the title in 1981 and lost the Intermediate Cup final the same year, and were given senior status by the county, sharing the title with Collier Row in 1983. Having played on the original Holloway Park, they moved across the road when the M40 was extended.

Slough Youth Centre was once on the site of Baylis School and when it moved to the new Community Centre in 1938 the team was formed. They joined the Slough Minors League just before War broke out, and afterwards they started in men's football, in the Slough and District League. They gained three promotions to reach the Premier Division where they were runners up in 1959, but further honours did not come and they entered the Windsor, Slough and District League in 1983. They lost the League Cup final in 1988, before joining the East Berks League, where they did the League and Cup double and were promoted to the Chiltonian League, gaining promotion in 1992. They won the League Cup and were league runners up before ground problems held them up, and so the amalgamation and move to Beaconsfield came about.

BRIMSDOWN ROVERS

Goldsdown Road, Enfield, Middx Tel: 0181 804 5491

Secretary and Press Graham Dodd 57 Roundmoor Drive,
Cheshunt, Herts EN8 9HU Tel: 01992 626820

Match Sec: Tony Beasley, 80 Cobham Rd, Fetcham,
Leatherhead, Tel: 01372 376820

Nickname: The Magpies

Colours: Black and White stripes

Capacity: 1,000

Seating: None

Covered standing: 50

Floodlights: Yes

Clubhouse on ground: Yes

Record attendance:
FA Cup 3rd Qual Rd v Chesham Utd 1991

DIRECTIONS

BR from Liverpool Street to Brimsdown (half mile away but not open Saturdays) or Southbury Road. By road off Green Street, itself off Hertford Road (A1010). Buses 191 or 307.

Honours

Enfield Alliance Division One 1948, League Cup 1949

Northern Suburban League 1953, 1957, 1958, 1968, 1969

London Spartan League Intermediate Div 2 B 1977

Division One: 1982, London Intermediate Cup 1983

Spartan League 1993, Spartan League Cup 1996

Tottenham Charity Cup 1995

Manager: Tony Faulkner, Assistant manager: Charlie Johnson

Chairman: Graham Dodd, Vice Chairman: Peter Anglis

Brimsdown Rovers was formed shortly after the last war by a group of Geordies, following a merger with a team called Durham Rovers. To this day the club's colours are the famous black and white stripes of Newcastle United and its mascot is a magpie. Some of the original team are still members of the club.

They began in the Enfield Alliance in 1937 and had three seasons on local parks until the War, then in 1947 they re-joined and were re-named, playing on King George V1 fields, jointly winning Division One. They won the League Cup twice and were runners up in the league twice in consecutive seasons and in 1950 joined the Northern Suburban League, winning promotion to the Premier Division. They had 25 seasons there, winning it six times, and during this spell they moved into their current ground, owned by the council, in 1958. They moved up to the Spartan League in 1976 and by 1982 had reached the Senior Division, where having gained the relevant status they were promoted to the Premier Division. Since then they have enjoyed success in League Cup and FA Vase, and have installed floodlights, and in 1992 they were runners up to Northwood in the league.

Their best season came in 1992-93 when they took the title and reached the final of the London Senior Cup. Last season they took the League Senior Cup, beating champions St Margaretsbury in the final.

BROOK HOUSE

Farm Park, Kingshill Ave, Hayes, Middx Tel: 0181 845 0110

Secretary: Barry Crump, 19 Bradenham Rd, Hayes, Middx UB4 8LP Tel: 0181 841 3959

Colours: Blue and white stripes

Clubhouse on ground: Yes

Seating: None

Covered standing: 75

Capacity: 500

Honours

Middlesex Junior Sunday Cup

Hayes and District Sunday League twice

League Cup twice

DIRECTIONS

From London or North Circular Road:
A40 Western Avenue to Target roundabout, turn left towards Hayes (A312), over White Hart roundabout towards Hayes, turn right at traffic lights in to Kingshill Avenue, ground 1 mile on right., Nearest BR station is Hayes & Harlington, then bus 90 or 195 to Brook House pub. Nearest tube is Northolt (central line), then bus to ground.

Brook House FC was formed in 1974, from a group of friends in a pub, and they entered a Sunday team. As most of them played for either Charville or Hayes North, they teamed up on a Sunday and success came in the Hayes and District League, ending with a win in the Middlesex Sunday Junior Cup.

They reached the Premier Division where they won the league and Cup double twice, before moving to Saturdays in 1982. They joined the now defunct South-West Middlesex League and after two seasons were founder members of the Middlesex County League in 1984.

Following four seasons in mid-table they gained senior status and moved to Division One of the London Spartan League in 1988. A final finish of fifth was enough for them to be promoted to the Premier.

Floodlights were installed in 1991, which has enabled the club to enter the FA Cup.

COCKFOSTERS

Cockfosters Sports Ground, Chalk Lane, Cockfosters, Barnet Tel: 0181 449 5833

Secretary: Mr Graham Bint, 15 Chigwell Park, Chigwell, Essex IG7 5BE Tel: 0181 500 7369

Match Sec: Mr Colin Bell, 24 Morris Way, London Colney, Herts AL2 1JL Tel: 01727 823458

Press officer: Alan Simmons, 14 The Poplars, Bramley Rd, Southgate, London N14 4HH Tel: 0181 440 7998

Nickname: Fosters,

DIRECTIONS

Ground on A111. M25 Jct 24 (Potters Bar) take A111 signed Cockfosters - ground 2 miles on right. Adjacent to Cockfosters underground station (Piccadilly Line). Bus 298 to Cockfosters station.

Colours: All Red

Capacity: 500,

Seating : None

Covered standing: 50

Floodlights: No but expected for 1997-98 season

Clubhouse on ground: Yes

Record attendance: 480 v Saffron Walden Herts Senior League in 1969

Biggest win: 10-1 v Rickmansworth Town 1968

Biggest defeat: 2-7 v Leggatts Old Boys 1968

Record appearances: Bob Davis 500+

Record scorer in one season: Stan Painer 42

Record goalscorer in aggregate: Peter Benham 194

Honours

London Intermediate Cup 1971 and 1990

Herts Senior County League 1979, 1981, 1984 and Div 1 in 1967

Aubrey Cup 1979 and 1985, Herts Intermediate Cup 1979

Northern Suburban League 1962, Div 1 1950 and 1961

Manager for 1996-97: Derek Townshend, Assistant manager: Glyn Macdonald

Chairman: Frank Brownlie

Local residents founded the club on the estate of Lady Bevan in 1921. They joined the Barnet League where they moved through the lower divisions before another local club, Cockfosters Juniors joined forces, enabling them to compete in the stronger Wood Green League. Again promotion was gained until the league itself was won along with the League Cup and the Barnet Cup, in 1939. After the War they joined the Northern Suburban Intermediate League where they reached Premier Division in 1947. Relegation followed but they persevered and in 1950 won the Premier Division title.Honours eluded the club during most of the 50's but in the 60's there began a decade of improvement. Firstly Division One and then the Premier Division titles went to Chalk Lane, before they joined the Herts Senior Cup which they also won three times, also taking the League Cup twice. 1979 saw Cockfosters take the treble of League, League Cup and Herts Intermediate Cup for the only time under former player Roy Reeder. The following nine seasons saw two more titles, two runners up places and an Aubrey Cup win. Throughout most of the 1980's the first and reserve teams were rarely out of the top four and in 1991 senior status was gained when the London Spartan League accepted them.

CROYDON ATHLETIC

Mayfield, off Mayfield Rd, Thornton Heath, Surrey Tel: 0181 664 8343

Secretary: Dean Fisher, 9 Kelvin Gardens, Croydon, Surrey Tel: 0181 667 1049

Match Sec: Alan McSweeney, 41 Canham Rd, South Norwood, SE25 Tel: 0181 771 2254

Nickname: The Rams

Colours: Maroon and white

Floodlights: Yes,

Seating: Yes

Covered standing: Yes,

Capacity: 2,000

Record win: 8-1 v Beckton Utd 1993

Record defeat: 1-9 v Yeading 1987

Record goalscorer in total: Graham Edginton

DIRECTIONS

From Norbury follow London Road towards Croydon, turn right into Headcorn Road, left into Silverleigh Road, right into Mayfield Crescent, right into Mayfield Road, left at end and follow road/path to ground. One mile from Norbury (BR). Buses 109, 154.

Honours

Wandsworth Town (Smallwoood Ath), South London League Junior Div 1949

Wandsworth and District League 1954, Wimbledon and District League Cup twice

Parthenon League twice, Surrey Senior League and Cup 1975

Croydon Athletic FC was formed in 1986 following the successful merger of two much older clubs, and was originally named Wandsworth and Norwood. Wandsworth FC were founded in 1948 and had played as a senior club in the Spartan League since 1976. They were originally known as Smallwood Athletic and began in the South London League, playing on Wimbledon Common Extension, winning the Junior Division at the first attempt. In 1953 they joined the Wandsworth and District League which they won, before switching to the Wimbledon League in 1954, where they enjoyed much success in their five seasons as members.

The club changed their name in 1960 and joined the Parthenon League, where they were champions twice, and then the Surrey Senior League, where they did the double in 1975. In 1977 they moved to the London Spartan League. The club have had a number of grounds, including Kimber Rd, Wandsworth, Wisley Gardens and Morfax Sports in Mitcham.

Norwood FC were an intermediate club founded a year before Wandsworth. Before playing in the Spartan League, Wandsworth were members of the Thornton Heath League, playing at Wandle Park and then Lloyd Park, in Croydon. In 1962 they moved to the Surrey Intermediate League, which later became the Surrey and South Eastern League, until the merger. When the merger was agreed work commenced on the ground with a pitch barrier and toilets, with a small covered stand. With senior status confirmed in 1986 the new club began and in 1989 finished runners up to Abingdon in the Premier Division on goal difference. In 1990 it was decided to change the club name to Croydon Athletic to create more local attention, and with the new name came floodlights in October 1990 and a new stand as the ground began to reach out towards Isthmian League standards. The Rams have come a long way in a short time and are getting closer than ever to getting on equal terms with their famous neighbours Croydon FC.

HANWELL TOWN

Reynolds Field, Perivale Lane, Perivale, Greenford , Middx Tel: 0181 998 1701

Secretary: John Wake, 38 Warwick Ave, South Harrow, Middx HA2 8RD Tel: 0181 422 1048

Colours: Black and white stripes

Nickname: The Town

Capacity: 2,000

Floodlights: Yes

Seating: Yes

Covered standing: Yes

Clubhouse on ground: Yes

Record attendance: 850 v Enfield Middlesex Senior Cup 1989

Biggest win: 10-0 v Brook House in London Spartan League

Record appearances: Phil Player

Record goalscorer in one season

Record goalscorer in total: Tony Pickering

DIRECTIONS

A40 Oxford road from London, exit B456 for Ealing, ground on corner of junction approached immediately via left turn into Perivale Lane. 3rd of a mile from Perivale tube station (central line).

Honours

Middlesex League Cup 1971 and 1977

London Spartan League 1984

London Senior Cup 1992 and 1993

Hanwell has seen football since 1898, with clubs such as Hanwell FC, Hanwell Old Nationals and Hanwell Mental Hospital, although the present club were formed in 1920, by a group of Geordies working in the area and to this date they still play in black and white stripes. Between 1924 and 1927 they were members of the London League, but records after that are not available, the club next appearing in 1948. They joined the Dauntless League and then progressed to the Harrow, Wembley and District League in 1954, where they stayed for 16 years. They moved to the Middlesex League in 1970, winning the League Cup a year later.

From the re-start in 1948 the club had played on the Ealing Central Sports Ground in Perivale, then in 1981 they obtained a long lease at their current home in Reynolds Field.

They were made senior in 1983 and joined the Spartan League which they won at the first attempt. Since then the club have installed floodlights and now enter both the FA Cup and FA Vase, and in the early 90's they dominated the London Senior Cup, the final of which was reached three times, winning twice.

HAREFIELD UNITED

Preston Park, Breakspeare Rd North, Harefield, Middx Tel: 01895 823474

Secretary: Terry Devereux, 72 Williamson Way, Rickmansworth, Herts Tel: 01923 711451

Colours: Blue and yellow

Nickname: The Hares

Seating: 150

Covered standing: Yes

Capacity: 2,000

Record attendance: 430 v Bashley FA Vase

DIRECTIONS

M25 junction 17, follow signs to Swakely corner then to Harefield A40. Denham (BR). Bus 347 from Watford.

Honours

Parthenon League 1965

Div 1 League Cup 1966

Middlesex League 1967, 1969, 1970, 1971

League Cup 1967 and 1969

Middlesex Premier Cup 1986

Harefield United are believed to have been formed in 1868, but little is known about the club other than that they played in the Uxbridge and District League before the war. They played for many years on an undeveloped ground which is still used for football today, called Taylor's Meadow, before moving to Preston Park.

They joined the Great Western Combination after the Second War and remained until moving to the Parthenon League in 1964, which they won at the first attempt. That league folded and the club moved to the Middlesex League, where they enjoyed their best moments to date, winning the title four times in five years and taking the League Cup twice. They took the gamble of moving up to the Athenian League in 1975, but strangely the nearest they came to honours was on the last day of the league's existence, when they lost the League Cup final to Wolverton Town.

Their elevation to the Isthmian League has not been a very successful one, the last major honour being the Middlesex Premier Cup in 1986. After a number of years of struggle they resigned and joined the Spartan League in the summer.

HARINGEY BOROUGH

Coles Park, White Hart Lane, N7 Tel: 0181 889 1495

Secretary: George Kilikita, Unit 12A,16-22 Seven Sisters Road, London N7 6A Tel 0181 368 2783

Match Secretary: Minos Perdios, 37 Stuart Avenue, Hendon, London NW9 7AU Tel 0181 201 5135

Colours: Green and White

ISLINGTON ST MARYS

Coles Park, White Hart Lane, N7 Tel: 0181 889 1495

Secretary: Nick Adams, 5 Hambledon Chase, 58 Croch Hill, London N4

Tel: 0171 263 1530 day 0171 354 1387 evenings

Match secretary Eddie Webb, 34 Bidwell Gardens, Bounds Green, London N11 Tel: 0181 881 0538

Colours: Black and red stripes

ALL GROUND DETAILS AS PER HARINGEY BOROUGH FC

HILLINGDON BOROUGH

Middlesex Stadium, Brakespear Rd, Ruislip, Middx Tel: 01895 639544

Secretary: Roy Lovell Tel:01753 654 756

Colours: White and blue

Nickname: Boro

Floodlights: Yes

Clubhouse on ground: Yes

Seating: Yes

Covered standing: No

Capacity: 1,500

Record win: 9-0 v Amersham Town 1994

Record fee received: £1,000 for Craig Johnson to Wealdstone

DIRECTIONS

From A40 take B467 (signed Ickenham), left at 2nd roundabout into Breakspear Road South, right after 1 mile by Breakspear pub - ground half mile on left. Nearest station is Ruislip. Bus U1 passes ground.

Hillingdon Borough FC were formed in 1990 when a Limited Company was set up by four directors of the old Borough club, plus the committee of Bromley Park Rangers FC, to try to re-establish the club, which was originally founded in 1872 as Yiewsley FC.

They turned professional in 1959 and joined the Southern League, and changed their name in 1964, dropping the Borough tag in 1981, but by then the fortunes were on the wane and in 1985 the ground was sold and the club merged with Burnham FC, who took over their place in the Southern League. The name disappeared soon after as Burnham reverted to their original name, from Burnham and Hillingdon.

Another club, Ruislip Town moved across the fence from their old ground in Brakespear Rd, to the newly built stadium and joined the Southern League in 1985, but it was a failure and after four seasons they dropped to the Hellenic League in 1989.

That year Chiltonian League side Bromley Park Rangers merged with them and Ruislip Park FC was born, but after one season and with the Ruislip connection gone, they moved across to the Spartan League, changing their name to Hillingdon Borough FC.

ST. MARGARETSBURY

Recreation Ground, Station Rd, Stanstead St Margarets Tel: 01920 870743

Secretary: Keith Myall, 30 Crib Street, Ware, Herts
SG12 9EX Tel: 01920 485067

Colours Red and black

Nickname: The Bury

Capacity: 1,000

Seating: 60

Covered standing: No

Floodlights : No

Clubhouse on ground: Yes

Biggest win: 15-1 v Sun Sports Herts County Lge 1949

Biggest defeat: 0-9 v Herts Police Herts Senior Co Lge 1989

Honours

East Herts League 1921 and Div 2 1920

Rolleston Charity Cup and Graphic Cup 1936

Waltham and District League 1947

Aubrey Cup 1972

Herts Senior Centenary Trophy 1993

Spartan League Cup 1996

DIRECTIONS

Harlow/Chelmsford exit from A10 to A414, take B181 at Amwell after 300 yds towards Stanstead Abotts - ground quarter mile on right. 300 yds from St Margaretsbury BR station (Liverpool Street - Hereford East line).

The club was formed in 1894 as Stanstead Abbots FC and retained the name until they moved to the current ground in 1962, on condition that the name be changed to comply with the wishes of the ground's previous owners when it was sold to the parish. They first played on the Mill Field in Capel Lane, part of an estate owned by the Buxton family. Prior to the Second War, they played in Herts County and East Herts Leagues and briefly after had a spell in the Waltham League before returning to the Herts County in 1948. Honours were few right through to 1991 when they returned to the top division having been relegated three years before.

After 44 years membership they moved to the Spartan League in 1992 when they won the Centenary Trophy defeating Sawbridgeworth at Ware FC, and in 1995 they finished runners up in the Premier Division, winning the championship last May, as well as reaching the final of the Senior Cup, where they lost to Brimsdown Rovers in a replay.

A Centenary book is available from the club, ring for details.

RUISLIP MANOR

Grosvenor Vale, off West End Rd, Ruislip, Middx

Tel: 01895 637487 office. If fixture is in doubt please use this number, 01895 636168

Secretary: Avice Horne, 49 Evelyn Close, Whitton, Twickenham, Middlesex TW2 7BL

Tel: 0181 898 3581

Chairman Mr M. Connors, 55 Shenley Ave, Ruislip, Middx HA4 6BT

Tel: 01895 634424 (H) 0171 548 6588 (B)

Press officer Steve Szymanski, 15 Grosvenor Vale, Ruislip, Middlesex.

Nickname: The Manor, Colours: Black and White

Capacity: 2,000

Covered seating: 100

Covered standing: 200, Clubhouse on ground: Yes

Record attendance: 2,000 v Tooting and Mitcham Utd FA Amateur Cup 1962

DIRECTIONS

From London: A40 to Ruislip, turn off on A4180 - right at roundabout into West End Road, right into Grosvenor Vale after a mile and a half - ground at end. From Ruislip Manor station (Metropolitan Line) turn left out of station, then first right into Shenley Avenue, third left into Cranley Drive - ground 150 yards on left. E2 bus (Ealing Broadway-Ruislip Station) is only bus that passes top of Grosvenor Vale.

Honours

Isthmian League Associate Members Trophy 1991

Athenian League Div 2 1973

Manager: Andy Waddock

Chairman: M.Connors, Vice Chairman: J.Evans

Ruislip Manor FC was founded in 1938 spending its first season in the Uxbridge League. They were founder members of the Middlesex League in 1939 and remained throughout the War, until 1946 when they left for the London League Division One. Another move occurred in 1947, when the club changed homes, from the playing fields in Sidmouth Drive to Grosvenor Vale. The first season there saw the club finish as runners up to Cheshunt after leading the table for most of the season, but there was no automatic promotion as only senior clubs were permitted into the top division. This status was finally given in 1950. Ruislip Manor were London League Premier Division runners up in 1952 behind West Thurrock and the following year they were third. After losing the League Cup final in 1954 the club moved to the stronger Spartan League, where they stayed until 1965, when despite a poor season, they were taken into the Second Division of the Athenian League replacing Histon. After a few seasons at the wrong end, there was a change and the title was won in 1973 and due to the Isthmian's expanding, Manor found themselves in the top division for 1973, where they came third. In 1977 the Isthmians again came to the rescue as the club finished bottom of the league, but with the Athenians reduced to one division they were reprieved. They stayed until the league disbanded in 1984, joining Division Two South of the Isthmian League. After a number of seasons they improved slightly, and were fifth in 1992, and a year later they were finally promoted as runner up to Worthing. Since then the league has been a struggle, as has the fight to maintain the grading required by the league regarding grounds. After finishing last but one in May, the club had resigned from the league, as much work needed to be done on the ground to obtain a B grading, but it was refused and for 1996 season the club are in the Spartan League.

TOTTENHAM OMADA

Barking FC, Lodge Ave, Dagenham, Essex Tel: 0181 595 6511

Secretary: Lindsay Byaram, 33 Adlington Close, Edmonton N18 Tel: 0181 341 5068

Colours: Gold and blue

GROUND DETAILS AS PER BARKING FC

Honours

Spartan League Div 2 1994

Division One: 1995

London Senior Cup 1996

The club was first formed in 1983 as Park Vale FC, in the Haringey and District Sunday League. After four years they moved to the Brooks Waltham League, where they soon reached the Premier Division. In 1991 they entered the Forest and District League which they won in 1993, whereupon they switched to Saturday football and joined Division Two of the Spartan League, changing their name to Tottenham Wine FC.

Playing at Wadham Lodge, Walthamstow they won Division Two and reached the semi-final of the London Junior Cup, and a season later, playing at Snakes Lane, Woodford, they won Division One, finishing the season at the CRS ground in Hainault. Having gained senior status, they reached the Premier Division and agreed a ground share with Haringey Borough, but with the new name came a new ground as they moved in with Barking FC. They won the London Senior Cup in April, beating Kingsbury Town in the final.

WOODFORD TOWN

Wingate-Leyton Stadium, Lea Bridge Rd, London E10 Tel: 0181 539 5405

Secretary: Bill Robertson, 2 Humphrey Close, Clayhill, Ilford, Essex Tel: 0181 550 6680

Colours: Red and white

Seating: Yes

Covered standing: Yes

Capacity: 2,000

Floodlights: Yes

Clubhouse on ground: Yes

DIRECTIONS

Lea Bridge Road is on the A104 and the ground is next to the Hare & Hounds pub.

WALTHAM ABBEY

Capershotts, Sewardstone Rd, Waltham Abbey, Essex Tel: 01992 711287

Secretary and Press Alex Myers, 88 The Weymarks,
Weir Hall Road, Tottenham Tel: 0181 808 2706

Colours: Red and Black,

Nickname: The Abbey.

Capacity: 2,000,

Seating: 400

Covered standing: No,

Floodlights: Yes

Clubhouse on ground: Yes

Record attendance: 1,806 v Tottenham Hotspur
Charity Match

Record appearances: Colin Winter

Record goalscorer in one season: Paul Holloway

DIRECTIONS

The ground is just off M25, junction 26 - just follow the signs for Waltham Abbey. The nearest station is Waltham Cross (BR Eastern Region) 3 miles away. 242 bus.

Honours

Abbey Sports, Northern Suburban League 1952

Waltham Abbey Rovers FC, Northern Suburban League 1958 and 1969

Beechfield Sports(Waltham Abbey) FC, Essex Junior Cup 1976

Watham Abbey FC

London Spartan League Div 1 1978

Senior Division 1979

Manager: John Ward

Assistant manager: Joe Collins

Chairman: Joe Collins

Waltham Abbey Youth Club first played football on Capershotts during the Second War, and in later years Abbey Sports and Waltham Abbey Rovers both shared the ground, gaining numerous honours in the Northern Suburban League. The two merged in the late sixties as Waltham Abbey United and they expanded later by building a new clubhouse. In 1974 there was another amalgamation when Beechfield Sports came on board, and as Beechfield Sports (Waltham Abbey) FC, they joined the London Metropolitan League, which became the London Spartan League.

In 1976 the club won the Essex Junior Cup, and later that summer dropped the Beechfield Sports tag on the advice of the FA. Two years later the club reached the final of the Essex Intermediate Cup and won the League's Division One title, and having gained senior status, were promoted.

In their first season they won the title without losing a game and again were promoted to the Premier Division, where they remain.

Recent seasons have seen many changes on and off the pitch, with floodlights installed in 1990 and the pitch being levelled, but sadly the club fell foul of Essex FA and lost their senior status. The league, however, allowed the club to remain at their current placing.

Minerva South Mids League

PREMIER DIVISION

	P	W	D	L	F	A	PTS
Arlesey Town	32	24	2	6	64	27	74
Hatfield Town	32	22	5	5	79	31	71
London Colney	32	21	5	6	88	34	68
Brache Sparta	32	20	8	4	56	24	68
Toddington Rovers	32	14	9	9	50	45	51
Royston Town(-3)	32	13	11	8	48	36	47
Hoddesdon Town	32	12	8	12	49	44	44
Milton Keynes	32	13	4	15	55	70	43
Potters Bar Town	32	11	9	12	56	63	42
Biggleswade Town	32	12	5	15	51	50	41
Welwyn	32	11	7	14	53	62	40
Langford	32	10	8	14	30	48	38
Buckingham Athl	32	9	6	17	43	63	33
Harpenden Town	32	8	8	16	42	56	32
Dunstable United	32	6	7	19	33	71	25
Shillington	32	5	9	18	42	60	24
Letchworth Garden City	32	1	9	22	33	88	12

SNR DIV FINAL

	P	W	D	L	F	A	PTS
Holmer Green	26	19	5	2	71	31	62
Leverstock Green	26	17	6	3	63	26	57
Bedford United	26	16	3	7	57	32	51
New Bradwell SP	26	14	5	7	69	43	47
Totternhoe	26	13	6	7	52	44	45
Tring Athletic	26	13	4	9	66	37	43
Houghton Town	26	9	8	9	40	33	35
Winslow United	26	7	8	11	43	57	29
Risborough R.	26	7	7	12	35	56	28
ACD	26	7	6	13	46	42	27
Amphill Town	26	7	6	13	39	62	27
Stony Stratford	26	6	5	15	39	67	23
The 61 FC	26	5	4	17	28	71	19
Kent Athletic	26	3	5	18	31	78	14

DIVISION ONE

	P	W	D	L	F	A	PTS
Mercedes-Benz	32	21	7	4	69	25	70
De Havilland	32	21	6	5	86	44	69
Walden Rangers	32	21	5	6	72	42	68
Leighton Athletic	32	18	4	10	87	51	58
Crawley Green	32	16	6	10	52	42	54
Bridger Packaging (-3)	32	14	8	10	77	56	47
Caddington	32	13	8	11	57	54	47
Bow Brickhill	32	13	6	13	56	55	45
Buckingham Utd	32	14	1	17	58	53	43
Emberton	32	10	11	11	58	55	41
Flamstead	32	9	13	10	47	55	40
Abbey National	32	11	5	16	53	70	38
Scot	32	9	10	13	50	61	37
Old Dunstablians	32	7	7	18	43	70	28
Old Bradwell U	32	6	8	18	67	89	26
Pitstone & I	32	6	7	19	38	84	25
Cranfield United	32	6	4	22	45	87	22

Lamb Meadow, Hitchin Rd, Arlesey, Beds Tel: 01564 731448

Sec and Press: John Albon, 13 St Johns Rd, Arlesey, Beds SG15 6ST Tel: 01462 731318

Nickname: The Blues

Capacity: 8,000

Seating: 120

Covered standing: 1,000

Floodlights: Yes

Clubhouse on ground: Yes

Record attendance: 2,000 v Luton Town Res. Beds Senior Cup Final 1906

Record appearances: Gary Marshall

DIRECTIONS

On main road through village. From Hitchin, ground 200 yards past Biggs Wall on left.

Honours

FA VASE 1995

South Mids League 1952, 1953, 1995, 1996, Div 2 1930, 1932, 1936

Beds Intermediate Cup 1958

South Mids Premier Shield 1965, Beds Senior Cup 1966 and 1979

Hinchingbrooke Cup 1978, 1980, 1982

Biggleswade Knock-out Cup 1978 and 1981

South Mids Challenge Trophy 1980, Beds Premier Cup 1984

United Counties League 1985 and Premier K-O Cup 1988, South Mids Floodlit Cup 1991

Manager: Robbie O'Keefe, Assistant Manager: Brian Williams

Chairman: John Milton, Vice Chairman: Scott Geekie

Arlesey Town celebrated their centenary in 1991 and produced a superb club history, detailing the club's ups and downs. Written by Malcolm Skillings and Tony Smith, copies are still available from the club, price £3 plus postage. Before the War the club played in the flourishing Biggleswade and District League, entering the knock-out Cup. The Blues were very successful in both, winning them on many occasions. During the 1920's they joined the Beds County League, which later became known as the South Midlands League. The birth of the modern era began in the late 40's when officials purchased Lamb Meadow for £500, with an adjoining area being bought in 1952 for the clubhouse.During the past decade Lamb Meadow has been transformed, with floodlights being installed, hard standing around the pitch and a new entrance drive. New dressing rooms followed, with a physio room, boardroom and kitchen, with a second stand. The old stand was sadly destroyed in gales but within months a new and better one had been built. On the pitch, fortunes have fluctuated since the War, with successive titles in 1952 and 1953 seeing the club join the London League. Naturally a greater amount of travelling was needed and although reasonably successful, after five seasons they returned to the South Midlands League. The next two decades saw two Beds Senior Cup wins, three Hinchingbrooke Cup wins and two League Cup wins, which again prompted a move, in 1982, to the United Counties League. After two seasons in mid table the Premier Division title came their way, under Dave Mosley, but his departure led to a barren spell where the club eventually returned once again to the SML.

Recent seasons have seen a dramatic upsurge, with Vase runs and league exploits culminating in an astonishing season in 1994-95 which saw the league title won, but overshadowed by a remarkable FA Vase success over Oxford City at Wembley. Having lost the semi-final first leg against Raunds Town 3-0, the Town won the return 5-0 after extra time to take their place in the final. Celebrations followed, as did the league title again in 1995-96 as Town reigned as top dogs.

FORMER GROUNDS

Arlesey's early years were spent on various farmer's fields, including one belonging to a Mr Papworth, another near the Three Counties Station, Long Meadow, Lamb Meadow and the Common. The Bury Meadow was next from around 1900, until another move to the Lamb. They were then evicted and were dormant for a while until returning to the Bury between the Wars.

BEDFORD UNITED

C/O Bedford Town FC, Meadow Lane, Cardington, Beds Tel: 01234 838448

Secretary: Graham Ford, 59 Southville Rd, Bedford Tel: 01234 346806

Colours: Blue and white   Nickname: United

GROUND DETAILS AS PER BEDFORD TOWN FC

Record attendance: 852 v Bedford Town SML Div 1 1992

Record appearances: Simon Fordham   Record goalscorer in total: Brian Fibbs

Honours

Bedford and District League; Division One; Beds Junior Cup; Biggleswade KO Cup; Bedford Charity Cup

BIGGLESWADE TOWN

Fairfield Rd, Biggleswade, Beds Tel: 10767 312374

Secretary: Graham Arkwright, 21 Willsheres Rd, Biggleswade,
Beds SE18 0BU Tel: 01767 316992

Brian Doggett, 49 Winston Crescent, Biggleswade, Beds
Tel: 01767 318307

Colours: All Green   Nickname: Waders

Capacity: 2,000   Seating: 250

Covered standing: 150   Clubhouse on ground: Yes

> ## DIRECTIONS
> **A1 North roundabout, left immediately after metal bridge into car park. 10 minutes walk from Biggleswade Railway Station.**

Honours

South Mids Lge 1924 and Div 1 1953

League Cup 1993, Premier Div Trophy 1992

Beds Premier Cup 1923 and 1928

Beds Senior Cup 1903, 1908, 1947, 1952, 1962, 1963, 1967, 1974

Hunts Premier Cup 1993, 1994, 1995; Hinchingbrooke Cup 1904 and 1993; South Mids Floodlit Cup 1996

North Beds Charity Cup 1908, 1910, 1923, 1924, 1925, 1926, 1927, 1934, 1950, 1953, 1955, 1958, 1963, 1965, 1968, 1969, 1974, 1992, 1995

Jess Piggott Trophy 1988, 1990, 1992, 1993; United Counties League Cup 1964 and 1974

Manager 1996-97: David Earl; Chairman: Maurice Dorrington

Biggleswade FC were formed in 1874 and began playing friendlies. They were founder members of the District League in 1902, and won it at the first attempt along with the Beds Senior Cup. They first entered the FA Cup in 1904, losing to Watford, then a Southern League side and in 1907 reached the fourth qualifying round. They stayed in the league until 1919, having supplemented fixtures by entering the Bedford League at the same time, and by the outbreak of War had won the leagues four times in all. 1920 saw them join the strong Northants League (now the UCL) and the highest position was third in 1935, although they won a subsidiary competition called the Northants Alliance in 1929.

After the Second War, the Waders spent five seasons in the Spartan League before rejoining the UCL in 1951. From there they had an eight year spell in the Eastern Counties from 1955, but found the going tough in East Anglia. Again, in 1964 they reverted to the UCL where they stayed until 1980, a season which is probably the worst ever. The club dropped into the South Midlands League Division One and after a number of years finally gained promotion to the Premier Division in 1987.

Floodlights came to Fairfield in 1989 and success was in the air, with a Hinchingbrooke Cup win and a Premier Cup win in 1992. The following season was a marvellous one with a Beds Premier Cup final and four trophies won, the South Mids League Cup, Hinchingbrooke Cup, Hunts Premier Cup and Jesse Piggott Trophy. Since then Town have won more cups as their fine spell continues.

BRACHE SPARTA

Foxdell Sports Ground, Dallow Rd, Luton, Beds LU1 1UP Tel: 01582 20751

Secretary: Maurice Franklin, 62 Katherine Drive, Dunstable, Beds Tel: 01582 661177

Colours: White and navy

Capacity: 400

Seating: 25

Covered standing: Yes

Clubhouse on ground: Yes

Record goalscorer in total: Pat Walsh

DIRECTIONS

Left off A505 to Dunstable into Chaul Lane at roundabout. Proceed across new relief road — ground entrance adjacent to Foxdell Junior School.

Honours

Luton and District League 1968, 1970, 1971, 1972

William Pease Trophy 1967, 1968, 1971, 1972

Beds Intermediate Cup 1972

Brache Sparta FC was founded in 1960 by seventy engineers based at Vauxhall Motors Engineering block, taking the name from the fact that the block was built on part of the Brache Estate and as Russian sides were popular, Sparta was attached. They joined the Luton and District League and by 1972 had reached the top division and had been champions four times and the League Cup five times.

Following this success and discussions with the council, the club moved to Foxdell and joined the South Midlands League in 1975 after members had built the facilities with the help of a grant.

After a spell where they twice had to rebuild after successful sides broke up, they moved to groundshare at Hitchin Town to comply with the all floodlight rule for the league, but happily that has now been rectified and they are back at Foxdell.

BUCKINGHAM ATHLETIC

Stratford Fields, Stratford Rd, Buckingham Tel: 01280 816945

Secretary: A. Miller, 4 Middlefield Close, Buckingham
Tel: 01280 822050

Colours: All Sky blue

Nickname: Swans

Capacity: 1,500

Seating: No

Covered standing: 200

Clubhouse on ground: Yes

Floodlights: Yes

Honours

South Midlands Lge Div 1 1986 and 1991

Div 1 League Cup 1991

North Bucks League 1985, and League Cup 1984

League Shield 1961

Berks and Bucks Junior Cup 1966

Buckingham Charity Cup 1970 and 1972

DIRECTIONS

From Milton Keynes take the A422 Stony Stratford-Buckingham Road — ground on left just before town centre. From Aylesbury, turn right at 1st roundabout, across 2nd roundabout, left at third — ground at bottom of hill on left.

Formed in 1933 as Buckingham Juniors and with no ground, all the early games were away friendlies. It was 1936 before a pitch was found, known as Timms Meadow and now known as Stratford Fields. They entered the Brackley and District League before switching to the North Bucks League for the first time.

In 1939 the club name was changed to Buckingham Athletic but the War curtailed fixtures for them until 1946, where they finished runner up in the Brackley League and third in the Leighton League, simultaneously. In 1947 they returned to the North Bucks with moderate success with a couple of runners up spots and three different pitches, but they finally found a permanent home on Bourton Road in 1950. They continued in the North Bucks where they were often beaten finalists in local cups without winning one until 1960 when they took their first North Bucks Shield, celebrating by moving back to the original home in Stratford Fields. In 1965 the club were accepted into the Hellenic League, from where they won the Berks and Bucks Junior Cup. In 1969 they were promoted and enjoyed a fine spell which saw them given senior status, but soon a decline set in and they returned to junior status and the North Bucks League. Work started on the changing rooms and clubhouse in 1982 and three years later they won their first ever championship, unbeaten, moving to the South Midlands League in 1985. They won Division One and reached two finals, but with the ground not ready for promotion they were denied, but with more work and a strong side, they were promoted as Division One champions in 1991 and with the stand complete, they moved up. Since then they have regained senior status but have struggled to get above mid table.

HARPENDEN TOWN

Rothampstead Park, Amenbury Lane, Harpenden Tel: 01582 715724

Secretary: Stephen Whiting, 169 Grove Rd, Harpenden, Herts AL5 1SY Tel: 01582 761606

Colours: Yellow and blue   Nickname: The Town

Capacity: 1,500   Seating: 25

Covered standing: 100

Clubhouse on ground: Yes

DIRECTIONS

A1081 to Harpenden. Turn left/right at George Hotel into Leyton Road. Turn left into Amenbury Road, then left again (50 yards) into 'Pay and Display car park — the club entrance is signposted through car park to opposite corner.

Honours

South Mids Lge 1962 and 1965, Champions Shield 1968,

League Cup 1971, Div 1 1990 Prem Div Trophy 1990

Herts County Lge 1912, 1950, 1952, 1954

Aubrey Cup 1921, 1929, 1951, 1952

Mid-Herts Lge 1910 and 1921

Pratt Cup 1907, 1909, 1911

Herts Junior Cup 1902, 1910, 1912, 1921, 1926

Herts Intermediate Cup 1953

Herts Charity Shield 1968

Bingham Cox Cup 1897, 1903, 1910, 1921

Managers for 1996-97: Mart Nicholls and Paul Woolfrey

Chairman: Alan King

Vice Chairman: Peter Eagles

Harpenden Town FC was formed as Harpenden FC in September 1891. In the early years they played in both Mid-Herts and Herts County Leagues having success in both. Cup success also came frequently with over a dozen trophies up to 1930. Easter Monday 1910 was particularly busy, for they won the Bingham Cox Cup in the morning and the Herts Junior Cup in the afternoon. They added the 'Town' to the name in 1909.

The 1950's was the next successful era as in six years the club won the Herts County League three times with three runners up spots and wins in Aubrey Cup and Intermediate Cup. After one more season Town joined the South Midlands League in 1957 and won the Premier Division twice in 1962 and 1965. Three years later they took two shields and the Challenge Cup was added in 1971, but that proved to be the last honour for two decades.

The 80's began disastrously with relegation and in 1989 they had reached rock bottom and were forced to apply for re-election. Major work was needed to rescue the club and under Lee Edwards and Alan King, 1989 became a year of success as first and reserve teams won trophies, the club returning to the Premier Division as champions. Floodlights were installed in 1990 along with the centenary stand. Since then the club have remained in the top flight and have returned to FA Vase action, although last season was disappointing.

HODDESDON TOWN

Lowfield, Park View, Hoddesdon, Herts Tel: 01992 463133

Secretary: Brenda Timpson, 82 Tolmers Rd, Cuffley, Herts EN6 4JY Tel: 01707 874028

Programme: Jane and Colin Sinden, 22 Hatley Rd, Wrestlingworth, Sandy, Beds Tel: 01767 631297

Press officer: Roger Merton, Roselands House, College Rd, Hoddesdon, Herts EN11 9DJ Tel: 01992 441410

Nickname : Lowfielders or Lilywhites

Capacity: 3,000, Seating: 250 new stand being built

Covered standing: Yes, Clubhouse on ground: Yes

Record attendance: 3,500 V West Ham United
Floodlight opener, 1973

Biggest win: 20-0 v Croxley Herts Challenge Cup 1889

Biggest defeat: 0-15 v Enfield (A)
FA Cup 2nd Qual Rd 1959

Record appearances: Stuart Parker, Record goalscorer in total: Bert Haynes approx 600 1918 - 33

DIRECTIONS

A10, A1170 and follow signs to town centre until left-hand fork signposted Broxbourne, right at 1st mini-roundabout into Cock Lane and 1st right is Park View. Ground on 200 yards left opposite Park Road. Nearest BR station is Broxbourne.

Honours

FA VASE WINNERS 1975, South Mids Challenge Trophy 1986, 1987, 1992

Spartan League 1971, Div 1 1936, Div 2 B 1928, League Cup 1971 and 1972

Herts Senior Cup 1887, 1888, 1890, Herts Charity Shield 1948, 1971, 1972, 1979

Herts Centenary Trophy 1987, South Mids Floodlit Cup 1990

Waltham Hospital Cup 1928, Perry Charity Cup 1922, 1931, 1932, 1933, 1934 jt, 1935, 1936 7 times

Manager 1996-97: Ray Greenall, Assistant manager: Jim Briggs

Chairman: Roger Merton, Vice Chairman: Stewart Edwards

Hoddesdon Town voted Programme of the Year in 1995 and runner up in 1996.

Hoddesdon are the second oldest club in Hertfordshire, beaten in age only by Bishop's Stortford. They were co-founders of the Herts FA back in 1885, as Hoddesdon FC, playing on a pitch on Mancers Field. Four years later, with a change of name, they moved to Lowfield, which other than for one season, has remained home. They were the first winners of the Herts Senior Cup, in 1887, and won it again in 1888 and 1890, losing the final in the other year. The early years were spent in the East Herts, and Herts County Leagues, and after the Great War, they moved to the Spartan League, where they stayed for over 50 years, gaining many honours. Between the Wars the local Perry Charity Cup was won seven times, as was the Spartan League Division Two and the Waltham Hospital Cup. 1936 saw the Division One title, but relegation came immediately. After the War Hoddesdon were elected to the Premier Division where they stayed as one of the top clubs for many years, winning the Charity Shield. The mid 60'ssaw an upturn in fortunes after a lean spell, finishing runners-up in the league, but their finest year to date came in 1969, when they took the treble of Spartan League, League Cup and Herts Charity Shield. retaining the two cups the following year and finishing runners up a further three years running. Lowfield saw floodlights as early as 1973, when West Ham provided the opposition in front of 3,500 people. Three times that amount saw Town play in the first ever Wembley FA Vase final in 1975, when they beat Epsom and Ewell 2-1. It proved to be the start of a fruitful period, for Town were elected to the powerful Athenian League in 1977, from where they won the Shield again, but within seven years the league had disbanded and Town joined the South Midlands League.

The last twelve years has seen the club win a number of trophies as they enjoyed a spell under manager Terry Scales whose eight years saw vast improvements on and off the field.

LANGFORD

Forde Park, Langford Rd, Henlow SG16 6AF Tel: 01426 816106

Secretary: Frank Woodward, 4 West View, Langford, Biggleswade, Beds SG19 9RT Tel: 01462 701015

Other matters: June Roberts, 22 Queensway, Langford Tel: 01462 700613

Colours: Red and white

Nickname: Reds

Capacity: 2,000

Seating: 50

Covered standing: 200

Clubhouse on ground: Yes

Record attendance: 450 v Queens Park Rangers on Aug 22nd 1985 club opening

Record fee received £1,400 Ian Phelan to Bedford Town in 1991

DIRECTIONS

Halfway between Langford and Henlow on A6001 Hitchin to Biggleswade Road. Bus 177 on main Hitchin-Biggleswade route stops right outside the ground.

Honours

South Mids Lge 1989 League Cup 1974 and 1976

Premier Div Trophy 1989 and 1995

Division One Trophy 1985

North Beds Charity Cup 1928, 1931, 1970, 1976, 1987, 1993, 1995

Beds and District League 1931, 1932, 1933

Beds Intermediate Cup 1969

Hinchingbrooke Cup 1973

Manager 1996-97: Gerald Rogers

Assistant Manager: Andy Wellings

Chairman: Mick Quinlan

Vice Chairman: Dave Boswell

The club was formed in 1910 and played in the Bedford League where they were champions three years running in the 30's. They had much cup success during that time, only losing the Senior Cup to Bedford Town in the final.

After the war they joined the South Midlands League but waited 37 years before taking the title, but there has been plenty of silverware elsewhere, including Intermediate and Charity Cups, the best spell being in the 70's under Roland Legate. Unfortunately they were later relegated for five years, but came back in 1985.

They took the Premier Division in 1989 along with the Premier Div Trophy and since then have added further trophies, and have enjoyed runs in the FA Cup and Vase.

Since forming the club have used many pitches in the village, moving to Forde Park, an old tip site, in 1984.

LETCHWORTH

Baldock Road, Letchworth, Herts SG6 2GN Tel: 01462 684691

Match Sec: Jeff Gates, 296 Archer Rd, Stevenage, Herts SG1 5HH Tel: 01438 759971

Football Sec: Darren Hazelwood, 44 Truemans Rd, Hitchin, Herts Tel: 01462 456088

Press: Steve Sheppard, 44 Romany Cl, Letchworth, Herts SG6 4JZ Tel: 01462 673105

Best contact when confirming fixture: Darren Hazelwood

DIRECTIONS

Junction 9 (A6141) off A1M straight over large roundabout, right at next roundabout, ground on right. From Luton (A505) through Hitchin, ground 3 miles after Hitchin. 2 miles from Letchworth Railway Station.

Nickname: The Bluebirds

Capacity: 3,000   Seating: 200

Covered standing: 200   Floodlights: Yes

Clubhouse on ground: Yes

HONOURS

Herts County League 1912, Spartan League 1930, 1936, 1952

Delphian League 1958, Athenian League 1975

Memorial Shield 1966 and 1967, Herts Senior Cup 1913, 1936, 1952

Herts Charity Shield 1923, 1948, 1988, 1992, East Anglian Cup 1977

Woolwich Cup 1982, Hitchin Cup 1982

Manager: Graham Hopkins, Assistant manager: Hendy Manning

Chairman: Adrian Earl, Vice Chairman: Graham Hopkins

Letchworth Football Club was formed back in 1906 and have in the past been known as Garden City FC, Letchworth Athletic, Letchworth Town and Letchworth Garden City. The club spent its early days in the Herts County League and then the Biggleswade League before moving briefly to the North Herts League in 1908. Interest was growing in the club and they moved from a rough pitch on Garth Road to Cashio Road, where they changed their name to Letchworth Athletic. They went back to the Herts County League and enjoyed champion success in 1912. A year later the club won the first of three Herts Senior Cups, the others coming in 1936 and 1952. 1922 saw them join the Bedfordshire County League before moving up to the Spartan League, in 1924, after which they added to their honours list twice before the War. They had by then moved to Jackmans Meadow in Baldock Road, where they play today. After hostilities they won the Charity Shield, beating Welwyn Garden City in the final, which saw the start of their slow rise up the football ladder. The route took in the Delphian League, where they were champions in 1958, the Corinthian League and then the Athenian League, in 1963. Around the War, they had become Letchworth Town, and in 1975 they became Letchworth Garden City and finally this year, Letchworth FC.

They finally took the Athenian League title in 1975, before moving up to the Isthmian League, although their 15 year membership was not a great success. In 1990 they lost their Isthmian status when finishing bottom and losing out on a play-off. Relegation meant a new challenge in the South Midlands League, but it has been a struggle with just the Herts Charity Shield to show for their efforts. Last season began with a change of name, to Letchworth FC. The club are proud to have not only a club photographer in Lynda Sheppard, but a club artist who regularly has her work in the match programme and is working on a watercolour of Baldock Road in 2016.

LONDON COLNEY

Cotlandswick, London Colney, Herts Tel: 01727 822132

Secretary: David Brock, 50 Seymore Rd, St Albans, Herts AL3 5HW Tel: 01727 761644

Colours: All Royal blue

Nickname: Blueboys

Capacity: 1,000

Seating: 30

Covered standing: 70

Clubhouse on ground: Yes

DIRECTIONS

From London Colney roundabout (junction of A414/A1081) take A414 towards Watford, after layby (300 yds) turn left (hidden turning marked 'Sports Ground') and follow around to gates. Three miles from St Albans (BR). Buses 84 & 358.

Honours

Herts Charity Shield 1962 and 1994

Herts Sen Centenary Trophy 1990 and 1995

Herts Intermediate Cup 1959, 1975, 1983

Herts Junior Cup 1955

South Midlands Lge Sen Div 1995

Challenge Trophy 1994

Herts Co Lge 1957, 1960, 1987, 1989, 1990

Division One 1923, 1954, 1955

Division Two 1920 and 1949

Aubrey Cup 1922, 1923, 1957, 1959, 1982

Bingham Cox Cup 1921, 1954

Mid Herts Benevolent Cup 1928, 1930, 1949

Mid Herts Benevolent Shield 1952, 1953, 1954, 1955

Mid Herts Charity Cup 1949

St Albans Playing Fields Cup 1963, 1974, 1976, 1981

Frank Major Trophy 1975 and 1976

London Colney FC was formed in 1907 and played from the start at the Recreation ground in Whitehorse Lane until moving to the old redundant Marconi ground in Cotlandswick in 1975. They played in both the Mid Herts and Herts County Leagues until 1954 when they left the former, and have enjoyed numerous successes, winning the County League three times in five years in the late eighties.

In 1992 they moved up to the South Midlands League where they were runners up in the Senior Division in the first year and further honours came in 1994 with the Challenge Cup and Charity Shield. They took the Centenary Trophy in 1995 as well as the Senior Division and last May finished as runners up to the now sadly defunct Hatfield.

MILTON KEYNES

Manor Fields, Bletchley, Milton Keynes

Secretary: Nesham Galloway, 22 Bascote, Tinkers Bridge, Milton Keynes, MK6 3DW

Tel: 0956 948829

Colours: Red and black stripes

Capacity: 3,000

Seating: 160

Covered standing: Yes

Clubhouse on ground: Yes

Record attendance: 250 v Bedford Town in 1994

DIRECTIONS

M1 junctions 13 or 14. Take the old A5 south to Fenny Stratford. 500 yards on the left go over the bridge opposite Belvedere Nursuries into Manor Fields. The ground is on the right.

Milton Keynes FC was founded in 1993 when the previous club Milton Keynes Borough was wound up with financial debts. They took over the tenancy of the Manor Fields, originally the home of Southern League Bletchley Town. After much work and with days to spare, the Company formed to run the club gained a lease on the ground and permission from league, and in the first season finished bottom, but the second season saw two cup finals, although both were lost. Last season saw the club end in mid table as they strive to settle down in a new league.

Milton Keynes Borough was founded as a Sunday side called Bowen Cameras, changing to Denbigh United soon after. On changing to Saturdays they took the name Belsize FC and joined the UCL, changing again to MK Borough in 1976. They were successful briefly before moving to the Hellenic and then South Midland Leagues, and after two nightmare seasons at the bottom they were runners up to Leighton Town in 1992.

A year later, despite a comfortable position, the club went under, only to re-form as Milton Keynes FC.

POTTERS BAR TOWN

Parkfield Centre, The Walk, Potters Bar, Herts EN6 1QN
Tel: 01707 654833

Secretary: Peter Waller, 26 Queen Anne Grove, Bush Hill Pk, Enfield EN1 2JR Tel: 0181 360 7859

Colours: Red and blue stripes

Nickname: The Scholars or Grace

Capacity: 2,000

Seating: 25

Covered standing: Yes

Clubhouse on ground: Yes

Record attendance: 400 v Barnet opening floodlights 1993

Biggest win: 19-0 v Arkley NL Comb 1965

Biggest defeat: 1-9 v Rolls Royce Aubrey Cup 1970

Record appearances: Mick Holson 708 1960-1989

Record goalscorer in total: Mick Gray 260

Honours

Herts Co Lge 1991, Div 1 1974 and 1982

Aubrey Cup 1991

Herts Intermediate Cup 1974

Barnet and Dist Lge Div 1 1962

Barnet Junior Cup 1962

North London Comb 1968

Barnet Charity Cup 1964

Potters Bar Charity Cup 1977

DIRECTIONS

M25 to junction 24, into Potters Bar on Southgate Road (A111), turn right into High Street at first lights, turn left into The Walk after half a mile, ground is on the right in the school.

The foundations for Mount Grace Old Scholars FC were laid in 1959, when the school's senior PE master helped form the club which joined the Barnet League in June 1970. Within a year they had won the league and cup double and when the league merged with the Finchley League to form the North London Combination, the Scholars fielded three teams in that league. 1968 saw the first and reserve teams both win their championships which saw the club admitted to the Herts County League Division Two which they won at the first attempt. By 1974 they had won the Premier Division and the Intermediate Cup, but they endured much strife in 1978 and the club almost went under suffering a humiliating season as all three teams were relegated. They survived and by 1982 were up again as Division One champions.

With a new clubhouse and a strong back room, the club progressed and reached the Aubrey Cup final and were accepted into the FA Vase, eventually doing the double in 1991, as well as reaching the third round of the Vase.

As the club moved into the South Midlands League, so the club name changed to Potters Bar Town and with a new stand and dug outs and floodlighting, to enable the club to stay in the top division.

They have since made their debut in the FA Cup and last season finished mid table in the Premier Division.

ROYSTON TOWN

Garden Walk, Royston, Herts SG8 7HP Tel: 01763 241204

Secretary: Trevor Glasscock, 39 Poplar Dr, Royston, Herts S98 7ER Tel: 01673 230783

Colours: White and black

Nickname: The Crows

Capacity: 4,000

Seating: 300

Covered standing: 300

Clubhouse on ground: Yes

Record attendance: 876 v Aldershot Town Isthmian League 1993

Biggest win: 13-2 v Addmult SML 1979

Biggest defeat: 0-9 v Bromley, Barnet and Stevenage Boro.

Record appearances Fred Bradley 713

Record goalscorer in total Trevor Glasscock 289 1968-1982

DIRECTIONS

From Baldock, A505 to Royston bypass, right at 2nd island onto A10 towards London, 2nd left is Garden Walk; ground 100 yds on left. From A11, exit 10 turning left onto A505, left at 1st island, 2nd left is Garden Walk. Ten mins walk from Royston (BR).

Honours

Herts Co.Lge 1977 and Div 1 1970 and 1973

South Midlands Lge Div 1 1978

Herts Charity Shield 1982 and 1990

Creake Shield 1921

Cambridge League Div 2 1930

Manager 1996-97: Paddy Butcher

Chairman: Tony Moulding

Vice Chairman: Bernard Brown

Formed way back in 1875, the Crows have played in the Buntingford and District League from 1919 to 1929, the Cambridgeshire League until 1948 and the Herts County League from then until 1960. They had two years in the South Midlands before returning to the Herts County until 1977 when they again moved to the SML. From there they moved up to the Isthmian League until taking a voluntary step down in 1994, back to the SML.

During that time the club used grounds at Newmarket Rd, Baldock Rd and Mackerall Hall before settling at Garden Walk in 1923. Their first major honour came in the Herts County League in 1970 and they went on to win it twice more in the 70's before moving on to the SML. They won the Charity Shield in 1983 and three years later accepted the invite to the Isthmians. Sadly they went down to the 3rd Division in 1991 and after falling foul of ground gradings and with meagre gates, they resigned to turn once again to the SML, under ex-Spurs star Tony Galvin.

TODDINGTON ROVERS

Barton Rovers FC, Sharpenhoe Rd, Barton-le-Clay, Beds Tel: 01582 882607

Secretary: To be announced

Colours: Black and white stripes   Nickname: Rovers

GROUND DETAILS AS PER BARTON ROVERS FC

Biggest win: 11-0 v Luton St Marys 1981   Biggest defeat: 0-9 v Bidwell 1957

Record appearances: George Stewart 1050   Record goalscorer in total: David Ashby

Honours

Luton and South Beds Lge Div 1 1930, 1931, 1932; Division Two 1929 and 1948, Division Three 1927 and 1989; Division Four 1926; Bedfordshire Junior Cup winners Cup 1931; South Midlands Lge Sen Div and League Cup 1994; Premier Division Cup 1996

The club was formed in 1894 as Toddington Stars and in 1898 joined the Luton and South Beds League as founder members where they stayed until 1989 when they moved up to the SML. In 1903 the name was changed to Toddington, but it was not until 1924 that they took the 4th Division title. Two seasons later, 'Rovers' went one better and were Div 3 champions. They won Division 2 three years running and the Beds Junior Cup, but then went 16 years before ending the drought with another Div 1 championship in 1947. The club then had a poor spell, enlivened by a couple of Cup finals which did not finish until the committee applied and were accepted into the South Midlands League, starting a five year run of success with the Senior Division championship and Cup and a runners up place in the Senior Division and Beds Senior Cup. Having been nomadic for a while, they are currently ground sharing with Barton Rovers.

WELWYN GARDEN CITY

Herns Lane, Welwyn Garden City Tel: 01707 328470

Secretary: Keith Browne, 12 Lemsford Rd, Hatfield,
Herts AL10 0DH Tel: 01707 251854

Colours: Maroon and white   Nickname: Citizens
Capacity: 1,500   Seating: Yes
Covered standing: Yes   Clubhouse on
ground: Yes
Record attendance: 600 v Welwyn Garden City

Honours

Herts Senior Centenary Trophy 1985
Herts Charity Shield 1928, 1987, 1988, 1995
South Midlands Lge 1974 and Div 1 1970 and 1982.

DIRECTIONS

From A1 follow signs for industrial area. Take one-way system opposite Avdel Ltd (signed Hertford B195), take 2nd exit off one-way system. Ground 400 yards on left. One and a half miles from Welwyn GC Railway Station.

Founded in 1921, Welwyn started their days in the Metropolitan League before moving to the Spartan League in 1927. That season saw the Charity Shield won, but it was after the Second War that with Harry Hibbs, the ex-England Goalkeeper as manager they entered the London League. 1954 saw a move back to the Spartans, but they were forced to drop down into County League football in 1959. They played at Springfields, but in 1968 moved to the new stadium at Herns Lane as a senior club.

In 1973 they moved to the South Midlands League, winning it at the first attempt, but by 1977 they had been relegated and it took until 1982, when they won Division One by a mile in scoring over 100 goals, to return. The late eighties saw lights come to the ground and a number of trophies including two wins of the Charity Shield, but since then the club have not set the league alight and were below mid-table last May.

VOTED NON-LEAGUE PROGRAMME OF THE YEAR FOR 1994/95 BY THE WIRRAL PROGRAMME CLUB.

HODDESDON TOWN FOOTBALL CLUB FOUNDED 1879

v SHILLINGTON
SMFL. PREMIER DIVISION
Saturday 13th APRIL 1996 K.O. 3.00 p.m.

OFFICIAL PROGRAMME 1995/96

MEMBERS OF THE MINERVA FOOTBALLS
SOUTH MIDLANDS FOOTBALL LEAGUE

60p

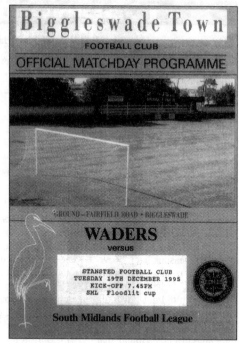

Biggleswade Town
FOOTBALL CLUB
OFFICIAL MATCHDAY PROGRAMME

GROUND—FAIRFIELD ROAD • BIGGLESWADE

WADERS
versus

STANSTED FOOTBALL CLUB
TUESDAY 19TH DECEMBER 1995
KICK-OFF 7.45PM
SML Floodlit cup

South Midlands Football League

MERCEDES-BENZ
FOOTBALL CLUB
FOUNDED 1967
AFFILIATED TO THE BERKS AND BUCKS FA

minerva® footballs

South Midlands Football League
Official Match Programme

The Barn, Downs Barn, Milton Keynes, Bucks

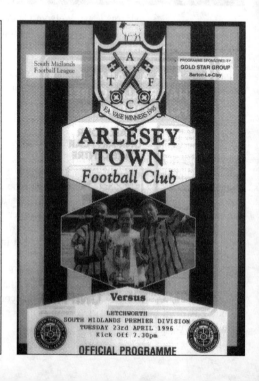

South Midlands Football League

PROGRAMME SPONSORED BY
GOLD STAR GROUP
Barton-Le-Clay

A T F C
F.A. VASE WINNERS 1995

ARLESEY TOWN
Football Club

Versus

LETCHWORTH
SOUTH MIDLANDS PREMIER DIVISION
TUESDAY 23rd APRIL 1996
Kick Off 7.30pm

OFFICIAL PROGRAMME

COMBINED COUNTIES LEAGUE

	P	W	D	L	F	A	PTS
Ashford Town (Middx)	42	32	7	3	111	36	103
Chipstead	42	30	4	8	102	44	94
Peppard	42	23	8	11	86	58	77
Merstham	42	22	9	11	89	66	75
Farnham Town	42	20	12	10	71	52	72
Godalming & Guildford	42	19	10	13	79	55	67
Reading Town	42	20	6	14	76	69	66
Feltham(-1)	42	18	10	14	94	86	63
Bedfont(+3)	42	18	6	18	67	64	63
Ash United	42	17	12	13	74	73	63
Westfield	42	17	11	14	69	67	62
Sandhurst Town	42	18	7	17	77	89	61
Netherne	42	16	12	14	78	64	60
D.C.A. Basingstoke	42	15	6	21	56	73	51
Eton Wick	42	13	11	18	71	81	50
Hartley Wintney	42	13	6	23	47	88	45
Viking Sports(+1)	42	11	9	22	58	85	43
Cranleigh	42	11	8	23	70	94	41
Cobham	42	12	4	26	59	84	40
Walton Casuals	42	10	8	24	46	67	38
Raynes Park Vale(-3)	42	10	7	25	58	97	34
Horley Town	42	6	9	27	49	95	27

ASH UNITED

Young's Drive off Shawfield Rd, Ash. Tel: 01252 20385

Secretary: Mr Alan Haberle, 30 Longfield Rd, Ash, Aldershot, Hants GU12 6NA. Tel: 01252 658351

Colours: Red and green

Capacity: 1,500

Seating: No

Covered standing: 300 overhang on clubhouse

Clubhouse on ground: Yes

Floodlights: Yes

Biggest win: 11-0 v Fleet Town 1986
and 11-0 v Yateley 1986

Biggest defeat: 1-9 v Chipstead

Manager 1996-97: Alex Smith-Gander

Assistant Manager: Gerry Kerrigan

Chairman: Bob Atkins

Vice Chairman: Cliff Foster

Programme : Gareth Watmore, 69 Longacre, Ash, Aldershot GU12 6RW Tel 657944

DIRECTIONS

Take A323 towards Ash, left into Shawfield Road, right into Ash Church Road, right at crossroads into Shawfield Road.

ASHFORD TOWN (MIDDLESEX)

Short Lane, Stanwell, Middx. Tel: 01784 245908

Secretary Alan Constable, 30 Marlborough Rd, Ashford, Middx TW15 3QA. Tel: 01784 885092

Nickname: The Ash Trees   Capacity 2,000

Seating/Æ None

Covered Standing: 75   Clubhouse On Ground: Yes

Record Attendance: 750 v Brentford July 20th 1986

Biggest Win: 12-0 v Horley.

Biggest Defeat: 0-7 v Tolworth Dec 3rd 1983

Record Appearances: Alan Constable 650.

Record Goalscorer In One Season:
Paul German 51 in 1995-96

Record Goalscorer In Total: Andy Smith

DIRECTIONS

M25 junction 13, take A30 towards London, third left after Ashford Hospital crossroads, ground is signposted on right after quarter mile down Short Lane.

Honours

Combined Counties League 1995 and 1996. Surrey Premier League 1989. Surrey Premier Cup 1990. Southern Combination Cup 1996.

Bar steward (full time) to check fixture Iain Messenger 01784 245908

Manager For 1996-97: Dave Kent.

Chairman: Bob Parker. Vice Chairman: Peter Heffernan

Press Officer: Dave Baker, c/o Club. Physio: Don Hanks

Clubhouse is open all day, seven days a week, with hot food on matchdays with patio and barbecue. The Secretary is always willing to swop Ashford programmes for other non-League.

Ashford Town FC was formed as recently as 1964 and first competed in the Hounslow and District League. The young team advanced through the divisions absorbing the old Staines Youth Club FC on the way. They were elected to the Surrey Intermediate League (Western) in 1967 and after one season of consolidation, worked their way to the Premier Division, winning league and cup honours on the way. Prior to the 1982-83 season, the Surrey County FC invited the club into the County Premier League.

From the start the club had always wanted its own ground and eventually a long lease was signed with Spelthorne Borough Council, enabling the club to move to Short Lane, Stanwell. From what was nothing more than a field, the facilities were quickly developed, with the first match taking place in February 1986.

The club now possess a modern clubhouse and the pitch is railed all round with cover for 75 and the floodlights were installed in September 1995.

In 1990 the club affiliated to both Middlesex and Surrey and in their last season as an Intermediate club, they reached the final of both County Cups, winning the Surrey version but losing to Willesden Hawkeye in Middlesex. Having finished runners up, they entered the Combined Counties as a senior team and have since enjoyed much success, finishing second in all three league competitions in 1994 before taking the league easily for the last two seasons.

BEDFONT

The Orchard, Hatton Road, Bedfont, Middlesex. Tel: 01 890 7264

Secretary and Press: Geoff Knock, 187 Northumberland Crescent, Bedfont, Middlesex TW14 9SR

Other contact: The Steward at the Football Club

Colours: Blue and Yellow

Capacity: 3,000

Seating: In process of being built

Covered Standing: Yes

Floodlights: Yes

Clubhouse On Ground: Yes

Record Attendance: 500

DIRECTIONS

Turn down Faggs Road opposite Hatton Cross station (Picadilly Line) on Great South Western Road (A30), then take a sharp right into Hatton Road. The ground is opposite the Duke of Wellington pub.

Honours

Combined Counties League Vase 1993

Harold Clayton Cup 1991

Surrey Premier League 1985 and 1987

Middlesex Premier League 1974 and 1977

Middlesex Intermediate Cup 1970 and 1977

Middlesex League Div 1 Cup 1972, 1979, 1980

Hounslow and District League Div 1 1987

Manager For 1996-97: Alan Humphries

Assistant Manager: Bob Barnes

Chairman: Alan Hale

Vice Chairman: Keith Stone

Bedfont FC were founded in 1900 as Bedfont Institute and in 1968 amalgamated with two other local clubs, Bedfont Rangers, founded in 1950, and Fairholme United, formed in 1953. They joined forces to become Bedfont FC. They were also joined in 1973 by Interharvester FC and in 1988 Bedfont Eagles were welcomed into the set up to complete the modern day club.

Bedfont run three teams, plus a Sunday side.

CHIPSTEAD

High Road, Chipstead, Surrey. Tel: 017375 53250

Secretary: G.Corner, 20 Sunnymede Avenue, Carshalton, Surrey. SM5 4JF. Tel: 0181 642 0827

Chairman: Keith Rivers 52B Oakhill Rd, Sutton, Surrey SM1 3AE Tel 0181 641 0955

Nickname: Chips

Capacity: 2,600   Seating: 45   Covered Standing: 60

Floodlights: Yes   Clubhouse On Ground: Yes

Record Attendance: 480

Biggest Win: 9-0   Biggest Defeat: 1-6

Record Appearances: Alan Dorrill

Record Goalscorer In One Season: Lee May   49

Record Goalscorer In Total: Billy Paterson

Record Fee Paid Or Received £12,000

DIRECTIONS

Brighton Road northbound, left into Church Lane, left into Hogcross Lane, right into High Road. One and a half miles from Chipstead Railway Station.

Honours

As senior club..Surrey Senior League Cup 1983, 1984, 1985. Combined Counties Challenge Cup 1987, 1991, 1993, 1995. Combined Counties League 1990

Manager For 1996-97: Dave Swindlehurst, Chairman and Press Officer: K. Rivers Vice Chairman: D. Parsons

Chipstead FC was formed in 1906 and the oldest club records, dated 1911, show that they were far from healthy, with survival relying on occasional whist drives. They changed at the White Hart pub after the Great War, and as things got easier they were able to hire an open topped lorry from a local builder to transport the players to away games. For 56 years the club played junior football, but having finished runners up in the County Junior Cup the previous year they then moved into the Surrey Intermediate League. In 1982 they became founder members of the re-formed Surrey Senior League and finished runners up three times, winning the League Cup three times, and keeping the cup for good.

After a long battle they were given senior status in 1986 and were promoted to the Combined Counties League where they took the title in 1990. Since then six League Cup finals have been reached, with entries into the FA Vase and FA Cup confirming their rise to prominence.

COBHAM

Leg O'Mutton Field, Downside Bridge Rd, Cobham, Surrey. Tel: 0181 397 0433

Secretary: Ken Reed, 29 Waterer Gardens, Tadworth, KT20 5PB. Tel: 01737 352641

Colours: All Red

Capacity: 2,000

Floodlights: No

Clubhouse on ground: Yes

Record attendance: 2,000 for Showbiz X1 in 1975

DIRECTIONS

A307 (Portsmouth Road) towards Leatherhead, right into Between Streets, right into Downside Road turn right opposite car park. Two miles from Cobham & Stoke D'Abernon Railway Station.

CORINTHIAN CASUALS

King George's Field, Hook Rise South, Tolworth, Surrey KT6 7NA Tel: 0181 397 3368

Secretary: Brian Wakefield, 5 Martingales Close,
Richmond Surrey TW10 7JJ Tel 0181 940 9208

Match Sec: Gerry Young, 227 Lynmouth Ave, Morden,
Surrey SM4 4RX Tel 0181 330 6643

Press: Geoff Brigden 32 West Ave, Wallington,
Surrey SM6 8PM Tel 0181 395 0593

Colours: White and navy blue   Nickname: Casuals

Capacity: 1,700   Seating: 126

Covered standing: 500   Clubhouse on ground: Yes

DIRECTIONS

A3 to Tolworth roundabout (The Toby Jug). Hook Rise is slip road immediately after the Toby Jug pub. Turn left under railway bridge after a quarter miles - ground immediately on right. Half mile from Tolworth (BR); turn left, continue to Toby Jug, then as above. K2 Hoppa bus from Kingston passes ground.

Honours

CORINTHIANS formed 1882

Sheriff of London Shield 1898 jt with Sheffield Utd, 1900 and 1904

THE CASUALS formed 1883

London Senior Cup 1887 jt

London Charity Cup 1891, 1894, 1897, 1901, 1905, 1907 jt, AFA Senior Cup 1908

FA AMATEUR CUP 1936, CORINTHIAN-CASUALS amalgamated 1939

FA AMATEUR CUP runners up 1956, Surrey Senior Cup 1954, Spartan League Sen Div 1986

General Manager 1996-97: Steve Bangs, 1st team Manager: Roger Speer,

Corinthian Casuals is possibly the most recognisable name in sport, although it only came about in 1939, through the merger of the two clubs who were formed within a year of each other in the 1880's.

Corinthians were founded by 'Pa' Jackson, a leading figure in the FA and he aimed to develop a club to challenge Scotland at International level. He called on all the best amateurs from Old Boys and Universities and within four years there were nine Corinthians in the England team. Casuals were even more exclusive, coming from Charterhouse, Eton and Westminster at first, although soon it went open to all public school and University players. They played in the first Amateur Cup final in 1894 and in 1905 founded the Isthmian League. In 1907 they were founder members of the Southern Amateur League and helped launch the AFA Senior Cup, winning the first tournament. After the Great War both clubs drew vast crowds, particularly in the FA Cup, with 60,000 seeing a replay with Millwall in 1930, at Stamford Bridge. Casuals won the Amateur Cup in 1936 after a draw with Ilford and Corinthians were regularly touring in Europe, but the gap with amateurs and pros was widening and Corinthians were suffering from not competing in leagues. The two clubs were close, often swapping players and talk of a merger was rife, but events elsewhere started the ball rolling, when the Crystal Palace was burned to the ground, taking Corinthian's HQ with it. The merger took place in 1939, but six days after Corinthian Casuals played their first Isthmian League match, Germany invaded Poland. The club was kept on and when competitve football returned they played on shared grounds, including Kingstonian, Chiswick Polytechnic, the Oval, Crystal Palace, Motspur Park, Wimbledon, Tooting and Mitcham and Molesey. In 1983 the league vetoed groundsharing and the club were forced to leave and join the Spartan League. In truth they had struggled as amateurs in a professional league, but happily the problem of never having had a home ground finally ended when Tolworth FC contacted the club to say that their clubhouse project was in trouble and would Casuals be interested. Three months later a deal was done and the Tolworth club was merged into Corinthian Casuals. The ground was fenced, the pitch enclosed and Corinthian Casuals could celebrate their first home and make plans to maybe return to the Isthmian League. In the summer of 1996 they left the Spartan League to play in the more localised Combined Counties League and are technically one step away from their goal.

COVE

Oak Farm, off Romayne Close, Cove, Farnborough Hants, GU14 8LB. Tel: 01252 543615

Secretary: Graham Brown, c/o Football Club
Tel: 01252 541152 (h)

Colours: Amber and black   Capacity: 3,500

Seating: 75   Covered standing: 400

Clubhouse on ground: Yes

Record attendance: 1,798 v Aldershot Town
Isthmian Lge 1993

Biggest win: 10-2 v Sway Feb 1974

Biggest defeat: 2-8 v Merrow 1969

Record appearances: Nigel Thompson 188

Record goalscorer in total: Nigel Thompson 164

Record fee paid £250 for Nick Horton to Egham Town in 1993

DIRECTIONS

Farnborough (BR) 2 miles; right into Union Street, right at lights into Prospect Rd, left into West Heath Road, right into Romayne close and follow signs to Cove F.C. Or, M3 jct 4, follow A325 signed Aldershot & Farnham. right into Prospect Ave (signposted Cove F.C and Farnborough Town FC), then as above.

Honours

Surrey Premier League 1950, 1952, 1954, 1964, 1968

League Cup 1960, 1961, 1970

Combined Counties League Cup 1982

Hampshire League Div 3 1977, Division 4 1974

Aldershot Senior Cup 1972, 1978, 1980, 1991, 1992

Southern Combination Floodlit Cup 1993

Aldershot Senior Shield 1938, 1939, 1947, 1972

Aldershot Senior League 1954 and Div 2 1933, 1938, 1939

Div 2 Cup 1951 and Div 4 Cup 1931

Cove FC were formed back in 1897, but most of their history has been spent in local football. They played in both the Farnham and Aldershot Junior Leagues with some success before entering the Aldershot Intermediate League in 1945 and Surrey Intermediate League in 1948. They were champions three years running but surprisingly returned to the Aldershot League which they won in 1954.

They had played from the start at Cove Green but in 1973 the club acquired the site of Oak Farm and began to fashion a clubhouse and ground, enabling them to join the Hampshire League in 1974 after a short spell in the Surrey Senior League. They won Division Four in 1975 and Division Three in 1978 and following a runners up spot in 1981 they were accepted into the old Surrey Senior League, which had become the Combined Counties, reaching the Premier Division after the league was reorganised.

Due to the development of the ground, Cove were elected to the Isthmian League in 1990, but it has been a struggle since and with ever more stringent gradings the club took the decision to drop back into the Combined Counties for this season.

CRANLEIGH

Snoxall Playing Fields, Knowle Lane, Cranleigh. Tel: 01483 275295

Secretary: Mark Edwards, 15 High Town Rd, Maidenhead, Berks SL6 1PA. Tel: 01628 783922

Colours: Blue and yellow

Nickname: Cranes

Capacity: 450

Seating: No

Covered standing: Yes

Clubhouse on ground: Yes

Floodlights: No

Record attendance: 450 v Crystal Palace Friendly 1989 and 285 v Hailsham Town FA Vase 1992

Biggest win: 9-1 v Merstham League Cup 1992

DIRECTIONS

A281 from Guildford towards Horsham, at Shalford take B2128 to Cranleigh High Street, right opposite Onslow Arms into Knowle Lane, ground half mile on left. Public transport: Guildford (BR) then bus 273 or 261.

Honours

West Sussex County Times Cup 1993

FARNHAM TOWN

Memorial Ground, Babbs Mead, West Street, Farnham, Surrey. Tel: 01252 715305

Secretary: Mrs Barbara Fripp, 70 Lower Farnham Rd, Aldershot, Hampshire GU12 4EA. Tel: 01252 28055

Colours: Claret and blue

Capacity: 2,000

Seating: No

Covered standing: Yes

Clubhouse on ground: Yes

Floodlights: Yes

Record attendance: 500 v Kingstonian

Surrey Senior Cup 1960

DIRECTIONS

Take A325 (West Street) at junction with A31 Farnham bypass, then first right. From Farnham (BR), left into Station Hill, left into Union Road, round Downing Street, left into West Street and Babbs Mead is 3rd left.

Honours

Combined Counties League 1991 and 1992

FELTHAM

Feltham Arena, Shakespeare Ave, Feltham, Middx TW14 9HY. Tel: 0181 384 5048

Secretary: John Cronk, 37 Ruskin Avenue, Feltham, Middx TW14 9HY. Tel: 0181 751 3663

Capacity: 10,000

Seating: 650

Covered standing: 500

Floodlights: Yes

Clubhouse On Ground: Yes

Record Attendance: 1,938 v Hampton Middlesex Senior Cup 1968

Record Appearance Holder: Paul Clarke 326

Record Goalscorer In Total: Paul Clarke 130

DIRECTIONS

BR to Feltham then 5 mins walk through Glebelands Park. Buses 90, 285, 117, 237, H24 or H25 to Feltham Station, or 116 to top of Shakespeare Avenue. By car: M3, M4, A312 Staines road towards Bedfont, second left is Shakespeare Avenue.

Honours

Surrey Senior League Cup 1966

Charity Cup 1964 and 1966

Southern Combination Cup

Feltham dropped the suffix "& Hounslow Borough" last season, four years after their amalgamation with Hounslow. Feltham FC were founded in 1946 as Tudor Park FC and competed under that name until 1962-63. They were originally members of the West Middlesex Sunday League but in 1949 they became affiliated to the Middlesex County FA and commenced playing on Saturdays in the Staines and District League. They were champions in 1951 and 1955 when they took a place in the Hounslow and District League before eventually moving up to the Parthenon League.

After moving to their present ground, Feltham FC was born and they turned senior, joining the Surrey Senior League. After five seasons they moved on to the Spartan League where they were runners up, and in 1973 they were promoted. Although winning no league honours, Feltham took the League Charity Cup in 1964 and 1966 as well as the League Cup the same year. In 1977, along with many other Athenians, they were elected to the Isthmian League, winning the Division Two championship in 1981. Three years later they went down, and had a couple of near misses in the Middlesex Charity Cup as their only consolation, until the merger with Hounslow.

For ten years Feltham's Arena ground has had an artificial surface, the running track around the ground having been dispensed with to accommodate it. With problems with that, and ground gradings, they resigned from the league in 1994, to play in the Combined Counties League. Last season saw them lose in the final of the Southern Combination Cup to Ashford Town, but with the prospect of a grass pitch returning, and major changes at the Arena, there is again hope for Feltham FC.

GODALMING AND GUILDFORD

Weycourt, Meadrow, Godalming, Surrey. Tel: 01483 417520

Secretary: Eddie Russell, 75 Drummond Rd, Guildford, Surrey GU1 4NX. Tel: 014835287

Nickname: The Weys,

Capacity: 1,500   Seating: 200,

Covered standing: No

Floodlights: Yes,

Clubhouse on ground: Yes

DIRECTIONS

A1300 from Guildford - carry on past Godalming Rugby Club and ground on right just after Burmah garage. Coming out of Godalming on A3100, ground on left by Leather Bottle pub. Three quarters of a mile from Farncombe BR station.

Record attendance: 600+ Ex-Guildford v Ex-Football League Tony Burge Benefit

Biggest win: 11-2 v Fleet Town

Record appearance holder: Paul Monger 322

Record goalscorer in total: Paul Hampshire 123

Honours

Combined Counties League 1984

Challenge Trophy 1983

Surrey Intermediate League Cup 1972

Manager for 1996-97: Mick Wollen, Assistant Manager: Chris Hatchwell

Chairman: Ron Rawlings, Vice Chairman: Dave Pullen

The club was formed in the early 50's by ex-pupils of Godalming County Grammar School who got together a team playing under the name of Godalming United FC from the 60's. In 1971 United joined forces with the ex-Surrey Senior League side Farncombe and took over the facilities at Weycourt. The club assumed the name of Godalming and Farncombe United and they played in the Surrey Intermediate League (Western Division). They had extensive work to do on the new pitch which was built on an old waste site, replacing the previous ground which is next door and now the site of Weycourt Sheltered Residence.

The club were successful in the Intermediate League, the reserves were runners up in B Div and the first team won the Premier Division Challenge Cup, and in 1978 they applied for senior status which was granted. The Combined Counties League accepted them for the 1979 season and a year later the name was changed to Godalming Town. As Town they won the league in 1984 after taking the Concours Trophy a year earlier, and the reserves have featured in their Cup final four times.

At the close of the 1991-92 season, the Guildford Football Appeal granted a sum of money to the club towards the erection of floodlights and in return the name of Guildford was incorporated into the club name.

On the sad demise of Addlestone FC, their stand and post and rails were purchased by the club and form part of the ground today.

HARTLEY WINTNEY

Memorial Playing Fields, Green Lane, Hartley Wintney, Hants. Tel: 01252 843586

Secretary: Ross Hilaire

Colours: Tangerine and black

Nickname: The Row

Capacity: 2,000

Seating: No

Covered standing: 200

Clubhouse on ground: Yes

Record attendance: Rothwell Town FA Vase 1992

Record appearances: Ray Shipman and Andy Spiers

Record goalscorer in total: Billy Bishop

Record goalscorer in season: Paul McMahon 60

Manager 1996-97: Ray Reagan and Martin Russell

Chairman: Fred Humphries

DIRECTIONS
A30 west through Camberley, left
at parade of shops at beginning of
village then sharp right - ground
on right. Two miles from
Winchfield Railway Station.

MERSTHAM

Merstham Rec, Weldon Way, Merstham, Redhill, Surrey. Tel: 01737 644046

Secretary: Matthew Boardman, 49 Orpin Rd, Merstham, Surrey RH1 3EX. Tel: 01737 212543

Other contact: Joe McElligott, 169 Albury Rd, Merstham Surrey. Tel: 01737 2121962

Colours: Amber and black,

Nickname: The Buzz

Capacity: 3,000,

Seating: 100

Covered standing: No, Clubhouse on ground: Yes

Floodlights: Yes, Record attend: 446 v Billericay Town

Biggest win: 11-0,

Biggest defeat: 1-9

DIRECTIONS

Leave Merstham village (A23) by School Hill, take 5th right (Weldon Way), clubhouse and car park 100m on right. Ground also accessible from Albury Road (2nd right off School). 10 mins walk from Merstham (BR); down School Hill, under railway bridge, fork left then right into Albury Road, ground entrance half way down on left.

Honours

Redhill and District League 1935, 1936, 1950, 1951

Combined Counties Elite Class Cup 1990, London Spartan League Cup 1980

Surrey Senior League 1972, Surrey Senior Charity Cup 1980

East Surrey Charity Cup 1981, Surrey Intermediate League East 1953

Manager for 1996-97: Joe McElligott, Assistant Manager: Martin Rosser, Chairman: Stan Baker

The history of Merstham Football Club dates back to 1892 when they played on a pitch at the old Merstham Lime Works which was between Joliffe Road, Lime Works Rd or Quarry Dean Lane. At the time the club had strong links with the Primary School and team pictures often adored the walls of the classrooms. In the early days players changed behind a hedge but after some time accommodation was found at the Joliffe Arms, later known as Detriots. In 1897 they were founder members of the Redhill and District League and just after the Great War they moved to the current ground at Albury Road, although it is believed they played under the Presidency of the Reverend Woodhouse they played at `The Weir', next to the current cricket ground. The Rec in those days was private land used for grazing cattle and in 1928 the landowner presented the top area to the town. Within a year the club were champions and a year from then they won the East Surrey Junior Cup. The ground began to take shape in 1933 when the Borough Council took over the running of the area, and the club prospered through 1935 and 1936 winning the league twice running, repeating it in 1950 and 1951. Merstham gained intermediate status and joined the Surrey Intermediate League, Eastern Section and they won the title in 1953. The Rec was developed first in 1960, after much hard work the dressing rooms and tea hut were installed with training lights and later in 1974 the small stand went in.

They did not win the league again but joined the Senior League in 1964, winning it in 1972 and stayed until 1978 when they moved to the Spartan League. After some cup success it was decided to return to the Senior League which had re-formed as the Combined Counties League and they were runners up in 1988, but 1990 was a fine year, as the club reached round four of the FA Vase, won the League Cup and were again runners up in the league. Also that year the floodlights were erected and switched on on November 22nd against Crystal Palace.

NETHERNE

Netherne Sports Club, Woodplace Lane, Hooley, Coulsdon, Surrey CR5 1YE. Tel: 01737 553580

Secretary: Steve Clark, 28 Lackford Rd, Chipstead, Surrey CR5 3TA. Tel: 01737 552200

Colours: Blue and black stripes

Capacity: 2,000

Seating: No

Covered standing: 50

Clubhouse on ground: Yes

Floodlights: No

Biggest win: 7-3 v Limpsfield Blues 1982

Biggest defeat: 1-8 v Springfield Hospital 1979

Record appearances: Steve Parker 600

Record goalscorer in total: Michael Rumble 350

DIRECTIONS

One mile from end of M32. Turn right off Brighton Road into Woodplace Lane, follow up hill for about half a mile, ground on left. Approx 20 mins walk from Coulsdon South station.

Honours

Surrey County Premier 1994

League Cup 1993

Surrey South Eastern Intermediate Comb 1989

Manager 1996-97: Graeme Crawford

Assistant Manager: John Fullick

Chairman: Steve Clark

Formed in 1968 as Reedham Park FC, they played in the now defunct Croydon Saturday League. The first pitch was at Higher Drive Rec in Purley with the majority of the players coming from the Old Lodge Lane area. The club were very progressive and and moved into the South Eastern Intermediate League in 1975, and with the merger of the Eastern and Southern Intermediates, they began the long climb, and a series of promotions ended with the Premier Division championship in 1989.

They were promoted to the Surrey Premier League and won the Sportsmanship Trophy twice and the Partington Cup in 1992, followed by the Premier League Cup in 1993 and the title in 1994.

After 26 years, four leagues and nine divisions they made it to senior football and joined the Combined Counties League.

The original name was derived from Reedham Orphanage which was near to the home pitch, and they soon moved to Sparrows Den in Addington, the Southern Railway Sports Club in Wallington and then to Netherne. The change of name was made in 1992 to identify with the area, Netherne being associated with the nearby hospital. The clubhouse was erected by hospital staff as a social club in 1952 and at one time had a running track around the pitch.

RAYNES PARK VALE

Grand Drive, Raynes Park, SW2. Tel: 0181 542 2193

Secretary: Paul Armour, 68 Oaks Avenue, Worcester Park, Surrey, KT4 8XD. Tel: 0181 337 4989

Capacity: 3000

Seating: 120

Covered standing: 170

Floodlights: Yes

Clubhouse on ground: Yes

Biggest win: 3-0 v Canterbury City FA Cup 1995

Biggest defeat: 0-8 v Cranleigh Comb Counties

Honours

Malden Vale

Surrey Senior League 1977

Southern Combination Cup 1978

Spartan League Cup 1981 and 1984

Combined Counties League and Concord Cup 1984

Manager for 1996-97: Glyn Stephens

Assistant manager: Peter Middleton

Chairman: Dave Brennan

Vice Chairman: Brian Davis

DIRECTIONS

Approach on the Kingston by-pass (A3). Take the West Coombe Lane exit (A238) east towards the city centre. Take the third turning on the right after the slip road back onto the A3, West Barnes Lane. Taunton Avenue is the first on the right. Bear left to the sports ground. (C2, page 120 London A-Z). Nearest station is Raynes Park.

Raynes Park Vale was founded after the merger of Malden Vale FC and Raynes Park FC in 1995.

Malden Vale were formed in 1967 and spent the first ten years in the North Surrey Youth League, Sunday Sportsman League, Thameside League and Surrey Combination, where a total of 37 honours were won. They took senior status in 1977 and joined the Surrey Senior League, winning it at the first attempt with the reserves completing a double. The following season the league was known as the Home Counties League but Vale moved to the Spartan League Premier Division. They finished fifth and also took the Southern Combination Cup. They were regularly in the top six in the Spartan League, ending as runners up twice, but they did win the League Cup in 1981 and 1984, losing the final in 82 and 83. They then returned to the old Surrey Senior League, by then known as the Combined Counties League winning it in 1984 along with the Concorde Challenge Cup (League Cup). After more success they joined the Isthmian League having had much work done on the ground to achieve the grading and in 1991 finished fourth and were promoted to Division Two.

Problems began to appear and rumours of a merger with a local junior side emerged and at the end of the 1994-95 season Vale were rock bottom with 5 wins in 42 games.

The merger of the two clubs went through and Raynes Park Vale played last season in the Combined Counties League, where they finished last but one.

READING TOWN

Reading Town Sports Ground, Scours Lane, Tilehurst, Reading, Berks. Tel: 01734 453555

Secretary: Patrick Monaghan 3, Penroath Ave, Reading, Berks RG30 2ED. Tel: 01734 571136

Colours: Black and red halves

Seating: Yes

Covered standing: Yes

Clubhouse on ground: Yes

DIRECTIONS
Out of Reading on Oxford road (A329), past Battle Hosp. Scours Lane 1st right after roundabout.

Reading Town FC began life as Lower Burghfield in 1966 and they stayed that way until the early 70's when, due to a loss of facilities, they moved to a new ground in Reading and were re-named XL United.

Playing in the Reading Combination, XL enjoyed a few seasons before in 1980, they secured a sponsorship deal with Vincents, the car dealer.

As Vincents United and then Reading Garage, they enjoyed its best seasons up to then, winning the Premier League in four out of five years, along with League Cup triumphs. Fittingly in 1984, the final year in the Combination, Reading Garage won the League championship, League Cup, Invitation Cup and All Champions Cup.

Moving into the Reading and District League the following year, Reading Garage were runners up and won the most prestigious trophy in local football, the Reading Senior Cup, at Elm Park.

In 1986 they were again runners up in league and Senior Cup, and three years later they moved on to a place in the Chiltonian League, as ITS Reading Town, finishing third.

Now known as Reading Town the club continue to look ahead to the future.

SANDHURST TOWN

Memorial Ground, Yorktown Rd, Sandhurst. Tel: 01252 873767

Secretary: John Parker, 24 Florence Rd, College Town, Camberley, Surrey. Tel: 01276 32308

Colours: Red and black

Nickname: Fizzers

Seating: No

Floodlights: No

Covered standing: No

Clubhouse on ground: Yes

DIRECTIONS
A30 westwards through Camberley, right at roundabout with traffic lights, past superstore turning right, left at next roundabout. Ground next to Town & Council offices and Community Sports Centre.

VIKING SPORTS

Avenue Park, Western Avenue, Greenford, Middx. Tel: 0181 578 2706

Secretary: John Bennett, 6 Bridge House, Boston Manor Rd, Brentford TW8 9LH. Tel: 0181 568 9047

Match Sec: Nigel Hicks 46 Castleton Rd, Eastcote, Middx HA4 9QL. Tel: 0181 429 1034

Press Sec: Fred Hyde, 6 Oakfield Gardens, Greenford, Middx UB6 8GD. Tel: 0181 575 2290

Colours: Tangerine and black

Nickname: Vikings

Capacity: 450,

Seating: 60

Covered standing: 140

Clubhouse on ground: Yes

Record attendance: 150 v Lambourn Sports

Biggest win: 8-0 v Aldermaston 1986

Biggest defeat: 2-7 v Hazells

Record goalscorer in one season: Frank Healy 37

Honours

Hellenic League Div 1 1986

Manager 1996-97: Terry Cross, Assistant Manager: Jim Curran

Chairman: Brian Lown, Vice Chairman: Kevan Lawton

> **DIRECTIONS**
> On London-bound carriageway of A40, 300 yds before Greenford flyover and slip road to A4127. 12 mins walk from Greenford (Central Line) station - turn right out of station and to A40 and turn right - ground quarter mile on right.

Official history of Viking Sports available from club £3 or abbreviated history available at £1, both celebrating clubs Golden Jubilee last year

The club began as a youth team formed by current President Roy Bartlett in 1945. They progressed through the old Dauntless Amateur League before joining the Nemean League in 1956. A tour of the Soviet Union was successfully negotiated and on returning the club took the league title. During this era the club moved from Churchfields to the Western Avenue in 1965. Four years later Vikings moved to the Middlesex League and in 1980 were accepted into the Hellenic League. Although just missing promotion in the second season, in 1986 the club were promoted as champions with the reserves also having a wonderful season.

Throughout the 80's much work went in to improve the facilities and senior status was granted in 1987, allowing them to enter the FA Vase and two Middlesex Cups. Sadly the old clubhouse was burned down in 1987 and with the handicap the club went down, but it was replaced in 1989 along with a small stand behind one goal. Due to the increasing cost of travelling, Vikings moved across to the Combined Counties League in 1991, where they remain, having finished runners up in 1995.

WALTON CASUALS

Franklyn Road Sports Ground, off Waterside Drive, Walton-on-Thames, Surrey. Tel: 01932 787749

Secretary: Stuart Roberts, 47 Foxholes, Weybridge, Surrey:
KT13 0BN Tel 01932 845923

Colours: Orange and white

Clubhouse on ground: Yes

DIRECTIONS

The easiest way to approach Walton-on-Thames is from junction 1 of M3 (from junction 12 of M25) where it is signposted south on A244. The ground is off Waterside Drive.

WESTFIELD

Woking Park, Kingfield, Woking, Surrey. Tel: 01483 771106

Secretary: Mick Lawrence, 19 Ash Road, Woking, Surrey GU22 0BJ Tel 01483 722182

Colours: Yellow and black

Capacity: 1,000

Floodlights: No

Seating: No

Clubhouse on ground: Yes

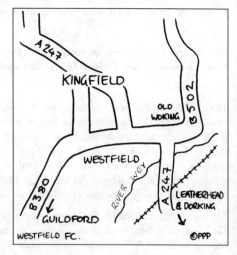

ENDSLEIGH MIDLAND COMBINATION

Premier Division

	P	W	D	L	F	A	PTS
Bloxwich Town	38	31	4	3	122	46	97
Coventry Sphinx	38	25	5	8	87	43	80
Massey-Ferguson	38	23	8	6	77	36	77
Knowle	38	21	10	7	87	49	73
Studley B.K.L.	38	17	11	9	93	64	62
Kings Heath	38	18	6	14	63	65	60
Wellesbourne	38	15	10	13	55	60	55
Southam United	38	13	14	11	69	63	53
Meir K.A.	38	15	10	13	72	72	53
Coleshill Town	38	14	9	15	76	66	51
Chelmsley Town	38	14	8	16	65	62	50
Upton Town	38	14	6	18	68	72	48
Ansells	38	12	10	16	64	81	46
Olton Royale	38	12	8	18	56	71	44
West Mids Fire	38	11	9	18	51	70	42
Alvechurch Villa	38	10	10	18	57	84	40
Highgate United	38	9	10	19	56	81	37
Handrahan Timb	38	9	10	19	46	71	37
Shirley Town	38	8	8	22	51	74	32
Northfield Town	38	3	6	29	33	123	15

Division One

	P	W	D	L	F	A	PTS
Richmond Swifts	32	26	5	1	92	18	83
Kenilworth Town	32	17	10	5	75	31	61
Bilston C C	32	18	7	7	78	41	61
Colletts Green	32	18	7	7	76	54	61
G.P.T. (Coventry)	32	19	3	10	84	47	60
Dudley Sports	32	16	8	8	63	39	56
Alveston	32	14	7	11	63	48	49
Polesworth N W	32	12	9	11	60	69	45
Newhall United	32	11	10	11	68	63	43
Monica Star	32	11	8	13	55	56	41
Holly Lane	32	9	11	12	43	53	38
Hams Hall	32	11	4	17	55	68	37
Kings N Ex-Ser	32	12	1	19	49	82	37
Thimbleml REC.	32	8	4	20	38	78	28
Barlestone St G	32	8	3	21	44	91	27
Fairfield Villa	32	6	4	22	27	75	22
Badsey Rangers	32	2	7	23	30	92	13

Division Two

	P	W	D	L	F	A	PTS
Continental Star	32	24	6	2	89	28	78
Enville Athletic	32	21	5	6	71	31	68
Brownhills Town	32	20	5	7	73	46	65
Cheslyn Hay	32	19	4	9	76	54	61
Earlswood Town	32	16	9	7	56	30	57
West Mids PlRes.	32	13	8	11	47	41	47
Bromsgrove Ran	32	12	8	12	63	59	44
Ledbury Town	32	11	9	12	71	50	42
Alvis S.G.L.	32	10	12	10	52	41	42
Coleshill Town Res.	32	12	6	14	49	61	42
Cadbury Athletic	32	11	6	15	36	49	39
Wolves Cas Res.	32	11	4	17	46	79	37
Blackheath Elec	32	8	8	16	40	49	32
Archdales	32	7	8	17	46	60	29
Burntwood	32	7	7	18	41	64	28
Albright & Wilson	32	6	6	20	35	81	24
Wellesbourne Res.	32	6	5	21	33	101	23

Division three

	P	W	D	L	F	A	PTS
Feckenham	34	27	5	2	102	26	86
Rich Sw Res.	34	25	4	5	89	29	79
Tipton Sports	34	21	5	8	68	30	68
Birmgham Vaults	34	20	8	6	62	38	68
Mitch & Butlers	34	16	9	9	74	44	57
Studley United	34	16	6	12	64	56	54
Cradley Heath	34	13	8	13	53	46	47
Kenilwor Ward	34	13	7	14	51	56	46
Dudley Sp Res.	34	14	3	17	48	55	45
Kings Heath Res.	34	13	2	19	53	79	41
Enville Ath Res.	34	10	8	16	47	60	38
Birchfield Sports	34	10	8	16	46	71	38
Tipton Rovers	34	10	7	17	51	59	37
Swan Sports	34	10	6	18	76	85	36
Studley B.K.L. Res.	34	9	6	19	45	71	33
Alvech V Res.	34	9	4	21	45	85	31
Barlestone Res.	34	8	7	19	35	81	31
Park Rangers	34	5	11	18	51	89	26

ALVECHURCH

Lye Meadow, Redditch Rd, Alvechurch, Worcs. Tel: 0121 445 2929

Secretary: Mr A Deakin, 58 Chesterfield Close, Northfield
B31 3TR Tel: 0121 411 1745

Colours: Gold and black   Nickname: The Church

Capacity: 3,000   Seating: Yes

Covered standing: Yes   Clubhouse on ground: Yes

Record attendance: 1,600 v Enfield FA Amateur Cup 1964

Biggest win: 7-1 v Redditch Utd

Biggest defeat: 1-8 v Halesowen Town

Record appearances: Kevin Palmer

Record goalscorer in total: Graham Allner

Record fee received: £28,000 for Andy Comyn
to Aston Villa in 1990

DIRECTIONS
M42 junction 2, left for Alvechurch (A441) at 1st island, pass right through Alvechurch - ground on left half mile after village. 10 mins walk from Alvechurch BR station. Birmingham-Redditch buses pass ground.

Honours

Southern League 1981

League Cup 1983 and Championship match 1981, West Midlands League 1974, 1975, 1976, 1977

League Cup 1974, 1975, 1978, Midland Combination 1963, 1965, 1967, 1972

League Cup 1965, 1966, 1968, 1969, 1972, Worcester Senior Cup 1973, 1974, 1977

Birmingham Senior Amateur Cup 1974, Birmingham Junior Cup 1966 and 1968

All above records apply to the original club formed in 1929 and folded in 1992

The current Alvechurch club rose from the ashes of Alvechurch FC, whose exploits in FA Cup and Amateur Cup are well documented. The original club were formed in 1929 and played in minor leagues on the Meadows before moving to Lye Meadow in 1957. They joined the Midland Combination in 1961 and in the 12 years of membership where four times champions and five times runners up, as well as reaching seven League Cup finals, winning five. Amongst all the success the club reached the quarter-finals of the Amateur Cup in 1965, going one better in 1966, and in 1971 played an 11 hour marathon FA Cup tie with Oxford City which is now in the Guinness Book of Records.

Alvechurch went on to win the Worcester Senior Cup in 1973 and joined the West Midlands League in the same year, winning the League, League Cup, Birmingham Senior Amateur Cup and Worcestershire Senior Cup in their first remarkable year. In the FA Cup they reached the 3rd round, losing to Exeter City.

Through to 1977 the club completed four successive championships as well as other League Cup and County Cup wins and entry to the Southern League was a formality. The club transferred Richard O'Kelly and Shaun O'Driscoll which brought in funds to build a stand at Lye Meadow and they soon won the Midland Division and clinched the championship by beating Dartford in the two leg final.

In 1983 the won the Southern League Cup as a Premier Division side and then were quiet until 1992 when financial problems came to the surface and they went under.

Lye Meadow was partially demolished, but a new club were formed and eventually Villa re-opened the ground and have begun to rebuild it and to bring top class football back to the village. For the new season the club have reverted back to the original name by dropping the Villa tag.

BILSTON COMMUNITY COLLEGE

At BILSTON TOWN FC Queen Street, Bilston, West Midlands. Tel: 01902 491498

Secretary: Jeff Calloway, 4 Mervyn Rd, Bradley, Bilston, West Mids Tel: 01902 491799

Colours: All Green

ALL GROUND DETAILS AS PER BILSTON TOWN IN SOUTHERN LEAGUE SECTION

BOLEHALL SWIFTS

Rene Road, Bolehall, Tamworth. Tel: 01827 62637

Secretary: Mike Simpkins, 22 Brambling, Wilnecote,
Tamworth, Staff B77 5PQ. Tel: 01827 283004

Colours: Yellow and black

Nickname: Swifts

Capacity: 2,000

Seating: 250

Covered standing: 250

Clubhouse on ground : Yes

Record attendance: 803 v Tamworth FA Cup 1995

Biggest win: 7-1 v Mile Oak Rovers April 1993

Biggest defeat: 0-8 v Solihull Boro 1991

Record appearances: Duane Mellors 196

Record goalscorer in total: Billy Oughton

DIRECTIONS

A51 signs south to Bolebridge island, left under railway arches into Amington Road, 4th left into Leedham avenue, fork right into Rene Road, ground on right by school. From Tamworth BR station walk up Victoria Road for three quarters of a mile and catch No. 3 or No. 6 mini-bus to Bolehall. Alight a Leedham Avenue or Rene Road and follow as above.

Honours

Mid Comb Div 2 and Challenge Vase 1985

Fazeley Charity Cup 1985

Manager 1996-97: Ron Tranter

Vice Chairman: W. Gould

In 1951 and 1952 Bolehall lads played friendlies but in 1953 they became affiliated and joined the Tamworth and Trent Valley League. They changed their name to the Swifts copying two local teams, Fazeley Swifts and Edingale Swifts who were a force at the time. In the first season they won Division Two and the Lady Agnes Cup and in 1961 moved to Rene Road, which is self owned. It was developed as a sports and social club in 1976 and has never looked back. The club moved to the Sutton League and then the Staffs County before joining the Midland Comb in 1980. They enjoyed their best season in 1985 when winning Division Two, the Challenge Vase and the Fazeley Charity Cup and in 1986 they moved up to the top division.

They were founder members of the Midland Alliance, and much work went on to bring Rene Road up to date, but sadly in May after a disastrous season the club returned to the Midland Combination.

COLESHILL TOWN

Pack Meadow, Packington Lane, Coleshill, Birmingham B46 3JQ. Tel: 01675 63259

Secretary: Neil Hamilton, 31 Fourfield Way, New Arley,
North Warks CV7 8PX Tel 01676 540488

Colours: All Green   Nickname: Coalmen

Capacity: 3,000   Seating: 50

Covered standing: No   Clubhouse on ground: Yes

Honours

Mercian League 1976

Walsall Senior Cup 1983

Midland Comb Div 2 1970

Invitation Cup 1970

Manager 1996-97: Martin Sockett

> **DIRECTIONS**
>
> A446 to A4117 towards Coleshill, Packington Lane forks from A4117, south of village and ground is 150 yds on right. M6 junction 4, 1 mile away.

Founded in 1894 they are one of the oldest clubs in the league. Most of their life was spent in local junior leagues but in 1964 Colehill Hall FC folded and their best players joined the Town, who then played at Memorial Park. As standards rose they joined the Mercian League and in 1968 the Midland Combination. Two years later they won Division Two but promotion was not granted until 1974 when they runners up. By that time the club had moved to Pack Meadow.

Since joining the Premier Division the best placing has been as runners up in 1984.

COVENTRY SPHINX

Sphinx Drive off Siddeley Avenue, Stoke Aldermoor, Coventry CV6 1JE. Tel: 01203 598148

Secretary: K.Whitehall, 34 Engleton Rd, Radford, Coventry CV6 1JE Tel: 01203 451361

Colours: Sky blue and navy blue

DAVID LLOYD AFC

Ansells Sports Club, Aldridge Rd, Perry Barr, Birmingham. Tel: 0121 356 4296

Secretary: Mr J.Cronin, 32 Whittleford Grove, Castle Bromwich, Birmingham B36 9SL Tel: 1021 747 9925

Colours: Blue and white

Capacity: 1,000

Seating: No

Covered standing: Yes

Floodlights: No

Clubhouse on ground: Yes

Honours

Midland Combination Div 2 1993

DAVID LLOYD AFC WERE FORMERLY KNOWN AS ANSELLS FC

HANDRAHAN TIMBERS

Mile Flat Sportsground, Mile Flat, Wallheath, Kingswinford. Tel: 01831 484755

Secretary: E.J. Smith, 47 Summercourt Sq, Kingswinford,
West Mids, DY6 9QJ

Tel: 01384 830149 (h) 01384 455333 (b)

Colours: Red and black   Nickname: Timbers

Seating: 40   Covered standing: 200

Clubhouse on ground: Yes   Floodlights: No

DIRECTIONS

Wall Heath is on the A449 south of Wombourne. Approach on the A458 from the west.

Honours

JW Hunt Cup 1993

Wednesbury Charity Cup 1992

Manager 1996-97: Glen Taylor and Nigel Kirkham

Chairman: John Smith

Formed in 1981 when the present ground was bought from British Steel by Mr Handrahan, formerly British Steel Cookley Works played in Wolverhampton Works and Staffs County League. Timbers joined the Midland Combination in 1986, being promoted in 1989 on the strength of their ground facilities. They were runners up in 1993 and gained promotion to the Premier Division.

HIGHGATE UNITED

The Coppice, Tythe Barn Lane, Shirley, Solihull, B90 1PH. Tel: 0121 744 4194

Secretary: G. Read, 23 Southam Road, Hall Green,
Birmingham, B28 8DQ Tel 0121 777 1786

Founded 1947

Nickname: The Gate   Colours: Red

Capacity: 2,000   Seating: 250

Standing: 500   Clubhouse on ground: Yes

Record attendance: approx 4,000 v Enfield
FA Amateur Cup quarter-final 1967

DIRECTIONS

A34 from City through Shirley, fork right B4102 (Tamworth Lane), half mile then right into Dickens Heath Road, then first right and the ground is on the left. 100 yds from Whitlocks End Railway Station.

Honours

FA AMATEUR CUP Semi-final 1967

Midland Combination 1973, 1974, 1975

Division Two 1967, 1969, 1972

League Cup 1973, 1974, 1976, 1977, 1985

President's Cup 1971 and 1986

Tony Allden Memorial Cup 1975

Invitation Cup 1969, 1972, 1986

West Midlands Alliance 1964

Birmingham Senior Cup 1974

KENILWORTH TOWN

Gypsy Lane, off Rouncil Lane, Kenilworth, Warws. Tel: 01926 50851

Secretary: Mr F. Breese, 188 Winsford Avenue, Allesley Park,
Coventry CV5 9NH Tel: 01203 678198

Colours: Red and white

DIRECTIONS

Gypsey Lane (off Rouncil lane), Kenilworth, Warks.

KINGS HEATH

Highgate United FC, The Coppice, Tythe Barn Lane, Shirley, Solihull, B90 1PH.
Tel: 0121 744 4194

Secretary: Dennis Ellis, 2 Willsbridge Covert, Druids Heath,
Birmingham B14 5YD Tel 0121 628 6019

Nickname: The Kings

ALL GROUND DETAILS AS PER HIGHGATE UNITED FC

Colours: Gold and black

DIRECTIONS

As Highgate United (see page 869).

Honours

South Birmingham Comb Div 1 1965

Presidents Cup and Jim Parker Cup 1965

Colin Cooke Trophy 1966

Birmingham Cut Shield 1969

Billie Wells Cup 1969

Mercian Butler Cup 1970

Aston Villa Shield, FH Ward Trophy, Mercian Div 1 1971

Mercian League Cup and FH Ward Trophy 1976

Mercian League and Senior Cup 1977

Worcestershire Senior Urn 1988

KNOWLE

Hampton Rd, Knowle, Solihull, Tel: 01564 779807

Secretary: Mr G. Phillips, 49 Circus Avenue,
Chelmsley Wood, Birmingham Tel 0121 770 9513

Nickname: Robins   Colours: Red and white

Floodlights: No   Capacity: 3,000

Seating: 75   Covered standing: 200

Record attendance: 1,000 for FA Vase match in 1980

DIRECTIONS

A41 Warwick Road from City, left at Wilsons Pub into Hampton Road, ground 200 yds on right. 1 mile from Dorridge (BR). Buses from Solihull.

Honours

Dr Nelson Charity Cup 1934

Henry Butler Cup 1936

West Bromwich Shield 1936

Evelyn Cecil Shield 1939

Birmingham Youth and Old Boys Senior Division 1949

Senior Cup 1949

Knowle Town FC were formed in 1926 at the Men's Institute, playing in the Birmingham Youth and Old Boys League. The first honours collected were in 1934 when they won the Dr Nelson Charity Cup and in 1936 they won the Henry Butler Cup and West Bromwich Shield. In 1939 the club took the prestigious Evelyn Cecil Shield but the War curtailed football and it was 1947 before the league re-commenced, with Knowle as a very strong side. In 1949 they completed the Senior League and Cup double.

In 1966 they joined the Worcester Combination and were runners up in Division Two in 1969, the first year it was the Midland Comb, and from the top division reached the final of the Birmingham Junior Cup. The next good spell was in 1982 when they got to the last eight of the FA Vase, and a year later the Robins merged with North Star Rangers, changing their name for a while to Knowle North Star, before taking the current title.

MASSEY FERGUSON

Massey-Ferguson Sports Ground, Banner Lane, Tile Hill, Coventry. Tel: 01203 694400

Secretary: L. Thomas, 730 Broad Lane, Coventry CV5 7BB

Tel: 01203 465476

Colours: Red and black

Honours

Midland Combination Challenge Vase 1994

Division Two 1994

DIRECTIONS

Tile Hill is on the west side of Coventry. Either approach along the B4101 from Coventry and the turning is on the right after the A45 or take the junction 15 exit of the M40 via A46. From the M42 take the A45 towards Coventry and follow the signs.

MEIR KA

Stanley Park, Hilderstone Road, Meir Heath, Stoke-on-Trent. Tel: 01782 388465

Secretary: Mr Stanley Tooth, 29 Colclough Rd,
Meir Heath, Stoke-on-Trent Tel: 01782 310145

Colours: Yellow and red

Nickname: Kings

Capacity: 2,000

Seating: Yes

Covered standing: Yes

Floodlights: Yes

Record win: 9-0 v Mile Oak Rovers
Midland Comb 1994

Record defeat: 0-9 v Wellesbourne Midland Comb 1995

Record goalscorer in total: W.Anderson

Record appearances: David Preston

DIRECTIONS

M6 junction 14, A34 to Stone, A520 from Stone, right (B5066) at Meir Heath, ground on right. 2 miles from Blythe Bridge Railway Station.

Honours

Staffs Senior League 1989 and 1991

Staffs FA Vase 1994

Walsall Senior Cup 1990

RICHMOND SWIFTS

Triplex Sports Ground, Eckershall Road, Kings Norton. Tel: 0121 458 4570

Secretary: Michael Rowley, 61 Derwent Drive, Priorslee,
Telford, Salop TF2 9QR Tel: 01952 200020

Colours: Red, white and black

DIRECTIONS

In Eckershall Road, Kings Norton.

SHIRLEY TOWN

Shirley Stadium, Tile House Lane, Shirley, Solihull, Tel: 0121 744 1560

Secretary: Brian Fox, 26 Claines Rd, Northfield, B31 2EE
Tel: 0121 475 4465

Founded: 1926

Colours: Maroon and white

DIRECTIONS
Take the A34 linking M42 junction 4 with Birmingham city centre (Stratford Road). Turn onto B4025 between Hall Green and Shirley (Solihull Lane) towards Solihull and Shirley BR station. The ground is one and a half miles on the left.

SOUTHAM UNITED

Banbury Rd Ground, Southam, Leamington Spa, Tel: 01926 812091

Secretary: R.J. Hancocks, 18 Warwick Rd, Southam, Leamington Spa Tel: 01926 813483

Nickname: The Saints

Colours: White and black

Capacity: 2,000

Seating: Yes

Floodlights: No

Covered standing: Yes

Record attendance: 1,500 v Coventry City Friendly 1990

Record win: 10-0 v Studley

Record Defeat: 1-7 v Kings Heath

Record goalscorer in total: Bob Hancocks

Record appearances: Bob Hancocks

DIRECTIONS
On righthand side of A423 Banbury Road heading south from Southam.

Honours:

Midland Combination Division 3 1981

Challenge Vase: 1981

STUDLEY BKL

Beehive, BKL Sports Ground, Abbeyfields, Birmingham Rd, Studley. Tel: 01527 853817

Secretary: K. Addis, 16 Ansley Close, Matchborough East, Redditch, B98 0AX Tel 01527 526454

Colours: Sky and navy blue   Nickname: Bees

Capacity: 1,000   Seating: Yes

Covered standing: Yes   Clubhouse on ground: Yes

Floodlights: No

Record appearances: Lee Adams

Record goalscorer in total: Kevin Rowlands

Honours

Midland Comb Div 1 1992

Div 2 Cup 1988

Smedley Crooke Cup 1992 and 1993

Studley began life in 1971 in Sunday football, known as BKL FC, they played in the Redditch and South Warwicks Comb for 15 seasons, then switched to Saturdays, joining Div 2 of the Midland Comb.

They won the Challenge Vase at the first attempt and a year later were promoted.

The Bees won the Smedley Crooke Cup twice running in 1991 and 1992 and won Division One of the league, moving to the Premier Division.

WELLESBOURNE

The Sports Field, Loxley Close, Wellesbourne CV36 9PD. Tel: 01789 842646

Secretary : Ted Forster, Brent House, Canal Lane, Hatton, Warws Tel: 01926 494507

Colours: Blue and white

Nickname: Bourne

Seating: 80

Covered standing: 20

Floodlights: No. (due 1997)

Clubhouse on ground: Yes

Honours

Midland Combination Div 1 1993

Presidents Cup `1992

Invitation Cup 1993 and 1995

WEST MIDLANDS FIRE SERVICE

The Glades, Lugtrout Lane, Solihull, Tel: 0121 705 8602
Secretary: Mr J. Clarke, 51 Stonebury Ave, Eastern Green, Coventry CV5 7FW Tel 01203 467997

Founded: 1947   Colours: Red and black
Capacity: 1,000   Seating: No
Covered standing: 150   Floodlights: No
Clubhouse on ground: No
Record appearances: Brian Farrell

Honours
Midland Combination Div 1 1995
Division Two 1988
President's Cup 1995
Jack Mould Trophy 1988
Fire Services National Cup 1990
Fire District Cup 1991

DIRECTIONS
M42, junction 5, towards Birmingham Airport. Leave at the next junction and at the island take the first exit, Catherine de Barnes Lane. The ground is half a mile on the left. Nearest station is Birmingham International. No buses pass the ground.

WORCESTER ATHLETICO

Nunnery Wood Sports Centre, Spetchley Rd, Worcester WR5 2NL
Tel: 01905 357842 (First few games may be played at Evesham United, please check)
Secretary: Don Roberts, 6 Gardens Close, Upton-on-Severn,
Worcs WR8 0LT Tel: 01684 593439
Any other contact address: David Boddy,
25 Common Road, Evesham, Worcs WR11 2NL
Tel: 01386 47302 or 01386 561350

Capacity: 1,000   Covered seating: 186
Covered standing: 50   Floodlights: Yes
Clubhouse on ground: Yes
Biggest win: 13-1   Biggest defeat: 0-17
Record attendance: 350 v Colletts Green Mid Comb 1994
Record appearance holder: Keith Angel
Record goalscorer in aggregate: Paul Buckley

DIRECTIONS
The club are currently sharing at Evesham United, but will move to their new ground in Spetchley Road, Worcester in the near future.

Honours
Midland Combination Div 2 1990; Jack Mould Trophy 1990
Worcester Junior Cup 1974 and 1989; Worcester Minor Cup 1925 and 1987
Manager for 1996-97 David Boddy, Chairman: Bill Jones; Vice chairman John Williams
Press officer: Graham Hill, 18 St Marks Close, Worcester, WR5 3DJ Tel 01905 351653
The name Worcester Athletico is a brand new one, and signals the beginning of a new era for the old Upton Town Football Club. Having played in local Malvern League football from their founding in 1904 to 1971, they then moved to the Worcester and District League until 1985, when for three years they were in the Kidderminster League. Having always played in the village of Upton on Severn at the Sports Field, they were forced due to lack of facilities, to ground share with Malvern Town for four seasons whilst in the Midland Combination, but due to that club reforming a reserve side, they were unable to stay. The club have made the bold decision to move into the Nunnery Wood Sports Centre in Spetchley Road, Worcester for this season, and have severed all connections with the village by changing the club name to Worcester Athletico.

Premier Division

	P	W	D	L	F	A	PTS
Wednesfield	36	28	6	2	95	30	90
Pelsall Villa	36	27	5	4	97	30	86
Lye Town	36	20	11	5	80	34	71
Stafford Town	36	19	10	7	79	35	67
Stourport Swifts	36	19	10	7	74	50	67
Bloxwich Strol	36	17	9	10	67	50	60
Walsall Wood	36	16	8	12	61	42	56
Gornal Athletic	36	16	7	13	55	42	55
Westfields	36	16	6	14	86	73	54
Ludlow Town	36	14	9	13	68	71	51
Ettings Holy Tr	36	11	9	16	62	80	42
Tividale	36	10	9	17	65	80	39
Lichfield City	36	9	10	17	43	65	37
Malvern Town	36	9	9	18	34	67	36
Brierley Hill Tn	36	10	4	22	49	73	34
Cradley Town	36	8	7	21	55	82	31
Wolves Casuals	36	9	4	23	53	108	31
Darlaston	36	5	11	20	40	86	26
Hill Top Rangers	36	4	6	26	34	99	18

Division One

	P	W	D	L	F	A	PTS
Goodyear	40	27	6	7	110	45	87
Wolves United	40	27	3	10	85	50	84
Rocester Res.	40	24	10	6	109	46	82
Morda United	40	26	4	10	87	54	82
Chasetown Res.	40	23	6	11	92	69	75
Bandon	40	22	7	11	94	57	73
Tipton Town	40	21	10	9	78	41	73
Rushall O Res.	40	21	4	15	98	70	67
Bilston United	40	17	10	13	92	84	61
Brereton Social	40	14	12	14	65	62	54
Moxley Rangers	40	16	8	16	70	64	53
Bromyard Town	40	16	5	19	70	67	53
Hinckley Ath Res.	40	15	4	21	71	84	49
Gornal Ath Res.	40	13	5	22	42	91	44
Great Wyrley	40	13	4	23	55	103	43
Mahal	40	12	6	22	61	89	42
Oldbury Utd Res.	40	11	7	22	68	87	40
Pershore Tn Res.	40	10	7	23	47	82	37
Tividale Res.	40	10	6	24	51	92	36
Cannock Chase	40	7	9	24	54	97	30
Sikh Hunters	40	6	5	29	50	115	20

BLOXWICH STROLLERS

Pelsall Villa FC, The Bush, Walsall Rd, Heath End, Pelsall, Walsall Tel: 01922 682018

Secretary: George Llewellyn, 7 Birchover Rd, Walsall Tel: 01922 614595

Colours: Black and white   Founded: 1888

Capacity: As Pelsall Villa   Clubhouse on ground: Yes

DIRECTIONS

As Pelsall Villa (see page 279).

Honours

Birmingham Combination 1925

Staffs County League South: 1985

Edge Cup and League Shield 1985

Walsall Senior Cup 1993

Also Walsall Charity Cup, Staffs Junior Cup, Walsall League

BRIERLEY HILL TOWN

The Dell Sports Ground, Bryce Rd, Pensnett, Brierley Hill, West Mids Tel: 01384 77289

Secretary: Bill Hughes, 13 Barnett Close, Kingswinford, West Mids DY6 9PN Tel: 01384 288855

Colours: Blue and white halves

Nickname: The Lions   Capacity: 5,000

Seating: 300   Covered standing: None

Clubhouse on ground: Yes

Record attendance: 800 v Wolverhampton Wanderers Friendly

Record fee received: Undisclosed for Neil Edwards to Wolverhampton Wanderers 1985

DIRECTIONS

At lights in the Brierley Hill High Street turn into Bank Street by Police Station. Proceed over bridge into Pensnett Road, ground three quarters of a mile on left by Paddy's Garage. Main entrance 120 yards in Bryce Road.

Honours

West Midlands League Div 1 and Div 1 Cup 1981

Brierley Hill Town were founded as Oldswinford FC in 1955 and played on a selection of grounds, including Field Lane, Wollescote Park, Swinford Common and South Road before they moved in with Brierley Hill Alliance at their Cottage Street ground in 1975.

Dudley Council sold the ground to Asda and it was developed and both clubs moved into the Dell Sports Ground in 1977. Sadly, Alliance folded with many debts in 1981, but Oldswinford continued at the Dell and won the League and Cup double in the First Division that year.

Dudley Met Council decided on a vast ground improvement for the Dell, which saw the club forced to play away on various grounds for two years, and when they moved back again the club changed its name to Brierley Hill Town in 1993. For this season the roles have been reversed for the club, as Dudley Town have moved into the Dell to groundshare, having moved out of their Round Oak home.

CRADLEY TOWN

Beeches View, Beeches View Avenue, Cradley, Halesowen Tel: 01384 569658

Secretary: David Attwood, 4 Birch Coppice, Quarry Bk, Brierley Hill, W.Mids DY5 1AP
Tel: 01384 637430

Press: Trevor Thomas, 41 Harmon Rd, Wollaston, Stourbridge Tel: 01384 441420

Colours: Red and black stripes

Nickname: Lukes, Capacity: 900

Seating: 200, Covered standing: 300

Clubhouse on ground: Yes

Record attendance: 1,000 Approx
Aston Villa Friendly

Biggest win: 9-1 v Wolverhampton Utd
West Mids Lge 1990

Biggest defeat: 0-8 v Ilkeston Town 1993

Record appearances: R.Hayward

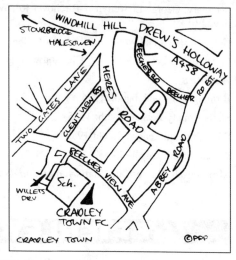

Record goalscorer in one season Jim Nugent 45 in 1970-71

Record goalscorer in total: R.Hayward

Record fee paid £1,000 for Darren Marsh from Oldswinford 1992

Record fee received £20,000 for John Williams to Swansea 1991

Honours

West Midlands League Div 1 1991

Midlands Comb Div 2 1973, President's Cup 1975 and 1976

Invitation Cup 1973, Metropolitan League 1971

Wednesbury Charity Cup 1991, Dudley Guest Hospital Cup 1972, 1973, 1976, 1991

Manager 1996-97: Trevor Thomas   **Assistant Manager: Terry Hetheridge**

Chairman: Graham Taylor   **Vice Chairman: Ronald Gosling**

Cradley Town were formed as a result of a merger between Albion Rovers and Haden Rangers in 1970, the two clubs being established around the time of the War. Albion began to develop the Beeches View ground and combined with Rangers ability to bring in good young players brought success. Originally the name was Albion Haden but this was changed to Cradley Town and in 1971 the club won the Metropolitan League which brought promotion to the Midland Combination. There were two runners up spots before they won Division Two, but the narrow pitch held them back, and so it was rectified along with the building of a clubhouse and small stand. After three years they switched to the West Midlands League and after applying for re-election they won the Second Division. Floodlights and a new stand were installed but recent years have seen the club go through some bad times which were brought on by financial problems.

DARLASTON TOWN

City Ground, Waverley Rd, Darlaston Tel: 0121 526 4423

Secretary: Mrs Kath Abley, 42 Addenbrooke St, Darlaston, West Midlands Tel: 0121 531 0487

Match secretary: Andrew Hickman, 31 Willenhall St, Darlaston, West Mids WS10 8NE Tel: 0121 568 7514

Colours: Blue and white stripes

Nickname: Blues

Capacity: 2,000

Seating: Yes

Covered standing: Yes

Clubhouse on ground: Yes

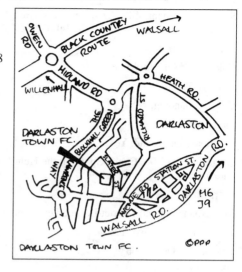

Honours

West Midlands League Div 1 and Div 1 Cup 1990

Birmingham Senior Cup 1973

Birmingham Vase 1991 and 1992

Birmingham Junior League 1908

Birmingham Combination 1911, 1938, 1946

Tillotson Cup 1937, 1938, 1939, 1946

Wednesbury League 1897, 1898, 1899, 1900, 1901

Manager 1996-97: Mendies Hylton

Chairman: Michael Howls

ETTINGSHALL HOLY TRINITY

Aldersley Stadium, Aldersley Rd, Tettenhall, Wolverhampton WV6 9NW Tel: 01902 751171

Secretary: Graham Mills, 27 Ashen Close, Sedgley,
Dudley, West Midlands DY3 3UZ Tel: 01902 662222

Nickname: Trins

Colours: Green and White

Seating: 500

Covered standing: No

Floodlights: Yes

Clubhouse on ground: Yes

Biggest win: 15-0 v Chubb Sports in the Hunt Cup,
date unknown

DIRECTIONS
A41 Tettenhall Road from
Wolverhampton, turn right into
Lower Street after five miles,
then right into Aldersley Road.

Honours

Wolverhampton and District League Div 1 and 2 Cup 1964, 1965, 1966

League Division Two: 1965

League Div One: 1966

Premier Division: 1981

AH Oakley Cup: 1981

Staffs County League Shield 1983 and 1984

Ike Cooper Cup: 1983 and 1984

Sporting Club award: 1982

JH Hunt Cup: 1983 and 1984

West Midlands League Sporting Club award 1986

Wolverhampton Cup: 1984

Joint Managers for 1996-97: David Caddick and Kenny Hall

Chairman: John O'Dell

Ettingshall's history has been traced back to the early 1900's, although the year of formation is usually stated as 1920. The club was formed as the name suggests, from members of the Ettinghall Holy Trinity Church which originally stood on the main road midway between Fighting Cocks and Bilston. The first side competed in the Wednesbury Church and Chapel League and then various local leagues before joining the Bilston Youth League in the early 1950's, later competing in the Wolverhampton and District Amateur League. After working their way through the divisions Trinity were accepted into the Staffs County League and spent three successful seasons picking up every trophy possible except the Premier Division title when in 1983 they missed it by one goal. The following season the progression was maintained when the club entered into Division 2 of the West Midlands League and in the first season were runners up and gained promotion to Division One, reaching the League Cup final in the first year. The highest league place was in 1989 when the club finished third narrowly missing promotion, before finally gaining promotion in 1995.

GORNAL ATHLETIC

Garden Walk Stadium, Lower Gornal, Dudley, West Midlands Tel: 01384 252285

Secretary: Keith Birch, 24 Dursley Close, Willenhall, West Mids. WV12 4DE Tel: 01902 410784

Colours: Yellow and green,   Nickname: Peacocks

Capacity: 3,000,   Seating: 100

Floodlights: Yes,   Covered standing: 500

Clubhouse on ground: Yes

Record fee received £1,500 for Gary Bell and George Andrews to Cardiff City 1966

Honours

West Midlands League Div 1 Cup 1993

Birmingham Vase 1992

DIRECTIONS

From Dudley take A459 to Sedgley past the Burton Road Hospital. 1st on the left at the Green Dragon public house on the B4175 (Jews Lane). Follow the road until you come to the Old Bull's Head, turn left into Rednall Road. 2nd left to Garden Walk.

HILL TOP RANGERS

Hadley Stadium, Wilson Rd, Smethwick, Warley Tel: 0121 434 4848

Secretary: Paul Allen, 14 Queen St, Wednesbury, West Mids Tel: 0121 566 5194

Match Sec: Angela Scott, 46 James Watt St, Hill Top, West Bromwich Tel: 0121 566 3597

Colours: Yellow and black

Biggest win: 15-0 v Ham Baker in 1984

Biggest defeat: 1-9 v West Brom Athletic 1981

Record goalscorer in total: Dean Cadman 175

Record appearances: Dave Scott 399

DIRECTIONS

Situated in Wilson Road, Smethwick.

Honours

West Mids Division Two: 1990

Mercian League: 1987

LYE TOWN

Stourbridge Rd, Lye, Stourbridge Tel: 01384 422672

Secretary: Mrs Audrey Ball, 76 Aretha Close, Crestwood Park, Kingswinford, West Mids DY6 8SW

Tel: 01384 839216

Match Secretary: Geoff Ball, same address

Colours: Blue and white halves

Nickname: Flyers

Capacity: 5,000

Seating: 200

Covered standing: 600

Clubhouse on ground: Yes

Record attendance 6,000 Brierley Hill Alliance

DIRECTIONS

On A458 Birmingham-Stourbridge road about 400yds after lights/cross-roads at Lye. From M5 jct 3 take the road marked Kidderminster as far as lights at bottom of Hagley Hill, right at island, 3rd turn off at next island 3rd turn off at cross-roads/lights, left, ground about 400yds on left. Quarter mile Lye Railway Station.

Honours

West Midlands League Premier Div Cup 1976

Midland Combination 1936

The club was formed in 1930 and initially played in the Worcestershire Combination. They joined the West Midlands League at the beginning of 1947 when it was the Birmingham and District League and are now the longest serving members.

Whilst never winning the title, Lye were runners up four times in five years at the end of the eighties and on two occasions only missed out on goal difference to Willenhall and Sutton Coldfield.

Last season they enjoyed a run which saw them finish third behind Wednesfield and Pelsall Villa.

From the start the club have played on a shared sports ground with Lye Cricket Club, with the pitch originally facing at right angles to its current position.

After the War the football side developed with two stands and dressing rooms where the clubhouse now is and is capable of holding 5,000; 1,000 less than the record crowd which saw a local derby with Brierley Hill Alliance in the 50's.

MALVERN TOWN

Langland Stadium, Langland Avenue, Malvern, Worcs. Tel: 01684 574068

Secretary: Glynne Knapper, 27 Alexandra Lane, Malvern, Worcs WR14 1JF Tel: 01684 574861

Match Sec: Dave Isley, 32 Howsell Rd, Malvern, Worcs Tel: 01684 567098

Colours: Claret and white

Capacity: 4,000

Seating: 150

Covered standing: 300

Clubhouse on ground: Yes

Record attendance: 1,221 v Worcester City FA Cup 1st Qual Rd Replay 1980

DIRECTIONS

From Worcester take main road to Malvern. When reaching Malvern turn left at 1st lights into Pickersleigh Ave, follow to Langland Arms Pub on left, left to Madresfield Road, 2nd left into Langland Ave ground 100yds on right 1 mile from Malvern Railway Station.

Manager 1996-97: Adrian Green

Assistant Manager: Dave Ilsley

Chairman: Reg Tandy

Vice Chairman: Paul Carter

Press Officer and Prog Ed: Dave Isley

Malvern Town were formed in 1947 and were originally known as Barnards Green FC. They first competed in the Worcester League, but soon progressed to the Worcester Combination in 1955.

In the first season they were champions as well as lifting the Worcestershire Junior Cup, but this was to be their last championship, although they were runners up to Highgate Utd in 1974.

They moved to the West Midlands League in 1979 and they have remained there, with 6th being their best finish in 1987.

The Worcestershire Senior Urn has proved the most lucrative competition, Town winning it in 1973, 74 and 75, and three times since. In the league, the club were forced to take demotion in 1992 due to a financial crisis, but with the re-structuring of the league, they are back in the Premier Division.

STAFFORD TOWN

Stafford Rangers FC, Marston Road, Stafford, Tel: 01785 42750

Secretary: Dave Rowley, 32 Lodge Rd, Brereton, Rugeley,
Staffs Tel: 01889 583000

Colours: All Red

Nickname: Reds

Capacity: As Stafford Rangers

Clubhouse on ground: Yes

Biggest win: 14-0 v Leek CSOB
Staffs Senior League 1988

Honours

West Midlands League Div 1 1994

Midland Combination Div 2 1979

Staffs Vase 1985 and 1993

Bourne Sports Trophy 1985

DIRECTIONS

From M6 junction 14, A34
(Stone) to roundabout,
straight over into Beaconside
take third right into Common
Road, ground one mile ahead
From Town Centre, follow
signs for B5066 (Sandon) turn
left by Lotus shoe factory.
Two miles from railway
station.

Stafford Town were formed in 1974 and began playing on Silkmore Lane in the Staffs County League North. They had just three years before trying their luck in the Midland Combination, moving to the better equipped Burton Manor Sports Ground in 1977. They were successful, winning Division Two in 1979, but returned to the County League for two years in 1982. After two further years the club moved on again and joined the Staffs Senior League, taking the Staffs FA Vase in the first season. Town were runners up in 1988 and were second in the league in 1992, a season when they also reached the semi-final of the Walsall Senior Cup. They won the Vase again in 1993 and moved up to the West Midlands League, winning Division 1 in 1994.

After leaving the Sports Ground in 1988 the club had three years at Riverway before moving to Rowley Park Stadium in 1991. After gaining promotion to the Premier Division the club entered into a groundshare agreement with Stafford Rangers to enable them to take their rightful place.

Marston Road – Stafford Town's borrowed home

STOURPORT SWIFTS

Walshes Meadow, off Harold Davis Drive, Stourport-on-Severn Tel: 01299 825188

Secretary: John McDonald, 65 Princess Way, Stourport-on-Severn, Worcs DY13 OEL Tel: 01299 822088

Press: Dave Watts 1 Elan Ave, Stourport-on-Severn, Worcs DY13 8LY Tel: 01299 823349

Nickname: Swifts   Capacity: 2,000

Seating: New 234 seater just built

Covered standing: 200   Clubhouse on ground: Yes

Record attendance: 4,000 v Birmingham City in Charity match.

Biggest win: 11-0 opponents not known

Biggest defeat: 1-7 opponents not known

Record appearances: Dave Brooks

Record goalscorer in one season: Martin Hallam

Record goalscorer in total: Simon Marsh

DIRECTIONS

Follow one-way system through Stourport sign posted Sports Centre. Go over River Severn Bridge, turn left into Harold Davies Drive. Ground is at rear of Sports Centre. Nearest rail station is Kidderminster.

Honours

West Mids Prem Div Cup 1993

Worcester Senior Urn 1992, 1993, 1994, 1995

Worcester Infirmary Cup 1993, 1994, 1995, 1996

Manager for 1996-97: Rod Brown, Assistant manager: Gary Wilde

Chairman: Chris Reynolds, Vice Chairman: Bill Inns

The clubs origins date back to 1882 when the first recorded games were played. These matches were practice games amongst themselves. The first competitive match was away at Kinver with Stourport winning 6-0, known then just as Swifts. The first home match was a local derby against Stourport Strollers.

The first real honours came in 1913 when both the Bromsgrove and Worcester Charity Cups were won and just prior to the Great War they reached the final of the County Cup, but lost.

After the War, Swifts finally won the cup three times between 1925 and 1927. The early days were spent in the Kidderminster and Worcester Leagues until joining the Midland Combination. More recently they have been members of the West Midlands League, although it is hoped that success in that league will lead to promotion to the Alliance.

The club have had a number of grounds, first playing on a field near the Station Hotel before some matches were played on Bewdley Road, near the New Inn. There were several more moves, to Moor Hall Park, Feathers Farm, and when the club reformed, Olive Grove, home of several previous Stourport clubs. Between the Wars Swifts used a ground at The Hawthorns, now covered by a Chain Makers and soon after World War Two they moved to Walshes Meadow, changing in the nearby Rugby Club.

LUDLOW TOWN

The Riddings, Riddings Rd, Ludlow, Salop Tel: 01584 875103

Secretary: Miss Kim Evans, 14 The Wildings, Riddings Rd,
Ludlow, Salop Tel: 01584 876579

Match Sec: John Nash, 58 Hucklemarsh Rd, Ludlow, Salop
Tel: 01584 874337

Colours: Red and black

Capacity: 1,000

Seating: No

Covered standing: Yes, 150

Clubhouse on ground: Yes

DIRECTIONS

From Kiddeminster road
A4117; straight over
roundabout into Henley Road,
2nd left into Sandpits Rd,
follow road for a quarter mile
until road bears round to the
left into Ridding Road -
ground immediately on right.

Honours

West Midlands League Div 1 Cup 1991

Shropshire County Challenge Cup 1994 and 1995

Presteigne Otway Cup 1991 and 1995

Manager 1996-97: Dave Meckin

Assistant Manager: Martin McKenzie

Coach: Bernard Mackey

Chairman: Peter Gwilliam

TIVIDALE

The Beeches, Packwood Road, Tividale, Warley, West Midlands Tel: 01384 211743

Secretary Paul Boswell, 34 Princes Road, Tividale, Warley
Tel 0121 520 3618

Chairman: Don Aston 18 Hollies Road, Tividale
Tel: 01384 850594

Colours: All Yellow

Nickname: The Dale

Capacity: 3,000

Seating: 200

Covered standing: 1,000

Clubhouse on ground: Yes

Record attendance 2,500 v Telford Utd FA Cup 1976

Biggest win: 18-0 v Darlaston 1969

Biggest defeat: 1-8 v Ilkeston Town 1992

Record fee received: £3,000 for Leroy May to Hereford Utd 1993

DIRECTIONS

Dudley Port Station to Burnt tree, left towards Birmingham, ground 1 mile on right. Or, M5 junction 2, follow Dudley signs A4123, after approx 2 miles turn left into Regent Road and left again into Elm Terraces, first left into Birch Crescent. Packwood Road is second left - ground at end of cul-de-sac.

Honours

West Midlands League Div 1 and Cup 1973

Premier Div Cup 1977

Wednesbury Charity Cup 1977

Manager 1996-97: Alan James

Assistant Manager: Gary Dunn

Chairman: Don Aston

Tividale FC was originally founded as the senior section of Tividale Hall Youth Club who played in the Handsworth and District League from 1953 to 1968. Tividale FC entered the senior section of that league in 1956 for four years. After two years without league football, they joined the Warwick and West Midlands Alliance, where they remained for four successful seasons until 1966 when they joined the newly formed West Midlands League Division One.

In 1973 they won the League and Cup double and were promoted to the Premier Division, and left the Community Centre ground in City Road to move to Packwood Road, renaming it The Beeches after the British Waterways official who leased them the land. In 1976 they enjoyed an FA Cup into the 4th qualifying round and in 1977 they won the Premier Division Cup and the Wednesbury Charity Cup.

During the 80's fortunes waned and in 1991 they were relegated, due to the lack of floodlights and a lack of ambition. The close season saw the manager of many players leave, but Tividale finished third and with floodlights installed, were back in the Premier Division.

WALSALL WOOD

Oak Park, Lichfield Rd, Walsall Tel: 01543 361084

Secretary: John Rousell, 19 Kinver Ave, Willenhall, West Mids Tel 01902 637711

Chairman: Robert Thomas Tel: 01543 361084

Colours: Red and black, Floodlights: Yes

Capacity: 1,000, Seating: 400

Covered standing: Yes, Clubhouse on ground: Yes

Record attendance: 800 v Aston Villa in 1980

Honours

Midland Combination 1952

League Cup 1980 (Walsall Sportsco)

League Cup 1955 and 1861

Birmingham Junior Cup 1977

Manager for 1996-97: Paul Madders

DIRECTIONS

Off A461 Walsall-Lichfield Road, 4 miles from Walsall town centre and 100 yds south of junction with A4152 Aldridge-Brownhills. If travelling via M6/M5 exit motorway at junction 7 (Post House) and continue on A34 towards Walsall before joining A4148 which connects with the A461. 4 miles from Walsall (BR) station - regular buses pass ground.

WEDNESFIELD

The Cottage Ground, Amos Lane, Wednesfield Tel: 01902 735506

Secretary: Mr R Thomas, 21 Stubley Drive, Wolverhampton

Colours: Red and white, Nickname: Cottagers

Capacity: 4,500, Seating: None

Covered standing: 250, Floodlights: Yes

Clubhouse on ground: Yes

Record attendance: 1,400

Biggest win: 9-1 , Biggest defeat: 1-6

Record appearances: Peter Calvin

Record goalscorer in one season: Jock Morrison

Record goalscorer in total: Jock Morrison

Honours

West Midlands League 1996, Division One 1977

Manager 1996-97: Kevin Haynes, Assistant Manager: Rob Morris, Chairman: Roger Thomas

DIRECTIONS

From Wolverhampton on the A4124 Wednesfield Road. Stay on road right through Wednesfield until island. Leave island at first exit (Wood End Road), left after about 200 yds into Amos Lane. Ground is on right, approx. 400 yds along. 3 miles from Wolverhampton BR station. Bus 559 to Wood End or 560 to Red Lion.

The club were formed in 1961 as Wednesfield Social and played chiefly in the Wolverhampton Amateur League until 1976. Home at that time was the St George's Playing Field, but their move when acquiring the old James Gibbon's Sports Ground meant a move to the West Midlands League Division One. The ground had a wooden pavilion with dressing rooms but little else and much work was done, especially after promotion which saw a post and rail and eventually floodlights, a stand and new dressing rooms. Wednesfield took the West Midlands championship in 1996, beating Pelsall Villa and Stourbridge Swifts, two early season favourites.

WESTFIELDS

Thorn Lighting Fittings Ltd, Holme Lacy Road, Rotherwas, Hereford.

Secretary: Andy Morris, 17 Fayre Oaks Green, Kings Acre, Hereford Tel: 01432 264711

Manager: Gary Stevens, 73 Quarry Road, Tupsley, Hereford

Nickname: The Fields   Capacity: 2,000

Seating: 100   Covered standing: None

Floodlights: Yes   Clubhouse on ground: No

Record attendance: 1057 v Hereford United

Biggest win: 11-1 v Coventry Sporting

Biggest defeat: 0-7 v Pelsall Villa

Record appearances: Phil Powell and Mark Tabb

Record goalscorer in one season: Paul Burton

Record goalscorer in total: Paul Burton

Record fee received: £4,000 for Alex Sykes from Mansfield Town

DIRECTIONS

Proceed 1 mile south from Hereford on A49, left in Home Lacy Road at Broadleys Inn, proceed 1 mile to Thorn Lighting Rotherwas, ground on the right on Rotherwas Industrial Estate. 2 miles from Hereford (BR).

Honours

Herefordshire Senior Challenge Cup 1986, 1989, 1992, 1996

West Midlands League Div 1 1987, West Midland League Div 2 Cup 1980 and 1984

Kington Challenge Cup 1984, 1986, 1987, 1990, 1992, , Kington Invitation Cup 1985, 86, 87, 96

Presteigne Otway Cup 1979, 1982, 1985, 1994

WFA Junior Cup 1980, Wye Guild Cup 1975 and 1978

Hereford Sunday League and Cup double 1976 and 1977

Division One 1972, Division One Cup 1974 and 1975, Division Three Cup 1973

Herefordshire League Division Two 1977 and Division Three 1976

Smart and Brown Cup 1968, Robert Biggart Memorial Trophy 1996

Manager: for 1996-97: Gary Stevens, Assistant manager: Sean Edwards

Westfields Football Club was formed in November 1966 when a group of lads from that area began cycling down to Widemarsh Common to play friendlies against others like Danish Bacon, Oxford Arms, Post Office and College Rovers. Now 30 years on they are still going and have elevated themselves to become one of the most successful amateur sides in Herefordshire. The lone survivor from that bunch of friends still at the club is Andy Morris, who is now Chief Executive. From those early days of friendlies, Westfields went into the Herefordshire Sunday League and won the Division Two League Cup in 1968. They spent ten enjoyable years in that league and won many trophies along the way. In 1973 they moved into the Worcester and District League, and were then running five teams, plus two on a Sunday and a youth side. Further progress was made when they moved to their present ground, the Thorn Lighting ground, in Rotherwas, in 1975.Three years later they moved to the West Midlands League, and continued to be successful, the best year being 1987 when the club reached the Fifth Round of the FA Vase. Lights were installed soon after as Westfields developed and last season was possibly the best ever with the Senior Challenge Cup, Robert Biggart Memorial Trophy, Kington Invitational Cup and HFA County Youth Cup all won. The club's ground was once a cricket ground owned by AEI, a company taken over by Thorn. Cricket ceased in the mid-sixties, but the old pavilion has been extended and is in use as changing rooms. At one time Hereford United used the ground for training.

WOLVERHAMPTON CASUALS

Aldersley Stadium, Aldersley Rd, Wolverhampton Tel: 01902 751171

Secretary: Michael Green, 63 St Philips Ave, Pennfields,
Wolverhampton Tel: 01902 333677

Colours: White and green

Founded: 1899

Seating: Yes

Covered standing: Yes

Capacity: Not known

Honours

West Mids League Div 1 1995

Division One League Cup 1986

DIRECTIONS

Take the M54 off the M6 to junction 2. Turn right onto the A449 to Stafford. The ground is half a mile on in Brinsford Lane. 2 miles from Billbrooke (BR). Stafford-Wolverhampton buses pass the ground.

WOLVERHAMPTON UNITED

Darlaston Town FC, Waverley Rd, Darlaston Tel: 0121 526 4423

Secretary: Liz Blatherwick, 38 Shape Rd, Ashmore Park,
Wednesfield, Wolverhampton Tel: 01902 728611

Match Sec: Graham Jones, 1 Davey Rd, Perry Barr,
Birmingham Tel: 0121 686 0967

Colours: Gold and black

Founded : 1976

GROUND DETAILS AS PER DARLASTON TOWN FC

Honours

West Mids League Div 1 Section B 1977

Division One League Cup 1977, 1982, 1994

Birmingham Vase: 1994

DIRECTIONS

M6 jct 10, onto A454 towards Willenhall, left at lights outside 'Lane Arms' into Bentley Road North. Follow the road down the hill and over rail and canal bridges to traffic lights. Cross over the lights into Richards Street and along into Victoria Road, 1st right into Slater Street. The ground is on the left but the entrance is next left in Waverley Road.

Supreme Division

	P	W	D	L	F	A	PTS
Oakham United	32	22	4	6	71	37	70
Glapwell	32	19	6	7	51	31	63
Heanor Town	32	19	5	8	70	41	62
Kimberley Town	32	17	6	9	70	56	57
Staveley M W	32	16	8	8	52	43	56
Long Eaton Utd	32	16	4	12	69	52	52
South Norm Ath	32	14	7	11	47	40	49
Case Sports	32	14	7	11	52	51	49
Gedling Town	32	13	8	11	57	42	47
Sandiacre Town	32	11	7	14	52	58	40
Harworth C I	32	12	3	17	55	76	39
Mickleover Sports	32	12	2	18	55	63	38
Rossington	32	10	7	15	49	59	37
Kiveton Park	32	9	5	18	40	61	32
Nettleham	32	5	13	14	34	55	28
Shirebrook Town	32	8	2	22	47	75	26
Thorne Colliery	32	6	4	22	26	57	22

Premier Division

	P	W	D	L	F	A	PTS
Killamarsh	34	26	3	5	111	46	81
Dunkirk	34	23	7	4	127	31	76
Graham St Prims	34	20	7	7	67	36	67
Nuthall	34	18	12	4	74	36	66
Clipstone Welfare	34	18	4	12	83	51	58
Sneinton	34	18	4	12	87	62	58
Radford	34	16	8	10	66	48	56
Askern Welfare	34	17	4	13	77	65	55
Shardlow St J	34	15	8	11	66	59	53
Hemsworth Tn	34	15	5	14	63	58	50
Sheffield Hall U	34	13	5	16	65	72	44
Mexborough Ath	34	10	9	15	64	77	39
Derby R R	34	11	5	18	62	78	38
Collingham	34	10	6	18	60	75	36
Stanton Ilkeston	34	10	5	19	54	79	35
Mickleover R.B.L.	34	9	4	21	42	86	31
Blackwell M W	34	2	8	24	44	125	14
Sheepbridge	34	2	2	30	34	162	8

CASE SPORTS

Cantley Park, Doncaster, South Yorkshire. Tel: 01302 535167

Secretary: Mr D.W. Henderson, 18 King George's Rd, New Rossington, Doncaster, South Yorks DN11 0PR Tel 01302 865027

Colours: All Red

Capacity: 1,000

Seating: No

Covered standing: 100

Clubhouse on ground: Yes

Floodlights: No

Record attendance: v Emley
Sheffield Senior Cup semi-final 1995

Honours

South-East Friendly League Div 2 and League Cup 1987

Doncaster and District Sunday Amateur League 1992, 93, 94

Division Two 1990, League Cup and Charity Shield 1993

Manager 1996-97: Steve Hinchcliffe, Assistant Manager: Bob McMimm, Chairman: Mr A. Wyman

DIRECTIONS

**Cantley Park, Doncaster.
Junction 3 off M18 White Rose Way, follow signs to racecourse. Right at racecourse roundabout to Bawtry Road (A638). Pass Doncaster Rovers and leisure centre on right. Left into Cantly Lane at Cantly traffic lights. 200 yds left into Ascot Avenue. Ground entrance opposite Beechers Brooke public house. Ground at end of drive.**

The club began as Co-op FC in the South East Friendly League and they changed the name to MS International and then Fabcon FC. The club has been called Case Sports for the past four seasons.After a successful spell in Sunday morning football, the club moved to Saturdays, joining the Central Midland League Premier Division. They gained promotion after finishing runners up and were also semi-finalists in the Sheffield Senior Cup and quarter-finalists in the League Cup.All the improvements to the ground, with fencing hard standing and stand have been completed by players and committee, and JI Case Social and Sports Club helped meet the costs.

DUNKIRK

The Ron Steel Sports Ground, Trentside Farm, Clifton Bridge, Nottingham. Tel: 01602 842147

Secretary: Steve Throssell, 24 Kingfisher Wharf, Castle Marina, Nottingham NG7 1GA. Tel: 0115 947 3903

Colours: Red and black, Capacity: 1,000, Seating: No

Covered standing: 150, Clubhouse on ground: Yes

Record attendance: 814 v Tiverton Town FA Vase

DIRECTIONS

Ring Road, Clifton Bridge (North End), Industrial Estate, Lenton Lane.

Honours

Notts Alliance Division One 1985

Division Two 1981, League Cup 1985

Notts Amateur League Premier Div and League Cup 1975

Notts Intermediate Cup 1985

Reformed after the War in 1946, they played their home games at Highfields in the Notts Amateur League.In 1975 a lease was agreed with Nottingham City Council for a new ground at Trentside Farm, near Clifton Bridge and after much hard work the ground was brought up to standard for the club to enter the Notts Alliance Division Two. Since then Dunkirk have progressed to the gain Senior Division status and they finished runners up three years running from 1989.The club has also had success in cups, winning the Alliance Senior Cup in 1988, beating Hucknall CW and have finished runners up in 1983 and 1991. In 1991 Dunkirk entered the FA Vase, and in 1993-94 they exceeded all expectations reaching the last 16 before losing to previous finalists Tiverton Town in front of a record crowd of 814. The football ground was named after the late Ron Steel who died in 1983, as a mark of respect for the sterling work he put in for the club and securing the lease for the ground.

GEDLING TOWN

Riverside Ground, rear of Ferry Boat Inn, Stoke Biddulph, Gedling, Notts. Tel: 01602 770258

Secretary: Paul Dobson, 26 Chevin Gardens, Top Valley Estate, Nottingham NG5 9ES. Tel: 0115 927 4790

Colours: Red and black, Capacity: 2, 000

Covered standing: 500, Club house on ground: Yes

Record attendance: 250 v Arnold Wakefield Floodlit Trophy 1992-93

Record appearances: G. Watson

Record goalscorer in total: Darren Terry

DIRECTIONS

From Notts County FC, A612 towards Southwell for 2 miles to Burton Joyce, Station Road, then Stoke Lane. Ground rear of Ferry Boat Inn.

Honours

Central Midlands Div 1 1991, Wakefield Floodlight Trophy 1993
Notts Amateur League 1990

Manager 1996-97: Jamie Brodie, Chairman: Roland Ash

Gedling Town Football Club were founded as R & R Scaffolding in 1986. They moved quickly through the Notts Amateur League before being elected to the Central Midlands League in 1991, whereupon they changed their name to Gedling Town. The club were successful in winning Division One at the first attempt and in 1992 they were runners up to Slack and Parr in the Premier Division. The first season in the Supreme Division saw the club finish sixth, winning the Wakefield Floodlit Cup beating Sheffield Aurora 2-0.

GRAHAM STREET PRIMS

Carriage and Wagon Welfare Club, Longbridge Lane, off Ascot Drive, Derby. Tel: 01332 571376

Secretary: Mr D Wright Tel 01332 765833

Colours: All Red Clubhouse on ground: Yes

Honours

Derbyshire FA Divisional Cup South 1972, 1973, 1976, 1977, 1979, 1980, 1981

Central Alliance League: 1971

East Midlands League Prem Div and League Cup 1979

Division 1: 1972

Derbyshire Premier League and League Cup 1981

DIRECTIONS

Approach Derby on the A52 from Ashbourne direction or from junction 25 of the M1. The A38 also serves Derby but the ground is on the east side near the baseball ground. Ascot Drive bridges London Road (A6) and Osmaston Road (A514) near Alvaston Park.

Manager 1996-97: S. Woodings, Assistant Manager: D. Tice

Chairman: D. Holmes, Vice Chairman: J. Toon

Graham Street Prims played their first game in September 1904. They were formed from a Primitive Methodist Church, hence the name and nickname, The Prims Graham Street is situated off Osmaston Road in Derby, close to the current home of Derby County. The Prims were disbanded in 1914 due to the First World War but in their first ten years boasted several players who went on to play League football, namely the Keetley brothers and Jimmy Bagshaw who eventually played for Notts County and England.

Prims did not re-form until 1953 but they soon won many honours including titles in Central Alliance, East Midlands and Derbyshire Premier Leagues. Their finest years were between 1971 and 1981 winning no less than 15 major honours including DFA Cups and 8 league titles.

HARWORTH COLLIERY INSTITUTE

Recreation Ground, Scrooby Road, Bircotes, Doncaster. Tel: 01302 750614

Secretary: Mr Tom Brogan, 30 Lindsay Rd, Harworth, Doncaster DN11 8QH. Tel: 01302 750132

Nickname: The Reds

Capacity: 2,000

Seating: No

Covered standing: 500

Clubhouse on ground: Yes

Record attendance: 350 v Congleton Town
FA Cup 1st Qualifying round 1988

Record Appearances: Robert Needham

DIRECTIONS

Off A1(M) at Blyth, head towards Bawtry for approx 2 miles, take third left, ground in village at top of hill on left. Or, from Doncaster to Bawtry them head for A1(M) and turn left after caravan site - ground at top of hill.

Honours

Wharncliffe Charity Cup 1961, 1963, 1975

Central Midlands League 1988

Challenge Cup 1987 and 1988

Floodlit Cup 1992 and 1996

Sheffield Senior League 1965 and 1975

Wakefield Floodlit Challenge Cup 992

Manager for 1996-97: Alan Needham, Assistant manager: Nigel Paczkowsk

Chairman: Paul Wilson 01302 744582

Best contact when confirming a fixture: Steve Owen 01302 750322

Press Officer: Mark Hickling, 22 Snipe Park Rd, Harworth, Doncaster Tel 01302 744569

Programme Editor: Steve Owen 13 Church Rd, Bircotes, Doncaster DN11 8DR Tel: 01302 750322

Founded in 1931, The Institute spent most of its early existence in local leagues before becoming members of the Yorkshire League briefly after the War. Later joining the Doncaster and Sheffield Senior Leagues, they enjoyed their most productive time in the 60's, winning the Wharncliffe Charity Cup in 1963 and the County Senior League in 1965, winning both in 1976.

The demand to move up into a higher sphere was met when the Yorkshire League accepted them back in 1977. Promotion was won and eventually the league was incorporated into the Northern Counties (East).

Harworth now play in the Supreme Division of the Central Midlands League which they dominated for a couple of years in the late eighties, winning it in 1988 and finishing runners-up in league and cup three times. Harworth CI name Paul Wilson, the former England semi-pro International amongst their most famous players.

894

HEANOR TOWN

The Town Ground, Mayfield Ave, Heanor, Derbys. Tel: 01773 713742 social club or 715815 boardroom

Secretary: Keith Costello, 45 Stainsby Ave, Heanor, Derbys, DE75 7EL. Tel: 01773 719446

Press Sec: Stan Wilton, 'Haven Holme', 57 Main Rd, Smalley, Ilkeston, Derbys DE7 6DS. Tel: 01332 880199

DIRECTIONS

North: M1 junction 27, A608. South: M1 junction 26, A610-A608.

Colours: White and black,   Capacity: 2,500

Seating: 200,   Covered standing: 1,200

Clubhouse on ground: Yes

Record attendance: 6,511 v Carlisle Utd FA Cup 1958

Biggest win: 16-2 v British Ropes 1956

Biggest defeat: 1-9 v Alfreton Town 1959 and 1995

Record appearances: Richard Preston 1988 to date

Record goalscorer in one season: Don Brown 72 1958-59, Record goalscorer in total: Brian Fidler 1963-68

Record fee received: £15,000 for Nigel Pearson

Honours

Central Midlands League and League Cup 1995, B.E. Webbe Removals Cup 1989

Derbyshire Senior Cup 1893, 1894, 1947, 1966, 1967, 1968, 1969, 1971, 1979

Central Combination 1934, Central Alliance Div One North 1956, 1957, 1958

Manager 1996-97: Bill Fossey, Assistant Manager: Jav Haslam

Chairman: John McCullough, Vice Chairman: Stan Wilton

Heanor Town's origins go back to sometime in 1883, their earliest known match being a friendly against Loscoe Rangers. By the end of the decade Heanor had become firmly established and joined the Derbyshire League winning the championship twice. After a successful run in the FA Cup Heanor joined the Midland League and in 1891-92 qualified to meet Aston Villa and despite Villa asking them to scratch as they were 'unknown in these parts', Heanor played at Perry Barr, losing 4-1. In 1897 the club moved back to the Derbyshire League but it soon folded and they had a further year in the Midland League before dropping to the Mid-Derbyshire League in 1901. Sadly the club folded in 1907, missing four seasons before re-forming, but they went with the legacy of a famous FA Cup tie with Bury in 1898, when 10,000 crammed in to the ground. When football started up again after the Great War Heanor were back and having played in the Notts and Derby League returned to it before once again having one year in the Midland League. It was not a wise move as despite crowds of 2, 000 the club were heavily in debt. They went back to the new Derbyshire League and ended the season as joint champions as well as winning six other trophies. In 1932 Heanor became founder members of the Central Combination and won it in 1935 but again they were bankrupt in 1937, and with the War in between it took until 1951 for them to again re-form.After one season of friendlies and one in the Notts Alliance they had seven years in the Central Alliance, backed by a strong Supporter's Club, and won Division One North in 1957. They retained the title a year later and in 1958 amid great excitement they reached the First round of the FA Cup for the first time in 59 years. 6,000 saw the match against Carlisle which was lost 5-1.In 1961 the Midland League was re-formed and for ten years they enjoyed a successful spell until moving to the West Midland League where they were runners up, but they again went back to the Midland League to try to re-capture their earlier success only to twice have to apply for re-election.

During that time they did dominate the Derbyshire Senior Cup, winning it five times in six years, but in the league they began in the Northern Counties East when the Midland was absorbed, and work was done at the ground, with a Social Club, seating in the Popular side stand and floodlights.

In 1987 Heanor switched to the Central Midlands League and have enjoyed their time so far, winning the BE Webbe Cup and finishing runners up when scoring over 100 goals and in 1995 they completed a treasured double by winning the League and League Cup.

KIMBERLEY TOWN

Stag Ground, Nottingham Road, Kimberley, Notts. Tel: 0115 9382788

Secretary: Stewart Brown, 14 Brendon Drive, Kimberley, Notts NG16 2JZ Te. 0115 9383542

Press Officer: George Brown, address as above

President: R.J. Penney 140 Newdigate Lane, Kimberley, Notts Tel: 0115 938 3542

Gen Manager: Brian Harrison 10 Nightingale Close, Nuthall, Notts

Colours: Blue and white,

Nickname: The Stags

Capacity: 2,500,

Seating: None

Covered standing: 100, Clubhouse on ground: Yes

Record attendance: 1,122 v Eastwood Town Midland Counties Lge 1976

Biggest win: 13-2 v Belper Town Res April 23rd 1959

Biggest defeat: 1-9 v Bridlington Trinity NCEL 1981

Record appearances: Denis Froggatt

Record goalscorer in one season: Graham Cutts

Record fee received £2,000 for Andy Hill to Derby County June 1981

DIRECTIONS

Through Nuthall from M1 jct 26 to Kimberley, ground entrance 150yds after Stag Inn 6 miles from Nottingham (BR). Trent Buses R11, R12, R13, 357 & 358 all stop outside the ground.

Honours

Notts Amateur League and League Cup 1952, Notts Alliance Division One 1955

Manager 1996-97: Julian Garmston, Chairman: George Giddens, Vice Chairman: Reg Izzard

The original Kimberley Town FC played in the Notts and District League before the turn of the century but disbanded in the early 1920's. A club was formed in 1948 with the title Kimberley YMCA and they played with distinction in the Notts Amateur League, finishing runners up in Division One in 1950 before doing the League and Cup double in 1952. In 1955 the club joined the Central Alliance and were placed in Division Two but when the YMCA closed they changed the name to Town and were again runners up in Division Two in 1958 and promoted. Invited to the Central Alliance Premier Division in 1961 they enjoyed their best spell in that and the East Midlands Regional League, although never winning a title. The nearest to any silverware was a League Cup defeat and a 4-0 defeat in the Notts Senior Cup final in 1965.

They were runners up in the EMRL in 1971 and were accepted into the Midland League, but they declined and were relegated and when the league was merged they found themselves at the bottom of Division Three.

Kimberley moved to the Central Midlands League as founder members but suffered two relegations until a social club and floodlights at the Stag Ground meant a revival and in 1992 they were back in the Supreme Division. Sadly the club's secretary Mr Horace Hibbert passed away in 1995 after 48 years involvement with the club.

LONG EATON UNITED

Grange Park, Station Rd, Long Eaton, Nottingham. Tel: 0115 9735700

Secretary: David Hampson, 4 Airedale Close,
Long Eaton, Nottm. NG10 3HW. Tel: 011597 26343

Press: Geoff Whitehead 01332 872849

Colours: Blue and white

Nickname: The Blues

Capacity: 3,000

Seating: None

Covered standing: 500

Clubhouse on ground: Yes

Floodlights: No

Record goalscorer in one season: G.Weston and G.Walker

Record goalscorer in total: S Holder

Record fee received £5,000 for Gary Birtles from Nottm Forest

DIRECTIONS

From Nottingham, A52 to roundabout by Bardills Garden Centre, left onto B63003 to T-junction & lights, right into Station Road, ground opposite Speedway Stadium. From M1 jct 25, A52 signed Nottingham, right onto B63003 at 1st roundabout then as above 2 miles from Long Eaton Railway Station.

Honours

Derbys Senior Cup 1965 and 1976

Central Alliance South 1959

Northern Counties East Div 1 South 1985

Manager 1996-97: Neil Lovell

Assistant Manager: Martin Dick

Chairman: Jim Fairley

Vice Chairman: Brian Webster

Long Eaton United FC were formed in 1956 and in 40 years have had their fair share of success. A lack of local support has always meant things have been tough and an unsympathetic local authority has held the club back. In spite of this the club have plans top go forward, as the founders did in the 50's. The first couple of years saw championships for both teams, indeed it was the reserves who had most of the glory in the 60's before the senior team won the Derby Senior Cup in 1965, beating Alfreton Town at the Baseball Ground. It was many years before the cup returned to Grange Road.

From 1961 United played in the Midland Counties League, achieving a second place in 1977, before the league was incorporated into the NCEL. United suffered by being excluded from the top division and they struggled until a new Chairman Jim Fairley, and manager Peter Johnson won the Division One title and lost the League Cup final to Alfreton after a replay. In 1989 United joined the Central Midlands Supreme Division but a lack of lights saw them go down. 1994 saw them back again and they still await floodlights in 1996, although an application has gone to the Lottery for a package involving lights, dressing rooms and a solid fence.

MICKLEOVER SPORTS

Mickleover Sports Ground, Station Rd, Mickleover, Derby. Tel: 01332 521167

Secretary: Derek Hewitt

Colours: Red and black stripes, Clubhouse on ground: Yes

Honours

Derby Senior League Section B 1953, Div1 Cup 1975

Premier Division Cup 1987

Derbyshire Junior Cup 1975 and 1981

Frank Andrew Memorial Trophy 1987

DIRECTIONS

Take Station Road from the Town Centre. Ground is on the right at the far end.

Mickleover Sports FC was originally founded in 1948 as Mickleover Old Boys playing in the Derby and District Senior League. For the next 44 years until their resignation in 1993 they were the longest serving members of the league. Following the development of new facilities at Station Road, the ambitions of the football club were understandably increased and it was this in mind that that an application was made to join the Central Midlands League. As Mickleover Sports an entirely new management team was drafted in and a final position of sixth for both teams was respectable.

A year later under Paul Spray and Bill O'Connor the club were promoted to the Supreme Division.

NETTLEHAM

Mulsanne Park, Field Close, Nettleham. Tel: 01522 750007

Gen Secretary: Stewart Timms, 5 Ash Tree Avenue, Nettleham, Lincoln LN2 2TQ. Tel: 01522 751140

Club Sec: John Wilson, 21 Chaucer Drive, Lincoln LN2 4LN
Tel: 01522 530566

Colours: Blue and Yellow   Nickname: Nettles

Capacity: 2,000   Seating: 100

Covered standing: 100   Clubhouse on ground: Yes

Record attendance: 1,200 v Aston Villa Floodlight opener

DIRECTIONS

A46 approx. 3 miles north of Lincoln, night at Brown Cow Pub, proceed past Church 2nd turning on right.

Honours

Village Trophy, Nursing Cup, Kelly Read Cup

Blakeney Hunt Cup, Joe Miller Trophy

Manager 1996-97: Ian Musson,
Assistant Manager: Jeff Alsopp, Chairman: Clive Mason

It is known that there was an original football club in Nettleham from around 1905. The team changed in the Half Way House pub at the top of Washdyke Hill and the pitch was at Grange-de-Lings, where it remained until 1946. The club disbanded for the Great War and the Second War but has been constant apart from those times. In 1948 the club moved its ground to the village, playing on what is known as Bill Bailey's Field on the Scothern Road, and changing at the White Hart Hotel, which necessitated a walk through the village to the pitch. However, the acquisition of land belonging to the church in the mid-70's saw the club to its present home in 1979, later to be named Mulsanne Park following the twinning with the French village. Nettleham continued to play in local leagues until 1981 when it moved into the Lincolnshire County League, gaining promotion in the first year. They stayed until joining the Central Midlands League in 1988 and in 1990 they moved up to the Supreme Division.

The club has developed considerably over the last 10 years and the facilities have allowed the club to play at their current level, with five senior sides, six juniors and a ladies team

NUTHALL

Birnam Park, off Eastwood By-pass, Eastwood, Nottm. Tel: to follow

Secretary: Tony Benniston, 117 Broad Lane, Brinsley, Nottm. Tel: 01773 712350

Colours: Sky and Navy blue   Nickname: The Larks

Capacity: 1, 000   Seating: No

Covered standing 200   Clubhouse on ground: Yes

Record attendance: 200+ v Arnold Town Notts Senior Cup

Biggest win: 9-0 v Shardlow St James 1993

Record appearances: Les Wild

Record goalscorer in total: Jack Paxton

DIRECTIONS

A610 southbound left southbound, right northbound.

Honours

Central Midlands League Premier Div 1994 Senior Div. 1985

East Midlands Regional League 1983, 1984 Knock-Out Cup 1982

Notts FA Intermediate Cup 1980, Notts Minor Cup 1983

Manager 1996-97: Andy Freeman, Assistant Manager: Andrew Robinson

Chairman: Alan Farmer, Vice Chairman: Ray Naylor

SANDIACRE TOWN

St Giles Park, Stanton Rd, Sandiacre, Nottingham NG10 5EP. Tel: 0115 9392880

Secretary Mel Williams, 38 Pasture Rd, Staplefore, Nottingham, NG9 8GL Tel 0115 9392415

Colours: Red and navy   Nickname: The Saints

Capacity: 2,000   Seating: None   Covered standing: 250

Floodlights: Yes   Clubhouse on ground: Yes

Biggest win: 12-0 v Ilkeston Town Res

Biggest defeat: 1-10 v Oakham United

Record appearances: Ged Le Blond 151

Record goalscorer in one season: Dave King 46 1992-93

Record goalscorer in total: Mark Robinson 56

DIRECTIONS

M1 junction 25, follow signs to Sandiacre passing Post House Hotel on right, straight over crossroads into Rushy Lane and towards Stanton, first right after 1000 yards into Stanton Road, ground at bottom after another 1000 yards. Trent buses from Nottingham to Derby alighting at Sandiacre Market Place — from traffic lights go along Town Street (canal on your right) eventually past Comet (on right) then left into Church Street, follow to Stanton and ground is 200 yards on right (total distance half mile).

Honours

Central Midlands League Premier Division and League Cup 1993

Manager 1996-97: Geoff Barrowcliffe, Chairman: John Ellis, Vice Chairman: Mark Warton

Sandiacre Town was formed in 1978 by Malc Turton and Pete Smith, who had previously run Ilkeston Town's under 14's. The first practice night saw over 150 youngster turn up and three teams were begun in the Notts Youth League. In 1979 it grew to five with a Saturday senior side entered into the Central Alliance League. In 1982 work began on the club Headquarters, with club members raising over half the £40,000 required. It was carried out with the help of Manpower Services Commission and was completed and opened in March 1984.The senior side moved on to the Central Midlands League but lost their place in 1989 because of the lack of facilities, but in 1991 the club merged with Lace Web United and finished second in the Premier Division and were re-admitted to the CML in 1992 where they did the double, winning the last 24 league and cup games. Sadly the sponsor and most of the team moved to Shepshed Albion and to make matters worse in 1993 the ground again did not meet with the league approval and for one season the club played at Kilburn Welfare. During 1994 the ground was enclosed and cover put up which was sufficient to go into the Supreme Division in 1994.

SHIREBROOK TOWN

Langwith Road, Shirebrook, Mansfield, Notts. Tel: 01623 742535

Secretary: S.P.Wall, 26 Carter Lane, Shirebrook, Mansfield, Notts. Tel: 01623 747638

Other contact: Mr T.Rowbottom 34 Slant Lane, Shirebrook, Notts.Tel: 01 623 74622

Nickname: The Brook

Capacity: 2,000

Seating: none

Covered Standing: 400

Floodlights: Yes

Clubhouse On Ground: Yes

Record Attendance: 2,200 v Mansfield Town Floodlight opener 1991

Biggest Win: 10-3

Biggest Defeat: 0-7 Newhall Utd Derbys Sen Cup 1988

Record Appearance Holder: G.Tennant

Record Goalscorer In One Season: M.Smith

Record Goalscorer In Total: S.Hill

Record Fee Received: £4,000 for Gary Castledine to Mansfield Town in 1991

DIRECTIONS

M1 junction 29, A617 to Mansfield, 2.5 miles, B6407 Shirebrook, through town to Langwith Road. Bus 81 from Chesterfield or 23 from Mansfield.

Manager For 1996-97: N.Moore

Assistant Manager: G.Charlesworth

Chairman: T.Rowbottom

Vice Chairman: K.Easom

Press Officer Mr T.Moore, 53 Valley Road, Shirebrook

The Town of Shirebrook has seen a number of teams come and go and Town are the latest having been in existence just 11 years. The original Town played at the same Welfare ground from 1911 until moving to a ground behind the White Swan pub. It had a large stand and once held 7,000 for a visit of Tranmere Rovers. It was turned into a greyhound track and is now under a housing estate. Shirebrook Colliery used the Welfare ground which is now owned British Rail Staff Association. The Colliery club became Town and they remain there playing in the Central Midlands League.

SOUTH NORMANTON ATHLETIC

Miners Welfare Ground, Lees Lane, South Normanton, Derbys. Tel: 01773 581491

Secretary: David Meredith, 5 Erica Drive, South Normanton, Derbys DE55 2ET Tel 01733 812566

Nickname: Athletic

Colours: Yellow and Blue

Capacity: 2,000

Seating: 150

Covered Standing 500

Floodlights: No

Clubhouse On Ground: Yes

Record Attendance: 409 v Heanor Town League Cup Jan 1st 1994

Biggest Win: 8-0 v Retford Rail in 1990, Shardlow St James in 1992 and again in 1993

Biggest Defeat: 1-7 v Sandiacre T 1993 and Alfreton Town in 1995

Record Appearances: Clice Churm 168

Record Goalscorer In One Season: Mick Bott and Wayne Hollis 32

Record Goalscorer In Total: Mick Kane

Clubshop manager: Kev Miles 9 Mansfield Rd, Sth Normanton, Derbys Tel 01773 510925

Honours

Alfreton and District Sunday League 1987 and Div 2 1984

Supplementary Shield 1985

WL Screen Bowl 1987

Mansfield Sunday League Premier Div Cup 1989

Manager For 1996-97: Andy Farby, Assistant Manager: Chris Lee

Chairman: Robert Ravenall, Vice Chairman: Eric Holland

DIRECTIONS

B6019 from the M1 exit 28. Turn right after 1 mile (in South Normanton) at Mobil garage into Market Street. After quarter of a mile turn left immediately after The Clock pub into Lees Lane. The ground is at the bottom. Alfreton & Mansfield Parkway BR staion is about 30 minutes walk away.

The current club were formed in 1980 and played in the Alfreton Sunday League until 1987, when they moved to the Mansfield Sunday League, much success being enjoyed in both. They turned to Saturday football in 1990 and joined the Central Midlands League where in 1994 they won promotion to the Supreme Division with healthy attendances culminating in a record crowd of over 400 against Heanor Town.

The Lees Lane ground is far older than the existing club, indeed there was a South Normanton Welfare who played in the strong Central Alliance League and folded in the early 70's. The ground opened as a recreational area in 1923 for the Colliery Welfare and expanded for football in 1937, long after the cycle track, the remains of which can still be seen in parts around the ground, fell into disuse.

After the club went under the ground was still used by junior clubs until the current club moved in and made great strides to improve the facilities.

STAVELEY MINERS WELFARE

Inkersall Road, Staveley, Chesterfield. Tel: 01246 471441

Secretary: Mr John Wilmot, 12 Winster Rd, Staveley, Chesterfield. Tel: 01246 476875

Other contact: Tony Barnes, 52 Curbar Curve, Inkersall, Chesterfield. Tel: 01246 474448

Press officer: Andrew Knowles Tel 01246 555064

Club shop: Rod Walker Tel: 01246 473655

Colours: Red and white

Nickname: The Welfare

Capacity: 5,000

Seating: 200

Covered standing: 400

Clubhouse on ground: No

Record attendance: 1,507

Biggest win: 14-0 v Abbeydale (a) 1991-92

Biggest defeat: 0-5 v Stocksbridge Park Steels (a) 1993-94

Record appearances: Andrew Knowles

Record goalscorer in one season: Paul Nicholls

Record goalscorer in total: Paul Nicholls

DIRECTIONS

M1 junction 30, follow A619 Chesterfield — Staveley is 3 miles from junction 3. Turn left at GK Garage in Staveley town centre into Inkersall Road — ground 200 yards on right at side of Speedwell Rooms. Frequent buses (47, 70, 72, 75, 77) from Chesterfield stop in Staveley town centre — 3 minutes walk to ground.

Honours

County Senior League Div 2 West 1993

and Division 3 West 1992

Chesterfield Amateur (Byron) League Cup 1990

Central Midlands League Premier 1995

Manager 1996-97: David Tromans, Assistant Manager: Phil Greaves

Chairman: Henry Ireson, Vice Chairman: Phil White

Staveley were formed as Staveley Nags Head FC in 1962, playing Sunday football. For three seasons they played friendly games against pub sides before joining the Mansfield Sunday League in 1965, playing the first ever game against Muschamps FC at Station Road, Barrow Hill.

In 1968 they moved to the Chesterfield Sunday League winning the title before the Saturday side was formed in 1989, playing in the Chesterfield Amateur Division One. They were runners up in the league and won the Byron League Cup and were runners up in both a year later. In 1991 the club moved into senior football and in the first year were champions of the Whitbread County Division 3, winning Division 2 a year later. The club were on the move and in 1993 they joined the Central Midlands Supreme Division.

The club play at the Welfare Ground which was home to a previous club under the same banner which played in the FA Cup in the late 40's.

THORNE COLLIERY

Miners Welfare Ground, Southfield Rd, Thorne, Doncaster. Tel: 01374

Secretary: Mr G Jones, Top Town Social Club, Fredrick St, Grimsby DN31 1RG Tel 01472 350554

Colours: Green and white

Capacity: 1,000

Seating: No

Covered standing: Yes

Clubhouse on ground: No

DIRECTIONS

Miners Welfare Ground, Southfield Road, Thorne, Doncaster.

Honours

Doncaster Senior League Premier Division 1989, 1990, 1991, 1992, 1993

Doncaster FA Challenge Cup 1990, 1991, 1992

Premier Division: 1993

Goole and Thorne Cup: 1987, 1988, 1989, 1991

Walker and Hall Trophy: 1988 and 1989

West Riding Challenge Cup: 1989 and 1993

Above: Sandiacre Town

Below: Staveley Miners Welfare

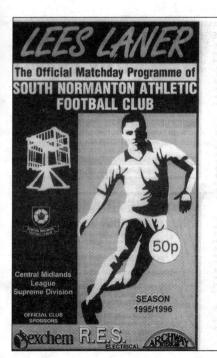

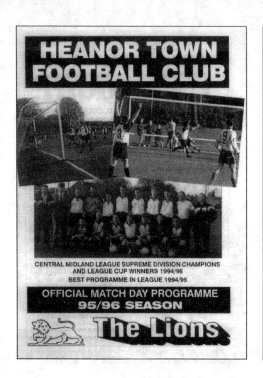

HEANOR TOWN FOOTBALL CLUB

CENTRAL MIDLAND LEAGUE SUPREME DIVISION CHAMPIONS
AND LEAGUE CUP WINNERS 1994/95
BEST PROGRAMME IN LEAGUE 1994/95

OFFICIAL MATCH DAY PROGRAMME
95/96 SEASON

The Lions

MICKLEOVER SPORTS
FOOTBALL CLUB
V
KIVETON PARK
Saturday 2nd March 1996
Kick-off 3.00 pm

Mickleover Sports Club

Sponsored by
McFLY'S HAIRDRESSING

50p

OFFICIAL PROGRAMME

Price £1-50

INCLUDES
ADMISSION

Lucky Number
27
£5.00 PRIZE

Thorne Colliery
FOOTBALL CLUB

Welcomes

CENTRAL MIDLANDS
V. CASE SPORTS
TUE. 26TH. DEC. 95.

1995/1996 Season

Thorne Colliery F.C.
Formed 1929
Moorends Welfare Ground, Grange Road, Moorends

Sponsored by
National Deposit Friendly Society

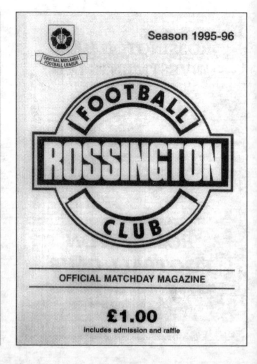

Season 1995-96

CENTRAL MIDLANDS
FOOTBALL LEAGUE

FOOTBALL
ROSSINGTON
CLUB

OFFICIAL MATCHDAY MAGAZINE

£1.00
Includes admission and raffle

	P	W	D	L	F	A	PTS
Barry Town	40	30	7	3	92	23	97
Newtown	40	23	11	6	69	25	80
Conwy United	40	21	13	6	101	58	76
Bangor City	40	21	6	13	72	65	69
Flint Town United	40	19	9	12	76	57	66
Caernarfon Town	40	16	13	11	77	59	61
Cwmbran Town	40	14	15	11	58	49	57
Inter Cardiff	10	14	12	14	62	62	54
Caersws	40	15	9	16	81	97	54
Connah's QN	40	13	14	13	68	63	53
Ebbw Vale	40	14	11	15	59	56	53
Llansantffraid	40	14	10	16	66	57	52
Porthmadog	40	13	11	16	56	62	50
Aberystwyth Town	40	13	9	18	60	68	48
Cemaes Bay	40	13	7	20	63	80	46
Holywell Town	40	12	7	21	53	74	43
Briton Ferry A	40	11	9	20	64	91	42
Rhyl	40	11	9	20	47	83	42
Ton Pentre	40	8	16	16	46	65	40
Afan Lido	40	9	9	22	33	71	36
Llanelli	40	8	9	23	50	88	33

ABERYSTWYTH TOWN

Park Avenue, Aberystwyth, Dyfed. Tel: 01970 612122

Secretary: Mr D.Steeds, Glen Rose, Brynmor Rd,
Aberystwyth, Dyfed SY23 2HX Tel 01970 624637

Chairman: Mr Derek Dawson, Tel 01970 624548

Colours: Green and black

Nickname: Seasiders

Capacity: 6,000

Seating: 250

Covered standing: 1,000

DIRECTIONS

From south: A487. 1st right at
Trefachan Bridge to roundabout, 1st
right with Park Avenue being 3rd right.
From north: A487 and follow one way
system to railway station, at
roundabout 1st left with Park Avenue
being 3rd right. 5 mins walk from
Aberystwyth Railway Station - follow
as above.

Record attendance: 4,500 v Hereford United
Welsh Cup 1971

Biggest win: 21-1 v Machynlleth Coastal League 1937

Biggest defeat: 1-20 v Caersws Mid-Wales League 1962

Record goalscorer in total: David Williams 476 in 433 games 1966-83

Record goalscorer in one season: Eddie Ellis 67 in 42 games in 1948-49

Record appearances David Whitney: 572 1961 - 1982

Honours

WELSH CUP WINNERS 1900

Welsh Intermediate Cup 1986 and 1988

Mid-Wales League 1923, 1924, 1926, 1927, 1928, 1933, 1949, 1950, 1959, 1984, 1985

League Cup: 1927, 1928, 1932, 1939, 1948, 1985, 1986

Welsh Amateur Cup 1931, 1933, 1970

Welsh League Division Two South 1952

Cambrian Coastal League 1933, 1934, 1935, 1936, 1937, 1950, 1957, 1959

League Cup: 1936, 1950, 1957

Central Wales Challenge Cup 1976, 1982, 1983, 1985, 1987, 1988

Manager: Meirion Appleton

BANGOR CITY

The Stadium, Farrar Rd, Bangor, Gwynedd. Tel: 01248 355852

Secretary: Mr A Griffiths, 12 Lon Y Bryn, Menai Bridge, Ynys Mon, Gwynedd Tel 01248 712820

Chairman: Mr G.P.Owen, Tel 01248 450373

DIRECTIONS

Old A5 into Bangor, 1st left before railway station, ground on left by garage

Colours: All Blue,   Nickname: Citizens

Capacity: 10,000,   Seating: 900

Covered standing: 2,000,   Clubhouse on ground : No

Record attendance 12,000 v AC Napoli
European Cup Winners Cup 1962

Honours

FA TROPHY Runners up 1984

Northern Premier League 1982 and League Cup 1969

President's Cup 1989 and Challenge Shield 1988, League of Wales 1994 and 1995

Welsh National League 1928, North Wales Coast League 1896

Welsh Cup 1889, 1896, 1962, , North Wales Challenge Cup 1927, 36, 37, 38, 47, 52, 58, 65, 68

Welsh Amateur Cup 1895, 1896, 1898, 1899, 1901, 1903, 1905, 1906, 1912

Welsh Junior Cup 1896, 1898, 1920, Alves Cup 1950 and 1960, Cookson Cup 1962, 69, 85, 87

Manager 1996-97: Kevin Langley

On December 18th 1876 at a meeting at the Magistrates room in the city, a club was formed that initially played both Association and Rugby Union. After a few years the club dropped the Rugby code, moved to a ground in the city centre and won the North Wales and Welsh Cups. They became founder members of the North Wales Coast Football League and won it three years later.

In 1898 they joined the Combination, and whilst members they provided the Welsh National side with ten players, and when the league folded in 1910, they moved to the North Wales Alliance until the War. The league was not revived and in 1921, having moved from Maes Y Dref to Farrar Rd to merge with the cricket club, they played in the Welsh National League, and from then until 1950 they were members of the North Wales Combination, Birmingham and District and Lancashire Combinations, before moving to the Cheshire League where they stayed for 18 years. They were twice runners up and won the Welsh Cup in 1962, beating Wrexham in the final, which saw them represent Wales in the European Cup Winners Cup. They drew AC Napoli in the 1st Round and beat them 2-0 in front of 12,000 at Farrar Rd, but lost 3-1 in Italy in front of 80,000. With no away goal rule, a replay was held at Arsenal, which they lost 2-1.

Bangor City were founder members of the Northern Premier League, winning the League Cup in the first season and in 1979 were invited to join the new Alliance Premier League. In 1980 they were relegated, for one season as they bounced back, but in 1984 they went down again. During that spell the club reached the FA Trophy final at Wembley, being the first Welsh club since Cardiff City in 1927 to play there. City and Northwich drew and in the replay at Stoke City, Bangor lost 2-1. The spell in the NPL lasted eight seasons during which time they were runners up to Shrewsbury Town in the Welsh Cup, and thereby qualified again for Europe. In the first round they beat Norway's Fredrickstad on away goals and drew Athletico Madrid in Round 2. Over 7,000 saw the home tie at Farrar Road before they lost in Madrid.

Bangor joined the League of Wales in 1992 and have won the title twice, enjoying more European action as a result.

BARRY TOWN

Jenner Park, Barry Road, Barry, South Glamorgan. Tel: 01446 735858

Secretary: Mr A Whelan, 132 Westward Rise, Barry, South Glamorgan Tel 01446 737188

Chairman: Mrs P O'Halloran, Tel 01222 641100 (b)

Nickname: Linnets or Dragons

Colours: Yellow and blue

Capacity: 3,000   Seating: Yes

Covered standing: Yes

Record attendance: 7,400 v Queens Park Rangers FA Cup 1st Round 1961

Record appearances: Basil Bright

Record goalscorer in total Clive Ayres

DIRECTIONS

M4 junction 33 via Wenvoe (A4050) to Barry. Left at 1st 2 roundabouts to Jenner Park. Nearest rail station is Cadoxton.

Honours

Welsh Cup Winners 1955 and 1995

Welsh Trophy 1995

Welsh League 1983, 1984, 1985, 1986, 1987, 1989, 1995

League Cup 1935, 1947, 1983, 1995

South Wales Senior Cup 1927, 1936, 1938, 1953, 1954, 1959, 1960, 1966, 1976, 1978, 1987, 1988, 1995

SA Brain Cup 1979, 1983, 1987

Manager For 1996-97: Gary Barnett

BRITON FERRY ATHLETIC

Old Road, Briton Ferry, West Glamorgan. Tel: 01639 812458

Secretary: c/o 262 Neath Road, Briton Ferry SA11 2SL

Chairman: Mr Graham Jenkins, Tel 01689 814762

Colours: Red and green quarters

Capacity: 1,750

Seating: 100

Covered standing: 300

Clubhouse on ground: Yes

Record win: 14-0 v Nantymoel Welsh League 1951

Record defeat: 0-10 v Ebbw Vale League of Wales 1993

Record attendance: 1,090 v Abergavenny Thursday Welsh League 1991

DIRECTIONS

M4 from Cardiff, on to A48 at roundabout (3rd exit) signed Briton Ferry, right at 1st traffic lights - ground half a mile on right.

Honours

Welsh League 1995

Div 2 1938, 1939, 1940, 1947, 1972

Manager: Paul Burrows

CAERNARFON TOWN

The Oval, Marcus Street, Caernarfon, Gwynedd Tel 01286 675002

Secretary: Mr W Gray-Thomas, Dorwyn, Bethel Rd, Caernarfon, Gwynedd Tel 01286 674482

Press Sec: Mr G. Lloyd Owen, Bod Aden, Bontnewydd, Caernarfon, Gwynedd, Tel 01286 830307

Colours: Yellow and green   Nickname: The Canaries

Capacity: 3,678   Seating: 178

Covered standing: 1,500   Clubhouse on ground: Yes

Record attendance: 6,002 v Bournemouth & Boscombe Ath FA Cup 1929

DIRECTIONS

Directions: A55 coast road to A487 bypass to Caernarfon. At inner relief road r'bout follow Beddlegert sign, then 2nd right — ground opposite. Nearest BR station is 9 miles distant at Bangor. Local buses to Hendre estate.

Biggest win: 16-2 v Holyhead 1939

Biggest defeat: 0-18 v Colwyn Bay in 1908

Record appearances Walter Jones 306 1906-1926

Record goalscorer in one season: Peter Reid 75 in 1928-29   Record goalscorer in total: Walter Jones 255

Honours

Lancashire Combination 1982; League Cup 1981; Welsh League North 1947, 1966, 1978, 1979; Alves Cup 1939, 1975, 1978, 1979; Cookson Cup 1957 and 1978; North Wales Combination 1933; Welsh National League 1927, 1930; North Wales Coast League 1912

Manager 1996-97: John Aspinall   Assistant Manager: Paul Bennett

Chairman: Mr G Lloyd Owen   Vice Chairman: Mr E Angel

The first football club in Caernarfon, known as Caernarfon Athletic was formed in September 1876 and played on various grounds before moving to the Oval in 1888. Five years later they folded, but two years later several former players began Caernarfon Ironopolis, and they reached the North Wales Coast League, winning it on two occasions and reaching two Welsh Cup semi-finals. Sadly, following a dispute with the league they too folded in 1903. The demise of Ironopolis resulted in some players forming Caernarfon Colts while others affiliated to the Caernarfon RWF. Both clubs played at the Oval and in 1906 they amalgamated to form Caernarfon United, the new club immediately being successful winning the Welsh and North Wales Amateur Cups.

After the Great War the demobbed players formed a new club which until 1926 played in the Coast League and then the Welsh League Division Two, with mixed fortunes. They employed a full time manager and turned professional, and Caernarfon Athletic, as they were known, were Division One champions in 1927 and 1930 and are still remembered for the FA Cup run of 1929 in which they defeated Darlington before losing to Bournemouth in a 2nd Rd Replay. A year later they too went into liquidation, but re-formed two years later and won the Welsh Combination before quitting over problems with using the Oval.

In 1937 a group of enthusiasts began Caernarfon Town FC and entered a team in the Welsh League North. It was the start of an unbroken 39 year membership as the town at last had a club which would last.

They won the championship in 1947 and 1966, but in 1976 internal; problems led to the club withdrawing from the league. In a matter of months the club had once again re-formed and took the league in 1978 and 1979 and after just missing the hat-trick in 1980, they were given permission to join the Lancashire Combination. They won that in 1981 and 1982, its last season, before it was absorbed into the new North-West Counties League, were promoted in the first season. In 1985 they were runners up and were elected to the Northern Premier League, and after a poor start, manager John King turned things round and in 1986-87 and club enjoyed their most successful FA Cup run, beating Stockport County and York City before losing in the 3rd Round to Barnsley in a replay.

King Left and Tommy Smith took over, but he soon departed and despite a run to the Welsh Cup semi-final, soon after they were relegated. After much conflict with the League of Wales and an unhappy spell when they were banned from playing at home, the club joined the League of Wales in 1995.

CAERSWS

Recreation Ground, Caersws, Powys. Tel: 01686 688753

Secretary: Mr T M Jones, 3 Hafren Terrace, Caersws, Powys, Tel 01686 688103

Chairman: Mr G Williams, Tel 01686 688258

Founded : 1887

Nickname: Bluebirds

Colours: Blue and white

Seating: 150

Covered standing: 300

Clubhouse on ground : No, in village

Record attendance: 2,795 v Swansea City Welsh Cup 1990

Record win: 20-1 v Aberystwyth Mid-Wales League 1972

Record goalscorer in total: Gareth Davies

DIRECTIONS
Entering Caersws (between Newtown & Llanidloes on A470) ground entrance on left by river bridge.

Honours

Welsh Amateur Cup 1961

Welsh Intermediate Cup 1989

Mid-Wales League 1960, 1961, 1963, 1978, 1983, 1986, 1989, 1990

League Cup 1980, 1983, 1988, 1990

Central Wales Challenge Cup 1978, 1983, 1988, 1990

Mongomeryshire Challenge Cup 1953, 1960, 1963, 1970, 1971, 1972, 1975, 1977, 1978, 1984, 1985, 1986, 1987, 1988, 1989, 1991, 1995

Montgomeryshire League 1978

Manager: Mickey Evans

CARMARTHEN TOWN

Richmond Park, Priory Street, Carmarthen

Secretary: Mr A Latham, 3 Maesdolau, Idole, Carmarthen SA32 6DQ Tel: 01267 232432

Chairman: Mr M Williams, Tel 01267 232372

Founded: 1953

Covered standing: 1,000

Seating: 300

Colours: Old Gold and black

Manager: Mr Wyndham Evans

DIRECTIONS

Carmarthen is situated where the A48 from the M4 meets the A40 heading east west.

CEMAES BAY

School Lane Stadium, Cemaes Bay, Anglesey. Tel: 01407 710600

Secretary: Mrs N.Hughes, 12 Maes Garnedd, Tregele, Cemaes Bay, Anglesey Tel 01407 710297

Chairman: Mr I Clews, Tel 01407 710728

Colours: Yellow and black stripes

Manager: Bryn Howes

DIRECTIONS

Approach Anglesey via Penrhosgarnedd by the A487, the A5 or the A55. From Menai Bridge head to Amlwch on the A5025. Cemaes is signposted from here.

CONNAH'S QUAY NOMADS

Halfway Ground, Connahs Quay, Deeside, Clwy. Tel: 01244 836784

Secretary: Mr R Hunter, 40 Brookdale Ave, Connahs Quay, Flint Tel 01244 831212

Chairman: Mr R Morris, Tel: 01244 812507

Colours: White and black

Nickname: Westenders

Capacity: 1,500

Seating: Yes

Covered standing: Yes

Clubhouse on ground: Yes

Record attendance: 1,500 v Rhyl
Welsh Cup semi-final 1993

Biggest win: 16-0 v Rhydymwym 1949

DIRECTIONS

On main coast road (A548) from Chester to Rhyl west end of Connah's Quay behind Halfway House.

Honours

WELSH AMATEUR CUP 1953 and 1955

North Wales Amateur Cup 1953 and 1955

North Wales Coast Challenge Cup 1981

Welsh Intermediate Cup 1981

Welsh Alliance Cookson Cup 1988

Manager 1996-97: Neville Powell

Connahs Quay FC was formed in 1946 by the Everton and Wales centre-half Tommy Jones. He formed a management committee and the first meeting, made up of local businessmen was held in a scout hut and from this was formed Connahs Quay Juniors. Permission was granted from the Northgate Brewery to play on the ground at the back of the pub which had been there for 80 years. They entered the Nortop Youth League and were so successful that in 1948 they formed a senior side to play in the Flintshire League. The youths won the Welsh Youth Cup in 1948 and peaked in 1951 when they reached the final of the Welsh Amateur Cup, only to lose to Treharris Athletic. In 1952 the name was changed to Nomads and they entered the Welsh League North Division One. They reached the final of the Welsh Cup only to lose to Chester at the Racecourse Ground and they were back there for the final of the Amateur Cup where they beat Caersws.

From this success came financial problems and they left to join the Halkyn League where they stayed until the Clwyd League was formed in 1975. The finest season since the 50's came in 1981 when the club won the Welsh Intermediate Cup, beating Newport YMCA 1-0. That season the club lifted seven trophies and got to the last eight of the Welsh Cup.

Nomads became founder members of the Cymru Alliance in 1990 and were also founder members of the League of Wales in 1992.

CONWY UNITED

Morfa Ground, Conwy, Gwynedd Tel 01492 573080

Secretary Mr C Jones, 'Iolyn', Iolyn Park, Conwy, Gwynedd Tel 01492 593496

Chairman: Mr G Rees Tel 01492 573243

Colours: Tangerine and black

Nickname: Musselmen

Capacity: 1,500

Seating: Yes

Covered standing: Yes

Clubhouse on ground: Yes

Record attendance: 850 v Bangor City League of Wales 1995

Biggest Win: 11-1 British Steel Shotton Welsh Cup 1979-80

Record goalscorer in total: Carl Dale

DIRECTIONS

Leave A55 on 1st slip road after river tunnel and turn left towards Conwy. Sharp left immediately after overhead railway bridge - ground 400 yds on left of Penmaen Road.

Honours

Welsh Alliance 1985 and 1986

Barritt Cup 1985

Jack Owen Cup 1982 and 1983

Quinton Hazell Trophy 1985

Welsh intermediate Cup 1982

North Wales Challenge Cup 1981,1983,1985

Gwynedd Cup 1984.

Manager 1996-97 J.Hulse

Conwy Town FC and Conwy British Legion FC amalgamated in 1977 to form the current club. The two clubs both played in the Vale of Conwy Youth League. Since the famous Borough United were formed from the amalgamation of Conwy and Llandudno Junction, there had been a shortage of Welsh League clubs in the area, but that changed as they were elected into the Welsh League North, which later became the Welsh Alliance. In 1882 they won the Intermediate Cup and went on to take the League title two years running in the mid eighties.

In 1990 they became founder members of the Cymru Alliance and later the League of Wales. The Morfa has developed recently from little more than a pitch to pleasant ground complete with stands and their playing in the League of Wales last May saw them venture into Europe via the Inter-Toto Cup.

CWMBRAN TOWN

Cwmbran Stadium, Henllys Way, Cwmbran, Gwent NP44 3XL. Tel: 01656 866192

Secretary: Mr P Dauncey, 36 Gregory Close, Pencoed, Bridgend, Mid Glam Tel 01656 861274

Press Officer Maurice Selway, 10 Hafod Rd, Ponthir, Newport, Gwent NP6 1GH Tel 01633 430065

Nickname: The Town, Colours: White and blue

DIRECTIONS

Approach Cwmbran on the A4042. From the south this road leads up from junctions 25 and 26 of the M4 at Newport.

Founded: 1951

Capacity: 8,500 reduced by safety certificate

Seating: 3,200,

Covered standing: None

Clubhouse on ground: Stadium lounge and catering

Record attendance: 8,148 v Manchester United Friendly 1994

Record win: 11-0 v Gwynfi Welsh League 1968

Record goalscorer in total: Graham Reynolds

Record appearances: Mostyn Lewis

Record fee paid: £1, 500 for Francis Ford from Briton Ferry Ath. 1993

Honours

League of Wales 1993

Welsh League Division One 1967

League Cup 1986 and 1991, Monmouthshire Challenge Cup 1955 and 1956

Gwent Senior Cup 1995 and 1996

Manager for 1996-97: Tony Wilcox, Coach: Roger Gibbins

President: John Colley, Vice Chairman: Clive Edwards

The first meeting of Cwmbran Town AFC took place at the Railway Inn, Llandowlais Street in August 1951, the club forming following the disbanding of Whiteheads AFC. The first season was spent in the Monmouthshire Senior League playing at Cwmbran Park.

They were runners up in the league in 1955, but went one better in the County Cup, winning it twice in 1955 and 1956. From there in 1960, Town joined the Welsh League and after several years on public parks they moved to the new Cwmbran Stadium in 1975. Results took a turn for the worst however, and in 1978 they were relegated to Division Two, and after a struggle the club began the climb back in 1982 as runners up, and although only finishing eighth a year later, they were invited to become founder members of the National Division, where they finished a best placing of third in 1987. In 1986 they were made full members of the FA of Wales and were chosen as one of 14 clubs to represent Wales in the FA Cup and Trophy.

1991-92 was a transitional period for the club and in the summer they were invited to become founder members of the new League of Wales. From there the club enjoyed success which was unimaginable a year earlier and after losing just one game from November onwards they were crowned champions after a win at Llanelli on May 3rd. The success saw them qualify to play in the European Champion Club Cup in 1993. The preliminary round saw them drawn against Cork City and in the home leg they were 3-0 up at half-time, only to concede two late goals. A 2-1 defeat in Cork saw them knocked out. Since then the emergence of a number of strong clubs in the league has seen Town fail to emulate the dream start they had, but they finished well above mid-table last season.

EBBW VALE

Eugene Cross Park, Ebbw Vale, Gwent. Tel: 01495 302995

Secretary: Mr D Coughlin, 107 Mount Pleasant Rd,
Ebbw Vale, Gwent Tel 01495 305993
Chairman: Mr J.Hopkins, Tel 01495 304796
Nickname: The Cowboys
Re-formed: 1950
Colours: Amber and black
Capacity: 10,000
Seating: 1,200
Covered standing: None
Record attendance: 1,762 v Wrexham
Welsh Cup 1989
Clubhouse on ground: Yes

DIRECTIONS

From A465 follow signs to Ebbw Vale, 1st left at next two roundabouts - ground on left.

Honours
WELSH CUP 1926
Welsh League 1988
Division One 1965
Southern Division 1953
Division Two East 1961
South Wales League 1904
South Wales Senior Cup 1905
Gwent Senior Cup 1925, 1927, 1929, 1933, 1946, 1951

Manager for 1996-97: John Lewis

FLINT TOWN UNITED

Cae y Caestel, March Lane, Flint. Tel: 01352 730982

Secretary: Glyn M Davies, 45 Bron y Wern, Bagillt, Flintshire CH6 6BS Tel: 01352 763571

Social Club Tel: 01352 762804

Nickname: The Silkmen

Colours: Black and White stripes

Capacity: 4,000,   Seating: 300

Covered Standing: nil

Clubhouse On Ground: Yes

Biggest Win: 15-0 v Rhos in 1952

Record Appearance: Glen Graham

Record Goalscorer In One Season: Steve Jones

Record Goalscorer In Total: Darren Emmitt

DIRECTIONS

Approaching Flint on A548 from Chester, turn right at signpost for Flint Castle. Ground to right of car park. Flint BR station and bus stops are adjacent to ground.

Honours

Welsh Senior Cup 1954, Runners up 1925

Welsh Amateur Cup 1948, Welsh non-League champions 1991

North Wales Challenge Cup 1991, North Wales Amateur Cup 1910, 1931, 1932, 1933, 1969

North Wales Coast Intermediate Cup 1987

Cymru Alliance 1991, Welsh League 1956, 1958, Cookson Cup 1989 and 1993

Alves Cup: 1954 and 1990, Clywd League 1979

Manager for 1996-97: Steph Rush, Assistant Manager: Timmy Williams

Chairman: Mr Alan Baines, Vice Chairman: Mr Graham George

Flint were founder members of the League of Wales.

The town of Flint is in the county of Clwyd, on the estuary of the River Dee, 12 miles from Chester.

The club's new ground is named Cae Caestel, (Castle Fields) and is not far from the spot where Flint played from 1886 to 1924. The ground is built on reclaimed land and until about five years ago it was marsh, with ponds and gutters and on high tides, water would reach the bottom goal. In 1908, the British Glanztoff Manufacturing Group opened a factory producing man made fibre in Flint and from there the club gets its nickname of the Silkmen. Their Holywell Road ground was originally Naylor's Field, but when the landowner died it was sold and the new owner decided to sell to Courtaulds, who in turn leased the rest to the council. From there Flint Town received the land for recreation in 1924. Six years later the football pitch had to be moved to accommodate an extension to the factory, and in 1952 it was given back to the council who granted the football club a 25 year lease. In 1994, the old ground was demolished and a new shopping complex built in its place.

The club itself has enjoyed much success since the club was formed in 1886, playing in a field close to the ground. They were runners up in the Welsh Amateur Cup in 1890 and have since won honours as they played in Clwyd, Welsh Alliance and Cymru Alliance Leagues amongst others.

HOLYWELL TOWN

Halkyn Road, Holywell, Clwyd, CH8 7WE Tel 01352 711411

Secretary: Mrs C Hughes, Bryn Awel, St James Place, Holway Rd, Holywell, Clwyd Tel 01352 714216

Colours: Red and White

Nickname: Wellmen

Capacity: 3,000

Seating: 300

Covered standing: 500

Clubhouse on ground: No

Record goalscorer in total: Neil Davies

DIRECTIONS

A55 Expressway to A5026 Holywell turn, turn right for ground just after Stanford Gate Hotel. Coming from town centre, turn left off ringroad at Victoria Hotel, past Police Station and turn left for ground at the surgery.

Honours

North Wales Coast Amateur Cup 1914, 1922, 1949, 1958

North Wales Coast Challenge Cup 1987

OCS League and Cup 1988

Welsh National League 1934

Dyserth League 1947

Waterfall Cup 1947

Alves Cup 1947, 1954

Welsh Alliance League 1953

Manager 1996-97: Glyn Griffiths

Chairman: Mr E Moore

Holywell Football Club were founded in 1906, and played in local leagues before joining the Welsh National League which they won in 1934. After the War returning servicemen built the Halkyn Road ground and re-established the club which played in the West Cheshire League and then Welsh League North until 1960. Later they had a brief spell in the Clywd League and the Cymru Alliance before joining the League of Wales.

INTER CABLE-TEL

Cardiff Athletic Stadium, Leckwith Road, Cardiff. Tel: 01222 225345

Secretary: Mr C Hicks, 48 Radyr Court Close, Llandaff, Cardiff Tel 01222 552679

Colours: White and black

Nickname: Seagulls

Seating: Yes

Covered standing: No

Clubhouse on ground: Yes

Record attendance: 1,500 v Cardiff City
 South Wales Senior Cup 1974

Biggest win: 11-1 v Abercynon

DIRECTIONS

The ground is clearly visible just west of Cardiff City's Ninian Park ground.

Honours in total for all clubs

Lake Utd merged with Rumney Rangers in 1984 to become AFC Cardiff, and they merged with Sully in 1990 to become Inter Cardiff. They changed their name to Inter Cable Tel in 1996

Corinthian Cup 1970, 1979

Welsh League Div 2 1972

South Wales Senior Cup 1981, 1982, 1986

Welsh League Div 1 1981

Premier Division 1984, 1986, 1990

Manager 1996-97: George Wood

Until the summer of 1990 the club had been known as Sully AFC. Under that name they enjoyed success rising through the Barry and District and South Wales Amateur Leagues, but the poor facilities at Burnham Avenue prevented them from reaching the Welsh League National Division despite much success in the lower divisions. Their ambition to move on was achieved in 1990 when AFC Cardiff went into liquidation and the chairman of Sully purchased their Cwrt-yr-Ala ground which allowed them to enter the National Division as Inter Cardiff.

1992 saw the birth of the League of Wales and the club became founder members, however facilities at the ground were not acceptable and through the lucrative sponsorship of Aspro Travel and Inter-European Airways the club moved into the superb Leckwith Stadium, next door to Ninian Park.

Through another deal, the club moved to Ninian Park and have subsequently played at Merthyr Tydfil and back at Leckwith Stadium.

On the pitch the club were runners up in 1993 and 1994 and have tasted Europe, playing a game in the UEFA Cup at Merthyr Tydfil.

LLANSANTFFRAID

Recreation Park, Treflan, Llansantffraid, Tel 01691 828112

Secretary: Mr A F Williams, 5 Maes y Garreg,
Llansantffraid, Powys

Tel: 01691 828535

Colours: Green and white

Nickname: The Saints

Capacity: 1,500

Seating: 120

Covered Standing: 100

Record attendance: 1,538 v Ruch Chorzow
European Cup Winners Cup 1996 at Wrexham

Record goalscorer in total: Andy Oakley

Record appearances: Derek Arthur

DIRECTIONS

A470 between Welshpool and Oswestry, left for Llansantffraid at Llnmyrdach, over bridge into village, left through village opposite silos, ground on right signed Community Centre.

Manager for 1996-97: Graham Breeze

Chairman: Mr E Jones

Honours

European Cup Winners Cup entrants 1996

Welsh Cup Winners 1996

League of Wales League Cup 1995

Cymru Alliance 1993

Welsh Intermediate Cup 1993

Central Wales Cup 1993

Montgomeryshire Amateur League 1969,1970,1971,1983,1987,1992,1993

League Cup 1963,1970,1971,1974,1976,1992

Emrys Morgan Cup 1973,1982,1983,1993

Presteigne Otway Cup 1993

Tommy Jarman Cup 1992 and 1993

Llansantffraid were caught in the national media spotlight earlier this season with their European Cup Winners Cup adventure. They qualified for the competition by sensationally beating Barry Town 3-2 on penalties after a 3-3 draw in last season's Welsh Cup Final at the National Stadium.

NEWTOWN

Latham Park, Newtown, Powys. Tel: 01686 626159

Secretary: Mrs S Reynolds, 19 Brynwood Drive, Milford Rd, Newtown, Powys Tel 01686 628089

Colours: Red and white

Nickname: Robins

Capacity: 5,000

Seating: Yes

Covered standing: Yes

Clubhouse on ground: Yes

Record attendance 5,002 v Swansea Town
Welsh Cup 1954

DIRECTIONS

A43 to Newtown, right at 1st lights into Back Lane & town centre - 400 yds left into Park Street, 500 yds right (at Library) into Park Lane - ground at end.

Honours

Welsh Cup Winners 1879, 1895

Runners Up 1886, 1888, 1897

Welsh Amateur Cup 1955

Central Wales League 1976, 1979, 1982, 1987, 1988

League Cup 1955, 1957, 1975, 1976, 1982, 1984

Arthur Barritt Cup 1987

Central Wales Cup 1975, 1981, 1993

Emrys Morgan Cup 1981

Manager 1996-97: Brian Coyne

Chairman: Mr K P Harding

Newtown are one of the oldest clubs in Wales, being formed in 1875 and are founder members of the Football Association of Wales. The club have a long and proud tradition and have progressed through to the Northern Premier League before returning to join the League of Wales, from where they qualified for Europe via UEFA Cup this July.

Back in 1877 they took part in the first ever Welsh Cup tie on October 13th against the Druids of Ruabon. Wrexham went on to win the Cup but the next year Newtown beat the favourites at Oswestry and were the first to receive the trophy which was only purchased a few months before.

Over the years the club has used a number of grounds, including the Cunnings, 24 Acres, the Racecourse Rec and Plantation Lane, but the committee of the club took the decision to purchase and construct the current Latham Park ground in the late 1940's and it was eventually opened on the 25th August 1951.

After playing in the Combination in the early days, Newtown joined the Central Wales League which they finally won for the first time in 1976, leaving the league for the Northern Premier League in 1990 after a further four titles. With six League Cup wins and wins in the Arthur Barritt, Emrys Morgan and Central Wales Cups, the Robins have enjoyed their fair share of success. Sadly a fire in 1989 destroyed the clubhouse and for a while caused serious problems but they bounced back and enjoyed a brief spell in English football before being persuaded to join the League of Wales. Their foray into Europe this July began with a 4-1 defeat by the Latvian champions Skonto Riga.

CPD PORTHMADOG

Y Traeth, Porthmadog, Gwynedd, Tel: 01766 514687

Secretary: Mr R I Griffiths, Llwyn Yr Eryr, Ynys, Criccieth, Gwynedd Tel 01766 810349

Colours: Red and Black

Nickname: Porth   Founded: 1884

Capacity: 4,000   Seating: 140

Covered standing: 400   Clubhouse on ground: No

Record attendance: 3,500 v Swansea Town
Welsh Cup 1965

DIRECTIONS
Y Traeth, Porthmadog. At town centre crossroads (by Woolworths) into Snowdon Street, pass RBL/Craft Centre onto unmade track, over railway line - ground on right.

Honours

Welsh Amateur Cup 1956,1957,1958.
North Wales Amateur Cup 1938,1957,1959,1963.
North Wales Coast Challenge Cup 1956, 1974, 1975, 1977, 1978. Welsh Alliance 1903,1938,1969,1975,1976,1990. Cookson Cup 1976 and 1990.
Barritt Cup 1978. Alves Cup 1966,1974, 1977

Manager for 1996-97 Colin Hawkins

Chairman Mr R J Havelock

RHYL

Belle Vue, Grange Road, Rhyl. Tel: 01745 338327

Secretary: Mr D Williams, 81a Dyserth Rd, Rhyl, Tel 01745 354773

Founded: 1883

Colours: White and navy

Capacity: 4,000   Seating: 200

Covered standing: 1, 000

Record attendance: 10,000 v Cardiff City Welsh Cup 1953

Clubhouse on ground: Yes

Record goalscorer in total: Don Spendlove

DIRECTIONS
A55 Expressway to Rhyl turn-off and follow signs through Rhuddlan. Follow signs for Sun Centre along.

Honours

Welsh Cup Winners 1952 and 1953.
Runners up 1930, 1937, 1993.
Welsh Amateur Cup 1973. Northern Premier League President's Cup 1985.
Cheshire County League 1948, 1951, 1972.
League Cup 1949, 1952, 1971. Division Two Shield 1982.
Cymru Alliance 1994. League Cup 1993

Joint managers for 1996-97: Jimmy Smith

Barry Roberts

TON PENTRE

Ynys Park, Sawmill Villas, Ton Pentre, Rhondda. Tel: (club) 01443 432813

Secretary: Mr P Willoughby, 37 Balley Street, Ton
Pentre, Rhondda Tel: 01443 438281

Nickname: Ton or The Bulldogs

Colours: All Red

Capacity: 2,500   Seating: 400

Covered standing: 800

Clubhouse on ground: Yes

Record attendance: 2,900 v Cardiff City
FA Cup Rd 1 1986

DIRECTIONS

A4058 Pontypridd to Treorchy Plain
road, left at Thames Rico Garage
then first left again. Ton Pentre
station is 400 yds from ground.

Honours

Welsh League Champions 1958, 1961, 1974, 1982, 1993

Welsh Amateur Cup 1952

South Wales Senior Cup 1948, 1961, 1962, 1974, 1984, 1993

Manager for 1996-97: John Emanuel

Chairman: Mr J Orrells

Football in Ton Pentre started prior to the turn of the century, around 100 years ago.

From 1909 to 1915 they played in the original Southern League, as they did after the War. In May 1922 Ton reached the final of the Welsh Cup, losing 2-0 to Cardiff City and in the following season they resigned from the Southern League and went back to the local Rhondda League. The present Ton Pentre side began in 1935 when they joined the Welsh League, where they won the championship five times.

After deciding not to join the new League of Wales in its first season, Ton won the Welsh League again as well as the South Wales Senior Cup and reversed their decision, finishing in third spot behind Bangor City and Inter Cardiff. Again in 1995 they finished third, meaning a venture into Europe, through the Inter-toto Cup.

WELSHPOOL

Maesydre Recreation Ground, Welshpool

Secretary: Mr J A Bartley, 24 Bryn Glas, Welshpool,
Powys Tel 01938 552131

Chairman: Mr M G Edwards

Manager: Mr Gareth Cadwallader

Colours: White and black

Welshpool are newcomers to the League of Wales this season, having been promoted from the PA Rowlands Cymru Alliance.

DIRECTIONS

Approach Welshpool (Y Trallwng) on
the A458 from the east via
Shrewsbury; the A483 from south and
north Wales and the west of England
and on the A458 from west Wales.
Welshpool BR station is on the
Birmingham-Aberystwyth line.

Jewson South Western League

	P	W	D	L	F	A	PTS
Truro City	34	26	4	4	99	27	82
Torpoint Athletic	34	23	8	3	81	32	77
Falmouth Town	34	22	4	8	89	35	70
Launceston	34	20	9	5	95	29	69
Bodmin Town	34	18	10	6	91	36	64
Penzance	34	18	5	11	64	43	58
Newquay	34	18	4	12	73	54	58
Holsworthy	34	17	5	12	58	43	56
Wadebridge Town	34	16	5	13	65	55	53
Saltash United	34	14	8	12	66	67	50
Porthleven	34	13	5	16	62	66	44
St Austell	34	10	5	19	57	79	35
Millbrook	34	9	7	18	40	59	34
Liskeard Athletic	34	9	6	19	58	96	33
Appledore & Bide	34	7	7	20	43	78	28
Tavistock	34	6	6	22	55	99	24
St Blazey	34	4	4	26	38	106	16
Okehampton Arg	34	4	2	28	24	143	14

BODMIN TOWN

Priory Park, Bodmin Tel: 01208 78165

Secretary: Martin Mullis, 24 Jubilee Terrace, Bodmin, Cornwall PL31 2QE Tel: 01208 77685

Colours: Yellow and black

Nickname: Black and ambers

Seating: 400

Covered standing: None

Clubhouse on ground: Yes

Biggest win: 14-1 v Bugle
South Western League Cup Aug 1988

Honours

South Western League 1991 and 1994

League Cup 1994

Cornwall Charity Cup 1987 and 1990

Manager 1996-97: Ricky Cardew

Assistant managers: Alan McSweeney and Phil Brown

Chairman: Colin Hooper

Vice Chairman: Paul Lee

DIRECTIONS

Just off town centre in large park complex, at rear of town car park.

FALMOUTH TOWN

Bickland Park, Bickland Vale, Falmouth, Cornwall Tel: 01326 375156

Nickname The Town, Capacity, 6,000

Seating, 300, Covered standing 1,200

Floodlights: Yes Clubhouse on ground: Yes

Record attendance: 6,300 v Oxford United
FA Cup 1st Round, Nov 3rd 1962

Biggest win: 13-0 v Penzance (A)
South-Western League Cup October 3rd 1964

Biggest defeat: 2-10 v Torquay Utd Res Sept 18th 1954

Record appearances: Keith Manley approx 580 1969-86

Record goalscorer in total: Joe Scott 204 1972-78

Record fee received: £12,000 for Tony Kellow to Exeter City in 1976

DIRECTIONS

Follow A39 to Tregoniggie Industrial Estate - will pass ground on left. One and a half miles from Penmere Halt (BR) on Falmouth-Truro branch line. Bus service from town centre.

Honours

Western League 1975, 1976, 1977, 1978

Western League Cup 1975

South-Western League 1962, 1966, 1968, 1971, 1972, 1973, 1974, 1986, 1987, 1989, 1990, 1992

South-Western League Cup: 1958, 1959, 1962, 1963, 1968, 1971, 1986, 1991, 1992, 1995

Cornwall Senior Cup: 1962, 1965, 1966, 1968, 1971, 1974, 1976, 1977, 1978, 1979

Cornwall Charity Cup: 1960, Cornwall Combination: 1984

St Austell Brewery Cup: 1990, 1992, 1994, 1995, 1996

Manager for 1996-97: David Ball, Assistant manager: Keith Barker

Chairman: Malcolm Newland, Vice Chairman: Paul Ashburn

Press officer: Mike Odgers 01209 715766

The club has two publications, the 12 year anniversary 1950-1971 and 15 years of Richard Gray 1960-1975 . Also there is an occasional fanzine AMFT (A Meesgae From Timmy). For more info contact club

There has been a Falmouth Town on and off since the turn of the century, playing for many years in the old Cornwall Senior League. In 1950 under the guidance of Ken Tewkesbury, senior football came to town and in 1958, having moved to Bickland Park they won their first major trophy when beating Newquay in the South-Western League Cup, retaining it 12 months later.

In 1962 the club achieved a unique record, winning the SWL Cup, the League championship and the Cornwall Senior Cup. The feat was repeated in 1968 and 1971. In 1962 the club staged the first FA Cup 1st Round tie in Cornwall when they lost narrowly to Oxford United in front of 8,000 and seven years later did it again, losing to Peterborough United. It was a boom time for Town, who took the South-Western League four years running from 1971 to 1974, deciding after the fourth to move up to the Western League. Incredibly the club won the double without losing a game and went on to win three more championships, making it eight in a row for manager Richard Gray, establishing a British record.

Despite the success, the club found the increased travel too much, and applied to re-join the South-western League only to have their application refused, and so after a season in the Cornwall Combination they returned. Since then success has continued with a total of 12 championships in the bag and national recognition after FA Vase runs. With a dozen or so League Cup wins and success in the Senior Cup, Falmouth are without question the most feared club in Cornwall.

FORMER GROUNDS...Recreation Ground, Union Corner (twice), Ashfield where the Shell-Mex depot is (and where rumour has it there is still some terracing to see), until the move to Bickland Park in 1957.

HOLSWORTHY

Upcott Fields, Holsworthy, Devon Tel: 01409 254295

Secretary: Rob Moores, Rydon View, Central Ave,
Holsworthy Tel: 01409 253982

DIRECTIONS

East or west: A3072
North or south: A388 into town
centre for Upcott Field.

Formed: 1891

Capacity: 1,000

Covered standing: Yes

Floodlights: Yes

Clubhouse on ground: Yes

Honours

Devon Junior Cup: 1939

Devon Senior Cup: 1954

Devon Premier Cup: 1972 and 1979

Plymouth and District League: 1969, 1970

Victory Cup: 1972, North Devon League 1976

Div 1 1924, Div 2 1938, Arlington Cup: 1938

North Devon Challenge Cup: 1950, Torridge Cup: 1939, 1976, 1979

Westward Ho! Cup: 1939, 1968, Sutton Vase: 1981

Hansen Cup: 1939, 65, 66, 67, 68, 69, 70, 78, 79, Hayward Shield: 1969, 1970, 1971, 1972, 1979

Kingsley League: 1929, 1976

Manager for 1996-97: Peter England.

LAUNCESTON

Pennygillam, Launceston, Cornwall Tel: 01566 773279

Secretary: Chris Martin, 3 Tavistock Rd, Launceston,
Cornwall Tel: 01566 776175

DIRECTIONS

Follow signs to Pennygillam
Industrial Est, just off main A30 -
ground 400yds on left.

Formed: 1891,   Nickname: The Clarets

Colours: Claret and Blue,   Capacity: 2,000

Seating: 150,   Covered standing: None

Floodlights: Yes,   Clubhouse on ground: Yes

Honours

Cornish Senior Cup 1900, 1901, 1983

South-Western League 1995

South-Western League Cup 1996

Manager: Roger Wakeham

Chairman: Keith Ellacott

Vice Chairman: Alan Bradley

LISKEARD ATHLETIC

Lux Park, Liskeard, Cornwall Tel: 01579 342665

Secretary: Adrian Wilton, Martina, Dawes Close, Dobwalls, Cornwall PL14 6JD Tel: 01579 20980

Vice Chairman Dave Rawlings, Bradwood, Woodgate Rd, Liskeard, Cornwall Tel: 01579 343200

Nickname: The Blues,   Colours: Blue and White,

Capacity: 2,500,   Seating: 100

Covered standing: 300,   Floodlights: Yes

Clubhouse on ground: Yes

Record attendance: 1,500 v Bournemouth

Biggest win: 11-0 v Holsworthy (H)

Biggest defeat: 1-12 v Newquay

Record appearances: Brian Bunney 632,

Record goalscorer in one season: T.Turner 59

Record fee received: £1,000 from Plymouth Argyle for Bradley Swiggs March 1984

DIRECTIONS

Take Tavistock Road (A390) from town centre, after 1/2 mile turn left on St Cleer Road (following signs to Lux Park Sports Complex) and the ground is 200 yards on left. Half mile from Liskeard station.

Honours

South-Western League 1977 and 1979

South-Western League Cup 1977 and 1979, Western League: 1988

Cornwall Senior Cup: 1905, 1984, 1985, 1986, 1989, 1994

Cornwall Charity Cup: 1922, 1980, Cornwall Junior Cup: 1906, 1914, 1927

East Cornwall Prem RAOB Cup 1968, East Cornwall Premier League 1985 and 1993

Plymouth and District League Div 2 1977 and Div 1 in 1960, Victory Cup 1961, Charity Cup 1960

Manager for 1996-97: Phil Sullivan, Assistant manager: Geoff Battams

Chairman: David Hick, Vice Chairman: Dave Rawlings

Football has been played in Liskeard since around 1890 although early references are not easy to come by. It is documented that Liskeard were one of eight clubs represented when the first Cornwall FA was formed in 1889 however. There is a mention in the local press of Liskeard YMCA reaching the Senior Cup Final of 1894 but to date it has not been defined as the current club. They club enjoyed occasional success until in 1921 a wooden stand was built at the cricket field, with dressing rooms underneath, but a year later the adjoining pitch was bought and created for £500, along with a bowling green, tennis courts and a cycle track. The football club moved in after the dividing hedge was taken away and on September 9th 1922, Woodland Villa were the visitors. The initial enthusiasm sadly waned until in 1935 the club folded with heavy debts. Rugby continued at Lux Park until after the Second War when during 1946 the Liskeard Athletic Football Club were formed. The East Cornwall Premier and Plymouth and District League were competed for until they moved up to the South-Western League in 1966. After a few years of consolidation the good times finally came to Lux Park when the League was won in 1977 and 1979 with runners-up spots in 76 and 78. Several Final appearances in the Senior Cup established the club as one to fear and eventually the club entered the Western League in 1979, winning it in 1988. For a number of years the club were rumoured, along with neighbours Saltash Utd, to be moving back to South-Western League football and in 1995 they resigned to cut costs and go back to their roots.

FORMER GROUNDS...Lux Cross, now covered by the Park View Estate, Evely's Field, situated roughly where the Post Office is now, and Liskeard Cricket Club, next door to Lux Park.

MILLBROOK

Mill Park, Millbrook, Cornwal, Tel: 01752 822113

Secretary: Bob Bell, 15 Carew Close, Crafthoe,
Cornwall Tel: 01503 230953
Colours: White and black
Nickname: The Brook   Seating: None
Covered standing: Yes
Capacity: Not known Record appearances: John Horne
Honours
Cornwall Charity Cup 1985. Cornwall Junior Cup 1976
Plymouth and District League 1981
Cornwall Charity Cup 1936, 1957, 1984
Herald Cup 1936, 1949
Manager for 1996-97: John Horne

DIRECTIONS
From Torpoint Ferry - 3 miles to Antony on A374, fork left, after 1 mile turn left again ad following B3247 to Millbrook (3 miles), take road marked 'Town Centre Southdown' right at mini roundabout after quarter mile, ground clearly visible. From Tamar Bridge - follow signs for Torpoint, 2 miles after Polbathic take right turning marked Millbrook, 5 miles to Millbrook then proceed as above.

NEWQUAY

Mount Wise, Newquay Tel: 01637 872935

Secretary: John Hawkey, 16 Higher Tower Rd, Newquay,
TR7 1QL Tel: 01637 871884

Nickname: The Peppermints,   Capacity: 4,000

Seating: 250,   Covered standing: 250

Floodlights: Yes,   Clubhouse on ground: Yes

DIRECTIONS
Half mile from Newquay station - follow 1-way system for 2 miles - ground signed on left just before Windsor Hotel. By road, turn right a mini roundabout following signs for beach (not town centre), left onto 1-way system.

Honours
Cornwall Senior Cup 1935, 1953, 1955, 1957, 1992.
Cornwall Charity Cup 1907, 1909, 1954, 1955, 1956, 1958, 1959, 1963, 1970, 1975, 1977, 1978, 1989. West Cornwall League 1907. Herald Cup 1935,: Senior League Div 1 Cup 1955. South-Western League Cup 1956 and 1989. South-Western League 1959, 1960, 1978, 1980, 1982, 1984, 1988. Cornwall Combination League 1973 and 1975

Manager: Graham Nicholls

Founded: Newquay FC from 1890 to 1903 , Newquay One and All FC 1903-1912, Newquay Rovers FC 1920-1937, Newquay Association FC 1946 to present
It is generally thought that Mr G R Card, a master at Newquay Grammar School was responsible for the introduction of soccer to the town. It was in January 1890, in the grounds of the Grammar School, today the site of the Pendennis Hotel in Mount Wise, that the first match took place under Association rules. Newquay FC did not play competitive football until 1986 when they were grouped with Truro, Camborne School of Mines, Illogan, St Agnes and Penzance in the Cornwall County Cup. They won their first trophy in 1907 beating Looe at Bodmin to take the Charity Cup. A milestone in the club's history was in 1921 when they were elected to the Plymouth and District League, but the financial burden was too great and they withdrew in 1927. In 1931 Newquay Rovers played in the newly formed Cornwall Senior League and in 1935 they completed the League and Cup double. Newquay FC was re-formed in April 1946 following a break during the Second War and the club played in the club joined the Senior League until 1951 when they joined the South-Western League as founder members. In 1959 another new senior league was formed, the Cornwall Combination, and they were founder members of that too, and the reserves have played there ever since. Back in 1922 the Newquay Urban District Council, under pressure from the general public to provide a football field, sought permission from the Ministry of Health to lease a piece of land, originally acquired for allotments and so Mount Wise was born. The club nickname of 'The Peppermints' evolved at the turn of the century and was first mentioned in 1906, alluding to the colours of red and white stripes which resembled the sweet. *Newquay FC's excellent official history, 'A Mixed Bag of Peppermints' by Sandra Biggin, is still available at the club.*

PENZANCE

Penlee Park, Penzance Tel: 01736 61964

Secretary: John Mead, 8 Chyancare, St Clare St, Penzance Tel: 01736 69066

Colours: Black and white

Nickname: Magpies

Seating: Yes

Covered standing: No

Floodlights: Yes

Clubhouse on ground: Yes

DIRECTIONS

Seafront road past harbour, after amusement arcade turn right at roundabout (Alexander Road), ground second right. Fifteen minutes walk from Penzance Railway Station.

Honours

Cornwall Senior Cup 1893, 1896, 1898, 1899, 1904, 1905, 1908, 1948, 1961, 1973, 1981

Cornwall Charity Cup 1948, 1949,

South Western League 1956, 1957, 1975

Cornwall Comb League Cup 1969

Cornwall Senior League Div 2 and Div 2 League Cup 1958

Cornwall Combination League Cup 1970

Cornwall Junior Cup West 1904, 1905, 1906, 1908, 1910

Manager for 1996/97: Martin Smith.

PORTHLEVEN

Gala Parc, Mill Lane, Porthleven Tel: 01208 574574

Secretary: Vidal James, 11 Primrose Close, Weeth Park, Camborne, TR14 7HS Tel: 01209 710618

Colours: Amber and black,   Nickname: Fishermen

Seating: No,   Covered standing: Yes

Clubhouse on ground: Yes

DIRECTIONS

Arriving from Penzance on A394, B3304 into Porthleven, ground on left immediately before town. Coming from Helston on B3304 ground on right as you exit town. Buses from Helston and Penzance.

Honours

Cornwall Combination 1960, 1964, 1966, 1967, 1979, 1989

League Cup: 1963, 1965, 1966, 1984, 1985, 1987

Cornwall Charity Cup 1971

George Evley Cup 1965, 1966, 1984, 1987

Cornwall County League Cup 1933 jt, 1934, 1935

Hannaford Cup 1946, 1947, 1948

Penzance Charity Cup 1948

West Cornwall Hospital Cup 1948

Cornwall Senior League Div 2, and Div 2 Cup jt 1957

Manager 1996-97: Trevor Mewton

SALTASH UNITED

Kimberley Stadium, Callington Rd, Saltash, Cornwall, Tel: 01752 845746

Secretary: Peter Gammage, 23 Spire Hill Park, Saltash, Cornwall

Colours: Red and white stripes, Nickname: The Ashes

Seating: 250, Covered standing: None

Capacity: 3,000, Clubhouse on ground: Yes

Floodlights: Yes

DIRECTIONS

First leg after crossing Tamar Bridge, through town centre, at top of town fork right at mini roundabout, ground 400 yds ahead on left.

Honours

Cornwall Senior League 1950 and 1951

Western League 1985, 1987, 1989

League Cup 1987 and 1988, Division One 1977

Merit Cup 1980 and 1988, South Western League 1954 and 1976, League Cup 1952, 1970, 1974

Cornwall Senior Cup 1951, 1975, 1982, 1988, 1991, 1993

Manager: Phil Towl

ST AUSTELL

Poltair Park, St Austell, Cornwall, Tel: 01726 77099

Secretary: Peter Beard, 24 Alexandra Rd, St Austell, Cornwall Tel: 01726 64138

Colours: White and black, Nickname: Lilywhites

Floodlights: No, Seating: 200

Clubhouse on ground: Yes, Covered standing: None

Capacity: 8,000

Record attendance: 15,000 v Penzance Cornwall Senior Cup final 1949

DIRECTIONS

Five minutes walk up hill from St. Austell Railway Station on left-hand side.

Honours

South Western League 1969

League Cup 1965, 1972, 1973, 1988

Cornwall Senior Cup 1912, 1913, 1914, 1934, 1939, 1946, 1947, 1964, 1969, 1972

Manager for 1996-97: John Peters

Assistant manager: Nigel Rowe

ST BLAZEY

Blaise Park, Station Road, St Blazey, Cornwall Tel: 01726 814110

Secretary: Martin Richards, 14 Landreath Place, St Blazey PL24 2JX Tel: 01726 817419

Nickname: Saints

Capacity: 3,500

Seating: 200

Covered standing: 500

Floodlights: Yes

Clubhouse on ground: Yes

Record attendance: 6,500 v St Austell Cornwall Senior Cup 1948-49

Biggest win: 15-0 v Tavistock (H) and Nanpean Rovers (A)

Biggest defeat: 0-14 v Wadebridge (A)

Record appearances: W.Isbell

Record goalscorer in total: B.Tallamy

DIRECTIONS

A390 Liskeard - St Austell road, turn into Station Road at lights in St Blazey village; ground 100 yards on left. One and a half miles from Par Main Line Station.

Honours

South-Western League 1955, 1958, 1963, 1964, 1981 1983

League Cup 1954, 1957, 1967 jt, 1982 1987

Cornwall Senior Cup 1936, 1950, 1954, 1956, 1958, 1960, 1963, 1987

Cornwall Charity Cup 1936, 1957, 1984

Herald Cup 1936, 1949

Manager: Gareth Lobb, Chairman: Harry Cooke, President: Ken Cocks

St Blazey AFC are celebrating their centenary this year, having been formed by Dr E S Davis who was one of the early members of the Cornwall FA.In the early days, the club began playing their football at junior level and soon won the Eastern Division Cup, the Cornwall Junior Cup and the Bodmin and District League Cup in 1909, a feat they repeated 12 months later. Their success prompted them to seek a higher level of football and senior status Between the Wars records are sketchy, but they did win two County Cups and in 1936 the Charity Cup, Senior Cup and Herald Cup were all won, they have gone on to win the County Cup a further six times.

They became founder members of the South Western League in 1951 where they have played ever since, winning the League six times and the League Cup five.

Saints were one of the first to install floodlights at Blaise Park which has a capacity of 3,000.

When formed the club played on a field which is adjacent to Blaise Park and from there they moved to a field in Back Lane, behind the Packhorse Hotel, and St Blaise Park was opened in 1906 where they played until the Great War when the pitch was dug up and sand taken to fill sandbags, the site having been on reclaimed land from a former estuary. The pitch was filled with rubbish and reseeded and while that was happening the club played at Kitts Moor, now known as Middleway.

The grandstand was built in 1930 and had a Royal Box added for the visit of Prince Phillip in 1957 for a Services match.

TAVISTOCK

Langsford Park, Crowndale Rd, Tavistock, Cornwall Tel: 01822 614447

Secretary: Phillip Lowe, 1 Bainbridge Ct, Colebrook,
Plymouth Tel: 01752 335273

Colours: Red and black   Nickname: Tavy

Seating: 200,   Covered standing: None

Capacity: 2,000,   Floodlights: Yes

Clubhouse on ground: Yes

DIRECTIONS

A368 from Plymouth, left after Ford garage into Crowndale Road, ground half mile on left.

Record attendance: 5,000 v Calstock in 1952,
Bedford Cup final

Record appearances: Alec Pethick 1,000 +

Record fee received: £1, 000 for Neil Langman to Plymouth Argyle Sept 1953

Honours

Devon Premier Cup 1991

Devon Senior Cup 1890, 1969, 1978, 1982

South Western League Cup 1969, Bedford Cup many times

Manager for 1996-97: Steve Metters, Assistant manager: Jerry Collins

Chairman: Doug Pethick

TORPOINT ATHLETIC

Mill Field, Mill Lane, Torpoint, Cornwall Tel 01752 812889

Secretary: Vic Grimwood, 43 Hemerdon Heights,
Plympton, Devon Tel 01752 344263

Colours: Gold and black stripes,   Seating: Yes

Clubhouse on ground: Yes,   Floodlights: No

DIRECTIONS

Bear left from Torpoint ferry, ground down hill on left after half a mile.

Biggest win: 16-0 v Marazion Blues Cornwall Senior Cup 1994

Honours

South-Western League 1965 and 1967

Cornish Senior Cup: 1897, 1906, 07, 09, 10, 20, 29, 33, 96

Cornwall Charity Cup 1996

The first football club in Torpoint was formed in 1887. Three of the founders, Messrs Stacey, Rose and Rowse all went on to County honours. In 1897 Torpoint won the Senior Cup for the first time and they have since won it on ten other occasions, the last being last season. In 1906 the club entered the FA Cup for the first time, and played Staple Hill at Home Park, winning a replay in Bristol but then losing to Radstock. In league football the club played for many years in the Plymouth and District League and joined the South-Western League in 1962. They were successful, winning the league twice and the Charity Cup three times, being runners up in the Senior and League Cups. During that time the club enjoyed many battles in the old Amateur Cup, where they played Harwich and Parkeston, Walton and Hersham, Corinthian Casuls, Wealdstone and Leyton, to name but a few Recent seasons have seen the club challenge for honours with the best and last year the FA Vase run brought glory, as did a runners-up spot in the league and the Senior and Charity Cups, in one of the best seasons the club has ever enjoyed.Torpoint Athletic have played on the Mill Ground since before the War, although for some 11 years from 1960 the ground was used exclusively for rugby, with the club having to play on the HMS Defiant pitch. The last 20 years or so has seen the clubhouse, new stand and changing rooms transform the ground into something acceptable to the senior league.

TRURO CITY

Treyew Rd, Truro, Cornwall Tel 01872 78853

Secretary: Ray Rowe, 5 Alverston Gardens, Truro, Cornwall Tel 01872 70684

Colours: Red and black,   Floodlights: Yes

Seating: Yes,   Covered standing: No

DIRECTIONS
On A39 bypass south of city. 10 mins walk from Railway Station: up hill and left at junction.

Honours

South Western League 1961, 1970, 1993, 1996

League Cup 1960 and 1967 jt, 1993

Cornwall Senior Cup 1895, 1902, 1903, 1911, 1924, 1927, 1928, 1938, 1959, 1967, 1970, 1995

Cornwall Charity Cup 1920, 29, 30, 31, 50, 65, 81

Cornwall Senior League 1932 and 1933

Manager: Leigh Cooper,
Assistant manager: Kenny Wills

WADEBRIDGE TOWN

Bodieve Park, Bodieve Rd, Wadebridge Tel: 01208 812537

Secretary Barry Cudmore, 3 Marine Terrace, Wadebridge, Cornwall PL27 7AJ Tel: 01208 812537

Colours: Red and white , Nickname: Bridgers

Capacity: 4,000, Seating: No,

Covered standing: 280, Clubhouse on ground: Yes

Floodlights: Awaiting planning approval

Record attendance: 2,800 v Saltash 1956

Biggest win: 10-0 v Holsworthy S.W. League 1988

Record appearances: Dave Blewett 760

Record goalscorer in one season: Dickie Endacott 66

DIRECTIONS
At junction of A39 and B3314 to east of Wadebridge.

Honours

South Western League Cup 1975, 1976, 1978, 1980, 1985

Cornwall Senior Cup 1980

Cornish Charity Cup 1927, 1934, 1952, 1964, 1973, 1976, 1982, 1985

Manager 1996-97: Nigel Menhennick, Assistant Manager: Robbie Black

Chairman: Dave Herring, Vice Chairman: Steve Cudmore

Wadebridge Town was founded in 1894 and during its early years played four or five games in a season.

The biggest game of every year was against the Devon and Cornwall Light Infantry who were based in Bodmin. The club first played in the Trevanion area and later moved to a pitch at Whiterock. Having moved to Bodieve Park in the early 20's the Charity Cup was won in 1927 for the first time. During the Second War, with most players away fighting, a team called Wadebridge Utd played friendlies against local sides. The team competed at Egloshayle Playing Field when the Bodieve Park became a corn field during the War and the grandstand was used as a barn. The club bought the ground in 1949, when big crowds were common for Cornwall Senior League matches and they entered the South Western League in 1951, a year after it formed. They were founder members of the East Cornwall Premier League in 1960. They were runners up in 1969, 1979 and 1980 and won the Cornwall Senior Cup in 1980.

COUNTY SENIOR CUPS

BEDFORDSHIRE PREMIER CUP
Holders Potton United

First Round

1 Kempston Rovers	v Brache Sparta	0-2
2 Biggleswade Town	v Langford	1-2
3 Potton United	v Arlesey Town	1-4
4 Dunstable United	v Shillington	0-4
5 Bedford Town	v Wotton Blue Cross	3-1
6 Stotfold	v Luton Town	2*3

2 Clubs with Byes Barton Rovers & Leighton Town

Second Round

1 Leighton Town	v Brache Sparta 3p4	0-0
2 Arlesey Town	v Bedford Town	0-1
3 Barton Rovers	v Luton Town	2-1
4 Shillington	v Langford	2-1

Semi-Finals

Brache Sparta	v Bedford Town	0-3
Barton Rovers	v Shillington	2-1

Final (Two Legs)

Bedford Town	v Barton Rovers	0-0
Barton Rovers	v Bedford Town	1-0

BEDFORDSHIRE SENIOR CUP
Holders Bedford Town

Preliminary Round

1 Wotton B Cross	v 61 FC Luton	5-1
2 Potton United	v Biggleswade Town	1-0
3 Stotfold	v Dunstable United	4-2
4 Langford	v Houghton Town	0-1

First Round

1 Kempston Rovers	v Totternhoe	0-2
2 Houghton Town	v Toddington Rovers	1-4
3 ACDFC	v Ampthill Town	1-3
4 Bedford Town	v Brache Sparta	2-1
5 Potton United	v Wootton Blue Cross	01
6 Stotfold	v Barton Rovers	2-4
7 Shillington	v Bedford United OAO	0-1
8 Leighton Town	v Arlesey Town	1-2

Second Round

1 Wootton Blue Cros	v Ampthill Town	1-3
2 Bedford United	v Bedford Town	0-4
3 Totternhoe	v Barton Rovers	1-3
4 Toddington Rovers	v Arlesey Town	1-2

Semi-Finals

1 Bedford Town v Ampthill Town 2-1
at Kempston Rovers FC Tuesday 5th March 1996
2 Barton Rovers v Arlesey Town 2-0
at Stotfold FC Wednesday 6th March 1996

Final Monday 6.5.96

Barton Roves v Bedford Town 0-1
at Kenilworth Road, Luton Town FC

BERKS & BUCKS SENIOR CUP
Holders Reading

2nd Qualifying Round (1st Not used)

1 Burnham	v Flackwell Heath	3-2
2 Thatcham Town	v Newport Pagnell Tn	7-0

First Round Proper

1 Maidenhead Utd	v Bracknell Town	1-0
2 Marlow	v Thatcham Town	0-2
3 Reading	v Slough Town	3-2
4 Chalfont St Peter	v Windsor & Eton	0-1
5 Abingdon Town	v Buckingham Town	2-1
6 Wycombe Wanderers	v Aylesbury United	1-2
7 Chesham United	v Hungerford Town	0-2
8 Burnham	v Wokingham Town	1-5

Second Round

1 Abingdon Town	v Reading	1-3
2 Thatcham Town	v Aylesbury United	0-2
3 Wokingham Town	v Hungerford Town	3-0
4 Windsor & Eton	v Maidenhead United	0-2

Semi Finals

Reading	v Wokingham Town	0-2
Maidenhead United	v Aylesbury United	2-2 0-4

Final Monday 6.5.96

Aylesbury United v Wokingham Town 0-1
at Aylesbury United FC

BERKS & BUCKS SENIOR TROPHY
Holders Lambourn Sports

First Qualifying Round

1 Wooburn Athletic	v Buckingham Ath	2-2 T-A
2 Reading Town	v Newport Pagnell	RT W-O
3 Penn & Tylers	v Milton Keynes	2-5
4 South Reading	v Finchampstead	1-3
5 Holmer Green	v Olney Town	3-1
6 Mortimer	v Martin Baker S&SSC	2-1

Tie Awarded to Wooburn Athletic after it was found
Buckingham Athletic had fielded an ineligible player.
22 Clubs with bye

Second Qualifying Round

1 Holmer Green	v Mortimer	1-0
2 Reading Town	v Winslow United	4-1
3 Amersham Town	v Forest Old Boys	2-1
4 Milton Keynes	v Finchampstead	1-0
5 Didcot Town	v Wooburn Athletic	0-1
6 Wraysbury	v Kintbury Rangers	2-1
7 Reading Exiles	v Chalfont Wasps	4-1
8 Wantage Town	v Old Paludians	3-0
9 Stocklake	v Risborough Rangers 1-1	3-1
10 New Bradwell St P	v Prestwood	10-1
11 Pitstone and I	v Beaconsfield SYCOB	1-4
12 Binfield	v Sandhurst Town	1-1 3-2
13 Abingdon United	v Milton United	2-0
14 Letcombe	v Broadmoor Social	1-2

2 Clubs exempt Eton Wick, Lambourn Sports

First Round Proper

1 Amersham Town	v Lambourn Sports	2-4
2 Reading Eiles	v Beaconsfield SYCOB	1-0
3 Wraysbury	v Reading Town	0-1
4 Stocklake	v Binfield	3-2
5 Holmer Green	v Wooburn Athletic	3-0
6 Abingdon United	v Broadmoor Special	1-4

| 7 Milton Keynes | v Eton Wick | 2-0 |
| 8 Wantage Town | v N Bradwell St Peter | 0-1 |

Second Round

1 Broadmoor Social	v Holmer Green	1-4
2 Stocklake	v Milton Keynes	1-2
3 Lambourn Sports	v New Bradwell St Peter	1-0
4 Reading Exiles	v Reading Town	2-3

Semi Finals

| Milton Keynes | v Lambourn Sports | 1-3 |
| Reading Town | v Holmer Green | 3-1 |

Final Saturday 27th April 1996

Lambourn Sports v Reading Town 1-2
at Thatcham Town FC

BIRMINGHAM SENIOR CUP
Holders Solihull Borough

First Round

1 Halesowen Harriers	v Racing Club Warwick		0-2
2 Knowle	v Tividale		4-3
3 Oldbury United	v Redditch United		4-0
4 Gornal Athletic	v Atherstone United	0-0	2-4
5 Brierley Hill Tn	v Darlaston		2-0
6 Lye Town	v Paget Rangers	1-1	2-1
7 Wednesfield	v Highgate United	1-1	3-1
8 Sutton Coldfield T	v Moor Green		2-4
9 Northfield Town	v West Midlands Police		1-3
10 Boldmere St Mich'	v Tamworth		1-4
11 Willenhall Town	v Stourbridge		1-0
12 Banbury United	v Evesham United		1-2
13 Cradley Town	v Dudley Town		1-4

19 Clubs with byes into the

Second Round

1 Bolehall Swifts	v Lye Town		0-4
2 Bedworth United	v Brierley Hill Town		5-0
3 Worcester City	v West Midlands Police		3-1
4 Sandwell Borough	v Birmingham City		1-2
5 Walsall	v Kings Heath		1-0
6 Evesham United	v Wednesfield		2-3
7 Burton Albion	v Nuneaton Borough		2-1
8 Tamworth	v Halesowen Town	1-1	2-1
9 Knowle	v Racing Club Warwick		2-1
10 V.S.Rugby	v Willenhall Town		3-1
11 Coleshill Town	v Solihull Borough		1-3
12 Wolverhampton W	v Oldbury United @OU		2-0
13 Aston Villa	v Stratford Town @SST		2-1
14 Atherstone United	v Coventry City		0-3
15 Moor Green	v Dudley Town		1-3
16 Hednesford Town	v West Bromwich Albion	2-3

Third Round

1 Wednesfield	v Bedworth United		0-3
2 Wolverhampton W	v Lye Town @LT		1-0
3 Dudley Town	v Birmingham City		0-3
4 Burton Albion	v Walsall @BA	0-0	0-3
5 Aston Villa	v Worcester City @WC		2-1
6 VS Rugby	v Coventry City		1-2
7 Knowle	v West Bromwich A	0-0	0-2
8 Solihull Borough	v Tamworth		1-0

Fourth Round

| 1 Solihull Borough | v West Brom Albion | 0-2 |

2 Walsall	v Coventry City	2-1
3 W'hpton Wanderers	v Birmingham City	2-3
4 Bedworth United	v Aston Villa	1-2

Semi-Finals

| Aston Villa | v West Bromwich Albion | 3-1 |
| Walsall | v Birmingham City | 0-1 |

Final Monday 6th May 1996,

Birmingham City v Aston Villa 2-0
at Birmingham City FC

CAMBS INVITATION CUP
Holders Wisbech Town

Preliminary Round

1 March Town Utd	v Great Shelford	0-2
2 Histon	v Foxton	1-5
3 Chatteris Town	v Soham Town Rangers	0-1
4 Newmarket Town	v Leverington Sports	4-2

First Round

1 Mildenhall Town	v Cambridge City		2-1
2 Ely City	v Newmarket T.	5pt 0-0	1-1
3 Chatteris Town	v Foxton		1-5
4 Wisbech Town	v Great Shelford		5-2

(Wisbech Town are removed from the Competition
and Great Shelford Re-instated.

Semi-Finals (Both at Histon FC)

| Foxton | v Ely City | 3-2 |
| Great Shelford | v Mildenhall Town | 1-2 |

Final Friday 3rd May

Foxton v Mildenhall Town 0-3
at Histon FC

CHESHIRE SENIOR CUP
Holders Witton Albion

First Round

1 Winsford United	v Hyde United	1-4
2 Vauxhall GM	v Cheadle Town	3-0
3 Northwich Victoria	v Runcorn	3-1
4 Congleton	v Stalybridge Celtic	2-6
5 Warrington Town	v Nantwich Town	6-1

3 Clubs with Byes Altrincham, Macclesfield Town
Witton Albion

Second Round

1 Vauxhall GM	v Macclesfield Town			0-4
2 Altrincham	v Warrington Town			4-0
3 Stalybridge Celtic	v Hyde United			0-3
4 Witton Albion	v Northwich Victoria			2-0

Semi Finals (Two Legs)

| Hyde United | v Macclesfield T | 2-1 | 1-1 | 3-2 |
| Witton Albion | v Altrincham | 1-1 | 2-1 | 3-2 |

Final Monday 6th May 1996

Hyde United v Witton Albion 1-3
at Altrincham FC

CORNWALL SENIOR CUP
Holders Truro City

First Round

1 Bude	v Helston Athletic		5-2
2 Ludgvan	v Mousehole		1-5
3 Marazion Blues	v Perranwell		0-5
4 Mullion	v St Ives Town	0-0	3-2
5 Nanpean Rovers	v RAS Culdrose		6-1

6 Pendeen Rovers	v Foxhole Stars	2-0
7 Roche	v Illogan RBL	0-0 1-0
8 St Agnes	v St Breward	4-0
9 Sticker	v St Cleer	3-5
10 Troon	v St Just	1-1 1-2

8 Clubs with byes and 14 clubs exempt

Second Round

1 Bude	v Millbrook	0-5
2 Bugle	v Padstow United	0-2
3 Callington	v Penryn Athletic	3-1
4 Camelford	v RAF St Mawgan	7-3
5 Launceston	v Truro City	0-0 1-2
6 Liskeard Ath	v Perranwell	0-0 4-1
7 Mousehole	v Porthleven	0-5
8 Mullion	v St Agnes	3-4
9 Nanpean Rovers	v Falmouth Town	0-9
10 Newquay	v St Cleer	4-0
11 Pendeen Rovers	v St Dennis	0-2
12 Penzance	v Bodmin Town	0-1
13 Riveria Coasters	v St Austell	1-4
14 St Blazey	v Roche	4-0
15 St Just	v Torpoint Athletic	1-5
16 Wadebridge Town	v Saltash United	1-4

Third Round

1 Falmouth Town	v Millbrook	4-1
2 Liskeard Athletic	v St Dennis	1-2
3 Newquay	v Callington	3-2
4 Padstow United	v St Blazey	0-1
5 St Agnes	v Porthleven	1-2
6 Saltash United	v Bodmin Town	4-3
7 Torpoint Athletic	v St Austell	3-2
8 Truro City	v Camelford	10-2

Quarter Finals

1 Falmouth Town	v Truro City	4-0
2 Newquay	v St Dennis	1-0
3 St Blazey	v Porthleven	1-1 0-5
4 Saltash United	v Torpoint Athletic	1-3

Semi-Finals

Falmouth Town	v Torpoint Athletic	1-2

at St Blazey FC

Newquay	v Porthleven	0-1

at Falmouth Town FC

Final Monday 8th April 1996

Porthleven	v Torpoint Athletic	1-1

at St Blazey FC

Final Replay Thursday 11th April 1996

Porthleven	v Torpoint Athletic	0-2

at St Blazey FC

CUMBERLAND SENIOR CUP
Holders Gretna

First Round

1 Sporting Museum	v Windscales	1-2
2 Mayport	v Windscales Res	WRs W-O
3 Cumbria Police	v Carlisle United Res	0-1
4 Whitehaven Soc	v Gilford Park	1-3
5 Wigton Harriers	v Whitehaven Rangers	2-3
6 Whitehaven Amts	v Penrith	

Second Round

1 Braithwaite	v British Steel	1-2
2 Gretna	v Gillford Park	3-2
3 Parton United	v Silloth	3-2
4 Penrith	v Aspatria Spartans	5-0
5 Windscales	v Langworthy	1-0
6 Whitehaven Rgrs	v Silloth Vets	3-3 5-3
7 Keswick	v Alston Town	7-1
8 Windscales Res	v Workington Res	0-2
9 Cleator Moor Cel	v New Victoria	5-2
10 Kirkoswald	v Whitehaven Amateurs	0-5
11 Greystoke	v Northbank	2-5
12 Whitehaven S Res	v Carlisle Utd Res	W W-O
13 Wetheriggs	v St Bees	6-1
14 Longtown	v Egremont St Mary's	3-1
15 Mirehouse	v Carlisle City	1-8
16 Abbeytown	v Workington	2-5

Third Round

1 Parton United	v Longtown	1-2
2 Wetheriggs	v Windscales	3-5
3 Gretna	v Workington Res	1-0
4 British Steel	v Whitehaven Soc Res	5-0
5 Whitehaven Amt	v Workington	0-3
6 Carlisle City @P	v Penrith	2-1
7 Whitehaven Rangers	v Keswick	0-3
8 Cleator Moor Celtic	v North Bank	5-3

Fourth Round

1 Carlisle City	v British Steel	5-0
2 Longtown	v Keswick	1-2
3 Workington	v Gretna	2-1
4 Cleator Moor Celtic	v Windscales	2-1

Semi-Finals

Cleator Moor Celtic	v Carlisle City	3-2
Keswick	v Workington	1-3

Final

Cleator Moor Celtic	v Workington	1-4

at Egremont att; 397

DERBYSHIRE SENIOR CUP HOLDERS
ALFRETON TOWN
Holders Alfreton Town

First Round

1 Glapwell	v Shardlow St James	1-3
2 Mickleover Sport	v Long Eaton United	3-0

Second Round

1 Graham St Prims	v Sheepbridge	8-2
2 Heanor Town	v Rolls Royce	2-0
3 Mickleover Sports	v Shirebrook Town	3-2
4 Mickleover RBL	v Sth Normanton Ath	2-5
5 Newhall United	v Shardlow St James	1-1 2-1
6 Sandiacre Town	v Blackwell MW	2-0
7 Staveley MW	v Stanton Ilkeston	3-1

9 Clubs Exempt Alfreton Town Belper Town, Borrowash Victoria, Buxton, Glossop North End, Gresley Rovers, Ilkeston Town , Matlock Town, Stapenhill to the

Third Round

1 Mickleover Sports	v Glossop North End	4-4 1-3
2 Sth Normanton Ath	v Belper Town	1-8

3 Staveley MW	v Gresley Rovers	1-4
4 Newhall @ Gresley	v Ilkeston Town	1-0
5 Alfreton Town	v Heanor Town	9-1
6 Borrowash Vics	v Graham Street Prims	0-1
7 Stapenhill	v Buxton	0-0 0-1
8 Matlock Town	v Sandiacre Town	8-2

Fourth Round

1 Belper Town	v Alfreton Town	4-3
2 Gresley Rovers	v Buxton	2-0
3 Glossop North End	v Newhall United	6-1
4 Graham St Prims	v Matlock Town	1-0

Semi-Finals

Gresley Rovers	v Glossop North End	3-0
Belper Town	v Graham Street Prims	2-0

Final (Two Legs) Thursday 9th May

Gresley Rovers	v Belper Town	0-0
Monday 13th May		
Belper Town	v Gresley Rovers	1-2

DEVON ST LUKES COLLEGE CUP
Holders Tiverton Town

First Round

1 Clyst Rovers	v Exmouth Town	6-3
2 Heavitree United	v Torrington	1-3
3 Ilfracombe	v Elmore	1-2

Fourth Round

1 Barnstaple Town	v Bideford	2-3
2 Clyst Rovers	v Crediton	6p7 2-2
3 Torrington	v Elmore	3-1
4 Tiverton Town	v Dawlish	1-2

(Crediton were found to have fielded ineligible players in the above match and were removed from the competition with Clyst Rovers being re-instate)

Semi-Finals

Clyst Rovers	v Torrington	0-2
Tiverton Town	v Bideford	1-2

Final Monday 6th May

Bideford	v Torrington	2-1
at Bideford FC		

DORSET SENIOR CUP
Holders Hamworthy Engineering

First Round

1 Holt United	v Portland United	0-2
2 Wareham Rangers	v Verwood Town	1-1 1-3
3 Hamworthy United	v Blandford United	1-1 1-2
4 Flight Refuelling	v Bournemouth Sports	0-1
5 Gillingham Town	v Sturminster Newton	1-1 1-4
6 Parley Sports	v Shaftesbury	0-7
7 Hamworthy Eng'ng	v Weymouth Sports	4-1

Second Round (Inc 9 Byes)

1 Dorchester Town	v Sturminster Newton	10-0
2 Verwood Town	v Wimborne Town	0-3
3 Allendale	v Shaftesbury	3-0
4 Weymouth	v Poole Town	5-1
5 Swanage T & H	v Sherborne Town	1-3
6 St Pauls Jersey	v Hamworthy Eng	1-0
7 Bournemouth Sp	v Portland United	2-1
8 Hamworthy Utd	v Bridport	0-2

Third Round

1 Weymouth	v Dorchester Town	0-2
2 Sherborne Town	v Wimborne	0-1
3 Bridport	v St Pauls Jersey	3-3 1-3
4 Bournemouth Sp	v Allendale	2-1

Semi- Finals

Wimborne Town	v St Pauls Jersey	0-2
Dorchester Town	v Bournemouth Sp	0-0 2-2 1-0

Final Tuesday 16th April 1996   att:362

Dorchester Town	v St Pauls	3-1
at Wimborne Town FC		

DURHAM CHALLENGE CUP
Holders Spennymoor United

First Preliminary Round

1 Billingham Town	v Darlington C S	5-0
2 Shotton Comrades	v Annfield Plain	2-1
3 Consett	v Jarrow FC	6-1
4 Boldon CA	v Norton-Stockton An	3-1
5 Harlepool BWOB	v Seaham Red Star	0-5
6 Easington Colliery	v Willington	1-0
7 Ryhope C A	v Whickham	0-1
8 Evenwood Town	v Dunston F.B	0-1
9 Horden C W	v Stanley United	3-2
10 Wolviston	v Birtley Town	2-3
11 Brandon United	v South Shields Cleadon	2-0
12 Washington	v South Tyneside Utd	
13 Peterlee	v Murton AFC	1-2

3 Clubs with Byes Sunderland Ryhope CW
Esh Winning Jarrow Roofing 16 Clubs exempt

First Round Proper

1 Hebburn	v Shotton Comrades	0-1
2 South Shields	v Cockfield	3-1
3 Ryhope CW	v West Auckland Town	0-4
4 Spennymoor Utd	v Birtley Town	3-2
5 Eppleton C W	v Brandon United	4-5
6 Murton	v Shildon	1-1 2-0
7 Bolton CA	v Easington CW	3-1
8 Whickham	v Durham City	0-4
9 Crook Town	v South Tyneside Utd	1-1 2-0
10 Tow Law Town	v Kennet Roker	4-0
11 Consett	v Washington Nissan	3-0
12 Dunston FB	v Billingham Synthonia	2-1
13 Esh Winning	v Bishop Auckland	2-3
14 Ferryhill Athletic	v Billingham Town	3-4
15 Jarrow Roofing	v Horden CW	5-1
16 Seaham Red Star	v Chester le St Town	1-3

Second Round

1 Brandon United	v Billingham Town	0-3
2 West Auckland Tn	v Bishop Auckland	1-5
3 South Shields	v Spennymoor United	0-3
4 Jarrow Roofing	v Durham City	0-1
5 Crook Town	v Dunston FB	0-1
6 Chester le St Tn	v Consett	3-2
7 Boldon C.A	v Tow Law Town	0-7
8 Murton	v Shotton Comrades	2-1

Third Round

1 Spennymoor Utd	v Tow Law Town	2-0
2 Bishop Auckland	v Murton	2-0

3 Billingham Town v Durham City 0-2
4 Chester le St Tn v Dunston 2-5
Semi Finals
Bishop Auckland v Durham City DC W-O
Dunston FB v Spennymoor United 0-1
(Bishop Auckland removed from the competition for fielding an ineligible player)
Final Monday 6th May 1996
Durham City v Spennymoor Utd 0-1
at Durham City FC

EAST RIDING SENIOR CUP
Holders Sculcoates Amateurs
First Round
1 Admiral Signs v Anlaby United 0-3
2 Youngs FC v Odeon FC 3-2
3 Dairycoates v Hull City 1-2
4 Bulmans v Smith & Nephew 4-1
Second Round 12 clubs with byes
1 Ideal Standard v Bulmans 1A1 2-1
2 Hull City v Sculcoates Amateurs 1-5
3 Anlaby United v Youngs 3-3 1-4
4 Westella & Willerby v Cottingham Sports 1-3
5 Hall Road Rangers v Hedon United 7-0
6 AFC Reckitts v Malet Lambert YC 3-2
7 Beverley OG's v Leconfield BOG W-O
8 North Ferriby Utd v Haltemprice 4-0
Third Round
1 Ideal Standard v Youngs FC 3-2
2 Beverley Old G's v Hall Road Rangers 0-1
3 Cottingham Sports v Sculcoates Amts 1-1 4V3
4 AFC Reckitts v North Ferriby United 3-1
Semi-Finals April 19963
(Cottingham Sports removed from the Competition for fielding an unregistered player in the third Round and their opponents Sculcoates Amateurs re-instated
Sculcoates Amateurs v Ideal Standard 3-2
at Hall Road Rangers FC
AFC Reckitts v Hall Rd Rangers 2-2 2-1
at Northern Foods
Final Monday 13th May 1996
Reckitts v Sculcoates Amateurs 3-3
at Hull City AFC
Replay Thursday, 16th May
Reckitts v Sculcoates Amateurs 1-2
at Hall Road Rangers FC

EAST RIDING COUNTRY CUP
Holders: Ward
First Round
1 Crown v Withernsea 2-2 2-4
2 Flamborough v Tickton 2-4
3 Hunmanby United v Driffield E I 2-1
4 Mkt Wieghton U v Rudston United 2nd 1-3
5 South Cave Utd v Holmpton United 4-2
6 North Cave v Filey Town 1-0
7 Bridlington LSC v Hilderthorpe 4-4 1-3
8 Rudston United v Bridlington Rovers 5-0
9 Stamford Bridge v Holme Rovers 1-5
10 Kingburn Athletic v Hornsea Town 7-1

11 Brandesburton v Middleton Rovers 4-1
12 Ward v Full Measure 11-1
Second Round
1 South Cave Utd v Kingburn Athletic 2-4
2 Brandesburton v Viking Panthers- 0-1
3 Rudston Utd 2nd v Rudston United 1-4
4 Tickton v North Cave 1-4
5 Holme Rovers v Hummanby United 9-0
6 Ward v Withernsea 10-0
7 Bridlington Tn v Little Driffield 9-0
8 Bridlington Tn Rs v Hilderthorpe AFC 0-6
Third Round
1 Hilderthorpe v Rudston United 2-1
2 Holme Rovers v Kingburn Athletic 4-2
3 Bridlington Town v Viking Panters 2-0
4 North Cave v Ward FC 2-2 1-6
Semi finals
Hilderthorpe v Bridlington Town 3-8
at Bridlington Town FC
Holme Rovers v Ward FC 2-5
at Stamford Bridge FC.
Final Saturday 4th May 1996
Bridlington Town v Ward 0-2
at Bridlington Town FC

ESSEX SENIOR CUP
Holders Grays Athletic
Preliminary Round
1 Brightlingsea Utd v Southend Manor 2-3
2 Concord Rangers v East Ham United 4-0
3 Clacton Town v Brentwood 0-1
4 Maldon Town v Hullbridge Sports 9-0
First Round
1 Burnham Ramblers v Woodford Town BR W-O
2 Concord Rangers v Romford 1-0
3 Basildon United v Harwich & Parkeston 1-2
4 Halestead Town v Brentwood 1-0
5 Bowers United v Tiptree United 0-3
6 Ford United v Maldon Town 1-0
7 Stanway Rovers v Waltham Abbey 3-1
8 Gt Wakering Rvrs v Stanstead 0-1
9 Southend Manor v Barkingside 0-2
23 Clubs seeded
Second Round
1 Wivenhoe Town v Billericay Town 3-3 1-2
2 Southend United v Canvey Island 6-0
3 Chelmsford City v Tilbury 3-0
4 Collier Row v Harlow Town 4-0
5 Stanway Rovers v Stansted 2-3
6 Concord Rangers v Colchester United 2-1
7 Leyton Pennant v Saffron Walden Town 2-1
8 Clapton v Halstead Town 1-4
9 Heybridge Swifts v Tiptree United 5-1
10 Aveley v Purfleet 0-3
11 Harwich Parkeston v Grays Athletic 2-3
12 Burnham Ramblers v Barkingside 0-1
13 Dngenham & R'dge v Leyton Orient 1-3
14 Witham Town v Hornchurch 2-1
15 Barking v Ford United 2-3

| 16 Braintree Town | v East Thurrock United | 2-1 |

Third Round

1 Barkingside	v Southend United	1-5
2 Grays Athletic	v Ford United	3-2
3 Halstead Town	v Heybridge Swifts	0-3
4 Braintree Town	v Chelmsford City	3-2
5 Collier Row	v Purfleet	0-1
6 Concord Rangers	v Leyton Orient	2-0
7 Leyton Pennant	v Billericay Town	3V2
8 Stansted	v Witham Town	3-4

(Leyton Pennant removed from Competition for fielding and ineligible player Billericay Town re-instated).

Fourth Round

1 Heybridge Swifts	v Billericay Town	1-3
2 Purfleet	v Southend United	2-4
3 Grays Athletic	v Witham Town	4-0
4 Braintree Town	v Concord Rangers	3-0

Semi Finals

| Braintree Town | v Southend United 1-1 | 1-0 |
| Grays Athletic | v Billericay Town | 0-2 |

Final Monday 22nd April 1996,

| Billericay Town | v Braintree Town | 1-2 |

at Dagenham & Redbridge FC

EAST ANGLIAN CUP
Holders Heybridge Swifts

Group 1 First Round

1 Hadleigh United	v Stowmarket Town	4p5 2-2
2 Felixstone P & Tn	v Ipswich Wanderers	3-6
3 Woodbridge Town	v Sudbury Town	0-1

Second Round Bye to this Round

| 1 Stowmarket Town | v Sudbury Town | 1-2 |
| 2 Cornard Utd -- | v Ipswich Wanderers | 1-3 |

Group Final

| Sudbury Town | v Ipswich Wanderers | 2-0 |

Group 2 First Round

1 Fakenham Town	v March Town United	2-1
2 Downham Town	v Holbeach United	1-2
3 Stamford AFC	v Spalding United	6p7 3-3

Second Round

| 1 Fakenham Town | v Spalding United | 1-0 |
| 2 Bourne Town-- | v Holbeach United | 0-2 |

Group Final

| Fakenham Town | v Holbeach United | 2-1 |

Group 2 First Round

1 Ely City	v Soham Town Rangers	1-3
2 Diss Town	v Mildenhall Town	2-0
3 Watton United	v Thetford Town	1-3

Second Round

| 1 Soham Tn Rangers | v Thetford Town | 4p3 4-4 |
| 2 Bury Town-- | v Diss Town | 2-0 |

Group Final

| Soham Town Rangers | v Bury Town | 4-0 |

Group 4 First Round

1 Royston Town	v Sawbridgeworth Town	4-1
2 Letchworth	v Saffron Walden Town	0-6
3 Ware	v Stansted	5-1

Second Round

| 1 Royston Town | v Ware | 0-2 |

| 2 Harlow Town-- | v Saffron Walden T | 6p2-2 |

Group Final A=Fog

| Ware | v Harlow Town | 0A0 1-0 |

Group 5 First Round

1 Eynesbury Rovers	v Potton United	7p8 1-1
2 Cambridge City	v Histon	6-0
3 Somersham Town	v St Ives Town	0-2
4 Warboys Town	v Biggleswade Tn	1A1 3-1

Second Round

| 1 Potton United | v St Ives Town | 2-0 |
| 2 Warboys Town | v Cambridge City | 2-4 |

Group Final

| Potton United | v Cambridge City | 0-2 |

Group 6 First Round

1 Harpenden Town	v Hoddesdon Town	2-0
2 Barkingside	v Hertford Town	5-1
3 St Albans City	v Romford	2-0

Second Round

| 1 Harpenden Town | v St Albans City | 1-2 |
| 2 Barking-- | v Barkingside | 4-0 |

Group Final

| St Albans City | v Barking | 1-0 |

Group 7 First Round

1 Concord Rangers	v Maldon Town	4-2
2 Burnham Ramblers	v Heybridge Swifts	0-3
3 Tiptree	v Southend Manor	5-2

Second Round

| 1 Concord Rangers | v Tiptree United | 2-0 |
| 2 Aveley-- | v Heybridge Swifts | 3-2 |

Group Final

| Concord Rangers | v Aveley | 2-0 |

Group & First Round

| 1 Colchester United | v Harwich & Parkeston | 5-0 |
| 2 Clacton Town | v Halstead Town | 1-2 |

Second Round

| 1 Colchester United | v Witham Town-- | 2-1 |
| 2 Braintree Town | v Halstead Town | 2-1 |

Group Final

| Colchester United | v Braintree Town | 3-4 |

Competition Proper Quarter-Finals

1 Braintree Town	v Ware	5-4
2 Concord Rangers	v Cambridge City	1-0
3 Fakenham Town	v Sudbury Town	1-2
4 St Albans City	v Soham Tn Rangers	1-0

Semi-Finals

| 1 Concord Rangers | v Sudbury Town | 0-2 |
| 2 Braintree Town | v St Alban City | 2-0 |

Final

Tuesday 7th May 1996 — Att: 643

| Braintree Town | v Sudbury Town | 3-0 |

at Braintree Town FC

ESSEX THAMES-SIDE TROPHY
Holders Purfleet

First Round

1 Witham Town	v Barkingside	2-1
2 Collier Row	v Hornchurch	3p2 1-1
3 Waltham Abbey	v Basildon United	0-1
4 East Thurrock Utd	v Canvey Island	1-2

5 Clapton	v Concord Rangers	0-3
6 Romford	v Ford United	3-1
7 Tilbury	v Gt Wakering Rovers	0-5
8 Burnham Ramblers	v Aveley	2-1
9 Southend Manor	v Bowers United	1-0

4 Clubs with byes Barking Billericay Town, Leyton Pennant, Tiptree United and 3 clubs exempt Purfleet, Chelmsford City, Grays Athletic

Second Round

1 Concord Rangers	v Southend Manor	1AO 2-1
2 Gt Wakering Rvrs	v Barking	3-2
3 Billericay Town	v Purfleet	0-2
4 Grays Athletic	v Romford	3-0
5 Witham Town	v Chelmsford City	2-1
6 Leyton Pennant	v Collier Row	2-1
7 Basildon United	v Canvey Island	1-3
8 Tiptree United	v Burham Ramblers	2-3

Third Round

1 Grays Athletic	v Great Wakering Rovers	2-1
2 Leyton Pennant	v Purfleet	6-2
3 Witham Town	v Burnham Ramblers	1-0
4 Canvey Island	v Concord Rangers	1-0

Semi Finals

| Witham Town @LP | v Leyton Pennant | 3-1 |
| Grays Athletic | v Canvey Island | 0-2 |

Final Sunday 12th May 1996

| Canvey Island | v Witham Town | 5-0 |

at Canvey Island FC

GLOS SENIOR CUP
Holders Cheltenham Town

First Round

| 1 Forest Green Rovers | v Gloucester City | 1-2 |

Semi-Finals A=Fog

| 1 Gloucester City | v Cinderford Town | 2AO 3-2 |
| 2 Cheltenham Town | v Yate Town | 2-0 |

Final Tuesday 2nd April

| Cheltenham Tn | v Gloucester City | 0-0 |
| at Cheltenham Town FC | | (3p1) |

GLOS SENIOR TROPHY
Holders Shortwood United

Preliminary Round

| 1 Stapleton | v Brockworth | 2-0 |

First Round

1 Mangotsfield Utd	v Shirehampton	1-3
2 Endsleigh @P	v Pucklechurch Sports	3-1
3 Broad Plain House	v Wotton Rovers	3-1
4 Bishops Cleeve	v Tuffley Rovers	0-3
5 Stapleton/Brock'th	v DRG (FP)	0-0 1-3
6 Broadwell Amt	v Ellwood	0-2
7 Bitton	v Hallen	1-1 3-1
8 Longwell Gn Abb	v Winterbourne United	0-1
9 Harrow Hill	v St Marks CA	1-2
10 Cirencester United	v Cheltenham Saracens	2-3
11 Patchway Town	v Old Georgians	0-1
12 Almondsbury Tn	v Cirencester Town	2-6
13 Totterdown Ath	v Cadbury Heath	1-3
14 Shortwood United	v Bristol Manor Farm	2-1
15 Frampton Athletic	v Smiths Athletic	1-0

| 16 Henbury Old Boys | v Fairford Town | 1-3 |

Second Round

1 Old Georgians	v Fairford Town	1-3
2 Ellwood	v Frampton Athletic	3-1
3 Bitton	v Tuffley Rovers	3-1
4 D R G	v Endsleigh	0-2
5 Shortwood United	v Cirencester Town	0-3
6 Ch't'ham Saracens	v Broad Plain House	2-1
7 Winterbourne Utd	v Shirehampton	2-1
8 Cadbury Heath	v St Marks C A	3-3 2-4

Third Round

1 Cirencester Town	v Fairford Town	3-2
2 St Marks C A @B	v Bitton	1-3
3 Cheltenham S'cens	v Winterbourne United	1-3
4 Ellwood	v Endsleigh	0-2

Semi-Finals

Winterbourne United v Cirencester Town 0-1
at Shortwood United AFC Tuesday 5th March
Endsleigh v Bitton 2-0
at Almondsbury Town FC Tuesday 19th March

Final Monday 6th May

Cirencester Town v Endsleigh 2-1
at Gloucester City AFC

HAMPSHIRE SENIOR CUP
Holders Havant Town

Preliminary Round

1 Aerostructures	v Hartley Wintney	4-0
2 AFC Lymington	v Hayling Island	4-0
3 AFC Totton	v Eastleigh	0-4
4 Bashley	v Paulsgrove	5-1
5 Basingstoke Town	v Pirelli General	8-0
6 Bass Alton Town	v Fleetlands	1-0
7 Bemerton HH	v Romsey Town	RT W-O
8 Brockenhurst	v AC Delco	3-1
9 Christchurch	v Ecchinswell	0-1
10 Cove	v Liss Athletic	4-2
11 East Cowes Vics	v Petersfield Town	2-1
12 Fareham Town	v Malshanger	5-4
13 Fleet Town	v Overton United	6-1
14 New Milton Tn	v Gosport Borough	1-2
15 New Street	v Cowes Sports	7-0
16 Sylvans Sports	v BAT Sports	6-0
17 Whitchurch Utd	v Netley Central Sports	0-3

15 Clubs with Byes

First Round

1 Aerostructures	v Moneyfields	2-1
2 Lymington AFC	v Sylvans Sports	2-1
3 Aldershot Town	v East Cowes Vic Ath	5-0
4 Andover	v Colden Common	3-1
5 Brockenhurst	v Winchester City	1-4
6 Cove	v Bashley	1-7
7 DCA Basingstoke	v Ecchinswell	5-1
8 Eastleigh	v Bass Alton Town	2-1
9 Fareham Town	v Basingstoke Town	1-3
10 Farnborough Town	v New Street	6-1
11 Fleet Town	v Blackfield & Langley	4-1
12 Gosport Borough	v Newport IOW	1-5
13 Horndean	v Bournemouth	0-1

14 Portsmouth RN	v Netley Central Sports	1-0
15 Romsey Town	v Havant Town	1-5
16 Waterlooville	v Ryde	4-0

Second Round

1 AFC Lymington	v Winchester City	4-0
2 Bahley	v Newport IOW	1-0
3 Basingstoke Town	v Havant Town	1A0
4 Bournemouth	v Andover	2-1
5 Eastleigh	v Aldershot Town	2-3
6 Farnborough Town	v DCA Basingstoke	1-4
7 Portsmouth RN	v Aerostructures	1-2
8 Waterlooville	v Fleet Town	2-1

The above match between Basingstoke Town & Havant Town was Abandoned after 87 minutes with Havant down to 7 players Result Stood

Third Round

1 Aerostructures	v Bashley	0-1
2 AFC Lymington	v Bournemouth	2-3
3 Basingstoke Town	v DCA Basingstoke	4-1
4 Waterlooville	v Aldershot Town	3-1

Semi-Finals

Bashley	v Waterlooville	0-1

at Eastleigh FC Wednesday 13th March 1996

Bournemouth	v Basingstoke Town	1-3

at Waterlooville FC Wednesday 6th March 1996

Final Tuesday 23rd April 1996

Basingstoke Town	v Waterlooville	2-0

at Southampton FC   Att; 850

HEREFORDSHIRE SENIOR CUP
Holders Hinton

Preliminary Round

1 Kington Town	v Pegasus Juniors	0-5

First Round Saturday

1 Leominster	v Ross Town	1-3
2 Colwall Rangers	v Westfields	WW-O
3 Ewyas Harold	v Conquest	1-3
4 Golden Valley	v Pegasus Juniors	0-7
5 Hereford Lads Club	v Hinton	0-5
6 Ledbury Town	v Fownhope	2-5
7 Wellington	v Woofferton	1-2
8 Weston	v Bromyard Town	1-5

Second Round

1 Conquest	v Ross Town 93	2-4
2 Hinton	v Woofferton	0-3
3 Fownhope	v Westfields	1-4
4 Bromyard Town	v Pegasus Juniors	3-6

Semi-Finals

Westfields	v Woofferton	1-0
Ross Town	v Pegasus Juniors	1-0

Final Monday 8th April 1996

Ross Town	v Westfields	2p4 2-2

at Hereford United FC

HERTS SENIOR CUP
Holders Watford

First Round

1 Sawbridgeworth Tn	v London Colney	1-4
2 Royston Town	v Hoddesdon Town	1-0
3 Welwyn Gdn City	v Hatfield Town	0-4

4 Potters Bar Town	v Hemel Hempstead	4-3
5 Cheshunt	v Ware	1-2
6 Hertford Town	v Tring Town	2-0
7 Harpenden Town	v Letchworth	2-3

Second Round

1 Barnet	v St Albans	3-0
2 Royston Town	v Boreham Wood	0-2
3 London Colney	v Ware	3-1
4 Letchworth	v Potters Bar Town	2-3
5 Bishop's Storford	v Berkhamsted Town	2-0
6 Stevenage Borough	v Watford @SB	0-0 3-4
7 Baldock Town	v Hatfield Town	3-1
8 Hertford Town	v Hitchin Town	0-6

Third Round

1 Hitchin Town	v Bishop's Storford	4-1
2 Watford	v Potters Bar Town	4-0
3 Boreham Wood	v Barnet	2-3
4 Baldock Town	v London Colney	4-3

Semi-Finals

1 Barnet	v Hitchin Town	1-0
2 Watford @BT	v Baldock Town	2-1

Final Monday 22nd April

Barnet	v Watford	2-1

at St Albans City FC

HERTS CENTENARY TROPHY
Holders London Colney

First Round

1 Somersett A V & F	v Leverstock Green	1-4
2 Bovingdon	v Wormley Rovers	0-2
3 St Peters	v Kings Langley	4-2
4 Sun Postal Sports	v Tring Athletic	2-0

Second Round

1 St Peters	v Cuffley	2-1
2 Colney Heath	v Leverstock Green	3-1
3 Oxhey Jets	v Welwyn	0-1
4 Met Police Bushey	v St Margaretsbury	4-1
5 Sandridge Rovers	v Chipperfield Co's	1A1 1-2
6 Bedmond Sports	v Agrevo Sports	0-4
7 Sun Postal Sports	v Elliott Star	1-2
8 Wormley Rovers	v Bragbury Athletic	4-3

Third Round

1 Wormley Rovers	v Chipperfield Corinthians	3-1
2 Agrevo Sports	v Elliott Star	2-1
3 Welwyn	v Mel Police Bushey	3-2
4 St Peters	v Colney Heath	2p4 2-2 3-3

Semi-Finals

1 Welwyn	v Colney Heath	0-2
2 Wormley Rovers	v Agrevo Sports	1-3

Final

Agrevo Sports	v Colney Heath	1-4

at Ware FC April 20th 1996

HERTS CHARITY CUP
Holders St Albans City

First Round

1 Boreham Wood	v Bishops Stortford	2-0
2 Hertford Town	v Hemel Hempstead	1-3
3 Cheshunt	v Tring Town	0-2
4 Baldock Town	v Berkhamsted Town	2-0

Second Round

1 St Albans City	v Ware	4-2
2 Stevenage Town	v Hitchin Town	3-0
3 Boreham Wood	v Baldock Town	BW W-0
4 Hemel Hempstead	v Tring Town	1-0

Semi Finals

1 Stevenage Borough	v Hemel Hempstead OAO 2-1
2 St Albans City	v Boreham Wood	2-0

Final Held over to pre-season 10.8.96
Stevenage Borough v St Albans City 4-2
@ St Albans City FC

HERTS CHARITY SHIELD
Holders Sawbridgeworth Town

First Round

1 Harpenden Town	v Letchworth FC @ L	4-0
2 London Colney	v St Margaretsbury	0-5
3 Royston Town	v Sawbridgeworth Town	0-4
4 Sun Sports	v Sandridge Rovers	0-1
5 Hatfield Town	v Tring Athletic	2-1
6 Welwyn Gdn City	v Hoddesdon Town	0-2

2 Clubs with Byes Leverstock Green, Potters Bar Town.

1 Potters Bar Town	v Leverstock Green	4-0
2 Hatfield Town	v Sandridge Rovers	1-2
3 Harpenden Town	v Hoddesdon Town	1-2
4 Sawbridgeworth Tn	v St Margaretsbury	2-1

Semi-Finals

1 Potters Bar Town	v Hoddesdon Town	4-0
2 Sandridge Rovers	v Sawbridgeworth Town	0-3

(Played at London Colney FC)

Final Thursday 9th May 1996
Potters Bar Town   v Sawbridgeworth Town   2-4
at Crofters End, West Rd, Sawbridgeworth Town FC.

Huntingdonshire Senior Cup
Holders Warboys Town

First Round

1 Somersham Town	v Warboys Town	0-2
2 Godmanchester Rvs	v Yaxley	0-2
3 Ramsey Town	v Hotpoint	1-0
4 St Ives Town	v Eynesbury Rovers	2-3

Second Round

1 Alconbury	v Eynesbury Rovers	0-3
2 Ramsey Town	v Bluntisham Rangers	3-1
3 Yuxley	v Warboys Town	0-2
4 St Neots Town	v Ortonians	6-1

Semi-Final Saturday 2nd March 1996

Eynesbury Rovers	v St Neots Town	2-0
Ramsey Town	v Warboys Town	0-2

Final Monday 6th may 3.00pm
Eynesbury Rovers   v Warboys Town   3-2
at Rowley Park Cambridge Rd St Neots Town FC

KENT FACIT SENIOR CUP
Holders Charlton Athletic

First Round

1 Tonbridge AFC	v Fisher	1-2
2 Dover Athletic	v Ashford Town	1-2
3 Bromley	v Millwall	1-1 4-1
4 Gravesend & Nfleet	v Margate	2-1
5 Welling United	v Deal Town	1-0

6 Sittingbourne	v Erith & Belvedere	3-3 5-2

Two clubs receive Byes Charlton Athletic and Gillingham

Second Round

1 Gillingham @B	v Bromley	4p3 1-1
2 Welling United	v Ashford Town	2-3
3 Sittingbourne	v Charlton Athletic	1-3
4 Fisher	v Gravesend & Northfleet	2-0

Semi-Finals

Ashford Town	v Gillingham	3-1
Fisher	v Charlton Athletic	4-8

Final Monday 6th May 1996,
Ashford Town   v Charlton Athletic   3-0
at Central Park, Sittingbourne FC att 1,200

KENT PLAAYA SENIOR TROPHY
Holders Deal Town

First Round

1 Beckenham Town	V Stansfield O & B	0-0 3-2
2 Greenwich Borough	V West Wickham	4-2
3 Sheppey United	V Woolwich Town	2-0
4 Cray Wanderers	V Whitstable Town	1-2
5 Kent Police	V Canterbury City	0-4
6 Thamesmead Tn	V Hythe United	4-2
7 Tunbridge Wells	V Corinthian	2-1
8 Midland Bank	V V C D Athletic	1-4
9 Chatham Town	V Crockenhill	4-2
10 Ramsgate	V Furness	0-4

Second Round

1 V C D Athletic	V Furness	0-2
2 Folkestone Invicta	V Dartford	0-1
3 Chatham Town	V Thames Polytechnic	9-2
4 Whitstable Town	V Faversham Town	3-0
5 Canterbury City	V Herne Bay	0-1
6 Slade Green	V Thamesmead Town	1-3
7 Beckenham Town	V Tunbridge Wells	1-3
8 Greenwich Borough	V Sheppey United	3-1

Third Round

1 Thamesmead Town	V Tunbridge Wells	2-1
2 Chatham Town	V Herne Bay	2*1
3 Whitstable Town	V Dartford	1*2
4 Furness	V Greenwich Borough	2-0

Semi-Finals

1 Dartford	V Furness	1-0
2 Thamesmead Town	V Chatham Town	0-4

Final Saturday 13th April 1996
Dartford v Chatham Town 3-0
at Welling United FC

LANCASHIRE ATS TROPHY
Holders Bamber Bridge

First Round

1 Atherton L R	V Bacup Borough	7-0
2 Barrow	V Fleetwood	3-1
3 Burscough	V Marine	3*3 0-2
4 Daisy Hill	V Nelson	2-1
5 Holker O B	V Blackpool Mechanics	6-0
6 Leigh RMI	V Atherton Collieries	1-0
7 Radcliffe Borough	V Great Harwood Town	3-1
8 Rossendale United	V Blackpool Rovers	0-3

Eight Clubs with Byes Accrington Stanley, Bamber,

Bridge, Chorley, Lancaster City, Clitheroe, Darwen, Morecambe, Southport, into the

Second Round

1 Accrington Stanley	V Radcliffe Borough	1*1	1-2
2 Atherton Rovers	V Chorley		1-2
3 Bamber Bridge	V Lancaster City		4*3
4 Blackpool Rovers	V Daisy Hill		1-2
5 Clitheroe	V Darwen	1A1	2-0
6 Holker Old Boys	V Barrow		1-2
7 Morecambe	V Leigh RMI		2-0
8 Southport	V Marine		1-0

Third Round

1 Bamber Bridge	V Diasy Hill	3-1
2 Clitheroe	V Chorley	2-3
3 Morecambe	V Radcliffe Borough	3-1
4 Southport	V Barrow	3-1

Semi-Finals

Bamber Bridge	V Chorley	3-0
Morecambe	V Southport	2-1

Final Wednesday 24th April 1996

Bamber Bridge v Morecambe		0-1
at Preston North End FC.	att;	1,708

LEICESTERSHIRE 'JELSON HOMES' SENIOR CUP
Holders Anstey Nomads

First Round

1 Earl Shilton Albion	V Kirby Muxloe	1-6
2 Cottesmore Amt	V Aylestone Park OB	0-1
3 Narboro & L'thorpe	V Asfordby Amateurs	2*3
4 Oadby Town	V Hemington	10-2
5 Blaby & Whetstone	V Holwell Sports	1-2
6 Saffron Dynamo	V Barlestone St Giles	4-1
7 Syston St Peters	V Downes Sports	2-3
8 United Collieries	V Burbage OB	1-6
9 Newfoundpool	V Friar Lane OB	2-1
10 North Kilworth	V Anstey Nomads	1*5

Second Round 4th Nov. **22 Clubs with Byes

1 St Andrews**	V Fosse Imps**	4-0
2 Anstey Nomads**	V Barwell**	0-1
3 Coalville Town**	V Harborough Town**	7-1
4 Slack & Parr**	V Thringstone MW**	0-1
5 L'boro**Dynamo	V Houghton Rangers**	6-0
6 Burbage OB	V Kirby Muxloe	1-3
7 Huncote S & S**	V Sileby Town**	3-1
8 Newfoundpool**	V Birstall United**	1-2
9 Saffron Dynamo	V Quorn**	2-1
10 Bardon Hill**	V Barrow Town**	0-2
11 Lutterworth**Tn	V Highfield Rangers**	0-3
12 Holwell Sports	V Hillcroft**	2-3
13 Oadby Town	V Anstey Nomads	4-1
14 Asfordby Amt	V Ibstock Welfare**	2-1
15 Downes Sports	V Stoney Stanton**	3-2
16 Leics**Constabulary	V Aylestone Park OB	2-1

Third Round

1 Huncote SSC	V Highfield Rangers	1-3
2 Thringstone MW	V Saffron Dynamo	2-1
3 Downes Sports	V Barwell	1-3
4 Loughboro Dynamo	V Leics Canstabulary	2-1

5 Oadby Town	V St Andrews	1-0
6 Birstall United	V Barrow Town	3-1
7 Kirby Muxloe	V Coalville	5-0
8 Asfordby Amateurs	V Hillcroft	4-1

Fourth Round

1 Barwell	V Highfield Rangers	3-0
2 Oadby Town	V Asfordby Amateurs	6-2
3 Thringstone MW	V Kirby Muxloe	1-5
4 Birstall United	V Loughborough Dynamo	4-2

Semi-Finals

Barwell	V Oadby Town	0-1
at Leicester United FC.		
Kirby Muxloe	V Birstall United	2-3
at Quorn FC.		

Final, Tuesday 2nd April

Birstall United v Oadby Town 1*0
at Holmes Park, Whetstone

LEICS WESTERBY CHALLENGE CUP
Holders Leicester City

First Round

1 Hinckley Athletic	V Oadby Town	0-3
2 Anstey Nomads	V Shepshed Dynamo	0-2
3 Holwell Sports	V Leicester United	1-4
4 Friar Lane OB	V Barrow Town	5-0

Second Round** 4 Clubs with byes

1 Barwell**	V St Andrews**	2-3
2 Friar Lane OB	V Leicester United	2-1
3 Shepshed Dynamo	V Hinckley Town**	1-0
4 Leicester City**	V Oadby Town	5-0

Semi-Finals March at Holmes Park, Whetstone

1 St Andrews	V Sheshed Dynamo	3-1
2 Friar Lane OB	V Leicester City	0-6

Final Monday 22nd April 1996

Leicester City v St Andrews 2-1
at Filbert Street, Leicester City FC.

LINCOLNSHIRE SENIOR CUP
Holders Grimsby Town

Section 'A'   **Won on the Toss of a coin

1 Grimsby Town	V Scunthorpe United	3-0
2 Gainsboro Trinity	V Scunthorpe United	3-0
3 Gainsboro Trinity	V Grimsby Town	0-0

Final Table

	P	W	D	L	F	A	Pts	GD
1 Grimsby Town**	2	1	1	0	3	0	5	+3
2 Gainsboro Trinity	2	1	1	0	3	0	5	+3
3 Scunthorpe United	2	0	0	2	0	6	0	-6

Section 'B'

1 Boston United	V Lincoln City	0-0
2 Grantham Town	V Lincoln City	1-2
3 Grantham Town	V Boston United	0-2

Final Table

	P	W	D	L	F	A	Pts	GD
1 Boston United	2	1	1	0	2	0	4	+2
2 Lincoln City	2	1	1	0	2	1	4	+1
3 Grantham Town	2	0	0	2	1	4	0	-3

Final. Tuesday 6th November 1995

Boston United v Grimsby Town 1-4
at York Road, Boston United FC.

LINCS SENIOR 'A' CUP
Holders Holbeach United

Preliminary Round

1 Bourne Town	V Mirrlees Blackstone	0-2
2 Immingham Town	V Boston Town	0-4
3 Brigg Town	V Spalding United	3-0
4 Stamford AFC	V Holbeach United	1-1 S W-O

*First Round** 4 Clubs with Byes*

1 Mirrlees Blackstone	V Brigg Town	0-3
2 Louth United**	V Nettleham**	1-2
3 Boston Town	V Stamford AFC	3-1
4 Lincoln United**	V Winterton Rangers**	4-0

Semi-Finals

Lincoln United	V Brigg Town	4-0
Boston Town	V Nettleham	2-1

Final Tuesday 16th April 1996

Lincoln United v Boston Town	2-1

at Ashby Avenue, Lincoln United FC

LINCS SENIOR 'B' CUP
Holders Immingham Blossom Way

First Round

1 Limestone Rangers	V Deeping Rangers	4-1
2 Louth Old Boys	V Appleby Frodingham	0-3
3 Hykeham Town	V Sleaford Town	4-1
4 Grimsby Amateurs	V Bottesford Town	4-1
5 Harrowby United	V Ruston Sports	0-3
6 Skegness Town	V Lincoln Moorlands	2-3
7 Barton Town OB	V Epworth Town	2-0
8 Wyberton	V Spilsby Town	W W-O

Second Round

1 Appleby Frod Ath	V Ruston Sports	2-1
2 Wyberton	V Barton Town OB	2-2 1-2
3 Grimsby Amateurs	V Lincoln Moorlands	1-2
4 Hykeham Town	V Limestone Rangers	2-0

Semi-Finals

Appleby Frodingham	V Lincoln Moorlands	2-0
Barton Old Boys	V Hykeham Town	3-0

Final Wednesday 13th March 1996

Appleby Frodingham v Barton OB	0-2

at, Winterton Rangers FC.

LIVERPOOL SENIOR CUP
Holders Tranmere Rovers

First Round

1 Bootle	V Prescot Cables	5-3
2 Burscough	V St Helens Town	1-2
3 Knowsley United	V Skelmersdale United	2-0

Second Round

1 Knowsley United	V Bootle	4-0
2 Southport	V Everton	3-3 0-2
3 Marine	V St Helens Town	1-0
4 Tranmere Rovers	V Liverpool	3-1

Semi-Finals By Saturday 30th March

Knowsley United	V Everton	0-2
Marine	V Tranmere Rovers	1-4

Final Held over to pre-season (First XI's) 31.7.96.

Everton v Tranmere Rovers	2-1

at Prenton Park, Tranmere Rovers FC

LONDON CHALLENGE CUP
Holders St Albans City

First Round

1 Uxbridge	V Hampton	0-2
2 Leyton Pennant	V Boreham Wood	5*5 3-2
3 Barking	V Fisher	2-1
4 Erith & Belvedere	V Tooting & Mitcham	1-6
5 Dulwich Hamlet	V Bromley	1-2
6 Welling	V Southall	12-0
7 Met Police	V Croydon	2-1
8 Collier Row	V St Albans City	2-1

Second Round

1 Bromley	V Barking	Bromley W-O
2 Tooting & Mitcham	V Welling United	2-1
3 Met Police	V Hampton	1-3
4 Leyton Pennant	V Collier Row	3-3 2*1

Semi-Finals

Leyton Pennant	V Hampton	2-1
Tooting & Mitcham	V Bromley	0-1

Final Wednesday 1st May

Bromley v Leyton Pennant	3*2

at The New Den, Millwall FC

LONDON SENIOR CUP
Holders Wingate & Finchley

First Round

1 Woolwich Town	V Hillingdon Borough	1*2
2 Tufnell Park	V East Ham United	5-0
3 Cray Wanderers @F	V Ford United	2*2 1-2
4 Thames Polytechnic	V Cockfosters	3-2
5 Bedfont	V St Margaretsbury	2*3
6 Civil Service	V Barkingside	2-0
7 Brimsdown Rovers	V Kingsbury Town	2-3
8 Hanwell Town	V Croydon Athletic	4-1
9 Clapton	V Woodford Town	3-1

Second Round

1 Willesden Hawkeye	V Corinthian Casuals	3-0
2 Hoddesdon Town	V Thames Polytechnic	3-2
3 Kingsbury Town	V Hillingdon Borough	1-0
4 Wingate & Finchley	V Civil Service	2-0
5 Tufnell Park	V Tottenham Omada	0-1
6 Eton Manor	V Hanwell Town	0-2
7 Thamesmead Town	V Ford United	2-0
8 St Margaretsbury	V Clapton	2*1

Third Round

1 Thamesmead Town	V Kingsbury	1-3
2 Hoddesdon Town	V Willesden Hawkeye	1-2
3 Tottenham Omada	V Wingate & Finchley	2-1
4 Hanwell Town	V St Margaretsbury	1-3

Semi-Finals

Willesden Hawkeye	V Kingsbury Town	1-1 1-3
St Margaretsbury	V Tottenham Omada	2*4

Final Saturday 20th April

Kingsbury T v Tottenham Omada	1-2

at Dulwich Hamlet FC

MANCHESTER PREMIER CUP
Holders Hyde United

First Round

1 Chadderton @SC	V Salford City	2-3

2 Radcliffe Borough	V Glossop North End	2-1
3 Curzon Ashton	V Mossley	2-1
4 Droylsden	V Flixton	2-4
5 Maine Road	'. Ashton United	1-0

3 Clubs with Byes Hyd United, Oldham Town, Trafford.

Second Round

1 Trafford	V Flixton	1*3
2 Salford City	V Radcliffe Borough	0-4
3 Curzon Ashton	V Oldham Town	2-1
4 Maine Road	V Hyde United	1*2

(Trafford are re-instated as Flixton were found to have fielded an ineligible player in the above match).

Semi-Finals

Curzon Ashton	V Trafford	6-2
Hyde United	V Radcliffe Borough	2-0

Final Tuesday 7th May 1996

Curzon Ashton v Hyde United   3p4 2*2
at Burnden Park, BoltonWanderers FC

OXFORDSHIRE SENIOR CUP
Holders Witney Town

First Round

1 A P Sports & S	V Chackendon Sports	0-2
2 Garsington	V Watlington	3-4
3 Worcs College OB	V Rover Cowley	4-1
4 Henley Town	V Launton Sports	4-0
5 Kidlington	V Easington Sports	8-1
6 Chipping Norton T	V Woodstock Town	2-2 1-3
7 Chinnor	V Old Woodstock	3-4
8 Headington Amt	V Eynsham AFC	5-5 2-3
9 Wheatley United	V Yarnton	0-4

7 Clubs With Byes Ardley United, Banbury United, Bicester United, Carterton Town, Clanfield, Peppard, Quarry Nomads

Second Round

1 Ardley United	V Peppard	0-2
2 Banbury United	V Old Woodstock	2-0
3 Bicester Town	V Kidlington	3-1
4 Carterton Town	V Checkendon Sports	6-0
5 Yarnton	V Clanfield	0-1
6 Watlington	V Woodstock Town	6-1
7 Worc's College OB	V Quarry Nomads	0-2
8 Eynsham AFC	V Henley Town	3-1

Third Round

1 Peppard	V Clanfield	2-1
2 Banbury United	V Eynsham AFC	4-3
3 Quarry Nomads	V Bicester Town	1-1 1-3
4 Watlington	V Carterton Town	0-2

4 Clubs Exempt Thame United, Witney Town, Oxford City, North Leigh

Fourth Round

1 Carterton Town	V Witney Town	0-1
2 Bicester Town	V Peppard	1-0
3 Thame United	V Banbury United	7-0
4 Oxford City	V North Leigh	3-1

Semi-Finals

Bicester Town	V Oxford City	1-2

at Thame United FC

Thame United	V Witney Town	3-0

at Oxford City FC

Final Wednesday 8th May 1996

Thame United v Oxford City		1-2

at Windmill Road, Thame United FC

SHEFFIELD & HALLAMSHIRE CUP
Holders Worksop Town

First Qualifying Round

1 Sheffield Bankers	V Mexborough Main St	3-2
2 Wath Saracens A	V Clifton Rovers	1-3
3 Kiverton Park	V Caribbean Sports	2-3
4 AshHousePhoenix	V Sheffield Abbeydale	2-1
5 Denaby & Cadeby	V Case Sports	1-2
6 A B M FC	V Wickersley Old Boys	2-1
7 Wombwell Town	V Grapes Nthn General	8-1
8 S & H Univ Union	V Harworth C Institute	4-2
9 Parramores Sports	V Yorkshire Main	3-1
10 Thurcroft D B	V Grimethorpe MW	0-2
11 Old Edwardians	V Swinton Athletic	0-5
12 Frecheville C A	V Mexboro Ath Oakhse	4-2
13 Hemsworth Town	V Sheffield Centralians	4-0
14 Avesta Sheffield	V Penistone Church	1-4
15 Elsecar Market H	V Killamarsh AFC	2-2 0-2
16 Throstles Ridgeway	V High Green Villa	1-5
17 Ecclesfield R R	V Woodsetts Sports	3-0
18 Treeton Welfare	V NCB Maltby MW	0-5
19 Oughtibridge WM	V Davy FC	2-0
20 Rossington FC	V The Wetherby	0-1

12 Clubs With Byes, Brodsworth, Denaby United, Emley, Frickley Athletic, Hallam, Maltaby MW, Parkgate, Rossingdon Main, Sheffield, Stocksbridge Park Steels, Worksop Town, Worsbrough Bridge MW,

First Round Proper

1 Hallam	V Clifton Rovers	5-1
2 Denaby United	V Hemsworth Town	3-1
3 Case Sports	V Ecclesfield Red Rose	0-3
4 Maltby MW	V Swinton Athletic	3-1
5 Sheffield Bankers	V Penistone Church	2-1
6 Grimethorpe MW	V Wombwell Town	5*1
7 Oughtibridge WMC	V Parkgate	2-1
8 Brodsworth	V Caribbean Sports	0*0 1-0
9 Worsbrough Br	V Ash House Phoenix	0-2
10 Killamarsh	V Sheff-Hallam Univ Un	5*4
11 Emley AFC	V Worksop Town	2-1
12 High Green Villa	V Stocksbridge Pk St	0*0 2-5
13 Frecheville CA	V NCB Maltby MW	2-1
14 Parramore Sports	V Sheffield	2-5
15 Rossington Main	V Frickley Athletic	2-8
16 The Wetherby	V A B M	2-1

Second Round

1 The Wetherby	V Frickley Athletic	1-3
2 Ecclesfield Red R	V Hallam	1-4
3 Frecheville C A	V Emley	1-0
4 Brodsworth	V Sheffield	1-0
5 Maltby MW	V Killamarsh Juniors	2-1
6 Grimethorpe MW	V Ash House Phoenix	4-2
7 Sheffield Bankers	V Oughtibridge WMC	1-2
8 Denaby United	V Stocksbridge Pk Steels	2-3

Third Round

1 Brodsworth	V Maltby MW		0-3
2 Frecheville C A	V Grimethorpe MW		1-3
3 Frickley Athletic	V Stocksbridge Pk	2*2	0-2
4 Hallam	V Oughtibridge WMC		3-2

Semi-Finals (Two Legs)

Grimethorpe MW	V Hallam		0-1 2-0 2-1
Maltby MW	V Stocksbridge P S	1-1 2-4	3-5

Final Wednesday 17th April

Grimethorpe MW 0
v Stocksbridge Park Steels 1
at Welfare Sports Ground, Huddersfield, Emley FC

SHROPSHIRE SENIOR CUP
Holders Shrewsbury Town

First Round

1 Ludlow Town	V Shifnal Town	0-3

Semi-Finals

1 Bridgnorth Town	V Telford United	1-2
2 Shifnal Town	V Shrewsbury Town	0-4

Final

at Buck's Head, Telford United FC
Telford United v Shrewsbury Town 0-2

SHROPSHIRE COUNTY CUP
Holders Ludlow Town

First Round

1 Wellington Amt	V Madeley Town		1-3
2 Newport	V Belle Vue OB		3-4
3 Lt Drayton Amt	V Snailbeach WS		3-1
4 Springvale Rovers	V Oakengates Town		0-3
5 Bandon Arms	V Bridgnorth Tn Res		7-3
6 Tibberton	V Church Stretton		2-3
7 Hadley Keys	V Wem Town	WT	W-O

9 Clubs with byes into

Second Round

1 Meole Brace	V Ellesmere Rangers	5-2
2 Brandon	V Ludlow Town Colts	3-2
3 Highley Welfare	V St Martins	6-0
4 Oakengates Town	V Morda United	3-1
5 L Drayton Rangers	V Belle Vue Old Boys	0-1
6 Whitchurch Alport	V Star Aluminium	2-1
7 Madeley Town	V Wem Town	2-3
8 Church Stretton	V Broseley	2-5

Third Round

1 Brandon	V Meole Brace		4-2
2 Belle Vue Old Boys	V Oakengates Town	3-3	2-1
3 Wem Town	V Broseley		4-1
4 Highley Welfare	V Whitchuch Alport		2-3

Semi-Finals

Whitchurch Alport	V Wem Town		4-1
Bandon	V Belle Vue OB	0-0	4-1

Final Thursday 4th April 1996

Bandon v Whitchurch Alport 3-1
at Gay Meadow Shrewsbury Town FC

SOMERSET PREMIER CUP
Holders Bath City

First Round

1 Chard Town	V Yeovil Town	0-2
2 Wellington	V Keynsham Town	1-2

Second Round

1 Taunton Town	V Welton Rovers		4-1
2 Bath City	V Keynsham Town		3-0
3 Minehead	V Paulton Rovers		0-4
4 Mangotsfield Utd	V Backwell United		3-1
5 Odd Down	V Frome Town		4-2
6 Weston Super Mare	V Clevedon Town	5p3	2*2
7 Brislington	V Yeovil Town		2-1
8 Glastonbury	V Bristol City		0-2

Third Round

1 Paulton Rovers	V Taunton Town		0-2
2 Odd Down	V Brislington		0-3
3 Bristol City	V Bath City		3*2
4 Weston S Mare	V Mangotsfield United		3-4

Semi-Finals

Bristol City	V Mangotsfield United	0-1
Brislington	V Taunton Town	1-0

Final Monday 6th May

Brislington v Mangotsfield Utd 6p5 1*1
at Clevedon Town FC

SOMERSET SENIOR CUP
Holders Brislington

First Round

1 Hengrove Athletic	V Weston Super Mare		1-0
2 Long Sutton	V Ilminster Town		1-0
3 Nailsea Town	V Hartcliffe Comm Cen		5*3
4 Highbridge United	V C T K Southside		3-0
5 Weston St John	V Portishead		1-0
6 Cheddar	V St George E in G		2-1
7 Bristol Spartak	V Nailsea United		4-6
8 Imperial	V Clandown		4-2
9 Welton Rovers	V Shepton Mallet Tn		0-2
10 Peasedown Ath	V Keynsham Cricketers		4-2
11 Brislington	V Congresbury	2p4 2*2	1*1
12 Wrington-Redhill	V Glastonbury	1*1	2-4
13 Winscombe	V P & W United		5*3
14 Westland Sports	V Castle Cary		0-1
15 Burnham United	V Clutton		4-0
16 Wellington	V Hartcliffe OB		3-1
17 Paulton Rovers	V Bishop Sutton		0-6
18 Clevedon United	V Radstock Town		2-4
19 Wells City	V Westland United		1-5
20 Frome Town	V Backwell United	3*3	0-6
21 Temple Cloud	V Larkhall Ath		0-7
22 Keynsham Town	V Street		2-7
23 Fry's Club	V Dundry Athletic		4-0
24 Tunley Athletic	V Clevedon Town		1-4
25 CleeveWest Tn	V Teyfant Athletic		3-2

Seven Clubs with Byes; Timsbury Athletic, Watchet
Town, Odd Down, Peasedown MYCOR, Saltford,
Bridgwater Town, Stockwood Green into the

Second Round

1 Backwell United	V Glastonbury		2-0
2 Larkhall Athletic	V Peasedown Athletic		1-2
3 Brislington	V Street		3-2
4 Saltford	V Winscombe		3-4
5 Long Sutton	V Nailsea United		1-0
6 Weston St John	V Stockwood Green	1-1	6-4

948

7 Imperial	V Cheddar	1-2
8 Bridgwater Town	V Clevedon Town	2-1
9 Bishop Sutton	V Nailsea United	1-2
10 Castle Cary	V Hengrove Athletic	0-2
11 Peasedown MYC	V Timsbury Athletic	0-2
12 Westland United	V Radstock Town	2-3
13 Burnham United	V Cleeve West Town	
14 Watchet Town	V Odd Down	3-1
15 Highbridge United	V Wellington Res	2-0
16 Shepton Mallet T	V Fry's Club	0-1

Third Round

1 Winscombe	V Cheddar	2-3
2 Timsbury Athletic	V Hengrove Athletic	1-2
3 Weston St Johns	V Brislington	2-1
4 Bridgwater Town	V Long Sutton	5-0
5 Watchet Town	V Nailsea United	0-2
6 Peasedown Athletic	V Highbridge United	1-1 3-0
7 Backwell United	V Fry's Club	3*3 0-2
8 Radstock Town	V Cleeve West Town	3-1

Fourth Round

1 Radstock Town	V Hengrove Athletic	0A0 0-3
2 Weston St John	V Fry's Club	4-3
3 Bridgwater Town	V Nailsea United	3-2
4 Peasedown Athletic	V Cheddar	14-1

Semi-Finals

Hengrove Athletic	V Peasedown Athletic	0*2
Bridgwater Town	V Weston St Johns	8-1

Final Monday 6th May 1996

Bridgwater Town v Peasedown Ath 2-0
at Winterfield Road, Paulton Rovers FC

STAFFORDSHIRE SENIOR CUP
Holders Stoke City

First Round

1 Bolehall Swifts	V Halesowen Harriers	1-2
2 Bilston Town	V Stourport Swifts	4-1
3 Stoke City	V Leek Town	2-3
4 Dudley Town	V Rocester	0-1
5 Kidsgrove Athletic	V Walsall Wood	2-0
6 Shifnal Town	V Oldbury United	0-4
7 Macclesfield Town	V Pelsall Villa	1-1 1-0
8 Eastwood Hanley	V Newcastle Town	1-5
9 Armitage	V Knypersley Victoria	3-1
10 Chasetown	V Stourbridge	1-1 0-4
11 Tamworth	V Lye Town	9-3
12 Stafford Rangers	V Rushall Olympic	0-2
13 Hednesford Town	V Willenhall Town	6-1

3 Clubs with a Bye, Boldmere St Michaels, Paget
Rangers, Port Vale, into

Second Round

1 Halesowen Harriers	V Kidsgrove Athletic	7*3
2 Bilston Town	V Oldbury United	4-0
3 Rocester	V Leek Town	2-3
4 Macclesfield Town	V Boldmere St Michaels	5-2
5 Armitage	V Hednesford Town	1-3
6 Paget Rangers	V Stourbridge	3-2
7 Rushall Olympic	V Newcastle Town	0-4
8 Port Vale @T	V Tamworth	1-4

Third Round

1 Macclesfield Town	V Bilston Town	1-2
2 Leek Town	V Halesowen Harriers	3-2
3 Paget Rangers	V Hednesford Town	2*1
4 Tamworth	V Newcastle Town	0-0 1-3

Semi-Finals

Bilston Town	V Leek Town	0-1
Newcastle Town	V Paget Rangers	2-1

Final First Leg

Newcastle Town v Leek Town	1-0

Second Leg

Leek Town v Newcastle Town	4*2

SUFFOLK PREMIER CUP
Holders Newmarket Town

Preliminary Round

1 Haverhill Rovers	V Bury Town	2-6
2 Woodbridge Town	V Hadleigh United	5-1
3 Felixstowe Port & T	V Cornard United	6-1

First Round

1 Sudbury Town	V Bury Town	1-2
2 Lowestoft Town	V Felixstowe Port & T	1-0
3 Sudbury Wanderers	V Newmarket Town	0-1
4 Woodbridge Town	V Stowmarket Town	5-1

Semi-Finals

Bury Town	V Lowestoft Town	2-1
Woodbridge Town	V Newmarket Town	2-2 3-0

Final Monday 6th May

Woodbridge Town	V Bury Town	0*0

Replay Thursday 9th May

Bury Town	V Woodbridge Town 5p4	0*0

SUFFOLK SENIOR CUP
Holders Grundisburgh

First Round

1 Mildenhall Tn Res	V Stowmarket Tn Res	3-1
2 Nicholians Loco	V Ashlea	2-2 0-3
3 Felixstowe P & T Rs	V Framlingham Town	0-1
4 Westerfield United	V Ipswich Wanderers	0-4
5 Grundisburgh	V Beccles Town	4-1
6 Long Melford	V Stonham Aspal	1-3
7 B Sugar Fonnereau	V Kirkley	1-0
8 Whitton United	V Haverhill Rovers Res	5-2
9 Sudbury Lucas Ath	V Achilles	2-7
10 Stanton	V Brantham & Stutton U	1-5
11 Haughley United	V Sudbury Wanderers Res	0-2
12 Lowestoft Tn Res	V BT Research	2-4
13 Saxmundham Sp	V Walton United	0-1
14 Bury Town Res	V Walsham le Willows	1-0
15 Needham Market	V Hailsworth Town	1-1 4-0
16 Brandon Town	V Oulton Broad & L Rail	0-4

Second Round

1 Framlingham Town	V Whitton United	1-0
2 Brantham & S Utd	V Bury Town Res	0-0 3-5
3 Needham Market	V Archilles	4-4 5-2
4 Mildenhall Town	V BS Fonnereau Ath	2-2 1-3
5 Ashlea	V Sudbury Wdrs Res	1-1 1-2
6 Stonham Aspal	V Grundisburgh	1-2
7 Ipswich Wanderers	V OB & Lowestoft Rail	4-1
8 Walton United	V BT Research	2-2 4-2

Third Round

1 Sudbury Wandrs Rs	V Ipswich Wanderers		1-4
2 BS Fonnereau Ath	V Bury Town Res		3-1
3 Grundiburgh	V Walton Utd	3*3 1*1	5p4
4 Framlingham Tn	V Needham Market	1*1	3-2

Semi-Finals

BS Fonnereau   V Grundiburgh   0-5
at Stowmarket Town FC

Framlingham Town   V Ipswich Wanderers   4-2
at Woodbridge Town FC

Final Tuesday 16th April 1996

Framlingham Town v Grundiburgh   0-3
at Portman Road, Ipswich Town FC

SURREY SENIOR CUP
Holders Sutton United

Second Qualifying Round

1 Raynes Park Vale	V Shene Old Grammarians	3-2
2 Dorking	V Leatherhead	0-4
3 Chipstead	V Ash United	6-0
4 Croydon	V Camberley Town	0-1
5 Netherne	V Old Suttonians	2-0
6 Cobham	V Farnham Town	2-3
7 Cranleigh	V Mersham	2-0
8 Walton Casuals	V Corinthian Casuals	0-2
9 Ashford Tn(Mx)	V Merton	3-1
10 Redhill	V Nat West Bank	3-1
11 Westfield	V Kew Association	2-1

Third Qualifying Round

1 Corinthian Casuals	V Ashford Tn(Mx)	2*2	5-2
2 Redhill	V Carshalton		2-3
3 Horley Town	V Cranleigh		0-1
4 Netherne	V Farnham Town		0-1
5 Camberley Town	V Godalming & Guildford		1-3
6 Raynes Park Vale	V Leatherhead		1-4
7 Westfield	V Chipstead	2-2	3-4

Three Clubs with Byes Banstead Athletic, Epsom & Ewell, Tooting & Mitcham United.

Fouth Qualifying Round

1 Corinthian Casuals	V Farnham Tn	0-0 1A0	2-0
2 Godalming & G'dfd	V Banstead Athletic	0-0	1-6
3 Carshalton @EE	V Epsom & Ewell		0-3
4 Horley Town	V Tooting & Mitcham U		1-4
5 Leatherhead	V Chipstead		1-0

Eleven Clubs exempt Carshalton Athletic, Chertsey Town, Crystal Palace, Egham Kingstonian, Metropolitan Police, Molesey, Sutton United, Walton & Hersham, Whyeleafe, Woking.

First Round

1 Egham Town	V Chertsey Town		2-4
2 Molesey	V Leatherhead		3-1
3 Tooting & Mitcham	V Sutton United		2-1
4 Carshalton Athletic	V Kingstonian	1-1	2-1
5 Banstead Athletic	V Metropolitan Police		1-2
6 Walton & Hersham	V Crystal Palace		0-3
7 Woking	V Epsom & Ewell		6-0
8 Corinthian Casuals	V Whyteleafe		1-0

Second Round

1 Chertsey Town	V Tooting & Mitcham U	1-3

2 Corinthian Casuals	V Carshalton Athletic	2-3
3 Met Police	V Crystal Palace	1-3
4 Woking	V Molesey	8-1

Semi-Finals

Tooting & Mitcham	V Carshalton Athletic		4-2
Crystal Palace @W	V Woking	0-0	1-4

Final Tuesday 23rd April 1996

Tooting & Mitcham v Woking   0-2
at Kingstonian FC

SUSSEX SENIOR CUP
Holders Brighton & Hove Albion

First Round

1 Selsey	V Hassocks		2-0
2 Bexhill Town	V Eastbourne United		2*1
3 Midhurst & Easebne	V Mile Oak		1-4
4 Broadbridge Heath	V Sidley United		1-4
5 Newhaven	V East Grinstead		4*2
6 Steyning Town	V Lewes		0-1
7 Bosham	V Saltdean United		0-4
8 Arundel	V Horsham YMCA	3*3	4-0
9 Withdean	V Chichester City		3*5
10 Littlehampton	V Lancing		2*3
11 East Preston	V Worthing United	0*0	1-0
12 Horsham	V Southwick		3*1

20 Clubs with Byes into the

Second Round

1 Pagham	V Eastbourne		2-0
2 Stamco	V Three Bridges		4-0
3 Bognor Regis Tn	V Sidley United		5-1
4 Saltdean United	V East Preston	1-1	0-2
5 Brighton & Hove	V Newhaven		6-1
6 Peacehaven & T	V Hastings Town		1-2
7 Chichester City	V Wick		0-3
8 Langney Sports	V Whitehawk		6-0
9 Lancing	V Crawley Town		0-4
10 Burgess Hill Town	V Shoreham		2-1
11 Worthing	V Oakwood		7-0
12 Ringmer	V Crowborough Athletic		2*1
13 Selsey	V Bexhill Town		3-2
14 Lewes	V Hailsham Town		3-2
15 Horsham	V Portfield		2-1
16 Mile Oak	V Arundel		2-0

Third Round

1 Brighton & Hove	V Bognor Regis Town		2*3
2 Pagham	V Worthing		1*2
3 Selsey	V Crawley Town		1-3
4 Horsham	V Ringmer		2-1
5 Hastings Town	V Stamco		2-1
6 Wick	V East Preston		1-0
7 Mile Oak	V Burgess Hill Town		0-4
8 Langley Sports	V Lewes		4-0

Quarter-Finals

1 Hastings Town	V Burgess Hill Town	4-0
2 Horsham	V Wick	0-1
3 Langney Sports	V Bognor Regis Town	2-1
4 Worthing	V Crawley Town	1-4

Semi-Finals

Crawley Town	V Wick	4-1
at Lancing FC		
Hastings Town	V Langley Sports	6-0
at Lewes FC		

Final Monday 6th May

Crawley Town v Hastings Town	0-1
at Worthing FC	

SUSSEX R U R CHARITY CUP
Holders Peacehaven & Telscombe

Preliminary Round

1 Whitehawk	V Eastbourne Town	3-1
2 Withdean	V Newhaven	3-6
3 Steyning Town	V East Preston	0-0 0-3
4 Wick	V Littlehampton Town	3-0
5 Selsey	V Broadbridge Heath	4-1

First Round

1 East Grinstead	V Oakwood	5-0
2 Three Bridges	V Ringmer	1-2
3 Burgess Hill Town	V Newhaven	4-1
4 Peacehaven & T	V Sidley United	4-1
5 Eastbourne Utd	V Crowborough Athletic	4-3
6 Hailsham Town	V Saltdean United	0-2
7 Stamco	V Langley Sports	3-1
8 Bexhill Town	V Whitehawk	2*3
9 Chichester City	V Midhurst & Easebourne	0-2
10 Southwick	V Pagham	1*1 1-0
11 Bosham	V Wick	2-4
12 Mile Oak	V Selsey	2-1
13 Hassocks	V Worthing United	4*2
14 Horsham YMCA	V Portfield	1-5
15 Shoreham	V Lancing	2-0
16 Arundel	V East Preston	3-1

Second Round

1 Ringmer	V Burgess Hill Town	0-1
2 Saltdean United	V Whitehawk	4-3
3 East Grinstead	V Eastbourne United	2-1
4 Stamco	V Peacehaven & Tels	0-1
5 Southwick	V Wick	0-2
6 Portfield	V Arundel	0*2
7 Midhurst & Easeb'ne	V Hassocks	2-1
8 Shoreham	V Mile Oak	6-1

Quarter-Finals

1 Burgess Hill Town	V Arundel	2-4
2 East Grinstead	V Peacehaven & Tels	0-3
3 Midhurst & E'bourne	V Saltdean United	3*3 0-10
4 Wick	V Shoreham	1-5

Semi-Finals

Peacehaven & Tels	V Arundel	5-1
Shoreham	V Saltdean United	0-1

Final Tuesday 5th March 1996

Peacehaven & Telscombe v Saltdean United		1-0
at Lancing FC		att;482

"WESTMORLAND GAZETTE" SENIOR CHALLENGE CUP
Holders Kendal United

First Round

1 Burton Thistle	V Appleby	0-3
2 Burneside	V Ambleside United	1-4
3 Grange Amateur	V Kirby Stephen	3-0
4 Milnthorpe Corr'ian	V Coniston	3-1
5 Staveley United	V Wetheriggs	2-1
6 Kendal County	V Lunesdale United	4-1
7 Shap	V Arnside	0-2

Second Round

1 Staveley United	V Kendal United**	2-3
2 Keswick**	V M Corinthians	2-3
3 Sedburgh**	V Arnside	7-0
4 Braithewaite**	V Kirby Lonsdale**	1-2
5 Grange Amateur**	V Windermere S C**	3-0
6 Endmoor KGR**	V Kendal County	5-0
7 Kirkoswald**	V Netherfield Res**	3-3 0-3
8 Appleby	V Ambleside United	2-4

Third Round

1 Ambleside United	V Kendal County	2-1
2 Milnthorpe Corr'ns	V Kirkby Lonsdale	4-1
3 Grange Amateurs	V Netherfield Res	2-3
4 Kendal United	V Sedburgh	1-1 3-1

Semi-Finals

Ambleside United	V Netherfield Res	5-5 0-5
Milnthorpe Co'thians	V Kendal United	3-0

Final Saturday 13th April

Netherfields Res v Milnthorpe Corinthians		0-0
at Parkside Road, Kendal, Netherfield FC		

Replay Saturday 20th April 1996

Milnthorpe Corinthian v Netherfield Res		2-1
at Milnthorpe Corinthians FC		

WEST RIDING COUNTY CUP
Holders Farsley Celtic

First Round

1 Liversedge	V Glasshoughton Welfare	0-1
2 Goole Town	V Guiseley	0-3
3 Garforth Town	V Ossett Albion	0-3
4 Yorkshire Amateur	V Selby Town	2-1

Second Round

1 Pontefract Coll's	V Glasshoughton Welf	0-2
2 Bradford Park Ave	V Ossett Albion	3-1
3 Guiseley	V Hatfield Main	3*3 2-0
4 Yorkshire Amateurs	V Thackley	0-2
5 Farsley Celtic	V Harrogate Town	3-2
6 Harrogate Railway	V Tadcaster Alb	8p7 1*1 2*2
7 Armthorpe Welfare	V Eccleshill Utd	1-2
8 Halifax Town	V Ossett Town	5-1

Fourth Round

1 Harrogate Railway	V Eccleshill Utd	
2 Thackley	V Guiseley	1*2
3 Glasshoughton MW	V Bradford Park Avenue	0-2
4 Farsley Celtic	V Halifax Town	1-0

Semi-Finals

Harrogate Railway	V Guiseley	1-3
Farsley Celtic	V Bradford Pk Ave	2A1 1-0

Final Wednesday 3rd April
Farsley Celtic v Guiseley 0-0 att;598
at West Riding Co FA Ground, Fleet Lane, Leeds
Replay Wednesday 10th April 1996
Farsley Celtic v Guiseley 2-3 att;440
at West Riding Co FA Ground, Fleet Lane, Leeds

WILTSHIRE PREMIER SHIELD
Holders Trowbridge Town

First Round

1 Warminster Town	V Bemerton Heath H	1-1 1-3
2 Calne Town	V Chippenham Town	1-2
3 Devizes Town	V Trowbridge Town	0-2

Second Round

1 Melksham Town	V Trowbridge Town	0-3
2 Chippenham Town	V Downton	2-0
3 Sw'don Supermarine	V Bemerton Heath H	3-4
4 Salisbury City	V Westbury United	3-2

Semi-Finals

Chippenham Town	V Bemerton Heath H'qps	2-1
Salisbury City	V Trowbridge Town	2-1

Final Wednesday 1st May
Chippenham Town v Salisbury City 0-2
at Westbury United FC

WILTSHIRE SENIOR CUP
Holders Purton

First Round

1 Wroughton	V Aldbourne Park	3-3 5-2
2 Burmah Castrol	V Amesbury Town	0-2
3 Biddestone	V Bromham	4-2
4 Highworth Town	V Tisbury United	2-1

12 Clubs with a Bye into the

Second Round

1 Purton	V Marlborough Town	7-1
2 Pewsey Vale	V Corsham Town	4-3
3 Highworth Town	V Bradford Town	4-0
4 Shrewton Town	V Biddestone	1-1 1-2
5 Dunbar Athletic	V Plessey Semics	2-0
6 Pinehurst	V Wootton Bassett Town	0-3
7 Malmesbury Vics	V Amesbury Town	1-3
8 Sanford	V Wroughton	2-3

Third Round

1 Wootton Bassett T	V Wroughton	2-0
2 Highworth Town	V Pewsey Vale	1-0
3 Amesbury Town	V Purton	3-1
4 Biddestone	V Dunbar Athletic	0-1

Semi-Finals

Amesbury Town	V Dunbar Athletic	3-1

at Pewsey Vale FC.

Highworth Town	V Wootton Bassett Town	3-1

at Swindon Supermarine FC

Final Wednesday 24th April
Amesbury Town v Highworth Town 0-3
at Melksham Town FC

WORCESTERSHIRE SENIOR CUP
Holders Bromsgrove Rovers

First Round

1 Evesham United	V Solihull Borough	2-2 1-2
2 Bridgnorth Town	V Halesowen Town	0-3
3 Stourbridge	V Redditch United	1-0
4 Sutton Coldfield T	V Dudley Town	0-1

Second Round

1 Worcester City	V Solihull Borough	0-2
2 Stourbridge	V Halesowen Town	1-0
3 Kidderminster H	V Dudley Town	2-1
4 Bromsgrove Rovers	V Moor Green	5-0

Semi-Finals

Solihull Borough	V Bromsgrove Rovers	2-2 1-3
Kidderminster Harriers	V Stourbridge	1-2

Final First Leg
Stourbridge v Bromsgrove Rovers 2-1
Second Leg
Bromsgrove Rovers v Stourbridge 3*1

Miscellaneous League Tables

ANGLIAN COMBINATION
Premier Division

	P	W	D	L	F	A	PTS
Horsford United	30	22	4	4	68	31	70
Madra United	30	22	2	6	76	28	68
Wroxham Res.	30	19	0	5	70	32	63
Diss Town Res.	30	19	2	9	62	35	58
Dereham Town	30	15	8	7	44	37	53
Ashlea	30	15	4	11	56	52	49
Lowestoft Tn Res.	30	14	3	13	52	47	45
Blofield United	30	12	4	14	68	55	40
Mulbarton Utd	30	10	7	13	57	66	37
St Andrews	30	9	8	13	47	54	35
Thorpe Village	30	10	4	16	38	53	34
Lakeford Rangers	30	8	5	17	48	74	29
Kirkley	30	8	4	18	33	78	28
Wymondham Town	30	6	9	15	49	61	27
Beccles Town	30	7	5	18	37	63	26
Newton Flotman	30	4	5	21	21	61	17

Division One

	P	W	D	L	F	A	PTS
Loddon United	30	18	6	6	71	34	60
Stalham Town	30	17	8	5	76	42	59
Fakenham T Res	30	14	10	6	62	35	52
Nth Walsham T	30	14	8	8	67	41	50
Oulton Broad	30	14	5	11	62	46	47
Coltishall HV	30	13	8	9	58	44	47
Gorleston Res	30	13	6	11	54	45	45
Poringland Wand	30	13	6	11	33	47	45
Brandon Town	30	12	8	10	49	50	44
Wortwell	30	10	7	13	43	57	37
Anglian Window	30	9	8	13	43	51	35
Mattishall	30	8	7	15	39	50	31
Gt Yarmouth Res	30	8	7	15	31	46	31
Hellesdon	30	9	4	17	34	81	31
Watton Utd Res	30	7	6	17	31	62	27
Bradenham Wan	30	6	6	18	28	52	24

Division Two

	P	W	D	L	F	A	PTS
Attleborough	30	21	9	0	82	22	72
Acle United	30	18	7	5	87	43	61
Caister United	30	17	3	10	63	38	54
Bradwell Scripts	30	17	3	10	69	46	54
Wells Town	30	16	6	8	51	35	54
Halvergate Utd	30	15	8	7	70	40	53
Cromer Town	30	15	7	8	83	62	52
Lakenheath	30	13	4	13	56	58	43
Hempnall	30	10	7	13	53	44	37
Holt United	30	11	4	15	56	72	37
Mundford	30	11	4	15	56	72	37
Bungay Town	30	9	8	13	53	66	35
Norwich Union	30	8	5	17	46	74	29
Sprowston Wan	30	6	5	19	44	87	23
South Walsham	30	6	3	21	44	82	21
Thetford Town	30	5	2	23	37	92	17

Division Three

Scole United	28	18	7	3	97	37	61
Sprowston Ath	28	17	5	6	70	44	56
Reepham Town	28	16	6	6	77	50	54
Swaffham T Res	28	16	5	7	66	28	53
Aylsham Wands	28	16	3	9	63	44	51
St Johns	28	15	5	8	53	38	50
Corton	28	13	4	11	64	55	43
CNSOBU	28	11	8	9	52	61	41
Thorpe SOB	28	13	1	14	50	50	40
Beccles Caxton	28	10	6	12	55	51	36
Norwich CEYMS	28	9	2	17	54	71	29
Norwich U Res	28	9	1	18	55	77	28
Southwold Town	28	8	3	17	53	74	27
East Harling	28	8	3	17	55	77	27
Dickleburgh	28	1	1	26	39	150	4

Division Four

Thetford Tn Res	28	23	1	4	116	30	70
Necton	28	20	6	2	91	25	66
Downham T Res	28	20	4	4	94	35	64
Martham	28	17	8	3	81	33	59
Sheringham	28	16	1	11	76	53	49
Saham Toney	28	13	4	11	53	43	43
Ditchingham	28	11	5	12	53	53	38
Costessey Sports	28	10	7	11	60	52	37
Long Stratton	28	11	4	13	42	48	37
Rocklands Utd	28	10	4	14	51	92	34
Shipdham	28	9	4	15	54	55	31
Morley Village	28	7	6	15	58	83	27
Harleston Tn	28	7	4	17	39	78	25
Ashill	28	4	3	21	33	108	15
Dilham	28	1	1	26	25	133	4

CHARRINGTON CHILTONIAN LEAGUE
Premier Division

	P	W	D	L	F	A	PTS
Binfield	30	25	1	4	97	30	76
Denham United	30	22	6	2	94	28	72
Quarry Nomads	30	19	4	7	64	40	61
A.F.C. Wallingford	30	18	6	6	89	53	60
Wraysbury	30	18	5	7	79	40	59
Stocklake	30	13	8	9	65	53	47
Old Paludians	30	14	1	15	58	50	43
Iver	30	13	3	14	43	44	42
Finchampstead	30	11	5	14	51	53	38
Martin Baker	30	10	7	13	48	51	37
Penn & T Green	30	10	7	13	40	57	37
Broadmoor Social	30	11	1	18	49	98	34
Henley Town	30	7	8	15	52	68	29
Wooburn Athletic	30	5	6	19	36	75	21
Prestwood	30	4	4	22	41	90	16
Chalfont Wasps	30	3	2	25	31	107	11

DEVON COUNTY LEAGUE

	P	W	D	L	F	A	PTS
Budleigh Salt	36	21	10	5	96	41	73
Stoke Gabriel	36	22	7	7	91	36	73
Willand Rovers	36	22	6	8	73	41	72
Dartmouth Utd	36	22	6	8	80	52	72
Alphington	36	19	6	11	85	46	63
Topsham Town	36	17	9	10	86	60	60
Teignmouth	36	19	3	14	93	67	57
Newton Abbot	36	16	8	12	66	55	56
Plymouth Cnd	36	16	6	14	68	58	54
Buckfastleigh R	36	12	11	13	62	66	47
Cullompton R	36	13	7	16	46	57	46
Elburton Villa	36	13	7	16	56	81	46
Plymouth Park	36	11	12	13	72	77	45
Plymstock Utd	36	12	8	16	54	63	44
Newton St Cyres	36	9	7	20	51	89	34
Ivybridge Town	36	10	4	22	55	95	34
Weston Mill OV	36	9	6	21	57	92	33
Ottery St Mary	36	8	6	22	43	111	30
Chagford	36	4	5	27	48	95	17

GLOUCESTERSHIRE COUNTY LEAGUE

	P	W	D	L	F	A	PTS
D.R.G.	34	23	7	4	74	30	76
Cadbury Heath	34	19	6	9	70	36	63
Broad Plain Hse	34	18	9	7	68	46	63
Brockworth	34	19	5	10	62	42	62
Bitton	34	15	11	8	63	37	56
Frampton Athl	34	14	9	11	53	49	51
Wotton Rovers	34	14	7	13	54	53	49
Patchway Town	34	13	6	15	51	62	45
Old Georgians	34	11	12	11	49	60	45
Henbury O B	34	11	10	13	49	55	43
St Marks C.A.	34	11	10	13	68	76	43
Totterdown P B	34	11	8	15	58	62	41
Ellwood	34	9	12	13	35	49	39
Broadwell Amat	34	9	9	16	38	60	36
Pucklechurch Sps	34	8	11	15	39	63	35
Stapleton	34	8	10	16	38	52	34
Smiths Athletic	34	8	5	21	45	62	29
Winterbourne Utd	34	6	11	17	43	63	29

HAMPSHIRE LEAGUE
Division One

	P	W	D	L	F	A	PTS
Colden Common	38	26	5	7	80	39	83
Netley Central	38	26	3	9	91	49	81
Romsey Town	38	23	6	9	95	43	75
Moneyfields	38	24	3	11	95	48	75
Fleetlands	38	23	6	9	84	45	75
New Street	38	21	7	10	71	52	70
Hayling United	38	21	6	11	58	42	69
Blackfield & L	38	18	5	15	85	71	59
Pirelli General	38	18	3	17	59	59	57
Malshanger	38	12	11	15	58	70	47
Horndean	38	13	7	18	54	60	46
Winchester City	38	12	9	17	62	75	45
Ecchinswell	38	11	9	18	59	78	42
Bass Alton Tn	38	10	11	17	64	84	41
A.C. Delco	38	12	5	21	54	88	41
New Milton Town	38	9	10	19	46	70	37
Liss Athletic	38	9	10	19	60	93	37
Overton United	38	10	5	23	39	76	35
Paulsgrove	38	9	5	24	61	84	29
Verwood Town	38	7	6	25	30	82	27

Division Two

	P	W	D	L	F	A	PTS
Locksheath	34	21	10	3	79	22	73
Stockbridge	34	20	10	4	87	51	70
Bishopstoke Soc	34	21	5	8	92	51	68
Brading Town	34	22	1	11	96	44	67
Vos Thornycroft	34	21	4	9	91	56	67
Fleet Spurs	34	18	6	10	76	53	60
Esso Fawley	34	16	10	8	79	44	58
Hilsea Club	34	16	7	11	84	55	56
Bishops Wal Tn	34	17	7	10	68	51	55
Otterbourne	34	15	7	12	69	58	52
Broughton	34	13	4	17	63	67	43
Hythe & Dibden	34	12	5	17	58	74	41
St Marys	34	12	4	18	60	71	40
Hedge End	34	11	3	20	56	98	36
Ludgershall Sp	34	7	7	20	58	104	28
Alresford Town	34	7	7	20	56	78	27
Compton	34	6	0	28	32	108	18
Basing Rovers	34	1	3	30	34	157	6

Division Three

	P	W	D	L	F	A	PTS
Ringwood Town	34	23	5	6	90	46	74
Tadley	34	22	6	6	80	43	71
Mayflower	34	18	8	8	84	43	62
Fleetlands Res.	34	18	8	8	68	45	62
Yateley Green	34	16	11	7	57	33	59
Hamble Club	34	16	10	8	55	33	58
Swanmore	34	15	9	10	53	57	54
Moneyfields Res.	34	11	12	11	60	52	45
Winchester Castle	34	12	8	14	68	69	44
A.F.C. Aldermas	34	12	8	14	60	70	44
Awbridge	34	11	10	13	46	42	43
Sherborne St J	34	11	7	16	64	70	40
Four Marks	34	10	8	16	60	84	38
Covies	34	11	4	19	52	80	37
Braishfield	34	7	13	14	40	61	34
Net Cen Sp Res.	34	6	9	19	53	82	27
Winchest C Res.	34	7	6	21	45	83	27
Bass Alton Tn Res.	34	7	5	22	45	90	26

HERTS SENIOR COUNTY LEAGUE
Premier Division

		W	D	L	F	A	PTS
Elliott Star	32	25	4	3	103	40	79
Met Pol Bushey	32	19	7	6	79	49	64
Colney Heath	32	20	2	10	78	52	62
Somersett AVE	32	19	3	10	71	55	60
Kings Langley	32	18	4	10	67	45	58
Sun Postal Sp	32	14	6	12	47	42	48
Chipperfield C	32	13	8	11	49	38	47
Agrevo Sports	32	13	7	12	73	68	46
Sandridge Rov	32	13	5	14	62	57	44
Welwyn	32	12	5	15	35	45	41
Cuffley	32	12	4	16	46	61	40
St Peters	32	10	7	15	57	67	37
Oxhey Jets	32	10	5	17	41	55	35
Bedmond Soc	32	9	8	15	40	57	35
Wormley Rov	32	11	2	19	40	66	35
Bovingdon	32	9	2	21	33	64	29
Bragbury Ath	32	2	7	23	38	98	13

Division One

	P	W	D	L	F	A	PTS
North Mymms	30	21	6	3	91	35	69
M.M.S. Dynam	30	20	2	8	79	43	62
Walkern	30	18	5	7	63	31	59
Emeralds	30	16	6	8	66	41	54
Bushey Rangers	30	16	5	9	74	44	53
Malex	30	16	5	9	47	41	53
Allensburys	30	16	4	10	73	53	52
Kimpton Rovers	30	14	5	11	58	59	47
Standon & Puck	30	13	4	13	67	64	43
Croxley Guild	30	12	4	14	76	64	40
Giffen Valmar	30	11	4	15	72	72	37
Evergreen	30	10	5	15	53	63	35
Kodak Hemel Hempstead	30	10	1	19	44	73	31
Sarratt	30	6	5	19	41	69	23
Codicote	30	5	7	18	31	64	22
St Ippolyts	30	1	2	27	25	144	5

Reserve Division One

	P	W	D	L	F	A	PTS
Sun Pos Sp Res.	28	22	4	2	106	26	70
Bovingdon Res.	28	18	3	7	98	42	57
Sanddge Rov Res.	28	18	2	8	66	30	56
Cuffley Res.	28	15	5	8	92	55	50
Met Pol Bsh Res.	28	14	6	8	80	51	48
Oxhey Jets Res.	28	13	5	10	55	42	44
Chipp Corin Res.	28	13	3	12	54	38	42
Bedmd Soc Res.	28	12	5	11	75	57	41
Wormley R Res.	28	11	6	11	47	56	39
St Peters Res.	28	11	3	14	62	70	36
Colney Heath Res.	28	9	6	13	49	76	33
Bragbury AthRes.	28	10	2	16	60	64	32
Walkern Res.	28	6	5	17	40	103	23
Welwyn Res.	28	4	3	21	31	85	15
Bushey RangRes.	28	4	2	22	22	142	14

Reserve Division Two

	P	W	D	L	F	A	PTS
Som AV & E Res.	26	21	4	1	102	22	67
Kings Lang Res.	26	18	5	3	76	28	59
North Mymms Res.	26	16	8	2	63	24	56
Elliott Star Res.	26	16	6	4	54	34	54
Agrevo Sp Res.	26	10	6	10	54	60	36
M.M.S. Dyn Res.	26	10	5	11	66	63	35
Kodak H H Res.	26	11	1	14	54	76	34
Sarratt Res.	26	11	0	15	49	58	33
Croxley Guild	26	9	5	12	43	51	32
Kimpton Rov Res.	26	9	5	12	35	47	32
Giffen Valmar Res.	26	7	3	16	49	81	24
Stan & Puck Res.	26	7	3	16	41	75	24
Evergreen Res.	26	4	4	18	32	60	16
Allensburys Res.	26	5	1	20	35	73	16

LEICESTERSHIRE SENIOR LEAGUE
Premier Division

	P	W	D	L	F	A	PTS
St Andrews	34	28	3	3	95	28	87
Oadby Town	34	27	2	5	122	40	83
Birstall United	34	21	7	6	60	37	70
Friar Ln O B	34	20	5	9	68	37	65
Kirby Muxloe	34	16	8	10	55	48	56
Ibstock Welfare	34	17	3	14	57	60	54
Burbage O B	34	15	7	12	64	64	52
Barrow Town	34	15	6	13	80	76	51
Anstey Nomads	34	14	7	13	87	69	49
Holwell Sports	34	14	5	15	74	59	47
Cottesmore Ams	34	12	4	18	62	84	40
Asfordby Am	34	11	6	17	44	61	39
Highfield Rangers	34	9	8	17	47	64	35
Downes Sports	34	10	4	20	54	79	34
Newfound W.MC.	34	9	5	20	45	76	32
Thringstone M W	34	8	7	19	40	69	31
Aylestne Pk O B	34	8	6	20	48	76	30
North Kilworth	34	3	5	26	37	111	14

Division One

	P	W	D	L	F	A	PTS
Quorn	36	33	3	0	134	16	102
Narboro & Little	36	23	4	9	92	53	73
Leics Cons	36	21	7	8	83	50	70
Coalville	36	21	4	11	91	56	67
Fosse Imps	36	18	9	9	75	58	63
Sileby Town	36	16	7	13	74	60	55
Saffron Dynamo	36	16	4	16	67	68	52
Anstey Town	36	13	10	13	48	49	49
Loughboro Dyn	36	13	8	15	78	74	47
Blaby & Whetst	36	12	9	15	44	59	45
Syston St Peters	36	12	8	16	57	73	44
United Collieries	36	14	2	20	71	90	44
Stoney Stanton	36	12	7	17	63	57	43
Huncote Sports	36	13	4	19	56	70	43
Lutterworth Tn	36	12	6	18	45	77	42
Bardon Hill	36	9	12	15	46	72	39
Earl Shilton Alb	36	8	8	20	66	97	32
Harboro Tn Imp	36	8	5	23	50	93	29
Houghton Rang (-3)	36	7	5	24	37	104	23

BOWVALE MIDLAND REGIONAL ALLIANCE
Division One

	P	W	D	L	F	A	PTS
Rowsley	32	21	7	4	76	33	70
Ilkeston Tn Res.	32	24	4	4	80	28	76
Belper United	32	20	5	7	79	40	65
Brailsford	32	18	5	9	67	37	59
Eastwood Tn Res.	32	15	7	10	63	44	44
Butterley Brick	32	16	4	12	58	45	52
Belper Tn Res.	32	14	9	9	68	47	51
Arnold Tn Res.	32	14	4	14	55	56	46
Matlock Tn Res.	32	12	7	13	51	56	43
Slack & Parr	32	15	1	16	41	55	46
Littleover Irone	32	13	3	16	46	54	42
Hucknall Tn Res.	32	10	3	19	40	58	33
Matlock Utd	32	9	3	20	48	71	30
Cromford	32	8	4	20	52	85	28
Selston	32	10	6	16	51	69	36
Holbrook St M	32	9	4	19	47	78	31
Blidworth W Res.	32	5	2	25	26	90	17

Division Two

	P	W	D	L	F	A	PTS
Gotham United	28	12	7	9	58	48	43
Draycott	28	15	5	8	67	47	50
Sutton	28	20	4	4	86	39	64
Wirksworth Town	28	18	4	6	81	44	58
Newark Town	28	14	4	10	51	44	46
Brailsford Res.	28	12	10	6	64	53	46
Belper United Res.	28	14	9	5	63	38	51
Selston Res.	28	9	5	2	33	21	32
Swanwick Pen Rd	28	11	5	12	50	54	38
Cromford Jnrs	28	12	3	13	58	58	39
Holbrook M W	28	8	3	17	49	75	27
Ridding St James	28	10	8	10	61	64	38
Slack & Parr Res.	28	8	2	18	45	72	26
Rolls R & Ass	28	6	3	19	52	89	21
Matlock Utd Res.	28	2	1	25	33	94	7

Division Three

	P	W	D	L	F	A	PTS
Arnold Town `A'	26	19	4	3	99	48	61
Heanor Athletic	26	15	5	6	66	42	50
Bridge Inn	26	19	3	4	102	51	60
Rowsley Res.	26	14	4	8	66	48	46
Swan Pen Rd Res.	26	11	6	9	51	52	39
Holbrk S M Res.	26	16	3	7	98	45	51
Sutton Trinity	26	11	4	11	60	61	37
Draycott Res.	26	9	4	13	51	71	31
Cotmanhay	26	8	5	13	50	78	29
New Eastwood	26	8	6	12	68	67	30
Brailsford `A'	26	9	3	14	49	61	30
Heanor Sports	26	6	7	13	55	71	25
Ashfield	26	5	2	19	38	99	17
Cromford Res.	26	3	2	21	42	101	11

MIDDLESEX COUNTY LEAGUE
Premier Division

	P	W	D	L	F	A	PTS
Willes(Const)	20	14	6	0	55	20	48
Osterley	20	14	2	4	50	24	44
Northfield C.A.V.	20	11	4	5	48	29	37
Hanworth Villa	20	10	3	7	42	37	33
New Hanford	20	9	5	6	49	30	32
Nth Green Utd	20	7	7	6	40	37	28
Spelthorne Sports	20	6	6	8	29	37	24
Pitshanger	20	6	3	11	29	49	21
Shamrock	20	5	5	10	31	38	20
Southgate	20	4	3	13	30	59	15
Hounslow Town	20	0	4	16	24	67	4

NORTHERN ALLIANCE
Premier Division

	P	W	D	L	F	A	PTS
Seaton Del Am	32	23	4	5	97	39	73
Carlisle City	32	19	10	3	85	23	67
Carlisle Gill Pk	32	20	6	6	62	23	66
Newc Ben Pk	32	21	3	8	73	41	66
Middlesbro `A'	32	17	7	8	79	37	58
West Allot Celtic	32	18	4	10	79	49	58
Ponteland United	32	15	7	10	73	39	52
Amble Town	32	15	6	11	81	58	51
Haltwh Cr Paints	32	14	5	13	52	58	47
Walker Central	32	13	5	14	59	62	44
Nth Shds St C	32	12	7	13	56	55	43
Westerhope	32	13	4	15	58	68	43
Winlaton	32	9	9	14	59	56	36
Blyth Seahorse	32	7	2	23	32	86	20
Spittal Rovers	32	5	6	21	27	71	18
Longbenton	32	4	1	27	29	156	13
Heaton Stanning	32	3	2	27	34	114	11

Division One

	P	W	D	L	F	A	PTS
Gosf Bohems	30	25	3	2	100	28	78
Walker Led Fos	30	21	5	4	73	32	68
Newbigg C W	30	20	4	6	83	41	64
Ryton	30	18	3	9	82	47	57
Orwin	30	17	4	9	83	50	55
Percy Main Am	30	15	5	10	75	55	50
Forest Hall	30	14	5	11	75	62	47
Shankhouse	30	14	5	11	78	70	47
Hebburn Reyrol	30	13	5	12	68	49	44
Swalwell	30	13	3	14	61	58	42
Dudley Welfare	30	10	5	15	67	79	35
Ash Hirst Prog	30	9	4	17	56	79	31
Procter & Gamble	30	7	4	19	42	81	25
Hexham Swinton	30	7	3	20	37	63	24
Wark	30	3	4	23	36	110	13
Wylam	30	3	0	27	26	138	9

Division Two

	P	W	D	L	F	A	PTS
Walbottle Mas	26	17	3	6	98	51	54
Heddon Inst	26	17	2	7	84	41	53
Highfields Utd	26	14	7	5	75	37	49
Newcastle B T	26	14	6	6	66	44	48
Northbank	26	15	2	9	100	60	47
Rutherford	26	12	6	8	72	44	42
Monks K.O.S.A.	26	12	5	9	74	54	41
Newcastle Univ	26	12	8	6	62	50	38
Otterburn	26	11	5	10	39	39	38
Wallington	26	6	6	14	42	68	24
Alnwick Ayd For	26	5	8	13	37	66	23
Shilbottle C W	26	4	5	17	27	78	17
Hexham Border	26	4	4	18	60	115	16
Marden Athletic	26	5	1	20	46	135	16

NOTTS ALLIANCE
Senior Division

	P	W	D	L	F	A	PTS
Rainworth M.W	30	19	8	3	83	40	65
Boots Athletic	30	20	4	6	75	41	64
Pelican	30	19	5	6	74	39	62
Hucknall R R	30	17	4	9	63	37	55
Greenwood Mead	30	16	3	11	46	51	51
John Player	30	14	5	11	54	42	47
Notts Police	30	13	5	12	59	47	44
Keyworth United	30	11	10	9	46	46	43
Cotgrave C W	30	11	4	15	46	56	37
Ruddington Utd	30	10	5	15	59	79	35
Thoresby C W	30	9	7	14	39	46	34
Welbeck C W	30	10	3	17	42	58	33
Southwell City	30	10	3	17	39	58	33
Wollaton	30	8	6	16	40	65	30
Basford United	30	8	3	19	41	60	27
G.P.T.	30	6	3	21	43	84	21

Division One

	P	W	D	L	F	A	PTS
Ollerton Town	30	19	7	4	66	28	64
Awsworth Villa	30	16	7	7	71	52	55
City & SherHosp	30	15	4	11	51	44	49
Abacus	30	14	6	10	46	43	48
Retford United	30	12	10	8	43	40	46
Linby C W	30	11	10	9	49	50	43
Boots Ath Res.	30	10	11	9	65	63	41
Teversal Grange	30	10	11	9	56	54	41
Rainth M W Res.	30	11	7	12	72	63	40
Bilsthorpe C W	30	11	6	13	58	68	39
Bestwood M W	30	11	5	14	53	58	38
Gedling M W	30	8	11	11	46	48	35
Worth'ton Simp	30	9	8	13	63	70	35
Clifton	30	9	4	17	51	72	31
Pelican Res.	30	7	8	15	54	65	29
Radcliffe Olympic	30	4	11	15	39	65	23

READING SENIOR LEAGUE
Senior Division

	P	W	D	L	F	A	PTS
Reading Exiles	22	17	2	3	49	18	53
Mortimer	22	16	4	2	56	23	52
Forest Old Boys	22	14	6	2	48	22	48
Checkendon Sp	22	12	4	6	55	34	40
Sutton Exiles	22	11	5	6	52	45	38
South Reading	22	8	2	12	45	50	26
A.F.C. Maidenhead	22	7	5	10	38	44	26
Woodley Yeoman	22	6	5	11	53	47	23
West Reading	22	6	5	11	38	45	23
Cookham Dean	22	5	5	12	29	50	20
Marlow United	22	4	4	14	29	46	16
Reading Old Bl	22	1	3	18	21	89	6

OXFORDSHIRE SENIOR LEAGUE
Premier Division

	P	W	D	L	F	A	PTS
Garsington	26	20	3	3	93	28	63
Worc Coll O B	26	20	2	4	73	26	62
Watlington	26	16	5	5	65	30	53
Adderbury Park	26	15	7	4	65	37	52
Eynsham	26	15	2	9	98	53	47
Chinnor	26	13	4	9	57	39	43
Old Woodstock	26	12	5	9	66	44	41
Oakley United	26	10	4	12	52	54	34
Launton Sports	26	10	2	14	48	71	32
Kennington	26	8	3	15	48	68	27
Chipp Nor Tn	26	7	5	14	47	70	26
Wheatley Utd	26	6	6	14	36	58	24
Woodstock Tn	26	3	2	21	25	117	11
Rover Cowley	26	1	2	23	35	108	5

Division One

	P	W	D	L	F	A	PTS
Charlton United	22	16	3	3	64	20	51
Fritwell	22	14	1	7	46	38	43
Marlborough	22	12	3	7	57	44	39
Botley United	22	9	7	6	37	36	34
Old Sales (Oxon)	22	10	3	9	54	47	33
Long Crendon	22	9	5	8	46	32	32
Horspath	22	9	3	10	51	45	30
Middleton Chen	22	8	2	12	45	45	26
Bletchington	22	6	5	11	30	42	23
Blackbird Leys.	22	6	4	12	32	61	22
John Radcliffe	22	6	3	13	37	54	21
Marston Saints	22	5	5	12	34	69	20

SURREY INTERMEDIATE LEAGUE WEST
Division One

	P	W	D	L	F	A	PTS
Haslemere	22	14	5	3	47	21	33
Frimley Green	22	14	3	5	42	28	31
Englefield Green	21	11	5	5	42	27	27
Worplesdon	22	11	4	7	52	33	26
Tongham	20	12	2	6	47	31	26
Horsley	22	9	5	8	60	46	23
Ewhurst	22	9	5	8	40	44	23
Badshot Lea	22	6	6	10	48	46	18
Marconi Resch	22	6	6	10	42	49	18
Windlesham Utd	22	6	4	12	31	61	16
Surrey Police	21	4	2	15	25	58	10
Woking Pk & H.	22	4	1	17	44	76	9

WEST HERTS LEAGUE
Premier Division

	P	W	D	L	F	A	PTS
Suburban Aerials	16	12	3	1	52	23	39
Kings Sports	16	10	3	3	45	23	33
Hemel H Rovers	16	10	3	3	38	27	33
B.K. Athletic	16	8	2	6	38	24	26
Leavesden Sp	16	7	5	4	36	25	26
Oxhey	16	8	2	8	43	37	20
Emeralds Res.	16	2	3	11	20	40	9
D.M.S. Builders	16	2	3	11	12	47	9
Albion Rovers	16	1	4	11	12	50	7

WORTHING AND DISTRICT LEAGUE
Premier Division

	P	W	D	L	F	A	PTS
Sompting	22	18	1	3	81	27	55
Northbrook	22	14	5	3	56	22	47
Eurotherm Dr	22	13	4	5	62	35	43
Maple Leaf Res.	22	13	2	7	58	33	41
Royal Mail	22	12	3	7	48	36	39
West Tarring	22	7	8	7	45	61	29
A.F.C. Lion	22	8	4	10	46	52	28
Russell Bourne	22	6	5	11	32	52	23
St Theresa's	22	6	3	13	35	61	21
Worthing Utd A	22	5	3	14	34	55	18
Inland Revenue	22	4	5	13	39	56	17
Worthing Civic	22	3	3	16	34	80	12

WEST SUSSEX LEAGUE
Premier Division

	P	W	D	L	F	A	PTS
Oving Social	20	15	4	1	49	22	49
South Bersted	20	11	5	4	41	22	38
Chichester Hosp	20	11	3	6	68	35	36
North Holmwd	20	10	3	7	49	41	33
A.F.C. Swan	20	8	7	5	37	23	31
Cowfold	20	9	2	9	34	32	29
Ferring	20	8	2	10	28	34	26
Roffey	20	6	3	11	28	42	21
Lancing United	20	6	3	11	26	44	21
Rustington	20	5	4	11	20	41	19
Wittering United	20	2	2	16	15	47	8

YEOVIL AND DISTRICT LEAGUE

	P	W	D	L	F	A	PTS
Henstridge Utd	20	15	3	2	71	24	48
Stoke	20	14	3	3	57	25	45
Baltonsborough	20	13	4	3	62	29	43
Tintinhull	20	12	2	6	48	23	38
Bradford Abbas	20	10	3	7	51	46	33
Milborne Port	20	9	3	8	48	38	30
Ash	20	8	2	10	37	43	26
Martock United	20	7	2	11	41	39	23
Wincanton Town	20	5	4	11	45	50	19
Ilchester	20	2	3	15	16	63	9
Westland Sp Res.	20	0	1	19	14	111	1

LIVERPOOL COUNTY COMBINATION
Division One

	P	W	D	L	F	A	PTS
Stockbridge	30	21	2	7	75	40	65
Waterloo Dock	30	20	4	6	89	36	64
Crawfords U B	30	20	4	6	55	38	64
Electric Supply	30	16	12	2	75	44	60
St Dominics	30	17	4	9	66	38	55
South Liverpool	30	16	4	10	61	32	52
Yorks Copper	30	13	7	10	69	50	46
Ayone	30	13	7	10	48	49	46
Mossley Hill	30	11	5	14	60	64	38
Ford Motors	30	11	4	15	43	56	37
Royal Seaforth	30	10	5	15	58	62	35
Lucas Sports	30	7	9	14	49	66	30
Earle	30	5	9	16	47	85	24
G.P.T. Plessey	30	6	5	19	54	95	23
Crystal Villa	30	6	1	23	38	79	19
British Rail	30	6	2	22	42	95	17

Division Two

	P	W	D	L	F	A	PTS
Eldonians	26	17	4	5	81	30	55
Selwyn	26	16	6	4	71	32	54
Bootle Res.	26	16	2	8	77	42	50
Halewood Town	26	16	2	8	71	46	50
Speke	26	15	3	8	61	39	48
Camadale	26	14	5	7	69	50	47
Rainhill Town (-3)	26	12	3	11	56	41	36
Cheshire Lines	26	10	1	15	55	58	31
Beesix	26	8	5	13	56	67	29
Elec Supp Res.	26	8	4	14	40	58	28
Maghull Res	26	8	6	12	38	41	27
British Rail Res.	26	8	1	17	40	85	22
Yorks Copp Res.	26	7	1	18	31	98	22
Avon Athletic	26	4	3	19	42	100	15

MANCHESTER LEAGUE
Premier Division

	P	W	D	L	F	A	PTS
Little Hulton Utd	30	22	4	4	78	37	70
Springhead	30	18	7	5	61	36	61
Abbey Hey W.M.C.	30	19	3	8	62	38	60
Highfield United	30	17	5	8	59	39	56
B.I.C.C.	30	14	10	6	60	43	52
Wythenshawe Town	30	16	4	10	50	33	52
Woodley S.C.	30	12	8	10	49	41	44
Mitchell Shackleton	30	11	10	9	55	48	43
Wythenshawe A	30	12	7	11	50	44	43
East Manchester	30	10	12	8	54	51	42
Atherton Town	30	12	5	13	54	53	41
Dukinfield Town	30	9	6	15	39	58	33
Stockport Georg	30	5	5	20	45	74	20
Monton Amats	30	5	5	20	37	73	20
Prestwich Heys	30	4	7	19	37	75	19
Sacred Heart	30	3	4	23	34	81	13

Division One

	P	W	D	L	F	A	PTS
Stand Athletic	26	18	5	3	83	25	59
Elton Ford	26	15	5	6	75	38	50
Manchester Royal	26	14	3	9	77	58	45
Breightmet United	26	12	9	5	59	42	45
Pennington	26	11	8	7	50	52	41
Whitworth Valley	26	11	7	8	68	66	40
Hollinwood	26	10	8	8	55	47	38
Old Altrinchamians	26	9	7	10	52	46	34
Ashton Athletic	26	7	9	10	37	48	30
Whalley Range	26	8	5	13	58	83	29
Coldhurst United	26	7	6	13	53	79	27
Milton	26	6	7	13	51	66	25
New Mills	26	6	6	14	54	85	24
Greater Man Pol	26	2	7	17	33	70	13

BRITISH SUGAR SUFFOLK AND IPSWICH LEAGUE
Senior Division

	P	W	D	L	F	A	PTS
Needham Market	30	23	4	3	87	25	50
Haughley United	30	23	2	5	88	31	48
Grundisburgh	30	20	4	6	64	28	44
Framlingham	30	13	11	6	63	42	37
B S Fonnereau	30	14	6	10	60	54	34
Stonham Aspal	30	15	3	12	50	45	33
Halesworth Town	30	10	8	12	50	46	28
Walton United	30	11	6	13	54	60	28
B.T. Research	30	12	3	15	47	50	27
Branth & Stutt	30	10	7	13	41	44	27
Achilles	30	9	6	15	43	69	24
Westerfield	30	8	6	16	38	62	22
Nicholians Loco	30	9	3	18	49	75	21
Walsham-le-W	30	8	5	17	35	62	21
Saxmundham Sp	30	5	9	16	31	65	19
Stanton	30	6	5	19	30	72	17

VAUX WEARSIDE LEAGUE
Division One

	P	W	D	L	F	A	PTS
Marske United	30	22	3	5	97	29	69
Jarrow Roofing (-3)	30	22	4	4	93	40	67
Birtley Town	30	15	6	9	60	49	51
South Tyne Utd	30	15	9	6	41	32	51
Ryhope C W	30	14	8	8	53	31	50
Windscale	30	13	7	10	69	54	46
Sunderland K R	30	12	5	13	56	55	41
Washington Niss	30	11	7	12	44	40	40
Annfield Plain	30	12	4	14	50	47	40
Boldon C A	30	12	6	12	59	50	39
Wolviston	30	10	4	16	48	60	34
Sth Sh Cleadon.	30	8	9	13	43	60	33
Jarrow	30	10	3	17	45	71	33
Hart'pool BWOB	30	11	2	17	46	66	32
Nth Shields Ath	30	7	5	18	34	74	26
S.C. Fulwell	30	5	0	25	36	116	15

Division Two

	P	W	D	L	F	A	PTS
Whitehaven Am	18	12	1	5	54	27	37
Stanley United	18	10	1	7	56	25	31
Harton & West	18	8	3	7	39	34	27
Washington Gl	18	8	2	8	39	30	26
Chilton Moor	18	6	3	9	22	47	21
Northallerton Ain	18	6	3	9	22	48	21
South Bank	18	4	5	9	15	36	17

TEESIDE STRONGARM LEAGUE

	P	W	D	L	F	A	PTS
Acklam Steel	30	23	6	1	92	31	75
Fishburn Park	30	18	8	4	69	38	62
Grange Boys Club	30	16	7	7	62	51	55
Nunthorpe Ath	30	16	8	6	79	43	53
Stockton Supp	30	14	6	10	60	57	48
Tees Comps	30	14	4	12	84	71	46
Dormans Ath	30	14	3	13	67	45	45
Thornaby Y C	30	12	8	10	66	49	44
Mannion Park	30	11	5	14	67	62	41
Stokesley S.C.	30	12	5	13	59	62	41
B.E.A.D.S. (-3)	30	11	5	14	54	61	35
Guisboro Tn Res.	30	7	6	17	41	77	27
Loftus West Rd	30	10	3	17	47	85	27
B.S.C. Redcar	30	7	2	21	40	74	23
New Marske SC	30	6	4	20	41	90	22
Richmond Town	30	4	8	18	45	78	20

CARLSBERG WEST CHESHIRE LEAGUE
Division One

	P	W	D	L	F	A	PTS
Poulton Victoria	30	22	6	2	91	26	50
Heswall	30	17	10	3	77	38	44
Cammell Laird	30	17	9	4	82	37	43
Merseyside Police	30	14	9	7	61	42	37
Christleton	30	13	9	8	48	41	35
Mersey Royal	30	8	15	7	44	48	31
Vauxhall	30	11	9	10	64	69	31
Capenhurst	30	8	14	8	52	50	30
Ashville	30	10	7	13	51	63	27
Bromborough Pool	30	9	6	15	36	44	24
Newton	30	8	8	14	52	71	24
General Chemicals	30	8	7	15	53	62	23
Moreton	30	8	7	15	46	60	23
Stork	30	8	5	17	44	71	21
Shell	30	5	6	19	41	92	16

Reserve Division

	P	W	D	L	F	A	PTS
Paulton Vic Res.	34	25	4	5	113	37	54
Capenhurst Res.	33	22	7	4	87	40	51
Upton Ath Ass	34	20	8	6	81	38	48
Heswall Res.	34	20	8	6	81	38	48
Castrol Social	34	16	9	9	72	53	41
West Kirkby	34	17	6	11	61	49	40
Vauxhall Res.	34	15	8	11	81	63	38
Christleton Res.	34	14	9	11	73	59	37
Willaston	34	12	11	11	59	52	35
Bromboro P Res.	34	12	8	14	61	80	32
Shell Res.	34	12	6	16	64	83	30
Ashville Res.	34	10	7	17	67	73	27
Mersey Royal Res.	34	11	5	18	64	73	27
Cammell Laird Res.	34	11	5	18	72	84	27
Manor Athletic	34	7	8	19	68	104	22
Stork Res.	34	9	4	21	50	87	22
Blacon Youth Club	34	8	4	22	48	86	20
Mersey Pol Res.	33	5	1	27	56	161	11

SKURRAYS WILTSHIRE LEAGUE
Division One

	P	W	D	L	F	A	PTS
Pinehurst	26	20	1	5	55	29	61
Biddestone	26	13	8	5	43	27	47
Aldbourne	26	14	3	9	60	46	45
Tisbury United	26	12	6	8	53	40	42
Melksh Tn Res.	26	11	5	10	39	31	38
Corsham Town	26	10	8	8	34	34	38
Devizes Tn Res.	26	10	6	10	34	29	36
Sanford	26	10	4	12	39	41	34
Bradford Town	26	9	6	11	36	39	33
Shrewton United	26	9	6	11	36	39	33
Burmah Castrol	26	6	13	7	38	38	31
Malmesbury Vic	26	7	8	11	32	37	29
Marlborough Tn	26	8	5	13	40	53	29
Pewsey V Res.	26	3	1	22	29	86	10

Division Two

	P	W	D	L	F	A	PTS
Southbrook Wal	27	20	4	3	82	22	64
Purton Res.	27	18	4	5	63	41	58
Wroughton	27	15	7	5	63	29	52
Chippen Tn Res.	27	14	4	9	43	34	46
Warm Tn Res.	27	12	4	11	48	40	39
Woot Bass Res	27	9	4	14	44	53	31
Bromham	27	8	5	14	35	51	29
Dunbar Athletic	27	8	3	16	35	55	27
Plessey Semics	27	7	2	18	20	53	23
Ames Town Res.	27	4	3	20	24	79	15

Division Three

	P	W	D	L	F	A	PTS
Raychem Spl	32	26	3	3	123	37	81
Shrewton U Res.	32	25	4	3	102	30	79
Marlboro T Res.	32	22	4	6	71	34	70
Aldbourne Res.	32	18	7	7	77	53	61
Chiseldon	32	18	4	10	85	66	58
Woott Bass Sp	32	14	5	13	73	66	47
Corsham T Res.	32	13	6	13	62	49	45
Pinehurst Res.	32	12	6	14	70	58	42
Sundstrand	32	11	8	13	59	68	41
Down Ampney	32	11	7	14	55	47	40
Ashton Keynes	32	10	8	14	62	77	38
Highworth Ath	32	9	9	14	53	74	36
Sanford Res.	32	10	5	17	46	85	35
Cricklade Town	32	7	5	20	52	115	26
Minety	32	6	6	20	51	94	24
Blunsdon United	32	5	8	19	37	77	22
West Swindon	32	4	7	21	42	91	19

Division Four

	P	W	D	L	F	A	PTS
P.F.C. Durrington	24	18	4	2	93	17	58
Southbrook Res.	24	18	4	2	76	32	58
Wroughton Res.	24	14	7	3	68	29	49
Malmes Vic Res.	24	13	5	6	63	38	44
Burmah Cas Res.	24	11	5	8	64	42	38
Biddestone Res.	24	11	2	11	45	45	35
Bradford Tn Res.	24	10	4	10	38	37	34
Dunbar Ath Res.	24	10	4	10	41	46	34
Box Rovers	24	9	6	9	56	54	33
Sherston Town	24	8	1	15	49	75	25
Marshfield	24	6	6	12	41	56	24
Bromham Res.	24	2	0	22	20	97	6
Royal Mail	24	2	0	22	24	110	6

MIKE SWANN INSURANCE BANBURY AND DISTRICT LEAGUE
Premier Division

	P	W	D	L	F	A	PTS
Ruscote Sports	16	14	2	0	63	16	30
Bloxham Athletic	16	12	2	2	58	18	26
Shipston Excel	16	11	2	3	52	18	24
Hook Norton	16	10	1	5	66	29	21
Wroxton Sports	16	4	3	9	34	54	11
Bishops Itchington	16	4	1	11	34	61	9
Sinclair United	16	4	1	11	20	52	9
Cropredy	16	3	2	11	33	57	8
Chacombe	16	2	2	12	30	86	6

TNT BATH AND DISTRICT LEAGUE
Premier Division

	P	W	D	L	F	A	PTS
Westgate	22	18	2	2	103	20	38
Odd Down A'	22	14	3	5	67	30	31
Bath C S	22	14	1	7	81	31	29
Freshford	22	12	1	9	59	53	25
Blue Bowl	22	9	6	7	51	51	24
Whiteway C.A.	22	9	4	9	42	49	22
Weston Wanderers	22	9	3	10	58	80	21
Aces	22	8	4	10	47	54	20
Bath University	22	9	2	11	45	58	20
Larkhall Ath`A'	22	6	4	12	43	78	16
Keynsham Gas	22	3	3	16	28	76	9
Imperial (Bristol)	22	3	3	16	32	87	9

BRISTOL DOWNS LEAGUE
Division One

	P	W	D	L	F	A	PTS
Sneyd Park	26	18	7	1	71	22	43
Clifton St Vincents	26	16	8	2	81	24	40
Clifton Rockets	26	14	7	5	74	46	35
St Judes Youth Club	26	16	2	8	59	47	34
K.G.C. Panels	26	10	9	7	57	53	29
The Albion	26	8	12	6	51	48	28
Tebby	26	11	6	9	41	42	28
Pump House	26	11	3	12	62	57	25
Torpedo	26	8	5	13	49	72	21
Springer Athletic	26	9	3	14	31	54	21
Retainers	26	6	6	14	35	54	18
D.D.A.S.	26	7	3	16	54	63	17
Ceramic Palace	26	7	3	16	52	62	17
Glenvic Sports	26	2	4	20	29	102	8

OFFICE VISIONS WELSH LEAGUE

	P	W	D	L	F	A	PTS
Carmarthen Tn	34	25	7	2	101	37	82
Haverfordwest C	34	23	7	4	116	34	76
Maesteg Park	34	20	8	6	73	47	68
Cardiff C S	34	19	6	9	82	47	63
Treowen Stars	34	18	6	10	67	46	60
Llanwern	34	15	7	12	57	56	52
Penrhiwceiber	34	14	9	11	69	58	51
Taffs Wells	34	14	9	11	66	63	51
Caldicot Town	34	14	4	16	60	68	46
A.F.C. Porth	34	11	10	13	57	67	43
Pontypridd Town	34	12	7	15	58	73	43
Risca United	34	12	6	16	50	67	42
Cardiff Corinth	34	11	7	16	46	56	40
Aberaman Ath	34	11	7	16	64	79	40
Abergavenny Th	34	10	8	16	50	62	38
Brecon Corinth	34	8	3	23	48	90	27
Ammanford	34	6	5	23	43	105	23
Caerleon	34	2	6	26	30	82	12

Division Two

	P	W	D	L	F	A	PTS
Grange Harl	30	21	2	7	97	58	65
Goytre United	30	19	6	5	84	36	63
Port Talbot Ath	30	19	5	6	69	32	62
Pontardawe Ath	30	21	3	6	77	37	58
B.P.	30	18	4	8	69	38	58
Porthcawl Town	30	15	7	8	61	32	52
Porth Tywyn S	30	13	8	9	51	35	47
Pontyclun	30	12	9	9	48	48	45
Bridgend Town	30	12	5	13	52	44	41
Caerau Athletic	30	12	5	13	46	45	41
Skewen Athletic	30	8	8	13	59	65	32
Fields Park P	30	9	3	18	46	71	30
Morriston Town	30	9	2	19	40	55	29
Blaenrhondda	30	6	7	17	50	79	25
Garw	30	7	1	22	30	84	22
Ferndale Athletic	30	1	1	28	27	166	4

Division Three

		W	D	L	F	A	PTS
Cardiff Institute	28	26	2	0	104	16	80
Treharris Athletic	28	23	3	2	118	30	72
Hoover Sports	28	22	3	3	102	27	69
Abercynon	28	16	2	10	66	55	50
Tonyrefail Welfare	28	16	1	11	73	71	49
Newport Y.M.C.A.	28	11	6	11	68	56	39
Monkton Swifts	28	11	5	12	71	56	38
Albion Rovers	28	11	5	12	48	52	38
Pont Blast Furn	28	10	3	15	63	77	33
Seven Sisters	28	10	2	16	48	57	32
Panteg	28	8	6	14	48	58	30
Milford United	28	9	2	17	63	66	29
South Wales C	28	9	1	18	38	67	28
Trelewis Welfare	28	5	2	21	42	108	17
Tondu Robins	28	1	1	26	19	175	4

CYNGHRAIR FFIGAR ABERYSTWYTH LEAGUE

	P	W	D	L	F	A	PTS
Bow Street	22	18	3	1			57
Tywyn & Bryn	22	13	6	3			45
Trawsgoed	22	14	2	6			44
Penrhync Res.	22	11	4	7			37
Talybont	22	12	1	9			37
Dolgellau A.A.	22	10	4	8			34
Bont	22	10	2	10			32
Aberystwyth	22	8	2	12			26
Padarn United	22	5	6	11			21
Llanon	22	6	2	14			20
Tregaron	22	5	3	14			18
Machynlleth Res.	22	2	1	19			7

Minor Club Directory

Clubs are listed with **League** followed by **Division**, **Secretary**, **Secretary's Address** and **Ground Address**.

ABACUS — Notts Alliance — 1 — Steven Bingley — 6 Brisbane Close, Mansfield, Notts NG19 8QZ. 01623 23072. — Sherwood Coll Ground, Debdale Lane, Mansfield Woodhouse, Notts.

ABBEY NATIONAL (MK) — South Midlands — 1 — Mike Burnside — 32 Falcon View, Greens Norton, Northants. NN12 8BT 01327 352095 B 01908 348210. Loughton Sports Club, Linceslade Grove, Milton Keynes, Bucks. 01908 690668.

ABERAMAN ATHLETIC — Welsh — 1 — Mr Brian Fear — 28 Mostyn Street, Abercwmboi, Aberdare, Wales, CF44 6BA, 01443 472858 — Aberaman A.F.C., Aberaman Park, Aberaman, Wales.

ABERCYNON — Welsh — 3 — Mr Jeffrey Dudley — 131 Abercynon Road, Abercynon, Mid-Glamorgan, CF45 4NE, 01443 741433 B:01222 868333 — Abercynon A.F.C., Parc Abercynon, Abercynon, Mid-Glamorgan, 01443 740238(grd) 740350(club).

ABERGAVENNY THURSDAYS — Welsh — 1 — Mr David John Morris — 48 Richmond Road, Abergavenny, Gwent, NP7 5RE, 01873 854730 B:01222 771260 — Abergavenny Thurs FC, Penypound Stadium, Abergavenny, Gwent, 01873 853906.

ACHILLES — S&I — S — Sue Cook — 47 Fairfield Road, Ipswich, Suffolk, IP3 9LB, 01473 720748 — Pauls & White S.C., Stone Lodge Lane, Ipswich, Suffolk, 01473 689044.

ACKLAM STEELWORKS — Teesside — Mr Peter Conley — 53 Roseberry Road, Longlands, Middlesbrough, Cleveland, TS4 2LJ, 01642 224266 — Acklam Steelworks, Park Road South, Middlesbrough, Cleveland, 01642 818717.

ACLE UNITED — Anglian Combination — 1 — Mr J H Goward — 18 Reve Crescent, Blofield Corner, Norwich, Norfolk, NR13 4RX, 01603 712947 — Acle United F.C., Bridewell Lane, Acle, Norfolk.

ACTON SHAMROCK — Middx — P — Mr Damien McCallion — 74 Balmoral Road, Harrow, Middlesex, HA2 8TB, 0181 422 7387 B:562 0817 — Shamrock Club, Horn Lane, Acton, Middlesex, W3, 0181 993 1270.

AGREVO SPORTS — Herts — P — Mr Stephen Sells — 5 Curlew Close, Berkhamsted, Hertfordshire, HP4 2HZ, 01442 876325 — Kitchener's Field, Castle Hill, Berkhamsted, Hertfordshire, 01442 864937.

ALBION ROVERS — Welsh — 3 — Mr Karl McCarthy — 30 Llanover Road Estate, Blaenavon, Gwent, NP4 9HP, 01495 792557 M:0585 195680 — Newport Stadium, Llangland Way, Newport, Gwent, 01633 280802.

ALDBOURNE — Wilts — S1 — Mr K Williams — Crown Hotel, Aldbourne, Marlborough, Wiltshire, SN8 2DU, 01672 540214 — Farm Lane, Aldbourne, Marlborough, Wiltshire.

ALLENDALE — Dorset — Rod Pope — 51 Dalkeith Rd, Corfe Mullen, Wimborne, Dorset, BH21 3PQ, 01202 602922 — Recotts Rec Gd, School Lane, Wimborne, Dorset.

ALPHINGTON — Devon — Mr Keith Phare — 23 Sussex Close, Exeter, Devon, EX4 1LP, 01392 58636 — Alphington FC, The Chronicles, Alphington, Exeter, Devon, 01392 79556.

ALSAGER — Mid-Cheshire — 2 — Steve Whittaker — 2 Lea Close, Sanbach, Cheshire, CW11 0HT, 01270 761810 B:01477 532116 — Town Ground, Woodpark, Alsager, Cheshire, 01270 882336.

ALVASTON ROVERS — MRA — 1 — Mr Stephen Pilkington — 12 Stiles Road, Alvaston, Derby, Derbyshire, DE24 0PG, 01332 756592 B:246898 — Meadow Lane P.F., Alvaston Park, London Rd, Alvaston, Derbyshire.

AMBLE TOWN — Northern Alliance — P — R Falkous — 30 George Street, Amble, Morpeth, Northumberland, NE65 0DW, 01655 711041 — Amble Running Track, Amble, Morpeth, Northumberland.

AMMANFORD — Welsh — 2 — Mr John Thomas — 154 Hendre Road, Capel Hendre, Ammanford, Dyfed, SA18 3LE, 01269 843712 B:01792 795157 — Rice Road, Bettws, Ammanford, Dyfed, 01269 592407.

AMPTHILL TOWN — South Midlands — S — Mr Eric Turner — 34 Dunstable Street, Ampthill, Bedfordshire, MK45 2JT, 01525 403128 — Ampthil Town FC, Woburn Rd, Ampthill, Beds, 01525 404440.

ANGLIAN WINDOWS — Anglian Combination — 1 — Mr T M Cann — 83 Beverley Road, Norwich, Norfolk, NR5 8AP, 01603 458745 — Horsford Manor, Cromer Road, Norwich, Norfolk, NR5 8AP, 01603 458745.

ANNFIELD PLAIN — Wearside — Mr Marshall Lawson — 24 Northgate, Annfield Plain, Stanley, County Durham, DH9 7HY, 01207 235879 — Derwent Park, West Road, Annfield Plain, County Durham.

ANSTEY TOWN — Leics — 1 — Mr Graham Ford — 99 Hollow Road, Anstey, Leicestershire, LE7 7FR, 0116 236 4170 B:0116 256 1613 — Anstey Town F.C., Leicester Road, Thurlaston, Leicestershire, 0116 236 8231.

ANSTY RANGERS — Sussex County — 3 — Tina Darbyshire — 6 Faulkners Way, Burgess Hill, West Sussex, RH15 8SB, 01444 233030 — Ansty Rangers F.C., Deaks Lane, Ansty, West Sussex, 01444 454010.

APPLEBY FRODINGHAM — Lincs — Mr M D Mumby, — 21 Messingham Road — Scunthorpe, North Lincs, DN17 2LL, 01724 840117 B:381371 — Brumby Hall, Ashby Road, Scunthorpe, North Lincs, 01724 843024.

APPLEDORE & BIDEFORD A.A.C. — Devon — Mr Eddie Nichols, — 14 Alexandra Terrace — Bideford, Devon, EX39 2PL, 01237 475493 — Appledore & Bide AAC, Marshford, Appledore, Devon, 01237 477099.

ARDLEY UNITED — Hellenic — 1 — Mr Nigel Adams — 139 Willow Drive, Bicester, Oxfordshire, OX6 9XF, 01869 325734 B:243215 — Ardley Sports Ground, , 01869 346429.

ARNOLD TOWN `A' — MRA — 1 — Mr G Stephen Barlow — 95 Plains Road, Mapperley, Nottingham, Nottinghamshire, NG3 5QT — 0115 952 9068, Burton Road P.F., Gedling, Nottingham, Nottinghamshire.

ASFORDBY AMATEURS — Leics — P — Mr Richard Smith — 17 Cheviot Drive, Shepshed, Leicestershire, LE12 9ED, 01509 502857 B:235566 — Hoby Road Spts Grnd, Hoby Road, Asfordby, Melton Mowbray, Leicestershire, 01664 434545.

ASHFIELD — MRA — 2 — Mr Dean Sharpe — 24 Cookson Street, Kirby-in-Ashfield, Nottinghamshire, NG17 8DZ, 01623 722536 — Ashfield F.C., Cowpasture Lane, Sutton-in-Ashfield, Nottinghamshire.

ASHILL — Anglian Combination — ` — Mr A Warby — 38 Swaffham Road — Watton, Thetford, Norfolk, IP25 6LA, 01953 882341 — Community Centre, Hale Round, Ashill, Norfolk.

ASHINGTON HIRST PROGRESSIVE — Northern Alliance — 1 — G Gibbons — 41 Hawthorn Road, Ashington, Northumberland, NE63 0SN, 01670 815218 — Ashington High Sch., Green Lane, Ashington, Northumberland.

ASHLEA — Anglian Combination — P — Mr S Gilder — 5 Back Lane, Lound, Lowestoft, Suffolk, NR32 5NE, 01502 731052 — Pitch One, Normanston Park, Lowestoft, Suffolk.

ASHTON KEYNES — Wilts — J3 — Mr G Mobley — 7 Richmond Court, Ashton Keynes, Wiltshire, SN6 6PP, 01285 861263 — Bradstone Spts Grnd, Rixon Gate, Ashton Keynes, Wiltshire.

ASHVILLE — West Cheshire — 1 — Mr Eddie Parker — 48a Upton Road, Claughton Village, Birkenhead, Wirral, L41 0DF, 0151 653 2297 — Villa Pk, Cross Lane, Wallesey Village, Wallesey, Merseyside, 0151 638 2127.

ASKERN WELFARE — Central Midlands — P — Miss Lynn Sudworth — Holly Croft, Main Street, Stillington, York, Yorks, YP6 1JU, 01347 810038 — Welfare Sports Gd, Doncaster Rd, Askern, Doncaster, 01302 700957.

ATTENBOROUGH — Notts Alliance — 1 — Terry Allen — 3 Firth Close, Arnold, Nottingham, Notts, NG5 8RU, 0115 920 0698 — Village Green, The Strand, Attenborough, Notts, 0115 925 7439.

ATTLEBOROUGH TOWN — Anglian Combination — 1 — Mr K A Parsons — Fernlee, Station Road, Spooner Row, Wymondham, Norfolk, NR18 9AH, 01953 603901 — Recreation Ground, Station Road, Attleborough, Norfolk, 01953 455365.

AVESTA SHEFFIELD — Sheffield — 2 — Mr Mark Cartledge — 63 Bonet Lane, Brinsworth, Rotherham, South Yorkshire, S60 5NF, 01709 372496 — Bawtry Road, Tinsley, Sheffield, South Yorkshire.

AWBRIDGE — Hampshire — 3 — Mr Mike Caws — 2 Copsewood Road, Bitterne Park, Southampton, Hampshire, SO18 1QU, 01703 551880 — Village Hall Field, Crossroads, Awbridge, near Romsey, Hampshire.

AWSWORTH VILLA — Notts Alliance — S — Keith Slaney — 24 Attewell Rd, Awsworth, Nottingham, Notts, NG16 2SY, 0115 930 2514 — Shio Park, Attewell Rd, Awsworth, Notts.

AYLESFORD — Kent County — 3W — Mr Mick Sands — Lantivet, Weavering Street, Weavering, Maidstone, Kent, ME14 5JP, 01622 734123 — Recreation Ground, Forstall Road, Aylesford, Kent.

AYLESFORD PAPER MILLS — Kent County — P — Mrs Lynda Casey — 41 Cobdown Close, Ditton, Kent, ME20 6SZ, 01732 849476 — Cobdown S&S Club, Station Road, Aylesford, near Ditton, 01622 716824.

AYLESTONE PARK OLD BOYS — Leics — P — Mr Brendon Tyrell — 7 Magnolia Close, Leicester Forest East, Leicester, Leicestershire, LE8 0JP 0116 238 7742 B:01455 292244, Dorset Avenue, Fairfield Estate, Wigston, Leicestershire, 0116 277 5307.

AYLSHAM WANDERERS — Anglian Combination — Mr P Hamilton — 6 Lancaster Gardens, Aylsham, Norwich, Norfolk, NR11 6LD, 01263 734904 — Sir Williams Lane, Aylsham, Norwich, Norfolk.

A.C. DELCO — Hampshire — 1 — Mr Brian Cook — 17 Hickory Gardens, West End, Southampton, Hampshire, SO30 3RN, 01703 470321 B:339662 — A.C. Delco Spts Grnd, Stoneham Lane, Eastleigh, Hampshire, 01703 613334.

A.C.D. TRIDON — South Midlands — S — Mr Terry Owen — 29 Elm Park Close, Houghton Regis, Dunstable, Bedfordshire, LU5 5PN, 01582 863273 — CD Tridon Sports Gd, High St North, Dunstable, Beds, 01582 678668.

A.F.C. ALDERMASTON — Hampshire — 3 — Mr Gareth Dew — 58 Portway — Baughurst, Tadley, Hampshire, RG26 5PE, 0118 982 7509 — Aldermaston Rec Soc., Aldermaston, Reading, Berkshire, RG7 4PR, 01734 824544.

A.F.C. BASINGSTOKE — Hampshire — 3 — T Purnell — 1 Byfleet Avenue, Old Basing, Basingstoke, Hampshire, RG24 7HD, 01256 23239 B:0171 580 6053 — War Memorial Park — Crossborough Hill, Basingstoke, Hampshire, .

A.F.C. EGERTON — Kent County — P — Mr Steve Parkes — 48 Oakdene Road, St Mary Cray, Orpington, Kent, BR5 2AN, 01689 818382 B:839516x364 — St Mary Cray Rec., Park Road, St Mary Cray, Kent.

A.F.C. GUILDFORD — Surrey — P — Mr Kevin Bookham — 104 Manor Road, Guildford, Surrey, GU2 6NR, 01483 36713 B:01344 713940 — Spectrum Leis Centre, Parkway, Guildford, Surrey, 01483 444777.

A.F.C. MAIDENHEAD — Reading — S — Mrs Donna Saunders — 63 Furze Platt Rd, Maidenhead, Berkshire, SL6 7NF, 01628 35994 B:01734 343280 — Cox Green School, Highfield Lane, Maidenhead, Berkshire.

A.F.C. NEWBURY — Hampshire — 1 — Mr Damien Hayden — 10 Nideggen Close, Thatcham, Berkshire, 01635 826540, — A.F.C. Newbury, Faraday Road, Newbury, Berkshire, RG13 2AD, 01635 40048.

A.F.C. RHONDDA — Welsh — 1 — Mr Ray Hacker — 57 High Street, Cymmer, Porth, Rhondda, CF39 9AR, 01443 684580, — A.F.C. Rhondda, Dinas Park, Dinas, Rhondda, 01443 688073.

A.F.C. WALLINGFORD — Chiltonian — P — E Gniadek — 17 Offas Close, Benson, Wallingford, Oxfordshire, OX10 6NR, 01491 838540 — , A.F.C. Wallingford, Hithercroft, Wallingford, Oxfordshire, 01491 835044.

A.F.C. ZENECA — Mid-Cheshire — 1 — Mrs Karen Black — 11 Beechwood Mews, Macclesfield, Cheshire, SK10 2SL, 01625 611937 — Mulberries Leis Cntr, Zeneca Pharms, Macclesfield, Cheshire, 01625 514040.

BANDON — West Midlands — 1B — Mr Steve Rogers — 33 Severn Street, Bridgnorth, Shropshire, WV15 6BB, 01746 765709 B:763135, Bandon Lane, — off Mill Street, Lowtown, Bridgnorth, Shropshire, 01746 763135.

BANWELL — Somerset — 3 — Chris Gibbons — 76 Blackthorn Gardens, Worle, Weston-super-Mare, North Somerset, BS22 0SA, 01934 512902 — Riverside Ground, Riverside, Banwell, North Somerset, 01934 820773.

BARDON HILL — Leics — 1 — Mr Adrian Bishop — 138 Bradgate Drive — Coalville, Leicestershire, LE67 4HG, 01530 815560 B:01455 822321, Bardon Close, Coalville, Leicestershire, 01530 815569.

BARDSEY — West Yorkshire — P — M Furlong — 7 The Drive, Crossgates, Leeds, West Yorks, LS15 8ER, 0113 2645693 H 01274 308098 — The Sportsfield, Keswick Lane, Bardsey, West Yorks, 01937 574286.

BARNTON – Mid-Cheshire — 1 — Michael Webster — 29 Townfield Lane, Barnton, Cheshire, CW8 4LH, 01606 781119 — Townfield, Townfield Lane, Barnton, Cheshire.

BARROW TOWN — Leics — P — Mr Paul Riley — 36 Palma Park, Shelley Street, Loughborough, Leicestershire, LE11 0LB, 01509 264840 — Riverside Park, Barrow Road, Quorn, Leicestershire, 01509 620650.

BARROW WANDERERS — West Lancs — 2 — Mr M Poole — 22 Conway Gardens, Walney Island, Barrow-in-Furness, Cumbria, LA14 3NZ, 01229 473734 — Lesh Lane, off Abbey Rd, Barrow-in-Furness, Cumbria, 01229 825224.

BARTON TOWN OLD BOYS — Lincs — Mr Peter Mitchell — 56 Brigg Road, Barton-on-Humber, North Lincs, DN18 5QR, 01652 632382 B:01472 355231 — Barton Old Boys F.C., Marsh Lane, Barton-on-Humber, North Lincs.

BARWICK — West Yorkshire — P — B J Kollesoff — Parklands, 3 Leeds Rd, Barwick in Elmet, Leeds, Yorks, LS15 4JE, 0113 281 2638 B 0113 2811201 — Back of Village Hall, Chapel Lane, HQ 0113 281 3065.

BASFORD UNITED — Notts Alliance — 1 — S Thompson — 2 Haddon Rd, West Bridgford, Nottingham, Notts, NG12 6EQ, 0115 914 1940 — Greenwich Ave, Bagnall Rd, Basford, Notts, 0115 942 3918.

BASING ROVERS — Hampshire — 3 — Mr Chris Dale — 13 Howard View, Basingstoke, Hampshire, RG22 6LF, 01256 26604 fax:469451 — Old Basing Rec., The Street, Old Basing, Hampshire, 01256 844254.

BASS ALTON TOWN — Hampshire — 1 — Mr Tony Hillman — 19a Beechwood Road, Alton, Hampshire, GU34 1RL, 01420 87103 B:541177x2362 — Bass Sports Ground, Anstey Road, Alton, Hampshire, 01420 82465.

BEARSTED — Kent County — 1W — Mr Julian Scannel — 24 Fauchons Lane, Bearsted, Maidstone, Kent, ME14 4AH, 01622 739072 B:01634 831118 — Bearsted Green, The Street,, Bearstead, Maidstone, Kent.

BEAUWATER — Kent County — 1W — Mr Robert Taylor — 24 Sun Lane, Gravesend, Kent, DA12 5HG, 01474 332208 B:01375 852729, — Beauwater Leis. Club, Nelson Road, Northfleet, Kent, 01474 336456.

BECCLES CAXTON — Anglian Combination — Mr J Moore — The Folly, Grove Road, Beccles, Suffolk, 01502 716709 — Caxton Meadow, Adj. Beccles Station, Beccles, Suffolk, NR34 9QH, 01502 712829.

BECCLES TOWN — Anglian Combination — 1 — Mr J Humby — 11 Station Road, Beccles, Suffolk, NR34 9QH, 01502 713776 — Beccles Town F.C., College Meadow, Beccles, Suffolk, 01502 712016.

BEDMOND SPORTS & SOCIAL — Herts — P — Christine Kelly — Hope Cottage, 33 Marlin Square, Abbots Langley, Hertfordshire, WD5 0EG, 01923 270557 — Toms Lane Rec Ground, Toms Lane, Bedmond, Hertfordshire, 01923 267991.

BEESTON ST ANTHONYS — West Yorkshire — P — M Browne — 42 Old Lane, Beeston, Leeds, Yorks, LS11 8AA, 0113 270 8408 — Beggars Hill, Beeston, 0113 270 7223.

BEESTON TOWN — Notts Alliance — 1 — Andy Meakin — 26 Redland Drive, Chilwell, Nottingham, Notts, NG9 5LE, 0115 967 7520 — Beeston Town, University Ground, Nottingham, Notts.

BELPER UNITED — MRA — P — Mr David Rees — 95 Elm Tree Avenue, Kilburn, Belper, Derbyshire, DE56 0NN, 01332 881635 — Alton Manor, Nailers Way, Belper, Derbyshire.

BELVEDERE — Kent County — 3W — Mr David Morgan — 11 Upton Road, Bexleyheath, Kent, DA6 8LS, 0181 303 8569 — Belvedere Spts Club, 101a Woolwich Road, Abbey Wood, London, SE2 0DY.

BENINGTON — Herts — 1 — Mr John Batchelor — 16 Cedar Close, Shefford, Bedfordshire, SG17 5RT, 01462 816114 — Benington Rec Ground, Town Lane, Benington, Hertfordshire.

BESTWOOD MINERS WELFARE — Notts Alliance — 1 — Andy Beeston — 114 Derbyshire Lane, Hucknall, Nottingham, Notts, NG15 GE, 0115 963 4665 — Bestwood Workshops, Park Rd, Bestwood Village, Notts.

BIDDESTONE — Wilts — S1 — Mr A Short — 1 Hartham Lane, Biddestone, Chippenham, Wilts, SN14 7EA, 01249 714724 — Cuttle Lane, Biddestone, Chippenham, Wiltshire, 0831 319248.

BIGGLESWADE UNITED — South Midlands — 1 — Tracey James — 17 Havelock Rd, Biggleswade, Beds, SG18 0DB, 01767 316270, — Second Meadow, Fairfield Rd, Biggleswade, Beds, 01767 600408.

BILSTHORPE COLLIERY WELFARE — Notts Alliance — 1 — Les Lee — 18 The Hollies, Rainworth, Mansfield, Notts, 01623 490053 — Bilsthorpe CW, Eakring Rd, Bilsthorpe, Notts.

BILSTON UNITED — West Midlands — 1B — Gillian Hartill — 13 Kinver Drive, Warstones Estate, Penn, Wolverhampton, West Midlands, WV4 4RR, 01902 653440, Parkfield Stadium, Rooker Avenue, Parkfields, W'hmpton, West Midlands, WV2 2DT, 01902 658645.

BINFIELD — Chiltonian — P — V Bradshaw — 21 Audley Way, Ascot, Berkshire, SL5 8EE, 01344 886144 — Binfield F.C., Stubbs Hill, Binfield, Berkshire, 01344 860822.

BIRSTALL UNITED — Leics — P — Mr Bob Garrard — 58 Halstead Road, Mountsorrel, Leicestershire, LE12 7HF, 0116 237 6886 B:0115 964 2366 — Birstall United F.C., Meadow Lane, Birstall, Leicestershire, 0116 267 1230.

BIRTLEY TOWN — Wearside — Mr Kevin McDonnell — 8 Leyburn Place, Birtley, Tyne & Wear, 0191 410 0495 — Birtley Spts Complex, near AEI Cables, Birtley, Tyne & Wear.

BISHOPS CLEEVE — Hellenic — 1 — Mr Phil Tustain — 7 Dale Walk, Bishops Cleeve, Gloucestershire, GL52 4PQ, 01242 674968 B:673333x2505 — Stoke Road, Bishops Cleve, Gloucestershire, 01242 676257.

BISHOPS WALTHAM TOWN — Hampshire — 2 — Mrs Margaret Weavil — 69 Oak Road, Ridgemede, Bishops Waltham, Hampshire, SO32 1ER, 01489 894952 — Priory Park, School Hill, Bishops Waltham, Hampshire.

BISHOPSBOURNE — Kent County — 1E — Mr Neil Carter — 43 Palm Tree Way, Lyminge, Folkestone, Kent, CT18 8JN, 01303 862687 B:01622 858888 — Canteen Meadow, The Street, Bishopsbourne, Kent.

BISHOPSTOKE SOCIAL — Hampshire — 1 — Mr Tony Boland — 34 Fryern Close, Chandlers Ford, Hampshire, SO53 2LF, 01703 364722 — Bishopstoke Soc. FC, Chickenhall Lane, Bishopstoke, Hampshire, 01703 612038.

BISLEY SPORTS — Surrey — P — Mr John Rose — 7 Orchard Close, West End, Woking, Surrey, GU24 9NS, 01483 480934, — Recreation Ground, Guildford Road, Bisley, Surrey.

BLABY & WHETSTONE ATHLETIC — Leics — 1 — Mrs Sandra C Morris — 10 Winchester Road, Blaby, Leicestershire, LE8 4HJ, 0116 277 3208, — Blaby/Whet Boys Club, Warwick Road, Whetstone, Leicestershire, 0116 286 4852.

BLACKBROOK — Somerset — 2 — Mr Rod Pepperell — 6 Sherford Terrace, Sherford, Taunton, Somerset, TA1 3SE, 01823 282892 — Blackbrook Pavilion, Blackbrook Way, Taunton, Somerset, 01823 333435.

BLACKFIELD & LANGLEY — Hampshire — 1 — Mr Ian Hore — 5 Foxhayes Lane, Blackfield, Southampton, Hampshire, 01703 893325 B:847659 — Gang Warily Rec Ctre, Newlands Road, Blackfield, Hampshire, SO45 1EA, 01703 847629.

BLACKROD TOWN — West Lancs — 1 — DG Almond — 40 Landedmans, Westhoughton, Bolton, Lancs, BL5 2QJ, 01942 793122 B 01253 303170, — Blackrod Comm Centre, Vicarage Rd, Blackrod, Lancs, 01204 692614.

BLACKWELL MINERS WELFARE — Central Midlands — P — Mr Julian Riley — 22 Glinton Avenue, Blackwell, Alfreton, Derbyshire, DE55 5HD, 01773 862411, — Welfare Ground, Primrose Hill, Blackwell, Alfreton, Derbys, 01773 811295.

BLACON YOUTH CLUB — West Cheshire — 2 — Mr Ron Paddock — 71 Blacon Avenue, Blacon, Chester, Cheshire, CH1 5BD, 01244 371240 — Cairns Crescent P.F., Blacon, Chester, Cheshire.

BLAENRHONDDA — Welsh — 3 — Wynford Ludlow — Marwyn, Abertonllwyd Street, Treherbert, Rhondda, CF42 5PF, 01443 771683, — Blaenrhondda A.F.C., Blaenrhondda Park, Blaenrhondda, Rhondda, 01443 774772.

BLANDFORD UNITED — Dorset — David Upshall — 18 Ramsbury Ct, Ramsbury Gardens, Blandford, Dorset, DT11 7UL, 01258 456125 B 01202 401300, — Recreation Ground, Park Rd, Blandford, Dorset.

BLOFIELD UNITED — Anglian Combination — P — Mr P Stevens — 25 Medeswell Close, Brundall, Norwich, Norfolk, NR13 5QG, 01603 717406 — Great Yarmouth Road, Blofield, Norwich, Norfolk, 01603 712576.

BOLDON COMMUNITY ASSOCIATION — Wearside — Mr George Pollard — 126 Horsley Hill Rd, South Shields, Tyne & Wear, 0191 454 6821 — Boldon Welfare, New Road, Boldon Colliery, Tyne & Wear.

BOLLINGTON ATHLETIC — Mid-Cheshire — 1 — Anthony Holmes — 1 Princess Drive, Bollington, Macclesfield, Cheshire, SK10 5ES, 01625 574913, — Recreation Ground, Bollington, Cheshire.

BOOKHAM — Surrey — P — Mr Gareth Mills — 5 Byron Place, Leatherhead, Surrey, KT22 8AX, 01372 378786 — Chrystie Rec. Ground, Dorking Road, Bookham, Surrey, 01372 459482.

BOOTS ATHLETIC — Notts Alliance — S — Ian Whitehead — 21 Rosthwaite Close, West Bridgford, Nottingham, Notts, NG2 6RA, 0115 981 2830 — Lady Bay, West Bridgford, Nottingham, Notts.

BOROUGH GREEN — Kent County — 3W — Mr Derrick Groom — Laburnum, Clearway, Addington, Kent, ME19 5BP, 01732 842557 — Recreation Ground, Maidstone Road, Borough Green, Kent.

BOROUGH UNITED — Kent County — 2W — Mr George W Johnson — 35 Green Walk, Crayford, Kent, DA1 4JP, 01322 527084 — Glentworth Club, Lowfield Street, Dartford, Kent, 01322 223676.

BORROWASH UNITED — MRA — P — W Ian Collins — 30 Margreave Road, Chaddesden, Derby, Derbyshire, DE21 6JD, 01332 739437 — Asterdale Spts Club, Borrowash Road, Spondon, Derbyshire, 01332 669688.

BOSHAM — Sussex County — 2 — Mr Richard Doncaster — 61 Manor Way, Southbourne, Emsworth, Hampshire, 01243 375184 — Recreation Ground, Walton Lane, Bosham, West Sussex, PO18 8QF, 01243 574011.

BOTTESFORD TOWN — Lincs — Mr Paul Herrick — 22a Rooklands, Scotter, Gainsborough, Lincolnshire, DN21 3TT, 01724 764183 — Birch Park, Ontario Road, Bottesford, Lincolnshire, 01724 871883.

BOURNEMOUTH SPORTS — Dorset — Mrs Lorraine Sansom — 42 Mallards Close, Bournemouth, Dorset, BH8 9PG, 01202 532723, — Bournemouth Sports, Chapel Gate, East Parley, Dorset, 01202 581933.

BOVINGDON — Herts — P — Mr David Rawson — 9 Granville Dene, Bovingdon, Hemel Hempstead, Hertfordshire, HP3 0JE, 01442 380223 — Green Lane, Bovingdon, Hemel Hempstead, Hertfordshire, 01442 832628.

BOX ROVERS — Wilts — J4 — Mr P Goulding — 20 Sunderland Close, Melksham, Wiltshire, SN12 6TZ, 01225 704988, — Box Rovers F.C., Recreation Ground, Box, Wiltshire.

BRADENHAM WANDERERS — Anglian Combination — Mrs P Rowley — 8 Roger Ride, Toftwood, Dereham, Norfolk, NR19 1SJ, 01362 697757 — Bradenham Wdrs F.C., Hale Road, Bradenham, Norfolk.

BRADFORD TOWN — Wilts — S1 — Mr C Lewis — 43 Tudor Drive, Trowbridge, Wiltshire, BA14 7NA, 01225 767425 — Trowbridge Town F.C., County Way, Trowbridge, Wiltshire, BA14 0DB, 01225 752076.

BRADING TOWN — Hampshire — 2 — Mr Mick Edmonston — Seawinds, Nunwell Street, Sandown, Isle of Wight, PO36 9DE, 01983 404770 — Brading Town F.C., Vicarage Lane, Brading, Isle of Wight, 01983 405217.

BRAGBURY ATHLETIC — Herts — 1 — Mr Ray Poulter — 292 Jessop Road, Stevenage, Hertfordshire, SG1 5NA, 01438 358078 — Brit. Aerospace S&S, Bragbury End, Stevenage, Hertfordshire, 01438 812985.

BRAILSFORD — MRA — P — Mr George Smith — 36 The Plain, Brailsford, near Ashbourne, Derbyshire, DE6 3BZ, 01335 361012, — Osmaston Polo Ground, Osmaston, Ashbourne, Derbyshire.

BRAISHFIELD — Hampshire — 3 — Mr Mick Tanner — 10 Avon Crescent, Romsey, Hampshire, SO51 5PY, 01794 523180 — Braishfield Rec Grnd, Braishfield, near Romsey, Hampshire.

BRAMHALL — Mid-Cheshire — 1 — Mrs Elaine Webster — 25 Kimberley Street, Edgeley, Stockport, Cheshire, SK3 8EB, 0161 477 7273 B 0161 285 8842 — Bramhall FC, Lumb Lane, Bramhall, Cheshire.

BRANDON TOWN — Anglian Combination — 1 — Mr P V Wright — c/o Breckland Roofing, Long Street, Great Ellingham, Attleborough, Norfolk, NR17 1LL, 01953 457545 F:457676(ev.), Remembrance P.F., Church Road, Brandon, Suffolk, 01842 813177.

BRANTHAM & STUTTON UNITED — S&I — S — Mr Michael Coombes — 4 Crowcroft Glebe, Nedging Tye, Ipswich, Suffolk, IP7 7LH, 01449 741201 — Brantham Social Club, New Village, Brantham, Suffolk.

BRECON CORINTHIANS — Welsh — 2 — Mr Geoff Buckingham — 67 Meadow Sweet Drive, St Mellons, Cardiff, South Glamorgan, CF30 0RD, 01222 796816 B:343061, — The Rich Field, The Watton, Brecon, Powys, 01874 624033.

BRENTFORD NEW INN — Middx — 1 — Mr Thomas Mackin — 86 Dukes Avenue, Chiswick, London, W4 2AF, 0181 995 0284 — White Lodge, Syon Lane, Osterley, Middlesex, 0181 758 1191.

BRERETON SOCIAL — West Midlands — 1A — Mr George Burton — 31 Leahall Lane, Brereton, Rugeley, Staffordshire, WS15 1JE, 01889 583358 — Red Lion Ground, Armitage Lane, Brereton, Rugeley, Staffordshire, 01889 585526.

BRERETON TOWN — West Midlands — 1A — Mr Sidney Littlewood — 3 Main Road, Brereton, Rugeley, Staffordshire, WS15 1DS, 01889 584574 — Ravenhill Rec. Park, Main Road, Brereton, Rugeley, Staffordshire, 01889 578255.

BRIDGE INN (ILKESTON) — MRA — 1 — Cobie J Weatherall — 12 Ribblesdale, Kirk Hallam, Ilkeston, Derbyshire, DE7 4GD, 0115 930 2848, — Windsor Crescent PF, Kirk Hallam, Ilkeston, Derbyshire.

BRIDGEND TOWN — Welsh — 2 — Mr Richard Harris — c/o Bridgend Town A.F.C., Coychurch Road, Bridgend, Mid-Glamorgan, CF31 3AP, 01656 661826 — Bridgend Town A.F.C., Coychurch Road, Bridgend, Mid-Glamorgan, CF31, 01656 662974(grd) 655097(club).

BRIDGER PACKAGING — South Midlands — 1 — Laurence Jack — 8 Lamb Meadow, Arlesey, Beds, SG15 6RY, 01462 835661 B 0181 905 1992 — Letchworth Corner, Muddy Lane, Letchworth, Herts.

BRITISH AEROSPACE CANBERRA — West Lancs — 2 — Mr SP Halse — 7 Chapman Rd, Hoddlesdon, Darwenn, Lancs, BB3 3LU, 01254 772687 B 01254 768681 — BAE Sports Club, British Aerospace, Samlesbury, Lancs, 01772 464351.

BRITISH SUGAR FONNEREAU — S&I — S — Mr David Knights — 16 Speedwell Road, Ipswich, Suffolk, IP2 0LP, 01473 601543 — British Sugar P.L.C., Sproughton Road, Ipswich, Suffolk, 01473 240202.

BRITISH TELECOM RESEARCH — S&I — S — Mr Alan Coleman — 22 Princes Road, Felixstowe, Suffolk, IP11 7QY, 01394 285355 — The Hollies, Straight Road, Bucklesham, Suffolk, 01473 659405.

BROADFIELDS UNITED — Middx — 1 — Mr David Bugden — 9 Parkfield Crescent, North Harrow, Middlesex, HA2 6LE, 0181 428 1152 B:0181 421 4739 — Broadfields, Headstone Lane, North Harrow, Middlesex, HA2 6NN.

BROADHEATH CENTRAL — Mid-Cheshire — 1 — David Murphy — 10 Green Drive, Timperley, Altrincham, Cheshire, WA15 6JW, 0161 718 0523 — Broadheath Cent FC, Viaduct Rd, Broadheath, Cheshire, 0161 928 5849.

BROADMOOR SOCIAL — Chiltonian — P — Mr Mick Roberts — 36 Constable Way, College Town, Sandhurst, Berkshire, GU17 8DH, 01276 609038 — Cricket Field Grove, Broadmoor Estate, Crowthorne, Berkshire, 01344 772612.

BROMBOROUGH POOL — West Cheshire — 1 — Mr Trevor Petterson — 102 Princes Boulevard, Higher Bebington, Wirral, L63 5LP, 0151 645 1642 — The Green, South View Road, Bromborough Pool, Wirral, 0151 645 3476.

BROMLEY GREEN — Kent County — 1E — Mr Ciaran McQuillan — 42 Falcon Way, Singleton Farm, Ashford, Kent, TN23 5UR, 01233 642941 B:617254 — Swan Cnte/Herbert Rd, South Willesborough, Ashford, Kent, 01233 610064.

BROMYARD TOWN — West Midlands — 1B — Mrs Nola Moses — 20 West Hill, Bromyard, Herefordshire, HR7 4EX, 01885 483530 — Delahay Meadow, Bromyard, Herefordshire, 01885 483974.

BROOMFIELD UNITED — Kent County — 1E — Mr Roger Cook — Flat 17, Francis Court, 117 High Street, Herne Bay, Kent, CT6 5LA, 01227 742480, — Patrixbourne Road, Bridge, near Canterbury, Kent.

BROUGHTON — Hampshire — 2 — Mr Tony Hammerton — 19 Plough Gardens, Broughton, Stockbridge, Hampshire, SO20 8AF, 01794 301495 B:301253, — Buckholt Road, Broughton, Stockbridge, Hampshire, 01794 301150 — .

BUCKFASTLEIGH RANGERS — Devon — Bob Haskell — 41 Moorland Gate, Buckfastleigh, Devon, TQ12 6TX, 01626 835386 — Buckfastleigh FC, Duckspond, Buckfastleigh, Devon, 01364 642853.

BUCKINGHAM UNITED — South Midlands — 1 — Stuart Mackey — 10 Gawcott Fields, Buckingham, Bucks, MK18 1TL, 01280 816903 — Buckingham Town FC, Ford Meadow, Buckingham, Bucks, 01280 816257.

BUDLEIGH SALTERTON — Devon — Nick Pannell — 33 Armytage Road, Budleigh Salterton, Devon, EX9 6SD, 01395 445877 — Football Ground, Greenway Lane, Budleigh Salterton, Devon, 01395 443850.

BUNGAY TOWN — Anglian Combination — Mr B Gower — 59 Garden Close, Bungay, Suffolk, NR35 1JE, 01986 892916, Maltings Meadow, Ditchingham, Bungay, Suffolk, 01986 894028.

BURNHAM UNITED — Somerset — P — Sandra Archibald — 115 Berrow Road, Burnham-on-Sea, Somerset, TA8 2PH, 01278 789111 M:0402 305048 — Burnham Road P.F., Cassis Close, Burnham-on-Sea, Somerset, 01278 794615.

BURNLEY UNITED — West Lancs — 1 — S Elliott — 6 Highfield Ave, Burnley, Lancs, BB10 1YB, 01282 414828 B 0161 834 3148 — Barden Sports Ground, Barden Lane, Burnley, Lancs.

BUSHEY RANGERS — Herts — 1 — Mr Rowland Marshall — 45 Blackwell Drive, Watford, Hertfordshire, WD1 4HP, 01923 461457 — Moatfield, Bournehall Lane, Bushey, Hertfordshire, 0181 386 1875.

BUSTLEHOLME — West Midlands — 1B — Suzanne Glover — 15 Swann Road, Hurst Hill, Coseley, Wolverhampton, West Midlands, WV14 9UP, 01902 659380, — Rayhall Lane, off Newton Road, Great Barr, Birmingham.

BUTTERLEY BRICK — MRA — P — Mr Michael Boam — 5 Valley Drive, Newthorpe, Nottinghamshire, NG16 2DT, 01773 715277 B:810132 — Waingroves Brickwrks, Peasehill Road, Ripley, Derbyshire, 01773 742287.

BUXTED — Sussex County — 3 — Mr P J Durrant — Haven, Station Rd, Isfield, East Sussex, TN22 5XB, 01825 750449, — Buxted Rec. Ground, Framfield Road, Buxted, East Sussex, 01825 732431.

B.A.C. PRESTON — West Lancs — 2 — Mr F Heaton — 22 Mill Lane, Fulwood, Preston, Lancs, PR2 2HD, 01772 724751 — BAC Sports Ground, South Meadow Lane, Preston, Lancs, 01772 464351.

B.E.A.D.S. — Teesside — Mr Dave Kane — 27 Edgeworth Court, Hemlington, Middlesbrough, Cleveland, TS8 9EP, 01642 596559, — Beechwood/Easterside, Spts Club, Marton Rd, Middlesbrough, Cleveland, 01642 311304.

B.P. LLANDARCY — Welsh — 2 — Mr Tony Williams — 17 Clos Glanlliw, Swansea, West Glamorgan, SA4 1DW, 01792 897205 B:322628, — B.P. Football Club, B.P. Sports Ground, Llandarcy, West Glamorgan, 01792 812036.

B.R.S.A. RETFORD — Lincs — Mr Mick Keeling — 18 Rutland Road, Retford, Nottinghamshire, DN22 7HF, 01777 703929 — B.R.S.A. Retford FC, Badworth Road, Retford, Nottinghamshire.

B.S.C. REDCAR WORKS — Teesside — Mr David Collins — 23 Welland Road, Redcar, Cleveland, TS10 1NR, 01642 491547, — B.S.C. Spts & Social, Dormanstown, Redcar, Cleveland, 01642 486691.

CADDINGTON — South Midlands — 1 — Leigh Glenister — 14 Elaine Gardens, Woodside, Luton, Bedfordshire, LU1 4DL, 01582 30502 — Caddington Rec Gd, Manor Rd, Caddington, 01582 450151.

CAERAU ATHLETIC — Welsh — 2 — Mr David Lewis — 19a Hermon Road, Caerau, Mid-Glamorgan, CF34 0ST, 01656 734388 — Caerau Football Grnd, Humphreys Terrace, Caerau, Mid-Glamorgan, 01656 732471.

CAERLEON — Welsh — 2 — Mr Ken Alden — 2 Conifer Close, Caerleon, Gwent, NP6 1RH, 01633 422390 — Caerleon F.C., Cold Bath Road, Caerleon, Gwent, 01633 420074.

CAISTER UNITED — Anglian Combination — Mr B Cork — 38 Upper Grange Crescent — Caister-on-Sea, Great Yarmouth, Norfolk, NR30 5AU, 01493 728988 — Caister P.F., off Allendale Road, Caister-on-Sea, Norfolk.

CALDICOT TOWN — Welsh — 1 — Mr Gordon Lewis — Taflan, 83 Newport Road, Caldicot, Gwent, NP6 4BS, 01291 422035 — Caldicot Town F.C., Jubilee Way, Caldicot, Gwent, 01291 422035.

CALVERTON TOWN — Notts Alliance — 2 — Derek Voce — 20 Ashdale Rd, Arnold, Nottingham, Notts, NG5 8BH, 0115 926 0120, — William Lee Mem Park, Park Rd East, Calverton, Notts, 0115 965 3097.

CAMMELL LAIRD — West Cheshire — 1 — Mr Ray Steele — 46 Croft Avenue, Bromborough, Wirral, L62 2BR, 0151 334 8998 — Kirklands, St Peters Road, Rock Ferry, Merseyside, 0151 645 5991.

CANNOCK CHASE — West Midlands — 1A — Mr Mark Clementson — 79 Stafford Road, Huntington, Cannock, Staffordshire, WS12 4NU, 01543 502177 B:0385 715120, W. Cannock Spts Cnte, Bradbury Lane, Hednesford, Cannock, Staffordshire, WS12 4EP, 01543 422141/425418.

CAPENHURST — West Cheshire — 1 — Mr Martin Williams — 157 Hope Farm Road, Great Sutton, South Wirral, L66 2TJ, 0151 339 8935 — Capenhurst Spts Grnd, Capenhurst Lane, Capenhurst, Merseyside, 0151 339 4101x613.

CARDIFF CIVIL SERVICE — Welsh — 1 — R A Fry — 4 Fairmead Court, Fairwater Court, Cardiff, South Glamorgan, CF, 01222 566762 B:880222, — Sanatorium Road, Leckwith, Cardiff, South Glamorgan, 01222 341181.

CARDIFF CORINTHIANS — Welsh — 1 — Mr Gerry Thomas — 9 Palace Road, Llandaff, Cardiff, South Glamorgan, CF5 2AF, 01222 212869 — Riverside Ground, Through Station Road, Radyr, Cardiff , South Glamorgan, 01222 843407.

CARIBBEAN SPORTS — Sheffield — P — Ashley Richards — 34 Louth Road, Greystones, Sheffield, South Yorkshire, S11 7AW, 0114 268 5314 B:269 3095 — The Common, Ecclesfield, Sheffield, South Yorkshire, S30 3WL.

CARLISLE CITY — Northern Alliance — P — D Ivison — 40 Skiddaw Road, Carlisle, Cumbria, CA2 5OS, 01228 316654 — Carlisle City F.C., Sheepmout Spts Cmplx, Carlisle, Cumbria, 01228 26569.

CARLISLE GILLFORD PARK — Northern Alliance — P — B Allen — 10 Rudchester Close, Sandsfield Park, Carlisle, Cumbria, 01228 26113 — Gillford F.C., Gillford Park, Carlisle, Cumbria, 01228 26449.

CARLTON ATHLETIC — West Yorkshire — P — R Hargreaves — 11 Newton Drive, Outwood, Wakefield, WF1 3HZ, 01924 826141 — Carlton Cricket Club, Town Street, Carlton, 0113 282 1114.

CARLTON D.C. — Notts Alliance — 2 — Robert Huckerby — 30 Vernon Avenue, Carlton, Nottingham, Notts, NG4 3FX, 0115 955 9120, — Carlton Hill Rec Gd, Carlton, Nottingham, Notts.

CARNFORTH RANGERS — West Lancs — 2 — Mr K Webster — 110 North Rd, Carnforth, Lancs, LA5 9LX, 01524 735322 b 0589 210528 — Close to town centre, .

CASTLE CARY — Somerset — 1 — Mr Charles Pike — Homedale, Weymouth Road, Evercreech, Somerset, BA4 6JB, 01749 830819 — Castle Cary F.C., Donald Pither Mem PF, Castle Cary, Somerset, 01963 351538.

CASTROL SOCIAL — West Cheshire — 2 — Mr Dave Bebbington — 490 Overpool Road, Whitby, Ellesmere Port, South Wirral, L66 2JJ, 0151 357 1979 B:01244 218201, — Castrol Spts & S.C., Chester Road, Whitby, Ellesmere Port, South Wirral, 0151 355 1730.

CHALFONT WASPS — Chiltonian — 1 — I Phillips — Stevens Mead, The Green, Chalfont St Giles, Buckinghamshire, HP8 4QA, 01494 875066, — Playing Fields, Bowstridge Lane, Chalfont St Giles, Buckinghamshire, HP8 4DF, 01494 875050.

CHARNOCK RICHARD — West Lancs — 1 — Graham Randle — 63 Broad Oak Lane, Penwortham, Preston, Lancs, PR1 0UY, 01772 496782 Mob 0831 880450 — Charter Lane, Charnock Richard, Lancs, 01257 794288.

CHEADLE HEATH NOMADS — Mid-Cheshire — 1 — George Gibbons — 3 Hurley Drive, Cheadle Hulme, Stockport, Cheshire, SK8 6DH, 0161 485 1343 B 0161 485 7694 — The Heath, Norbreck Ave, Cheadle, Cheshire, 0161 282 6574.

CHECKENDON SPORTS — Reading — S — Ernie Smith — 10 Emmens Close, Checkendon, Reading, Berkshire, RG8 0TU, 01491 681575, — playing Fields, Checkendon, Reading, Berkshire.

CHEDDAR — Somerset — 2 — Mr Mark Higginbotham — 2 Mewswell Drive, Cheddar, Somerset, BS27 3LL, 01934 744102 — Bowdens Park, Draycott Road, Cheddar, Somerset, 01934 743736.

CHELTENHAM SARACENS — Hellenic — 1 — Mr R Attwood — 179 Arle Rd, Cheltenham, Gloucestershire, GL51 8LJ, 01242 515855 — Petersfield Park, Tewkesbury Rd, Cheltenham, Glos, 01242 584134.

CHESLYN HAY — Midland Combination — 1 — Mr Ivor Osborne — 16 Littlewood Lane, Cheslyn Hay, Walsall, WS6 7EJ, 01922 414755 — Oak Park, Lichfield Road, Walsall, West Midlands, 01543 361084.

CHESSINGTON & HOOK UNITED — Surrey — P — Mr Alan Warwick — 38 Hartfield Road, Chessington, Surrey, KT9 2PW, 0181 397 1843 — Chessington/Hook FC, Chalky Lane, Chessington, Surrey, 01372 729892.

CHESTER NOMADS — Mid-Cheshire — 2 — Ritz Ritzema — 22 Cross Green, Upton, Chester, Cheshire, CH2 1QR, 01244 379791 B 01244 347972, — Garrison Ground, Eaton Rd, Handbridge, Cheshire.

CHIPPERFIELD CORINTHIANS — Herts — P — Mr Stephen Hall — 3 Rowley Close, Oxhey, Watford, Hertfordshire, WD1 4DT, 01923 253803 — Chipperfield Cor. FC, Queens Street, Chipperfield, Hertfordshire, 01923 269554.

CHIPSTEAD (KENT) — Kent County — 2W — Mr David R Houston — 31 Chevening Road, Chipstead, near Sevenoaks, Kent, TN13 2RZ, 01732 452798 — Chevening Road, Chipstead, near Sevenoaks, Kent, TN13 2RZ.

CHISLEHURST — Kent County — 2W — Mr Harry W Martin — 3 Berwick Crescent, Sidcup, Kent, DA15 8HU, 0181 302 3542 — Flamingo Park, A20 (London Bound), Sidcup By-Pass, Kent.

CHOBHAM — Surrey — P — Mrs Daisy Walley — 8 Brook Green, Chertsey Road, Chobham, Surrey, GU24 8PN, 01276 858039 — Chobham Rec. Ground, Station Road, Chobham, Surrey, 01276 857876.

CHORLTON TOWN — Mid-Cheshire — 1 — Jim Calderbank — 21 South Meade, Timperley, Altrincham, Cheshire, WA15 6QL, 0161 959 1156 B 0161 969 4600 — Harry Dalton PF, Brantingham Rd, Chorlton.

CHRISTLETON — West Cheshire — 1 — Mr Ken Price — 35 Canadian Avenue, Hoole, Chester, Cheshire, CH2 3HQ, 01244 313513 — Little Heath, Christleton, Chester, Cheshire, 01244 332153.

CHURCHILL CLUB — Somerset — 2 — Mr Neil Hickman — Dolberrow, New Road, Churchill, North Somerset, BS19 5NW, 01934 852858 — Churchill F.C., Ladymead Lane, Churchill, North Somerset.

CIPPENHAM VILLAGE — Chiltonian — 2 — A Duncan — 29 Mainprize Road, Bullbrook, Bracknell, Berkshire, RG12 2RE, 01344 489425, — The Green, Cippenham, Slough, Berkshire, 01628 660885.

CIRENCESTER UNITED — Hellenic — 1 — Mr G Varley — 95 Vaisey Rd, Cirencester, Gloucestershire, GL7 2JW, 01285 657836 b 01285 862617 — Four Acres, Chesterton Lane, Cirencester, Glos, 01285 885460.

CITY OF NORWICH S.O.B.U. — Anglian Combination — Mr N Podolski — 3 Aspen Way, Cringleford, Norwich, Norfolk, NR4 6UA, 01603 502559, — C.N.S.O.B.U., Britannia Barracks, Norwich, Norfolk.

CITY & SHERWOOD HOSPITALS — Notts Alliance — 1 — Alan Bird — 72 Bilborough Rd, Bilborough, Nottingham, Notts, NG8 4DW, 0115 928 5507 — M.O.D., Chilwell, Nottingham, Notts, 0115 925 4811.

CLANDOWN — Somerset — 2 — Tracey Pearson — 37 Goldney Way, Temple Cloud, near Bristol, North Somerset, BS18 5DU, 01761 453573 — Thyme Field, Clandown, near Bath, North Somerset, 01761 434274.

CLANFIELD — Hellenic — 1 — Mr J Osborne — 70 Lancut Rd, Witney, Oxfordshire, OX8 5AQ, 01993 771631, Radcot Road, Clanfield, Oxon, 01367 810314.

CLEEVE WEST TOWN — Somerset — 2 — Mr Stephen Minns — 11 Barnards Close, Yatton, Bristol, North Somerset, BS19 4HZ, 01934 833008 B:0117 963 9389 — King George 5th P.F., Meeting House Lane, Cleeve, North Somerset, 01934 832173.

CLEVEDON UNITED — Somerset — P — Mr Dudley White — 2 Orchard Road, Clevedon, North Somerset, BS21 6JT, 01275 872978 — Clevedon United F.C., Coleridge Vale, Clevedon, North Somerset, 01275 871878.

CLIFTON — Notts Alliance — 1 — Keith Elliott — 61 Greencroft, Clifton Estate, Nottingham, Notts, NG11 8GJ, 0115 921 5401, — Green Lane, Clifton Estate, Nottingham, Notts, 0115 984 4903.

CLIFTON ROVERS — Sheffield — 2 — Mr Stephen Gorrill — 11 Broom Road, Broom, Rotherham, South Yorkshire, S65 2SN, 01709 518801 B:01246 26026 — 1, Clifton Rovers F.C., Silverwood M.W., Rotherham, South Yorkshire.

CLIPSTONE WELFARE — Central Midlands — P — Mr Barry Clarke — 40 Church Road, Clipstone, Mansfield, Nottinghamshire, NG21 9DG, 01623 640829, — Lido Ground, Clipstone West West, Mansfield, Notts, 01623 655674.

CLUTTON — Somerset — 3 — Mr Harry Marsland — 9 Maynard Terrace, Clutton, near Bristol, North Somerset, BS18 4PL, 0761 453064 — Warwick Fields, Upper Bristol Rd A37, Clutton, nr Bristol, North Somerset.

COALVILLE — Leics — 1 — Mr Robert Brooks — 17 Ashland Drive, Coalville, Leicestershire, LE67 3NH, 01530 833269 — Owen Str. Spts Grnd, Owen Street, Coalville, Leicestershire, 01530 833365.

CODICOTE — Herts — 1 — Mr Richard Hunt — 68a Vaughan Road, Stotfold, Hitchin, Hertfordshire, SG5 4EN, 01462 835623 — John Clements Mem Gd, Bury Lane, Codicote, Hertfordshire.

COLDEN COMMON — Hampshire — 1 — Mr Mark Budden — 44 Orchard Close, Colden Common, Winchester, Hampshire, SO21 1ST, 01962 713813 B:01703 613151, — Colden Common Rec., Main Road, Colden Common, Hampshire, 01962 712365.

COLLINGHAM — Central Midlands — P — Mr G Williams — 47 Dukes End, Collingham, Newark, Nottinghamshire, NG23 7LD, 01636 892189 B:893175 — Collingham FC, Station Rd, Collingham, Newark, Notts, 01636 892303.

COLNEY HEATH — Herts — P — Mr Martin Marlborough — 16 Meadway, Colney Heath, St Albans, Hertfordshire, AL4 0PT, 01727 824820 — Pavilion Rec. Ground, High Str, Colney Hth, St Albans, Hertfordshire, 01727 826188.

COLTISHALL H.V. — Anglian Combination — 1 — Mr N R Everett — What's On, Church Street, Coltishall, Norwich, Norfolk, NR12 7DJ, 01603 736211 — Rectory Road, Coltishall, Norwich, Norfolk.

COMPTON — Hampshire — 3 — Mr Mick Allerton — 28 Keats Close, Olivers Battery, Winchester, Hampshire, SO22 4HR, 01962 869574 — Shepherds Lane, Compton Down, Winchester, Hampshire, 01962 712083.

CONEY HALL — Surrey — P — Mr Bill Lennox — 1 Southway, Hayes, Kent, BR2 7NR, 0181 325 0298 B:0171 895 5754 — Coney Hall F.C., Tie Pigs Lane, West Wickham, Kent, 0181 462 9103.

CONGRESBURY — Somerset — 1 — Mr Irving Prowse — Wood View, Wrington Road, Congresbury, near Bristol, North Somerset, BS19 5AN, 01934 832004 B:01275 858383, Broadstones P.F., Stonewell Lane, Congresbury, North Somerset, 01934 832150.

COOKHAM DEAN — Reading — S — Rory Gavin — 46 Chiltern Rd, Maidenhead, Berkshire, SL6 1XA, 01628 832997 B:01235 821177 — Alfred Major Rec Gd, Hillcrest Ave, Cookham Rise, Berkshire.

CORESTONE SERVICES — West Midlands — 1A — Kamlesh Patel — 34 Wyrley Road, Wednesfield, Wolverhampton, West Midlands, WV11 3NY, 01902 632644 — Wolverhampton Utd FC, Prestwood Road West, Wednesfield, W'pton, West Midlands, 01902 730881.

CORTON — Anglian Combination — Mr P Allison — 9 West Side Close, Lowestoft, Suffolk, NR32 4NS, 01502 508626 — Village Playing Fld, Long Lane, Corton, Suffolk.

COSTESSEY SPORTS — Anglian Combination — Mr A Page — 57 Sunny Grove, New Costessey, Norwich, Norfolk, NR5 0EJ, 01603 742749, Breckland Park, Breckland Road, New Costessey, Norfolk.

COTGRAVE COLLIERY WELFARE — Notts Alliance — S — Kevin Whitehead — 51 Crosshill, Cotgrave, Nottingham, Notts, 0115 989 4043, Cotgrave Welfare, Cotgrave, Nottingham, Notts.

COTMANHAY — MRA — 2 — Mr Christopher C Colley — 47 Pavilion Road, Cotmanhay, Ilkeston, Derbyshire, DE7 8UQ, 0115 930 2691 M:0589 466977 — , Pavilion Road P.F., Cotmanhay, Ilkeston, Derbyshire.

COTTESMORE AMATEURS — Leics — P — Mr Kevin Nimmons — 17 Redwing Close, Oakham, Rutland, LE15 6DA, 01572 724582 B:01780 62351 — Rogues Park, Main Street, Cottesmore, Rutland, 01572 813486.

COTTINGHAM — United Counties — 1 — Mr V Keefe — 24 Westbury Walk, Corby, Northants, NN18 0AE, 01536 202114 B:267438 — Cottingham F.C., Berryfield Road, Cottingham, Northants, 01536 770051.

COVIES — Hampshire — 3 — Mr John Marchment — 4 Linstead Road, Cove, Farnborough, Hampshire, GU14 9HH, 01276 34254 — Queens Road Rec., North Camp, Farnborough, Hampshire.

COXLODGE SOCIAL CLUB — Northern Alliance — 2 — L W Ramsey — 28 Coxlodge Road, Gosforth, Newcastle-upon-Tyne, Tyne & Wear, NE3 3UZ, 0191 285 0782 — Coxlodge Comm Ground, Gosforth, Newcastle-upon-Tyne, Tyne & Wear.

CRAWLEY GREEN SPORTS — South Midlands — 1 — Neil Ludlow — 159 Cutenhoe Rd, Luton, Beds, LU1 3NQ, 01582 486802 — Recreation Gd, Crawley Green Rd, Luton, Beds, 01582 451058.

CROMER TOWN — Anglian Combination — Mr J R Baker — 32 Salisbury Road, Cromer, Norfolk, NR27 0BW, 01263 514405, — Cabbell Park, Mill Road, Cromer, Norfolk, 01263 512185.

CROMFORD — MRA — 1 — Mr Keith S Bonsall — 23 Tor View Rise, Cromford, Derbyshire, DE4 3RA, 01629 822759 B:733621x403, — Cromford Meadows, Mill Road, Cromford, Derbyshire.

CROMFORD JUNIORS — MRA — 1 — Mr Kenneth Doxey — 6a Water Lane, Wirksworth, Derbyshire, DE4 4DZ, 01629 822035 B:823948 — Lea Green, Lea, Matlock, Derbyshire, 01629 534561.

CROXLEY GUILD ASTRALS — Herts — 1 — Mr David Rickman — 18 Tudor Walk, Watford, Hertfordshire, WD2 4PA, 01923 490836 — Croxley Guild of Spt, The Green, Croxley Green, Hertfordshire, 01923 770534.

CROYDON MUNICIPAL OFFICERS — Surrey — P — Mr Tony Osborn — 15 Long Lane, Croydon, Surrey, CR0 7AR, 0181 656 6120 B:0973 367850 — Russell Hill R'voir, Pampisford Road, Purley, Surrey, 0181 660 9720.

CUFFLEY — Herts — P — Mr David Chapman — 51 Woodlands Road, Hertford, Hertfordshire, SG13 7JF, 01992 582358 — King George's P.F., Northaw Road East, Cuffley, Hertfordshire, 01707 875395.

CULLOMPTON RANGERS — Devon — Mr K Norman — 37 Headwear Rd, Cullompton, Devon, EX15 1NN, 01884 33539 — Cullompton FC, Speeds Meadow, Cullompton, Devon, 01884 33090.

DALTON UNITED — West Lancs — 1 — G Turner — 3 Yarl Meadow, Rossefield, Barrow-in-Furness, Cumbria, LA13 9SJ, 01229 831287 B 01229 873773, Railway Meadow, Beckside Road, Dalton-in-Furness, Cumbria, 01229 462799.

DARTMOUTH UNITED — Devon — Debbie Smith — 3 Archway Drive — Dartmouth, Devon, TQ6 9TE, 01803 833791 — Dartmouth Utd FC, Longcross, Dartmouth, Devon, 01803 832902.

DAVY — Sheffield — 1 — Mr John Watson — 16 Greengate Lane, Woodhouse, Sheffield, South Yorkshire, S13 7PZ, 0114 254 8397 B:244 9971x4860, — Davy Spts & Soc Club, Prince of Wales Road, Darnall, Sheffield, South Yorkshire.

DE HAVILLAND — South Midlands — 1 — Mr R Ridgway — 85 Garden Avenue, Hatfield, Hertfordshire, AL10 8LH, 0707 267327 — De Havilland Sports, Comet Way, Hatfield, Herts, 01707 263204.

DENHAM UNITED — Chiltonian — P — R Lee — 7 Newcroft Close, Hillingdon, Middlesex, UB8 3RH, 01895 254207, — Denham United F.C., Oxford Road, Denham, Buckinghamshire, 01895 238717.

DEPORTIVO GALICIA — Middx — 1 — Mr Eddie Cagigao — 26 Bedford Road, Harrow, Middlesex, HA1 4LZ, 0181 863 0072, — Burlington Danes, School, Du Cane Road, London, W12.

DERBY ARMS — MRA — 2 — Mr John Draper — 34 Milward Road, Loscoe, Heanor, Derbyshire, DE75 7JX, 01773 762747 B:01332 676336 — Lockton Avenue P.F., Lockton Avenue, Heanor, Derbyshire.

DERBY ROLLS ROYCE — Central Midlands — P — Mr A Burns — 67 Field Rise, Littleover, Derby, Derbyshire, DE23 7DF, 01332 767332 — Rolls Royce Rec Gd, Moor Lane, Derby, Derbys, 01332 249167.

DEREHAM TOWN — Anglian Combination — P — Mr M Henman — 17 Hillcroft Avenue, Toftwood, Dereham, Norfolk, NR19 1NF, 01362 692242 — Aldiss Park, Norwich Road, Dereham, Norfolk, NR20 3AL, 01362 693677.

DICKLEBURGH — Anglian Combination — Mr T J Leeder — Trev-Icia, Norwich Road, Dickleburgh, Diss, Norfolk, IP21 4NR, 01379 741444 — Harvey Lane P.F., Dickleburgh, Diss, Norfolk.

DILHAM — Anglian Combination — Mr K Sidell — No. 1 Ivy Farm, Dilham, North Walsham, Norfolk, NR28 9PN, 01692 536263 — Recreation Ground, near Cross Keys P.H., Dilham, Nth Walsham, Norfolk, 01692 536144.

DITCHINGHAM ROVERS — Anglian Combination — Mr C Simpson — 20 Beccles Road, Bungay, Suffolk, NR35 1HY, 01986 894841 — Wainford Road, Pirnough Street, Ditchingham, Norfolk.

DORMANS ATHLETIC — Teesside — Mr Don Hall — 52 Westbourne Road, Linthorpe, Middlesbrough, Cleveland, TS5 5BJ, 01642 817771, Dormans Ath. Club, Oxford Road, Middlesbrough, Cleveland, 01642 817099.

DOUGLAS HIGH SCHOOL OLD BOYS — Isle of Man — Mr Malcolm Lewis — 14 Beech Tree Avenue, Birch Hill Park, Onchan, Isle of Man, IM3 3QM, 01624 620928 B:683776 F:68684, The Bowl, King George V Park, Douglas, Isle of Man.

DRAYCOTT — MRA — 1 — Mr John Capps — 67 Walter Street, Draycott, Derby, Derbyshire, DE72 3NU, 01332 873451 — Hopwell Road, Draycott, Derby, Derbyshire.

DRAYTON WANDERERS — Chiltonian — 1 — D Mitcham — 30b Bathurst Walk, Iver, Buckinghamshire, SL0 9AZ, 01753 655013 — Cowley Rec. Ground, Cowley High Road, Cowley, nr Uxbridge, Middlesex, 01895 258269.

DUNDRY ATHLETIC — Somerset — 3 — Mr Steve Saunders — 74 Meadowside Drive, Whitchurch, Bristol, BS14 0NS, 01275 830085 — Dundry Playing Field, Crabtree Lane, Dundry, near Bristol, North Somerset, 0117 964 5536.

DUNTON GREEN — Kent County — 3W — Mrs Joyce Williams — 20 Dane Road, Otford, Sevenoaks, Kent, TN14 5NN, 01959 522892 — London Road Rec., Dunton Green, Sevenoaks, Kent.

D.C.A. BASINGSTOKE — Chiltonian — P — Mr Mick Davis — 451 Abbey Road, Popley Abbeys, Basingstoke, Hampshire, RG24 9EN, 01256 468873 M:0385 903424, Whiteditch P.F., Sherbourne Road, Basingstoke, Hampshire, 01256 814618 club:844866.

EAGLEY — West Lancs — 1 — MJ Hackin — 260 Darwen Rd, Bromley Cross, Bolton, Lancs, BL7 9JG, 01204 595863, — Eagley Sports Comp, Dunscar Bridge, Bolton, Lancs, 01204 306830.

EALING ASSYRIANS — Middx — 1 — Wilson Jaso — 1 Locarno Road, Greenford, Middlesex, UB6 8SN, 0181 578 6707 — Osterley Spts & Soc., Tentelow Lane, Southall, Middlesex, 0181 574 3774.

EARL SHILTON ALBION — Leics — 1 — Mr Adrian Knight — 19 Waverly Road, Blaby, Leicestershire, LE8 3HH, 0116 278 5042 B:0116 260 0081 — oneycroft Park, New Street, Earl Shilton, Leicestershire, 01455 844277.

EASINGTON SPORTS — Hellenic — 1 — Terry Horley — 25 Bath Road, Banbury, Oxfordshire, OX16 0TU, 01295 252939 — Addington Rd, Easington Estate, Oxon, 01295 257006.

EAST BERGHOLT UNITED — S&I — S — Mr Daryl Butcher — 23 Gravel Pit Lane, Brantham, Manningtree, Suffolk, CO11 1NX, 01206 391953 — East Bergholt Utd FC, Gandish Road, East Bergholt, Suffolk, (Carriers Arms 01206 298392).

EAST HARLING — Anglian Combination — Mrs D Jubb — 7 Drakes Close, East Harling, Norwich, Norfolk, NR16 2JB, 01953 717128, — Memorial Fields, Church Street, East Harling, Norfolk, 01953 718251.

EAST LEAKE ATHLETIC — Notts Alliance — 2 — Andrew Fletcher — 35 Manor Farm Meadow, East Leake, Loughborough, Leics, LE12 6LL, 01509 852087, — Costock Rd, East Leake, Loughborough, Leics.

ECCLESFIELD RED ROSE — Sheffield — P — Mr Alf Goodison — 202 High Street, Ecclesfield, Sheffield, South Yorkshire, S30 3XF, 0114 246 8286 — Civil Serv. Spts Grd, Green Lane, Ecclesfield, South Yorkshire.

EDENBRIDGE UNITED — Kent County — 2W — Mr Chris Bradford — 109 New Farthingdale, Dormansland, near Lingfield, Surrey, RH7 6RF, 01342 832854 B:01732 865322, Recreation Ground, Lingfield Road, Edenbridge, Kent, 01732 862435.

ELBURTON VILLA — Devon — Steve Ware — 34 Cofton Hill, Cockwood, Starcross, Devon, 01626 890464, Elburton Villa, Haye Rd, Elburton, Devon, 01752 480025.

ELLIOTT STAR — Herts — P — Mr Ray Capper — 28 Alban Crescent, Boreham Wood, Hertfordshire, WD6 5JF, 0181 207 3940 — G.E.C. Sports Ground, Rowley Lane, Boreham Wood, Hertfordshire, 0181 953 5087.

ELSECAR MARKET HOTEL — Sheffield — 2 — Mr David Kilner — 12 Wentworth Road, Elsecar, Barnsley, South Yorkshire, S74 8EP, 01226 — Armroyd Lane, Elsecar, Barnsley, South Yorkshire, S74 8EP, 01226 749120.

ELTHAM PALACE — Kent County — 2W — Mr Darren Walker — 24 Sussex Road, Sidcup, Kent, DA14 6LG, 0181 302 6514 — Beaver Wood Lodge, Beaverwood Road, Chislehurst, Kent, 0181 300 0635.

EMBERTON — South Midlands — 1 — Mr R L Dugdale — 9 Stone Court, West Lane, Emberton, nr Olney, Buckinghamshire, MK46 5ND, 01234 711004, — The Playing Field, Emberton, Nr Olney, Beds, 01234 713748.

EMERALDS — Herts — 1 — Mr Mick Wigg — 1 Flatfield Road, Bennetts End, Hemel Hempstead, Hertfordshire, HP3 8EX, 01442 394442, — Watford Irish Club, Wiggenhall Road, Watford, Hertfordshire, 01923 462332(bar).

ENGLEFIELD GREEN ROVERS — Chiltonian — 1 — A Beasley — 8a Manorcroft Road, Egham, Surrey, TW20 9LU, 01784 435042 B:0956 247115 — Engefield Gn Rvrs FC, Coopers Hill Spts Gd, Englefield Green, Berkshire.

EPWORTH TOWN LC — Lincs — Mr Geoff Yeardley — 9 Hayfield Close — Haxey, near Doncaster, North Lincs, DN9 2NT, 01427 753257 — South Axholme School, Burnham Road, Epworth, North Lincs.

ESSO FAWLEY — Hampshire — 2 — Mr Alan Haws — 40 Hollybank Road, Hythe, Southampton, Hampshire, SO45 5FQ, 01703 843402, — Esso Recreation Club, Long Lane, Holbury, Hampshire, 01703 893750.

ETON WICK — Chiltonian — P — Mr Neil Morrell — Kingsway Utd Reform Ch., Church Street, Slough, Buckinghamshire, SL1 1SZ, 01753 823822, — Haywards Meadow, Eton Wick, Slough, Berkshire, 01753 852749.

EVERGREEN — Herts — 1 — Mr Dennis McCrystal — 76 Woodmere Avenue, Watford, Hertfordshire, WD2 4LW, 01923 465750 — Evergreen F.C., Southway, Abbots Langley, Hertfordshire, 01923 267812.

EX BLUES — Kent County — P — Mr Malcolm H D Harvey — 29 Crown Lane, Bromley, Kent, BR2 9PG, 0181 464 4815 — Ex Blues F.C., Wellcome, Beckenham, Kent.

EYNSFORD — Kent County — 1W — Mr Eddie Walkling — 76 Pollyhaugh, Eynsford, Kent, DA4 0HF, 01322 863673, — Harrow Meadow, Bower Lane, High St, Eynsford, Kent.

FARLEIGH ROVERS — Surrey — P — Mrs Valerie Willcocks — 238 The Glade, Shirley, Croydon, Surrey, CR0 7UJ, 0181 406 3494 — Parsonage Field, Harrow Road, Farleigh, Surrey, 01884 626483.

FARNBOROUGH OLD BOYS GUILD — Kent County — 2W — Mr Victor Farrow — 17 Arundel Drive, Orpington, Kent, BR6 9JF, 01689 832966, — Farnborough Spts Cl., High Street, Farnborough, Kent, 01689 86294.

FENISCOWLES — West Lancs — 1 — A L Akeroyd — 12 Quakerfields, Darwen, Lancs, BB3 OD4, 01254 706931, — Livsey Branch Rd, Feniscowles, Lancs, 01254 208210.

FERNDALE ATHLETIC — Welsh — 3 — K J Jones — 12 Graig Terrace, Ferndale, Rhondda, CF43 3EU, 01443 756214, — Ferndale Athletic FC, Recreation Ground, Maerdy, Rhondda.

FIELDS PARK PONTLLANFRAITH — Welsh — 2 — D P Chiplin — 1 Williams Street, Ynysddu, Newport, Gwent, NP1 7GY, 01495 200349, — stwyn Park, Pontllanffraith, Blackwood, Gwent, 01495 224512.

FINCHAMPSTEAD — Chiltonian — P — R Bradley — 14 Webb Court, Wokingham, Berkshire, RG40 5YR, 01734 892908 — Memorial Ground, Finchampstead Park, Finchampstead, Berkshire, 01734 732890.

FISHBURN PARK — Teesside — Mr Ian Lai — 9 Pinewood Close, Whitby, North Yorkshire, YO21 1LR, 01947 600066 B:602021, — Tur.   .l Ground, Upgang Lane, Whitby, North Yorkshire, 01947 603193.

FLAMSTEAD — South Midlands — 1 — Mrs Susan Hayward — Greenways, Old Watling Street, Flamstead, St Albans, Hertfordshire, AL3 8HN, 01582 841213 — Flamstead Sports Ass, Friendless Lane, Flamstead, Herts, 01582 841307.

FLEET SPURS — Hampshire — 2 — Mr Clive Filkins — 5 Byron Close, Fleet, Hampshire, GU13 9QD, 01252 627385 F:01958 228350, — Fleet Spurs F.C., Ancells Farm, Fleet, Hampshire.

FLEETDOWN UNITED — Kent County — 2W — Mr Brian Wakeman — 670 Princes Road, Dartford, Kent, DA2 6JG, 01322 228680 B:392550 — Wood Lane, Green St., Green Road, South Darenth, Kent, 01322 221006.

FLEETLANDS — Hampshire — 1 — Mr David Bell — 72 White Hart Lane, Portchester, Fareham, Hampshire, PO16 9BQ, 01705 843869 — Fleetlands F.C., Lederle Lane, Gosport, Hampshire, 01329 239723.

FLEETWOOD HESKETH — West Lancs — 2 — Mr B Charnock — 6 Parbold Close, Burscough, Lancs, L40 7TS, 01704 895588, Fylde Rd, Southport, Merseyside, 01704 27968.

FLIGHT REFUELLING, — Dorset — Harry Doyle — 27 Fairview Crescent, Broadstone, Poole, Dorset, BH18 9AP, 01202 698393 — Merley Park, Merley Lane, Wimborne, Dorset, 01202 885773.

FOREST — Sussex County — 3 — Mrs Gill Holtquist — 117 Ifield Drive, Ifield, Crawley, West Sussex, RH11 0EA, 01293 522846 — Roffey Spts & S.C., Spooners Road, Roffey, West Sussex, 01403 210221.

FOREST HALL — Northern Alliance — 1 — G Willis — 4 Lythe Way, Benton, Newcastle-upon-Tyne, Tyne & Wear, NE12 8LP, 0191 215 1226 — Palmersville Com Ctr, Forest Hall, Newcastle-upon-Tyne, Tyne & Wear, 0191 268 7081.

FOREST OLD BOYS — Reading — S — Bob Hulett — 10 Ramsbury Drive, Earley, Reading, Berkshire, RG6 7RT, 01734 663514 M:0374 230964 — Holme Park, Sonning Lane, Sonning, Berkshire.

FOSSE IMPS — Leics — 1 — Mr Ivan Colbourne — 55 Harrowgate Drive, Birstall, Leicestershire, LE4 3GQ, 0116 267 1424, — Co-op Ground, Birstall Road, Leicester, Leicestershire, 0116 267 4059.

FOUR MARKS — Hampshire — 3 — Mr Simon C Annetts — 5 Thorn Court, Four Marks, near Alton, Hampshire, GU34 5BY, 01420 562570 B:0181 759 8929 — Uplands Lane Rec., Brisslands Lane, Four Marks, Hampshire.

FRAMLINGHAM TOWN — S&I — S — Mrs Fiona Whatling — 46 College Road, Framlingham, Woodbridge, Suffolk, IP13 9ES, 01728 723524 — Sports Field, Badlingham Road, Framlingham, Suffolk, 01728 724038.

FRANKLANDS VILLAGE — Sussex County — 3 — Mrs Linsey Worsfold — 151a Franklands Village, Haywards Heath, West Sussex, RH16 3RF, 01444 416475 — Hardy Memorial P.F., Franklands Village, Haywards Heath, West Sussex, 01444 440138.

FRECHEVILLE COMMUNITY ASSOC. — Sheffield — P — Mr David Taylor — 75 Gleadless Avenue, Sheffield, South Yorkshire, S12 2QG, 0114 264 9754, — Frecheville C.A., Silkstone Road, Sheffield, South Yorkshire, S12.

FRECKLETON — West Lancs — 1 — Mrs Lorainne O'Reilly — 37 Wades Croft, Freckleton, Preston, Lancs, PR4 1SU, 01772 634773 — Hodgson Memorial Gd, Bush Lane, Freckleton, Lancs, 01772 679139.

FRY CLUB — Somerset — P — Mr Alan Taylor — Laburnum Cottage, Cockers Hill, Compton Dando, Bristol, BS18 4JX, 01761 490350, — Fry Club, Somerdale, Keynsham, Bristol, 0117 937 6500/6501.

FULWOOD AMATEURS — West Lancs — 1 — Mr LMC Waller — 10 Woodlands Crescent, Barton, Preston, Lancs, PR3 5HB, 01772 864019 — Nr Ingol,0.5mile M6, .

GARSTANG — West Lancs — 2 — Mr S G Freeman — 116 Dorchester Rd, Garstang, Preston, Lancs, PR3 1EE, 01995 602514 B0125325212 X2123 — Riverside, Off High Street, Garstang, Lancs, 01995 601586.

GARW — Welsh — 3 — Mr Ray Smiles — 48 Blaengarw Road, Blaengarw, Bridgend, Mid-Glamorgan, 01656 870487 — Garw Football Club, Blandy Park, Pontycymmer, Mid-Glamorgan, 01656 870438(matchdays only).

GEDLING MINERS WELFARE — Notts Alliance — 1 — Maureen Chambers — 8 Fraser Rd, Carlton, Nottingham, Notts, NG14 1NJ, 0115 961 2994 — Plains Rd, Mapperley, Nottingham, Notts, 0115 926 6300.

GENERAL CHEMICALS — West Cheshire — 1 — Mr Vincent O'Brien — 1 Martindale Grove, Runcorn, Cheshire, WA7 2TU, 01928 577810, — Pavilions Club, Sandy Lane, Weston Point, Runcorn, 01928 590508.

GIFFEN WHEATHAMPSTEAD — Herts — 1 — Mr John Welch — 26 St Edmunds Walk, St Albans, Hertfordshire, AL4 0BJ, 01727 868827 — Lemsford Vill. Hall, Brocket Road, Lemsford, Hertfordshire, 01707 333548.

GILLINGHAM TOWN — Dorset — David Ayles — 37 Sylvan Way, Bay Road, Gillingham, Dorset, SP8 4EQ, 01747 822065 — Gillingham Town FC, Hardings Lane, Gillingham, Dorset, 01747 823673.

GLAXO — West Lancs — 2 — Mr M Simpson — 10 Croft Park Grove, Barrow-in-Furness, Cumbria, LA13 9NJ, 01229 870142 b01229582261x2116 — Glaxo Sports Club, North Lonsdale Rd, Ulverston, Cumbria, 01229 582261.

GOSFORTH BOHEMIANS — Northern Alliance — P — B Dale — 118 Newton Road, High Heaton, Newcastle-upon-Tyne, Tyne & Wear, NE7 7HN, 0191 281 1403, Benson Park, Brunton Park Estate, Gosforth, Tyne & Wear.

GOTHAM UNITED — MRA — 1 — Mr Allan Pearson — 3 Holland Close, Gotham, Nottingham, Nottinghamshire, NG11 0JA, 0115 983 0581 B:01332 364299, Memorial P.F., Nottingham Road, Gotham, Nottinghamshire.

GOYTRE UNITED — Welsh — 1 — Mr Boris Suhanski — 20 Goytre Crescent, Port Talbot, West Glamorgan, 01639 886826 — Glenhafod Park, Goytre, Port Talbot, West Glamorgan, 01639 898983.

GRANGE HARLEQUINS — Welsh — 1 — Mr Malcolm Stammers — 26 Eddystone Close, Carlton Gardens, Grangetown, Cardiff, South Glamorgan, CF1 7EB, 01222 667978, Cardiff Ath. Stadium, Leckwith, Cardiff, South Glamorgan, 01222 225345.

GRANGETOWN BOYS CLUB — Teesside — Mr Brian Honeywell — 11 Ambleside Road, Normanby, Middlesbrough, Cleveland, TS6 0DY, 01642 458208 — Grangetown Y.C.C., Trunk Rd, Grangetown, Middlesbrough, Cleveland, 01642 455435.

GRAPES NORTHERN CENTRAL — Sheffield — 1 — Mr Ian Lemons — 6 Champion Road, Shiregreen, Sheffield, South Yorkshire, S5 0JR, 0114 240 3640 B:275 2757 — Civil Serv. Spts Grd, Green Lane, Ecclesfield, South Yorkshire.

GREAT WYRLEY — West Midlands — 1A — Mr Dennis Holford — 79 Broadstone Avenue, Bloxwich, Walsall, West Midlands, WS3 1JA, 01922 493423 — Hazelbrook, Hazel Lane, Gt Wyrley, Walsall, West Midlands, 01922 410366.

GREENWAYS — Kent County — P — Mr William Miller — 14 Cygnet Gardens, Northfleet, Kent, DA11 7DN, 01474 560913, — Beauwater Leis. Club, Nelson Road, Northfleet, Kent, 01474 336456.

GREENWOOD MEADOWS — Notts Alliance — S — Brian Hall — 34 Sullivan Close, Marmion Estate, Nottingham, Notts, NG3 2HX, 0115 958 2459 — Old Lenton Lane, Clifton Bridge, Nottingham, Notts, 0115 986 5913.

GRIMETHORPE MINERS WELFARE — Central Midlands — P — Arthur Gill — 7 Duke Street, Grimethorpe, Barnsley, Grimethorpe, South Yorkshire, 01226 711544, — Welfare Ground, Cemetery Rd, Grimethorpe, Yorks.

GRIMSBY & IMMINGHAM AMATEURS — Lincs — Mr Norman Shackleton — 42 Campden Crescent, Cleethorpes, North Lincs, DN35 7UL, 01472 698351 — Spts & Social Club, Blossom Way, Immingham, North Lincs.

GROVE UNITED — Mid-Cheshire — 1 — Bernard Jordan — 25 Beanleach Rd, Hazel Grove, Stockport, Cheshire, SK7 4LD, 0161 456 2542 — Half Moon Lane, Offerton, Stockport, Cheshire.

GRUNDISBURGH — S&I — S — Mr Malcolm Harris — 70 Post Mill Gardens, Grundisburgh, Woodbridge, Suffolk, IP13 6UP, 01473 735422, — The Playing Field, Grundisburgh, Woodbridge, Suffolk, 01473 738234.

GWYNFI UNITED — Welsh — 3 — Mr David Walters — 144 Jersey Road, Blaengwynfi, Port Talbot, West Glamorgan, SA13 3TF, 01639 851506 B:01656 733431, Gwynfi United A.F.C., Gwynfi Welfare, Blaengwnfi, West Glamorgan, 01639 850313.

G.N. KHALSA — West Yorkshire — P — A Wisdom — 17 Bayswater Terrace, Leeds, LS8 5QL, 0113 235 1445 B 01904 606486 — Prince Phillip Cntre, Scott Hall Avenue, Leeds, HQ 0113 2622380.

G.P.T. — Notts Alliance — 1 — Roger Marshall — Sports Office, GPT, Beeston, Nottingham, Notts, NG9 1LA, 0115 943 3669 — Trent Vale Rd, Beeston, Nottingham, Notts, 0115 925 8320.

HALESWORTH TOWN — S&I — S — Mr Paul Collier — 98 Dukes Drive, Halesworth, Suffolk, IP19 8DR, 01986 872015 — Dairy Hill P.F., Bungay Road, Halesworth, Suffolk, 01986 875564.

HALLEN — Hellenic — 1 — Charmaine Phillips — 145a Station Road, Henbury, Bristol, Avon, BS10 7LZ, 0117 970 1754, — Moorhouse Lane, Hallen, Bristol, 0117 950 2265.

HALLS — Kent County — 3W — Mr Stephen Challis — 2 Princes Avenue, Dartford, Kent, DA2 6NE, 01322 292557 — Princes Golf/Leis Cb, Darenth Road, Dartford, Kent, DA1 1LZ, 01322 276565.

HALSTEAD — Kent County — 2W — Mrs Ann Lynch — 44 Watercroft Road, Halstead, Kent, TN14 7DP, 01959 534509 — Halstead Rec. Ground, Station Road, Halstead, Kent.

HALTWIIISTLE CROWN PAINTS — Northern Alliance — P — R Skeet — 14 Westgate, Haltwhistle, Northumberland, NE49 9AF, 01434 321271 — Bardon Mill Spts Grd, Bardon Mill, Northumberland, (1996-97 only).

HALVERGATE UNITED — Anglian Combination — Mr A Broom — 40 Churchill Road — Great Yarmouth, Norfolk, NR30 4NH, 01493 850451 — Playing Field, Wickhampton Road, Halvergate, Norfolk.

HAMBLE CLUB — Hampshire — 3 — Mr Harry Noice — 55 The Oaks, Bitterne, Southampton, Hampshire, SO19 7RP, 01703 398370 — Mount Pleasant P.F., Hamble Lane, Hamble-le-Rice, Hampshire.

HAMWORTHY ENGINEERING — Dorset — Ray Willis — 52 Heckford Rd — Poole, Dorset, BH15 2LY, 01202 773290, — Hamworthy Rec Club, Magna Road, Canford Magna, Dorset, 01202 881922.

HAMWORTHY UNITED — Dorset — Roy Mitchener — 68 St Mary's Rd, Poole, Dorset, BH15 2LL, 01202 676128 — County Ground, Blandford Close, Hamworthy, Poole, Dorset, 01202 674974.

HANLEY TOWN — Mid-Cheshire — 2 — Alma Rhodes — 98 Greasley Rd, Abbey Hulton, Stoke on Trent, Staffs, ST2 8JB, 01782 543020 — Abbey Lane, Bucknall, Stoke On Trent, Staffs, 01782 267234.

HANWELL VIADUCT — Middx — 1 — Mr Kevin Kavanagh — 44 Chestnut Grove, South Ealing, Middlesex, W5 4JS, 0181 579 7983 B:0171 617 4306 — Old Creightonians, Tentelow Lane, Southall, Middlesex, 0181 574 4941.

HANWORTH VILLA — Middx — P — Mr David Brown — 104 Kiln Park Road, Kingston, Surrey, KT2 5JZ, 0181 546 5979 B:751 4424, — Rectory Meadow, Park Rd, Hounslow Rd, Hanworth, Middlesex.

HARLESTON TOWN — Anglian Combination — Mr G N Page — 4a Station Road, Harleston, Norfolk, IP20 9ES, 01379 853929 — Rec/Mem Leisure Ctre, off Wilderness Lane, Harleston, Norfolk, 01379 854519.

HARROW HILL — Hellenic — 1 — Geoff Tuffley — Westfield Ct, Heywood Rd, Cinderford, Gloucestershire, GL14 2RU, 01594 542421 — Harrow Hill FC, Larksfield Rd, Harrow Hill, Glos, 01594 543873.

HARROW ST MARY'S — Middx — 1 — Mr David Campbell — 11 Walford Road, Uxbridge, Middlesex, UB8 2NF, 01895 272473 B:277432 — Harrow Rec. Ground, Roxborough Road, Harrow, Middlesex.

HARTLEPOOL BOYS WELFARE O.B. — Wearside — Philip Jordan — 473 Catcole Rd, Hartlepool, Cleveland, TS25 2RA, 01429 870015 — Grayfield Enclosure, Jesmond Road, Hartlepool, Cleveland.

HARTLEPOOL UNITED `A' — Northern Alliance — P — S Bagnall — 19 Wolsingham Road, Gosforth, Newcastle-upon-Tyne, Tyne & Wear, 0191 284 3889, — Victoria Park, Clarence Road, Hartlepool, Cleveland, TS24 8BZ, 01429 222077.

HARTON & WESTHOE C.W. — Wearside — Graham Bass — 76 Stanhope Rd, South Shields, Tyne & Wear, 0191 454 4798 B:0191 564 1552, — Harton & Westoe CWFC, Harton Coll. Welfare, South Shields, Tyne & Wear.

HASLINGDEN ST MARY'S — West Lancs — 2 — Mr M Molloy — 4 Rifle Street, Haslingden, Rossendale, Lancs, BB4 6NR, 01706 229337 B 01706 215351 — Townsend Street, , 01706 221814.

HAUGHLEY UNITED — S&I — S — Mr Alan Sparkes — 17 Wayside Close, Stowmarket, Suffolk, IP14 2DY, 01449 676828 — Haughley United F.C., King George V P.F., Haughley, Suffolk, 01449 673460.

HAVERFORDWEST COUNTY — Welsh — 1 — Mr Clifford Saies — 46 Wesley Place, Trecwn, Haverfordwest, Dyfed, SA62 5XD, 01348 840083 — Haverfordwest Co. FC, The Bridge Meadow, Haverfordwest, Dyfed, 01437 762082/ 769048(m'days).

HAWKENBURY — Kent County — 2W — Mr Malcolm Foy — 2 Chieveley Drive, Tunbridge Wells, Kent, TN2 5HF, 01892 533679 B:540255 — Hawkenbury Rec. Grnd, Hawkenbury Road, Tunbridge Wells, Kent.

HAYES ST CLARETS — Middx — 1 — Mr Paul Treanor — 310 Balmoral Drive, Hayes, Middlesex, 0181 848 3500, — Pitshanger Park, Scotch Common, Ealing, Middlesex.

HAYLING UNITED — Hampshire — 1 — Mrs Shirley Westfield — L'Ancresse, 14 Harold Road, Hayling Island, Hampshire, PO11 9LT, 01705 463305 B:492472 — Hayling United F.C., Hayling Park, Hayling Island, Hampshire.

HAYWARDS HEATH TOWN — Sussex County — 3 — Pat Bucknell — 79 Priory Way, Haywards Heath, West Sussex, RH16 3NS, 01444 457726 — Hanbury Park Stadium, Allen Road, Haywards Heath, West Sussex, 01444 412837.

HEANOR SPORTS — MRA — 2 — Mr Christopher J Parkins — 11 Kerry Drive, Smalley, Ilkeston, Derbyshire, DE7 6ER, 01332 781084 — Heanor Sports F.C., Nottingham Road, Ripley, Derbyshire.

HEATH HAYES — West Midlands — 1A — Mr Peter Francis — 191 Hednesford Road, Heath Hayes, Cannock, Staffordshire, 01543 277177 — Coppice Colliery Grd, Newlands Lane, Heath Hayes, Cannock, Staffordshire.

HEATON STANNINGTON — Northern Alliance — 1 — J R Grounsell — 73 Cleveland Gardens, High Heaton, Newcastle-upon-Tyne, Tyne & Wear, NE7 7QH, 0191 266 7464 — Newton Park, Newton Road, High Heaton, Tyne & Wear, NE7 7HP, 0191 281 9230.

HEBBURN REYROLLE — Northern Alliance — 1 — G Taylor — 29 Crawley Avenue, Hebburn, Tyne & Wear, NE31 2LT, 0191 483 4537 — Hebburn Spts Ground, Victoria Road West, Hebburn, Tyne & Wear.

HEDDON INSTITUTE — Northern Alliance — 1 — N A D Anderson — 14 Aquila Drive, Heddon-on-the-Wall, Newcastle-upon-Tyne, Tyne & Wear, NE15, 01661 853136, Newburn Leis. Centre, Grange Road, Newburn, Newcastle-upon-Tyne, Tyne & Wear.

HEDGE END — Hampshire — 2 — Mr Martin J Oliver — 25 Blossom Close, Botley, Southampton, Hampshire, SO30 2FR, 01489 786308 B:01705 754820, — Norman Rodaway P.F., Heathhouse Lane, Hedge End, Hampshire.

HELLESDON — Anglian Combination — 1 — Mr J Watson — 58 Northcote Road, Norwich, Norfolk, NR3 4QE, 01603 413486, — Hellesdon Comm. Ctre, Woodview Road, Hellesdon, Norwich, Norfolk, 01603 427675.

HEMPNALL — Anglian Combination — Mr R C Youngman — Dorchester, Sunnyside, Woodton, Bungay, Suffolk, NR35 2LY, 01508 482237, — Hempnall F.C., Bungay Road, Hempnall, Norfolk.

HEMSWORTH TOWN — Central Midlands — P — Mr Mike Pickering — 1 Sycamore Road, Hemsworth, nr Pontefract, West Yorkshire, WF9 4PD, 01977 613974 — Sports Complex, Kirkby Rd, Hemsworth, Yorks, 0836 553519.

HENGROVE ATHLETIC — Somerset — P — Mr Graham Close — 112 Allerton Crescent, Whitchurch, Bristol, BS14 9PX, 01275 835700 — Norton Lane, Whitchurch, Bristol, North Somerset, 01275 832894.

HENLEY TOWN — Chiltonian — P — A Kingston — 50 Birdhill Avenue, Reading, Berkshire, RG2 7JU, 0118 967 0196 — Henley Town F.C., Mill Lane Spts Grnd, Henley-on-Thames, Oxfordshire, 01491 411083.

HERSHAM R.B.L. — Surrey — P — Mr Ron Shields — 75 Homefield Road, Walton-on-Thames, Surrey, KT12 3RE, 01932 246724 — Coronation P.F., Molesey Road, Hersham, Surrey, 01932 223037.

HERTFORDSHIRE POLICE ATHLETIC — Herts — 1 — Mr Ian Moody — 41 Grove Meadow, Welwyn Garden City, Hertfordshire, AL7 2BE, 01707 373904 — Police Headquarters, Stanborough Road, Welwyn Garden City, Hertfordshire.

HESKETH BANK — West Lancs — 2 — Mr D Hand — 93 Sidney Ave, Hesketh Bank, Preston, Lancs, PR4 6PD, 01772 813247 B 01772 854768 — Nr Church, Hesketh Bank.

HESWALL — West Cheshire — 1 — Mr Jake O'Hara — 13 Reedville Road, Bebington, Wirral, L63 2HS, 0151 644 0459 B:343 1600x3493 — Gayton Park, Brimstage Road, Heswall, Wirral, 0151 342 8172.

HEXHAM BORDER COUNTIES — Northern Alliance — 2 — M Scandle — 10 St Wilfred's Road, Hexham, Northumberland, NE46 3EA, 01434 601757 — Hexham Border Cos FC, Wentworth Park, Hexham, Northumberland.

HEXHAM SWINTON — Northern Alliance — 1 — D Tiffin — 8 Valebrook, Hexham, Northumberland, NE46 2BQ, 01434 604573 — Hexham Swinton F.C., Wentworth Park, Hexham, Northumberland.

HIGH GREEN VILLA — Sheffield — P — Mr Trevor Staples — 41 Woodburn Drive, Chapeltown, Sheffield, South Yorkshire, S30 4YT, 0114 246 8560 B:246 8981 — High Green P.F., Mortomley Close, Sheffield, South Yorkshire.

HIGHFIELD RANGERS — Leics — P — Mr Maurice J Christian — 18 Blanklyn Avenue, Leicester, Leicestershire, LE5 5FA, 0116 273 4002 B:0116 253 1122, 443 — Gleneagles Ave., Rushey Mead, Leicester, Leicestershire, 0116 266 0009.

HIGHFIELDS UNITED — Northern Alliance — 2 — B Dytor — 43 Newfields, Berwick-on-Tweed, Northumberland, TD15 1SJ, 01289 305342, — Pier Park, Pier Road, Berwick-on-Tweed, Northumberland.

HILSEA — Hampshire — 2 — Mr Terry Harwood — 147 Manners Road, Southsea, Portsmouth, Hampshire, PO4 0BD, 01705 785140, — Sailing Centre, Eastern Road, Portsmouth, Hampshire, 01705 670119.

HOLBROOK — Central Midlands — P — Peter Begent — 22 Grasmere Close, Stapenhill, Burton on Trent, Staffs, DE15 9DS, 01283 540583 B 01283 512345 — Welfare Ground, Shaw Lane, Holbrook, Derbys, 01332 880259.

HOLBROOK ST MICHAELS — MRA — P — Mr Geoffrey Hartshorn — Oxford House, 11 Lime Avenue, Ripley, Derbyshire, DE5 3HD, 01773 744770 — Holbrook Park, Mellors Lane, Holbrook, Derbyshire.

HOLMER GREEN — South Midlands — S — John Anderson — 1 Jason Street, Cressex Rd, High Wycombe, Bucks, HP12 4TT, 01494 446128 — Holmer Green FC, Watchet Lane, Hoilmer Green, Bucks, 01494 711485.

HOLMESDALE — Surrey — P — Mr Mark Hayes — 45 Acacia Road, Mitcham, Surrey, CR4 1SF, 0181 715 7679 B:01689 893232 — John Ruskin P.F., Coombe Lodge, Oaks Road, Shirley, 0181 654 3804.

HOLT UNITED — Anglian Combination — Mr B Owen — 10 Mill Streetz, Holt, Norfolk, NR25 6LB, 01263 713914 — Sports Centre, Kelling Road, Holt, Norfolk.

HOOVER SPORTS — Welsh — 2 — Mr Philip Flye — 17 Bryn Carwyn, Dowlais, Merthyr Tydfil, Mid-Glamorgan, CF48 3DY, 01685 359857 B:725555 — Merthyr Tydfil F.C., Penydarren Park, Merthyr Tydfil, Mid-Glamorgan, 01685 725568 G:384102 F:382882.

HORBURY TOWN — West Yorkshire — P — J Mosalski — 21 Blake Hall Drive, Mirfield, Leeds, West Yorks, WF14 9NL, — Slazenger Sports SC, Southfields, Addingford, Horbury, West Yorks, WF4 5BH, 01924 274228.

HORNCASTLE TOWN — Lincs — Mr Dale Johnson — 41 Banovallum Gardens — Horncastle, Lincolnshire, LN9 6PN, 01507 527684 — The Wong, Boston Road, Horncastle, Lincolnshire.

HORNDEAN — Hampshire — 1 — Mrs G Berry — 74 Five Heads Road, Horndean, Hampshire, PO8 9NZ, 01705 591698 — Five Heads Park, Five Heads Road, Horndean, Hampshire, 01705 591363.

HORSFORD UNITED — Anglian Combination — P — Mr G Soanes — 5 Bulwer Road, Buxton, Norwich, Norfolk, NR10 5HG, 01603 278156 — Horsford United F.C., Village Hall Rec., Horsford, Norfolk.

HOUGHTON TOWN — South Midlands — S — Ken Dye — 9 Luxembourg Close, Luton, Bedfordshire, LU3 STD, 01582 563378, — Houghton Town AC, Park Road North, Houghton Regis, Beds, 01582 864862.

HOVETON WHERRYMEN — Anglian Combination — Mr R J Gates — Charmouth, Norwich Road, Smallburgh, Norfolk, NR12 9NS, 01692 536544 B:580126, — Playing Field, Stalham Road, Hoveton, Norfolk.

HUCKNALL ROLLS ROYCE — Notts Alliance — S — Adrian Ward — 7 Redwood Court, Hucknall, Nottingham, Notts, NG16 6NN, 0115 953 8491 — Watnall Rd Sports Cl, Watnall Rd, Hucknall, Notts, 0115 963 0134.

HUNCOTE SPORTS & SOCIAL — Leics — 1 — Mr David Russell — 72 Sycamore Way, Littlethorpe, Leicestershire, LE9 5HU, 0116 284 1952 — Huncote Spts & Soc., Enderby Lane, Thurlaston, Leicestershire, 01455 888430.

HUNTINGDON UNITED — United Counties — 1 — Mr Steve Thresh — 41 Maple Drive, Huntingdon, Cambridgeshire, PE18 7JE, 01480 417146 — Sapley Park, Stoneley Close, Huntingdon, Cambridgeshire, 01480 417202.

HURSTPIERPOINT — Sussex County — 3 — Mr Paul A John — 16 Church Close, Burgess Hill, West Sussex, RH15 8EZ, 01444 247183 — Fairfield Rec Ground, Cuckfield Road, Hurstpierpoint, West Sussex, 01273 834783.

HYKEHAM TOWN — Lincs — Mr Colin Edwards — 5 Landsdowne Avenue — Rookery Lane, Lincoln, Lincolnshire, LN6 7PU, 01522 520857 — Memorial P.F., North Hykeham, Lincoln, Lincolnshire, 01522 680193.

HYTHE & DIBDEN — Hampshire — 2 — Mr Tony Moyst — 105 Hobart Drive, Hythe, Southampton, Hampshire, SO45 6FD, 01703 847335 — Ewart Recreation Grd, Jones Lane, Hythe, Hampshire, 01703 845264.

IDEN — Kent County — 1E — Mr Gerard Say — 18 Parkwood, Iden, Rye, East Sussex, TN31 7XE, Iden Playing Fields, Iden, Rye, East Sussex.

IFIELD — Sussex County — 3 — Mr Robert Anderson — 1 Old Orchards, Church Road, Worth, Crawley, West Sussex, RH10 7QA, 01293 886215 — Ifield Sports Club, Ifield Green, Rusper Road, Crawley, West Sussex, 01293 536569.

ILMINSTER TOWN — Somerset — 1 — Mr R J Parkin — 2 Herne Rise, Ilminster, Somerset, TA19 0HU, 01460 52344 — Ilminster Town F.C., Recreation Ground, Ilminster, Somerset, 01460 54756.

IMPERIAL — Somerset — 1 — Mr Ivor Grimstead — 567 Wells Road, Whitchurch Park, Bristol, BS14 9BA, 01275 837273 — Bristol Imperial SC, West Town Lane, Whitchurch, Brislington, 01275 546000.

IPSWICH ATHLETIC — S&I — S — Mr Clive Wilkinson — 13 Atherton Road, Ipswich, Suffolk, IP2 9LD, 01473 687469 — John Player Spts Grd, Halifax Road, Ipswich, Suffolk, 01473 687685.

IRCHESTER UNITED — United Counties — 1 — Mr P Mayhew — 52 Castle Way, Barton Seagrave, Northants, 01536 518542 — Irchester United FC, Alfred Street, Irchester, Northants, 01933 312877.

IVER — Chiltonian — P — S Law — 59 Grange Way, Iver, Buckinghamshire, SL0 9NT, 01753 819780, — Lee Barton, High Street, Iver, Buckinghamshire, 01753 651248.

IVYBRIDGE TOWN — Devon — Chris Pattison — Clearmont, Crescent Rd, Ivybridge, Devon, PL21 0BP, 01752 892119 — Ivybridge Town, Erme Valley, Ivybridge, Devon.

JARROW — Wearside — Mr Calum McAuley — 56 Beaconside, Cleadon Village, South Shields, Tyne & Wear, 0191 455 5924, — Perth Green C.A., off Inverness Road, Jarrow, Tyne & Wear.

JOHN PLAYER — Notts Alliance — S — Ron Walton — 27 St Margarets Ave, Aspley Lane, Nottingham, Notts, NG8 5GD, 0115 929 2027 — John Player FC, Aspley Lane, Nottingham, Notts, 0115 929 4244.

KENNINGTON — Kent County — 1E — Mr Martin Smith — The Gables, Sandyhurst Lane, Ashford, Kent, TN25 4PE, 01233 628586 B:813234 — Kennington Crick. Cb, Ulley Road, Kennington, Ashford, Kent.

KENT ATHLETIC — South Midlands — S — Felix Maguire — 114 Fourth Avenue, Luton, Beds, LU3 3BU, 01582 583659 — Kent Social Club, Tenby Drive, Leagrave, Beds, 01582 582723.

KESGRAVE — S&I — S — Mrs Aveline Ainslie — 7 Bell Lane, Kesgrave, Ipswich, Suffolk, IP5 7JG, 01473 625685 — Kesgrave Comm. Assoc, Twelve Acre Approach, Kesgrave, Suffolk.

KEYNSHAM CRICKETERS — Somerset — P — Mr Martin Palmer — 20 Chandos Road, Keynsham, Bristol, BS18 2DB, 0117 985 9019 M:0585 514995 — Cadbury Schweppes, Somerdale, Keynsham, Bristol, 0117 937 6500/6501.

KEYWORTH UNITED — Notts Alliance — S — Maurice Simpson — 25 Waddington Drive, Wilford Hill, West Bridgford, Notts, N2 7GT, 0115 923 2921 — Platt Lane, Keyworth, Nottingham, Notts, 0115 937 5998.

KILLAMARSH JUNIORS — Central Midlands — P — Mr Philip Bright — 17 Marrison Drive, Killamarsh, Sheffield, South Yorkshire, S31 8HF, 0114 248 2763 — Athletic Club & Inst, 284 Sheffield Rd, Killamarsh,Sheffield, Yorks, 0114 248 4390.

KIMBERLEY MINERS WELFARE — Notts Alliance — 2 — Graham Rowley — 47 Noel Street, Kimberley, Nottingham, Notts, NG16 2NF, 0115 938 9151 — Digby Street, Kimberley, Nottingham, Notts, 0115 938 2124 Welfare.

KIMPTON ROVERS — Herts — 1 — Mr Neil Matthews — 30 Commons Lane, Kimpton, Hitchin, Hertfordshire, SG4 8QG, 01438 832625 — Kimpton Rec. Ground, High Street, Kimpton, Hitchin, Hertfordshire.

KINGS LANGLEY — Herts — P — Mr Brian Aldersley — 49 Diamond Road, Watford, Hertfordshire, WD2 5EN, 01923 461869 — Kings Langley F.C., Hemel Hempstead Road, Kings Langley, Hertfordshire.

KINGTON TOWN — West Midlands — 1B — Mrs P Shaw — Kington Town F.C., Park Road Ground, Kington, Herefordshire, 01544 231007, — Kington Town F.C., Park Road Ground, Kington, Herefordshire, 01544 231007.

KIRKHAM & WESHAM — West Lancs — 1 — E Picton — 4 St Michaels Rd, Kirkham, Preston, Lancs, PR4 2TQ, 01772 686264 — Recreation Ground, Coronation Rd, Kirkham, Lancs.

KIRKLEY — Anglian Combination — P — Mr G Reynolds — 79 May Road, Lowestoft, Suffolk, NR32 2DJ, 01502 566867 — Kirkley Rec. Ground, Walmer Road, Lowestoft, Suffolk, 01502 513549.

KIVETON SPORTS — Sheffield — 1 — Mr Dave Shepherd — 8 Broomhill Avenue, Worksop, Nottinghamshire, S81 7QP, 01909 484568 — Kiveton Park M.W., Hard Lane, Kiveton Park, South Yorkshire.

KNARESBOROUGH TOWN — West Yorkshire — P — I J Pickles — 3 Farndale Rd, Knaresborough, West Yorks, HG5 ONY, 01937 845845 B 0860 834258 — Knaresborough Town, Manse Lane, 01423 868560.

KNATCHBULL — Kent County — P — Mr David G Howie — 13 Charminster, Washford Farm, Ashford, Kent, TN23 2UH, 01233 611207 B:01634 240463 — Hatch Park, off A20, Mersham, near Ashford, Kent, 0585 663171(matchdays).

KNOCKHOLT — Kent County — 1W — Mr Ray Thurlow — 37 Whitethorne Avenue, Coulsdon, Surrey, CR5 2PQ, 0181 668 1418 — Knockholt Vlge Club, Main Road, Knockholt, Kent, 01959 532468.

KNUTSFORD — Mid-Cheshire — 1 — Keith Jones — 20 Townfields, Knutsford, Cheshire, WA16 8DR, 01565 755711, — Knutsford FC, Manchester Rd, Knutsford, Cheshire.

KODAK HEMEL HEMPSTEAD — Herts — 1 — Mr Brian Pollard — The Laurels, Wood Rising Lodge, High Street, Green, Hemel Hempstead, Hertfordshire, HP2 7AA, 01442 256720, Wood Lane End, off Maylands Avenue, Hemel Hempstead, Hertfordshire, 01442 242597.

LAKEFORD RANGERS — Anglian Combination — P — Mr R J Watling — 6 Cressener Close, Hellesdon, Norwich, Norfolk, NR6 5RF, 01603 405032 B:592528 — Marlingford Spts Grd, Easton Road, Marlingford, Norfolk.

LAKENHEATH — Anglian Combination — Mrs Peta Gyte — 5 Covey Way, Lakenheath, Suffolk, IP27 9HJ, 01842 860979 — Lakenheath F.C., Wings Road, Lakenheath, Suffolk, 01842 860221.

LANCASHIRE CONSTABULARY — West Lancs — 1 — Mr E Thistlethwaite — 7 Willow Grove, Hambleton, Lancs, FY6 9ED, 01253 700153 B 01253 293933 — Police HQ, Saunders Lane, Hutton, Lancs.

LANSIL — West Lancs — 1 — Mrs K Price — 34 Wellington Rd, Bowerham, Lancaster, Lancs, LA1 4DN, 01524 849834 Mob 0402 233482 — opp Nelson Works, Caton Rd, Lancaster, Lancs.

LAVERSTOCK & FORD — Hampshire — 3 — Chris R Dare — 22 Beechcroft Road, Laverstock, Salisbury, Wiltshire, SP1 1PF, 01722 329395, — 23 Church Road, Laverstock, Salisbury, Wiltshire, 01722 327401.

LEAVES GREEN — Kent County — 3W — Mr Paul Douglas — 125 Sundale Avenue, Selsdon Village, South Croydon, Surrey, CR2 8RX, 0181 657 8249 B:684 4395 — Hayes Country Club, West Common Road, Hayes, Kent, 0181 462 2324.

LEAVESDEN SPORTS — Herts — 1 — Sue Edwards — 13 The Square, North Watford, Watford, Hertfordshire, WD2 5ND, 01923 246139 — Bricket Wood, Country Club, Lye Lane, Bricket Wd, Hertfordshire.

LEICS CONSTABULARY — Leics — 1 — Ian Leacy — 6 Lena Drive, Groby, Leicester, Leicestershire, LE6 0FJ, 01530 243110 — Police Headquarters, St Johns, Enderby, Leicestershire, 0116 248 2198(matchdays only).

LEIGHTON ATHLETIC — South Midlands — 1 — Lin Scott — 1 Meadow Way, Leighton Buzzard, Beds, LU7 8XN, 01525 853680 — Memorial Playing Fld, Mentmore Rd, Linslade, Beds, 01525 370469.

LEMINGTON UNITED SOCIAL — Northern Alliance — P — A Findlay — 14 Tewkesbury Road, West Denton Park, Newcastle-upon-Tyne, Tyne & Wear, NE15 8UU, 0191 267 6493, Cowgate New Tavern, Ponteland Road, Cowgate, Tyne & Wear.

LEOMINSTER TOWN — West Midlands — 1B — Mr Roger Weaver — 19 Castlefields, Leominster, Herefordshire, HR6 8BG, 01568 614450 — Bridge Street Park, Bridge Street, Leominster, Herefordshire, 01568 611172.

LETCOMBE — Hellenic — 1 — Mr Desmond Williams — 8 Larkdown, Wantage, Oxfordshire, OX12 8HE, 01235 764130 B:763061 — Letcombe F.C., Bassett Road, Letcombe Regis, Berkshire, 01235 768685.

LEVERSTOCK GREEN — South Midlands — S — Mr S D Robinson — 11 Connaught Close, Hemel Hempstead, Hertfordshire, HP2 7AB, 01442 65734 — Pancake Lane, Leverstock Green, Hemel Hempstead, Herts, 01442 246280.

LEYLAND MOTORS ATHLETIC — West Lancs — 1 — Mr K Pownall — 10 Elswick Rd, Leyland, Lancs, PR5 3BH, 01772 495217 — Leyland Motors FC, Thurston Rd, Leyland, Lancs, 01772 422400.

LIMESTONE RANGERS — Lincs — Mr Michael Patrick Harty — 3 Brook Street, Hemswell, Gainsborough, Lincolnshire, DN21 5UJ, 01427 668382 B:01724 864307 — Limestone Rangers FC, Hollowgate Hill, Willoughton, Lincolnshire.

LINBY COLLIERY WELFARE — Notts Alliance — 1 — Frank Taylor — 6 Beech Avenue, Hucknall, Nottingham, Notts, NG15 7FH, 0115 952 9633 — Church Lane, Linby Village, Linby, Notts.

LINCOLN MOORLANDS — Lincs — Mr Tim Walshaw — 19 Spilsby Close, Hartsholme Field, Lincoln, Lincolnshire, LN6 3YX, 01522 501229 — Moorlands Spts Grnd, Newark Road, Lincoln, Lincolnshire.

LINGFIELD — Sussex County — 3 — Mr Ian Tomsett — 8 Orchard Cottages, St Piers Lane, Lingfield, Surrey, RH7 6PN, 01342 835089 — Lingfield F.C., Godstone Road, Lingfield, Surrey, 01342 834269.

LINOTYPE — Mid-Cheshire — 1 — Brian McGuinness — 36 Barrington Rd, Altrincham, Cheshire, WA14 1HJ, 0161 929 0021 B 0151 652 1527 — British Airways Club, Clay Lane, Timperley, Cheshire, 0161 980 7354.

LISS ATHLETIC — Hampshire — 1 — Mr W E Moseley — 3 Yew Tree Place, Liss, Hampshire, GU33 7ET, 01730 894631 — Newman Collard, Hill Brow Road, Liss, Hampshire, 01730 894022.

LITTLE EATON — MRA — 1 — Mr Alan Machell — 68 Alfreton Road, Little Eaton, Derby, Derbyshire, DE21 5DD, 01332 832751 B:01773 761266, — St Peters Park, Little Eaton, Derby, Derbyshire.

LITTLEMOOR — Mid-Cheshire — 2 — Stanley McQuarrie — 96 Mottram Towers, Mottram St, Hillgate, Stockport, Cheshire, SK1 3NY, 0161 474 0257, Ward Street, St Mary's Way, Stockport, Cheshire.

LITTLEOVER IRONGATE — MRA — P — Mr Martin Bayliss — 28 Whittlebury Drive, Littleover, Derby, Derbyshire, DE23 7BF, 01332 510486 B:0116 253 6725, — University of Derby, off Western Road, Mickleover, Derbyshire.

LLANWERN — Welsh — 1 — Mr Michael Bourne — 709 Chepstow Road, Newport, Gwent, 01633 282967 B:832097, — B.S.C. Sports Ground, Spytty Road, Newport, Gwent, 01633 273790.

LOCKSHEATH — Hampshire — 1 — Mr Mick Harrison — 30 Whitebeam Road, Hedge End, Hampshire, SO30 0PZ, 01489 784470 F:578515 B:574519 — Warsash Road, Titchfield Common, Fareham, Hampshire, PO14 4JX, 01489 600932.

LODDON UNITED — Anglian Combination — P — Mr A Cook — 4 Crossway Terrace, Loddon, Norwich, Norfolk, NR14 6JY, 01508 528115, — George Lane P.F., Loddon, Norwich, Norfolk, 01508 528497.

LOFTUS WEST ROAD S.C. — Teesside — Mr Simon Whitwell — 10 Hareball Close, Skelton, Saltburn, Cleveland, TS12 2FE, 01287 652135 — Rosecroft School, Rosedale Lane, Loftus, Cleveland.

LONG ASHTON — Somerset — 2 — Mr Christopher Downing — 8 Longford Avenue, Westbury-on-Trym, Bristol, BS10 5LL, 0117 950 7625, — Long Ashton Rec., Keedwell Hill, Long Ashton, North Somerset.

LONG STRATTON — Anglian Combination — Mr J Harvey — 3 Norwich Road, Long Stratton, Norwich, Norfolk, NR15 2PG, 01508 530962 — Manor Road P.F., Long Stratton, Norwich, Norfolk.

LONG SUTTON — Somerset — 1 — Mr Robert Sams — Brookside, Crowds Lane, Long Sutton, Langport, Somerset, TA10 9NR, 01458 241395 — Recreation Ground, Long Sutton, Langport, Somerset.

LONGBENTON — Northern Alliance — 1 — J Fawcett — 7 Glencoe Avenue, Southfield Green, Cramlington, Northumberland, NE23 6EH, 01671 715772 — Longbenton F.C., Burradon Rec. Centre, Burradon, Tyne & Wear.

LONGWELL GREEN ABBOTONIANS — Somerset — P — Mr George Threader — 6 Little Dowles, Cadbury Heath, Bristol, BS15 5AW, 0117 967 0306 — Longwell Green C.A., Shellards Road, Longwell Green, Bristol.

LOSTOCK GRALAM — Mid-Cheshire — 2 — Andrew Hough — 44 Shelley Ave, Wincham, Northwich, Cheshire, CW9 6PH, 01565 733383 — Slow and Easy Hotel, Manchester Rd, Lostock Gralam, Cheshire.

LOUGHBOROUGH DYNAMO — Leics — 1 — Mr Max Hutchinson — 3 Wythburn Close, Loughborough, Leicestershire, LE11 3SZ, 01509 266092 B:612144, — Loughborough Dyn. FC, Nanpantan Spts Grnd, Loughborough, Leicestershire, 01509 237148.

LOUTH OLD BOYS — Lincs — Mr Mark Shackleton — 12 Tudor Drive, Louth, Lincolnshire, LN11 9EE, 01507 602929 — L.S.A. Sports Ground, London Road, Louth, Lincolnshire.

LUDGERSHALL SPORTS — Hampshire — 2 — Mr Steve Winstone — 57 Wood Park, Ludgershall, Andover, Hampshire, SP11 9NS, 01264 791193 B:735371, — Astor Crescent, Ludgershall, Andover, Hampshire, 01264 398200.

LUTON OLD BOYS — South Midlands — 1 — Roland Dodge — 5 Brunel Rd, Luton, Beds, LU4 0RX, 01582 601705 B 394771 — Luton Old Boys FC, Dunstable Rd, Luton, Beds, 01582 582060.

LYDD TOWN — Kent County — P — Mr Peter Sisley — 21 The Fairway, Littlestone, Romney Marsh, Kent, TN28 8PJ, 01797 366101 — The Rype, Manor Road, Lydd, Kent.

LYTHAM ST ANNES — West Lancs — 2 — Mr S Broomfield — 84 Lytham Rd, Warton, Preston, Lancs, PR4 1XE, 01772 632392 B 01772 855058, — Lytham Cricket Club, Church Rd, Lytham St Annes, Lancs, 01253 734137.

MALEX — Herts — 1 — Mr David Kyte — 2nd Floor, Walbrook House, 23 Walbrook, London, EC4N 8LA, 0181 340 2096 — International Univ., The Avenue, Bushey, Watford, Hertfordshire.

MACKWORTH UNITED — MRA — 2 — Mrs Ann Spray — 5 Embankment Close, Mackworth, Derby, Derbyshire, DE22 4HF, 01332 517321 B:365711 — Mackworth College, Prince Charles Ave., Mackworth, Derby, Derbyshire, 01332 340045.

MADRA UNITED — Anglian Combination — P — Mr P Bugdale — 101 Colindeep Lane, Sprowston, Norwich, Norfolk, NR7 8EQ, 01603 483283, — Madra Sports Field, Knapton, near North Walsham, Norfolk, 01263 721870.

MAESTEG PARK ATHLETIC — Welsh — 1 — Mr David Griffiths — 3 Padleys Close, Maesteg, Mid-Glamorgan, CF34 0TX, 01656 733000 B:684699x4640 — Maesteg Park A.F.C., Tudor Park, Maesteg, Mid-Glamorgan, 01656 732029.

MAGDALA AMATEURS — Notts Alliance — 2 — Alan Gilmour — 9 Adbolton Grove, West Bridgford, Nottingham, Notts, NG2 5AR, 0115 982 1071 — Civil Service Sports, Wilford Lane, West Bridgford, Notts, 0115 981 1418.

MAGNET SPORTS — West Yorkshire — P — M Howcroft — 45 Willow Rise, Tadcaster, South Yorks, LS24 9LG, 01937 833756 B 01937832361X228 — R/O Magnet Sp Club, Queens Gardens, Tadcaster, 01937 833435.

MAHAL — West Midlands — 1B — Rajinder Singh Daley — 248 Portland Road, Edgbaston, Birmingham, West Midlands, B17 8LR, 0121 429 9935, — Hadley Stadium, Wilson Road, Smethwick, Warley, West Midlands, 0121 434 4848.

MAIDSTONE UNITED — Kent County — 1W — Mr George Gritty — 6 Morella Walk, Lenham Road, Maidstone, Kent, ME17 2JX, 01622 859964, — The Athletic Ground, London Rd (rear MFI), Maidstone, Kent, 0860 296121(matchdays).

MALPAS — Mid-Cheshire — 1 — Bernard Lloyd — 15 Springfield Ave, Malpas, Cheshire, SY14 8QD, 01948 860812 B 01948 860395 — Malpas Sports Club, Oxhey, Wrexham Rd, Malpas, Cheshire, 01948 860662.

MALSHANGER — Hampshire — 1 — Mr Fred Norris — 9 Goddard's Firs, Oakley, Basingstoke, Hampshire, RG23 7JL, 01256 781697 M:0831 666884, — The Sportsfield, Malshanger, Basingstoke, Hampshire, 01256 780285.

MANNION PARK — Teesside — Mr Michael Andrew — 12 Fieldview Close — Port Clarence, Middlesbrough, Cleveland, TS2 1TN, 01642 564363 — Mannion Pk Rec. Club, Broadway, Grangetown, Middlesbrough, Cleveland, 01642 453701.

MANOR ATHLETIC — West Cheshire — 2 — Mr Stewart Galtress — 3 Centurion Close, Meols, Wirral, L47 7BZ, 0151 632 3211 B:641 4036, — Unilever Spts Ground, Bromborough, Wirral, Merseyside.

MARSKE UNITED — Wearside — Mr Ian Rowe — 19 High Row, Loftus, Saltburn-by-the-Sea, Cleveland, TS13 4SA, 01287 643440 — Mount Pleasant, Mount Pleasant Ave., Marske-by-Sea, Cleveland, 01642 471091.

MARTHAM — Anglian Combination — Mr C Tungate — 46 Ormesby Road, Caister-on-Sea, Great Yarmouth, Norfolk, NR30 5LB, 01493 721773 B:01603 406372, — Coronation Rec. Grnd, Rollesby Road, Martham, Norfolk, 01493 740252.

MARTIN BAKER SPORTS — Chiltonian — P — W Wright — Hillside Cottage, Tilehouse Lane, Denham, Buckinghamshire, UB9 5DD, 01895 832977 — Martins Field, Tilehouse Lane, Denham, Buckinghamshire, 01895 833077.

MASTERCOLOUR — Kent County — 3W — Mr Barrie Pickett — 100 Ridgeway, Pembury, Tunbridge Wells, Kent, TN2 4ET, 01892 823464 B:536655 — Putlands S&L Centre, Pascalls Court Road, Paddock Wood, Kent, 01892 838290.

MATLOCK UNITED — MRA — P — Mrs Yvonne Duchar — 2 Beech Cottage, Main Road, Lea, Matlock, Derbyshire, DE4 5GJ, 01629 534022, — Cavendish Road P.F., Cavendish Park, Matlock, Derbyshire.

MATTISHALL — Anglian Combination — 1 — Mrs J Bugg — 42 Rayners Way, Mattishall, Norwich, Norfolk, NR20 3NQ, 01362 850500 — Mattishall P.F., South Green, Mattishall, Norwich, Norfolk, 01362 850246.

MAYFLOWER — Hampshire — 2 — Mr Chris Papadatos — 5 Albion Close, Portchester, Fareham, Hampshire, PO16 9EW, 01329 510623 B:01705 722709, — Clarence Ground, Clarence Pier, Southsea, Hampshire, 01705 824246.

MERCEDES-BENZ — South Midlands — S — Bob Flight — Mercedes Benz (U.K.) Ltd, Mercedes Benz Centre, Tongwell, Milton Keynes, Buckinghamshire, MK15 8BA, — The Barn, Pannier Place, Downs Barn, Milton K, Bucks, 01908 245158.

MERSEY ROYAL — West Cheshire — 1 — Mr Dave Lawson — 7 Mount Park, Higher Bebington, Wirral, L63 5RD, 0151 608 2261 M:0589 406331, — Unliver Spts Ground, Bromborough, Wirral, Merseyside.

MERSEYSIDE POLICE — West Cheshire — 1 — George Todd — 14 Crowther Street, St Helens, Merseyside, WA10 4NH, 01744 755845 B:0151 777 6615, — Police Club, Fairfield, Prescot Road, Liverpool, L7 0JD, 0151 228 2352 F:259 6997.

METROPOLITAN POLICE (BUSHEY) — Herts — P — Jim Howard — Met. Police Sports Club, Aldenham Road, Bushey, Hertfordshire, WD2 3TR, 01923 674373, — Met. Police Sp. Club, Aldenham Road, Bushey, Hertfordshire, WD2 3TR, 01923 243947.

MEXBOROUGH ATHLETIC — Central Midlands — P — Mr Neville Wheeler — 15 Holmshore Drive, Sheffield, South Yorkshire, S13 8UJ, 0114269 4142 b 0114239 9824 — Mexboro. Football Gd, New Oxford Rd, Mexborough, South Yorkshire, 01709 583426.

MEXBOROUGH MAIN STREET — Sheffield — P — Mr Tony Hough — 4 Cranswick Way, Conisborough, Doncaster, South Yorkshire, DN12 3AY, 01709 866479 B:01302 382416 — Mexboro. Football Gd, Hampden Road, Mexborough, South Yorkshire, 01709 570739.

MICKLEOVER R.B.L. — Central Midlands — P — Mr Ray Taylor — 15 Inglwood Avenue, Mickleover, Derby, Derbyshire, DE3 5RT, 01332 515047 — Ypres Lodge, Western Rd, Mickleover, Derbys, 01332 513548.

MIDDLESBROUGH `A' — Northern Alliance — P — Mrs K Nelson — Cellnet Riverside Stadium, Middlesbrough, Cleveland, TS3 6RS, 01642 207003 — Norton & Stocton AFC, Station Road, Norton, Stockton, Cleveland, 01642 530203.

MILFORD UNITED — Welsh — 3 — Mr Ken Lowe — 17 Milton Crescent, Pill, Milford Haven, Pembrokeshire, SA73 2QS, 01646 692194 — Milford United F.C., Marble Hall Road, Milford Haven, Pembrokeshire, 01646 693691.

MILL END UNITED — Middx — P — Mr Barry Horwood — 17 Middleton Road, Mill End, Rickmansworth, Hertfordshire, WD3 2JE, 01923 446529 — Mill End Spts & S.C., Penn Road, Mill End, Rickmansworth, Hertfordshire, 01923 776892.

MILNTHORPE CORINTHIANS — West Lancs — 2 — Mr C Davidson — 27 Beetham Rd, Milnthorpe, Cumbria, LA7 7ON, 01595 62884 B 01539 818731 — Strands Lane, Milnthorpe, Cumbria, 015395 64640.

MILTON ATHLETIC — Kent County — P — Mr Paul Duffin — 18 Hales Road, Tunstall, Sittingbourne, Kent, ME10 1SR, 01795 471260 B:01438 734654 — U.K.P. Sports Ground, Gore Court Road, Sittingbourne, Kent, 01795 477047.

MOND RANGERS — West Cheshire — 1 — Beverley Crilly — 26 Perrin Avenue, Weston Point, Runcorn, Cheshire, WA7 4BJ, 01928 575938 B:792269 — Pavilions Club, Sandy Lane, Weston Point, Runcorn, 01928 590508.

MONEYFIELDS — Hampshire — 1 — Mr Peter Shires — 242 Grafton Street, Mile End, Portsmouth, Hampshire, PO2 7LH, 01705 645813 B:611363 — Moneyfields Lane, Copnor, Portsmouth, Hampshire, 01705 665260.

MONKTON SWIFTS — Welsh — 3 — Mr Maurice William Jones — 27 North Street, Pembroke Dock, Pembrokeshire, 01646 682143 — Monkton Lane, Monkton, Pembroke, Pembrokeshire, 01646 683735.

MOONSHOT ATHLETIC — Kent County — 2W — Mr Joe Collymore — 37 Vaughan Williams Close, Deptford, London, SE8 4AW, 0181 691 2543 — Fordham Park, Pagnell Street, New Cross, London, SE14.

MORDA UNITED — West Midlands — 1A — Gwilym Williams — 2 Sunnyside, Morda, Oswestry, Shropshire, SY10 9NP, 01691 657783 B:652385 — Weston Road, Morda, Oswestry, Shropshire, 01691 659621.

MORETON — West Cheshire — 1 — Mr Jeff Lloyd — 46 Burrell Drive, Moreton, Wirral, L46 0TQ, 0151 677 9840, — Moreton F.C., Elm Grove, Hoylake, Merseyside.

MORLEY VILLAGE — Anglian Combination — Miss Mandi Bowhill — 214 Sawyers Lane, Suton, Wymondham, Norfolk, NR18 9JH, 01953 603578 — Golf Links Road, Morley St Peter, Wymondham, Norfolk.

MORRISTON TOWN — Welsh — 3 — Lynford Owens — Flat 59, Llanllienwen Close, Morriston, Swansea, West Glamorgan, SA6 6LY, 01792 791740 — The Dingle Field, Morriston, Swansea, West Glamorgan, 01792 702033.

MORTIMER — Reading — S — Steve Dell — 30 Croft Rd, Mortimer, near Reading, Berkshire, RG7 3TS, 01734 333821 M:0860 454166 — Alfred Palmer Mem PF, West End Rd, Mortimer, Berkshire.

MULBARTON UNITED — Anglian Combination — P — Mr J T Eastell — Erengon, 1 Cuckoofield Lane, Mulbarton, Norwich, Norfolk, NR14 8AZ, 01508 570832 B:01603 612362, — Mulberry Park, Mulbarton, Norwich, Norfolk, 01508 570626.

MUNDFORD — Anglian Combination — Mr J E Marston — 16 Impson Way — Mundford, Thetford, Norfolk, IP26 4JU, 01842 878339 — The Glebe, Mundford, Thetford, Norfolk.

MURSLEY UNITED — South Midlands — 1 — Roger Gurnett — 6 Station Rd, Mursley, Milton Keynes, Bucks, MK17 0SA, 01296 720505, — Mursley FC, Station Rd, Mursley.

M.M.S. DYNAMICS — Herts — 1 — Mr Simon Watson — 32 The Paddocks, Stevenage, Hertfordshire, SG2 9TU, 01438 311065 — MMS Space Syst. Spts, Fairview Road, Stevenage, Hertfordshire, 01438 736284.

NAILSEA TOWN — Somerset — 3 — M C Nicholls — 5 Killarney Avenue, Burnham-on-Sea, Somerset, TA8 1NB, 01278 789513 — Fryeth Way, Pound Lane, Nailsea, North Somerset.

NAILSEA UNITED — Somerset — P — Mr John Hobbs — 4 Kingston Road, Nailsea, North Somerset, BS19 2RD, 01275 855432 — Grove Sports Ground, Old Church, Nailsea, North Somerset, 01275 856892.

NARBOROUGH & LITTLETHORPE — Leics — 1 — Mr Ronald Bexley — 53 Trinity Road, St Johns, Narborough, Leicestershire, LE9 5BW, 0116 286 2818 — Ray Hurd Pavilion, Leicester Road, Narborough, Leicestershire, 0116 275 1855.

NEASDEN — Middx — 1 — Ms K Henry — 17 Oxgate Court, Coles Green Road, London, NW2 7EU, 0181 830 5754 — Chalkhill Youth CC, Poplar Grove, Wembley, Middlesex, HA9 9DR, 0181 904 1974.

NECTON — Anglian Combination — Mrs S Ashman — The Willows, Cranes Corner, Great Fransham, Dereham, Norfolk, NR19 2HX, 01362 687581 — Necton Playing Field, Tuns Road, Necton, Norfolk.

NESTLE ROWNTREES — West Yorkshire — P — G Wordsworth — 51 The Village, Stockton on the For, York, YO3 9UF, 01904 400588 — Mille Crux, Haxby Road, York, 01904 623933.

NETHERFIELD — Northern Premier — 1 — Mr Andrew Roe — 4 Lowther Park, Kendal, Cumbria, LA9 6RS, 01539 731680 B:582390, — Netherfield F.C., Parkside Road, Kendal, Cumbria, LA9 7BL, 01539 727472 C:722469.

NETLEY CENTRAL SPORTS — Hampshire — 1 — Mr R W Crompton — 47 Station Road, Netley Abbey, Southampton, Hampshire, SO31 5AE, 01703 452049l — Station Road Rec., Netley Abbey, Southampton, Hampshire, 01703 452267.

NEW BRADWELL ST PETER — South Midlands — S — Mr L Smith — 47 Rowle Close, Stantonbury, Milton Keynes, Buckinghamshire, MK13 7AT, 01908 319522, — Recreation Gd, Bradwell Rd, New Bradwell, 01908 313835.

NEW BRIGHTON — West Cheshire — 2 — Mr Russell Holmes — 10 Rudgrave Square, Wallasey, Wirral, L44 0EL, 0151 638 9506 B:5684 — Harrison Drive, Wallasey Village, Wallasey, Merseyside.

NEW EASTWOOD — MRA — 2 — J Nicholas Walters — 5 Brandreth Drive, Giltbrook, Nottinghamshire, NG16 2UN, 0115 945 8449 — Codnor Miners Welf., Goose Lane, Codnor, Derbyshire.

NEW HANFORD — Middx — P — Mr Eamonn Murphy — 21 Rosewood Avenue, Greenford, Middlesex, UB6 7QP, 0181 902 0943 — , Drayton Fields, Greenford Avenue, Greenford, Middlesex, 0181 578 5831.

NEW MARSKE SPORTS CLUB — Teesside — Mr Peter Whitaker — 28 High Street, Marske, Redcar, Cleveland, TS11 7BE, 01642 486770 — New Marske Spts Club, New Marske, Redcar, Cleveland, 01642 479808.

NEW MILTON TOWN — Hampshire — 1 — Mr Malcolm J Smith — 4 Kestral Drive, Mudeford, Christchurch, Dorset, BH23 4DE, 01425 277565 — Fawcetts Field, Lymington Road, New Milton, Hampshire.

NEW ROMNEY — Kent County — 1E — Mr Darryl Masters — 44 Fernbank Crescent, Folkestone, Kent, CT19 5SF, 01303 253961, — New Romney F.C., Station Road, New Romney, Kent, 01797 362956.

NEW STREET — Hampshire — 1 — Mrs F Joy Waterman — Jorin Bay, 2 Pine Walk, Andover, Hampshire, SP10 3PW, 01264 362751 B:01980 674454 — Foxcotte Park, Charlton Down, Andover, Hampshire, 01264 358358.

NEWARK TOWN — MRA — 1 — Mr Keith Asher — 115 Grove Street, Balderton, Newark, Nottinghamshire, NG24 3AR, 01636 686077 B: 01522 584537 — The Stadium, Elm Ave, London rd, Newark, Nottinghamshire.

NEWBIGGIN CENTRAL WELFARE — Northern Alliance — 1 — G Penman — 37 King George's Road, Newbiggin-by-the-Sea, Northumberland, NE64 6HS, 01670 854278 — Newbiggin Welfare, Cleveland Terrace, Newbiggin-by-the-Sea, Northumberland.

NEWCASTLE BENFIELD PARK — Northern Alliance — P — G J Martin — 2 The Fold, Eastfield Estate, Walker, Newcastle-upon-Tyne, Tyne & Wear, NE6 4XL, 0191 263 5237 — Benfield Park, Benfield Road, Newcastle-upon-Tyne, Tyne & Wear.

NEWCASTLE BRITISH TELECOM — Northern Alliance — 2 — J Weatherstone — 6 Cheadle Avenue, Hardian Park, Wallsend, Northumberland, NE28 2QP, 01670 262 0758 — Civil Service Sports, Darsley Park, Whitley Road, Benton, Tyne & Wear.

NEWCASTLE UNIVERSITY — Northern Alliance — 2 — R Garlick — 194 Sandyford Road, Newcastle-upon-Tyne, Tyne & Wear, 0191 232 2834 — Cochrane Park, Etherstone Avenue, Newcastle-upon-Tyne, Tyne & Wear.

NEWPORT Y.M.C.A. — Welsh — 3 — Mr Mark Davies — 15 Lodge Hill, Caerleon, Gwent, NP6 1DA, 01633 422907 B:862020 — Y.M.C.A. Grounds, Mendalgief Road, Newport, Gwent, 01633 263387.

NEWTON — West Cheshire — 1 — Mr Alan Dabner — 41 St David Road, Claughton, Birkenhead, Merseyside, L43 8SW, 0151 653 2151 B:227 2151 — Millcroft, Frankby Road, Greasby, Wirral, 0151 677 8282.

NEWTON ABBOT — Devon — Mr Roy Perkins — 21 Prospect TerraceNewton Abbot, Devon, TQ12 2LN, 01626 61596 — Devon FA HQ, Coach Rd, Newton Abbot, Devon, 01626 335011.

NEWTON ABBOT SPURS — Devon — Mr M Hayman — Newsagents, Dolphin Square, Bovey Tracey, Devon, TQ13 9AL, 01626 832505, — Newton Abbot Spurs, Recreation Ground, Newton Abbot, Devon, 01626 65343.

NEWTON FLOTMAN — Anglian Combination — 1 — Mr N Harrod — 158 Norwich Road, New Costessey, Norwich, Norfolk, NR5 0EH, 01603 746507 B:622494 — N.F. Village Centre, Grove Way, Newton Flotman, Norfolk.

NEWTON ST CYRES — Devon — Mr Roger Dymond — 12 New Estate, Newton St Cyres, near Exeter, Devon, EX5 5AR, 01392 851719, — Recreation Ground, Newton St Cyres, Nr Exeter, Devon, 01392 851546.

NICHOLIANS LOCOMOTIVE — S&I — S — Mr Raymond Storey — 28 Maidenhall Approach, Ipswich, Suffolk, IP2 8NX, 01473 688577 — Y.M.C.A. Rugby Club, Rushmere Road, Ipswich, Suffolk, (Loco Club 01473 688708).

NOMADS — Kent County — 3W — Mr Les R C Holmes — 51 Church Street, Edenbridge, Kent, TN8 5BQ, 01732 865258 — Great Mowshurst Farm, Four Elms Road, Edenbridge, Kent.

NORCROSS & WARBRECK — West Lancs — 2 — Mr S Lee — 100 St Andrews Rd South, St Annes, Lancs, HY8 1PS, 01253 720363 B 01253 331335 — 200 yds from 2nd Rb, from M55.

NORTH GREENFORD UNITED — Middx — P — Mr John Bivens — 1 The Green, Sarratt, Hertfordshire, WD3 6AY, 01923 270057 — Berkeley Fields, Berkeley Avenue, Greenford, Middlesex, 0181 422 8923.

NORTH KILWORTH — Leics — 1 — Mr Raymond Bell — 3 High Street, North Kilworth, Lutterworth, Leicestershire, LE17 6ET, 01858 880758, — Rugby Road, North Kilworth, Lutterworth, Leicestershire, 01858 880890.

NORTH MYMMS — Herts — P — Mick Fitt — 61 Holloways Lane, North Mymms, Hatfield, Hertfordshire, AL9 7NU, 01707 269790 — Welham Green Rec., Dellsome Lane, Welham Green, Hertfordshire, 01707 266972/260338.

NORTH SHIELDS ATHLETIC — Wearside — David Thompson — 38 Barnstaple Rd, North Shields, Tyne & Wear, NE29 8QF, 0191 259 0249 — Ralph Gardner Park, West Percy Road, Chirton, Nth Shields, Tyne & Wear.

NORTH SHIELDS ST COLUMBAS — Northern Alliance — P — A J Baird — 23 Balkwell Avenue, North Shields, Tyne & Wear, NE29 7JN, 0191 258 0833 — Purvis Park, St John's Green, Percy Main, Tyne & Wear.

NORTH WALSHAM TOWN — Anglian Combination — 1 — Mr J Hick — 9 Millard Close, North Walsham, Norfolk, NR28 0HH, 01692 404557, — Sports Centre, Greens Road, North Walsham, Norfolk, 01692 406888.

NORTHBANK — Northern Alliance — 2 — B Lancaster — 25 South Street, Carlisle, Cumbria, CA1 2EW, 01228 39383 — Carlisle City F.C., Sheepmount Spts Cplx, Carlisle, Cumbria, 01228 26569.

NORTHERN SOCIAL CLUB — Northern Alliance — 2 — D Fish — 15 Fairfield Drive, North Seaton, Ashington, Northumberland, 01670 811975, — Northern Social F.C., Newbiggin Spts Centre, Newbiggin-by-the-Sea, Northumberland.

NORTHFIELD C.A.V. — Middx — P — Mr Graham O'Dell — 5 Olympic Way, Greenford, Middlesex, UB6 8NQ, 0181 575 3745 — Yeading F.C. Annexe, Beaconsfield Road, Hayes, Middlesex, UB4 0SL, 0181 848 7362/7369 F:561 1063.

NORTHOLT SAINTS — Middx — 1 — Mr Simon Dunleavy — 59 Hollowfield Walk, Islip Manor, Northolt, Middlesex, UB5 5SX, 0181 841 3285 — Lord Halsbury's S&SC, Eastcote Lane, Northolt, Middlesex, 0181 841 0475.

NORTON WOODSEATS — Sheffield — 2 — Mr Malcolm Hutchby — 43 Manor Park Crescent, Sheffield, South Yorkshire, S2 1WX, 0114 264 4603 — Norton Woodseats FC, Coach & Horses Grnd, Dronfield, Derbyshire, 01246 413469.

NORWICH C.E.Y.M.S. — Anglian Combination — Mr N D Laws — 14 Eastern Road, Thorpe St Andrew, Norwich, Norfolk, NR7 0UJ, 01603 437229 — Hilltops Spts Centre, Swardeston, Norwich, Norfolk.

NORWICH ST JOHNS — Anglian Combination — Mr T Franklin — 35 Falcon Road (East), Salhouse Road, Norwich, Norfolk, NR7 8XZ, 01603 429026 — Cringleford Rec., Oakfields Road, Cringleford, Norfolk.

NORWICH UNION — Anglian Combination — Mr C McCullough — 10 Glenburn Court, Sprowston, Norwich, Norfolk, NR7 8DR, 01603 402242 B:622200, — Pinebanks, School Lane, Harvey Lane, Thorpe, Norfolk.

NOSTELL MINERS WELFARE — West Yorkshire — P — R Winfield — 13 Edward Drive, Outwood, Wakefield, Yorks, WF1 2LL, 01924 826408 — Miners Welfare Gd, New Crofton, Wakefield, HQ 01924 862348.

NOTTINGHAMSHIRE POLICE — Notts Alliance — S — John Beeston — 17 Alandene Ave, Watnall, Nottingham, Notts, NG16 1HH, 0115 938 2110 B0115942099X4560 — Police Training Cnt, Epperstone, Nottingham, Notts.

NUNTHORPE ATHLETIC— Teesside — Mr Kevin Levitt — 131 Burlam Road, Middlesbrough, Cleveland, TS5 5AX, 01642 824332 — Recreation Club, Guisborough Lane, Nunthorpe, Cleveland, 01642 313251.

N.C.B. MALTBY MINERS WELFARE — Sheffield — 2 — Mr Jim Plant — c/o 5 Gaitskill Close, Maltby, Rotherham, South Yorkshire, S66 7JR — Maltby Miners Welf., Muglet Lane, Maltby, Rotherham, South Yorkshire, 01709 812462(matchdays).

N.P.I. — Kent County — 3W — Mr Chris Booth — 30 Granville Road, Tunbridge Wells, Kent, TN1 2NX, 01892 534248, — Tonbridge Farm, Longmead, Darenth Rd, Tonbridge, Kent, 01892 534248.

OAKWOOD — Kent County — P — Mr Peter J Mannering — 24 Ellenswood Close, Otham, Maidstone, Kent, ME15 8SG, 01622 862482, — Honey Lane, Otham, Maidstone, Kent.

OCEAN INN — Kent County — 2E — Mr Alan Roots — Flat 2, 4 High Street, Dymchurch, Romney Marsh, Kent, TN29 0NG, 01303 872814 B:260551x2122 — St Mary's Road Rec., Dymchurch, Romney Marsh, Kent.

OLD BEXLEIANS — Kent County — 3W — Mr Robert Carter — 67 Westbrooke Road, Welling, Kent, DA16 1PS, 0181 301 0791 — Bexley Grammar Sch., Danson Lane, Welling, Kent.

OLD BRADWELL UNITED — South Midlands — 1 — David Bird — 24 Loughton Rd, Bradwell Village, Milton Keynes, Buckinghamshire, MK13 9AA, 01908 315947 — Abbey Rd, Bradwell Village, Milton Keynes, Bucks, 01908 312355.

OLD DUNSTABLIANS — South Midlands — 1 — Craig Renfrew — 75b Princes St, Dunstable, Beds, LU6 3AS, 01582 471794 — Lancot Park, Dunstable Rd, Totternhoe, Beds, 01582 663735.

OLD EDWARDIANS — Sheffield — 2 — Mr Brian Colley — 20 Ashland Road, Sheffield, South Yorkshire, S7 1RJ, 0114 281 9438, — Bawtry Rd Rec Centre, Tinsley, Sheffield, South Yorkshire.

OLD PALUDIANS — Chiltonian — P — P Holt — 14 Lime Close, Wokingham, Berkshire, RG41 4AW, 01734 890815 — Stanley Jones Field, Berry Hill, Taplow, Maidenhead, Berkshire, 01628 21745.

OLLERTON TOWN — Notts Alliance — S — Jack Graham — 73 Petersmith Drive, New Ollerton, Mansfield, Notts, NG22 9SD, 01623 863127 — Walesby Lane, New Ollerton, Nottingham, Notts.

ORWIN — Northern Alliance — 1 — B C Burn — 40 Helmsley Drive, Rosehill, Wallsend, Tyne & Wear, 0191 287 1046 — Rising Sun Welfare, Kings Road North, Wallsend, Tyne & Wear.

OSTERLEY — Middx — P — Mr Christopher Clapham — 132 Eastbourne Road, Brentford, Middlesex, TW8 9PG, 0181 568 4660, White Lodge Club, Syon Lane, Osterley, Middlesex, 0181 758 1191.

OTFORD UNITED — Kent County — 2W — Mrs Margaret Smith — 13 Rye Lane, Otford, Kent, 01959 522927, — Recreation Ground, High Street, Otford, Kent, 01959 524405.

OTTERBOURNE — Hampshire — 2 — Mr Robin J Broom — 249 Passfield Avenue, Eastleigh, Hampshire, SO50 9NB, 01703 328992 B:395147 — Oakwood Park, off Oakwood Avenue, Otterbourne, Hampshire, 01962 714681.

OTTERBURN — Northern Alliance — 2 — J Cowens — Greenchesters Farm, Otterburn, Northumberland, NE19 1JG, 01830 520471, — Otterburn F.C., R.T.C. Sports Centre, Otterburn, Northumberland.

OTTERSHAW — Surrey — P — Mr Steve Caswell — 2 Chaworth Road, Ottershaw, Surrey, KT16 0PE, 01932 872133 M:0836 602381 — Woodham Court S.C., Martyrs Lane, Woodham, Woking, Surrey, 01483 763375.

OTTERY ST MARY — Devon — Mr Ray Dack — 13 Vaughan Rise, Whipton, Exeter, Devon, EX1 3UD, 01392 422190 — Ottery St Mary FC, Washbrook Meadows, Ottery St Mary, Devon, 01404 813539.

OUGHTIBRIDGE WAR MEMORIAL SPORTS CLUB — Sheffield — P — Mr Barry Eustace — 25 Broomfield Road, Stocksbridge, Sheffield, South Yorkshire, S30 5AR, 0114 288 5853 — Station Lane, Oughtibridge, Sheffield, South Yorkshire.

OULTON BROAD & LOWESTOFT RAILWAY — Anglian Combination — 1 — Mr I McMeekan — 618 London Road South, Lowestoft, Suffolk, NR33 0LF, 01502 563018 — Kirkley High School, Kirkley Run, Lowestoft, Suffolk.

OVERTON UNITED — Hampshire — 1 — Mrs Anita Wheeler — 3 Lordsfield Gardens, Overton, Hampshire, RG25 2EW, 01256 771241 B:770770 — Recreation Centre, Bridge Street, Overton, Hampshire, 01256 770561.

OXHEY JETS — Herts — P — Mr John Elliott — 7 Brampton Road, South Oxhey, Watford, Hertfordshire, WD1 6PF, 0181 428 6382 — Chilwell Gardens, South Oxhey, Watford, Hertfordshire, 0181 421 4965.

PADDOCK WOOD TOWN — Kent County — 1W — Mrs Joan Inhester — 17 Newton Gardens, Paddock Wood, near Tonbridge, Kent, TN12 6AJ, 01892 833766, — Memorial P.F., Maidstone Road, Paddock Wood, Kent.

PADIHAM — West Lancs — 2 — Mr C Barker — 40 Carter Street, Burnley, Lancs, 01282 452395 — Well St, close to, Hare and Hounds ph, 01282 773742.

PANTEG — Welsh — 3 — Mr Colin Davies — 54 Monmouth House, Cwmbran, Gwent, NP44 1QU, 01633 877131 B:01222 771411 — Panteg House, Greenhill Road, Griffithstown, Gwent.

PARK STREET VILLAGE — Herts — 1 — Mr William Whinnett — 1 Sturmer Close, St Albans, Hertfordshire, AL4 0BN, 01727 844825 — Park Street Rec., Park Street Lane, Park Street, Hertfordshire.

PARLEY SPORTS — Dorset — Mrs Pat Coombes — 332 Christchurch Rd, West Parley, Ferndown, Dorset, BH22 6SN, 01202 578546 — Parley Sports Club, Christchurch Rd, West Parley, Dorset, 01202 573345.

PARRAMORE SPORTS — Sheffield — P — Mr Frank Wilkinson — 64 Slate Street, Sheffield, South Yorkshire, S2 3HB, 0114 249 8594 — Davy Spts & Soc Club, Prince of Wales Road, Sheffield, South Yorkshire.

PAULSGROVE — Hampshire — 2 — S J Cox — 22 Alameda Road, Purbrook, Waterlooville, Hampshire, PO7 5HD, 01705 785110, — Grove Cb, Marsden Rd, Allaway Avenue, Paulsgrove, Hampshire, 01705 324102.

PEASEDOWN ATHLETIC — Somerset — P — Mr Dave Wilkinson — 52 Clandown Road, Paulton, Somerset, BS18 5SF, 01761 412450 M:0802 646253, — Miners Welfare Park, Peasedown St John, Bath, Somerset, 01761 437319(club club).

PEDIGREE PETFOODS — Leics — 1 — Mr Jim Freeman — 40 Kestrel Road, Melton Mowbray, Leicestershire, LE13 0AY, 01664 500282 B:410808, — Sports Ground, Saxby Road, Melton Mowbray, Leicestershire.

PEGASUS JUNIORS — Hellenic — 1 — Mr Brian C James — 7 Loder Drive, Hereford, Herefordshire, HR1 1DS, 01432 274982 B:01568 612367, — Essex Arms, Widemarsh Street, Hereford, Herefordshire, 01432 268705.

PELICAN — Notts Alliance — S — Dave Eastwood — 42 Chetwin Rd, Bilbrough, Nottingham, Notts, NG8 4HN, 0115 913 8345 — Brian Wakefield SG, Lenton Lane, Nottingham, Notts, 0115 986 8255.

PENISTONE CHURCH — Sheffield — 1 — Mr David Hampshire — 36 Park Avenue, Penistone, Sheffield, South Yorkshire, S30 6DN, 01226 764689, — Memorial Ground, Church View Road, Penistone, South Yorkshire, S30 6AT.

PENN & TYLERS GREEN — Chiltonian — P — K Croxon — 10 Beaconsfield Mews, Holtspur Top Lane, Beaconsfield, Buckinghamshire, HP9 1BF, 01494 670694 — French School Meadow, Elm Road, Penn, Buckinghamshire, 01494 815346.

PENRHIWCEIBER RANGERS — Welsh — 1 — Mrs Catherine Pritchard — 8 Hughes Street, Miskin, Mountain Ash, Mid-Glamorgan, 01443 477631 — Glasbrook, Glasbrook Terrace, Penrhiwceiber, Mid-Glamorgan, 01443 473368.

PEPPARD — Chiltonian — P — Mr Chris Boyles — 14 Redwood Avenue, Woodley, Reading, Berkshire, RG5 4DR, 0118 969 9488 B:01235 524326, — Bishops Wd Spts Cnte, Horsepond Road, Sonning Cmn, Reading, Berkshire, 01734 722675.

PERCY MAIN AMATEURS — Northern Alliance — 1 — G Marsh — 32 Selkirk Way, Chirton Park, North Shields, Tyne & Wear, NE29 8DD, 0191 258 0202 — Purvis Park, St John's Green, Percy Main, Tyne & Wear.

PHOENIX — Sheffield — P — Mr Trevor Cottam — 41 Pleasant Road, Sheffield, South Yorkshire, S12 2BD, 0114 239 0897 — Phoenix Spts Complex, Brinsworth, Rotherham, South Yorkshire.

PHOENIX SPORTS — Kent County — 1W — Mr Martyn Cole — 91 Hurst Road, Northumberland Heath, Erith, Kent, DA8 3EW, 01322 350750, — Phoenix Sports Club, Mayplace Road East, Bexleyheath, Kent, 01322 526159.

PILKINGTON — Mid-Cheshire — 2 — Paul Pinder — 629 Eltonhead Rd, Sutton Heath, St Helens, Merseyside, WA9 5SX, 01744 816158 B 0151 420 9752, Pilkington FC, Ruskin Drive, St Helens, Merseyside, 01744 22893.

PIRELLI GENERAL — Hampshire — 1 — Miss Bernice Fox — 31 Spring Close, Fair Oak, Eastleigh, Hampshire, SO50 7BB, 01703 693537 M:0402 139613, — Jubilee Spts Ground, Chestnut Avenue, Eastleigh, Hampshire, 01703 612721.

PITSHANGER — Middx — P — Mr Chris Green — 14 Silver Birch Close, Ickenham, Middlesex, UB10 8AP, 01895 231796 B:0802 636516 — Pitshanger F.C., Scotch Common, Ealing, Middlesex, 0181 991 9826.

PITSTONE & IVINGHOE — South Midlands — 1 — Jay Edlam — 22 Maud Janes Close, Ivinghoe, Leighton Buzzard, Bedfordshire, LU7 9ED, 01296 668663 — Recreation Ground, Pitstone, Beds, 01296 661271.

PLATT UNITED — Kent County — 1W — Mr Glenn N Broad — The Lilacs, Rowhill Road, Hextable, Kent, BR8 7RL, 01322 662452 B:01634 240463, — Stonehouse Field, Longmill Lane, Platt, Kent.

PLYMOUTH COMMAND — Devon — Maurice Launce — 57 Chaucer Way — Brake Farm, Crownhill, Plymouth, Devon, PL5 3EQ, 01752 700168 — Millbay Park, West Hoe Road, Plymouth, Devon, 0589 296662.

PLYMOUTH PARKWAY — Devon — Mr S Cadmore — 25 Dudley Gdns — Eggbuckland, Plymouth, Devon, PL6 5PE, 01752 782661, — Plymouth Parkway FC, Parkway, Ernesettle,Plymouth, Devon, 01752 363080.

PLYMSTOCK UNITED — Devon — Dave Baskwill — 334 Fort Austin Ave — Crownhill, Plymouth, Devon, PL6 5TG, 01752 706284 — Plymstock Utd FC, Dean Cross, Plymstock, Devon, 01752 406776.

PONTARDAWE ATHLETIC — Welsh — 2 — Mr Joseph Krem Szczesnian — 13 Flynnonwen, Hill Rise Park, Clydach, West Glamorgan, SA6 5DX, 01792 845263 B:654091 — Recreation Ground, Trading Estate, Pontardawe, West Glamorgan, 01792 642228.

PONTELAND UNITED — Northern Alliance — P — L McMahon — 1 Wardle Drive, Annitsford, Cramlington, Northumberland, NE23 7DB, 0191 250 0463 — Ponteland United FC, Ponteland Leis. Ctre, Ponteland, Northumberland.

PONTLOTTYN BLAST FURNACE — Welsh — 3 — Mr Barry Horsman — Wordesley, Gwerthonor Road, Gilfach, Bargoed, Mid-Glamorgan, CF8 8JS, 01443 831606, — Welfare Ground, Hill Road, Pontlottyn, Mid-Glamorgan, 01685 841305.

PONTYCLUN — Welsh — 2 — Mr Peter Shilton — 3 Lilac Drive, Chandlers Reach, Llantwit Fardre, Mid-Glamorgan, CF38 2PH, 01443 217305 B:Cdf 753271x3023, — vor Park, Cowbridge Road, Pontyclun, Mid-Glamorgan, 01443 222182.

PONTYPRIDD TOWN — Welsh — 2 — Mr Ray Robinson — 199 Bryntirion, Mountain Ash, Mid-Glamorgan, CF45 4PJ, 01443 472900 — Pontypridd Town F.C., Ynysangharad Park, Pontypridd, Mid-Glamorgan, 01443 486571.

POOLE TOWN — Hampshire — 1 — Mr Bill Read — 15 Addison Close, Romsey, Hampshire, SO51 7TL, 01794 517991 — Petersham Lane, Gants Gommon, Holt, Wimborne, Dorset, 01258 840379.

PORINGLAND WANDERERS — Anglian Combination — 1 — Mr Ben Casey — 8 Malten Close, Poringland, Norwich, Norfolk, NR14 7RW, 01508 493791, — Poringland Mem Field, Poringland, Norwich, Norfolk, 01508 495198.

PORT TALBOT ATHLETIC — Welsh — 1 — Mr John Dawkins — 28 Morrison Road, Sandfields Estate, Port Talbot, West Glamorgan, 01639 897912 B:813663, — Victoria Park, Victoria Road, Aberavon, Pt Talbot, West Glamorgan, 01639 882465.

PORTH TYWYN SUBURBS — Welsh — 2 — Mr Colin Jenkins — 25 St Mary's Rise, Burry Port, Dyfed, SA16 0SH, 01554 832109 B:01792 222234, — arc Tywyn, Woodbrook Terrace, Burry Port, Dyfed, 01554 833991(grd) 833471(club).

PORTHCAWL TOWN — Welsh — 2 — Mr Steve Harris — 18 Mary Street, Porthcawl, Mid-Glamorgan, CF36 3YA, 01656 786496 B:788038 — , Porthcawl Town AFC, Locks Lane, Porthcawl, Mid-Glamorgan, 01656 784804.

PORTISHEAD — Somerset — P — Mr Brian Hobbs — 13 St Peters Road, Portishead, Bristol, North Somerset, BS20 9QY, 01275 847612 — Bristol Road P.F., Portishead, Bristol, North Somerset, 01275 847136.

PORTLAND UNITED — Dorset — David Camp — 23 Four Acres, Weston, Portland, Dorset, DT5 2JG, 01305 821816 — New Grove Corner, Crove Rd, Portland, Dorset, 01305 861489.

POULTON TOWN — West Lancs — 1 — Mr D Sponder — 11 Fairfield Ave, Poulton-le-Fylde, Lancs, FY6 7DR, 01253 890284 — Cottam Hall PF, Blackpool Old Rd, Poulton-le-Fylde, Lancs.

POULTON VICTORIA — West Cheshire — 1 — Mr Harry Deery — 15 Dorset Drive, Irby, Wirral, L61 8SX, 0151 648 2903 — Victoria Park, Rankin Street, Wallasey, Merseyside, 0151 638 3559.

POYNTON — Mid-Cheshire — 1 — Paul Burch — 24 Brookfield Ave, Poynton, Cheshire, SK12 1HZ, 01625 871205 B 0161 834 4319 — Poynton FC, London Rd North, Poynton, Cheshire, 01625 875765.

PRESTON WEST END — West Lancs — 2 — Mr S Robinson — 12 Hurstway, Fulwood, Preston, Lancs, 01772 715907 B 01254 768067, — Close to Shawes Arms, London Rd, Preston.

PRESTWOOD — Chiltonian — P — R Martin — 27 Westrick Walk, Prestwood, Great Missenden, Buckinghamshire, 01494 864744, — Honor End Lane, Prestwood, Great Missenden, Buckinghamshire, 01494 865946.

PROCTER & GAMBLE MONKSEATON — Northern Alliance — 1 — R Woods — 15 Rayleigh Drive, Wideopen, Newcastle-upon-Tyne, Tyne & Wear, 0191 256 2988 — Monkseaton Comm H.S., Monkseaton, Whitley Bay, Northumberland.

PURTON — Hellenic — 1 — Mr Nick Webb — 4 Glevum Close, Purton, Swindon, Wiltshire, SN5 9HA, 01793 770242 B:852451 — Purton F.C., The Red House, Purton, Wiltshire, 01793 770262.

QUARRY NOMADS — Chiltonian — P — K Dolton — 58 Pitts Road, Headington, Oxfordshire, OX3 8AZ, 01865 450256, — Quarry Nomads F.C., St Margarets Road, Headington, Oxford, 0802 865367.

QUEENS KEEP — Hampshire — 3 — Mr Donald Campbell — 81 Lumsden Avenue, Shirley, Southampton, Hampshire, SO15 5EJ, 01703 781362 B:792106, — Civil Service Club, off Malmesbury Road, Shirley, Southampton, Hampshire, 01703 771950.

QUEEN'S HOTEL — Sheffield — 2 — Mr John Mills — 11 Norwood Avenue, Maltby, Rotherham, South Yorkshire, S66 8JG, 01709 813609 — Braithwell &, Micklebring, Main Str, Braithwell, South Yorkshire.

RADCLIFFE OLYMPIC — Notts Alliance — 2 — C Johnson — 2 The Firs, Holme Pierrepoint, Nottingham, Notts, NG12 2LT, 0115 933 3791, — Wharf Lane, Radcliffe-on-Trent, Nottingham, Notts.

RADFORD — Central Midlands — P — Mr Malcolm Goodwin — , 0115 978 1587, Radford FC, Radford Rd, Radford, Notts, 0115 942 3250.

RADSTOCK TOWN — Somerset — 1 — Mr Graham Seymour — 12 Wesley Avenue, Radstock, Somerset, 01761 437889, — Southfield Rec. Grnd, Frome Hill, Radstock, Somerset, 01761 435004.

RAINWORTH MINERS WELFARE — Notts Alliance — S — Alan Wright — 10 Faraday Rd, Mansfield, Notts, NG18 4ES, 01623 24379 B 01623 553237, — Rainworth MW, Kirklington Rd, Rainworth, Notts.

READING EXILES — Reading — S — M J Aust — 24 Aylesham Close, Tilehurst, Reading, Berkshire, RG3 4XG, 01734 421453 B:01734 561881 — Palmer Park Stadium, Wokingham Rd, Reading, Berkshire.

REEPHAM TOWN — Anglian Combination — Mr D W Norris — 12 Silver End, Reepham, Norwich, Norfolk, NR10 4LH, 01603 870634 Car:0860 290264, — Stimpsons Piece Rec., Reepham, Norwich, Norfolk.

RETFORD UNITED — Notts Alliance — 1 — Jeff Lamb — 18 Northumbria Drive, Retford, Nottingham, Notts, DN22 7PR, 01777 705833 — Oaklands, off London Rd, Retford, Notts.

RICHMOND TOWN — Teesside — Mr Geoff Hunter — 49 Willance Grove, Richmond, North Yorkshire, DL10 4HA, 01748 822657 B:873709/873745 — Earls Orchard P.F., Sleegill, Richmond, North Yorkshire.

RIDDINGS ST JAMES — MRA — 1 — Mrs Vickie Newey — 21 Spanker Lane, Nether Heage, Derbyshire, DE56 2AT, 01773 853358 B:01629 580602, — The Park, West Street, Riddings, Derbyshire.

RINGWOOD TOWN — Hampshire — 2 — Mrs S Crewe — 278 Windham Road, Bournemouth, Dorset, BH1 4QU, 01202 398975(inc f) B:557544, — The Clubhouse, Long Lane, Ringwood, Hampshire, 01425 473448.

RISBOROUGH RANGERS — South Midlands — S — Mr Derrick J Wallace — 42 Ash Road, Princes Risborough, Buckinghamshire, HP27 0BQ, 01844 345179 — Windsor, Horsenden Lane, Princes Risborough, Bucks, 01844 274176.

RISCA UNITED — Welsh — 1 — Ann Luckwell — 19 Maple Gardens, Pontymister, Risca, Gwent, NP1 6AR, 01633 613434 B:812259, — Ty-Isak Park, Pontymister Road, Risca, Gwent, 01633 615689(c) 615081(ground).

ROBIN HOOD ATHLETIC — West Yorkshire — P — G Hart — 16 Belfry Ct, Outwood, Wakefield, WF1 3TY, 01924 820635 — Behind Coach & Horse, Rothwell Haigh, Leeds, 0113 282 1021.

ROBINSONS — Somerset — 1 — Mr Martin Shipway — 32 Fraser Street, Bedminster, Bristol, BS3 4LY, 0117 985 1872 — Robinsons Spts Grnd, St Johns Lane, Bedminster, Bristol, 0117 966 4183.

ROCKLAND UNITED — Anglian Combination — Mr S J Fisher — 17 Rectory Road — Rocklands, Attleborough, Norfolk, NR17 1XA, 01953 483501 — Rocklands P.F., Rocklands, Attleborough, Norfolk.

ROLLS ROYCE & ASSOCIATES — MRA — 2 — Mr Graham Smedley — 22 Hindscarth Crescent, Mickleover, Derby, Derbyshire, DE3 5NN, 01332 511388 B:661461x4773 — Rolls Royce Spts Grd, Merril Way, Allenton, Derby, Derbyshire, 01332 249167(groundsman).

ROSS TOWN — Hellenic — 1 — Tim Barnard — Apsley House, Whitchurch, Ross-on-Wye, Herefordshire, 01600 890722 b 012856 59866 — Cinderford Town FC, Causeway Ground, Hilldene, Cinderford, Glos, 01594 822039.

ROSSINGTON — Central Midlands — P — Mr Ian Wilson — The Wickets, 3 Holly Close, Rossington, Doncaster, South Yorkshire, DN11 0XX, 01302 867221 — Welfare Ground, West End Lane, Rossington, Yorks, 01302 868272.

ROTHWELL ATHLETIC — West Yorkshire — P — D Amann — 28Haigh Rd, Rothwell, Leeds, Yorks, LS26 0NH, 0113 282 7322 B 0113 271 4420, — Royds Lane, Rothwell, Leeds, Yorks, HQ 0113 282 0723.

ROUNDHEAD — Reading — S — Eric Wise — 63 St Saviours Rd, Reading, Berkshire, RG1 6EJ, 01734 610063 — Prospect Park, Liebenrood Road, Reading, Berkshire.

ROWSLEY — MRA — P — Mr Kevin P Wagstaff — 91 Northwood Lane, Darley Dale, Matlock, Derbyshire, DE4 2HR, 01629 734584, — Rowsley Rec. Ground, School Lane, Rowsley, Derbyshire.

RUDDINGTON UNITED — Notts Alliance — S — John Fisk — 3 Savages Rd, Ruddington, Nottingham, Notts, NG11 6EW, 0115 984 2552, — The Elms Park, Loughborough Rd, Ruddington, Notts, 0115 984 4976.

RUSTHALL — Kent County — 1W — Mr Keith Brownson — 13 Bretland Road, Rusthall, Tunbridge Wells, Kent, TN4 8PS, 01892 536544 — Jockey Farm, Nellington Road, Rusthall, Tunbdge W., Kent.

RUSTON SPORTS — Lincs — Mr P S Dickson — 42 Fontwell Crescent, Lincoln, Lincolnshire, LN6 7LE, 01522 684738, — R.M.S.C. Club, Newark Road, Lincoln, Lincolnshire, 01522 680057.

RUTHERFORD NEWCASTLE — Northern Alliance — 2 — S Coxon — 6 Hollydene, Kibblesworth, Gateshead, Tyne & Wear, NE11 0NR, 0191 410 9604, — Farnacres, Coach Rd, Lobley Hill, Gateshead, Tyne & Wear.

RYE UNITED — Kent County — 1E — Mr Barry Goodsell — 15 Spring Hill, Northiam, near Rye, East Sussex, TN31 6PX, 01797 253208, — Sydney Allnut Pav., Cricket/F'ball Salts, Rye, East Sussex, 01797 223855.

RYHOPE COLLERY WELFARE — Wearside — Ray Hartley — 2 Stannington Gardens, Tunstall, Sunderland, Tyne & Wear, 0191 528 2939 — Ryhope Recreation Pk, Ryhope Str., Ryhope, Sunderland, Tyne & Wear, 0191 521 2843.

RYLANDS — Mid-Cheshire — 1 — Ian Finchett — 31 Elizabeth Drive, Padgate, Warrington, Cheshire, WA1 4JQ, 01925 816911, — Rylands AFC, Gorsey Lane, Warrington, Cheshire, 01925 625700.

RYTON — Northern Alliance — 1 — L Robson — 31 Park View Gardens, Runhead, Ryton, Tyne & Wear, NE40 3JD, 0191 413 7628 — Clara Vale Rec Grnd, Clara Vale, Crawcrook, Tyne & Wear.

SAFFRON DYNAMO — Leics — 1 — Mr Bob King — 14 Bramley Close, Broughton Astley, Leicester, Leicestershire, LE9 6QU, 01455 284270 B:554101, — Saffron Dynamo F.C., Cambridge Road, Whetstone, Leicestershire, 0116 284 9695.

SAHAM TONEY — Anglian Combination — Mr J Knights — 35 Grovebury Close — Brundall, Norwich, Norfolk, NR13 5NJ, 01603 714362, — Pavilion, Pages Lane P.F., Saham Toney, Norfolk.

SALTFORD — Somerset — 1 — Mr Colin Baker — 2 St Cadoc House, Keynsham, Bristol, BS18 1HD, 0117 986 6183 — Playing Fields, Norman Road, Saltford, Avon, 01225 873725.

SANDRIDGE ROVERS — Herts — P — Mr Graham Hardwick — 21 Woodcock Hill, Sandridge, St Albans, Hertfordshire, AL4 9EF, 01727 855334, — Spencer Rec. Ground, Sandridge, St Albans, Hertfordshire, 01727 855159/835506.

SANTOS — MRA — 1 — Mr Anthony Bull — 160 Matlock Road, Chaddesden, Derby, Derbyshire, DE21 4QB, 01332 675122 — Parkers Piece, City Road, Derby, Derbyshire.

SARRATT — Herts — 1 — Mick Warner — Colinwood, 45 Church Lane, Sarratt, near Rickmansworth, Hertfordshire, WD3 6HN, 01923 264618, — King George V P.F., King Georges Avenue, Sarratt, Hertfordshire.

SCOLE UNITED — Anglian Combination — Mr D Hill — 30 Ransome Avenue, Scole, Diss, Norfolk, IP21 4EA, 01379 740696 — Ransome Avenue P.F., Scole, Diss, Norfolk, 01379 741204.

SCOT — South Midlands — 1 — Mrs Ann Land — 18 Coleridge Close, Bletchley, Milton Keynes, Buckinghamshire, MK3 5AFU, 01908 372228 — SCOT FC, Selbourne Ave, Bletchley, Bucks, 01908 368881.

SEAFORD TOWN — Sussex County — 3 — Mr M Webster — 113 Lexden Drive, Seaford, East Sussex, BN25 3JF, 01323 899218, — Crouch Gardens, East Street, Seaford, East Sussex, 01323 892221.

SEATON DELAVAL AMATEURS — Northern Alliance — P — V Donnelly — 6 Hollymount Square, Bedlington, Northumberland, 01670 829464 — Seaton Delaval AFC, Wheatridge Park, Seaton Delaval, Northumberland.

SELSTON — MRA — P — Mr Mark Pearce — 4 Rutland Road, Westwood, Jacksdale, Nottinghamshire, NG16 5JQ, 01773 609886 — Parish Hall Ground, Mansfield Road, Selston, Nottinghamshire.

SEVEN SISTERS — Welsh — 3 — Mr David Herdman — 11 Pen-Y-Banc, Seven Sisters, Neath, West Glamorgan, 01639 700843 — Welfare Ground, Church Road, Seven Sisters, Neath, West Glamorgan, 01639 700354.

SEVENOAKS TOWN — Kent County — P — Mr Eddie Diplock — 23 Holly Bush Lane, Sevenoaks, Kent, TN13 3TH, 01732 454280, — Greatness Park, Seal Road, Sevenoaks, Kent, 01732 741987(Sat. pm only).

SHAFTESBURY — Dorset — Mrs Alison Marsh — 16 Jeanneau Close — Shaftesbury, Dorset, SP7 8PQ, 01747 855832, Cockrams, Coppice Street, Shaftesbury, Dorset, 01747 853990.

SHANKHOUSE — Northern Alliance — 1 — S Ramsey — 6 Brinkburn Avenue, Cramlington, Northumberland, NE23 6TB, 01670 715943 — Shankhouse F.C., Bates Welfare, Seaton Delaval, Northumberland.

SHARDLOW ST JAMES — Central Midlands — P — Mr Reg Symcox — 22 West End Drive, Shardlow, Derby, Derbyshire, DE7 2GY, 01332 792733, — The Wharf, Shardlow, Derby, Derbys, 01332 799135.

SHEEPBRIDGE — Central Midlands — P — Mr Allan Staniforth — 11 Grasmere Close, Newbold, Chesterfield, Derbyshire, S41 8EG, 01246 20554 — , GKN Sports Ground, Newbold Rd, Newbold, Derby, 01246 234282.

SHEERNESS EAST — Kent County — 1E — Mr Jonathan Longhurst — 5 Week's Court, Mountfield, Queensborough, Sheppey, Kent, ME11 5DB, 01795 667758 B:668515, — Sheerness East WMC, 47 Queensborough Rd, Sheerness, Kent, 01795 662049.

SHEERWATER — Surrey — P — Mr Trevor Wenden — 14 Byrefield Road, Guildford, Surrey, GU2 6UD, 01483 38686, — Blackmore Crescent, Sheerwater Estate, Woking, Surrey.

SHEFFIELD BANKERS — Sheffield — 1 — Mr Peter Gray — 71 Carr Road, Walkley, Sheffield, South Yorkshire, S6 2WY, 0114 281 7687 — Sheff. Transport SC, Meadowhead, Sheffield, South Yorkshire.

SHEFFIELD CENTRALIANS — Sheffield — 2 — Mr Chris Gribben — 63 Lockwood Avenue, South Anston, Sheffield, South Yorkshire, S31 7GQ, 01909 562030 B:0114 272 4036, Woodbourn Stadium, 3 Stadium Way, Sheffield, South Yorkshire, S9.

SHEFFIELD HALLAM UNIVERSITY — Central Midlands — P — Stephen Wright — 198 Home Lane, Mainbridge, Sheffield, Yorks, 0378 481483 — Aurora Sports Gd, Bawtry Rd, Brinsworth, Yorks, 01709 372613.

SHEFFIELD LANE TOP — Sheffield — 2 — Mr Des Barlow — 29 Strawberry Avenue, Sheffield, South Yorkshire, S5 9GP, 0114 245 5265 — Forgemasters S & SC, Shirecliffe Road, Sheffield, South Yorkshire, S5.

SHELL — West Cheshire — 1 — Mr Joseph Davies — 35 Glencoe Road, Great Sutton, South Wirral, L66 4NA, 0151 339 0652 — Chester Road, Whitby, Ellesmere Port, South Wirral, 0151 200 7080/ 7050.

SHEPTON MALLET TOWN — Somerset — P — Mr Ken Hurrell — 3 Buckland Road, Shepton Mallet, Somerset, BA4 5TQ, 01749 344037 — Old Wells Road P.F., West Shepton, Shepton Mallet, Somerset, 01749 344609.

SHERBORNE ST JOHN — Hampshire — 3 — Mrs Jean Barton — 34 Pitcairn Close, Basingstoke, Hampshire, RG24 9BD, 01256 819802 — Charles Chute Rec., 2 Vyne Road, Sherborne St John, Hampshire.

SHERBORNE TOWN — Dorset — Malcolm Bartlett — 5 Wessex Rd, Stalbridge, Dorset, DT10 2PF, 01963 362880 — Raleigh Grove, The Terrace PF, Sherborne, Dorset, 01935 816110.

SHERBURN WHITE ROSE — West Yorkshire — P — Mrs S Inglis — 21 Deighton Avenue, Sherburn in Elmet, Leeds, Yorks, LS25 6BR, 01977 683089 — Recreation Gd, Finkle Hill, Sherburn in Elmet, Yorks, Emer Cont 01977 684953.

SHERINGHAM — Anglian Combination — Mr P R Bacon — 33 Nelson Road, Sheringham, Norfolk, NR26 8BX, 01263 823625 — Recreation Ground, Weybourne Road, Sheringham, Norfolk.

SHIELDFIELD SOCIAL CLUB — Northern Alliance — 2 — W Tindle — 43 Kinross Drive, North Kenton, Newcastle-upon-Tyne, Tyne & Wear, NE3 3JQ, 0191 285 4094 — Longbenton Comm Col., Longbenton, Newcastle-upon-Tyne, Tyne & Wear.

SHINEWATER ASSOCIATION — Sussex County — 3 — Mr Brian Dowling — 79 Harebeating Drive, Hailsham, East Sussex, BN27 1JE, 01323 442488 — Shinewater Lane, Milfoil Drive, Nth Langney, E'brne, East Sussex, 01323 765880.

SHIPDHAM — Anglian Combination — Mr R F Knights — Park Cottage, High Street, Shipdham, Thetford, Norfolk, IP25 7PA, 01362 820420 — Bullock Park, Mill Road, Shipdham, Thetford, Norfolk.

SHIREHAMPTON — Somerset — P — Mr Chris Hawker — 11 Lux Furlong, Sea Mills, Bristol, BS9 2QB, 0117 940 1067 — Recreation Ground, Penpole Lane, Shirehampton, Bristol, 0117 923 5461.

SHOTTERMILL — Surrey — P — Mr Ian Munday — 20 Erles Road, Liphook, Surrey, GU30 7BW, 01428 724986 F:722868, — Shottermill F.C., Woolmer Hill Spts Gd, Haslemere, Surrey, 01428 643072.

SIDLESHAM — Sussex County — 3 — Mr Peter Turner — 64 Hawthorn Road, Bognor Regis, West Sussex, PO21 2DD, 01243 822860 — Recreation Ground, Sidlesham, Chichester, West Sussex, 01243 641538.

SIKH HUNTERS — West Midlands — 1A — Mr Ronald Parker — 118 Alexandra Road, Fulbrook, Walsall, West Midlands, WS1 4A3, 01922 448995 — Hazelbrook, Hazel Lane, Gt Wyrley, Wyrley, West Midlands, 01922 410366.

SKEGNESS TOWN — Lincs — Mr Allan Gray — The Cedars Hotel, 7 Algartha Road, Skegness, Lincolnshire, PE25 2AG, 01754 763722, — Skegness Town F.C., Burgh Road, Skegness, Lincolnshire, 01754 764385.

SKEWEN ATHLETIC — Welsh — 2 — Mr John Harris — 22 Goshen Park, Skewen, Neath, West Glamorgan, SA10 6PT, 01792 423637, — Tennant Park, Skewen, Neath, West Glamorgan.

SLACK & PARR — MRA — P — Mr Roy W Withers — 1 Meynell Road, Long Eaton, Nottingham, Nottinghamshire, NG10 1AF, 0115 972 6170 B:01509 672306, Behind S&P Factory, Long Lane, Kegworth, Leicestershire.

SLEAFORD TOWN — Lincs — Mr John W Drew — 35 Durham Avenue, Sleaford, Lincolnshire, NG34 8UD, 01529 305099 — Sleaford Town F.C., Boston Road, Sleaford, Lincolnshire, 01529 306959(c - Market Place).

SLOUGH HEATING — Chiltonian — 1 — J Lake — 1 Hardymead Court, Kingsmead Road, Loudwater, Buckinghamshire, HP11 1JS, 01494 464147 — Stoke Park P.F., Northern Road, Slough, Buckinghamshire, 01753 694750.

SMETHWICK RANGERS — West Midlands — 1B — Mohan S Gill — Plot 8, Falcon Rise, Middlesmoor, Wilnecote, Tamworth, Staffordshire, B77 4PL, 01827 282901 B:62187, Parkfield Stadium, Rooker Avenue, Parkfields, W'pton, West Midlands, 01902 658645.

SNEINTON — Central Midlands — P — Mr Paul Shelton — 28 Freda Close, Gedling, Nottingham, Nottinghamshire, NG4 4GP, 0115 987 7527 b 0115 977 3371, — Sneinton FC, Stoke Lane, Gedling, Notts, 0850 155460.

SNODLAND — Kent County — 1W — Mr Terry M Reeves — 136 Townsend Road, Snodland, Kent, ME6 5RN, 01634 240076 — Potyn's Field, Paddlesworth Road, Snodland, Kent, 01634 243961.

SNOWDOWN COLLIERY WELFARE — Kent County — 1E — Mr Alan Jones — 121 St Radlgund's Road, Dover, Kent, CT17 0LA, 01304 211856 — Spinney Lane, Aylesham, Canterbury, Kent.

SOMERSETT AMBURY V. & E. — Herts — P — Mr John Venables — 156 Crossbrook Street, Cheshunt, Hertfordshire, EN8 8JY, 01992 636991 — The V & E Club, Goffs Lane, Cheshunt, Hertfordshire, 01992 624281.

SOUTH BANK — Wearside — Dave Di Marco — 146 Oxford Rd, Linthorpe, Middlesbrough, Cleveland, TS5 5EL, 01642 826514 — Mannion Park, Broadway, Trunk Rd, Grangetown, Cleveland.

SOUTH READING — Reading — S — David Spiller — 5 Village Close, Whitley Wood, Reading, Berkshire, 01734 864989 B:01734 871604, — Whitley Wood Rec Gd, Basingstoke Rd, Reading, Berkshire.

SOUTH SHIELDS CLEADON S.C. — Wearside — Mr Charlie Appleby — 49 Tynedale Road, South Shields, Tyne & Wear, 0191 454 5724, — Jack Clark Park, Horsly Hill Road, South Shields, Tyne & Wear.

SOUTH TYNESIDE UNITED — Wearside — 1Martin Lynn — 261 Sunderland Rd — South Shields, Tyne & Wear, 0191 455 5145 — Monkton Stadium, Dene Terrace, Jarrow, Tyne & Wear.

SOUTH WALES POLICE — Welsh — 3 — Derrick Price — 6 Salem Row, Gwaelod-Y-Garth, Cardiff, South Glamorgan, CF4 8HX, 01222 813511 B:888704 — Police Sports Ground, Waterton, Bridgend, Mid-Glamorgan, 01656 655555.

SOUTH WALSHAM — Anglian Combination — Mrs J Bruce — 24 Borton Road, Blofield Heath, Norwich, Norfolk, NR13 4RU, 01603 714220, — South Walsham F.C., The Playing Field, South Walsham, Norfolk.

SOUTHGATE — Middx — P — Joanne George — 47 Streamside Close, Edmonton, Middlesex, N9 9XB, 0181 345 5431 — Tottenhall Rd Sp. Gd, Tottenhall Road, Palmers Green, Middlesex, N13, 0181 888 1542.

SOUTHWELL CITY — Notts Alliance — S — Pat Johnson — 63 The Ropwalk, Southwell, Nottingham, Notts, NG25 0AL, 01636 812594 — War Memorial Rec Gd, Bishops Drive, Southwell, Notts, 01636 814386.

SOUTHWOLD TOWN — Anglian Combination — Mr R W Hart — 23 Thistledown, Lowestoft, Suffolk, NR33 8SN, 01502 568382 — Southwold Town F.C., Southwold Common, Southwold, Suffolk.

SPELTHORNE SPORTS — Middx — P — Veronica Higgins — 5 Hogarth Avenue, Ashford, Middlesex, TW15 1QB, 01784 242447 — Spelthorne Spts Club, 296 Staines Rd West, Ashford, Middlesex, TW15 1RY, 01932 783625.

SPITTAL ROVERS — Northern Alliance — P — G Burn — 7 Sea Road, Spittal, Berwick-on-Tweed, Northumberland, TD15 1RN — Spittal Rovers F.C., Newfields, Berwick-on-Tweed, Northumberland.

SPORTING KHALSA — West Midlands — 1A — Manjit S Gill — 23 Greenslade Road, Brookhouse, Walsall, West Midlands, WS5 3QH, 01922 640891 B:1902 716911, — Cannock Spts Stadium, Pye Green Road, Cannock, Staffordshire, 01543 571898.

SPRINGFIELDS — West Lancs — 1 — Mr T Threlfall — 63 Kilworth Height, Fulwood, Preston, Lancs, PR2 3NH, 01772 718959 — SSRA Sports Ground, Dodney Drive, Lea, Preston, Lancs, 01772 726131.

SPROWSTON ATHLETIC — Anglian Combination — Mr C Thomson — 11 Fairfields, Cawston, Norwich, Norfolk, NR10 4AS, 01603 871404 — Sprowston Spts & SC, Blue Boar Lane, Sprowston, Norwich, Norfolk.

SPROWSTON WANDERERS — Anglian Combination — Mr H Murphy — 20 Impala Close, Sprowston, Norwich, Norfolk, NR6 7PN, 01603 412069, — Barkers Lane, Sprowston, Norwich, Norfolk, 01603 404042.

ST ANDREWS — Anglian Combination — P — Mr V Hatchett — 53 Cheyney Avenue, Salhouse, Norwich, Norfolk, NR13 6SA, 01603 721286, — Thorpe Rec. Ground, Laundry Lane, Thorpe, Norfolk, 01603 300316.

ST FRANCIS HOSPITAL — Sussex County — 3 — Mr Colin Mansbridge — 9 Pinehurst, Burgess Hill, West Sussex, RH15 0DG, 01444 244197 — St Francis Hospital, Colwell Lane, Haywards Heath, West Sussex, 01444 441881.

ST GEORGE EASTON-IN-GORDANO — Somerset — 3 — Mrs Glenis Jones — 29 Newsome Avenue, Pill, Bristol, BS20 0DW, 01275 372875 — Court Hay, Easton-in-Gordano, Bristol, North Somerset.

ST GEORGE'S (WROTHAM) — Kent County — 3W — Mr John Underdown — 01732 884390, Old Recreation Grnd, Old London Road, Wrotham, Sevenoaks, Kent.

ST MARGARETS — Kent County — 1E — Mr William Hay — 28 The Freedown, St Margarets-at-Cliffe, near Dover, Kent, CT15 6BD, 01304 852386, — Alexander Field, Kingsdown Road, St Marg.-at-Cliffe, Kent.

ST PETERS — Herts — P — Mr John Lister — 32 Thirlestane, Lemsford Road, St Albans, Hertfordshire, AL1 3PE, 01727 850246 — William Bird P.F., Toulmin Drive, St Albans, Hertfordshire, 01727 852401.

STALHAM TOWN — Anglian Combination — P — Mr H Nicholson — Three Windows, Brumstead Road, Stalham, Norwich, Norfolk, NR12 9DE, 01692 581529 B:580513, Recreation Road, off St Johns Road, Stalham, Norwich, Norfolk.

STANDON & PUCKERIDGE — Herts — 1 — Natasha Wildman — 96 Downhall Ley, Buntingford, Hertfordshire, SG9 9JT, 01763 272490, — Station Road, Standon, near Ware, Hertfordshire, 01920 822489.

STANSFELD O & B CLUB — Kent County — P — Mr Edward Ellis — 40 Tilbrook Road, Kidbrooke, London, SE3 9QE, 0181 319 0903 B:0171 614 7087 — St James Squash & LC, 35 Marvels Lane, Grove Park, London, SE12, 0181 851 3522.

STANTON ILKESTON — Central Midlands — P — Mrs S Smedley — 4 Queens Ave, Ilkeston, Derbys, DE7 4DL, 0115 932 3772, — Hallam Fields, Hallam Field Lane, Ilkeston, Derbys, 0115 932 3244.

STOCKBRIDGE — Hampshire — 1 — Mr Graham Howard — 1 Moat Cottages, Longstock, Stockbridge, Hampshire, SO20 6EP, 01264 810753 B:01264 782222, — Recreation Ground, High Street, Stockbridge, Hampshire.

STOCKLAKE — Chiltonian — P — T Exton — 116 Narbeth Drive, Aylesbury, Buckinghamshire, HP20 1PZ, 01296 415780 — Stocklake S & SC, Haywards Way, Aylesbury, Buckinghamshire, 01296 23324.

STOCKTON SUPPORTERS — Teesside — Susan Gardner — 25 Brotton Road, Thornaby, Stockton, Cleveland, TS17 8EP, 01642 645032, — Teesdale Park, Acklam Rd, Thornaby, Stockton, Cleveland, 01642 606803.

STOCKWOOD GREEN — Somerset — 1 — Mr Simon Llewellyn — 12 Cogsall Road, Stockwood, Bristol, BS14 8NP, 01275 831929, Old Knowle C.C., Stockwood Lane, Stockwood, Bristol, 01275 838811.

STOKE GABRIEL — Devon — Anne Faulkener — 5 Barn Park, Stoke Gabriel, Totnes, Devon, TQ9 6SR, 01803 782481 — GJ Churchward Mem Gd, Stoke Gabriel, Totnes, Devon, 01803 782223.

STOKESLEY S.C. — Teesside — Mr Peter Grainge — 77 Darnton Drive, Easterside, Middlesbrough, Cleveland, TS4 3RF, 01642 316691 — Stokesley Spts Club, Broughton Road, Stokesley, North Yorkshire, 01642 710051.

STONEBRIDGE TOWN — Middx — P — Mr Nick Christie — 45 Lee Road, Perivale, Greenford, Middlesex, UB6 7BS, 0181 810 5196 — Wembley Park Spts/SC, Wembley Park, Forty Lane, Wembley, Middlesex.

STONEY STANTON — Leics — 1 — Mr Brian Chapman — 54 John Bold Avenue, Stoney Stanton, Leicester, Leicestershire, LE9 4DN, 01455 274295 B:557652, — Highfields Farm, Huncote Road, Stoney Stanton, Leicestershire, 01455 274295.

STONHAM ASPAL — S&I — S — Mr Eric Cousins — 2 Holly Green, Mickfield, Stowmarket, Suffolk, IP14 5LH, 01449 711884 — Delsons Meadow, Three Crossways, Stonham Aspal, Suffolk, 01449 711051.

STONY STRATFORD TOWN — South Midlands — S — Mr Maurice J Barber — 26 Boundary Crescent, Stony Stratford, Milton Keynes, Buckinghamshire, MK11 1DF, 01908 567930 — Stony Stratford FC, Ostlers Lane, Stony Stratford, Bucks, 01908 562267.

STORK — West Cheshire — 1 — Mr Steve Carter — 7 Elm Road, Bebington, Wirral, L63 8PF, 0151 645 6697 B:933 7565 — Unilever Spts Ground, Bromborough, Wirral, Merseyside.

STORRINGTON — Sussex County — 3 — Mr Keith Dalmon — 4 End Cottages, Storrington Rd, Amberley, Arundel, West Sussex, BN18 9LX, 01798 831887, — Storrington F.C., Recreation Ground, Storrington, West Sussex, 01903 745860.

STREET — Somerset — P — Mr Mark Clarke — 1 Deerswood Gardens, Street, Somerset, BA16 9PY, 01458 442249, — The Tannery Ground, Middlebrooks, Street, Somerset, 01458 448227 B:445987.

STURMINSTER MARSHALL — Dorset — David Miller — 8 Blaney Way, Corfe Mullen, Wimborne, Dorset, BH21 3HG, 01202 602366 — Sturminster Marshall, Churchill Close, Sturminster Marshall, Dorset.

STURMINSTER NEWTON UNITED — Dorset — Richard Frear — 44 Green Close, Sturminster Newton, Dorset, DT10 1BL, 01258 473036, — Barnetts Field, Honeymead Lane, Sturminster Newton, Dorset.

STYAL — Mid-Cheshire — 2 — Alan Jones — 1 Oak Brow Cottages, Altrincham Rd, Styal, Wilmslow, Cheshire, SK9 4JE, 01625 530270 — Styal FC, Altricham Rd, Styal, Cheshire, 01625 529303.

SUN ALLIANCE — Sussex County — 3 — Mr Steve Jenkins — 33 Owlscastle Close, Horsham, West Sussex, RH12 5YA, 01403 256697, — Sunallon Sports Club, North Heath Lane, Horsham, West Sussex, 01403 253814.

SUN POSTAL SPORTS — Herts — P — Mr Alan Cowland — 132 Bushey Mill Lane, Watford, Hertfordshire, WD2 4PB, 01923 233045, — Sun Postal Sports FC, Bellmount Wood Ave., Watford, Hertfordshire, 01923 227453.

SUNDERLAND KENNEK ROKER — Wearside — Adrian Forster — 42 Sunnybrow, Silsworth, Sunderland, Tyne & Wear, 0191 521 4007, — Silksworth Welfare, Blind Lane, Silksworth, Tyne & Wear.

SUTTON — MRA — P — Mr Peter Crich — 4 Sandfield Road, Kirby-in-Ashfield, Nottinghamshire, NG17 9FN, 01623 755404 — Mansf. Hoisery Mills, Mansfield Road, Sutton-in-Ashfield, Nottinghamshire.

SUTTON ATHLETIC — Kent County — 1W — Mr John F Wills — 6 Somerset Road, Dartford, Kent, DA1 3DP, 01322 222540 — Parsonage Lane, Sutton-at-Hone, near Dartford, Kent, 01322 280507.

SUTTON EXILES — Reading — S — Michael Charles — 32 Eastwood Rd, Woodley, Reading, Berkshire, RG5 3PY, 01734 448130, — Cantley Park, Milton Rd, Wokingham, Berkshire, 01734 793188.

SUTTON TRINITY — MRA — 2 — Mr Raymond Townsend — 42 Sherwood Road, Sutton-in-Ashfield, Nottinghamshire, NG17 1GU, 01623 440107 — Sutton Lawn, off Station Road, Sutton-in-Ashfield, Nottinghamshire.

SWALWELL — Northern Alliance — 1 — R J Robinson — 17 Milton Road, Swalwell, Newcastle-upon-Tyne, Tyne & Wear, NE16 3JD, 0191 421 1661 — Avenue Ground, Old Hexham Road, Swalwell, Tyne & Wear.

SWANMORE — Hampshire — 3 — Mrs L Chapman — Green Brae, Swanmore Road, Swanmore, Hampshire, 01489 894246 — Recreation Ground, New Road, Swanmore, Hampshire.

SWANSCOMBE UNITED — Kent County — 2W — Mrs Yvonne Howard — 49 Alexandra Road, Gravesend, Kent, DA12 2QG, 01474 329077, — Broomfield Rd Sp Pav, The Grove, High Str., Swanscombe, Kent, 01322 3822242.

SWANWICK PENTRICH ROAD — MRA — 1 — Mr Brian Kerry — 12 Reynolds Avenue, Ripley, Derbyshire, DE5 3FB, 01773 749704, — Swanwick Pent. Rd FC, Highfield Road, Swanwick, Derbyshire.

SWILLINGTON MINERS WELFARE — West Yorkshire — P — F Boon — 39 Neville Grove, Swillington, Leeds, Yorks, LS26 8QN, 0113 286 7833 B 2701107 X 3888 — Welfare Sports Gd, Wakefield Rd, Swillington, Yorks, 0113 286 2188.

SWINTON ATHLETIC — Sheffield — 1 — Mr Fred Bradshaw — 58 Piccadilly Road, Swinton, Mexborough, South Yorkshire, S64 8LF, 01709 582806 — Swinton Miners Welf., Park Road, Swinton, Mexborough, South Yorkshire.

SYSTON ST PETERS — Leics — 1 — Mr Dennis Stringer — 15 Unicorn Street, Thurmaston, Leicester, Leicestershire, 0116 269 8037 B:269 6391 — Memorial Park, Necton Street, Syston, Leicestershire, 0116 269 8110.

TADLEY — Hampshire — 2 — Mr Michael G Miller — Meadow View, West Heath, Baughurst, Hampshire, RG26 5LE, 01256 850700 — Tadley Football Club, The Green, Tadley, Hampshire.

TAFFS WELL — Welsh — 1 — Mr Ray Toghill — 38 Heol Berry, Gwaelod-Y-Garth, Taffs Well, Mid-Glamorgan, CF4 8HB, 01222 811356 B:811080, — Rhiwddar, Parish Road, Taffs Well, Mid-Glamorgan.

TEES COMPONENTS — Teesside — Mr Bryan Kitchen — 151 Guisborough Road, Nunthorpe, Middlesbrough, Cleveland, TS7 0JQ, 01642 311358 B:444720 — Recreation Ground, Machine Lane, North Skelton, Cleveland.

TEIGNMOUTH — Devon — Vince Breslan — 31 Kingsway, Teignmouth, Devon, 01626 773551, Teignmouth FC, Coombe Valley, Teignmouth, Devon, 01626 776688.

TEMPEST UNITED — West Lancs — 1 — Mr P Bennett — 441 Bolton Rd, Westhoughton, Bolton, Lancs, BL5 3BJ, 01942 810244 — Tempest Rd, Chow Moor Village, Lostock, Lancs, 01942 811938.

TEMPLE CLOUD — Somerset — 3 — Mr Steven Coles — 3 Downsway, Paulton, Somerset, BS18 5XE, 01761 412420, — Cameley P.F., Temple Cloud, Bristol, North Somerset.

TEN EM BEE ELMS — Kent County — 1W — Mr Clinton Rhule — 6 Waddon Close, Croydon, Surrey, CR0 4JT, 0181 680 6893 — Ladywell Running Trk, Silvermere Road, Catford, London, SE6.

TENTERDEN ST MICHAELS UTD — Kent County — P — Mr Sam Stevens — Kent House, Ashford Road, St Michaels, Tenterden, Kent, TN30 6PY, 01580 762703 B:0345 125749, Recreation Ground, High Street, Tenterden, Kent.

TEVERSAL GRANGE — Notts Alliance — 1 — Kevin Newton — 8 Vere Avenue, Sutton-in-Ashfield, Notts, NG17 2DS, 01623 511402, Teversal Grange Inn, Carnarvon Street, Teversal, Notts, 01623 442021.

TEYNHAM & LYNSTED — Kent County — P — Mr Colin Page — 2 Foxgrove, Milton Regis, Sittingbourne, Kent, ME10 2DW, 01795 426675, Pitch 1, Central Pk, Sittingbourne F.C., Eurolink, Sittingbourne, ME10 3SB, 01795 475547 F:430776.

THAMES POLYTECHNIC — Kent County — P — Mrs Shirley R Jarvis — 31 Monkton Drive, Welling, Kent, DA16 3JU, 0181 854 5509, — Thames Poly F.C., Kidbrooke Lane, Eltham, London, SE9 6TA, 0181 850 1221.

THE 61 F.C. — South Midlands — S — Mr Richard Everitt — 44 Somersby Close, Luton, Bedfordshire, LU1 3XB, 01582 485095, — Kingsway Ground, Beverley Rd, Luton, Beds, 0421 365236.

THE BEECHES — Mid-Cheshire — 2 — David Corrigan — 7 Burrows Ave, Haydock, St Helens, Merseyside, WA11 0DE, 01744 757273 — Cowley High School, Wynne Road, St Helens, Merseyside.

THE WETHERBY — Sheffield — 1 — Mr Raymond Lyne — 18 Ashley Grove, Aston, Sheffield, South Yorkshire, S31 0AB, 0114 287 6483 B:270 1866 — Swallownest M.W., Swallownest, Sheffield, South Yorkshire.

THETFORD ROVERS — Anglian Combination — Mr E R Zipfel — 24 Williamson Crescent, Thetford, Norfolk, IP24 3BE, 01842 755781 — Thetford Road F.C., Euston Park, near Thetford, Norfolk.

THOMSON ATHLETIC — Sussex County — 3 — Mrs Tracy Lucas — 24 Manorfields, Bewbush, Crawley, West Sussex, RH11 8GN, 01293 851800(pm only) — Thomson Athletic FC, Tinsley Lane, Three Bridges, West Sussex, 01293 515797.

THORESBY COLLIERY WELFARE — Notts Alliance — S — Brian Wathall — 29 First Ave, Edwinstowe, Nottingham, Notts, NG21 9NZ, 01623 823885, — Welfare Ground, Fourth Avenue, Edwinstowe, Notts.

THORNABY YOUTH CLUB — Teesside — Mr Geoffrey Kirk — 9 Tipton Close, Thornaby, Stockton, Cleveland, TS17 9QF, 01642 676516 — Dene School, Baysdale Road,, Thornaby, Stockton, Cleveland.

THORNTON CLEVERLEYS INTER — West Lancs — 2 — Mr D Stanborough — 19 Calder Ave, Thornton Cleverleys, Lancs, FY5 2TP, 01253 865814 — International SC, Gamble Rd, Thornton, Lancs.

THORPE SCHOOL OLD BOYS — Anglian Combination — Mr M Howe — 28 Julian Road, Spixworth, Norwich, Norfolk, NR10 3QA, 01603 898549, — Thorpe School, Laundry Lane, Thorpe, Norfolk.

THORPE VILLAGE — Anglian Combination — P — Mr A Meek — 8 Birchwood, Thorpe, Norwich, Norfolk, NR7 0RL, 01603 435985 — Thorpe Rec. Ground, Laundry Lane, Thorpe, Norwich, Norfolk, 01603 300316.

THROSTLES RIDGEWAY — Sheffield — 1 — Mr John Flower — 78 Kilvington Road, Sheffield, South Yorkshire, S13 8AH, 0114 265 6468 B:01709 378153, — Ridgeway Spts Centre, Main Road, Ridgeway, South Yorkshire.

THURCROFT DOUBLE BARREL — Sheffield — 1 — Mr John Murphy — 71 Katherine Road, Thurcroft, Rotherham, South Yorkshire, S66 9HF, 01709 545232 B:0114 269 0791 — Thurcroft Welfare, New Orchard Road, Thurcroft, Rotherham, South Yorkshire.

TIMSBURY ATHLETIC — Somerset — 2 — Mr Martyn Sage — 3 Newmans Lane, Timsbury, Bath, Somerset, BA3 1JA, 01761 471290 — Recreation Ground, North Road, Timsbury, Somerset.

TIPTON SPORTS & SOCIAL — Midland Combination — 2 — Mr W Andrews — 42 Ambleside Close, Bradley, Bilston, West Midlands, WV14 0SN, 01902 497404 — Brinsford Lane, Coven, Wolverhampton, West Midlands, 01902 782314.

TONBRIDGE INVICTA — Kent County — 3W — Mr Bill Warner — 4 Plane Walk, Tonbridge, Kent, TN10 3QS, 01732 364579 B:01892 514044 — Swanmead Spts Ground, Swanwead Way, Cannon Lane, Tonbdge, Kent, 01732 350473.

TONBRIDGE RANGERS — Kent County — 2W — Mr John Turner — 10 Lambeth Close, Lordswood, Chatham, Kent, ME5 8YL, 01634 666922, — Woodlands Walk, Shipbourne Road, Tonbridge, Kent.

TONYREFAIL WELFARE — Welsh — 3 — Mr Peter Jones — 13 Rees Street, Treorchy, Rhondda, Mid-Glamorgan, CF42 6PL, 01443 773460 — Tonyrefail Welf. AFC, The Welfare Park, Tonyrefail, Mid-Glamorgan, 01443 670387(after match only).

TOPSHAM TOWN — Devon — Sue Bulled — 207 Topsham Rd, Exeter, Devon, EX2 6EN, 01392 421703, — Topsham Town FC, Coronation Field, Topsham, Devon, 01392 873678.

TOTTERNHOE — South Midlands — S — Mr J Basterfield — 41 Park Avenue, Totternhoe, Dunstable, Bedfordshire, LU6 1QF, 01582 667941 — Totternhoe FC, Recreation Ground, Totternhoe, Beds, 01582 606738.

TOWN HALL SCRIPTS — Anglian Combination — Mr A Algar — 7 Lincoln Avenue, Gorleston, Great Yarmouth, Norfolk, NR31 7NL, 01493 657278 — , Southtown Common, Suffolk Road, Southtown, Gt Yarmth, Norfolk.

TREETON WELFARE — Sheffield — 1 — Mr Graham Shaw — 28 Fox Lane — Frecheville, Sheffield, South Yorkshire, S12 4WR, 0114 265 0806 B:01246 417691, — Treeton Welfare, Washfield Lane, Treeton, South Yorkshire.

TREHARRIS ATHLETIC — Welsh — 2 — Mr Mike Casey — 10 Windsor Road, Edwardsville, Treharris, Mid-Glamorgan, CF46 5NP, 01443 411153 — Athletic Ground, Commercial Terrace, Treharris, Mid-Glamorgan.

TRELEWIS WELFARE — Welsh — 3 — Kyrien K Thomas — 16 Gwerna Crescent, Maesycwmmer, Hengoed, Mid-Glamorgan, CF8, 01443 812030, — The Welfare Ground, Trelewis, Treharris, Mid-Glamorgan.

TREOWEN STARS — Welsh — 1 — Archie Davies — 19 Meredith Terrace, Newport, Gwent, NP1 4FN, 01495 245494 — Treowen Stars F.C., Bush Park, Treowen, Gwent, 01495 248249.

TRING ATHLETIC — South Midlands — S — Mr Ralph Griffiths — 42 Bedgrove, Aylesbury, Buckinghamshire, HP21 7BD, 01296 26425 — Tring Athletic FC, Miswell Lane, Tring, Herts, 01442 828331.

TUNLEY ATHLETIC — Somerset — 3 — Mr Christopher Reeves — 10 Martock Road, Keynsham, Bristol, BS18 1XA, 0117 985 1788, — Tunley Athletic F.C., The Recreation Grnd, Tunley, Somerset.

TURTON — West Lancs — 1 — Ernest Charnock — 15 Crown Point, Edgworth, Bolton, Lancs, BL7 0BD, 01204 852608 — Moorfield, Edgworth, Bolton, Lancs.

UCKFIELD TOWN — Sussex County — 3 — Mr Ian Bohemen — 32 Farriers Way, Uckfield, East Sussex, TN22 5BY, 01825 767781 — Uckfield Town F.C., Victoria Pleas. Grds, Uckfield, East Sussex, 01825 769400.

UNITED COLLIERIES — Leics — 1 — Mr John Meason — 29 Standard Hill, Coalville, Leicestershire, LE67 3HN, 01530 810941, — 1 Terrace Road, Ellistown, Coalville, Leicestershire, 01530 230159.

UNITY — Reading — S — Trevor Lowe — 161 Cotswold Way, Tilehurst, Reading, Berkshire, RG31 6ST, 01734 455133 B:0800 282030 — , Cintra Park, Cintra Avenue, Reading, Berkshire.

UNIVERSITY OF KENT — Kent County — 1E — Mrs Irene Simmonds — Sports Federation, Sports Centre, University of Kent, Canterbury, Kent, CT2 7NL, 01227 475455 F:768027 — The Playing Fields, University of Kent, Canterbury, Kent.

UPTON ATHLETIC ASSOCIATION — West Cheshire — 2 — Mr Barry Gaulton — 24 St Marks Crescent, Whitby, Ellesmere Port, South Wirral, L66 2XD, 0151 339 1504 B:357 5326 — Cheshire County S&SC, Plas Newton Lane, Chester, Cheshire, CH2 1PR, 01244 318167.

U.I.W. CARDIFF — Welsh — 2 — Mr Paul Smith — 8 Mendip Road, Llanrumney, Cardiff, South Glamorgan, 01222 777662 B:585917 — U.W.I.C., Cyncoed Road, Cardiff, South Glamorgan, 01222 551111.

VANDYKE — Surrey — P — Mr Gordon McLeod — 8 Rose Avenue, Mitcham, Surrey, CR4 3JS, 0181 646 4175 — London Fire Brigade, Banstead Road, Ewell, Surrey, 0181 394 1946.

VAUXHALL MOTORS — West Cheshire — 1 — Carole Paisey — 26 South Road, West Kirby, Wirral, L48 3HQ, 0151 625 6936 — Rivacre Road, Hooton, Ellesmere Port, South Wirral, 0151 327 2115/ 328 1114.

VERWOOD TOWN — Hampshire — 2 — Mrs Judith Fry — 19a Noon Hill Road, Verwood, Dorset, BH31 7DB, 01202 822828 B:823333, — Pottern Park, Pottern Way, Verwood, Dorset.

VICKERS CRAYFORD DARTFORD . — Kent County — P — Mr Gary Dillon — 5 Ladds Way, Swanley, Kent, BR8 8HN, 01322 669057 — VCD Spts & Soc. Club, Oakwood, Old Road, Crayford, Kent, 01322 524262.

VICKERS S.C. — West Lancs — 1 — Mrs B Knagg — 53 Hibbert Rd, Barrow-in-Furness, Cumbria, LA14 5AF, 01229 831785 — Vickers SC, Hawcoat Lane, Barrow-in-Furness, Cumbria, 01942 811938.

VIRGINIA WATER — Surrey — P — Mr Stephen Webb — 13 Melrose Avenue, Whitton, Twickenham, Surrey, TW2 7JF, 0181 894 6754 B:844 2020, — The Timbers, Crown Road, Virginia Water, Surrey, 01344 843811.

VOSPER THORNYCROFT — Hampshire — 2 — Mr Peter Prinn — 454 Bursledon Road, Sholing, Southampton, Hampshire, SO19 8QQ, 01703 403829(9-3)M:0589 225596 — Vosper Thornycroft, Portsmouth Road, Bursledon, Hampshire, SO19 9PW, 01703 403829.

WAKEFIELD — West Yorkshire — P — Mrs S Dean — 2 Malham Rd, Eastmoor, Wakefield, Yorks, WF1 4HN, 01924 383792, Wooley Colliery, , 01226 385095.

WALBOTTLE MASONS — Northern Alliance — 1 — N Aikman — 16 Knightside Walk, Chapel Park Estate, Newcastle-upon-Tyne, Northumberland, NE5 1TN, 0191 229 0147, Newburn Leis. Centre, Grange Road, Newburn, Newcastle-upon-Tyne, Tyne & Wear.

WALDEN RANGERS — South Midlands — 1 — Irene Oodian — 9 Garfield Ct, Handcross Rd, Luton, Bedfordshire, LU2 8JZ, 01582 483090 — Recreation Ground, Breachwood Green, Nr Luton, Beds, 01483 833332.

WALKER CENTRAL — Northern Alliance — P — B Mulroy — 31 Dalton Crescent, Byker Wall, Newcastle-upon-Tyne, Tyne & Wear, NE6 2DA — Monkchester Rec., Walker, Newcastle-upon-Tyne, Tyne & Wear.

WALKER LEDWOOD FOSSE — Northern Alliance — P — K Slade — 59 Moorland Crescent, Walkergate, Newcastle-upon-Tyne, Tyne & Wear, NE6 4AT, 0191 276 1519, — Miller's Dene, Walkergate, Newcastle-upon-Tyne, Tyne & Wear.

WALKERN — Herts — P — Ann Huggins — The Coach House, Todds Green, Stevenage, Hertfordshire, SG1 2JE, 01438 759171, — Walkern Spts/Rec Grd, Julilee Pavilion, High Street, Walkern, Hertfordshire, 01438 861615.

WALLINGTON — Northern Alliance — 2 — Mrs S Thurlbeck — 4 The Birches, Scots Gap, Morpeth, Northumberland, 01670 774679 — Oakford Park, Scots Gap, Morpeth, Northumberland.

WALMER ROVERS — Kent County — 2E — Mr Bernard Skinner — 131 Downs Road, Deal, Kent, CT14 7TF, 01304 361832 — Marke Wood, Dover Road, Walmer, Kent, 01304 374160.

WALSHAM-LE-WILLOWS — S&I — S — Mr Robert Newman — 3 The Walks, Stanton, Bury St Edmunds, Suffolk, IP31 2BX, 01359 250973 — Walsham Sports Club, Summer Road, Walsham-le-Willows, Suffolk, 01359 259298.

WALTON UNITED — S&I — S — Mr Richard Cooper — 24 Seaton Road, Felixstowe, Suffolk, IP11 3BP, 01394 275753 — Walton Rec. Ground, Recreation Road, Felixstowe, Suffolk.

WAREHAM RANGERS — Dorset — Mrs Carole White — 18 Folly Lane, Wareham, Dorset, BH20 4HH, 01929 551765, — Wraeham Rec Gd, Worgret Rd, Wareham, Dorset.

WARK — Northern Alliance — 2 — J Armstrong — 12 St Michaels Mount, Wark, Hexham, Northumberland, NE48 3NA, 01434 230382, — Wark Sports Club, Wark, Hexham, Northumberland, 01434 230259.

WASHINGTON GLEBE — Wearside — Mr Robert Robson — 24 Talbot Close, Glebe, Washington, Tyne & Wear, NE38 7RH, 0191415 1893 b:0374 233027 — Washington Glebe FC, Wash. Glebe Welfare, Washington, Tyne & Wear.

WASHINGTON NISSAN — Wearside — Mr Harry English — 193 Newcastle Road, Fulwell Mill, Sunderland, Tyne & Wear, 0191 548 7194, — Washington Nissan FC, Nissan Spts Complex, Washington, Tyne & Wear.

WATCHET TOWN — Somerset — 2 — Mr David Knight — 11 Bay View, Watchet, Somerset, TA23 0EY, 01984 634329, — Memorial Ground, Doniford Road, Watchet, Somerset, 01984 631041.

WATH SARACENS ATHLETIC — Sheffield — 1 — Mr Jim Mower — 163 Oak Road, Wath-on-Dearne, Rotherham, South Yorkshire, S63 7JX, 01709 876464, — Wath Sports Ground, Moor Lane, Wath-on-Dearne, South Yorkshire.

WELBECK COLLIERY WELFARE — Notts Alliance — S — Ron Turner — 75 Hamilton Drive, Warsop, Mansfield, Notts, NG20 0EY, 01623 847738 — Elksley Rd, Meden Vale, Mansfield, Notts, 01623 842611 colls 842267 welf.

WELLS CITY — Somerset — P — Mr Norman W Church — 48 Mount Pleasant Avenue, Wells, Somerset, BA5 2JQ, 01749 674347, — The Athletic Ground, Rowden Road, Wells, Somerset, 01749 679971.

WELLS TOWN — Anglian Combination — Mrs A Finch — The Bungalow, c/o Alderman Peel School, Market Lane, Wells-next-the-Sea, Norfolk, NR23 1RB, 01328 711768 — Wells Town F.C., Beach Road, Wells-next-the-Sea, Norfolk, 01328 710907.

WELWYN — Herts — P — Mr Malcolm Temple — 11 Copper Beeches, Oaklands, Welwyn, Hertfordshire, AL6 0SS, 01438 840873 — Welwyn Playing Field, Ottway Walk, London Road, Welwyn, Hertfordshire, 01438 714183.

WEST ALLOTMENT CELTIC — Northern Alliance — P — J Jackson — 4 Rosewood Crescent, Seaton Sluice, Whitley Bay, Northumberland, NE26 4BL, 0191 237 0416 — Whitley Bay F.C., Hillheads Park, Whitley Bay, Northumberland, 0191 252 9570 f:251 3680.

WEST KIRBY — West Cheshire — 2 — Mr John Gossage — 40 Milton Road, West Kirby, Wirral, L48 5ES, 0151 625 5221, — Marine Park, Greenbank Road, West Kirby, Wirral, 0151 625 7734.

WEST READING — Reading — S — Mrs Sue Porton — 6 Hampstead Court, Grovelands Rd, Reading, Berkshire, RG30 2QQ, 01734 504034 — West Reading F.C., Victoria Rec. Ground, Reading, Berkshire.

WESTERFIELD UNITED — S&I — S — Mr Clive Mitchell — 24 Malvern Close, Ipswich, Suffolk, IP3 9BH, 01473 714623 — S.E.H. Sports Centre, Humber Doucy Lane, Rushmere, Suffolk.

WESTERHAM — Kent County — 1W — Mr Doug Sayers — 16a The Gree, Westerham, Kent, TN16 1AX, 01959 563163 — King George P.F., Costells Meadow, Quebec Av, Westerham, Kent, 01959 561106.

WESTLAND SPORTS — Dorset — Tony Kent — c/o Yeovil Town FC, Huish Park, Yeovil, Somerset, BA22 8YS, 01823 413752 — Westkand Sports Gd, Westbourne Close, Yeovil, Somerset, 01935 703810.

WESTLAND UNITED — Somerset — P — Mr Gary Coles — 31 The Crescent, Worlebury, Weston-super-Mare, North Somerset, BS22 9SR, 01934 624173 M:0589 543473, Westland Spts Club, Winterstoke Road, Weston-super-Mare, North Somerset, 01934 632037.

WESTON MILL OAK VILLA — Devon — Mr John Davey — 74 Molesworth Rd, Plympton, Plymouth, Devon, PL7 4NU, 01752 348301 — Westom Mill OV FC, The Mill, Plymouth, Devon, 01752 363352.

WESTON ST JOHNS — Somerset — 1 — Mr Ray Williams — 69 Kingfisher Road, Worle, Weston-super-Mare, North Somerset, BS22 8TZ, 01934 514029 — Weston St Johns F.C., off Coleridge Road, Weston-super-Mare, North Somerset, 01934 622456.

WEYMOUTH SPORTS — Dorset — Alan Burt — 32 Preston Rd, Weymouth, Dorset, DT3 6PZ, 01305 833256, — Weymouth College, Cranford Avenue, Weymouth, Dorset, 01305 208859 or 208860.

WHINNEY HILL — West Lancs — 2 — Mr DW Keeley — 19 Sandy Lane, Accrington, Lancs, BB5 2AT, 01254 387938 B 01254 301333 — Half mile from, Clayton-le-Moors.

WHITCHURCH ALPORT — Mid-Cheshire — 1 — Robert Dutton — 7 Nessina Grove, Crewe, Cheshire, CW2 8EL, 01270 663015, — Yockings Park, Whitchurch, Cheshire, 01948 667415.

WHITEHAVEN AMATEURS — Wearside — Harry Upton — 14 Foxhouses Rd, Whitehaven, Cumbria, CA28 8AF, 01946 61750 B:019467 80878, — County Sports Field, Coach Road, Whitehaven, Cumbria.

WHITKIRK WANDERERS — West Yorkshire — P — D J Nutter — 17 The Crescent, Leeds, Yorks, LS15 7SL, 0113 294 5408 B 0113 283 3591 — Whitkirk S & S Club, Selby Rd, Whitkirk, Leeds, Yorks, 0113 264 6623.

WHITLEY LODGE SNOOKER — Northern Alliance — 2 — J Shaxon — 4 Dolphin Court, Newcastle-upon-Tyne, Tyne & Wear, NE4 2BR, 0191 272 5466 — Monkseaton Comm H.S., Monkseaton, Whitley Bay, Northumberland.

WICKERSLEY OLD BOYS — Sheffield — 1 — Mr Clive Davis — 12 Willow Drive, Sunnyside, Rotherham, South Yorkshire, S66 0QA, 01709 545477 — Sorby Way, Wickersley, Rotherham, South Yorkshire.

WICKHAM PARK — Kent County — 3W — Mr Phil O'Rourke — 17 Broughton Avenue, Hayes, Kent, BR2 7PL, 0181 462 6975 — Wickham Pk Spts Club, Pickhurst Rise, West Wickham, Kent, 0181 777 2550.

WIGAN COLLEGE — West Lancs — 2 — Mr M Draper — 15 Broadlands, Shevington, Wigan, Lancs, WN6 8DH, 01257 421495 B:01254 55101x475 — Christopher Park, Standish Lower Gd, Wigan, Lancs.

WILLAND ROVERS — Devon — Mr A L Jarrett — 2 College Court, Uffculme, Cullompton, Devon, EX15 3EQ, 01884 841210 — Willand Rovers FC, Silver Street, Willand, Devon, 01884 841210.

WILLASTON — West Cheshire — 2 — Mr Peter Lloyd Armstrong — 22 Deeside, Whitby, Ellesmere Port, South Wirral, L65 6RQ, 0151 200 2068 B:355 3984 — Johnston Rec. Ground, Neston Road, Willaston, South Wirral.

WILLESDEN CONSTANTINE — Middx — P — Mr Dwight John — 29 Tangmere Gardens, Northolt, Middlesex, UB5 6LS, 0181 845 9887, — Alperton Sports Grnd, Alperton Lane, Alperton, Middlesex, 0181 997 9909/ 0589 158604.

WILMSLOW ALBION — Mid-Cheshire — 1 — David Elliott — 10 Tranmere Drive, Handforth, Wilmslow, Cheshire, SK9 3BW, 01625 549524 — Oakwood Farm, Styal Rd, Styal, Wilmslow, Cheshire, 01625 535823.

WINCHESTER CASTLE — Hampshire — 3 — Mr Alan Rutter — 79 South Ham Road, Basingstoke, Hampshire, RG22 6AA, 01256 842689 M:0378 119282 — Hants CC Sports Grnd, Petersfield Rd (A31), Chilcomb, Winchester, Hampshire, 01962 866989.

WINCHESTER CITY — Hampshire — 1 — Mr Geoffrey Cox — 9 Burnetts Gardens, Horton Heath, Eastleigh, Hampshire, SO50 7BY, 01703 693021 B:01252 845545 — Hillier Way, Abbotts Barton, Winchester, Hampshire, 01962 863553.

WINDSCALE — Wearside — Mr Geoff Turrell — 65 Leathwaite, Loop Road South, Whitehaven, Cumbria, CA28 7UG, 01946 62229 — Windscale F.C., Falcon Field, Egremont, Cumbria.

WINLATON HALLGARTH — Northern Alliance — P — G S Batey — 6 Wylam View, Winlaton, Tyne & Wear, NE21 4RJ, 0191 414 7970 — Shibdon Park, Shibdon Road, Blaydon-on-Tyne, Tyne & Wear.

WINSCOMBE — Somerset — P — R S Liddiard — 2 Ash Close, Winscombe, North Somerset, BS25 1HT, 01934 843396 — Recreation Ground, The Lynch, Winscombe, North Somerset, 01934 842720(cricket club).

WINSLOW UNITED — South Midlands — S — Mr David F Ward — 28 Park Rd, Winslow, Buckingham, Buckinghamshire, MK18 3DL, 01296 713210, — Recreation Ground, Elmfields Gate, Winslow, Bucks, 01296 713057.

WIRKSWORTH TOWN — MRA — P — Mrs Alison R Pearson — 10 Ian Avenue, Wirksworth, Derbyshire, DE4 4AZ, 01629 825184, — Anthony Gell School, Wirksworth, Derby, Derbyshire.

WITTERSHAM — Kent County — 2E — Mr Cecil Packham — 3 Forge Meads, Wittersham, near Tenterden, Kent, TN30 7PE, 01797 270239, — Wittersham Spts Grnd, Poplar Road, Wittersham, Kent.

WOLLATON — Notts Alliance — S — Andrew Moon — 150 Wollaton Vale, Wollaton, Nottingham, Notts, NG8 2PL, 0115 928 1215, — Wollaton CC, Wollaton Rd, Wollaton, Notts, 0115 928 9746.

WOLVISTON — Wearside — Mr Keith Simpson — 14 Lodore Grove, Acklam, Middlesbrough, Cleveland, TS5 8PB, 01642 823734, — Metcalfe Park, Wynyard Road, Wolviston, Cleveland, TS22 5NE.

WOMBWELL MAIN — Sheffield — 2 — Mr Ian Woodall — 15 Loxley Avenue, Wombwell, Barnsley, South Yorkshire, S73 8NU, 01226 756744 B:751237 — Hough Lane, Wombwell, Barnsley, South Yorkshire.

WOMBWELL TOWN — Sheffield — P — Mr John Hunt — 10 Ryton Avenue, Wombwell, Barnsley, South Yorkshire, S73 0SD, 01226 210420 — Wombwell Sporting C., Station Rd, Wombwell, Barnsley, South Yorkshire, 01226 752128.

WOOBURN ATHLETIC — Chiltonian — P — B Nash — 10 Philip Drive, Flackwell Heath, Buckinghamshire, HP10 9JB, 01628 523293, — Wooburn Park, Town Lane, Wooburn Green, Buckinghamshire, 01628 520772/ 819201.

WOODLEY YEOMAN — Reading — S — Bob Brodrick — 44 Hilltop Rd, Earley, Reading, Berkshire, RG6 1DA, 01734 612278 B:01628 486644 — Woodford Park, Haddon Drive, Woodley, Berkshire.

WOODNESBOROUGH — Kent County — 1E — Mr Geoff Hunt — Hillcross Farm, Eastry, Sandwich, Kent, CT13 0NY, 01304 611311 B:611532, — Hillborough, Eastry Road, Woodnesborough, Kent, 01304 614721.

WOOTTON BASSETT TOWN — Hellenic — 1 — Mr Rod Carter — 14 Blackthorn Close, Wootton Bassett, Swindon, Wiltshire, SN4 7JE, 01793 851386, — Gerard Buxton Sp Gd, Rylands Way, Wootton Bassett, Wilts, 01793 853880.

WORCESTER PARK — Surrey — P — Mr Frank Thompson — 6 Courtenay Road, Worcester Park, Surrey, KT4 8RY, 0181 335 3379 B:0973 366693, — Worcester Park F.C., Green Lane, Worcester Park, Surrey, 0181 337 4995.

WORLE — Somerset — 2 — Mr David Brine — 44 Beach Road, Kewstoke, Weston-super-Mare, North Somerset, BS22 9UU, 01934 625585, — Worle Rec. Ground, Station Road, Worle, Weston-super-Mare, North Somerset.

WORMLEY ROVERS — Herts — P — Mr David Smith — 19 Nursery Gardens, Enfield, Middlesex, EN3 5NG, 0181 804 3608, — Wormley Sports Club, Church Lane, Wormley, Hertfordshire, 01992 460650.

WORTHINGTON SIMPSONS — Notts Alliance — 1 — Antony Allam — 11 Graham Close, Balderton, Newark, Notts, NG24 3EW, 01636 72430 — Lowfields Works, off Hawton Lane, Balderton, Notts, 01636 702672.

WORTWELL — Anglian Combination — 1 — Mr I Fisher — 18 Chestnut Road, Pulham St Mary, Diss, Norfolk, IP21 4RA, 01379 608401, — Wortwell P.F., opposite Bell P.H., Wortwell, Norfolk.

WRAYSBURY — Chiltonian — P — J Rice — 77 Grange Way, Iver, Buckinghamshire, SL0 9NT, 01753 652780, — Wraysbury F.C., Memorial Ground, Wraysbury, Buckinghamshire, 01784 482155.

WRINGTON-REDHILL — Somerset — 3 — Mr Brian David Bull — 4 Church Road, Redhill, Bristol, North Somerset, BS18 7SQ, 01934 862027 — Recreation Ground, Silver Street, Wrington, North Somerset.

WYBERTON — Lincs — Mrs Chris Scrupps — 52 Deldale Road, Wyberton, Boston, Lincolnshire, PE21 7BT, 01205 367756, — Causeway, Wyberton, Boston, Lincolnshire, 01205 353525

WYMONDHAM TOWN — Anglian Combination — P — Mr M B Utting — 52 Mill Lane, Attleborough, Norfolk, NR17 2NW, 01953 453146 — Wymondham Town F.C., Kings Head Meadow, Wymondham, Norfolk, 01953 607326.

WYRE VILLA — West Lancs — 1 — Mr G Bradley — Park Farm, Burned House Lane, Preesall, Poulton-le-Fylde, Lancs, FY6 0PQ, 01253 810637 B 01253 810637 — Stalmine Village, Nr Knott End, 01253 701468.

YARNTON — Hellenic — 1 — Amanda Kirk — 11 Saw Close, Chalgrove, Oxfordshire, OX44 7TW, 01865 891088 — Marsh Rd Sports Gd, Marsh Rd, Yarnton, Oxon, 01865 842037.

YATELEY GREEN — Hampshire — 2 — Mr Alan Baynes — 7 Borderside, Yateley, Camberley, Surrey, GU17 7LJ, 01252 870725, — Yateley Rec. Ground, Reading Road, Yateley, Camberley, Surrey.

YATTON ATHLETIC — Somerset — 3 — Mr Paul Faiers — 20 Carice Gardens, Clevedon, North Somerset, BS21 5DG, 01275 340299 — Hangstones P.F., Stowey Road, Yatton, North Somerset.

YORK RAILWAY INSTITUTE — West Yorkshire — P — S M Alford — 12 St Gilesway, Copmanthorpe, York, YO2 3XT, 01904 702407 B 488507 — York RI, New Lane, Acomb, York, 01904 798930.

YORKSHIRE MAIN — Sheffield — 2 — Mr Dennis Tymon — 22 Pamela Drive, Warmsworth, Doncaster, South Yorkshire, DN4 9RP, 01302 852455 — Edlington Lane, Edlington, Doncaster, South Yorkshire.

ZENITH WINDOWS — Anglian Combination — Mrs S Marsh — 358 Holt Road, Horsford, Norwich, Norfolk, NR10 3EG, 01603 898616 B:401923x222 — Rhone Poulenc SC, Low Road, Hellesdon, Norfolk

KEY:

MRA = Midland Regional Alliance

S&I = Suffolk and Ipswich League

Index

Contents	2
Intro	3
FA Cup Results	8
FA Vase Results	14
FA Trophy Results	19
Aberystwyth Town	908
Abingdon Town	712
Abingdon United	364
Accrington Stanley	456
Aerostructures	291
AFC Lymington	292
AFC Totton	293
Aldershot Town	714
Alfreton Town	458
Almonsbury Town	365
Alnwick Town	627
Altrincham	23
Alvechurch Villa	866
Amesbury Town	440
Amersham Town	820
Andover	294
Arlesey Town	835
Armthorpe Welfare	591
Arnold Town	592
Arundel	334
Ashfield United	593
Ashford Town	90
Ashford Town (Middx)	850
Ashington	628
Ashton Town	576
Ashton United	502
Atherstone United	92
Atherton Collieries	551
Atherton Laburnum Rovers	504
Aveley	787
Aylesbury United	666
B.A.T. Sports	295
Backwell United	421
Bacup Borough	576
Baldock Town	94

Bamber Bridge	460
Banbury United	366
Bangor City	909
Banstead Athletic	761
Barking	762
Barkingside	821
Barnstaple Town	422
Barrow	462
Barry Town	910
Barwell	269
Bashley	180
Basildon United	809
Basingstoke Town	718
Barton Rovers	716
Bath City	26
Beaconsfield Slough Youth Club Old Boys	822
Beckenham Town	312
Bedfont	851
Bedford Town	763
Bedford United	836
Bedlington Terriers	629
Bedworth United	136
Belper Town	594
Bemerton Heath Harlequins	295
Berkhamsted Town	720
Bexhill Town	335
Bicester Town	367
Bideford	423
Biggleswade Town	836
Billericay Town	722
Billingham Synthonia	630
Billingham Town	631
Bilston Community College	867
Bilston Town	138
Bishop Auckland	464
Bishop Sutton	440
Bishop's Stortford	668
Blackpool Mechanics	577

Blackpool (Wren) Rovers	552
Blakenall	270
Blidworth Welfare	595
Bloxwich Town	271
Bloxwich Strollers	877
Blyth Spartans	466
Bodmin Town	926
Bognor Regis Town	724
Boldmere St Michaels	272
Bolehall Swifts	867
Bootle	553
Boreham Wood	670
Borrowwash Victoria	596
Bosham	335
Boston Town	382
Boston United	468
Bournemouth	296
Bourne Town	384
Bowers United	809
Brache Sparta	837
Brackley Town	368
Bracknell Town	764
Bradford Park Avenue	506
Braintree Town	788
Brandon United	632
Brentwood	810
Bridgnorth Town	273
Bridgwater Town	424
Bridport	425
Brierley Hill Town	877
Brigg Town	597
Brightlingsea United	228
Brimsdown Rovers	823
Brislington	426
Bristol Manor Farm	427
Briton Ferry Athletic	910
Broadbridge Heath	336
Brockenhurst	297
Brodsworth Miners Welfare	598

Bromley	672	
Bromsgrove Rovers	29	
Brook House	824	
Buckingham Athletic	838	
Buckingham Town	182	
Bugbrooke St Michaels	385	
Burgess Hill Town	336	
Burnham	369	
Burnham Ramblers	811	
Burscough	554	
Burton Albion	96	
Burton Park Wanderers	386	
Bury Town	229	
Buxton	470	
Caernarfon Town	911	
Caersws	912	
Calne Town	429	
Camberley Town	790	
Cambridge City	98	
Canterbury City	313	
Canvey Island	726	
Carmarthen Town	913	
Carshalton Athletic	674	
Carterton Town	370	
Case Sports	892	
Castleton Gabriels	577	
Cemaes Bay	913	
Chadderton	556	
Chalfont St Peter	765	
Chard Town	429	
Chasetown	274	
Chatham Town	314	
Chatteris Town	230	
Cheadle Town	578	
Chelmsford City	100	
Cheltenham Town	102	
Chertsey Town	676	
Chesham United	728	
Cheshunt	766	
Chester-le-Street Town	633	
Chichester City	337	
Chippenham Town	430	
Chipstead	852	
Chorley	472	
Christchurch	298	
Cinderford Town	184	
Cirencester Town	186	
Clacton Town	231	
Clapton	791	
Clevedon Town	188	
Clitheroe	557	
Clyst Rovers	441	
Cobham	852	
Cockfosters	825	
Cogenhoe United	387	
Coleshill Town	868	
Collier Row & Romford	767	
Concord Rangers	812	
Congleton Town	508	
Connah's Quay Nomads	914	
Consett	635	
Conwy United	915	
Corby Town	140	
Corinthian Casuals	853	
Corinthian	315	
Cornard United	232	
Cottingham	388	
Cove	854	
Coventry Sphinx	868	
Cowes Sports	299	
Cradley Town	878	
Cranleigh	855	
Crawley Down Village	337	
Crawley Town	104	
Cray Wanderers	316	
Crediton United	441	
Crockenhill	317	
Crook Town	636	
Crowborough Athletic	338	
Croydon	730	
Croydon Athletic	826	
Curzon Ashton	510	
Cwmbran Town	916	
Dagenham & Redbridge	678	
Daisy Hill	579	
Darlaston Town	879	
Dartford	190	
Darwen	558	
Daventry Town	389	
David Lloyd Sports	868	
Dawlish Town	442	
Deal Town	318	
Denaby United	599	
Desborough Town	390	
Devizes Town	442	
Didcot Town	371	
Diss Town	233	
Dorchester Town	106	
Dorking	768	
Dover Athletic	32	
Downham Town	234	
Downton	300	
Droylsden	512	
Dulwich Hamlet	680	
Dudley Town	142	
Dunkirk	892	
Dunston Federation Brewery	637	
Durham City	638	
Ebbw Vale	917	
Easington Colliery	639	
East Cowes Victoria Athletic	301	
East Grinstead	339	
East Ham United	813	
East Preston	340	
East Thurrock United	792	
Eastbourne Town	341	
Eastbourne United	340	
Eastleigh	302	
Eastwood Hanley	559	
Eastwood Town	514	
Eccleshill United	600	
Edgware Town	769	
Egham Town	770	
Elmore	431	
Ely City	235	

Emley	474	Gedling Town	893	Harworth Colliery Institute	894
Endsleigh	372	Glapwell	602	Haslingden	582
Enfield	682	Glasshoughton Welfare	602	Hassocks	342
Eppleton Colliery Welfare	634	Glastonbury	445	Hastings Town	116
		Glossop North End	560	Hatfield Main	606
Epsom & Ewell	793	Gloucester City	108	Havant Town	202
Erith & Belvedere	192	Godalming & Guildford	857	Haverhill Rovers	243
Esh Winning	640	Gorleston	238	Hayes	44
Ettingshall Holy Trinity	880	Gornal Athletic	861	Heanor Town	895
Eton Manor	814	Gosport Borough	303	Heavitree United	446
Evenwood Town	641	Graham Street Prims	893	Hebburn	644
Evesham United	144	Grantham Town	146	Hednesford Town	47
Exmouth Town	443	Gravesend & Northfleet	110	Hemel Hempstead Town	772
Eynesbury Rovers	391	Grays Athletic	684	Hendon	688
Fairford Town	373	Great Harwood Town	520	Herne Bay	323
Fakenham Town	236	Great Wakering Rovers	815	Hertford Town	796
Falmouth Town	926	Great Yarmouth Town	239	Heybridge Swifts	690
Fareham Town	194	Greenwich Borough	322	Higham Town	394
Farnborough Town	35	Gresley Rovers	112	Highgate United	869
Farnham Town	855	Gretna	522	Highworth Town	374
Farsley Celtic	516	Guisborough Town	643	Hillingdon Borough	829
Faversham Town	319	Guiseley	480	Hill Top Rangers	861
Felixstowe Port & Town	237	Hadleigh United	240	Hinckley Athletic	276
		Hailsham Town	341	Hinckley Town	148
Feltham	856	Halesowen Harriers	275	Histon	244
Ferryhill Athletic	642	Halesowen Town	114	Hitchin Town	692
Fisher Athletic	196	Halifax Town	41	Hoddesdon Town	840
Flackwell Heath	794	Hallam	604	Holbeach United	395
Fleet Town	198	Hall Road Rangers	603	Holker Old Boys	561
Flint Town United	918	Halstead Town	241	Holywell Town	919
Flixton	518	Hampton	732	Holsworthy	928
Folkestone Invicta	320	Handrahan Timbers	869	Horden Colliery Welfare	645
Ford Sports	392	Hanwell Town	827	Hornchurch	797
Ford United	814	Harefield United	828	Horsham	773
Forest Green Rovers	200	Harlow Town	795	Horsham YMCA	343
Formby	580	Harpenden Town	838	Hucknall Town	607
Frickley Athletic	476	Harrow Borough	686	Hullbridge Sports	815
Frome Town	444	Harrowby United	393	Hungerford Town	774
Furness	321	Harrogate Town	524	Huntingdon United	396
Gainsborough Trinity	478	Harrogate Railway Athletic	605	Hyde United	482
Garforth Town	601			Hythe United	324
Garswood United	581	Hartley Wintney	858	Ilford	816
Gateshead	38	Harwich & Parkeston	242		

Ilfracombe Town	447	London Colney	843	Nantwich Town	565
Ilkeston Town	150	Long Buckby	399	Needham Market	250
Inter Cable-Tel	920	Long Eaton United	897	Nelson	584
Ipswich Wanderers	245	Lordswood	324	Netherfield	532
Irchester United	397	Louth United	609	Netherne	860
Islington St Mary's	829	Lowestoft Town	246	Nettleham	898
Jarrow Roofing		Ludlow Town	886	Newcastle RTM	649
Boldon CA	645	Lye Town	862	Newcastle Town	566
Kempston Rovers	398	Macclesfield Town	55	Newhaven	347
Kenilworth Town	870	Maghull	583	Newmarket Town	251
Kettering Town	49	Maidenhead United	738	Newport AFC	122
Keynsham Town	448	Maine Road	563	Newport Pagnell Town	401
Kidderminster Harriers	52	Maldon Town	247	Newport (I.O.W.)	206
Kidsgrove Athletic	562	Maltby Miners Welfare	610	Newquay	930
Kimberley Town	896	Malvern Town	883	Newtown	922
Kingsbury Town	798	Mangotsfield United	432	Northallerton	650
Kings Heath	870	March Town United	248	Northampton Old	
King's Lynn	118	Margate	204	Northamptonians Chenecks	402
Kingstonian	694	Marine	490	Northampton Spencer	403
Kintbury Rangers	375	Marlow	740	Northampton Vanaid	404
Knowle	871	Massey-Ferguson	871	North Ferriby United	611
Knowsley United	484	Matlock Town	530	North Leigh	377
Knypersley Victoria	277	Meir K.A.	872	Northwich Victoria	61
Lambourn Sports	376	Melksham Town	449	Northwood	801
Lancaster City	486	Merstham	859	Norton & Stockton	
Lancing	344	Merthyr Tydfil	120	Ancients	651
Langford	841	Metropolitan Police	777	Norwich United	252
Langney Sports	345	Mickleover Sports	898	Nuneaton Borough	124
Larkhall Athletic	448	Middlewich Athletic	584	Nuthall	899
Launceston	928	Midhurst and		Oakwood	348
Leatherhead	775	Eastbourne United	346	Odd Down Athletic	433
Leek CSOB	582	Mildenhall Town	249	Oldbury United	278
Leek Town	488	Mile Oak	347	Oldham Town	585
Leigh RMI	526	Millbrook	930	Olney Town	405
Leighton Town	776	Milton Keynes	844	Osset Albion	612
Letchworth	842	Minehead	449	Osset Town	613
Lewes	799	Mirrlees Blackstone	400	Oxford City	696
Leyton Pennant	734	Molesey	742	Paget Rangers	154
Lincoln United	528	Moor Green	152	Pagham	349
Liskeard Athletic	929	Morecambe	58	Parkgate	614
Littlehampton Town	346	Morpeth Town	647	Paulton Rovers	434
Liversedge	608	Mossley	564	Peacehaven &	
Llansantffraid	920	Murton	648	Telscombe	350

Pelsall Villa	279	Ryhope Community		Spennymoor United	494
Penrith	567	Association	653	Squires Gate	587
Penzance	931	Saffron Walden Town	816	St Albans City	700
Pershore Town	280	Salford City	570	St Austell	932
Peterlee Newtown	651	Salisbury City	126	St Blazey	933
Petersfield Town	304	Saltash United	932	St Helens Town	571
Pewsey Vale	450	Saltdean United	354	St Ives Town	410
Pickering Town	615	Sandhurst Town	862	St Leonards Stamcroft	208
Pontefract Collieries	616	Sandiacre Town	899	St Margaretsbury	830
Portfield	351	Sandwell Borough	283	St Neots Town	411
Porthleven	931	Sawbridgeworth Town	817	Stafford Rangers	168
Porthmadog	923	Seaham Red Star	654	Stafford Town	884
Portsmoth Royal Navy	304	Selby Town	618	Staines Town	702
Potters Bar Town	845	Selsey	354	Stalybridge Celtic	73
Potton United	406	Sharnbrook	408	Stamford	412
Prescot Cables	568	Sheffield	619	Stansted	818
Prudhoe Town	651	Sheppey United	326	Stantondale	587
Purfleet	698	Shepshed Dynamo	164	Stanway Rovers	255
Racing Club Warwick	156	Shifnal Town	284	Stapenhill	285
Radcliffe Borough	534	Shildon	655	Staveley Miners	
Ramsbottom United	585	Shirebrook Town	900	Welfare	902
Ramsey Town	407	Shirley Town	873	Stevenage Borough	76
Ramsgate	325	Shoreham	355	Steyning Town	358
Raunds Town	158	Shortwood United	378	Stocksbridge Park	
Raynes Park Vale	861	Shotton Comrades	656	Steels	536
Reading Town	862	Sidley United	356	Stockton	658
Redditch United	160	Sittingbourne	128	Stotfold	414
Redhill	352	Skelmersdale United	586	Stourbridge	170
Rhyl	923	S & L Corby	413	Stourport Swifts	885
Ringmer	353	Slade Green	327	Stowmarket Town	256
Rocester	281	Slough Town	67	Stratford Town	286
Romsey Town	305	Soham Town Rangers	253	Studley BKL	874
Rossendale United	569	Solihull Borough	166	Sudbury Town	130
Rossington Main	617	Somersham Town	254	Sudbury Town Reserves	257
Rothwell Town	162	Southall	802	Sudbury Wanderers	257
Rothwell Corinthians	408	Southam United	873	Sutton Coldfield Town	172
Royston Town	846	Southend Manor	817	Sutton United	704
Ruislip Manor	831	South Normanton		Swaffham Town	258
Runcorn	492	Athletic	901	Swindon Supermarine	379
Rushall Olympic	282	Southport	70	Tadcaster Albion	620
Rushden & Diamonds	64	South Shields	657	Tamworth	174
Ryde Sports	306	Southwick	357	Taunton Town	435
		Spalding United	409	Tavistock	934

Telford United	79	Waterlooville	214	Woking	85
Tetley Walker	587	Watton United	262	Wokingham Town	754
Thackley	621	Wealdstone	804	Woodbridge Town	265
Thame United	744	Wednesfield	888	Woodford Town	832
Thamesmead Town	328	Wellesbourne	874	Woolwich Town	331
Thatcham Town	307	Wellingborough Town	416	Wootton Blue Cross	418
Thetford Town	259	Wellingborough		Worcester City	132
Thorne Colliery	903	Whitworths	417	Worcester Athletico	875
Thrapston Venturas	415	Wellington	451	Workington	542
Three Bridges	359	Welling United	82	Worksop Town	544
Tilbury	778	Welshpool	924	Worsbrough Bridge	
Tiptree United	260	Welton Rovers	452	Miners Welfare	623
Tiverton Town	436	Welwyn Garden City	847	Worthing United	361
Tividale	887	Wembley	782	Worthing	756
Toddington Rovers	847	West Auckland Town	660	Wroxham	266
Tonbridge Angels	210	Westbury United	439	Yate Town	222
Ton Pentre	924	Westfield	864	Yaxley	419
Tooting & Mitcham		Westfields	889	Yeading	706
United	746	West Midlands Police	287	Yeovil Town	708
Torpoint Athletic	934	Weston-Super-Mare	216	Yeovil Town Reserves	452
Torrington	438	Weymouth	218	Yorkshire Amateur	624
Tottenham (Omada)	832	Whickham	661		
Trafford	572	Whitby Town	662		
Tring Town	803	Whitchurch United	308		
Trowbridge Town	212	Whitehawk	359		
Truro City	935	Whitley Bay	540		
Tuffley Rovers	380	Whitstable Town	330		
Tunbridge Wells	329	Whitton United	263		
Uxbridge	748	Whyteleafe	752		
Vauxhall G.M.	573	Wick	360		
Viking Sports	863	Willenhall Town	288		
V. S. Rugby	176	Willington	663		
Wadebridge Town	935	Wimborne Town	309		
Walsall Wood	888	Wingate	806		
Waltham Abbey	833	Winsford United	496		
Walton & Hersham	750	Winterton Rangers	622		
Walton Casuals	864	Wisbech Town	264		
Wantage Town	381	Witham Town	783		
Warboys Town	261	Withdean	361		
Ware	780	Witney Town	220		
Warminster Town	450	Witton Albion	498		
Warrington Town	538	Wivenhoe Town	784		
Washington	659	WM Fire Service	875		